I0128617

CHICKASAW
An Analytical Dictionary

CHICKASAW
An Analytical Dictionary

by
Pamela Munro
and
Catherine Willmond

University of Oklahoma Press : Norman

By Pamela Munro

Mojave Syntax (New York, 1976)

(with Katherine Siva Sauvel) *Chem'ivillu' (Let's Speak Cahuilla)* (Los
Angeles and Banning, Calif., 1981)

(ed., with John Haiman) *Switch-Reference and Universal Grammar*
(Amsterdam and Philadelphia, 1983)

(with Maurice L. Zigmond and Curtis G. Booth) *Kawaiisu: A Grammar and
Dictionary, with Texts* (Los Angeles, 1990)

(with Susan E. Becker, et al.) *Slang U.* (New York, 1991)

(with Catherine Willmond) *Chickasaw: An Analytical Dictionary* (Norman,
1994)

(with Catherine Willmond) *Let's Speak Chickasaw: Chikashshanompa'
Kilanompoli'* (Norman, 2009)

Library of Congress Cataloging-in-Publication Data

Munro, Pamela.
  Chickasaw: an analytical dictionary / Pamela Munro and Catherine Willmond.
     p.   cm.
  Includes bibliographical references and index.
  ISBN 978-0-8061-2687-6 (paper)
  1. Chickasaw language—Dictionaries—English.   2. English language—Dictionaries—
Chickasaw.   I. Willmond, Catherine, 1922–   II. Title.
PM801.Z5M85   1994
497'.5—dc20

94-12872
CIP

The paper in this book meets the guidelines for permanence and durability of the
Committee on Production Guidelines for Book Longevity of the Council on Library
Resources, Inc. ∞

Copyright © 1994 by Pamela Munro and Catherine Willmond. Published by the
University of Oklahoma Press, Norman, Publishing Division of the University. Manu-
factured in the U.S.A.

CONTENTS

PREFACE

This is a dictionary of Chickasaw, a language of the Muskogean family of American Indian languages now spoken primarily in the Chickasaw Nation of south-central Oklahoma. The Chickasaws are one of the Five Tribes of Oklahoma (traditionally known as the Five Civilized Tribes), having been moved to Indian Territory there by the federal government in the 1830s. Our dictionary consists of several introductory sections, which explain the structure and use of the dictionary; a Chickasaw-English section, with main entries for Chickasaw words, including definitions, grammatical information, etymologies, cross-references, and examples; and an English-Chickasaw index.

While this book primarily reflects the speech of Catherine Willmond, who grew up near McMillan, Oklahoma (a community in western Marshall County), every effort has been made to present additional varieties of spoken Chickasaw. Other speakers whose usage has been extensively recorded (and who have helped us in many other ways as well) include Frankie Alberson, Adeline Brown, Vera Virgie Brown, Willie Byars, Onita Carnes, the late Mina Christie, the late Cora Lee Collins, Lizzie Frazier, Lorene Greenwood, Emily Howard, Mary James, Luther John, the late Tecumseh John, the late Jeff Johnson, the late Martha Johnson, the late Maybell Lacher, Caroline Milligan, the late Tennie Pettigrew, Eloise Pickens, the late Clarence Porter, Leola Porter, Flora Reed, Lee Fannie Roberts, Mary Ella Russell, Minnie Shields, the late Hattie Stout, Thomas Underwood, and Adam Walker. These speakers represent areas of the Chickasaw Nation from Kingston in the south to Byng or Happyland (near Ada) in the north, and from Davis or Ardmore in the west to Fillmore and Wapanucka in the east; their ages at the time of our work ranged from the late thirties to the late nineties. All are native speakers of Chickasaw, with the exception of Mr. Byars, a native speaker of Choctaw who learned Chickasaw as a young man. Still others, including Edna Baken, Pauline Brown, the late Patsy Byars, Frank Christie, the late Jackson Collins, Joyce Cripps, Josie Crow, Pauline Fillmore, Thomas Frazier, Geraldine Greenwood, the late Amos James, Rose Jefferson, Annie Orr, Bill Pettigrew, the late Dan Pettigrew, the late Binum Pickens, John Puller, and Fanny Underwood, have shared their knowledge of Chickasaw, providing valuable additional help with or comments on our studies. We are very grateful to all of these people.

A number of other sources suggested words for possible inclusion here. The most important of these was Jesse and Vinnie May (James) Humes's *Chickasaw Dictionary*, which reminded Mrs. Willmond of many words, some of them older words no longer in common use. Since the Choctaw and Chickasaw languages are very closely related, we consulted Choctaw sources as well, and many of these, particularly Cyrus Byington's *Choctaw Dictionary*, Allen Wright's *Chahta Leksikon*, Ben Watkins's *Choctaw Definer*, and several works by T. Dale Nicklas (and his associates), suggested other Chickasaw words to include. In addition, a number of Choctaw speakers from Oklahoma,

Mississippi, and Los Angeles, including Aaron Baker, Juanita Baker, Rosie Billy, Laura Carney, Gus Comby, Edith Gem, Jincy Ingram, Ollie Jack, Leona Jefferson, McDonnell Johnson, Levi Jones, Marie McKinney, Reba Meashintubby, Florence Nelson, Paul Perkins, the late Tillie Perkins, the late Steven Roberts, Semiah Robinson, the late Julia Thomas, Julia Timms, Henry Tubby, Gladys Wade, Hanson Wade, Frances Willis, and especially the late Josephine Wade, Adam Sampson, and the late Buster Ned (who helped in many other ways as well), taught us Choctaw words whose Chickasaw equivalents appear in our dictionary.

Many other people in Oklahoma, Mississippi, and Los Angeles have helped us to prepare this version of our dictionary. The late Reverend Oliver Neal deserves very special thanks for introducing me to Mrs. Willmond in 1977. We are grateful for the encouragement of the administration of the Chickasaw Nation of Oklahoma under Governors Overton James and Bill Anoatubby. During the early stages of our work, Lynn Gordon and Charles Ulrich often gave us four much appreciated extra ears and lots of other support. Aaron Broadwell and Jack Martin helped with the preparation of the index, and Karen Wallace and JP Munro provided valuable editorial assistance. Allen Munro gave us computer support and other good help and comments. We also thank Stephen Anderson, Fern Appel, Janet Scott Batchler, Jerry Bennett, William Bright, Rhonda Brown, Brenda Carnes, Felicia Carnes, Bonnie Chiu, Barbara Clum, David Costa, the late James Crawford, William Davies, Betty Dodd, John Drayton, Larry Dunn, Emil Farve, the late Harry Folsom, Bonnie Glover, Brunetta Bernard Griffith, Joe Griffith, Mary Haas, Heather Hardy, Cindy Huston, Norma John, Dan Kempler, Margaret Langdon, Ann Lewis, Benjamin Marquez, Irene Marquez, Ramona Marquez, William (Mac) McGalliard, Vera McGilberry, Wanda Ned, Sarah Nestor, T. Dale Nicklas, Doris Payne, Jane Russell, Teresa Spörk, Laura Welch, Robert Williams, Andreas Wittenstein, Harvey York, Jean York, the students in four UCLA classes that studied Chickasaw with Mrs. Willmond, and everyone else who has encouraged or assisted in our research, which has been funded by the Academic Senate and Department of Linguistics of the University of California, Los Angeles, and by the National Science Foundation (A Chickasaw Dictionary, 1987-89), with additional assistance from the American Indian Studies Center of UCLA (through a grant to Charles Ulrich).

We hope you enjoy using the dictionary.

PAMELA MUNRO

Los Angeles

¶1. A GUIDE TO THE DICTIONARY

¶1.1 Writing Chickasaw

The orthography, or spelling system, used in this dictionary is adapted from those used previously for Chickasaw and Choctaw in Oklahoma. In our spelling system, each Chickasaw sound has just one spelling, and each spelling has one standard pronunciation (although variations may be possible). Like any other spelling system, Chickasaw spelling works according to its own set of rules, which must be learned. (A complete list of the Chickasaw alphabet is given for reference just before the Chickasaw-English portion of the dictionary.)

The basic sounds of the Chickasaw language include ', a, aa, a̱, b, ch, f, h, i, ii, i̱, k, l, lh, m, n, ng, o, oo, o̱, p, s, sh, t, w, y. Many of these letters and letter combinations (two letters used together to indicate a single sound) represent about the same sounds as in English, but there are some differences, of course, which you will need to pay attention to if you want to have good Chickasaw pronunciation.

The vowel sounds a, i, and o are normally pronounced roughly as in Spanish, with a as in English *father*, i as in *police*, and o as in *Ohio*. The long vowels aa, ii, and oo are written double, and the nasal vowels a̱, i̱, and o̱ (pronounced with the air released through the nose) are written with an underline (in some other books, you may see the nasal vowels written in italics).

As in other orthographies for Chickasaw and Choctaw, ch represents [č] (roughly as in English *church*), sh [š] or [ṣ] (a sound similar to that in English *shake*, but with more of a whistle to it on occasion), and lh [ɬ]. Lh is the hardest Chickasaw sound for English speakers to learn to pronounce, and the best way to learn to say it is to listen to a Chickasaw speaker. Lh may sound a bit like l and h or l and sh pronounced at the same time. If you say an English word which begins with a *kl* sound, such as *Klondike*, the sound just after the *k* is very much like a Chickasaw lh—so if you can say *Klondike* without the *k* you'll be fine. (Some younger speakers replace the difficult Chickasaw lh sound with *th*, as in English *thin*, but this is not usually considered a correct pronunciation by older people.) ' (the apostrophe) represents the glottal stop sound [ʔ] (a catch in the throat, as in the middle of English *uh-uh*, meaning "no"), which is contrastive in all but initial and postconsonantal positions in Chickasaw. Ng is [ŋ] (as in *sing*), a sound derived in Chickasaw when n k comes before b, l, m, or n. (As in English, Chickasaw n has the same ng sound in any word where it comes immediately before k, but in these words we just write nk.) Each of the consonant sounds listed above except for ' and ng may be doubled (long or geminate) in Chickasaw words.

A few additional pronunciation rules will help make your pronunciation of the Chickasaw vowel sounds even more natural. Chickasaw has a Rhythmic Lengthening rule by which non-final even-numbered short non-nasal vowels in most sequences of consonant-vowel, consonant-vowel syllables are lengthened, coming to sound almost as long as the vowels that are written long. Thus, for example, the vowel of the second syllable of the word **pilachi** "send" (which has three consonant-vowel syllables, **pi, la,** and **chi**) is almost as long as a long **aa** sound. When the prefix **sa-** is added to form the four-syllable word **sapilachi** "he sends me", however, it is the vowel of the **pi** syllable that is pronounced with a lengthened vowel (because now it is even-numbered); in this word, the **la** syllable includes a shorter **a** sound. (For more about Rhythmic Lengthening, see ¶2.3.4 of The Structure of Chickasaw Words, the next section of the dictionary. References to the introductory sections of the dictionary always begin with the ¶ symbol.) Short vowels which are not lengthened by this rule may have a laxer pronunciation, with short **a** pronounced as in English *sofa*, short i as in *bit*, and short o like the *oo* in *book*. The sequence **ay** before a consonant may be pronounced as in English *bay*, and the sequence **oy** (or especially **oyyo**) may sound like a long *u* (as in *lunar)* or, for some speakers, like a French *u* or German *ü* sound. Nasal vowels ordinarily sound quite long. In some words, such as **pichchạa** "barn", a nasal vowel is followed by an oral vowel of the same quality, producing an extra-long vowel that loses its nasal quality in the middle. In a few words, such as **ittialbi'** "lips", an i and a come together in the middle of a word (because of the loss of an earlier h); this **ia** combination is often pronounced like the *e* of English *bet* or the *a* of English *bat*.

We write a hyphen in words where two similar vowel sounds come together (such as **aa-albinachi'** "camp"), in certain compounds and derived words (such as **nit-oshi'** "baby bear") to show their special pronunciation (see ¶2.542), and in a few words (such as **tashan-kachi** "to be coiled like a spring") in which an **n** before **k** has the normal n sound, not the sound **ng**. Other than this, Chickasaw words in the dictionary are never hyphenated, except in a few rare cases where a word is too long for its line. When you see a hyphen in a Chickasaw word, you know that it represents something concerning pronunciation.

Some vowels in certain Chickasaw verbs have an accent (indicated in the dictionary with a ´ over the vowel letter, or, in certain verb forms where two consonants follow an accented vowel (¶2.61), with a ^ over that vowel). Accent is marked only in main entries and cross-references in the dictionary, not in example sentences or in etymologies. Chickasaw nouns do not have distinctive accent, and both they and unaccented verbs are always stressed on their last syllable.

Some words borrowed from English and other languages that are often used in Chickasaw speech are included in the dictionary. Most of these use standard Chickasaw sounds, but a few are pronounced with sounds that are not normally used in Chickasaw, including d (as in English *dog*), e (as in English *bed*), g (as in English *get*), j (as in English *jug*), r (as in English *rug*), u (as in English *use*), v (as in English *vote*), and z (as in English *zip*). The complete Chickasaw alphabet with all these additions, in order, is ', a, aa, ạ, b, ch, d, e, f, h, i, ii, ị, k, l, lh, m, n, ng, o, oo, ọ, p, r, s, sh, t, u, v, w, y, z. This order is followed in alphabetizing the Chickasaw words in the dictionary, with letter combinations treated as single elements in the alphabet. Thus, for example, any word starting with **o** (even **owwa** "to moo") will be alphabetized before any word starting with **oo** (even **oochi** "to draw water"), since **o** precedes the letter combination **oo** in the alphabet.

¶1.2 The form of dictionary entries

All full entries in the dictionary follow a standard form. First comes the Chickasaw word or phrase, in **boldface** type; next, the definition; next, grammatical information, if any (in parentheses); next, grammatical features, if any [as listed below, each one in separate brackets]; next, the etymology [in brackets]; next, cross-references to related forms {in braces}; and finally (following a §), any examples. The format and abbreviations used in the dictionary entries are explained below. Variant pronunciations are listed immediately after the main entry, either in boldface or (if they are used only by certain speakers) in normal type.

Some entries do not include a definition: entries for variant pronunciations are listed with a reference to the main entry beginning with "see"; words that are used only as subparts of a longer phrase are listed with a reference to that full phrase ("in —"); and verb grades and certain other derived forms have a brief reference to the verb or noun stem from which they are derived. Verb and noun stems that never occur as independent words are listed in <angles> with a reference to the entries in which they appear.

Occasional words may be used either as nouns or as verbs. Identical words of different parts of speech have separate entries in the dictionary.

¶1.3 Definitions

A Chickasaw noun is defined with an English noun. The entry for a noun may indicate information about possession and sometimes will include an example, an etymology, or a cross-reference.

A Chickasaw verb is defined with an English verb (given in the infinitive "to" form) whose subject matches that of the Chickasaw verb. The main entry for each Chickasaw verb gives information regarding agreement and may also indicate selectional restrictions, derived or related forms, suppletive alternants, other grammatical information, and etymology. Examples are given for many verbs, showing their inflection and use in sentences.

Definitions for words of other classes (adverbs, interjections, and so forth) work similarly.

In general, no definition is given for non-main entries, whether they are derived forms of main entries, otherwise non-occurring words that are part of longer main entries, variant pronunciations, or non-independent stems (listed in <angles>).

Chickasaw grammatical morphemes (prefixes, suffixes, and so forth that combine with dictionary entries to form longer words) are not listed in the dictionary; they are indexed in ¶2.7.

¶1.4 The representation of Chickasaw agreement patterns

¶1.41 Chickasaw verbs indicate the person and number of non-third-person subjects and objects with one or two of several different sets of agreement markers, which are described and exemplified in ¶2.2. Agreement is indicated in parentheses following a verb's definition, using the abbreviations "I" (for the -li, ish-, il- agreement set), "II" (for the sa-, chi-, po- agreement set), and "III" (for the am-, chim-, pom- agreement set).

¶1.411 An intransitive verb that can be used with only one associated argument (noun phrase), its subject, is followed by "(I)" if it marks a pronominal subject with a marker from the I set, for example, and with "(II)" if it marks its subject with a II set prefix. Transitive verbs that can be used with two sets of markers show the subject first, then, after a semicolon, the object: thus "(I;II)" indicates a verb that marks a pronominal subject with an affix from the I set and a pronominal object with an affix from the II set. Here is a simple example:

apila   to help (I;II)

The definition shows that the verb apila "to help" marks its subject with a I marker and its object with a II marker. (The sample entries given in this introduction are generally shorter and less complete than the full entries in the dictionary.) According to the description of the I and II markers in ¶2.2, you know that this verb can be used in sentences such as Ishapila "You help him", Achipilali "I help you", Apopila "He helped us", and so on. Whenever you can use a prefix to show a subject or object, you can use a noun instead, so you also know that this verb can be used in sentences such as Hattakat ihooa apila "The man helps the woman", with a subject noun hattak "man" and an object noun ihoo "woman" (case marking on nouns is discussed in ¶2.51). In most types of sentences, nouns are not required, however, so Apila "He helps her" is a complete sentence by itself. (There is no gender in Chickasaw, so Apila can also mean "He helps him", "She helps him", "She helps her", and so forth.)

Several other abbreviations are used. "3" shows that a given sentence role can be filled only by a third-person nominal, so "(II;3)", for example, follows a transitive verb that marks its subject with a II set prefix, but whose object can only be a noun, while "(3;II)" follows a verb whose subject is a non-agreeing noun, but whose object can be indicated by a II set prefix. "N" indicates hypothetical (ak-, chik-, etc.) agreement (used with certain negative verbs), and "IR" is used to indicate the special form of I agreement used with certain reciprocal (itti-) verbs. Some verbs have different meanings according to which of several agreement patterns is used: in such cases, the listing of the agreement pattern follows each definition. When more than one agreement pattern may be used for a given verb for the same meaning, a slash (/) separates the alternative agreement patterns. Here are some more examples of how agreement patterns are indicated in the dictionary:

(I;III) — I subject; III object
(III) — III subject
(I;3) — I subject; nominal (non-agreeing) object
(3;III) — nominal (non-agreeing) subject; III object
(I / II) — either a I subject or a II subject may be used

There are many other agreement patterns. For verbs taking more than one non-subject argument, abbreviations like the following are used:

(I;3;3) — I subject; nominal first object; nominal second object
(I;3;3;3) — I subject; nominal first object; nominal second object; nominal third object
(I;II;3) — I subject; II first object; nominal second object
(I;III;3) — I subject; III first object; nominal second object

In the first and second cases, only the I subject can be marked on the verb, and the non-subject arguments do not agree, but in cases like the next two, it is not necessarily clear from a verb's definition which argument will trigger agreement.

For a small number of verbs, no subject word or marking is allowed. Inflection of these verbs is marked with "(—)".

All verbs that include III agreement are listed in the dictionary with a form of the dative prefix (im-, in-, or i̱-).

¶1.412 Only one non-subject argument, which we consider the first object, may trigger agreement in Chickasaw. For all verbs that have an agreeing first object and one or more other arguments, we have indicated the agreeing non-subject argument in the verb's definition with a raised circle (°), as follows:

ima   to give to ° (I;III;3)

This definition shows that **ima** takes a subject (marked with a I affix), a first object, marked with a III prefix, and an additional noun object. The first object is the one to whom something is given (as shown by the position of the ° in the definition), and the second object is the thing given. Following the rules in ¶2.2, you can make up sentences like **Issamatok** "You gave it to me" and **Imali** "I give it to him". There is an important point to note here. There is no way to show a non-third-person gift with an agreeing prefix on this verb. Thus, it is not possible to say "I gave you to him" or "He gives me to you" with a simple Chickasaw sentence. Although such sentences sound fine in English, they are not possible in Chickasaw, so it is important to pay attention to the parenthesized information that tells you how to use each verb.

Here is another example, showing that in some cases two separate verbs allow you to express two kinds of objects:

aholhchifochi   to name after ˚ (I;II;3) §
Lynn asaholhchifoshtok. She named
Lynn after me.
ahoochifochi   to name ˚ after (I;II;3) §
Lynn asahoochifoshtok. She named me
after Lynn.

As these entries show, the agreeing first object of **aholhchifochi** is the person after whom someone else was named; the agreeing first object of **ahoochifochi** is the person who was named after someone else. In these entries, example sentences follow § after the definition.

There are a few verbs for which either of two arguments may (on different occasions) be the agreeing first object. These have definitions containing two ˚s, as in

ayoppachichi   to make ˚ greet ˚ (I;II;3) §
Ihoo yamma asayoppachishtok. She
made me greet that woman, She made
that woman greet me.

For verbs like **ayoppachichi**, either the one who is made to greet someone or the one someone is made to greet may be the agreeing object. But you still cannot mark both of these at once: it is not possible to say "She made you greet me", with two agreeing objects, for example.

An object noun may be marked with an accusative case marker (¶2.51) or left unmarked, according to the speaker's judgment. If a verb takes more than one object, as in the examples just discussed, only one of these may be so marked. However, the speaker may choose any of the objects as the accusative object. Thus, for instance, both **Ihoot Lynna ofi' imatok** and **Ihoot ofi'a Lynn imatok** mean "The woman gave Lynn a dog"; the sentence used would depend on the speaker's feelings and on what had already been discussed. (In a strange context, both sentences might also mean "The woman gave Lynn to the dog", but this would be highly unlikely in the real world.) This example shows that the accusative object is not necessarily the same as the agreeing first object, since the accusative object of **ima** may be either the recipient or the gift but the agreeing first object can be only the recipient. When an object noun is unmarked it must appear directly before the verb, unlike an accusative-marked object, which may undergo movement rules.

¶1.413 A few verbs take only such unmarked "objects" or, as we will refer to them, complements; these are not normal objects, since they may not be marked accusative, never show pronominal agreement, and are not subject to the movement rules optionally undergone by normal objects. (Some such complements may not be proper nouns or may not be modified or definite.) Here is an example:

xiv

nakshobi   to smell bad (like a dog, fish, or
blood) (II); to smell bad like (a dog, fish,
or blood) (II;3C)

This definition shows that **nakshobi** is often used intransitively, with a II-marked subject, as in **Sanakshobi** "I smell bad". It can also be used with a noun complement (indicated with "3C"), as in **Ofi' sanakshobi** "I smell bad like a dog". But this complement noun (which may be seen as syntactically incorporated) cannot be marked accusative and is not a normal object.

With a few verbs, such 3C complements are required:

a   to be (II;3C) (<ya> when prefixed;
requires an overt preceding noun
complement) § Chikashsha' saya. I am a
Chickasaw. | Hattak yammat minko'
attook. That man was a chief (long ago).

Nakshobi can be used with or without an unmarked complement, but **a** must have one; **saya** "I am" is not a complete sentence.

¶1.414 There is a class of verbs in Chickasaw that take a different kind of complement from the unmarked complements described above. These verbs have either III- or II-marked subjects, and their complements are always suffixed with -at. Entries for these verbs have their agreement pattern listed as "(III;3-at)" or "(II;3-at)", as in

imittola   to drop (III;3-at)

The sentence **Lynn ịholissaat amittola** "I dropped Lynn's book" has a III-marked subject (shown with the prefix **am+**); the complement **Lynn ịholisso** "Lynn's book" is marked with **+at**. Verbs whose entry includes a nominal complement suffixed with **+at** are listed as in

chipotaat imatta   to have a baby (III)

The subject of this expression goes before the whole phrase, the **+at** noun is invariant, and the verb has a III prefix agreeing with the subject. Thus **Ihooat chipotaat imatta** means "The woman had a baby", and **Chipotaat amatta** means "I had a baby".

Verbs such as **imittola** that are listed in the dictionary as taking 3-at complements reflect the operation of the lexically triggered Oblique Subjectivalization rule. Two other types of Chickasaw sentences have 3-at complements, Possessor Raising sentences and "have" sentences.

Intransitive verbs marked [+PR] may occur in sentences in which a possessor of their subject becomes a derived subject, and the original semantic subject is a 3-at complement. Thus the [+PR] verb **illi** "to die" may occur not only in expected possessed subject sentences such as **Ihoo imofi'at illitok** "The woman's dog died" but also sentences such as **Ihooat ofi'at imillitok**, in which the possessor **ihoo** "woman" is the subject, the former possessed subject **ofi'** "dog" is a 3-at complement, and the verb rather than the possessed noun has a III prefix agreeing with the subject (possessive phrases are described in ¶2.264). Many [+PR] verbs also allow a second, less common type of Possessor Raising, as in **Ihooat imofi'at illitok**, in which the III possessive prefix remains on the possessed noun. (Because color verbs show only this type of Possessor Raising, this is referred to as Color Possessor Raising, and verbs which may undergo this process are marked [+CPR].) All three sentences, both the original unraised version and the two Possessor Raising versions, are logically equivalent, though speakers use Possessor Raising sentences to indicate greater saliency of the (usually human) possessor in a discourse situation. Both I and II subject intransitive verbs participate in Possessor Raising but these rules are lexically restricted. We are sure that we have not marked all the verbs that can undergo these rules.

Chickasaw "have" sentences also include 3-at complements. Some "have" verbs are listed in the dictionary as in

> **iwáyya'a**   to have (sg. obj. that rests on
> four legs (or wheels) or is thought of as
> having a flat upper surface with open
> space beneath) (III;3-at)

Iwáyya'a is derived from the positional/existential verb **wáyya'a** and is used in sentences like **Ihooat ofi'at iwayya'a** "The woman has a dog" or **Ofi'at awayya'a** "I have a dog". Such sentences include a subject, a 3-at noun, and a verb with a III prefix. "Have" sentences may be formed with any positional/existential verb, and only the most common of them, such as **iwáyya'a**, are listed in the dictionary. There is a clear semantic difference between the presumed intransitive source and the "have" sentence, which is used to assert possession, not existence.

All of the 3-at constructions described in this section have certain syntactic similarities. Despite its case marking, the 3-at noun, while an underlying semantic subject at some level, is not a surface subject. For example, it cannot trigger the use of the plural subject prefix **hoo-** (¶2.432) or the diminutive suffix **-a'si** (¶2.451) or same- and different-subject switch-reference marking (¶2.493)—each of these properties is controlled by the new derived subject. There are serious restrictions on the degree to which the 3-at noun may be modified, and it may take only neutral nominative **-at** marking. Moreover, the 3-at noun must appear overtly in the sentence (unlike any normal subject noun, which can be pronominalized) and may not be moved from its position immediately before the verb.

¶1.415 The indicated inflection regularly appears on the last element of a verbal expression consisting of more than one word (unless that last element is the negative auxiliary **ki'yo**, which never takes subject or object marking). For example,

lhimpat ittola   to fall on one's face (I / II)

shows that "I fall on my face" may be **Lhimpat ittolali** (I marking) or **Lhimpat sattola** (II marking) but that the first word of the phrase, **lhimpat**, does not receive any subject marking. Any entry consisting of more than one word will have agreement markers added to its last word unless the definition indicates otherwise.

Some longer verbal phrases depart from the regular pattern by showing agreement marking on a word other than, or in addition to, the final one. This is indicated, for instance, as (I , —) for a two-word verbal expression irregularly taking I subject agreement on its first element (in such entries, the comma separated by spaces separates the inflection used on each word of the phrase), as in

tochchí'na bíyyi'ka   to be in (scattered)
groups of three (I , —) § Hashtochchi'na
biyyi'katok. You were in scattered
groups of three.

As the example sentence in the entry shows, the I subject prefix for "you (pl.)", **hash-**, goes on the first word of the verbal expression, and the second is unmarked. For still other expressions, subject agreement may appear on one element (usually the last) and object agreement on another (usually the first), as in

atalkachit máa   to be leaning against (pl.
subj.) (II = obj. , I = subj.) § Achitalkachit
iimaatok. We leaned against you.

As the example shows, the object "you" is marked in the first word with the II prefix **chi-**, while the subject "we" is marked on the second word with the I prefix **ii-**. (The Structure of Chickasaw Words gives more details concerning how the form of these prefixes changes in different words.)

Some verbal expressions that are phonologically a single word are inflected as though they contained more than one word. The division between the components of such expressions is indicated in the etymology, which follows an entry in square brackets. In most cases, inflection follows the regular rules for multiword expressions, so that verbal agreement markers are used on the last word of the expression. Thus

ishtanompoli   to talk about (I;II) [isht
*anompoli]

xvii

is inflected with I subject and II object prefixes attached to its second element, **anompoli**, following the instrumental preverb **isht**, so **Ishtiichinompoli** is "We talk about you". The * in the etymology indicates the beginning of the element to which agreement markers can be attached, in this case **anompoli**. A * appears in the etymology of every verb entry to which agreement markers are added in a non-standard way.

¶1.416 Idiomatic verbal expressions consisting of a complete subject and predicate are given an English translation containing a "for" infinitive, as in

> **yaaknaat wina'kachi** for there to be an
> earthquake, for the earth to shake

No agreement is indicated for such expressions (since they include a subject); their verbs can be inflected for aspect and modality like any other predicate. The +at noun in such expressions functions like any other subject noun.

¶1.417 Certain expressive predicates containing the verb **aachi** "to say" are listed as follows:

> **pas pas pas aachi** to make a slapping
> sound (expressive) (I)

Such predicates (which may be shortened to include two occurrences of the expressive syllable or word, rather than three) are most commonly not inflected at all, but the verb **aachi** can receive person, aspect, and modality affixes, or can be used with a III prefix indicating an indirect object. Such expressions are not used in subordinate clauses or other complex sentences and are generally heard only in special discourse situations, for instance when the speaker is talking directly to babies or small children.

¶1.418 "Cha expressions" include two verbs, the first of which ends in the conjunctive suffix **-cha**. Both verbs are inflected for subject. For more information about the form of -cha words, see ¶2.4.93.

¶1.42 For many nouns, the form of possessive prefixes is indicated in parentheses following the definition: "(IIp)" for II possessive prefixes (generally inalienable, referring primarily to body parts and kinship terms); "(IIIp)" for III possessive prefixes (generally alienable, referring to acquired items, although some body parts and kinship terms also use these prefixes); "(Ip)" for the rare I possessive. A noun that always occurs with an obligatory III possessive prefix is marked "(oIIIp)". If the form of the noun changes irregularly when it is possessed, this is also indicated. In noun phrases more than one word long, the possessive prefix is added to the first word of the phrase; any exceptions to this rule are noted with an example.

The use of III prefixes on nouns not marked for a different kind of possession is regular. If there is no parenthesized indication of the sort of possessive marking a noun takes, you may assume it takes III prefixes.

¶1.5 Syntactic and morphological features and other information

The parenthesized agreement information for many verbs is followed by one or more of the following syntactic or morphological features that indicate whether the verb undergoes certain phonological or syntactic rules, its interaction with certain other words, or the particular complementation structure it selects:

[+CPR]: the verb may undergo the Color Possessor Raising rule, with its logical (underlying) subject retaining +at marking and its derived possessor subject subject-marked, but without derived III agreement on the verb

[E]: the verb is used with an Equi (same-subject) complement unmarked for subject with no suffix

[E+kat]: the verb is used with an Equi complement unmarked for subject with a +kat suffix

[E+t]: the verb is used with an Equi complement unmarked for subject with a +t suffix

[+HM]: the verb has a reduced form with a nasalized vowel derived by the HM rule

[+OPR]: the verb may undergo the Object Possessor Raising rule whereby the possessor of the logical (underlying) object acquires argument status and triggers III agreement on the verb (the derived III-prefixed [OPR] verbs are cross-referenced, if they do not occur independently with another meaning)

[+PR]: the verb may undergo the Possessor Raising rule, with its logical (underlying) subject retaining +at marking and its derived possessor subject subject-marked and triggering III agreement on the verb (the derived III-prefixed [PR] verbs are cross-referenced, if they do not occur independently with another meaning)

[-SC]: the verb does not follow the regular Strident-Coronal cluster formation rule (because of rhythmic lengthening of final -chi syllable)—see ¶2.37

[+SC]: the verb follows the Strident-Coronal rule (despite possible expectations to the contrary)

[±SC]: the verb may behave either as a [+SC] or a [-SC] verb

[+T]: the verb is normally or often followed by the taha/tahli perfective/completive auxiliary

[+taha]: the verb may be used with the taha auxiliary to express a plural subject

Many verbs are followed by information regarding related forms, given in {}'s. This information is given in the following order: v1 or v2 (¶2.4422), grades (¶2.6), suppletive forms, and other related words of interest. See the Abbreviations section for the various abbreviations used in these sections.

¶1.6 Usage and variation

The dictionary entries indicate several types of interdialectal variation. Some words are pronounced differently by different speakers. Others are considered by many speakers to be certainly or probably Choctaw rather than Chickasaw, although they are often used by Chickasaw speakers.

The great majority of the entries in the dictionary follow Mrs. Willmond's pronunciation and usage, and instances where other speakers agree with her (the great majority of documented cases) are not explicitly indicated. (Thus this dictionary can give only an impressionistic picture of the complete usage of other speakers.) When another Chickasaw speaker's different pronunciation or usage is included in the dictionary, it is identified with the speaker's initials, as follows:

AB	Adeline Brown
AJ	Amos James
AW	Adam Walker
CC	Cora Lee Collins
CM	Caroline Milligan
CP	Clarence Porter
EP	Eloise Pickens
ER	Mary Ella Russell
FA	Frankie Alberson
FR	Flora Reed
HS	Hattie Stout
JC	Jackson Collins
JJ	Jeff Johnson
LF	Lizzie Frazier
LG	Lorene Greenwood
LJ	Luther John
LP	Leola Porter
LR	Lee Fannie Roberts
MC	Mina Christie
MJ	Mary James
MtJ	Martha Johnson
ML	Maybell Lacher
MS	Minnie Shields
OC	Onita Carnes
PB	Patsy Byers
PBr	Pauline Brown
RJ	Rose Jefferson
TJ	Tecumseh John
TP	Tennie Pettigrew

TU	Thomas Underwood
VB	Vera Virgie Brown
WB	Willie Byars

"CW" is used in cases where Mrs. Willmond's usage is explicitly contrasted with that of other speakers. Another speaker may use a word that shares one or more syllables with Mrs. Willmond's word and thus might be viewed either as a similar but different word (entered and indexed separately in the dictionary) or as a mere variant of the same word (listed under the main entry, Mrs. Willmond's word). The decisions we made about how to list such words may have been arbitrary.

Although Choctaw and Chickasaw are similar languages that share a considerable amount of vocabulary, there are many words that speakers consider to belong properly only to one language or the other. Words marked "(Ct.)" are used by Mrs. Willmond in Chickasaw conversation but identified by her as properly Choctaw rather than Chickasaw. Words marked "(Ct.?)" are considered to be possibly Choctaw. These abbreviations are not used for words not used by Mrs. Willmond, many of which could be similarly classified.

Usually, other speakers' variant pronunciations or definitions are not cross-referenced or indexed. Information concerning the agreement patterns used with verbs documented only for other speakers and not known by Mrs. Willmond is often incomplete.

Some entries are marked with additional usage information. The label "(rare)" is used for words or, most often, forms of words that Mrs. Willmond felt should be marked as extremely unlikely to be used in normal discourse. If a word is considered to be nearly archaic it is marked "(old word)". Many euphemisms are marked as such. A few words are marked as "(slang)"; these are most often lighthearted direct translations of English idioms. Finally, some words marked "(Bible word)" are considered to be derived from the standard translation of the Bible into Choctaw and in some cases may actually be Choctaw words; such words are used only in sermons or very formal speaking.

¶1.7 Other parts of the dictionary entry

Etymologies are indicated in brackets ([ ]'s). Etymologies indicate the sources of words borrowed into Chickasaw from other languages and the parts that make up complex words. Many of these parts and the rules governing how they combine are discussed in ¶2; ¶2.7 includes a complete list of the grammatical morphemes that appear in our etymologies. In general, if a word has its own entry with an etymological breakdown at its main entry in the dictionary, this etymology is not repeated if the word occurs elsewhere as part of other, longer entries.

Examples follow § after a word's definition and other grammatical information. Subsequent examples are separated by straight lines (I 's).

Words that are unattested independently are indicated in angles (<>'s)—

these are all part of or forms of some word that is attested but are not used alone in the form given.

¶1.8 The English-Chickasaw index

Following the Chickasaw-English dictionary is an English-Chickasaw index. Each main entry in our dictionary appears at least once in the index, and entries that have many or complicated English translations are listed a number of times. Variant pronunciations and grade forms of verbs are not indexed, unless they have additional meanings that cannot be predicted from those of the main entry.

The English-Chickasaw Index is not a dictionary itself, as far less information is given in that section than in the main Chickasaw-English section. When you look up a word in the index, you should be sure to check its entry in the main section, especially if more than one Chickasaw equivalent of the English word is given. Fine shades of meaning and usage and other important information are not given in the index; to find out about these things, it is important to consult the main entry for each word in the Chickasaw-English Dictionary.

When two or more Chickasaw words appear after an English entry word in the index, they are listed in alphabetical order, not in order of importance or acceptability. Occasionally, however, a Chickasaw word is only a very peripheral equivalent of the English entry. These words are listed after all other entries, after the English word *also* (in italics). Remember to check words taken from the index in the main section of the dictionary to determine exactly how they are used in sentences.

¶1.9 The selection of the words in the dictionary

Some people may wonder why we chose to include some of the words in the dictionary. Although some words refer to things or actions that it may bother some readers to think about, we want to present a complete picture of the Chickasaw language, with all the words it contains, in order to help preserve it for future generations of speakers and for study by Chickasaw people and scholars. We have tried to include every Chickasaw noun and verb stem that we have heard in the course of our research. However, there are many Chickasaw words that are not listed in the dictionary.

First, Chickasaw is a language in which very long and complex words—often used to express the equivalent of whole English sentences—are built up from simpler ones by adding prefixes and suffixes. We could not list all of the possible words of Chickasaw, but section ¶2 of the dictionary explains many of the ways longer Chickasaw words are formed from the stems listed in the dictionary. This section will also help you to understand the structure of words that occur in the example sentences in the dictionary.

A number of traditional Chickasaw names are listed in the dictionary, but Chickasaw versions of English names are not listed. (Many of these are used in example sentences in the dictionary, although we have not written all

xxii

names in Chickasaw spelling.) A few rules will help you convert English names to Chickasaw pronunciation and spelling. First, a glottal stop sound (') is added at the end of any English name that ends in a vowel: thus, the Chickasaw for "Onita" is **Onita'**. Next, a final *r* in an English name longer than one syllable is not pronounced in Chickasaw, and the name is treated as if it ended in a vowel. Usually English final *er* will sound like Chickasaw final **a'**, so "Lester", for example, is pronounced **Lesta'**. Finally, **s** after another consonant at the end of a word is dropped: "Pickens" is pronounced **Pikken**. This rule works even when the English s sound is not spelled with an *s*: thus, "Alex" is pronounced **Alek**. The last few examples show that you have to make some spelling changes when going from English to Chickasaw: the name "Buster" should perhaps be spelled **Basta'**, for example, since the first vowel of the English word is pronounced like a Chickasaw short **a**, but it may look better to you to write **Busta'**. If this seems confusing, do not worry. You can spell English names as usual and simply pronounce them the way Chickasaw speakers do.

There are also undoubtedly many ordinary Chickasaw words that should be included in the dictionary but were missed. If you are a Chickasaw speaker or are learning the language, you should keep a list of additional Chickasaw words you discover that are not listed here. (Of course, if you are looking for a word and you do not find it in the Chickasaw-English section, you should also check the English-Chickasaw Index.) Your list may be a valuable document about the language someday.

THE STRUCTURE OF CHICKASAW WORDS

¶2.1 Introduction

A good dictionary of English includes almost all the words of the language actually used by most speakers. In addition to listing nouns, verbs, adjectives, and so forth, an English dictionary gives all the additional forms that are used in sentences, such as plurals of nouns; *-ed*, *-s*, and *-ing* forms of verbs; and *-er* and *-est* forms of adjectives. It would be much harder to list all the words in a language like Chickasaw, in which a single verb word usually corresponds to a complete English sentence. All Chickasaw verbs change not only according to the time to which they refer (as in English), but also according to their subject and object and whether they are negative. Many additional sentence elements, such as "will", "may", and "yet", which are separate words in English, are expressed as part of the verb in a Chickasaw sentence. A Chickasaw verb such as **lhiyohli** "to chase" has more than thirty different forms varying only for subject, object, and negativity. When the time or other features of an event change, the verb word changes as well, so that there may be hundreds of forms of a single verb.

No dictionary that you could hold in your hands, then, could list all the words of Chickasaw. In this dictionary, we give only the simplest forms, or stems, of nouns, verbs, and other words. The stem of a noun is the form that a speaker would use to identify an object (What is that? —**Nita'**, "A bear"), and the stem of a verb is the form that can be used to give a simple command to one person (**Lhiyohli!**, "Chase it!"). The various forms of nouns and verbs that are used in sentences are generally predictable (when you know the rules), so we do not list them for each stem. This part of the dictionary will help you to understand how nouns and verbs change as they are used in sentences and to see the relationships between many of the words in the dictionary. ¶2.2 below describes the ways in which verbs show different subjects and objects and nouns show different possessors. ¶2.3, ¶2.4, and ¶2.5 describe other ways that nouns and verbs change as they are used in sentences.

Many Chickasaw verbs have forms called "grades" that are used to convey additional meaning about the event or state to which the speaker refers or the speaker's view of it. Grades are made not by adding something to the beginning or end of a verb but by accenting one of the verb's vowels and altering the sounds of the verb in a regular way. For instance, the n-grade of "to chase" is **lhiyóhli**, with an accented nasalized **ó** vowel; an n-grade always includes either added nasalization or an added n or m. ¶2.6 describes grade formation.

Finally, ¶2.7 gives a list of the different prefixes and suffixes used to build the Chickasaw words in the dictionary and in the examples presented to illustrate the use of many of these words. Studying these examples will give you a clearer idea of how both simple and complex Chickasaw words are used in sentences.

¶2.2 Pronominal agreement marking

Like English verbs, Chickasaw verbs "agree" with their subjects, but in Chickasaw this phenomenon is much more extensive. Chickasaw makes use of four major series of non-third-person pronominal agreement affixes, prefixes and a suffix that specify subject and object on verbs and possessor on nouns, in what has been termed an "active" inflectional system.

The first three of these series (named with roman numerals) are parallel to each other in that each can be used to indicate the subject of an affirmative intransitive verb. The I affixes are used primarily for indicating semantically active intransitive subjects and most transitive subjects. II prefixes can indicate non-active intransitive subjects, most transitive objects, and a few transitive subjects. III prefixes indicate indirect and direct objects as well as subjects, most of which could be viewed as semantic datives. All three series can be used on nouns to indicate possessors, with III prefixes used for most alienable possessors and II prefixes used for most inalienable possessors. This characterization of the three series is semantically based, and the affixation structure of the majority of Chickasaw verbs can, indeed, be predicted from their semantics. However, the particular agreement pattern used with any given single verb must be lexically specified. The terms "active" and "stative" used here refer only to the semantic features of a given verb, not to its inflectional pattern.

The fourth series of pronominal affixes is the N series, used with hypothetical and certain negative verbs. A fifth series, IR, is used on certain reciprocal verbs.

The dictionary specifies which series are used with different verbs, as explained in ¶1.4. Specific verb words with agreement affixes added are generally not included in the dictionary unless they have unexpected meanings.

¶2.21 The Chickasaw I affixes are

1sg.	2sg.	1pl.	1spl.	2pl.
-li	ish-	il- / ii- (kil- / kii-)	iloo- (kiloo-)	hash-

The first-person singular affix -li is the only suffix in the pronominal agreement system. There are no third-person affixes. The first-person plural affix varies according to the sound that follows it: il- is used before a vowel, ii- before a consonant. In addition, many speakers allow or prefer variant first-person plural affixes beginning with k, kil- and kii-, which appear to be derived from the N affix series. The "special" first-person plural affix iloo- (or, for some speakers, kiloo-) is used relatively rarely (or not at all, by some speakers), and it is not yet clear what conditions its use, since oppositions such as dual-plural, paucal-multiple, collective-distributive, and inclusive-exclusive do not adequately characterize the difference between it and the regular first-person plural affix.

Here is an example of a Chickasaw I subject verb, **malli** "to jump": **Mallili**

"I jump"; **Ishmalli** "You jump"; **Malli** "He jumps, She jumps, It jumps, They jump"; **Iimalli** (or **Kiimalli, Iloomalli,** or **Kiloomalli**) "We jump"; **Hashmalli** "You all jump". These single words (like most of the verb words in Chickasaw) are complete simple sentences that may be translated in several ways. **Mallili** can also be translated as "I am jumping" or even "I jumped", for example.

¶2.211 The Chickasaw sound **sh** regularly becomes **s** before **s,** so the prefixes **ish-** and **hash-** become **is-** and **has-** before an **s** sound. This happens most often when these prefixes precede the first-person singular II series prefix **sa-** (¶2.22), as in **Issathána** "You know me", but also occurs before verb stems that begin with **s,** as in **Issatabli** "You spread it".

¶2.212 A number of Chickasaw short verbs (those consisting of a short vowel, a single consonant, and another short vowel) have irregular prefixed inflections, which vary according to the initial vowel of the verb. (In each case, the suffixed first-person singular form and the unaffixed third-person form are unaffected.)

There are two patterns for short verbs beginning with **a.** One involves deletion of the initial **a** of the verb. Thus **abi** "to kill" has the following I prefixed forms: **Ishbi** "You kill him", **Iibi** (or **Kiibi**) "We kill him", **Hashbi** "You all kill him". **Ala** "to arrive", **apa** "to eat (something)", and (for many speakers) **amo** "to gather, mow" work the same way. The short verbs **ani** "to pour (into a container)" and **aya** "to go" (and **amo,** for some speakers) double their consonant when they have a I prefix: **Ishanni** "You pour it", **Ilanni** "We pour it". In addition, the first vowel of **aya** changes to **i** in I-prefixed forms like **Ishiyya** "You go" and **Iliyya** "We go".

For most speakers, the short verb **ishi** "to get, to take, to catch" is replaced by **í'shi** when it has a I prefix: **Ishili** "I take it", **Ishí'shi** "You take it", **Ishi** "He takes it, She takes it, They take it", **Ilí'shi** "We take it", **Hashí'shi** "You guys take it".

The special first-person plural prefix **iloo-** or **kiloo-** is normally added directly to an unchanged short verb stem. Occasionally, though, these prefixes are pronounced with a following **h** when they precede a short verb. Thus, "We kill him" may be **Kilooabi** or **Kiloohabi**.

¶2.22 The Chickasaw II prefixes are

1sg.	2sg.	1pl.	1spl.	2pl.
sa-	chi-	po-	hapo-	hachi-

These prefixes indicate the subject of II subject verbs such as **lhinko** "to be fat": **Salhinko** "I am fat", **Chilhinko** "You are fat", **Lhinko** "He is fat, She is fat, It is fat, They are fat", **Polhinko** and **Hapolhinko** "We are fat", **Hachilhinko** "You all are fat". The same prefixes are used to show the object of verbs such as **hayoochi** "to find", as in **Sahayoochi** "He finds me", **Chihayoochi** "He finds you", **Pohayoochi** or **Hapohayoochi** "He finds us", and **Hachihayoochi** "He finds you all". The special first-person II prefixes are used (or, more often, not used) similarly to the equivalent I prefixes.

As already shown, Chickasaw does not distinguish the gender or number of a third-person subject or object of most verbs in simple sentences (but see ¶2.432 below). Any "he" in translations can be replaced by "she" or "they" (or, when appropriate, "it"), just as any "him" can be replaced by "her", "it", or "them". Consequently, the simple sentence **Hayoochi** can be translated into English as "He finds him", "He finds her", "He finds it", "He finds them", "She finds him", "She finds her", "She finds it", "She finds them", "It finds her", "They find it", and so on.

A I prefix comes before a II prefix: **Iichihayoochi** "We find you", **Hashpohayoochi** "You all find us". The combinations of **ish-** and **hash-** plus **sa** are **issa-** and **hassa-** (see ¶2.211): **Issahayoochi** "You find me", **Hassahayoochi** "You all find me".

¶2.221 The initial **i** of a verb stem like **ibishshano** "to have a cold" is lost after a II prefix: **Sabishshano** "I have a cold", **Chibishshano** "You have a cold", **Pobishshano** or **Hapobishshano** "We have colds", **Hachibishshano** "You all have colds".

With verb stems beginning with **a**, such as **abika** "to be sick", the prefix is added to the word between the initial **a** and the rest of the stem: **Asabika** "I am sick", **Achibika** "You are sick", **Apobika** "We are sick".

An extra **a** appears at the beginning of a verb word with a II prefix whose stem starts with **o**, such as **okcha** "to wake up". Once again, the II prefix follows this **a**, but its vowel drops before the **o** of the verb stem: **Achokcha** "You wake up" (from **a** plus **chi** plus **okcha**, with the **i** of **chi** dropped), **Asokcha** "I wake up", **Apokcha** "We wake up". (Any short vowel is deleted before an added **o** or **a**.)

The **a** added before a verb stem beginning with **a** or **o** is lost when the verb has both a I and a II prefix. Thus **apila** is "to help", **Asapila** is "He helps me", and **Issapila** is "You help me"; **ollali** is "to laugh at", **Achollali** is "He laughs at you", and **Kiichollali** is "We laugh at you".

The two II prefixes beginning with **ha**, **hapo-** and **hachi-**, are only used at the beginning of a word. When another prefix or other part of a word would precede these elements, the simple prefixes **po-** and **chi-** are used. Thus, these two **ha** prefixes are never used after a I prefix or with a verb stem beginning with **a** or **o**.

¶2.222 The short verbs **abi** "to kill" and **apa** "to eat" lose their **a** after a II prefix: **Sabi** "He kills me", **Chibi** "He kills you", **Pobi** "He kills us", **Hapopa** "He eats us", **Hachipa** "He eats you all".

Verb stems that begin with **aa** vary according to how they are used with II prefixes. When the initial **aa** is an added locative prefix (¶2.44121), a II prefix follows it: thus, **aafammi** "to whip in (a place)", has forms such as **Aasafammi** "He whips me in it" and **Aachifammi** "He whips you in it". With some verb stems starting with **aa**, such as **aabi** "to paint, put on grease", the II prefix is also added after the **aa**: **Aachibi** "He paints you". With others, such as **aaissachi** "to leave behind", the II prefix appears after an initial **a** and the prefix vowel is lengthened: **Asaaissachi** "He leaves me behind", **Achii-issachi** "He leaves you behind", **Apooissachi** "He leaves us behind". Examples with II prefixes are included in the dictionary entries for all such verb stems to show how each one works. (Once again, ha- prefixes are not used after **aa**.)

A few verb stems beginning with **ho**, such as **hottopa** "to hurt", irregularly drop this syllable after a II prefix: **Sattopa** "I hurt", **Chittopa** "You hurt", **Pottopa** "We hurt". Dialect variation affects such forms: some speakers say **ittopa** instead of **hottopa**, and others use **holhpokonna** in place of **ilhpokonna** "to dream".

¶2.23 The Chickasaw III prefixes are complexes of pronominal elements plus the dative prefix im- (¶2.44122). A prefix from this set replaces the dative prefix on such words to indicate a non-third-person. At the beginning of a word, before a vowel or the consonants **b** or **p**, these prefixes have the following forms:

1sg.	2sg.	1pl.	1spl.	2pl.
am-	chim-	pom-	hapom-	hachim-

The pronominal portions of these prefixes (before the **m**) are identical to the II prefixes, except in the first-person singular, where **a-** appears instead of **sa-**. Once again, the "special" first-person prefixes are rare.

Verb stems that are used with III prefixes are listed in the dictionary with the dative prefix im- attached. An example is the III subject verb **imalhchiba** "to be slow", which has the forms **Amalhchiba** "I am slow", **Chimalhchiba** "You are slow", **Imalhchiba** "He is slow, She is slow, They are slow", and **Pomalhchiba** "We are slow". III prefixes also may express the object of a verb stem like **imanompoli** "to talk to": **Amanompoli** "He talks to me", **Imanompoli** "He talks to him, They talk to her", **Hachimanompoli** "He talks to you all".

¶2.231 The dative prefix im- and the III agreement prefixes vary according to what follows them. Before **t**, **ch**, and **k**, the **m** of these prefixes becomes **n** (with **nch** and **nk** pronounced as in English words such as _bench_ and _bank_). Thus, **intakho'bi** "to be lazy" includes **in**, a form of the dative prefix, and takes III prefixes: **Antakho'bi** "I am lazy", **Chintakho'bi** "You are lazy". Before all other consonants, the vowel of the prefix plus the **m** is replaced by the corresponding nasal vowel. **Ihollo** "to love", which includes the **i-** form of the dative prefix, for example, is used in sentences like **Ahollo** "He loves me", **Pohollo** "He loves us", and **Hachihollo** "He loves you all".

Like a II prefix, a III prefix appears after a I prefix on a verb: **Ishpomanompoli** "You talk to us", **Iichihollo** "We love you". Prefixes beginning with ha- are not used after another prefix. After a I prefix (or an N prefix; see ¶2.241), the first singular prefix am- (an-, **a**-) becomes **sam**- (san-, **sa**-). As described above, ish- and hash- become is- and has- before the **s** of this prefix: **Hassamanompoli** "You all talk to me", **Issahollo** "You love me".

xxix

In general, III prefixes can be used to mark a non-third-person dative only if the dative prefix comes at the beginning of the verb stem (¶2.44122). However, a III prefix may either precede or follow the locative prefix **aa-** (¶2.44121).

No Chickasaw verb word can have both a II prefix and a III prefix at the same time.

¶2.232 When a dative prefix is used on a word beginning with a short vowel plus **b** plus another vowel, an **m** is added before the **b**. For example, **abi** "to kill" has the dative prefix stem **imambi** "to kill for"; **ibishshano** "to have a cold" is related to **imimbishshano** "to have a cold for". This rule does not affect verb stems beginning with a long vowel plus **b**: **aabi** "to paint", **imaabi** "to paint for".

When a dative prefix is added to a short verb beginning with **a**, the resulting derived stem always has two consonants after the **a**. With **imambi** "to kill" the added **m** provides the extra consonant; with other short verbs, the verb's consonant is doubled: **imalla** "to arrive for", **imammo** "to mow for", **imanni** "to pour for", **imappa** "to eat for", **imayya** "to eat for".

Usually a dative prefix has a nasalized vowel before **m**: **i̱malli** "to jump for". However, in a few verb stems, such as **immi** "to belong to", the dative prefix appears as **im** before **m**.

¶2.24 The Chickasaw N prefixes are used on verbs with the hypothetical prefix **ik-**. The N prefixes are complexes of pronominal plus hypothetical elements. A prefix from this set replaces the hypthetical prefix to indicate certain non-third-persons.

1sg.	2sg.	1pl.	1spl.	2pl.
ak-	chik-	kil- / kii-	kiloo-	hachik-

The pronominal portions of most of these prefixes are similar to those in the III prefixes. The first-person plural N prefixes look like I prefixes, however. As with the I prefixes, **kil-** is used before a vowel and **kii-** before a consonant. However, unlike the first-person plural I prefixes, the first-person plural N prefixes always start with **k-**.

¶2.241 The most common use of the N prefixes is on negative forms of verbs that mark their subjects with I markers in the non-negative. In addition to the **ik-** hypothetical prefix, all negative verbs include a negative suffix **-o**, before which the final vowel of the verb stem is deleted. Here are some examples of the use of N prefixes, using the verb stem **malli** "to jump" in its negative stem form **ikmallo**: **Akmallo** "I don't jump", **Chikmallo** "You don't jump", **Kiimallo** (or **Kiloomallo**) "We don't jump", **Hachikmallo** "You all don't jump".

When a verb stem ends with a single consonant plus a vowel, a glottal stop (') is added before that consonant in the negative: **halili** "to touch" has the negative stem **ikhali'lo** and derived forms like **Akhali'lo** "I don't touch it" and **Chikhali'lo** "You don't touch it".

A long (non-nasalized) vowel is shortened before a non-final ': thus, hayoochi "to find" has negative forms Ikhayo'cho "He doesn't find it", Chikhayo'cho "You don't find him", and so on. Phonetically, this shortening is somewhat variable, but there is no contrast between phonetically long and short vowels before non-final '. (The example shows that although ch is written with two letters, it is a single Chickasaw sound, so a ' must be added before the ch in the negative.)

When a verb stem ends with a vowel plus mb, mp, nt, nch, or nk, its negative forms have a nasalized vowel plus ' plus b, p, t, ch, or k. Impa is "to eat"; "He doesn't eat" is Iki'po; konta is "to whistle"; Akko'to is "I don't whistle".

A few verbs, such as tikbayka "to be a dance leader", include the diphthong ay before their (single) final consonant. In negative forms of these verbs, ' is added before the final consonant k: Iktikbay'ko "He is not a dance leader". However, a double yy before a final vowel counts as a sequence of two consonants, so no ' is used: thus, kayyo is "to be full, satisfied" and Ikkayyo is "He isn't full".

The dative prefix im- and all II and III object prefixes follow N prefixes: Ikihollo "He doesn't love him", Ikchihollo "He doesn't love you"; Akchihayo'cho "I don't find you". The first-person III prefix becomes sam- after an N prefix: Iksamanompo'lo "He doesn't talk to me", Chiksahollo "You don't love me". The a before II prefixes in verbs whose stem begins with a or o is lost after an N prefix: Kiichipi'lo "We don't help you", Chikpollo'lo "You don't laugh at us".

The examples presented so far have only illustrated negatives of verbs that indicate their subjects with I affixes. The negative of verbs that are used with II or III subject prefixes is made in a similar way, using ik- and -o. Thus, the negative stem of ibishshano is ikibishsha'no, the negative stem of abika is ikabi'ko, and the negative stem of imalhchiba is ikimalhchi'bo. But these negative stems are not used with the N prefixes. Instead, the regular II and III prefixes follow ik- in the negative of such verbs: Iksabishsha'no "I don't have a cold", Ikchibishsha'no "You don't have a cold"; Iksabi'ko "I'm not sick", Ikchibi'ko "You're not sick"; Iksamalhchi'bo "I'm not slow", Ikpomalhchi'bo "We're not slow".

¶2.242 Short verbs that lose their initial a after a I prefix also lose it after an N prefix: Ikbo "He didn't kill him", Aklo "I didn't arrive", Hachikpo "You all didn't eat it".

Most accented verbs are grades derived from simpler unaccented verb stems (see ¶2.6 below), but there are a few verb stems that always have an accent. Most grades are not used in the negative but are replaced by the negative of the corresponding unaccented verb stem: thus, the negative of ithána "to know" is ikitha'no. When an accented verb without a corresponding unaccented stem is used in the negative, no ' is added to it. Thus, íla is "to be different" and "It's not different" is Ikílo.

The negative of most verb stems is formed regularly according to the rules above and consequently is not given in the dictionary. Negative stems are listed only when they are irregular or when they have an unexpected meaning. Negative stems that are irregular or have an unexpected meaning appear in the dictionary with hypothetical **ik-** and the negative suffix **-o**.

¶2.243 N prefixes are also used on hypothetical verb words, which contain ik- but neither -o nor the inserted ' that goes with -o. Hypotheticals are translated with "let" and have a final '. Thus, **Ikhayoochi'!** means "Let him find it!", **Iksahopoba'!** is "Let me be hungry!", **Akchimanompoli'!** is "Let me talk to you!", and **Kiimalli'!** means "Let's jump!" Some speakers use a plain final vowel: **Ikhayoochi!, Akchimanompoli!, Iksahopoba!, Kiimalli!** There are no hypothetical verb words beginning with **chik-** or **hachik-**.

¶2.25 Verb stems that contain the reciprocal prefix itti- may be inflected in two ways. A reciprocal verb stem like **ittihayoochi** "to find each other" may take I and N prefixes as expected: **Ilittihayoochi** "We find each other", **Hashittihayoochi** "You all find each other", **Ikittihayo'cho** "They don't find each other", and so on. Alternatively (and in fact more commonly) the verb stem may use IR inflection, in which the **it** of the reciprocal prefix is deleted after the I or N prefix: **Iitihayoochi** "We find each other", **Hashtihayoochi** "You all find each other", **Iktihayo'cho** "They don't find each other". (A dative prefix used on a reciprocal stem may also form a similar combination, **inti-**.) The type of agreement used is indicated in the dictionary for all verb stems beginning with **itti-**.

¶2.26 Possession is marked on nouns using the same three sets of prefixes described in ¶2.21-¶2.23; cf. ¶1.42. (The N and IR prefixes are never used to indicate possession. Third-person plural **hoo-** [¶2.432] is not used on possessed nouns.)

¶2.261 Nouns referring to body parts and family members generally express possession with II prefixes agreeing with their possessor. **Foni'** means "bone" or "his bone, her bone, its bone, their bone"; "my bone" is **safoni'**; and "your bone" is **chifoni'**. II prefixes follow the same rules on nouns as on verbs: **ishki'** "mother, his mother", **poshki'** "our mother"; **oshi'** "son, his son", **asoshi'** "my son".

¶2.262 Most other nouns, and some that semantically would be expected to fall in the II prefix class, have a dative prefix in the possessed form. **Holisso** means "book", while the possessed form, **iholisso** "his book", includes a dative prefix. Non-third-person possessors are shown with III prefixes: "my book" is **aholisso**; "your book", **chiholisso**. Some nouns, such as **inki'** "father, his father", always include a dative prefix.

¶2.263 A few complex derived nominalizations, such as **aaittapiha'** "group; descendants", indicate possession with I prefixes. Thus **ilaaittapiha'** means "our group, our descendants", and **ishaaittapiha'** means "your group, your descendants". "My group" is **aaittapihali'**—the I suffix -li is added before the ' at the end of the word, if there is one. The kil- and kii- variants of the first-person plural I prefixes are not used to indicate possession.

¶2.264 Possessor nouns (which are always unmarked) precede appropriately marked possessed nouns: **chipota iholisso** "the child's book", **John ishki'**

"John's mother".

¶2.3 Some important phonological rules

There are a number of important phonological rules and processes that affect the pronunciation and often the spelling of Chickasaw words in sentences.

In addition to the rules discussed below, several others are described elsewhere in ¶2. These include the rule by which **sh** becomes **s** before **s** (¶2.211), the rule deleting **a** after a I or N prefix and before a short verb or a II prefix (¶2.212, ¶2.221), the rule deleting any vowel before **a** or **o** (¶2.221), the nasal assimilation rule (¶2.231), the rule adding **m** between a short vowel after a dative prefix and a following **b** (¶2.232), long vowel shortening before non-final **'** (¶2.241), medial **t** deletion (¶2.42), and compounding processes (¶2.542). There are also other Chickasaw rules that we will not discuss here.

¶2.31 The last vowel of a Chickasaw word is generally stressed, unless the word has an accent or is part of certain questions. The strongest stress is on the final word of a phrase or sentence.

¶2.32 According to the H rule, a sequence of a vowel plus **h** before a consonant, especially **b, m, n, l, w,** or **y,** is often (or, for some speakers, usually or always) pronounced like the corresponding long vowel. Thus, for example, **lohmi** "to hide" may sound like **loomi.** We do not write these long vowel variants of such Chickasaw verb stems in this dictionary, because the negative of these stems shows that they end in two consonants plus a vowel—the negative of **lohmi** is **iklohmo** (occasionally pronounced as **ikloomo**), with no added **'**. In contrast, a verb like **toomi** "to shine", contains a long vowel and is never pronounced with an **h**; the negative of **toomi** is **ikto'mo.**

¶2.33 There are two types of Chickasaw verb stems that end in **lli.** Some such verb stems, many of which have related forms containing the sound **t,** often sound as if they end in **tli** (this may sound more like *dli*). For instance, **lhayilli** "to wet (something)", related to **lhayita** "to be wet", is sometimes pronounced as **lhayitli.** Other Chickasaw verb stems ending in **lli,** such as **palli** "to be hot", are never pronounced with **tli.** In order to distinguish these two types of **lli** verb stems, we list a variant with **tli** for all verb stems of the first type.

In grades where a nasalized vowel precedes the **lli** (see ¶2.63 and ¶2.64 below), the **lli**'s in both types of verb stems are pronounced in the same way (with either the **lli** or the **tli** pronounciation), so we give only the **lli** spelling. Similarly, when **ll** occurs in other positions in a word, there is no distinction between **ll** and **tl** pronunciations.

¶2.34 Rhythmic Lengthening is the most important and pervasive rule of Chickasaw phonology.

To see how it operates, start by dividing a word into syllables, each of which begins with a single consonant: for instance, **Lhayita** "It is wet" is syllabified as **lha-yi-ta** (lh is two letters, but it is a single consonant!); **Salhayita** "I am wet" is syllabified as **sa-lha-yi-ta; Hapompoyo** "He looks around" is **ha-**

pom-po-yo; **Hapompoyoli** "I look around" is **ha-pom-po-yo-li**; **Baafa** "He stabs him" is **baa-fa**; **Baafali** "I stab him" is **baa-fa-li**; **Chibaafa** "He stabs you" is **chibaa-fa**; **Toksali** "He works" is **tok-sa-li**; **safoni'** "my bone" is **sa-fo-ni'** and so on. (Recall that letter combinations like lh and sh are single consonants.) Words beginning with vowels have initial syllables beginning with vowels. In the rare case in which two separate vowel sounds come together, the second one begins a new syllable.

Each syllable can be identified as light (a single short vowel or a consonant plus a short vowel) or heavy (a long vowel, a nasalized vowel, or a vowel followed by one or two consonants—any of which may have a preceding consonant). According to the Rhythmic Lengthening rule, the vowel of every second light syllable in a sequence of light syllables (counting from the left) is lengthened unless it is the last syllable in the word. Several of the words above have rhythmically lengthened vowels, which we will write here with italicized capital letters: **lhay*I*ta, salh*A*yita, hapompoy*O*li, saf*O*ni'**. Rhythmically lengthened vowels sound similar to long vowels but are slightly shorter in duration for most speakers.

Although words like **hapompoyo, baafali**, and **toksali** include sequences of two light syllables, the second syllables in those sequences are not lengthened, because they are at the end of the word. However, as **hapompoy*O*li** shows, when a suffix is added such syllables are no longer at the end, so they can be lengthened. In **Hapompoy*O*tok** "He looked around" (which includes the **-tok** suffix, ¶2.461), **Baafal*I*tok** "I stabbed him", and **Toksal*I*li** "I worked" these same vowels are lengthened.

The Rhythmic Lengthening rule is very important, because it causes words that look very similar when they are written, such as **lhayita** and **salhayita**, to be pronounced with a completely different rhythm. Syllables with rhythmically lengthened vowels are heavy syllables, which is important for other phonological rules as well.

Only certain parts of a Chickasaw word may be affected by Rhythmic Lengthening or can be thought of as within the domain of this rule. These include stems, II prefixes, and certain suffixes, especially the first-person singular I suffix -li and -tok (¶2.461), -ta (¶2.481), and -chi (¶2.443). (See also ¶2.67 below.) However, I, III, and N prefixes are not counted as part of sequences of light syllables to which Rhythmic Lengthening can apply, so, for example, the second vowel of a word like **Ishap*I*la** "You help him" will never be lengthened. Instead, the light syllable count begins with the first vowel of the verb stem **apila**. The **ha** at the beginning of the II prefixes **hapo-** and **hachi-** also is not included in the light syllable sequence, so, for example, "We are wet" is pronounced **Hapolh*A*yita**. The applicative prefixes **im-** and **on-** (¶2.44122, ¶2.44126) are also not included in the Rhythmic Lengthening domain. A full list of the suffixes in the Rhythmic Lengthening domain is given at the end of this section.

Rhythmic Lengthening interacts in a complicated way with some rules that delete certain vowels or syllables. For instance, consider a word such as

"You help us", Ishp*O*pila. The stem **apila** "to help" has the II prefix **po-** added after its first **a-**, and the I prefix **ish-** goes at the front: **ish-** plus **a** plus **po-** plus **pila**. The **a** plus **po** sequence is one in which Rhythmic Lengthening can apply, so the **a** of **p*O*** is lengthened. But the first **a** in such a word always drops between a I and a II prefix (¶2.221). When the word is pronounced, then, the first **a** is deleted and the vowel of **po** is lengthened: Ishp*O*pila "You help us". Another such example is iss*A*pila "You help me", in which, in addition to the changes just described, the **sh** of **ish-** becomes **s** before **s** (¶2.211),

Several short verbs (¶2,212) behave exceptionally with regard to the Rhythmic Lengthening rule. The short dative prefix verb **ima** "to give" is an exception to many of the statements above, since, for example, Ish*I*ma "You give it to him" and Im*A*li "I give it to him" are words in which I and III prefixes count as part of the Rhythmic Lengthening sequence of light syllables. Similarly, **ona** "to get there" and **ola** "to crow" both include I and III prefixes in the Rhythmic Lengthening domain (Ish*O*na "You get there", Am*O*la "He crows for me"), although when a I prefix precedes a III prefix, it is not part of the Rhythmic Lengthening sequence (Ishim*O*na "You get there to him"). **Ishi** "to get" also treats an added III prefix as part of the Rhythmic Lengthening domain: Im*I*shi "He gets it for her".

Because the effects of the Rhythmic Lengthening rule are regular, we do not write lengthened vowels in our spelling system, but it is important to keep the rule in mind while pronouncing words. Here is a complete list of the consonant-initial suffixes that are included in the Rhythmic Lengthening domain (such that a preceding even-numbered light syllable vowel will be lengthened, or that their vowel will be lengthened after a preceding odd-numbered light syllable): -chi / -chichi (¶2.443), -ka (¶2.4422), -ka' (¶2.541), -ki- (¶2.482), -li (¶2.21), -li (¶2.4422), -mank*o̱* (¶2.463), -po- (¶2.4421), -ta (¶2.471), -tok (¶2.461), and -tokat / -tok*a̱* / -tokoot / -tok*o̱* (¶2.493). No suffixes beginning with h are included in the Rhythmic Lengthening domain, nor are any noun suffixes (though II prefixes on nouns may trigger the rule). Suffixes whose affixation always produces a heavy syllable, such as -m (¶2.472), -ttook (¶2.461), or -cha (¶2.494), fail to interact with the rule, but it is worth noting that some suffixes that appear quite similar to others in the list above are never included in the Rhythmic Lengthening domain, such as -kat / -k*a̱* (¶2.493), the aforementioned verb suffix -kaash, and a number of verb suffixes with initial h.

¶2.35 According to the rule of Li Deletion, a **li** syllable at the end of a verb stem is deleted between a heavy syllable that includes a long, lengthened, or nasalized vowel or a vowel plus **h** or **'** and a suffix beginning with a single **t, ch,** or **n.** Thus, verb stems like **kooli** "to break", **halili** "to touch" (hal*I*li with lengthening), **tonnon*ó*li** "to roll around", **tasahli** "to yell", and **bo'li** "to hit" lose their final **li** before suffixes like -tok (¶2.461), -ta (¶2.481), -chi (¶2.443), -cha (¶2.494), -na (¶2.494), and -t (¶2.495). For example, **tasahli** has forms such as **Tasahtok** "He yelled" and **Tasahta?** "Is he yelling?". Li Deletion may result in fairly complex consonant sequences: thus **Bó'htok** is "She (finally) laid it down", from **bó'hli**, the ggr. (¶2.61) of **bohli** "to lay down", plus **tok**. The key is that the li syllable in **tasahli**, **bó'hli**, and other verb stems of this type is not rhythmically lengthened, so it is deleted. A lengthened li syllable, in contrast, is not deleted, so the li remains in **Toksalltok** "He worked". Even a non-lengthened **li** is not deleted, however, if it follows a consonant other than **h** or **'**: **Bashlitok** "He cut it".

Li is not always treated in the same way at the end of a given verb stem, depending on the structure of the word in which that stem appears. Thus li is deleted from **halili** "to touch" in **Halitok** "He touched it" but not in **Sahalilitok** "He touched me" (pronounced **sahAlilltok**, with a rhythmically lengthened li syllable). Similarly, although there is no deletion in **Toksalitok**, deletion occurs in the hn-grade of **toksali**, **toksaháli** (¶2.63), as in **Toksahátok** "He worked again and again".

Note that only li syllables at the end of verb stems (often reflecting the v2 formative, ¶2.4422) are affected by Li Deletion. The first-person singular I suffix -**li** (¶2.21) is not affected by this rule, even in a word such as **Pisalitok** "I looked at it" (pronounced **pisAlitok**), where the li is not rhythmically lengthened and appears before **tok**.

Some speakers occasionally fail to apply Li Deletion, but for most it is completely regular. See also ¶2.37.

¶2.36 The Strident-Coronal rule works somewhat like Li Deletion. This rule deletes a non-lengthened vowel (possibly only **a** or **i**) between a single **s**, **sh**, **lh**, or **ch** and a following suffix beginning with **t**, **n**, **l**, or **ch**, either at the end of a word or followed immediately by a vowel. Thus, a vowel is deleted following an **s**, **sh**, **lh**, or **ch** that is preceded by a long, lengthened, or nasalized vowel or a vowel plus **h** or **'**. For instance, the **a** in **hǫsa** "to shoot at" is deleted in a word like **Hǫsli** "I shoot at him"; since it is preceded by a heavy syllable, it is not lengthened.

This rule results in the same sort of alternations that result from Li Deletion. The second **a** in **NalhAtok** "He was shot" is not deleted because it is rhythmically lengthened, but the same vowel is not lengthened, and thus is deleted, in **SanAlhtok** "I was shot".

Most speakers apply the Strident-Coronal rule completely regularly between verb stems and suffixes, and it occasionally seems to have applied within derived words. However, unlike Li Deletion, the Strident-Coronal rule does not apply in the derivation of causative verbs like **hǫsachi** "to make (someone) shoot at". (See also ¶2.37.)

¶2.37 After the Strident-Coronal rule applies, some clusters of **ch** plus a following consonant would be expected, but these are changed to **sht**, **shl**, **shch**, and **shn** by the Ch-Sh rule. For example, **hilhachi** "to make (someone) dance" has forms such as **HilhAshli** "I make him dance", **HilhAshtok** "She made him dance", and **Hilha'shcha** "She made him dance and she..." (this last word includes the suffix -**cha**; see ¶2.494). This rule is completely regular for all speakers. (The only consonant **ch** may occur before is another **ch**, in words whose dictionary entries have a double **chch**, such as **kochcha** "to go out", or in a g-grade (¶2.61), such as fáchcho'pa, the ggr. of fachopa "to be open (of a pocket knife)". A chch sequence is never produced by the Strident-Coronal rule.)

Normally only every other vowel in a sequence of light syllables is rhythmically lengthened, but in one case lengthened vowels can occur in two adjacent syllables. This happens when Li Deletion deletes the li between two light syllables, as in malichi "to drive, make (something or someone) run", from malili "to run" plus the causative suffix -chi (see ¶2.443). The end of malichi sounds similar to the end of toksalichi "to make (someone) work". When another suffix is added, however, the difference is clear. "I make him work" is ToksalIshli (with the Strident-Coronal and Ch-Sh rules applying to the non-lengthened chi syllable), but "I drive it" is MalIchIli. Only some causatives of verb stems ending in -li work in this way. These verb stems are marked [-SC] (indicating that the Strident-Coronal rule does not apply in them) in the dictionary.

¶2.38 The N rule works similarly to the Strident-Coronal rule but is less well understood. This rule deletes a vowel (possibly only i or a) between a single n preceded by a heavy syllable and a following suffix beginning with t or ch, followed by a vowel, as in Hopoontok "She cooked it", a form of hopooni "to cook".

The N rule does not appear to be productive for most speakers.

¶2.39 The HM rule operates in certain suffixed forms of verbs that end in a vowel plus hm plus a vowel or, in a few cases, 'm plus a vowel. In such forms, the vowel before the h or ' is nasalized and the m-plus-vowel is deleted. Thus, for example, the verb yahmi "to do" becomes yah in forms such as Yahtok "He did it" (including -tok, ¶2.461). This rule applies before suffixes that begin with a single coronal consonant, like those listed in ¶2.35. Occasional examples suggest that the rule may sometimes apply before other suffixes as well.

The HM rule is lexically triggered. Some verbs, such as lohmi "to hide (something)", do not show this alternation: Lohmitok "He hid it". Verbs such as yahmi are marked in the dictionary as [+HM], and HM variants such as <yah> are listed, with cross-references.

¶2.4 Verb structure

A Chickasaw verb word may have as many as five or six main parts (and each of these may have several subparts): a preverb (one of the proclitic elements in ¶2.42); one or two agreement prefixes (¶2.43); the verb stem itself (¶2.44); one or two viewpoint suffixes (¶2.45); and one or more tense/aspect and modality suffixes (¶2.46). Thus Ishchissolitok "I hit you with it" is a complete sentence in one verb word with five parts: the instrumental preverb isht-, the second-person singular II agreement prefix chi-, the verb stem isso, the first-person singular I viewpoint suffix -li, and the perfective tense/aspect suffix -tok. The complex verb word Ishchissolitoka "that I hit you with it", as in the sentence Ishchissolitoka ithana "He knows that I hit you with it", has these same five parts plus a final -**a** (or more properly -**ka**) complementizer that shows that this subordinate verb has a different subject from the next verb of its sentence (¶2.493). Dictionary verb entries, in general, include only stems (¶2.44) or preverb stems (combinations of elements from ¶2.42 and ¶2.44). Thus, the verb stem **isso** "to hit" is listed in the dictionary, as is the preverb stem **ishtisso** "to hit with", but the verb words **Ishchissolitok** and **Ishchissolitoka** are not.

Along with ¶2.2, ¶2.3, and ¶2.6, then, this section clarifies the relationships between the verb stems in the dictionary and the ordinary verb words speakers use and the connections among different verb stems. ¶2.41 below covers the use of "bare" verbs, while questions, negatives, and non-main verbs are considered in ¶2.47-.49. (As a careful study of the dictionary entries and the discussion below show, the order of verbal elements we present here is modified in certain cases.)

¶2.41 Sometimes a verb word used in conversation is identical to the verb stem listed in the dictionary. Bare verbs (dictionary stems used alone) are used for many neutral affirmative statements. A bare verb, or a bare verb with an agreement marker from ¶2.2, can express an ongoing action or state or convey a habitual or generic statement. In many cases, a bare verb can also refer to an event in the recent past.

Bare verbs are also used for affirmative imperatives, as in **Malli!** "Jump!". Such imperatives may have object prefixes, but never subject prefixes. (Some speakers use a prefix **ho-** for imperatives with a plural subject. Other types of imperatives are described in ¶2.484 and ¶2.496.)

Bare verbs are also used in certain complex constructions (¶2.49).

In the Choctaw language, which is very similar to Chickasaw, the verbs we describe here as "bare" (and any verbs that would end in a final vowel in Chickasaw) have a suffix -**h**. It is likely that this suffix was once also used in Chickasaw, since some Chickasaw speakers occasionally add a final -**h** to vowel-final or bare verbs, and an -**h** occasionally appears between two vowels in strings of suffixes that may originally have been sequences of separate words. There is similar evidence that nouns that are pronounced today as vowel-final may originally have also ended in h (¶2.511), as do many of the corresponding Choctaw nouns. An alternative analysis of Chickasaw would thus have been to write all words that appear here as vowel-final with final **h**. We have chosen an analysis and spelling that more closely reflect speakers' pronunciation.

¶2.42 Preverbs are used at the beginning of many Chickasaw verbs. Chickasaw has an instrumental preverb and five directional preve⁻bs. All preverbs end in the participial suffix -**t** (¶2.495; complete etymologies are in the dictionary) and, like other participles, may be said as separate words. Usually they are pronounced and written as one word with the verbs (including all agreement prefixes) they precede. Preverbs that end in **sht** lose their -**t** before a following consonant.

¶2.421 The instrumental preverb **isht** is used in verb stems such as **ishtisso** "to hit with", as in **Ishtishisso** "You hit him with it" or **Ishtakisso** "I don't hit him with it". The final -t of **isht** drops before a consonant: **Ishchikisso** "You don't hit him with it". In turn, the **sh** of **ish** becomes **s** before another **s**: **Issasso** "He hits me with it". (**Issasso** also means "You hit me". Perhaps because of this ambiguity in the interpretation of verbs starting with **issa-**, some speakers do not apply the **sh** to **s** rule in instrumental verbs, and thus would pronounce "He hits me with it" as **Ishsasso**.)

Verb stems with **isht** generally have one more argument (person or thing involved with the action) than the corresponding verb stem without **isht**. Usually, this added argument is the instrument with which the action named by the verb is performed, but there are several additional unexpected uses of **isht**. With verbs of communication, **isht** means "about", as in **ishtanompoli** "to talk about". A verb of motion with a preceding **isht** means "bring" or "take": **isht** plus **aya** "to go" is "to take".

Any object used with an **isht** verb word is indicated with a prefix on the verb stem following **isht**: **Ishtachinompoli** "He talks about you"; **Ishtapoya** "She takes us"; **Ishtimanompoli** "He talks to her about it". "About" objects and other objects added because of the presence of **isht** are marked with II prefixes.

Verb stems with **isht** usually have meanings that can easily be predicted from those of the verb without **isht**, but in a few cases these meanings are unexpected. In some cases, the verb stem cannot be used without **isht**.

¶2.422 The five directional preverbs add generally adverbial notions to the verb stems that follow them but do not involve the addition of extra arguments. **Osht** and the much rarer **asht** specify action performed in the direction of the speaker (and for this reason are often avoided with a first-person subject). **Pit**, in contrast, specifies action performed in a direction away from or emanating from the speaker (and for this reason is common or preferred on verb words with a first-person subject). **Oot** usually means "to go and —", while the rarer **at** usually means "to come and —", although these meanings may vary with certain verb stems.

Like **isht**, the directional preverbs precede any prefixes on the verbs that follow them. **Osht** and **asht** change before consonants, losing their final **t** as **isht** does.

The use of **osht, pit**, and **oot** is extremely productive, and we are sure not all verb stems that can be used with these preverbs are included in the dictionary. **At** probably can be used with more verb stems than those we list. **Asht** occurs only with a few intransitive verbs of motion.

¶2.423 The preverb is always first in a verb word. There is no evidence that any of the directional preverbs can co-occur with each other, but **isht** may rarely appear after a directional preverb.

¶2.43 Agreement prefixes and the hypothetical prefix **ik-** follow the preverb in a verb word.

¶2.431 First come the I or N prefixes or the hypothetical prefix **ik-** (¶2.21, ¶2.24; see ¶2.48 below for more about negative verb words). The IR variants of the I prefixes (¶2.25) combine in a special way with the reciprocal prefix **itti-** (¶2.4411 below).

¶2.432 As noted in ¶2.2, there are no I, II, III, or N affixes that specifically indicate that a verb word has a third-person subject (or object). However, the **hoo-** prefix may be added to a verb word with a third-person plural subject (regardless of its agreement class): **Hoohilha** "They are dancing" (I subject verb), **Hoolhinko** "They are fat" (II subject verb), **Hoointakho'bi** "They are lazy" (III subject verb). **Hoo-** follows the hypothetical prefix **ik-**: **Ikhoohi'lho** "They aren't dancing".

The exact discourse constraints on the use of **hoo-** are not yet well understood. **Hoo-** interacts in different ways with participle-plus-verb constructions (¶2.495).

¶2.433 The II and III prefixes come next, whether they are used to express subjects or objects. (Sections ¶2.22 and ¶2.23 explain how these sets of prefixes combine with different sorts of verb words.) **Ikhoosapi'so** "They don't see me" is an example of a verb word with **ik-**, **hoo-**, and a II prefix.

¶2.44 Next comes the verb stem. There are two types of verb stems, basic stems and derived stems. The basic stem (¶2.442) is a complete verb stem by itself. Prefixes (¶2.441) or a suffix (¶2.443) may be added to it to form more complex derived stems. All recorded examples of each type of stem are included in the dictionary.

¶2.441 Two types of prefixes are used in derived verb stems. The order in which they are presented below is typical, but there are a number of cases in which it is reversed.

¶2.4411 The reflexive prefix is **ili-**, and the reciprocal prefix is **itti-**: combined with **pisa** "to look at, see", these give **ilipisa** "to look at oneself" and **ittipisa** "to look at each other". Chickasaw verb stems with either of these prefixes use I inflection for non-third-person subjects and generally have one fewer argument than the corresponding stem without the prefix.

Sometimes speakers avoid reflexive verb words because they sound similar to "we" subject verbs with the I prefix **il-**: thus, **Ilollali** can mean either "We laugh at him" or "He laughs at himself". Verb stems that start with a vowel followed by a single consonant, however, have a pronunciation difference between these forms: **Ilapila** "We help him" is pronounced **ilap͞Ila** (because its il-, the I prefix, is not part of the rhythmic lengthening sequence), while reflexive **Ilapila** "He helps himself" is pronounced **il͞Apila** (because its il-, from the reflexive prefix ili-, is part of the rhythmic lengthening sequence).

A preceding I or N prefix may combine with reciprocal **itti-** as a IR prefix (¶2.25). Some verb stems containing itti-, such as **ittihaalalli** "to marry", may take II object prefixes, but this is not true of verb stems containing ili-. Dative **im-** or a III prefix (or its IR variant) may precede either prefix, as in **imilipilachi** "to send oneself to", but see ¶2.44122.

Not all verb stems may be used with the reflexive and reciprocal prefixes, and verbs with these prefixes sometimes have unexpected meanings. A few

xl

verbs have irregular reflexive or reciprocal stems.

¶2.4412 There are several applicative prefixes that can be added to other verb stems to derive new verb stems that, like those containing the instrumental preverb isht- (¶2.421), generally have one more argument than the original verb stem. Occasionally more than one of these prefixes can occur in a single derived stem.

With one exception (¶2.44121), agreement prefixes always precede the applicative prefixes. There are occasional irregularities of form and meaning in the use of these prefixes that are indicated in the dictionary entries.

¶2.44121 The general locative prefix aa- is added to a verb stem for which a third-person locative or source argument is specified: hilha "to dance", aahilha "to dance in, at"; fammi "to whip", aafammi "to whip in, at"; ikbi "to make", aaikbi "to make from".

Aa- precedes a II or, usually, a III prefix on the verb word: Aasafammi "He whips me in it", Aa-antaloowa "She sings to me in it" (¶2.222, ¶2.44122).

Since aa- precedes a II prefix and a I prefix precedes aa-, we might guess that a sentence such as "You whip me there" would begin with a sequence of ish- plus aa- plus sa-. However, most speakers put such prefixes together with familiar combinations like issa- for ish- plus sa- (¶2.211, ¶2.22), giving Issaafammi.

There is an unexpected and as yet poorly understood non-locative use of aa- on verbs with the conjunctive suffixes -cha and -na (¶2.494) translated with "when", as in Ishaano'scha yaalitok "When you went to sleep I cried". Such verbs do not have an added locative argument.

In a few verb stems aa- is replaced by aay- or ay-.

¶2.44122 The dative prefix im- (or in- or i-, depending on what follows) generally marks either subjects or objects in a variety of semantic roles. Non-third-person datives are marked with III prefixes (¶2.23), with the dative or III prefix changing according to the first sound of the following verb stem, as described in ¶2.231.

There are several types of Chickasaw verb stems with dative prefixes. The dative prefix may appear on a verb that could also be used on its own to refer to performing the same action "to" or "for" someone. For instance, anompoli means "to talk", and imanompoli is "to talk to". Other verb stems, such as intakho'bi "to be lazy" and ihollo "to love", always occur with their dative prefix. Verb stems of both types are listed in the dictionary with their dative prefixes.

Dative prefixes are also used on verbs in Possessor Raising and Object Possessor Raising structures. Such dative prefix forms are listed in the dictionary with cross-references to the non-raised verb stem. The dative prefix is always the first element of derived raising verb stems. Thus, for example, the Object Possessor Raising form of ibaafokhi "to put in with" is imimbaafokhi, with im- added at the beginning of the verb (m is added between the i and b of ibaa, as discussed in ¶2.232).

Another prefix may precede the dative prefix in verbs such as ilimpilachi "to send to oneself" (with reflexive ili, ¶2.4411), **ibaainchompa** "to buy for (someone) with" (with comitative ibaa-, ¶2.44123), and **aaintaloowa** "to sing to (someone) in" (with locative **aa**, ¶2.44121).

A III prefix can be used with the verb stem to show a non-third-person dative only when the dative prefix im- comes first in the derived stem, except when the preceding element is locative aa-. Thus a III prefix can be used with a verb like **imanompoli** "to talk to" or **ihollo** "to love" or with a derived Object Possessor Raising verb such as **imimbaafokhi** (in all of which the dative prefix comes first) or with **aaintaloowa** (where the dative prefix follows aa-) , but not with verbs such as **ilimpilachi** or **ibaainchompa**, in which another element precedes the dative prefix. The dictionary gives examples of the use of such verbs.

¶2.44123 The comitative prefix is **ibaa-**, as in **ibaahilha** "to dance with". The comitative "with" argument is indexed with a II prefix: **Sabaahilha** "He dances with me".

With most transitive verbs, the comitative argument performs the action with the subject: thus, the dictionary definition of **ibaanalhlhi** is "to shoot (someone) with (a co-subject°)", indicating that the added noun indexed with the II prefix shoots along with the subject. (¶1.41 explains the use of the ° symbol.) With some verbs, however, the comitative argument is a co-object: thus, **ibaatoksalichi** means "to make (someone) work with (a co-object°)", indicating that the added noun indexed with the II prefix is made to work along with the other object.

¶2.44124 The "from" prefix **imaa-** indicates a human source, as in **hobachi** "to copy", **imaahobachi** "to copy from". The "from" argument is indicated with a III prefix: **Amaahobachi** "He copies from me".

¶2.44125 The **okaa-** prefix indicates a third-person "into" or "in" argument, as in **malli** "to jump", **okaamalli** "to jump into"; **hilichi** "to stand (something) up", **okaahilichi** "to stand (something) up in". A II prefix used with such a verb stem precedes okaa-: **Asokaahilichi** "He stands me up in it".

¶2.44126 The **on-** prefix indicates an "on" argument, as in **apa** "to eat (something)", **onapa** "to eat on". On- varies in pronunciation depending on the following verb stem similarly to the dative prefix (see ¶2.231): **bínni'li** "to sit", **ombínni'li** "to sit on"; **kahli** "to put (two things) down", **onkahli** "to put (two things) down on"; **hika** "to step", **ohika** "to step on"; **omalli** "to jump on".

A human argument indexed by on- is often translated by "in the direction of" or "about": **habishko** "to sneeze", **ohabishko** "to sneeze at, in the direction of"; **loshka** "to tell a lie", **oloshka** "to lie about". This argument is indicated by a II prefix: **Asoloshka** "He lies about me".

In a few cases the on- argument is a subject: **onna** "to dawn", **ononna** "to have it get to be dawn on one, to stay out all night".

¶2.44127 There is an additional applicative prefix **a-**, which occurs in many verb stems in the dictionary but is seldom added productively to a basic stem. The most easily described use of a- is to mean "against" in verb stems such as

apiichiffi "to throw (something) against (something), making it splat", from **pichiffi** "to make (something) splat" (the change of **i** to **ii** here is typical).

As explained in ¶2.221, **a-** precedes the II prefixes.

¶2.442 The basic stem of a Chickasaw verb is the smallest part of it that can be used alone with all the derivational prefixes and suffixes removed. Some basic stems cannot be analyzed further, but many are related to other basic stems in regular ways. There are three important types of basic stem internal structure.

¶2.4421 Many basic stems contain prefix formatives, elements that cannot be used alone or freely added to existing verb stems but that have consistent meaning, such as **bak-** (referring to the head or face), **chok-** (referring to the mouth or head), **nok-** (referring to the throat or emotions), **osh-** (referring to the head or hair), **tok-** or **tak-** (referring to the mouth or lips), **yak-** (meaning "this"), **yok-** or **ok-** (referring to water; from **oka'** "water"), and **ok-** or **okk-** (meaning "sideways"; perhaps connected with **okaa-** "into", ¶2.44125). These prefix formatives have a modifying or adverbial meaning in verb stems such as **nokshila** "to be hoarse", from **nok-** plus **shila** "to be dry", or **okkawaatali** "to put across sideways", from **okk-** plus **awaatali** "to put across". In some cases, the part of the verb stem following the prefix formatives cannot occur by itself.

Another basic stem formative that is more difficult to understand is **-po-**, which appears to convey a certain affective intensity. This formative is not always a prefix but appears at different points in the verb structure.

¶2.4422 Verb pair relationships are also part of basic stem structure. The first member of a verb pair, known as the v1, usually ends in **a**, while the second, the v2, usually ends in **li**. (In some verbs, the mark of the v1 is **ka**, not **a**.) In addition, or alternatively, the v1 may include an **l** (which may convey a passive meaning), usually after its first vowel. The v2 is usually, though not always, used with one more argument than the v1. The relationship between the two verbs is sometimes causative. Here are some examples of v1-v2 pairs:

albi "to be painted"	**aabi** "to paint"
basha "to be operated on"	**bashli** "to cut"
chokma "to be good"	**chokmali** "to improve"
fokha "to be in"	**fokhi** "to put in"
ishtanompa "to be said about"	**ishtanompoli** "to talk about"
kola "to be dug"	**kolli** "to dig"
talakchi "to be tied"	**takchi** "to tie"

As these examples show, there may also be changes in vowels between the v1 and the v2.

In addition, there are several other regular changes. The v1 formative **l** appears as **lh** when it comes before **ch**, **f**, **k**, **p**, or **t**. After **b**, **f**, **lh**, **m**, **n**, or **w**, the **l** of **li** changes into a copy of this preceding consonant. Before **li**, **p** becomes **b** and **t** becomes **l** (though see ¶2.33 above). Here are some more examples:

alhtoba "to be paid"	atobbi "to pay"
bashafa "to be cut"	bashaffi "to cut"
lhakófa "to be one left"	lhakóffi "to be safe"
lhatapa "to spill"	lhatabli "to spill"
nalha "to be shot"	nalhlhi "to shoot"
olhchi "to be drawn (of water)"	oochi "to draw (water)"
olhkomo "to be mixed"	okommo "to mix"
tiwa "to open (of a door)"	tiwwi "to open (a door)"
wakaa "to fly"	wakiili "to make fly"

Usually the causative suffix -chi cannot be added to either a v1 or v2. Sometimes, however, a v2 may include -chi along with a form of the v2 ending:

falama "to go back"	falammichi "to take back"

A cross-reference to a verb's v1 or v2 is given along with other related words in {}'s following the verb's dictionary definition. Occasionally, a given v2 may be associated with two different v1's.

¶2.4423 Most Chickasaw verb stems do not change to show that their subjects or objects are singular (sg.) or plural (pl.), although the agreement markers with which they are used may change, but some indicate these differences with changes in the basic stem. For example, some singular v1's replace their last syllable with hli to indicate a plural subject: kinafa "to fall, be cut down (sg.)", kinahli "to fall, be cut down (pl.)". Often verb stems with plural arguments are shorter than those referring to singulars: achoosholi "to stick in (sg. object)", achoshli "to stick in (pl. object)". In some cases, there is no apparent relationship between the verb stems at all: kanchi "to sell, throw away (sg. object)", fimmi "to throw away (dl. object)", lhatabli "to throw away (tpl. object)". As this example shows, verb stems may vary not only for singular (exactly one) versus plural (two or more) but also for singular versus dual (dl., exactly two) versus triplural (tpl., three or more). The dictionary gives many examples of verb stems with different forms for different numbers of arguments.

¶2.443 The regular causative suffix in Chickasaw is -chi. This suffix may be added to many Chickasaw verb stems, both transitives (verb stems with an object) and intransitives, although not, in most cases, the v1's and v2's described in ¶2.4422. Normal causatives have one more argument than the corresponding non-causative stem. Their subject is marked with a I affix and their object with either II or III, depending on the type of agreement used for the subject of the original verb stem. Alternatively, II or III agreement on a -chi causative verb may indicate an object of the original verb stem, with the subject of that verb stem (the causee) indicated by a non-agreeing third-person nominal.

Causatives of a few verb stems whose next-to-last syllable is heavy have the suffix -chichi rather than -chi.

In a few cases, the causative suffix appears to be added to a noun rather than a verb stem, as with pinha' "seed for planting", pinhachi "to save as seed for planting" and salhkona "guts", salhkonachi "to gut". There are other cases where the addition of -chi does not seem to have a causative meaning, as with apilachi "to assist", related to apila "to help".

¶2.45 There are three viewpoint suffixes in Chickasaw, which come between the verb stem and the tense/aspect and modality suffixes.

¶2.451 The diminutive suffix -a'si (occasionally -o'si) is used on verb words with a diminutive subject, at the speaker's option in appropriate discourse contexts. The use of this suffix is more common among female speakers.

A few verbs , such as iskanno'si "to be little" and tilofa'si "to be short", include the diminutive suffix as part of their derived stem, in all contexts for most speakers, so this suffix is included on the dictionary entries for such verb stems. Normally, however, the use of diminutive stems is highly context-specific, and speakers' judgments about appropriate uses vary widely. In general, then, we do not list diminutive stems of verbs in the dictionary.

The two main processes that refer to verb stems and that might help to clarify whether -a'si should be included as part of the stem are negative stem formation (¶2.241) and grade formation (¶2.6), but these processes differ somewhat in their treatment of the diminutive suffix.

It is extremely rare for negatives to include the diminutive suffix (most verbs that include diminutives use periphrastic negation with ki'yo, ¶2.481), but when they do, negative -o follows the diminutive (which always appears as -o's-), so the diminutive should be considered part of the derived stem. Thus, for instance, Ikcha'ho'so means "He's not too tall", from chaaha "to be tall", and ikhi'lho'so is the negative diminutive of hilha "to dance" (note that the negative stems contain an added ' in the usual position).

Grade formation never includes the diminutive. A verb that includes a diminutive suffix in its dictionary stem entry loses the diminutive in all grades, so the n-grade of iskanno'si, for example, is iskánno.

¶2.452 The second suffix in this category is the first-person singular I suffix -li (¶2.21), which follows the diminutive suffix. Like the diminutive suffix, -li is not included in the stem for grade formation: Talohówali "I sing all the time", Hihílhli "I dance all the time" (hn-grades, ¶2.63; the Strident-Coronal rule applies in the second word). (Of course, -li does not appear with negative verbs.)

¶2.453 The negative suffix -o is also a viewpoint suffix, since, like the other two suffixes in this category, -o is added to verb stems (as in words with the diminutive suffix, the resulting words may be thought of as a type of derived stem), preceding all other suffixes in the verb word. As described in ¶2.241, negative stems in -o are used with N prefixes. Combinations of negative stems with following suffixes are described in ¶2.48.

¶2.46 Each of the tense/aspect and modality endings in this section can be used alone following a Chickasaw verb stem (with or without a preverb, prefixes, and a viewpoint suffix) in a main clause verb word. The standard tense/aspect endings in ¶2.461 and the standard modal endings in ¶2.4621 can, in addition, be combined with other endings in this section and in ¶2.47-¶2.49.

¶2.461 There are two standard tense/aspect suffixes in Chickasaw. They do not co-occur. These two suffixes may be seen as opposed to the lack of a suffix (or the presence of a zero suffix). As described in ¶2.41, verbs without a tense/aspect suffix refer to the present or to the recent past.

The perfective -tok suffix has a complex aspectual meaning that is difficult to pin down. Explicitly active verbs referring to events in the (relatively recent) past usually include -tok. On stative verbs, however, -tok does not necessarily suggest a reference to the past. The use of this suffix seldom seems to be required with affirmative verb words, except when the clause contains the adverb oblaashaash "yesterday".

The -ttook suffix refers to the remote past, any time from some years before the present back to mythic time.

These two suffixes may be combined with standard modal suffixes (¶2.4621) and with the evidential modal suffixes (¶2.464). They are also used in negative and non-main verb words (¶2.48, ¶2.49).

¶2.462 The standard Chickasaw modals all contain the sequence a'. There are three principal suffixes that can be combined with various other suffixes and several less common suffixes. Because these suffixes start with a, they usually condition the deletion of any preceding vowel (¶2.221).

¶2.4621 The three main modal suffixes are -a'chi, -a'ni, and -a'hi. Incompletive -a'chi is used on all normal futures: Hilha'chi "He will dance". Potential -a'ni appears on statements of possibility and, occasionally, ability: Hilha'ni "He may dance". Convictional -a'hi is relatively uncommon in simple sentences but is used on statements reflecting the speaker's firm belief rather than sure knowledge, generally about the future.

One of the standard tense/aspect suffixes (¶2.461) may appear after any of these modals, altering the time reference of the modal statement, as in Hilha'chitok "He would have danced (but he didn't get the chance)", Hilha'ntok "He could have danced (but he didn't show up)", Hilha'hitok "He should have danced (it was his duty)". (The Strident-Coronal rule (¶2.36) does not apply to the suffix -a'chi, as shown in the complex modal suffix -a'chitok, for example. This fact indicates a complex analysis for this suffix, with a probable derivation from non-occurring <-a'li> (an actual suffix in Choctaw) plus -chi. The word Hilha'ntok illustrates the operation of the N rule (¶2.38).) In addition, the standard modals may appear before the evidential tense suffix (¶2.463), the evidential modal suffixes (¶2.464), and the other suffixes in ¶2.47-¶2.49.

Epistemic modal statements indicating a conclusion or deduction by the speaker (most often translated into English with "must") are formed with

-ha'ni added to a complete statement ending in a bare verb, a modal, or tense/aspect -tok or -ttook. After a consonant this suffix is -a'ni, homophonous with and perhaps the same as the potential suffix (see the discussion of h in ¶2.41). Here are some examples of epistemic modal sentences: **Hilhaha'ni** "He/they/people must be dancing (I can hear the music)", **Hilhatoka'ni** "He must have danced", **Hilhattooka'ni** "He must have danced long ago", **Hilha'chitoka'ni** "I guess he was supposed to dance, It must have been the case that he would have danced (if given the chance)", **Ikayyokitoka'ni** "He must not have gone", **Hilha'chiha'ni** "They must be going to dance (I can see everything set up)", **Akhi'lhokísha'chiha'ni** "I might not have danced yet (at that future time)".

¶2.4622 There are a number of additional less common modal suffixes. -A'cho is a stronger variant of -a'chi (possibly expressing a promise about the future). -A'shki is translated with "should" or "must". This suffix is used to express strong commands (which, however, always have a second-person subject prefix). Unlike the -a' modals in ¶2.4621, these two suffixes may not be followed by tense/aspect or subordinating suffixes.

Another -a' modal is described in ¶2.481.

¶2.463 There are two evidential tense suffixes. These are used roughly equivalently to bare verbs or verbs marked with perfective -tok on verbs referring to events or states that the speaker can personally vouch for.

The present evidential suffix -shki is used on verbs referring to ongoing events or currently true states of which the speaker has direct personal knowledge. **Holissochishki** "They are writing it (now, I know)" and **Ikishkoshki** "He's not drinking (now, I know)" constitute affirmations by the speaker as to the truth of these statements. -Shki does not combine with modal suffixes (¶2.4621).

The past evidential suffix -manko is used on verbs referring to past events or states that the speaker has personally witnessed. This suffix can follow one of the standard modal suffixes, as in **Aya'chimanko** "He was going to go (I know)". Like-shki, -manko may follow a negative verb (¶2.48; see also ¶2.482).

Each of these suffixes must be the last suffix in its word.

¶2.464 A Chickasaw exclamation has a verb followed by h plus a nasalized copy of the verb's last vowel: **Chokmaha!** "It's good", **Malililihi!** "I ran!", **Ishissoho!** "You hit him!" Exclamations are never negative. The h-nasalized vowel ending is always the last suffix in its word.

¶2.465 Two less well understood suffixes are used to express complex tense/aspect and modal ideas, in combination with suffixes indicating past reference. -Hchaa, which must be followed by -tok or -ttook, indicates a perfect or a past habitual notion, as in **Pisalihchaatok** "I have seen it, I used to see it". -Chayni, which must follow -tok or -ttook, marks a verb that refers to an event regarding which the speaker had no control or direct knowledge, something that occurred accidentally or is known about by hearsay, as in **Ishilitokchayni** "I took it (must have taken it) by accident" or **Illittookchayni**

"He must have died long ago". The combinations of these two suffixes with -tok or -ttook can in turn be followed by modal or other suffixes, as in Pisahchaatoka̱ ithá̱nali "I know he used to see him" or Illitokchayna'chiha'ni "Maybe she'll already have died (when I get there)".

¶2.47 Chickasaw questions calling for a yes or no response generally include a question suffix. Those calling for a longer response include a question word. The verb word in this type of question may have a question suffix or may be like an ordinary verb word, with no ending or one of the suffixes in ¶2.461-¶2.4621. The question suffixes may follow a modal suffix (¶2.4621) or a negative verb (¶2.48). Question suffixes are always the last element in their word.

¶2.471 The standard Chickasaw question suffix is -ta: **Chokmata?** "Is it good?", **Ishmalila'chita?** "Will you run?", **Malita?** "Is he running?" (Li Deletion applies). The question suffix may follow a modal suffix but is not used in combination with -tok or -ttook. Occasionally this suffix is omitted from neutral questions in casual speech.

In a focus question containing a noun with an interrogative case marker (¶2.513), there is no question ending on the verb: **Ofi'ta ishhoyo?** "Are you looking for a *dog*?", "Is it a dog that you're looking for?"

¶2.472 Neutral questions referring to the past end in -tam, a combination of -ta plus past question -m: **Chokmatam?** "Was it good?", **Ishmalitam?** "Did you run?"

In a past focus question containing a noun with an interrogative case marker (¶2.513), the verb word ends simply in -m: **Oblaashaashta pi̱slim?** "Was it yesterday that I saw him?", **Konihat chikisilim?** "Did the *skunk* bite you?"

¶2.473 Questions that contain a question word usually have a verb word with no suffix or with one of the suffixes in ¶2.461 or ¶2.4621. Nominal question words generally have an interrogative case marker (¶2.513), so the verbs of past questions containing question words may also end in the past question -m (¶2.472).

Chickasaw has a great many different question words, examples of which are given in the dictionary. There are question verbs, such as **katihmi** "to do (what)", in addition to the nominal question words. Nominal question words and question verbs used in direct questions belong to the class of interrogatives, which are marked "(int.)" in the dictionary. Such words include the interrogative formative t (like the t in **katihmi**).

Chickasaw has similar classes of indefinites ("(ind.)") and inferentials ("(inf.)"). Nouns and verbs of these classes include the indefinite/inferential formative n in place of the interrogative t. For instance, **kanihmi** may be an indefinite verb "to do (something)" or an inferential verb "to do (what)" (used in an indirect or embedded question). Examples of the use of such words are in the dictionary.

¶2.474 There is a poorly understood suffix -**hay'm** (usually pronounced with a vowel like that of English *bet*, and thus one of the most difficult

Chickasaw morphemes to phonemicize) that occurs in questions with a past or completed sense containing the word "ever", such as **Malilihay'm?** "Did he ever run?" Most likely this suffix is composed of some modal element plus **-m**. Tense/aspect and other modal suffixes are not used in **-hay'm** questions.

¶2.48 Chickasaw negative verbs are quite complex. Negative verb stems are derived with the **ik-** hypothetical prefix and the **-o** suffix (¶2.241); N prefixes express the equivalent of a I subject, as in **Akmallo** "I don't jump". (See also ¶2.453.)

As noted already, negative verb stems (with no non-third-person prefixes or post-stem suffixes) are listed in the dictionary when they are irregular either in form or in meaning.

¶2.481 Negation may be expressed periphrastically with the negative auxiliary **ki'yo**, which follows a verb word, as in **Mallili ki'yo** "I don't jump".

The verb word before **ki'yo** may include a standard tense/aspect or modal suffix (¶2.461, ¶2.462), as in **Mallila'chi ki'yo** "I won't jump".

Two modal suffixes, **-a'** "ever" and **-'** "can", are used only on verbs preceding **ki'yo**: **Mallila' ki'yo** "I don't ever jump, I never jump (perhaps I never bother), I can't jump (temporarily)", **Mallili' ki'yo** "I can't jump (it's impossible—perhaps I have no legs)".

Speakers are more comfortable using inflected negatives with certain verbs and periphrastic negatives with others, but most verbs can be negated either way. Periphrastic negation is somewhat more common with stative verbs. There is usually no difference in translation between the two types of negative verbs.

¶2.482 Tense/aspect, modal, question, and non-main clause suffixes always follow negative **-o** and may either follow or precede **ki'yo**. It seems to be much more common for negative verb words referring to the past to end in perfective **-tok** (¶2.461) than it is when such verb words are not negative. The linking suffix **-ki-** is added to negative verbs in **-o** before most suffixes, including those in ¶2.461-¶2.463, and ¶2.47: **Akmallokitok** "I didn't jump"; **Ikchokmokittook** "He wasn't good (long ago)"; **Ikchokmokita?** "Isn't it good?", **Ikayyokimankǫ** "She didn't go (I know)", and **Akmalloka'chi** "I won't jump". (The i of **-ki-** drops before a vowel: ¶2.221.) **-Ki-** is also used between **ki'yo** and the same group of suffixes: **Mallili ki'yokitok** "I didn't jump"; **Mallila' ki'yokittook** "I never jumped (long ago)". The **-ki-** linker is not used before any suffix that begins with **h** or before the non-main clause suffixes in ¶2.49, except for participial **-t** (¶2.495). Before participial **-t** and one other suffix, present evidential **-shki** (¶2.463), **-ki-** use is variable: **ikhi'lhokit / ikhi'lhot** "dancing", **Ikishkoshki /Ikishkokishki** "He's not drinking (now, I know)".

Usually, a suffix following **ki'yo** has a more general sense than one before **ki'yo**, and a modal after **ki'yo** may have only an epistemic reading: thus compare **Impatok ki'yo** "He didn't eat (at the last meal)", **Impa ki'yokitok** "He didn't eat (when he was sick)"; **Sipokna'chi ki'yo** "He won't (get to) be old",

Sipokni ki'yoka'chi "He won't (turn out to) be old, It won't be the case that he's old".

¶2.483 A few suffixes are used only in negative constructions. Examples include the modals **-a'** and **-'** (¶2.481) and **-ísha** "yet" (a rare accented suffix), as in **Akmallokísha** "I didn't jump yet" or **Chaaha ki'yokísha** "He's not tall yet".

¶2.484 Negative hortatives end in **-nna** but have no other negative marking: **Mallinna!** "He mustn't jump!" The most common type of negative hortative is a negative imperative, such as **Ishmallinna!** "Don't jump!" or **Chissikopanna!** "Don't be mean!" Unlike positive imperatives, these words always include a prefix indicating the subject.

¶2.49 Verb words in Chickasaw complex sentences may have a variety of endings.

In a Chickasaw sentence with two clauses, the second one generally has the form of a simple main clause while the first usually has one of the endings in this section. Usually, but not always, these non-main first clauses are translated into English with subordinate clauses, but we will refer to them here simply as non-main clauses. Many non-main clauses may be postposed after the main clause, but a few must occur immediately before the main clause. We will survey only a few of the most important Chickasaw non-main-clause endings and constructions in this section.

Each of the suffixes in this section is always final in its word. In general, verb words with the non-main-clause endings in this section are not complete sentences and may not be used on their own (but note ¶2.492 and ¶2.496).

A few types of Chickasaw complex sentences include an unsuffixed complement verb, either with or without agreement marking, such as the first word in **Hilha mihali** "I try to dance". Such unsuffixed verbs can be identified as non-main verbs because they may not freely be postposed, and they do not express the neutral assertion of a normal bare verb (¶2.41). Verbs like **miha** that select this type of complement are so marked (¶1.5) and exemplified in the dictionary.

Many complex sentences appear in the dictionary's examples. The dictionary also includes entries for a few complex verb phrases that consist of a non-main verb word with one of the suffixes in this section, followed by another verb stem.

¶2.491 The **-hookya** suffix is used to connect two sentences that are translated into English with "but": **Intakho'bihookya ayoppa** "He's tired but he's happy". Since **-hookya** follows the first verb rather than the second, however, its meaning is closer to that of "although". After a consonant, **-hookya** appears as **-ookya**, and occasionally it is reduced to **-kya**. Most often, **-hookya** follows a verb unmarked for tense, aspect, and modality, but this is not always the case, and **-hookya** may occur following any suffix in ¶2.46 that need not be final in its word.

¶2.492 There are two evidential complementizer suffixes in Chickasaw,

1

dubitative -hchi̱ (as in Alahchi̱ "Maybe he's coming") and desiderative -hookmano (as in Alahookmano "I hope he's coming"). These suffixes may follow tense/aspect and modal suffixes (¶2.461, ¶2.4621). The h of these suffixes drops after a consonant.

As the examples suggest, verb words with these two suffixes are most often used alone to express a speaker's doubt or hope. However, they are also used in complex constructions, followed by certain other verbs, as in **Lynnat Charlesat alahookmano anhi** "Lynn hopes that Charles is coming". The particular complement structure used with a given verb is indicated (as described in ¶1.5) and exemplified in its dictionary entry.

¶2.493 The great majority of Chickasaw non-main clauses are marked with switch-reference suffixes that are differentiated according to whether their subjects are the same as or different from the subject of the main clause with which they are associated. There are several pairs of same- and different-subject suffixes, with same-subject suffixes ending in t and different-subject suffixes ending in a nasalized vowel.

Same-subject **-kat** and different-subject **-ka̱** are the general Chickasaw complementizers, for example, but there are many other such pairs. Same-subject **-hootokoot** and different-subject **-hootoko̱** mean "because". Same-subject **-hookmat** and different-subject **-hookma̱** mean "if". Two pairs of complementizers are specified to reflect whether or not the clause they mark is realized relative to the main clause, realis **-hmat** and **-hma̱** and irrealis **-kmat** and **-kma̱**. **-Tokoot** and **-toko̱** are backgrounding suffixes. Each of these suffixes may follow a full verb, with subject and object marking, which often includes a modal suffix (¶2.4621) and occasionally a tense/aspect suffix (¶2.461). The combination of -tok plus -kat or ka̱ has only one k (-tokat, -toka̱) rather than the expected two.

In general, switch-reference verb words are marked with subject agreement. There are a few exceptions to this generalization (perhaps only involving -kat or -ka̱?) in constructions with particular main verbs, as indicated in the dictionary.

¶2.494 Another pair of switch-reference suffixes, conjunctive same-subject **-cha** and different-subject **-na** (usually used to translate two clauses connected with "and" or "and then" in English), look and work differently from those above.

Verb stems used before these suffixes have a ' inserted in their penultimate (next-to-last) syllable under the same conditions as the negative -o verbs discussed in ¶2.241: **A'pacha**... "She ate it and she..."; **Ishmallicha**... "You jumped and you..."; **Kiiko̱'tacha**... "We whistled and we...". Regular rules apply before these suffixes, since the addition of the ' makes the penultimate syllable of the verb stem heavy: **Hi'lhcha**... "He danced and he..." (the Strident-Coronal rule applies); **Ilolla'cha**... "We laughed and we..." (Li Deletion applies).

All conjunctive verb words are marked with subject agreement. The conjunctive suffixes change when they follow the first-person singular I suffix **-li**

li

or negative -o—in this case, the same-subject suffix is -t, and the different-subject suffix is shown by nasalizing the i of the -li suffix or the -o: **Mallilit**..."I jumped and I..."; **Mallili̠**... "I jumped and someone else...". The **'** is still inserted in the verb stem: **Hi'lhlit**... "I danced and I...".

Conjunctive verbs never have tense/aspect or modal suffixes.

Dictionary entries consisting of one verb plus -cha followed by another verb stem are labeled as "cha expressions" as a reminder of their unusual inflection.

¶2.495 The Chickasaw participial suffix is -t. This is a same-subject suffix with no corresponding different-subject form, used much like an English modifying -ing participle to mark a verb that modifies the action of the main verb. Participles that modify the action of a main verb in this way are almost always formed from semantically active verbs. Participles used with following auxiliary verbs, however, may be semantically stative. Some participles are irregular in their form. As noted in ¶2.482, negative participles may or may not include the linker -ki-. Many dictionary entries include participles.

Participles modifying lexical verbs generally are not marked with subject agreement unless they are negative: negative participles always show N subject agreement. Participles formed from II and III subject verbs show subject agreement before many auxiliaries, unlike participles formed from I subject verbs: **Potikahbit taha** "We are all tired out" shows II agreement on the participle, while the corresponding **Apat kiitahli** "We're eating it all up" shows I agreement on the auxiliary. The plural subject prefix **hoo-** (¶2.432) appears on a main lexical verb, even when it is preceded by a participle, as in **Lohmit hooholissochitok** "They wrote hiding it, They wrote secretly", but appears on the participle before at least some auxiliaries, as in **Hoolohmit ishtayatok** "They started to hide it".

¶2.496 Occasionally a non-main verb word with a second-person subject is used alone to express a command. The usual endings used this way are different-subject irrealis -km**a̠**, same-subject conjunctive -cha, and, for some speakers, different-subject conjunctive -na. (These constructions are probably short for longer sentences: **Ishhilhakm**a̠... "You might dance and...", **Ishhi'lhacha**... "You dance and...".)

¶2.5 Noun inflection and derivation

Chickasaw noun inflection is much less complex than Chickasaw verb inflection. The most important types of noun inflection include suffixation for case (¶2.51) and affixation to indicate possession (¶2.26). Most Chickasaw nouns do not have plural forms (¶2.53). Complex nouns are formed from verbs by several processes (¶2.54). All forms of Chickasaw independent pronouns are given in the dictionary.

¶2.51 Nouns have an unmarked stem, which is listed in the dictionary. In a sentence, a noun may be nominative, accusative, oblique, or unmarked (in stem form). (Some examples of case-marked nouns in sentences are given in ¶1.4.) There are several different sets of case suffixes whose use is governed by discourse factors, and a few suffixes that do not vary for case.

Inflected forms of nouns are not listed in the dictionary. Inflected pronominal forms are identified as subjects ("subj."), which are nominative in form, or nonsubjects ("nonsubj.)", which are accusative.

¶2.511 The neutral forms of the case suffixes are nominative -at, accusative -a, and oblique -ak: for instance, hattak "man, person" has the inflected forms hattakat, hattaka, and hattakak, and ofi' "dog" has the forms ofi'at, ofi'a, and ofi'ak.

Nouns that end in a vowel take the same endings: koni "skunk" has the forms nominative koniat, accusative konia, and oblique koniak; chola "fox", the forms chola-at, cholaa, chola-ak. (When two similar vowels come together, as in words like chola-at, a hyphen is written between them to distinguish short a plus short a [two syllables], for instance, from long aa [one syllable].) The rule deleting a vowel before an added a or o (¶2.221) does not apply in these noun forms, perhaps providing evidence that they actually end in (silent) h (¶2.41). In fact, speakers occasionally insert an h at the end of a vowel-final noun before a neutral case ending.

In a noun whose next-to-last syllable is heavy (see ¶2.34) and whose last syllable ends with a vowel or vowel plus ', this final vowel or vowel plus ' may be dropped before the case endings. When a noun-final vowel or vowel plus ' is dropped in nominative or oblique forms, the case endings have long vowels: nominative -aat instead of -at and oblique -aak instead of -ak. Thus, chokfi "rabbit" has the nominative forms chokfiat or chokfaat, chipota "child" has the nominative forms chipota-at or chipotaat, bissa' "blackberry" has the accusative forms bissa'a or bissa, and minko' "chief" has the oblique forms minko'ak or minkaak. The forms with deleted vowels are used more frequently.

¶2.512 The contrastive case endings are nominative -akot and accusative -ako. Thus, the nominative contrastive form of ofi' is ofi'akot. After a noun whose next-to-last syllable is heavy (¶2.34) and whose last syllable ends with a vowel or vowel plus ', the final vowel or vowel plus ' of the noun is dropped and the a of the ending is lengthened; thus, the nominative contrastive form of chokfi is chokfaakot, and the accusative contrastive form is chokfaako. Contrastive forms are used to emphasize a noun; they can often be translated with "It's___that...". There is no oblique contrastive ending.

¶2.513 The interrogative case endings are nominative -haat and accusative -hta or -hta. (The h in these endings is deleted after a consonant.) Thus, the interrogative (int.) forms of chokfi are chokfihaat and chokfihta, and the interrogative forms of hattak are hattakaat and hattakta. Interrogative nouns are focused in questions (as in "Was it a man who hit you?"; see ¶2.481-¶2.482); the same endings appear on nominal question words, such as nominative nantahaat "what?" in a question. Oblique interrogative nouns end in -akta.

¶2.514 The indefinite case endings are nominative -hmat and accusative -hma. These endings appear on indefinite (ind.) words, such as nannahmat "something". There is no oblique indefinite ending. Words with these endings are used only in affirmative sentences; in negative sentences, they are replaced by indefinites with the -hookya "any/every" ending (¶2.524).

¶2.515 The focus/inferential case endings are nominative -hoot and accusative -ho̱. These endings are used on focused nouns, especially those modified by adjectival verbs, and on inferential (inf.) words. Aside from their special endings, inferential words are formally identical to indefinites; they appear in subordinate questions. An example is accusative **nannaho̱** "what", as in **Nannaho̱ ishpi̱stoka̱ itha̱nali** "I know what you saw". There is no oblique focus/inferential ending.

¶ 2.516 A few noun phrases are identified in the dictionary as clausal nouns (cln.). Although semantically simple, these phrases take case marking that makes them look syntactically like embedded clauses, generally including the general complementizers (¶2,492), with same-subject -kat functioning as a nominative case ending and different-subject -ka̱ functioning as an accusative case ending. A final ' at the end of a clausal noun drops before endings are added. For instance, **nakshish filammi'** means "branch (of a tree)". This clausal noun is used as a subject in sentences such as **Nakshish filammikat lowa** "The branch is burning", and as an object in sentences such as **Nakshish filammika̱ pi̱sli** "I see the branch".

¶2.52 There are a few other syntactic endings that can occur on Chickasaw nouns.

¶2.521 -Akya "too" follows a subject noun: **Waakaat ishto. Issoba-akya ishto** "Cows are big. Horses are big too". No additional case marking is used with -akya. After a noun whose next-to-last syllable is heavy (¶2.34) and whose last syllable ends with a vowel or vowel plus ', the final vowel or vowel plus ' of the noun is dropped, and the a of the ending is lengthened: **waakaakya** "cows too...".

¶2.522 The Chickasaw topic marker is -hookano (-ookano after a consonant). This suffix may follow a noun in any case role, usually at the beginning of the sentence, but it is most common with subjects. Topic nouns are not case marked.

¶2.523 The -aash "aforementioned" suffix is used on unmarked forms of nouns the speaker has used before in a conversation, as in **ihooaash** "the aforementioned woman". Focus case markers are used after -aash: **ihooaashoot** is the nominative "aforementioned woman", for instance.

On a time word, -aash indicates a reference to the past: **Tuesdayaash** "last Tuesday". A corresponding reference to the future is shown with an irrealis suffix (¶2.493), sometimes in oblique form: **Tuesdaykma̱, Tuesdaykmak** "next Tuesday".

¶2.524 The suffix -hookya (-ookya after a consonant) follows an indefinite or inferential word to express "every" (in an affirmative sentence) or "any" (in a negative sentence). Thus **nannahookya** is "everything" or "anything". -Hookya is also used on other noun words to express a meaning such as "everything like" or "anything like", as in **Ofi'ookya sakisili** "Everything like a dog bites me" or **Ofi'ookya chibannata?** "Do you want anything like a dog?". This ending does not show case marking.

¶2.53 Most Chickasaw nouns do not have plural forms, so **ihoo**, for instance, can mean either "woman" or "women", although only the first meaning is listed in the dictionary. A few complex nouns that include verb stems that change depending on the number of their subject do have singular and plural forms, such as **naafkaatakka'li'** "hanger" (where one article of clothing hangs), **naafkaatakohli'** "hangers" (where several articles of clothing hang). Plural English translations are generally used in definitions only for nouns of this type. An exception is nouns such as **bala'** "beans, peas", which are almost always used in a mass sense; these also may have a mass definition.

A collective plural may be expressed by a lexical noun followed by **alhiha'**.

¶2.54 Many noun stems in the dictionary are basic nouns, which, like basic verb stems, have no internal structure. Some nouns, however, are derived from verbs, and some are compounds.

¶2.541 Several suffixes are used to derive nouns from verb stems. The most important nominalizer is -**'**, which has a very general meaning: **taloowa'**, from **taloowa** "to sing", means either "song" or "singer". Another similar nominalizer is -**ka'**.

¶2.542 Compounds are combinations of two (or more) separate words. A common element of Chickasaw compounds is the word **oshi'** "son", which is used to form words referring to small objects or offspring. For example, **akankoshi'** "chick, egg" is a compound of **akanka'** "chicken" and **oshi'**. As this word shows, a vowel (or vowel plus **'**) at the end of the first member of a compound usually drops. Many elements of compound words do not combine to form sequences of light syllables that can be rhythmically lengthened (¶2.35), but others do. "Colt", a compound of **issoba** "horse" and **oshi'**, may be pronounced either way, as **IssobOshi'** with a lengthened **o** or as **Issob-oshi'** with no lengthening. In the first case, **sobo** counts as a sequence of two light syllables, but in the second, the sequence starts with **oshi'** (as indicated by the hyphen), so there is no lengthening. A hyphen is always used whenever Rhythmic Lengthening is blocked within a compound word.

Verbs can also occur in compounds. Many compound nouns have a noun as their first element and a modifying verb as their second, as in **nashobokchamali'** "grey wolf", which includes the noun **nashoba** "wolf", the verb **okchamali** "to be blue or green", and the nominalizer -**'**. The noun at the beginning of some compounds specifies the object or some other complement of the verb. Thus, **waakaatakchi'** "rodeo grounds" means literally "(place) where (people) rope cows", containing **waaka'** "cow" plus the locative prefix **aa-** added to the verb **takchi** "to tie, rope", and the nominalizer -**'**.

Chickasaw also has some compound verbs, which we will not survey here.

¶2.6 Verb grades

Chickasaw verb stems have "grades", derivatives with accented vowels that indicate various aspectual changes. The meanings of these derived verb forms are usually predictable from the meaning of the verb stem that serves as the base for grade formation. There are five standard grades, the g-grade, h-grade, hn-grade, n-grade, and y-grade, and several less common grades. Not every grade may be formed from each verb stem. All known grades are listed in the dictionary, but there are certainly others that we have not listed or that might be used by other speakers but not by Mrs. Willmond.

It is well known that Western Muskogean grades usually involve alteration of the penultimate (next-to-last) syllable of the base, generally through gemination or doubling of consonants, vowel nasalization, or insertion of h or '. Usually the penultimate syllable of a grade is accented, although in the usual form of the g-grade (¶2.61) the accent falls on the syllable before this one. However, Chickasaw has six other grades that have not previously been described (¶2.66), characterized by reduplication or copying of various consonants or syllables and insertion of other segmental material, in some of which the accent falls on the fourth syllable from the end of the verb stem.

In addition to the aspectual meanings described for each grade below, many of the standard grades (especially the g-grade and hn-grade) have lexicalized uses for indicating nonsingular number agreement, or other unpredictable meanings. These are indicated in the dictionary.

Some verbs occur only in grades, with no corresponding unaccented stem. For some of these verb stems (usually those with several related forms) a hypothesized unaccented stem is listed in <>'s, indicating that it does not occur alone. However, it is not always possible to know what the base of a given grade is or even which of several grades a particular accented verb may be.

The base for grade formation is usually a verb stem. With short verbs (¶2.212) and two-syllable verb stems beginning with i, however, the base may include an agreement prefix. Thus while isso "to hit" has the normal hn-grade ihísso (¶2.63), the hn-grade of Sasso "He hits me" is Sahásso: the II prefix sa- is included in the base. Similarly, pisa "to look at, see" has a non-geminated ggr. pí'sa (¶2.61), but since Sapisa "He looks at me" has three syllables, not two, it forms a geminated ggr., Sáppi'sa. Verbs in which the rule of Li Deletion (¶2.35) has applied before the causative suffix -chi (¶2.443), particularly those marked with the feature [-SC] (¶2.37), generally base their grades on an underlying form that includes the li syllable that is deleted on the surface. Thus, for example, malichi "to make run", from malili "to run" plus -chi, has the hngr. malilihínchi, formed from the base <malilichi>. (Li Deletion does not occur in the hngr., because the stem-final li comes before h, not ch.) On the other hand, some such verbs may also treat the surface verb form as the base—so an alternate hngr. of malichi is malihínchi. Occasionally a grade is formed from another grade rather than from an unaccented stem.

The grade system in Chickasaw is not completely regular or productive. Speakers vary as to where and how often they use grade forms of verbs. Although most occurring grades are formed regularly according to the rules below, there are many irregular grades. The most common irregularities involve unexpected or failed gemination or consonant doubling and missing or unexpected h's and "s. A long vowel in the penultimate syllable of a base verb is usually, but not always, shortened in a grade form.

We are not committed to the descriptions below as a formal analysis; instead, we have attempted to present the basics of grade formation as simply as possible for the language user. A few additional facts about grades are given in ¶2.67. The examples here are presented as typical illustrations; many additional grade forms are in the dictionary.

¶2.61 The g-grade (geminated grade or ggr.) of a semantically active verb is usually translated "finally" (normally when used after kaniht "finally"); the ggr. of a stative verb is usually translated "kind of" or sometimes "very". Some ggrs. have unexpected meanings, as indicated in the dictionary.

The ggr. is the Chickasaw grade form with the most variation, both predictable and irregular. There are two basic types of ggrs. In the first type, the geminated ggr., there is gemination or doubling of one of the base verb's consonants, and the accent falls on the antepenultimate syllable of the ggr. (two syllables before the final syllable). In the second type, the non-geminated ggr., there is no gemination, and the accent falls on the penultimate syllable. The shape of the verb determines how its ggr. is formed.

A ggr. of a verb of three or more syllables in which a single consonant precedes the penultimate (next-to-last) vowel generally has a geminated ggr.: the next-to-last consonant of the verb is doubled or geminated, the vowel before that consonant is accented, and ' is inserted before the last consonant. The ggr. of halili "to touch", for instance, is hálli'li; the ggr. of chofata "to be clean" is chóffa'ta.

When there are two consonants after the penultimate vowel, no ' is inserted in a geminated ggr. Thus, the ggr. chilakbi "to be dry and cracked" is chíllakbi, and the ggr. of holiitobli "to treasure" is holíttobli (a long vowel is always shortened before a doubled consonant in a geminated ggr.).

When there are two consonants before the penultimate vowel, a non-geminated ggr. is always used: there is no consonant doubling, and the penultimate vowel (followed by ', if there is only one consonant after it) is accented. Thus, the ggr. of ibishshano is ibishshá'no, and the ggr. of toksali "to work" is toksá'lo. Ggrs. of two-syllable verb stems are similar: á'pa is the ggr. of apa, and bá'sha is the ggr. of basha "to be cut, to be operated on".

A non-geminated ggr. of a verb whose penultimate vowel is followed by mb, mp, nt, nch, or nk includes a nasalized vowel plus ' plus b, p, t, ch, or k respectively. Thus the ggr. of konta is kǫ́'ta. When the penultimate vowel is followed by a different sequence of two consonants, ' is inserted if the first of these consonants is f, h, l, lh, m, n, s, sh, w, or y. Thus, the ggr. of imponna "to be good at something" is impó'nna, the ggr. of achaknaski "to turn on one's side" is achakná'ski, and the ggr. of nalhlhi "to shoot" is ná'lhlhi. When ' is added before hp, ht, hch, or hk, the h deletes: thus, the ggr. of lhihka "to blow one's nose" is lhí'ka, and the ggr. of yamihchi "to do" is yamí'chi. Before any other sequence of two consonants, ' is not inserted, and the penultimate vowel is pronounced with a falling accent (^). Thus, the ggr. of **okcha** "to wake up" is **ôkcha**, and the ggr. of **nannabli** "to swallow" is **nannâbli**.

(There are some similarities between the formation of non-geminated ggrs. and the formation of the negative [¶2.241] or conjunction [¶2.494] stem, but these processes do work differently. Any sequence of two consonants before a verb's final vowel [except for the nasal sequences **mb**, **mp**, **nch**, **nk**, or **nt**] blocks insertion of ' in the negative or conjunction stem, as shown by **ikimponno** "he's not good at it" and **achaknaskicha...** "he turned on his side and...". Also, negative and conjunction stems are not accented.)

A long vowel in the base verb's penultimate syllable is usually shortened in the ggr.: thus **aachi** "to say" has the ggr. **á'chi**. Some ggrs. are exceptions to this rule: for instance, the ggr. of **yaachi** "to make (someone) cry" is **yáa'chi**.

A number of verb stems have irregular ggrs., as an inspection of the dictionary will show. In particular, many verb stems that might be expected to have geminated ggrs. have non-geminated ggrs., especially when these stems include a prefix. For instance, the ggr. of **asilli** "to pin (several) on" is **así'lli**, not <ássilli> (this verb includes the prefix a-, ¶2.44127), and the ggr. of **ilibi** "to kill oneself" is **ilí'bi**, not <ílli'bi> (this verb includes the prefix ili-, ¶2.4411). A few verbs for which geminated ggrs. would be expected allow both types of ggr.: thus, either **píshshoffi** or **pishó'ffi** may be the ggr. of **pishoffi** "to skin, scrape". In a few cases (all involving verbs containing **li** before the causative suffix -chi), the syllable before the antepenultimate syllable is geminated: for example, the ggr. of **atakalichi** "to chain" is **atákkali'chi**.

A few verbs with non-geminated ggrs. have variant forms with an accented penultimate vowel followed by a geminated consonant. These forms have specially lexicalized meanings. Thus, for example, **oklhili** "to be night" has the (rare) regular non-geminated ggr. **oklhí'li** and the variant ggr. **oklhílli** "to be very dark".

Chickasaw number verbs such as **tochchí'na** "to be three in number" and **talhlhá'pi** "to be five in number" resemble geminated ggrs., except that they are written with penultimate accent. Accent is somewhat variable in these words—sometimes they are pronounced with the (expected) antepenultimate accent and sometimes they appear to have no accent. Most of these verbs do not have related non-grade forms but a few do: the base form of **pokkó'li** "to be ten in number", **pokoli**, is used in decade numerals, and **chakkó'li** "to be nine in number" is derived from the archaic **chakali** "to be pregnant".

Many of the other Chickasaw grades described below are built on or similar to ggrs.

¶2.62 The h-grade (hgr.) has an inserted **hh** following an accented copy of a verb base's penultimate vowel, with a ' before the base's last consonant: thus, the hgr. of **chofata** is **chofáhha'ta**. No ' appears if the penultimate vowel is followed by more than one consonant: thus, for example, the hgr. of **banna** "to want" is **báhhanna**. Hgrs. are normally made only from semantically stative verbs and, like the ggr., usually have an intensive or emphatic meaning ("very") or a "kind of" meaning. Most hgrs. look similar to geminated ggrs. (¶2.61) of stems containing h; they are also very similar to ygrs. (¶2.65).

When the penultimate syllable of a verb base includes a nasalized vowel or a vowel plus mb, mp, nch, nt, or nk, a nasalized vowel plus ' appears after the hh of the hgr., with a plain vowel before the hh. Thus the hgr. of masǫfa "to be bald" is masóhhǫ'fa, and the hgr. of lhinko "to be fat" is lhíhhi'ko.

There is a type of variant hgr. used in a few verbs of motion or position, in which a single h appears after the accented penultimate vowel of the base. If there are two consonants after the inserted h, it is followed by a copy of the accented vowel. These hgrs. (which resemble the Choctaw hgr. in form and meaning) have a "quickly" meaning, or express a resultant state. Thus, the variant hgr. of filita "to turn (oneself) around" is filíhta "to turn around quickly", and the variant hgr. of achaknaski "to turn on one's side" is achaknaháski "to be lying on one's side, keep turning on one's side".

A few other verb stems have irregular hgrs.

¶2.63 An hn-grade (hngr.) has its penultimate vowel followed by an inserted h plus an accented nasalized copy of that vowel and refers to repeated or habitual action (often with the following auxiliary bíyyi'ka "all the time"). (Hngrs. of stative verbs are not normally used as the only verb in a sentence.) Thus, the hngr. of halili is halihíli, the hngr. of tofa "to spit" is tohǫ́fa, and the hngr. of malli is mahálli. When the penultimate vowel of the verb base is nasal, the vowel before the h of the hngr. is non-nasal: thus, the hngr. of masǫfa "to be bald" is masohǫ́fa.

When the consonant following the penultimate vowel of a verb stem is b or p, an accented copy of that vowel plus m instead of a nasalized vowel is used: thus, the hngr. of apa is ahámpa and the hngr. of abi is ahámbi. Similarly, when the consonant after the next-to-last vowel of a verb stem is ch, k, or t, an accented vowel plus n is used, as in pilahánchi, the hngr. of pilachi "to send"; alihínkchi, the hngr. of alikchi "to doctor"; or chofahánta, the hngr. of chofata.

In hngrs. of verb stems whose next-to-last vowel is followed by bb, chch, kk, pp, or tt, these consonant sequences are shortened: atohómbi is the hngr. of atobbi "to pay", kohóncha is the hngr. of kochcha "to go out", hohómpi is the hngr. of hoppi "to bury", and so forth. Other doubled consonants normally remain long in the hngr., but a few verb stems that end in a doubled lhlh, ss, or shsh plus a vowel have an hngr. with a single lh, s, or sh: thus, alhpihíshi is the hngr. of alhpishshi "to pillow one's head on".

For a verb stem whose penultimate vowel is followed by kb, kl, km, kn, kw, or ky, the hngr. includes an accented vowel plus ng plus b, l, m, n, w, or y: ihíngbi is the hngr. of ikbi "to make", ahángmi is the hngr. of akmi "to freeze"; lahángna is the hngr. of lakna "to be yellow"; and ichchohóngwa is the hngr. of ichchokwa "to be cold".

Verb stems that end in h plus b, m, l, n, w, or y have an hngr. that looks as if its base did not include the h: thus, tohómbi is the hngr. of tohbi "to be white" and bohǫ́li is the hngr. of bohli "to lay down".

Usually the hngr. of a verb stem whose penultimate vowel is long has a short vowel before the h: thus, the hngr. of **baafa** "to stab" is **baháfa**, and the hngr. of **aachi** "to say" is **ahánchi**. For a few verb stems, however, the hngr. keeps its long vowel: thus, the hngr. of **labaachi** "to talk all the time" is **labaahánchi**.

¶2.64 The n-grade (ngr.) has its penultimate vowel accented and nasalized. Thus, the ngr. of **halili** is **halį́li** and the ngr. of **tofa** is **tǫ́fa**. The ngr. of a stative verb often has a comparative translation: thus, **chofánta** means "to be cleaner". The ngr. of an active verb usually refers to an action that was ongoing at the same time as another action. The ngr. of a positional verb refers to remaining or being left in that position.

Most of the rules for hngrs. (¶2.63) also apply in ngrs. Thus, for example, the ngr. of **pilachi** is **pilánchi**; the ngr. of **kochcha** is **kóncha**; and the ngr. of **lakna** is **lángna**. However, verb stems that end in h plus a consonant plus a vowel keep the h in the ngr.: the ngr. of **tohbi** is **tǫ́hbi**, and the ngr. of **bohli** is **bǫ́hli**.

¶2.65 The y-grade (ygr.) has an inserted **yy** following an accented copy of the verb base's penultimate vowel, with a ' before the base's last consonant: the ygr. of **chofata** is **chofáyya'ta**. The ' appears after the penultimate vowel any time that vowel is followed by a single consonant or by two consonants of which the first is f, h, l, lh, m, n, s, sh, w, or y. Thus, for instance, the ygr. of **banna** "to want" is **báyya'nna**, and the ygr. of **kawaski** "to be hard" is **kawáyya'ski**. (This use of ' presents a contrast with the hgr. [¶2.62], which otherwise often resembles a ygr. with hh instead of **yy**. Ygrs. also look like geminated ggrs. [¶2.61] of stems containing a y.) Ygrs. of semantically stative verbs usually have an intensive meaning. Ygrs. of semantically active verbs are less common, but may have a resultative stative meaning. Thus, the ygr. of **holo** "to put on (shoes)" is **hóyyo'lo** "to wear (shoes)".

When the penultimate syllable of a verb base includes a nasalized vowel or a vowel plus mb, mp, nch, nt, or nk, a nasalized vowel plus ' appears after the **yy** of the ygr., with a plain vowel before the **yy**. Thus the ygr. of **masofa** "to be bald" is **masóyyǫ'fa** and the ygr. of **lhinko** "to be fat" is **lhíyyį'ko**.

¶2.66 The six other Chickasaw grades are far less common, and have not been previously reported or investigated in the literature. These include the kl-grade, several different reduplicated grades (in which a consonant or a whole syllable is copied later in the word), and the extended grade. A number of these grade forms are used primarily or exclusively with the prefix **itti-** (¶2.25, ¶2.4411), which normally has a reciprocal meaning but in these verbs appears to refer to sounds. These grades differ from the standard grades in that all are formed from verb stems of a particular shape (each ending in either a, chi, or li, and in some cases with other particular features); they may not be productively formed from other types of verb stems. These grades sometimes are irregularly formed (¶2.667), and their meanings often cannot be predicted (as the dictionary entries make clear).

¶2.661 The kl-grade (klgr.) is formed from a base consisting of a consonant-vowel-consonant plus a copy of the same vowel, a ', and **chi**, such as **baka'chi** "to make a noise with wood". Most such base verbs refer to making sounds, and the meaning of the derived klgr. is about the same or may be somewhat more intensive. Many klgr. stems are used only or frequently with the prefix **itti-** (which also often appears with the **'chi** base verb). The second consonant of the base is geminated and the vowel before it accented, and **kli** is inserted before the final **'chi** of the verb stem. Thus, **baka'chi** has the klgr. **bákkakli'chi** "to hit (making a sound)", also in **ittibákkakli'chi** "to make a knocking or hammering sound"; and **chobo'chi** "to splash" and **ittichobo'chi** "to make a splashing sound" have the klgr. **ittichóbbokli'chi**.

¶2.662 The reduplicated chi-grade (rcgr.) is usually formed from the same base as the klgr. and also refers to sounds. The consonant and vowel before the **'chi** are reduplicated and accented. Thus, the rcgr. of **baka'chi** is **bakaká'chi** "to hammer". Many rcgr. stems have an **itti-** prefix, in words such as **ittibakaká'chi** "to make a knocking or hammering sound".

¶2.663 The reduplicated initial grade (rigr.) is usually formed from a verb stem with a structure like that of **pattala** "to be short", ending in a geminate consonant plus a short vowel, a single consonant (perhaps always **l** or **n**?), and **a**; generally the first two vowels in such verbs are the same. The initial consonant of the verb stem is copied after its last consonant, followed by an accented nasalized copy of the verb stem's first vowel (with a following **y** if that vowel is **i**, or **w** if that vowel is **o**). Thus, the rigr. of **pattala** is **pattalpáa**, the rigr. of **missila** "to have a big stomach" is **missilmíya**, and the rigr. of **poffola** "to inflate" is **poffolpówa** "to puff oneself out like a toad". As the last example shows, an rigr. may have a specialized meaning, although most are intensives.

¶2.664 The reduplicated li-grade (rlgr.) is similar to the rigr (¶2.663) but is formed from a verb stem ending in a sequence of consonant plus vowel plus consonant plus vowel plus **li**. The next-to-last consonant (always **l**?) of the verb stem is geminated, a ' is added after the penultimate vowel, and the initial consonant and an accented nasalized copy of the first vowel of the verb stem's ending sequence is added before the final **li**. Thus, **shokmalla'máli** is the rlgr. of **shokmalali** "to be shiny", and **shikkilli'kíli** is the rlgr. of **shikkilili** "to be on tiptoe". Rlgrs. are very rare.

¶2.665 The reduplicated medial grade (rmgr.) is usually formed from a verb stem with a ggr. (¶2.61) that conveys a stative meaning made from a base with three consonant-vowel syllables, usually ending in **li** but occasionally in **a, ka'chi,** or **kalhchi**. The second consonant of this base is geminated (except after a long vowel) and the whole middle syllable is reduplicated with a nasalized accented vowel (or an accented vowel plus **n** before **k**). Thus, the rmgr. of **binili** "to sit down", **bínni'li** "to be sitting down (sg.)" is **binniníli** "to sit around (sg.)"; the rmgr. of **shamalli** "to squeeze into a tight space (sg.)", **shámma'li** "to be stuck (sg.)" is **shammamáli** "to wiggle around, try to squeeze through somewhere (sg.)"; the rmgr. of **shámmohli** "to be stuck (dl.)" is **shammomóli** "to wiggle around, try to squeeze through somewhere (dl.)";

and the rmgr. of **tono'kalhchi** "to roll" is **tonnonónkalhchi** "to roll around". As the last examples show, the middle syllable of the base may end with **h** or **'**, but these sounds are lost in the grade. An rmgr. usually refers to distributed or repeated action or a distributed state.

¶2.666 The extended grade (xgr.) is normally formed from a v1 (see ¶2.4442) ending in **a**. The penultimate vowel of such a verb stem (plus a **y** if that vowel is **i** or a **w** if that vowel is **o**) is copied between its last consonant and final **a**, and a standard ggr. (¶2.61) is formed from this extended base. Thus, the xgr. of **shila** "to be dry" is **shílli'ya** (the ggr. of the extended base <shiliya>), the xgr. of **aloota** "to fill, be filled" is **alótto'wa** (extended base <alootowa>), and the xgr. of **pattala** is **pattálla'a** (extended base <pattala-a>). (Some speakers pronounce words with final **a'a** with **a'ha**.) The meaning of an xgr. is similar to that of a ygr.

¶2.667 Perhaps because the non-standard grades in this section are very rare and are formed only from verbs of restricted shapes, there are some ir-regular formations, especially in terms of which syllable or consonant-vowel sequence is doubled in the reduplicated grades. For instance, the rlgr. of **wakchalali** "to put one's legs apart" is **wakchalla'wáli** (instead of the expected <wakchalla'cháli>), and the rigr. of **chiffola** "to be bent into a circle" is **chiffolfówa** "to slither like a snake" (instead of the expected <chiffolchówa> or <chiffolchíya>).

¶2.67 The Rhythmic Lengthening rule (¶2.35) does not apply into syllables affected by grade formation (thus the first **a** of the hngr. **hilhaháli** is not lengthened). The syllable preceding an affected syllable may be lengthened, however, as in the rcgr. **ittibAkaká'chi**, and the last syllable of a grade may count as the first syllable of an odd-even sequence: **hilhaháli***l***tok**.

In general, negatives are not formed from grades. See ¶2.242. Negated grade words may be followed by the negative auxiliary ki'yo (¶2.481).

Note that impossible or non-occurring grades are not listed in the Dictionary.

¶2.7 Chickasaw prefixes and suffixes: A summary list

In this section we present an alphabetical list of the Chickasaw prefixes and suffixes that appear in the etymologies of entries in the dictionary (given in []'s in the dictionary entries) and the dictionary examples. Prefix formatives used in certain types of stems (¶2.4421, ¶2.473) are included as well, but most basic stem formatives are not listed. Complete words (including non-actual words in <>'s) that have their own entries in the dictionary are not included in this list. Thus, for example, the preverbs (¶2.42) do not appear in the list here, since they may be pronounced as separate words. The list includes most variants of the prefixes and suffixes discussed in the preceding sections, al-though a few variants produced by clear-cut phonological rules are omitted.

The identifications given here are quite brief, with references to the main section in which the prefixes and suffixes listed are described above. (A few elements not discussed above have no such references.) Prefixes and suffixes are identified here according to whether they are used on nouns, verbs, or other types of words. These identifications refer to the category to which a given prefix or suffix can be added, not to the ultimate type of word on which such prefixes or suffixes can appear. For example, the comitative prefix **ibaa-** can be added only to verbs, but nouns such as **ittibaapishi** "brother, sister" can later be derived from such verbs, so it would not be correct to say that **ibaa-** may be seen only on verbs.

-' nominalizing verb suffix (¶2.541); hortative verb suffix (¶2.243); negative modal verb suffix ("(not)...can") (¶2.481)

a- applicative verb prefix (¶2.44127)

-a vl formative (¶2.4422)

-a' negative modal verb suffix ("(not)...ever") (¶2.481)

-a'chi modal verb suffix (¶2.4621)

-a'cho modal verb suffix (¶2.4621)

-a'hi modal verb suffix (¶2.4621)

-a'ni modal verb suffix (¶2.4621); variant of -ha'ni (¶2.4621)

-a'si diminutive verb suffix (¶2.451)

-a'shki modal verb suffix (¶2.4622)

ak- 1sg. N verb prefix (¶2.24)

-ak oblique noun suffix (¶2.511)

-akot nominative/same-subject contrastive noun or relative clause suffix (¶2.512)

-ako accusative/different-subject contrastive noun or relative clause suffix (¶2.512)

-akya "too" noun suffix (¶2.521); variant of -hookya (¶2.491)

am- lsg. III verb and noun prefix (¶2.23)

an- variant of am- (¶2.231)

-at nominative noun suffix (¶2.511)

aa- locative applicative verb prefix (¶2.44121)

-aak variant of -ak (¶2.511)

-aakot variant of -akot (¶2.512)

-aako variant of -ako (¶2.512)

-aakya variant of -akya "too" (¶2.521)

-aash aforementioned noun suffix (¶2.523)

-aat variant of -at (¶2.511); variant of -haat (¶2.513)

aay- variant of aa- (¶2.44121)

a- variant of am- (¶2.231)

-a accusative noun suffix (¶2.511)

bak- prefix formative (refers to the head or face) (¶2.4421)

-cha same-subject conjunctive verb suffix (¶2.494)

-chayni modal verb suffix (¶2.465)

chi- 2sg. II verb and noun prefix (¶2.22)

-chi causative verb suffix (¶2.443)

-chichi variant of -chi (¶2.443)

chik- 2sg. N verb prefix (¶2.24)

chim- 2sg. III verb and noun prefix (¶2.23)

chim- variant of chim- (¶2.231)

chok- prefix formative (refers to the mouth or head) (¶2.4421)

chi- variant of chim- (¶2.231)

-chi variant of hchi (¶2.492)

-h bare verb suffix (¶2.41)

-ha'ni epistemic modal verb suffix (¶2.4621)

hachi- 2pl. II verb and noun prefix (¶2.22)

hachik- 2pl. N verb and noun prefix (¶2.24)

hachim- 2pl. III verb and noun prefix (¶2.23)

hachin- variant of hachim- (¶2.231)

hachi- variant of hachim- (2.231)

hapo- special 1pl. II verb and noun prefix (¶2.22)

hapom- special 1pl. III verb and noun prefix (¶2.23)

hapon- variant of hapom- (¶2.231)

hap̲o̲- variant of hapom- (¶2.231)

hash- 2pl. I verb (occasionally noun) prefix (¶2.21)

-hay'm "ever" question verb suffix (¶2.474)

-haat nominative interrogative noun suffix (¶2.513)

-h̲a̲ exclamation verb suffix (¶2.464)

-hchaa perfect/habitual verb suffix (¶2.465)

-hch̲i̲ dubitative verb suffix (¶2.492)

hi- cardinal number prefix

-h̲i̲ exclamation verb suffix (¶2.464)

-hmat same-subject realis verb suffix (¶2.493); nominative indefinite noun suffix (¶2.514)

-hm̲a̲ different-subject realis verb suffix (¶2.493); accusative indefinite noun suffix (¶2.514)

hoo- 3pl. subj. verb prefix (¶2.432)

-hookano topic noun suffix (¶2.522)

-hookmano desiderative verb suffix (¶2.492)

-hookmat same-subject "if" verb suffix (¶2.493)

-hookm̲a̲ different-subject "if" verb suffix (¶2.493)

-hookya "but" verb suffix (¶2.491); "every"/"any" noun suffix (¶2.524)

-hoot nominative focus/inferential noun suffix (¶2.515)

-h̲o̲ accusative focus/inferential noun suffix (¶2.515); exclamation verb suffix (¶2.464)

-hta accusative interrogative noun suffix (¶2.513)

-ht̲o̲ predicate nominal noun interrogative suffix

ibaa- comitative applicative verb prefix (¶2.44123)

ik- hypothetical verb prefix (¶2.24)

il- 1pl. I verb (occasionally noun) prefix (¶2.21)

iloo- special 1pl. verb (occasionally noun) prefix (¶2.21)

ili- reflexive verb prefix (¶2.4411)

im- dative applicative verb and noun prefix (¶2.23, ¶2.44122)

imaa- "from" applicative verb prefix (¶2.44124)

in- variant of im- (¶2.231)

ish- 2sg. I verb (occasionally noun) prefix (¶2.21)

itti- reciprocal verb prefix (¶2.4411)

ii- variant of il- (¶2.21)

i- variant of im- (¶2.231)

-ísha "yet" verb suffix (¶2.483)

-k nominal formative (variant of -ka' ?)

-ka v1 formative (¶2.4422)

-ka' nominalizing verb suffix (¶2.541)

-kat same-subject subordinating verb suffix (¶2.493); nominative clausal noun suffix (¶2.516)

-kaash aforementioned verb suffix

-k̲a̲ different-subject subordinating verb suffix (¶2.493); accusative clausal noun suffix(¶2.516)

-ki- negative linker verb suffix (¶2.482)

kil- 1pl. N verb prefix (¶2.24); variant of il- (¶2.21)

kiloo- special 1pl. N verb prefix (¶2.24); variant of iloo- (¶2.21)

kii- variant of kil- (¶2.24, ¶2.21)

-kmak irrealis oblique time word suffix (¶2.523)

-kmat same-subject irrealis verb suffix (¶2.493)

-km̲a̲ different-subject/accusative irrealis verb and time word suffix (¶2.493, ¶2.523)

-kya variant of -hookya (¶2.491), -akya (¶2.521)

-l- v1 formative (¶2.4422)

-li 1sg I verb (occasionally noun) suffix (¶2.21, ¶2.452); v2 formative (¶2.4422)

-lh- variant of -l- (¶2.4422)
-m past question verb suffix (¶2.472)
-mankǫ past evidential verb suffix (¶2.463)
-n- indefinite/inferential formative (¶2.473)
-na different-subject conjunctive verb suffix (¶2.494)
nok- prefix formative (refers to the throat or the emotions) (¶2.4421)
-nna negative hortative verb suffix (¶2.484)
-o negative verb suffix (¶2.241, 2.453)
-o'si variant of -a'si (¶2.451)
ok- prefix formative (refers to water) (¶2.4421); prefix formative ("sideways") (¶2.4421)
okaa- "in" applicative verb prefix (¶2.44125)
on- "on" applicative verb prefix (¶2.44126)
osh- prefix formative (refers to the head or hair) (¶2.4421)
-ookano variant of -hookano (¶2.522)
-ookmano variant of -hookmano (¶2.492)
-ookmat variant of -hookmat (¶2.493)
-ookma variant of -hookma (¶2.493)
-ookya variant of -hookya (¶2.491, ¶2.524)
-oot variant of -hoot (¶2.515)
-ǫ variant of -hǫ (noun suffix) (¶2.515)
po- 1pl. II verb and noun prefix (¶2.22)

-po- intensive formative (¶2.4421)
pom- 1pl. III verb and noun prefix (¶2.23)
pon- variant of pom- (¶2.231)
pǫ- variant of pom- (¶2.231)
sa- 1sg. II verb and noun prefix (¶2.22)
sam- variant of am- (¶2.231)
san- variant of sam- (¶2.231)
sǫ- variant of sam- (¶2.231)
-shki present evidential verb suffix (¶2.463)
-t participial verb suffix (¶2.495)
-t- interrogative formative (¶2.473)
-ta question verb suffix (¶2.471); variant of -hta (¶2.513)
-tǫ variant of -htǫ
tak- prefix formative (refers to the mouth or lips) (¶2.4421)
tok- prefix formative (refers to the mouth or lips) (¶2.4421)
-tok perfective verb suffix (¶2.461)
-tokat perfective same-subject subordinating verb suffix (¶2.493)
-toka perfective different-subject subordinating verb suffix (¶2.493)
-tokoot backgrounding same-subject subordinating verb suffix (¶2.493)
-tokǫ backgrounding different-subject subordinating verb suffix (¶2.493)
-ttook remote past verb suffix (¶2.461)
yak- prefix formative ("this") (¶2.4421)
yok- prefix formative (refers to water) (¶2.4421)

BIBLIOGRAPHY

i. Works Cited in A Guide to the Dictionary

Byington, Cyrus. 1915. *A Dictionary of the Choctaw Language*. Ed. J. R. Swanton and H. S. Halbert. Bureau of American Ethnology Bulletin 46. Washington, D.C.: Government Printing Office. [Reprinted 1973, Oklahoma City Council of Choctaws; 1978, St. Clair Shores, Mich., Scholarly Press.]

Humes, Rev. Jesse, and Vinnie May (James) Humes. 1973. *A Chickasaw Dictionary*. [Ada, Okla.:] The Chickasaw Nation.

Jacob, Betty, Dale Nicklas, and Betty Lou Spencer. 1977. *Introduction to Choctaw*. Durant, Okla.: Choctaw Bilingual Education Program, Southeastern Oklahoma State University.

Nicklas, T. Dale. 1979. *Reference Grammar of the Choctaw Language*. Durant, Okla.: Choctaw Bilingual Education Program, Southeastern Oklahoma State University.

Watkins, Ben. 1892. *Complete Choctaw Definer: English with Choctaw Definition*. Van Buren, Ark.: J. W. Baldwin. [Reprinted 1972, Nashville, Southeastern Indian Antiquities Survey.]

Wright, Allen. 1880. *Chahta Leksikon: A Choctaw in English Definition for the Choctaw Academies and Schools*. St. Louis: Presbyterian Publishing Co.

ii. Some Additional References on Chickasaw Grammar

Munro, Pamela. 1984. "The Syntactic Status of Object Possessor Raising in Western Muskogean." In *Proceedings of the Tenth Annual Meeting of the Berkeley Linguistics Society*, ed. C. Brugman, et al., pp. 634-49. Berkeley: BLS.

Munro, Pamela. 1987. "Some Morphological Differences Between Chickasaw and Choctaw." In *Muskogean Linguistics*, ed. P. Munro, *UCLA Occasional Papers in Linguistics* 6, pp. 119-33. Los Angeles: Department of Linguistics, University of California.

Munro, Pamela. In preparation. "Chickasaw." In *The Native Languages of the Southeastern United States*, ed. J. Scancarelli and H. Hardy, *Studies in the Anthropology of North American Indians*. Lincoln: University of Nebraska Press.

Munro, Pamela, and Lynn Gordon. 1982. "Syntactic Relations in Western Muskogean: A Typological Perspective." *Language* 58: 81-115.

Munro, Pamela, and Charles H. Ulrich. 1984. "Structure-Preservation and Western Muskogean Rhythmic Lengthening." In *Proceedings of the Third Annual West Coast Conference on Formal Linguistics*, ed. M. Cobler, et al., pp. 191-202. Stanford, Calif.: Stanford Linguistics Association.

ABBREVIATIONS

The following abbreviations are used in the dictionary entries. (See ¶1.6 for a complete list of the abbreviations used to identify individual Chickasaw speakers' usage.)

3	non-agreeing third-person	int.	interrogative
3C	non-agreeing third-person complement (cannot be omitted)	IR	reciprocal I agreement set
		klgr.	kl-grade
		N	hypothetical agreement set
an.	animate	ngr.	n-grade
aux.	auxiliary	nonhum.	non-human
cln.	clausal noun	nonsubj.	non-subject
[+CPR]	verb may undergo Color Possessor Raising rule	nonsubr.	non-subordinate
		obj.	object
[-CPR]	verb does not undergo Color Possessor Raising rule	[OPR]	dative prefixed verb used in OPR construction
(Ct.)	word is probably Choctaw, according to Catherine Willmond	[+OPR]	verb may undergo Object Possessor Raising rule
		[-OPR]	verb does not undergo Object Possessor Raising rule
(Ct?)	word is possibly Choctaw, according to Catherine Willmond		
		pl.	plural (two or more)
dl.	dual (exactly two)	[PR]	dative prefixed verb used in PR construction
[E]	verb takes an unsuffixed Equi complement	[+PR]	verb may undergo Possessor Raising rule
[E+kat]	verb takes an Equi complement with +kat suffix	[-PR]	verb does not undergo Possessor Raising rule
		prt.	participle formed with -t
[E+t]	verb takes an Equi complement with +t suffix	rcgr.	reduplicated chi-grade
		rigr.	reduplicated initial grade
		rmgr.	reduplicated medial grade
ggr.	g-grade		
hgr.	h-grade	[-SC]	verb does not follow Strident-Coronal rule
[+HM]	verb undergoes HM rule	[+SC]	verb follows Strident-Coronal rule
hngr.	hn-grade		
hum.	human	sg.	singular (exactly one)
I	I agreement set	spl.	special (first-person) plural
II	II agreement set		
III	III agreement set	subj.	subject
inan.	inanimate	subr.	subordinate
ind.	indefinite	[+T]	verb often is used with
inf.	inferential		

lxix

	tahli/taha auxiliary	v1	v1 of verb pair
[+taha]	verb may be used with	v2	v2 of verb pair
	taha auxiliary for plural	var.	variant
	subject	xgr.	extended grade
tpl.	triplural (three or more)	ygr.	y-grade

SYMBOLS USED IN THE DICTIONARY

The following symbols are used in the dictionary entries. All of these are explained further in section §1 above, as the references below show. They are listed approximately in the order in which they might be encountered within a typical dictionary entry.

< > Angles enclose word-like elements that cannot be pronounced separately without added material (§1.2, §1.7) or, in this introduction, elements that do not occur in Chickasaw.

° A raised circle marks the argument in a verb's definition that triggers II or III object agreement (§1.4).

( ) Parentheses enclose the abbreviations used to specify agreement class (§1.4).

; A semicolon separates agreement indications for different arguments, with subject always coming first: thus, "(I;II)" indicates a I subject, II object (§1.4).

/ A slash separates alternative agreement frames: thus, "(I / II)" indicates either a I or a II subject (§1.4).

, A comma (with surrounding spaces) separates agreement marking on separate elements of complex verbs: thus, "(I , I)" indicates that each of the two words in a complex verb is marked for a I subject; "(II = obj. , I;II)" indicates that the first such word is marked for a II object, while the second is marked for a I subject and (the same) II object (§1.4).

— A horizontal line specifies that a given agreement role, generally subject, cannot be filled: for example, (—) indicates a subjectless verb (§1.4).

[] Brackets enclose grammatical features specified for some words in the dictionary. More commonly, they enclose etymologies: information on the source of borrowings and on the structure of complex words or expressions (§1.2, §1.7).

* A star marks the element to which agreement marking is added in the etymology of a complex verb (§1.4).

{ } Braces enclose grammatical information and derived or related forms (§1.2, §1.7).

§ A section mark introduces examples within a dictionary entry (§1.2, §1.7) or, in this introduction, precedes section numbers.

| A vertical line separates different examples within a dictionary entry (§1.7).

THE CHICKASAW ALPHABET

Below is a list of the letters and letter combinations used to write Chickasaw in the alphabetical order used in the dictionary. (The pronunciation of the sounds these letters and letter combinations represent is explained in section ¶1.1.)

'	lh
a	m
aa	n
a̲	ng
b	o
ch	oo
d	o̲
e	p
f	r
g	s
h	sh
i	t
ii	u
i̲	v
j	w
k	y
l	z

The vowels a, i, and o come in three varieties, short (written with an ordinary vowel letter), long (written with two of the same vowel letter), and nasal (written underlined), each of which is considered a completely separate sound. These different vowel sounds are alphabetized in the order short, long, nasal. Vowels may be accented or marked with either a ´ or a ^ over the vowel. Accent marks are ignored in the alphabetical order, except when two words differ only in that one includes an accented vowel but the other does not: in this case, the word without the accent comes first.

Each two-letter combination in the list above represents a different sound and is alphabetized separately. Thus, a word beginning with **ab**, such as **abooha** "house", comes before a word beginning with **aab**, such as **aabi** "to paint", because the first sound of the first word is **a**, while the first sound in the second word is **aa**, which follows **a** in the alphabet.

The sounds (and letters) **d, e, g, j, r, u, v,** and **z** are used only in words Chickasaw has borrowed from other languages, mainly English. The sounds ' and **ng** cannot be used at the beginning of Chickasaw words. All the other consonant sounds of Chickasaw (and the letters that represent them) may occur doubled, as in **hollosi** "to be pounded", which contains a double **l** sound, or **kochcha** "to go out", which contains a double **ch**. Unlike long vowels, doubled consonants are not alphabetized separately. Thus, **hollosi** comes before **holmo** "to be roofed".

Chickasaw-English Dictionary

a

a to be (II;3C) (<ya> when prefixed;
deleted when no prefix or suffix is
used; <oo> when there is no prefix
and suffix is +t, +tok, +tokmat,
+tokma, +kmat, +kma, +ta, +tam,
+to, +kat, or +ka; requires an overt
preceding complement noun) §
Chikashsha' saya. I am a Chickasaw.
| Chahta chiyata? Are you
Choctaw? | Alikchi' poya'chi. We
are going to be doctors. | Hattak
yammat minko' attook. That man
was a chief (long ago).
á'lbi ggr. of albi
á'lmo ggr. of almo
á'lhto ggr. of alhto
á'ni ggr. of ani
á'pa ggr. of apa
á'ya ggr. of aya
aba' up; something above ground
level: upstairs, ceiling
aba' anompa anompoli' see aba'
anompishtanompoli'
aba' anompishtanompoli', aba'
anompa anompoli' preacher [aba'
anompa (isht) anompoli+']
aba' aya to go up, go upstairs (I)
aba' bínni'li to sit up high (I)
Aba' Binni'li', Abaabinni'li' God in
Heaven [(aba' binni'li)+']
Aba' Chaaha' highest Heaven
[chaaha+']
aba' ishtaloowa' hymn [isht
taloowa+']
aba' pí'la ggr. of aba' pílla, <aba pila>
aba' píhhi'la hgr. of aba' pílla, <aba'
pila>
aba' pila up
<aba' pila> in aba pilachi {ggr. aba'

pí'la, (var.) aba' pílla; hgr. aba'
píhhi'la}
aba' pilachi to roll up (one's sleeves),
pull up (one's dress), raise
(something) (I;3) [<aba' *pila>+chi]
aba' pílla way up
aba' pílla to be up: pulled up, sticking
up (of hair, for instance) (3)—var.
ggr. of <aba pila> {ggr. aba' pí'la;
hgr. aba' píhhi'la}
Aba' Pinchitokaka' Our Lord, Our
God [from the Choctaw Bible: pim+
(=pom+) Chitokaka']
Aba' Pinki' God our Father [from the
Choctaw Bible: pim+ (=pom+) inki']
Aba' Yaakni' Heaven
abá'ni ggr. of abaani
abaksha', (AB, WB, MS, TJ) abaksho',
(ER) habaksho', (LF) habaksho'
chicken snake
abakshowahángli hngr. of
abakshowakli
abakshowakli to toss one's head,
throw one's head back (I) [a+bak+]
{ggr. abakshówwakli; hngr.
abakshowahángli; ngr.
abakshowángli; abakshowali}
abakshowali to put one's head way
back, put one's chin in the air (I)
[a+bak+] {ggr. abakshówwa'li; ngr.
abakshowáli; abakshowakli}
abakshowángli ngr. of abakshowakli
abakshowáli ngr. of abakshowali
abakshówwa'li ggr. of abakshowali
abakshówwakli ggr. of abakshowakli
abalalli, abalatli to grow over, grow
together with (of crabgrass on a
lawn, for example) (3;3) [a+balalli]
abalatli see abalalli

aballaka' following, after (an an. or
moving obj.—in a line, usually not
immediately behind) (II)
{aballak<u>a</u>li'} § asaballaka': after me
aballaka' finha to be last (I) §
Aballaka' finhalitok. I was last.
aballaka' finha last § Aballaka' finha
alalitok. I came last.
aballak<u>a</u>li' (moving) along behind,
(moving) along in back of,
following (an an. or moving obj.)
{aballaka'}
aballakshi', ishtaballakshi' last child
in a family [(isht) aballaka' oshi']
<aban-kachi> in aban-kachit m<u>a</u>a
{v2. abanni; ygr. aban-k<u>a</u>yya'chi}
aban-kachit m<u>a</u>a to be lying on,
perpendicular to (tpl. subj.) (II =
obj. , I = subj.) [<aban-kachi>+t] {sg.
ab<u>a</u>nna'a, abaana, dl. aban-
k<u>a</u>yya'chi} § Asaban-kachit
hashm<u>a</u>a. You're all lying on me.
aban-k<u>a</u>yya'chi to be lying on,
perpendicular to (dl. subj.) (I;II)—
ygr. of <aban-kachi> {sg. ab<u>a</u>nna'a,
abaana; tpl. aban-kachit m<u>a</u>a}
ab<u>a</u>nna'a to be lying on,
perpendicular to (sg. subj.) (I;II)—
xgr. of abaana {v2. <ab<u>a</u>nna'li>; dl.
aban-k<u>a</u>yya'chi; tpl. aban-kachit
m<u>a</u>a}
<ab<u>a</u>nna'li> in ittab<u>a</u>nna'li—ggr. of
abaanali {v1. ab<u>a</u>nna'a}
abanni to lay, throw (pl. obj.) across
(I;3;3) {v1. <aban-kachi>; sg. obj.
abaanali}
<abannichi> in ittabannichi
[abanni+chi]
ab<u>a</u>wwa'a to be out of alignment, not
to lie flat; to put one's head up or
slightly back (I)—ggr. of abaawaa
abayya to go from one (indef. obj.) to
another (I;3) (usually in part.)
[aba'+aya ?] § Chokka' abayyalitok. I

went from one house to another.
abayyachi to go along by; to go from
one (obj.) to another (I;3) (often in
part.) {hngr. abayyah<u>a</u>nchi; abayya} §
Ihoo yammookano hattak
abayyahanchi. That woman goes
from man to man, That woman
keeps going from one man to
another. | Abookoshi' abayyachit
<u>a</u>atok. He went along the riverbank.
abayyat n<u>o</u>wa, abayyachit n<u>o</u>wa to go
from one (obj.) to another (I;3)
[abayya/abayyachi+t] § Johnat
chokka' abayyat n<u>o</u>wa. John goes
from one house to another.
Abaabinni'li' see Aba' Binni'li'
abaana to flop across, flop over (sg.
subj.) (I;II) {v2. abaanali; xgr.
ab<u>a</u>nna'a; dl. aban-k<u>a</u>yya'chi; tpl.
aban-kachit m<u>a</u>a; ootabaana}
abaanabli to go over, across (sg.
obj.)—for instance, to go over the
edge of (a pot), as a liquid does
when it boils over (I;II) {v1.
abaanapa; hngr. abaanah<u>a</u>mbli: to go
over and over; pl. obj. abaanapo'li}
abaanah<u>a</u>mbli to go over and over—
hngr. of abaanabli
abaanali to put, lay (sg. obj.°) across,
crossing, down on (I;II;3) {v1.
abaana; ggr. <ab<u>a</u>nna'li>; pl. obj.
abanni; ilabaanali: to shoulder (a
burden); ishtilabaanali: to confess,
take the blame}
abaan<u>a</u>mpa ngr. of abaanapa
abaanapa to go over, run over; to
pass (of time, for example) (3) {v2.
abaanabli, abaanappichi; ngr.
abaan<u>a</u>mpa} § Nittakat abaanapatok.
The day passed. | afammi
abaanampak<u>a</u>... over a year ago, a
year having gone by...
abaanapo'li to go over (pl. obj.) (I;II)
{sg. obj. abaanabli; rmgr.}

abaanappopóli} § Apobaanapo'tok. He went over us.

abaanappí'chi ggr. of abaanappichi

abaanappichi to put over (I;II); to run over, take too much time (of a speaker) (I) {v1. abaanapa; ggr. abaanappí'chi}

abaanappopóli to go over one after another (I;II)—rmgr. of abaanapo'li

abaani to barbecue (I;II) {v1. albani; ggr. abá'ni, ábba'ni}

abaanompa, abaanompa' word of God, gospel [aba' anompa/anompa']

abaanompa' anoli to preach (I)

abaanompa' taloowa' gospel music, gospel songs

abaanompa' toshooli' preacher [toshooli+']

Abaanompa' Yimmi' Christian [yimmi+']

abaanompishtanompoli to preach (I) [abaanompa' isht *anompoli]

abaanompishtanompoli' preacher, minister [abaanompishtanompoli+']

abaanompishtimanompoli to preach to (I;III) [abaanompa' isht *imanompoli]

abaanompittanaha' religious meeting, prayer meeting [abaanompa' ittanaha']

abaanompi'shi' minister, missionary [abaanompa' i'shi+']

abaatalahchaa', (AB) abaatalashsha, (CM) abaatalaschaaha', (WB) yabashchaa' daddy-long-legs (IIIp: imambaatalahchaa') [aba' ?]

abaawaháa hngr. of abaawaa

abaawaa to go up, rise (I) [aba' waa ?] {v2. abaawiili; ggr. abáwwa'a; hngr. abawaháa}

abaawaachi to raise (I;II) [abaawaa+chi]

abaawiili to lift, pick up, raise (usually, over one's head) (I;II); to pull up (a dress, skirt, or shirt) (I;3) [+OPR] [aba' wiili] {v1. abaawaa; ngr. abaawíli}

abaawíli ngr. of abaawiili

abaayo'wa, (CP) abaayochi to gallop (of a horse, for instance) (I) {hngr. abaayohówa}

abaayo'wachi to make (a horse, etc.) gallop (I;II) [abaayo'wa+chi]

abaayohówa hngr. of abaayo'wa

ábba'ni ggr. of abaani

ábbi'ka ggr. of abika

ábbilhlhi ggr. of abilhlhi

abi to kill; to abort (I;II) (short verb) [+OPR: imambi] {v1. <albi>; hngr. ahámbi; neg. ikbo; imambi: to beat (in a game), to kill for; ittibi: to fight; <ambi>} § Ishbitok. You killed him. | Akbokitok. I didn't kill him. | Chibila'chi. I'll kill you.

abi'chi to poke (the fire) (I;3) (Ct?) [+SC]

<abichi> in aa-abichi' [abi+chi]

<abiha> in iabisowa' {v2. abihli; albi'ha, <albiha>}

abihínka hngr. of abika

abihíli hngr. of abihli

abihílhlhi hngr. of abilhlhi

abihli to put, pack (dl. obj.') in (I;II;3) [-OPR] {v1. albí'ha, <abiha>, <albiha>; hngr. abihíli; ngr. abíhli; sg. obj. fokhi; tpl. obj. ani (put in), abihpoli (pack); imambihli: to put in, pack (dl. obj.) for}

abihpoli to load, pack (tpl. obj.) (I;3) [abihli +po+] {v1. abilhpowa; dl. obj. abihli; imambihpoli: to load, pack for}

abika, abiika to be sick; to be menstruating, be in labor (of a woman) (II) [+PR: imambiika] [-CPR] [abi+ka ?] {ggr. ábbi'ka; hngr. abihínka; ngr. abínka; ygr. abíyyi'ka;

abika'

imambiika: to be sick for}
abika' sick person; sickness [abika+']
abika' halili to catch a sickness (I)
abika' imaahalili, imaahalili to catch
a sickness from (I;III) [imaa+halili] §
Lynnat amaahalitok, Lynnat abika'
amaahalitok. Lynn caught it from
me.
abika' ihalili to catch a sickness from
(I;III) [im+halili] § Lynnak abika'
ihalililitok. I caught it from Lynn.
abika' shaali' ambulance [shaali+']
abikachi, abiikachi to make
(someone) sick (I;II) {ggr. abiiká'chi;
hngr. abikahánchi} § Asabikashtok,
Asabiikachitok. She made me sick.
abikahánchi hngr. of abikachi
abikakat impállammi to have a
serious illness (II , III) [abika+kat] §
Asabikakat ampallammi. I was
seriously ill.
abik-apiisachi' nurse [abika+'
apiisachi+']
abikaa-asha' hospital [abika+' aa-
asha']
abikimilhkoochi to make hysterical,
send into a fit of shaking (I;III) [-SC]
[abikimilhkooli+chi] § Abika
chiksamilhko'cho. You didn't make
me hysterical.
abikimilhkooli to be hysterical, have
a shaking fit (III) [abika
*im+<ilhkooli>] § Abikamilhkooli.
I was hysterical.
abikoppolo' epidemic, plague, really
serious disease (AIDS, for instance)
[abika+' oppolo+']
abila to melt onto, be soldered onto
(3;3) [a+bila] {v2. abilili; abilachi} §
Kendi'at holisso abilatahatok. The
candy melted onto the paper.
abilachi to solder, melt (something)
onto (I;3;3) [abila+chi]
abilili to solder (something) onto

(I;3;3) [a+bilili] {v1. abila}
abilhlhi to train (plants) on stakes
(I;3) {v1. albilha; ggr. ábbilhlhi; hngr.
abihílhlhi} § Bala' abilhlhilitok. I
staked the beans.
abilhpowa to be packed (Ct) (3) [+T]
{v2. abihpoli}
abínka ngr. of abika
abíyyi'ka ygr. of abika
abiika see abika
abiiká'chi ggr. of abikachi, abiikachi
abiikachi see abikachi
abiikami, (FA, CM, LR) abiikama,
(WB) abiikamo, (MJ) abiikammi,
(AB, LF) abiikamma to be sickly,
sick all the time (3) (often used in
the negative) [abika mina ?, abika
yahmi ?]
abiitippichi to press down on (I;II); to
press * against (I;II;3)
[a+<bitippichi>]
abíhli ngr. of abihli
abokkisa' door (the swinging part)
[abooha+okkisa']
abokkisa' tikba' front door
abokkisaayo'kli' doorknob [abokkisa'
aa+yokli+']
abokkisishkasa'chi' door knocker
[abokkisa' isht kasa'chi+']
abokkol-anonka' forest [abokkoli'
anonka']
abokkoli to be bushy (nonhum. subj.)
(3) {ygr. abokkóyyo'li}
abokkoli' thicket [abokkoli+']
abokkóyyo'li ygr. of abokkoli
aboknoha, aboknowa to be swaddled,
wrapped up in; to playfully wrap
oneself up in (II;3); to be wrapped
around (3;II); to have wrapped
around oneself (II;3-at) {v2.
aboknohli; ngr. aboknóha} §
Naachaat Alek aboknowatahatok.
The quilt is wrapped around Alex. I
Alekat naachi aboknowatahatok,

Alekat naachaat aboknowatahatok.
Alex is wrapped in a quilt.
aboknohli to swaddle, wrap up ° in
(I;II;3) {v1. aboknoha; hngr.
aboknohóli; ngr. aboknóhli}
aboknowa see aboknoha
aboknóhli ngr. of aboknohli
abooha, aboowa house (IIIp:
imambooha) {abooha}
abooha aba' upstairs, upper floor
abooha apootaka' see
aboohapootaka'
abooha aachokoshkomo' playhouse
[aa+chokoshkomo+']
abooha ashaka' backyard; in back of
the house
abooha ashaka' okkisa', (WB, MJ)
okkisa' abooha ashka' back door
abooha chaffo' the other room (not
the one we are in)
abooha chofalli' janitor,
housecleaner [chofalli+']
abooha fóyyokhi to keep (someone)
in the house, confine to the house
(I;II) § Abooha safoyyokhitok. She
kept me in the house.
abooha holisso lapali', holisso abooha
lapali' wallpaper [lapali+']
abooha ikbi' carpenter, house builder
[ikbi+']
abooha iksaachi' carpenter
[iksaachi+']
abooha ittabaana' see
aboohattittabaana'
abooha ittintakla' see
aboohattintakla'
abooha ihiyohli' vertical supporting
beams in a house [im+hiyohli+']
abooha kallo' jail [kallo+']
abooha lapa'li' side room added onto
a house [lapali+']
abooha lhipa' old house [lhipa+']
abooha naksika' wall
abooha nannaa-asha' furniture

[nanna aa-asha+']
abooha nannishtaa-asha' courthouse
[nanna isht aa-asha+']
abooha nota' crawl space
abooha notinto'wa' foundation (of a
house) [nota' im+to'wa+']
abooha pakna' roof, ceiling
abooha tannap on the other side of
the house; in the other room
Abooha Tohbi' (CP), (LF) Abooha
Toobi' the White House (LF),
Washington, D. C. (CP) [tohbi+']
abooha' see yaakni' cholok abooha'
[abooha+']
aboohalbi', aboowalbi' house paint
[abooha albi']
aboohapootaka', abooha apootaka'
side of the house (usually, on the
outside); wall (either inside or
outside)
aboohattintakla', abooha ittintakla'
hall (in a house)
aboohattittabaana', abooha ittabaana'
log cabin [abooha (itti') ittabaana+']
{itti' ittabaana' abooha}
aboohishpihli' vacuum cleaner
[abooha isht pihli+']
aboohishtachifa' mop [abooha isht
achifa+']
aboohishtaasha'na' lock on the door
of a house [abooha isht
aa+ashana+']
aboohishtaasha'na' iksaachi'
locksmith [iksaachi+']
abookoshi, (ER, MC) bookoshi, (FA)
abookoshi', (AB) abokshi' river,
creek [oshi']
abookoshi apotaka' riverbank
abookoshi hina' aalhopolli' bridge
(WB) [aa+lhopolli+']
Abookoshi Homma' the Red River
[homma+']
abookoshi shila' dry riverbed
[shila+']

7

abookoshi' in Lokchok Abookoshi'
[abookoshi+']
abooshi' little house; bathroom,
outhouse; closet [abooha oshi']
abooshi' aya to go to the bathroom (I)
abooshollichi to shatter against, crack
into many pieces against (I;II;3); to
break, crack open (pecans, hard-
boiled eggs) so that the shell and
meat are mingled together (I;3)
[+OPR] [a+boshollichi] § Lynn
iwinda akankoshi'
abooshollichilitok, Lynna winda'
akankoshi' imabooshollichilitok. I
shattered eggs against Lynn's
window.
aboowa see abooha
aboowa bo'li' woodpecker (LF)
[bo'li+']
aboowalbi' see aboohalbi'
<acha'pa> in ittacha'pa
<achaffa> in ilachaffa , ittachaffa
[a+chaffa] {<achaafowa>}
achákka'a to be attached to (sg.
nonhum. subj.) (3;3)—xgr. of
achaaka {dl. achakkáyya'chi; tpl.
achakkachit máa}
<achakkachi> in achakkachit máa,
ittachakkachi {ygr. achakkáyya'chi}
achakkachit máa to be attached to
(tpl. nonhum. subj.) (3;3)
[<achakkachi>+t] {sg. achákka'a; dl.
achakkáyya'chi}
achakkáyya'chi to be attached to (dl.
nonhum. subj.) (3;3)—ygr. of
<achakkachi> {sg. achákka'a; tpl.
achakkachit máa}
achakli to make (pl. nonhum. obj.)
longer, wider (I;3) {sg. obj. achaakali}
achakná'ski ggr. of achaknaski
achaknaháski to be lying on one's
side, keep turning on one's side (I);
to lie on one's side in (a place)
(I;3)—var. hgr. of achaknaski

achaknaháski hngr. of achaknaski
achaknáhhaski hgr. of achaknaski
achaknaski to turn on one's side (I)
[naksi'] {ggr. achakná'ski; hgr.
achaknáhhaski, (var.)
achaknaháski; hngr. achaknaháski;
ngr. achaknáski; ygr.
achaknáyya'ski: to be crooked,
sideways (3); achaknahaski}
achaknaskichi to turn (mainly
nonhum. obj.) on its side (I;II)
[achaknaski+chi]
achaknaskichit bohli to turn (mainly
hum. obj.) on its side (I;II)
[achaknaskichi+t] § Achaknaskichit
sabohtok. She turned me on my
side.
achaknáyya'ski to be crooked,
sideways, lying on its side (of a box,
for instance) (3)—ygr. of achaknaski
achaknáski ngr. of achaknaski
achánka to be increased, higher (of
prices), to be longer (of a string with
more tied onto the end, for
instance)—ngr. of achaaka
achánkahma, ootachánkahma again
(Ct) [(oot) achanka+hma] §
Achankahma issolitok. I hit him
again.
achapa, achaapa to talk back to,
answer back, sass at; to argue with;
to vote against, petition against; to
compete against (I;II) {v2.
<achapali>; ggr. áchcha'pa: to face;
ittachapa, ishtachapa}
<achapali> in ittachapali {v1. achapa}
<achapo'li> in ittachapo'li
<achapo'wa> in ittachapo'wa
<achaabli> in ittachaabli
<achaafowa> in ittachaafowa
[a+<chaafowa>] {<achaffa>}
<achaafoochi> in ittachaafoochi
[a+chaafoochi, <achaafowa>+chi]
achaaha to be used to (II;3) [+T]

[a+chaaha ?] {ikacha'ho; imachaaha: to be used to (a person)}
achaahachi to get (someone) used to one (I;II) [achaaha+chi]
achaaka to grow, sprout (nonhum. subj., unless preceded by chaahakat) (3) {v2. achaakali; ggr. áchcha'ka; ngr. achánka: to be increased, higher, longer; xgr. achákka'a} § chaahakat achaaka: to grow tall
achaakali to add another piece onto; to make wider, longer (I;II) [a+chakali] {v1. achaaka, achákka'a; ngr. achaakáli: to increase, lengthen; pl. obj. achakli}
achaakáli to increase (prices), lengthen (a string, for instance) (I;3)—ngr. of achaakali
achaakí'ssa ggr. of achaakissa
achaakissa to stick onto, be stuck onto (3;II); to have stuck on to one (II;3-at) (best with an overt II prefix) [a+chakissa] {ggr. achaakí'ssa; ittachaakissa} § Ithanali holissaat asachaakissakat. I know the paper stuck on to me.
achaakissachi to stick, glue (something) onto ° (I;II;3) [achaakissa+chi] § Holisso achichaakissachilitok. I stuck the paper onto you.
achaamapa to vibrate and make a noise, to echo (3); to hear an echo (or a loud noise in a tunnel), to have one's head ring (II) [a+chamapa]
achaapa see achapa
áchcha'ka to grow a little (for instance, of a weed)—ggr. of achaaka § chaahakat áchcha'ka: to grow tall (I)
áchcha'pa to face, be straight across from—ggr. of achapa
áchchi'li ggr. of achiili

áchcho'li ggr. of acho'li
achifa, achiifa to wash (I;II) {v1. alhchifa} § Achichifalitok, Achichiifalitok. I washed you.
achifachi to wash off, wash out; to rinse (I;II) [achifa+chi]
achilihínta hngr. of achilita
achilita to bother, pester (I;II) [a+chilita] {ggr. achílli'ta; hngr. achilihínta; ygr. achilíyyi'ta}
achilíyyi'ta ygr. of achilita
achílli'ta ggr. of achilita
achiifa see achifa
achiilakbi to dry onto (3;II) [a+chilakbi] § Lokchokat asachiilakbitahatok. The mud has dried onto me.
achiili to lay (eggs) (I;II) [a+chiili] {ggr. áchchi'li}
acho'li to sew, to stitch up a wound (I;II) {v1. alhcho'wa; ggr. áchcho'li}
achohóshli hngr. of achoshli
achokkobbi to be used only to, to cling to, to be dependent on, to stay with; to love (I;II) [a+<chokkobbi>] {imachokkobbi}
achokkobbichi to get (someone, such as a baby°) used to (a person, such as a babysitter°) (I;II;3) [achokkobbi+chi] {ilachokkobbichi} § Lynn asachokkobbichitok. She got Lynn used to me, She got me used to Lynn.
achokmalichi to treat well (I;II) [a+chokmali+chi] {ngr. achokmalínchi: to be careful with, treat pretty well}
achokmalicho'si to be easy, gentle with (I;II) [achokmalichi+o'si] § Achichokmalishlo'sachi. I'll be gentle with you. | Achokmalishlo'stok, Achokmalicho'slitok. I was easy with him.

9

achokmalínchi

achokmalínchi to be careful with,
treat pretty well—ngr. of
achokmalichi
achokmí'lhka ggr. of achokmilhka
achokmíhhilhka hgr. of
achokmilhka
achokmihílhka to be kneeling (I)—
var. hgr. of achokmilhka
achokmihilhkat bínni'li to sit on
one's heels, kneel with one's
buttocks resting on one's heels (sg.
subj.) (I) [achokmihilhka+t] {dl.
achokmihilhkat chí'ya; tpl.
achokmihilhkat binohmáa}
achokmihilhkat binohmáa to sit on
one's heels, kneel with one's
buttocks resting on one's heels (tpl.
subj.) (I) (see binohmáa)
[achokmihilhka+t] {sg.
achokmihilhkat bínni'li; dl.
achokmihilhkat chí'ya} §
Achokmihilhkat binoht iimaa.
We're sitting on our heels.
achokmihilhkat chí'ya to sit on one's
heels, kneel with one's buttocks
resting on one's heels (dl. subj.) (I)
[achokmihilhka+t] {sg.
achokmihilhkat bínni'li; tpl.
achokmihilhkat binohmáa}
achokmihílhka hngr. of
achokmilhka
achokmilhka, (CC, ER, CM, TJ)
chokmilhka, (AB) chokbilhka, (WB)
chombilhka to kneel down, get on
one's knees (I) {ggr. achokmí'lhka;
hgr. achokmíhhilhka, (var.)
achokmihílhka; hngr.
achokmihílhka; ygr.
achokmíyyi'lhka; achokmihilhka:
to be kneeling}
achokmilhkachi to make (someone)
kneel (I;II) [achokmilhka+chi]
achokmíyyi'lhka ygr. of
achokmilhka

achónna'chi to persevere, keep on; to
stand it, be able to take it (a
situation) (I)
<achoshkachi> in achoshkachit máa,
chofak-oshi' aachoshkachi' {ygr.
achoshkáyya'chi}
achoshkachit máa to be stuck into,
plugged into; to follow around, stick
to (tpl. subj.) (II = obj. , 3)
[<achoshkachi>+t] {v2. achoshli; sg.
achóshsho'wa; dl. achoshkáyya'chi}
§ Asachoshkachit maa. They're
sticking into me (of acupuncture
needles, for example).
achoshkáyya'chi to be stuck into,
plugged into; to follow around, stick
to (dl. subj.) (3;II)—ygr. of
<achoshkachi> {v2. achoshli; sg.
achóshsho'wa; tpl. achoshkachit
máa}
achoshli to stick, plug (pl. patient
obj.) into, throw (knives) at * (I;II;3)
{v1. achoshkáyya'chi (dl. subj.),
achoshkachit máa (tpl. subj.); hngr.
achohóshli; sg. patient obj.
achoosholi} § Bashpo asachoshlitok.
He threw knives at me.
achóshsho'wa to be stuck into,
plugged into; to follow around, stick
to (sg. subj.) (3;II)—xgr. of achoosha
{v2. achoosholi; dl.
achoshkáyya'chi; tpl. achoshkachit
máa} § Asachoshsho'wa. He's
following me around, sticking close
to me.
achoosha to stick into, get stuck into
(3;II) {xgr. achóshsho'wa}
achoosholi to stick, plug (sg. patient
obj.) into *, to throw (a knife) at *
(I;II;3) {v1. achóshsho'wa; pl. patient
obj. achoshli} § Issachoosholitok.
You stuck it into me.
achọ'chaba', (MC, TJ) hachọ'chaba',
(HS) hachọ'choba', (TP)

10

achǫ'choba', (CM) hachonchaba' alligator

afacha to get barred (somehow) (3) {xgr. afáchcha'a}

afachali to bar (a door, especially with a stick across it) (I;3) {v1. afáchcha'a}

afáchcha'a to be barred (of a door) (3)—xgr. of afacha {v2. afachali}

afahámmi hngr. of afammi

afama to meet, encounter (especially, by chance?) (I;II) [+OPR] [a+fama ?] {v2. afammi?; afaama}

<afamachi> in ittafamachi [afama+chi]

afammi to be another year old, to have a birthday (II) [a+fammi ?] {v1. afama?; ggr. áffammi; hngr. afahámmi} § Asafammitok. I was another year old.

afammi year (can be used with a following number verb (I) to tell someone's age) {afammi chaffa'si: to be one year old (I / II)} § Afammi toklotok. He was two years old. | Afammi oshtali. I'm four years old. | Afammaat taha. The year's gone, The year's over.

afammi chaffa'si to be one year old (I / II) § Afammi chaffa'sli, Afammi sachaffa'si. I'm one year old.

Afammi Himitta' New Year, New Year's Day [himitta+']

afammi himona' this year

afammi kánnohmi to be so many years old (ind.), to be how old (inf.) (II) [+HM], <afammi kánnǫh> {int. afammi katohmi} § Afammi chikannohmikạ ithạnali. I know how old you are.

<afammi kánnǫh> [HM] of afammi kánnohmi

afammi katohmi to be how old (int.) (II) [+HM], <afammi katǫh> {ind.-inf. afammi kánnohmi} § Afammi chikatǫhta? How old are you?

<afammi katǫh> [HM] of afammi katohmi

<afammichi> in ittafammichi

<afamo'chi> in ittafamo'chi

<afamo'li> in ittafamo'li

afánnali'chi to be nosy, poke into things (I)—ggr. of afaana'chi

afánnalhchi to be barred (of a door, for example) (3) {v2. afaanali}

afanní'chi ggr. of afannichi

afannichi to twist (something) (I;II) {ggr. afanní'chi}

afaama to meet, pick up (especially, by arrangement?) (I;II) {afama}

afaana'chi to be a detective, investigate, find out about (I;II) {ggr. afánnali'chi; to be nosy, poke into things (I)}

afaanali to bar (a door) (I;3) {v1. afánnalhchi}

afaapo'wa, (ML, MJ) afaapa, (ER) hafaapa to yawn (I), (ML, MJ) (I / II) {hngr. afaapohǫ́wa}

afaapohǫ́wa hngr. of afaapo'wa

áffammi ggr. of afammi

áffinni, afí'nni ggr. of afinni

áffolli ggr. of afolli

afihínni hngr. of afinni

<afímmo'pa> in ittafímmo'pa {v2. <afímmobli>}

<afímmobli> in ittafímmobli {v1. <afímmo'pa>}

afina to be stuck in (of a door in the frame or a stick in a hole, for instance), to be stuck in crosswise as a brace or reinforcement (3;3) {v2. afinni; xgr. afínni'ya}

<afinha> in ilafinha

<afin-kachi> in afin-kachit máa {ygr. afin-káyya'chi}

afin-kachit máa to be placed crosswise on as braces (tpl. subj.) (3;3) [<afin-kachi>+t] {sg. afínni'ya;

11

afin-káyya'chi

dl. afin-káyya'chi}
afin-káyya'chi to be placed crosswise
on as braces (dl. subj.) (3;3)—ygr. of
<afin-kachi> {sg. afínni'ya; tpl. afin-
kachit máa}
afinni to stick (a lever or pry bar) in;
to place (pl. obj.) crosswise as a brace
or reinforcement for; to stick
(mainly pl. obj.) in (I;3;3) {v1. afina;
ggr. áffinni, afí'nni; hngr. afihínni;
sg. obj. afinili} § Abokkisa'a itti'
afinnit tiwwilitok. I pried open the
door with a stick, I stuck in a stick
and opened the door.
afínni'ya to be really stuck in, stuck
tight in; to be placed crosswise on as
a brace (sg. subj.) (3;3)—xgr. of afina
{v2. afiinili; dl. afin-káyya'chi; tpl.
afin-kachit máa}
afiinili to place (sg. obj.ʾ) crosswise
on or in; to brace with (sg. obj.ʾ)
(I;II;3) {v1. afínni'ya; pl. obj. afinni} §
Itti' asafiinilitok. He put me up in a
tree.
afiitipa to have a tight chest, to be
unable to breathe (II)
afiitipat illi to die as a result of
witchcraft, to be bewitched and die
(3) [afiitipa+t] {fatpo'}
afo'pa' in ishkin afo'pa'
afo'si grandfather (vocative) (IIIp) §
imafo'si': his grandfather
afohólli hngr. of afolli
<afokhi> in afokhi'chi, ittafokhi
[a+fokhi]
afokhi'chi to wear underneath (I;3)
[+SC] § Naafka lo'bo' afokhi'shli. I
wear a shirt underneath.
afolli to make boiled dumplings
from (I;II) {v1. alhfola; ggr. áffolli;
hngr. afohólli}
afóllo'pa ggr. of afoolopa
afóllobli ggr. of afoolobli
<afowa> in ilaafowa {v2. <alhfowa>}

<afoyopa> in ilafoyopa [a+foyopa]
afoolobli to crowd around, form a
circle around (pl. subj.) (I;II) {v1.
afoolopa; ggr. afóllobli}
afooloblichi to put (a fence) around ˙
(I;II;3) [afoolobli+chi]
afoolohómpa hngr. of afoolopa
afoolómpa ngr. of afoolopa
afoolopa to go around (something)
(I;II) {v2. afoolobli; ggr. afóllo'pa;
hngr. afoolohómpa; ngr.
afoolómpa; afoolopo'wa}
afoolopo'wa to go around
(something stationary), to avoid
(I;II) {afoolopa}
aha' anhi to be careful (WB) (I) (Ct)
ahá'mmi ggr. of ahammi
ahahámmi hngr. of ahammi
ahaksichi to cheat, make a mistake
affecting (I;II) [a+haksichi]
ahala'li' see ishtahala'li'
ahalaa in nannishtahalaa {ggr.
ahálla'a; ngr. ahaláa}
ahaláa in ishtahaláa—ngr. of ahalaa
ahálla'a in nannishtahálla'a—ggr. of
ahalaa
ahalla'ta', (MJ) ahalla'ta' type of
medicinal plant (CW, CC): life
everlasting (WB, MJ), snow in the
mountains (AB)
ahalhlhichi to kick around (I;II)
[a+halhlhi+chi]
ahámbi hngr. of abi, aabi
ahammi to anoint (I;II); to anoint ˙
with (I;II;3) [a+hammi] {ggr.
áhhammi, ahá'mmi; hngr.
ahahámmi} § Niha asahammitok.
He anointed me with oil.
ahámpa hngr. of apa
ahánchi hngr. of aachi
ahánta to stay, remain—hngr. of atta
ahángmi hngr. of akmi
aháyyo'chi in nannishtaháyyo'chi
<ahaalahlínchi> in

12

ittahaalahlínchi—ngr. of ahaalaachi
ahaalaachi to peep at, look at secretly
(like a peeping Tom) (I;II) [-SC]
[a+halahli+chi ?] {ngr.
<ahaalahlínchi>}
ahaa so there!, serves you right!
ahálbi hngr. of albi
aháni hngr. of ani
aháshwa hngr. of ashwa
aháya hngr. of aya
áhhammi ggr. of ahammi
áhhi'ka to owe (something) on
(I;3;3)—ggr. of ahiika § Chokka'
yappa ta'osso kanihka ahhi'kalikat
i'ma. I still owe a lot of money on
this house.
ahi', ayi' potato
ahi' api' potato vine
ahi' awaalhaali' french fries
[awaalhaali+']
ahi' aaholokchi' potato patch
[aa+holokchi+']
ahi' alhlhi' type of light-skinned
sweet potato [alhlhi+']
ahi' champoli' sweet potato (any of a
number of varieties), yam
[champoli+']
ahi' himona', ahi' himona' waa'
freshly dug potatoes [waa+']
ahi' homma' red potatoes
[homma+']
ahi' imissosh potato bug; (ML)
ladybug [im+issosh]
ahi' ishkin eye of a potato
ahi' lhibowa', (TP) ahi' lhobowa',
(LP) ahi' lhoboha' Irish potatoes
[lhibowa+']
ahi' lhobowa' champoli' sweet
potatoes (TP) [champoli+']
ahi' palaska' mashed sweet potatoes
ahi' pinha' seed potato
ahi' pokta' double potato
ahi' tohbi' white potatoes [tohbi+']
ahi'ka' debt [ahiika+']

ahi'ka' atobbit inkashoffi see atobbit
inkashoffi
ahínta ngr. of ahiita
ahishlhacho'li' potato masher [ahi'
isht lhacho'li+']
ahiika to charge, use credit to buy
(I;II) [a+hika] {ggr. áhhi'ka: to owe
on}
ahiikachi, (ER) ahi'kachi to extend
credit for (a purchase) to ˚, to let
(someone˚) buy (something) on
credit (I;II;3) [ahiika+chi] § Impa'
achihiikachili. I let you buy the food
on credit.
ahiina, ayiina, ayna to go with, be
with, be in the same group as, stay
with, be involved with (I;II) {ayina}
§ Toklocha chaffa oot ayiinakmat
tochchi'na. Two plus one is three.
ahiinachi to make (someone˚) stay
with (someone˚) (I;II;3) {ngr.
ahiinánchi} § Irenea
achihiinachilitok. I made Irene stay
with you, I made you stay with
Irene.
ahiinánchi ngr. of ahiinachi
ahiita to go behind (I;II) {ngr. ahínta;
aahiitánka}
ahiitánka to be behind, be hidden by
(I;II) {ahiita}
<ahoba> in ittahoba {v2. <ahobbi>;
ahooba}
ahobba'li in ishtahobba'li ki'yo
<ahobbi> in ahobbichi, ilahobbi,
ittahobbi {v1. ahooba, <ahoba>}
ahobbichi to pretend (someone or
something˚) to be (someone else˚)
(I;II;3); to accuse falsely, to imagine
about falsely, get the wrong idea
about (I;II); to pretend [+0 comp] (I)
{v1. ahooba; <ahobbi>} § Charles
achihobbichilitok. I pretended
Charles was you, I pretended you
were Charles. | Asahobbichi. He

accused me falsely, He pretended it (the culprit) was me, He had the wrong idea about me. | Ishhilha ahobbichilitok. I pretended you were dancing.

aholhchi'fo to be named for, to take the name of, to have the same name as (I;II) [a+holhchifo]

aholhchifochi to name after ° (I;II;3) [aholhchi'fo+chi] {ahoochifochi} § Lynn asaholhchifoshtok. She named Lynn after me.

aholhtinachi to include in a group to make up a required number (I;II) [a+holhtina+chi] {ahotihnachi}

ahómba ngr. of ahooba

ahonalha to be crucified (3) [analha] {v2. ahonalhlhichi} § Chihoowoshi'at ahonalhattook. Jesus was crucified.

ahonalhlhichi to crucify (3;3) [analhlhichi] {v1. ahonalha}

ahopoochi to be jealous of (someone°) with regard to (another person) (I;II;3) [±SC] [a+hopoo+chi] {ishtahopoochi} § Ihoo yamma achihopoochilitok, achihpooshlitok. I'm jealous of you and your relationship with that woman.

ahotihnachi to count in, include in the count (I;II) [a+hotihna+chi] {aholhtinachi}

ahóyyo'ba ygr. of ahooba

ahooba to look like, resemble, seem like (I;II) [a+<hoba>] {v2. <ahobbi>, ahobbichi; ngr. ahómba; ygr. ahóyyo'ba; hobachi; ittihooba, <ahoba>, ahobbichi} § Achihoobali. I look like you. | Yammakot ahomba. That's more like it.

ahooba'li in ishtahooba'li ki'yo, ishtikahooba'lo, ikimahooba'lo {ngr. ahoobáli}

ahoobachi to make ° resemble ° (I;II;3) [ahooba+chi] § Elizabeth Taylor asahoobachi. She made me look like Elizabeth Taylor, She made Elizabeth Taylor look like me.

ahoobáli in ishtahoobáli ki'yo—ngr. of ahooba'li

ahoochifochi to name ° after (I;II;3) [a+hochifo+chi] {aholhchifochi} § Lynna asahoochifoshtok. She named me after Lynn.

akallo to be tight, be stuck (of a door) (3); to be tight on, be a tight fit for (3;II); to have (something) tight (II;3-at / II;3); to be stuck in (II;3) [a+kallo] {ggr. ákkallo; ngr. akállo} § Ambalaafkaat asakallokat sanokhanglo. I'm sad my pants are tight, that I have tight pants. | Lynnat balaafka akallo. Lynn has tight pants. | Tali' aaittintaklaako asakallotok. I got stuck in between the rocks.

akallochi to tighten (I;3) [akallo+chi] {ngr. akallónchi}

akallónchi ngr. of akallochi

akalhali to break, burst (eggs, peaches) against (I;3;3) [a+kalhali]

akanaa to be parted (of hair) (3) {v2. akaniili}

akanaachi to part (hair in general—perhaps on a wig) (I;3) [-SC] {hngr. akanaahánchi; imakanaachi: to part (someone's) hair}

akanaahánchi hngr. of akanaachi

akaniya to go off with (and marry) (I;3) [a+kaniya] {v2. alhkaniya ?; ngr. akaníya: to love, be willing to go off with; ggr. akánni'ya: not to be able to do things right, not to think right}

akaniili to part one's hair (I); to part (one's hair) (I;3) {v1. akanaa; imakanili: to part (someone else's)

hair} § Akaniili, Sapạshi' akaniilili.
I parted my hair.
akaníya to love, be crazy about, be
willing to go off with—ngr. of
akaniya
akanka' chicken {short form: kanka'}
akanka' basoowa' striped chicken
species [basoowa+']
akanka' chakwokoli', (MJ) akanka'
chakwoko'li' bearded chicken
species, with prominent feathers
under its beak [chakwokoli+']
akanka' hishi' chicken feathers
akanka' holisso' spotted chicken
species, (MJ) guinea hen, (ER)
Wyandotte chicken [holisso+']
akanka' homma' Rhode Island Red
[homma+']
akanka' inchokạ'to' tomato (TJ)
[im+chakạ'to']
akanka' ishtimittibi', akankishtittibi'
rooster spurs [akanka'
(im+)ishtittibi']
akanka' ittibi' fighting cock [ittibi+']
akanka' ịhoshottika',
akankịhoshottika', (MJ) kanka'
ịshottika' castor bean plant
[im+hoshottika']
akanka' lakna' yellow chicken
species [lakna+']
akanka' losa' black chicken species
[losa+']
akanka' nakni', akạnakni' rooster
akanka' niha' chicken fat [niha+']
akanka' nipi' chicken meat
akanka' sinti' chicken snake (CM)
akanka' tiik hen
akanka' tohbi' White Rock chicken
[tohbi+']
akanka' yalhkobo'li', (AB) akank
yaalhkobo'li' tailless chicken
species
akankabi', (LR) akanka' abi', (MJ)
akanka'bi' chicken hawk [akanka'
abi+']
akankabi' hasimbish homma',
hasimbish homma' red-tailed
hawk [homma+']
akankabiskanno' type of small hawk
[akankabi' iskanno+']
akankabishto' type of hawk
[akankabi' ishto+']
akankalaata' setting hen [akanka'
alaata+']
akankapa' chicken snake (ER)
[akanka' apa+']
akankawaalhaali' fried chicken
[akanka' awaalhaali+']
akankhishfili'ta', (AB)
akankishfilli'ta', (MJ)
akankoshfili'ta' frizzly chicken, a
curly-feathered chicken species
[akanka' hishi' filita+']
akankholisso' guinea fowl, guinea
hen [akanka' holisso+']
akankimbala' chick-peas (joke)
[akanka' im+bala']
akankimilhlha' wild chicken
[imilhlha+']
akankimimpa' tomato (VB) [akanka'
im+impa+']
akankimpinak aa'lhto' chicken crop
(MJ) [akanka' im+(pinak aalhto')]
akankimpoffola' chicken crop (used
by children as a balloon) [akanka'
impoffola']
akankinchakaffa' chicken gizzard
[akanka' inchakaffa']
akankinchakwa', (ER) chakwa'
chicken pox, (ER) measles [akanka'
<inchakwa'>]
akankinchofak rooster's spurs
[akanka' im+chofak]
akankinchokka' chicken house
[akanka' im+chokka']
akankintakọloshi' (MC, CP), (LP)
kanka' intakọloshi' tomato
[akanka' im+takọloshi']

akankiskanno', (AB) akanka'
iskanno' bantam chicken [akanka'
iskanno+'] {pl. akank sawa'}
akankishki' mother hen [akanka'
ishki']
akankishniha' (WB), (CM)
akankishniya', (LR, TP)
kankishniha', (WB)
akankishkishniha' tomato [akanka'
isht niha+' ?, akanka' ishkish
niha+'—last version is perhaps
only a joke]
akankishniha' okchi' ketchup (WB)
akankishtalhfola' chicken dumpling
[akanka' isht alhfola+']
akankishtashiila chicken and
dumplings, chicken soup [akanka'
isht ashiila]
akankishtittibi' see akanka'
ishtimittibi'
akankittibi'chi' type of plant (wooly
violet?) [akanka' ittibichi+']
akankihashintak rooster's comb
[akanka' im+hashintak]
akankihomi' gall on chicken liver
[akanka' im+homi']
akankihoshottika' see akanka'
ihoshottika'
akankosh-apa' chicken snake (EP)
[akankoshi' apa+']
akankoshchahali' chicken species
with a crest that looks like hair
sticking up [akanka' oshchahali+']
akankoshchiloli' frizzly chicken—
same as akank hishfili'ta' [akanka'
oshchiloli+']
akankoshi' chicken's egg; chick
[akanka' oshi']
akankoshi' awaalhaali' fried egg
[awaalhahli+']
Akankoshi' Aalohmi', Akankoshi'
Aalohmi' Nittak see Akankoshi'
Lohmi' Nittak
akankoshi' aalhto' egg carton
[aalhto+']
akankoshi' aatahaka' very small egg
(possibly the last that particular
chicken will lay) [aa+taha+ka']
akankoshi' bo'kalhchi' scrambled
eggs [bo'kalhchi+']
akankoshi' hofanti' chick (used for
clarification if akankoshi' alone
would be confusing) [hofanti+']
{akankoshi' lombo'}
Akankoshi' Hoyo' Nittak Easter
[hoyo+']
akankoshi' ishbo'kalhchi' see
akankoshishbo'kalhchi'
akankoshi' lobo', (CC) akankoshi'
lobona' boiled egg: especially, hard-
boiled egg
akankoshi' lobona' hard-boiled egg
(CC, TJ) [lobona+']
Akankoshi' Lohmi' Nittak,
Akankoshi' Aalohmi', Akankoshi'
Aalohmi' Nittak, (TP) Kankoshi'
Lohmi' Nittak, (TP) Kankoshi'
Aalohmi' Easter [(aa+)lohmi+']
akankoshi' lombo' chicken's egg
(used for clarification if akankoshi'
alone would be confusing)
[lombo+'] {akankoshi' hofanti'}
akankoshi' toklo' double-yolked egg
[toklo+']
akankoshintohbi' egg white
[akankoshi' im+tohbi+']
akankoshilakna' egg yolk
[akankoshi' im+lakna+']
akankoshishbo'kalhchi', akankoshi'
ishbo'kalhchi' egg beater [isht
bo'kalhchi+']
akankpihcha', (AB) akanka' pishcha'
short-legged chicken species
akanksawa' bantam chickens—pl. of
akankiskanno' [akanka' sawa+']
akánni'ya not to think anything, not
to be able to do things right (II)—
ggr. of akaniya

akanomi in ishtakanomi
akassanachi to push (someone's)
head over to one side, make
(someone) lean his head over to
one side (I;II) [-SC] [akassanali+chi]
akassanali to have one's head bent
over to one side, lean one's head
over to one side (I) [*akka <sanali>
?] {ggr. akassánna'li}
akassánna'li ggr. of akassanali
<akashkoli> in ittakashkoli {v1.
<akashkowa>}
<akashkowa> in ittakashkowa {v2.
akashkoli}
akatolhlhi to cut off along with
(something else—for instance,
flowers, when cutting weeds) (I;3;3)
[a+katolhlhi]
akaabá'lli ggr. of akaaballi
akaaballi, akaabatli to play akaaballi'
(I) {ggr. akaabá'lli}
akaaballi' game in which a little stick
like a hockey stick is used to hit a
ball (something like golf?)
[akaaballi+']
akaaballichi to play akaaballi' (I)
[akaaballi+chi]
akaabatli see akaaballi
akaanihmichi in ishtakaanihmichi
[a+kanihmichi]
<akaashabli> in ittakaashabli {v1.
askaashapa}
akaashámpa ngr. of akaashapa
akaashampa' branch, unit, subgroup
[akaashampa+']
akaashapa to split off from, be a
branch of (I;II) [a+kashapa] {v2.
<akaashabli>; ngr. akaashámpa;
ittakaashapa}
akállo ngr. of akallo
akanakni' see akankanakni'
akchalhpi' in itti' akchalhpi'
akchomakpí'la, hakchomakpí'la, (LF)
akchonnokpí'la to be upside

down—ggr. of akchomakpila,
hakchomakpila
akchomakpíhhi'la hgr. of
akchomakpila
akchomakpihíla hngr. of
akchomakpila
akchomakpila, hakchomakpila, (LR)
akchomappila to turn (oneself)
upside down (I) {ggr.
akchomakpí'la, hakchomakpí'la: to
be upside down; hgr.
akchomakpíhhi'la; hngr.
akcomakpihíla; ngr. akchomakpíla;
ygr. akchomakpíyyi'la}
akchomakpilachi, hakchomakpilachi
to turn (something) upside down
(I;II) [akchomakpila+chi]
akchomakpíyyi'la, (AW)
akchobappíyyi'la ygr. of
akchomakpila
akchomakpíla ngr. of akchomakpila
<akchosh> in ilbakchosh, iyyakchosh
akí'chi ggr. of akihchi
akihchi to put down, bring down,
drop (I;II) [akka'+chi ?] {ggr.
ákkihchi, akí'chi; hngr. akihínchi}
akihínchi hngr. of akihchi
akiilawa, (CC) ilakiilawa to belch,
burp (I / II)
akiilawachi to burp (a baby), make
burp (I;II) [akiilawa+chi]
akiiliili to burn so as to ignite a larger
fire, to start a fire with or on (I;II)
[a+kilili] § Asakiiliitok. He started a
fire on me (He put a match to my
skirt, for instance, and a bigger fire
started from there).
akka to go down, recede (of the
ocean) (3) [+T] {v2. <akkaali>; ngr.
ánka}
akka' floor; down {akihchi}
akka' aya to go down, descend; to go
down, lessen (of a swelling) (I)
akka' ishshokmalachi' floor polish,

wax [isht shokmalachi+']
akka' lhatabli to spill on the ground,
on the floor (liquid or pl. obj.) (I;3)
akka' ootittola see akkootittola
akka' ootkaha see akkootkaha
akka' ootlhatapa see akkootlhatapa
akka' patalhpo' rug, carpet, pallet (for
sleeping on the floor) [pattalhpo+']
akka' patalhpo' ishbo'wa' carpet
beater [isht bo'wa+']
akka' pila down
akka' pílla way down
akka' tákka'li to crouch down, sit on
one's haunches (sg. subj.) (I) {dl.
akka' tákkohli; tpl. akka' takoht
máa}
akka' tákkohli to crouch down, sit on
one's haunches (dl. subj.) (I) {sg.
akka' tákka'li; tpl. akka' takoht
máa}
akka' takoht máa to crouch down, sit
on one's haunches (tpl. subj.) (I) {sg.
akka' tákka'li; dl. akka' tákkohli}
akka' wayowat máa to crouch down,
stoop over, bend over (tpl. subj.) (I)
{sg. akka' wáyya'a; dl. akka'
wáyyo'wa}
akka' wáyya'a to crouch down, stoop
over, bend over (sg. subj.) (I) {dl.
akka' wáyyo'wa; tpl. akka' wayowat
máa}
akka' wáyyo'wa to crouch down,
stoop over, bend over (dl. subj.) (I)
{sg. akka' wáyya'a; tpl. akka'
wayowat máa}
akka'si taloowa to sing low, have a
low singing voice (I) [akka+a'si+ho]
akkachi to calm (someone) down,
make (someone) behave (I;3); to
lower (I;II) {ngr. akkánchi: to lower,
turn down} [akka+chi]
ákkallo ggr. of akallo
akkánchi to lower, turn down—ngr.
of akkachi

<akkaachi> in ilakkaalincho'si
[<akkaali>+chi] {ngr. akkaalínchi}
<akkaali> in akkálo'si, akkali',
<akkaachi> {v1. akka; ngr. <akkáli>}
akkaalínchi to humble, put down (a
person) (I;II)—ngr. of <akkaachi>
akkaanohówa hngr. of akkaanowa
akkaanówa to be walking, to be on
foot (I) [*akka' aa+nowa] {hngr.
akkaanohówa}
akkaayínka, (TJ) akkaahínka to be on
foot (I) [*akka' aa+hika] §
Ishakkayyinka. You are on foot.
akkaayinkat áa to hitchhike (I , I)
[akkaayinka+t] § Ishakkaayinkat
ishaatok. You hitchhiked.
<akkáli> ngr. of <akkaali>
akkali' (moving) down [<akkali>+']
{akka'} § Akkali' aatok. He's going
along down there.
akkálo'si to be humble (in a religious
sense), to be kind (I / II)
[<akkali>+o'si]
ákkihchi ggr. of akihchi
akkohówa to go down, descend (dpl.
subj.) (I); to get off (dpl. subj.) (I;3)—
hngr. of akkowa {sg.-dl.-nondpl.
akkowa}
akkoshwayaachi to bring down, bend
down (sg. obj. with limbs, such as a
tree branch) (I;3) [akka'
*oshwayaachi] § Itti'
akkoshtishwayaachinna! Don't
bend down the tree!
akkowa to go down, get down,
descend (sg. subj.) (I); to get off (a
bus, for instance) (sg. subj.) (I;3)
[+taha] {hngr. akkohówa (dpl. subj.);
aakkowa: to get down from}
akkowachi to make go down, put
down, set down, pull down (I;II)
[±SC] [akkowa+chi] {hngr.
akkowahánchi}
akkowahánchi hngr. of akkowachi

akkootittola, akka' ootittola to fall
down, fall to the ground (sg. subj.) (I
/ II) [akka' oot *ittola] {dl.
akkootkaha; tpl. akkootlhatapa} §
Akkootittolalitok,
Akkootsattolatok. I fell to the
ground.
akkootkaha, akka' ootkaha to fall
down, fall to the ground (dl. subj.)
(I) [akka' oot *kaha] {sg.
akkootittola; tpl. akkootlhatapa} §
Akkootiikahatok. We (two) fell
down.
akkootlhatapa, akka' ootlhatapa to
fall down, fall to the ground (tpl.
subj.) (I) [akka' oot *lhatapa] {sg.
akkootittola; dl. akkootkaha} §
Akkootiilhatapatok. We (all) fell
down.
akmi, (TP, MC, ML) hakmi to be
frozen; to congeal (II) {ggr. âkmi;
hngr. ahángmi; ngr. ángmi; ygr.
áyyakmi; ayakmi}
âkmi ggr. of akmi
akmichi to freeze (I;II) [akmi+chi]
akónno'fa to be really close to (I;II)
akostinichi to find out about, learn
about for sure (I;II) [a+kostiini+chi]
akoobá'ffi ggr. of akoobaffi
akoobaffi to break (long obj.) against
˚ (I;II;3) [a+kobaffi] {ggr. akoobá'ffi} §
Itti' asakoobaffitok. He broke the
stick against me by hitting me with
it.
akooli to break (compact obj.) against
˚ (I;II;3) [a+kooli] § Akankoshi'
asakootok. They threw eggs against
me and broke them.
aktampi', haktampi', (AB) hatampi'
armpit (IIp) § sahaktampi',
asaktampi': my armpit
aktampi' hishi' armpit hair (IIp) §
asaktampi' hishi': my armpit hair
akya too, as well (subj.) § Bonnie

akya Doris Pam tawwa'a pistok.
Bonnie (too) saw Doris and Pam.
ala to come, arrive; to get here, be
here; to be born (I); to come here to,
arrive at (a place) (I;3) (short verb)
[+PR] [+CPR] [+taha] {hngr. ahála;
ngr. ála;neg. iklo; imalla: to come
to, <alla>} § Ishlatok. You arrived. |
Aklokitok. I didn't get here.
alaháwwi hngr. of alawwi
alaknachi to turn yellow, ripen (of a
plant) (3) [a+lakna+chi]
alalli, alatli to patch (a lot of holes in)
(pl. obj.) (I;3) {sg. obj. alaatali;
ittalalli} § Naafka alallitahlilitok. I
patched a lot of dresses.
<alapalínchi> in imalapalínchi
<alatkachi> in ittalatkachi,
ittalatkachit máa {ygr.
<alatkáyya'chi>}
<alatkáyya'chi> in ittalatkáyya'chi—
ygr. of <alatkachi>
alatli see alalli
alátta'a to be on top of (especially, of
one of two pieces of paper, with the
edges lined up) (3;3)—xgr. of alaata §
Holissaat yappa alatta'a. The paper
is on top of this one.
alawachi to gather, mass (in a place)
(pl. subj.) (3) [a+lawa+chi] § Hattakat
alawachitok. People gathered.
alawwi to stain (3;3) [a+lawwi] {hngr.
alaháwwi} § Takolaat salbak alawwi.
The peach stained my hand.
alawwichi to stain (3;3) [alawwi+chi]
alaata to be patched; to set (of a hen)
(3) {v2. alaatali; xgr. alátta'a}
alaatali to patch; to line, face (a
garment) (sg. obj.) (I;3) {v1. alaata;
pl. obj. alalli}
alaatassachi to crush, flatten ˚ against
(I;II;3) [a+latassa+chi] § Abooha
pootaka' asalaatassachitok. He
crushed me against the wall.

alba wild plant, weed
alba balalli' vine [balalli+']
alba haloppa', (WB) alba halappa'
type of low bush with stickers and
yellow flowers; (WB) briar
[haloppa+']
alba homi' bitter weed (another
name for alba' lakna') [homi+'] §
Waakaat alba homi' apatok. The
cow's been eating bitter weed.
alba lakna' bitter weed (same as alba
homi'); yellow weed (type of plant
for which Yellow Hill near
Durwood is named) [lakna+']
alba lowak type of poisonous plant (a
low shrub with pretty red flowers),
sometimes called fireweed
alba pakali' wildflower
alba pishokchi', (CM) pishokchi' alba'
milkweed
alba tono'li', alba tonolli'
tumbleweed [tonolli+']
albani to be barbecued (II) {v2. abaani}
Albaamo' Alabama Indian (or
perhaps an Indian from some other
group); (CP) Black Chickasaw
albi to be painted, to have paint on,
to be greased up (II); to be painted
on (something) (of paint) (3;3) {v2.
aabi; ggr. á'lbi; hngr. ahálbi; ngr.
álbi}
<albi> in issapishtalbi {v2. abi}
albi' paint [albi+']
albí'ha, albí'ya to be put in, shut up
(dl. subj.) (I)—ggr. of <albiha> {v2.
abihli; sg. fokha; tpl. albihat máa}
albí'ya see albí'ha
<albiha>, <albiya> in albihat máa,
ishkin albiha' {v2. abihli; ggr.
albí'ha, albí'ya}
albihat máa, albiyat máa to be shut
up, put in (tpl. subj.) (I)
[albiha/albiya+t] {sg. fokha; dl.
albí'ha}

albihílli hngr. of albilli
albilli, albitli to put on more than
one additional (covering, layer) (I;3);
to do over and over (I) (usually
used in part.) {v1. <albita>; hngr.
albihílli; albitili: to put on another
(layer); albítti'ya, ittalbilli} § Albillit
amasihilhlha. She asks me the
same thing over and over, She asks
me again and again.
albillit ayowa, albitlit ayowa to glean
(produce left behind by the
harvesters) (I;3) [albilli+t]
albilha to be trained on poles (of
plants) (3) {v2. abilhlhi} §
balalbilha': pole beans
albimpishokchi' white plant sap [alba
im+pishokchi']
albina to be a camping place, be a
place to stay (3) {imalbina: to be a
camp for}
albinachi to make a camp, stay the
night (I) [albina+chi] § aalbinachi':
camp
<albita> in imalbita {v2. albilli,
albitili; xgr. albítti'ya}
albitichi to rinse (I;II) [+SC]
[albitili+chi]
albitili to put on another (coat,
covering, layer); to repeat once,
double (I;3); to do again (I) (usually
used in part.) {v1. albita, albítti'ya;
albilli: to put on more than one
additional (layer); ittalbitili} § Albitit
aabitok. He put on another coat of
paint, He painted on another layer.
| Naafokha albitilitok. I put on
another dress (over my first one). |
Lynn ishkina albitit issolitok. I hit
Lynn again in the eye, I hit Lynn's
eye again.
albitit achifa to rinse, wash again (I;II)
[albitili+t] § Albitit asachifatok. He
washed me again.

albitkachi to be put on over others (of patches, for example) (3) [+T]

albitli see albilli

albitlit ayowa see albillit ayowa

albítti'ya to be put on over another (of an article of clothing) (3) {v2. albitili}—xgr. of <albita>

<albiya> see <albiha>

albiyat máa see albihat máa

albokchi' plant sap [alba okchi']

alboppolo' marijuana, weed [alba oppolo+']

alikchi to act as a doctor (I) {imalikchi: to doctor (someone)}

alikchi' doctor [alikchi+']

alikchi' hattak yokolli' psychiatrist, shrink (a joke) [yokolli+']

alikchihoo' woman doctor [alikchi' ihoo+']

alikchimmi' magical item, part of an Indian doctor's paraphernalia [alikchi' immi']

alikchishokcha doctor's medical bag [alikchi' im+shokcha]

alii, aliiho ouch!

aliichi to cultivate (a plant) (I;3) [-SC] [a+liichi]

aliiho see alii

<alla> in imalla [ala]

állo'ta ggr. of aloota

almo to be mowed, cut (3) [+PR] {v2. amo; ggr. á'lmo}

alokoli in ootalokoli

alokoochi to gather to see (I;3) [+T] [alokoli+chi]

aloktowachi to let (water) stand so that it becomes clear (I;3) [aloktowali+chi]

aloktowali, (TJ) anoktomali, (TP, MC) anoktomali, (VB, WB) noktawali, (MJ) oktamali, (CP) anoktawali, (AB, TU) anoktowali to be clear, transparent (of water, especially standing water) (3) {ggr.

aloktówwa'li: to be clear (especially of running water)}

aloktówwa'li to be clear (of water, especially running water)—ggr. of aloktowali}

alolli, alotli to fill (pl. obj.) (I;3) (Ct?) {sg. obj. alootoli}

aloshkachi to tell half-truths about, suggest falsehoods about (I;II) [a+loshka+chi]

alóshsho'ma to be determined, have one's mind made up (I) [a+loshoma]

alotli see alolli

alótto'li ggr. of alootoli

alótto'wa to fill (3;3); to be full; to have a full diaper (3)—xgr. of aloota § Takolaat talhpak alotto'wa. Peaches fill the basket, The basket is full of peaches.

alowa, aloowa to burn up with, catch fire from (I;II) [a+lowa] § Achilowalitok, Achiloowalitok. I burned up with you.

aloota to be full; to fill (3); to fill (3;3) {v2. alootoli; ggr. állo'ta; xgr. alótto'wa} § Talhpakat aloota. The basket is full. | Takolaat talhpak aloota. Peaches fill the basket.

alootoli to fill up (sg. obj.) (I;II); to fill (sg. obj.) with (I;3;3); to defecate in (one's pants or diaper) (I;3) {v1. aloota; ggr. alótto'li; hngr. alootohóli; pl. obj. alolli} § Takola talhpak alootolilitok. I filled the basket with peaches.

alootolit anoli to tell in full, tell the whole story (I) [alootoli+t]

aloowa see alowa

aloowachi to burn (something) up with ˙ (I;II;3) [aloowa+chi] § Ti'wat nosilitoka abooha asaloowachitok. They burned the house with me lying asleep in it.

<alhata>

<alhata> in alhata', ittalhata {v2.
alhatali}
alhata' cooked in liquid—preceded
by a noun, in complex expressions
[<alhata>+'] § tanchi' alhata': corn
cooked in liquid | nipi' alhata':
meat cooked in liquid
alhatali to cook (meat or walnuts in a
stew, for example) in liquid (I;3) {v1.
<alhata>}
<alhatta> in ishkinat alhatta
alhchaba, (TP) ashchaba bridge
alhchiba to be a long time, to be late
(—); for a (relatively) long time, a
longer time (aux.) {hngr.
alhchihímba; ngr. alhchímba: to be
later; ygr. alhchíyyi'ba} § Toksahalili
alhchibatok. I worked a longer time.
| Alhchimbatahakma
pisla'chiaakayni. I'm going to see
him later.
alhchibachi to be slow, take one's
time, waste time (I) [alhchiba+chi]
alhchifa to be washed (II) {v2. achifa}
alhchímba to be later, after a while—
ngr. of alhchiba § Haatoko
poshnookano alhchimbatahaho
iimintittok. Then we came back
later.
alhchimba'si a little while
[alhchimba+a'si]
alhchíyyi'ba ygr. of alhchiba
alhcho'wa to be sewn, sewed; to have
stitches (II) {v2. acho'li}
alhchoba mountain
alhchóna, alhchóna'si to be cheap,
inexpensive (II) [alhchona+a'si]
{chonna}
alhchóna'si see alhchóna
alhchonachi to make cheap, reduce
the price of (I;3) [alhchona+chi] {ngr.
alhchonánchi: to make cheaper}
alhchonánchi to make cheaper—ngr.
of alhchonachi

alhfabi' left (opposite of right)
{alhfa'bi} § salbak alhfabi': my left
hand
alhfabi' pila to the left, on the left §
Alhfabi' pila ayalitok. I went left.
alhfa'bi to be left-handed (I / II)
alhfa'bika' left side (3p) [alhfa'bi+ka']
§ abooha alhfa'bika' pila: on the left
side of the house
alhfola to be cooked, boiled:
especially, to be made into a
dumpling, be cooked in a dumpling
(II) {v2. afolli}
alhfola' dumpling [alhfola+'] §
panki' alhfola': grape dumpling
<alhfowa> in chofak yaalhfowa' {v1.
<afoha>}
alhibli to cover (pl. inan. obj.) (for
instance, plants, to guard against a
freeze, or corpses) (I;3) {v1.
alhipkachi, alhipkachit máa; sg. obj.
alhiipili}
alhiha', alhiya' two or more (used
only with a preceding an. noun or
noun phrase) § illi' alhiha': dead
ones | chipota alhiha': children |
Chomak howasa' alhihat ikayyo'bo.
Tobacco chewers are disgusting.
alhihlínchi ngr. of alhihchi—usually
used as prt. § Alhihlisht ootayali
manko. Stripping the leaves off (the
brush), I was going (fast).
alhihlisht prt. of alhihlinchi
alhipkachi to be covered (tpl. subj.)
(3) (used primarily in the negative)
[+T] {v2. alhibli; ygr. alhipkáyya'chi:
dl.; sg. alhíppi'ya, alhiipa;
alhipkachit máa}
alhipkachit máa to be covered (inan.
tpl. subj.) (3) [alhipkachi+t] {v2.
alhibli; sg. alhíppi'ya, alhiipa; dl.
alhipkáyya'chi}
alhipkáyya'chi to be covered (inan.
dl. subj.) (3)—ygr. of alhipkachi {v2.

alhibli; sg. alhíppi'ya, alhiipa; tpl. alhipkachit máa}
alhíppi'ya to be covered, especially, with a lid (sg. subj.) (II)—ggr. of <alhiipiya>, xgr. of alhiipa {v2. alhiipili; ngr. alhiipíya; dl. alhipkáyya'chi; tpl. alhipkachi, alhipkachit máa; alhiipi'ya'}
alhiya' see alhiha'
alhiichi to strip the leaves from (I;3) [a+lhiichi] {ngr. alhihlínchi}
alhiipa to be covered: especially, to have one's head covered (sg. or hum. subj.) (II) [a+lhipa ?] {v2. alhiipili; xgr. alhíppi'ya; dl. alhipkáyya'chi; tpl. alhipkachi, alhipkachit máa}
alhiipi'ya' top, lid, cover (3p) [alhippi'ya+'] § aaimpalhiipi'ya': tablecloth
alhiipili to cover (sg. or hum. obj.) (I;II); to cover ° with (I;II;3) {v1. alhiipa; pl. obj. alhibli} § Naachi achilhiipililitok. I covered you with a quilt.
<alhiipiya> in alhiipi'ya' {ggr. alhíppi'ya; ngr. alhiipíya; alhiipa}
alhiipíya ngr. of <alhiipiya> {ggr. alhíppi'ya}
alhkaháyya hngr. of alhkayya
alhkaniya to be forgotten (II); to be left behind (3) {v2. akaniya ?; ggr. alhkánni'ya; imalhkaniya: to forget}
alhkánni'ya ggr. of alhkaniya
alhkayya to be sad (II) [kayya ?] {hngr. alhkaháyya; ngr. alhkáyya: to be just about to cry}
alhkayya' patha' spreading adder (type of snake) (CP, MC) [alhkayya+' patha+']
alhkayyachi to make sad (I;II) [alhkayya+chi]
alhkáyya to be sad, to be just about to cry—ngr. of alhkayya

<alhkona> in alhkona', anonkalhko'na', pitalhko'nacha aya [from French alconand ?] {ygr. alhkóyyo'na: to wear (a skirt)}
alhkona' skirt [<alhkona>+'; from French alconand ?]
alhkona' iklanna'si half-slip
alhkona' wahhala' hoopskirt [wahhala+']
alhkona' wihhila' hoopskirt [wihhila+']
alhkóyyo'na to wear (a skirt) (I;3)—ygr. of <alhkona> § Alhkona' homma' alhkoyyo'nalitok. I wore a red skirt.
alhoopó'lli ggr. of alhoopolli
alhoopohólli hngr. of alhoopolli
alhoopolli, alhoopotli to have diarrhea (II) [a+lhopolli] {ggr. alhoopó'lli; hngr. alhoopohólli}
alhoopollichi to give (someone) diarrhea, to give (someone) a laxative (I;II) [alhoopolli+chi] {ishtalhoopollichi'}
alhoopotli see alhoopolli
alhpatak wide winnowing basket
alhpash big wooden spoon used in the old days for stirring pishofa; (TP, MJ) oar
alhpí'sa to be right, proper, correct (I); to fit (of clothes) (3;II); enough (aux.)—ggr. of alhpisa {v2. alhpíssa'li; aalhpi'sa} § Impalikat alhpi'sa. I eat enough.
alhpí'shi ggr. of alhpishshi § Kaniht alhpi'shtok. He finally laid his head down.
alhpíhhi'shi hgr. of alhpishshi, <alhpishi>
alhpihíshshi, alhpihíshi hngr. of alhpishshi, <alhpishi>
<alhpila> in alhpila' {v2. apila}
alhpila' help [<alhpila>+']
alhpila' ima to give help, assistance

to (I;III)

alhpila' ishi to get help, be on welfare (I)

alhpisa to be measured: for instance, to be weighed and bagged, of cotton (II) [+T] {v2. apiisa; ggr. alhpí'sa: to be right (I), to fit (3;II), enough (aux.); ngr. alhpísa: to be rich; ygr. alhpíyy'sa: to fit well (3;II)}

alhpisa yard (measurement); bushel—used with a following number § alhpisa chaffa: one yard, one bushel

alhpisa'chi to make right, to correct, to straighten out (I;II) [+SC] [alhpi'sa+chi]

alhpíssa'li to make right, correct (I;II) {v1. alhpí'sa}

<alhpishi> in alhpishichi—var. grade base for alhpishshi {hgr. alhpíhhi'shi; hngr. alhpihíshi; ngr. alhpíshi}

alhpishichi, alhpishshichi to pillow (someone's*) head on * (I;II;3) [<alhpishi>/alhpishshi+chi]

alhpishshi to lay one's head on, pillow one's head on (I;II) {ggr. alhpí'shi; hgr. alhpíhhi'shi; hngr. alhpihíshshi, alhpihíshi; ngr. alhpíshshi, alhpíshi; ygr. alhpíyyi'shi: to have one's head on; var. grade base <alhpishi>}

alhpishshi' pillow [alhpishshi+']

alhpishshi' ishokcha, alhpishshishokcha pillow case [im+shokcha]

alhpishshishokcha see alhpishshi' ishokcha

alhpíyyi'sa to fit well (3;II)—ygr. of alhpisa

alhpíyyi'shi to have one's head (pillowed) on—ygr. of alhpishshi

alhpísa to be rich (II) [+CPR] [-PR]—ngr. of alhpisa

alhpíshshi, alhpíshi ngr. of alhpishshi, <alhpishi>

alhpóllo'sa ggr. of alhpolosa

alhpolosa to be daubed on, smeared on (3;II); to have (a substance) daubed on one's face (anim. subj., best with overt subj. prefix) (II;3-at) {v1. apoolosli; ggr. alhpóllo'sa} § Lokchokat asalhpollo'sakat ithanali, Lokchokat asalhpollo'saka ithanali. I know I've got mud daubed on my face, I know there's mud on my face.

alhposha to be roasted, baked, toasted (II) {v2. aposhli}

alhpooba to be delivered, born (II) {v2. apooba}

alhpooyak bundle, luggage (Ct?)

alhtaha to be ready, done, completed (of a thing) (3) {v2. atahli}

alhtakla to be widowed, orphaned (II) {ataklama}

alhtakla' widow, orphan [alhtakla+']

alhtaklaa-asha' orphanage [alhtakla' aa-asha']

alhtipo to be tented, covered (like a covered wagon) (3) [+T] {v2. atiipoli}

alhtipo' tent [<alhtipo>+']

alhto to be put into a container, to be shut up (in prison, for instance) (usually nonhum. subj.) (3) {ngr. álhto: to remain; ggr. á'lhto; ngr.+ygr. áyyalhto}

alhtó'ka ggr. of alhtoka

alhtoba to be paid for (3) [-PR] [-CPR]; to substitute for, replace (I;II) {v2. atobbi; ngr. alhtómba} § Chihoowoshi'at apolhtobat illittook. Jesus died for us, in place of us. | Impa'at alhtobatayya'a. The food is paid for.

<alhtobo'wa> in ittalhtobo'wa {v2. <atobo'li>}

alhtohónka hngr. of alhtoka

alhtoka to be elected, appointed; to
get the job (II) {v2. atookoli; ggr.
alhtó'ka; hngr. alhtohónka; ngr.
alhtónka; xgr. <alhtókko'wa>}
<alhtókko'wa> in alhtókko'waka—
xgr. of alhtoka {v2. atookoli}
alhtókko'waka ithána to know for
sure (I) [<alhtokko'wa>+ka] §
Alhtokko'waka ishithanata? Do
you know for sure?
alhtómba ngr. of alhtoba
alhtónka ngr of alhtoka
amahchi see amaachi
amákka'li in ishtamákka'li,
ilamákka'li
amasali to run (lose dye) onto (3;3)
[a+masali] § Anaafkaat chinaafka
amasalitok. My dress ran onto your
dress.
amaachi, amahchi to fan (I;II) [±SC]
[a+mahli+chi]
<ambi> in imambi [abi]
amiitá'ffi ggr. of amiitaffi
amiitaffi to cut a hole into
(something) and make a hole in
(what was underneath); to make a
hole in (something) while making a
hole in (something else) (I;II;3)
[a+mitaffi] {ggr. amiitá'ffi}
<ammo> in imammo [amo]
ámmo'na to be first, to be oldest (I);
to be the first time (3) (usually subr.)
§ Lynnat yappat ammo'naho
hilhatok. This is the first time Lynn
has danced.
ammo'na' oldest one (in a family)
[ammo'na+']
ámmohmi to be out of it (II); never
(aux. used after a negative verb
+k(i), usually pronounced as a
single word) [+HM], <ámmoh> §
Asammohtokoot binni'lili. I'm
sitting (feeling) out of it. |
Ikayyokammohtok. He never did

go.
<ámmoh> [HM] of ámmohmi
amo to mow (I;3) (short verb) [+OPR]
{v1. almo; neg. ikmo, ikammo;
imammo: to mow for, <ammo>} §
Ishmo, Ishammo. You mow it. |
Kiimokitok, Kilammokitok. We
didn't mow it.
amosholi to make a pig out of
oneself, be greedy (II); to eat
greedily, be greedy for (II;3) {ngr.
amoshóli; ygr. amoshóyyo'li;
amóshsho'li} § Paskaak asamosholi.
I eat bread like a pig.
amoshóyyo'li ygr. of amosholi
amoshóli ngr. of amosholi
amóshsho'li to try hard (I) [ggr. of
a+mosholi] {amosholi;
ittamóshsho'li}
ámpa ngr. of apa
ampohko'li' trumpet vine
(medicinal plant)
amposhaa-asha' kitchen shelves,
china cupboard [amposhi' aa-asha']
amposhaachifa' see amposhi'
aalhchifa'
amposhi' dishes
amposhi' aalhchifa', amposhaachifa',
(TP, OC) amposhi' aalhchifa', (TP)
amposhaalhchifa', (ER) amposhi'
aachifa', (MJ) ampshi' aa-achifa'
dishpan, dishwasher [amposhi'
aa+achifa/alhchifa+']
amposhi' aaholhponi', (OC)
amposhi' aalhponi' ovenproof
dish [aa+holhponi+']
amposhi' falaa' platter [falaa+']
amposhi' holiitopa' china
[holiitopa+']
amposhi' ontalla'a' place mat
[on+talla'a+']
amposhi' ontalohli to set the table (I)
amposhi' shokkawwa'li' drinking
glass; glass (material)

amposhi'at ontalowa

[shokkawwa'li+']
**amposhi'at ontalowa, amposhi'at
ontaloha** for the table to be set
[amposhi'+at]
amposhimpatha' plate [amposhi'
im+patha+']
amposhishkasho'kalhchi' dish towel
[amposhi' isht kashookalhchi+']
amposhishtachifa' dishwashing
detergent [amposhi' isht achifa+']
amposhishtalhchifa' dishrag
[amposhi' isht alhchifa+']
<ana'> in ana'ak, ana'akot, ana'ak̲o̲,
ana'at, ana'aakayni, ana'a̲—see ano'
ana'ak me (nonsubj.; rare)
[<ana'>+ak]
ana'akot , anaakot I (emphatic subj.)
[<ana'>+akot]
ana'ak̲o̲, anaak̲o̲ me (emphatic
nonsubj.) [<ana'>+ak̲o̲]
ana'at I (subj.; rare) [<ana'>+at]
ana'aakaynihaat, anaakaynihaat I
myself (int. subj.; rare)
[<ana'>+aakayni+haat] §
Anaakaynihaat ayalim? Did I
myself go? (perhaps I was drunk, so
I really don't remember).
ana'aakaynihoot, anaakaynihoot I
myself (focus subj.)
[<ana'>+aakayni+hoot] §
Ana'aakaynihoot taloowali. I
myself sang.
ana'aakaynih̲o̲, anaakaynih̲o̲ me
myself (focus nonsubj.)
[<ana'>+aakayni+h̲o̲] §
Anaakaynih̲o̲ amasilhlhatok. He
asked me myself.
ana'aakayniht̲a̲, anaakayniht̲a̲ me
myself (int. nonsubj.)
[<ana'>+aakayni+ht̲a̲] §
Anaakayniht̲a̲ asasilhlham? Did he
ask about me myself?
ana'a̲ me (nonsubj.; rare) [<ana'>+a̲]
<anahli> in ittanahli

anakshowa, (TJ) anakshoha to have
one's hair singed or burned off; to
singe or burn off one's hair
(accidentally) (II) {v2. anakshooli}
anakshooli to singe, burn the hair off
(I;II) {v1. anakshowa}
analha to be nailed (inan. subj.) (3);
to be nailed onto (3;3) [a+nalha] {v2.
analhlhichi; ggr. ánna'lha;
ahonalha} § naaishtanalha': nail
analhlhí'chi ggr. of analhlhichi
analhlhichi to nail ° to (I;II;3)
[a+nalhlhi+chi] {v1. analha; ggr.
analhlhí'chi; ahonalhlhici}
<anaachi> in ittanaachi
anaakaynihat see ana'aakaynihat
anaakaynihoot see ana'aakaynihoot
anaakaynih̲o̲ see ana'aakaynih̲o̲
anaakayniht̲a̲ see ana'aakayniht̲a̲
anaakot see ana'akot
anaak̲o̲ see ana'ak̲o̲
<anaalhchi> in ittanaalhchi
anchi to cover oneself (I) {ggr. á'chi;
ygr. áyya̲'chi: to have a cover, have
as a cover; pitanchi} § N̲aachih̲o̲
ayya'chi. He's covered with a quilt,
He has a quilt as a cover.
ánchi to make noise (I)—ngr. of
aachi {neg. ika'cho}
anchíchchi'chi ggr. of anchichichi
anchichi to cover (I;II) [anchi+chi]
{anchichichi}
anchichichi to cover (I;II); to cover °
with (I;II;3) [+SC] [anchi+chichi]
{ggr. anchíchchi'chi; anchichi} §
N̲aachi achinchichishlitok. I
covered you with a quilt.
anhi to want, desire, love; to expect
(someone) (I;II); to wish, hope
[+hookmano comp.] (I) {ygr.
áyyanhi} § Janat Charlesat
alahookmano anhi. Jan wishes
Charles would come.
<anhichi> [anhi+chi] {ngr. anhínchi;

neg. ikanhi'cho}
anhínchi to like, (HS) love (I;II)—
ngr. of <anhichi> {neg. ikanhi'cho}
anhit anokfilli to wish [+hookmano
comp.] (I) [anhi+t] § Alahookmano
anhit anokfillili. I wish he'd come.
ani to produce, bear fruit (3); to pour,
put (tpl. or mass obj.") into (a
container) (I;II;3); to stuff (a turkey
or pillow) (I;3) (short verb) [+OPR]
{ggr. á'ni; hngr. aháni; ngr. áni; sg.
obj. fokhi; dl. obj. abihli; imanni: to
pour for} § Ishannitok. You poured
it in. | Kaaa niha anila'chi. I'm
going to put gas in the car.
ani' crop, fruit, produce [ani+']
<anipaachi> in ittanipaachi
aniichi to fester, have pus (3) [+SC]
[ani+chi ?]
ánka ngr. of akka
ánna'lha ggr. of analha
annowa to be out, known (of news),
to be known about, told about (II)
{v2. anoli; annoya}
annowachi, annoyachi to announce
publically, to put the facts (about) in
the paper (I;II)
[annowa/annoya+chi]
annowishto to be well-known (II)
[*annowa ishto] § Achinnowishto.
You are famous, well-known.
annoya to be out, known (of news),
to be known about, told about (II)
(Ct?) {v2. anoli; annowa}
annoyachi see annowachi
ánno'li ggr. of anoli
ano' me (nonsubj.) (<ana'> before all
endings, ino' in the expression
ishno' ino' iitawwa'a) § ana'ak: me
| ana'at: I (rare) | ana'a: me (rare) |
ana'akot: I (emphatic) | ana'ako: me
(emphatic) | ana'aakayni: to be, do
myself, to do to myself
anohóli hngr. of anoli

anokfihílli hngr. of anokfilli
<anokfila> in imaanokfila,
ishtimaanokfila {v2. anokfilli}
anokfilli to think about, miss (I;II); to
think, engage in thinking (I) {v1.
<anokfila>; hngr. anokfihílli;
imanokfila} § anhit anokfilli: to
wish
anokpilifa to be inside out (TJ)
anokpiliffi to turn inside out (TJ)
anoktobafa in asilhlhat anoktobafa
{v2. anoktobaffichi}
anoktobaffi in issot anoktobaffi,
anoktobaffichi
anoktobaffichi to miss (a target) in
throwing (I;II) [anoktobaffi+chi] {v1.
anoktobafa}
anoktoklo to be in doubt, be of two
minds about something (II); to be
uncertain about, be disappointed by
(II;3) [a+nok+toklo]
anompchokoshpa see anompaat
chokoshpa
anompchokoshpa' see anompa
chokoshpa'
anompa language; word
anompa in ishtanompa {v2.
anompoli}
anompa chokoshpa see anompaat
chokoshpa
anompa chokoshpa',
anompchokoshpa',
anonchokoshpa' gossip (story),
rumor; newspaper [(anompa
chokoshpa)+']
anompa chokoshpa' anoli to tell an
untrue story, spread gossip (I)
anompa chokoshpali to spread
rumors, to gossip (I)
anompa chokoshpali' tattletale,
gossip (person) [chokoshpali+']
anompa falama' answer (noun)
[falama+']
anompa falama' ishi, anompa

falama' í'shi to get an answer
(especially, in a letter) (I)

anompa falammichi to answer, give
an answer (I) {anompifalammichi:
to answer (someone)}

anompa falappo' gossip (WB)
[falappo+']

anompa ishtiktimayyo to have an
argument or discussion (3RN) [isht
*iktimayyo] {anompa ishtittimayya
ki'yo}

anompa ishtittimayya ki'yo to have
an argument or discussion (I / IR);
to have an argument with (I;II) [isht
*ittimayya] {anompa ishtiktimayyo}
§ Anompa issatimayya ki'yokitok.
He had an argument with me.

anompa ittimapiisa see
anompittimapiisa

anompa kallo' onhochi to sentence;
to impose a serious responsibility
on (of someone administering an
oath of office, for example) (I;II)
[kallo+'] § Anompa kallo'
achonhochilitok (abooha kallo'
chifokha'chiho). I sentence you (to
be imprisoned).

anompa kobaffi to break one's word,
promise (I) {imanompa kobaffi}

anompa pisa to read in the paper or
in a book (I)

anompa shaali' delegate (noun)
[shaali+']

anompa toshooli' translator
[toshooli+']

anompalhpisa' promise (noun)
[anompa alhpisa+']

anompalhpisa' ima to promise, to
give one's word to (I;III)

anompapiisa to promise (I) [anompa
*apiisa] {hngr. anompapihísa} §
Anompishapiistok. You promised.

anompaat chokoshpa, anompa
chokoshpa, anompchokoshpa,

anonchokoshpa for there to be a
rumor [anompa+at] § Anompaat
chokoshpa illitoka. There's a rumor
that he died, There's a rumor about
his death.

anompaat inchokoshpa to be the
subject of rumor (III)
[im+(anompaat chokoshpa)>
anompaat *inchokoshpa] § Felicia-
at anompaat inchokoshpatok. There
was a rumor about Felicia, Felicia
was rumored about.

anompaat intayolhkomo to speak
nonsensically or with unnecessary
repetition (like a senile person) (III)
[anompa+at im+ittayolhkomo] §
Anompaat antayolhkomotaha. I
was speaking like a senile person.

anompilbashsha' prayer (normally
used only in the expressions below)
[anompa ilbashsha+']

anompilbashshanompoli to pray (I)
[anompilbashsha' *anompoli] §
Anompilbashshilanompolitok. We
prayed.

anompilbashshasilhha to pray (I)
[anompilbashsha' *asilhha] §
Anompilbashsha' chikasilhhokitok.
You didn't pray.

anompilbashshimanompoli to pray
to (I;III) [anompilbashsha'
*imanompoli] § Chihoowaak
anompilbashshilimanompoli. We
pray to God.

anompilbashshishtanompoli to pray
for (I;II) [anompilbashsha' isht
*anompoli] § Anompilbashshisht-
achinompolilitok. I pray for you.

anompimapihísa hngr. of
anompimapiisa

anompimapiisa to promise (I;III)
[im+(anompapiisa)> anompa
*imapiisa] {hngr. anompimapihísa}
§ Anompittimapiistok. They

promised each other.

anompimoppani to curse (someone) (I;III) [anompa *im+oppani] §
Anompamoppanitok. He cursed me.

anompimoppanichi to curse (someone) (I;III) [anompa *im+oppanichi]

anompinchokoshpa to be rumored about (III) [anompa *im+chokoshpa] {anompaat inchokoshpa} § Anompanchokoshpatok. I was rumored about.

anompinchokoshpali to talk about, spread rumors about (I;III) [anompa *im+chokoshpali] § Anompissanchokoshpalitok. You spread rumors about me.

anompinkobaffi to break one's word, break a promise (I;III) [anompa *im+kobaffi] § Anompa chinkobaffila'chi. I'll break my word to you.

anompintoshooli to translate (speech) for (a speaker or a hearer) (I;III) [anompa *intoshooli] § Anompishintoshootok. You translated for him.

anompishtombohli to spread stories about (I;II) [anompa isht *ombohli] {anompombohli, ishtombohli} § Anompishtissombohtok. You spread stories about me.

anompittimapiisa, anompa ittimapiisa to make a spoken agreement, promise each other (I / IR) [itti+(anompimapiisa)> anompa *ittimapiisa] § Anompiitimapiistok. We made a spoken agreement.

anompifalammichi to answer (someone), send an answer to (I;III) [anompa *im+falammichi] § Anompishifalammichitam? Did

you answer her?

anompila anompoli to speak in tongues (as a religious experience) (I) [anompa ila]

anompilhafi to sign a document (I) [anompa *ilhafi] § Anompishilhafitok. You signed.

anompó'li ggr. of anompoli

anompohóli hngr. of anompoli

anompoli, (CC) anampoli to talk, speak; to coo, babble (of a baby) (I); to speak, say (a word) (I;3) [+CPR] [-PR] [anoli +po+ ?] {v1. anompa; ggr. anompó'li; hngr. anompohóli; ngr. anompóli}

anompolichi to make (someone) talk (I;II) [anompoli+chi]

anompombohli to spread stories or accusations about (I;II) [anompa *ombohli] {anompishtombohli, ishtombohli} § Anompachombohtam? Did he spread stories about you?

anomponchokoshpali to gossip about (I;II) [anompa *onchokoshpali] § Anompishonchakoshpalitokchayni. You gossip about her.

anompoppá'ni ggr. of anompoppani

anompoppani to curse, swear, use bad language (I) [anompa *oppani] {ggr. anompoppá'ni} § Anompishoppaninna. Don't curse.

anompoppanichi to curse, swear, use bad language (I) [anompa *oppanichi] § Anompikoppani'chokitok. He didn't curse.

anompóli ngr. of anompoli

anonchokoshpa see anompaat chokoshpa

anonchokoshpa' see anompa chokoshpa'

anonka' in, inside (II); inside, insides

anonka' fokha'

(IIp) {anonkaka'; anonkali'} §
asanonka': inside me; my insides
anonka' fokha' underwear [fokha+']
anonkaka' way inside, deep in (II);
inside, insides (IIp) [anonka'+ka'] §
asanonkaka': inside me; my insides
anonkaka' pitpolho'ma' facing (of a
garment) [pit polhoma+']
anonkak̲a̲li' (moving) in, (moving)
inside {anonkaka'}
anonkalatta'a' lining (of a garment)
anonkalhko'na' slip, petticoat
[anonka' alhkona']
anonk̲a̲li' (moving) in, (moving)
inside {anonka'} § Yaakni'
anonk̲a̲li' aaittan̲o̲wa'chi. They're
going to go through the earth
(building the subway).
anosi to go to sleep on, sleep next to
(I;II) [a+nosi]
anoshkonna to fix ° up with °, to
like ° as a possible mate for °
(especially, one's child) (I;II;3)
[a+noshkonna] § Lynn̲a̲
achinoshkonnali. I like you as a
mate for Lynn, I like Lynn as a mate
for you.
an̲o̲li to tell; to tell on, tell about (I;II)
{v1. annowa, annoya; ggr. ánn̲o̲'li;
hngr. anoh̲ó̲li; ilan̲o̲li: to tell on
oneself}
an̲o̲wa', (MJ) anwa again, another
time; another one, the other (often
precedes a subj.) § An̲o̲wa' issoli. I
hit him twice, I hit him another
time. | An̲o̲wa' kowi'at alatok,
Kowi'at an̲o̲wa' alatok. Another cat
came, The cat came again.
ánta to stay, to live (sg. subj.); to be
there (used on the telephone) (I); to
be doing (an action which can be
done in a stationary position,
preceded by hngr. verb +cha) (sg.
subj.) (I) [+PR] [+CPR]—ngr. of atta

{dl. áshwa; tpl. áyya'sha (stay, live,
be doing), ás̲h̲a (stay)} §
Ishtaloh̲ó̲wacha ishántatok. You
were singing. | Peeweeat antata? Is
Peewee there? (on the phone) |
Ikánto. She didn't stay.
antachichi to make stay behind (I;II)
[anta+chichi] {ngr. antachínchi: to
leave behind}
antachínchi to leave behind—ngr. of
antachichi § ibaa-antachínchi to
leave with (a co-obj.)
ángmi ngr. of akmi
apa to eat (something) (I;II) [+OPR]
{ggr. á'pa; hngr. ahámpa; ngr. ámpa;
neg. ikpo; imappa: to eat
(something) for, <appa>}
apakchíllo'fa ggr. of apakchilofa
apakchilofa to cling to, hang on to,
cuddle up to (usually in ggr.) (I;II)
{ggr. apakchíllo'fa}
apakfó'lli ggr. of apakfolli
apakfoha, apakfowa to be wound
around (sg. subj.) (3;II) [+T] {v2.
apakfohli; dl. apakfohkáyya'chi; tpl.
apakfowat m̲á̲a, apakfohkachit m̲á̲a;
apakfowalhchi}
apakfohchi to put (something
around °, wind (something) around
° (several times) (I;II;3); to go
around, especially while hanging
on (I;II) [-SC] [apakfohli+chi] {hngr.
apakfohlihínchi: to go around
many times; ngr. apakfohlínchi}
<apakfohkachi> in apakfohkachit
m̲á̲a, ittapakfohkachi {ygr.
apakfohkáyya'chi}
apakfohkachit m̲á̲a to be wrapped
around (tpl. subj.) (II = obj. , 3 =
subj.); to have (tpl. 3-at) wrapped
around one (II;3-at) (with overt II
prefix only) [<apakfohkachi>+t] {sg.
apakfoha; dl. apakfohkáyya'chi;
apakfowat m̲á̲a} § Ishtamalhchi'ba

30

nampanaa'at asapakfohkachit
maakat. I'm sad that the strings are
wrapped around me.
apakfohkáyya'chi to be wrapped,
wound around (dl. subj.) (3;II)—ygr.
of <apakfohkachi> {sg. apakfoha;
tpl. apakfowat máa, apakfohkachit
máa}
apakfohli to wind (a string, for
instance) around ° (I;II;3); to wind
into a ball (I;3) {v1. apakfoha,
apakfowalhchi; hngr. apakfohóli;
ngr. apakfóhli; ygr. apakfóyyo'hli;
apakfolli} § Nampanaa'
asapakfohtok. He wound the string
around me.
apakfohlihínchi to go around many
times—hngr. of apakfohchi
apakfohlínchi ngr. of apakfohchi
apakfohóli hngr. of apakfohli
apakfohólli hngr. of apakfolli
apakfolli to wind up (I;3); to wrap,
wind (something) around ° (I;II;3)
{v1. apakfoota; ggr. apakfó'lli; hngr.
apakfohólli; ygr. apakfóyyo'lli: to
have wrapped around; apakfohli} §
Polona achipakfollili. I wrapped the
string around you.
apakfowa see apakfoha
apakfowalhchi to be wound, tangled,
wrapped around (3;II); to be tangled,
wrapped up in (II;3-at) [+T] {v2.
apakfohli; apakfowa} § Ithanali
nampanaa'at asapakfowalhchitokat,
Ithanali nampanaa'at
asapakfowalhchitoka. I know I'm
tangled up in the string, the string is
wrapped around me. | Kowi'at
nampanaa'at apakfowalhchitaha.
The cat is tangled up in the string.
apakfowat máa to be wrapped,
wound around (tpl. subj.) (II = obj ,
3 = subj.); to have (tpl. 3-at) wrapped
around one [apakfowa+t] {sg.

apakfoha; dl. apakfohkáyya'chi;
apakfohkachit máa} § Apopakfowat
maa. They are wrapped around us.
apakfóyyo'hli ygr. of apakfohli
apakfóyyo'lli to have wrapped
around, to wear wrapped around—
ygr. of apakfolli
apakfóyyo'ta to wrap around, be
wrapped around (once) (3;II)—ygr.
of apakfoota (sg. subj.)
apakfoota to go around once, to walk
around, to put one's arms around;
to fit, go around (sg. subj.) (I;II) {v2.
apakfolli; ygr. apakfóyyo'ta: to wrap
around, be wrapped around (3;II);
ootapakfoota}
apakfóhli ngr. of apakfohli
apákko'ta ggr. of apaakota
<apalli>, <apatli> in ittapalli [a+palli]
<apalhlhi> in ittapalhlhi [a+palhlhi]
apanaa to be wound, twisted around
(3;3) [a+panaa] § Polonaat itti'
apanaatayya'ha. The string is
twisted around the stick.
apanaachi to twist up (with
something), to set (one's hair—
especially, by twisting one's hair on
rags to form ringlets) (I;3) [-SC]
[apanaa+chi] {hngr. apanaahánchi} §
Sapashi' apanaachilitok. I set my
hair (by twisting it with something).
apanaahánchi hngr. of apanaachi
<apanni> in ittapanni, apannichi
apannichi to twist (something); to
catch (a rabbit, by poking a stick into
its hole against its flesh, twisting it
to catch the skin, and pulling out
the rabbit along with the stick) (I;II)
[<apanni>+chi] {panaa, paniili}
<apánta> in apantat—ngr. of
<apaata>
apantat next to (II) (Ct) [<apanta>+t] §
Asapantat binni'tok. He sat next to
me.

31

apat pisa to taste (I;II) [apa+t] § Apat
sapiistok. He tasted me.
<apatkachi> in ittapatkachi
<apatkalhchi> in ittapatkalhchi
<apatli> see <apalli>
<apatohli> in ittimaapatohli
apátta'a to be next to (especially, of
plots of land) (3;3)—xgr. of <apaata>
[a+patta'a] {v2. <apátta'li>;
imaapátta'a}
<apátta'li> in imaapátta'li—ggr. of
apaatali {v1. apátta'a}
apaakó'lli ggr. of apaakolli
apaakolli, apaakotli to fix
(something) so that it is folded
around (something else'), to fold or
bend (something) around ' (I;II;3)
[a+pakolli] {v1. apaakota; ggr.
apaakó'lli} § Tali' achipaakollilitok.
I fixed the metal to go around you, I
folded the metal around you.
apaakollichi to hem (I;II)
[apaakolli+chi] {v1. apaakotalhchi}
apaakota to be folded around, bent
around (I;II) {v2. apaakolli; ggr.
apákko'ta} § Kaa-at itti' yamma
apakko'tatok. The car was folded
around that tree.
apaakotalhchi to be hemmed (II) {v2.
apaakollichi}
apaakotli see apaakolli
apaalhá'lli ggr. of apaalhalli
apaalhalli, apaalhatli to split open
(into two pieces) against ' (I;II;3)
[a+palhalli] {ggr. apaalhá'lli} §
Takolo asapaalhallitok. He split the
peach open by hitting me with it.
apaalhatli see apaalhalli
apaaniili to twist (something)
around (I;3)
<apaata> {v2. apaatali; ngr. <apánta>;
xgr. apátta'a}
apaatali to put next to ' (I;II;3); to add
on to the side of (I;3) [+OPR] {v1.

<apaata>, apátta'a; ggr. <apátta'li>;
ittapatli}
api' stem, trunk, tree (always
preceded by the name of a plant; in
names of some specific plants, the
order of api' and plant name may be
reversed) § tiyak api', api' tiyak:
pine tree | itti' api': tree trunk
apiha to follow, come with (pl. subj.)
(I;II) {v2. <apihli>; ggr. áppi'ha; ngr.
apíha; apiichi} § Asapihat
ayatahatok. They all came with me.
apihchi to make a leader (I;II); to put
' in charge of (I;II;3); to hoe, put dirt
on: especially, to put up furrows of
dirt to protect (new plants) (I;3) [-SC]
[<apihli>+ chi / a+pihchi] {hngr.
apihlihínchi; ngr. apihlínchi} §
Chipota achipihchila'chi. I'll send
the children with you, I'll put you
in charge of the children. | Ahi'
apihchilitok. I hoed the potatoes.
<apíhhihcha> in ittapíhhihcha
[a+<pihhihcha>]
apihíla hngr. of apila
<apihli> in apihchi [a+pihli ?] {v1.
apiha}
apihísa hngr. of apiisa
apihlihínchi hngr. of apihchi
apihlínchi ngr. of apihchi
apila, (ER, OC) apiila to help; to vote
for (I;II); to help (someone) do
[+unmarked postposed ka comp.]
(I;II) [-OPR] [a+pila ?] {ggr. áppi'la;
hngr. apihíla; ngr. apíla; apiilachi} §
Sashkaat asapilatok chipota ipitaka.
My mother helped me feed the
baby.
apila' helper [apila+']
<apilachi> in ilapilachi [apila+chi]
{apiilachi}
apínka to be still on the cob (of corn)
(3) [api'+ka] {tanchi' apinka}
apissa to be straight (II) [+CPR] [+PR]

{v2. apissali; ggr. áppissa; ngr. apíssa}

apissali to straighten (I;II) [apissa+li] {v1. apissa; ngr. apiss_a_li: to go straight across}

apissali'chi to aim at, not miss (I;II) [apissali+chi]

apissat aya to go upstream (I) [apissa+t] § Apissat ishiyatam? Did you go upstream?

apissat minti to go downstream (I) [apissa+t]

apiss_a_li to go straight across, not to follow a curve (I) (often used in prt.)—ngr. of apissali

apiss_a_t aya to take a shortcut, go straight through (I) [apiss_a_li+t] § Apiss_a_t ayalitok Madill ayalikat. I took a shortcut through Madill.

apistikih_i_li hngr. of apistikili

apistikili to pester, bother, tease; to touch, fondle (I;II) [tikili] {ggr. apistíkki'li; hngr. apistikih_i_li}

apistíkki'li in ishtapistíkki'li—ggr. of apistikili

apiichiffi to splat (something) on (I;II;3) [a+pichiffi] § Akankishniha' achipiichiffilitok. I splatted a tomato on you, I splatted you with a tomato.

apiilá'chi ggr. of apiilachi

apiilachi to support, give assistance (such as welfare) to (I;II) [apila+chi] {ggr. apiilá'chi; ngr. apiilánchi} § _A_hattak_a_ apiilachili. I'm supporting my husband.

apiilánchi to assist—ngr. of apiilachi

apiilanchi' vice-president [apiilanchi+']

apiisa to measure (I;II); to plan, propose (to do something) (I) [a+pisa] {v1. alhpisa; ggr. áppi'sa; hngr. apihísa; ngr. apísa; imapiisa: to tell one's plan; anompapiisa} §

Ayala'chit apiisli. I plan to go, I propose to go.

apiisachi to watch; to take care of (I;II) {ngr. apiisánchi} [a+pisa+chi]

apiisánchi ngr. of apiisachi

apíha ngr. of apiha

apíla ngr. of apila

apísa ngr. of apiisa

apíssa ngr. of apissa

apoh_ó_lli hngr. of apolli

apolli, apotli to line (sg. obj.) up with (edge to edge, not in a stack) (I;3;3) {v1. apoota; hngr. apoh_ó_lli; apootoli}

apollí'chi ggr. of apollichi

apollichi to spy on (I;II) [a+<pollichi>] {v1. apoota ?; ggr. apollí'chi}

apólhlho'ma to be folded inside (3;3) {v2. apoolhommi}

aponnachi in ishtaponnachi [a+<ponna>+chi] {imponna}

apónta to be next to (I;II) (Ct)—ngr. of apoota {apótto'wa}

aponta' next to (rel N) (Ct) [aponta+']

aposli (WB), (LF) apasli to chink (the cracks in a log cabin) {apoolosli}

aposhli to roast, bake, parch, toast (I;II) {v1. alhposha}

<apotkachi> in apotkachit m_á_a, ittapotkachit m_á_a {ygr. apotkáyya'chi}

apotkachit m_á_a to be next to (tpl. subj.) (3;3) [<apotkachi>+t] {sg. apótto'wa; dl. apotkáyya'chi}

apotkáyya'chi to be next to (dl. subj.) (I;II)—ygr. of <apotkachi> {sg. apótto'wa; tpl. apotkachit m_á_a} § Asapotkayya'chi. They (two) were next to me.

apotli see apolli

apótto'wa to be next to (sg. subj.) (I;II)—xgr. of apoota {v2. apootoli; dl. apotkáyya'chi, tpl. apotkachit

máa}
apooba to deliver (a baby), to raise
(chickens, for instance) (I;II) {v1.
alhpooba}
apoolosa to be chinked (of a long
cabin) (WB) {nanna apoolosa'}
apoolosli, (AB, MJ, LP, ER, LR)
ishtapoolosli to put, daub
(something like mud) on one's face;
to stucco, plaster, mortar, daub
(mud, etc.) on: especially, to chink
(the cracks in a log cabin) (I:3); to put
(dirt, etc.) on (someone's°) face
(I;II;3) [losa ?] {v1. alhpolosa,
apoolosa; aposli} § Lokchok
achipooloslilitok. I daubed your face
with mud.
apoolha to get comfortable, stop
crying (II) {v2. apoolhali; ngr.
apólha}
apoolhachi to comfort, make
comfortable (I;II) [apoolha+chi] {ngr.
apoolhánchi: to make more
comfortable}
apoolhali to quiet, comfort
(someone); to make (someone) stop
crying (I;II) {v1. apoolha; ngr.
apoolháli}
apoolhánchi to make more
comfortable—ngr. of apoolhachi
apoolháli ngr. of apoolhali
apoolhó'mmi ggr. of apoolhommi
apoolhommi to fold inside (I;3;3)
[a+polhommi] {v1. apólhlho'ma;
ggr. apoolhó'mmi}
apoota in ootapoota, ootittapoota
[a+<pota>] {v2. apolli, apollichi ?;
ngr. apónta; xgr. apótto'wa}
apootaka' side (of an inan. obj.) (3p);
next to (II) [apoota+ka'] {apootakali'}
§ aboopootaka': the side of the
house | asapootaka': next to me
apootakaachi to edge (a lawn), draw a
line beside (I;3)—used mainly in

ngr. [-SC] [<apootakaali>+chi] {ngr.
apootakaalínchi: to go along the
side; apootaka'}
<apootakaali> in apootakaachi {ngr.
<apootakáli>}
apootakaalínchi to go along on the
side—ngr. of apootakaachi, used
mainly in prt.
apootakaalísht going along on the
side [apootakaalinchi+t] §
Apootakaalisht aatok. He was going
along on the side.
<apootakáli> in apootakali'—ngr. of
<apootakaali>
apootakali' (moving) beside
[<apootakáli>+'] {apootaka'}
apootoli to put ° next to ° (mainly
hum. obj.?) (I;II;3) {vl. apótto'wa;
apolli}
apofachi to blow at, blow on (I;II)
[a+pofa+chi] {hngr. apofahánchi;
ngr. apofánchi} § Asapofachitok. He
blew at me.
<apóla> in ilapóla
apólha ngr. of apoolha
<appa> in imappa [apa]
áppi'ha ggr. of apiha
áppi'la ggr. of apila
áppi'sa ggr. of apiisa
áppissa ggr. of apissa
Appo'si' Grandma, Granny,
Grandmother (vocative or referring
to one's own grandmother)
[(s)a+ippo'si'] § Appo'saat nosi.
Granny is asleep.
Appo'sishto' Great-grandma, Great-
grandmother (vocative or referring
to one's own great-grandmother)
[(s)a+ippo'sishto']
<asánna'a> in ittasánna'a—xgr. of
<asaana>
asánna'li ggr. of asaanali
<asaana> in ittasaana {ggr. <ássa'na>;
xgr. <asánna'a>}

<asiitoha>

asaanali to face (I;II) [a+ <sanali>]
{ittasaanali; ggr. asánna'li}
asaanalichi to make (someone˚) face
(something) (I;II;3) [asaanali+chi]
<as<u>a</u>wachi> in ishtas<u>a</u>wachi'
[a+s<u>a</u>wachi]
así'lli ggr. of asilli
asih<u>í</u>lli hngr. of asilli
asih<u>í</u>lhha, asih<u>í</u>lhlha hngr. of asilhha
asilli, asitli to pin (pl. obj.—usually,
with safety pins) on (so that they are
hanging down, like tails pinned on
the donkey) (I;3;3) {ggr. así'lli; hngr.
asih<u>í</u>lli; sg. patient obj. asiitili;
asiitohli}
asilhha, asilhlha to ask (a question,
favor, etc.) (I;3); to ask for (a woman
in marriage, from her father, for
instance) (I;II) {hngr. asih<u>í</u>lhha,
asih<u>í</u>lhlha; ngr. as<u>í</u>lhha, as<u>í</u>lhlha;
silhlhi} § anompilbashsha asilhha:
to pray | Asasilhhatok. He asked for
me (from my father).
asilhhat anoktobafa, asilhlhat
anoktobafa to ask for
unsuccessfully (especially, for the
hand of) (II = obj. , I = subj.)
[asilhha+t] § Achisilhhat
anoktobafatam? Did he ask for your
hand (and get turned down)? |
Ta'osso asilhhat anoktobafalitok. I
asked unsuccessfully for money.
asilhlha see asilhha
asilhlhat anoktobafa see asilhhat
anoktobafa
asilhpoh<u>ó</u>wa hngr. of asilhpowa
asilhpowa to ask around about, ask a
lot of questions about (I;II) [asilhha
+po+] {hngr. asilhpoh<u>ó</u>wa;
imasilhpowa: to ask around of}
<asitkachi> {ygr. asitkáyya'chi;
<asotkachi>}
asitkáyya'chi to be pinned on (of
safety pins) (dl. subj.) (3;II)—ygr. of

<asitkachi> {sg. asítti'ya; tpl.
asiitowat m<u>á</u>a}
asitli see asilli
asítti'li to tie (a mean dog, for
instance) all the time—ggr. of
asiitili
asitti't <u>á</u>a to follow around (sg. subj.)
(II = obj. , I) [asitti'li+t] {dl. asitti't
tánnowa} § Asasitti't <u>a</u>a. He's
following me around.
asitti't tánnowa to follow around (dl.
subj.) (II = obj. , I) [asitti'li+t] {dl.
asitti't <u>á</u>a} § Pilla asasitti't
hashtannowa. You two are just
following me around.
asítti'ya to be tied (of a dangerous
dog, for instance) (3); to be pinned
on (of a safety pin) (sg. subj.) (3;II); to
have pinned onto one (II;3-at) (with
overt II prefix only); to hang onto
(I;II)—xgr. of asiita {v2. asiitili; dl.
asitkáyya'chi; tpl. asiitowat m<u>á</u>a;
isht asiiti'ya} §
bakshiyammashtasitti'ya': safety pin
| Ith<u>a</u>nali chofakoshi'at
asasitti'yakat, Ith<u>a</u>nali chofakoshi'at
asasitti'yak<u>a</u>. I know the pin is
pinned onto me. | Issasitti'yanna.
Don't hang onto me.
asiita to hang on to (sg. subj.) (I;II)
[a+sita] {v2. asiitili; xgr. asítti'ya; dl.
asotkáyya'chi; tpl. asotkachit m<u>á</u>a;
ootasiita}
asiita tanned leather [< asiita, because
it is hung?]
asiita holba' imitation leather
asiita iksaachi to tan leather (I)
asiitili to pin, tie (sg. patient obj.—
usually, a safety pin) on, to ˚ (I;II;3)
[a+sitili] {v1. asiita, asítti'ya; ggr.
asítti'li: to tie all the time; pl.
patient obj. asiitohli, asilli}
<asiitoha>, <asiitowa> in asiitowat
m<u>á</u>a, tali' ishtasiitoha' {v2. asiitohli}

asiitohǫ́li hngr. of asiitohli
asiitohli to pin (pl. patient obj.—
usually, safety pins) on ˚ (I;II;3); to
button (a garment) (I;3)
[a+<sitohli>] {v1. asitkayya'chi (dl.),
asiitowat mą́a (tpl.), <asiitoha>;
hngr. asiitohǫ́li; ngr. asiitǫ́hli; sg.
patient obj. asiitili; asilli} §
Achisiitohlili. I pinned them on
you.
<asiitowa> see <asiitoha>
asiitowat mą́a to be pinned on (of
safety pins) (tpl. subj.) (II = obj. , 3 =
subj.) [<asiitowa>+t] {sg. asítti'ya; dl.
asitkáyya'chi}
asiitǫ́hli ngr. of asiitohli
asį́lhha, asį́lhlha ngr. of asilhha,
asilhlha
askoffa, (LF) iskofa, (WB) skofa belt
askoffachi, (WB) skofachi to put on
(a belt) (I;3) [askoffa+chi] {ygr.
askoffáyya'chi: to wear (a belt)} §
Yammakǫ askoffachit pisa! Try on
that one!
askoffáyya'chi to wear (a belt)—ygr.
of askoffachi
askoffishtasitti'ya' (ordinary) belt
buckle [askoffa isht asitti'ya+']
askoffontalla'a' ornamental belt
buckle [askoffa ontalla'a+']
asonnak, (WB, LF, ER) asoonak, (MJ)
osannak, (AB) asaanak tin
asonnak amposhi' tin plate
asonnak aaholhponi' pot
[aa+holhponi+']
asonnak banna'ta' tuba [banata+']
asonnak ola' brass band [ola+']
asonnak palassa' dishpan [palassa+']
asonnak patassa' dishpan (Ct?)
[patassa+']
asonnak patha' any big flat pan—
roasting pan, dishpan [patha+']
asonnak pathalhiipi'ya' pan lid
[asonnak patha' alhiipi'ya']

asonnak tobbalhiipi'ya' lard can lid
[asonnak tobbi' alhiipi'ya']
asonnak tobbi', (MC) asoonak tohbi'
bucket, trash can, tin can, lard can
[tohbi+']
asonnak tobbi' ishtiwwi' can opener
[isht tiwwi+']
asonnak tobbi' okishtolhchi' metal
well bucket [oka' isht olhchi+']
<asotkachi> in asotkachit mą́a {ygr.
asotkáyya'chi; <asitkachi>}
asotkachit mą́a to hang onto (tpl.
subj.) (II = obj, I) [<asotkachi>+t] {sg.
asiita; dl. asotkáyya'chi}
asotkáyya'chi to hang onto (dl. subj.)
(I;II)—ygr. of <asotkachi> {sg. asiita;
tpl. asòtkachit mą́a} §
Issasotkayya'chinna! Don't (you
two) hang onto me!
asoonaktoshi' tin can (CC) [asonnak
tobbi' oshi']
<ássa'na> in ittássa'na—ggr. of
<asaana>
<asha> in ashaachi, aa-asha, iksho
(short verb?) {ngr. ásha; ygr.
áyya'sha; sg. atta; dl. ashwa; prt. asht
?}
ashahánchi hngr. of ashaachi
ashahą́ma hngr. of ashama
ashama to stick, burn on, scorch (of
food) (3) [+PR] {v2. ashamali; ggr.
áshsha'ma; hngr. ashahą́ma; ygr.
asháyya'ma; imashama} § Bala'at
amashamatok. My beans scorched.
ashamachi to cause (something) to
burn on, scorch (food) (I;3)
(preferred to ashamali)
[ashama+chi]
ashamali to cause (something) to
burn on, scorch (food) (I;3) {v1.
ashama}
ashana to be locked (3) [a+shana] {v2.
ashannichi; ggr. áshsha'na;
ashanalhchi}

ashanalhchi to be locked (3) {v2.
ashannichi; ashana}
ashánchi ngr. of ashaachi
ashanní'chi ggr. of ashannichi
ashannichi to lock; to tighten, twist
shut; to wind (a clock) (I;3) {v1.
ashana, ashanalhchi; ggr.
ashanní'chi}
asháyya'ma ygr. of ashama
ashaachi to put up, down (tpl. or
mass obj.), to put (tpl. or mass obj.)
in a pile (I;II) [<asha+chi] {ggr.
áshsha'chi; hngr. ashahánchi; ngr.
ashánchi; sg. obj. bohli; dl. obj.
kahli; ootashaachi: to take (tpl. obj.)
there; atashaachi: to bring (tpl. obj.)
here}
ashchokkowa to enter, come in (to,
this way) (I;3); to open the door and
come in (this way) (I) [asht
*chokkowa] § Ashtishchokkowatok.
You came in (to it) gradually.
<ashikkílli'li> in ittashikkílli'li
[a+shikkilli'li]
ashímpa ngr. of ashippa
ashippa to be dried up, boiled away
(3) [+T] [a+shippa] {v2. ashippali;
ngr. ashímpa}
ashippachi to boil down (I;3)
[ashippa+chi] {ashippali}
ashippali to boil down (jam, for
example) (I;II) {v1. ashippa}
ashiyaháma hngr. of ashiyama
ashiyama, (TJ) ashi'yama, (MJ)
ashaama to have a splinter (II) {ggr.
ashíyya'ma; hngr. ashiyaháma;
hashiyama}
ashíyya'ma ggr. of ashiyama
ashiichi to tie ° to, burden ° with; to
tie ° in (to a highchair, for
example); to lace ° up in (a corset,
for example) (I;II;3) [-SC] {v1.
ashiiyalhchi; hngr. ashiilihínchi}
ashiikoono'li to knot (something)

onto ° (I;II;3) [a+shikoono'li] {v1.
ashiikoono'wa} § Ishtalakchi'
asashiikoono'tahtok. He knotted a
string onto me.
ashiikoono'wa to be knotted onto
(3;II); to have (something) knotted
onto one (II;3-at) [a+shikoono'wa]
{v2. ashiikoono'li}
ashiila to coat, melt into, stick onto,
dry onto (3;II); to have sticking onto
one (II;3-at) [a+shila] § Lynnat
holissaat ashiila. Lynn has a paper
sticking onto her.
ashiila dumpling; soup; stew; mush
ashiilihínchi hngr. of ashiichi
ashiiyalhchi to be tied into; to have
tied on, be burdened with; to be
laced up with, girdled in (II;3); to be
tied onto (3;II); to have tied on (II;3-
at) {v2. ashiichi} § Aaombiniili'
asashiiyalhchitahatokot ithanali. I
know I'm tied into the chair. |
Lynnat nampanaa'at ashiiyalhchi.
Lynn has a string tied on her. |
Nampanaa'at kowoshi'
ashiiyalhchi. The string is tied onto
the kitten.
ashkanalli to move this way (I) [asht
*kanalli] {ngr. ashkanálli} §
Ashtishkanallinna! Don't move
this way!
ashkanálli ngr. of ashkanalli
ashkochcha to open the door and
come out (this way) (I) [asht
*kochcha]
ashmalli to jump down (this way) (I)
[asht *malli]
ashokafa to come off along with (of
paint which peels off when tape is
removed, for instance) (3;3)
[a+shokafa] {v2. ashokaffi}
ashokaffi to remove along with
(paint along with tape, for example)
(I;3;3) [a+shokaffi] {v1. ashokafa}

<ashokaachi>

<ashokaachi> in ittashokaachi
<ashoma> in ittashoma
[a+<shoma>]
<ashommi> in ittashommi
[a+<shommi>]
ashshá'chi ggr. of ashshachi
áshsha'chi ggr. of ashaachi
áshsha'ma ggr. of ashama
áshsha'na ggr. of ashana
ashshachi to sin (I) {ggr. ashshá'chi;
hngr. ashshahánchi; aaishshachi';
imashshachi: to sin against}
ashshahánchi hngr. of ashshachi
asht prt. of <asha>? {ashchokkowa;
ashkochcha; ashmalli; ashtakkowa;
ashtittola; ashtoyya}
ashtakkowa to come down (this way)
(I) [asht *akkowa] §
Ashtishakkowatam? Did you come
down (here)?
ashtittola to fall out, fall through
(this way) (sg. subj.) (I / II) [asht
*ittola] § Ashtittolalitok,
Assattolatok. I fell out (this way).
ashtoyya to climb up (this way) (I)
[asht *toyya] § Ashtishtoyyanna!
Don't you climb up (here)!
ashwa to live in (dl. subj.) (I;3) {ngr.
áshwa: to be in (a location); hngr.
aháshwa; sg. atta; tpl. <asha>,
áyya'sha}
at prt. of ala [ala+t]
atahli to prepare (I;3) [a+tahli] {v1.
alhtaha; ngr. atáhli: to get ready,
finish up; imatahli: to prepare
(hum. obj.)}
<atahpoli> in atahpolichi, ilatahpoli
[po+atahli]
atahpolichi to decorate, dress
(someone) up (I;II) [<atahpoli>+chi]
<atakali> in atakalichi, ittatakali
[a+takaali] {ggr. atákka'li; rmgr.
ataakakáli}
atakalichi to chain, put a chain on (a

door, gate): especially, to solder a
chain onto; to hook (something like
a screen door); to latch (I;3)
[<atakali>+chi] {ggr. atákkali'chi}
atakchí'chi ggr. of atakchichi
atakchichi to tie something onto, put
a tail on (I;II) [a+takchi+chi] {ggr.
atakchí'chi}
atákka'li to hang onto, hang from,
hang onto the skirts of, cling to (sg.
subj.) (I;II); to be hooked (of a latch)
(3)—ggr. of <atakali> [a+takka'li]
{dl. atákkohli; tpl. atakoht máa;
rmgr. ataakakáli}
atákkali'chi ggr. of atakalichi
atákkohli to hang onto, hang onto
the skirts of, cling to (dl. subj.)
(I;II)—ggr. of <atakohli> {sg.
atákka'li; tpl. atakoht máa}
ataklá'ma ggr. of ataklama
ataklá'mmi ggr. of ataklammi
ataklahámmi hngr. of ataklammi
ataklama to be busy; to be delayed,
held up (II) {v2. ataklammi; ggr.
ataklá'ma; alhtakla}
ataklammi to bother, pester; to delay,
hold up (I;II) {v1. ataklama; ggr.
ataklá'mmi; hngr. ataklahámmi}
<atakohli> in atakoht máa,
atakohmáa [a+takohli] {ggr.
atákkohli; rmgr. ataakokóli}
atakohmáa to hang onto (tpl. subj.)
(I;II) [atakoht maa] § Ilatakohmáa.
We're hanging on.
atakoht máa to hang onto, hang onto
the skirts of, cling to (tpl. subj.) (II =
obj. , I = subj.) [<atakohli>+t] {sg.
atákka'li, ataakakáli; dl. atákkohli,
ataakokóli; atakohmáa} §
Achitakoht iimaa'chi. We'll hang
onto you.
<atalakchi> in ittatalakchi
[a+<talakchi>]
<atalkachi> in atalkachit máa {ygr.

38

atalkáyya'chi}
atalkachit máa, atayyalkachit máa to
lean against (tpl. subj.) (II = obj. , I =
subj.) [<atalkachi>+t] {sg. atáyya'a;
dl. atalkáyya'chi} § Achitalkachit
iimaatok. We leaned against you.
atalkáyya'chi to lean against (dl.
subj.) (I;II)—ygr. of <atalkachi> {sg.
atáyya'a; tpl. atalkachit máa,
atayyalkachit máa}
atalhlhichi to blaze (a tree) (I;3)
[a+talhlhi+chi]
atamowa to go off with (pl. subj.), go
crazy over (3;3) [+taha] [a+tamowa]
atannalhchi to have something
twisted, snarled in one's hair (II); to
be ornamented with twists,
especially crochet (3); to have
tangled (3;3) {v2. atannichi} §
Asatannalhchitaha. I have
something twisted in my hair. |
Sapashaat hashintaka
atannalhchitaha. My hair has a
brush tangled in it.
atannichi to ornament, pretty
(something) up, by twisting
something around (for instance, by
crocheting around the edge) (I;3); to
snarl, twist something in: especially,
to twist a brush in the hair (I;II)
[a+tanni+chi] {v1. atannalhchi} §
Asatannichi. She snarled
something in my hair.
atappí'chi ggr. of atappichi
atappichi to herd, drive, follow
home (I;II) {ggr. atappí'chi}
atashaachi to bring (pl. obj.) here (I;II)
[at *ashaachi]
ataya to go by here (I) [at *aya]
atáyya'a to lean against (sg. subj.)
(I;II)—xgr. of ataaya {v2. ataayali; dl.
atalkáyya'chi; tpl. atalkachit máa,
atayyalkachit máa}
atayyalkachit máa see atalkachit máa

ataachi, hataachi to turn color while
ripening (of fruit or vegetables) (3)
[<hata>+chi ?]
ataakakáli to hang onto (sg. subj.)
(I;II) {dl. ataakokóli; tpl. ataakoht
máa}
ataakokóli to hang onto (dl. subj.)
(I;II) {sg. ataakakáli; tpl. ataakoht
máa}
ataapo'chi to distract, get in the way
of (I;II) (Ct?)
ataapolichi to distract, go in front of,
make things hard for (I;II) (Ct?) {ngr.
ataapolínchi}
ataapolínchi ngr. of ataapolichi
ataaya to lean against (I;II) {xgr.
atáyya'a; v2. ataayali}
ataayali to lean (something) against '
(I;II;3) {v1. atáyya'a, ataaya}
atáhli to get ready, finish up (I)—ngr.
of atahli
atchokkowa to enter, (come and)
come in to (I;3) [at *chokkowa] §
Atishchokkowatam? Did you come
in (to it)?
athoyo to come and get (I;II) [at
*hoyo] § Atsahoyo. He's coming to
get me.
atíllo'fa ggr. of atiilofa
atílhlhi'fa to be cut off evenly (3); to
be lined up even with the edge of
(3;3) {v2. atiilhiffi} § Folosh yammat
aaimpa' atilhlhi'faho ishbohli! You
put that spoon so that it was lined
up even with the edge of the table!
atimpilachi to come and get and send
for ' (I;III;3) [at *impilachi] § Holisso
atchimpilachila'chi. I'll come and
get the book and send it for you.
atittola to fall down (here) (sg. subj.)
(I / II) [at *ittola] {dl. atkaha; tpl.
atlhatapa} § Atittolalitok,
atsattolatok. I fell down.
atiilofa to be broken off in (3;II)

atiiloffi

[a+tilofa] {v2. atiiloffi; ggr. atíllo'fa} §
Bashpaat asatiilofatok. The knife is
broken off in me.
atiiloffi to break off in ° (I;II;3)
[a+tiloffi] {v1. atiilofa} § Alikchaat
bashpo asatiiloffitok. The doctor
broke the knife off in me.
atiilhiffi in atiilhiffichi, issot atiilhiffi
{v1. atílhlhi'fa}
atiilhiffichi in issot atiilhiffichi
[atiilhiffi+chi]
atiipoli to put an awning or tent over
(I;II); to make a tent (I) {v1. alhtipo}
atkaha to fall down (here) (dl. subj.)
(I) [at *kaha] {sg. atittola; tpl.
atlhatapa}
atkochcha to come out (I) [at
*kochcha]
atlhatapa to fall down (here) (tpl.
subj.) (I) [at *lhatapa] {sg. atittola; dl.
atkaha} § Athashlhatapatok. You all
fell down (here).
<atoba> in ilatoba, ittatoba {v2.
atobbi}
<atobachi> in ilatobachi
atobachi to be grown over by (a tree
or its bark—of a grafted limb, for
instance) (3;3) [+T] § Tali' yammat
itti' atobachitaha. That metal has
been overgrown by the tree.
atobbi to pay for (I;3); to pay (an
amount) for (I;3;3); to be punished,
pay for something (I) {v1. alhtoba,
<atoba>; ggr. áttobbi; hngr.
atohómbi; ngr. atómbi; imaatobbi} §
Ta'osso pokko'liho̱ atobbilitok ofi'
yamma̱. I paid ten dollars for the
dog.
atobbí'chi ggr. of atobbichi
atobbichi to make (someone°) pay
(an amount) (I;II;3); to make
(someone°) pay (an amount) for
(I;II;3;3); to punish (I;II) [atobbi+chi]
{ggr. atobbí'chi} § Asatobbichi. He

made me pay.
**atobbit inkashoffi, ahi'ka' atobbit
inkashoffi** to pay off a debt for (I;III)
[atobbi+t]
<atobo'chi> in ittatobo'chi
<atobo'wa> in ittatobo'wa {v1.
<alhtobo'wa>}
atochchí'na to be the third (I)
[a+tochchi'na] {ishtatochchí'na}
atochchi'nachi to do for the third
time (I); to make (someone or
something) the third in a group
(I;II) [atochchi'na+chi]
atohno to make (someone) do
something, to order (I;II) [a+tohno]
{hngr. atohó̱no}
atohnochi to order (to do something)
(I;II); to sic, set (a dog) on ° (I;II;3)
[atohno+chi]
atohómbi hngr. of atobbi
atohó̱no hngr. of atohno
atókko'li to attempt to kill, to
target—ggr. of atookoli
atókkoli'chi to aim at, not miss—ggr.
of atookolichi [+SC]
atokla to be the second (I); to be one
removed from the present (3)
[a+toklo] {ngr. atóngla: to occur a
second time; atoklánchi, ishtatokla}
§ hashi' atoklakaash: last month |
wiik atoklakma̱: next week
<atoklachi> [atokla+chi] {ngr.
atoklánchi; <atoklochi>}
atoklánchi to do for the second time
(I)—ngr. of <atoklachi>
<atoklochi> [a+toklo+chi] {ngr.
atoklónchi; <atoklachi>}
atoklónchi to have as one's second
(I;II)—ngr. of <atoklochi>
{imatoklónchi} § Hattakat
asatoklonchi. The man has me as
his number two.
atómbi ngr. of atobbi
atóngla to occur a second time (3)—

40

ngr. of atokla § Atonglahma sattola.
I fell for the second time.
atonhi see atooni
atookoli to elect, appoint, nominate
(I;II) {v1. alhtoka, <alhtókko'wa>;
ggr. atókko'li: to attempt to kill;
ittaatookoli}
atookolichi to appoint (I;II) {ggr.
atókkoli'chi: to aim at}
atoonchi see atoonichi, atochi
atooni, atonhi to guard (the door)
(I;3) (usually used in prt. with a
following verb) {ishtatooni} §
Okhisa' atoonit binni'lilitok. I sat
guarding the door.
atooni' guardian, person in charge
[atooni+'] § amatooni': my guardian
atoonichi, atoonchi to make a
guardian (I;II) [±SC] [atooni+chi;
influenced by atochi] {imatoonichi:
to make (someone) a guardian for}
atoonichi, atoonchi see atochi
atoonihínchi hngr. of atochi
<atooshafa> [a+toshafa] {ngr.
atoosháfa}
atoosháfa to be broken off, be a part
of (something bigger), be a chip off
(some old block) (I;II)—ngr. of
<atooshafa>
ató'chi ggr. of atochi
ató'li to post bond for (I;II) (TJ)—ggr.
of <atoli>
atochi, atoonichi, atoonchi, (TJ)
atolichi to mortgage, put up as
security (I;II) [-SC] [<atoli>+chi] {ggr.
ató'chi; hngr. atoonihínchi;
atoonichi}
atofalaa' see atofalla'a'
atofalaa' imilhlha' hishi' patha'
wide-leaved variety of wild onion
(WB) [patha+']
atofalaa' kosoma'si' garlic (CC)
[kosoma+a'si+']
atofalla'a', atofalla'ha', atofalaa',

(WB, TP, MJ) tofalaa', (HS)
hatofalla'a', (FA, TJ) hatofala', (AB)
hatofalaa' onion [falaa+', or
perhaps laa+'] {short form: tofalaa'}
atofalla'a' homi' garlic [homi+']
atofalla'a' himona' green onion
atofalla'a' homma' red onion,
Bermuda onion [homma+']
**atofalla'a' ililawachi', atofalla'a'
ilalawachi',** (MJ) tofalaa' laalawachi'
winter onion
[ililawachi/ilalawachi+']
atofalla'a' imilhlha' wild onion
[imilhlha+']
atofalla'a' lakna' yellow onion
[lakna+']
atofalla'a' okchamali' green onion
[okchamali+']
atofalla'a' shobbokoli' prairie onion
[shobbokoli+']
atofalla'a' tohbi' white onion
[tohbi+']
atofalla'ha' see atofalla'a'
<atoli> in atochi {ggr. ató'li}
atoshpalichi to make (someone)
hurry (I;II)
atta to be born (I); to live in (I;3) (sg.
subj.) {ggr. átta; hngr. ahánta; ngr.
ánta: to stay, live; dl. ashwa; tpl.
<asha>, áyya'sha; imatta: to be born
to, to give birth}
âtta ggr. of atta
áttobbi ggr. of atobbi
awa and—used only in numbers
from eleven to nineteen, twenty-
one to twenty-nine, thirty-one to
thirty-nine, etc. {táwwa'a} § pokoli
toklo awa tochchí'na: twenty-three
(twenty and three)
awa chaffa, pokkó'li awa chaffa, (EP)
pokko'laachaffa, (CP) pokolachaffa
eleven; to be eleven in number (3);
(LG) six § Chahtaat awa chaffatok.
There were eleven Choctaws.

awa chakká'li, pokkó'li awa
chakká'li, (EP) pokko'laachakká'li,
(CP) pokolachakká'li nineteen; to
be nineteen in number (3)
awa hanná'li, pokkó'li awa hanná'li,
(EP) pokko'laahanná'li, (CP)
pokolahanná'li sixteen; to be
sixteen in number (3)
awa ontochchí'na, pokkó'li awa
ontochchí'na, (EP)
pokko'laaontochchí'na, (CP)
pokolontochchí'na eighteen; to be
eighteen in number (3)
awa ontoklo, pokkó'li awa ontoklo,
(EP) pokko'laaontoklo, (CP)
pokolontoklo seventeen; to be
seventeen in number (3)
awa oshta, pokkó'li awa oshta, (LR,
LF, MJ) awoshta, (EP)
pokko'laaoshta, (CP) pokoloshta
fourteen; to be fourteen in number
(3)
awa talhlhá'pi, pokkó'li awa
talhlhá'pi, (EP) pokko'laatalhlhá'pi,
(CP) pokolatalhlhá'pi fifteen; to be
fifteen in number (3)
awa tochchí'na, pokkó'li awa
tochchí'na, (EP)
pokko'laatochchí'na, (CP)
pokolatochchí'na thirteen; to be
thirteen in number (3); (LG) eight
awa toklo, pokkó'li awa toklo, (EP)
pokko'laatoklo, (CP) pokolatoklo
twelve; to be twelve in number (3);
(LG) seven
awá'lli ggr. of awalli
awalli, awatli to lay (pl. obj.) across
(I;II) {ggr. áwwalli, awá'lli; sg. obj.
awaatali}
<awashshálla'a> in ittawashshálla'a
[a+washshalla'a]
<awashshállo'wa> in
ittawashshállo'wa
<awatkachi> in awatkachit máa {ygr.

awatkáyya'chi}
awatkachit máa to be laid across (tpl.
subj.) (I;3) [<awatkachi>+t] {sg.
awátta'a; dl. awatkáyya'chi}
awatkáyya'chi to be laid across (dl.
subj.) (I:3)—ygr. of awatkáyya'chi
{sg. awátta'a; tpl. awatkachit máa} §
Yammako kilawatkayya'chi. We
were laid across that one.
awatli see awalli
awátta'a to be laid across (I;3); to just
lie around anyhow, anywhere (like
a bum) (sg. subj.) (I)—xgr. of awaata
{v2. awaatali; dl. awatkáyya'chi; tpl.
awatkachit máa; iwa'ta',
okkowwátta'a}
awaala'chi to put a ruffle on (I;II)
[+SC] {v1. awaala'kachi,
awaala'kalhchi}
awaala'kachi to be ruffled (3) (Ct?)
{v2. awaala'chi}
awaala'kalhchi to be ruffled, flounced
(II) {v2. awaala'chi}
awaalhahchi see awaalhaachi
awaalhahli to be fried, cooked, done
(II)
awaalhaachi, awaalhahchi to fry (I;II)
[-SC] [awaalhahli+chi]
awaata in hashi'at awaata, hashi'at
himona' awaata, ootawaata {v2.
awaatali; xgr. awátta'a}
awaatali to lay (sg. obj.) across (I;II)
{v1. awaata, awátta'a; pl. obj. awalli}
awishipa' fringe {shibli} § Anaafkaat
awishipa'at ayya'sha. My dress has a
fringe.
áwwali'chi to follow along after, be
right behind (I;II) {iláwwi'li,
táwwa'a}
áwwalli ggr. of awalli
aya to go to (I;3); to go to the
bathroom, defecate; to walk, in
baseball (WB) (I); to get (aux.,
preceded by II or III subj. verb +t,

more common in the negative)
(short verb, replaced by <ayya> with
III or N prefix, by <iyya> with I
prefix) [+PR] [-CPR] [+taha] {ggr. á'ya;
hngr. aháya; ngr. áya; neg. ikayyo;
imayya: to go for} § Oklahomma'
ishiyyatam? Did you go to
Oklahoma? I Iliyya, kiliyya. We go.
I Ayali. I'm going; Goodbye. I Aya'
ki'yo. She is constipated (never
goes). I Sasipoknit aya. I'm getting
old. I Sasipoknit aya ki'yo. I'm not
getting old. I Akayyokitok. I didn't
go.
aya' chaffa to be one-way (3) [aya+'] §
Hina' yappat aya' chaffa. This street
is one-way.
aya' ki'yo to be constipated, never go
(to the bathroom) (I) [aya+a']
ayachi to make go, send off (a letter,
for instance—not a person) (I;3)
[aya+chi]
ayahámmi hngr. of ayammi
ayakaa to follow, leave after (I;II) {ggr.
ayákka'a; ngr. ayakáa; pl.
<ayakowa>; ayyakayya}
ayakáa ngr. of ayakaa
ayakaat aya to follow, go after (II =
obj. , I) [ayakaa+t] § Asayakaat
ayatok. He followed me, He went
after me.
ayákka'a ggr. of ayakaa
ayákka'at ittánno'wa to follow (dl.
subj.) (II = obj., IR = subj.)
[ayakka'a+t] {ayákko'wat
ittánno'wa}
<ayákko'wa> in ayákko'wat
ittánno'wa—ggr. of <ayakowa>
ayákko'wat ittánno'wa to follow (dl.
subj.) (3;3) {ayákka'at ittánno'wa}
ayakmi to freeze onto (3;3); to have
(something) frozen on (II;3)
[a+akmi]
ayakmichi to solder, freeze to (I;3;3)

[ayakmi+chi]
<ayakowa> in ittayakowa,
ittayákko'wat ittánno'wa {ggr.
<ayákko'wa>; sg. ayakaa}
ayali I'm going; good-bye [aya+li]
ayalli to cost (an amount) (3;3) §
Issoba-at talhipa chaffa ayallitok.
The horse cost $100.
ayalli' price [ayalli+']
ayalli' chaaha to be high priced, have
a high price (3) § Issoba yappat
ayyalli' chaaha. This horse is priced
high.
ayalli' chaahachi to charge high
prices (I) ; to charge high prices for
(I;3) § Impa' ayalli' chaahachi. She
charges high prices for food.
ayalli' imombohli to put a price on
(something) for ˙ (I;III;3)
[im+(ayalli' ombohli) > ayalli'
*imombohli] § Ayalli'
amombohtok. He priced it for me.
ayalli' ombohli to put a price on,
assess, bid on (I;3)
ayalli'at inchaaha to charge high
prices (III) [ayalli'+at im+chaaha] §
Lynnat ayalli'at inchaaha. Lynn's
prices are high, Lynn charges a lot. I
Ayalli'at chinchaaha' salami. You
charge too high prices.
ayallishto to be expensive (II); to be
expensive in (a store) (of a product)
(3;3) [ayyalli' *ishto] § Nannakat
aachompa' yamma ayallishto.
Things are expensive in that store.
ayammi to season with (primarily
salt, pepper), especially by shaking
on the seasoning (I;II:3) [a+yammi]
{hngr. ayahámmi} § Ashiila hapi'
ayammilitok. I seasoned the soup
with salt (most likely by shaking it
on).
ayáshsha'chi ggr. of ayaashachi
ayaapaháli hngr. of ayaapahli

ayaapahli to stalk, sneak up on (I;II)
{hngr. ayaapaháli}

ayaasinti' (MJ, TJ, CC), (WB) aaysinti'
eel [sinti']

ayaashachi to crowd, swarm around
(used about people converging on a
food table, for example) (pl. subj.)
(I;II) {ggr. ayáshsha'chi; hngr.
ayaashahánchi}

ayaashahánchi hngr. of ayaashachi

ayalhlhi to be really true (3) {ggr.
áyyalhlhi; álhlhi}

ayalhlhichi to do as one is told (I); to
act on, obey (a command, for
instance) (I;3) [ayalhlhi+chi] {ngr.
ayalhlhínchi; alhlhihchi} § Lynn
imanompa ayalhlhichilitok. I acted
on Lynn's word.

ayalhlhínchi ngr. of ayalhlhichi

ayi' see ahi'

ayí'li ggr. of ayiili

ayímmi'ta ggr. of ayiimita

ayina too, as well § Ofi' ayina abitok.
She killed a dog too.

ayina, ayna to be too (subr. only?—
usually as ayinakat (too subj.),
ayinaka (too obj.), with no
agreement marking) {ahiina,
ayinínchi} § Ano' aynakat
malililitok. I ran too. | Ishno'
ayinaka chihololli. I love you too.

ayiichi to wash (someone's) hair (I;II)
[-SC] [ayiili+chi] {hngr. ayiilihínchi;
ngr. ayiilínchi}

ayiili to wash one's hair; to clean
oneself in the dust (of a bird) (I); to
wash one's hair with (a medicine,
for instance) (I;3) {ggr. ayí'li, áyyi'li}

ayiilihínchi hngr. of ayiichi

ayiilínchi ngr. of ayiichi

ayiimillí'chi ggr. of ayiimillichi

ayiimillichi to cheer, say hoorah for
(I;II) {v1. ayiimita; ggr. ayiimillí'chi}

ayiimillichi' cheerleader

[ayiimillichi+']

ayiimita to jump or bounce up and
down (for instance, in anticipation)
(II) {v2. ayiimillichi; ggr. ayímmi'ta;
ishtayímmi'ta}

ayiina see ahiina

ayinínchi to add, have in addition:
especially, to have as an additional
sexual partner (I;II) {ayina} § Naachi
ayinisht ishtayatok. She took the
quilt along too (as well as the other
things she had).

ayna see ayina, ahiina

ayó'lhlha ggr. of ayolhlha

<ayoba> {ggr. áyyo'ba; ngr. ayómba}

ayobba'li ki'yo to mess up, deface
(I;3); to do poorly, not do well (I)
{ikayobba'lo} § Ishnowakat
ishayobba'li ki'yo. You can't walk
well.

ayohómpa hngr. of ayoppa

ayohǫ́wa hngr. of ayoowa

<ayokommo> in ittayokommo
[aa(y)+okommo]

ayokpanichi see ayoppanichi

ayokpánni'chi see ayoppánni'chi

ayoli to stop precipitating (—)
(preceded by verb +t or +kat) {ggr.
áyyo'li} § Ombat ayoli. It stopped
raining.

<ayolhkomo> in anompaat
intayolhkomo, ittayolhkomo
[aa(y)+olhkomo]

<ayolhkomochi> in ittayolhkomochi

ayolhlha, (AB) ahooyolhlha, (MJ)
oyolhlha to be lucky, have good
luck, have something good happen
(II); to have good luck with, be lucky
enough to get (I;II) {ggr. ayó'lhlha} §
Issoba asayolhlha. I have good luck
with horses. | Hattak ikayolhlho.
She couldn't get a man.

ayómba to be good, better; to be above
it all (II)—ngr. of <ayoba> {neg.

ikayyo'bo}
ayómba ki'yo ngr. of áyyoba ki'yo
ayómpa ngr. of ayoppa
ayoppa, (MC) naayoppa to be happy
(II) [+PR], [+CPR] {v2. <ayoppali>;
ggr. áyyoppa; hngr. ayohómpa; ngr.
ayómpa}
ayoppachi to speak to, greet; to bow
to; to praise, worship; (AB, MJ) to
shake hands with (I;II) [ayoppa+chi]
{hngr. ayoppahánchi; ngr.
ayoppánchi: to like, love}
ayoppachichi to make ° shake hands
with °, make ° greet ° (I;II;3)
[ayoppachi+chi]
ayoppahánchi hngr. of ayoppachi
<ayoppali> in ishtayoppali {v1.
ayoppa}
ayoppánchi, (ER) ayokpánchi to like,
love (I;II) [+OPR] {neg.
ikayoppa'cho}—ngr. of ayoppachi
ayoppanichi, ayokpanichi to fail to
do right by, do badly by, mess up; to
beat up (I;II) {ggr. ayoppánni'chi,
ayokpánni'chi} [aa(y)+oppani+chi]
ayoppánni'chi, ayokpánni'chi ggr. of
ayoppanichi
ayoppitahámmi hngr. of
ayoppitammi
ayoppitammi to cross paths with,
meet face to face (I;II) {ggr.
ayoppíttammi; hngr.
ayoppitahámmi}
ayoppitammichi to make (someone)
pass another person without
speaking (I;II) [ayoppitammi+chi]
ayoppíttammi ggr. of ayoppitammi
ayoppolachi, yoppolachi, (ER)
ayoopolachi, (ER) yoopolachi to
tease, make fun of, tell jokes about
(I;II) [a+yoppola+chi]
ayoppóllo'ka ggr. of ayoppolo'ka
ayoppolo'ka to be ruined, wrecked
(3); to have an accident (II) (usually

in ggr.) {ggr. ayoppóllo'ka; oppolo}
ayoshkammi to flirt with; to bewitch,
put a spell on (I;II) § ittayoshkammi
to flirt with, have sex with
<ayoshkóllo'li> in ittayoshkóllo'li
<ayoshkolochi> in ittayoshkolochi
ayowa, aywa to pick, gather (fruit,
corn, etc.—pl. obj.); to embezzle,
steal little by little; to pick up, give a
ride to, select for a team (pl. obj.)
(I;3) {ggr. áyyo'wa; hngr. ayohówa;
aayoowa, ayoowa}
ayowachi to make ° gather (I;II;3)
[ayowa+chi]
ayoowa to pick up, give a ride to,
select for a team (pl. obj.) (I;II) (rare)
{ayowa, aayoowa}
aywa see ayowa
<ayya> in imayya, ikayyo, nanna
ayya [aya]
<áyya'ma> in ishtáyya'ma
áyya'sha to exist, to be located, to be
there, to live there; to stay there (tpl.
subj.) (I); to be doing (something in
a stationary position) (preceded by
hngr. verb +cha) (tpl. subj.) (I); to be
a group of (a certain number,
generally one higher than ten)
(preceded by number verb +oot)
(I)—ygr. of <asha> {ngr. ásha; sg.
atta (live, be there), ánta (stay, be
doing); dl. ashwa (live, be there),
áshwa (stay, be doing); aa-asha} §
Talohowacha ayya'shtok. They were
singing. | Awa chaffoot ilayya'sha.
There are eleven of us.
ayyabi to be ugly (II) [+CPR] [-PR]
{hgr. ayyáhha'bi; ngr. ayyámbi}
ayyabichi to worsen the condition of:
especially, to beat up again (I;II)
[ayyabi+chi]
ayyáhha'bi hgr. of ayyabi
ayyakahájyya hngr. of ayyakayya
ayyakayya to follow (the lead of),

ayyakáyya

follow around (I;II) {hngr. ayyakaháyya; ngr. ayyakáyya; ayakaa}
ayyakáyya ngr. of ayyakayya
áyyakmi ygr. of akmi
ayyámbi ngr. of ayyabi
áyyanhi ygr. of anhi
áyya'chi to have a cover on, be covered (I); to have as a cover, be covered with (I;3)—ygr. of anchi § Naachiho ayya'chi. He's covered with a quilt.
áyyalhlhi ygr. of álhlhi or ggr. of ayalhlhi (used only in the negative) § Ayyalhlhi ki'yoha'ni. It's not really true.
áyyalhto to be loaded (of a gun) (3)— ygr. of álhto
áyyi'li ggr. of ayiili
áyyo'ba in áyyo'ba ki'yo, ikayyo'bo— ggr. of <ayoba>

áyyo'ba ki'yo to be bad, disgusting (II) {ngr. ayómba ki'yo}
áyyo'ka in chaffa áyyo'ka, toklo áyyo'ka, tochchí'na áyyo'ka, oshta áyyo'ka {ayyoka}
áyyo'li ggr. of ayoli
<**áyyo'pi**> in ishtáyyo'pi
áyyo'wa ggr. of ayowa
ayyobba'li ki'yo to mess up, deface (I;3); to say bad things about (I;II) {ikayyobba'lo} § Asayyobba'li ki'yo. He talked bad about me.
ayyoka in ilayyoka, ittimilayyoka {áyyo'ka}
áyyoppa ggr. of ayoppa
ayyoshta to be the fourth (I) {ggr. áyyoshta; ishtayyoshta}
áyyoshta ggr. of ayyoshta
Ayyoshta' Thursday (TP) [ayyoshta+']
ayyoshtachi to do something for a fourth time (I) [ayyoshta+chi]

a a

aa oh, ah (exclamation)
aa-abi to kill some of (I;3); to kill in (a place) (I;3;3) [+OPR] [aa+abi] I Chokfi kani'ka aa-abitok. He killed some of the sheep. I Idaho' hattak aa-abitok. He killed a man in Idaho.
aa-abichi' goalpost (for instance, in a stickball game) [aa+abi+chi+']
aa-achifa to wash in (I;3;3) [aa+achifa]
aa-achokmilhka to kneel in (a place) (I;3) [aa+achokmilhka]
aa-afama, aa-afaama to meet in, meet at (I;II;3) [aa+afama/afaama] § Holissaapisa'ak aa-asafaamatok, Holissaapisa'ak aa-asafamatok. He met me at school.
aa-afaama see aa-afama
aa-akaaballi to play akaaballi' in (a place) (I;3) [aa+akaaballi]
aa-akkowa see aakkowa
aa-aksho' memorial service [iksho ?]
aa-akshochi, aakshochi to have a memorial service for (someone several years dead, whose name is not mentioned afterwards) (I;3) [aa-aksho'+chi]
aa-akshochi' memorial service [aa-akshochi+']
aa-akshochi' imáyya'sha to have a memorial service (III) § Chahtaat aa-akshochi' imayya'shtokoot ishtaalhopollicha tamowatahatok. The Choctaws had a memorial service; when they were done with it they went away.
aa-akshochi' ishtáyya'sha to have a

memorial service (pl. subj.?) (3)
[isht *ayya'sha]
aa-albani' barbecue [aa+albani+']
aa-albinachi to make camp in (a
place) (I;3) [aa+albinachi]
aa-albinachi' campsite, camphouse
(at a church or dance ground),
motel [aa-albinachi+']
aa-albinachi' ikbi to make camp (I)
aa-albinachi' ishtalhtipo' tent
aa-alhchifa to be washed in (a place)
(3;3) [aa+alhchifa]
aa-alhto' see aalhto'
aa-ani to pour some of (a liquid or
collection of small objs.) into (a
container); to put into (a container)
in (a place); to put (something) in a
container in (a place) (I;3;3) [aa+ani]
§ Oka'a̱ ishtakafa' aa-anilitok. I
poured some of the water into the
cup.
aa-anompoli to talk on (the
telephone) (I;3) [aa+anompoli] §
Talaanompa' ishaa-anompoli? Are
you talking on the phone?, Are you
on the phone?
aa-apa to eat some of (I;3); to eat
(something) in (a place) (I;3;3)
[+OPR] [aa+apa] § Paska̱ aa-apalitok.
I ate some of the bread. | JPa̱ paska
imaa-apalitok. I ate some of JP's
bread.
aa-asha, aasha to live, make one's
home in (tpl. subj.) (I;3) [aa+<asha>]
{sg. aatta; dl. aashwa} § Yammako̱
tashka-chipota'at aa-ashattook.
There used to be soldiers there.
aa-asha' place where things are—
generally preceded by a noun
{nannaa-asha'} [aa-asha+'] §
amposhaa-asha': kitchen shelves |
nafkaa-asha': closet | holissaa-asha':
bookcase | abikaa-asha': hospital
aa-awaalhahli to be fried in (a place)

(3;3) [aa+awaalhahli] § Nipi'
yammat kochcha' aa-awaalhahtok.
That meat was fried outdoors.
aabachi, (ER) albichi to point at (I;II)
{v1. <aabalhchi>; imaabachi: to
point out to, to teach} §
Achiaabachitok. He pointed to you.
<aabalhchi> in imaabalhchi {v2.
aabachi}
aabanna to want (something) from,
want (something) out of an
undertaking (II;3) [aa+banna] §
Ta'osso aachibannata? Do you want
to get money out of it?
aabanna finha to really need (I;3 , —)
§ Nipi'ako̱ aasabanna finhatok. I
really need meat.
aabaptismo to be baptized in (a place)
(I;3 / II;3) [aa+baptismo] § Canada-ak
aabaptismolitok, Canada-ak
aasabaptismotok. I was baptized in
Canada.
aabaptismochi to baptize ˚ in (a
place) (I;II;3) [aa+baptismochi]
aabaptismochi' baptismal font
[aa+baptismochi+']
aabasha to have an operation in, be
cut in, operated on in (a place) (II;3)
[aa+basha] § Ardmore abika' aa-
asha' aasabashtok. I had my
operation in Ardmore hospital.
aabashli to cut in (a place) (I;3;3)
[aa+bashli]
aabi to paint, grease, smear (I;II); to
rub, smear (hand cream, grease,
medicine) on (someone˚) (I;II;3)
{v1. albi; hngr. ahámbi; imaabi: to
paint for} § Asabitok. He painted
me.
aabichili' spout or lip (of a pitcher)
[aa+bichili+']
aabilhpowa' holder [aa+abilhpowa+']
§ nannaabilhpowa': pocket
aabiniili' tono'chi' (ER), (MJ)

ambiniili' tono'kachi' rocking chair {aaombiniili'}

aachaffa to be in (a group, gang); to be for, agree with (a candidate or other leader) (I;3) [aa+chaffa] § Reaganak ilaachaffa. We're for Reagan.

aachaffa' one of (a group) (IIp); member (of a group) [aachaffa+'] § yammako̲ aachaffa': one of them | apoaachaffa': one of us | aachaffa' alhiha': members

aachalhka to gamble, play cards in (a place) (I;3) [aa+chalhka]

aachi to say (especially, about the doings of another), to mean (I;3); to give an order; to be in charge, have the say-so (I) {hngr. ahánchi; ngr. ánchi} § Ho̲sa'chi aashli ho̲stok. I made him shoot it. | Ishho̲sa'chi aashli ishho̲stok. I made you shoot it, I ordered you to shoot it and you did. | Mashkooki'at "ifa" aachikat, "ofi'" aachi. "Ifa" means "dog" in Creek, When a Creek says "ifa", he means "dog." | Nantahta aachi? What does it mean?

aachika' the one called (used following a name or a word from another language) [aachi+ka'] § Josephat falamat Nazareth aachikako̲ ayattook. Joseph went back to the place called Nazareth.

aachokfanni to spin around in (a place) (I;3) [aa+chokfanni]

aachokkaamala to spin around in (a place) (I;3) [aa+chokkaamala]

aachokkillissa' abandoned, lonely place [aa+chokkillissa+']

aachokmilhka' kneeler (to kneel on, in a Catholic church) [aa+achokmilhka+']

aachokoshkomo' playground, bingo hall [aa+chokoshkomo+']

aachokoshkomo' abooha' amusement arcade, playhouse [abooha+']

aachompa to buy from, at (an establishment) (I;3;3) [aa+chompa] § Safewayak paska aachompalitok. I bought the bread at Safeway.

aachompa' town; store, trading post [aachompa+']

aachompa' foshi' sparrow, "town bird" (AB, ER)

aachompishto' big store: department store, supermarket [aachompa' ishto+']

aachoshkachi' see chofak-oshi' aachoshkachi'

aafa'pa' swing, hammock (noun)

aafalakto' intersection—place where a tree (especially) or a road branches; crotch [aa+falakto+'] § itti' aafalakto': crotch of a tree

aafálla'ma to go to (a place) and come back all the time (I;3) [aa+fálla'ma]

aafammi hashi' birth month (IIp) [aa+afammi] {imaafammi nittak, imaafammi'} § aachifammi hashi': your birth month, the month of your birth

aafilima to have a relapse (after an illness) (II) {ggr. aafílli'ma} § Asafilimatok. I had a relapse.

<aafilito'chi> in ishtaafílito'chi'

aafílli'ma ggr. of aafilima

aafinha to be important (I) [aa+<finha>] {ngr. aafínha; nannakat aafinha}

aafínha ngr. of aafinha

aafoha to rest, to sit and rest in (a place) (I;3) [aa+foha]

aafoha' rest stop, rest area [aafoha+']

aafohachi to let (someone') rest in (a place) (I;3;3) [aafoha+chi]

aafowa to try to get, contend for (I;3) {imaafowa, ittimaafowa} § Paska champoli' aafowalikya aki'shokimanko. I was trying to get the cookie but I didn't get it.

aafoyopa' air hole, vent [aa+foyopa+']

aahabina to get, receive (something) at (I;3;3) [aa+habina] § Yammako impa' aahabinalitok. I got food there (for instance, at a welfare distribution).

aahala'li' strap {ishtaahala'li'}

aahaloppachi' razor strop, stone used to sharpen a knife on [aa+haloppachi+']

aahalha'bli' stirrup, pedal [aa+halhabli+']

aahalhlhi' treadle [aa+halhlhi+']

aahashtahli', aahashtaali', (TP) aaashtaali' window [aa+hashtahli+']

aahika' stopping place [aa+hika+'] § itti' chanaa malili' aahika': train depot

aahikki'ya' someone who is always standing in a particular place; place to stand [aa+hikki'ya+']

aahilha to dance in, dance at (I;3) [aa+hilha] § Charlesat amamboha pakna' aahilhatok. Charles danced on the roof of my house.

aahilha' dance place, dance ground, disco [aahilha+']

aahiika' credit (on account) [aa+ahiika+'] § Amahiikat chokma. My credit is good.

aahobachi to copy from (I;3) [aa+hobachi] {imaahobachi: to copy from (a person)}

aahola'fa' outhouse (vulgar term) [aa+holafa+']

aaholba to be haunted (of a house) (3) [+PR] [aa+holba]

aaholbachi' photography studio; (CC) camera [aa+holbachi+']

aaholissochi to write in (a book, etc.) (I;3) [+OPR]; to write (something) in,

at (a location) (I;3;3) [aa+holissochi] § Chimamboha anonka holisso aaholissochilitok. I wrote the letter in your house. | Lynn iholissa aaholissochilitok, Lynna holissimaaholissochilitok. I wrote in Lynn's book.

aaholissochi' desk, place for writing [aa+holisso+chi+']

aaholitto'pa' holy place [aa+holitto'pa+']

Aaholitto'paka' Heaven, glorious place [aa+holitto'pa+ka']

Aahollonkso' joke name sometimes used for Ahloso, Oklahoma ("farting place") [aa+hollokso+']

aaholloppi' graveyard [aa+holloppi+']

aaholhfo to come out of, sprout from (the ground) (3;3) [aa+holhfo]

aaholhponi' cooking place or instrument—kitchen, stove, pot [aa+holhponi+']

aahonkopa to steal from (a place or institution) (I;3;3) [+OPR] [aa+honkopa] § Lynn inki' imbanka ta'osso aahonkopalitok, Lynn inka ta'osso bank imaahonkopalitok. I stole money from Lynn's father's bank.

<aahoshontika> see <aahoshottika>

aahoshontika' see aahoshottika'

aahoshontínka see aahoshottínka

<aahoshottika>, <aahoshontika> in aahoshottika', aashoshontika' [aa+hoshottika] {ngr. aahoshottínka, aahoshontínka}

aahoshottika', aahoshontika' shady area [<aahoshottika>+']

aahoshottínka, aahoshontínka to be shady (3)—ngr. of <aahoshottika>

aahoshowa' urinal, bedpan, chamber pot [aa+hoshowa+']

aaibaachaffa to be in (a group, gang)

aaibbisọwa'

with (pl. obj.) (I;II) [aa+ ibaa+chaffa]
§ Aapobaachaffa. He's in a gang
with us.
aaibbisọwa' see aybisọwa'
aaikbi to make from (I;3;3) [aa+ikbi]
{inchokka' aaikbi} § Hapọ'lo' tii
aaikbilitok. I made tea from the
hapọ'lo' weed.
aaikbichi to spread (of a skin
problem) (3) [aa+ikbi+chi] § Hichi'at
aaikbichit ishtayya. The boils are
starting to spread.
aaiklanna to be right in there with
them, to go along with the crowd
(and what they do) (I) [aa+iklanna]
aaiklọ́ha, aaiklọ́wa to be brave,
famous; to be a bully, be mean (I); to
really do, to do well (I) (used with I-
subj. verb +kat); really, well (aux.)
(used with II- or III-subj. verb +kat)
{imaaiklọ́ha: not to be afraid of} §
Ishtaloowakat ishaaiklọwatam?
Were you really singing (loud,
well)? | Antakho'bikat aaikọwa. I
was really lazy. | Salhpokonnakat
aaiklọwa. I really dreamed.
aaiklọ́wa see aaiklọ́ha
aaiksaachi to make in (a place) (I;3;3)
aailipisa to see oneself in (I;3)
[aa+ilipisa] § Aainchaa'
aailipisalitok. I saw myself in the
mirror.
aailipisa' (ER, CC, VB), (JC) ilipisa',
(WB) ilapisa' mirror (Ct?)
[aa+ili+pisa+']
aailishạfi to shave (oneself) in (a
place) (I;3) [aa+ilishạfi]
aailli to die in (a place) (II;3) [aa+illi] §
Yappak aapolla'chi. We're going to
die here.
aailli' goalpost (WB) [aa+illi+']
aaimanni to pour for ˚ in (I;III;3)
[aa+imanni] § Abooha anonkaakọ
tii aachimannitok. He poured tea

for you in the house.
aaimaachompa to buy from ˚ in
(I;III;3;3) [aa+imaa+chompa]
aaimaaiksaachi to make for
(someone) in (a place) (I;III;3;3) §
Yammak naafka
aachimaaiksaashtok. He made the
dress for you there.
aaimilhlha to get scared in (a place)
(III;3) [aa+imilhlha]
aaímmo'ma, aaimọ́ma in
ishtaaímmo'ma, ishtaaimọ́ma
aaimọmochi to get used to (a place)
(III;3) {imọmochi} [aa+im+ọmochi]
§ Abooha aa-amọmochitaha. I got
used to the house.
aaimpa to eat in (I;3) [aa+impa]
aaimpa', aaị'pa' table [aa+impa+']
aaimpa' ittintakla' leaf of a table
aaimpalhiipi'ya' tablecloth [aaimpa'
alhiipi'ya']
aaimpishkasho'kalhchi' duster
[aaimpa' isht kashookalhchi+']
aaimpiyyi', aaị'piyyi' table leg
[aaimpa' iyyi']
aaimpompatkachi' place mat
[aaimpa' ompatkachi+']
aainchaa', (CC) aainchaaha', (TJ, TP)
aainchaha' mirror
aainchaa' bíyyi'ka to be all glass, be
shiny (of a mirrored or glass wall,
for instance) (3)
aainchompa to buy for ˚ in (I;III;3;3)
[aa+im+chompa]
aaintaloowa to sing to ˚ in (a place)
(I;III;3) [aa+im+taloowa] §
Yammakọ aa-antaloowatok. He
sang to me there.
aaintapa' in ipashi' aaintapa'
aaissa to get well, heal, be back to
normal (II) [aa+issa] {ngr. aaíssa} §
Asaissa. I got well.
aaissachi, (LG) issachi, (OC, CC, TP)
sachi to quit (I), to leave (I;II) [+E]

50

[aaissa+chi ?] § Toksali aaissachilitok. I quit working. | Apoissa'shcha ayatok. He left us and went away.

aaisso to hit ˙ in (a place) (I;II;3) [aa+isso]

aaishi to take away, to subtract (I;3); to take from (I;3;3) [aa+ishi] § Tochchi'natoko toklo ishaaishikma chaffa'si. Three take away two is one, Given three, if you take away two, there's just one.

aaishko to drink some of (I;3) [+OPR]; to drink from (a container), drink in (a place) (I;3;3) [aa+ishko] § Alekat pishokchi' ishtaka'fa' aaishko. Alex drinks milk from a cup. | JPa pishokchi' imaaishkolitok. I drank some of JP's milk.

aaishko', nannaaishko' bar, saloon; cup, glass [aa+ishko+']

<**aaishshachi**> in aaishshachika', nannaaishshachi' [aa(y)+ashshachi]

aaishshachika' hell; sin [<aaishshachi>+ka']

aaithana to learn one's way around (I;3) [aa+ithana] {ngr. aaithána: to know one's way around}

aaithána to know one's way around—ngr. of aaithana

aaittachakkachi' joint § ilbak aaittachakkachi': arm, hand, or finger joint

aaittachakkachi' ompatkachi', (WB) aaittachakkachi' ompatali' lath

aaittafama to meet (each other) in, have a meeting in (pl. subj.) (I;3) [aa+ittafama]

aaittanaha', aaittanaa' church

aaittanaa' see aaittanaha'

aaittanaachi to pile up around (I;3;3) [-SC] [aa+ittanaachi] § Lokfi' itti' aaittanaachilitok. I piled dirt around the tree.

aaittanowa' see hattak aaittanowa'

aaittapiha', aaittapihaka' group, gang (who are usually together); descendants, younger kinfolk (Ip) [(aa+)ittapiha+'/ka'] {ittapihaka'} § Aaittapihali' alhihaak ibaa-ayalitok. I went with the members of my group.

aaittapihaka' see aaittapiha'

aaittasiitilichi to pin (something) to (I;3;3); to pin, tie together (I;3) [aa+itti+asiitili+chi]

aaittáwwa'a to be partners (pl. subj.) (3) [aa+ittawwa'a]

aaittawwa'a' partner (Ip) [aaittawwa'a+'] § aaittawwa'ali': my partner | ishaaittawwa'a': your partner

aaittí'wa to lie next to (usually nonhum. obj.) (sg. subj.) (I;II) [aa+<itti'wa>] § Achiti'watok. He's lying next to you (talking to a dog).

aaittibaachaffa to all be in one gang or group together; to all agree (I) [itti+(aaibaachaffa)] § Hashaaittibaachaffa. You all agree, you're all in it together.

aaittibi to fight in, on (a location) (I;3) [aa+ittibi] § Topa hashaaittibinna! Don't fight on the bed!

aaittihaalalli to get married in, on (a location) (I;3) [aa+ittihaalalli] § Piini' aaittihaalallitok. They got married on a boat.

aaittimanompoli' walkie-talkie [aa+itti+im+anompoli+']

aaittipisa to see each other in (I;3) [aa+ittipisa] § Albuquerque'ak ilaaittipistok. We saw each other in Albuquerque.

aaittola to fall from (I;3 / II;3) [aa+ittola] § Takolaat itti' aaittolatok. A peach fell from the tree. | Itti' aaittolalitok, Itti' aasattolatok. I fell from the tree.

aai̱'pa' see aaimpa'

aai̱'piyyi' see aaimpiyyi'

aai̱la in ishtaai̱la [aa+i̱la]

aai̱ssa ngr. of aaissa

aakaha in aakahat má̱a, ootaakaha [aa+kaha] {ygr. aakáyya'ha}

aakahat má̱a to be lying (real sick), to be (dead and) laid out in (a place) (tpl. subj.) (I;3) [aakaha+t] {sg. aatí'wa; dl. aakáyya'ha}

<aakallohónchi> in ittaakallohónchi

aakana'li to move aside, move out of the way (pl. subj.) (I) {sg. aakanalli}

aakanalli to move aside, move out of the way (sg. subj.) (I) [aa+kanalli] {pl. aakana'li}

aakanihma'nikat ithá̱na to know what to do (I , I) (with 'I' subj., first word is aakanihmila'nikat) [aakanihmi+a'ni+kat] § Aakanihmila'nikat akitha̱'no. I don't know what to do.

aakanihmi to do something in (a place) (I;3); to happen in (a place) (3;3); to do (something) in (a place) (I;3;3) [+HM], <aakani̱h> (may be used with "still" aux. to say that someone is still the same) [aa+kanihmi] {int. aakatihmi} § Nannahmat yammako̱ aakani̱htok. Something happened there. | Aakanihmilitokat immo'ma. I'm still doing it there, I'm still the same.

aakaniya in malit aakaniya

<aakani̱h> [HM] of aakanihmi

aakánnakli to move out of the way (I) [aa+kannakli] {aakanalli, imaakánnakli}

aakatihmi to do (what) in (a place) (I;3;3) [+HM], <aakati̱h> [aa+katihmi] {ind. aakatihmi} § Katiyakta nanta aakati̱htok? What

did he do where?

<aakati̱h> [HM] of aakatihmi

aakatolhlhi to cut off (pl. obj.) (I;3) [aa+katolhlhi] {sg. obj. aatabli}

aakayni (emotive aux.; usually nonsubr.; may act as a suffix on preceding verb) § Malili aakayni!, Malilaakayni! It runs! | Ala aakayni! He's here! | Malili aakayntam? Did it start? | Alali aakayni! I'm here! | Malili aakayntoka̱ amano̱tok. He told me that it did, in fact, start.

aakaynihoot own (subj.; follows a noun) [aakayni+hoot] § Sashki' aakaynihoot sahayoshtok. My own mother found me.

aakayniho̱ own (nonsubj.; follows a noun) [aakayni+ho̱] § Ampaska aakayniho̱ apalitok. I ate my own bread.

aakáyya'ha to be lying (real sick), be (dead and) laid out in (a place) (dl. subj.) (I;3)—ygr. of <aakaha> {sg. aatí'wa; tpl. aakahat má̱a}

aakilaa' wick (of a candle or lamp) [aa+kilaa']

aakkowa, aa-akkowa to get down from, get down off of, descend from; to go down, descend in (a place) (I;3) [aa+akkowa]

aakochcha to go out of, move out of (I;3) [aa+kochcha]

<aakola'> see tobaksaakola'

aakoloffi to cut off a part of (I;3) [+OPR] [aa+koloffi] § Charlesak paska ishimaakoloffitok. You cut off a part of Charles's bread.

aakshochi see aa-akshochi

<aalak> in imaalak

<aalami> in imaalami

aalashpali' wall heater [aa+lashpali+']

aalaachi to go along beside (a river)

(I;3) [-SC] {ngr. aalaalínchi}
aalaalínchi ngr. of aalaachi
aalohmi to hide (something) in (I;3;3) [aa+lohmi] § Istiwa'a̱ aaimpa' nota'ak aalohmilitok. I hid the key under the table.
aaloma to hide in (I;3) [aa+loma] § Aaimpa' nota'ak aalomalitok. I hid under the table.
aaloma' hiding place (to hide oneself in) [aaloma+']
aalowa' hellfire [aa+lowa+']
aalta' altar [from the English]
aalhatabli to spill (something) from (I;3;3) [aa+lhatabli] {v1. aalhatapa; ngr. aalhatámbli}
aalhatapa to spill from (3;3) [aa+lhatapa] {v2. aalhatabli} § Oka'at ishtakafa' aalhatapatok. Water spilled from the cup.
aalhlhi to be the last, be all (3) {ngr. álhlhi: to be true; ishtaalhlhi; ootaalhlhi} § Yammakot aalhlhi. That's all.
aalhopo'li to go out through (pl. subj.) (I;3) [aa+lhopo'li] {sg. aalhopolli}
aalhopolli to cross over (on an overpass, for instance), to go out through (I;3) (sg.-dl. subj.); to go through with, be through with (I) (sg.-dl.-pl. subj) [E+t] [aa+lhopolli] {pl. aalhopo'li} § Anompolit ishaalhopollita? Are you through talking? | Winda' aalhopollili. I went out through the window.
aalhopolli', (AB) itti' basha' aalhopolli' bridge [aa+lhopolli+']
aalhopollichi to put (a road, for example) through (I;3;3) [aalhopolli+chi] § Ihooat i̱yaaknaak hina' aalhopollichitok. The woman put a road through her land.
aalhpi' straight handle—only used

in complex expressions [aa+<olhpi>+'] § bashpo aalhpi': knife handle | ishpiha' aalhpi': broom handle | ishkalla'fa' aalhpi': rake handle
aalhpí'sa to think one is doing the right thing; to be righteous; to be fair (I) [+CPR] [-PR] [aa+alhpi'sa]
aalhpi'sa' right (opposite of left) [aalhpi'sa+']
aalhpi'schokoshkomo to play fair (I) [aalhpi'sa *chokoshkomo] § Aalhpi'sishchokoshkomo. You play fair.
aalhponi' kitchen [aa+holhponi+']
aalhto', aa-alhto', nannalhto' container, cage [aa+alhto+']
aamalli to jump from, jump off, jump out of (I;3) [aa+malli]
aamallittakali to jump off, jump out of (I;3) [aa+<mallittakali>] § Alhchaba pakna' ishaamallittakatam? Did you jump off the bridge?
aambiniili' see aaombiniili'
aaminko to be president in, to be a leader in (I;3) [aa+<minko>] § Tom Bradleyat Los Angelesa̱ aaminko. Tom Bradley is the leader in Los Angeles.
aaminti to come from, come in from (I;3) [aa+minti] § Charlesat ta'osso aamintat imi̱'ma. Charles has money coming in (from some place). | Oklahomma'ak aaminti. She comes from Oklahoma.
aanalha to be nailed on (of a nonhum.) (3) [aa+analha]
aani to leave some of, not to take all of (tpl. inan. or liquid obj.) (I;3) {ani; ibaani; imaani}
aaniha okchi' see pishokchi' aaniha' okchi'
aanihichi' cotton gin [aa+nihichi+']

53

aanokchí'to to depend on (I;II)—ggr.
of <aanokchito> {ngr. aanokchínto;
ygr. aanokchíyyi'to} §
Achinokchi'tolitok. I depended on
you. | Chihoowa
ishaanokchi'tokma achipila'hi. If
you depend on God He will help
you.

aanokchínto ngr. of <aanokchito>,
aanokchí'to

<aanokchito> [aa+nokchito] {ggr.
aanokchí'to; ngr. aanokchínto; ygr.
aanokchíyyi'to}

aanokchíyyi'to ygr. of <aanokchito>,
aanokchí'to

<aanokfila> in imaanokfila
{anokfilli, <anokfila>}

aanosi' bed (WB) [aa+nosi+']

aanosi' abooha hotel

aanowa to walk on, leave tracks or
footprints on; to walk in (a location)
(I;3) [aa+nowa] § Shinok
aanowalitok. I left footprints on the
sand.

aaoka'mi', aayoka'mi' washbasin,
sink [aa(y)+okaami+']

aaokaami to wash one's face in (I;3)
[aa+okaami]

Aaokchaa', (Ct) Aayokchaa' Heaven
[aa(y)+okchaa+']

Aaokchaa' Itti' Tree of Life (Bible
expression)

<aaokla'> in imaaokla' [aa+okla+']

aaokloboshli to be baptized in (a
place) (I;3) [aa+okloboshli] § Canada-
ak aaokloboshlilitok. I was baptized
in Canada.

aaokloboshli' baptistry, baptismal
tank [aa+okloboshli+']

aaokloboshlichi to baptize ˙ in (a
place) (I;II;3) [aa+okloboshlichi]

aaoklhilika' dark place; hell
[aa+oklhili+ka']

aaollali to laugh in (I;3); to laugh at ˙

in (3;II;3) [aa+ollali]

aaolhti' heater, chimney; see lowak
aaolhti' [aa+olhti+']

aaolhti' ihikki'ya' andiron, fire dog
[im+hikki'ya+']

aaolhti' ihi'li' andirons, fire dogs (set
of two) [im+hi'li+']

aaombaayo'chi' trampoline
[aa+ombaayo'chi+']

aaombiniili', aambiniili', (ER)
aabiniili' chair; toilet
[aa+on+biniili+']

aaombiniili' aatayya'a' back of a chair
[aa+atayya'a+']

aaombiniili' chanalli' wheelchair
[chanalli+']

aaombiniili' falaa' sofa, bench, pew
[falaa+']

aaombiniili' faya'kachi', (CM)
aambiniili' fayyakachi', (MJ)
aambiniili' faya'kachi' rocking
chair [faya'kachi+']

aaombiniili' ihikki'ya' chair leg
(WB) [im+hikki'ya+']

aaombiniiliyyi' chair leg
[aaombiniili' iyyi']

aaombitka' massage parlor
[aa+ombitka+']

<aaonchololi> in ishtaaonchololi'

aaoncholowa in ishtaaoncholowa

aaoppoloka', aaoppolo'ka' hell
[aa+oppolo+ka']

aaoshkannapa to have an accident in
(a location) (II;3) [aa+oshkannapa] §
Yammak aasoshkannapatok. I had
an accident there.

aaowwatta to hunt in (a place) (I;3)
[aa+owwatta]

aaohika', aayohika', aayoka'
doorstep; rung of a ladder
[aa+on+hika+']

aaohikki'ya', aaoki'ya' pulpit
[aa+ohikki'ya+']

aaoholissochi to write on

(something) placed on top of (something else) (I;3;3) [aa+on+holissochi] § Holissa itti' basha' aaoholissochilitok. I wrote on the paper on top of the board.
aaọmalli to jump on ˙ in (I;II;3) [aa+ọmalli] § Aalhponi'ak aaissọmallitok. You jumped on me in the kitchen.
aaọmalli' trampoline [aa+om+malli+']
aapakfoha' reel, spool [aa+apakfoha+']
aapakna' pílla way up there; up the hill [aa+pakna']
aapalammi to be in a depression, be a difficult place to live (3) [aa+palammi] {ggr. aapállammi}
aapalaska' cookie sheet, griddle, bread pan [aa+<palaska>+']
aapállammi ggr. of aapalammi
aapallichi' frying pan [aa+pallichi+']
<aapatachi> in imaapatachi
aapichi to favor, consider precious (3;II) (only in prt. or ngr.) {ngr. aapínchi; ilaapichi, ishtaapichi} § Aapichit boyyohli. She keeps it because it's precious to her.
aapisa to see ˙ from, see ˙ in (I;II;3) [aa+pisa] {ngr. aapísa; pitaapisa} § Charlesa winda' ishaapistam? Can you see Charles from the window?
aapisa' sample [aapisa+']—used only in complex expressions § naalhilafa' aapisa': cloth sample | sholosh aapisa': shoe sample
aapísa ngr. of aapisa
aapollichi to play with (sexually), fondle (someone of the opposite sex) (I;II) [aa+<pollichi>] § Asapollichi bannatok. He wants to fondle me.
aapolhoma' fold line (on a document, for example)

[aa+polhoma+'] § ilbak aapolhoma': the inside of the elbow
aaponta to borrow, withdraw (from inan.), borrow at (I;3) [aa+ponta] § Bankak aapontali. I withdrew it from the bank.
aasanali to be opposed to, be against; to run (for office) against (I;II) [aa+<sanali>] {ggr. aasánna'li} § Asasanali. He is opposed to me. | Achisanalili. I'm running against you.
aasánna'li ggr. of aasanali
aash, aashọ in, on (a past date or time) [aash+họ] {aachi ?; mashshaasho} § 1985 aashọ: in 1985 | April the first aashọ: on (this past) April the first | Tuesday aash: on (last) Tuesday
aasha see aa-asha
<aasha'na'> in ishtaasha'na'
aashala'li' slide, sliding board [aa+shala'li+']
aashobohli', (AB) aashobooli' chimney, flue, smokestack, pipe; fireplace [aa+shobohli+']
aashoppala' light, lamp; light bulb; flash, flashbulb; headlight [aa+shoppala+']
aashoppala' alhiipi'ya' lampshade
aashoppala' alhto' battery
aashoppala' homma' red light, stoplight, traffic signal [homma+']
aashoppala' niha' lamp oil, coal oil [niha+']
aashoppala' ọwayya'a' lampshade [ọwayya'a+']
aashoppala' talakchi' lantern
aashọ see aash
aashọ'ka to kiss ˙ in (a place) (I;II;3) [aa+shọ'ka] § Aalhponi'ak aasashọ'katok. He kissed me in the kitchen.
aashọ'ka' nipple (CC) [aa+shọ'ka+']

55

aashwa to live, make one's home in
(dl. subj.) (I;3) [aa+ashwa] {sg. aatta;
tpl. aa-asha}

aatabli to cut, cut off (sg. obj.) (I;3); to
do too much, to do to excess (I) [E+t]
(used with preceding I subj. verb:
'eat', 'sleep', 'drink', 'work') {v1.
aatapa; pl. obj. aakatolhlhi} § Impat
aatablilitok. I ate too much.

aatahaka' in akankoshi' aatahaka'

aatakafa to have something dipped
out; to have a dip (of a road) (3)
[aa+<takafa>] {v2. aatakaffi}

aatakaffi to dip out, skim (one cup,
spoon, or dipper full) from (a
container) (I;3;3); to cut into
(material) too much (I;3) [aa+takaffi]
{v1. aatakafa; aatakli: to dip out
more than one cup}

aatakaali to hang onto, especially
after reaching (I;II) [aa+takaali] {ggr.
aatákka'li; <aatakohli>} §
Asatakatok. He reached over and
hung onto me. | Ilaatakatok. We
hung onto it.

aatákka'li to hold onto (sg. subj.)
(I;II)—ggr. of aatakaali {dl.
aatákkohli; tpl. aatakohmáa}
[aa+takka'li] § Asatakka'tok. He
held onto me.

aatákkohli to hold onto (dl. subj.)
(I;II)—ggr. of <aatakohli> {sg.
aatákka'li; tpl. aatakohmáa} §
Asatakkohtok. The two of them
held onto me.

aatakli to dip out (more than one cup
or dipper of) from (I;3;3) [aa+takli]
{aatakaffi: dip (one cup) from}

aataklit lha'li to bail (water) out of (a
boat) (I;3;3) [aatakli+t] § Piini'a oka'
aataklit lha'lilitok. I bailed water
out of the boat.

<aatakohli> in aatakohmáa {ggr.
aatákkohli; aatakaali}

aatakohmáa to hold onto (tpl. subj.)
(II = obj. , I = subj.) [aatakohli+t maa]
§ Asatakohmaa. They held onto me.

aataloowa' song book; psalm
[aa+taloowa+']

Aataloowa' Holisso, (EP) Aataloowa'
Holisso' the Book of Psalms
[holisso+']

<aatambli> in ishtaatambli

aatámpa to be big, loose (3) [+PR]
[-CPR]; to be big, loose on (3;II); to be
left over, to be too much, too many
(I) [E+kat]—ngr. of aatapa
{imaatampa} § Lawakat kilaatampa.
There are too many of us. |
Naafkaat asatampa. The dress is big
on me.

aatángla to be among (3;3) (Ct) (used
only in subr. clause) {ibaatángla}

aatangla' in the group, among the
company (Ct) [aatangla+']

aatapa to be cut off (sg.) (3); too, too
much (aux.) (used following II or III
subj. verb +t) {v2. aatabli; ngr.
aatámpa: to be too big on (3;II); to be
too many (I)} § Salhinkot aatapa.

aatapichi to do too much (I) [E+t]
(used with preceding I subj. verb:
'eat', 'drink', 'sleep', 'work', 'think
about') {ngr. aatapínchi} § Nost
ishaatapishtam? Did you sleep too
much?

aatapínchi ngr. of aatapichi

aatayya'a' back (of a chair, sofa)
[aa+atayya'a+']

aatí'wa to be lying (real sick), be (dead
and) laid out in (a place) (sg. subj.)
(I;3) [aa+ti'wa] {dl. aakáyya'ha; tpl.
aakahat máa; aato'wa}

<aatiya> in aatiyaka', imaatiya

aatiyaka', ishtaatiyaka' generation
[(isht) <aatiya>+ka+']

aato'li to play ball in (a place) (I;3)
[aa+to'li]

aato'li' ball field, baseball diamond [aato'li+']

aato'wa to lie in (a place); to be lying (real sick), be (dead and) laid out in (a place) (sg. hum. subj.) (I;3) [aa+to'wa] {aatí'wa}

aatoba to be made from (I;3) [aa+toba]

aatofa to spit in, on (a designated location) (I;3) (rare) [aa+tofa]

aatofa' spitoon [aatofa+']

aatoftowa' spitoon [aa+toftowa+']

aatoklha to flirt, be a flirt (I); to flirt with, joke around with; to play with (I;II) § Achitoklhatam? Did he flirt with you?

aatoklhakafa' gymnasium [aa+toklhakafa+']

aatoksali to work in (a place) (I;3) [aa+toksali]

aatoksali' prison, penitentiary [aatoksali+']

aatoksali'at inkaniya to get fired, lose one's job (III) [aatoksali'+at] § Aatoksali'at ankaniya'chikat ithanali. I know I'm going to lose my job.

aatoliyya' see aatoloyya'

aatoloyya', aatoliyya' ladder, stairs, fire escape [aa+<toloyya>+']

aatono'li to roll around in (a place) (I;3) [aa+tono'li]

aatonolli to roll around in (a place) (I;3)[aa+tonolli]

aatoyya to climb on (a person) (I;II) [aa+toyya] § Kowi'at achitoyyatam? Did the cat climb on you?

aatoyya' ramp [aatoyya+']

<aatookoli> in ittaatookoli {atookoli}

aatoomika' in the sun, out in the sun [aa+toomi+ka']

aatta to live, make one's home in (sg. subj.) (I;3) [aa+atta] {dl. aashwa; tpl. aa-asha}

aattattook holisso birth certificate (Ip,

—) [aa+atta+ttook] § Aattalittook holissaat ankaniyatok. My birth certificate is lost. I Ishaattattook holissohma ishi'shtam? Did you get your birth certificate?

aawiha to move out of (a place) (I;3) [aa+wiha] § Lynn inchokkaak aawihalitok. I moved out of Lynn's house.

aawihíli hngr. of aawihli

aawihli to take (sg. obj.) from ° (I;II;3) [aa+<wihli>] {hngr. aawihíli; pl. obj. aawihpoli} § Holisso achiwihlila'chi, Aachiwihlila'chi. I'll take the book from you. I Poshki' apowihtok, Aapowihtok. He took our mother from us.

aawihpoli to take, get (pl. obj.) from (I;II;3); to take everything away from, repossess things from (I;II) [aa+wihpoli] {sg. obj. aawihli} § Achiwihpolitok, Aachiwihpolitok. He took them from you, He took everything away from you. I Poshki' aapowihpolitahtok, Apowihpolitahtok. He took us from our mother.

aayahánta to stay around, be always around, stay watching (sg. subj.) (I;II) [aa(y)+ahanta] {dl. aayashwahánchi; pl. aayashahánchi}

Aayahanta' name of I. Hunter Pickens [aayahanta+']

aayashahánchi to stay around, be always around, stay watching (pl. subj.) (I;II) {sg. aayahánta; dl. aayashwahánchi}

aayashwahánchi to stay around, be always around, stay watching (dl. subj.) (I;II) {sg. aayahánta; pl. aayashahánchi}

aayaa to cry in (a place) (I;3) [aa+yaa]

aayimma to be about, to concern (3;3C) (requires an overt preceding

complement noun) § Janeako
ishno' aayimmaka imanotok. He
told Jane about you. | Holissaat
Lynn aayimmaho ishtanompatok.
The book was about Lynn. |
Josephine aayimmatok. It was about
Josephine.

aayimmi' believer in, adherent to (a
faith) [aa+yimmi+'] § Holinessak
aayimmi' saya. I'm a believer in the
Holiness faith, I'm a member of the
Holiness Church.

aayoka'mi' see aaoka'mi'

aayokachi' police station
[aa+yokachi+']

aayo'kli' (curved) handle on the side
of something (a cup, trunk, etc.);
railing; handlebars [aa+yokli+']

Aayokchaa' see Aaokchaa'

aayopi to swim in (I;3) [aa+yopi]

aayopi' bathtub, swimming pool
[aayopi+']

aayoppolo' trash (WB)
[aay+oppolo+'] {hayompolo'}

aayoppoloka' hell, hellfire
[aay+oppolo+ka+']

aayoowa to select (the best) from a
group (I;3) [aa+ayowa?]

aayohika', aayoka' see aaohika'

a

á'chi ggr. of anchi

a'chi' shawl, cape [a'chi+']

áa to go along, go around, walk (sg.
subj.) (I); to go around, walk around
in (a general location) (I;3) {dl.
tánno'wa, tpl. tanówa} § Okla pila
aalitok. I was walking around
downtown. | Aacha tikahbitahtok.
He's getting tired walking. | Aat
loshkatok. He goes around telling
lies.

ahaa yes

ála to come from there to here, to be
stretched, reach (inan. subj.) (3)—
ngr. of ala

<alak> in imalak

álbi ngr. of albi

alhakoffitok excuse me (I made a
mistake) [am+lhakoffi+tok]

álhlhi to be true, to tell the truth
(I)—ngr. of aalhlhi {ygr. áyyalhlhi
(used only in the negative);
ayalhlhi: to be really true; imálhlhi:
to be true, faithful to}

álhlhi ila it's really different
(exclamation)

alhlhi' truth [alhlhi+']

**alhlhi' anoli, alhlhi' aachi, alhlhi'
miha** to tell the truth (I)

alhlhi' aachi see alhlhi' anoli

alhlhi' miha see alhlhi' anoli

alhlhínchi to obey, do what one has
been told (even if the order or
suggestion was made in fun) (I)
{imalhlhínchi: to obey, do what
(someone) says}

álhto to be inside, to be some inside,
to remain (I)—ngr. of alhto {ygr.
áyyalhto} § Alhto. There's some
there, There's some in there. |
Charlesat tashpishofa amposhi'
alhto oshtaho apatok. Charles ate
(the contents of) four bowls of
pishofa.

áni ngr. of ani

ásha to remain, stay, be left (lying or
in some other position) (tpl. subj.)
(I)—ngr. of <asha> {sg. tówa (lying),

ánta; dl. ká̲ha (lying), á̲shwa}; might, might have to (aux., used with preceding verb +kmaka'chikya) § Itti̲sh yappa̲ ishilikmaka'chikya a̲shakat amilhlha. I'm afraid I might have to take this medicine. | Ika̲shokitok. They didn't stay.

ashaka', (ER, TP, WB) a̲shka', (LF) aashaka' back (of the body) (3p); right in back of (II) [a̲sha+ka'] § asaa̲shaka': in back of me | apoa̲shaka': in back of us |

ima̲shaka': buttocks, rear end

ashaka̲li' (moving) behind § Aahikki'yali a̲shaka̲li' ootayatok. He went behind where I was standing.

á̲shwa to be located; to stay, remain; to be left (dl. subj.) (I)—ngr. of ashwa {sg. ánta (stay, be located), tó̲wa (stay, be left); tpl. áyya'sha (stay, be located), á̲sha (stay, be left); ká̲ha}

áya ngr. of aya

b

ba' or (conjunction used between two complete but parallel sentences or, less often, between two noun phrases); so (used to introduce a question formed with +ta) § Kaafi'ak chibanna ba' tiiak chibanna? Do you want coffee or tea? | Tii ba' kaafi' katimpi chibanna? Which do you want, tea or coffee? | Brendaakat yamihshtok ba' Feliciaakat yamihshtok. Either Brenda did it or Felicia did it. | Ba' tii ishishkokat i̲'mata? So you're still drinking tea?

Ba' ishlata! Hello!, So you've come! (response to this greeting, used by the one arriving, is I̲i alali!) [ish+(a)la+ta]

ba'k ba'k ba'k aachi see bak bak bak aachi

bá'fa ggr. of baafa

bá'nna ggr. of banna

ba's ba's ba's aachi see bas bas bas aachi

bá'sha ggr. of basha

bá'shli ggr. of bashli

bachali to talk too much, talk about

nothing (I) {imbachali: to tell off}

bachali to hail (OC) {bachalosha}

bachalosha to sleet; to have sleet in (of a place) (3) {bachali} § Oklahomma'at bachaloshatok. It's sleeting in Oklahoma, Oklahoma has sleet.

bagi' buggy, carriage [from the English]

baha to have more than one hole (3) [+T] {v2. bahli}

bahafa see baafa

bahá̲li hngr. of bahli

bahá̲nna hngr. of banna

bahá̲sha hngr. of basha

báhhanna to be always craving—hgr. of banna

bahli to stab (more than once), punch more than one hole in (I;II); to poke (the fire) (I;3) {v1. baha; baafa: to stab once, punch one hole in}

bak bak bak aachi, ba'k ba'k ba'k aachi to make a knocking or hammering sound (expressive) (I) {baka'chi}

baka'chi to make a noise with wood (I) [+SC] {hngr. baka'lihínchi; klgr. bákkakli'chi; rcgr. bakaká'chi; bak

59

bak bak aachi}
baka'lihínchi hngr. of baka'chi
bakaká'chi to hammer, peck like a
woodpecker, make a noise with
wood (I)—rcgr. of baka'chi
bakbak woodpecker [bak bak bak
aachi]
bakbak ishkobo' homma' type of
redheaded woodpecker [homma+']
bakbak ishto' type of big woodpecker
[ishto+']
bakchi' in ishkin bakchi'
bakhitibli to go backwards, move
back, slip back (I); to be a backwater
(of water) (3) [bak+ <hitibli>] {ngr.
bakhitímbli; bakhitiipo'li}
bakhitiblichi to back up (a car, for
example) (I;3) [bakhitibli+chi] {ngr.
bakhitiblínchi}
bakhitiblínchi ngr. of bakhitiblichi
bakhitímbli ngr. of bakhitibli
bakhitiipo'chi to tell to go backwards,
make go backwards, push back (I;II)
[-SC] [bakhitiipo'li+chi]
bakhitiipo'li to go backwards, walk
backward (I) [bak+<hitiipo'li>]
{rmgr. bakhitiipopóli; bakhitibli}
bakhitiipopóli to keep going
backwards (I)—rmgr. of
bakhitiipo'li
bákkakli'chi to hit (I;II)—klgr. of
baka'chi
baklosochi to paint (someone's face)
(I;3); to paint the face of (I;II)
[baklosoli+chi]
baklosoli to have a dirty face; to have
one's face painted (II) [bak+<losoli>]
{ggr. baklósso'li; ngr. baklosóli; ygr.
baklosóyyo'li}
baklosóyyo'li ygr. of baklosoli
baklosóli ngr. of baklosoli
baklósso'li ggr. of baklosoli
bakshakachi to sharpen (a stick) to a
point (I;3) [-SC] [bakshakali+chi]

bakshakali, (CC) bokshakali to be
pointed (3); (AB) to be rounded on
the end; (CC) to be crooked
[bak+<shakali>]
bakshiyahámmi hngr. of
bakshiyammi
bakshiyama diaper
<bakshiyama> {v2. bakshiyammi;
bakshiyama}
**bakshiyama holisso aatoba', holisso
bakshiyama aatoba', holisso
bakshiyama** disposable diaper
[aa+toba+']
bakshiyamashtasitti'ya' safety pin,
diaper pin [bakshiyama isht
asitti'ya+']
bakshiyammi to put (a diaper) on
(oneself) (I;3) [bak+<shiyammi>]
{v1. <bakshiyama>; ggr.
bakshíyyammi: to have a diaper on;
hngr. bakshiyahámmi}
bakshiyammichi to put a diaper on
(someone) (I;II) [bakshayammi+chi]
{hngr. bakshiyammihínchi}
bakshiyammihínchi hngr. of
bakshiyammichi
bakshíyyammi to have (a diaper)
on—ggr. of bakshiyammi
baktasali to have a blaze on the
forehead (of a horse) (3)
[bak+<tasali>] {ggr. baktássa'li}
baktasachi to paint a blaze on the
forehead of (a horse) (I;3) [-SC]
[baktasali+chi]
baktássa'li ggr. of baktasali
bakwoshochi to put whiskers on
(someone) (I;II) [±SC]
[bakwosholi+chi]
bakwosholi to have a hairy face (II)
[bak+<wosholi>] {ggr.
bakwóshsho'li; chakwokoli}
bakwóshsho'li ggr. of bakwosholi
bala' beans, peas
bala' alaknachi', bala' laknachi' wax

beans; half-dried beans (Kentucky wonder, for instance) [alaknachi+']

bala' albilha', balalbilha' pole beans, climbing beans [bala' albilha+']

bala' awaalhaali' refried beans [awaalhaali+']

bala' balalli' climbing beans [balalli+']

bala' bilama' vanilla bean [bilama+']

bala' bolbo' ahooba'sika' kidney beans (PB) [imbolbo' ahooba+a'si+ka'; translation from English]

bala' champoli' sweet pea (flower) (joke) [champoli+'; translation from English]

bala' chaaha' bush beans (MJ) [chaaha+']

bala' falaha' losa' whippoorwill beans (ER) [falaha+' losa+']

bala' falaa', (ER) **bala' falaha',** (OC) bala' falaya' peas; (ER) black-eyed peas; (OC) pole beans (?), (ML) crowder peas [falaa+']

bala' falaa' ishkin losa' black-eyed beans [losa+']

bala' falaa' ittitikili', (MJ) bala-titikili' crowder peas [ittitikili+']

bala' falaa' shobbokoli' crowder peas (ER) [shobbokoli+']

bala' hakshop losa' purple hull peas [losa+']

bala' hakshop okchamali' purple hull peas (WB) [okchamali+']

bala' hika' yellow-meat low-growing beans, runner beans, (ML) wax beans, (ER) bush beans, (LR) Kentucky wonder beans [hika+']

bala' himona', bala' himona' waa' green beans, snap beans [waa+']

bala' holisso' speckled peas [holisso+']

bala' holhfo' bean sprout [holhfo+']

bala' homma' red beans; pinto beans;

kidney beans [bala' homma+']

bala' ishkin losa' (ER, OC, ML, CC, MJ), bal-ishkin losa' (WB) black-eyed beans [losa+']

bala' ittakallochi', (CP) bala' takallochi' crowder peas [itti+akallochi+']

bala' itti' albilha' bean pole (ER) [albilha+']

bala' itti' aatoyya' climbing beans [aa+toyya+']

bala' itti' shawwa aatoyya' Kentucky wonder beans [aa+toyya+']

bala' ihina' row of beans [im+hina']

bala' kendi', kendi' bala' jelly beans

bala' lakna' yellow beans; (CC) wax beans [bala' lakna+']

bala' laknachi' see bala' alaknachi' [laknachi+']

bala' laalawachi' crowder peas [ilalawachi+']

bala' losa' black beans [losa+']

bala' losayyi' type of butter beans; (WB) purple-hulled peas [losayyi+']

bala' lhibowa' English (green) peas [lhibowa+']

bala' malli' jumping beans [malli+']

bala' okchamali', balokchamali' green, fresh-picked beans; string beans (?) [okchamali+']

bala' okmiloli', balokmiloli', (ML) bala' okmillo'li' type of peas: monkey peas (CC), speckled peas (ML) [bala' okmiloli+']

bala' onchololi' bean sprouts [onchololi+']

bala' patha' lima beans, especially large ones; butter beans [patha+']

bala' patha' sawa'si' baby limas [sawa'si+']

bala' sawa' tohbi' see bala' tohbi' sawa'

bala' sinti' snake beans, very long green beans, yard beans

bala' shila' dry beans [shila+']
bala' shiwaa' striped peas [shiwaa+']
bala' shotik pila' type of peas [pila+']
bala' takassali' green (not dried)
  beans
bala' tohbi', (CC, TP, MJ, OC, ER) bala'
  toobi' navy beans; (CC) northern
  white beans, speckled beans
  [tohbi+']
bala' tohbi' iskano' small white
  beans (WB) [iskano+']
bala' tohbi' ishto' lima beans
  [ishto+']
bala' tohbi' sawa', bala' tohbi'
  sawa'si', bala' sawa' tohbi' field
  peas; baby lima beans; small white
  beans, such as small navy beans
  [tohbi+' <sawa>+']
bala' tohbi' sawa'si' very small white
  beans
bala' waaka' type of red and white
  spotted peas [waaka+']
bala' woksho' velvet beans
  [woksho+']
bala'chi to drag (someone) on the
  ground; to make crawl (I;II) [-SC]
  [bala'li+chi]
bala'li to crawl (I) {ggr. bálla'li; rmgr.
  ballaláli; balalli}
balalbilha' see bala' albilha'
balalli, balatli to grow on the ground
  like a vine or squash plant (3) [+T]
  {ggr. bállalli; balla'li}
balalli' vine [balalli+']
balatli see balalli
bala-tombi' iskanno' very small
  white beans (WB) {bala' tohbi'
  sawa'}
balaafka' see balaafokha'
balaafka' chawwala' shorts
balaafka' toba' denim [toba+']
balaafokchamali' blue jeans, blue
  pants [balaafka' okchamali+']
balaafokha', balaafka', (AB) abaalafka'

pants, trousers; underpants
  [aballaka' aa+fokha+']
balishtalbilha' bean pole [bala' isht
  albilha+']
balishto' lima beans, butter beans
  (WB)
bálla'li ggr. of bala'li
ballaláli to be always crawling
  around (I)—rmgr. of bala'li
bállalli ggr. of balalli
balokchamali' see bala' okchamali'
balokchi' bean juice—soy milk, for
  instance
balokmiloli' see bala' okmiloli'
balop slippery elm, slick elm
baná'lli ggr. of banalli
banaha see banaa
banaha', banaa' banaha
  (Chickasaw/Choctaw tamale)
  [banaa+']
banalli, banatli to roll (something)
  up (usually, in a loose roll) (I;3) {v1.
  banata; ggr. bánnalli, baná'lli}
banallichi to roll (something) up
  (usually, tightly and securely) (I;3);
  (CM) to knead [banalli+chi]
banata to be crumpled up, wrinkled
  (II) {v2. banalli; ggr. bánna'ta}
banatli see banalli
banaa, banaha to be rolled up in
  something (+T) (II)
banaa' see banaha'
Bani' Chickasaw man's name
  (anglicized as Bunny or Barney)
baniya dam; to be dammed (TP)
banka originally; from birth (aux.;
  generally used only of humans) §
  Chokma bankatok. He was born
  good, He was good from birth. |
  Hopooli bankatok. I was jealous
  from birth.
banna to want (II;3); to want to (II)
  [+E] (when same subj. complement
  is I or II subj., it must be [E]; III subj.

same subj. complement need not be
[E]); to want (an event or state) (II)
(prec. different subj. verb +a'ni)
{ggr. bá'nna; hgr. báhhanna: to be
always craving; hngr. baha̲nna; ngr.
ba̲nna; ygr. báyya'nna; neg. ikbanno}
§ Hilha sabanna. I want to dance. |
Chaaha sabanna. I want to be tall. |
Chokmishto sabanna,
Anchokmishto sabanna. I want to
be healthy. | Chichaaha'ni sabanna.
I want you to be tall.
bánna'ta ggr. of banata
bannachi to make * want, to tempt *
with (I;II;3) [banna+chi]
bannakat yawoolínchi to be itching
to (II , II) [E] § Pisa chibannakat
chiyawooli̲shta? Were you itching
to see him?
bánnalli to roll (someone or
something) (I;II) [+T]—ggr. of
banalli
baptismo to be baptized, christened
(with water on the forehead,
usually as an infant—for instance,
as done by Methodists) (I) [+CPR]
[+PR] [from English baptism,
perhaps influenced by Spanish
bautismo]
baptismochi to baptize, christen (in
the Methodist way) (I;II)
[baptismo+chi]
bas bus [from the English]
bas bas bas aachi, ba's ba's ba's aachi
to make the sound of wood
creaking or breaking (expressive) (I)
{basaachi}
basa'chi see basaachi
basak basak basak aachi to make the
sound of wood creaking or breaking
(expressive) (I)
basasá'chi to creak, crack (of a house,
for example) (3)—rcgr. of basaachi
basaachi, basa'chi to creak, crack (of a

house settling, or in an earthquake,
for example); to sound like
something burning (3) {ggr.
bássa'chi; hngr. basaahánchi; klgr.
<bássakli'chi>; rcgr. basasá'chi; bas
bas bas aachi, basak basak basak
aachi}
basaahánchi hngr. of basaachi
<basmo> in imbasmo
basóyyo'wa ygr. of basoowa
basoowa to be striped (II) [+CPR]
[+PR] {ggr. básso'wa; ygr.
basóyyo'wa}
basoowachi to stripe, put stripes on
(I;II) [basoowa+chi]
bássa'chi ggr. of basaachi
<bássakli'chi> in ittibássakli'chi—
klgr. of basaachi
básso'wa ggr. of basowa
basha to be sawed; to be operated on,
to have an operation (II) {v2. bashli;
ggr. bá'sha; hngr. baha̲sha; bashafa}
bashá'ffi ggr. of bashaffi
bashafa to be cut (II) {v2. bashaffi;
hngr. bashaha̲fa; basha}
bashaffi to cut (I;II) {v1. bashafa; ggr.
bashá'ffi, báshshaffi; hngr.
bashaha̲ffi; ngr. basha̲ffi; bashli}
bashaha̲fa hngr. of bashafa
bashaha̲ffi hngr. of bashaffi
bashanchik sumac {basho̲'kchi'}
bashanchik homma' type of sumac
[homma+']
bashanchik tohbi' type of sumac
[tohbi+']
basha̲ffi ngr. of bashaffi
bashili to be cloudless, fine; to clear
up (of the sky, weather) (3)
bashli to cut, saw, amputate; to
operate on (especially, to perform a
caesarian on); to mow (grass) (I;II)
[+OPR] {v1. basha; ggr. bá'shli; prt.
basht; bashaffi}
bashlicha chipotaaishi to deliver a

baby by caesarian section (I)
[bashli+cha chipota *aaishi]
bashǫ'kchi', (MC) bashǫ'chi' type of
tall weed with large fragrant white
flowers, used for medicine (queen
anne's lace?) {bashanchik}
bashpaalhpi' knife handle [bashpo
aalhpi']
bashpihaloppa' sharp edge of a knife
blade [bashpo im+haloppa+']
bashpo knife [basha/bashli +po+]
bashpo chakchaki' big knife with a
serrated edge [chakchaki+']
bashpo falaa' kitchen knife, butcher
knife [falaa+']
bashpo falaa' ishtittibi' sword [isht
ittibi+']
bashpo ishtimpa' table knife [bashpo
isht impa+']
bashposhi' pocket knife [bashpo
oshi']
báshshaffi ggr. of bashaffi
bashshi to be a crybaby, cry all the
time (II) [-PR] {ygr. báyya'shshi;
ilbashsha, tabashi}
bashshishokcha' crybaby [bashshi
im+shokcha+']
basht prt. of bashli
bashtabli to cut with a knife (I;3)
[basht *tabli] § Basht ishtablitok.
You cut it with a knife. | Basht
iktablokitok. He didn't cut it with a
knife.
bati' type of sumac (LF)
bayahálli hngr. of bayalli
bayalli, bayatli to go along in separate
rows or lines (at a bank or
supermarket checkout, for example,
or while picking cotton) (pl. subj.)
(I); to line up in (a place) (pl. subj.)
(I;3) {v1. báyya'ta; ggr. báyyalli;
hngr. bayahálli}
bayatli see bayalli
báyya'nna ygr. of banna

báyya'shshi ygr. of bashshi
báyya'ta to go along different paths to
the same goal, to converge on a goal
from different directions (pl. subj.)
(3) (Ct?) {v2. bayalli}
báyyalli ggr. of bayalli
baafa, bahafa to stab (once); to punch,
make one hole in (I;II) {ggr. bá'fa;
bahli: to stab more than once,
punch more than one hole in)
okkaabaafa}
baafachi to make ° stab ° (I;II;3)
[baafa+chi]
baafalallak morning glory
baaksalhto' in tii baaksalhto' [baaks
(from English box) + alhto+']
baanit bonnet, sunbonnet [from the
English]
Baatambi' Chickasaw man's name
baayo'chi to bounce (a ball); to
bounce on, to push down on (a
spring or something with springs)
(I;3) [-SC] {v1. baayo'kachi; hngr.
baayo'lihínchi; imbaayo'chi: to
bounce (someone); ombaayo'chi: to
bounce on}
baayo'kachi to go up and down (like
waves); to have springs, be bouncy
(3) {v2. baayo'chi; hngr.
baayo'kahánchi; paayo'kachi}
baayo'kahánchi hngr. of baayo'kachi
baayo'kalhchi to bounce (of a ball) (3)
{v2. baayo'chi; paayo'kalhchi}
baayo'lihínchi hngr. of baayo'chi
bánna ngr. of banna
beptaayzi to baptize (ER)
bí'la ggr. of bila
bichchala' short form of ibichchala'
bíchcho'ta ggr. of bichota
bíchcholli ggr. of bicholli
bichili to pour (I;3) (Ct)
bicho'kachi to be flexible, limber,
flimsy (I) {hngr. bicho'kahánchi;
bichota}

bichó'lli ggr. of bicholli
bicholli, bichotli to bend (sg. obj.)
(I;II) {v1. bichota; ggr. bíchcholli,
bichó'lli; pl. obj. bichoto'li}
bichota to be crooked, bent (sg. subj.)
(II) [+PR] [+CPR] {v2. bicholli; ggr.
bíchcho'ta; ygr. bichóyyo'ta; pl.
bichoto'wa; bicho'kachi}
bichotli see bicholli
bichoto'li to bend a lot (for instance,
with pliers), bend (pl. obj.) (I;3) {v1.
bichoto'wa; sg. obj. bicholli}
bichoto'wa to be crooked, bent (of a
piece of wire that cannot be
straightened, for instance;
especially, to be bent in several
places); to be crooked, bent (pl. subj.)
(3) {v2. bichoto'li; sg. bichota}
bichóyyo'ta ygr. of bichota
bihi' mulberry
bihi' api' mulberry tree
<bikili> in nokbikili
bila to melt, be melted, thaw,
dissolve (II) [+PR] [-CPR] {v2. bilili;
ggr. bí'la}
bila' shila', (WB) bila-shila' pork
crackling [bila+' ('grease' in
Choctaw)]
<bilachi> in abilachi, ittabilachi
[bila+chi]
bilama to smell good, have a
fragrance (II) {ggr. bílla'ma; ngr.
biláma; ygr. biláyya'ma}
bilamachi to make smell good, to
perfume (I;II) [bilama+chi] {hngr.
bilamahánchi}
bilamahánchi hngr. of bilamachi
biláyya'ma ygr. of bilama
biláma ngr. of bilama
bilili to melt, thaw, dissolve (I;II) {v1.
bila}
bílla'ma ggr. of bilama
bílli'ya always, everlastingly (aux.,
preceded by verb +na or bare verb)

{biika} § Ithanali chinkanali
billi'ya'chikat. I know I'll be your
friend always.
bilo'chi to masturbate (someone)
(I;II) [±SC] {ilibilo'chi; biloffi}
bilo'chit nowa to be promiscuous,
run around (I) [bilo'chi+t]
biloffi to masturbate (I) {hngr.
bilohóffi; bilo'chi; imbiloffi}
bilohóffi hngr. of biloffi
Bilokshi' Biloxi Indian; exclamation
used by Mississippi Choctaws (WB)
<bilhipa> in ombilhipa {ggr.
bílhlhi'pa}
bílhlhi'pa to kneel (pl. subj.) (I)—ggr.
of <bilhipa>
Bini'cha loshka! Sit down and tell
lies! (an invitation to gossip)
[biniili+cha]
biniichi to make sit down; to leave
behind (a child, something in a bag,
something round) (sg. obj.) (I;II)
[-SC] {biniili+chi} {pl. obj. binohchi}
biniili to sit down (punctual) (sg.
-dl.subj.) (I); to sit down in (a place)
(sg.-dl. subj.) (I;3) {ggr. bínni:li: to be
sitting; ngr. biníli; rmgr. binniníli;
dl.-tpl. binohli; bin-kachi; Hobinili!}
§ Hoobiniitok. They (two) sat down.
biníli ngr. of biniili
bínka to be like (someone) in (3;II)
[E]; each of two, each of two groups
(aux.)—ngr. of biika § Charlesat
chaaha chibinka manko. Charles
was tall like you. | Onkof chaffa
binka imalitok. I gave (the two of
them) one persimmon each. |
Toklo binkakmat oshta. Two plus
(times?) two is four.
binka' one of the same type (IIp)
(used with a preceding noun;
mainly predicative) [binka+'] §
Ella'at Chikashsha sabinka'. Ella is a
Chickasaw like me.

65

bin-kachi to shimmer in the heat or as part of a mirage; to throb (3) {hngr. bin-kahánchi; biniili} § Pallikat bin-kahanchi. It shimmered in the heat. | Sachonkashat bin-kachi. My heart is throbbing.

bin-kahánchi hngr. of bin-kachi

bínni'li to sit, be sitting (sg. subj.) (I) [+PR] [-CPR]—ggr. of biniili {dl. chí'ya; tpl. binohma̲a̲}

binni't ilhpokonna to sit dreaming, to daydream (II) [binni'li+t] § Binni't chilhpokonna. You daydreamed.

binnini̱li to sit around (sg. subj.) (I)—rmgr. of biniili

binohchi to make sit down, set down (pl. obj) (I;II) [±SC] [binohli+chi] {sg. obj. biniichi}

binohli to sit down (punct.) (mainly tpl. subj., also dl.) (I) [+taha] {sg., dl. biniili}

binohma̲a̲ to be sitting down (tpl. subj.) (I) [binoh(li)+t *ma̲a̲] {sg. bínni'li; dl. chí'ya}

biskit biscuit [from the English]

bissa' type of berry (blackberry, perhaps also raspberry)

bissa' akka' balalli', bissa' balalli', (JC) bissa' bala'li', (WB) bissakka', (WB, CC, ML) bissakkaabalali', (CC, ML) biskaabalali' dewberry [bissa' akka' balalli+']

bissa' balalli' see bissa' akka' balalli'

bissa' chaaha' tall blackberry plant [chaaha+']

bissa' hika' type of large blackberry, (ER) dewberry [hika+']

bissa' okchamali' blueberry (ER) [okchamali+']

bissapi' berry vine [bissa' api']

bishalhchi to drip; to leak (of breast milk); to be mushy (3) {v2. bishlichi}

bishlichi to strain, squeeze out (a liquid); to pump (one's breasts) (I;3) {v1. bishalhchi; imbishlichi: to milk} § lhitoffit bishlichi: to squeeze out the juice from

bit bit (money)—mainly used in complex expressions below [from the English]

bit hanna'li six bits, seventy-five cents

bit oshta four bits, fifty cents

bit toklo two bits, twenty-five cents

<bitippichi> in abiitippichi {v1. bitiipa>

bitiipa to put out a hand to break one's fall (I) {v2. <bitippichi>; bitka}

bitka to press down or feel with one's open hands alternately, especially when crawling on hands and knees (I) {bitiipa, ombitka}

bitkat hoyo to look for (in the dark) (I;II) [bitka+t] § Bitkat sahoyotok. He looked for me in the dark, He felt around for me in the dark.

bitkat pisa to see by touch (of a blind person) (I;II) [bitka+t]

biya' beer [from the English]

bíyyi'ka to have (something) all over one (II;3); all the time, always (aux.—usually used with preceding ngr. or hngr.), all around, scattered (aux.—used with preceding number)—ygr. of biika § Niha sabiyyi'ka. I have grease all over. | Ankaarat okti' bíyyi'ka. My car has snow all over it. | Saniha biyyi'ka. I'm greasy all the time. | Iloshta biyyi'ka. We were (scattered) in groups of four. | Talohówa biyyi'kakat itha̲nali. I know I sing all the time. | Alhpila' chibannahookma̱ Chihoowaat achipila'hi biyyi'ka. If you need help God will always help you.

biyyo̱'ka' strawberry

biibi', (LF) biibii baby [from English
baby]
<biibli> in nokbiibli
biibosi' little baby [biibi'+o'si+']
biika to be just, only (pl. subj.) (I;3)
(must be used with a preceding
noun with pl. reference) {ngr. bínka;
ygr. bíyyi'ka; bílli'ya} § Ihoo
biikatok. It was only women. I Ihoo
iibiikakat ilithana. We know that
we were only women.
<biipa> in nokbiipa
<biipo'li> in nokbiipo'li
<biipo'wa> in nokbiipo'wa
biitop short form of ibiitop
biits beets [from the English]
bo'chi to churn, to beat (eggs); to
make waves in (water) (I;3) [-SC]
[bo'li+chi] {v1. bo'kalhchi; ggr.
bó'chi; hngr. bo'lihínchi; ngr.
bo'línchi}
bo'chit lha'li to splash (something)
around (for instance, from a bucket)
(I;3) [bo'chi+t]
bó'hli ggr. of bohli
bo'kahálhchi hngr. of bo'kalhchi
bo'kalhchi to be beaten (of eggs), to be
splashed; to come in waves (of
water) (3) {v2. bo'chi; hngr.
bo'kahálhchi}
bo'li to beat, pound; to beat up; to hit
(pl. subj.) (I;II) {v1. bo'wa; sg. isso
(hit)}
bo'lihínchi hngr. of bo'chi
bo'línchi hngr. of bo'chi
bo'wa to be beat up (II) {v2. bo'li;
hngr. bohówa}
bohli to put down, lay down, put to
bed; to bury; to put (money) in the
bank (sg. obj.) (I;II) {ggr. bó'hli; hngr.
bohóli; ngr. bóhli: to lay
(something) down for a while; ygr.
bóyyo'hli: to keep, preserve; dl.-tpl.
obj. kahli (lay down), tpl. obj.

ashaachi (put down in a heap), ani}
bohóli hngr. of bohli
bohówa hngr. of bo'wa
bohpohóli hngr. of bohpoli
bohpoli to go around picking fights;
to throw rocks (I) [po+bohli] {hngr.
bohpohóli}
boka', (CC) booga' bogeyman, booger
[from the English]
bokafa to burst (of a large balloon), to
go boom, to be crushed with the
fingers (of a large bug, for example)
(sg. subj.) (II) {v2. bokaffi; ggr.
bókka'fa; hngr. bokaháfa; pl.
bokahli}
bokaffi to burst (something large); to
crush (a large bug, for instance) with
the fingers (sg. obj.) (I;II) {v1. bokafa;
hngr. bokaháffi; pl. obj. bokahchi,
bokli}
bokaháfa hngr. of bokafa
bokaháffi hngr. of bokaffi
bokaháli hngr. of bokahli
bokahchi to burst (large things) (pl.
obj.) (I;3) [±SC] [bokahli+chi] {sg. obj.
bokaffi}
bokahli to burst, pop open (of large
things) (pl. subj.) (3) {hngr. bokaháli;
sg. bokafa}
bókka'fa ggr. of bokafa
bokkaháa hngr. of bokkaa
bokkaa, bokkaha to beat up (I;II); to
hit (in baseball) (WB) {hngr.
bokkaháa}
bokkaha see bokkaa
bokli to burst (large things, or things
which make a loud noise) (pl. obj.)
(I;3) {sg. obj. bokaffi}
bokoffa' gnat, (TP) type of very small
mosquito, (AB) buffalo gnat
bokshíkko'fa to be in a big bundle—
ggr. of bokshikofa
bokshiko'li to bundle (pl. obj.),
bundle (mass or pl. obj.) into a

number of bundles (I;3) {v1.
bokshiko'wa; sg. obj. bokshikoffi}
bokshiko'wa to be bundled up (pl.
subj.) (3) {v2. bokshiko'li; sg.
bokshikofa}
bokshikofa to be in a bundle, be
bundled, balled up (and wrinkled
up) (sg. subj.) (II) {v2. bokshikoffi;
ggr. bokshíkko'fa: to be in a big
bundle; ngr. bokshikǫ́fa; ygr.
bokshikóyyo'fa; pl. bokshiko'wa}
bokshikoffi to bundle, ball up (and
wrinkle) (sg. obj.) (I;II) {v2.
bokshikofa; pl. obj. bokshiko'li}
bokshikóyyo'fa ygr. of bokshikofa
bokshikǫ́fa ngr. of bokshikofa
bokyóffǫ'li ggr. of bokyofǫli
bokyofǫli to make faces; to have an
ugly face (3) [bak+] {ggr. bokyóffǫ'li}
bolbo' in bala' bolbo' ahooba'sika',
imbolbo'
bóllokta ggr. of bolokta
bolokta to be round, spherical (II) (Ct)
{ggr. bóllokta; ngr. bolónkta; ygr.
bolóyyokta}
bolónkta ngr. of bolokta
bolóyyokta ygr. of bolokta
boshó'lli ggr. of bosholli
boshohǫ́lli hngr. of bosholli
bosholli, boshotli to be cracked; to be
crumbly, crumbled; to be ruined (3)
{ggr. bóshsholli, boshó'lli; hngr.
boshohǫ́lli; ngr. boshǫ́lli} §
namboshsholli': garbage
boshollichi to crack (something) into
pieces (I;3) [bosholli+chi]
boshotli see bosholli
boshǫ́lli ngr. of bosholli
boshshal bushel [from the English]

bóshsholli ggr. of bosholli
Boshto Chickasaw man's name (CC)
boshto' type of oak tree (overcup
oak?)
bota to be ground up (3) {v2. botoli}
botoli to grind fine, like flour,
especially by pounding in a wooden
mortar (I;II) {v1. bota} § Kitti'
aabotolili. I ground it in a wooden
mortar.
bowafa to sink, settle (of ground) (3)
[+T]
boyafa to fall out, shed (of hair,
feathers) (3); to shed, have the hair
or feathers fall out (especially,
seasonally) (sg. subj.) (II); to have
(hair) come out, shed (3;3) [+CPR]
[+PR] {v2. boyaffi; hngr. boyahǫ́fa; pl.
boyahli} § Kowi'at hishi'at boyafa.
The cat's hair shed. | Kowi'
nannahmat hishi' boyafa. Some cat
shed hair.
boyaffi to pull out hair or feathers
(especially of a hog or chicken, after
scalding the skin) (I;II) {v1. boyafa}
boyahǫ́fa hngr. of boyafa
boyahǫ́li hngr. of boyahli
boyahǫ́lli to have the hair coming
out (of an animal) (3)
boyahli to shed, have the hair or
feathers fall out (of animals—pl.
subj.) (3) {hngr. boyahǫ́li; sg. boyafa}
<boyolli> in iliboyolli
bóyyo'hli to keep, preserve—ygr. of
bohli
Book Chickasaw man's nickname [<
Ct book "river"]
bǫ́hli to lay (something) down for a
while—ngr. of bohli

ch

cha'lh cha'lh cha'lh aachi see chalh
chalh chalh aachi
chá'lhlhi ggr. of chalhlhi
cha'm cha'm cha'm aachi see cham
cham cham aachi
cha'sh cha'sh cha'sh aachi see chash
chash chash aachi
Chabi' man's nickname (anglicized
as Chubby)
chaffa one; to be one in number, to
be the one, to be the other (sg. subj.)
(I) [+PR] {ygr. cháyya'ffa} § Anaakot
chaffali. I'm the one, I'm the other
one.
chaffa áyyo'ka to do one by one, to be
one each (3) (when subr., this verb
can refer to a non-third-person, but
it is never marked for a non-third-
person subj.) § Chaffa ayyo'kat
iliyyatok. We left one by one. |
Chipota chaffa ayyo'kakat onkof
chaffa biyyi'ka apatok. Each of the
children ate one persimmon.
chaffa bíyyi'ka to be (scattered) alone
(pl. subj.) (I , —) § Iichaffa
biyyi'katok. We were scattered
about, each alone by himself.
chaffa'si only one; to be only one in
number; to be the only one; to be
alone (sg. subj.) (II) [chaffa+a'si] §
Sachaffa'si. I'm alone, I'm the only
one.
chaffí'chi ggr. of chaffichi
chaffichi to send away, run off; to fire,
lay off (sg. obj., or one at a time) (I;II)
{ggr. chaffí'chi; hngr. chaffihínchi}
chaffihínchi hngr. of chaffichi
chaffo' another one, the other one,
the mate (for instance, of a pair)
[chaffa]
chafi'nachi in ishchafi'nachi {fi̱'chi}
chahá̱la hngr. of cha̱la

chahá̱lhlhi hngr. of chalhlhi
cháhha'ha, cháhha'a hgr. of chaaha
cháhha̱'la hgr. of cha̱la
Chahta' Choctaw person
Chahta' kallo' full-blooded Choctaw
(Ct) [kallo+']
Chahta' losa' slang name for
chalhha' losa' bird [losa+']
Chahtanompa', Chahtimanompa the
Choctaw language [Chahta'
anompa+']
Chahtihoo' Choctaw woman
[Chahta' ihoo+']
Chahtimanompa see Chahtanompa'
Chahtı̱yaakni' the Choctaw Nation
of Oklahoma [Chahta' im+yaakni']
Chahtoshi' Choctaw child [Chahta
oshi']
<chakaffa'> in inchakaffa'
chakali to be pregnant, great with
child (3) (Ct) {ggr. chakká'li}
chaka̱'to' tomato
chakbakachi to rip the clothes off
(someone) (I;II) [±SC]
[chakbakali+chi]
chakbakali to be naked (MJ) {ggr.
chakbákka'li}
chakbákka'li to be naked (II)—ggr. of
chakbakali
chakchaki to be scalloped or
sawtoothed (3)
chakchakichi to scallop, make the
edge (of something) have a
scalloped or sawtooth pattern (by
cutting it or putting on rickrack)
(I;3) [chakchaki+chi]
chakihı̱ssa, chakihı̱sa hngr. of
chakissa, <cakisa>
<chakisa> var. grade base of chakissa
{hngr. chakihı̱sa; ngr. chakı̱sa; ygr.
chakíyyi'sa}
chakissa, (WB) chakassa to be sticky

(II); to be not done on the inside (of bread) (3) {ggr. chákkissa; hngr. chakihíssa, chakihísa; ngr. chakíssa, chakísa; ygr. chakíyyi'sa; <chakisa>}

chakissachi to make (something) sticky (I;II) [chakissa+chi]

chakíyyi'sa ygr. of chakissa, <chakisa>

chakíssa, chakísa ngr. of chakissa, <chakisa>

chakká'li nine; to be nine in number (I)—ggr. of chakali

chakká'li áyyo'ka to be in groups of nine (I , —)

chákkissa ggr. of chakissa

chaklit chocolate, cocoa [from the English]

chaklit losa' chocolate [losa+']

chaklit palli' hot chocolate, cocoa [palli+']

<chakwa'> in akankinchakwa'

chakwihili' possum (JJ)

chakwókko'li ggr. of chakwokoli

chakwokoli to have a large beard (3) [chok+] {ggr. chakwókko'li; ngr. chokwokóli; ygr. chakwokóyyo'li; bakwosholi}

chakwokóyyo'li ygr. of chakwokoli

chakwokóli ngr. of chakwokoli

Chalakkanompa' see Chalakkimanompa'

Chalakki' Cherokee

Chalakkihoo' Cherokee woman [Chalakki' ihoo+']

Chalakkimanompa', Chalakkanompa' Cherokee language [Chalakki' (im+)anompa+']

Chalakkiyaakni' the Cherokee Nation of Oklahoma [Chalakki' im+yaakni']

chalantak buckeye (CC) [Choctaw chalatak "woodpecker" ?]

chalbakko' (TJ, TP, WB), (CC, MJ)

chalbako' sucker (fish); (MJ) bass

chalokloha' see chaloklowa'

chaloklowa to gobble like a turkey (I)

chaloklowa', chalokloha' turkey [chaloklowa+']

chaloklowa' akanka' turkey-headed chicken (ER)

Chaloklowa' Hilha' Turkey Dance

chaloklowa' ibilhkan turkey wattles

chaloklowa' imilhlha' wild turkey [imilhlha+']

chaloklowa' imissap June bug [im+issap]

chaloklowa' ittish type of mint—the leaves were soaked in water for a medicinal wash

chaloklowa' okchamali' see chaloklowokchamali'

chaloklowokchamali', chalokloha' okchamali' peacock [okchamali+']

chalh chalh chalh aachi, cha'lh cha'lh cha'lh aachi to make the sound of little parts rattling (in a toy, for instance) (expressive) (I) {chalha'chi}

chalha to be cut (pl. subj.) (3) [+T] {v2. chalhlhi; sg. chalhafa; chalhahli}

chalha'chi to make noise; to rattle (3) [-SC] {klgr. <chálhlhakli'chi'>; rcgr. <chalhalhá'chi'>; chalhaachi, ittichalhlhalhaachi, chalh chalh chalh aachi, chalhak chalhak chalhak aachi}

chalhafa to be cut (with scissors) (sg. subj.) (3) {v2. chalhaffi; pl. chalha, chalhahli}

chalhaffi to cut (sg. obj.) (with scissors) (I;3) {v1. chalhafa; pl. obj. chalhlhi}

chalhahli to be tattered, all cut up (with scissors), to be cut up (pl. subj.) (3) {sg. chalhaffi; chalha}

chalhak chalhak chalhak aachi to make the sound of little parts rattling (in a toy, for instance) (expressive) (I) {chalha'chi} <chalhalhá'chi> in ittichalhalhá'chi—rcgr. of chalhá'chi

chalhaachi to make noise (for instance, of children playing with little cars) (I) {hngr. chalhaahánchi: to rattle, clatter; chalha'chi, ittichalhalhá'chi}

chalhaahánchi to make noise, rattle, clatter (of metal things) (3)—hngr. of chalhaachi

chalhha', (MJ) chalhlha' blackbird

chalhha' ishto' large type of blackbird with a red spot on each wing [ishto+']

chalhha' losa' blackbird (another name for chalhha') [losa+'] {Chahta' losa'}

chalhka to gamble with cards, play cards (especially, for money) (I)

chalhka' card player; (WB) cards, dice [chalhka+'] <chálhlhakli'chi> in ittichálhlhakli'chi—klgr. of chalha'chi

chalhlhi to cut (pl. obj.) (with scissors); to cut into strips (I;3) [+T] {vl. chalha; ggr. chá'lhlhi; hngr. chahá̱lhlhi; sg. obj. chalhaffi}

cham cham cham aachi, cha'm cha'm cha'm aachi to make the sound of glass breaking, of things banging or rattling around inside something, or of tinkling (as of the bell on an ice-cream cart) (expressive) (I) {chama'chi}

chama'chi to make a sound with a metal obj. (I) [+SC] {klgr. chámmakli'chi; rcgr. chamamá'chi; cham cham cham aachi, chamak chamak chamak aachi; chamapa}

chamahámpa hngr. of chamapa

chamak chamak chamak aachi to make the sound of glass breaking, of things banging or rattling around, or of a tinkling bell (expressive) (I) {chama'chi}

chamamá'chi to make a noise with metal; to ring (I)—rcgr. of chama'chi [+SC]

chamapa to hit together and make noise (of pans) (3) {hngr. chamahámpa}

chamaachi to ring (for example, of a telephone) (3) {hngr. chamaahánchi; samaachi}

chamaahánchi hngr. of chamaachi

chámmakli'chi to make a noise (I)— klgr. of chama'chi

champó'li ggr. of champoli

champóhho'li hgr. of champoli

champohó̱li hngr. of champoli

champoli to be sweet, to taste good; to have a taste (II) [+CPR] [-PR] {ggr. champó'li; hgr. champóhho'li; hngr. champohó̱li; ngr. champó̱li; ygr. champóyyo'li; inchampoli: to like the taste of; chonkash champoli'}

champolichi to sweeten (I;3) [champoli+chi]

champóyyo'li ygr. of champoli

champó̱li ngr. of champoli

chanaha see chanaa

chanahá̱lli hngr. of chanalli

chanahli to roll, spin, rotate (of a wheel, drum, globe) (3) {chanalli}

chanakbi to be crooked (3) {ggr. chánnakbi; ygr. chanáyyakbi}

chanalli, chanatli to roll (for instance, of a car or wagon left on a hill) (3) [+taha] {ggr. chánnalli; hngr. chanahá̱lli; chanahli, chanaa}

chanallichi to roll, spin (something) (I;3) [chanalli+chi]

chanalloshi' toy wagon, buggy (Ct?)

71

[chanalli oshi']

chanatli see chanalli

chanáyyakbi ygr. of chanakbi

chanaa, chanaha to roll, spin (for instance, of a wheel) (3) {chanalli}

chanaa malili' see itti'chanaa malili'

chanaa malili' apiisachi' conductor [apiisachi+']

chanaa malili' aahika' railway station, depot [aa+hika+']

chanaa malili' chaffichi' engineer [chaffichi+']

chanaa malili ishnọwa' engineer

chanaa malili' lowak imooti', lowak imooti', (WB) chanaa malili' lowak imonti fireman (on a train) [im+ooti+']

chanaa malili-malichi' engineer [chanaa malili' malichi+']

chanaa malili-patassa' flatcar (WB)

chanaachi to make spin, roll (I;3) [±SC] [chanaa+chi]

chank haloppa' cucumber (AB) [ishtokchank haloppa+']

chánnakbi ggr. of chanakbi

chánnalli ggr. of chanalli

chapchap type of small woodpecker (AB, WB, MJ)

chash chash chash aachi, cha'sh cha'sh cha'sh aachi to make a rattling or rustling sound (expressive) (I) {<chasha'chi>}

chashak chashak chashak aachi to make a rattling or rustling sound (expressive) (I) {<chasha'chi>}

<chasha'> in sintinchasha' {<chasha'chi>}

<chasha'chi> in ittichasha'chi {klgr. <cháshshakli'chi>; rcgr. <chashashá'chi>; chash chash chash aachi, chashak chashak chashak aachi, <chasha'>}

<chashashá'chi> in ittichashashá'chi—rcgr. of

<chasha'chi>

<cháshshakli'chi> in itticháshshakli'chi—klgr. of <chasha'chi>

chashshanak nape, base of the neck (where the bone sticks up) (HS)

<chashwa> in inchashwa

chawwáhha'la hgr. of chawwala

chawwala to show a lot of leg: to be very tall (of a man), to be too short (of a dress) (3) [+PR]—often used in prt. {hgr. chawwáhha'la; ngr. chawwála; xgr. chawwálla'a} § Chawwalat aamanko. He's going along looking very tall.

chawwalili to make short (in the leg: for instance, to shorten a skirt) (I;3) {ngr. chawwalíli}

chawwalíli ngr. of chawwalili

chawwálla'a to show a lot of leg, be long in the thighs (of a new-born colt, for example): to be too short (of a skirt), to wear skirts too short (of a woman), to be really tall (of a man) (3) (often used in part.)—xgr. of chawwala

chawwála ngr. of chawwala

cháyya'ffa ygr. of chaffa

cháyya'ha ygr. of chaaha

cháyya'la ygr. of chala

chaafoha'si see chaafowa'si

<chaafowa> in chaafowa'si, chaafoochi, ittachaaafowa [chaffa]

chaafowa'si, chaafoha'si to be just a few, to be some (I) [<chaafowa>+a'si] {ngr. chaafówa, chaafóha; ittachaafowa}

chaafoochi to pick the best one from a group; to distribute one each (I;3) [+/-SC] [<chaafowa>+chi] {ittachaafoochi; chaffo'; oka'at chaafoochi} § Paska champoli' chaafoochilitok. I gave out one cookie each.

chaafoochit aayoowa to pick the best
from a group (I;3) [chaafoochi+t]
chaafǫwa, chaafǫha ngr. of
chaafowa'si
chaaha to be tall (II); to be high (of
prices, temperatures) (3) [+CPR]
[+PR] {hgr. cháhha'ha, cháhha'a;
ngr. cháha; ygr. cháyya'ha}
chaahachi to make tall (I;II); to
increase, make (prices) high (I;3)
[chaaha+chi] {ngr. chaahánchi}
chaahakat achaaka to grow taller (I /
II / II, —) [chaaha+kat] {ggr.
chaahakat áchcha'ka} § Sachaahakat
achaakakat ithanali, Chaahakat
asachaakakat ithanali. I know I grew
taller. | Chaahakat ishachaaka. You
grew taller.
chaahakat áchcha'ka ggr. of
chaahakat achaaka
chaahánchi ngr. of chaahachi
chaaha taloowa to sing high, have a
high singing voice (I) [chaaha+a]
Chaali' Chickasaw man's name [<
Eng. Charlie]
<chaamo'> in iyyinchaamo'
cha'a to be pounded (3) [+T] {v2.
cha'li}
cha'li to chop, pound; to break up
(dirt) (I;3) {v1. cha'a}
cháha to be taller—ngr. of chaaha
chahollo' see chaholo'
chaholo', chahollo', (MJ) chaalo'
bluebird (?)
chala to be starched, to be stiff with
dirt or another substance (II) {hgr.
cháhha'la; hngr. chahála; ygr.
cháyya'la}
chalá'chi ggr. of chalachi
chalachi to starch (I;II) [chala+chi]
{ggr. chalá'chi}
chashpo in chashpo mishshaash,
chashpochi, chashpohma
chashpo mishshaash, nittak chashpo

mishshaash long ago, at one time,
in earlier days
chashpochi to shorten, hasten the
end of (3;3) (used almost exclusively
in proverbial expressions like the
following) [chashpo+chi] § Hattakat
nittak chashpochihoot ayya'sha'hi.
Man is going to make the day
shorter (used about daylight saving
time, or metaphorically to refer to
the coming Judgment Day).
chashpohma, nittak chashpohma
long ago, in earlier days
[chashpo+hma]
chek check (payment) [from the
English]
cheli', jeli' jelly, preserves [from the
English] § panki' cheli' grape jelly
chí'ya to sit, be sitting (dl. subj.) (I)
{hngr. chihíya: to sit around (dl.);
ngr. chíya; sg. bínni'li; tpl.
binohmáa}
chibaali sparks (CM) [chipasli]
chiffohǫla hngr. of chiffoola
chiffola to be bent into a circle, bent
over, curled up (3) {v2. chiffololi;
rigr. chiffolfǫwa; xgr. chifǫllo'wa;
chiffoola}
chiffolachi to bend (wood, for
instance) (I;3) [chiffola+chi]
chiffolfǫwa to slither like a snake
3)—rigr. of chiffola
chiffolkachi to slither like a snake (3)
chifǫllo'wa to lie doubled up,
crooked (I)—xgr. of chiffola
chiffololi to bend (something) (I;3)
{v1. chiffola}
chiffoola to wiggle like a worm (I)
{hngr. chiffohǫla; chiffola}
chihaksibish patha a mild insult
("you've got ears like an
elephant's") [chi+haksibish]
chihasimbish an insult (short for
chihasimbish falaa)

73

chihasimbish falaa

chihasimbish falaa, chihasimbishat
falaa an insult ("you've got a long
tail") [chi+hasimbish(+at)]
chihíya to sit around (dl. subj.)—
hngr. of chí'ya
chihmi to act like, be like, seem like,
feel like (I;3C); to be as much as
(I;3C) [E+kat], [+kat] [+HM], <chih>
(requires an overt preceding
complement noun) {chohmi} §
Chipota ishchihmi. You're like a
child. | Himitta' chihmili. I act
young, like a young one. | Ano'
chihmi. He's acting like me. |
Naahollihoo' chihmi ki'yo. She
doesn't act like a white lady. |
Hopookat ishno' chihmili,
Hopoolikat ishno' chihmili. I'm
jealous like you. | Shimmanoolaat
Florida ayya'shakat Oklahomma'
ayya'shaka' chihmaakayni. The
Seminoles in Florida are like the
ones in Oklahoma. | Hopookat
ishno' chihmili aakayni. I'm as
jealous as you.
chihmihchi to treat ° like (I;II;3C)
[chihmi+chi ?] {must be used with
an overt noun complement} §
Chipota sachihmihshtok. He treated
me like a child.
Chihoowa God
Chihoowa Aba' Binni'li' God
Chihoowa aayoppachi' altar
[aa+ayoppachi+']
Chihoowa Chitokaka' God
Chihoowa imanompaalhpisa' God's
commandment
Chihoowa Imaapihlichika' Heaven,
God's Realm (Bible expression) [<
Ct imaapihlichika']
Chihoowa Imobyaka' Impa' the
Lord's Supper, communion
[im+(obyaka' impa')]
Chihoowa inannalhpisa' God's law,

commandment [im+nannalhpisa']
Chihoowa Inannalhpisa' Yimmi'
Christian [yimmi+']
Chihoowa inaaholittompishtatta' see
naaholittompishtatta'
Chihoowa inaaholittompishtaa-asha'
see naaholittompishtaa-asha'
Chihoowa inaalhpisa' rainbow
("God's promise") (ER)
[im+nannalhpisa']
Chihoowa Inaayimmi' believer in
God, Christian [im+naayimmi']
Chihoowa inaanoli' prophet
[im+nanna anoli+'] {Chihoowaak
inaanoli'}
Chihoowa inittak holitto'pa
religious holiday [im+nittak]
Chihoowa iyaakni' the whole world
[im+yaakni']
Chihoowa kalakshichi to blaspheme,
take the Lord's name in vain (I)
Chihoowa naaishtimaaholitto'pa'
the glory of God [nanna isht
im+aa+holitto'pa+']
Chihoowa Pinchitokaka' God [from
Choctaw pim (= pom) +
Chitokaka']
Chihoowaak inaanoli' prophecy
[Chihoowa+ak im+nanna anoli+']
{Chihoowa inaanoli'}
Chihoowimanompa anompoli to
speak in tongues (as part of a
religious experience) (I) [Chihoowa
im+anompa]
Chihoowimaapihlichika' God's
kingdom [Chihoowa
im+aapihlichika']
Chihoowoshi' Jesus, the Son of God
[Chihoowa oshi']
Chihoowoshi' Imaafammi'
Christmas
chik word used to call chickens
(repeated many times, quickly)
[from English chick?]

74

Chikashsha, (FA) Chikashsha' Chickasaw person

Chikashsha finha' full-blooded Chickasaw (MJ) [finha+']

Chikashsha kallo' full-blooded Chickasaw (ER) [kallo+']

Chikashshanompa', Chikashsha imanompa' Chickasaw, the Chickasaw language [Chikashsha anompa+']

Chikashshalhlhi' full-blooded Chickasaw (AB) [Chikashsha alhlhi+']

Chikashshihoo' Chickasaw woman [Chikashsha ihoo+']

Chikashshiklanna' someone who is half Chickasaw [Chikashshiklanna+']

Chikashshimanompa' see Chikashshanompa'

Chikashshiminko' the Governor of the Chickasaw Nation of Oklahoma [Chikashsha im+minko']

Chikashshiyaakni' the Chickasaw Nation of Oklahoma [Chikashsha im+yaakni']

Chikashshoshi' Chickasaw child [Chikashsha oshi']

chikimba although supposedly, planning to; nothing! § Aya chikimba, ishtoksala'chi; Ishiyya chikimba, ishtoksala'chi. Though (you were) intending to go, you're going to (have to) work; Go nothing—you've got to work. | Aachompa' ayali chikimba, chokoshkomolitok; Aachompa' aya chikimba chokoshkomolitok. Although (I was) supposed to go to the store, I played; Go to the store nothing, I played instead. | Madonna chikimba, foshi'at taloowatok! Madonna nothing—a bird was singing!

chikkibbi to be all piled up (3); to push to get into (a crowded space, like a store or bus) (I) {hngr. chikkihímbi; <chokkobbi>}

chikkibichi to pile up (I;3) [chikkibbi+chi]

chikkihímbi hngr. of chikkibbi

Chiklin Chickasaw man's name

chiko'li to play with, pull on (someone's) hair (I;II); to tease, rat (one's hair) (I) {v1. chiko'wa} § Chichiko'lili. I play with your hair.

chiko'wa to be all sticking up; to be teased, ratted (of hair) (3) {v2. chiko'li}

chilabli to be rough (of hands, for instance), to have something be rough (II) [+PR] [+CPR] {ggr. chíllabli; hngr. chilahámbli; ngr. chilámbli; ygr. chiláyyabli}

chilablichi to roughen (I;II) [chilabli+chi]

chilahámbli hngr. of chilabli

chilahángbi hngr. of chilakbi

chilakbi to be dry and cracked (of mud, for example); to be crusted, dried onto a surface (II) {ggr. chíllakbi; hngr. chilahángbi; ygr. chiláyyakbi}

chilámbli ngr. of chilabli

chilanto type of bird (CC)

chiláyyabli ygr. of chilabli

chiláyyakbi ygr. of chilakbi

chili' chili [from the English, or possibly the Spanish]

chili' ibalhto' chili powder

chilichi to make crumbs of (I;3) [-SC] [chilili+chi]

chilihínta hngr. of chilita

chilili to be crumbs, to be crumbly (3)

chilínta ngr. of chilita

chilita to try, keep on, persevere (I) {ggr. chílli'ta; hngr. chilihínta; ngr. chilínta} § Chilli'talikya taloowala'

75

chilịsa'

ki'yokitok. I keep trying but I never can sing.
chilịsa' chipmunk, (EP) flying squirrel
chíllabli ggr. of chilabli
chíllakbi ggr. of chilakbi
chílli'ta to keep on (trying unsuccessfully, or doing the wrong thing)—ggr. of chilita
chíllokka ggr. of chilokka
chillowa to be off the cob (of corn) (3) [+T] {chilokka}
Chilo'na' Chickasaw woman's name
chilohónka hngr. of chilokka
chilokka to shell (corn) (I;3) {ggr. chíllokka, chilôkka; hngr. chilohónka; ngr. chilónka; chillowa}
chilôkka ggr. of chilokka
chilónka ngr. of chilokka
chilhạ'kbi' (TJ), (CC, ER, WB, MJ) chilhạ'bi', (LF) chiklhạ'bi', (LR) chilhlhạ'bi' copperhead
chilhlhạ'li to have a cyst or other hard swelling beneath the surface of the skin (3) § Salbakat chilhlhạ'li. There's a lump under the skin of my hand, My hand has a cyst.
chimli' fireplace [< English chimney]
chímmikli'chi to attack, hit suddenly (I;II) § Sachimmikli'shtokạ ithạnali. I know I had a sudden attack (a sharp pain, charley horse, etc., attacked me).
chinaafalla'ha' black haw (tree sp.)
chincha' ginger [from the English]
chincha' pallaska' gingerbread
chinchis bedbug (MJ) [from Spanish chinche]
chinchokma, chinchokmata hello; how are you? [2s+inchokma(+ta)]
chinchokmata see chinchokma
chínnoffi ggr. of chinoffi
chino'li to pinch a lot, pinch (pl. obj.)

(I;II) {v1. chino'wa; sg. obj. chinoffi}
chino'wa to be pinched a lot, be pinched (pl. subj.) (II) [+T] {v2. chino'li; sg. chinofa}
chinofa to be pinched: especially, to have one's skin pinched (sg. subj.) (II) {v2. chinoffi; pl. chino'wa}
chinofa'si, chino'fa'si a pinch, a little bit [chinofa+a'si] § Hapi chinofa'si ishibaanikmạ. Put in a pinch of salt.
chinoffi to pinch (sg. obj.) (I;II) [-OPR] {v1. chinofa; ggr. chínnoffi; hngr. chinohóffi; pl. obj. chino'li} § Chimofi' chinoffitok. He pinched your dog.
chinohóffi hngr. of chinoffi
chinokko' middle of the upper back; (EP) back of the head (IIp) § chichinokko': the middle of your upper back
chínto to be bigger (II)—ngr. of ishto, <chito>
<chintochi> [chinto+li+chi] {ngr. chintolínchi}
chintolínchi to make bigger (I;II)—ngr. of <chintochi>
chipasli to emit sparks (of a fire) (3) {lowak chipasli}
chipaslichi see lowak chipaslichi
chipónta, chipónta'si to be smaller, younger, as one was when a child (II)—ngr. of chipota'si [chiponta+a'si]
chipónta'si see chipónta
chipota child
chipota ammo'na' oldest child [ammo'na+']
chipota habina to adopt a child; to get pregnant (I)
chipota habinachi to give up a child to for adoption (I;II); to give up a child for adoption (I) [(chipota habina)+chi]
chipota hayoochi to get pregnant

76

(often, accidentally) (I) § Chipota
hayooshtokoot ittihaalalla'chi.
She's going to get married because
she got pregnant.
chipota holba' baby doll
chipota holhkopa' illegitimate child
whose father is not known
[holhkopa+']
chipota ima to give up a child for
adoption to (I;III)
chipota inki' toklo' child whose
father is not known because its
mother had two lovers [toklo+']
chipota ippo'si', chipotippo'si'
midwife
chipota ishtayyo'pi' youngest child
[ishtayyo'pi+']
chipota kobolli' family of children
closely spaced in age
chipota loma' illegitimate child
whose father is not known [loma+']
chipota nakni' boy
chipota nakni' toklo' twin boys
[toklo+']
chipota noti' baby teeth
chipota sho'li to have a baby (I) §
Chipota sho'la'chi. She's pregnant,
She's going to have a baby.
chipota tiik girl
chipota tiik toklo' twin girls [toklo+']
chipota toklo' twins, twin children
[toklo+']
chipota'si to be young, little (rare) (3)
[chipota+a'si] {ngr. chipónta,
chipónta'si}
chipotabi to have an abortion (I)
[chipota *abi] § Chipotishbitam? Did
you have an abortion?
chipotalhtakla' orphan, abandoned
child; latchkey child
chipotammo'na' first child (in a
family) [chipota ammo'na+']
chipotapiisachi' baby sitter [chipota
apiisachi+']

chipotapooba to deliver a baby, act as
a midwife (I) [chipota *apooba] §
Chipot-ishapoobatok. You delivered
a baby.
chipotaa-asha' children's ward (in a
hospital) [chipota aa-asha']
chipotaachokoshkomo' playpen
[chipota aa+chokoshkomo+']
chipotaafokha' stroller, baby carrier
[chipota aa+fokha+']
chipotaapishi' nipple on a baby bottle
[chipota aa+pishi+']
chipotaat imala to have a baby, give
birth (III) [chipota+at] § Chipotaat
amala. I had a baby.
chipotaat imánta ngr. of chipotaat
imatta
chipotaat imatta to have a baby, give
birth (III) [chipota+at] {ngr. chipotaat
imánta} § Chipotaat amattakat
itha̱nali. I know I'm having a baby.
chipotaat imilli to have a miscarriage
(III) [chipota+at]
chipotaat inkaniya to have a
miscarriage, lose a baby (III)
[chipota+at] § Chipotaat
ankaniyatok. I had a miscarriage.
chipotaat inti'wa to have a baby, give
birth (III) [chipota+at] § Dorisat
chipotaat inti'watok. Doris had a
baby.
chipotikhofa̱'to' blue baby or other
baby born alive but with serious
health problems (one that probably
won't live) [chipota ikhofa̱'to+']
chipotimapooba to deliver the baby
of (I;III) [chipota im+apooba] §
Chipotissamapoobatok. You
delivered my baby.
chipotimaafa'pa' baby swing
chipotimaaishi to perform an
abortion on (euphemistic) (I;III)
[chipota *imaaishi] § Alikchaat
chipotamaaishitok. The doctor did

77

chipotimaaombiniili' chaaha'

an abortion on me, I had an abortion.
chipotimaaombiniili' chaaha' highchair [chipota im+aaombiniili' chaaha+']
chipotinkali fontanel, baby's soft spot [chipota im+kali]
chipotintopa crib, cradle [chipota in+topa]
chipotippo'si' see chipota ippo'si'
chipotishki' mother (mainly used predicatively) [chipota ishki'] § Chipotishki' toba sabanna. I want to become a mother.
chipotishki' aa-asha' maternity ward (in a hospital)
chipotishtáa to be pregnant (I) [chipota isht *aa] § Chipotishtishaa. You're pregnant.
chipoti'sha'chit abika to be in labor (I = subj. , II = subj.) [chipota i'shi+a'chi+t] § Chipoti'shla'chit asabika. I'm in labor.
chipotoppolo' bad kid, poorly behaved child [chipota oppolo+']
chipsi', jipsi' gypsy [from the English]
chisiya to be polka-dotted, spotted (of a dress, for instance) (old word) (3) (may be used after a color verb) [+PR] [+CPR] {neg. ikchisiyyo} § Naafkaat chisiya. The dress is polka-dotted. | Naafkaat losa chisiyatok. The dress had black spots.
chiskilik, (TP) tiskilik blackjack (type of oak tree)
chisha', (TP) tisha' post oak
chishak dew
chishanko arbor, built (often of willows) for shade outdoors
chishanko toba' willow; any material used to build an arbor [toba+']
chishkish! an insult [chi+ishkish]
chishkish losa, chishkish losa', chishkishat losa an insult

[chi+ishkish(+at) losa+']
chitta sister (one family's word) (LR, MS) [from the English?]
Chittialbi' falaa! Pouty face!, You pouter! (joking comment used to a child who's pouting) [chi+ittialbi']
<chito> in Chitokaka', hichito, nokchito [from Choctaw chito "big"] {ngr. chínto; ishto}
Chitokaka' in Aba' Pinchitokaka', Pinki' Chihoowa Chitokaka', Chihoowa Chitokaka', Chitokaka' Imaafammi' [<chito>+ka+ka']
Chitokaka' Imaafammi', (ER) Chitokaka' Afammi' Christmas (Ct?), (ER) Easter
chii takchi'sha it has to be that way [+a'chi]
chiichi', (AB) chi'chi, (MS, EH) chiichi milk (children's word) [pishokchi']
chiiki to be early; to be earlier or quicker than expected (with reference to an event, time, or state, although generally not one with the speaker as subj.) (—) § Chiikitok. It was early. | Chi'kina alatok. He came early.
chiiki áyya'shahmat..., chiiki áyya'shahmat aachikat..., chiiki áyya'shahmat ishtanompolikat aachikat..., chiiki áyya'shakat aachikat..., chiiki áyya'shakat ishtanompolikat aachikat..., chiiki pílla áyya'shakaash..., chiiki pílla áyya'shahmat..., chiiki pílla áyya'shahmat aachikat..., chiiki áyya'shahmat ishtanompolikat aachikat... once upon a time (it was told that, they say that)... (formulas for beginning a traditional story, regardless of its subj.) [ayya'sha+hmat/kat/kaash ((ishtanompoli+kat) aachi+kat)] §

78

Chiiki áyya'shahmat
ishtanompolikat aachikat Chokfaat
abikattook. Once upon a time (they
say) Rabbit was sick (long ago).
chiiki' early, earlier than expected
[chiiki+'] § Chiiki' alalitok. I came
early.
chiikihma, nittak chiikihma in
earlier days [chiiki+hma]
chiiko'si' quickly [chiiki+o'si+'] §
Chiiko'si' tii ishtamalla. Bring me
some tea quickly.
chiili to lay (eggs), (CC) set on (eggs)
(I;3) {achiili}
Chiisas Jesus [from the English]
<chih> [HM] of chihmi
chifalakto' an insult
[chim+falakto+']
chilhilafa a cuss word
[chim+lhilafa—a pun on holafa?]
chíya ngr. of chí'ya
cho'b cho'b cho'b aachi see chob chob
chob aachi
<cho'li> in incho'li
chó'lhlhi ggr. of cholhlhi
cho'mi to be together (of more than
two) (I); to be together with (pl.
subj.) (I;3) (mainly subr.) [+HM],
<cho'> § Busta' kiicho'tok. It was
us, together with Buster. | Pam
Doris Dan cho'maat ittibo'li. Pam
and Doris and Dan (together) hit
each other. | Lynn iicho'maat
iichipistok. We, together with Lynn,
saw you.
chó'nna ggr. of chonna
<cho'wa> in incho'wa
**chob chob chob aachi, cho'b cho'b
cho'b aachi** to make a splashing or
swishing sound in water
(expressive) (I) {chobo'chi}
<chóbbokli'chi> in
ittichóbbokli'chi—klgr. of chobo'chi
chobo'chi to splash (a liquid) (I;3)

[-SC] {klgr. <chóbbokli'chi>; rcgr.
<chobobó'chi>; chob chob chob
aachi, chobok chobok chobok aachi,
choboowachi}
<chobobó'chi> in ittichobobó'chi—
rcgr. of chobo'chi
chobok chobok chobok aachi to make
a splashing or swishing sound in
water (expressive) (I) {chobo'chi}
choboowachi to make a bubbling,
gurgling sound (of a waterfall or the
tide, for example, or a child blowing
into milk) (I) {hngr.
choboowahánchi; ngr.
choboowánchi; chobo'chi}
choboowahánchi hngr. of
choboowachi
choboowánchi ngr. of choboowachi
chofá'lli ggr. of chofalli
chofahálli hngr. of chofalli
chofak see chofaak
chofalli, chofatli to clean, clean up
(something) (I;II) {v1. chofata; ggr.
chóffalli, chofá'lli; hngr. chofahálli}
chofánta ngr. of chofata
chofata to be clean (II) [+PR] [+CPR]
{v2. chofalli; ggr. chóffa'ta; ngr.
chofánta; ygr. chofáyya'ta}
chofatli see chofalli
chofáyya'ta ygr. of chofata
chofaak, chofak fork; pitchfork
chofaak haloppa' awl, ice pick
[haloppa+']
chofaak ishtimpa' fork [isht impa+']
chofaak yaalhfowa', (EP) chofaklhwa'
spurs [chofaak iyyi'
aa+<alhfowa>+']
chofaakoshi' pin; safety pin [chofaak
oshi']
chofaakoshi' aachoshkachi'
pincushion [aa+<achoshkachi>+']
chofaakoshi' ilontala'li' pin
(ornament), brooch, badge, medal
chofaakoshi' ishtoopo'li', (AB)

chofak-oshi' naaishtacho'wa' ishtoopo'li' thimble [isht toopo'li+']
chofaakoshi' naaishtalhcho'wa' see naaishtalhcho'wa'
chofaakoshi' oshkibbi'li' straight pin (with a little head) [oshkibbi'li+']
chóffa'ta ggr. of chofata
chóffalli ggr. of chofalli
chohmi to act like, be like (I;3) (used only with a preceding noun and following negative ki'yo); kind of (aux.) [+HM], <choh> § Ishno' chohmili ki'yo. I don't act like you. | Chimissikopali chohmi. I'm kind of mean to you. | Issikopa chohtok. He was kind of mean. | Ithanali hopooli chohmikat. I know I'm kind of jealous.
chohmo'si just a little (aux.) [chohmi+o'si]
chohómpa hngr. of chompa
chohólhlhi hngr. of cholhlhi
chohónna hngr. of chonna
chokaani nihi' flyspeck (CC) {chokaano}
chokaanishtabi' fly swatter [chokaano isht abi+']
chokaano, (WB, VB, CC, ER, AW) chokaani, (MC) chokaan, (AB, OC, LF, LJ, EP, TP, LR, HS) chokaana, (CP) chokaana', (MJ) chokkaani, (CM) chokaani' fly (the insect)
chokaano ishyokachi' flypaper [isht yokachi+']
chokaanokchamali', (TP) chokaanokchama'li' blue fly, green fly [chokaano okchamali+']
chokaanoshi' small maggot, fly egg [chokaano oshi']
chokcho' in koni chokcho'
chokfá'nni ggr. of chokfanni
chokfahánni hngr. of chokfanni
chokfalhpooba' sheep [chokfi

alhpooba']
chokfalhpoobapiisachi' shepherd [chokfalhpooba' apiisachi+']
chokfalhpooboshi' lamb [chokfalhpooba' oshi']
chokfanni to spin around, be spun around (I) {ggr. chokfá'nni; hngr. chokfahánni}
chokfannichi to spin (something) around (I;II) [chokfanni+chi]
Chokfaat Achiili for it to be Easter (when the rabbit lays eggs—a joke) [chokfi+at] § Chokfaat Achiilikma... on Easter (in the future)...
chokfi rabbit, sheep
Chokfi Chickasaw man's nickname
chokfi haksobish falaa' jackrabbit (WB) [falaa+']
chokfi haksobish falaa' okchamali' blue jackrabbit (WB) [okchamali+']
chokfi hishi' wool
chokfi hishi' falaa' long-haired sheep (WB) [falaa+']
chokfi ishto' sheep (LP) [ishto+']
chokfi lakna', (AB, WB) chokfaalakna' swamp rabbit [lakna+']
chokfi loma' wild rabbit [loma+']
chokfi losa' black sheep (WB) [losa+']
chokfi palhki' jackrabbit [palhki+']
chokfi woksho' long-haired sheep [woksho+']
chokfiyammi, (ER) chokfayammi, (AB) chokfiyyomi, (CM) chokfiimi, (WB) chokfiyama, (MJ) chokfimmi, (TJ) chokfihommi to hiccup (II / I) [chok+]
chokfiyyi' rabbit's foot (for instance, used as a good-luck charm) [chokfi iyyi']
chokfisholosh type of medicinal plant with pink flowers [chokfi im+sholosh]
chokfokchamali', (WB) chokfi-

haksobish falaa' okchamali' type of rabbit, (WB) blue jackrabbit [chokfi (haksobish falaa+') okchamali+']

chokfóllo'ha to be half drunk—ggr. of chokfoloha

chokfoloha, chokfolowa to be dizzy (II) [chok+foloha] {v2. chokfolohli; ggr. chokfóllo'ha: to be half drunk}

chokfolohli to make dizzy (I;II) {v1. chokfoloha}

chokfolowa see chokfoloha

chokfoshi' baby rabbit [chokfi oshi']

chokfoshtaka'li', (WB) chokfoshtakali', (AB) chokfashtaka'li', (MC) chokfi oshtaka'li' cottontail rabbit

chokka' house, home

chokka' lokoli' neighbors; houses grouped together in a bunch § chinchokka' lokoli': your neighbors

chokka' naa-alhtoka' constable

chokka' pakna' roof

chokka' poto'ni' toad (AB) [potooni+'] {chokkato'chi'}

chokka-chaffa' family (IIIp: inchokka-chaffa') [chokka' chaffa+']

chokkala'bolo', chokbila'bolo', (ER) chakbolo'bolo', (ML) chokbala'bolo', (MS) chokbilo'bilo', (CC) chokbilo'bolo', (LR, HS) chakbilo'bilo', (CP, MJ) chakbolombolo', (AB, TJ) chokbolo'bolo', (WB) chokbila'bilo', (LP) chokbolo'bolo', (CC) chokfilo'bolo', (VB) chokkabo'bolo', (EP) chokwala'bolo' whippoorwill, (CC) screech owl

chokkala'bolo' bala', (WB) chokbilambilo' bala' whippoorwill beans

chokkapiisachi' apartment house manager [chokka' apiisachi+']

chokkato'chi' toad (AB) [chokka' atochi+'] {chokka' potooni'}

chokkayá'lli ggr. of chokkayalli

chokkayahálli hngr. of chokkayalli

chokkayahli to drool (I) {chokkayalli}

chokkayalli, chokkayatli to drool, slobber (I) [chok+] {ggr. chokkayá'lli; hngr. chokkayahálli; ngr. chokkayálli; chokkayahli, shokha' chokkayalli'}

chokkayálli ngr. of chokkayalli

chokkayatli see chokkayalli

<chokkaalaha> see <chokkaalaa>

chokkaalaha' see chokkaalaa'

<chokkaalaa>, <chokkaalaha> in inchokkaalaa, chokkaalaa' [chokka' aa+ala ?]

chokkaalaa', chokkaalaha' guest, visitor

chokkaamahála hngr. of chokkaamala

chokkaamala to spin around, be spun around (I) [chok+] {hngr. chokkaamahála; ngr. chokkaamála; malli?}

chokkaamalachi to spin (something) around (I;II) [chokkaamala+chi]

chokkaamála ngr. of chokkaamala

chokkiksaachi' carpenter [chokka' iksaachi+']

chokkilissa to be quiet, not saying anything (I) [+CPR] [+PR] [chokka' illa issa?] {ggr. chokkíllissa; ngr. chokkilíssa; inchokkilissa: to be lonely}

chokkilíssa ngr. of chokkilissa

chokkilissachi to shut (someone) up, make quiet (I;II) [chokilissa+chi] {ngr. chokkilissánchi}

chokkilissánchi ngr. of chokkilissachi

chokkíllissa ggr. of chokilissa

chokkimponta' landlord [chokka' imponta+']

chokkishto' building, big house [chokka' ishto+']

<chokkobbi>

<chokkobbi> in achokkobbi, imachokkobbi, imachokkobbichi {chikkibbi}

chokkohǫwa to go into (dpl. subj.)— hngr. of chokkowa {sg.-dl.-nondpl. chokkowa}

chokkowa to go into (I;3) [+taha] {hngr. chokkohǫwa (dpl. subj.); ngr. chokkǫwa: to be caught inside}

chokkoyya'li' in shokha' chokkoyya'li'

chokkǫwa to be caught inside—ngr. of chokkowa

choklhí'li ggr. of choklhiili

choklhíhhi'li hgr. of choklhiili

choklhihı̨li hngr. of choklhiili

choklhíyyi'li ygr. of choklhiili

choklhiili to smile, grin (I) [chok+] {ggr. choklhí'li; hgr. choklhíhhi'li; hngr. choklhihı̨li; ygr. choklhíyyi'li}

chokma to be good, nice (II); to act good (I); to be a good (example of one's role or profession) (II;3) (in this meaning, a noun is required); really, good and, well (aux.) [-CPR] [+PR] {v2. chokmali; ngr. chóngma; ygr. chóyyokma; inchokma: to feel good; <chokmaka>} § Inkaat alikchi' chokma. His father is a good doctor. | Holissopisachi' chichokma'chi. You're going to be a good teacher. | Asokcha chokma. I'm really awake. | Chokmat sanostok, Sanost chokmatok. I slept well. | Hashi'at aloota chokma. The moon is good and full. (MJ)

chokma imalhta is it okay, suitable?, is he okay?, is she okay? (3) § Yappat chokma imalhta? Is it okay? | Bonnieat chokma imalhtam? Was Bonnie okay, suitable?, Was it okay (regarding Bonnie)?

chokma imilahobbi to act good to (I;III) § Chokma amilahobbitok. He

acted good to me.

chokma ímmo'ma, (AB) chokmímmo'ma still okay! (a response to the greeting chinchokmata)

chokma'si to be pretty (II) [chokma+a'si] [+PR] [+CPR] {inchokma'si}

chokmahookay okay, you're welcome (response to yakookay) [chokma+<hookay>]

<chokmaka> in inchokmánka, ishtinchokmaka [chokma+ka] {v2. chokmali}

chokmali to improve, make good (nonhum. obj.) (I;3) {v1. chokma, <chokmaka>}

<chokmánka> in inchokmánka

chokmat ánta ngr. of chokmat atta

chokmat asilhha to really ask, to look into something carefully (I) [chokma+t] {chokmat imasilhha} § Chokmat ishasilhhatam? Did you really ask?

chokmat atta to behave well, act good (I) [chokma+t] {ngr. chokmat ánta} § Chokmat antali. I act good.

chokmat imasilhha to really ask (someone), to question carefully (I;III) [im+(chokmat asilhha)] § Chokmat issamalhha'chita? Are you really going to question me carefully?

chokmata hello; how are you? [chokma+ta]

<chokmishto> in inchokmishto

chokoshkó'mo ggr. of chokoshkomo

chokoshkohǫmo hngr. of chokoshkomo

chokoshkomo, (TJ) cho'shkomo to play; to nip playfully (of a pet) (I); to play (an instrument, a game) (I;3) [-PR] [-CPR] {ggr. chokoshkó'mo; hngr. chokoshkohǫmo}

chokoshkomo-apiisachi' referee
[chokoshkomo apiisachi+']
chokoshkomochi to make play (I;II);
to make go, wind up (a toy, etc.) (I;3)
[chokoshkomo+chi]
chokoshpa story (MC, TP)
chokoshpá'li ggr. of chokoshpali
chokoshpachi to spread gossip (I)
[chokoshpa+chi] {inchokoshpachi}
chokoshpachi' gossiper
[chokoshpachi+']
chokoshpali to gossip, say things
without foundation (I) {ggr.
chokoshpá'li; inchokoshpali: to
gossip about, gossip to}
chola fox
chola homma' red fox [homma+']
chola oshi' see chol-oshi'
cholok hole
cholok biyyi'ka to be hollow, empty
inside; to have a lot of holes (3)
cholok ishtiwa' ishtaafilito'chi'
keyhole [isht aa+filito'chi+']
cholokchama'li' grey fox [chola
okchamali+']
<chololi> in onchololi
choloshi' see chol-oshi'
chol-oshi', choloshi', chola oshi'
baby fox
cholha to be cut for shingles (of
wood, for instance) (3) [+T] {v2.
cholhlhi}
cholha' see itti' cholha'
cholhkan, (CC, MC, MJ, CP)
choklhan, (AW) ishtolhkan spider
{toklhan}
cholhkan apa' spider wasp [apa+']
cholhkan hala'li', (TP, MJ) cholhkan
hola'li', (CP) cholhkan ola'li'
spider web
cholhkan ishto' big spider, tarantula
[ishto+']
cholhkan losa' black widow spider
[losa+']

cholhkan oshi' baby spider
cholhlhi to make (wood) into
shingles (I;3) {v1. cholha; ggr.
chó'lhlhi}
chomak tobacco
chomak apa' tomato worm [apa+']
chomak aaholbona' cigarette paper
[aa+holbona+']
chomak aapofa' pipe (EH, AW)
[aa+pofa+']
chomak bota' snuff [bota+']
chomak hishi' tobacco leaves
chomak hoboona to roll a cigarette (I)
chomak holba' type of weed that
looks like tobacco
chomak holbona' cigarette, especially
a hand-rolled one [holbona+']
chomak ishokcha tobacco pouch
[im+shokcha]
chomak palaska' chewing tobacco
[<palaska>+']
chomak pofa to smoke, smoke
tobacco (I)
chomak pofa' cigarette [(chomak
pofa)+']
chomak pofa' ishto' cigar [ishto+']
chomak shana' chewing tobacco in a
long, twisted piece [shana+']
chomak shoboochi to blow out
smoke playfully, blow smoke rings
(I) [-SC]
chomak shoti', (MJ) chomak shotik
pipe
chompa to buy (I;II) [+OPR] {hngr.
chohómpa; inchompa: to shop for,
buy for; imaachompa: to buy from}
§ Katimpi ofi' inchompatok?
Which one's dog did he buy?
chompachi to make ˚ buy ˚ (I;II;3)
[chompa+chi]
chona'sha' water moccasin (snake)
(AB, TJ, TP)
chonkash, (FA) ichonkash heart (IIp)
{imichonkash}

83

chonkash akkálo'si to be humble (3)
chonkash champoli' sweetheart
(joking slang) [translation of the
English: champoli+']
chonkash holba' heart shape
chonkash hottopa' heart attack
[hottopa+']
chonkash hottopa' hayochi to have a
heart attack (I)
chonkash hottopat illi to die of a
heart attack (II) [hottopa+t] §
Chonkash hottopat salla'chi. I'm
going to die of a heart attack.
chonkash ishtanokfilli to think about
something in one's heart (IIp , I)
{imichonkash ishtanokfilli}
chonkash kallo person whose mind
is set, unyielding person §
Chonkash kallo saya. My mind is
made up, I won't change, I'm an
unyielding person.
chonkash kallochi to refuse to
change one's mind after having
made a decision (IIp, I) {ilikallochi}
§ Sachonkash kallochilitok. I
hardened my heart, refused to
change my mind.
chonkash yohbi to have a peaceful
heart: to be calm, to keep going on
with things (IIp , —)
chonkashat hottopa to have a heart
attack (IIp, II) [chonkash+at] §

Sachonkashat sattopatok. I had a
heart attack.
chonkashat yaháa to feel very sorry,
be crying inside (IIp = subj.)
[chonkash+at] § Pisa sabannakat
sachonkashat yahaa. I wanted to see
it, so I felt very sorry.
chonna to be skinny (II) [+CPR] [+PR]
{ggr. chó'nna; hngr. chohónna; ngr.
chónna; ygr. chóyyo'nna}
chonokko' upper back (IIp)
chóngma to be better (II)—ngr. of
chokma
chowaala', chowahala', (CM)
chowahla', (WB, var.) chohwala',
(MJ) chomahala', (VB) chawala
cedar, (CC) Christmas tree
chowahala' see chowaala'
chóyyo'nna ygr. of chonna
chóyyokma ygr. of chokma
choocho' hog (baby talk) [shokha']
<cho'> [HM] of cho'mi
cho'ki' martin, purple martin (type
of bird)
cho'ki' losa' type of black bird [losa+']
cho'ti' frog
cho'ti' nakni' bullfrog (VB)
cho'ti' okchamali' type of edible frog
(AB) [okchamali+']
cho'tishto' big frog [cho'ti' ishto+']
<choh> [HM] of chohmi
chónna ngr. of chonna

d

daala' see taala'

f

fá'mmi ggr. of fammi
fabahása hngr. of fabassa, <fabasa>
fabahássa hngr. of fabassa
<fabasa> var. grade base for fabassa
{hngr. fabahása; ngr. fabása}
fabassa to be straight, thin; to stand
erect (II) [-PR] [-CPR] {ggr. fábbassa;
hngr. fabahássa, fabahása; ngr.
fabássa, fabása; <fabasa>, fáhha'ko}
fabása ngr. of fabassa, <fabasa>
fabássa ngr. of fabassa
fábbassa ggr. of fabassa
fáchcho'pa to be open (of a
switchblade)—ggr. of fachopa
fachobli to open (a pocketknife or
switchblade) (I;3) {v1. fachopa}
fachopa to open (of a switchblade) (3)
{v2. fachobli; ggr. fáchcho'pa: to be
open (of a switchblade)}
fahámpa hngr. of faapa
faháli hngr. of fahli
faháma hngr. of fama
fahámmi hngr. of fammi
fáhha'ko, (CC) fanko to be a long bare
obj. with something coming out of
the top (of a tree with no lower
limbs, like a palm tree, an
unfeathered arrow, or a tufted tail,
for example—or, by extension (or as
a joke?), a person with a naked body
and hair at the top) (3) {fabassa}
fahli to shake (with wrist action),
shake down (a thermometer, for
instance), to shake (one's head),
wave (one's hand), wag (one's tail)
(I;3) {hngr. faháli}
fakit turkey (taboo word, not used
any more) (Ct)
fákko'pa ggr. of fakopa
fakobli to have buds come out (for
instance, of trees) (3); to open (sg.
obj.—for instance, a peach or pecan)

(I;3) {v1. fakopa; pl. obj. fakohchi}
fakohchi to take off the green hulls
from (pecans — pl. obj.) (I;3) [-SC]
[fakohli+chi] {sg. obj. fakobli}
fakohli to open (of pecans, peaches,
or cotton pods, for example—pl.
subj.) (3) {hngr. fakohóli; sg. fakopa}
fakohóli hngr. of fakohli
fakopa to open (of a pecan or peach,
for example—sg. subj.) (3) {v2.
fakobli; ggr. fákko'pa; pl. fakohli}
fala crow
fala imilhlhali' scarecrow
[imilhlhali+']
fala ishto' type of big crow; raven
[ishto+']
falakna' yellow squirrel (AB) [fani'
lakna+']
falaha see falaa
falaháa hngr. of falaa
falaháma hngr. of falama
falakto to be forked, branched (of a
tree), to be cloven, split (of hooves);
to have a fork or crotch (insulting if
applied to people) (II) {ggr. fállakto}
falama to return, come back, be back;
to turn around, not to go the whole
way (I) {v2. falammichi; ggr.
fálla'ma; hngr. faláma;
fashkálla'ma; ootfalama} § Falamat
shoppalatok. The lights came back
on.
falama' see anompa' falama'
falammi north
Falammi, Falammi Hattak
Republicans, the Republican party;
the North, Northern soldiers (in
the Civil War)
Falammi Fochik the North Star
Falammi Hattak see Falammi
falammi nita' polar bear
falammi pila, falammi pílla north

falammi pílla

(direction) § Falammi pilla ayatok.
He went north. I Falammi pila-at
kapassa, Falammi pillaat kapassa.
It's cold in the north.
falammi pílla see falammi pila
Falammi Pílla the North Pole
falammichi to put back, return, take
back (an erring spouse, for instance,
or a defective product—sg. obj.) (I;II)
{v1. falama; part.: falammisht; pl.
obj. falamo'chi}
falammisht prt. of falammichi
falammisht isso to hit back (I;II) §
Falammisht sassotok. She hit me
back.
falammisht ittibi to fight back, fight
back at (I;II / IR;3) § Falammisht
pottibitok. They fought back at us.
falammishtithana' compass
[falammi isht ithana+']
falamo'chi to return, take (pl. obj.)
back (I;3) [+SC] {sg. obj. falammichi}
falamo'sht acho'li to sew a zigzag
stitch on a sewing machine, to sew
back and forth in one place (I)
[falamo'chi+t]
Falanchi' French person [from the
English]
Falanchi' Chahta' Louisiana
Choctaw
falappo to be untrue, be gossip (WB)
{fatpoli}
faláyya'a, faláyya'ha ygr. of falaa
falaa, falaha to be long (sg. or hum.
subj.) (II) [+PR] [+CPR] {v2. falili;
ggr. fálla'a, fálla'ha; hngr. faláha;
ngr. faláa; ygr. faláyya'a, faláyya'ha;
pl. faloha}
falaachi to make long, lengthen (I;II);
(LF, ER) to grow (a beard) [-SC]
[falaa+chi] {ngr. falaahánchi: to
make longer}
falaahánchi to make longer—ngr. of
falaachi

falaanosi' type of plant; (WB)
mayapple [fala aa+nosi+']
faláa ngr. of falaa
Falisko' Frisco, San Francisco [from
the English]
faliili to make long, lengthen (I;II);
(AB, ER) to grow (a beard) {v1. falaa;
ngr. falíli}
falíli ngr. of falili
fálla'a, fálla'ha ggr. of falaa
fálla'ma in aafálla'ma, ootfálla'ma—
ggr. of falama
fállakto ggr. of falakto
fállo'ha ggr. of falowa
faloha, falowa to be long (pl. subj.) (3)
{ggr. fállo'ha; ngr. falóha; ygr.
falóyyo'ha; sg. falaa}
falohachi, falowachi to make long,
lengthen (pl. obj.) (I;3) [faloha+chi]
{ngr. falowánchi}
fal-oshi' baby crow [fala oshi']
falowa see faloha
falowachi see falohachi
falowánchi ngr. of falohachi
falóyyo'ha ygr. of faloha
falóha ngr. of faloha
fama to be whipped (II) [+CPR] [+PR]
{v2. fammi; hngr. faháma}
fammi to whip (I;II) {v1. fama; ggr.
fá'mmi; hngr. fahámmi}
fammichi to make ° whip ° (I;II;3)
[fammi+chi]
fanalhchi' wing (IIp)
fani' squirrel
fani' hasimbish type of plant
(probably medicinal)
fani' lakna' fox squirrel (ER)
[lakna+']
fani' losa' black squirrel [losa+']
fani' shobboko'li' grey squirrel
fani' wakaa', (WB) fani-wakaa' flying
squirrel (CC) [wakaa+']
fanishapha' mistletoe [fani'
im+shapha']

86

fanní'chi ggr. of fannichi
fannichi to sting or burn (something) (of a plant like a nettle, or of certain types of insects) (3;II); to sting with a stinging plant (I;II) {ggr. fanní'chi; fannik}
fannik type of stinging plant; (MJ) bull nettle {fannichi}
fannik ishto' type of nettle (bull nettle?) [ishto+']
fannik sawa' type of small plant with burning leaves
fanokchama'li', (AB) fani' okchamali' grey squirrel [fani' okchamali+']
fan-oshi' baby squirrel [fani' oshi']
fashkalammi, (MJ) foshkalammi to turn inside out, turn over (sg. obj.) (for example, to flip a pancake) (I;3) {v1. fashkálla'ma; ggr. fashkállammi; pl. obj. fashkalamo'li}
fashkalamo'li to turn over, turn inside out (pl. obj.) (I;3) {v1. fashkalamo'wa; sg. obj. fashkalammi}
fashkalamo'wa to turn around in different directions (I); to be turned over, be turned inside out (pl. subj.) (3) {v2. fashkalamo'li; hngr. fashkalamohówa; sg. fashkálla'ma} § Amaanokfila-at fashkalamo'wa. My mind keeps turning around, I can't make up my mind.
fashkalamohówa hngr. of fashkalamo'wa
fashkálla'ma to be inside out (of clothes, for instance), be turned over (sg. subj.) (3); to look around in all directions (I) {v2. fashkalammi; pl. fashkalamo'wa; falama}
fashkállammi ggr. of fashkalammi
fata'chi to jerk, shake (something) around (I;II) [-SC] {v1. fata'kalhchi;

hngr. fata'lihínchi; klgr. <fáttakli'chi>; rcgr. fatatá'chi; ilifata'chi: to shake oneself}
fata'kahálhchi hngr. of fata'kalhchi
fata'kalhchi to swing, wave (of a flag, for instance) (3) {v2. fata'chi; hngr. fata'kahálhchi}
fata'lihínchi hngr. of fata'chi
fatabli to have dandruff (of the head, or of hair), to be dandruffy, flaky all over (of a person); (MJ) to have dirt rolling off one's body, even after washing (II) {ggr. fáttabli; hngr. fatahámbli; ngr. fatámbli; ygr. fatáyyabli}
fatahámbli hngr. of fatabli
fatámbli ngr. of fatabli
fatatá'chi to shake oneself (noisily, like a dog) (3)—rcgr. of fata'chi {ittifatatá'chi}
fatáyyabli ygr. of fatabli
fatpo magic; magical power
fatpo ishchokoshkomo to do magic tricks (I) [isht *chokoshkomo] § Fatpo ishtishchokoshkomota? Do you do magic?
fatpo í'shi to have magical powers (I) § Alikchi'at fatpo i'shi. An Indian doctor has magical powers.
fatpo takaali' charm worn on a string around the neck (AB) [takaali+']
fatpo shaali' magician [shaali+']
fatpoli to talk (possibly, to talk seriously—about business, for example, or to get news after a long absence) (I) {ifatpoli; fatpo}
fáttabli ggr. of fatabli
fattahála hngr. of fattaala
<fáttakli'chi> in ittifáttakli'chi—klgr. of fata'chi
fattalfáa to walk with the hips and shoulders swinging; to walk like a penguin, with the arms out stiff (I)—rigr. of fattaala

fattaala to scramble up (a steep surface) (I) {hngr. fattaha̱la; rigr. fattalfa̱a}

faya'chi to shake, push (for instance, so as to make a noise, or so that something will fall) (I;II) [-SC] {i̱faya'chi: to rock in a cradle; faya'kachi}

faya'kachi to go back and forth—wave in the wind, shake in an earthquake, rock (in a chair or cradle), sway while standing (I) {hngr. faya'kahánchi; faya'chi, faya'kalhchi} § Faya'kachili. I'm rocking (myself in a chair). | aaombiniili' faya'kachi': rocking chair

faya'kahánchi hngr. of faya'kachi

faya'kalhchi to rock back and forth, sway (because of illness, for example) (II) {ngr. faya'ka̱lhchi; faya'kachi}

faya'ka̱lhchi ngr. of faya'kalhchi

fayyí'chi ggr. of fayyichi

fayyichi to flick, drip (water, for example, off the fingers) (I;3) {ggr. fayyí'chi}

<faali> see ilbak i̱faali

faapa to swing (in a swing); to swing, wave (of a flag, for instance); (WB) to strike, hit a foul ball (in baseball) (sg. subj.) (I) {v2. faapichi ?; hngr. fahámpa; pl. faapo'wa} § Faapa chaffa, faapa toklo, faapa tochchi'na, ishkochcha! One, two, three strikes, you're out!

faapichi to throw, throw around; to swing (something); to push in a swing (sg. obj., once) (I;II), to strike, hit a foul ball (in baseball) (I) {v1. faapa ?; pl. obj. faapo'chi}

faapo'chi to throw; to jerk, swing around; to push in a swing (pl. obj., or more than once) (I;II) [±SC]

[<faapo'li>+chi] {hngr. faapo'lihínchi; i̱faapo'chi; oshti̱faapo'chi: to throw to; sg. obj. faapichi}

<faapo'li> in faapo'chi {v1. faapo'wa}

faapo'lihínchi hngr. of faapo'chi

faapo'wa to flap in the breeze; to wave (of flags); to swing, hang (on monkey bars, for instance) (sg.-dl.-tpl. subj.) (I / II) {v2. <faapo'li>; hngr. faapoho̱wa; rmgr. faapopo̱wa; sg. faapa}

faapoho̱wa hngr. of faapo'wa

faapopo̱wa to wave, swing in the breeze (3)—rmgr. of faapo'wa

fí'mmi ggr. of fimmi

fihi̱mmi hngr. of fimmi

fikfihíya hngr. of fikfiya

fikfiya to chatter, make a noise like a squirrel (I) {hngr. fikfihíya}

<filammi> in i̱filammi, filammi', itti̱filammi

filammi' branch—used in a complex cln., such as abookoshi' filammi', naksish filammi' [<filammi>+'] {filamo'li'}

<filamo'li> in filamo'li', itti̱filamo'li, i̱filamo'li

filamo'li' branches—used in a complex cln., such as abookoshi' filamo'li', nakshish filamo'li' {filammi'}

fili'chi to turn (something) (I;3) [+SC] (if turning is part of an attempt to open something), [-SC] (if just fiddling around)

fili'ta to be on wrong, be inside out (of a shirt, for example) (3) [+CPR] [-PR] {ggr. fílli'ta; filita, itti̱fili'ta}

filíhhi'ta hgr. of filita

filihínta hngr. of filita

filíhta to turn around quickly—var. hgr. of filita

filihtikahchi, filittikahchi to turn

around quickly (I) {filíhta}
filillí'chi ggr. of filillichi
filillichi to turn (something):
especially, to turn (a switch or knob)
on or off, to turn (something) over
(I;II) {v1. filita; ggr. filillí'chi}
filita to turn, to turn around, turn
over (once); to turn one's head
(once); to be turned around, turned
over, twisted (I) {v2. filillichi; ggr.
fílli'ta: to have one's head turned
all around, to be inside out, to be
turned on (of a light or switch); hgr.
filíhhi'ta, (var) filíhta: to turn
quickly; hngr. filihínta; filito'wa: to
turn more than once; fili'ta}
filito'chi to turn (pages, food in the
microwave) (I;3) [±SC]
[<filito'li>+chi] {hngr.
filito'lihínchi; rcgr. filitoto'chi}
<**filito'li**> in filito'chi {v1. filito'wa}
filito'lihínchi hngr. of filito'chi
filito'wa to turn one's head or body
(more than once) (I) {v2. <filito'li>;
rmgr. filitotówa; filita: to turn once}
filitotó'chi to keep turning (a drying
sweater, for instance) around or
over (I;3)—rcgr. of filito'chi
filitotówa to turn completely around
more than once, turn over and
over, keep turning (I)—rmgr. of
filito'wa
filittikahchi see filihtikahchi
fílli'ta to be inside out, turned on,
turned around—ggr. of filita, fili'ta
Filli'ta' Chickasaw family name
fimmi to get rid of, throw out, let out
(dl. obj.) (I;II) {ggr. fí'mmi; hngr.
fihímmi; sg. obj. kanchi; pl. obj.
lha̱'li, lhatabli; fímmo'pa,
<fímmobli>}
fímmo'pa to be scattered all over
(nonhum. subj.) (3) {v2.
<fímmobli>; ittafímmo'pa}

<**fímmobli**> in ittafímmobli {v1.
fímmo'pa}
fincha eel (TU) {okfincha}
finha too (aux.) (used in the
negative) {ngr. fínha: to show off (I);
aafinha} § Sachaaha finha ki'yo,
Sachaaha ikfinho. I'm not too tall.
<**finhachi**> in ilifinhachi
fi'chi, (AB) ishtafi̱'chi to pick (one's
teeth) (I;3) [-SC]
fínha to put on airs, show off, be a
daredevil; to bluff(I)—ngr. of finha
§ Fínhali. I'm a daredevil, I'm
showing off, I'm bluffing.
fochchanashik, fohchanashik, (HS)
fo'chanashi', (MS) **foschanashik**
wasp {fohi'}
fochchanashik ilhpichik wasp nest
fochik star
fochik holba' star shape
fochik ilontalaali' sheriff's badge
shaped like a star [ilontalaali+']
fochik ishto' evening star, morning
star [ishto+'] § Fochik ishtat fochik
ishto'. The morning star is the
evening star.
fochik malili' comet, shooting star,
meteor [malili+']
Fochik Ontoklo' the Seven Stars,
Pleiades [ontoklo+']
fochik shobohli' smoking star—an
omen of war to come [shobohli+']
fochosh duck
Fochosh Hilha' Duck Dance, a
Choctaw dance also danced by
Chickasaws
fochosh hishi' woksho' duck down
[woksho+']
fochosh ishki' mother duck
fochosh-oshi' duckling; duck egg
[fochosh oshi']
foha to rest; to retire (I) [-PR] [-CPR]
fohachi to make rest, retire, let rest
(I;II) [foha+chi] § Safohachitok. They

retired me, I retired.
fohchanashik see fochchanashik
fohi', (LF) fowi' bee; honey
fohi' bila' beeswax; (AB, ER) honey;
(CM) syrup [bila+']
fohi' ilhpichik, fohilhpichik bees'
nest, beehive (in nature);
honeycomb; wasp nest
fohi' inkapittani' queen bee
fohi' ishki' queen bee
fohi' ihashintak honeycomb (ER)
fohi' iminko' queen bee
fohi' lakna' yellowjacket, (CP)
bumblebee [lakna+']
fohi' oshi' baby bee
fohi' wiha' swarm of bees [wiha+']
fohilhpichik see fohi' ilhpichik
fohinchampoli', (VB) fohi'
inchampoli' honey [fohi'
im+champoli+']
fohinchokka' manmade beehive
[fohi' im+chokka']
fohkol type of bumble bee; (TJ)
hornet
fohli, (AB, ER) fooli to lick (I;II)
{hngr. fohóli; ngr. fóhli}
fohóli hngr. of fohli
fohómmi to howl (of the wind) (AB)
fokha to be in (sg. subj.), to put on
(clothes) (I;3); to get dressed (I); to be
about (a certain time or extent) (I;3);
to be about like (with reference to a
certain quality) (I;3); about (aux.)
{v2. fokhi; ngr. fónkha; ygr.
fóyyokha: to wear (sg.-dl.-tpl. subj.),
be in (sg. subj.); dl. albí'ha; tpl.
albihat máa} § Alalitokma nittak
toklo fokha. I've been here about
two days. | Affammi' pokko'li
ishfokha'si. You're only about ten. |
Sachaahakat yappa fokha'chi. I'm
going to be about this tall. |
(Ishtokat) ishno' fokhali. (With
regard to size) I'm about like you. |

Nannahmat sashkin foyyokha.
There's something in my eye. |
Shokchaako foyyokhali. I'm in the
sack. | Naafokha hoofokhatok.
They put on their dresses.
fokhá'chi ggr. of fokhachichi
fokhachichi, (AB, MJ, ER, LR)
fokhichichi to dress (someone) (I;II)
[fokha+chichi] {ggr. fokhá'chi}
fokhachisht pisa, fokhachishpisa to
try (something) on (someone') (II =
obj. , I;3) [fokhachichi+t pisa] §
Naafka safokhachishpisatok. She
tried the dress on me.
fokhakaash about (referring to time
that has passed) [fokha+kaash] §
Nittak toklo fokhakaash pislitok. I
saw him about two days ago.
fokhakma about (referring to time in
the future) [fokha+kma] § Nittak
toklo fokhakma pisala'chi. I'll see
him in about two days.
fokhat pisa to try on (clothing) (I;3)
[fokha+t]
fokhi to put (sg. obj.') into (a
container) (I;II;3); to put on (gloves)
(I;3) {v1. fokha; ygr. fóyyokhi: to
keep in, have hidden in (I;3;3); to
wear gloves (I); dl. obj. abihli; tpl.
obj. ani}
fokkol type of snail (CP); leech (CP)
{okfokkol}
folfo' in ishkobo' folfo'
fóllo'ka'chi ggr. of folo'kachi
fóllo'ta ggr. of folota
folo'kachi to get around fast (I) {ggr.
fóllo'ka'chi; hngr. folo'kahánchi;
folo'kalhchi}
folo'kahánchi hngr. of folo'kachi
folo'kalhchi to go around, wind (of a
mountain road, for example) (3)
{folo'kachi}
foloha to be drilled, ground up (3)
{v2. folohli}

folohli to drill, to grind (corn, for instance) (I;II) {v1. foloha; hngr. foloh**ó**li; ngr. fol**ó**hli}
folohónta to be wound up, to go around—hngr. of folota
folohó**li** hngr. of folohli
folohtokahchi, folottokahchi to turn around quickly (especially of a wheeled vehicle) (3)
folollí'chi ggr. of folollichi
folollichi to turn (something), pull around (I;II) {v1. folota; ggr. folollí'chi}
folónta ngr. of folota
folop shoulder, area below the shoulder blade; forequarter (IIp)
folosh spoon
folosh chinto' soup spoon, tablespoon [chinto+']
folosh falaa' kitchen spoon [falaa+']
folosh ishtimpa' teaspoon [isht impa+']
folosh naaishtapiisa' measuring spoon [nanna isht apiisa+']
folosh-ata' clam [folosh <hata>+']
folosh-ata' aatoba' pearl [aa+toba+']
folosh-oshi' teaspoon [folosh oshi']
folota to turn around, to turn, to curve (I); to turn in at, stop by (a place) (I;3) {v2. folollichi; ggr. f**ó**llo'ta; hngr. folohónta: to be wound up, to go around; ngr. folónta}
foloto'chi to steer (a vehicle) (I;3) [+SC] {hngr. foloto'lihínchi; rcgr. folototó'chi}
foloto'lihínchi hngr. of foloto'chi
foloto'wa to follow a squiggly course, to zigzag (I) {rmgr. folototówa}
folototó'chi to turn all the time, keep turning (I;3)—rcgr. of foloto'chi
folototówa to turn, weave (3)—rmgr. of foloto'wa
folottokahchi see folohtokahchi

foloochi to grind (WB) [folohli+chi]
foló**hli** ngr. of folohli
fomoowachi to make a noise like the noise of a tornado (I) {hngr. fomoowahánchi}
fomoowahánchi hngr. of fomoowachi
foni' bone (IIp)
foni' bíyyi'ka, foni' biika skeleton
foni' biika see foni' bíyyi'ka
foni' hottopa arthritis
foni' hottopa i'shi to have arthritis
foni' hottopa' tish rubbing alcohol (ER) [(foni' hottopa)+']
foni' illa skeleton; skin and bones § Benjieat chonnahma polla, foni' illa. Benjie is very skinny, he's just skin and bones.
foni' kooli to crack one's knuckles (IIp, I) § Safoni' koolili. I cracked my knuckles.
foni' lha'li' dice (WB) [lha'li+']
fonka in misha' fonka, ola' fonka [fonkha ?]
fónkha ngr. of fokha
fosh-ato'chi', (MJ) foshi' ato'chi', (HS) fashshato'chi', (LF) fosh-ato'chi', (WB) foshto'chi' mockingbird [foshi' ato'chi+' ?]
foshhommak, (AB, CC, WB) foshkommak, (JC) foshkomok, (WB) foshkomma', (LF) foshi' homma' redbird, cardinal [foshi' homma+k]
foshi' bird
foshi' anompoli' parrot; (ER) mockingbird [anompoli+']
foshi' aalhto' birdcage
foshi' chaaha', (JJ) foshchaaha' crane [foshi' chaaha+']
foshi' hina' type of bird that walks around on the ground after dark
foshi' hishi' feather
foshi' hishi' ishholissochi' quill pen

foshi' hishi' nannishwilooli'

[isht holissochi+']
foshi' hishi' nannishwilooli' feather
duster [nanna isht wilooli+']
foshi' hishi' woksho' down, soft
feathers [woksho+']
foshi' homma' redbird, cardinal (CC)
[homma+'] {foshhommak}
foshi' ishkalasha' hasimbish
scissortail (ER) [translation from
English]
foshi' palhki' roadrunner [palhki+']
foshi' taloowa' mockingbird (RJ)
[taloowa+']
foshi' tolhposhi' snowbird (LF)
foshi' yaaya' type of crying bird (CC)
[yaa+']
fosh-ibichchala' beak, bill [foshi'
ibichchala']
foshi-hoyo' bird dog, retriever (WB)
[foshi' hoyo+']
foshilhpichik, (ER, CC) foshi'
impichik bird's nest [foshi'
(im+)ilhpichik]
foshinchokka' birdhouse, birdcage
[foshi' im+chokka']
foshiyyi' type of holly (winterberry?
yaupon?) [foshi' iyyi']
fosh-oshi' baby bird; (CC)
hummingbird [foshi' oshi']
fottatak yellowhammer
fowabbi, foyabbi, (MJ) fohaabi to have
an allergic reaction (a rash or

swelling) (II) [fohi' abi]
fowabbichi, foyabbichi to cause an
allergic reaction (I;II) [fowabbi+chi]
foyabbi see fowabbi
foyabbichi see fowabbichi
<foyo'chi> in ilifoyo'chi
foyohómpa to be breathing, be
alive—hngr. of foyopa
foyómpa ngr. of foyopa
foyopa to breathe (I) {ggr. fóyyo'pa: to
give a sigh of relief; hngr.
foyohómpa: to be breathing, be
alive; ngr. foyómpa; ilafoyopa}
foyopachi to make breathe, to give
artificial respiration to (I;II)
[foyopa+chi]
foyopat intaha to be out of breath (III)
[foyopa+t im+taha] § Foyopat
antaha. I'm out of breath.
foyopishtithana' stethoscope [foyopa
isht ithana+']
fóyyo'pa to give a sigh of relief—ggr.
of foyopa
fóyyokha to wear, be in—ygr. of
fokha [-OPR]
fóyyokhi to hide, have hidden (sg.
obj.) (I;3); to wear gloves (I)—ygr. of
fokhi § abooha foyyokhi: to confine
in the house
footi see vooti
fóhli ngr. of fohli

g

gidap, gitap get up, giddiyup (said to a
horse) [from the English]

h

ha'aa no
há'lhlhi ggr. of halhlhi
há'mmi ggr. of hammi
hábbi'na to apologize—ggr. of habina
{ihábbi'na}
habihína hngr. of habina
habihíshko hngr. of habishko
habina, habiina to receive as a
present (I;II) {v1. halbina; ggr.
hábbi'na: to apologize; hngr.
habihína; ihabiina: to receive for,
beg for; imaahabina: to get as a
present from}
habinachi to give to ° as a present; to
adopt out (a child) to °, give up to °
for adoption (I;II;3) [habina+chi]
{hngr. habinahánchi}
habinahánchi hngr. of habinachi
habishko to sneeze (II / I) [-PR] {hngr.
habihíshko; ohabishko: to sneeze at}
habishkochi to make sneeze (I;II)
[habishko+chi]
habiina see habina
hachik suitcase
hachishnaakaynihaat you yourselves
(int. subj.)
[hachishno'+aakayni+haat] §
Hachishnaakaynihaat hashpisam?
Did you see him yourselves?
hachishnaakaynihoot you
yourselves (focus subj.)
[hachishno'+aakayni+hoot] §
Hachishnaakaynihoot
hashyamihshtok. You did it
yourselves.
hachishnaakayniho you yourselves
(focus nonsubj.)
[hachishno'+aakayni+ho]
hachishnaakaynihta you yourselves
(int. nonsubj.)
[hachishno'+aakayni+hta] §
Hachishnaakaynihta hachipisam?

Did she see you yourselves?
hachishnaak you (pl.), you all
(nonsubj.; rare) [hachishno'+ak]
hachishnaakot you (pl.), you guys,
you all (contrastive subj.)
[hachishno'+akot]
hachishnaako you (pl.), you guys,
you all (contrastive nonsubj.)
[hachishno'+ako]
hachishnaat you (pl.), you all (subj.;
rare) [hachishno'+at]
hachishna you (pl.), you all
(nonsubj.; rare) [hachishno'+a]
hachishno' you (pl.), you guys, you
all (nonsubj.)
hahálhlhi hngr. of halhlhi
hahámmi hngr. of hammi
hahánka hngr. of hahka
hahánksi hngr. of haksi
hahánglo hngr. of haklo
háhhaksi hgr. of haksi
hahka, (FA, AB, TJ) hakha, (MJ, MS)
hakka to pant (I) [+CPR] [-PR] {hngr.
hahánka}
hahtaayi' (TJ), (CM) haatayyi'
buckeye
hahtok, (LF) hattok, (WB) halhtok
red root (type of medicinal plant)
hakashtap, (TJ) akashtap trash; wood
chips (old word) {hashtap}
hakbó'li ggr. of hakboli
hakboli to be green mold, to have
green mold; to stay in one place so
long as to be moldy (II) {ggr.
hakbó'li; hgr. hakbóhho'li; hngr.
hakbohóli; ngr. hakbóli; ygr.
hakbóyyo'li}
hakbóyyo'li ygr. of hakboli
hakbóli ngr. of hakboli
hakchin penis (IIp) (Ct)
hakchintalop male genitals (IIp)
[hakchin (in)talop]

hakchish pubic hair (IIp)
hakchomakpí'la see akchomakpí'la
hakchomakpila see akchomakpila
hakchomakpilachi see
 akchomakpilachi
haklo to listen to, to hear (I;II) {ggr.
 hâklo; hngr. hahánglo; ngr. hánglo:
 to hear, to listen to; ygr. háyyaklo;
 hapowánglo, hapowaklo}
hâklo ggr. of haklo
hakló'chi ggr. of haklochi
haklochi to get (someone) to listen,
 mind; to give (someone) the news
 (in person) (I;II) [haklo+chi] {ggr.
 hakló'chi; haklochichi}
haklochichi to make ° hear, let °
 hear (I;II;3) [haklo+chichi]
 {haklochi}
haknip, (AW) aknip body (IIp)
haknip bíyyi'ka to be naked (3)
haknip illi' see hattak haknip illi'
haknip illi' hayoochi to be
 (completely) paralyzed (I) § Haknip
 illi' hayooshlitok. I am paralyzed.
haknip tannapat illi for half one's
 body to be paralyzed (IIp = possr. ,
 — , —); to be paralyzed on half of
 one's body (IIp = subj. , — , —)
 [tannap+at] § Sahaknip tannapat
 illikat, illika ithanali. I know that I
 am paralyzed on half of my body,
 half of my body is paralyzed. |
 Lynnat haknip tannapat illi. Lynn is
 paralyzed on half of her body.
haksaa-asha' insane asylum [haksi+'
 aa-asha']
haksi to be drunk; to be crazy, insane
 (II) [+PR] [+CPR] {ggr. hâksi; hgr.
 háhhaksi; hngr. hahánksi; ngr.
 hánksi; ygr. háyyaksi}
hâksi ggr. of haksi
haksi'shcha ayowat intahli to
 completely cheat ° out of (II = obj. ,
 — , I;III;3) (cha expression; includes

haksichi and [ayowa+t im+tahli]) §
 Naahollaat hattak api' homma'
 haksi'shcha nanna moma ayowat
 intahtok. The white man cheated
 the Indian out of everything. |
 Pohaksi'shcha ayowat pontahtok.
 He completely cheated us out of it.
haksibish, (AW) aksibish ear (IIp)
haksibish cholok opening in the
 external ear
haksibish falaha' type of medicinal
 plant (CC) [falaa+']
haksibish falaa' donkey [falaa+']
**haksibish falaa' iskanno', haksibish
 falaaskanno'** little donkey, burro
 [iskanno+']
haksibish ishto' elephant (CC)
 [ishto+']
haksibish lhitihli' ear wax (IIp)
 [lhitihli+'] § sahaksibish lhitihli':
 my ear wax
haksibish patha' elephant [patha+']
Haksibish Patha' (pet name, possibly
 mildly insulting)
haksibish takaali' earring (IIIp)
 [takaali+'] § ahaksibish takaali': my
 earring
haksichi to get (someone) drunk; to
 cheat, trick, deceive (I;II) [haksi+chi]
 {ngr. <haksínchi>}
<haksínchi> ngr. of haksichi {prt.
 haksisht}
haksit kánni'ya to be crazy, forgetful;
 to be sex-crazed (3)
haksisht unexpectedly; to the
 surprise of (II = obj.)—prt. of
 <haksínchi> § Sahaksisht
 kaniyatok. He went away (and I
 didn't expect it), He went away, to
 my surprise. | Haksisht onalitok. I
 arrived unexpectedly.
haksobachi to make too much noise
 for (I;II) [+SC]
hakson area slightly above and in

front of the ear (IIp)

hakson wakla' type of large mole; (WB) gopher

hakshish root; tendon (IIp)

hakshish apissa'li' type of plant with a root that is chewed to settle an upset stomach (MJ) [apissali+']

hakshish falakto' type of root that smells like licorice and is boiled and used for medicine (sweet anise? sweet fennel?) [falakto+']

hakshop close-fitting outer covering: skin, shell, bark, rind (IIp) § holisso hakshop: the cover of the book

hakshop okchanki' rawhide, untanned skin [okchanki+']

hakshop shila' scab [shila+']

hakshop tabli to circumcise (IIp = obj. , I = subj.)

hakshop tapa' circumcised male [tapa+']

haktampi' see aktampi'

hala'li to take by the handle, to take by the hand (I;II); to take (the hand) of ˙ (I;II;3) {ggr. hállalli: to hold hands with; halahli, halalli} § Sahal'tok, Salbak sahala'tok. He took me by the hand, He took my hand.

halaháli hngr. of halahli

halahálli hngr. of halalli

halahli to tug, pull (I;II) {hngr. halaháli; halalli}

halaht abaawiili to pull up (a quilt, for example) (I;3) [halahli+t]

halaht ishkochchi to pull out (I;II) [halahli+t] § Halaht issakochchatok. He pulled me out.

halaht ishtona to lead (I;II) [halahli+t] § Issoba-a halaht oka' aa-ashaka ishtishonokya oka' ishishkochicha' ki'yo. You can lead a horse to water but you cannot make him drink. | Halaht

ishtasonatok. He led me.

halaht lhifi to pull down on (a vine or branch), stripping off the leaves and fruit (I;3) [halahli+t]

halaht oshwayaachi to grab (especially, by the hair) and pull down (of women fighting, for instance) (I;II) [halahli+t osht wayaachi] § Halaht ossawayaachitok. She grabbed me and pulled me down.

halalli, halatli to pull (I;II); to have a charley horse or cramp (II); (MS) to have a seizure {ggr. hállalli; hngr. halahálli; ngr. halálli; ittihaalalli: to get married; hala'li; halahli}

halalli' charley horse, cramp (IIp) [halalli+']

halallichi to hitch (a horse or dog) to (a wagon) (I;3;3) [halalli+chi]

halambabi to have ringworm (II) [halambo' abi] § Sahalambabi. I have ringworm.

halambo red, scaly, venomous lizard

halambo tish type of medicinal plant (CP)

halasbi (CC, MJ, AB, ER, TP, TJ), (VB) halosbi, (WB) halasmi to be slippery (Ct?) {talasbi}

halatli see halalli

hala'bosha', (MJ) hala'bosha' bat (animal)

halbabi' cataracts (MC)

<halbi'> in ittihalbi'

halbina to be given away, given up (3) {v2. habina, habiina}

halbina' present, gift [halbina+']

halichi to make ˙ touch ˙, to touch ˙ with ˙ (I;II;3) [+SC] [halili+chi] {haliichi} § Sahalilishtok. He made me touch it, He made it touch me.

halihíli hngr. of halili

halili, haliili to touch, feel; to reach out to touch (I;II) [+OPR] {ggr.

hálli'li; hngr. halih_íli; ngr. hal_íli: to brush, touch (briefly, or by accident); imaahalili, _ihalili}

halit pisa to feel (something to test it) (II = obj. , I = subj.) [halili+t] § Chihalit pisalitok. I felt you (to see how you would feel).

haliichi to make ° touch °, to touch ° with ° (I;II;3) [-SC] [halili+chi] {halichi} § Sahaliichitok. He made me touch it, He made it touch me.

haliilawi', (HS, ER) hal_ilawi' type of big bullfrog, (ER) snapping turtle

haliili see halili

hal_íli to brush, touch (briefly, or by accident)—ngr. of halili

hállakli'chi to pull, jerk (something) (I;II); to jump, jerk, startle (II) [+SC] {halalli} § Sahallakli'chikat ith_anali. I know I jerked, startled. I Lynnat sahallakli'chik_a ith_anali. I know Lynn jerked me.

hállalli to hold hands with (I;II); to hold (someone's hand), to hold (something) by the handle (I;3)— ggr. of hala'li, halalli § Sahallallitok. He held hands with me. I Salbak hallallitok. He held my hand.

hálli'li ggr. of halili

hallito hello (Ct)

hálloppa ggr. of haloppa

halma to be ironed (3) {v2. hammi}

halohómpa hngr. of haloppa

halómpa ngr. of haloppa

haloppa, (WB) halappa to be sharp (II), to be scratchy (of wool material, for instance) (3); (LR, LF, AB, ER, CC, MJ) to be pointed [+PR] [+CPR] {ggr. hálloppa; hngr. halohómpa; ngr. halómpa; ygr. halóyyoppa}

haloppachi to sharpen (I;II) [haloppa+chi]

halowa (AB, MJ), (CC) haliwa', (JC) halowi', (JC) holowi' soft-shelled

turtle (AB, MJ), snapping turtle (CC, JC)

halóyyoppa ygr. of haloppa

halha to be kicked (II) [+T] {v2. halhlhi; halhapa}

halhabli to kick (sg. obj.), kick once (I;II) [+OPR] {v1. halhapa; pl. obj. halhlhi}

halhapa to be kicked (sg. subj.) (II) {v2. halhabli; halha}

halhlhi to kick (pl. obj.), to kick a lot (I;II); to pedal (I) {v1. halha; ggr. há'lhlhi; hngr. hah_álhlhi; sg. obj. halhabli; ahalhlhichi}

<hama> in naashhama' {v2. hammi}

hammi to press, iron (I;3) {v1. halma, <hama>; ggr. há'mmi; hngr. hah_ámmi}

<hammichi> in t_ish ishtilihammichi'

hanaawi'li to put on, wear (a scarf, bandolier, or beaded sash) over one shoulder and diagonally across the chest (I;3)

hanaawi'li' sash worn diagonally [hanaawi'li+']

hanaawiichi to put a (sash, etc.) diagonally on (someone°) (I;II;3) [hanaawi'li+chi]

hankha', (MJ) hanka' big, scary night bird (Ct?)

hánksi ngr. of haksi

hanná'li, hánna'li six; to be six in number (I) [+PR]

hánna'li see hanná'li

hanná'li áyyo'ka to be in groups of six (I)

hánglo to hear, listen to—ngr. of haklo

hapayyá'mmi ggr. of hapayyimmi

hapayyíhhi'ma hgr. of hapayyima

hapayyih_íma hngr. of hapayyima

hapayyih_ímmi hngr. of hapayyimmi

hapayyima, (CC, ER, TP) hapayoma,

(HS) hapayomi, (WB) hapoyama, (MJ) hapayomma to be salty (II) {v2. hapayyimmi; ggr. hapayyí'ma; hgr. hapayyíhhi'ma; ngr. hapayyihíma; hapi homi}
hapayyimmi to salt (something) (I;II) [hapi yammi ?] {v1. hapayyima; ggr. hapayyí'mmi, hapayyá'mmi; hngr. hapayyihímmi}
hapayyí'ma ggr. of hapayyima
hapayyí'mmi ggr. of hapayyimmi
hapaanokfila, hapaanokfila', (AW) apaanokfila type of bug that swarms in a cloud; small whirlwind, dust devil
hapaanokfila' see hapaanokfila
hapaanokfilishto' large hapaanokfila bug; large whirlwind [hapaanokfila ishto+']
<hapashi> see hapashshi
hapashshi to be tame (II) (<hapashi> in neg. and occasionally conj.) {ggr. háppa'shshi} § Ikhapa'shokisha. It's not tame yet.
hapashshi' tame one [hapashshi+']
hapashshichi to tame; to break (a horse); to pet, stroke, caress (I;II) [hapashshi+chi]
hapi salt
hapi aafohli' salt lick [aa+fohli+']
hapi aalhto' salt shaker
hapi chino'fa'si a pinch of salt [chinofa+a'si]
hapi homi to be salty (AB) {hapayyima}
hapi kallo' rock salt [kallo+']
hapi kapassa' epsom salts [kapassa+']
hapi poshi' salt
hapompohóyo hngr. of hapompoyo
hapompoyo to watch out, look behind one, look around (I) {hngr. hapompohóyo; ngr. hapompóyo; negs. ikhapompo'yo, ikhapompoyyo; ihapompoyo: to

watch out for, take care of; hopoo}
hapompoyo' spy [hapompoyo+']
hapompóyo ngr. of hapompoyo
haposhnaak us (many), us all (nonsubj.) [haposhno'+ak]
haposhnaakaynihaat we ourselves (many) (int. subj.) [haposhno'+aakayni+haat]
haposhnaakaynihoot we ourselves (many) (foc. subj.) [haposhno'+aakayni+hoot]
haposhnaakayniho us ourselves (many) (foc. subj.) [haposhno'+aakayni+ho]
haposhnaakaynihta us ourselves (many) (int. nonsubj.) [haposhno'+aakayni+hta]
haposhnaakot we (many), we all (contrastive subj.) [haposhno'+akot]
haposhnaako us (many), us all (contrastive nonsubj.) [haposhno'+ako]
haposhnaat we (many), we all (subj.; rare) [haposhno'+at]
haposhno' us (many), us all (nonsubj.) [ha+poshno']
hapoyoksa to be clever, wise (II) {ihapoyoksa}
hapo'lo' type of weed boiled for tea (several varieties—including mint?)
hapowaklo, (MJ) hapónklo to listen, hear, mind, obey (I) (usually used in imperative) {ngr. hapowánglo: to be able to hear just a little; neg. ikhapowaklo: to go deaf; ihapowánglo: to mind, obey (someone); haklo} § Hapowaklo! Listen!
hapowánglo to be able to hear just a little—ngr. of hapowaklo
háppa'shshi ggr. of hapashshi
hasi' vagina (IIp)
hasimbish, (OC) asimbish tail (IIp);

train (on a dress)

hasimbish chanaa', (MJ) hasimbish chanaha' scorpion [chanaa+']

hasimbish falaa see chihasimbish falaa

hasimbish foni' tailbone (IIp) § sahasimbish foni': my tailbone

hasimbish homma' see akankabi' hasimbish homma'

hasimbish iksho' bobtail (born that way) [iksho+']

hasimbish tapa' bobtail (with its tail cut) [tapa+']

hason (TJ, ER) hasolo' type of water creature; (TJ) leech; (ER) water bug

hashahᶐa hngr. of hashaa

hasháyya'a ygr. of hashaa

hashaa, (OC, CM) hashaaya to be angry (II) [+PR] [+CPR] {v2. hashiili; hngr. hashahᶐa; ngr. hashᶐa; ygr. hasháyya'a; ịhashaa: to be angry at}

hashaachaffa' spreading adder (CM) [chaffa+']

hashaachi to make angry (rare) (I;II) [-SC] [hashaa+chi]

hashaakonohli' see hashaakonoli'

hashaakonoli', hashaakonohli', (WB) hashaakanalli', (MJ) hashi' aakonoli', (ER) hashaakonolli' ring around the moon, (ER) rainbow

hashaakochcha', (TP) ashaakochcha', ashaakochchaka' (TP, CC) east [hashi' aa+kochcha+']

hashaakottola' west [hashi' aa+okattola+']

hashaanokpila' rainbow (WB)

hashaaobya, (CC) ashaaobya', hashi' aaobya (TP) west [hashi' aa+obya]

hashaapatha', (MJ) hashaapatta', (AW) ashaapatta' spreading adder [hashaa patha+']

hashaatabookoli' south [hashi' aa+tabookoli+']

Hashaatabookoli' Imma' the South,

the Southern side (in the Civil War) (WB)

hashᶐa ngr. of hashaa

hashi' sun; month; moon

hashi' abika (AB, WB), (VB, LF, CM) hashi' ishtabika, (MS) hashi' imambiika to menstruate, have a period

hashi' abika', (LP) hashi' imambiika' menstrual period [(hashi' abika)+']

hashi' alootiklanna half moon (LF) [aloota + iklanna]

hashi' awaata see hashi'at awaata

hashi' awaata' new moon [hashi' awaata+']

hashi' ayoppachi' sun worshiper [ayoppachi+']

hashi' himoona new moon (LF)

hashi' holhtina' calendar

hashi' illi' eclipse (of the sun or moon) (cln.) [illi+'] {hashi'at illi} § Hashi' illika pislitok. I saw the eclipse.

hashi' ittakashkowa' see hashittakashkowa'

hashi' kanallaat imambaanapa to have one's time be up, to go over one's time, to talk too long (III) [(hashi' kanalli)+at; im+abaanapa]

hashi' kanallaat intaha to have one's time be up (III) [im+(hashi' kanallaat taha)] § Hashi' kanallaat chintaha! Your time is up!

hashi' kanallaat taha for the time to be up [(hashi' kanalli)+at]

hashi' kanalli hour, time

hashi' kanalli to be (number) o'clock (with a following number verb) (—); to have it be (number) o'clock (of a place) (3) § Hashi' kanalli pokko'li. It's ten o'clock. | Hashi' kanalli pokko'chiklanna, pokko'cha iklanna. It's ten-thirty. | Oklahommaat hashi' kanalli toklo.

It's two o'clock in Oklahoma.
**hashi' kanalli ishtithana',
shikaishtithana'** clock, watch
[hashi' kanalli isht ithana+']
**hashi' kanalli ishtithana'
ishtalakchi', shikaishtithana'
ishtalakchi'** watchband [isht
talakchi+']
hashi' kanalli ishtithana' ola' alarm
clock [ola+']
hashi' kanalli kaniya fokha for it to
be what time (inf.) {int. hashi'
kanalli katiya fokha} § Hashi'
kanalli kaniya fokhaka amanootok.
He told me what time it was.
hashi' kanalli kánnohmi for it to be
what time (inf.) (becomes <hashi'
kanalli kannoh>) {int. hashi'
kanalli katohmi} § Hashi' kanalli
kannohka ithanali. I know what
time it is.
<hashi' kanalli kannoh> see hashi'
kanalli kánnohmi
hashi' kanalli katiya fokha for it to be
what time (int.) {inf. hashi' kanalli
kaniya fokha}
hashi' kanalli katohmi for it to be
what time (int.) (becomes <hashi'
kanalli katoh>) {inf. hashi' kanalli
kánnohmi} § Hashi' kanalli
katohta? What time is it?
<hashi' kanalli katoh> see hashi'
kanalli katohmi
**hashi' ninak aa', hashi' ninak, hashi'
nakaa'** moon [ninak aa+']
hashi' pakali' sunflower [pakali+']
hashi' tilikpi see hashi'at tilikpi
hashi' toomi see hashi'at toomi
hashi'at aloota for there to be a full
moon [hashi'+at]
hashi'at awaata, hashi' awaata for
there to be a new moon; (ER) for
there to be a half moon); (WB) for
there to be a full moon [hashi'+at]

{awátta'a}
hashi'at bolokta for there to be a full
moon (AB)
**hashi'at himona' awaata, hashi'at
himonawaata** for there to be a new
moon [hashi'+at]
hashi'at himonawaata see hashi'at
himona' awaata
hashi'at iklanna'si, (MJ) **hashi'at
iklanna** for there to be a half moon
[hashi'+at]
hashi'at illi for there to be an eclipse
(of the sun or moon) [hashi'+at]
{hashi' illi}
hashi'at ittalata for there to be an
eclipse (MJ)
**hashi'at ittayoppitammi,
hashittayoppitammi** for there to be
an eclipse (of the sun or moon)
[hashi'(+at) ittayoppitammi]
hashi'at kaniya for there to be no
moon [hashi'+at]
hashi'at kaniyat ishtaya for the
moon to be in its last quarter
[hashi'+at]
hashi'at kochcha for the sun to rise
[hashi'+at] § Hashi'at kochchakma
chipisla'chi. I'll see you at sunrise,
when the sun rises.
hashi'at lowachi for the sun to burn
(someone) (II = obj.) [hashi'+at] §
Ithanali hashi'at salowachitoka. I
know I got a sunburn.
hashi'at lhibokta for there to be a full
moon [hashi'+at]
hashi'at oka' oochi for there to be
bars of light and shadow stretching
between clouds and the earth
[hashi'+at]
hashi'at oklhili for there to be an
eclipse; (WB) for it to be the dark of
the moon [hashi'+at]
hashi'at tilikpi, hashi' tilikpi for
there to be a full moon; for there to

be an eclipse [hashi'+at]
hashi'at toomi, hashi' toomi to be
sunny, for the sun to shine
[hashi'+at] § Hashi' toomikat
chokma. It's pretty when the sun is
shining.
hashintak comb (for combing hair or
holding it in place); brush
haship area between the breasts (IIp)
haship foni' breastbone, (EP)
collarbone (IIp) § sahaship foni': my
breastbone
hashittakashkowa', hashi'
ittakashkowa' month
hashittayoppitammi see hashi'at
ittayoppitammi
hashiyaháma hngr. of hashiyama
hashiyama, (TJ) hashi'yama, (MJ)
hashaama to have a splinter (3)
{hngr. hashiyaháma; ashiyama}
hashiili to make angry (I;II) {v1.
hashaa}
hashonkani' fruit fly, (TP, TJ, CC)
gnat
hashoomala, (TJ) hasho̱'mala, (WB,
AB) hashoomala', (TP) asho̱mala,
(LP) ashoomala, (CM) ashoomala'
cottonwood
hashoomala pofalli' cottonwood
seeds [pofalli+']
hashshan, (CC) haashan, (AB) hashan
type of edible weed, (CC, AB) ton
grass, (AB) pepper grass
hashshok, (CC) haashok grass; hay
hashshok aa-asha' hayloft
hashshok aa-ashaachi' hay barn
[aa+ashaachi+']
hashshok bashli to cut, mow grass (I)
hashshok haloppa', (MJ) shokha'
haloppa' type of plant with little
stickers or burrs (smaller than
shommatik) (brown sedge?
sandbur?) [haloppa+']
hashshok holokchi' lawn; cultivated

grass [holokchi+']
hashshok impisa' see impisa'
hashshok ishkachiili' grass clippers
hashshok ishkalla'fa' buck rake
(piece of farm machinery pulled by
a horse or tractor)
hashshok ishtamo',
hashshokshtamo' grass cutter,
scythe [hashshok isht amo+']
hashshok kallo' Johnson grass
[kallo+']
hashshok loposhki' type of grass
with fine, soft plumes [loposhki+']
hashshok pata' crabgrass [<pata>+']
hashshok shila' dried hay [shila+']
hashshok talakchi' bale of hay
[talakchi+']
hashshokshtamo' see hashshok
ishtamo'
hashtahli to get light, become light;
to be bright (—); to be bright, light in
(a location) (3) [hashi' tahli] {ngr.
hashtáhli; ygr. hashtáyyahli: to get
light a long way off, to be light very
early in the morning} § Aboohaat
hashtahli. The house is bright, It's
bright in the house.
hashtaht minti to be after midnight,
but before dawn: especially, to be
just before dawn (—) [hashtahli+t]
hashtap dead leaves or other debris
in a creek bed
hashtáyyahli to get light a long way
off, to be just before dawn, very
early in the morning—ygr. of
hashtahli   ·
hashtayyahlo'si to be just getting
light a long way off, to be just before
dawn (—) [hashtáyyahli+o'si]
hashtáhli ngr. of hashtahli
hashtola', (TP) ashtola' winter
[hashi' ittola+']
hashtola' ato̱falla'a' winter onions
hashtola' yanha' pneumonia

100

[yanha+']
hashtola' yanha' í'shi to have
  pneumonia (I)
hashtolammo'na' the beginning of
  winter [hashtola' ammo'na+']
hashtola-panki' possum grapes (WB)
  [hashtola' panki']
<hata> in okkata, shokhata, possibly
  ataachi, folosh-ata'
hatalhposhik, (CP, TP, CC, MJ, MC,
  HS, WB) talhposhik, (EH)
  hatalhpakko, (AW) tashposhik
  butterfly, moth
hatalhposhik ishyokachi' butterfly
  net [isht yokachi+']
hataachi see ataachi
hata'lobo' tadpole [lobo']
hatafo, (TP) hataafo, (AW) atafo, (MJ)
  hatafo' grasshopper
hatip hips; small of the back, lower
  back (IIp)
hatiimimi' type of small bee or
  hornet; (TJ) June bug
hattak person; man, male person
hattak abaanompishtanompoli' male
  preacher
hattak abi' murderer [abi+']
hattak apa' cannibal [apa+']
Hattak Api' Homma', (ML) Api'
  Homma', (WB) Hattak Nipi'
  Homma' Indian [homma+']
hattak api' homma' aa-asha' Indian
  reservation
Hattak Api' Homma' alhlhi' full-
  blooded Indian (VB) [alhlhi+']
Hattak Api' Homma' Iyaakni' Indian
  Territory [im+yaakni']
hattak api' homma' naapiisa' Indian
  judge
hattak api' homminchokka' Indian
  home (house of standardized design
  built on Indian land and
  maintained for residents by the
  tribal government) [Hattak Api'

Homma' im+chokka']
hattak api' hommisholosh
  moccasins [Hattak Api' Homma'
  im+sholosh]
hattak apiisachi' conductor (on a
  train) [apiisachi+']
hattak aa-asha' park
hattak aabinohli' living room
  [aa+binohli+']
hattak aaittanowa', aaittanowa'
  sidewalk
Hattak Aakapassaa-asha', Hattak
  Aakapassa' Aa-asha' Eskimos
  [aa+kapassa aa-asha']
hattak aanoksitili' gallows
  [aa+noksitili+']
hattak bashli' surgeon [bashli+']
hattak binoochi' usher [binoochi+']
hattak chokkimponta' landlord,
  renter [chokka' imponta+']
hattak foni' skeleton
hattak haknip illi', haknip illi'
  paralyzed person [illi+']
hattak hapoyoksa' gentleman; well-
  behaved, smart person; wise man
  (in the parable) [hapoyoksa+']
Hattak Hapoyoksa' Wise Men, Magi,
  Kings (in the Christmas story)
hattak hawi' male prostitute
hattak himitta' teenage boy, young
  man (older than hattak himittachi')
  [himitta+']
hattak himittachi' young teenage boy
  [himittachi+']
hattak holba', takholba' doll;
  mannequin; picture, statue,
  representation (of a person)
  [holba+']
hattak holba' aaiksaachi' darkroom
  [aa+iksaachi+']
hattak holba' aalhto' see holba'
  aalhto'
hattak holba' aapisa', hattak
  holbaapisa' television [aa+pisa+']

hattak holbaafokha' picture frame
[hattak holba' aa+fokha+']
hattak holbaapisa' see hattak holba'
aapisa'
hattak holitto'pa' see holitto'pa'
hattak holhpali' type of caterpillar
[holhpali+']
hattak hotihna' census [hotihna+']
hattak ibaanosit nọwa to go with lots
of men, be promiscuous (of a
woman) (I) [ibaanosi+t]
hattak ihoo iklanna' hermaphrodite
[iklanna+']
hattak ihoo ilahobbi' transvestite
[ilahobbi+']
hattak ihoo toba' transvestite; male
homosexual [toba+']
hattak ikhali'lo' virgin
[ik+halili+o+']
hattak illapa', (CP) hattak illi' apa'
armadillo, "grave digger" [apa+']
hattak illi', takilli' dead person,
corpse [illi+']
hattak illi' aa-asha' graveyard
hattak illi' aafo'kha' coffin
[aa+fokha+']
hattak illi' intiyyo'bi' see hattak
illintoyyo'bi'
hattak illi' ishshaali' ambulance [isht
shaali+'] {hattak illi' shaali'}
hattak illi' ọhikki'ya' gravestone (sg.)
[ọhikki'ya+'] {pl. hattak illi'
ọhiyohli'}
hattak illi' ọhiyohli' gravestones—
pl. of hattak illi' ọhikki'ya'
[ọhiyohli+']
hattak illi' shaali', takilli' shaali'
hearse, ambulance; undertaker
[shaali+'] {hattak illi' ishshaali'}
hattak illintoyyo'bi', hattak illi'
intiyyo'bi', (HS) tak illi' imitoobi',
(ER) illi' intiyyobi', (AB) hattak illi'
intiyyobi' coffin [illi'
im+ittoyyobbi']

hattak imilhlha' wild Indian
[imilhlha+']
hattak immo'ma' midget
Hattak Imosak Chạ'a' person of a
certain old Chickasaw clan (TJ)
[im+osak chạ'a+']
Hattak Inchiisha' Wayya'a' person of
a certain old Chickasaw clan (TJ)
[im+chiisha' wayya'a+']
Hattak Issi' Inchiisha' Koba'fa'
person of a certain old Chickasaw
clan [im+chiisha' kobafa+']
hattak issikopa' criminal [issikopa+']
hattak ittasita', hattak nannittasita'
gambler [nanna ittasita+']
hattak ịnaapiisa' judge
[im+naapiisa']
hattak losa', tak losa', losa' black
person, African American [hattak
losa+']
Hattak Losa' Aa-asha' Africa
Hattak Losa' Ịyaakni' Africa
[im+yaakni']
hattak losa' nakni' black man
hattak losa' toksali' black slave
hattak los-ihoo', los-ihoo' black
woman [hattak losa' ihoo+']
hattak losiklanna' person who is half
black [hattak losa' iklanna+']
hattak losishkobo' black-eyed susan
(flower) [hattak losa' ishkobo']
hattak los-oshi' black child [hattak
losa' oshi']
hattak lowak moshoochi' fireman
[moshoochi+']
hattak mọma the world, all people,
everyone (cln.) § Hattak mọmakat
ithạnattook presidentat nalhakạ.
Everyone knew that the president
got shot.
hattak nakni' man, male person
hattak nannimaalami' business man
[nanna imaalami+']
hattak nannithana' wise man [nanna

ithana+']
hattak nannittasita' see hattak
ittasita'
hattak nannokchamal-apa'
vegetarian [nanna okchamali+'
apa+']
Hattak Okakmi' Okaa-asha' Eskimos
hattak oppani' someone under a
spell, someone bewitched
[oppani+']
Hattak Oshi' Jesus Christ (the Son of
Man)
hattak pihcha' midget
hattak pokta' Siamese twins
hattak sawa' Indian spirit guide or
"leprechaun" (another name for
iyaaknasha') [<sawa>+']
hattak sawintopa soft, green, mossy
area in the woods [hattak sawa'
im+topa]
hattak shawi' monkey, ape
Hattak Shawi' person of the old
Chickasaw raccoon clan
hattak shaali', chanaa malili' hattak
shaali' passenger car (on a train),
bus [shaali+']
hattak sholop bogeyman (WB)
hattak taloowa' singer [taloowa+']
hattak toklo' twins: especially, adult
twins [toklo+']
hattak toksali' employed person,
worker [toksali+']
hattak yoka' prisoner, slave [yoka+']
hattak yoshoba' sinner [yoshoba+']
hattakat imáyya'sha to have a
husband, be married (of a woman)
(III) [hattak+at]
hawaháshko hngr. of hawashko
hawáhhashko hgr. of hawashko
hawashko to be sour, to smell sour
(for example, of milk) or rotten (of
fruit, for instance) (II) {ggr.
háwwashko: to be really sweaty, to
smell strongly of sweat; hgr.

hawáhhashko; hngr. hawaháshko;
ngr. hawáshko; ygr. hawáyya'shko}
hawashkochi to make sour (I;3)
[hawashko+chi]
hawáyya'shko ygr. of hawashko
hawáshko ngr. of hawashko
<hawi> in hawi', hawichi, hawit
nowa
hawi' prostitute —normally used as
part of a compound expression, or
with an associated verb or subj.
noun [<hawi>+'] {hattak hawi',
ihoo hawi', hawi' abooha, hawichi}
§ Hawi' chiya. You're a prostitute. I
Yammakot hawi'. That one's a
prostitute.
hawi' abooha brothel, house of
prostitution
hawi' abooha apiisachi to keep a
house of prostitution (I)
hawi' ikbi to make into a prostitute
(I;II)
hawichi to prostitute, bring into a life
of prostitution (I;II) [<hawi>+chi]
hawit nowa to walk the streets as a
prostitute does (I) [<hawi>+t] §
Hawit ishnowatoka'ni. You must
have been a prostitute, You must
have walked the streets.
háwwashko to be really sweaty, to
smell strongly of sweat—ggr. of
hawashko
<hayahánka> in hayahánkat áa—
hngr. of <hayaka>
hayahánkat áa to walk around
wearing a really thin dress (I)
[<hayahanka>+t] § Hayahánkat
ishaa. You're going around with a
see-through dress on.
<hayaka> in hayaka', hayahánkat aa
{hngr. <hayahánka>}
hayaka' way off somewhere, out in
the boondocks [<hayaka>+']
hayaka' bíyyi'ka to be deserted (3) §

103

hayi

Yaaknaat hayaka' biyyi'ka. The land is deserted.
hayi, (CC) **hayyi,** (CM) **haayi,** (CP) **hakaayi'** walnut
hayi alhpooba' cultivated walnuts; English walnuts [alhpooba+']
hayi api' type of hard black walnut
hayi imilhlha' wild walnuts [imilhlha+']
hayi'chi to stomp (grapes or quilts in a washtub, for instance) (I;3) [-SC] {v1. hayi'kalhchi; ngr. hayi'línchi; rcgr. hayiyí'chi}
hayí'ffi ggr. of hayiffi
hayi'kalhchi to be soft, mushy (of rotten or crushed produce, for instance) (3) [+T] {v2. hayi'chi}
hayi'línchi ngr. of hayi'chi
hayifa, (WB, LF, LJ, LP, LR, MS, AW) **hayofa** to be out of shape, out of alignment, lopsided; to have one leg shorter than the other (II) {v2. hayiffi; ggr. háyyi'fa; hngr. hayihífa}
hayiffi to make lopsided (I;II) {v1. hayifa; ggr. háyyiffi, hayí'ffi; hngr. hayihíffi}
hayihífa hngr. of hayifa
hayihíffi hngr. of hayiffi
hayihíma hngr. of hayima
hayima, hayimo to be muddy (3) {ggr. háyyi'ma; hngr. hayihíma; ngr. hayíma; ygr. hayíyyi'ma}
hayimachi to make (dirt, land) muddy (by putting water on it) (I;3) [hayima+chi]
hayimo see hayima
hayip pond, lake, tank
hayip ishto' lake, dam [ishto+']
hayiyí'chi to walk in, slosh in (mud or something mushy) (I;3)—rcgr. of hayi'chi
hayíma ngr. of hayima
hayoha, hayowa to be sifted (3) [+T] {hayowalhchi}

hayompolo', (TJ) **haayonkpolo',** (ER) **hayo͟'polo'** weed; trash (Ct?) [oppolo] {aayoppolo', nannoppolo'}
hayowa see hayoha
hayowalhchi to be sifted, picked over (II); to be cleaned (of corn) (3) {v2. hayoochi; hayoha}
hayowani', (TP) **haywani'** worm (usually, an above-ground species)
Hayowani' Abookoshi Hauwani Creek
hayowani' holhpali', (CP) **holhpali'** type of caterpillar [holhpali+']
hayowani' lhipa' tent caterpillar [lhipa+']
hayowani' shoppala' glowworm
hayowani' woksho' caterpillar [woksho+']
hayoochi to find (I;II); to get, catch, have (a sickness) (I;3) [+SC]
hayoochi, (MJ) **hayo'chi** to sift (I;II); to clean (corn) (I;3) [-SC] {v1. hayowalhchi; hayoha}
hayoochichi to faint, have a convulsion or seizure (II) [+CPR] [-PR]; to be mad, of a dog (3) [-CPR] [-PR]
hayoochichichi to make faint (I;II) [hayoochichi+chi]
háyyaklo ygr. of haklo
háyyaksi ygr. of haksi
háyyi'fa ggr. of hayifa
háyyiffi ggr. of hayiffi
háyyi'ma ggr. of hayima
haa what? I beg your pardon?
haa chikimba what nothing!—you heard me
Haalooso Ahloso (place near Ada, Oklahoma)
haalo͟shi', (HS) **haaloshi',** (TP) **aaloshi'** rice [from Spanish arroz]
haatokya look! behold! lo! § Haatokya! Pisa! Lo! Behold!
haayonkpolo' (TJ), (ER) **hayo͟'polo'**

trash
haa see aa
haha, (LF) haa, (MS) hiha to groan,
grunt (I)
hí'ka ggr. of hika
hí'li to stand, be standing up (dl.
subj.) (I); to stand, be standing in (dl.
subj.) (I;3)—ggr. of <hili> {hngr.
hihíli: to stand around (dl. subj.); sg.
híkki'ya; tpl. hiyohmáa, hiyoht
máa}
hí'lha ggr. of hilha
hichabbi to have a boil come up on
one's skin (II); (ER) to have a sty
[hichi' abi]
hichakka'li' nine times
[hi+chakka'li+'] § Hichakka'li'
aashlitok. I said it nine times.
híchchi'to ggr. of hichito
hichi' boil (on the skin) (IIIp)
hichínto ngr. of hichito
<hichintochichi> [hichinto+chichi]
{ngr. hichintochínchi;
hichintolínchi, hichitolichi}
hichintochínchi to make (pl. obj.)
bigger (I;3)—ngr. of
<hichintochichi>
<hichintolichi> [<hichitoli>+chi]
{hngr. hichintolihínchi; ngr.
hichintolínchi}
hichintolihínchi hngr. of
<hichintolichi>
hichintolínchi to make (pl. obj.)
bigger (I;3)—ngr. of <hichintolichi>
{hngr. hichintolihínchi;
hichintochichi, hichitolichi}
hichito, (ML, CC) hochito to be big
(pl. subj.) (II) [+CPR] [+PR]
[hoo+<chito>] {v2. <hichitoli>; ggr.
híchchi'to; ngr. hichínto; ygr.
hichíyyi'to; sg. ishto} [hoo+ishto]
hichitochi to make (pl. obj.) big (I;II)
[hichito+chi] {ngr. hichitónchi;
hichitolichi}

<hichitoli> in hichitolichi, hichitolit
ishpisa' {v1. hichito; ngr. hichitóli:
to make bigger; <hichintoli>}
hichitolichi to make (pl. obj.) big (I;3)
[<hichitoli>+chi] {ngr.
hichitolínchi; hichitochi}
hichitolínchi ngr. of hichitolichi
hichitolishpisa' magnifying glass
[<hichitoli> isht pisa+']
hichitónchi ngr. of hichitochi
hichitóli to make bigger (I;II)—ngr. of
<hichitoli>
hichíyyi'to ygr. of hichito
hich-oshi' little boil [hichi' oshi']
hihanna'li' six times [hi+hanna'li+']
hihínka hngr. of hika
hihíli to stand around—hngr. of hí'li
hihílha hngr. of hilha
hika to stop, cease; to step; to stand
up (punctual) (I); to stop in, stop at
(a place) (I;3) [-PR] [-CPR] {v2. <hili>;
ggr. hí'ka; hngr. hihínka; ngr.
hínka: to stop, do less; xgr. híkki'ya;
akkaayínka, tikbayka}
hika! whoa!
hikannohmi' a few times, a number
of times (ind.); how many times
(inf.) {int. hikatohmi'}
[hi+kannohmi+'] § Hikannomi'
taloowalitok. I sang a few times. |
Hikannohmi' taloowatoka ithanali.
I know how many times he sang.
hikatohmi' how many times (int.)
{ind.-inf. hikannohmi'}
[hi+katohmi+'] § Hikatohmi'
ishtaloowam? How many times did
you sing?
hikíya to stand back, stay back, be left
standing (sg. subj.) (I)—ngr. of
híkki'ya
híkki'ya to stand, be standing (sg.
subj.) (I); to stand, be standing in (sg.
subj.) (I;3)—xgr. of hika [+PR] [-CPR]
{ngr. hikíya: to stand back, stay back;

rmgr. hikkikíya; dl. hí'li; tpl.
hiyohmáa, hiyoht máa}
hikkikíya to stand and walk around
(sg. subj.) (I)—rmgr. of híkki'ya
<hili> in hilichi {v1. hika; ggr. hí'li}
<hiliya> in ihiliya
hilichi to stand (something) up,
make stand up (mainly sg. obj.); to
stop (a car, horse); to cock (a gun)
(I;II) [+SC] [<hili>+chi] {pl. obj.
hiyohchi}
hiloha, hilowa thunder; to thunder
(3) {hngr. hilohóha, hilohówa} §
Loksaat chikisilikmat
ikchitalhoffi'cho hilowakma'chi. If
a turtle's biting you he won't let go
till there's thunder (old saying).
hilohóha, hilohówa hngr. of hiloha
hilowa see hiloha
hilowifoshi', (MJ) hilowa foshi'
scissortail (bird), scissortailed
flycatcher [hilowa im+foshi']
hilha to dance; to spin (of a top) (I); to
dance (a particular dance) (I;3) [+PR]
[+CPR] {ggr. hí'lha; hngr. hihílha;
ngr. hílha} § Ittimolabi' Hilha'
hilhatok. They danced Changing
Partners.
hilha' dance; dancer [hilha+']
Hilha' Falama' name of a dance
[falama+']
hilha' intikbayka' see intikbayka'
hilha'chi' top (toy) [hilhachi+']
hilhachi to make dance; to spin (a
top) (I;II) [hilha+chi] {ggr.
hílhlha'chi}
hílhlha'chi ggr. of hilhachi
himínta ngr. of himitta
himitta to be new; to be stylish,
fashionable (of clothes) (3); to be
young (II) [+PR] [+CPR] {ngr.
himínta; ygr. himíyyitta: to be brand
new}
himitta'si to be a teenager (II)

[himitta+a'si]
himittachi to make young, renew,
renovate, make over (I;II); to have
arrived at one's teenage years, to be
13 or 14 years old (II) [himitta+chi]
{ngr. himittánchi: to be younger}
himittánchi to be younger (II)—ngr.
of himittachi
himíyyitta to be brand new—ygr. of
himitta
himmak nittaki see himmaka'
nittakika
himmaka', himmaka now, finally,
after (some point of reference)
[himmaka+'(+a)] § Himmakattook.
It was much later (than an earlier
time under discussion).
himmaka' nittak, (ER, AB) himmak
nittak today; the present day §
Himmaka' nittakat nittak chokma.
Today is a nice day.
**himmaka' nittakika, himmaka
nittakika,** himmak nittaki this
morning, today in the morning
[nittaki+ka]
himmaka' obyaka this evening
[obya+ka]
himmaka' pila, himmaka' pílla (to
be) in the future (relative to now or
some other reference point), from
now on, from then on § Mosesat
antakat himmaka' pillattook.
When Moses was around it was
much later [than when Noah was].
| himmaka' pilakma... in the
future...
himmaka'ma now (and in the past
too); again, still; the next time, the
second time
himmaka see himmaka'
himmaka nittakika see himmaka'
nittakika
**himmako'sa, himmako'sak,
himmako'saako** just now (a very

short time ago in the past)
[himmako'si+a/ak/ako]
himmako'si in himmako'si finha,
himmako'sa
himmako'si finha, himmako'si
finhaka right now, very shortly (in
the immediate future) [finha+ka]
himmakoklhilika, makoklhilika
tonight [himmaka' oklhili+ka]
hímmo'na to wait in vain—ggr. of
himóna, <himona>
<himona> in himona', himonachi,
himonali {ggr. hímmo'na; ngr.
himóna; <himonna>?}
himona' in afammi himona', ahi'
himona', bala' himona', tanchi'
himona' [<himona>+']
himonachi to renovate (I;3) (Ct?)
[<himona>+chi]
himonala' newborn [himona' ala+']
§ chipota himona': newborn baby
himonali to happen quickly (—) §
Himonatok. It happened quickly.
himonali' suddenly [himonali+'] §
Himonali' sattolatok. Suddenly I
fell down.
himóna to wait (I)—ngr. of
<himona> {ggr. hímmo'na: to wait
in vain; ihimóna: to wait for}
<himonna> in himonna',
himonna'si, himonnahma...
{<himona>?}
himonna', himonna'si,
himonna'sikkano, himonnookano
once [himonna+'/a'si/ookano] §
Himonnookano onalitok. I've been
there once (recently).
himonna'si to happen once (—)
[himonna+a'si] § Himonna'si
hilhalitok. I only danced once.
himonna'si, himonna'sikkano,
himonnookano see himonna'
himonnahma..., himonnahma
aachikat... once upon a time...

[himonna+hma aachi+kat]
himonofanti' newly hatched
[himona' hofanti+'] § akankoshi'
himonofanti': newly hatched chick
hina' road
hina' aa-abaanabli' overpass
[aa+abaanabli+']
hina' aaittabanna'a' crossroad,
intersection [aa+ittabanna'a+']
hina' aaittifilammi' fork (in a road)
[aa+ittifilammi+']
hina' aalhopolli' overpass,
underpass, tunnel [aalhopolli+']
hina' aatakafa' road with a dip in it
[aatakafa+']
hina' ishtontono'kalhchi', hina'
ishtontono'chi' steamroller
hina'at aaittabánna'a for there to be a
crossroad or intersection in (a place)
[hina'+at] § Yamma fokhaako
hina'at aaittabanna'a minattook.
Long ago there used to be a
crossroad around there.
hinishto' highway, main road [hina'
ishto+']
hínka to stop, do less—ngr. of hika §
Ishimpakat ishhinka'ni. You
should eat less.
hin-oshi' trail, path [hina' oshi']
hipokko'li' ten times [hi+pokko'li+']
<hisa> in okhisa' {pisa}
hishi' fur; body hair (used following
the name of a body part); feather;
leaf, needle (of a plant, used
following the name of a plant) (3p)
§ salbak hishi': the hair on my arm,
my arm hair | itti' hishi': leaf, tree
leaf | chowaala' hishi': cedar
needles
hishi' loposhki' down (feathers)
[loposhki+']
hitalhlha'pi' five times
[hi+talhlha'pi+']
<hitibli> in bakhitibli {<hitiipo'li>}

<hitiipo'li>

<hitiipo'li> in bakhitiipo'li
{<hitibli>, <hitiipopóli>}
<hitiipopóli> in bakhitiipopóli
{<hitiipo'li>}
hitochchi'na' three times
[hi+tochchi'na+']
hitokla' twice [hi+tokla+']
hiyohchi to stand (pl. obj.) up, make
stand up, plant (seedlings) (pl. obj.)
(I;II) [±SC] [<hiyohli>+chi] {sg. obj.
hilichi}
<hiyohli> in hiyohchi, hiyoht maa,
notaahiyohli', ohiyohli
hiyohmáa to stand, be standing up
(tpl. subj.) (I); to stand, be standing
in (tpl. subj.) (I;3) [hiyoht *maa] {sg.
híkki'ya; dl. hí'li} § Kiihiyohmaa.
We are standing up.
hiyoht máa to stand, be standing up
(tpl. subj.) (I); to stand, be standing
in (tpl. subj.) (I;3) [<hiyohli>+t] {sg.
híkki'ya; dl. hí'li; hiyohmáa} §
Hiyoht iimaa. We are standing up.
hiyontochchi'na' eight times
[hi+ontochchi'na+']
hiyontoklo' seven times
[hi+ontoklo+']
hiyoshta' four times [hi+oshta+']
hiyyawa chaffa' eleven times (WB)
[hi+(awa chaffa)+']
hílha ngr. of hilha
hó'fka ggr. of hofka
hó'lmo ggr. of holmo
ho'mi, hoomi, (AW) oomi you're
welcome; yes, okay, all right
{<ohmi>}
hó'mi ggr. of homi
hó'mma ggr. of homma
hó'mo ggr. of homo
hó'yo ggr. of hoyo
hó'yya ggr. of hoyya
<hoba> in ahooba, hobachi, hobak,
ittihoba {v1. holba}
hobachi to copy, imitate; to take a

picture of (I;II) [<hoba>+chi]
hobak sterile, infertile person or
animal {<hoba>}
hobak ikbi to sterilize, fix (I;II)
hobak ishtikbi' birth control device:
especially, birth control pills;
sterilization method [isht ikbi+']
hobasht aaishi, (TP) hobachit aaishi
to copy (I;3) [hobachi+t]
hobasht imaaishi, (TP) hobachit
imaaishi to copy from (I;III)
[hobachi+t]
Hobinili! Sit down! (imperative
only; to pl. subj.) [hoo+biniili]
hoboona, (ER) hobana to wrap (I;II)
{v1. holbona}
hóchchi'fo ggr. of hochifo
hochifo to name (someone°) (a
name) (I;II;3); to select, name to a
team; to call by name (I;II); to say (a
word), call (someone's) name (I;3)
{v1. holhchifo; ggr. hóchchi'fo;
hngr. hochihífo} § Lynn
chihochifola'chi. I'll name you
Lynn.
hochifochi to make (someone) say
(something) (only used with
reference to children) (3;3;3)
[hochifo+chi]
hochihífo hngr. of hochifo
hofaháya hngr. of hofahya
hofahya to be embarrassed, ashamed,
shy, bashful, timid (II); to be
embarrassed, ashamed to, to be shy
about [+a'ni+kat ss comp.] (II); to be
embarrassed, ashamed that [+ka
comp.] (II) [+PR] [+CPR] {v2.
hofahyali; hofaháya} § Sahofahya
ayala'nikat. I'm ashamed to go. |
Katahaat hofahyatok Lynnat
Charles kisilika? Who was
embarrassed that Lynn bit Charles?
hofahyachi to embarrass (I;II)
[hofahya+chi]

hofahyali to embarrass (I;II) {v1. hofahya}

hofanti to grow; to hatch, be born (II) [-CPR] [+PR] {ggr. hóffa'ti; hngr. hofahánti; neg. ikhofa'to}

hofanti' type of bug (CM)

hofantichi to raise (animals), bring up, rear (I;II) [hofanti+chi]

hofantikat ona to become an adult, be grown up (I) [hofanti+kat] {ngr. hofantikat óna}

hofantikat óna ngr. of hofantikat ona

hofka to air, air (something) out (I;II) {v1. holofka; ggr. hó'fka; hngr. hohófka}

hofkachi to be painful, to have pins and needles (for instance, because a part of one's body has been asleep) (II) {hngr. hofkahánchi}

hofkahánchi hngr. of hofkachi

hofkaháa hngr. of hofkaa

hofkaa, (VB, CC, MJ, WB, TP) ofkaa to have a sticker or thorn (in one); (ER, TP, WB, CC, MC) to have a splinter (II); to have (a sticker or thorn) sticking in one (II;3) {hngr. hofkaháa} § Anaakot shommatik sahofkaa. I have a shommatik sticking in me.

hofobi to be deep (3) [-PR] [-CPR]

hofobichi to make deep (I,3) [hofobi+chi]

hohómpi hngr. of hoppi

hohónkchi hngr. of hokchi

hohónkso hngr. of hokso

hohófka hngr. of hofka

hohólba hngr. of holba

hohólo hngr. of holo

hohólhfo hngr. of holhfo

hohólhpa hngr. of holhpa

hohómi hngr. of homi

hohómma hngr. of homma

hohósa hngr. of hosa

hohósi hngr. of hosi

hohóyya hngr. of hoyya

hokaffi see okaffi {pl. obj. hokaachi}

hokaachi to seine, catch (fish) in a net (pl. obj.) (CP) {sg. obj. hokaffi}

hokchi to plant (seeds) (I;3) {v1. holokchi; hngr. hohónkchi; ngr. hónkchi}

holafa to defecate (I) {ggr. hólla'fa; hngr. holaháfa; ngr. holáfa}

holaháfa hngr. of holafa

holáfa ngr. of holafa

holba to be photographed (II) {v2. <hoba>; hngr. hohólba; ngr. hólba; ahooba}

holba' imitation; representation, picture, photograph, statue (IIp: picture of) [holba+'] § kitoba holba': plastic bottle | iyyi' holba': artificial leg | saholba': my picture: a picture of me

holba' aalhto', hattak holba' aalhto' photograph album

holba' chokmaho toba see holba'at chokmaho toba

holba'at chokmaho toba, holba' chokmaho toba to photograph well, have one's picture turn out good (I) [holba'+at chokma+ho] § Holba'at chokmaho tobalitokoot i'shlitok. My picture turned out good so I kept it. | Holba'at chokmaho tobalitoko chokma'si. My picture turned out good and it's pretty.

holbachi to photograph (I;II) [holba+chi]

holbona, (ER) holbana to be wrapped up; to coil up, be coiled up (of a snake) (II) {v2. hoboona; ygr. holbóyyo'na}

holbóyyo'na ygr. of holbona

holihísso hngr. of holisso

holissamposhi' paper plate [holisso amposhi']

holissaa-asha' see holisso aa-asha'

holissaaishi' post office [holisso aaishi']

holissaaittola' post office (old word) [holisso aa+ittola+']

holissaalhto' see holisso aalhto'

holissaapisa' school [holisso aapisa'] § aholissaapisa': my school

holissaat inkashofa to get a divorce (III) [holisso+at] § Holissaat ankashofatok. I got a divorce.

holissikbi to make a will (also: to make a book) (I) [holisso *ikbi] § Holisso ishikbitam? Did you make a will?

holissimikbi to make a will for (3;3) [holisso *im+ikbi]

holissinkashoffi see holisso inkashoffi

holissintoshooli to read, preach to (I;III) [holisso *intoshooli] § Holissishintoshootok. You preached to them.

holissilhafi see holisso ilhafi

holisso to be written; to have marks or spots, be spotted (3) [+PR] [+CPR] {ggr. hóllisso: to be spotted (II); hngr. holihísso; ngr. holísso; ygr. holíyyi'sso; ibaaholisso}

holisso paper, book, page

holisso abooha lapali' see abooha holisso lapali'

holisso aa-asha', holissaa-asha' library; bookcase

holisso aaishi' post office box [aa+ishi+']

holisso aaishi' holhtina' post office box number

holisso aalhto', holissaalhto' mailbox, post office box; mailbag; bookcase

holisso aataloowa' song sheet, song book [aa+taloowa+']

holisso bakshiyama aatoba' see bakshiyama holisso aatoba'

holisso chokoshpa' newspaper [chokoshpa+']

holisso fóyyokha to be in the paper (of a name, picture, or story) (3) § Lynn holba'at holisso foyyokhatok. There was a picture of Lynn in the paper. | Saholhchifoat holisso foyyokha. My name is in the paper. | Lynn ittihalallitokchaynina holisso foyyokhatok. It was in the paper that Lynn got married.

holisso holba' photocopy

holisso holbachi to copy a book or paper: especially, to make a Xerox or photocopy (I)

Holisso Holitto'pa', (ML) Holissolitto'pa' Bible [holisso holitto'pa+']

holisso hotihna to count votes (I)

holisso inkashoffi, holissinkashoffi to get a divorce from (I,III) [im+(holisso kashoffi)> holisso *inkashoffi] § Holisso inkashoffilitok. I got a divorce from him.

holisso ishshaali' mailbag [isht shaali+']

holisso ishtakallo'chi' paper clip, staple

holisso ishtaya', holisso ishtayachi' stamp [ishtaya/ishtayachi+']

holisso ishtayachi' see holisso ishtaya'

holisso ishtiwwi' letter opener [isht tiwwi+']

holisso ittibaapisa to go to school together (I / IR) [itti+ibaa+(holisso pisa)> holisso *ittibaapisa] § Holisso iitibaapisatttook. We went to school together (some time ago).

holisso ihotihna to count the votes for (a candidate) (I;III) [im+(holisso hotihna)> holisso *ihotihna] § Bush holisso ilihotihna'chi. We'll count

the votes for Bush.
holisso ịlhạfi, holissịlhạfi to vote for (I;III); to sign, make one's mark on (I;3) § Holisso ạlhạfitok. He voted for me.
holisso kallo' cardboard [kallo+']
holisso kashofa' divorce [kashofa+']
holisso kashofa' ishi to get a divorce (I)
holisso kashofa' imishi to get a divorce from (I;III) § Holisso kashofa' chimishila'chi. I'll get a divorce from you.
holisso kashoffi to get divorced (I) {holisso inkashoffi}
holisso loposhki' paper money [lopposhki+']
holisso lhopolli to graduate (I) § Holisso ishlhopollitam? Did you graduate?
holisso mi finha' original (of a document—not a copy)
holisso nanna ishtạlhlhi' will (document) [isht ạlhlhi+']
holisso nannishtilawwichi' sandpaper [nanna isht ilawwichi+']
holisso nannishtithạna' license, certificate [nanna isht ithạna+']
holisso onaa-asha' bookcase [on+aa-asha+']
holisso pisa to study, go to school; to look at books, papers (I)
holisso pisa' student [(holisso pisa)+']
holisso pisachi to teach; to show books, papers to (I;II) [(holisso pisa)+chi]
holisso shaali' mail truck [shaali+']
holisso shokmalali' tinfoil, aluminum foil [shokmalali+']
holisso toba to be written down, be recorded (3) § Poholhchifoat holisso toba'chi. Our names will be recorded. | ...Chikashshanompa'at

holisso toba'chih**o**.... ...for the Chickasaw language to be recorded....
holisso toshooli to read (I)
holisso toshooli' preacher, teacher [(holisso toshooli)+']
holissó'chi ggr. of holissochi
holissochi to write, to write in (I;3) [holisso+chi] {ggr. holissó'chi; hngr. holissohónchi}
holissochi' secretary (especially, in an organization or club) [holissochi+']
holisso-pisachi' schoolteacher [(holisso pisachi)+'] § ịholisso-pisachi' his teacher
holitta fence, (stone) wall [hollitta]
<holitta> (verb) in holittachi {ggr. hóllitta}
holitta shokolbika' ịhikki'ya' corner fencepost [im+hikki'ya+']
holitta' in tali' haloppa' holitta' [<holitta>+']
holittachi to fence in (an area) (I;3) [<holitta>+chi] {ịholittachi: to fence in (a person)}
holittịhikki'ya' fence post [holitta im+hikki'ya+']
holítto'pa to be precious, holy—ggr. of holiitopa
holitto'pa', hattak holitto'pa' prophet, holy person, preacher [holitto'pa+']
holíttobli ggr. of holiitobli
holittokkisa' gate [holitta okkisa']
holíyyi'sso ygr. of holisso
holiitobli to treasure, take care of, love, hang on to (I;II); to pass (a motion), accept (minutes) (I;3) {v1. holiitopa; ggr. holíttobli; ngr. holiitómbli: to prefer, favor}
holiitoblichi to dedicate (I;II) [holiitobli+chi]
holiitóhho'pa hgr. of holiitopa
holiitómbli to prefer, favor—ngr. of

111

holiitómpa

holiitobli
holiitómpa ngr. of holiitopa
holiitopa to be rich (II); to be passed (of a motion), accepted (of minutes) (3) {v2. holiitobli; ggr. holítto'pa: to be precious, holy; hgr. holiitóhho'pa; ngr. holiitómpa; ygr. holiitóyyo'pa}
holiitóyyo'pa ygr. of holiitopa
holísso ngr. of holisso
hólla'fa ggr. of holafa
hollabi to be sick (generally with a headache or nosebleed) as a result of being around a woman having a period or a woman who has just given birth (usually used of a man) (II) (AB, WB, MJ, ER, LR, MS) [*<hollo> abi]
<hollappi> in hollappi', holappichi
hollappi' in tanchi' hollappi' [<hollappi>+']
hollappichi to cook (corn) on the cob (I;II) [<hollappi>+chi]
hollashki to look like vomit; to be stringy, slimy (like overcooked okra) (3)
hóllisso to be spotted, freckled, checked (II)—ggr. of holisso
hóllitta to be fenced (3)—ggr. of <holitta>
<hollo> in hollabi, ihollo, imihollo, ishtahollo', naahollo, Nittak Hollo'
hollonkso' fart, flatulation (IIIp) {honkso; shotik ihollokso'}
hollonkso' aloota, (AB) honkso' aloota to have gas (II) § Hollonkso' asalootatok. I had gas.
holloppi to be buried (II) {v2. hoppi}
hollosi to be pounded (of dried foods, like meat or grain) (II) {v2. hosi} § nipi' hollosi': hash
holmo to be roofed (3) [+PR] [+CPR] {v2. homo; ggr. hó'lmo}
holo to put on (shoes or other

footwear) (I;3) {hngr. hohólo; ygr. hóyyo'lo: to have on (shoes)}
holochi to put (shoes or footwear) on (someone°) (I;II;3), to shoe (a horse, for instance) (I;3) [holo+chi]
holofka to be aired (II) {v2. hofka; hngr. holohófka}
holohófka hngr. of holofka
holokchi to be planted (covered with dirt) (of seeds, for example) (3) {v2. hokchi}
holot pisa to try on (shoes) (I;3) [holo+t] § Sholosh holot pisalitok. I tried on the shoes.
holhaano horsefly
holhchifammo'na' first name [holhchifo ammo'na+']
holhchifo, (CC, HS) olhchifo name (IIp)
holhchifo to be named (a certain name) (II;3) {v2. hochifo; ggr. holhchí'fo; hngr. holhchihífo}
holhchifo inno'chi' dog tags (identity necklace)
holhchifo intakaachi to put (someone's) name down, to vote for (I;III) [-SC] § Holhchifo antakaachitok. He voted for me, He put down my name.
holhchifo intakaachi, holhchifo takaachi to sign one's name (IIp , I) [±SC] § Saholhchifo takaashlitok, Saholhchifo intakaashlitok. I signed my name.
holhchifo ishtaalhi' last name, family name
holhchifo takaachi see holhchifo intakaachi (sign one's name)
holhfo to sprout, grow (3) [+CPR] [+PR] {hngr. hohólhfo; iyalfolfo'}
holhfochi to grow (a beard) (ER) [holhfo+chi]
<holhkopa> in holhkopa' {v2. honkopa}

holhkopa' something stolen or from an unknown source; bastard, illegitimate child [<holhkopa>+']

holhpa to burn, get burned, get a shock (II); to get burned by, burn oneself on (something hot) (II;3) {v2. holhpali; hngr. hohólhpa; hoshba} § Ithanali asonnak patha' yamma saholhpa'chikat. I know I'm going to burn myself on that pan.

holhpaháli hngr. of holhpali

holhpali to burn (something); to give a shock to (I;II) {v1. holhpa; hngr. holhpaháli}

holhpohóni hngr. of holhponi

holhponi to be cooked, boiled (II) {v2. hopooni; hngr. holhpohóni}

holhtáhha'pi hgr. of holhtapi

holhtánnaffo to be braided (of hair, etc.) (3) {v2. hotaanaffo}

holhtapi to be strung (of beads) (3) [+T] {v2. hotampi; hgr. holhtáhha'pi}

holhtihína hngr. of holhtina

holhtina to be counted; to be numbered, be marked with a number (3) {v2. hotihna; hngr. holhtihína}

holhtina hanna'li' tochchi'na 666 (type of patent medicine with these numbers on the bottle) [hanna'li+']

holhtina' number [holhtina+']

holhtina' ishchokoshkomo' checkers (WB)

holhtina-chaffaho ikbi to score: to make a run (in baseball), make a basket (in basketball), etc. (I) [holhtina' chaffa+ho]

holhtofa to come untied, be untied, get released (mainly sg. subj.) (II) {v2. hotoffi} [+PR] [+CPR] {hngr. holhtohófa; pl. hotohli}

holhtohófa hngr. of holhtofa

holhtohósi hngr. of holhtosi

holhtosi to be caught on a hook; to be seduced with a medicinal charm (II) {v2. hotósi; hngr. holhtohósi}

homi to be strong-tasting, bitter, hot and spicy (II) {ggr. hó'mi; hngr. hohómi; ngr. hómi; ygr. hóyyo'mi}

homichi to make bitter, make spicy (I;3) [homi+chi] {ngr. homínchi}

homínchi ngr. of homichi

homma to be red (II) [+CPR] {ggr. hó'mma; hngr. hohómma; ngr. hómma; ygr. hóyyo'mma}

homma losayyi to be maroon, dark red (II) § Homma salosayyi. I am dark red.

homma tokbakali to be pink, peach-colored (II)

homma' in homma' losa', hommahomma' [homma+']

homma' losa' black pepper [losa+']

homma' losa' api' type of plant that smells like black pepper

homma' losa' aalhto' see homma' losaalhto'

homma' losaalhto', homma' losa' aalhto' pepper shaker

hommachi to make red (I;II) [homma+chi]

hommahángbi hngr. of hommakbi

hommahomma' red pepper (the spice), chile, cayenne pepper [homma' homma+']

hommahomma' ani' pepper (fruit) [ani+']

hommahomma' champoli' sweet pepper, bell pepper [champoli+']

hommahomma' homi' hot pepper [homi+']

hommahomma' lakna' yellow pepper [lakna+']

hommahomma' okchamali' green pepper [okchamali+']

hommakbi to be red all over (II)

113

{hngr. hommahángbi}
hommayyi to be an odd shade of red, especially maroon or dark red (II)
homo to roof, put a roof on (I;3) [+OPR] {v1. holmo; ggr. hó'mo} § Ofinchokka' homo. He put a roof on the doghouse.
honkó'pa ggr. of honkopa
honkohómpa hngr. of honkopa
honkopa to steal, to kidnap (I;II); to cheat (in a game, for instance) (I) {v1. <holhkopa>; ggr. honkó'pa; hngr. honkohómpa}
honkopa' thief
hónkso to pass gas, fart, break wind, flatulate (I) {hngr. hohónkso; neg. ikhokso}
hopaháyi hngr. of hopayi
hopákki'chi ggr. of hopaakichi
hopánki ngr. of hopaaki
hopayi to concentrate on something (perhaps so hard that one appears to be inattentive to what is going on around one) (I) {hngr. hopaháyi; ihopayi: to tell (someone's) fortune; hopaaki}
hopayi' fortune-teller, gypsy, prophet [hopayi+']
hopáyya'ki ygr. of hopaaki
hopaaki to be long ago, far away (3) {ggr. hóppa'ki; ngr. hopánki; ygr. hopáyya'ki; hopayi}
hopaaki áyya'shahmat…, hopaaki pílla áyya'shakaash…, hopaaki pílla áyya'shahmat aachihmat…, hopaaki píllakaash…, hopaaki píllakaash áyya'shahmat aachihmat… once upon a time… [pilla(+kaash) ayya'sha+hmat aachi+hmat]
hopaakichi to go far away (I) [hopaaki+chi] {ggr. hopákki'chi; ihopaakachi: to go far from}
hopaakishpisa' telescope, binoculars [hopaaki isht pisa+']

hopó'ni ggr. of hopooni
hopoba to be hungry, to starve (II) [+PR] [+CPR] {ggr. hóppo'ba: to crave for food; hgr. hopóhho'ba; hngr. hopohómba; ngr. hopómba; ygr. hopóyyo'ba}
hopobat illi to starve to death (II) [hopoba+t] § Hopobat sallitok. I starved to death.
hopóhho'ba hgr. of hopoba
hopohómba hngr. of hopoba
hopohǫ́ni hngr. of hopooni
hopohǫ́o hngr. of hopoo
hopómba ngr. of hopoba
hopóyyo'ba ygr. of hopoba
hopóyyo'ha, hopóyyo'wa ygr. of hopoo
hopoo, (MC, MS) hopoowa, (ER, CM) hopooya to be jealous, suspicious (I); to be jealous of, suspicious of, to suspect (I;II) [-OPR] {ggr. hóppo'wa; hngr. hopohǫ́a; ygr. hopóyyo'ha, hopóyyo'wa; hapompoyo}
hopoobachi to starve (someone) (I;II) [hopoba+chi]
hopoobachit abi to starve (someone) to death (I;II) [hopoobachi+t] § Hopoobachit sabitok. She's starving me to death.
hopoochi to make ˚ jealous of ˚ (I;II;3) [-SC] [hopoo+chi]
hopooni to cook (I;II) {v1. holhponi; ggr. hóppo'ni, hopó'ni; hngr. hopohǫ́ni}
hopoonichi to make ˚ cook ˚ (I;II;3) [hopooni+chi]
hóppa'ki ggr. of hopaaki
hoppi, (EP) hohpi to bury (I;II) {v1. holloppi; hngr. hohómpi}
hóppo'wa ggr. of hopoo
hóppo'ba to crave for food—ggr. of hopoba
hóppo'ni ggr. of hopooni
hosi, (MJ) hossi to pound (corn or

other dried material) in a wooden
mortar (I;II) {v2. hollosi; hngr.
hohǫ́si}
hosiino bumblebee, (CC) hornet
hoski cattail (WB)
hosǫlo (AB, CC), (JC, MJ) hasǫlo
leech (AB, CC, MJ), snail (CC, JC)
hosha to have sexual intercourse
with, to mate with (I;II) (somewhat
vulgar expression, not usually used
by women) {hoshowa}
hoshba to be scorched (3) [+PR] {v2.
hoshbali; holhpa}
hoshbahą́li hngr. of hoshbali
hoshbali to scorch (something),
overcook (I;3) {v1. hoshba; hngr.
hoshbahą́li}
hoshinko to be chapped (3) [+CPR]
[-PR]; to have chapping (II) [-CPR]
[-PR] {ggr. hóshshị'ko; ngr.
hoshínko; ygr. hoshíyyị'ko}
hoshinkochi to make itchy, irritate
(someone's) skin (3;II)
[hoshinko+chi] § Nạachaat
sahoshinkochitok. The quilt makes
me feel itchy.
hoshíyyị'ko ygr. of hoshinko
hoshohǫ́wa hngr. of hoshowa
hoshollak bran, hulls of grain, small
ears of corn (used for feed)
{hoshollo'}
hoshollo' in ishkin hoshollo', paska
hoshollo', tanchi' hoshollo'
{hoshollak}
hoshonnachi to have a boil, bite,
rash, pimple (II) {hngr.
hoshonnahánchi; ygr.
hoshonnáyya'chi}
hoshonnachi' (TJ), (LF) hoshonnachi'
homma' measles [hoshonnachi+'
(homma+')]
hoshonnahánchi hngr. of
hoshonnachi
hoshonnáyya'chi ygr. of

hoshonnachi
hoshonti to be a cloud; to be cloudy
(of a place); to be obscured by clouds
(of the sun, for instance) (3) {ggr.
hóshshǫ'ti: to be hazy, a little
cloudy; ygr. hoshóyyǫ'ti;
hoshottika}
hoshonti cloud (usually cln.)
hoshontichi to be hazy (of the sky,
weather, a place) (3) [hoshonti+chi]
hoshontikachi to make an arbor,
shade (I) ; to make an arbor, shade
(in a location) (I;3) [hoshottika+chi]
{ịhoshontikachi: to make an arbor
or shade for; ǫhoshontikachi: to cast
shade on}
hoshontikachi', (ER, TP) hoshontika,
(OC) shontik shadow (IIp)
[hoshontikachi+']
hoshottika to be shady (3) {ngr.
hoshottínka; hoshonti}
hoshottika' porch, balcony (even
without a roof); shed, lean-to;
awning; roofed outdoor gathering
place [hoshottika+']
hoshottika' hattak aa-asha' shelter
hoshottika' ihoo aa-asha' women's
shelter (for battered women, for
instance)
hoshottikachi to put up a shade (I)
[hoshottika+chi]
hoshottikịhiyohli' porch poles
[hoshottika' im+hiyohli+']
hoshottínka ngr. of hoshottika
hoshowa to urinate (I) {ggr.
hóshsho'wa; hngr. hoshohǫ́wa; ngr.
hoshǫ́wa; hosha}
hoshóyyǫ'ti ygr. of hoshonti
hoshǫ́wa ngr. of hoshowa
hóshshị'ko ggr. of hoshinko
hóshsho'wa ggr. of hoshowa
hóshshǫ'ti ggr. of hoshonti
hotahámpi hngr. of hotampi
hotampi to string (beads) (I;3) {v1.

holhtapi; ggr. hótta'pi; hngr. hotahámpi}

hotaaná'ffo ggr. of hotaanaffo

hotaanaffo to braid (I;3) {vl. holhtánnaffo; ggr. hotaaná'ffo; hngr. hotaanaháffo; ihotaanaffo: to braid (someone's hair)}

hotaanaháffo hngr. of hotaanaffo

hotí'hna ggr. of hotihna

hotihína hngr. of hotihna

hotihna to count (I;II); to figure, do math (I) {vl. holhtina; ggr. hotí'hna; hngr. hotihína; ngr. hotíhna}

hotihnachi to make ° count ° (I;II;3) [hotihna+chi]

hotíhna ngr. of hotihna

hotoffi to untie (sg. obj.) (I;II) {vl. holhtofa; ggr. hóttoffi; hngr. hotohóffi; ngr. hotóffi; pl. obj. hotohchi}

hotohchi to untie (pl. obj.) (I;3) [hotohli+chi] {sg. obj. hotoffi}

hotohli to be untied (pl. subj.) (3) [+PR] {sg. holhtofa; ngr. hotóhli; pl. obj. hotohchi} § Sholoshat chihotohli. Your shoes are untied.

hotohónti hngr. of hotonti

hotohóffi hngr. of hotoffi

hotohólhko hngr. of hotolhko

hotolakna to be dirty, dingy, yellowed; to be yellowish, "flesh" color, tan (3) [+CPR] [-PR] [hottok lakna ?]

hotolhkilli', hotolhko illi' whooping cough [hotolhko illi+']

hotolhkilli' í'shi to have whooping cough (I)

hotolhko, (CC, MC, ER, TP) hotilhko to cough (II / I) [+PR] [+CPR]; to cough up (I;3) {ggr. hóttolhko; hngr. hotohólhko; ygr. hotóyyo'lhko} § Issish hotolhkoli. I coughed up blood.

hotolhkochi to make cough (I;II) [hotolhko+chi]

hotolhkottish, (AB) hotilhkottish cough medicine [hotolhko ittish]

hotonti frost; to be frost; to have frost (of a place) (3) {ggr. hótto'ti; hngr. hotohónti; ngr. hotónti}

hotóyyo'lhko ygr. of hotolhko

hotóffi ngr. of hotoffi

hotosi to catch on a hook; to seduce, win the affection of (especially, by the use of medicine); (HS) to catch with a net (I;II) {vl. holhtosi}

hotosichi to cause ° to catch ° on a hook, cause ° to seduce ° (I;II;3) [hotosi+chi]

hótta'pi ggr. of hotampi

hottó'pa ggr. of hottopa

hóttoffi ggr. of hotoffi

hottóhho'pa to hurt all the time— hgr. of hottopa

hottohómpa hngr. of hottopa

hottok ashes: especially, unsifted ashes

hottok aalhto' ashtray

hottok hoyya' another name for hottok okchi' [hoyya+']

hottok lakna' sulphur

hottok okchi' water strained through blackjack oak ashes—used as a flavoring for hominy (also called hottok hoyya')

hottok poshi' ashes: especially, sifted ashes

hóttolhko ggr. of hotolhko

hottómpa to have one's feelings hurt—ngr. of hottopa

hottómpakat aalhlhi to be really hurt (II , —) (see hottopa) [hottómpa+kat] § Sattompakat aalhlhi. I was really hurt.

hottopa, (TP) ittopa to hurt, have a pain; to be hurt (II) (works like <ittopa> after any II prefix) [+PR]

[+CPR] {ggr. hottó'pa; hgr. hottóhho'pa; hngr. hottohómpa; ngr. hottómpa: to have one's feelings hurt; ygr. hottóyyo'pa} § Sattopa. It hurts me; I hurt. | Chittopata? Are you hurt?
hottopachi, (TP) ittopachi to hurt (someone) (I;II) (<ittopachi> after any II prefix) [hottopa+chi] {ngr. hottopánchi: to break (someone's) heart} § Sattopashtok. He hurt me.
hottopakmat nokhammi'chi to feel labor pains (II = subj., II = subj.) (ho- is lost after any II prefix—see hottopa) [hottopa+kmat] Chittopakmat chinokhammi'cha'chi. You'll feel the pain of labor.
hottopánchi to break (someone's) heart—ngr. of hottopachi
hottopánchikat aalhlhi to really break (someone's) heart (I;II , —) (ho- is lost after any II prefix—see hottopa) [hottopánchi+kat] § Issattopanchikat aalhlhitokoot issabokkaatok. You broke my heart and beat me up.
hottóyyo'pa ygr. of hottopa
hottó'ti ggr. of hotonti
howahása hngr. of howasa
howasa, (FA) wasa to chew (I;II) {ggr. hówwa'sa; hngr. howahása} § Howastok. He chewed it.
howasachi to make ° chew ° (I;II;3) [howasa+chi]
howihínta hngr. of howita
howínta ngr. of howita
howita, (WB also) howiita to vomit (II / I) [+PR] [-CPR]; to vomit (something), vomit up (I;II) {ggr. hówwi'ta; hngr. howihínta; ngr. howínta}
howitachi to make ° vomit ° (I;II;3) [howita+chi] {hngr. howitahánchi}

howitahánchi hngr. of howitachi
hówwa'sa ggr. of howasa
hówwi'ta ggr. of howita
hoyá'no, hoyá'hno ggr. of hoyahno
hoyahno to sweat (II) [-PR] [-CPR] {ggr. hoyá'no, hoyá'hno; hngr. hoyaháno; yanha}
hoyo to look for, look up, hunt (unsuccessfully) (I;II) (<hoyyo> when used with an N prefix or conj. suffix) {ggr. hó'yo; hngr. hohóyo; prt. hoyot, hoot; neg. ikhoyyo}
hoyo'kni', (CC, CP, MC, HS, JJ) hoyokni', (ML, TP) hoyyokni', (MJ, AW) hoyokni' frog, toadfrog
hoyo'knishto' big toadfrog, (LF) bullfrog [hoyo'kni' ishto+']
hoyopa to be mean, vicious (of a dog, for instance) (3)
hoyot, hoot prt. of hoyo
hoyot aya to hunt, go look for (I;II) {hoot aya}
hoyya to drip, leak out, strain through (3); (CC) to sprinkle [-CPR] [-PR] {ggr. hó'yya; hngr. hohóyya}
hoyyachi to make drip, to strain (something): especially, to hang up (a jelly bag or bag of wet blackjack oak ashes) and let the water drip out (for instance, to make hottok okchi') (I;3) [hoyya+chi]
<hoyyo> see hoyo
hóyyo'lo to have (footwear) on, wear (footwear)—ygr. of holo § Sholosh chaaha'o hoyyo'lo. He's wearing boots.
hóyyo'mma ygr. of homma
hóyyo'mi ygr. of homi
hoo yes (old word) (Ct) {<oo>}
<hookay> in chokmahookay, yakookay [from Choctaw hookay "indeed"]
hoomi see ho'mi
hoot see hoyot

117

hoot aya

hoot aya to hunt, go look for (I;3)
{hoyot aya}
hólba ngr. of holba {ittihólba}
hómi ngr. of homi
hómma ngr. of homma
hosa to shoot at (someone); to fire (a

gun), to shoot (marbles) (I;II) {hngr.
hohósa; ngr. hósa} § Ikho'sokitok.
She didn't shoot at him.
hósa ngr. of hosa
hosachi to cause ˚ to shoot at ˚ (I;II;3)
[hosa+chi]

i

í'lli ggr. of illi
í'ma ggr. of ima
í'mmi ggr. of immi
í'ssa ggr. of issa
í'sso ggr. of isso
í'shko ggr. of ishko
í'shto ggr. of ishto
iabisọwa', iyyaabisọwa', (AB)
iyyaabiyasawa', (MJ) iyyiibisama',
(MC) ibiisawa', (CC, TJ, CM)
biisawa', (CP) iibiisawa', (HS)
iyyibiisọwa' socks, stockings (IIIp)
[iyyi' (aa+)<abiha> sawa+'] {ilbak
aabihli'}
iabisọwa' ishtalakchi' garter
iabisọwa' ishyo'kli' garter [isht
yokli+']
iabisọwa' loposhki' silk socks, silk
stockings [loposhki+']
ibalhto to be in with (3;3) [ibaa+alhto]
{ggr. íbbalhto; ngr. ibálhto} § Lokfaat
oka' ibalhto. There's still dirt in
(with) the water.
ibayyi niece, nephew (IIp)
ibayyihoo' niece (IIp) [ibayyi ihoo+']
ibaa-abi to kill along with (a co-
subj.˚), to help (someone˚) butcher
(I;II;3) [ibaa+abi]
ibaa-abika to be sick along with (I;II)
[ibaa+abika]
ibaa-achifa to wash along with (a co-
subj.˚) (I;II;3) [ibaa+achifa]
ibaa-afama to meet (someone) along

with (a co-subj.˚) (I;II;3)
[ibaa+afama]
ibaa-ahánta hngr. of ibaa-ánta
ibaa-akkowa to go down with,
descend with (I;II) [ibaa+akkowa]
ibaa-akkowachi to help ˚ put down,
put down along with (a co-subj.˚)
(I;II;3) [ibaa+akkowachi]
ibaa-ala to arrive along with (I;II)
[ibaa+ala]
ibaa-amo to mow along with (a co-
subj.˚) (I;II;3) [ibaa+amo]
ibaa-ani to put in along with (a co-
subj.˚) (I;II;3) [ibaa+ani] {ibaani}
ibaa-anokfilli to think with (I;II)
[ibaa+anokfilli] § Issabaa-
anokfilla'shki! You should think
(about it) with me!
ibaa-anompoli to talk with, have a
conversation with (I;II)
[ibaa+anompoli]
ibaa-ánta to live with, be with (I;II)—
ngr. of ibaa-atta [ibaa+anta] {hngr.
ibaa-ahánta; dl. ibaa-áshwa; pl. ibaa-
áyya'sha}
ibaa-antachichi to leave behind with
(a co-obj. or subj.˚) (I;II;3)
[ibaa+antachichi] {ngr. ibaa-
antachínchi}
ibaa-antachínchi ngr. of ibaa-
antachichi
ibaa-apa to eat along with (a co-
subj.˚) (I;II;3) [ibaa+apa]

118

ibaa-apila to help with (a co-subj.˹)
(I;II;3) [ibaa+apila]
ibaa-apiisachi to watch with (a co-
subj.˹), help ˮ watch (I;II;3)
[ibaa+apiisachi]
ibaa-atta to live with, room with (sg.
subj.) (I;II) [ibaa+atta] {ngr. ibaa-ánta}
ibaa-aya to go with; to go out (on a
date) with (I;II) [ibaa+aya]
ibaa-ayowa to help ˮ pick, pick with
(a co-subj.˹) (I;II;3) [ibaa+ayowa]
ibaa-áyya'sha to be (located) with (pl.
subj.) (I;II) [ibaa+ayya'sha] {sg. ibaa-
ánta; dl. ibaa-áshwa} §
Hashpobaaáyya'sha. You guys are
with us.
ibaa-áshwa to be with (dl. subj.) (I;II)
[ibaa+ashwa] {sg. ibaa-ánta; pl. ibaa-
áyya'sha}
ibaabiniichi to make (sg. patient
obj.˹) sit with (a co-obj.˹); to help ˮ
make (sg. patient obj.) sit, make (sg.
patient obj.) sit with (a co-subj.˹)
(I;II;3) [ibaa+biniichi] {pl. patient obj.
ibaabinohchi}
ibaabinohchi to make (pl. patient
obj.) sit with ˮ, set (pl. patient obj.)
with (a co-obj.˹); to help ˮ make (pl.
patient obj.) sit, to make (pl. patient
obj.) sit with (a co-subj.˹) (I;II;3)
[ibaa+binohchi] {sg. patient obj.
ibaabiniichi}
ibaabo'li to beat up along with (a co-
subj.˹) (I;II;3) [ibaa+bo'li]
ibaabohli to put down along with (a
co-obj.˹), to help (a co- subj.˹) put
down (I;II;3) [ibaa+bohli]
ibaachaffa to go along with, do the
same as, be with; to be loyal to (I;II);
to go along with (a co-subj.˹)
regarding (I;II;3) [ibaa+chaffa] §
Reaganak pobaachaffa. He goes
along with us regarding Reagan. |
Hooibaachaffa. They go along with

it.
ibaachaffichi to send with (a co-obj.˹)
(I;II;3) [ibaa+chaffichi]
ibaachalhka to play cards for money
with (I;II) [ibaa+chalhka]
ibaachokoshkomo to play along with
(I;II) [ibaa+chokoshkomo]
ibaachokoshkomochi to make play
with (a co-obj.˹) (I;II;3); to help (a co-
subj.˹) make play (I;II;3)
[ibaa+chokoshkomo+chi]
ibaachompa to pay for with ˮ, go in
with ˮ on, buy with ˮ (I;II;3)
[ibaa+chompa]
ibaafama to be whipped along with
(I;II) [ibaa+fama]
ibaafammi to whip along with (a co-
subj. or obj.˹) (I;II;3) [ibaa+fammi]
ibaafokha to wear (the same clothes)
as, share (clothes) with (a co-subj.);
to join with (sg. subj.) (I;II)
[ibaa+fokha] {ngr. ibaafónkha; ygr.
ibaafóyyokha: to be with, be among}
ibaafokhi to put in (sg. obj.) along
with (a co-obj. or subj.˹) (I;II;3)
[+OPR] [ibaa+fokhi] {ngr.
ibaafónkhi} § Lynn iholissa yamma
ibaafokhitokchayntok, Lynna
holisso yamma
imimbaafokhitokchayntok. He put
Lynn's book in along with that one.
ibaafónkha ngr. of ibaafokha
ibaafónkhi ngr. of ibaafokhi
ibaafóyyokha to be among, be with—
ygr. of ibaafokha
ibaahabina to get, receive along with
(a co-subj.˹) (I;II;3) [ibaa+habina]
ibaahaklo to hear (inan. obj.) along
with (a co-subj.˹) (I;II;3) [ibaa+haklo]
{ngr. ibaahánglo: to hear (anim.
obj.) with (a co-subj.)}
ibaahaksi to get drunk with, be as
crazy as (I;II) [ibaa+haksi]
ibaahalalli to pull along with (a co-

119

subj.') (I;II;3) [ibaa+halalli]

ibaahalili to touch along with (a co-subj.') (I;II;3) [ibaa+halili]

ibaahánglo to hear (anim. obj.) along with (a co-subj.')—ngr. of ibaahaklo

ibaahí'li to stand with, stick up for (dl. subj.) (I;II) [ibaa+hi'li] {sg. ibaahíkki'ya; pl. ibaahiyohmáa}

ibaahíkki'ya to stand with, stick up for (sg. subj.) (I;II) [ibaa+hikki'ya] {dl. ibaahí'li; pl. ibaahiyohmáa}

ibaahilha to dance with (I;II) [ibaa+hilha]

ibaahilhachi to make dance with (a co-obj.'); to help ° make dance, make dance with (a co-subj.') (I;II;3) [ibaa+hilhachi]

ibaahiyohmáa to stand with, stick up for (pl. subj.) (II = obj., I) [ibaa+hiyohmaa < ibaa+(hiyoht *maa)] {sg. ibaahíkki'ya; dl. ibaahí'li} § Sabaahiyoht hashmáa? Are you going to stand with me?

ibaahofantichi to raise, rear with (a co-obj. or subj.') (I;II;3) [ibaa+hofantichi]

ibaaholisso to have one's name recorded with, to be registered with (I;II) [ibaa+holisso]

ibaaholhtina to join with, be numbered with (a group or pl. obj.) (I;II) [ibaa+holhtina]

ibaahoppi to bury along with (a co-obj. or subj.'): especially, to bury (a body) on top of (another) in the same grave (I;II;3) [ibaa+hoppi]

ibaahotihna to help count, to count along with (a co-subj. or obj.') (I;II;3) [ibaa+hotihna]

ibaahottopa to get hurt along with (I;II) [ibaa+hottopa]

ibaahowasa to chew along with (a co-subj.') (I;II;3) [ibaa+howasa]

ibaahoyo to look for along with (a co-subj.') (I;II;3) [ibaa+hoyo]

ibaahosa to shoot along with (a co-subj.'), help ° shoot (I;II;3) [ibaa+hosa]

ibaaikbi to make along with (a co-subj.') (I;II;3) [ibaa+ikbi]

ibaailli to die along with (I;II) [ibaa+illi]

ibaaima to give, pass out (food, for example) along with (a co-subj.') (I;II;3) [ibaa+ima]

ibaaimilhlha to be scared with (I;II) [ibaa+imilhlha]

ibaaimmi to own with ° (I;II;3) [ibaa+immi]

ibaaimpalammi to go through hardship with (I;II) [ibaa+impalammi]

ibaaimpalammichi to treat badly along with (a co-subj. or obj.') (I;II;3) [ibaa+impalammichi]

ibaainchompa to buy for with ° (I;II;3;3) [ibaa+inchompa] § Lynna T.V. chibaainchompalitok. I bought Lynn a T.V. with you.

ibaainkatabli to trap along with (a co-subj. or obj.') (I;II;3) [ibaa+inkatabli]

ibaainkatapa to be trapped along with (I;II) [ibaa+inkatapa]

ibaaintakho'bi to be lazy with (I;II) [ibaa+intakho'bi]

ibaaintaloowa to sing for along with (a co-subj.') (I;II;3) [ibaa+intaloowa]

ibaaipita to feed along with (a co-subj.'), help ° feed (I;II;3) [ibaa+ipita]

ibaaisso to hit along with (a co-subj.') (I;II;3) [ibaa+isso]

ibaaishi to take along with (a co-subj.') (I;II;3) [ibaa+ishi]

ibaaithána to know with (a co-subj.') (I;II;3) [ibaa+ithana]

ibaaittí'wa see ibaatí'wa

ibaaittola to fall down with (on

purpose) (I;II) [ibaa+ittola]
<ibaakaha> in ibaakahat máa
[ibaa+kaha] {v2. ibaakahli; ygr.
ibaakáyya'ha}
ibaakahat máa to lie with (tpl. subj.)
(II = obj. , I) [<ibaakaha>+t] {sg.
ibaatí'wa; dl. ibaakáyya'ha} §
Sabaakahat hashmaa. You guys are
lying down with me.
ibaakahli to lay down (pl. obj.) with
(a co-subj. or obj.') (I;II;3)
[ibaa+kahli] {v1. <ibaakaha>}
ibaakaniya to go, run away, take off
with (I;II) [ibaa+kaniya]
ibaakáyya'ha to lie with (dl. subj.)
(I;II)—ygr. of <ibaakaha>
[ibaa+kayya'ha] {sg. ibaatí'wa; tpl.
ibaakahat máa}
ibaakisili to bite along with (a co-
subj.') (I;II;3) [ibaa+kisili]
ibaakolli to dig along with (a co-
subj.') (I;II;3); to dig around (a tree,
house, etc.) (I;3) [ibaa+kolli]
ibaalohmi to hide (something) along
with (a co-obj. or subj.') (I;II;3)
[ibaa+lohmi]
ibaamalli to jump along with (I;II)
[ibaa+malli]
ibaamallichi to make jump along
with (a co-obj. or subj.') (I;II;3)
[ibaa+malli+chi]
ibaanalli to swallow (pl. patient)
along with (a co-subj.') (I;II;3)
[ibaa+nalli]
ibaanalha to be shot along with (I;II)
[ibaa+nalha]
ibaanalhlhi to shoot along with (a co-
subj.') (I;II;3) [ibaa+nalhlhi]
ibaanannabli to swallow along with
(a co-subj.') (I;II;3) [ibaa+nannabli]
ibaani to add some more to, put
some more in (I;3;3) [ibaa+ani ?]
{prt. ibaant; ibaa-ani; ittibaani} §
Ashiila hapi ibaanilitok. I put more

salt in the soup.
ibaanokhánglo to be sad with,
sympathize with (I;II)
[ibaa+nokhanglo]
ibaanosi to sleep with (literal and
euphemistic) (I;II) [ibaa+nosi]
ibaanosichi to put to sleep with (a co-
subj. or obj.') (I;II;3) [ibaa+nosi+chi]
ibaanowa to walk along with; to go
out (on a date) with; to be dating, be
going with; to have an affair with,
commit adultery with (I;II)
[ibaa+nowa]
ibaanowachi to walk (a dog, for
instance) along with (a co-obj. or
subj.') (I;II;3) [ibaa+nowachi]
ibaant prt. of ibaani
ibaant hotihna to add on, count in
with (I;3)
ibaaokaamalli to jump into with °
(I;II;3) [ibaa+okaamalli]
ibaaona to get there along with (I;II);
to arrive at (there) along with °
(I;II;3) [ibaa+ona] § Chinchokka'
Lynn ibaaonalitok. I got to your
house with Lynn.
ibaaowwatta to hunt with (I;II)
[ibaa+owwatta]
ibaapassáa to spank along with (a co-
subj.'), help ° spank (I;II;3)
[ibaa+passaa]
ibaapilachi to send with (a co-subj. or
obj.') (I;II;3) [ibaa+pilachi]
ibaapishi to suck, nurse with (I;II)
[ibaa+pishi] {ittibaapishi}
ibaapísa to be a witness for (I;II); to
see with (a co-subj.') (I;II;3)
[ibaa+pisa]
ibaaponta to borrow with (a co-
subj.') (I;II;3); to co-sign with (I;II)
[ibaa+ponta]
ibaashooli to carry with, hug with (a
co-subj.') (I;II;3) [ibaa+shooli]
ibaatahángla hngr. of <ibaatakla>,

<ibaatakla>

ibaatángla
<ibaatakla> {hngr. ibaatahángla; ngr.
ibaatángla; ygr. ibaatáyyakla}
ibaatalaali to set (one's possession)
next to that of; to set (something) up
with (a co-subj. ") (I;II;3)
[ibaa+talaali] § Ammi'
chibaatalaalili. I put mine next to
yours, I set up mine with you.
ibaataloowa to sing with (I;II)
[ibaa+taloowa]
ibaataloowachi to make sing with (a
co-subj. or obj. ") (I;II;3)
[ibaa+taloowachi]
ibaatángla to go, be with, among
(I;II)—ngr. of <ibaatakla> {hngr.
ibaatahángla; ygr. ibaatáyyakla,
ibaatáyyangla}
ibaatáyyakla ygr. of <ibaatakla>,
ibaatángla
ibaatáyyangla ygr. of ibaatángla
{ibaatáyyakla}
ibaatí'wa, ibaaittí'wa to lie with, be
located (lying) with; to sleep with
(euphemistic) (sg. subj.) (I;II)
[ibaa+ti'wa/itti'wa] {dl.
ibaakáyya'ha; tpl. ibaakahat máa} §
Foloshat ishtakafachi' ibaati'wa.
The spoon is (lying) with the cup.
ibaatikahbi to be tired with (I;II)
[ibaa+tikahbi]
ibaatikahbichi to wear out, make
tired along with (a co-subj. ") (I;II;3)
[ibaa+tikahbichi]
ibaatobbi to pay for (something) with
(a co-subj. "), to go in together with
(a co-subj. ") on (I;II;3) [ibaa+atobbi]
ibaatoksali to work along with (at a
job) (I;II) [ibaa+toksali]
ibaatoksalichi to make work with (a
co-obj. ") (I;II;3) [ibaa+toksalichi]
ibaawakiili to fly (something) along
with (a co-subj. or obj. ") (I;II;3)
[ibaa+wakiili]

ibaawiichi in ishtibaawiichi
ibaayahmi to do (along) with (a co-
subj.) (I;II) [+HM], <ibaayah>
[ibaa+yahmi]
ibaayakohli to stick one's finger in (a
little hole in) (I;3) {hngr.
ibaayakohóli} § Aboohapootakaka'
ibaayakohlili. I stick my finger in (a
hole in) the wall.
ibaayakohóli hngr. of ibaayakohli
ibaayamihchi to do (along) with (I;II)
[ibaa+yamihchi]
ibaayáa to be with, go with (I;II)
[ibaa+aa] § Iksabaayaokitok. He
didn't go with me.
<ibaayah> [HM] of ibaayahmi
ibaayimmi to believe with, be of the
same belief as (I;II) [ibaa+yimmi]
ibaayokachi to help catch (pl. patient)
along with (a co-subj. ") (I;II;3)
[ibaa+yokachi] {sg. patient ibaayokli}
ibaayokli to help catch (sg. patient)
along with (a co-subj. ") (I;II;3)
[ibaa+yokli] {pl. patient ibaayokachi}
ibaayopi to swim with (a co-subj. ") in
(I;II;3) [ibaa+yopi] § Oka'
ishibaayopitok. You swam with
him (in the water).
ibaayopichi to bathe (along) with (a
co-obj. or subj. ") (I;II;3)
[ibaa+yopichi, ibaayopi+chi]
ibálhto ngr. of ibalhto
íbbalhto ggr. of ibalhto
<ibi> in ittibi, ilibi {abi}
ibichchala', ibihchala', (CC)
ibishchala' nose, beak, bill (of a hat)
(IIp) {short form: bichchala'}
ibichchala' alhiipi'ya' surgical mask
ibichchala' cholok nostril (IIp) §
sabichchala' cholok: my nostril
ibichchala' ibayakohli to pick one's
nose (IIp , I)
ibichchala' inkooli to give (someone)
a bloody nose (IIp = obj. , I;III)

[im+(ibichchala' kooli)> ibichchala'
*inkooli]
ibichchala' issish lhatapa,
ibichchala'at issish lhatapa to have
a nosebleed (IIp = subj.) §
Sabichchala'at issish lhata'pacha
sashshoka' achifalitok. I had a
nosebleed and then washed my face.
ibichchala' kooli to give (someone) a
bloody nose (IIp = obj. , I) §
Sabichchala' koolihookya
ikkobaffokitok. He gave me a
bloody nose but he didn't break it.
ibilhkan snot; growth on a turkey's
beak (IIp) § waak ibilhkan cooked
okra (a joke)
ibilhkanat lhatapa to have a runny
nose (IIp = subj.) [ibilhkan+at] §
Sabilhkanat lhatapakat ithạnali. I
know my nose is running.
ibish projection from a roundish
obj.: especially the neck of a gourd
or squash or a nipple on a bottle (3p)
ibishshá'no ggr. of ibishshano
ibishshachi' bangs (on hair) (IIp)
ibishshahạ́no hngr. of ibishshano
ibishsháhha'no hgr. of ibishshano
ibishshano to have a cold, have the
flu (II) [+PR: imimbishshano]
[+CPR] {ggr. ibishshá'no; hgr.
ibishsháhha'no; hngr.
ibishshahạ́no; ngr. ibishshạ́no; ygr.
ibishsháyya'no} § Sabishshano. I
have a cold. | Chipotaat
amimbishshano. My child has a
cold.
ibishsháyya'no ygr. of ibishshano
ibishshạ́no ngr. of ibishshano
ibiitop end (of a hair, rope) (3p)
{short form: biitop}
ichchohóngwa hngr. of ichchokwa
ichchokwa to be cold, chilled (of
people) (II) [+PR] [+CPR] {v2.
ichchokwali; hngr. ichchohóngwa;

ngr. ichchóngwa; ygr.
ichchóyyokwa}
ichchokwali to give a chill to (I;II)
{v1. ichchokwa}
ichchóngwa ngr. of ichchokwa
ichchóyyokwa ygr. of ichchokwa
<ichonkash> in imichonkash
ihayya' daughter-in-law; (HS) sister-
in-law (IIp) (Ct?)
íhhishto hgr. of ishto
ihímpa hngr. of impa
ihíngbi hngr. of ikbi
ihịlli hngr. of illi
ihísso hngr. of isso
ihíshko hngr. of ishko
ihíshto hngr. of ishto
ihoo, (AW) yohoo woman, female
{<ihoo'>}
ihoo abaanompishtanompoli' lady
preacher
ihoo alhtakla' widow, (MJ) orphan
woman
ihoo hattak ikimiksho', (CC) ihoo
hattak imiksho' woman who has
never been married, (CC) widow
[ikimiksho+']
ihoo hattak ilahobbi' homosexual
woman, lesbian [ilahobbi+']
ihoo hattak imilli' widow [im+illi+']
ihoo hawi' prostitute
ihoo hawi' apiisachi' madam (in a
house of prostitution) [apiisachi+']
ihoo hawi' intoksali' pimp
[intoksali+']
ihoo hawi' ittanahli' pimp
[ittanahli+']
ihoo hawi' piichi' pimp
ihoo himitta' young woman, teenage
girl (older than ihoo himittachi')
[himitta+']
ihoo himittachi' young teenage girl,
12 to 14 years old [himittachi+']
ihoo holitto'pa' nun [holitto'pa+']
ihoo ibaanosit nǫwa to be

ihoo imambiika'

promiscuous (of a man), to sleep
around with women (I) [ibaanosi+t]
ihoo imambiika' menstrual period
(ER) [imambiika+']
ihoo imiabisọwa' stockings, panty
hose [im+iabisọwa']
ihoo imiabisọwa' loposhki' silk
stockings [loposhki+']
ihoo inchokkiksho' bag lady,
homeless woman [im+chokka'
iksho+']
ihoo intoba to live with, have a
relationship with (another man) (of
a homosexual man) (I;III) [im+toba]
ihoo iyaalhipa bonnet (WB)
[im+yaalhipa]
ihoo kashiiho', ihoo kashiiyo' old
woman
ihoo minko' lady president, lady
governor, queen
ihoo tabashi' widow, especially one
in ritual seclusion (according to an
old custom)
ihoo toklo' twin women [toklo+']
ihoo yoka' female prisoner [yoka+']
ihoo' in alikchihoo', hattak los-
ihoo', ibayyihoo', ipok ihoo'
[ihoo+']
ihooat imáyya'sha to have a wife, be
married (of a man) (III) [ihoo+at] §
Ihooat amayya'sha. I'm married, I
have a wife. | Charlesat ihooat
imayya'sha ki'yo. Charles isn't
married.
ihooat ootimokfaha to have a
woman over, have a woman come
to one's house (III) [ihoo+at] §
Ihooat ootamokfaha. I had a
woman over.
<ihooba> in ittihooba {ahooba}
ikacha'ho to be lonesome, be
homesick (N+II)—neg. of achaaha
{ishtikacha'ho}
ikahooba'lo to put down, think

poorly of (IN;II) [+OPR]
{ikimahooba'lo: not to like}
ikalhchibo'so to be just a while (—) §
Iki'poka'chi ikalhchibo'sokạ. He
won't eat for a little while.
ikalhchibo'so, ikalhchibo'sohọ for a
while, not for long
[ikalhchibo'so+họ] § Ikalhchibo'so
anompolitok. He talked for a while.
ikalhpi'so to be wrong (IN / N+II)—
neg. of alhpi'sa § Akalhpi'sokitok,
iksalhpi'sokitok. I was wrong.
ikammo neg. of amo
ikanhi'cho neg. of anhínchi
ikayobba'lo to mess up, deface (IN; 3);
to talk bad about (IN;II) {ayóbba'li
ki'yo}
ikayoppa'cho neg. of ayoppánchi
ikayyo neg. of aya
ikayyo'bo to be bad, evil, obscene
(3N) [+PR] [+CPR]—neg. of ayyoba
ikaaimọ́no in ishtikaaimọ́no
ikbanno neg. of banna
ikbi to make, create (I;II); to make ˙
into (I;II;3) {ggr. íkbi; hngr. ihíngbi;
ngr. íngbi} § Paska sakbitok. She
made me into bread. | Istokchank-
apa' pikkal ikbilitok. I made the
cucumbers into pickles.
îkbi ggr. of ikbi
ikbo neg. of abi
ikcha'ho to be short (N+II) [+CPR]
[-PR]—neg. of chaaha
ikchampo'lo to be tasteless, without
flavor (3N)—neg. of champoli
ikchisiyyo neg. of chisiya
ikfala'o to be short (N+II) [+CPR]
[+PR]—neg. of falaa
ikfo'ko in naafka ikfo'ko
ikhapompo'yo, ikhapompoyyo negs.
of hapompoyo
ikhapọwaklo, (TJ) ikhaponhaklo to
go deaf (IN)—neg. of hapọwaklo
{hapowánglo}

124

ikhofa'to neg. of hofanti
{chipotikhofa'to'}
ikhokso neg. of hónkso
ikholbo not to act like (IN;II)—neg.
of holba {ahooba} § Akchiholbo. I
don't act like you.
ikhoyyo neg. of hoyo, hoyya
<ikiksho> see iksho
ikiliyay'lo to hate oneself (IN)
[ili+ikyay'lo]
ikima'lo, ikimallo negs. of imalla
ikima'mo, ikimammo negs. of
imammo
ikima'no, ikimanno negs. of imanni
ikima'po, ikimappo negs. of imappa
ikimachonna'cho not to be able to
stand what happens to (IN;III)
ikimahooba'lo not to like (someone)
for what he does(3N; III)—[OPR] of
ikahooba'lo § Ahattakat
hopoonilika iksamahooba'lo. My
husband doesn't like my cooking,
My husband doesn't like me for my
cooking. | Paska iksamahooba'lo.
He doesn't like my bread.
ikimallo see ikima'lo
ikimalhpi'so to be sad (N+III) [-PR]
[-CPR]—neg. of imalhpi'sa
ikimambo see ikima'bo
ikimammo see ikima'mo
ikimanno see ikima'no
ikimappo see ikima'po
ikimayyo'bo [PR] of ikayyo'bo; in
ishtikimayyo'bo
ikima'bo, ikimambo negs. of imambi
ikimbaati'yo, ikimbaatiyyo negs of
imbaatiya
ikimiksho not to have (N+III;3-at /
(rare) N+III;3); not to have any
(N+III) [im+iksho] § Chipota
chikayoppa'chokmat
ikchimikshoka'shki. If you don't
like kids you shouldn't have any.
ikimitha'no neg. of imithana,

imithána
ikimo'no not to get enough of
(N+III;3-at) [im+iko'no] {ngr.
ikimóno; imona ki'yo} | Impa'at
iksamo'no. I didn't get enough
food, There wasn't enough food for
me.
ikimóno not to have gotten enough;
to have one's feelings hurt
(N+III)—ngr. of ikimo'no {imóna
ki'yo} § Iksamono. I didn't get
enough, My feelings were hurt.
ikímpo in ishtikímpo
ikinchokmo to feel bad (N+III)—neg.
of inchokma
ikinka'no neg. of <inkana>, inkána
ikinkanihmo neg. of inkahnihmi
{nannishtikinkanihmo}
ikitha'no neg. of ithana, ithána
ikittiyay'lo, iktiyay'lo to hate each
other (pl. subj.) (INR) [itti+ikyay'lo]
§ Hachiktiyay'lo. You all hate each
other.
ikifala'o [PR] of ikfala'o
ikihaklo not to listen to, to disobey
(IN;III)—neg. of ihaklo § Sashka
akihaklokitok. I disobeyed my
mother. | Iksahaklokimanko. He
was disobeying me.
ikihapowaklo to disobey (IN;III)—
neg. of ihapowánglo
ikiyay'lo [OPR] of ikyay'lo § Chipota
iksayay'lo. She hates my child.
ikkallo to be loose (of a tooth); to be
limber, not stiff (3N)—neg. of kallo
ikkanihmikya, kanihmikya no
matter what [ik+kanihmi+kya ?] §
Ikkanihmikya ayala'chi. No matter
what (happens), I'm going.
ikko drink (children's language) (LF)
[ishko]
ikkosti'no to be funny, to act funny
(N+II)—neg. of kostini §
Iksakosti'nokimanko. I was acting

iklanna

funny.

iklanna to be half, to be in the middle (3); to be half past (an hour— preceded by hashi' kanalli plus the number of the hour +cha) § Hashi' kannalli pokko'cha iklanna. It's ten-thirty. | Iklannakat Chikashsha poya. Half of us are Chickasaws.

iklanna' half-breed [iklanna+'] § Iklanna' saya. I'm a half-breed. | Chikashshiklanna': person who is half Chickasaw

iklanna'si to be (only, just) half (3) [iklanna+a'si]

iklawwi'cho to be behind (in a race, for example), to be soft (of music) (IN)—neg. of lawwi'chi

iklo neg. of ala {ngr. ínglo: (3)} § Inglo tanglana ootfalamala'chi. I'll go over there and back while she's not here.

Ikloon, Loon Chickasaw man's name

ikmo neg. of amo

iknakno to fail to act like a man, to be a sissy (male subj.) (N+II)—neg. of nakni

iknokchi'to to be wild, undisciplined (N+II)—neg. of nokchito § Iksanokchi'tokitok. I was wild.

iknokwayyo to be brave, unafraid (N+II) [ik+nokwaya+o] [-PR] [-CPR]—neg. of nokwaya

iko'no not enough (aux)—neg. of ona § Impalikat iko'no. I don't eat enough.

<ikoyyo> in shakchikoyyo'—neg. of <oyya>

ikpi'so to be blind (IN)—neg. of pisa

ikpo neg. of apa

Iksa' Christian

Iksa' ibaafokha to join a church, become a Christian (I)

Iksa' ilayyoka different religious

denominations

iksa' piichi' deacon § Iksa' piichi' saya. I'm a deacon.

iksá'chi ggr. of iksaachi

iksahánchi hngr. of iksaachi

iksala'mo in impa' iksala'mo—neg. of salami

iksánchi hngr. of iksaachi

iksaa to be made (3) [+T] {iksaachi}

iksaachi to make, fix; to develop (photographs) (I;3) [iksaa+chi] [+SC] [-OPR] {ggr. iksá'chi; hngr. iksahánchi; ngr. iksánchi}

ikshami'lo neg. of <shamila>, shamíhhi'la

iksho not to exist, not to be, not to be there, not to be here (N+II) (with a II or III prefix, this verb works as if it were <ikiksho>) [+PR] [+CPR] {ggr. íksho; ngr. ínksho; ikimiksho: not to have}—neg. of <asha> § Iksaksho. I don't exist, I'm not there. | Iksho. She's not here (said to a caller on the phone). | Ikchikshokittook. Long ago you didn't exist. | Ikpoksho. We're not there. | Ikchinksho tanglaka ishtayatok. She took him while you were gone.

íksho ggr. of iksho

ikshokat without (subj.) [iksho+kat] § Ashilaat hapi ikshokat ikchampo'lo. Soup without salt doesn't taste good.

ikshoppaya'lo neg. of shoppayali

ikshoppayyo neg. of shoppaya

iksho without (nonsubj.) [iksho+ho] § Ta'osso iksho aachompa' ayalitok. I went to the store without money. | Niha iksho paskalitok. I made bread without lard.

iktiholbo to clash, not match (of colors, clothes) (3N)—neg. of ittihólba

126

iktiyay'lo see ikittiyay'lo
iktoshpo to be slow (IN) [+CPR]
[-PR]—neg. of toshpa
ikyay'lo to hate (IN;II) [+OPR]
[ik+yayli+o]
ilabaanachi to help (someone) put (a
burden) on his shoulders (I;3;3)
[±SC] [ilabaanali+chi]
ilabaanali to shoulder (a burden),
carry (sg. obj.) on one's shoulders
(I;3) [ili+abaanali] {ggr. ilabánna'li;
pl. obj. shaali}
ilabánna'li ggr. of ilabanali
ilabiika'si bílli'ya to be sickly (ER)
[ili+abiika+a'si]
ilaboknohli to roll oneself up,
bundle up against the cold (I); to
wrap oneself up in (I;3)
[ili+aboknohli] {hngr. ilaboknohóli;
ngr. ilaboknóhli} § Naachi
ilaboknohlili. I wrap myself in the
quilt.
ilaboknohóli hngr. of ilaboknohli
ilaboknóhli ngr. of ilaboknohli
ilachaffa, ilachaffa'si to be the only
one, to be just one in number; to be
an only child (sg. subj.) (I)
[ili+a+chaffa]
ilachaffa bíyyi'ka to be scattered
around alone, not in groups (3)
ilachaffa'si see ilachaffa
ilachaahachi to try to get used to a
situation (I) [ili+achaahachi]
ilachokkobbichi to make (someone)
like oneself, make (someone) get
used to oneself (I;3)
[ili+achokkobbichi ?] §
Ilachokkobbichilitok. I got him used
to me, I got him to like me.
ilafoyopa to suck in, inhale (I)
[ili+a+foyopa] {ilifoyopa}
ilahobbi to pretend, act like, become
(I;3) [+/- E]; to be proud, pretentious,
smart alecky (I) [ili+<ahobbi>] {ygr.

ilahóyyo'bi} § Taloowa
ishilahobbitok, Ishtaloowa
ishilahobbitok. You pretend to sing.
| Ishno' ilahobbilitok. I acted like
you.
ilaholhchifochi to name oneself (a
certain name), take the name; to
give (someone) one's own (first or
last) name (I;3) [ili+aholhchifochi] §
Chiholhchifoako
ilaholhchifoshlitok. I changed my
name to yours, I took your name.
ilahóyyo'bi ygr. of ilahobbi
ilahoochifochi to name (someone)
after oneself (I;3) [ili+ahochifochi]
ilakkaalinchi see ilakkaalincho'si
ilakkaalíncho'si, ilakkaalínchi to
humble oneself (I) {<akali>,
akalo'si} § Ilakkaalincho'slitok,
ilakkaalishlitok, ilakkaalishlo'stok.
I humbled myself.
ilalawachi to grow out at the sides (of
a plant) (3) [ili+alawachi]
ilamákka'li to be never satisfied (3)
[ili+amakka'li] {ishtilamákka'li}
ilamóshsho'li to work hard, do one's
best (I) [ili+amoshsho'li]
ilanakshooli to singe or burn off
one's hair (deliberately) (I)
[ili+anakshooli]
ilanoli to confess, tell on oneself (I)
[ili+anoli]
ilapakfolli to roll oneself up in (I;3)
[ili+apakfolli] {ygr. ilapakfóyyo'lli:
to be rolled up in}
ilapakfóyyo'lli to be rolled up in—
ygr. of ilapakfolli
ilapila to help oneself (I) [ili+apila]
ilapilachi to take on as a helper, to
have (someone) help oneself (I;3)
[ilapila+chi] § Lynna ilapilashla'chi.
I'm going to have Lynn to help me.
ilapofachi to blow on one's hands to
cool or warm them (I) [ili+apofachi]

127

ilapóla to be pigheaded, stubborn (I) [-PR] [-CPR] § Ilapólacha ikayyokitok. He was stubborn and didn't go.

ilashiichi to lace oneself up, fasten one's girdle (I) [±SC] [ili+ashiichi]

ilatahpoli to fix oneself up, get dressed up nice (I) [ili+<atahpoli>] § ishtilatahpoli': jewelry, ornament

ilatahpolichi to fix (someone) up, dress (someone) up nice (I;II) [ilatahpoli+chi] § Salatahpolishtok. She dressed me up nice.

ilatoba to restrict oneself, not spend much on oneself, not use much, take good care of one's things, keep to a budget (I); to save, put aside, keep back (I;3) [ili+<atoba>] {ngr. ilatómba}

ilatobachi to reproduce oneself (of plants such as winter onions) (3) [ili+<atobachi>]

ilatobbi to pay for oneself: especially, to post bail for oneself (I) [ili+atobbi]

ilatómba ngr. of ilatoba § Ikilatómbo. He didn't save it.

ilatookoli to appoint oneself; to volunteer (I) [ili+atookoli]

<ilawiili> in ilawiit {ggr. iláwwi'li; ngr. <ilawíli>}

ilawiit along (prt.) [<ilaawiili>+t] § Ilawiit ishtasalatok. He brought me along. | Ilawiit aatok. He went along.

<ilawíli> in imilawíli—ngr. of iláwwi'li, <ilawiili>

iláwwi'li to live with, shack up with, be with, stay with (I;II) (not used with first-person obj.)—ggr. of <ilawiili> {ngr. <ilawíli>; áwwali'chi, táwwa'a}

ilayoppa in ishtilayoppa

ilayyoka to be different (in tribe, race, color), to have different ways (3) [ili+ayyoka]

ilayyokha to be stingy (3)

ilaabi to rub in (medicine, cream, grease) to one's skin (I;3) [ili+aabi]

ilaafinha to be proud of oneself, conceited (I) [ili+aafinha]

ilaafowa to resist, pull back (of a mule, for example); to refuse to go along with authority (I) [ili+aafowa] {imilaafowa}

ilaafowa ikbanno to resist, be stubborn; to refuse to go (N+II) § Ilaafowa iksabanno. I refuse to go.

ilaaiksaachi to fix oneself up, dress up; to have oneself fixed, sterilized (of either a man or woman) (I) [+SC] [ili+aa+iksaachi]

ilaapakayni, ilaapakayniho him himself, her herself, them themselves (nonsubj.; rare) [ilaapo'+aakayni(+ho)]

ilaapakaynihaat he himself, she herself, they themselves (subj., int.) [ilaapakayni+haat] § Ilaapakanynihaat iksaachim? Did he make it himself?

ilaapakayniho see ilaapakayni

ilaapakaynihoot he himself, she herself, they themselves (subj.) [ilaapakayni+hoot]

ilaapakilloot he and he alone, she and she alone, they and they alone

ilaapakit see ilaapakaynit

ilaapakya he himself also, she herself also, they themselves also [ilaapo'+akya]

ilaapichi to take care of oneself (I) [ili+aapichi] {ngr. ilaapínchi; ishtaapichi, ishtilaapichi}

ilaapilla to be lonely (3) [ilaapo' illa] § Lynnat ilaapillakat ithana. Lynn knows she's lonely.

ilaapínchi ngr. of ilaapichi

ilaapit by itself, by himself, by herself; see ilaapakaynit

ilaapit holhfo to come up by itself (of a seed that was dropped accidentally, not planted) (3)
ilaapit ikbi' something homemade (especially, furniture) [ikbi+'] § Aaimpa' yappat ilaapit ikbi'. This table is homemade.
ilaapo' himself, herself, themselves; by himself, by herself, by themselves; on his own, on her own, on their own; he himself, she herself, they themselves (very rare as subj.); own (most commonly used preceding a possessed noun) § Pamat ilaapo' holba' Josephine pisashtok. Pam showed Josephine a picture of herself, her own picture. | Lynnat ilaapo' inchokka' akaynit ahanta. Lynn lives in her own house. | Ilaapo' nakfish abitok. He killed his own brother. | Lynnat ilaapo' alatok. Lynn came by herself (alone, on her own initiative). | Ilaapat ayinatok. He himself was involved too. | Ilaapo' ilibitok. He killed himself on his own initiative.
ilaatabli in ishtilaatabli [ili+aatabli]
ilaatapichi in ishtilaatapichi [ili+aatapichi]
ilaayokha in ishtilaayokha
ilbá'shshsa, ilbá'sha ggrs. of ilbashsha
ilbáchchi'fa ggr. of ilbachifa
ilbachifa to wash one's hands (I) [ilbak achifa] {ggr. ilbáchchi'fa}
ilbachifachi to wash (someone's) hands (I;II) [ilbachifa+chi]
ilbaháshsha, ilbaháshsa hngrs. of ilbashsha
ilbáhhashshsa hgr. of ilbashshsa
ilbak arm, hand (IIp)
ilbak alotto'wa handful (IIp) {ilbak alhto} § Tili'ko' salbak alotto'wa ishilitok. I took a handful of flour.

ilbak apakfo'li' bracelet (IIIp) [apakfolli+'] § amilbak apakfo'li': my bracelet
ilbak apakfo'li' apakfolli to put on a bracelet (I) {ygr. ilbak apakfo'li' apakfóyyo'li: to wear a bracelet}
ilbak apakfo'li' apakfóyyo'li to wear a bracelet—ygr. of ilbak apakfo'li' apakfolli
ilbak apakfo'li' imapakfolli to put a bracelet on (someone) (IIIp = obj. , — , I;III) [im+ (ilbak apakfo'li' apakfolli)> ilbak apakfo'li' *imapakfolli] § Salbak apakfo'li' amapakfollitok. He put a bracelet on me.
ilbak api' forearm (IIp) {iyyapi'} § salbak api' my forearm
ilbak ayyoshta, (ER) ilbak ayyoshto' fourth finger [ayyoshta]
ilbak aabihli' muff [aa+bihli+']
ilbak aaittachakkachi', (TP) ilbak aattachakha' knuckle; (TP) wrist (IIp) § salbak aaittachakkachi': my knuckle
ilbak aapolhoma' inside of the elbow (IIp) § salbak aapolhoma': the inside of my elbow
ilbak alhto, ilbak alhto'si handful {ilbak alotto'wa} § Tilli'ko' ilbak alhto'si ishilitok. I took a handful of flour.
ilbak fo'kha' see ilbak fokhi'
ilbak fo'khi', ilbak fo'kha', (WB) ilbak fokka' glove, mitten, muff (IIIp); (WB, MJ) ring [fokhi/fokha+'] § amilbak fokhi': my glove
ilbak fo'khi' shiipa' rubber glove [shiipa+']
ilbak fo'khi' to'wishyokachi' see to'wa' ishyokachi'
ilbak fo'khishtittibi' boxing glove [ilbak fo'khi' ishtittibi+']
ilbak fokka' to'li' baseball glove

ilbak ilbak shalbi'yaafokha'

(WB) [to'li+']
ilbak ilbak shalbi'yaafokha' ring
finger (IIp) [ilbak (ilbak shalbi'ya'
aa+fokha+')] § salbak ilbak
shalbi'yaafokha': my ring finger
ilbak iklanna' middle finger (IIp)
[iklanna+']
ilbak illi' butterfingers, clumsy
person [illi+'] § Ilbak illi' saya. I'm a
butterfingers.
ilbak impasa'chi to clap for [-SC] (IIp
= subj. , I;III) § Salbak
impasa'chilitok. I clapped for him.
ilbak impatha', ilbak patha' palm of
the hand (IIp) [ilbak (im+)patha+'] §
salbak impatha', salbak patha': my
palm
ilbak inki' thumb (LF)
ilbak inkofi, (MJ) inkofi, (TP) inkofi',
(HS) ilbak-ofi' elbow (IIp) [im+kofi']
§ salbak inkofi: my elbow
ilbak intakchi to put handcuffs on
(IIp = obj. , I;III)
ilbak ishki' see ilbakshki'
ilbak ishtalakchi' handcuffs, sling
[isht talakchi+']
ilbak ishtanompoli to use American
Sign Language or another sign
language of the deaf (IIp = subj. , I)
[isht *anompoli]
ilbak ishtanoli to gesture; to use
Indian sign language (IIp = subj. , I)
[isht *anoli] § Salbak ishtanolili. I
gesture.
ilbak ishtimanompoli to sign to (IIp
= subj. , I;III) [im+(ishtanompoli)>
isht *imanompoli]
ilbak ishtimanoli to gesture to (IIp =
subj. , I;III) [im+(ishtanoli)> isht
*imanoli]
ilbak ishtincho'wa' handwritten
material
ilbak ishtiwaa to beckon to:
especially, to beckon to (someone)

to come (IIp = subj. , I;III) [isht
*iwaa]
ilbak ifahli, ilbak oshtifahli to wave
one's hand to (IIp = subj. , I;III)
[(osht) *ifahli] § Lynnak salbak
ifahlilitok. I waved to Lynn. I
Lynnat ilbak oshtafahtok. Lynn
waved to me.
ilbak ifokhi to put (secretly) into
(someone's*) hand (IIp = obj. ,
I;III;3) § Lynnat ta'ossoho salbak
afokhitok. Lynn slipped the money
into my hand.
ilbak imosak, (CP) ilbak masak wrist
(IIp) § salbak imosak: my wrist
ilbak ishanni to twist (someone's)
arm (IIp = obj. , I;III) [im+(ilbak
shanni)> ilbak *ishanni]
ilbak lopi' bone marrow of the hand
or arm (IIp) § salbak lopi': the bone
marrow of my arm
ilbak lho'fa' glove (CC) [lhofa+']
ilbak nannishtaabachi' see ilbak
naaishtaabachi'
**ilbak naaishtaabachi', ilbak
nannishtaabachi', ishtaabachi',** (ER)
ilbak ishtalbichi', (AB) ilbak
ishtaabalhchi' index finger (IIp)
[nanna isht aabachi+'] § salbak
naaishtaabachi': my index finger
ilbak oshtifahli see ilbak ifahli
ilbak pakna' back of the hand (IIp)
ilbak pasa'chi to clap the hands (IIp,
I) [-SC]
ilbak patha' see ilbak impatha'
ilbak pochokko' fist (IIp) § salbak
pochokko': my fist
ilbak shalbi'ya', ilbak-oshi' albi'ha'
ring (IIIp) [ilbak-oshi' albi'ya+'] §
amilbak shalbi'ya': my ring
ilbak shanni to twist (someone's)
arm (IIp = obj. , I) {ilbak ishanni}
ilbak sho'ka, ilbakshki' sho'ka to
suck one's thumb (IIp, I) § Salbak

shọ'kali. I suck my thumb.

ilbak takchi to put handcuffs on (IIp = obj. , I)

ilbak toklọ alotto'wa double handful (IIp) [toklo+họ] § Tilli'ko' salbak toklọ alotto'wạ ishilitok. I took a double handful of flour.

ilbakchosh fingernail (IIp) [ilbak <akchosh>]

ilbakchosh ishhommachi' (red) nail polish (IIp) [isht hommachi+'] § salbakchosh ishhommachi': my nail polish

ilbakchosh ishkatolhlhi' nail clippers [isht katolhlhi+']

ilbakchosh ishshoochi' nail file [isht shoochi+']

ilbak-oshi' finger (sometimes, specifically, little finger) (IIp) [ilbak oshi']

ilbak-oshi' albi'ha' see ilbak shalbi'ya'

ilbak-oshi' awaatali' finger (AB) [awaatali+']

ilbak-oshi' aapolhoma' inside of the knuckle joint (IIp) § salbak-oshi' aapolhoma': the inside of my knuckle joint

ilbak-oshi' ittintakla' space between the fingers (IIp)

ilbakshki', ilbak ishki' thumb (IIp); (LF) third finger

ilbakshki' shọ'ka see ilbak shọ'ka

<ilbasha> in ilbashachi; var. grade base for ilbashsha {ggr. ilbá'sha; hngr. ilbahásha; ngr. ilbásha; ilbashsha}

ilbashachi, (LF) ilbashshachi to abuse, mistreat (I;II) [<ilbasha>+chi] {ggr. ilbáshsha'chi, ilbáshsha'cho'si} § Ilbashsha'cho'sli ki'yo. I don't mistreat him.

ilbashsha, ilbashsha'si, (MJ) ilbasha to be poor, pitiful, impoverished (II)

[+CPR] [+PR] {ggr. ilbá'shsha, ilbá'sha; hgr. ilbáhhashsha; hngr. ilbaháshsha, ilbahásha; ngr. ilbáshsha, ilbásha; ygr. ilbáyya'shsha; ilbashachi, <ilbasha>} § Chibashsha'si! Poor you!

ilbashsha' poor one, poor thing [ilbashsha+']

ilbáshsha'chi ggr. of ilbashachi

ilbáshsha'cho'si ggr. of ilbashachi [ilbashsha'chi+o'si]

ilbashsha'si see ilbashsha

ilbáyya'shsha ygr. of ilbashsha

ilbáshsh, ilbásha ngrs. of ilbashsha

ilbolbo', (LJ, EH) bolbo' kidney; (EH) bladder (IIIp: imbolbo', inbolbo' [used with all III prefixes]; ịlbolbo' [follows a noun]) § waak ilbolbo': beef kidneys | ambolbo', anbolbo': my kidney

ilí'bi ggr. of ilibi

ilí'pa ggr. of ilipa

ilibaklosochi to paint one's face (I) [-SC] [ili+baklosochi]

ilibanna in ishtilibanna

ilibi to kill oneself (I) [ili+abi] {ggr. ilí'bi}

ilibilamachi to put on perfume (I) [ili+bilamachi] {ishtilibilamachi'}

ilibilo'chi to masturbate (of a man) (I) [±SC] [ili+bilo'chi]

ilibo'li to hit oneself (I) [ili+bo'li]

iliboyaffichi to shed one's feathers (of a chicken) (MJ) [ili+boyaffi+chi]

iliboyaachi to scratch out one's hair (of a dog, for instance) (3) [ili+boyahli+chi]

iliboyolli, iliboyotli to pull out one's feathers to make a nest (of a bird, for instance) (3)

iliboyotli see iliboyolli

ilichakbakachi to strip (oneself) naked (I) [-SC] [ili+chakbakachi]

ilichakbakachi' stripper

[ilichakbakachi+']

ilifata'chi to shake oneself (of a dog) (3) [ili+fata'chi]

ilifaya'chi to be proud; to swagger (I) [ili+faya'chi]

ilifinhachi to think one can do anything, to be proud, to be a daredevil, to set oneself up above others, to be a smart aleck (I) [ili+finha+chi]

ilifoyo'chi to be proud; to be frisky; to swagger, to swing from side to side while walking (I)

ilifoyopa to take a breath, inhale (I) (Ct?) [ili+foyopa] {ilafoyopa}

ilihaklochichi to make (someone) listen to himself (I;3) [(ili+haklo)+chichi]

ilihaksichi to show off, to act silly, crazy (I) [ili+haksichi]

ilihaksichit ishnǫwa see ilihaksichit nǫwa

ilihaksichit nǫwa, ilihaksichit ishnǫwa to have fun, carouse, go out on the town (I) [(isht) ilihaksichi+t (isht) *nǫwa]

ilihalalli to back out, pull out; not to want to do something; to refrain from doing something (I) [ili+halalli]

<ilihammichi> in tish ishtilihammichi' [ili+hammi+chi]

ilihofahyachi to blame, reproach oneself (I) [ili+hofahyachi]

ilihopohǫo, ilipohǫo hngr. of ilihopoo, ilipoo

ilihopoo, ilipoo to be extremely fearful or suspicious (I) [ili+hopoo] {ggr. ilihóppo'wa; hngr. ilihopohǫo, ilipohǫo; ngr. ilihopǫo, ilipǫo: to be careful}

ilihopǫo, ilipǫo to be careful—ngr. of ilihopoo, ilipoo

ilihóppo'wa ggr. of ilipoo, ilihopoo

ilihottopachi to hurt oneself (I) [ili+hottopachi]

iliká'lli ggr. of ilikalli

ilikalli to scratch oneself (I) [ili+kalli] {ggr. iliká'lli}

ilikallochi to be hardhearted, unresponsive; not to listen when spoken to; to refuse to reconsider a decision (I) [ili+kallochi] {chonkash kallochi}

ilikasho'chi to wipe oneself off (I) [ili+kasho'chi]

ilikbi in oshi' iksho' ilikbi

ilikostinichi to repent, make a confession; to be saved (in a religious sense), get religion (I) [ili+kostinichi] {ggr. ilikostínni'chi}

ilikostínni'chi ggr. of ilikostinichi

ililataffi to stub one's toe (I) [ili+lataffi] {hngr. ililatahą́ffi}

ililawachi' in atǫfalaa' ililawachi'

ililohmi to hide oneself away, stay in the house all the time (for instance, to conceal one's pregnancy) (I) [ili+lohmi]

ililowachi to burn oneself (I) [ili+lowachi]

ililhiyohli to chase oneself (I) [ili+lhiyohli]

ililhǫfi to shed one's skin (of a snake) (3) [ili+lhǫfi]

ililhpokonna in ishtililhpokonna

ilima to give oneself to, give up to (of a wife to her husband, for instance); to give to oneself (rare) (I;3) [ili+ima]

ilimalikchi to doctor oneself (I) [ili+imalikchi]

ilimalhkaniya to forget oneself (I) [ili+imalhkaniya]

ilimanompoli to talk to oneself (I) [ili+imanompoli]

ilimihachi to always refuse things, to think one's too good for things (3) [ili+mihachi] {ggr. ilimíhha'chi; ishtilimihachi}

ilimpilachi to send (something) to oneself (I;3) [ili+impilachi]

ilincho'li to put on war paint or stage makeup, to tattoo oneself (I) [ili+incho'li]

ilintaloowa to sing to oneself (rare) (I) [ili+intaloowa]

ilipa to eat oneself (I) [ili+apa] {ggr. ilí'pa}

ilipafi to enter a contest or fight, be a candidate or contestant (especially, with the expectation of winning) (I) [ili+pafi]

ilipilachi to send oneself (I) [ili+pilachi]

ilipisa to see oneself (I) [ili+pisa] {ngr. ilipísa}

ilipisachi to show (someone) to himself (I;3); to show oneself naked, appear naked (I) [ilipisa+chi/ili+pisachi]

ilipísa ngr. of ilipisa

ilipohǫo hngr. of ilihopohǫo

iliposilhlha, iliposilhha to indulge in self-pity, try to get sympathy (I) [ili+po+asilhlha]

ilipoo see ilihopoo

ilipǫo see ilihopǫo

ilisatapo'li to stretch; to spread the wings (of a bird) (I) [ili+satapo'li]

ilisso to hit oneself (I) [ili+isso]

ilissochichi to make (someone) hit himself (I;3) [(ili+isso)+chichi]

ilishanaayo'chi to walk with a wiggle (I) [±SC] [ili+shanaayo'li+chi]

ilishaachi to scratch oneself, scratch an itch (I) [ili+shaachi] {hngr. ilishaalihínchi; ngr. ilishaalínchi}

ilishaalihínchi hngr. of ilishaachi

ilishaalínchi ngr. of ilishaachi

ilishafi to shave (oneself) (I) [ili+shafi]

ilishǫ'kachichi to make (someone) kiss, suck himself (I;3) [(ili+shǫ'ka)+chichi]

ilishtochichi to make oneself big (for instance, by putting a pillow in one's stomach) (I) [ili+ishtochichi]

ilitobachi to turn oneself into (an animal) (usually, because one is a witch) (I;3) [ili+tobachi]

ilitobasht nǫwa' type of witch who always appears in the form of a specific animal (used with a preceding animal name) [ilitobachi+t nǫwa+'] § ofi' ilitobasht nǫwa': dog witch

ilitohbichi to make oneself white: especially, to put on face powder (I) [ili+tohbichi]

iliwilooli to shake oneself (of a dog, for instance) (I) [ili+wilooli]

iliwiikichi to weigh oneself (I) [ili+wiikichi]

iliyimmichi to psych oneself up, get mentally prepared (I) [ili+yimmichi] {imiliyimmichi: to challenge}

iliyokachi to turn oneself in (at a police station) (I) [ili+yokachi]

ilihofahya to be ashamed of oneself (I) [ili+ihofahya]

ililánchi to change oneself (on the outside) (I) [ili+ilanchi]

iliyimmi to be a smart aleck, to think one can do anything (I) [ili+iyimmi]

illa to be just, only, alone (3;3C) (requires an overt preceding complement noun); just (aux.) {illi} § Ihoo illatok. It's just a woman. I Poshno' illa. It's just us. I Janat imalhkaniyatok ilaapo' hooillaka. Jan forgot that it was just them alone. I JPat affammi' tochchi'na'si illa. JP is only three years old. I Sapisa illakat sathana. They just look at me and they know me.

illi

illi to die (II) [+PR] [+CPR] {ggr. í'lli;
hngr. ihílli; ygr. íyyi'lli; illa}
illi' death; dead person [illi+']
illichi to kill (a plant) deliberately
(I;II) [illi+chi] {issot illichi, ittillichi,
noklhitoffit illichi} § Chillichila'chi.
I'm going to kill you (talking to a
plant).
Illit Falamat Taani', (TJ) Falamat
Taani' the Resurrection [illi+t
falama+t taani+']
illit ittola to fall dead (II) § Illit
sattola'chi. I'll fall dead.
illitokat falamat taani see illitokoot
falamat taani
illitokmat falamat taani to rise from
the dead (used of someone now
alive) (II, — , I) [illi+tokmat
falama+t] § Chillitokmat falamat
ishtaana'chi. You'll rise from the
dead.
illitokoot falamat taani, illitokat
falamat taani to rise from the dead,
for the dead to rise (3)
[illi+tokoot/tokat falama+t] § Nittak
Ishtayyo'pikma illitokoot falamat
taana'chi. On the Judgment Day
they will rise from the dead.
ilokchina to be pink, healthy-
looking; to be happy, healthy, lively;
to keep going, be able to do things;
(of a horse) to prance (II) {ngr.
ilokchína; ygr. ilokchíyyi'na}
ilokchíyyi'na ygr. of ilokchina
ilokchína ngr. of ilokchina
iloktanichi to show off, try to attract
attention (I) [ili+oktanichi]
ilollali to laugh at oneself (I)
[ili+ollali]
ilollalichi to make (someone) laugh
at himself (I;3) [ili+ollalichi]
ilombitka to press on one's skin with
one's hands (I) [ili+ombitka]
ilombítti'pa to place one's hands on

one's waist, have one's arms
akimbo (I) [ili+ombitti'pa]
ilonhochi to be guilty; to confess,
take the blame (I) [ili+onhochi]
{imilonhochi: to take the blame for}
ilontala'li' bow tie [ilontalaali+']
ilontalaali to put (something) on
oneself (in one's hair or buttonhole,
for example) (I;3) [ili+ontalaali] {ggr.
ilontálla'li: wear on oneself} §
Nampakali' ilontalaalilitok. I put
on a flower (in my hair or
buttonhole, for instance).
ilontálla'li to wear, have
(something) on oneself (in one's
hair or buttonhole, for example)—
ggr. of ilontalaali
iloshshowanchichichi to make
(someone) smell himself (I;3)
[ili+oshshowanchichichi]
ilohoshontikachi to shade oneself (I)
[ili+ohoshontikachi]
ilohoshowa to urinate on oneself (I)
[ili+ohoshowa]
ilolhatabli to spill (something) on
oneself (I;3) [ili+olhatabli] § Lynnat
oka' ilolhatablitok. Lynn spilled
water on herself.
ilhko'chi to shake (something) (I;II)
[-SC] [ilhko'li+chi]
ilhko'kóli to move, shake (I)—rmgr.
of ilhko'li
ilhko'li to move, shake, vibrate (I); to
beat (of the heart) (3) [+PR] {rmgr.
ilhko'kóli; ilhkóyyokli, <ilhkooli>}
§ Yaaknaat ilhko'tok. There was an
earthquake, the earth shook.
ilhkóyyokli to jerk, make a sudden
movement (I)
ilhkoyyokli'chi to jerk, bump against
(I;II) [ilhkoyyokli+chi] §
Salhkoyyokli'shna tiiat
anlhatapatok. He bumped against
me and I spilled the tea.

134

<ilhkooli> in abikimilhkooli
[ilhko'li]
ilhpichik nest (IIIp: i̱lhpichik)
ilhpita to be fattened, ready for
market; to get money free, be on a
pension (II) {v2. ipita}
ilhpitachi to fatten (for market, for
example) (I;II) [ilhpita+chi]
ilhpókkonna, ilhpokó'nna ggr. of
ilhpokonna
ilhpokohónna hngr. of ilhpokonna
ilhpokonna, (MJ, TP, CC)
holhpokonna to dream (II); to
dream that (+cha/na comp.; 'I' subj.
only) (II) [+CPR] [-PR] (for speakers
using holhpokonna, ho- is lost after
any II prefix) {ggr. ilhpókkonna,
ilhpokó'nna; hngr. ilhpokohónna;
ngr. ilhpokónna} § Salhpokonna.
I'm dreaming. | Salhpokonnatok
Lynnat Charles kisi'na. I dreamed
that Lynn bit Charles. | Lynnat
ilhpokonnakat Charles kisili
imahoobatok. Lynn dreamed that
she bit Charles, Lynn dreamed and
imagined that she bit Charles.
ilhpokonna' dreamer [ilhpokonna+']
ilhpokónna ngr. of ilhpokonna
ima to give to '; to bequeath to ',
leave to ' in one's will; to adopt
out, give up (a child) for adoption to
' (I;III;3); to make an offering (I)
{ggr. í'ma; hngr. ihíma; ngr. íma} §
Kani̱ht A'matok. He finally gave it
to me.
imaboshollichi [OPR] of aboshollichi
imachaaha to get used to (a person)
(I;III) [+T] [im+achaaha]
imacho'li to sew for ' (I;III;3)
[im+acho'li]
imachokkobbi to get used to, be close
to, love (a person) (I;III)
[im+achokkobbi]
imachokmilhka to kneel to (I;III)

[im+achokmilhka]
imafama [OPR] of afama
imafo'si' grandfather (oIIIp)
[im+afo'si+']
imafo'sishto' great-grandfather
(oIIIp) [imafo'si' ishto+']
imahánta hngr. of imánta
imáhhi'ka to owe (money) to ' on
(I;III;3;3), to get on credit for ' (I;III;3)
[im+ahhi'ka] § Lynna̱ chokka'
yappa̱ ta'osso imahhi'kalikat i̱'ma. I
still owe Lynn money on this
house. | Lynna̱ TV imahhi'kalitok.
I bought Lynn a TV on credit.
imahiita to get, be in front of (I;III)
[im+ahiita]
imahobbichi to give (someone) the
wrong idea (I;III); to suggest
incorrectly to (I;III) [0 comp]
[im+ahobbichi] § Lynnat holissaat
ayya'shtok amahobbi'shna
ayalitokookya ikshokitok. Lynn said
there were books there, and I went,
but there weren't any.
imaholítto'pa in ishtimaholítto'pa
imahooba to have it seem like (III;3);
to think, imagine (III) [0 comp]
[im+ahooba] § Charlesat Lynnat Jan
pi̱stok imahoobatok. Charles thinks
Lynn saw Jan. | Ishno'
amahoobatokat sanokfonkha. I
remember that it seemed like you to
me.
imakanaachi to part (someone's')
(hair) (I;III;3) [-SC] [im+akanaachi]
imakaniili to part (someone's')
(hair) (I;III;3) [im+akaniili]
imakkálo'si to be kind to (I;III)
[im+akkálo'si]
imalapalínchi to cosign, be a
guarantor (for a loan, insurance
policy) for (I;III); to add, attach for '
(I;III;3) [im+alapalinchi]
imalbilli, imalbitli to put more than

imalbina

one additional (layer, article of
clothing) on (someone˘) (I;III;3)
[im+albilli] {imalbitili: to put an
additional (layer) on} § Naafka
amalbillitok. She put still another
dress on me.
imalbina to be a camp for (3;III);
make camp in (III;3-at) [im+albina] §
Lynnat pichcha̲a-at imalbina. Lynn
made her camp in a barn.
imalbinachi to stay all night with
(I;III) [im+albinachi]
imalbita to have an additional
disease as well as the original one
(III) {v2. imalbitili}
imalbitili to put an additional (layer,
article of clothing) on (someone˘)
(I;III;3); to do the same thing again
to (I;III) [im+albitili] {v1. imalbita;
imalbilli: to put more than one
additional (layer) on} § Carmen
naafka imalbitililitok. I put another
dress on Carmen. | Amalbititok.
She did it to me again.
imalbitli see imalbilli
imalikchi to doctor (someone) (I;III)
[im+alikchi]
imalla to come to, to be born to (I;III),
to give birth to (hum. subj.) (III;3-at)
[im+ala] {negs. ikimallo, ikima'lo}
imálla'mi in nannimálla'mi ki'yo
imalmo [PR] of almo
imalótto'wa to have a full diaper (III)
[im+alotto'wa]
imalhchí'ba ggr. of imalhchiba
imalhchiba to be slow, late (III)
[im+alhchiba] {ggr. imalhchí'ba; ygr.
imalhchiyyi'ba: to be lonely, to have
nothing to do}
imalhchibachi to make late, to make
it take a long time for (I;III)
[imalhchiba+chi] {ggr.
imalhchíbba'chi: to annoy, irritate,
give a pain to}

imalhchíbba'chi to annoy, irritate,
give a pain to—ggr. of
imalhchibachi § Lynnat
amalhchibba'chi. Lynn gives me a
pain. | Lynn imalhchibba'shli. I
give Lynn a pain.
imalhchíyyi'ba to be lonely, to stay
home alone; to be bored, not to
have anything to do—ygr. of
imalhchiba
imalhcho̲nachi to give a good price
to ˘ on (I;III;3) [im+alhcho̲nachi] §
Lynnat ofi' amalhcho̲nachitok.
Lynn gave me a good price on the
dog.
imalhfabi' left side (oIIIp)
[im+alhfabi'] § Chichonkashat
chimalhfabi' pila. Your heart is on
your left side.
imalhkanihíya hngr. of imalhkaniya
imalhkaniya to forget; to put out of
one's mind (III;3) [im+alhkaniya]
{hngr. imalhkanihíya}
imalhkaniyachi to make ˘ forget
(I;III;3) [imalhkaniya+chi] § Holissa̲
issamalhkaniyachitok. You made
me forget the book.
imalhpi'sa to have enough of, to
have had enough of (III;3-at / III;3)
[im+alhpi'sa] {neg. ikimalhpi'so}
imalhpooba to be born to (3;III), to
give birth to (III;3-at) [im+alhpooba]
imalhta see chokma imalhta
imalhtaha to be ready (usually hum.
subj.) (III) [im+alhtaha] {v2.
imatahli; ngr. imalhtá̲ha; ygr.
imalhtáyya'ha}
imalhtáyya'ha ygr. of imalhtaha
imalhtá̲ha ngr. of imalhtaha
imalhtoba to be paid to (3;III); to be
paid, get paid (III;3-at) [im+alhtoba]
{ngr. imalhtómba}
imalhtómba ngr. of imalhtoba
imambaanabli to let (something) go

over, have (something) go over: for
instance, to let (a liquid) boil over
(III;3-at) [im+abaanabli] {v1.
imambaanapa} § Irene imoatmealat
chimambaanablitok. You let Irene's
oatmeal boil over.
imambaanapa to have (a period of
time) pass without one's noticing,
to miss a commitment during (a
period of time) (III;3-at)
[im+abaanabli] {v2. imambaanabli}
§ Nittakat amambaana'pacha
akayyokitok. I had the day pass
without my noticing it and didn't
go, I missed a commitment during
the day and didn't go.
imambaani to barbecue for (I;III;3)
[im+abaani]
imambaatalahchaa' poss. of
abaatalahchaa'
imambaawiili [OPR] of abaawiili
imambi to kill for ˚ (I;III;3); to win
(I); to beat (in a game or contest)
(I;III); to win from ˚ (I;III;3) [im+abi]
{negs. ikimambo, ikima'bo} § Pamat
amambitok. Pam beat me. |
Imambilitok. I won. | Ta'osso
talhlha'pi chimambilitok. I won
five dollars from you. |
Iksama'bokitok. He didn't beat me.
imambihíli hngr. of imambihli
imambihli to put (dl. obj.) in for ˚
(I;III;3) [im+abihli] {hngr.
imambihíli; ngr. imambíhli: to
leave (dl. obj.) for}
imambihpoli to pack for ˚ (I;III;3)
[im+abihpoli]
imambiika to be sick for, to be sick
and thus affect (I;III) [im+abiika]
imambiitippichi to press (something)
down for ˚ (I;III;3) [im+abiitippichi]
imambíhli to leave (dl. obj.) for ˚—
ngr. of imambihli {sg. obj. ifónkhi;
tpl. obj. imáni} § Paska champoli'

chimambihlilitok. I left two cookies
for you.
imambooha poss. of abooha
imammo to mow for ˚ (I;III;3)
[im+amo] {negs. ikimammo,
ikima'mo}
imanhi to wish something good for,
to wish well (I;III) [im+anhi] {ygr.
imáyyanhi} § Chimanhili. I wished
for you, I wished good for you.
imanhínchi to like (someone's
behavior) (I;III) [im+anhinchi] §
Chimanhishli. I like what you do.
imanni to pour for ˚ (I;III;3) [im+ani]
{negs. ikimanno, ikima'no; ngr.
imáni: to leave (tpl., mass, or liquid
obj.) for}
imannoya to be told (to) (3;III); to
know, have been told (III;3-at); to
know (III) [im+annoya] §
Iksamanno'yo. I don't know. |
Lynnat anompaat imannoyatok.
Lynn knows the word.
imannoyachi to go tell (someone˚)
(something) (I;III;3) [imannoya+chi]
imanokfilli to think for, make
decisions for (I;III) [im+anokfilli]
imanompa word, promise, language
(oIIIp) [im+anompa]
imanompa inkobaffi to break one's
word or promise to (IIIp = subj.,
I;III) [im+(imanompa kobaffi)>
imanompa *inkobaffi] §
Chimanompa issankobaffitok. You
broke your word to me.
imanompa kobaffi to break one's
word or promise (IIIp, I)
imanompaat kobafa for a comment
or suggestion to be ignored; to have
one's comment or suggestion
ignored (IIIp = subj.) [imanompa+at]
§ Charlesat imanompaat kobafatok.
Charles's ideas were ignored.
imanompoli to talk to (I;III) [+OPR]

137

imanoli

[im+anompoli] § Chihattaka
imanompolila'cho, Hattaka
chimimanompolila'cho. I'm going
to talk to your husband.
imanoli to tell; to tell (someone) to
(do something), to order; to teach
(I;III); to tell (something, such as a
story) to ° (I;III;3) [im+anoli]
imánta to give birth to (a child); to
have (a relative) (III;3-at) [im+anta]
{hngr. imahánta}
imantachínchi to leave (a child) with
° for care (I;III;3) [im+antachinchi]
<imapatohli > in ittimapatohli
imapaatali [OPR] of apaatali
imapihíla hngr. of imapila
imapila to help ° out with, to give °
support for (I;III;3) [im+apila] {hngr.
imapihíla} § Anchipota amapilatok.
He's helping me out, supporting
me in my expenses for the baby.
imapilachi to give ° support for, to
help ° out with (I;III;3)
[im+apilachi] {hngr. imapilahánchi}
imapilahánchi hngr. of imapilachi
imapissa [PR] of apissa
imapiisa to promise, propose (to do
something) to (I;III) (used with a
preceding verb +a'chit) [im+apiisa]
§ Ayala'chit Lynn imapiisli. I
promised Lynn to go.
imapooba to deliver (a child) of °, to
deliver (someone's°) (child) (I;III;3)
[im+apooba]
imapoolhali to quiet (a baby) for °
(I;III;3) [im+apoolhali]
imappa to eat (something) for °
(I;III;3) [im+apa] {negs. ikima'po,
ikimappo}
imasilhha, imasilhlha to ask for
from °, beg for from °: especially, to
ask permission to marry from ° (a
father, for example) (I;III;3)
[im+asilhha] § Hattak yammat

Georgea Marie imasilhhatok. That
man asked George for permission to
marry Marie.
imasilhlha see imasilhha
imasilhpowa to ask a question of
(I;III) [im+asilhpowa]
imashama to be sick after overeating
(III) [im+ashama ?]
imashana to be locked in (a building)
(III;3-at) [im+ashana] §
Chimambohaat amashanatok. I was
locked in your house.
imashanalhchi to be locked in (a
building) (III;3-at) [im+ashanalhchi]
imashannichi to lock (someone) up,
lock (someone) in (I;III)
[im+ashannichi]
imashaachi to put down (tpl. or mass
obj.) for ° (I;III;3) [im+ashaachi] {ggr.
imáshsha'chi: keep (tpl. of mass
obj.) for}
imáshsha'chi to keep (tpl. or mass
obj.) for—ggr. of imashaachi
imashshachi to sin against (I;III)
[im+ashshachi]
imatahҙli hngr. of imatahli
imatahli to get (someone) ready (I;III)
[im+atahli] {v1. imalhtaha; hngr.
imatahҙli; ngr. imatáhli}
imatáhli ngr. of imatahli
imatoklónchi to be a second one for
(3;3) [im+atoklonchi] § Ihoo
yammakot hattak imatoklonchi.
That woman is the man's second
(woman).
imatonhi see imatooni
imatoonchi see imatoonichi
imatooni, imatonhi, (CP)
nannimatooni to post bail for (I;III);
to guard (a house) for ° (I;III;3)
[im+atooni] {ngr. imatóni,
imatónhi}
imatoonichi, imatoonchi to appoint
(someone) as a guardian for °

138

(I;III;3); to post bail for (I;III) [-SC]
[im+atoonchi] {ngr. imatoonínchi}
imatoonínchi ngr. of imatoonichi
imatóni, imatónhi ngr. of imatooni
imatta to be born to (I;III); to give
birth to (III;3-at) [im+atta]
imayallishto to charge high prices
(III) [im+ayallishto] § Lynnat
imayallishtokat Charlesa immayya.
Lynn charges higher prices than
Charles does.
imayalhlhínchi to obey, do the
bidding of (I;III) [im+ayalhlhichi]
imayoppa [PR] of ayoppa
imayoppánchi to be proud of (I;III); to
like (someone's°) (behavior or
possession) (I;III;3) [im+ayoppanchi]
{neg. ikimayoppa'cho} § Chokka'
chimayoppashli. I like your house. |
Chimayoppashlitok. I'm proud of
you. | Ishtaloowaka
chimayoppashli. I like your singing.
imayoppáni'chi to misdirect,
confuse, interrupt (I;III); to mess up,
ruin (something) for ° (I;III;3)
[im+ayoppani'chi]
imayoppolo'ka to be ruined, to lose
all one's money (III)
[im+ayoppolo'ka]
imayya to go to for (someone°)
(I;III;3) [im+<ayya>] {ggr. ímmayya:
to be ahead of (I;III); ngr. imáya} §
Oklahomma' issamayya'chi? Will
you go to Oklahoma for me?
imáyya'sha to have (tpl. or mass 3-
at), to give birth to (many)
(especially, of an animal); to have (a
wife or husband) (III;3-at); to have,
organize (a gathering or ceremony)
(III;3) [im+ayya'sha] {sg. 3-at.
intálla'a, iwáyya'a; dl. 3-at.
intállo'wa, iwáyyo'wa} § Aa-
akshochi' pomayya'shtok. We had a
memorial service. | Oka'at

amayya'sha. I have water.
imayyabi [PR] of ayyabi
imayyabichi to make it worse for (for
instance, to beat up again) (I;III)
[im+ayyabichi]
imayyachi to lie in wait for (I;III)
imáyyanhi ygr. of imanhi
imáyyalhlhi (Ct?)—ygr. of imalhlhi
imaa-akshochi to have a memorial
service for, following an old custom
(I;III) [im+aa-akshochi] {ishtimaa-
akshochi}
imaa-apa [OPR] of aa-apa
imaabachi to teach (someone°)
(something) (I;III;3); to teach to,
teach how to (+ unmarked 0 or +ka
comp.) (I;III) [im+aabachi] {v1.
imaabalhchi; hngr. imaabahánchi;
ngr. imaabánchi} §
Chikashshanompa issamaabachi.
You teach me Chickasaw. |
Sashkaat naafka acho'lika
amaabachitok. My mother taught
me to sew dresses. | Allenat JP
hilha imaabachitok, Allenat JP
hilhaka imaabachitok. Allen taught
JP to dance.
imaabahánchi hngr. of imaabachi
imaabalhchi to practice, rehearse
(III;3); to be practiced, trained for
something one has been taught; to
be trained (III); to be trained to (III)
[E+0] {v2. imaabachi} § Taloowa'
pomaabalhchitok. We rehearsed the
song. | Chahtimanompa'
amaabalhcha'chitokoot Brighter
Day ayalitok. I went to Brighter Day
to practice Choctaw. | Nanna hosa
amaabalhchitok. I was trained to
shoot.
imaabánchi ngr. of imaabachi
imaabanna to want from ° (3;III;3)
[imaa+banna] § Pamat ta'osso
amaabanna. Pam wants money

139

imaabi

from me.
imaabi to paint, smear for ' (I;III;3)
[im+aabi]
imaachi to say to ' (I;III;3) [im+aachi]
§ Yakookay imaashlitok. I said
thank you to him.
imaachompa to buy from ' (I;III;3)
[im+aa+chompa]
imaafammi', imaafammi' nittak
birthday (oIIIp) [im+<aafammi>+']
imaafammi' nittak see imaafammi'
imaafowa to contend with ' for, try
to get before ' (I;III;3) [im+aafowa] §
Paska champoli' chimaafowalitok.
I'm trying to get the cookie before
you do.
imaahabiina to get as a present from
' (I;III;3) [imaa+habiina]
imaahaklo to hear from (orally or in
writing) (I;III) [imaa+haklo] {ngr.
imaahánglo}
imaahalili see abika imaahalili
imaahánglo ngr. of imaahaklo
imaahhi'ka to buy from ' on credit
(I;III;3) [imaa+ahhi'ka]
imaahobachi to copy from (a person)
(I;III;3) [imaa+hobachi]
imaaholba to be sensitive to the
presence of spirits (III); to be
sensitive to the presence of spirits
in (a place) (III;3-at) [im+aaholba] §
Lynnat chokka' yammat imaaholba.
Lynn feels that that house is
haunted, Lynn is sensitive to the
presence of spirits in that house.
imaaholissochi [OPR] of aaholissochi
imaahonkopa to steal from ' (I;III;3)
[imaa+honkopa]
imaaiklóha, imaaiklówa to act
bravely toward, stand up to, not to
fear; to be mean to (I;III)
[im+aaikloha]
imaaiklówa see imaaiklóha
imaaiksaachi, imiksaachi to make

(something) over for ', to alter for '
(I;III;3) § Irene inaafka
imaaiksaashlitok. I made over
Irene's dress for her (someone other
than Irene).
imaaishi to take away from ', take (a
covering, for example) off ' (I;III;3);
to perform an abortion on
(euphemistic) (I;III) [imaa+ishi]
imaaishko [OPR] of aaishko
imaaithana to learn from (I;III); to
learn to, learn how to from
(+unmarked ka/0 comp.) (I;III)
[imaa+ithana] § Sashkaako tanchi'
hopooni imaaithanalitok,
Sashkaako tanchi' hopoonika
imaaithanalitok. I learned to cook
corn from my mother.
imaakallo in nannakat ishtimaakallo
imaakana'li to dodge, move away
from (pl. subj.) (I;III) [imaa+kana'li]
{sg. imaakanalli}
imaakanalli to dodge, move away
from (sg. subj., hum. obj.) (I;III)
[imaa+kanalli] {pl. imaakana'li}
imaakánnakli to dodge (hum. obj.)
(I;III) [im+aakannakli]
imaakoloffi [OPR] of aakoloffi
imaalahámi hngr. of imaalami
imaalak see imalak
imaalami to have business; to go to
the bathroom; to hustle (III) {hngr.
imaalahámi; nannimaalami}
imaaloma to hide from ' in (I;III;3)
[im+aaloma] § Lynna Charles
imamboha imaalomalitok. I hid
from Lynn in Charles's house.
imaalhlhi to be tired, worn out (III)
[im+aalhlhi]
imaalhlhichi to wear (someone) out
(I;III) [imaalhlhi+chi]
imaalhpí'sa to have been born that
way (with a certain physical
condition) (III) § Chimaalhpi'sta?

140

Were you born like that?

imaanokfila mind (noun) (oIIIp) [im+<anokfila>]

imaanokfila filito'wa see imaanokfila-at filito'wa

imaanokfila ilánchi to change one's mind (IIIp , I) § Chimaanokfila ishilanchi biyyi'ka. You're always changing your mind.

imaanokfila-at fashkalamo'wa to have one's mind keep turning around, not be able to make up one's mind (IIIp = subj.) [imaanokfila+at] § Amaanokfila-at fashkalamo'wakat ithanali. I know I can't make up my mind.

imaanokfila-at filito'wa, imaanokfila filito'wa to be capricious, changeable, to say one thing and then say another, to go back on one's commitments (IIIp = subj.) [imaanokfila+at] § Amaanokfila-at filito'wakat ithanali. I know I'm capricious.

imaanokfila-at ikimiksho to be completely out of one's mind (IIIp,III) [+CPR] [-PR] [imaanokfila+at] § Amaanokfila-at iksamiksho. I'm completely out of my mind.

imaanokfila-at iksho to be silly, crazy, absentminded (IIIp = subj.) [+CPR] [-PR] [imanokfila+at] § Amanokfila-at iksho. I'm silly.

imaanokfila-at inkaniya see imaanokfilinkaniya

imaanokfila-at imóma not to be retarded, not to be crazy (IIIp, III) [imaanokfila+at] {imaanokfila-at móma} § Ithanali amaanokfila-at amomakat. I know I'm not retarded.

imaanokfila-at kaniya to think only about one thing; to be crazy (IIIp =

subj.) [imaanokfila+at]

imaanokfila-at móma not to be retarded, not to be crazy (IIIp = subj.) [imaanokfila+at] {imaanokfila-at imóma} § Ithanali amaanokfila-at momakat. I know I'm not retarded.

imaanokfila-at toklo to be of two minds about, to be unable to make up one's mind (IIIp = subj.) [imaanokfila+at]

imaanokfila-at yohbi bíyyi'ka, imaanokfila-at yohbi chokma to have one's mind be calm, peaceful, at rest (IIIp = subj.) [imaanokfila+at] § Amaanokfila-at yohbi chokmakat ithanali. I know my mind is at rest.

imaanokfila-at yohbi chokma see imaanokfila-at yohbi bíyyi'ka

imaanokfilinkaniya, imaanokfila-at inkaniya to be crazy (IIIp , III / III;3-at) [imaanokfila-at *inkaniya] § Amaanokfila-at ankaniyakat ithanali. I know I'm crazy. | Imaanokfilinkaniya, Imanokfila-at inkaniya. He's crazy.

imaaokla' family, people, group, gang; member of one's family, group (oIIIp) [im+aa+okla+'] § amaaokla' alhiha': the members of my gang, my fellow gang members

imaaolabi to get, take away from ˙ (I;III;3) [imaa+olabi]

imaapatachi to put (something) next to ˙ (I;III;3) [-SC] [im+aa+patali+chi] <imaapatohli> in ittimaapatohli

imaapátta'a to be located beside (the land) of (someone's˙) (of a parcel of land) (3;III;3) [im+aa+apatta'a] {imaapátta'li} § Iyaaknaat ayaaknaak amaapatta'a. His land is located beside my land.

imaapátta'li to be beside (I;III) [im+<apatta'li>] {imaapátta'a}

imaapihlichika' in Chihoowa

141

imaaponta

Imaapihlichika'
imaaponta to borrow from ˚ (I;III;3)
[imaa+ponta]
imaatámpa to be too big or loose for
(3;III); to have (something) too big
on one, to have (something) as a
leftover (III;3-at) [im+atampa] §
Paskaat chimaatampatam? Did you
have leftover bread?
imaatiya to go along with, listen to
(Ct) (I;III) [imaa+itti+aya ?] {ngr.
imaatíya; imbaatiya}
imaatíya ngr. of imaatiya
imaatobbi to pay to ˚ (I;III;3); to pay
back, get revenge (I;III) [im+atobbi]
{ggr. imaatôbbi}
imaatôbbi ggr. of imaatobbi
imaawí'ki ggr. of imaawiiki
imaawiiki in ishtimaawiiki,
nannakat imaawiiki {ggr.
imaawí'ki}
imaayopi to swim in for ˚ (I;III;3)
[im+aayopi]
imalak, imaalak brother-in-law
(oIIIp)
imalako'si' sister-in-law (TP)
[imalak+o'si+']
imálhlhi to be true to, faithful to
(I;III); to have be faithful to (III;3-at)
[im+alhlhi] {ygr. imáyyalhlhi}
imalhlhínchi to obey, do as one was
told (even if the order was not
seriously intended) (I;III)
[im+alhlhinchi]
imáni to leave (tpl., mass, or liquid
obj.) for ˚—ngr. of imanni {sg. obj.
ifónkhi; dl. obj. imambíhli} § Oka'
issamana'shki. Leave some of the
water for me.
imásha to have (tpl. or mass 3-at)
left; to leave behind (tpl. 3-at) (III;3-
at) [im+asha] {sg. 3-at intaláa,
intówa, iwayáa; dl. 3-at intalówa,
inkáa, iwayówa} § Shokkola'at

chimasha. You've got some sugar
left (in a pile). | Aaombiniili'at
amashtok. I left the (three or more)
chairs.
imashaka' buttocks, rear end, behind
(oIIIp) [im+ashaka'] § amashaka':
my buttocks, my behind
imáshwa to have (children) (dl. 3-at)
(III;3-at) [im+áshwa] § Chipotaat
imashwatok. She has (two)
children.
imáya ngr. of imayya
imbachali to tell off, talk mean to
(I;III) [im+bachali]
imbaka'chi to knock on (a door) (I;3);
to knock on (someone's˚) (door)
(I;III;3) [+SC] [im+baka'chi] {hngr.
imbaka'lihínchi} | Lynn imokkisa'
imbaka'shlitok, Lynna okkisa'
imbaka'shlitok. I knocked on
Lynn's door.
imbaka'lihínchi hngr. of imbaka'chi
imbalaafka' ohoshowa to wet one's
pants (IIIp,I) [im+balaafka'
*on+hoshowa]
imbaptismo [PR] of baptismo
imbaptismochi to baptize (someone)
for ˚ (I;III;3) [im+baptismochi]
imbasmo to kiss (WB) (I;III)
[im+<basmo>; from French baise-
moi] § Chimbasmo sabanna. I want
to kiss you.
imbasoowa [PR] of basoowa
imbashli to cut for ˚ (I;III;3); to
castrate, fix (a male animal),
perform a vasectomy on (a man)
(I;III) [im+bashli]
imbaani to put more (liquid) in a
container for ˚ (I;III;3) [im+ibaani]
imbaatiya to go along with, agree
with, be loyal to; (VB, TJ, ER, WB)
to obey (I;III) [im+ibaa+itti+aya]
{negs. ikimbaati'yo, ikimbaatiyyo;
imaatiya, ishtimbaatiya}

imbaayo'chi to rock (someone) (in a rocking chair) (I;III) [im+baayo'chi]
imbichili to pour (something) for (someone˚) (I;III;3) (Ct) [im+bichili]
imbichota [PR] of bichota
imbila [PR] of bila
imbiloffi to masturbate (someone) (I;III) [im+biloffi]
imbínni'li to sit around, sit by while (someone) works (of an old or disabled person, for example) (sg. subj.) (I;III) [im+binni'li] {dl. inchí'ya; tpl. imbinohmáa}
imbinohmáa to sit around, sit by while (someone) works (tpl. subj.) (3;3) (see binohmáa) [im+bihohmaa] {sg. imbínni'li; dl. inchí'ya}
imbishalhchi to be milked (of a cow) (III) [+T] {v2. imbishlichi}
imbishchit prt. of imbishlichi
imbishlichi, (AB, WB) bishlichi to milk (a cow, for instance), squeeze out milk from; to fondle (a woman's) breasts (I;III) {v1. imbishalhchi; prt. imbishchit, imbishlichit} § waakimbishlichi: to milk a cow
imbo'li to knock on (a door) (I;3); to knock on (someone's˚) (door) (I;III;3) [im+bo'li]
imbohli to lay down (sg. obj.) for (I;III;3) [im+bohli] {ygr. imbóyyo'hli: to keep (sg. obj.) for}
imbolbo' poss. of ilbolbo' (oIIIp)
imbosholli to crack, shatter (III;3-at) [im+bosholli] § Amposhi'at chimbosholli. You cracked the dish.
imboshollichi in ta'osso imboshollichi
imboyafa [PR] of boyafa
imbóyyo'hli to keep (sg. obj.) for ˚— ygr. of imbohli
imí'lli ggr. of imilli
imí'lha ggr. of imilhlha

imí'shko ggr. of imishko
imichchokwa [PR] of ichchokwa
imichonkash poss. of chonkash (oIIIp)
imichonkash ishtanokfilli to think about something in one's heart (IIIp , I)
imihílha, imihílhlha hngrs. of imilhlha, <imilha>
imihoo wife (oIIIp) [im+ihoo]
imikbi to make for ˚ (I;III;3) [im+ikbi] § Paska amikbitok. She made bread for me.
imiksaa to be made for (3;III); to have made for one (III;3-at) [im+iksaa] § Asayoppa naafka yappat amiksaatokat. I'm happy that I had this dress made for me.
imiksaachi, imaaiksaachi to make for ˚, fix for ˚, make over for ˚ (I;III;3) [im+iksaachi]
imiláffo'wa ggr. of imilaafowa
imilahobbi to be mean, to brag, to show off to (I;III) {ygr. imilahóyyobbi}
imilahóyyobbi ygr. of imilahobbi
imilatómba to reserve for ˚, save for ˚ (I;III;3) [im+ilatómba] § Aaimpa' iichimilatomba'chi. We'll reserve a table for you.
imilawíli ngr. of imiláwwi'li
imiláwwi'li to keep (a child) with one for ˚ (someone, for a few days or on a regular basis) (I;III;3) [im+ilawwi'li] {ngr. imilawíli} § Lynna Evan imilawílilitok. I kept Evan for Lynn (for a few days). | Lynnakot JP amilawwi'li. Lynn keeps JP for me.
imilaafowa to resist, to be stubborn or obstinate toward, not to want to go with (I;III) {ggr. imiláffo'wa}
imilbashsha to ask, beg (often, while kneeling) (I;III) [im+ilbashsha] {ygr.

imilbáyya'shsha}
imilbáyya'shsha ygr. of imilbashsha
imilipilachi to send oneself to (I;III)
[im+ili+pilachi]
imilipóo to be careful with, to watch
oneself around (I;III) [im+ilipoo]
imiliyimmichi to challenge, pick a
fight with, act tough to (I;III)
[im+ili+yimmichi]
imilli to lose (a game), be beaten (III);
to lose (a race, game) (III;3-at)
[im+illi] {ggr. imí'lli, ímmi'lli} §
Tennisat amilli. I lost at tennis.
imilonhochi to take the blame for,
confess falsely so as to save (I;III)
[im+ilonhochi]
<imilha> var. grade base for
imilhlha {ggr. imí'lha; hngr.
imihílha; ngr. imílha; malhata}
<imilhkooli> in abikimilhkooli
[im+<ilhkooli>]
imilhlha to be scared, wild, afraid
(III); to be scared, afraid to
[E+a'nikat] [-PR] [-CPR] {v2.
imilhlhali; ggr. imí'lha, ímmilhlha;
hngr. imihílha, imihílhlha; ngr.
imílha, imílhlha; ygr. imíyyi'lha;
<imilha>, malhata} § Amilhlhatok
Charles imanompola'nikat. I was
scared to talk to Charles.
imilhlhabi to be a scaredy-cat (III)
[imilhlha abi] {hngr.
imilhlhahámbi; ngr. imilhlhámbi;
ygr. imilhlháyya'bi}
imilhlhabi' scaredy-cat [imilhlhabi+']
imilhlhahámbi hngr. of imilhlhabi
imilhlhali to scare, to scare off (I;III)
{v1. imilhlha}
imilhlhámbi ngr. of imilhlhabi
imilhlháyya'bi ygr. of imilhlhabi
imimanompoli to talk to (someone)
for (someone') (I;III;3); to interpret
for (I;III) [im+imanompoli] § Lynna
chimimanompolila'cho. I'll talk to

Lynn for you.
imimaatobbi to pay for (someone), to
post bail for (I;III); to pay
(someone') for (I;III;3)
[im+imaatobbi] § Amimaatobbi. He
paid for me (for instance, paid my
admission), posted bail for me. I
Nipi' chimimaatobbila'chi. I'll pay
you for the meat.
imimbaafokhi [OPR] of ibaafokhi
imimbaakolli to dig around (a tree,
house) for ' (I;III;3) [im+ibaakolli]
imimbalhto to have (one's
belonging) in with (III;3-at;3)
[im+ibalhto] § Ishithanata
chimimpa'at amimpa'a
chimimbalhtotokat? Did you know
that your groceries were in with my
groceries?
imimpa to have a meal (especially, a
party) for (I;III) [im+impa] § Lynnat
ittihaalalla'chihootoko Lynn
ilimpa'chi. Because Lynn was going
to get married we had a party for
her.
imincho'li to make marks on for '
(I;III;3) [im+incho'li]
iminno'chi' necklace, dog collar
(oIIIp)
imintakho'bi to be tired of, sick of
(I;III) [im+intakho'bi]
imipita [OPR] of ipita
imissa to let (someone) do
something: especially, to go to bed
with (a man), let (a man) have his
way, or to let (a daughter) go with a
man (I;III) (with a verb telling what
action was allowed, imissa is subr.
and followed by +na; alternatively,
imissa may be used with a subr.
clause with a different subj. +a'chi
+ka) [im+issa] § Amissana
hilhalitok. She let me dance. I
Lynnak ishimissa'shki! Let Lynn do

it! | Chimissali̱ ishhilha'shki. I'm
going to let you dance. | Ihoo
yammat iksamissokittook hina'
aalhopollichila'chika̱. That woman
wouldn't let me put the road
through.
imissikopa to be mean to (I;III)
[im+issikopa]
imishi to take from ˚, take for ˚; to
get for ˚ (I;III;3) [im+ishi]
imishko to take (medicine) for ˚
(especially, of a child who will take
medicine only at the request of
certain adults) (I;III;3) [im+ishko]
{ggr. imí'shko, ímmishko}
imishto to be too big for (3;III); to
have be too big for (III;3-at)
[im+ishto]
imithana to come to understand
(someone) (I;III) [im+ithana] {ngr.
imitha̱na: to understand}
imithá̱na to understand (someone)
(I;III) {neg. ikimitha'no}—ngr. of
imithana
imittibi to fight for, on the same side
as (I;III) [im+ittibi]
imittihaalalli to get married for, get
married to please (I;III)
[im+ittihaalalli]
imittimanompoli to read to ˚ (I;III;3)
[im+ittimanompoli]
imittola to drop, let fall (sg.-dl. 3-at)
(III;3-at) [im+ittola] {tpl., mainly
inan. 3-at. i̱lhatapa}
imíyyi'lha ygr. of imilhlha
imí̱'ma to have (anim. subj.—see
i̱'ma) (III;3-at) [im+i̱'ma] § Ofi'at
abokissaat imi̱'ma. The dog has a
(dog) door, There's a door for the
dog.
imí̱'shi to keep for ˚ (I;III;3)
[im+i̱'shi]
imi̱hollo to be off limits, proscribed,
forbidden to (of a food or drink)

(3;III) (an overt noun obj. must be
postposed); to have (a food or drink)
forbidden to one (III;3-at)
[im+i̱hollo] {imi̱hollochi: to forbid
to consume} § Nipi'at
ami̱hollohootokoot apala' ki'yo.
Since meat is off limits for me, I
never eat it. | Nipi'at imi̱hollo
Lynna̱. Meat is forbidden to Lynn.
imi̱hollochi to forbid ˚ to consume
(I;III;3); to forbid certain activities to
(a menstruating woman) (I;III)
[imi̱hollo+chi] § Alikchaat paska̱
ami̱hollochitok. The doctor said I
couldn't eat bread.
imi̱la to feel bad (3) [im+i̱la]
imi̱lahchohmi to have one's feelings
hurt, be in a huff (III) [+HM],
<imi̱lahcho̱h> (usually used in a
cha expression) [imi̱la chohmi] §
Ami̱lacho̱hcha ayalitok. I went off
in a huff.
<imi̱lahcho̱h> [HM] of
imi̱lahchohmi
imí̱lha, imí̱lhlha ngrs. of imilhlha
imi̱naano̱li to be a witness or
interpreter for (I;III) [im+im+nanna
ano̱li] § Ami̱naano̱tok. She was my
witness.
imi̱naano̱li' witness for, interpreter
for (someone), witness, interpreter
(oIIIp) [imi̱naano̱li+']
Imma' in Hashaatabookoli' Imma'
ímmayya to be ahead of (I;III); to be
more than (I;III) [E+kat] (used to
express a comparison)—ggr. of
imayya § Chaahakat issammayya.
You're taller than me.
ímmayya banna to want to be better
than everyone else, to be a smart
aleck (sg. subj.) (II) {pl.
ittimmayya'chi banna} § Immayya
sabanna. I want to be better than
everyone, I'm a smart aleck.

145

ímmayya'chi to pass; to excel over; to beat up (I;III) [+SC] {ittímmayya'chi}
immi to belong to (I;III); to have, own (III;3-at) {v1. ima ?; ggr. í'mmi} § Akchimmokisha. I don't belong to you yet. | Ofi'at ammikat asayoppaha. I'm happy that I finally own the dog.
immi' possession, thing (oIIIp); sex organ (oIIIp); owner (with preceding 3-at) [immi+'] § Aboohaat ammi'. The house is mine, The house is my possession, The house is my thing. | Ofi'at immaat inkaniyatok. The dog's owner is away. | John immi': John's thing, John's possession, John's sex organ
ímmi'lli ggr. of imilli
ímmi'lha ggr. of imilhlha, <imilha>
immishko ggr. of imishko
immit ishi to adopt (III = subj , I;3) [immi+t] § Ammit ishilitok. I adopted him.
ímmo'ma to be the same (I); still (aux.); again (aux.) {móma ?; prt. immo̱'t: (going) straight on; ishtaaímmo'ma} § Sanokfoyyokhakat immo'ma. I still remember it. | Immo'mali. I'm the same.
immo'ma' midget, little one (it never changes) [immo'ma+'] § hattak immo'ma': midget | waak immo'ma': small cow
immo̱'t (going) straight on, without stopping—prt. of ímmo'ma § Immo̱'t ayatok. He went straight on. | Immo̱'t onala'chi. I'll arrive there without stopping, I'll go there nonstop.
immo̱'t folota, immo̱'t ootfolota to make a home run (I) [(oot) *folota]
immo̱'t ootfolota see immo̱'t folota
imó'na ggr. of imona

imokattola to fall into (something) in order to get away from or avoid (someone˙) (I;III;3); to drop into (III;3-at;3) [im+okattola] § Oka' imokattolalitok. I fell into the water to get away from him. | Lynn iholissaat oka' amokatto'lacha ishkochchalitok. I dropped Lynn's book into the water and (then) I got it out.
imokaahika [OPR] of okaahika
imokaahowita [OPR] of okaahowita
imokcha [PR] of okcha
imokcháa [PR] of okcháa
imokfaha to appear, show up in front of (I;III) [im+okfaha]
imokfahchi to show (something) to (someone˙), let (someone˙) see (something) (I;III;3) [im+okfahchi] § Issamokfahchinna! Don't let me see it!
imokkawalli, imokkawatli to put up more than one barricade against (I;III) [im+okkawalli] {imokkawaatali}
imokkawaatali to go by in front of; put up one barricade against (I;III) [im+okkawaatali] {imokkawalli}
imokkawatli see imokkawalli
imoklhilichi to put in the dark, make it dark for (I;III) [im+oklhilichi]
imokshílli'ta to be closed in, behind a closed door (nonhum. subj.) (3) [im+okshilli'ta]
imokshitta to close (a door) against (someone˙, especially, so that he can't get out) (I;III;3) [im+okshitta] § Abokkisa' imokshittalitok Irenea. I closed the door against Irene.
imoktabli to block against ˙ (I;III;3); to block (I;III) [im+oktabli] {v1. imoktapa} § Hina' imoktablilitok. I blocked the road against him.

imoktani to appear to (in a vision) (I;III); to have a vision of (III;3-at) [im+oktani] {ngr. imoktáni}
imoktanichi to reveal (a fact or situation) to (I;III) [im+oktanichi] § Chihoowaat chokfalhpoobapiisachi' alhiha chipota aati'waka imoktanichittook. God revealed to the shepherds where the baby was lying.
imoktapa to have (something) blocked, be blocked by (III;3-at); to be blocked, stopped (III) [im+oktapa] {v2. imoktabli}
imoktáni ngr. of imoktani
imola to crow, make noise for (3;3) [im+ola]
imolhchi [PR] of olhchi
imolhti to have a fire built for one (III); to have (a fire) built for one (III;3-at) [im+olhti]
imomoppolo, (MJ) imimokpolo, (ER) imomoppolo, (EP) imimoppolo to be crippled (III) [+T] [im+im+oppolo; im+iyyi'+im+oppolo; imoma oppolo?]
imomoppolo', (HS) imiyyonkpolo', (WB) imoppolo', (CC) imompolo' cripple [imomoppolo+']
imona to go (somewhere over there) to ˚ (I;III;3); to have (someone) go to one (III;3-at) {ggr. imó'na}
imontochchí'na [PR] of ontochchí'na
imontoklo [PR] of ontoklo
imoppani [OPR] of oppani
imoppóllo'ka ggr. of imoppoloka
imoppolo [PR] of oppolo
imoppolohónka hngr. of imoppoloka
imoppoloka to answer back, get mad at, be mean to (I;III) [im+oppoloka] {ggr. imoppóllo'ka; hngr. imoppolohónka}

imoshchiloli [PR] of oshchiloli
imoshchooni to bow to, nod at (I;III) [im+oshchooni] § Iksamoshcho'no. He didn't bow to me.
imoshta [PR] of oshta
imowwatta to hunt for the benefit of (I;III) [im+owwatta]
imootaalhlhika' edge (ER) [im+ootaalhlhika']
imooti to build (a fire) for ˚ (I;III;3) [im+ooti]
imohika [OPR] of ohika
imohilha [OPR] of ohilha
imolabi to want (something) from ˚ (I;III;3); to tell to behave, exact obedience from (I;III); to forbid, keep from doing (I;III) [im+olabi] {ngr. imolámbi; ootimolabi, ittimolabi} § Ikayyoka'chiho imolabilitok. I forbade him to go.
imolámbi ngr. of imolabi
imolhatabli [OPR] of olhatabli
<imóma> in ishtaaimoma
imomochi to get used to, accustomed to (III;3) [+T]; to have a habit (III) [im+omochi] {ishtimomochi}
imomolhchi [PR] of omolhchi
imóna ki'yo not to have enough (III) [im+ona]
imonowa [OPR] of onowa
imoshi' uncle: mother's brother (oIIIp) {moshi'}
impa to eat, have a meal, dine (I) [+PR] [+CPR] {ggr. í'pa; hngr. ihímpa; ngr. ímpa; ishtikímpo ?}
ímpa ngr. of impa
impa' food, groceries [impa+']
impa' asonnak tobbaalhto' canned food
impa' aa-asha' food store
impa' iksala'mo not to eat too much (IN) § Impa' aksala'mo. I didn't eat too much.
impachichi to make (someone) eat

Impaka'li'

(I;3) [impa+chichi]
Impaka'li' Chickasaw woman's
name (CP) [im+Paka'li']
impalahánta hngr. of impalata
impalahámmi hngr. of impalammi
impalammi to be seriously affected;
to be depressed, have it bad; to be
mourning (III) [im+palammi] {ggr.
impállammi; hngr. impalahámmi}
§ Achibikakat chimpallammi.
You're real sick. I Haksitokot
impallammi. He has a hangover,
He really drank.
impalammichi to treat badly (I;III)
[impalammi+chi]
impalata to be mean to (I;III) {hngr.
impalahánta; ygr. impaláyya'ta}
impaláyya'ta ygr. of impalata
impállammi ggr. of impalammi
impalli to be hot; often, to be sexually
aroused (an. subj.) (III) [im+palli]
impalhki to outwalk, leave behind,
be too fast for (I;III) [im+palhki]
impanaa [PR] of panaa
impasa'chi to applaud, clap for (I;III)
[im+pasa'chi]
impassaa [OPR] of passaa
<impashooli> in ishtimpashooli'
impaalhto' crop (of a fowl) (AB, MJ)
[impa' aalhto']
impaapi' father, daddy (oIIIp) [from
English pappy ?]
impihlí'chi ggr. of impihlínchi
impihlínchi to come in to watch
(children—pl. obj.) for ˚ (I;III;3)
[im+pihlinchi] {ggr. impihlí'chi} §
Lynnat Doris inchipota
ampihlinchikma ayala'chi. When
Lynn comes in to watch Doris's kids
for me, I'll go.
impilachi to send to ˚ (I;III;3)
[im+pilachi]
impilihísa hngr. of impilisa
impilisa to fondle, play with

(sexually), molest (I;III) [im+pilisa]
{hngr. impilihísa; ngr. impilísa}
impilísa ngr. of impilisa
impisa', hashshok impisa', (WB)
impisa, (ER) impissa', (AB) impissa
beargrass (said to look up one's
dress or pants when it clings to the
legs) [im+pisa+' (reanalyzed)]
impishi to nurse from (one's mother
or a wet nurse) (I;III) [im+pishi]
impishichi [OPR] of pishichi
impó'nna ggr. of imponna
impoffola' crop (of a fowl)
[im+poffola+'] {akankimpoffola',
poffóllo'wa}
impoffololi to inflate, blow up for ˚
(I;III;3) [im+poffololi]
impohónna hngr. of imponna
impokkó'li [PR] of pokkó'li
impokpoki [PR] of pokpoki
impokpokichi in oka' impokpokichi
[im+pokpokichi]
imponna to be smart, clever (III); to
know how to do (well) (III)
[E+kat/ka] [im+<ponna>] {ggr.
impó'nna; hngr. impohónna; ygr.
impóyyo'nna} § Hilhakat amponna,
Hilhaka amponna. I know how to
dance (well).
imponnachi to teach (I;III); to teach
how to [+unmarked ka/0 comp.]
(I;III) [imponna+chi] § Hilha
amponnachitok, Hilhaka
amponnachitok. He taught me to
dance.
imponta to lend, rent to ˚ (I;III;3); to
rent to ˚ for (a sum) (I;III;3;3)
[im+ponta] § Anchokka' Charles
impontalitok ta'osso oshtaho. I
rented my house to Charles for four
dollars.
impotooni to watch (a house) for ˚
(I;III;3) [im+potooni]
impóyyo'nna ygr. of imponna

imvooti to vote for (I;III) [im+vooti] § Issamvootitam? Did you vote for me?

inbolbo' poss. of ilbolbo' (oIIIp)

inchaffa to do for the first time (III) [E+t] [im+chaffa] {ittinchaffa} § Toksalit anchaffatok. I worked for the first time. | Waaka' abit ponchaffatok. We killed a cow for the first time.

inchaffichi [OPR] of chaffichi {oshtinchaffichi}

inchakaffa', (MJ) chakaffa' gizzard (oIIIp) [im+<chakaffa'>]

inchakká'li [PR] of chakká'li

<inchakwa'> in akankinchakwa'

inchalha to be marked with a cut in the ear (of a cow—to show ownership) (3) [-PR] [im+chalha] {v2. inchalhlhi}

inchalhlhi to mark (a cow) with a cut in the ear (to show ownership) (I;3) [im+chalhlhi] {v1. inchalha}

inchama'chi to make a noise with metal (for instance, by hitting pans together) (I); to make a noise with metal and thus move or charm (animals) (I;3) [im+chama'chi]

inchampoli to like the taste of, enjoy (III;3) [im+champoli] § Paska anchampoli. I like bread.

inchanaa' wheel, tire (oIIIp) [im+chanaa+'] § itti' chanaa inchanaa': wagon wheel, the wagon's wheel

<inchasha'> in sintinchasha'

inchashwa part of the back, area between the shoulders (oIIIp)

inchashwa' sinew from the back (of an animal, especially a hog, cow, or squirrel), or string made from such a sinew (o3p) {inchashwa}

inchawwala to have one's skirt be too short (III) [im+chawwala]

inchaafoochi see intachaafoochi

inchaaha [PR] of chaaha

<inchaamo'> in iyyinchaamo'

inchí'ya to sit around, sit by while (someone) works (dl. subj.) (3;3) {sg. imbínni'li; tpl. imbinohmáa} [im+chi'ya]

inchilabli [PR] of chilabli

inchisiya [PR] of chisiya

inchiiki to have it be too early for one (III) [im+chiiki] § Anchiika'chikat ithanali. I know it'll be too early for me.

incho'li to brand, mark, tattoo, vandalize (I;III) {v1. incho'wa}

incho'wa to be marked, vandalized, tattooed, branded (III) {v2. incho'li} § Aboohaat incho'wa. The house is vandalized.

incho'wa' sign [incho'wa+']

inchofata [PR] of chofata

inchokka' home, (possessed) house (oIIIp) [im+chokka'] § chinchokka': your home

inchokka' aaikbi to make one's home in (something other than a normal house) (IIIp , I;3) [aa+ikbi] § Alhchaba nota'ak anchokka' aaikbilitok. I make my home under a bridge.

inchokkachaffa' family (oIIIp) [inchokka' chaffa+']

inchokkachaffa' holhchifo clan name (oIIIp)

inchokkapanta' see inchokkaponta'

inchokkaponta', inchokkapanta' neighbor (oIIIp)

inchokkaalaa, inchokkaalaha to visit (I;III) [im+<chokkaalaa>] § Ikinchokkaala'okitok. He didn't visit her.

inchokkiksho' hobo, bum [inchokka' iksho+']

inchokkilissa to be sad, lonely (III)

149

[im+chokkilissa] {ggr. inchokkíllissa}

inchokkíllissa ggr. of inchokkilissa

inchokma to like to (III) [E], [E+kat]; to be healthy (III) [im+chokma] {ngr. inchongma: to be well; neg. ikinchokmo: to feel bad} § Hilhakat anchokma. I like to dance. | Alekat ollali inchokma. Alex likes to laugh.

inchokma'si to be pretty: especially, to be dressed up pretty (III) [im+chokma'si]

inchokmahánka hngr. of inchokmaka

inchokmaka in ishtinchokmaka [im+<chokmaka>] {hngr. inchokmahánka; ngr. inchokmánka}

inchokmánka to feel fine (III) —ngr. of inchokmaka {hngr. inchokmahánka} § Anchokmankacha antalikat i'ma. I feel fine and I'm still alive.

inchokmishto to be healthy (III) [im+chokma+ishto]

inchokoshpachi to gossip about, to gossip to (I;III) [im+chokoshpachi]

inchokoshpali to gossip about, to gossip to (I;III) [im+chokoshpali]

inchompa to shop for °, buy for ° (I;III;3) [im+chompa]

inchóngma to be well—ngr. of inchokma

inkaba'chi to knock on (someone's°) (door); to rouse (someone°) by knocking on (the door) (I;III;3); to knock on (someone's door); to knock on (someone's) door (I;3) [+SC] [im+kaba'chi] § Lynna okkisa' inkaba'shlitok, Lynn imokkisa' inkaba'shlitok, Lynna inkaba'shlitok. I knocked on Lynn's door.

inkaha' foundation (oIIIp) [im+kaha+'] § Abooha inkaha'at tali'. The foundation of the house is rock.

inkalli to scratch (a part of (someone's°) body that he can't reach), scratch (something) for ° (I;III;3) [im+kalli] § Sanaalhchaba ankalli! Scratch my back!

inkallo to have an erection (III); to be really hard on (I;III) [im+kallo] § Sashki' anki' tawwa'at ankallohootoko kaniya' ayala' ki'yo. My mother and father are really hard on me; that's why I never go anywhere.

inkamaa [PR] of kamaa

inkámmo'sha ggr. of inkamosha

inkamosha to be nauseated by, disgusted by (I;III) [im+kamosha] {ggr. inkámmo'sha} § Impa' inkamoshli. I was nauseated by the food. | Chinkamoshli. You nauseate me, disgust me, I am nauseated by, disgusted by you.

<inkana> in ittinkana {ngr. inkána; neg. ikinka'no}

inkanalli to get away from, to dodge, avoid (I;III) [im+kanalli] § Ankanalli! Get away from me!

inkanchi to sell to ° (I;III;3) [im+kanchi]

inkanihmi to do (something) for ° (ind.) (I;III;3) [+HM], <inkanih> [im+kanihmi] {int. inkatihmi} § Nanna ankanihtok. He did something for me.

inkaniya to go, be away from (sg. subj.) (I;III); to lose, to have (one's candidate) lose (sg. 3-at) (III;3-at) [im+kaniya] {pl. subj./3-at intamowa} § Alek holba'at ankaniyatok. I lost my picture of Alex. | Lynnat ankaniya. Lynn (my

candidate, whom I voted for) lost. |
imaanokfila-at inkaniya: to be crazy,
lose one's mind | wiikaat inkaniya:
to lose weight
<inkani'chi> in ishkin inkani'chi
<inkanih> [HM] of inkanihmi
inkánnohmi to have several
(especially, men, women, romantic
interests), to have how many
(especially, men, women) (ind.)
(III;3-at) [+HM], <inkannoh>
[im+kannohmi] {int. inkáttohmi} §
Jamesat ihooat inkannohmika
ithanali. I know how many women
James has.
<inkannoh> [HM] of inkánnohmi
inkano'mi cross-cousin (child of
one's mother's brother or one's
father's sister), distant cousin (at
least a second cousin) (oIIIp)
{ittinkano'mi}
inkapassa to be cold, to feel cold (an.
subj.) (III) [im+kapassa]
inkapittani' boss, head, president,
general (o3p) [im+<kapittani'>—
from English captain or Spanish
capitán] § nannaaiksaachi'
inkapittani': the boss of the factory
inkasa'chi to knock on (someone's°)
(door) (especially, using a door
knocker), to rouse (someone°) by
knocking on (the door) (I;III;3) [±SC]
[im+kasa'chi] § Abokkisa'
ankasa'chitok. She knocked on my
door (with the knocker).
inkashabli to share with °, give to
(one person°); to divide (sg., whole
obj.) with ° (I;III;3) [im+kashabli]
{pl. III obj. inkashkoli}
inkashapa to get a share, receive
(III;3-at) [im+kashapa]
inkashkoli to divide among (several
people°) (I;III;3) [im+kashkoli] {sg.
III obj. inkashabli; ittakashkoli}

inkashofa to be absolved, forgiven
(for instance, of a Catholic who has
been to confession) (III)
[im+kashofa] {v2. inkashoffi}
inkashoffi to forgive (I;III)
[im+kashoffi] {v1. inkashofa}
inkatabli to forbid (someone to do
something), to ground (someone),
to trap or head off (someone), to
stop (someone's) progress;
traditionally, to block (people) from
the yard of a house where someone
is doctoring (of the doctor's
assistant) (I;III) {v1. inkatapa}
inkatapa to be forbidden, grounded;
to be blocked, headed off (III) {v2.
inkatabli}
inkatapo'chi to try to stop (I;III) [±SC]
[inkatapo'li+chi]
inkatapo'li to try to stop (I;III)
[im+<katapo'li>]{ggr. inkatáppo'li}
inkatáppo'li ggr. of inkatapo'li
inkatihmi to do (what) for ° (I;III;3)
[+HM], <inkatih> [im+katihmi] §
Nantahta ishinkatihtok? What did
you do for him?
inkatimpi to be which one for (rare;
mainly used as a somewhat rude
'for you' question) (3;III)
[im+katimpi] {ind. inkanihmi} §
Ihooat chinkatimpita? Which
woman is for you?
<inkatih> [HM] of inkatihmi
inkatolhlhi to cut (pl. obj.) for °
(I;III;3) [im+katolhlhi] § Alek
ilbakchosh inkatolhlhilitok. I cut
Alex's nails.
inkáttohmi to have how many
(especially, men, women, romantic
interests) (int.) (III;3-at) [+HM],
<inkáttoh> [im+kattohmi] {ind.
inkánnohmi} § Ihooat
chinkattohta? How many women
do you have?

<inkáttoh>

<inkáttoh> [HM] of inkáttohmi
inkawaski [PR] of kawaski
inkaalli to call for (I;III) [im+kaalli]
inkáa to leave (dl. obj., lying) (III;3-at) [im+kaa] {sg. 3-at intówa; tpl. 3-at imásha} § Itti'at ankáatok. I left (two) sticks (lying).
inkána to act friendly toward, be friends with (I;III)—ngr. of <inkana> {neg. ikinka'no}
inkana' friend (oIIIp) [inkana+']
inki' father (of a person, not an animal) (oIIIp)
Inki' Oshi' Shilombish Tochchi'na the Trinity: Father, Son, and Holy Ghost
inki' toba' stepfather (oIIIp) § anki' toba': my stepfather
inkihli to wipe (a child) after defecation (I;III) [im+kihli]
inkilish penis (oIIIp)
inko'si' uncle, father's brother; (CC) grandfather (oIIIp) [inki' o'si+']
inkobafa [PR] of kobafa
<inkobaffi> in anompinkobaffi
inkochcha [PR] of kochcha
inkofi in ilbak inkofi [im+kofi]
inkofollichi to make steam for (someone with breathing difficulties) (I;III) [im+kofollichi]
inkoloffi to break off a part of for ° (I;III;3) [im+koloffi] § Charlesak paska ishinkoloffitok. You broke off part of the bread for Charles.
inkonta to whistle at (I;III) [im+konta]
inkosoma [PR] of kosoma
inkostini to impress; to outsmart (I;III) {ngr. inkostíni} [im+kostini]
inkostíni ngr. of inkostini
inkowa to break (sg. compact obj.) (III;3-at) [im+kowa] {pl. 3-at inkookowa} § Lynnat amamposhi'at inkowa. Lynn broke

my plate.
inkookoli to break (pl. compact objs.) for ° (I;III;3) [im+kookoli] {sg. obj. inkooli}
inkookowa to break (pl. compact objs.) (III;3-at) [im+kookowa] {sg. 3-at inkowa} § Lynnat imalhkaniyatok amamposhi'at inkookowatahatokat. Lynn forgot that she had broken my plates.
inkooli to break (sg. compact obj.) for ° (I;III;3) [im+kooli] {pl. obj. inkookoli}
ínksho ngr. of iksho
inni in lowak inni, toomi inni
innó'chi ggr. of innochi
inno'chi' necklace, necktie (IIIp) [inno'chi+'] § iminno'chi': his necktie
innochi to put on (a necklace, scarf) (I;3) {ggr. innó'chi; ygr. innóyyo'chi: to wear (a necklace, scarf)}
innochi' handkerchief, scarf (iminnochi': IIIp) [innochi+']
innochi' homma' bandanna
<innoti'> see noti'
innóyyo'chi to wear (a necklace, scarf)—ygr. of innochi
ino' in ishno' ino' iitawwa'a {ano'}
inonka' voice (IIp) {anonka' ?} § sanonka': my voice
inonka' chokmali to clear one's throat (IIp, I)
inonka' hottopa, inonkaat hottopa to have a sore throat (IIp, II) [inonka'+at] § Sanonka' sattopa, Sanonkaat sattopa. I have a sore throat.
inonkaat hottopa see inonka' hottopa
inonkopoolo', (CC) nonkapola' throat, Adam's apple (IIp) [inonka' oppolo+' ?]
intachaafoochi, inchaafoochi to

divide up among ° (usually, giving one each) (I;III;3) [im+ittachaafoochi] § Paska hachintachaafoochila'chi. I'll divide the meat among you.

intaha to be out of, to have run out of (III;3-at) [im+taha] § Lynnat tili'kaat intahatok. Lynn is out of flour.

intakashshi' milt, spleen (especially, of a pig) (oIIIp)

intakashkoli to divide among (more than two°) (I;III;3) [im+ittakashkoli] § Nipi' pontakashkolitok. She divided the meat among us.

<intakaali'> in iyyintakaali'

intakchi to tie for ° (I;III;3); to brake, stop (a car, wagon) (I;3) [im+takchi] {v1. intallakchi}

intakho'bi to be lazy (III) {ygr. intakhóyyo'bi}

intakho'bichi to make lazy, bore, wear out (I;III) [intakho'bi+chi]

intakhóyyo'bi ygr. of intakho'bi

<intakla'> in ittintakla'

intalaali to place, put out (sg. inan. patient obj., standing on a flat bottom) for ° (I;III;3) [im+talaali] {ngr. intalá̱li: to leave for; pl. patient obj. intalooli}

intalá̱a to leave (sg. inan. obj., standing on a flat bottom) (III;3-at) [im+tala̱a] {dl. 3-at. intalǫ́wa; tpl. 3-at. imá̱sha} § Amalhkani'yacha asonnak tobbi'at antala̱atok. I forgot and left the bucket (standing).

intalá̱li to leave (sg. inan. obj., standing on a flat bottom) for—ngr. of intalaali

intalbitili to put another (layer) on (someone°) (I;III;3) [im+ittalbitili] {intalbitli: to put more than one additional (layer) on}

intalbitli to put more than one

additional (layer) on (someone°) (I;III;3) [im+ittalbitli] {intalbitili: to put another (layer) on}

intálla'a to have (sg. inan. obj., standing on a flat bottom) (III;3-at) [im+talla'a] {dl. 3-at. intállo'wa; tpl. 3-at. intalowat má̱a}

intallakchi to be braked (of a car), to be locked (of wheels) (3) [im+tallakchi] {v2. intakchi} ·

intállo'wa to have (dl. inan. obj., standing on flat bottoms) (III;3-at) [im+tallo'wa] {sg. 3-at. intálla'a; tpl. 3-at. intalowat má̱a} § Ishtakafaat antallo'wa. I have (two) cups.

intalop testicles (oIIIp) (Ct?)

intalowat má̱a to have (tpl. inan. obj., standing on flat bottoms) [im+(talowat ma̱a)] (III;3-at , —) {sg. 3-at. intálla'a; dl. 3-at. intállo'wa} § Ishtakafaat antalowat ma̱a. I have (more than two) cups.

intalooli to put out, place (pl. inan. obj., standing on flat bottoms) for ° (I;III;3) [im+talooli] {ngr. intalǫ́li: leave (standing) for; sg. patient obj. intalaali}

intaloowa to sing for: especially, to lead in singing, show how to sing (I;III); to sing (a song) for °, lead ° in singing (a song) (I;III;3) [im+taloowa]

intaloowachi to make sing for ° (I;III;3); to make sing (a song) for ° (I;III;3;3) [im+taloowachi]

intalǫ́li to leave (pl. inan. obj., standing on flat bottoms) for °— ngr. of intalooli

intalǫ́wa to leave (dl. inan. obj., standing on flat bottoms) (III;3-at) [im+talǫ́wa] {sg. 3-at. intalá̱a; tpl. 3-at. imá̱sha} § Lynnat asonnak tobbi'at intalo̱watok. Lynn left the (two) buckets (standing).

intalhlhá'pi

intalhlhá'pi [PR] of talhlhá'pi
intalhoffi to go off, pull away from
(I;III); to drop, let fall (III;3-at)
[im+talhoffi]
intamowa to go away from (pl. subj.)
(I;III); to lose (pl. 3-at) (III;3-at)
[+taha] [im+tamowa] {sg. subj./3-at
inkaniya} § Holissaat antamowatok,
antamowatahatok. I lost my (two)
books. I Holissaat tamowat
antahatok. I lost my (three or more)
books.
intanap (MJ, TJ), (CM, EP) intanapi
enemy (oIIIp) [im+tanap]
intannap the other side of; on the
other side of (o3p) [im+tannap] §
hina' intannap: on the other side of
the street I holisso intannap: the
other side of the paper
intapa to break (sg. long obj.) in two
(III;3-at) [im+tapa] § Lynn
ishtalakchaat antapatok. I broke
Lynn's rope.
intapalhalli to cut in half for ° (I;III;3)
[im+ittapalhalli] § Tak olo
pontapalhallitok. He cut the peach
in half for us.
intapalhlhi to cut in three or more
pieces for ° (I;III;3)
intasahli to holler, scream to (I;III)
[im+tasalhli] § Lynnak
intasahlilitok asapila'chiho. I
screamed to Lynn for help.
intí'wa to have (something lying); to
give birth to (hum. subj.) (III;3-at)
[im+ti'wa] § Charles iholissaat
anti'wa. I've got Charles's book
(lying down).
intibá'lli ggr. of intiballi
intiballi, intibatli to avoid, to miss
(on purpose?) (I;III); to miss
(without knowing it?) (III;3-at)
[im+<tiballi>] {ggr. intíbballi,
intibá'lli; tiballichi}

intiballichi to make (someone) miss
(I;III) [intiballi+chi] § Charlesat
antiballichitok. Charles made me
miss.
intibatli see intiballi
intíbballi ggr. of intiballi
intikba older sibling of the same sex
as oneself; older first cousin of the
same sex as oneself (oIIIp) § antikba:
my older brother (if a man is
speaking), my older sister (if a
woman is speaking)
intikba iklanna' older half-sibling of
the same sex as oneself (oIIIp)
[iklanna+']
intikba toba' older step-sibling of the
same sex as oneself (oIIIp)
intikbáy'ka ggr. of intikbayka
intikbayka to be a dance or song
leader for (I;III) {ggr. intikbáy'ka}
[im+tikbayka]
intikbayka', hilha' intikbayka' dance
leader [intikbayka+']
intikili to touch (something) because
there is little room to maneuver
(3;3) [im+tikili] {ggr. intíkki'li: to
hold up, support} § Kaa-at holitta
intikili. The car touched the fence
(because there was no room for it to
get by).
intikiichi to prop up with (I;3;3) [±SC]
[im+tikiichi] § Yamma itti'
intikiichilitok, intikiishlitok. I'm
propping that one up with a stick.
intíkki'li to hold up, support—ggr. of
intikili
intilhaa, intilhaha to run (in a race)
against; to run from, bolt with (pl.
subj.) (I;III); to have (horses) run
from, bolt with one (3-at;III)
[im+tilhaa] {v2. intilhili} § Brenda-
at asoba-at intilhaatok. My horses
bolted with Brenda, Brenda had my
horses run away from her.

154

intilhili to run, shoo (pl. obj.) off
from ˚ (I;III;3) [im+tilhili] {v1.
intilhaa} § Chokaan intilhililitok. I
shooed the flies away from him.
intishooko'chi to make a rustling
sound with (paper, usually) for ˚ (to
amuse a baby, for example) (I;III;3)
[±SC] [im+ittishooko'chi] § Chipota
holisso intishooko'chilitok. I
rustled the paper for the baby.
intiwa to have (a door or gate) open
for one (III;3-at) [im+tiwa] §
Okkisa'at anti'wacha kochchalitok.
The door was open for me and I got
out.
intiwwa'pa [PR] of tiwwa'pa
intiwwi to open for ˚ (I;III;3)
[im+tiwwi]
intiibli to reinjure a sore spot (of
someone's) (I;III) [im+tiibli] {v1.
intiipa; intiipo'li}
intiik sister (of a man); female first
cousin (of a man) (oIIIp) [im+tiik]
intiik iklanna' half-sister (of a man)
(oIIIp) [iklanna+'] § antiik iklanna':
my half-sister (a man says this)
intiik toba' stepsister (of a man)
(oIIIp) [toba+']
intiipa to reinjure one's own sore
spot (III); to reinjure (a part of one's
body) (III;3-at) [im+<tiipa>] {v2.
intiibli; intiipo'wa} § Salbakat
antiipatokat ithanali. I know I hit
my sore hand again.
intiipo'li to keep on reinjuring
(someone) (I;III); to keep on
reinjuring (someone˚) in (a body
part) (I;III;3) {v1. intiipo'wa; intiibli}
[im+tiipo'li] § Ilbak intiipo'lili. I
keep hitting him in his hand.
intiipo'wa to keep being reinjured in
(a body part) (III;3-at)
[im+<tiipo'wa>] {v2. intiipo'li;
intiipa} § Benjieat ilbakat

intiipo'wa. Benjie keeps getting his
hand hurt.
intįfa [PR] of tįfa
into'wa to lie down to have sexual
intercourse with (sg. subj.) (I;III)
[im+to'wa]
intoba in nanna ataklama' intoba
intochchí'na [PR] of tochchí'na
<intohbi'> in akankoshintohbi'
intohǫno hngr. of intohno
intohno to throw out, make go (I;III)
[im+tohno] {hngr. intohǫno; ngr.
intǫhno}
intoklo [PR] of toklo
intoksali to work for, do work for
(I;III); to work out for (refers either
to a situation, or to the effect of
some magic or charm) (—;III)
[im+toksali] § Chintoksalika
achiyoppata? Are you happy that it
worked out for you?
intoksali' slave, employee (oIIIp)
[im+toksali']
<into'lhka'> in iyyinto'lhka'
Into'lhka-losishto' (pet name for a
child) (MJ) [iyyinto'lhka' losa
ishto+']
intono'chi to roll (a ball, for instance)
to ˚ (I;III;3) [im+tono'chi]
intoshaffi to break off a piece of for ˚;
to divide up (land) into plots for ˚
(I;III;3) [im+toshaffi] § Paska
antoshaffitok. He broke off a piece of
the bread for me.
intoshli to cut up for ˚ (I;III;3)
[im+toshli] § Irenea nipi'
intoshlilitok. I cut up the meat for
Irene.
intoshooli to interpret, explain, or
translate to or for (I;III)
[im+toshooli] {ggr. intóshsho'li}
intóshsho'li ggr. of intoshooli
intǫhno ngr. of intohno
intǫwa to leave (sg. inan. obj., lying)

(III;3-at) [im+towa] {dl. 3-at inkáa; tpl. 3-at imásha} § Lynn iholissaat antowatok. I left Lynn's book (lying).

íngbi ngr. of ikbi

ínglo ngr. of iklo

<ipa> in ilipa, ittipa [apa] {ishtikímpo ?}

ipashaaiksaachi' beauty parlor [ipashi' aa+iksaachi+']

ipashaaoshchilo'chi' beauty parlor [ipashi' aa+oschilochi+']

ipashi' (head) hair (IIp) {short form: pashi'}

ipashi' alhiipi'li', pashalhiipi'li', (CM) pashalhiipi'ya' hairnet

ipashi' aaintapa' barbershop [aa+im+tapa+']

ipashi' holba' wig, hairpiece (IIp) § sapashi' holba': my wig

ipashi' ishtakallo'chi' see ipashishtakallo'chi'

ipashi' ontalla'a', ipashontalla'a' barrette (IIp)

ipashi' tabli' barber [tabli+']

ipashishtakallo'chi', ipashi' ishtakallo'chi' hairpin, bobby pin (IIp)

ipashishtasiiti'li', ipashishtasiiti'ya' barrette (IIp)

ipashishtasiiti'ya' see ipashishtasiiti'li'

ipashishtoshchilochi' curling iron [ipashi' isht oshchilochi+']

ipashishtoshchiloli' curlers [ipashi' isht oshchiloli+']

ipashontalla'a' see ipashi' ontalla'a'

ipihínta hngr. of ipita

ipínta ngr. of ipita

ipita to feed ˚ to ˚, give (food or something to drink˚) to ˚ (I;II;3); to feed, give something to eat or drink to; to support, care for (I;II) [+OPR] {v1. ilhpita; hngr. ipihínta; ngr.

ipínta; apa} § Lynnat nipi' sapitatok. Lynn fed me the meat. | Nannimilhlha' chipitala'chi. I'm going to feed you to the monster. | Lynna chipota imipitalitok. I fed Lynn's baby.

ipitat haksichi to get (someone˚) drunk on (I;II;3) (sounds best if the intoxicating drink is specified) [ipita+t] § Biya' ipitat sahaksichi. He got me drunk on beer.

ipishik breast (IIp) {pishi}

ipishik ibitop nipple

ipok grandchild (IIp)

ipok ihoo' granddaughter (IIp) § sapok ihoo' : my granddaughter

ipok nakni' grandson (IIp) § popok nakni': our grandson

ipok tiik granddaughter (HS, TP), daughter-in-law (ER)

ippo'si' grandmother (IIp) {appo'si'}

ippo'sishto' great-grandmother (IIp) {appo'sishto'}

ippolhchi', (CC) ipposhchi', (WB) ipolhchi' son-in-law, (HS, TP, WB) father-in-law, (CC) daughter-in-law (IIp)

ippolhchihoo' daughter-in-law (IIp) [ippolhchi' ihoo+']

iská'nno ggr. of <iskanno>

iskahánno hngr. of <iskanno>

iskáhhanno hgr. of <iskanno>

<iskanno> in iskanno'si, iskannochi {ggr. iská'nno; hgr. iskáhhanno; hngr. iskahánno; ngr. iskánno}

iskanno'si to be little, small (sg. subj.) (II) [+CPR] [-PR] [<iskanno>+o'si] {pl. sawa'si; ggr. iská'nno; hgr. iskáhhanno; hngr. iskahánno; ngr. iskánno}

iskannochi to make (sg. obj.) small (I;II) [<iskanno>+chi] {ngr. iskannónchi: to make smaller; pl. obj. sawachi} iskannónchi to make smaller—ngr. of iskannochi

iskánno to be smaller—ngr. of <iskanno>

isolash, (LR) isolosh tongue (IIp) {short form: solash}

isolash falaa to stick out one's tongue (IIp = subj) (cannot be embedded or further inflected) § JPat isolash falaa. JP is sticking out his tongue. I Chisolash falaa. You're sticking out your tongue.

isolash faliili to stick out one's tongue (IIp = subj, I) § Chisolash ishfaliitok. You stuck out your tongue.

isolash ifaliili to stick out one's tongue at (IIp = subj, I;III) [im+falilii]

isolash-oshi' uvula (IIp) [isolash oshi']

issa to finish, be done (I) [E+t] {ggr. í'ssa; ngr. íssa} § Impat ishissatok. You finished eating.

issap louse (IIIp)

issap ishtalbi' fine-tooth comb (IIIp) [isht <albi>+']

issap nihi' nits, louse eggs

issi' deer; billy goat

issi' hakshop buckskin

issi' imilhlha' deer [imilhlha+']

issi' ishatanni deer tick (AB) [im+shatanni]

issi' kosoma' goat [kosoma+']

issi' kosoma' nakni' billy goat

issi' kosoma' notakhish goatee

issi' kosomimpishokchi' niha' cheese [issi' kosoma' im+pishokchi' niha']

issi' lapish faloha' buck with full-grown horns [faloha+']

issi' nakni' buck; billy goat

issi' tiik doe; she-goat, nanny goat

issíkko'pa ggr. of issikopa

issikohómpa hngr. of issikopa

issikómpa ngr. of issikopa

issikopa, (MJ) issakopa, (AB) sikopa, (AW) sokopa to be mean, vicious, cruel (II) {ggr. issíkko'pa; hngr. issikohómpa; ngr. issikómpa; ygr. issikóyyo'pa; imissikopa: to be mean to}

issikopachi to make mean, teach to be mean (I;II) [issikopa+chi] § Sassikopachitahtok. That taught me to be mean.

issikopalichi to make mean, make act mean (I;II) [issikopa+li+chi]

issikóyyo'pa ygr. of issikopa

issim-ahi' deer potatoes (plant with purple flowers whose root is used as a medicine for swelling) [issi' im+ahi']

issimittish type of medicinal plant (WB) [issi' im+ittish]

issish blood (IIp / IIIp); blood (in general) § sassish, amissish: my blood I Issish howitalitok. I threw up blood.

issish alotto'wa' full blood, full-blooded Indian (EP) [alotto'wa+']

issish aaishi to bleed, take blood from (IIp = obj. , I) § Chissish aaishila'chi. I'll take blood from you.

issish ishko' bloodsucker, leech; doctor or technician who draws blood [ishko+']

issish ihina' blood vessel—vein, artery (IIp) [im+hina'] § sassish ihina': my vein

issish lhatapa to bleed; to be bleeding, to have internal bleeding; to menstruate, have a period (IIp, —) {issishat lhatapa} § Sassish lhatapakat ithanali. I know I'm bleeding. I Salbakat issish lhatapa. My hand is bleeding.

issish shalahli' blood clot that's

starting to set

issish shǫ'ka' bloodsucker, leech [shǫ'ka+']

issishat hika for one's blood to clot (IIp) [issish+at] § Sassishat hikaka̲ itha̲nali. I know my blood clotted, I know I have a blood clot.

issishat lhatapa to bleed (IIp, —) [issish+at] {issish lhatapa} § Sassishat lhatapakat itha̲nali. I know I'm bleeding.

issishkin type of small bird (AW) [issi' ishkin]

isso to hit (I;II); to hit (in baseball) (I) {ggr. í'sso; hngr. ihísso; ngr. ísso} § Sahasso. He keeps hitting me. | Kani̲ht sa'ssotok. He finally hit me.

issoba horse; sawhorse (IIIp: i̲soba) {short form: soba}

issoba aaipita' piini' horse trough

issoba basoowa' zebra [basoowa+']

issoba chaaha' giraffe [chaaha+']

issoba imo'ma' Shetland pony

issoba ipa̲shi' mane

issoba ishki' mother horse

issoba itti' ibitop aaimpa' giraffe [aa+impa+']

issoba i̲sholosh horseshoe (MC) [im+sholosh]

issoba i̲shoptilhi'li' type of medicinal plant (probably a large variety of horsemint) [im+shoptilhi'li']

issoba kamaa' zebra [kamaa+']

issoba kapali' bit (for a horse) [kapali+']

issoba kapali' ishhalalli' bridle [isht halalli+']

issoba kapali' ishtalakchi' bridle

issoba kobokshi' camel [kobokshi+']

issoba lakna' palomino [lakna+']

Issoba Losa' a bad name for one person to call another [losa+']

issoba malli' bucking bronco [malli+']

issoba nokhistap falaa' giraffe [falaa+']

issoba oshpishichi' nursing mother horse

issoba sa̲wa', soba sa̲wa' pony [issoba sa̲wa('si)+']

issoba shaapoli' harness

issoba shiwaa' zebra [shiwaa+']

issoba tossoola' bucking bronco [tossoola+']

issobimato̲falaa' garlic [issoba im+(h)ato̲falaa']

issobimbala' lima beans; (AB) buckeye [issoba im+bala']

issobimilhlha' wild horse [issoba imilhlha+']

issobinchokaana horsefly (TP) [issoba im+chokaano]

issobinchokka' barn [issoba im+chokka']

issobinno'chi' horse collar [issoba inno'chi']

issobinnochi' bell (of any type) [issoba innochi+']

issobintako̲lo horse apples (bois d'arc fruit) [issoba im+tako̲lo]

issobintali' lapali' horseshoe [issoba im+tali' lapali+']

issobishfama', soba ishfama', soba ishfammi' horsewhip [issoba isht fama/fammi+']

issobishliichi' plow (pulled by a horse) [issoba isht liichi+']

issobishliili' plow (pulled by a tractor or by hand) [issoba isht liili+']

issobimilhlha' wild horse [issoba imilhlha+']

issobi̲naachi horse blanket [issoba im+na̲achi]

issobi̲sholosh horseshoe [issoba im+sholosh]

issobombiniili' cowboy; rodeo rider [issoba ombiniili+']

issobompatalhpo' saddle blanket;

saddle [issoba on+patalhpo']
{sontalhpo'}
issob-oshi', issoboshi', sob-oshi' baby
horse, colt [issoba oshi']
issóchchi'chi ggr. of issochichi
issochichi to make ° hit ° (I;II;3)
[isso+chichi] {ggr. issóchchi'chi}
issot anoktobaffi, issot anoktobaffichi
to hit without knocking down (I;II)
[isso+t] § Issot asanoktobaffi'shna
kaniyalitok. He hit me (without
knocking me down) and went off.
issot anoktobaffichi see issot
anoktobaffi
issot atiilhihíffi hngr. of issot
atiilhiffi
issot atiilhiffi to hit without
knocking down (I;II) [isso+t] {hngr.
issot atiilhihíffi; issot atiilhiffichi} §
Issot asatiilhiffitok. He hit me but
didn't knock me down.
issot atiilhiffichi to hit without
knocking down (I;II) [isso+t] {issot
atiilhiffi} § Issot atiilhiffi'shna
malililimankó. He hit me and I ran.
issot bohli to kill (I;II) [isso+t] § Issot
iksabohlokimankó. He didn't kill
me.
issot illichi to knock out (I;II) [isso+t]
§ Issot sallichitok. He knocked me
out.
issot ittapakolli to hit in the stomach
and thus cause to double over (I;II)
[isso+t] § Issot sattapakollitok. He
hit me in the stomach and made
me double over.
issot nokbiibli to knock the breath
out of (I;II) [isso+t] § Issot
sanokbiiblitok. He knocked the
breath out of me.
issot noktiibli to knock the breath
out of (I;II) (Ct?) [isso+t] {issot
nokbiibli}
ssot tiballichi to hit wrong, hit the

wrong way (I;3) [isso+t] § To'wa'
issot tiballichilitok. I hit the ball
wrong.
issotkochi' thickener [isht
sotkochi+']
issosh insect, worm (parasite), bug
{short form: sosh} § issosh isolash:
the bug's tongue
issosh abi' exterminator [abi+']
issosh bíyyi'ka to have bugs (for
instance, of flour) (II) § Issosh
chibiyyi'ka! You've got bugs!
issosh homma' bedbug, red ant
[homma+']
issosh hommishto' fire ant [(issosh
homma') ishto+']]
issosh itti' apa' termite [apa+']
issosh itti' toshbichi' termite
[toshbichi+']
issosh ilawa, issoshat ilawa to have
worms (III) [im+lawa] § Issosh
alawa. I have worms.
issosh loksi', (WB) issosh loksi'
holba' ladybug, potato bug
issosh losa' black ant [losa+']
issosh palaska' bread made with
infested flour [<palaska>+']
issosh patha' type of big beetle
[patha+']
issosh shoppala' lightning bug (WB)
issoshat ilawa see issosh ilawa
issoshtilli' moth balls, bug spray
[issosh isht illi+']
istokchank, stokchank, (VB)
ostokchank watermelon [osto
okchanki]
istokchank bila'ma',
istokchangbila'ma', (ER)
ostokchangbila'ma',
istokchangbila'ma', (TP)
changbila'ma' cantaloupe
[bilama+']
istokchank kallo' white watermelon
[kallo+']

159

istokchank nihi' watermelon seeds (boiled to make a medicine for stomach trouble) (LF)

istokchankapa', (TP) tokchankapa' cucumber; pickle [istokchank apa+']

istokchangbila'ma' see istokchank bila'ma'

istokchanglakna', (CC) istokchank lakna' yellow watermelon, (CC) pumpkin [istokchank lakna+']

istoof, stoof stove [from the English]

ishbanna to want (someone, probably as a possible spouse) for (someone) (II;3;3) [isht *banna] § Onita'a hattak yammak issabannatok. I want that man for Onita.

ishbilamachi' flavoring [isht bilama+chi+'] § paska champoli' ishbilamachi' vanilla or any cake flavoring

ishbo'chi' beater, mixer [isht bo'chi+']

ishbo'kalhchi', nannishbo'kalhchi' beater [(nanna) isht bo'kalhchi+']

ishbo'wa' something to hit with [isht bo'wa+'] § nannishbo'wa': hammer I akka' patalhpo' ishbo'wa': carpet beater I to'wishbo'wa': baseball bat

ishchafi'nachi to pick (one's teeth) (WB) [isht *chafi'nachi] {fi'chi}

ishchakká'li to be ninth (I) [isht *chakka'li] § Ishtishchakka'li. You're ninth.

ishchalhka' playing card [isht chalhka+']

ishcha'li' kitchen mallet [isht cha'li+']

ishchokkaamala' hula hoop [isht chokkaamala+']

ishchokkowa to bring ° into (I;II;3) [isht *chokkowa] § Abooha issachokkowatok. He brought me into the house.

ishchokoshkomo',

nannishchokoshkomo' toy [isht chokoshkomo+']

ishfama' switch (for whipping) [isht fama+']

ishfama' falaa' long switch, whip [falaa+']

ishfilillichi' spatula, pancake turner; faucet [isht filillichi+']

ishfilito'chi' spatula, pancake turner [isht filito'chi+']

ishfilli'chi' crank [isht filli'chi+']

<ishfi'chi'> in notishfi'chi'

ishfolota', ishfoloto'chi' steering wheel [isht folota/foloto'chi+']

ishfoloto'chi' see ishfolota'

ishfoyopa' oxygen tube, cannula [isht foyopa+']

ishhaksi to get drunk on, get high on (II;3); to go crazy over (something) (II;3); to go crazy over (a person) (I;II) [isht *haksi] § Ishchihaksilitok. I went crazy over you.

ishhaksi', nannishhaksi' addict [(nanna) ishhaksi+']

ishhánna'li to be sixth (I) [isht *hanna'li] § Ishtishhanna'li. You're sixth.

ishhashaa, ishhashaha to be jealous of, angry (because of jealousy) about (II;3) [isht *hashaa/hashaha] § Ishchihashaata? Are you angry about him?

ishhayowalhchi' sifter [isht hayowalhchi+']

ishhayoochi' sifter [isht hayoochi+'] {shayowachi}

ishholbachi' camera, (CC) film [isht holbachi+']

ishholbachi' fo'kha' film [fokha+']

ishholissochi' pen, pencil, chalk [isht holissochi+']

ishholissochi' tohbi' (white) chalk [tohbi+']

ishholmo' roofing material [isht

holmo+']
ishholmo' into'wa', (WB) ishholmo'
onto'wa' roof beams; (WB) rafters
[im+to'wa+']
ishholmo' ihiyohli' rafters
[im+hiyohli+']
ishholhtosi' bait, trap [isht
holhtosi+']
ishhopaakachi to take (far) away
(from some situation) (I;II) [isht
*hopaakachi] § Issahopaakachitok.
He took me away from it. |
Ishhopaakachili. I take it far away.
ishhottómpa to have a broken heart,
be deeply hurt (about something)
(II) (see hottopa) [isht *hottompa] §
Issattompatok. I was deeply hurt.
ishhottopachi' weapon, something
to hurt people with [isht
hottopachi+']
ishhowitachi' emetic (such as pure
lard) [isht howitachi+']
ishi to take, get (I;II); to answer the
telephone, get it (I) (ishi is replaced
by í'shi if immediately preceded by a
I or N prefix) [-OPR] {ggr. í'shi; hngr.
ihíshi; ngr. íshi; imishi: to take
from} § holisso kashofa' ishi: to get
a divorce
<ishkaha> in ishkahat máa [isht
*kaha] {ygr. ishkáyya'ha}
ishkahat máa to each lie with (tpl.
subj.) (I;3) [<ishkaha>+t] {sg.
ishtittí'wa; dl. ishkáyya'ha} §
Naachi ishkahat hashmáa. You all
each lie with your own quilt.
ishkala'fa' rake [isht <kalafa>+']
ishkala'fa' aalhpi' rake handle
ishkalasha' scissors [isht kalasha+']
ishkalasha' chakchaki' pinking
shears [chakchaki+']
ishkalasha' iskanno'si' nail scissors,
embroidery scissors, or any small
pair of scissors [iskanno'si+']

ishkapassali' air conditioner [isht
kapassali+']
ishkasa'chi' castanets [isht
kasa'chi+']
ishkasho'kalhchi',
nannishkasho'kalhchi' towel;
kleenex [(nanna) isht
kasho'kalhchi+']
ishkáyya'ha to each lie with (dl.
subj.) (I;3)—ygr. of <ishkaha> [isht
*kayya'ha] {sg. ishtittí'wa; tpl.
ishkahat máa}
ishki' mother (of a person or animal)
(IIp) § akankishki': mother hen |
ofi' ishki': mother dog
ishki' holba' unfit mother, mother
who doesn't take care of her kids
Ishki' Oshta' old-time Indian law or
religion [oshta+']
Ishki' Oshta' aaittanaha' old-time
Indian religious service
ishki' toba' stepmother, (MJ)
mother-in-law (IIp) [toba+'] §
sashki' toba': my stepmother
ishkihli' toilet paper [isht kihli+']
ishkin eye (IIp); hard head in a
pimple
ishkin afo'pa' sty in the eye (CP)
ishkin albiha' contact lenses
[<albiha>+']
ishkin bakchi' eye mucus (IIp) §
sashkin bakchi' : my eye mucus
ishkin finha ishpísa see ishkin
ishpísa
ishkin hakshop alhiipa', ishkin nipi'
alhiipa' cataract (WB) [alhiipa+']
ishkin hishi' eyelash, eyebrow (WB,
HS); eyelash (MC, ER) (IIp)
ishkin hishi' ishtihli' tweezers [isht
tihli+']
ishkin holba' glass eye (IIp) § sashkin
holba': my glass eye
ishkin homma' pinkeye,
conjunctivitis [homma+']

ishkin hoshollo'

ishkin hoshollo' eyelash; eyebrow, eyelash (TP) (IIp) § sashkin hoshollo': my eyelash
ishkin hoshollo' holba' false eyelashes
ishkin imalikchi' eye doctor, optometrist [im+alikchi']
ishkin imokaabaafa to punch in the eye (IIp = obj. , I;III) [im+okaabaafa] § Sashkin amokaabaafa. He punched me in the eye.
ishkin inkani'chi to wink at (ER, AB)
ishkin intakchi to blindfold (IIp = obj. , I;III) § Sashkin antakchitok. He blindfolded me.
ishkin ishpisa', ishkinshpisa' eyeglasses [ishkin isht pisa+'] (IIIp: ishkin ishpisa', ishkinshpisa') § ashkinshpisa': my glasses
ishkin ishpisa' losa' sunglasses, dark glasses [losa+']
ishkin ishpísa, ishkin finha ishpísa to see with one's own eyes (IIp = subj. , (—), I;II) [isht *pisa] § Sashkin finha ishchipíslitok. I saw you with my very own eyes.
ishkin koyohli to rub one's eyes (IIp , I) § Sashkin koyohlili. I rub my eyes.
ishkin lobo' eyeball (IIp) § sashkin lobo': my eyeball
ishkin nipi' alhiipa' see ishkin hakshop alhiipa'
ishkin okchi' tear (IIp) § sashkin okchi': my tear
ishkin okchi' minti to cry (IIp = subj.) § Atofalla'ha' loffishlit sashkin okchi' mintitok. When I peeled the onions I cried.
ishkin okchi'at lawa to have one's eyes water, to have watery eyes (IIp = subj.) [(ishkin okchi')+at] § Sashkin okchi'at lawatokoot pisala' ki'yo. I couldn't see because my eyes were watering.

ishkin okkawatali to cross one's eyes, make oneself go cross-eyed (IIp , I) {ggr. ishkin okkawátta'li}
ishkin okkawátta'li ggr. of ishkin okkawatali
ishkin osho'ba', (TP) ishkin yoshoba' eyebrow; (TP) eyebrow (IIp) § chishkin osho'ba': your eyebrow
ishkin tannap pila ishpisa, ishkin tannap pilashpisa to make eyes at, wink at (IIp = subj., —, (—), I;II) [pila isht *pisa] § Chishkin tannap pilashtishpisatok. You made eyes at him.
ishkinat alhatta to have a cataract (ER) [ishkin+at a+<hata> ?]
ishkinat intamowa to be blind in both eyes (IIp , III) [ishkin+at im+tamowa] § Sashkinat antamowa. I'm blind in both eyes.
ishkinat okkawaata for one's eyes to be crossed (IIp); to be cross-eyed (IIp = subj., —) [ishkin+at] {ggr. ishkinat okkáwwa'ta} § Sashkinat okkawaata. I am cross-eyed. I Lynnat ishkinat okkawaatakat ishtikimalhpi'so. Lynn is unhappy that she's cross-eyed.
ishkinat okkáwwa'ta ggr. of ishkinat okkawaata
ishkinat talha to have a cataract (ER) [ishkin+at]
ishkinat tannap pila'si to be one-eyed (IIp = subj. , —) [ishkin+at] § Ihooat ishkinat tannap pila'si. That woman is one-eyed.
ishkinshpisa' see ishkin ishpisa'
ishkish sex organ (penis, vagina); buttocks (IIp); an insult; (LF) rectum § Chishkish! Your ass! (an insult)
ishkish cholok rectum (IIp)
ishkish losa in chishkish losa
ishkish losa' an insult or cuss word [losa+']

ishko to drink; to take (liquid
medicine) (I;II) [+OPR] {ggr. í'shko;
hngr. ihíshko; ngr. íshko}
ishko'si' aunt; stepmother, aunt (HS)
(IIp) [ishki'+o'si']
ishkobo' head (IIp); train engine
ishkobo' apakfo'li' bandeau,
headband [apakfolli+']
ishkobo' folfo' place on the top of the
head where the hair grows out from
(LF) {iyalfolfo'}
ishkobo' foni' skull (IIp)
ishkobo' hili'shcha filita to turn a
somersault or cartwheel (IIp, I, I)
[hilichi+cha] § Sashkobo' hili'shlit
filitalitok. I turned a somersault. |
Chishkobo' ishhili'shcha
ishfilitatok. You turned a
somersault.
ishkobo' homma' plant with red,
yellow, or orange flowers, used for
medicine; (WB) butterfly weed; (CP)
copperhead (snake) [homma+']
ishkobo' homma' pakali' type of
medicinal plant (perhaps the same
as ishkobo' homma'), (CP)
(different from ishkobo' homma')
ishkobo' homma' tish red liniment
(one brand had an Indian head on
the bottle) (ER)
ishkobo' hottopa see ishkobo'at
hottopa
ishkobo' kallo' person who won't
take no for an answer; hardheaded,
stubborn person [kallo+']
ishkobo' lopi' brain (IIp) §
chishkobo' lopi': your brain
shkobo' oshmasholi to be bald (IIp =
subj.) (CP) § Sashkobo' oshmasholi.
I'm bald.
shkobo' Toklo Hilha' name of a
dance
shkobo'at hottopa, ishkobo' hottopa
to have a headache (IIp = subj. , II)

[ishkobo'+at] § Sashkobo'at
sattopacha chokka' ayalitok,
Sashkobo' satto'pacha chokka'
ayalitok. I went home because I had
a headache.
ishkoboka' head, leader—chief,
mayor, or governor, for instance
(IIIp: ishkoboka', imishkoboka')
[ishkobo'+ka']
ishkoboka' apilachi', ishkoboka'
apilanchi' assistant (IIIp:
ishkoboka' apilachi')
[apilachi/apilanchi+']
ishkochcha to take out, bring out (sg.
obj.) (I;3) [isht *kochcha] {pl. obj.
kochchaakaali} §
Ishtishkochchatam? Did you take it
out?
ishkochichi to make ° drink
(especially through the use of
physical force) (I;II;3) [ishko+chichi]
§ Issobaa halaat oka' aa-ashaka
ishtishonokya oka' ishishkochicha'
ki'yo. You can lead a horse to water
but you cannot make him drink.
ishkot haksi to get drunk (II)
[ishko+t] § Ishkot chihaksitok. You
got drunk.
ishlaa' hoe [isht laa+']
ishlaa' aalhpi' hoe handle
ishliichi' plow [isht liichi+']
ishlhopolli to take across, through
(I;II) [isht *lhopolli]
ishmalli to jump along carrying
(someone) (I;II) [isht *malli]
ishmalhaha see ishmalhaa
ishmalhata to be surprised and
happy (II) [isht *malhata] {ggr.
ishmálhlha'ta} §
Ishchimalhlha'taha! You're
surprised and happy!
ishmalhaa, ishmalhaha to be jealous
over, jealous about (I;II) [isht
*malhaa/malhaha] §

163

Issamalhaatok. He was jealous over me.

ishmálhlha'ta ggr. of ishmalhata

ishmáa to get (I) [E+t] (used with I subj. verbs); get (aux.) (used with II or III subj. verbs +t) [isht *maa] § Palhkit ishtishmaa. You're getting faster. | Sasipoknit ishmaakat ithanali. I know I'm getting older.

ishminti to bring ° to (I;II;3) [isht *minti] § Yappak issamintitok. He brought me here.

ishnaak you (sg., nonsubj.) [ishno'+ak]

ishnaat you (sg., subj.) [ishno'+at]

ishnaakaynihaat you yourself (sg., int. subj.) [ishno'+aakayni+haat] § Ishnaakaynihaat ishiksaachim? Did you make it yourself?

ishnaakaynihoot you yourself (sg., focus subj.) [ishno'+aakayni+hoot] § Ishnaakaynihoot ishhilhatok. You yourself danced.

ishnaakayniho you yourself (sg., focus nonsubj.) [ishno'+aakayni+ho]

ishnaakaynihta you yourself (sg., int. nonsubj.) [ishno'+aakayni+hta]

ishnaakot you (sg., emphatic subj.) [ishno'+akot]

ishnaako you (sg., emphatic nonsubj.) [ishno'+ako]

ishna you (sg., nonsubj.) [ishno'+a]

ishno' you (sg., nonsubj.)

ishno' ino' iitáwwa'a (it's) you and I, (it's) you and me [ano', ii+tawwa'a]

ishnokhamihínchi hngr. of ishnokhámmi'chi

ishnokhámmi'chi to be impatient (about an upcoming event) (II) [isht *nokhammi'chi] {hngr. ishnokhamihínchi}

ishnosi' sedative, sleeping pill [isht nosi+']

ishnosi'chi' see ishnosichi'

ishnosichi to give (an anaesthetic) to °, put ° to sleep with (an anaesthetic) (I;II;3) [isht *nosichi] § Ishnosi'chi' ishchinosishtok. They put you to sleep with ether.

ishnosichi', ishnosi'chi' ether [ishnosichi+']

ishno'wa' walker (for a child or crippled person to walk with) [isht nowa+']

ishnowa to drive (a car): especially, to be able to drive (a car) (I;3 [isht *nowa] § Kaa ishtishnowa'hi biyyi'ka? Can you drive a car?

ishnowa' driver [ishnowa+']

ishpiha' broom (for sweeping) [isht piha+']

ishpiha', (MJ) alba ishpiya' broom weed (used for brooms, or boiled for a medicinal tea used for coughs)

ishpiha' aalhpi' broomstick

ishpokkó'li to be tenth (I) [isht *pokko'li] § Ishtishpokko'li. You're the tenth.

ishpokko'li' tenth (noun), tenth part [ishpokko'li+'] § ishpokko'li' tochchi'na: three tenths

ishponta to borrow (money) on, to use as security for (I;3;3) [isht *ponta]

ishshimohli', ishshimoha' local anaesthetic [isht shimohli/shimoha+']

ishshoka' face, cheeks (IIp) {short form: shoka'}

ishshoka' albi' makeup, cosmetics

ishshoka' alhiipi'ya', to'wa' aachokoshkomo' ishshoka' alhiipi'ya' face mask (in baseball)

ishshoka' holba' mask

ishshoka' incho'li to put on makeup or war paint (IIp , I) § Sashshoka' incho'lilitok. I put on makeup, I

made up my face.
**ishshoka' ishtincho'li', ishshoka'
ishtincho'wa'** war paint, makeup,
face paint [ishtincho'li/isht
incho'wa+']
ishshoka' ishtincho'wa' see
ishshoka' ishtincho'li'
**ishshoka' ishtohbichi',
ishshokishtohbichi'** face powder
[isht tohbi+chi+']
ishshoka' oppanit pisa to make a face
at (IIp = subj. , —, I;II) [oppani+t] §
Ishshoka' oppanit sapistok. He
made a face at me. | Sashshoka'
oppanit pisalitok. I made a face at
him.
ishshoka'at incho'wa to be made up,
have one's face painted (IIp = subj.)
[ishshoka'+at]
ishshokishtohbichi' see ishshoka'
ishtohbichi'
ishshokmalachi' in akka'
ishshokmalachi'
isht prt. of ishi; (preverb) with, about
ishtaballakshi' see aballakshi'
ishtabi'chi' poker (for the fire) (Ct?)
[isht abi'chi+']
ishtachapa to argue with (I;II) [isht
*achapa] § Ishtasachapa. He argued
with me.
ishtachaaha to like, really love:
especially, to really like to have
around (II;3); to like, really love
(first- or second-person obj. only)
(I;II) [isht *achaaha] {neg.
ishtikacha'no} §
Ishtachichaahalitok. I really like
you, I love having you around. |
Ishtasachaaha. I really love it.
shtachifa to wash with (I;3;3) [isht
*achifa]
shtachifa' washcloth, washrag,
sponge; soap (IIIp: ishtachifa')
[ishtachifa+']

ishtahalaa in nannishtahalaa {ggr.
ishtahálla'a; ngr. ishtahaláa}
ishtahaláa to be concerned in the
matter of, have something to do
with (II;3-at)—ngr. of ishtahalaa
[isht *ahalaa] § Lynnat yaaknaat
ishtahalaa'chi. Lynn's going to be
concerned in the matter of the
property.
ishtahálla'a in nannishtahálla'a—
ggr. of ishtahalaa
ishtahammi to anoint ˚ with (I;II;3)
[isht *ahammi] § Niha
ishtasahammitok. He anointed me
with oil.
ishtahánta hngr. of ishtánta
ishtaháyyo'chi in
nannishtaháyyo'chi
ishtahála hngr. of ishtala
ishtaháya hngr. of ishtaya
ishtahollifatpo' devil's power, bad
magic [ishtahollo' im+fatpo']
ishtahollo' witch (man or woman)
[isht a+<hollo>+']
ishtahollo' ishokcha small bag
holding a magic charm worn
around the neck for protection
against spells [im+shokcha]
ishtaholloppolo' bad witch
[ishtahollo' oppolo+']
ishtahopoochi to be jealous of (I;II)
(LF) [isht *ahopoochi]
ishtahooba'li ki'yo to mock, make
fun of, discourage (I;II) [isht
*ahooba'li] {ngr. ishtahoobáli ki'yo;
ishtikahooba'lo}
ishtahoobáli in naaishtahoobáli
ishtahoobáli ki'yo ngr. of
ishtahooba'li ki'yo
ishtaka'fa', ishtakafa' cup, dipper
[isht <takafa>+']
Ishtaka'fa', Ishtakafa', Oka' Ishtakafa'
the Big Dipper [ishtaka'fa']
ishtaka'fa' lokosh see lokosh

165

ishtaka'fa'
ishtaka'fa' naaishtapiisa', ishtakafa'
naaishtapiisa' measuring cup
[nanna isht apiisa+']
ishtakafa', Ishtakafa' see ishtaka'fa',
Ishtaka'fa'
ishtakafa' toba' gourd [toba+']
ishtakallo'chi' fastener, clamp §
holisso ishtakallo'chi' paper clip,
staple
ishtakallochi to stop up (something)
with (I;3;3) § Holissa cholok
ishtishakallochi. You plugged the
hole with paper.
ishtakallochi' stopper, plug
[ishtakallochi+']
ishtakaniya in pi'scha ishtakaniya
ishtakanomi to be a clown (I) [isht
*akanomi] § Ishtishakanomi. You
are a clown.
ishtakanomi' clown [ishtakanomi+']
ishtakanomit nọwa to clown around
(I) [ishtakanomi+t] § Ishtakanomit
nọwalitok. I clowned around.
ishtakaanihmichi to vandalize; to
say suggestive things to, sexually
abuse, seduce (I;II) [isht
*akaanihmichi] §
Ishtasakaanihmichi banna. He
wanted to seduce me.
ishtakchi to tie ° with (I;II;3) [isht
*takchi] § Ishtalakchi'
ishchitakchila'chi. I'm going to tie
you up with a rope.
ishtakkowa to bring down (I;II) [isht
*akkowa] § Ishtasakkowatok. He
brought me down.
ishtakkowa' parachute
[ishtakkowa+']
ishtala to bring here (I;II); to bring °
to (a place) (I;II;3) (I and N prefixes
work as with ala; II prefixes work as
with normal a-initial verb) [isht
*ala] {hngr. ishtahála} § Ishtasalatok.

He brought me. I Ishtishlatok. You
brought him.
ishtalakchi' rope, cord, yarn; leash
(IIIp: ishtalakchi') [isht talakchi+'] §
ilbak ishtalakchi': sling, handcuffs
ishtalakchi' malli to jump rope (I) §
Ishtalakchi' kiimalli. Let's jump
rope.
ishtaloshkachi to lie about (old word)
(I;II) [isht *aloshkachi] §
Ishtachiloshkachilitok. I lied about
you.
ishtaloowa to sing about (I;II) [isht
*taloowa] § Ishtissataloowatok. You
sang about me.
ishtaloowa' in aba' ishtaloowa'
ishtalhchifa to be washed with,
washed in (II;3) [isht *alhchifa] §
Chiisas imissish
ishtasalhchifattook. I was washed in
Jesus's blood.
ishtalhchifa' soap, detergent (IIIp:
ishtalhchifa') [isht alhchifa+']
ishtalhchifa' homi' lye soap [homi+']
ishtalhchifa' pokpoki' soap bubble
(especially, one floating in the air)
ishtalhlhá'pi to be fifth (I) [isht
*talhlha'pi] § Ishtishtalhlha'pi.
You're fifth.
ishtalhlhi' in ittishtalhlhi',
nannishtalhlhi'
ishtalhopo'li' pin, brooch
ishtalhoopolli' , (WB)
tishtalhoppolli' laxative (such as
castor oil or black draught) [(ittish)
isht alhoopolli+']
ishtalhoopollichi' laxative (such as
castor oil or black draught) [isht
alhoopollichi+']
ishtalhpila' monetary assistance:
especially, welfare or public
assistance [isht alhpila']
ishtalhpóllo'sa ggr. of ishtalhpolosa
ishtalhpolosa to be daubed all over

(3;II); to be daubed all over with, to be slathered with (II;3-at) (anim. subj., best with overt subj. prefix)— usually used in ggr. [isht *alhpolosa] {v1. ishtapoolosli; ggr. ishtalhpóllo'sa} § Lokchokat ishtasalhpollo'sakat ith<u>a</u>nali, Ishtasalhpollo'sak<u>a</u> ith<u>a</u>nali. I know that the mud got daubed all over me, I was slathered with mud.
ishtalhtipo' canvas; awning, tent [isht alhtipo']
ishtalhtipo' abooha tent used to live in
ishtalhtoba to be paid (of money) for (3;3); to be paid for with (3;3-at) [isht *alhtoba] {v2. ishtatobbi} § Ta'ossohoot impa' ishtalhtobatok. The money was paid for the food. | Impa' yammat ta'ossohoot ishtalhtobatok. This food was paid for with the money.
ishtamákka'li to be never satisfied (II / I) [isht *amakka'li] {ishtilamákka'li} § Ishtasamakka'li, Ishtamakka'lili. I'm never satisfied.
ishtamaachi' electric fan, air conditioner [isht amaachi+']
ishtamo' mower, cutter [isht amo+'] § hashshok ishtamo' grass cutter, scythe
ishtani', nannishtani' funnel [(nanna) isht ani+']
ishtannowa to be talked about, told on (II) [isht *annowa]
ishtannowa story (TJ)
ishtanokfih<u>i</u>lli hngr. of ishtanokfilli
ishtanokfilli to think about (I;II); to think about or consider ˚ (as a potential mate) for ˚ (I;II;3) [isht *anokfilli] {hngr. ishtanokfih<u>i</u>lli} § Lynnak<u>o</u> ishtachinokfillilitok. I'm thinking about Lynn (as a wife) for you.

ishtanompa to be talked about (II); to be about (3;II) [isht *anompa] § Holissaat Lynn ishtanompa. The book is about Lynn.
ishtanompoli to talk about (I;II) [isht *anompoli] § Ishtasanompoli. They're talking about me. | Himonahm<u>a</u> hattakat takombish falaa' ayowatok aachih<u>o</u> ishtilanompola'chi.... Now we're going to talk about what is said concerning a man who was picking pears....
ishtanoshkonna to like (someone) as a possible mate for ˚, to fix ˚ up with (I;II;3) [isht *anoshkonna] § Ishtasanoshkonnatok. She fixed me up with him.
ishtánta to fool with, toy with, fondle (I;II) [isht *anta] {hngr. ishtahánta}
ishtapanni to twist (something) around (something) (I;3;3) [isht *apanni] {ishtapaaniili} § Sap<u>a</u>shi' naalhila'fa' ishtapannitahlilitok. I twisted my hair around rags, I set my hair on rags.
ishtapaaniili to twist (sg. obj.) around (something) (I;3;3) [isht *apaaniili] {apanni}
ishtapistíkki'li to pick on, tease (I;II) [isht *apistikki'li] {neg. ishtikapistiki'lo}
ishtapiisa to judge ˚ as, evaluate ˚ as (I;II;3); to pass ˚ off as (I;II;3) [isht *apiisa] § Hattak hapoyoksa' ishtachipiisla'chi. I would judge you to be a wise man. | Chahtihoo' ishtachipiisla'chi. I'm going to pass you off as a Choctaw woman.
ishtaponnachi, nannishtaponnachi to be clever, smart (I) [(nanna) isht *aponnachi] {imponna}
ishtapoolosli to slop, slather ˚ with (I;II;3) [isht *apoolosli] {v2.

ishtasawachi'

ishtalhpolosa} § Lokchok
ishtachipooloslili. I slather you with
mud.
ishtasawachi', nannishtasawachi'
knickknacks, little ornaments
[(nanna) isht <asawachi>+']
ishtasiiti'ya' fastener (such as a
buckle or a hook and eye) [isht
asitti'ya+']
ishtasha'na' lock (IIIp: ishtasha'na')
[isht ashana+']
ishtatobbi to pay (money) (I;3); to pay
for with (money) (I;3;3) [isht *atobbi]
{v1. ishtalhtoba}
ishtatochchí'na to be third (I) [isht
*atochchi'na]
ishtatokla to be second (I) [isht
*atokla]
ishtatoonchi see ishtatochi
ishtatooni to mortgage, get money
out of (I;3) [isht *atooni] § Chokka'
ishtatoonitok. He mortgaged the
house, got money out of the house.
ishtatoonichi see ishtatochi
ishtatochi, ishtatoonchi,
ishtatoonichi to mortgage for (I;3;3)
[±SC] [isht *atoonichi] § Anchokka'
ta'osso ishtatoshlitok. I mortgaged
my house for money.
ishtawaalhahli to be fried with, fried
in (3;3) [isht *awaalhahli] § Ahi'
yappat niha ishtawaalhahli. These
potatoes were fried in lard.
ishtaya, ishtayya to drive (a car) (I;3);
to take ° to (a place) (I;II;3); to start,
begin to (used with preceding I subj.
verb) (I) [E+t]; get, start, begin (used
with preceding II or III subj. verb +t)
(aux.) [isht *aya/ayya] {hngr.
ishtaháya} § Imissikopat ishtayyali.
I'm starting to be mean to him. |
Sassikopat ishtayya. I'm starting to
be mean, I'm getting mean. |
Oklahomma' ishtasayatok. She took

me to Oklahoma.
ishtayachi in holisso ishtayachi',
naki' ishtayachi' [isht *ayachi]
ishtayili' shampoo [isht ayili+']
ishtayímmi'ta to jump up and down
(for instance, in anticipation)—ggr.
of ishtayiimita
ishtayiimita to enjoy, be happy about
a situation (II) [isht *ayiimita] {ggr.
ishtayímmi'ta: to jump up and
down in anticipation} §
Ishtasayiimita. I was really happy.
ishtayobáli ki'yo ngr. of ishtayóbba'li
ki'yo
ishtayóbba'li ki'yo to make fun of, to
be mean, rude to, to cuss out (I;II);
not to do right at all (3) [isht
(*ayobba'li ki'yo)] {ngr. ishtayobáli
ki'yo] § Ishtasayobba'li ki'yokitok.
They made fun of me. | Nowakat
ishtayobba'li ki'yo. He can't walk
right at all.
ishtayómba to look better, be better (I
/ II)—ngr. of ishtáyyo'ba [isht
*ayomba] {neg. ishtikayyo'bo} §
Ishtasayomba, ishtayombali. I look
better.
ishtayómba ki'yo ngr. of ishtáyyo'ba
ki'yo
ishtayoppa to be happy about, proud
of (II;3) [isht *ayoppa] {v2.
ishtayoppali}
ishtayoppali to make (someone°)
happy with, please (someone°) with
(something, especially that one has
brought) (I;II;3) [isht *ayoppali] {v1.
ishtayoppa] § Nipi'
ishtachiyoppalilitok. I pleased you
by bringing you meat.
ishtayoppolachi to joke about (I;II)
[isht *ayoppolachi]
ishtayya see ishtaya
ishtáyya'ma to be the same (I / II);
still (aux.) (usually used with hngr.

168

or ngr. +kat); again (aux.) (used with verb +kat) [isht *ayya'ma] §
Ishtayya'mali, Ishtasayya'ma. I'm the same. I Ihissokat ishtayya'ma. He's still hitting him. I Issolikat ishtayya'ma. I hit him again.

ishtáyya'sha to have, organize (a gathering or ceremony) (tpl. subj.) (I;3) [isht *ayya'sha] {imáyya'sha} § Piknik ishtilayya'shtok. We had a picnic.

ishtáyyo'ba in ishtáyyo'ba ki'yo {ngr. ishtayómba}

ishtáyyo'ba ki'yo to be disgusting looking, be bad (II) [isht *ayyo'ba] {ngr. ishtayómba ki'yo} § Ishtachiyyo'ba ki'yo. You're disgusting looking.

ishtáyyo'pi to be last (I) [isht *ayyo'pi] § Ishtishayyo'pi. You're the last (for instance, the last child in your family).

ishtayyo'pi last one [isht ayyo'pi] § Ishtayyo'pi poya. We're the last ones.

ishtayyoshta to be fourth (I) [isht *ayyoshta] {ilbak ishtayyoshto'}

ishtaa-abi' goalpost (WB) [isht aa-abi+']

ishtaabachi' see ilbak naaishtaabachi'

ishtaabi to paint ° with, smear ° with (I;II;3) [isht *aabi] § Ishtissabinna! Don't smear me with it!

ishtaabi' grout, (MJ) plaster [ishtaabi+']

ishtaabini'li' seat, bottom, rear end (Ip) [isht aa+biniili+'] § ishtaabini'lili': my seat, my rear

ishtaachoosho'wa' see iyyobi' ishtaachoosho'wa'

ishtaafilito'chi' faucet handle, knob on a TV [isht aa+filito'chi+']

ishtaahala'li', aahala'li' curved handle (on top of a suitcase, purse, bucket) [isht aa+halali+']

ishtaahikki'ya' above-ground root, place where a plant goes into the ground; person or thing always standing in the same place with something (for instance, a flower seller) [isht aa+hikki'ya+']

ishtaahoshowa' organ for urination (in male or female): penis, urethra (IIIp: ishtaahoshowa') [isht aa+hoshowa+']

ishtaahoshowa' hakshop foreskin

ishtaaímmo'ma to be that way (3)— ggr. of ishtaaimómo [isht *aaimmo'ma]

ishtaaimóma to be that way (I) [isht *aaimoma] {ggr. ishtaaímmo'ma: (3)}

ishtaaíla to be different, unusual, extraordinary; to have funny ways (I / II) [isht *aa+ila] § Ishtaailali, ishtasaaila. I'm different.

ishtaakkowa to bring °, help ° down from, off of (I;II;3) [isht *aakkowa] § Bas ishtaakkowalitok. I helped her off the bus.

ishtaakochcha to bring, help out of (I;3;3) [isht *aakochcha] § Yaakni' cholok ishtaachikochchalitok. I helped you out of the hole.

ishtaalhlhi to be last (in any group— for instance, to be the youngest child in a family) (I) [isht *aalhlhi]

ishtaalhlhi' last; last one [ishtaalhlhi+'] § Ishtaalhlhi' impalitok. I ate last. I Ishtaalhlhi' saya. I am last.

ishtaalhopolli to bring through, get or be through with (I) [E+t] [isht *aa+lhapolli] § Anompolit ishtaalhopollili. I finished talking.

<ishtaaonchololi> in ishtaaonchololi' [isht aa+onchololi] {v1. ishtaaoncholowa}

ishtaaonchololi'

ishtaaonchololi' descendent (of
someone now dead); bunch, family,
clan [<ishtaaonchololi>+'] §
Willmond ishtaaonchololi': the
Willmond bunch—that is, the
descendents of some Willmond
ancestor
ishtaaoncholowa to be the (relatively
remote) descendent of (3;3) [isht
*aaoncholowa] {vl.
<ishtaaonchololi>}
ishtaaoncholowa' (relatively remote)
descendent (may be used
predicatively with Ip marking)
[ishtaaoncholowa+'] § Aayahanta'
Pikkin ishtaaoncholowa' saya,
Aayahanta' Pikkin
ishtaaoncholowali'. I am a
descendent of I. Hunter Pickins.
ishtaaohikki'ya', ishtaayohikki'ya'
base, foot, pedestal [isht
aa+on+hikki'ya+']
ishtaapichi to spoil, do everything
for, wait on hand and foot; to love
(a child, pet); to favor (one child
over others) (I;II) [isht *aapichi]
{ngr. ishtaapínchi} § Ishtachiaapichi.
She really loves you, spoils you. |
Sashkaat ishtasa-aapichittook. My
mother did everything for me.
ishtaapínchi ngr. of ishtaapichi
ishtaasha'na' lock [isht aa+shana+']
ishtaatabli to do too much (I) [isht
*aatabli] {ngr. ishtaatámbli}
ishtaatakaali' hinge, ring for hanging
[isht aa+takaali+']
ishtaatámbli ngr. of ishtaatabli
ishtaatámpa to be crazy (I) [isht
*aatampa]—ngr. of ishtaatapa §
Ishtishaatampa. You're crazy.
ishtaatapa to do too much (I) [E+t]
(used with preceding I subj. verb:
'eat', 'drink', 'sleep', 'work'); too
(aux.) (follows a II or III subj. verb +t

or +kat) [isht *aatapa] {ngr.
ishtaatámpa: to be crazy} §
Antakho'bikat ishtaatapa. I'm too
lazy. | Nost ishtishaatapatam? Did
you sleep too much?
ishtaatapichi to do too much (I) [E+t]
(used with preceding I subj. verb:
'eat', 'drink', 'sleep', 'work') [isht
*aatapichi] § Impat
ishtaatapishlitokoot asabikatok. I ate
too much so I'm sick.
ishtaatiyaka' see aatiyaka'
ishtaatta in nannishtaatta
ishtaayohikki'ya' see
ishtaaohikki'ya'
ishtáa to carry off, take along with
one, have with one; to drive (a car)
(I;3); to go around with (something)
in (a place) (I;3;3) (sg. subj.) [isht *aa]
§ Holisso ishtishaakat i'mata? Do
you still have the book with you? |
Lynnat holissa okla pila ishtaatok
chayntok. Lynn must have walked
around with a book downtown. |
Lynn inkaa'ako ishtaalitok. I drove
Lynn's car.
ishtalhlhi' important document,
such as a deed or receipt [isht
alhlhi+']
ishtibaawiichi to help bring, help
move (I;3;3) [+SC] [isht
*ibaa+wiichi] § Itti'
ishtibaawiishlitok. I helped him
move the wood.
ishtikacha'ho to be lonely for
(N+II;3) [isht *ikacha'ho]—neg. of
ishtachaaha § Sashki'
ishtiksacha'ho. I'm lonely for my
mother.
ishtikahooba'lo to mock, make fun
of (IN;II) [isht *ikahooba'lo]
{ishtahooba'li ki'yo} §
Chihoowoshi'
ishtikahooba'lokittook. They

170

mocked Christ.
ishtikapistiki'lo neg. of
ishtapistíkki'li
ishtikayoppo to be sad (II) [isht
*ikayoppo] § Ishtiksayoppokitok. I
was sad.
ishtikayyo'bo to be bad: especially, to
be disgusting looking; to be spoiled
(of children) (II) [isht *ikayyo'bo]
{ishtayómba ki'yo, ishtayyoba ki'yo}
§ Ishtiksayyo'boho! I'm disgusting
looking!
ishtikaaimóno to be discouraged
(N+II) [aa+(ishtikimono)]> isht
*ikaaimono] §
Ishtikaasamonokitok. I am
discouraged.
ishtikimalhpi'so to be sad about,
lonely for (III;3) [isht *ikimalhpi'so]
§ Amihooak ishtiksamalhpi'so. I'm
sad about, lonely for my wife.
ishtikimayyo'bo not to look good on
(of clothing) (3;III); not to look good
in (clothing), to have (clothing) not
look good (III;3-at) [isht
*ikimayyo'bo] § Naafka yappat
ishtiksamayyo'boka'chikat ithanali.
I know this dress is going to look
bad on me. | Naafka yammat Irenea
ishtikimayyo'bo. That dress doesn't
look good on Irene. | Ireneat naafka
yammat ishtikimayyo'bo. Irene
doesn't look good in that dress.
ishtikimbaati'yo, ishtikimbaatiyyo
negs. of ishtimbaatiya
ishtikimóno to be discouraged
(N+III) [isht *ikimonho]
{ishtikimaaimóno} §
Ishtiksamonokitok. I am
discouraged.
ishtikímpo to be ashamed of, to be
disgusted by (someone) (IN;II) (used
only in the subj. and obj. forms
listed) [isht *ikimpo] § Ishtakimpo. I

am ashamed of him, I am disgusted
by him. | Ishtikimpo. He is
ashamed of her. | Ishtakchimpo. I
am ashamed of you. |
Ishtikhooimpo. They are ashamed
of him. | Ishtikchimpo. She is
ashamed of you. |
Ishtiksampokitok. He is ashamed of
me.
ishtilabanna'li' suspenders, shoulder
straps [isht ilabanna'li+']
ishtilabaanali to take the blame,
confess falsely (I) [isht *ilabaanali]
ishtilachifa' washcloth (IIIp:
ishtachifa') [isht ili+achifa+']
ishtilahobbi to show off (one's
clothes or appearance) (I;3) [isht
*ilahobbi] § Naafka
ishtilahobbilitok. I showed off my
dress.
ishtilakallo'chi' girdle, corset [isht
ili+akallochi+']
ishtilamákka'li to act spoiled, behave
badly: especially, to be picky, difficult
to satisfy (I) [isht *ilamakka'li]
{ishtamákka'li}
ishtilamaachi' fan (used in the hand)
[isht ili+amaachi+']
ishtilatahpoli' jewelry, ornament
[isht ilatahpoli+']
ishtilayoppa to get something for
oneself out of (I;3); to get everything
for oneself (I) [isht *ilayoppa] §
Ishnaakilloot yaakni' yamma
ishtishilayoppatok. You were the
only one who got something for
yourself out of that land.
ishtilaaiksaachi' makeup [isht
ilaaiksaachi+']
ishtilaapichi to take care of oneself (I)
[isht *ilaapichi] {ngr. ishtilaapínchi}
ishtilaapínchi ngr. of ishtilaapichi
ishtilaatabli to do too much (I) [E+t]
(used with a preceding I subj. verb:

ishtilaatámbli

'eat', 'drink', 'sleep', 'work') [isht
*ilaatabli] {ngr. ishtilaatámbli} §
Ishkot ishtilaatablilitok. I drank too
much.
ishtilaatámbli ngr. of ishtilaatabli
ishtilaatapichi to do too much (I)
[E+t] (used with a preceding I subj.
verb: 'eat', 'drink', 'sleep', 'work')
[isht *ilaatapichi] § Toksalit
ishtishilaatapishtok. You worked
too much.
ishtilaayokha to be stingy with (I;3)
[isht *ilaayokha]
{nannishtilaayokha} § Nipi'
ishtishilaayokha. You're stingy with
meat.
ishtilibanna to want to do
(something) in place of someone
else); to be ambitious (I) [isht
*ili+banna]
ishtilibilamachi' perfume [isht
ilibilamachi+']
ishtilibo'li to knock into (things—
mainly pl. obj.; for instance, of a
drunkard) (I;3) [isht *ili+bo'li] §
Ishtishilibo'tok. You knocked into
things.
ishtilihaksichi to clown around (I)
[isht *ilihaksichi]
ishtilihammichi' in tish
ishtilihammichi'
ishtilihopoo, ishtilipoo to stay at
home out of fear (I); to be careful
with, to keep (money, a baby) at
home (I;3) [isht *ilihopoo/ilipoo]
{ngr. ishtilipóo} § Ta'osso
ishtishilipoo. You keep money at
home.
ishtilikasho'chi' napkin, kleenex,
towel [isht ili+kashoochi+']
ishtililhpokonna to dream about
oneself (I) [isht *ililhpokonna]
ishtilimihachi to complain, be
dissatisfied (I) [isht *ili+mihachi]

{ggr. ishtilimíhha'chi} §
Ishtishilimihachi. You complain.
ishtilimíhha'chi ggr. of
ishtilimihachi
ishtilincho'li' eyebrow pencil (IIIp:
ishtilincho'li') [isht *ilincho'li+']
ishtiliposilhha to be sorry for oneself
(I) [isht *iliposilhha] §
Ishtishiliposilhha. You're feeling
sorry for yourself.
ishtilipoo see ishtilihopoo
ishtilipóo ngr. of ishtilihopoo
ishtilisso to bump into (I;II) [isht
*ili+isso] § Ishchilissoli. I bumped
into you.
ishtilishafi' razor [isht ilishafi+']
ishtilishafi' aahaloppachi' razor strop
[aa+haloppachi+']
ishtilitohbichi' talcum powder;
powder puff [isht ilitohbichi+']
ishtilli to die from, die of (II;3) [isht
*illi] § Toshabi' ishtillitok. He died
of the measles.
ishtilombitka' see itti' ishtilombitka'
ishtilonhochi to take the blame (I)
[isht *ilonhochi]
ishtiloshontika'chi',
ishtilohoshontika'chi' umbrella,
parasol [isht ilohoshontikachi+']
ishtilhpokonna to dream about (I;II)
[isht *ilhpokonna] §
Ishchilhpokonnalitok. I dreamed
about you.
ishtimachaaha to be pleased with
(something) for ° (I;III;3) [isht
*imachaaha] {ishtachaaha}
ishtimaholítto'pa to be a tightwad
(III); to be tight with (III;3) [isht
*imaholitto'pa] § Charlesat ta'osso
ishtimaholitto'pa. Charles is tight
with money.
ishtimakanomit nowa to clown
around in place of (III = obj. , I)
[im+(ishtakanomit nowa)>

172

ishtimakanomit *nowa] §
Ishchimakanomit nowala'chi. I'll
clown around for you, in your
place.
ishtimalla to bring to, bring for °
(I;III;3) [isht *imalla]
ishtimalhchiba to be stuck with,
slowed down by (III;3) [isht
*imalhchiba] § Ithanali chipota
ishtamalhchiba'chikat. I know I'm
going to be stuck with the kids.
ishtimalhkaniya to forget with the
aid of (III;3); to forget everything
while (forms cha expression with
preceding verb) (III) [isht
*imalhkaniya] § Hattak yamma
ahattak ishtamalhkaniyatok. I
forgot my husband because of that
man. | Toksa'cha ishtimalhkaniya.
He forgot everything while he was
working.
ishtimalhtoba to be paid to (3;III) [isht
*imalhtoba]
ishtimanompoli to talk to ° about
(I;III;3) [isht *imanompoli]
ishtimayya to bring to, bring for, take
to, take for (someone°) (I;III;3) [isht
*imayya]
ishtimaa-akshochi to have a
memorial service for (I;III) [isht
*imaa-akshochi] § Ishchimaa-
akshocha'chi. They'll have a
memorial service for you.
ishtimaakallo in nannakat
ishtimaakallo
ishtimaanokfihíla hngr. of
ishtimaanokfila
ishtimaanokfila to think about,
worry about (III;3) [isht
*imaanokfila] {hngr.
ishtimaanokfihíla}
ishtimaatámpa ngr. of ishtimaatapa
ishtimaatapa to be mean to (I;III) [isht
*imaatapa] {ngr. ishtimaatámpa}

ishtimaatobbi to pay (someone°)
with (goods) (I;III;3) [isht
*imaatobbi] § Akankoshi'
ishtimaatobbilitok. I paid him with
a chicken.
ishtimaawí'ki ggr. of ishtimaawiiki
ishtimaawiiki to be a burden to (I;III);
to be burdened (III) [isht
*im+aa+wiiki] {ggr. ishtimaawí'ki}
§ Ishtchimaawiikili. I'm a burden to
you.
ishtimaawiikichi to burden
(someone) (I;III) [isht
*imaawiiki+chi]
ishtimbaatiya to go along with
(someone); to let (someone,
especially a child) get away with
something (I;III) [isht *imbaatiya]
{negs. ishtikimbaati'yo,
ishtikimbaatiyyo}
ishtimilahobbi to show off
(something) to °, brag about to °
(I;III;3) [isht *imilahobbi]
ishtimona to breed (an animal) with
(another animal) (I;3;3); to take to,
bring to, bring for (someone over
there°) (I;III;3) [isht *imona]
ishtimomochi to be used to it, be
used to a situation (III); to be used to
(something) (III;3) [isht *imomochi]
§ Holisso yappako
ishtamomochitayya'ha. I've gotten
used to this book.
ishtimpashooli' feelers, antennae (of
an insect) (WB) [isht
im+pashooli+']
ishtincho'wa to be tattooed, marked,
branded with (a design) (III;3-oot)
[isht *incho'wa] § Sashakbaat
nampakali holba'oot ishtincho'wa.
My arm has a flower tattooed on it.
ishtincho'wa' letter (of the alphabet),
figure [ishtincho'wa+']
ishtinchohóngma hngr. of

ishtinchokma

ishtinchokma
ishtinchokma to like to (III) [E],
[E+kat] [isht *inchokma] {hngr.
ishtinchohóngma} § Hilhakat
ishtanchokma. I like to dance. |
Ollali ishtanchokma. I like to laugh.
ishtinchokmá'ka ggr. of
ishtinchokmaka
ishtinchokmahánka hngr. of
ishtinchokmaka
ishtinchokmaka to like it, have
everything be okay, have it feel
good (III) [isht *inchokmaka] {ggr.
ishtinchokmá'ka; hngr.
ishtinchokmahánka; ngr.
ishtinchokmánka}
ishtinchokmánka ngr. of
ishtinchokmaka
ishtintalakchi' brake [isht
intalakchi+']
ishtittachapa to argue together about
(pl. subj.) (I;3 / IR;3) [isht *ittachapa]
§ Ta'osso ishtiitachapatok. We
argued about money.
ishtittanaha to have a meeting about
(pl. subj.) (IR;3 / I;3) [isht *ittanaha]
§ Impa' ishtiitanahatok,
ishtilittanahatok. We had a meeting
about the food.
ishtittanaha' meeting, rally
[ishtittanaha+']
ishtittaamowa, ishtittitamowa to run
off together (pl. subj.) (3) [isht
*ittaamowa/ittitamowa]
ishtittaanokfilli to think about each
other (I / IR) [itti+(isht anokfilli)>
isht *ittaanokfilli]
ishtittaapichi to help each other (I /
IR) [isht *ittaapichi]
ishtittí'wa to lie with, lie down with
(sg. subj.) (I;3) [isht *itti'wa] {dl.
ishkáyya'ha; tpl. ishkahat máa} §
Naachi ishtitti'wali. I lay down with
a quilt.

ishtittibaanokfilli to come to an
agreement concerning (I;3 / IR;3)
[isht *ittibaanokfilli] § Ihoo
ishtiitibaanokfillitok. We agreed
about the woman.
ishtittibi to fight with, fight over (I;II
/ IR;3) [isht *ittibi] § Ana'ak
issattibitok. They were fighting over
me. | Bashpo ishtittibitok. They
were fighting with knives, They
were fighting over the knife.
ishtittibi' sword, shield [ishtittibi+']
ishtittibo'li to hit each other with (I;3
/ IR;3) [isht *ittibo'li]
ishtittibo'li' boxing gloves
[ishtittibo'li+']
ishtittichalha'chi' baby's rattle [isht
ittichalha'chi+']
ishtittihállalli to hold to (a law,
treaty); to keep an old promise (pl.
subj.) (I;3 / IR;3) [isht *ittihallalli] §
Ishhashtihallalla'chi. You all will
hold to it, abide by it.
ishtittilisso to bump into each other,
bump together (IR) [isht *ittilisso]
ishtittimayya in anompa
ishtittimayya ki'yo
ishtittisso to collide, hit each other
(once) with (I;3 / IR;3) [isht *ittisso]
§ Kaa ishtittissotok. They bumped
into each other's cars.
ishtittishoochi to rub (something)
together (I;3 / IR;3) [isht
*ittishoochi]
ishtittitamowa see ishtittaamowa
ishtittola to fall with (I;II) [isht
*ittola] § Holisso ishtittolalitok. I
fell with a book. | Issattola. He fell
with me.
ishtiwa' key [isht tiwa+']
ishtiwa' ikbi' locksmith [ikbi+']
ishtjhaksi to show to ', turn up with
for ' unexpectedly, all of a sudden
(I;III;3) (mainly subr.; with +na) [isht

174

*ihaksi] (ygr. ishtiháyyaksi) §
Ta'osso ishtahaksina ishilitok. He
turned up with the money for me
all of a sudden, and I got it. |
Ishchihaksili ishishimanko. I
suddenly showed it to you, and you
took it. | Holissa ishtishihaksina
pisatam?, Ishtishihaksina holissa
pisatam? Did he suddenly see the
book you were concealing?, Did he
see the book as you suddenly
showed it to him?
ishtihashaa to be jealous of (I;III) [isht
*ihashaa]
ishtiháyyaksi ygr. of ishtihaksi
ishtihohólba hngr. of ishtiholba
ishtiholba to have nightmares about,
think one has seen (III;3) [isht
*iholba] (hngr. ishtihohólba) §
Lauraak ishtaholbatok. I have
nightmares about Laura.
ishtihopaakichi to take away from °
(I;III;3) [isht *ihopaakichi] § Chipota
ahattak ishtihopaakichilitok. I took
the children away from my
husband.
ishtíla to be different, look different
(II) [isht *ila]
ishtimalhaa, ishtimalhaha to be
jealous, envious of (I;III) [isht
*i+malhaa/ i+malhaha]
ishtimóma to have all of (III;3); to do
all (III) [isht *imoma] § Nipi'a
ishtamómatok. I had all of the
meat.
ishto to be big (II) [+CPR] [+PR] (ggr.
í'shto; hgr. íhhishto; hngr. ihíshto;
ngr. chínto (preferred), íshto; ygr.
íyyi'shto; pl. subj. hichito)
ishtochichi to make big (I;II)
[ishto+chichi] (ngr. ishtochínchi)
ishtochínchi ngr. of ishtochichi
ishtoksali' tractor [isht toksali+']
ishtokshili'ta' door (the moving

part); shutter [isht okshilitta+']
ishtokshili'ta' aayo'kli' doorknob
[aa+yokli+']
ishtoktani', ishtoktani' sign,
billboard [isht oktani/oktani+']
ishtoktani' holisso, ishtoktani'
holisso document: especially, a
deed [isht oktani/oktani+']
ishtoktani' see ishtoktani'
ishtoktani' holisso see ishtoktani'
holisso
ishtombohli to accuse (I;II) [isht
*ombohli] (anompombohli,
anompishtombohli) §
Ishtachombohlilitok. I accused you.
ishtona to bring, take (over there)
(I;II); to bring °, take ° to (a place
over there) (I;II;3) [isht *ona] §
Yamma ishtasonatok. He brought
me there.
ishtonhochi to accuse, blame; to
gossip about (I;II) [isht *onhochi] §
Ishtasonhochitok. They blamed me.
ishtonittola to be falsely accused, to
be blamed (II) [isht *on+ittola] §
Ithanali ishtasonittolatokat. I know
that I was falsely accused.
ishtontí'wa to be blamed, implicated
(II); to be blamed, implicated by (II;3-
at) [isht *on+ti'wa] § Benjieakot
anompa yammakot ishtonti'wa.
Benjie was implicated by that
testimony.
ishtontochchí'na to be eighth (I) [isht
*ontochchi'na] §
Ishtishontochchi'na. You're eighth.
ishtontoklo to be seventh (I) [isht
*ontoklo] § Ishtishontoklo. You're
seventh.
ishtontono'kalhchi' in
paskishtontono'kalhchi'
ishtossoola to carry while bucking (of
a horse) (I;II) [isht *tossoola]
ishtohíkki'ya to stand on (I;3) [isht

ishwakaa'

*on+hikki'ya] § Sashkobo'
ishtohikki'yali. I stood on my head.
ishwakaa' see nannishwakaa'
ishwihpoli to rob ° using (I;II;3) [isht
*wihpoli] § Tanampo'
ishwihpolitok. He robbed her with a
gun, at gunpoint.
ishyaa to cry about, mourn (I;II) [isht
*yaa] § Ishchiyaatok. He mourned
for you (with crying).
ishyo'kli' gripping clip, such as an
alligator clip [isht yokli+']
ishyokachi' in alhposhik ishyokachi'
ishyoppola to play around with, toy
with, not be serious about (I;II) [isht
*yoppola]
ithá'na ggr. of ithana
ithahána hngr. of ithana
ithana to get to know, find out,
recognize (I;II); to learn to (I) [E+0]
{ggr. ithá'na; hngr. ithahána; ngr.
ithána: to know, understand, know
how; ygr. itháyya'na} § Holissochi
ithanalitok. I learned to write.
ithanachi to teach to ° (I;II;3); to
introduce ° to ° (I;II;3) [ithana+chi]
§ Chikashshanompa sathanachi.
She teaches me Chickasaw. I
Charlesa sathanashtok. She
introduced me to Charles, She
introduced Charles to me.
itháyya'na ygr. of ithana
ithána to know, understand [-OPR];
to know how to [E+kat]; to feel (an
earthquake)—ngr. of ithana {neg.
ikitha'no} § Taloowakat ithanali. I
know how to sing. I Yaaknaat
wina'kachitoka ishithanatam? Did
you feel the earthquake?
iti mouth (IIp)
iti intakchi to gag (IIp = obj, I;III) §
Sati antakchitok. He gagged me.
iti takchi to gag (IIp = obj. , I) § Sati
takchitok. He gagged me.

itihalbi' see ittihalbi'
itokchaat lawa, itokchi' lawa to
salivate (for a food) (IIp = subj.)
[itokchi'+at] § Impa' pisalikat
satokchaat lawatahatok. When I
saw that food I salivated.
itokchaat pokpoki, itokchi' pokpoki
to foam at the mouth (IIp = subj.)
[itokchi'+at] § Chitokchaat
pokpokitok. You were foaming at
the mouth. I Satokchi' pokpokikat
ithanali. I know I foamed at the
mouth.
itokchi' saliva (IIp) [iti okchi']
itokchi' lawa see itokchaat lawa
itokchi' lawachi to make (someone)
salivate (of the experience of eating
a sour-tasting food) (IIp = obj. , 3)
[(itokchi' lawa)+chi> itokchi'
*lawachi] § Pikkal apalika satokchi'
lawashtok. Eating the pickle made
me salivate.
itokchi' pokpoki see itokchaat
pokpoki
ittabalahálli to keep walking around
aimlessly—hngr. of <ittabalalli>,
ittabállalli
ittabalalli to grow together (of
ground-growing plants like
crabgrass) (3) [itti+abalalli] {ggr.
ittabállalli: to mill around; hngr.
ittabalahálli}
ittabállalli, ittabállatli to mill around,
walk around aimlessly or in a group
(pl. subj.) (I / IR)—ggr. of ittabalalli
{hngr. ittabalahálli}
ittabállatli see ittabállalli
ittaban-kachit máa to be crossed:
especially, to be laid overlapping on
the ends perpendicular to each
other (like the logs in a log cabin)
(tpl. subj.) (3) [itti+aban-kachi+t] {dl.
ittabánna'a}
ittabánna'a to be crossed (of legs,

176

sticks, etc.) (dl. subj.) (3)
[itti+abanna'a] {v2. ittabaanali,
ittabánna'li; tpl. ittaban-kachit máa}
ittabánna'li to punish (crimes)
following the philosophy of "an eye
for an eye, a tooth for a tooth" (3;3)
[itti+<abanna'li>] {v1.
ittabánna'a}—ggr. of ittabaanali §
Chikashshaakot nannaka
ittabanna'liminattook. The
Chickasaws used to punish things
by "an eye for an eye".
ittabanni to build (a house) log-cabin
style (IR;3) [itti+abanni]
{ittabannichi} § Abooha
ittabannitok. They built a log cabin.
ittabannichi to build (a house) log-
cabin style (I;3 / IR;3)
[itti+<abannichi> ?] § Abooha
ittabannichit ayatahatok. They went
to build a log cabin.
ittabaana to be made with wood
stacked with the ends overlapping
(of a fence or pen) (3) {v2.
ittabaanali} § Holittaat
ittabaanatáyya'ha. The fence is
made of wood stacked with the ends
overlapping. | aboohattittabaana':
log cabin
ittabaanali to make (dl. obj.) cross, to
place (dl. obj.) so that one crosses
the other: especially, to cross (one's
legs) (I;3 / IR;3) {v1. ittabaana; ggr.
ittabánna'li: to punish "eye for an
eye" style} § Sayyi' ittabaanalilitok. I
crossed my legs.
ittabi' (MJ, WB), (ER) tabi' cane,
walking stick (Ct?)
ittabihli to fit (pl. obj.) together (I;3 /
IR;3) [itti+abihli]
ittabila to melt together (pl. or mass
obj.—of candy, for example) (3)
[itti+abila] {v2. ittabilili}
ittabilachi to melt (pl. or mass obj.)

together (I;3) [ittabila+chi]
ittabilili to melt (pl. or mass obj.)
together (I;3) [itti+abilili] {v1.
ittabila}
ittaboknohli to tangle up, bunch up
(a string, for instance—sg. obj.) (I;3)
{v1. ittaboknowa; pl. obj.
ittaaboknohli}
ittaboknowa to be tangled (of a
string—sg. subj.) (3) {v2.
ittaboknohli; pl. ittaaboknowa}
ittacha'pa' mate (of one of a pair of
shoes, gloves, earrings, etc.)
[ittachapa+']
ittachaffa to be the same, be alike (3);
to each get (I;3 / IR;3)
[itti+<achaffa>] {ittachaafowa} §
Nannilanolikat ittachaffatoko
ilithanatok. We found out that we
had told the same story, that what
we told was the same. | Naafka
iitachaffatok. We each got a dress. |
Naafkaat ittachaffaho iichompatok.
We bought dresses that were alike.
ittachahámpa hngr. of ittachapa
ittachakali to put (two separate
things) together (dl. obj.) (I;3 / IR;3)
{v1. ittachákka'a; pl. obj. ittachakli}
ittachákka'a to be attached, joined
together (dl. subj.) (3)
[itti+achakka'a] {v2. ittachakali; tpl.
ittachakkachit máa}
ittachakkachi to be made of a
number of different items put
together (for instance, of a pieced
quilt or a cinderblock wall) (3)
[itti+<achakkachi>] {ittachakkachit
máa} § Naachaat ittachakkachi. The
quilt is pieced.
ittachakkachit máa to be joined
together (tpl. subj.) (3)
[ittachakkachi+t] {dl. ittachákka'a;
pl. obj. ittachakli}
ittachakli to add together, put

together, bring together the ends of (pl. obj.), to piece (a quilt) (I;3 / IR;3) {dl. obj. ittachakali; ittachakkachit máa}

ittachámpa to be the same on both sides—ngr. of ittachapa

ittachapa to argue, debate (dl. subj.); to bring up an old issue, support a rejected candidate; to face each other (I / IR) [itti+achapa] {v2. ittachaabli, ittachapali; ggr. ittáchcha'pa; hngr. ittachahámpa; ngr. ittachámpa: to be the same on both sides; tpl. ittachapo'wa; ishtachapa; ittacha'pa}

ittachapali to bring (opponents) together (in a boxing match, for example) (3;II) {v1. ittachapa; ggr. ittacháppa'li}

ittachapo'li to sort (shoes, for example) into pairs (I;3 / IR;3) [itti+achapo'li]

ittachapo'wa to brawl, argue, all talk at once (tpl. subj.) (I / IR); to be sorted into pairs (3) [itti+<achapo'wa>] {dl. ittachapa}

ittacháppa'li ggr. of ittachapali

ittachaabli to make up a pair with (something that doesn't match) (IR;3 / I;3) {v1. ittachapa}

ittachaafowa to get one each (I;3 / IR;3) [itti+<achaafowa>] {ittachaffa} § Paska champoli' iitachaafowatok. We got one cookie each.

ittachaafoochi to divide up, give away (especially, one each); to separate ; to sort into pairs (I;II / IR;3) [-SC] [ittachaafowa+chi/ itti+<achaafoochi>] {hngr. ittachaafoolihínchi; ngr. ittachaafoolínchi; intachaafoochi: to divide among}

ittachaakissa to stick together (of pieces of candy, for example—not of people) (3) [itti+achaakissa]

ittáchcha'pa ggr. of ittachapa

ittachokkobbi to be used to each other (3) [itti+achokkobbi] {ittaachokkobbi}

ittafama to meet, get together, have a fight, have a meeting (pl. subj.) (I / IR); to meet, get together with; to have a fight with, defend oneself against (I;II / IR;3) [itti+afama] {v2. ittafammichi; ittafamo'li} § Sattafama. He had a fight with me, He had to defend himself against me.

ittafamachi to invite (dl. obj.) to meet each other (I;II) [itti+afama+chi] {pl. obj. ittafammichi, ittafamo'chi}

ittafammichi to invite, have over (pl. obj.) (especially, all at once ?) (I;3 / IR;3) {v1. ittafama; dl. obj. ittafamachi; ittafamo'chi}

ittafamo'chi to assemble, invite (pl. obj.) (especially, from different areas or on different occasions ?) (I;II / IR;3) [ittafamo'li+chi] {dl. obj. ittafamachi; ittafammichi}

ittafamo'li to assemble, gather (pl. subj.) (I / IR) {ittafama}

ittafímmo'pa to be scattered all over (pl. subj.) (I / IR)—ggr. of ittafimopa [itti+a+fimmo'pa/ itti+<afimmo'pa>] {v2. ittafímmobli}

ittafímmobli ggr. of ittafimobli

ittafimobli to scatter all over (pl. nonhum. obj.) (I;3 / IR;3) [+T]— usually used in ggr. [itti+a+<fimmobli>] {v1. ittafimopa, ittafímmo'pa; ggr. ittafímmobli}

ittafimopa to be scattered all over (3) [+T]—usually used in ggr. {v2. ittafímmobli; ggr. ittafímmo'pa: (I / IR)}

ittahaalahlínchi to watch, take care of (pl. obj.) (IR;3) [itti+<ahaalahlinchi>] § Shokcha ittahaalahlįshlitokoot chaffaat ankaniyatok. Because I was taking care of a lot of bags I lost one.

ittahiina to stick together, stay together (perhaps because of being scared) (I / IR) [itti+ahiina]

ittahoba to be gathered, piled up (of wood, for example) (3) (Ct?) {v2. ittahobbi}

ittahobbi to gather, pick up and put all in one place, make a collection of; to give an offering of (money) (I;3 / IR;3) {v1. ittahoba}

ittahobbi' offering, collection (in church) [ittahobbi+']

ittahobbi' hoyo to take an offering, take up a collection (in church, or for someone unfortunate) (I)

ittahoochifochi to give (one's children) the same name (pl. subj., of two mothers, for example) (I;3 / IR;3) [itti+ahoochifochi]

ittakallochi' in bala' ittakallochi' [itti+akallochi+']

ittakánni'ya to be committed, to really do it, not to let anyone stop one, to make it work (primarily sg. subj.) (I); to make it work with (someone), stick with (someone) (primarily sg. subj.) (I;3); to be committed to each other (pl. subj.) (I / IR) [itti+akanni'ya]

ittakashkoli to divide up, share (tpl. subj.) (I;3 / IR;3) [itti+a+kashkoli] {v1. ittakashkowa}

ittakashkowa to get a share of, split up among oneselves (I;3 / IR;3) [itti+a+kashkowa] {v2. ittakashkoli} § Paska iitakashkowatok. We split the bread among ourselves.

ittakatolhlhi to cut (a string, for example) into short pieces (I;3 / IR;3) [itti+akatolhlhi]

ittakaashabli to share, get an equal amount (dl. subj.) (I;3 / IR;3) [itti+a+kaashabli] {v1. ittaakashapa}

ittakaashapa to split up, split apart, be split up, be divided (I / IR) [itti+akaashapa] {v2. ittakaashabli}

ittakoba', (CC) ittakomba stomach; tripe (IIp) {short form: takoba'} § waak-ittakoba' beef tripe

ittakoba' kisili' stomach ache [kisili+']

ittakoba' kisili' hayoochi to get a stomach ache (I)

ittakoba' kisili' i'shi to get a stomach ache (I)

ittakoba' loksi' stomach ulcer; appendix (ER) (IIp) § sattakoba' loksi': my ulcer

ittakoba' malli' stomach ulcer [malli+']

ittakoba' sokbish folds between the legs and the trunk, under the stomach; groin (IIp) § sattakoba' sokbish: the folds under my stomach

ittakónno'fa to fight with (sg. subj.) (I;II) [itti+akonno'fa] § Sattakonno'fa. He fought with me.

ittalahálli hngr. of ittalalli

ittalalli, ittalatli to stack, put (pl. obj.) one on top of the other, align the edges of (I;3 / IR;3) [itti+<alalli>] {v1. ittalaata; hngr. ittalahálli; dl. obj. ittalaatali; ittalatkachi, ittalatkachit máa}

ittalatkachi to be piled up, to have the edges lined up (tpl. subj.) (3) [itti+<alatkachi>] {v2. ittalalli; dl./ygr. ittalatkáyya'chi; ittalaata, ittalatkachit máa}

ittalatkachit máa to be piled up, have the edges lined up (tpl. subj.) (3) [ittalatkachi+t] {dl. ittalatkáyya'chi}

ittalatkáyya'chi to be one on top of

179

ittalatli

the other (dl. subj.) (3)—ygr. of
ittalatkachi {tpl. ittalatkachi,
ittalatkachit máa; ittalátta'a}
ittalatli see ittalalli
ittalátta'a to be piled up, doubled
over (dl. subj.) (3)—xgr. of ittalaata
[itti+alatta'a] {v2. ittalaatali; tpl.
subj. ittalatkachi, ittalatkachit máa;
ittalatkáyya'chi}
ittalaata to be doubled up, folded
over (3) [itti+alaata] {v2. ittalaatali,
ittalalli; ggr. ittálla'ta; xgr. ittalátta'a}
ittalaatali to make double, to make a
double thickness, put one on top of
the other (dl. obj.) (I;3) [itti+alaatali]
{v1. ittalátta'a; pl. obj. ittalalli}
ittalaatassachi to press together,
flatten (I;3 / IR;3) [itti+alaatassachi]
ittalbihílli hngr. of ittalbilli
ittalbilli, ittalbitli to put on more
than one additional (layer, article of
clothing) (I;3 / IR;3) [itti+albilli]
{hngr. ittalbihílli; ittalbitili: to put
on an additional (layer)}
ittalbitili to put on an additional
(layer, article of clothing) (I;3 / IR;3)
[itti+albitili] {ittalbilli: to put on
more than one additional (layer)}
ittalbitkachi to be stacked, piled up (3)
ittalbitli see ittalbilli
ittalikchi', itti' alikchi', (AB) talikchi'
cherry tree
ittálla'ta ggr. of ittalaata
ittalhata dish containing two
ingredients cooked together in
liquid—only used in a complex cln.,
with two preceding nouns
[itti+<alhata>] § tanchi' nipi'
ittalhata dish consisting of corn and
meat cooked together | Tanchi'
osak ittalhataka chibannata? Do you
want corn and nuts cooked together
in liquid?
ittalhatali to cook (something)

together with (another thing) in
liquid (IR;3;3) [itti+alhatali]
{ittalhata} § Nipi' ittalhatalilitok
bala'a. I cooked the beans together
with the meat in liquid.
ittalhtobo'wa to take turns, trade off
(pl. subj.) (I / IR) {v2. <ittatobo'li>;
ittatobo'wa}
ittamóshsho'li to try hard; to get
married, get together (especially, no
matter what happens) (I / IR); to
marry, get together with (especially,
no matter what happens) (I;II / IR;3)
[itti+amoshsho'li]
ittanaha, ittanaa to have a church
meeting, service; to be a
congregation (I / IR) {v2. ittanahli}
ittanaha', ittanaa' meeting,
congregation; church [ittanaha+']
ittanaháli hngr. of ittanahli
ittanahishto' camp meeting
[ittanaha' ishto+']
ittanahli to gather, collect, make a
pile of (I;II / IR;3) {v1. ittanaha;
hngr. ittanaháli; ngr. ittanáhli} §
Brenda'at issosh ittanahli. Brenda
collects bugs.
ittanaa see ittanaha
ittanaa' see ittanaha'
ittanaachi to gather, bring together in
one place; to assemble (people) (of a
deacon) (I;3 / IR;3) [-SC]
[ittanahli+chi] {v1. ittanaalhchi;
hngr. ittanaahánchi}
ittanaahánchi hngr. of ittanaachi
ittanaalhchi to pile up, gather; to be
piled up, be gathered (3) [+T] {v2.
ittanaachi}
ittanáhli ngr. of ittanahli
ittanipahchi see ittanipaachi
ittanipaachi, ittanipahchi to take the
arms and legs off, dismember
inexpertly (I;3) [+T]
ittánno'wa see tánno'wa

180

ittannonka' wilderness [itti' anonka']
ittanohǫ́wa see tanohǫ́wa
ittanǫ́wa in nǫwat ittanǫ́wa; see tanǫ́wa
ittapá'lli ggr. of ittapalli
ittapahánni hngr. of ittapanni
ittapakchíllo'fa to cuddle up to each other (I / IR) [itti+apakchillo'fa] {ittaapakchíllo'fa}
ittapakfohkachi to be tangled up (3) [itti+<apakfohkachi>]
ittapakfohli to wind into a ball (3;3) [itti+apakfohli] {ittapakfolli}
ittapakfolli to wind into a ball (I;3) [itti+apakfolli] {ittapakfohli}
ittapákko'ta ggr. of ittapaakota
ittapalli, ittapatli to piece (a quilt with a design), sew together (clothes, etc.—pl. obj.) (I;3 / IR;3) [itti+<apalli>] {v1. (dl.) ittapátta'a, (tpl.) ittapatkachi; ggr. ittapá'lli, ittáppalli; dl. obj. ittapaatali; apaatali} § Nạachi' ittapallili. I pieced the quilt.
ittapalli' pieced quilt, especially one with a pieced design [ittapalli+']
ittapalhlhi to cut or split in more than two pieces (I;3 / IR;3) [itti+a+palhlhi]
ittapanaa to be twisted together (3) [itti+apanaa] {v2. ittapanni}
ittapanaachi to twist (two threads, for instance) together (I;3 / IR;3) [ittapanaa+chi]
ittapanni to twist together (threads, for instance) (I;3 / IR;3) [itti+<apanni>] {v1. ittapanaa; hngr. ittapahánni}
ittapatkachi, ittapatkalhchi to be pieced, sewn together (mass or tpl. subj.) (3) {v2. ittapalli; dl. subj. ittapátta'a} § Nạachaat ittapatkachi. The quilt is pieced.
ittapatkachi' pieced quilt

[ittapatkachi+']
ittapatkalhchi see ittapatkachi
ittapatli see ittapalli
ittapátta'a to be sewn together (of two pieces) (dl. subj.) (3)—xgr. of <ittapaata> [itti+apatta'a] {v2. ittapalli; tpl. subj. ittapatkachi}
ittapaakolli to bend, double over (I;3 / IR;3); to dent each other (3) [itti+apaakolli] {v1. ittapaakota; issot ittapakolli}
ittapaakota to be bent over, folded over, doubled over, hunched over (3) [itti+apaakota] {v2. ittapaakolli; ggr. ittapákko'ta}
ittapaalhalli to cut or split in two (I;3 / IR;3) [itti+apaalhalli] § Takolo ittapalhallila'chi. I'm going to cut the peach in two.
ittapaaniili to twist (dl. obj.) together (I;3 / IR;3) [itti+apaaniili]
<ittapaata> in naaittapa'ta' {v2. ittapaatali; xgr. ittapátta'a}
ittapaatali to sew (dl. obj.) together (I;3 / IR;3) [itti+apaatali] {v1. <ittapaata>; pl. obj. ittapalli}
ittapiha to go, come, be together; to be kin, to be related (I / IR) [itti+apiha] {ggr. ittáppi'ha: to go, come together; ngr. ittapíha: to go, come together}
ittapihaka' younger kin, descendants, relatives (especially grandchildren) (Ip / IIp); associates, fellow gang members (usually pl.) (IIp) [ittapiha+ka'] § Sattapihaka' chiyattook. You used to be related to me, You used to be my relative. I Chittapihaka' sayattook. I used to be related to you, I used to be your relative. I Pottapihakaakǫ pistiliyatok, Ilittapihakaakǫ pistiliyatok. We went to see our relatives.

181

ittapíhhihcha

ittapíhhihcha to be very small, to be midgets (pl. subj.) (I / IR) {sg. subj. píhhihcha} § Iitapihhihcha. We're midgets.
ittapila to help each other, work together (pl. subj.) (I / IR) [itti+apila]
ittapíha to go, come together—ngr. of ittapiha
ittapolli, ittapotli to lay together, bring together (tpl. obj.), bring together the ends of (I;3 / IR;3) [itti+apolli] {dl. obj. ittapootoli}
<ittapotkachi> in ittapotkachit máa [itti+<apotkachi>] {ygr. ittapotkáyya'chi}
ittapotkachit máa to be closely attached together (tpl. subj.) (I) [<ittapotkachi>+t] {dl. ittapotkáyya'chi}
ittapotkáyya'chi to be closely attached together (dl. subj.) (I / IR)—ygr. of <ittapotkachi> {tpl. ittapotkachit maa]
ittapotli see ittapolli
ittapótto'wa to go everywhere together, be parallel, be attached together (I / IR); to be tied to, go everywhere with, be parallel to, be attached to (I;II) [itti+apotto'wa]
ittapoota in ootittapoota [itti+apoota] {v2. ittapootoli}
ittapootoli to put (dl obj.) next to each other; to bring the ends of (two things) together (I;II / IR;3) [itti+apootoli] {v1. ittapoota; pl. obj. ittapolli}
ittáppalli ggr. of ittapalli
ittáppi'ha to go, come together—ggr. of ittapiha
ittasánna'a xgr. of ittasaana
ittássa'na ggr. of ittasaana
ittasaana to have a fight, face to face (I / IR) {v2. ittasaanali; ggr. ittássa'na; xgr. ittasánna'a}

ittasaanali to face each other (in a fight) (I / IR) [itti+asaanali] {v1. ittasaana; ggr. ittasánna'li; isanali'}
ittasiita to bet with (I;II / IR;3); to bet with ˚ on ˚ (I;II;3 / IR;3;3); to gamble, have a bet (I / IR) [itti+asiita] § Lynnako chittasiitalitok. You and I had a bet on Lynn, I had a bet with Lynn on you.
ittasiitohóli hngr. of ittasiitohli
ittasiitóhli ngr. of ittasiitohli
ittasiitili, tasiitili to close (a safety pin), button a button on (a garment) (sg. obj.) (I;3 / IR;3) [itti+asiitili] {pl. obj. ittasiitohli}
ittasiitohli, tasiitohli to close (safety pins), pin, button (pl. obj.); to button more than one button on (I;3 / IR;3) [itti+asiitohli] {hngr. ittasiitohóli; ngr. ittasiitóhli; sg. obj. ittasiitili} § Naafkishto' tasiitohlili. I buttoned the (buttons on the) coat.
ittássa'na to (finally) have a fight (I / IR)—ggr. of ittasaana
ittashikkílli'li to be pagoda shaped, pointed (of houses in Chinatown or highway cones, perhaps); to be sitting so that just the heads are visible (of children, for example) (pl. subj.) (3)
ittashiichi to tie together; to sew together just any old way (I;II / IR;3) [-SC] [itti+ashiichi] {v1. ittashiiyalhchi}
ittashiikoono'li to knot (strings) together (I;3 / IR;3) [itti+ashiikoono'li] {v1. ittashiikoono'wa}
ittashiikoono'wa to be knotted together, tangled up (3) [itti+ashiikoono'wa] {v2. ittashiikoono'li}
ittashiiyalhchi to be tied together, to

182

be sewed up wrong, to be all tangled up (3) [itti+ashiiyalhchi] {v2. ittashiichi}
ittashohǫ́mmi hngr. of ittashommi
ittashokaffi to take apart (dl. obj.) (I;3 / IR;3) [itti+ashokaffi] {pl. obj. ittashokaachi}
ittashokahlihínchi hngr. of ittashokaachi
ittashokahlínchi ngr. of ittashokaachi
ittashokaachi to take (something) apart (I;3 / IR;3) [-SC] [itti+a+shokahli+chi] {hngr. ittashokahlihínchi; ngr. ittashokahlínchi; dl. obj. ittashokaffi}
ittashoma to be mixed up, shuffled (pl. subj.) (3); to be all different colors (inan. subj.) (3); to be a racially mixed group (pl. subj.) (I / IR) [+T] [itti+<ashoma>] {v2. ittashommi; ggr. ittáshsho'ma}
ittashommi to mix up, shuffle, put away in the wrong place (I;II / IR;3) [itti+<ashommi>] {v1. ittashoma; ggr. ittáshshommi; hngr. ittashohǫ́mmi}
ittashommit anompoli to mix in (another language) while talking (I;3) [ittashommi+t] § Oshpaanimanompa' ayna ittashommit ishanompolitok. You mixed in some Spanish too.
ittáshsho'ma ggr. of ittashoma
ittáshshommi ggr. of ittashommi
ittatakali to be tangled (3) [itti+atakali]
ittatakchichi to tie (pl. obj.) together (I;II / IR;3) [iiti+atakchichi]
ittatalakchi to be tied with each other, have a tie score (IR) [itti+atalakchi]
ittatoba to trade to ° for (I;II;3;3 /

IR;3;3;3); to trade ° for (I;II;3 / IR;3;3); to trade with each other (I / IR) [itti+<atoba>] § Asoba Lynn iwaaka' chittatobala'ni. I'll trade you my horse for Lynn's cow. | Iitatoba, ilittatoba. We traded. | Sashkaat ahi' shokcha a̲lhto' sattobatok. My mom traded me for a sack of potatoes.
ittatobbí'chi ggr. of ittatobbichi
ittatobbichi to change (dl. obj.) around, exchange, to make (dl. obj.) change places (I;II / IR;3) [itti+atobbichi] {ggr. ittatobbí'chi; pl. obj. ittatobo'chi}
ittatobo'chi to take turns with, to take (lovers, children one is caring for) in turn, to switch back and forth between, to change around (pl. obj.) (I;II / IR;3) [±SC] [<ittatobo'li>+chi] {dl. obj. ittatobbichi}
<ittatobo'li> in ittatobo'chi {v1. ittalhtobo'wa, ittatobo'wa}
ittatobo'wa to take turns, trade off (IR) {v2. <ittatobo'li>; ittalhtobo'wa}
ittawashshálla'a to be bushy (pl. subj.) (3) [itti+a+washshalla'a] {ittawashshállo'wa}
ittawashshállo'wa, ittawashshállo'ha to be bushy (pl. subj.) (3) [itti+a+washshallo'wa] {ittawashshálla'a}
ittayákko'wa to be lined up (dl. subj.) (I / IR)—ggr. of ittayakowa
ittayakmichi to solder (things) together (I;3 / IR;3) [itti+ayakmichi]
ittayakowa to be lined up, be in single file (pl. subj.) (I / IR) [itti+<ayakowa>] {ggr. ittayákko'wa: to be lined up (dl. subj.)}
ittayaapahli to sneak up on each other (3) [itti+ayaapahli] {ittaayaapahli}
ittayokmíllo'li to look at each other

ittayokommo

with interest (I / IR) [itti+
aa(y)+okmillo'li]
ittayokommo to mix up (ingredients,
things in the wrong place, etc.) (I;3 /
IR;3) [itti+aa(y)+okommo]
ittayokommochi to mix (dry
ingredients) (I;3 / IR;3)
[ittayokommo+chi]
{ittayolhkomochi}
ittayolhkomo to be mixed up, in a
mishmash (3) [itti+aa(y)+olhkomo]
ittayolhkomochi to mix (dry
ingredients) (I;3 / IR;3)
[ittayolhkomo+chi]
{ittayokommochi} §
Iitayolhkomocha'chi. We're going
to mix the dry ingredients.
ittayoppachi to speak to each other (I)
{ngr. ittayoppánchi; ittaayoppachi}
ittayoppánchi to like each other—
ngr. of ittayoppachi
ittayoppitahámmi ngr. of
ittayoppitammi
ittayoppitammi to meet face to face
and go on by, to pass going in
opposite directions (I / IR)
[itti+ayoppitammi] {hngr.
ittayoppitahámmi}
ittayoppitammichi to make (things,
or their ends) overlap (I;3 / IR;3); to
make (people) just pass each other
without stopping (of parents
keeping young lovers apart, for
example) (I;II) [ittayoppitammi+chi]
ittayoshkammi, (MJ) tishkammi to
flirt, make love, have sexual
intercourse (pl. subj.) (I / IR)
[itti+ayoshkammi]
ittayoshkóllo'li to be cut off short (of
trees in a clearing) (pl. subj.) (3)
[itti/itti'? +aa(y)+oshkololi]
ittayoshkolochi to cut off (trees) short
to make a clearing (pl. obj.) (3;3)
[itti/itti'?+aa(y)+ oshkolochi]

ittaabasha' sawmill [itti' aa+basha']
ittaaboknohli to tangle up (several
strings—pl. obj.) (I;3 / IR;3)
[itti+aboknohli] {v1. ittaaboknowa;
sg. obj. ittaboknohli}
ittaaboknowa to be all tangled up (pl.
subj.) (3) [itti+aboknowa] {v2.
ittaaboknohli; sg. ittaboknowa}
ittaachokkobbi to be used to each
other (I / IR) [itti+achokkobbi]
{ittachokkobbi}
ittaachokmalichi to treat each other
well (I / IR) [itti+achokmalichi]
ittaafaana'chi to investigate each
other (I / IR) [itti+afaana'chi]
ittaaholhchifochi to name (pl. obj.)
after each other (I;3 / IR;3)
[itti+aholhchifochi]
ittaakallohónchi to be packed in (of
people in a small space, for
example) (I / IR)
[itti+aa+kallhohonchi]
ittaakassanachi to push each other's
heads to the side (I / IR)
[itti+akassanachi]
ittaakostinichi to find out about each
other (I / IR) [itti+akostinichi]
ittaalhchi', (TP) ittaaschi', (WB, CC)
taalhchi', (TJ) taahchi', (MJ)
ittaashchi' shoulder (IIp)
ittaalhchi' foni' shoulder blade
ittaamowa in ishtittaamowa
ittaanokfilli in ishtittaanokfilli
ittaapakchíllo'fa to cuddle up to each
other (I / IR) [itti+apakchillo'fa]
{ittapakchíllo'fa}
ittaapichi in ishtittaapichi
ittaapollichi to fondle each other (of
adults, especially homosexuals) (I /
IR) [itti+aapollichi]
ittaaposhli to roast each other (I / IR)
[itti+aposhli]
ittaapoolosli to daub (something) on
each other's faces (I;3 / IR;3)

[itti+apoolosli]
ittaapoolhali to comfort each other (I / IR) [itti+apoolhali]
ittaapofachi to blow at each other (I / IR) [itti+apofachi]
ittaataklammi to bother each other (I / IR) [itti+ataklammi]
ittaatáyya'a to lean against each other (I / IR) [itti+atayya'a]
ittaatohnochi to sic (a dog or dogs, for example) on each other (I;3 / IR;3) [itti+atohnochi] § Ofi' iitaatohnochitok. We sicked the dog on each other.
ittaatookoli to appoint each other (I / IR) [itti+atookoli]
ittaatoshpalichi to hurry each other (I / IR) [itti+atoshpalichi]
ittaayaapahli to sneak up on each other (I / IR) [itti+ayaapahli] {ittayaapahli}
ittaayoppachi to greet each other (I / IR) [itti+ayoppachi] {ittayoppachi}
itti' tree, wood, stick
itti' akchalhpi' bark chips
itti' alikchi' see ittalikchi'
itti' alhpisa' rick (unit) of wood [alhpisa+']
itti' amposhi' wooden bowl
itti' api' tree trunk
itti' aabashli' sawmill, sawhorse [aa+bashli+']
itti' aabo'li' stickball goalposts [aa+bo'li+']
itti' aaholhfo' huckleberry (CC) [aa+holhfo+']
itti' basha', (WB) ti-basha' board, plank [itti' basha+']
itti' basha' tali-hina' aalhopolli' aahilichi' railroad crossing guard (WB) [tali' hina' aalhopolli+' aa+hilichi+']
itti' bosholli' sawdust
itti' chanaa, itti' chanaha wagon (IIIp:

inti' chanaa)
itti' chanaa inchanaa' wagon wheel [im+chanaa]
itti' chanaa inchanaa' iwashshalaka' spoke of a wheel [im+washshala+ka']
itti' chanaa ishtalhtipo' covered-wagon cover
itti' chanaa ishto', itti' chanaashto' wagon [ishto+']
itti' chanaa malili', chanaa malili', (WB) naa malili' railroad train [malili+']
itti' chanaa malili' aa-abaanabli' railroad bridge [aa+abaanabli+']
itti' chanaa malili' aahika' railroad station, depot [aa+hika+']
itti' chanaa malili' hasimbish caboose
itti' chanaa malili' hina' aabaanapo'li' railroad crossing [aa+abaanapoli+']
itti' chanaa malili' ihina' railroad track [im+hina']
itti' chanaa malili' ihina' inkaha' railroad tie
itti' chanaa oshi', (MJ, CC) chanaa oshi' little (toy) wagon; wheelbarrow
itti' chanaa palhki', chanaa palhki' car, automobile [palhki+']
itti' chanaashto' see itti' chanaa ishto'
itti' chanaalhtipo' covered wagon [itti' chanaa alhtipo']
itti' chaaha' telephone pole [chaaha+']
itti' cha'li' type of woodpecker [cha'li+']
itti' cholha' shingles (for a roof) [<cholha>+']
itti' falakto' yoke (for cattle); slingshot [falakto+']
itti' falakto' innóyyo'chi to be yoked

itti' folosh

(of cattle) (3)
itti' folosh wooden spoon
itti' hakshish root of a tree
itti' hakshish ishcha'ha' see itti' hakshishcha'ha'
itti' hakshishcha'ha', itti' hakshish ishcha'ha' grubbing hoe [isht chaa+']
itti' hobak tree that doesn't bear fruit
itti' holokchi' cultivated tree [holokchi+']
itti' ishcholha' large axe used for cutting shingles [isht cholha+']
itti' ishno'wa', (LF, MJ) itti' ishnowa' crutch, cane; stilts [isht nowa+']
itti' ishtaabachi' pointer (for use in a classroom, for instance) [isht aabachi+']
itti' ishtilombitka', ishtilombitka', (AB) itti' ishtombitka' cane (to walk with); crutches
itti' ittabaana' abooha, ittittabaana' abooha, (EP) itti' ittabaana' log cabin [itti+abaana+'] {aboohattittabaana'}
itti' ittabaana' holitta fence made of zigzagged overlapping logs [itti+abaana+']
itti' ittikisili' see itti' tikisili'
itti' ihiyohli' wooden poles or supports [im+hiyohli+']
itti' kafi' sassafras tree
itti' kati see kati
itti' kobolli' twigs [kobolli+']
itti' kolofa barrel, wooden bucket
itti' kolofishto', (TP) toklofishto' barrel [itti' kolofa ishto+']
itti' lakna' bois d'arc [itti' lakna+']
itti' laknani' horse apple (bois d'arc fruit) [itti' lakna' ani']
itti' lombo see itti' lombo'
itti' lombo', itti lombo log (not split) [lombo+']
itti' nakni' tree that doesn't bear fruit

or have flowers
itti' naksish branch (of a tree)
itti' okchama'li' type of medicinal plant (used for a drink like sassafras) [okchamali+']
itti' okchi' sap
itti' olhti' firewood [olhti+']
itti' oshkololi' (CC), (ER, TP) toshkololi', (TJ) tishkololi', (LR) itti' ishkololi' clearing where the trees are cut off a few feet high; (CC, MJ, TJ, TP, ER, LR) stump [oshkololi+']
itti' palha' split wood; fence post [palha+']
itti' palha' holitta rail fence
itti' patalhpo' wooden floor or platform, porch, bridge
itti' sokbish bottom of a tree trunk, where it grows out of the ground
itti' shalalli' sled (especially, for hauling wood) [shalalli+']
itti' shawwa bush; limbs cut from a tree
itti' shawwa illi' see itti' shawwilli'
itti' shawwilli', itti' shawwa illi' dead brush [itti' shawwa illi+']
itti' shinap ash tree
itti' shipafa' splinter [shipafa+']
itti' sholosh wooden shoe
itti' tali' petrified wood
itti' tapa' log [tapa+']
itti' tayokhana' cross, crucifix
itti' tayokhana' aatakaachi to crucify (I;3) [-SC] [aa+takaachi]
itti' tayokhana' takaachi to crucify (I;II) [-SC]
itti' tikisili', itti' ittikisili' any tree whose limbs rub together—used to make medicine for blue babies [ittikisili+']
itti' tiyya' pole beans, bush beans (CC) [toyya+']
itti' tiik tree that bears fruit
itti' tohbi' sycamore, birch, (TJ, ER,

186

MJ) cottonwood [tohbi+']
itti' toshbi' issọsh, (AB) itt<u>o</u>shbi'
iss<u>o</u>sh type of white worm (termite
larva?) used to doctor ringworm
itti'shi' , (AB, WB) itti' hishi' (tree)
leaf [itti' hishi']
ittí'wa in ishtittí'wa, aaittí'wa,
ibaaittí'wa {tí'wa}
ittialbaat falaa see ittialbi' falaa
ittialbi', ittihalbi', itihalbi' lip (IIp) [iti
<halbi'>]
ittialbi' falaa, ittialbaat falaa to pout,
stick out one's lower lip (IIp = subj.)
[ittialbi'+at] § Chittialbaat falaakat
ishith<u>a</u>nata? Did you know you're
pouting?
ittialbish, ittihalbish, (AB) talbish
navel (IIp)
ittialbish ishtalakchi' umbilical cord
ittialbishhommachi' lipstick [ittialbi'
isht hommachi+']
ittibaka'chi to make a knocking or
hammering sound (I / IR) [+SC]
[itti+baka'chi] {hngr. ittibakahánchi:
to make a noise like a wagon or like
hail on a wooden roof (3); klgr.
ittibákkakli'chi; rcgr. ittibakaká'chi}
ittibakaánchi see ittibakahánchi
ittibakaká'chi to make a knocking or
hammering sound (I / IR)—rcgr. of
ittibaka'chi [+SC] [itti+bakaka'chi]
ittibakahánchi, ittibakaánchi to make
a noise like a wagon or like hail
hitting a wooden roof (3)—hngr. of
ittibaka'chi
ittibákkakli'chi to make noise (for
instance, falling down like a drunk
person or knocking against wood) (I
/ IR)—klgr. of ittibaka'chi
[itti+bakkakli'chi]
ittibalhto to be all together, all in one
place all mixed up (inan. subj.) (3)
[itti+ibalhto] {ggr. ittíbbalhto; ngr.
ittib<u>á</u>lhto: to be all together (I); ygr.

ittibáyya'lhto}
ittibasa'chi to make a creaking
sound; to make a crackling sound
(like a fire) (I / IR) [itti+basa'cni]
{klgr. ittibássakli'chi; rcgr.
ittibasasá'chi}
ittibasasá'chi to creak (of a tree limb
when it's breaking) (3)—rcgr. of
ittibasa'chi [+SC] [itti+basasa'chi]
ittibássakli'chi to make a creaking
sound (I / IR)—klgr. of ittibasa'chi
[+SC]
ittibáyya'lhto ygr. of ittibalhto
ittibaa-anokfilli to think about
something together (I / IR)
[itti+ibaa-anokfilli]
ittibaa-áyya'sha to live together (of a
great variety of people) (I / IR)
[itti+ibaa-áyya'sha]
ittibaabinohchi to make sit together
(I;II / IR;3) [-SC] [itti+ibaabinohchi] §
Pottibaabinohchitok. They made us
sit together.
ittibaachaffa to come together,
assemble; to agree (I / IR)
[itti+ibaachaffa]
ittibaachaffa' group, gathering,
assembly [itti+ibaachaffa+']
ittibaachompa to buy together, go in
together on (I;3 / IR;3)
[itti+ibaa+chompa]
ittibaafokha to wear one another's
clothes (I;3 / IR;3) [itti+ibaafokha]
ittibaaholisso to be registered
together: especially, to have one's
names registered together (IR)
[itti+ibaaholisso]
ittibaaishi to be partners, go half-and-
half with regard to (I;3 / IR;3)
[itti+ibaaishi]
ittibaakahli to arrange, lay down
together (pl. obj.) (I;3 / IR;3)
[itti+ibaakahli]
ittibaakahlínchi ngr. of ittibaakaachi

ittibaakaachi to arrange, put together, mix (I;3 / IR;3) [ittibaakahli+chi] {hngr. ittibaakaalihínchi; ngr. ittibaakahlínchi}

ittibaakaachit anompoli to mix in (other languages) while talking (I;3) [ittibaakaachi+t]

ittibaakaalihínchi hngr. of ittibaakaachi

ittibaani to mix, mix up, combine; to put together, add together (I;II / IR;3) [itti+ibaani] § Toklo tochchi'na ittibaanikma talhlha'pi. Two and three are five, If two and three are added, it's five.

ittibaanokfilli to come to an agreement (I / IR) [itti+ibaa+anokfilli]

ittibaanosi to sleep together (euphemistic) (I / IR) [itti+ibaanosi]

ittibaapishi to be siblings, be animals from the same litter (pl. subj.) (I / IR); to be a sibling to (I;II) [itti+ibaapishi] § Yammakot sattibaapishi. She is my sister.

ittibaapishi brother, sister, cousin (often in a religious sense: brother or sister in Christ); animal from the same litter (as oneself); first cousin (IIp / (rare) Ip) [itti+ibaapishi] § Sattibaapishi atok. He was my brother. | Ittibaapishi poya. We are brothers. | ittibaapishili alhiha': my brothers and sisters (term of address that might be used by a minister) | Pottibaapishi pistiliyatok, Ilittibaapishi pistiliyatok. We went to see our brothers and sisters.

ittibaapishi iklanna' half-brother, half-sister (IIp) [iklanna+']

ittibaapishi pila first cousin (TP)

ittibaapishi toba' stepbrother, stepsister (especially, of the opposite sex) (IIp) [toba+'] § sattibaapishi toba': my stepbrother, stepsister

ittibaatobbi to share expenses on (I;3 / IR;3) [itti+ibaatobbi] § Impa' iitibaatobbitok. We shared expenses on food, We paid for the food together.

ittibaayóhhokli hgr. of ittibaayokli

ittibaayokli to grab onto; to attack (pl. subj.) (I;II / IR;3) [itti+ibaayokli] {ggr. ittibaayôkli: support, hold up; hgr. ittibaayóhhokli}

ittibaayôkli to hold onto, hold up, support—ggr. of ittibaayokli

ittibálhto to be all together (I)—ngr. of ittibalhto § Ittibalhtot iliyatok. We all went together.

ittíbbalhto ggr. of ittibalhto

ittibi to fight (sg/pl subj), kill each other (pl subj) (I / IR) [itti+abi] § Ittibilitok. I fought.

ittibichi to make fight (I;II / IR;3) [ittibi+chi]

ittibikolofa, (TP) tibokolofa', (MS) ittibi' kolofa stump [itti' abi kolofa+' ?]

ittibinka' a similar one to, another like (IIp / Ip) (always preceded by a noun) [itti+binka+'] {binka'} § Chikashsha' sattibinka'at yammak anta. A Chickasaw like me lives there. | Chikashsha' pottibinka', Chikashsha' ilittibinka': Chickasaws like us

ittibo'li to hit each other: especially, to box, have a boxing match (I / IR) [itti+bo'li]

ittichaffa to have one, to have the same (pl. subj.) (IR;3) [itti+chaffa] § Inki' iitichaffa. We had (one and) the same father.

ittichalha'chi to make a rattling, banging, or clanking sound (for instance, playing with a chain or throwing pans) (I / IR) [+SC] [itti+chalha'chi] {klgr. ittichálhlhakli'chi; rcgr. ittichalhalhá'chi}

ittichalhalhá'chi to rattle, make a rattling sound (of or with a rattle or a box with something in it, for example); to clank, make a clanking sound (I / IR)—rcgr. of ittichalha'chi

ittichalhaahánchi to rattle around and make noise (for example, of a noise maker attached to the wheel of a bicycle) (3) [itti+chalhaahanchi]

ittichálhlhakli'chi to make a rattle or clanking sound (of or with pans, for instance) (I / IR)—klgr. of ittichalha'chi

ittichama'chi to make the sound of dishes rattling (I / IR) [-SC] [itti+chama'chi] {hngr. ittichamahánchi: to make the sound of hail hitting a metal roof (3); klgr. ittichámmakli'chi; rcgr. ittichamamá'chi}

ittichamahánchi to make the noise of hail hitting a metal roof (3)— hngr. of ittichama'chi

ittichamamá'chi to make the sound of dishes rattling (I / IR)—rcgr. of ittichama'chi [+SC] [itti+chamama'chi]

ittichámmakli'chi to rattle, bang things together (I / IR)—klgr. of ittichama'chi [itti+chammakli'chi]

ittichasha'chi to make a rattling or rustling sound (I / IR) {klgr. itticháshshakli'chi; rcgr. ittichashashá'chi}

ittichashashá'chi to rattle (of a rattlesnake) (3); to make a rattling or rustling sound (I / IR)—rcgr. of ittichasha'chi

itticháshshakli'chi to make a sound with paper, a plastic bag, or dead

leaves (I / IR)—klgr. of ittichasha'chi [+SC]

ittichiko'li to pull each other's hair (as women do when they fight) (I / IR) [itti+chiko'li]

ittichóbbokli'chi to make a splashing sound, to make things splash each other (I / IR)—klgr. of ittichobo'chi [+SC]

ittichobo'chi to make a splashing sound (for instance, by jumping into water) (I / IR) [+SC] [itti+chobo'chi] {klgr. ittichóbbokli'chi; rcgr. ittichobobó'chi}

ittichobobó'chi to splash, make a splashing sound (I / IR); to splash (a liquid) (I;3 / IR;3)—rcgr. of ittichobo'chi [+SC]

ittifata'chi to make a noise flapping or shaking oneself (of an animal) [itti+fata'chi] (3) {klgr. ittifáttakli'chi; rcgr. ittifatatá'chi}

ittifatatá'chi to make a flapping sound or the sound of shaking oneself (of an animal) (3)—rcgr. of ittifata'chi [±SC] {ngr. ittifatata'línchi}

ittifatata'línchi ngr. of ittifatatá'chi

ittifáttakli'chi to make a noise by dragging a lumpy thing, such as a person or a bag of sand or by shaking something (I / IR)—klgr. of ittifata'chi

ittifokha to fit onto (of a lid, for instance) (3;3) [itti+fokha] {v2. ittifokhi; ygr. ittifóyyokha: to be fitted onto}

ittifokhi to fit on (a piece or lid) (sg. obj.) (I;3 / IR;3) [itti+fokhi] {v1. ittifokha}

ittifon forehead (IIp)

ittifonat ishto to have a high forehead, a high hairline (IIp =

189

subj.) [ittifon+at]

ittifóyyokha to fit onto, be fitted onto—ygr. of ittifokha

ittihaklo to hear each other, listen to each other (especially when practicing an oral performance) (I / IR) [itti+haklo]

ittihaksichi to cheat each other (I / IR) [itti+haksichi]

ittihala'li to take each other's hands (I / IR) [itti+hala'li]

ittihalbi' see ittialbi'

ittihalbish see ittialbish

ittihaliili to touch each other (I / IR)

ittihállalli to be together (of a group), to agree (pl. subj.); to hold hands (I / IR) {ittihalálli}—ggr. of ittihaalalli

ittihayoochi to find each other; to live together, shack up (I / II) [itti+hayoochi]

ittihaalá'lli ggr. of ittihaalalli

ittihaalalli, ittihaalatli to get married, be married (I / IR); to marry (I;II / IR;3) [itti+halalli] {ggr. ittihaalá'lli, ittihállalli; ngr. ittihaalálli: to be together, to agree}

ittihaalalli' holisso marriage license, marriage certificate [ittihaalalli+']

ittihaalallichi to marry (a couple—of a minister, for example) (I;II / IR;3) [ittihaalalli+chi]

ittihaalatli see ittihaalalli

ittihaalálli to be together (of a group), to have a relationship, to agree (pl. subj.) (I / IR) {ittihállalli}—ngr. of ittihaalalli

ittihímpa hngr. of ittipa

ittihoba to be the same, to look like each other (I / IR) [itti+<hoba>] {ngr. ittihómba; ahooba}

ittihómba ngr. of ittihoba

ittihosha to have sexual intercourse (pl. subj.) (I / IR) [itti+hosha]

ittihottopachi to hurt each other (I / IR) [itti+hottopachi]

ittihoyo to look for each other (as in hide and seek, for instance) (I;II / IR;3) [itti+hoyo]

ittihoyochi to make look for each other (I;II / IR;3) [ittihoyo+chi]

ittihólba to match, go together (of colors, clothes) (3) [itti+holba] {neg. iktiholbo}

ittikaba'chi to make a knocking sound (I / IR) [±SC] [itti+kaba'chi] {klgr. ittikábbakli'chi; rcgr. ittikababá'chi}

ittikababá'chi to make a knocking sound (I / IR)—rcgr. of ittikaba'chi

ittikábbakli'chi to knock things together, make a knocking sound (I / IR)—klgr. of ittikaba'chi [itti+<kabbakli'chi>]

ittikalha'chi to make a noise (of someone walking upstairs or moving furniture, or of birds in the attic, or a wagon coming) (I / IR) [+SC] {klgr. ittikálhlhakli'chi; rcgr. ittikalhalhá'chi}

ittikalhalhá'chi to make a noise (of someone walking upstairs or moving furniture, or birds in the attic, or a wagon coming) (I / IR)—rcgr. of ittikalha'chi [itti+kalhalha'chi]

ittikálhlhakli'chi to make a noise (as while moving furniture) (I / IR)—klgr. of ittikalha'chi

ittikama'chi to make a clatter (I / IR) [+SC] {klgr. ittikámmakli'chi; rcgr. ittikamamá'chi}

ittikamamá'chi to make a clatter (I / IR)—rcgr. ittikama'chi

ittikámmakli'chi to make a clatter, bang things (like pans) together (I / IR)—klgr. of ittikama'chi [itti+kammakli'chi]

ittikasa'chi to make a noise with

marbles (I / IR) [itti+kasa'chi] [+SC] {klgr. ittikássakli'chi; rcgr. ittikasasá'chi}

ittikasasá'chi to make a noise with marbles (I / IR) [+SC]—rcgr. of ittikasa'chi [itti+kasasa'chi]

ittikássakli'chi to make a noise with marbles; to play marbles (I / IR)—klgr. of ittikasa'chi [+SC]

ittikasha'chi to make a noise eating crunchy things (I / IR) [+SC] {klgr. ittikáshshakli'chi; rcgr. ittikashashá'chi}

ittikashashá'chi to make a noise eating crunchy things (I / IR)—rcgr. of ittikasha'chi [+SC]

ittikáshshakli'chi to make a noise eating crunchy things, to chew noisily (I / IR)—klgr. of ittikasha'chi [+SC]

ittikisili to bite each other (I / IR) [itti+kisili]

ittikisilichi see noti' ittikisilichi

ittikóbbokli'chi to hit something made of wood; to make a noise inside a wooden box (I / IR)—klgr. of ittikobo'chi [+SC]

ittikobo'chi to make the sound of something knocking around in a wooden box (I / IR) [+SC] {klgr. ittikóbbokli'chi; rcgr. ittikobobó'chi}

ittikobobó'chi to make the sound of something knocking around in a wooden box (I / IR)—rcgr. of ittikobo'chi [+SC]

ittikómmokli'chi to make noise banging (I / IR)—klgr. of ittikomo'chi [itti+kommokli'chi]

ittikomo'chi to make noise banging (I / IR) [-SC] [itti+komo'chi] {hngr. ittikomo'lihínchi; klgr. ittikómmokli'chi; ngr. ittikomo'línchi; rcgr. ittikomomó'chi}

ittikomo'lihínchi hngr. of ittikomo'chi

ittikomo'línchi ngr. of ittikomo'chi

ittikomomó'chi to make noise banging (I / IR)—rcgr. of ittikomo'chi [+SC] [itti+komomo'chi]

ittilá'wwi ggr. of ittilawwi

ittilapali, (ER) ittilapoli to have sexual intercourse (pl. subj.) (I / IR) [itti+lapali]

ittilapoli to have sexual intercourse (pl. subj.) (ER) [itti+<lapohli>] {ggr. ittiláppo'li (ER); ittilapali}

ittiláppo'li ggr. of ittilapoli (ER)

ittilasa'chi to smack one's lips, pop gum, eat noisily (I / IR) [+SC] {klgr. ittilássakli'chi; rcgr. ittilasasá'chi}

ittilasasá'chi to smack one's lips, pop gum, eat noisily (I / IR)—rcgr. of ittilasa'chi [+SC]

ittilássakli'chi to smack one's lips, pop gum, eat noisily (I / IR)—klgr. of ittilasa'chi [+SC]

ittilawwi to be even with, to equal, to be as much as, to have a tie score with (I;II / IR;3); to be even (I / IR); to be set (of a clock) (3) {ggr. ittíllawwi, ittilá'wwi; ngr. ittilá̲wwi: to be level} § Sachaahakat Jan ittilawwili. I'm as tall as Jan.

ittilawwí'chi ggr. of ittilawwichi

ittilawwichi to set (a clock), to make even, smooth (I;3 / IR;3) [+SC] [ittilawwi+chi] {ggr. ittilawwí'chi; ngr. ittilawwínchi; ittillawi'chi}

ittilawwichit tan̲ówa to march, walk in step (pl. subj.) (I) [ittilawwichi+t]

ittilawwínchi ngr. of ittilawwichi

ittilá̲wwi to be level—ngr. of ittilawwi

ittilisso in ishtittilisso [itti+ili+isso]

ittillawi'chi to get even with, get revenge; to get up even with (in

191

position); to have a tie score with
(I;II / IR;3) [+SC] {ggr. ittilláwwi'chi;
ittilawwichi}
ittíllawwi ggr. of ittilawwi
ittilláwwi'chi ggr. of ittillawi'chi
ittillichi to kill each other (I / IR)
[itti+illichi]
ittilhóchchokli'chi to slurp, make a
slurping noise (I / IR)—klgr. of
ittilhocho'chi [+SC]
ittilhocho'chi to slurp, make a
slurping noise (I / IR) [±SC] {klgr.
ittilhóchchokli'chi; rcgr.
ittilhochochó'chi}
ittilhochochó'chi to slurp, make a
slurping noise (I / IR)—rcgr. of
ittilhocho'chi [+SC]
ittilhókkokli'chi to make the noise
of something flying around inside a
box (usually of a bird) (3)—klgr. of
ittilhoko'chi [+SC]
[itti+lhokkokli'chi]
ittilhoko'chi to make the noise of
something inside a paper or
cardboard box (I / IR) [+SC] {klgr.
ittilhókkokli'chi; rcgr.
ittilhokokó'chi}
ittilhokokó'chi to make the noise of
something inside a paper or
cardboard box (I / IR)—rcgr. of
ittilhoko'chi [+SC]
ittima to give to each other, exchange
(I;3 / IR;3) [itti+ima]
ittimachaaha to get used to each
other (3) [itti+imachaaha]
ittimachokkobbi to get used to each
other (I / IR) [itti+imachokkobbi]
ittimalikchi to doctor each other (I /
IR) [itti+imalikchi]
ittimalhallichi to scare each other (I /
IR) [itti+malhallichi]
ittimanompoli to talk together (I /
IR); to talk with (I;II / IR;3); to read
(mainly sg. subj.) (I); to read

(something) (I;3 / IR;3)
[itti+im+anompoli]
{imittimanompoli: to read to} §
Sattimanompolitok. He talked with
me. | Holisso ittimanompolili. I'm
reading a book.
ittimappa to eat each other's, to eat
for each other (I;3 / IR;3)
[itti+imappa] § Paska ittimappa.
They ate bread for each other, They
ate each other's bread.
ittimasalichi to have the colors run
together (of clothes) (3)
ittimasilhpowa to ask each other
questions (I / IR) [itti+imasilhpowa]
ittimayya to be uneven, not to be at
the same position or level (of stairs,
for example) (3) [itti+imayya] {ggr.
ittímmayya; ngr. ittimáya}
ittimayyachi to have a race, race
against each other (IR); to race
(horses, for instance) (3;3); to make
uneven (for instance, to build stairs
or make a skirt with an uneven
hem) (IR;3) [ittimayya+chi] {ggr.
ittímmayya'chi} § Issoba
ittimayyacha'chi. They're going to
race the horses.
ittimaachi to say to each other (IR)
[itti+imaachi]
ittimaafowa to contend with one
another for (I;3 / IR;3)
[itti+imaafowa]
ittimaapatohli to be lined up side by
side (I / IR)
ittimáya ngr. of ittimayya
ittimbasmo to kiss each other (IR)
(WB) [itti+imbasmo]
ittimbaayo'chi to seesaw (I / IR) [±SC]
[itti+im+baayo'chi]
ittimilayyoka to be different (in tribe
or race, for example), to be of a
number of different groups; to be
different from each other (tpl. subj.)

(I / IR) [itti+im+ilayyoka] {dl. subj.
ittimi̱la}
ittimilínka, ittimilínka'si to be near
each other (I / IR)
[itti+milinka+a'si]
ittimilínka'si see ittimilínka
ittimilhlhali to scare each other (I /
IR) [itti+imilhlhali]
ittimiti'chi to make a running sound
(3) [+SC] [itti+miti'chi]
{ittimitití'chi, ittimíttikli'chi}
ittimitití'chi to make the sound of
walking without shoes (I / IR) [+SC]
[itti+mititi'chi] {ittimiti'chi}
ittimíttikli'chi to make the sound of
walking without shoes or of hitting
pillows (I / IR); to hit each other,
making a noise (pl. subj.) (I / IR)
[+SC] [itti+mittikli'chi] {ittimiti'chi}
ittimi̱la to be different from (I;II /
IR;3); to be different from each other
(dl. subj.) (I / IR); to have different
(I;3 / IR;3) [itti+imi̱la] {tpl. subj.
ittimilayyoka} § Sattimi̱la. He's
different from me. | Inki' iitimi̱la.
We had different fathers.
ittimi̱la toklo to be two different
colors, be two-tone (3)
ittimi̱lachi to make different, alter,
change (I;II / IR;3) [ittimi̱la+chi]
{ngr. ittimi̱lánchi}
ittimi̱lánchi ngr. of ittimi̱lachi
ittímmayya ggr. of ittimayya
ittímmayya'chi ggr. of ittimayyachi
ittímmayya'chi banna to want to be
better than everyone else, think
oneselves to be better than
everyone else, to be smart-alecks (pl.
subj.) (II) § Ittimmayya'chi pobanna.
We're smart-alecks, We think we're
better than everyone else.
ittimoppoloka to be mad at each
other, to fight all the time (I / IR)
[itti+imoppoloka] {ngr.

ittimoppolónka}
ittimoppolónka ngr. of
ittimoppoloka
ittimo̱labi to fight over (I;3 / IR;3)
[itti+imo̱labi] § Ishchokoshkomo'
ilittimo̱labi. We fought over a toy.
Ittimo̱labi' Hilha' Changing
Partners—name of a Choctaw dance
also danced by Chickasaws, in
which dancers "steal" partners of
the opposite sex [ittimo̱labi+'
hilha+']
ittimpalammi to race (I / IR); to race
(horses, for instance), race with (I;II)
[itti+impalammi] §
Ittimpalammilitok. I raced against
her.
ittimpalammichi to race (horses, for
instance), make race (I;II / IR;3)
[ittimpalammi+chi] § Ofi'
ittimpalammichitok. He raced dogs.
| Pottimpalammichitok. He made
us race.
ittimpilachi to send (things) to each
other (I;3 / IR;3) [itti+impilachi] §
Holisso iitimpilachi. We send each
other books.
ittinchaffa to have the same (parent)
(I;3); to be the same (3) [itti+inchaffa]
§ Ishki' ilittinchaffa. We have the
same mother. | Nannilano̱likat
ittinchaffatoko̱ ilithanatok. We
found out that we had told the
same story, We found out that the
our tellings had been the same.
ittinchaffa̱li' on the same (used with
a preceding time word) § Nittak
ittinchaffa̱li' hasha̱shwattook. You
two were born on the same day.
ittinkana to make up, reconcile (I /
IR); to make up, reconcile with (I;II
/ IR;3) [itti+<inkana>] {ngr.
ittinká̱na: to be friendly; ygr.
ittinká̱yya'na} § Sattinkanatok. He

193

made up with me.
ittinkano'mi to be cousins (I / IR); to
be a cousin of (I;II / IR;3)
[itti+inkano'mi] § Yammat
sattinkano'mi. She is my cousin.
ittinkáyya'na ygr. of ittinkana
ittinkána to be friendly, act like
friends (I)—ngr. of ittinkana
ittinkana' (respective) friends (Ip /
IIp) [ittinkana+'] § Ilittinkana' atok,
Ittinkana' poyatok. We used to be
friends. | Pottinkana' pistiliyatok,
Ilittinkana' pistiliyatok. We went to
see our friends.
ittintakla' area between (close objs.);
between, in between (close objs.),
specifically, in between one's legs
(II) {ittintaklaka'; ittintaklali'} §
Sattintakla' lhipollitok. He went
between my legs. | abooha
ittintakla': in between the houses;
hallway | Chittintakla' moma
pisatok! He's looking at everything
between your legs!
ittintaklaka' area between (close
objs.); between, in between (close
objs.) (3) [ittintakla'+ka'] {ittintakla';
ittintaklakali'}
ittintaklakali' (moving) between
(close objs.) (3) {ittintaklaka';
ittintaklali'}
ittintaklali' (moving) between (close
objs.) (3) {ittintakla'; ittintaklakali'}
§ Chokka' ittintaklali' aatok. He
went between the houses (very
close together, as in a narrow alley).
ittintángla while (aux.; used only in
subr. clause following ngr.) {tángla}
§ Anompolili ittintanglahmat nipi'
oshwashlitok. While I was talking I
sniffed at the meat. | Holissoshli
ittintanglahma nositok. While I
was writing he went to sleep.
ittintilhaa to race, run against one

another, run in an election (pl.
subj.) (I / IR) [itti+intilhaa] §
Ilittintilhaa, Iitintilhaa. We're
running in the election.
ittintilhaachi to run, race (pl. obj.)
against each other (I;II / IR;3) [±SC]
[ittintilhaa+chi] {hngr.
ittintilhaahánchi} §
Pottintilhaachitok. He raced us
against each other.
ittintilhaahánchi hngr. of
ittintilhaachi
ittintilhili to run, race against each
other (pl., usually nonhum. obj.)
(I;3 / IR;3) [itti+im+tilhili]
ittipa to eat each other (as cannibals
are said to do) (I / IR) {hngr.
ittihímpa}
ittipasa'chi to clap one's hands (I /
IR); to clap (the hands) (I;3 / IR;3)
[+SC] [itti+pasa'chi] {klgr.
ittipássakli'chi; ngr. ittipasa'línchi;
rcgr. ittipasasá'chi} § Ittipasa'shli,
salbak ittipasa'shli. I clap my hands.
| Polbak iitipa'shtok, Polbak
ilittipa'shtok. We clapped our
hands.
ittipasa'línchi to make a little noise,
clap the hands—ngr. of ittipasa'chi
ittipasasá'chi to make a little noise by
clapping or slapping (I / IR)—rcgr.
of ittipasa'chi [+SC] [itti+pasasa'chi]
ittipássakli'chi to make noise (for
instance, by flapping one's wings,
pounding on the table, splashing in
the bathtub, clapping) (I / IR)—klgr.
of ittipasa'chi [+SC]
[itti+passakli'chi]
<ittipata'chi> {klgr. ittipáttakli'chi;
rcgr. ittipatatá'chi}
ittipatatá'chi to make a sound with
one's feet (I / IR) [+SC]—rcgr. of
<ittipata'chi> [itti+patata'chi]
ittipáttakli'chi to walk barefoot (used

of someone fairly heavy) (I / IR)—
klgr. of <ittipata'chi> [+SC]
ittipisa to see each other (I / IR)
[itti+pisa]
ittipisachi to show (something) to
each other (IR;3); to take off one's
clothes in front of each other (I /
IR); to make (pl. obj.) look at each
other (IR;3)
[itti+pisachi/ittipisa+chi]
ittipita to feed each other (I / IR); to
feed each other (something) (I;3 /
IR;3) [itti+ipita]
ittisaka'chi to make a noise with
marbles (I / IR) [+SC] [itti+saka'chi]
{klgr. ittisákkakli'chi; rcgr.
ittisakaká'chi}
ittisakaká'chi to make a noise with
marbles (I / IR)—rcgr. of ittisaka'chi
[+SC] [itti+sakaka'chi]
ittisákkakli'chi to make a noise with
marbles (I / IR)—klgr. of ittisaka'chi
[+SC] [itti+sakkakli'chi]
ittisso in ishtittisso [itti+isso]
ittishbasha' saw (noun) [itti' isht
basha+']
ittishbasha' noti' sawteeth
ittishkatolhlhi' pruning shears [itti'
isht katolhlhi+']
ittishkola' chisel [itti' isht kola+']
ittishno̱**wa'** stilts; crutches [itti' isht
n**o̱**wa+']
ittishóchchokli'chi to crinkle (paper)
(I;3 / IR;3) [+SC]
[itti+shochchokli'chi]
ittishóffokli'chi to make the sound
of paper crinkling (I / IR)—klgr. of
ittishofo'chi [+SC]
ittishofo'chi to crinkle (paper) (I;3 /
IR;3); to sizzle (of a hot stove when
water drops on it) (3) [+SC] {klgr.
ittishóffokli'chi; rcgr.
ittishofofó'chi}
ittishofofó'chi to crinkle paper, make

a crinkling sound (I / IR)—rcgr. of
ittishofo'chi [+SC]
ittishókkokli'chi to make a noise
with paper (of mice in a bag, for
instance) (I / IR)—klgr. of
ittishoko'chi [+SC]
ittishoko'chi to make a rustling
sound with, to rustle, crinkle
(paper) (I;3 / IR;3) [±SC] {hngr.
ittishoko'lihínchi; klgr.
ittishókkokli'chi; rcgr.
ittishokokó'chi}
ittishoko'lihínchi hngr. of
ittishoko'chi
ittishokokó'chi to crinkle paper (I /
IR)—rcgr. of ittishokokó'chi [+SC]
[itti+shokoko'chi]
ittishola'chi to make a dragging,
scraping sound (I / IR) [+SC] {klgr.
ittishóllakli'chi; rcgr. ittisholalá'chi}
ittisholalá'chi to make a dragging,
scraping sound (I / IR)—rcgr. of
ittishola'chi [+SC]
ittishóllakli'chi to make a dragging,
scraping, or scratching sound (I /
IR)—klgr. of ittishola'chi [+SC]
ittishóllokli'chi to make a noise with
little bells (I / IR)—klgr. of
ittisholo'chi [+SC]
ittisholo'chi to make a dragging
noise, or a noise like crickets (I / IR)
[+SC] [itti+sholo'chi] {klgr.
ittishóllokli'chi; rcgr.
ittishololó'chi}
ittishololó'chi to make a noise like
that of little bells on baby shoes (I /
IR)—rcgr. of ittisholo'chi [+SC]
[itti+shololo'chi]
ittishoyyo't tano̱**wa** to walk with the
arms around each other's shoulders
(pl. subj.) (I) [itti+shoyyo'li+t] §
Ittishoyyo't iitan**o̱**watok. We
walked with our arms around each
other's shoulders.

195

ittishoochi to rub together: especially, to wear from rubbing against each other (3 / 3R) [-SC] [itti+shoochi] {hngr. ittishoolihínchi}
ittishooli to wrestle (I / IR) [itti+shooli]
ittishoolihínchi hngr. of ittishoochi
ittishshafi' plane (for wood) [itti' isht shafi+']
ittishtalha', ittishtalhlhi' drawknife: two-handled tool for smoothing wood [itti' isht talha/talhlhi+']
ittitaamowa in ishtittaamowa
ittithana to introduce oneselves (pl. subj.) (I / IR) [itti+ithana]
ittithanachi to introduce (pl. obj.) (I;3 / IR;3); to introduce (someone°) to ° (I;3;3 (most likely) / IR;3;3 / I;II;3) [ittithana+chi] § Charlesa Lynn ittithanashlitok. I introduced Lynn to Charles. | Charlesa sattithanashtok. He introduced me to Charles, He introduced Charles to me.
ittitamowa in ishtittitamowa
ittitikili to cuddle up to each other, be touching each other (dl. subj.) (I / IR) [itti+tikili] {ggr. ittitíkki'li: to be side by side; ngr. ittitikíli; tpl. ittitiko'li}
ittitikilichi to make (dl. obj.) touch each other (I;3 / IR;3) [ittitikili+chi] {pl. obj. ittitikoochi}
ittitikíli ngr. of ittitikili
ittitíkki'li to be next to one another, be side by side, be so close as to be touching (dl. subj.)—ggr. of ittitikili
ittitíkkohli to be touching (dl. subj.) (I / IR) {hngr. ittitikohóli; ngr. ittitikóhli; tpl. ittitikoht máa}—ggr. of <ittitikohli>
ittitikohchi see ittitikoochi
<ittitikohli> in ittitikoht máa, ittitikoochi {ggr. ittitíkkohli; hngr.

ittitikohóli; ngr. ittitikóhli}
ittitikohóli hngr. of <ittitikohli>, ittitíkkohli
ittitikoht máa to be touching (tpl. subj.) (I) [ittitikohli+t] {dl. ittitíkkohli} § Ittitikoht iimáatok. We were touching.
ittitikoochi, ittitikohchi to make (pl. obj.) touch each other (I;3 / IR;3) [<ittitikohli>+chi] {dl. obj. ittitikilichi} § Ittitikoochit iibinoochitok. We made them sit real close together (so that they were touching).
ittitikóhli ngr. of <ittitikohli>, ittitíkkohli
ittitimimí'chi to make a noise like a bumblebee (I / IR) [+SC] [itti+timimi'chi]
<ittitipi'chi> {klgr. ittitíppikli'chi; rcgr. ittitipipí'chi}
ittitipipí'chi to walk barefoot (of someone fairly light) (I / IR)—rcgr. of <ittitipi'chi> [+SC]
ittitíppikli'chi to walk barefoot (of someone fairly light) (I / IR)—klgr. of <ittitipi'chi> [+SC]
ittitómmokli'chi to beat on a leather-covered drum (I / IR)—klgr. of ittitomo'chi
ittitomo'chi to beat on a leather-covered drum (I / IR) {klgr. ittitómmokli'chi; rcgr. ittitomomó'chi}
ittitomomó'chi to beat on a leather-covered drum (I / IR)—rcgr. of ittitomo'chi [itti+tomomo'chi]
ittitoopo'li to push against each other (pl. subj.) (I / IR) [itti+toopo'li]
ittitoopolóli to push and shove each other (I / IR) [itti+toopopoli]
ittittabaana' abooha' see itti' ittabaana' abooha
ittiwasha'chi to make a noise,

especially a rattle (I / IR)
[itti+washa'chi] {klgr.
ittiwáshshakli'chi; rcgr.
ittiwashashá'chi}
ittiwasha'chi' rattlesnake; rattle
(noun) [ittiwasha'chi+']
ittiwashanchi' snake: especially,
rattlesnake
ittiwashashá'chi to rattle, make a
rattling sound (I / IR)—rcgr. of
ittiwasha'chi [itti+washasha'chi]
ittiwashasha'chi' rattle (for music or
for a baby) [ittiwashasha'chi+']
ittiwáshshakli'chi to make a rattling
sound (I / IR)—klgr. of
ittiwasha'chi [+SC]
ittiwini'chi to rumble, rev (of a
motor) (3) [itti+<wini'chi>] {rcgr.
ittiwininí'chi; winiihachi}
ittiwininí'chi to rumble, rev (of a
motor) (3)—rcgr. of ittiwini'chi
ittiya mouth (IIp) (VB) [iti]
ittiyokli to wrestle (IR) (ER)
[itti+yokli]
ittiyyo'bi' see ittoyyo'bi'
ittifalama to get back together,
reconcile (pl. subj.) (I / IR)
[itti+ifalama]
ittifalammichi to reconcile, bring
back together (pl. obj.—a couple, for
instance) (I;II / IR;3)
[itti+ifalammichi] §
Pottifalammichitok. She brought us
back together, reconciled us.
ittifatpoli to talk together (pl. subj.) (I
/ IR); to talk with (I;3 / IR;3)
[itti+ifatpoli]
ittifilammi to separate (from each
other), go apart (dl. subj.); to
separate, divide itself (I / IR)
[itti+ifilammi] {tpl. ittifilamo'li} §
Abookoshi'at ittifilammi. The river
divides into (two) branches.
ittifilammí'chi ggr. of ittifilammichi

ittifilammichi to separate (dl. obj.—
for instance, eggs, combatants) (I;II /
IR;3) [ittifilammi+chi] {ggr.
ittifilammí'chi} §
Pottifilammichitok. She separated
us.
ittifilamo'chi to separate (pl. obj.), to
put (pl. obj.) into separate groups
(I;3 / IR;3) [ittifilamo'li+chi]
ittifilamo'li to separate, go in
different directions (tpl. subj.) (I /
IR) [+taha] {dl. ittifilammi}
ittifili'ta to be turned out (of feet), to
be on wrong (of shoes) (3)
[itti+im+fili'ta]
ittihollo to love each other (pl. subj.)
(I / IR) [itti+ihollo]
ittihollochi to make (pl. obj.) love
each other (I;II / IR;3) [ittihollo+chi]
§ Pottihollochitok. He made us love
each other.
ittihonkopa to cheat each other (I /
IR) [itti+ihonkopa]
ittiloma to hide from each other,
play hide and seek (I / IR)
[itti+iloma]
ittilomaka to commit adultery (I /
IR); to commit adultery with (3;3)
[itti+ilomaka] § Ihoo yammak
ittilomakatok. He committed
adultery with that woman.
ittimalhata to scare each other; to be
scared of each other (I / IR)
[itti+imalhata]
ittimilínka, ittimilínka'si to be close,
friendly with each other; to live
close together, be close neighbors (I
/ IR) [itti+imilinka+a'si]
ittimilínka'si see ittimilínka
ittinannayya to make peace, forgive
each other (pl. subj.) (I / IR)
[itti+im+(nanna ayya)]
ittinókko'wa to argue with each
other (I / IR) [itti+inokko'wa]

ittịnokshoopa to be afraid of each other (I / IR) [itti+ịnokshoopa]

ittịsanali' enemies (of each other); enemies (IIp / Ip) [itti+ịsanali'] § pottịsanali', ilittịsanali': our enemies

ittịsánna'li to be enemies, to be political opponents (I / IR) [itti+ịsanna'li]

ittịsh medicine {short form: tịsh}

ittịsh ani to give an injection to, vaccinate (I;II) § Alikchaat ittịsh asanitok. The doctor gave me a shot.

ittịsh aa-asha' drugstore; medicine cabinet

ittịsh aakanchi' drugstore [aa+kanchi+']

ittịsh bila' castor oil [bila+']

ittịsh homi' quinine [homi+']

ittịsh homma' red liniment; iodine [homma+']

ittịsh ima to give medicine to, medicate (I;III) § Alikchaat ittịsh amatok. The doctor medicated me.

ittịsh lhibowa', (AB) tịsh lhobowa' pill [lhibowa+']

ittịsh lhibowa' ishtilihaksichi' birth control pill (joke expression) [isht ilihaksichi(t nọwa)+']

ittịsh oppolo' poison, narcotic [oppolo+']

ittịshanaa to be on wrong (for instance, of shoes on the wrong feet, buttons in the wrong holes) (3) [itti+im+shanaa] {v2. ittịshaniili}

ittịshaniili to put on wrong, put together wrong (so things won't go together right—for instance, getting buttons in the wrong holes) (I;3 / IR;3) [itti+im+shaniili] {v1. ittịshanaa} § Ạsholosh ittịshaniilili, Ạsholosh ittịshaniit hololitok. I put my shoes on wrong.

ittó'la ggr. of ittola

ittohọ́la hngr. of ittola

ittokaamichi to wash each other's faces (dl. subj.) (I / IR) [itti+okaamichi] {pl. ittookaamichi}

ittokchali to wake each other up (I / IR) [itti+okchali]

ittola to fall (sg.-pl. anim. subj.) (II); (sg. anim. subj.) (I); (sg. inan. subj.) (3) [-PR] [-CPR] {ggr. ittó'la; hngr. ittohọ́la; inan. dl. kaha; inan. pl. lhatapa; ootittola: to fall down}

ittolat folo'kachi to run around like crazy (I) {hngr. ittolat folo'kahánchi} [ittola+t]

ittolat folo'kahánchi hngr. of ittolat folo'kachi

ittollali to laugh at each other (pl. subj.) (I / IR) [itti+ollali]

ittonchololi' new growth on a tree [itti' onchololi+']

ittonhochi to blame each other (I / IR) [itti+onhochi]

ittontalkachi to be stacked (tpl. subj.—of cups, for instance) (3) [+T] {ygr. ittontalkáyya'chi; ittontalkachit máa}

ittontalkachit máa to be stacked (tpl. subj.—of cups, for instance) (3) [ittontalkachi+t] {dl. ittontalkáyya'chi}

ittontalkáyya'chi to be stacked on top of each other (dl. subj.—of cups, for instance) (3)—ygr. of ittontalkachi {tpl. ittontalkachi, ittontalkachit máa}

<ittopa> see hottopa

<ittopachi> see hottopachi

ittoyyo'bi', ittiyyo'bi' trunk, chest, coffin [itti']

ittookaaillichi in oka' ittookaaillichi

ittookaamichi to wash each other's faces (pl. subj.) [itti+ okaamichi] {dl. ittokaamichi}

ittoonashaachi to put (pl. or mass obj.) on each other (I;3 / IR;3) [itti+onashaachi] § Shinok ittoonashaachi. They put sand on each other.

ittoonittola to fall on each other (I / IR) [itti+onittola]

ittoonokmiloli to ogle each other, look at each other with interest (I / IR) [itti+onokmiloli] {ggr. ittoonokmíllo'li}

ittoonokmíllo'li ggr. of ittoonokmiloli

ittoloshka to lie about each other (pl. subj.) (I / IR) [itti+oloshka] § Iitoloshkatok. We lied about each other.

ittolha'li to throw (a liquid) on each other (I;3 / IR;3) [itti+ olha'li] § Oka' iitolha'tok, Oka' ilittolha'tok. We threw water on each other.

iyoba happen to, chance to (aux.) (used only in subr. clauses) § Pitaapisali iyo'bacha chipislitok. I happened to be looking out and I saw you. | Alatok iyobookma pisala'chi. I'll see if he has happened to arrive.

<iyya> see aya

iyyakchosh toenail (IIp); hoof (3p) [iyyi'+<akchosh>]

iyyapi' lower leg (IIp) [iyyi' api']

iyyaa-asha' large kettle on little feet—used as washpot or for cooking pishofa [iyyi' aa-asha']

iyyaabisowa' see iabisowa'

iyyaat ittabánna'a to cross one's legs (IIp = subj) [iyyi'+at]

iyyaat ittifili'ta to toe out, turn one's toes out (IIp = subj) [iyyi'+at]

iyyaat kawwana to be bowlegged (IIp = subj) [iyyi'+at] {iyyinchamaat kawwana}

iyyashka' see iyyi' ashaka'

iyyi' foot, leg (IIp); foot (measure of length) (always followed by a quantifier) § Itti' yappat iyyi' tochchi'na. This stick is three feet long.

iyyi' ashaka', iyyashka' hind leg

iyyi' bíyyi'ka to be barefoot (IIp = subj.) § Sayyi' biyyi'kmat asayompa. I'm happy if I'm barefoot.

iyyi' hishi' hair on the legs (IIp) § sayyi' hishi': the hair on my legs

iyyi' holba' wooden leg; footprint (IIp) § chiyyi' holba': your wooden leg, your footprint

iyyi' impatha' see iyyimpatha'

iyyi' ittabaanali to cross one's legs (IIp, I) [itti+abaanali] § Chiyyi' ishtabaanalitam? Did you cross your legs?

iyyi' kawwana' bowlegged person [kawwana+'] {iyyaat kawwana}

iyyi' lawa' see iyyi-lawa'

iyyi' lopi' marrow of a leg or foot bone (IIp)

iyyi' nota' bottom of the hoof (of a cow, sheep, horse, pig, etc.)

iyyi' pakna' instep (IIp)

iyyi' patha' see iyyimpatha'

iyyi' tako'bish, (MS) intako'bish, (LR) iintako'bish heel (IIp) § chiyyi' tako'bish: your heel

iyyi' tannapat falaakat iklawwi'cho to have one leg shorter than the other (IIp = subj.) [tannap+at falaa+kat] § Sayyi' tannapat falaakat iklawwi'chokat sanokhanglo. I'm sad that I have one leg shorter than the other.

iyyi' tannapat tilofa'si to have one leg shorter than the other (IIp = subj) [tannap+at] § Chiyyi' tannapat tilofa'si. You have one leg shorter than the other.

iyyi' tikba' foreleg

íyyi'lli

íyyi'lli ygr. of illi
íyyi'shto ygr. of ishto
iyyi-lawa', iyyi' lawa' centipede [iyyi'
lawa+']
iyyimpatha', iyyi' impatha', iyyi'
patha' sole of the foot (IIp); paw,
bottom of the foot (of an animal
without hooves) [iyyi' im+patha+']
§ sayyi' impatha': the sole of my
foot
iyyinchamaat kawwana to be
bowlegged (IIp = subj)
[iyyinchamo'+at] {iyyaat kawwana}
iyyinchamo' lower leg: shin, calf (IIp)
iyyintakaali' calf of the leg; (LF) ankle
[iyyi' im+takaali+']
iyyinto'lhka', (ER) iyyi' into'lhka',
(LF, LR) iinto'lhka', (TJ) iito'lhka',
(LP) iyyi' to'lhka', (EH, CM, MS)
iito'lhka', (MJ) into'lhka', (VB)
iyyonto'lhka', (AW) iyyi' itolhka',
(CP) intolhko' knee (IIp)
iyyishki' big toe (IIp) [iyyi' ishki']

iyyimosak, (AB, MJ, TJ, CM, LP, ER,
LR, MS) iyyi' mosak, (HS) imosak,
(CP) iyyi' masak, (AW) iyyi' osak
ankle (IIp) [iyyi' im+osak ?] {ilbak
imosak}
iyyobi' thigh (IIp); ham
iyyobi' aaishto' top of the thigh (IIp)
[aa+ishto+']
iyyobi' aaittachakka'a' hip bone (IIp)
iyyobi' hakshish hamstring (IIp)
iyyobi' ishtaachoosho'wa' outer part
of the hip, above the hip joint (IIp)
[isht aa+achoshsho'wa+']
iyyobi' ishtoka' buttocks (LF)
[ishto+ka']
iyyobittintakla' (a woman's) private
parts (IIp) [iyyobi' ittintakla']
iyyop son-in-law (IIp)
iyyop ihoo' daughter-in-law (IIp) §
sayyop ihoo': my daughter-in-law
iyyoshi' toe other than the big toe
(IIp) [iyyi' oshi']

ii

iikowa' work party (where people
come to share a job and get paid
with a free meal)
iikowa' apiisa to plan or hold a work

party or bee (I)
Iili' Chickasaw woman's name
Iista' Easter (TJ, HS) [from the
English]

i

i'ma to be located, exist (attached to a
flat surface) (3); to be located, exist
on (a flat surface, such as a wall or
ceiling) (3;3); to have (inan. subj.)
(3;3-at); to be the same (sg. subj.) (I);
still (aux.—usually used with ngr.
or hngr.), again (aux.) {imi'ma} §

Hattak holbaat i'ma. There's a
picture (there on the wall). |
Yammako i'ma. There's one there.
| Chokkaat abokkissaat i'ma. The
house has a door. | I'mali. I'm still
the same, just as I was. |
Chokoshkomokat i'ma. They're

still playing.

í'pa ggr. of impa

í'shi to keep, hold, have in one's hands (I;II) [+OPR]—ggr. of ishi

ifahli see ilbak ifahli

ifalakto' crotch (off-color expression) (oIIIp) [im+falakto+']

ifalama to come back, return to (I;III) [im+falama]

ifalammí'chi ggr. of ifalammichi

ifalammichi to do the same back to, get revenge on (I;III); to return (something) to °, give (something) back to ° (I;III;3) [im+falammichi] {ggr. ifalammí'chi} § Issassotoko chifalammichilitok. You hit me and I did it back to you.

ifalaa [PR] of falaa

ifalaaka' gallbladder (LF) [im+falaa+ka']

ifama [PR] of fama

ifatpohóli hngr. of ifatpoli

ifatpoli, (WB) ifahpoli to talk to (I;III) [im+fatpoli] {itr. ifatpohóli}

ifaya'chi to rock (someone—in a cradle, for instance) (I;III) [±SC] [im+faya'chi]

ifaapo'chi to push in a swing (I;III) [im+faapo'chi]

ifilahámmi hngr. of ifilammi

ifilammi to get away from, separate from, leave (sg.-dl. subj.) (I;III) [im+<filammi>] {ggr. ifíllammi; hngr. ifilahámmi; tpl. subj. ifilamo'li}

ifilammí'chi ggr. of ifilammichi

ifilammichi to take (sg. obj.) away from ° (often as a result of legal action) (I;III;3) [ifilammi+chi] {ggr. ifilammí'chi; pl. obj. ifilamo'chi}

ifilamo'chi to separate (pl. obj.) from, take (pl. obj.) away from (I;III;3) [ifilamo'li+chi] {sg. obj. ifilammichi}

ifilamo'li to go off from, leave (tpl.

subj.) (I;III) {sg.-dl. subj. ifilammi}

ifíllammi ggr. of ifilammi

<ifili'ta> in ittifil'i'ta

ifinha in nannishtifinha

ifokhi to put (sg. obj.) in for ° (I;III;3) [im+fokhi] {ngr. ifónkhi: to leave for}

ifokkol cowlick (CP) [im+fokkol]

ifóllo'ta ggr. of ifolota

ifolota to make a turn so as to avoid (something far off or moving) (I;III) [im+folota] {ggr. ifóllo'ta}

ifónkhi to leave (sg. obj.) for—ngr. of ifokhi {dl. obj. imambíhli; tpl. obj. imáni}

ihábbi'na to coax, beg; to apologize to—ggr. of ihabina

ihabina to receive for ° (I;III;3); to coax (I;III) [im+habina] {ggr. ihábbi'na: to coax, beg ; to apologize}

ihaklo to listen to and obey (I;III) [im+haklo]

ihaksi to get drunk for (I;III); to be deceived by (I;III) (used in a +na subr. clause) [im+haksi] {ygr. iháyyaksi} § Chihaksili ishkaniyatokchayni. I was deceived by you and you took off, You deceived me and took off.

ihaksina ibaanosi to seduce (I = subj , I;II) (na expression) [ihaksi+na ibaa+nosi] § Ahaksina ibaanosilitok. I seduced her, She was deceived by me and I slept with her.

ihalili to touch for ° (I;III;3) [im+halili]

ihaloppa [PR] of haloppa

ihalhabli to kick for ° (I;III;3) [im+halhabli]

ihanná'li [PR] of hanná'li

ihapashshi to act nice to (someone, especially after a period of anger) (3;III) [im+hapashshi]

ihapompohóyo hngr. of ihapompoyo

ihapompoyo to watch out for, take care of (I;III) [im+hapompoyo] {ngr. ihapompóyo; hngr. ihapompohóyo}

ihapompoyo' bodyguard (oIIIp) [ihapompoyo+'] § ahapompoyo' my bodyguard

ihapompóyo ngr. of ihopompoyo

ihapowánglo to mind, obey (someone) (I;III) [im+hapowanglo] {neg. ikihapowaklo}

ihapowanglochi to make (someone) mind (someone˚) (I;III;3) [ihapowanglo+chi]

ihapoyoksa to outsmart (I;III) (Ct?) [im+hapoyoksa]

ihashaa, ihashaha to be angry at (I;III) [im+hashaa/hashaha]

ihattak husband (oIIIp) [im+hattak]

iháyyaksi ygr. of ihaksi

ihichito [PR] of hichito

ihíkki'ya to support, hold up (for instance, of a pole holding up a tree limb or clothesline) (3;3) [im+hikki'ya] § Itti' yammat naafkaatakkohli' ihikki'ya. That pole is holding up the clothesline.

ihilichi to stand up, plant (sg. obj.) for ˚ (I;III;3) [im+hilichi] {pl. patient obj. ihiyohchi}

ihiliya to get bawled out (III)

ihilha to dance for (I;III) [im+hilha]

ihilhachi to spin (a top) for ˚ (I;III;3) [im+hilhachi]

ihimitta [PR] of himitta

ihímmo'na to wait in vain for—ggr. of ihimóna

ihimóna to wait for (I;III) [im+himona] {ggr. ihímmo'na: to wait in vain for}

ihina' row, furrow [im+hina']

ihiyo'li' onto'wa' horizontal beams [im+<hiyohli>+' onto'wa+']

ihiyohchi to stand up, plant (pl. obj.) for ˚ (I;III;3) [im+hiyohchi] {sg.

patient obj. ihilichi}

ihó'lba ggr. of iholba

ihó'llo ggr. of ihollo

ihofahya to be ashamed of, be ashamed about (someone) (I;III); to be ashamed to (do something) because of (someone connected with the action) [+a'nikat ss comp.] (I;III) [im+hofahya] § Ihofahyali imanompola'nikat. I'm ashamed (about him) to talk to him.

ihofanti [PR] of hofanti

iholba to see a mirage, have a vision, have a nightmare, think one has seen something (III) [im+holba] {ggr. ihó'lba}

iholbachi to fool (I;III) [iholba+chi]

iholisso [PR] of holisso

iholissochi to write to ˚, write for ˚ (I;III;3) [im+holissochi]

<iholitta> in iholittachi [im+<holitta>} {ggr. ihóllitta}

iholittachi to fence in (I;III) [<iholitta>+chi] § Chokkak iholittachilitok. I fenced in the house, I put a fence around the house. I Aholittachitok. He fenced me in, He fenced in my house, He fenced in my things.

iholitto'pa to be precious, mean a lot to (I;III); to hold dear, consider precious (III;3-at)—ggr. of iholiitopa} § Iholitto'pali. I am precious to him.

iholiitopa to hoard, be stingy with (III;3) [im+holiitopa] {ggr. iholítto'pa: to be precious to} § Lynnat ta'osso iholiitopa. Lynn is stingy with money.

ihóllitta to be fenced in (III)—ggr. of <iholitta> § Ahollitta. I'm fenced in.

ihollo to love (I;III); to be stingy with, be greedy for (something) (III;3) [im+<hollo>] {ggr. ihó'llo; ygr. ihóyyo'llo} § Ahollo. He loves me. I Ta'osso ahollo. I'm stingy with money.

ihollochi to be stingy with (a person) (I;III) [ihollo+chi] § Benjieat chipotaak ihollochitok. Benjie was stingy with the child.

iholmo [PR] of holmo

iholhfo [PR] of holhfo

iholhtina' roll number (of an original enrolled member of one of the Five Civilized Tribes) (oIIIp) [im+holhtina']

iholhtofa [PR] of holhtofa

ihomi' gall, bile; (AB) gall bladder (oIIIp) [im+homi+']

ihomo to put a roof on (a house) for ° (I;III;3) [im+homo] § Lynnat imofi' inchokka' ihomola'ni bannana ihomolitok. Lynn wanted me to put a roof on her dog's house and I did it for her.

ihonkopa to steal from °, to steal for ° (I;III;3); to cheat (I;III) [im+honkopa] § Charlesa paska ihonkopalitok. I stole the bread from Charles, for Charles.

ihopayi to tell (someone's) fortune (I;III) [im+hopayi]

ihopaakichi to go off a ways from (I;III) [im+hopaakichi]

ihopo'ni' cook (n.) [im+hopooni+']

ihopoba [PR] of hopoba

ihopoo [OPR] of hopoo

ihoshba [PR] of hoshba

ihoshottikachi to make shade for (I;III) [im+hoshottikachi]

ihotaanaffo to braid (someone's°) (hair) (I;III;3) [im+hotaanaffo]

ihotohli [PR] of hotohli

ihotolhko to cough for (a doctor, for instance) (I;III) [im+hotolhko]

ihottopa [PR] of hottopa

ihowita [PR] of howita

ihóyyo'llo ygr. of ihollo

ii yes

ii alali yes, I've come (response to greeting ba' ishlata?) [ala+li]

ila to be different, unusual, unmatched (I / II) [-PR] [-CPR] {ittimíla} § Ilali, Asila. I'm different.

ila' a different one, a unique one, another one, one of a group [ila+'] § Ila' saya. I'm different, I don't belong to that group.

ila'o kaali to get a wrong number (when telephoning) (I) [ila'+ho]

ilachi to make different, alter (I;3) [ila+chi] {hngr. ilahánchi; ngr. ilánchi: (I;II), to change (I)}

ilahánchi hngr. of ilachi

ilaháwwi hngr. of ilawwi

<ilakna'> in akankoshilakna'

ilánchi to make different, alter (I;II); to change (oneself) (I)—ngr. of ilachi (I;II)

ilashpa to feel hot (III) (Ct?) [im+lashpa]

ilawashki [PR] of lawashki

ilawwi to sting (of salt, acid, on broken skin) (3;III) [im+lawwi] {hngr. ilaháwwi} § Hapiat alawwitok. The salt stung me.

ilitiha [PR] of litiha

ilbolbo' poss. of ilbolbo'

ilohmi to hide (something) from ° (I;III;3) [im+lohmi] § Ishchokoshkomo' alohmitok. She hid the toy from me.

ilokfi-toba [PR] of lokfi-toba

iloma to hide from, be hidden from (I;III) [im+loma]

ilomaka to have as a secret lover, have on the side (I;III)

iloposhki [PR] of loposhki

iloshka to lie to (I;III) [im+loshka]

iloshkat haksichi to deceive (III =

obj , I;II) [iloshka+t] § Aloshkat
sahaksichitok. He deceived me, He
lied to me and took me in.
iloshoma to lose (a relative or close
friend) in death (III;3-at)
[im+loshoma] § Maryat Georgeat
iloshomatok. Mary lost George (her
husband). I Sashkaat aloshomatok.
I lost my mother.
ilhaha to be bled (medicinally) (3)
[im+<lhaha>] {v2. ilhahli}
ilhahli to bleed (someone, as a
medical procedure) (I;III) [i+lhahli]
{v1. ilhaha}
ilhakoffi to be safe from, get away
from, escape from, avoid (I;III); to
make a mistake, to make an error
(in baseball) (III) [im+lhakoffi]
ilhatapa to drop (tpl., nonhum.,
usually inan. 3-at), to spill
(especially, by accident) (III;3-at)
[im+lhatapa] {sg.-dl. 3-at. imittola} §
oka'at ilhatapa: to urinate on
oneself I Lynnat kaafi'at ilhatapa.
Lynn spilled the coffee. I
Amposhi'at alhatapatok. I dropped
the dishes.
ilhayita [PR] of lhayita
ilha'a to spill (accidentally), to let (a
liquid) slop out of a container (III;3-
at) [im+lha'a] § Chipotaat tiiat
ilha'a. The child spilled the tea.
ilhafi in anompilhafi, holissilhafi
ilhimishko [PR] of lhimishko
ilhonklhowa to grunt at (I;III)
[im+lhonklhowa]
ilhpichik poss. of ilhpichik
imalili to run away from (I;III)
[im+malili]
imalli to jump for (I;III) [im+malli]
imalhaha see imalhaa
imalhata to be scared of, to be
surprised by (I;III) [im+malhata]
imalhaa, imalhaha to be angry at, to

act grouchy toward (I;III)
[im+malhaa]
imasali to be healed (3) [im+masali]
imasofa [PR] of masofa
imaami' mother (oIIIp) [im+maami']
imiha to bawl out, criticize (I;III)
[im+miha] {hngr. imihiha}
imihachi to tell off (I;III) [imiha+chi]
imihiha hngr. of imiha
imilínka, imilínka'si to be close to,
friendly with (I;III) [i+milinka+a'si]
imilínka'si see imilínka
iminti to ejaculate (III) [im+minti]
imocholi to wink at (I;III) (MJ)
[im+mocholi]
imosak in ilbak imosak, iyyimosak,
shakba' imosak [im+osak ?]
imoshmoli to wink at (I;III)
[im+moshmoli]
imoshooli [PR] of moshooli
imóma to be all there, not defective
(of a newborn baby or a person
alleged to be crazy) (3) [im+moma]
imomachit táyya'ha (AB), imomachit
kaniya to be used to it (III , —)
[im+momachi+t]
inakfi' brother (of a woman); male
first cousin (of a woman) (oIIIp)
{nakfish}
inakfi' toba' stepbrother (of a
woman) (oIIIp)
inakfiklanna' half-brother (of a
woman) (oIIIp) [inakfi' iklanna+']
inampila to fix, adjust (something)
for (someone°), to put (something)
on (someone°) (I;III;3)
[im+nampila] {ngr. inampíla} §
Tikba-takaali' inampilalitok. I put
the apron on her.
inampíla ngr. of inampila
{pitinampíla}
inaapiisa to order (legally), to
sentence to do something, to put on
probation (I;III)

inaanoli', inanoli' witness
[im+nanna anoli+'] {iminaanoli'}
inaithana', nannimaaithana' disciple
(oIIIp) [im+nanna (aa+)ithana+'] §
Chihoowoshi' inaithana': Jesus
Christ's disciple
inamihachi to tell off, to criticize
(someone's) possessions (I;III)
[*im+nanna mihachi] §
Issanamihachi. You told me off.
inanoli' see inaanoli'
iniha [PR] of niha
inihachi to grease for ˚ (I;III;3)
[im+nihachi] § Lynn imaapallaska'
chinihashla'chi. I'll grease Lynn's
bread pan for you.
inihi' testicles (oIIIp) [im+nihi']
inihi' ishyo'kli' jock strap, athletic
supporter (oIIIp) [isht yokli+']
inokhánglo to pity, feel sorry for,
have mercy on (I;III)
[im+nokhanglo]
inókko'wa to yell at, bawl out (I;III)—
ggr. of inokowa
inokowa to yell at, bawl out (I;III) (Ct)
[im+<nokowa>] {ggr. inókko'wa}
inokshohómpa hngr. of
inokshooopa
inokshómpa ngr. of inokshoopa
inokshóyyo'pa ygr. of inokshoopa
inokshoopa to be afraid of (someone)
(I;III); to be afraid to (do something)
because of (someone connected
with the action) [+a'nikat ss comp.]
(I;III) [im+<nokshoopa>] {hngr.
inokshohómpa; ngr. inokshómpa;
ygr. inokshóyyo'pa} § Charlesat
chimanompola'nikat
chinokshoopa. Charles is afraid to
talk to you.
inokwaya to hate to talk to, be
reluctant to talk to (I;III)
[im+nokwaya]
inona [PR] of nona

inosi [PR] of nosi
inoshkonna to like (someone for the
way he does something) (I;III)
[im+noshkonna] § Holissochilika
anoshkonnatok. He likes the way I
write, He likes me because of how I
write.
inowa to go see, to visit: especially,
perhaps, to court (I;III) [im+nowa]
inowoot áa, inowat áa to court, go
visit (III = obj. , I) [inowa+hoot/t] §
Anowoot aa. He comes courting
me.
iriidi to read to ˚ (I;III;3) [im+<riidi>
(from the English)] § Chiriidila'chi.
I'll read it to you.
isanali to be opposed to, be against
(I;III) [im+<sanali>+'] {ggr.
isánna'li} § Asanali. He's against
me.
isanali' enemy (oIIIp) [isanali+'] §
ittisanali': enemies of each other
isánna'li to be against, opposed to
(I;II)—ggr. of isanali § Asasanna'li.
He's against me. | Achisanna'li.
He's against you.
isatabli to straighten, smooth out
(something) for ˚ (I;III;3)
[im+satabli]
isoba poss. of issoba
issa ngr. of issa
isso ngr. of isso
ishakabli [PR] of shakabli
ishaniili to make crooked for ˚, mess
up for ˚ (I;III;3) [im+shaniili] § Lynn
imaaombiniili' issashaniilinna!
Don't mess up Lynn's chair for me!
Ishaaki' Chickasaw family name—
anglicized as Sharkey or Ensharkey
ishafi [OPR] of shafi
ishi ngr. of ishi
ishila [PR] of shila
ishilli to wash, groom, comb the hair
of (I;III); to comb for ˚ (I;III;3)

205

ishippali

[im+shilli] § A̱shilli, Sap̱ashi'
a̱shilli. She combed my hair. | Ofi'
i̱shillilitok. I combed the dog's hair.
i̱shippali to blow on for ° (I;III;3)
[im+shippali] § Sashkaat nipi'
a̱shippalitok. My mother blew on
the meat for me.
ishi̱fa [PR] of shi̱fa
íshko ngr. of ishko
ishkoboka' poss. of ishkoboka'
i̱shobohchi to smoke out (rabbits, for
instance); to send smoke signals to
(I;III) [-SC] [im+shobohchi]
i̱shoha, i̱showa [PR] of shoha, showa
i̱shoppalá̱li to leave on a light for
(I;III) [im+shoppala̱li]
i̱shoppálla'a [PR] of shoppálla'a
i̱shoppaya' lights, lungs (of an
animal, such as a hog) (WB)
[im+shoppaya+']
i̱shoppayachi to make (a burden)
light for ° (I;III;3) [im+shoppayachi]
{ngr. i̱shoppayánchi}
i̱shoppáyya'a [PR] of shoppáyya'a
i̱showa see i̱shoha
ishtilachifa' poss. of ishtachifa',
ishtilachifa'
iwá'a ggr. of i̱waa (call)
iwahá̱a hngr. of i̱waa (call)
i̱wakaa [PR] of wakaa
i̱wakchalali to spread one's legs for
(in a sexual sense) (I;III)
[im+wakchalali]
i̱wayaachi to place (sg. obj. on a flat
bottom or on four legs) for ° (I;III;3)
[im+wayaachi] {pl. patient obj.
i̱wayoochi}
i̱wayá̱a to leave (sg. obj. on a flat
bottom or on four legs) (III;3-at)—
ngr. of i̱wáyya'a {dl. 3-at i̱wayó̱wa;
tpl. 3-at imá̱sha} § Lynnat
aaombiniili'at i̱waya̱atok. Lynn left
the chair.
i̱wayowat má̱a to have (tpl. 3-at, on

flat bottoms or on four legs) set up
(III = subj. , — ;3-at) {sg. 3-at
i̱wáyya'a; dl. 3-at i̱wáyyo'wa} §
Aaombiniili'at a̱wayowat ma̱a. I
have chairs (set up).
i̱wayoochi to place (pl. obj. on four
legs or flat bottoms) for ° (I;III;3)
[im+wayoochi] {sg. patient obj.
i̱wayaachi}
i̱wayó̱wa to leave (dl. obj. on four
legs or flat bottoms) (III;3-at) {sg. 3-at
i̱wayá̱a; tpl. 3-at imá̱sha}
i̱wáyya'a to have (sg. obj. that rests
on four legs (or wheels) or is
thought of as having a flat upper
surface with open space beneath)
(III;3-at) [im+wayya'a] {ngr. i̱wayá̱a:
to leave; dl. 3-at i̱wáyyo'wa; tpl. 3-at
i̱wayowat má̱a} § Danat kaarat
i̱wayya'a. Dan has a car.
i̱wáyyo'wa to have (dl. objs. resting
on four legs (or wheels) or flat
bottoms) (III;3-at) [im+wayyo'wa]
{ngr. i̱wayó̱wa: to leave; sg. 3-at
i̱wáyya'a; tpl. 3-at i̱wayowat má̱a}
i̱waa to call (I;III) {ggr. i̱wá'a; hngr.
i̱wahá̱a}
i̱waa [PR] of waa
i̱waachi to make (a plant) grow for °
(I;III;3) [im+waachi]
i̱waaka [PR] of waaka
i̱wa̱'ta', (AB) imaskawa̱'ta, (AB)
i̱skawa̱'ta wide area across one's
body, such as the hips or (AB, TJ)
collarbones (oIIIp) {awátta'a,
okkowwátta'a}
i̱wí'li in oshti̱wí'li, piti̱wi'li—ggr. of
i̱wiili
i̱wihhiila to attract the attention of by
waving one's arms and jumping
around (I;3) [im+wihhiila]
i̱wilili [PR] of wilili
i̱wiiki to have (something) be too
heavy for one (III;3-at) [im+wiiki] §

Ittoyyo'baat a̱wiiki' salamikat ith̲a̱nali. I know the box is too heavy for me.
iwiikichi to burden (someone) (I;III) [im+wiiki+chi] § A̱wiikichitok. He burdened me, gave me a burden.
iwiili in piṯi̱wiili, oshṯi̱wiili [im+wiili] {ggr. i̱wí'li}
iwoshwoki [PR] of woshwoki
iwoochi to bark for (I;III) [-SC] [im+woochi]
I̱yaaknasha' mythical little spirit companion creature or "leprechaun" [im+yaakni' <asha>+']
i̱yaaknasha' aachokoshkomo' large, green, mossy clearing [aa+chokoshkomo+']
i̱yaaknasha' intopa small, green, mossy clearing [im+topa]
iyalfolfo', (LR) i̱folfo', (AB, WB) yaafolfo', (MJ) aafolfo' cowlick; place on the crown of the head where the hair grows out in a circle (oIIIp) {holhfo}
iyamihchi to do to (I;III)

[im+yamihchi]
iyámmohmi to act in a certain way toward, to do for (I;III) [+HM], <iyámmo̱h> [im+yammohmi] § I̱yammo̱hcha ayoppa. She's happy doing it for him. | I̱yammohmili. I do it for her, I act that way to her.
<iyámmo̱h> [HM] of iyámmohmi
iyatofa [PR] of yatofa
iyaa [PR] of yaa
iyí'mmi ggr. of iyimmi
iyilhipa [PR] of yilhipa
iyimmi to trust, believe (someone); to believe in (I;III) [im+yimmi] {ggr. iyí'mmi}
iyoka [PR] of yoka
iyokota [PR] of yokota
iyopi to swim, take a bath (as entertainment) for (I;III) [im+yopi]
iyopichi to bathe (someone) for ° (I;III;3); to bathe (someone) for (someone°) in (water) (I;III;3;3) [im+yopichi] {oka' iyopichi}
iyoppola to kid, tease, tell a joke to (I;III) [im+yoppola]

j

jeli' see cheli'

jipsi' see chipsi'

k

ka'b ka'b ka'b aachi see kab kab kab aachi
ká'lli ggr. of kalli
ká'llo ggr. of kallo
ka'lh ka'lh ka'lh aachi see kalh kalh kalh aachi
ka's ka's ka's aachi see kas kas kas

aachi
ka'sh ka'sh ka'sh aachi see kash kash kash aachi
ká'wwi ggr. of kawwi
ká'yya ggr. of kayya
kab kab kab aachi, ka'b ka'b ka'b aachi to make the sound of knocking or

kaba'chi

hammering (expressive) (I)
{kaba'chi}
kaba'chi to make noise with wood
(perhaps by hitting two sticks
together or knocking on a door; to
bang on a white man's drum) (I)
[-SC] {hngr. kaba'lihínchi; klgr.
<kábbakli'chi>; ngr. kaba'línchi;
rcgr. kababá'chi; kab kab kab aachi,
kabak kabak kabak aachi}
kaba'lihínchi hngr. of kaba'chi
kaba'línchi ngr. of kabba'chi
kababá'chi to make a knocking or
hammering sound (I)—rcgr. of
kaba'chi
kabak kabak kabak aachi to make the
sound of knocking or hammering
(expressive) (I) {kaba'chi}
<kábbakli'chi> in ittikábbakli'chi—
klgr. of kaba'chi
kabi' boy (member of one's family:
son, brother, etc.), sonny (often used
as a term of address) {kabosh}
Kabi' Chickasaw man's name or
nickname, anglicized as "Cubby"
kabosh boy (member of one's family:
son, brother, etc.) [kabi' oshi']
kachaha, kachaa to be cut out (for
instance, of a pattern), cut up (II)
[+T] {v2. kachiili}
kachaa see kachaha
kachi see bint kachi
kachihíli hngr. of kachiili
kachiili to cut with scissors (I;II) {v1.
kachaha; hngr. kachihíli}
kafali to straddle (a bicycle, tree limb,
etc.), especially in an undignified
manner; to get stuck (between two
surfaces) (sg. subj.) (I;3) {ggr. káffa'li;
dl. kafohli; tpl. kafoht máa} § Tali'
kafalilitok. I straddled the rock. |
Tali' ittintakla' kafalilitok. I got
stuck between two rocks.
káffa'li ggr. of kafali

káffohli ggr. of kafohli
kafi' coffee (Ct) [from the English]
kafi', (ER, CC, LF) itti' kafi' sassafras
kafohli to straddle; to get stuck
(between two surfaces) (dl. subj.)
(I;3) {ggr. káffohli; sg. kafali; tpl.
kafoht máa}
kafoht máa to straddle; to get stuck
(between two surfaces) (tpl. subj.)
(I;3) [kafohli+t] {sg. kafali; dl.
kafohli}
kaha in akkootkaha, inkaha', kahat
máa, lokfi' kaha', oshtonkaha,
ootkaha, ootonkaha, pitkaha {v2.
kahli; ngr. káha; ygr. káyya'ha; sg.
inan. ittola (fall); pl. inan. lhatapa}
kahánchi hngr. of kanchi; see bint
kahánchi
kahat máa to lie down (tpl. subj.) (I);
to lie down in (a location) (I;3)
[kaha+t] {sg. ti'wa; dl. kayya'ha} §
Kahat iimaatok. We're lying down.
kaháli hngr. of kahli
kahállo hngr. of kallo
kaháwwi hngr. of kawwi
káhhallo hgr. of kallo
káhhayya hgr. of kayya
kahli to make lie down, lay down,
lay out (pl. obj.) (I;II) {v1. kaha;
hngr. kaháli; ngr. káhli; sg. obj.
bohli} § Kaht potahtok. He made us
all lie down.
kala' color (for instance, as a feature
of a color television) [from the
English]
<kalafa> in ishkala'fa' {v2. kalaffi}
kalaffi to rake (I;3) {v1. <kalafa>;
hngr. kalaháffi; kalli}
kalaháffi hngr. of kalaffi
kalakshi to be degraded, lowest of the
low (II) {ygr. kaláyyakshi}
kalakshichi to degrade, demean (I;II)
[kalakshi+chi]
kaláyyakshi ygr. of kalakshi

208

kali well (in the ground)
Kali Chito' Big Well—name of a
Choctaw church [<chito>+']
{Kalishto'}
kali foloha', kali folowa' pipe that
goes down a hole drilled for a well
[foloha+']
kali folowa' see kali foloha'
kali hofobi' deep well, specially dug
well [hofobi+']
Kali Homma' Kalihoma, Red Spring
(Chickasaw Nation park)
[homma+']
kali okshalli', (WB) kali okshayalli'
spring
kali palli' hot spring [palli+']
Kali Showa' Sulphur [showa+']
Kali Toklo' Twin Wells—name of a
church near Kalihoma [toklo+']
kali walhaali' bubbling source of a
spring; hot spring [walhaali+']
kalishto' well dug by hand [kali
ishto+']
Kalishto' Chickasaw name of Kali
Chito'
kalli to scratch (a part of one's body)
(I;3) {ggr. ká'lli; kalaffi}
kallo to be hard, firm; to be difficult;
to set, gel; to be tight; to be stiff; to be
erect (of a penis) (3) [+CPR] [+PR]
{ggr. ká'llo; hgr. káhhallo; hngr.
kahállo; ngr. kállo; ygr. káyya'llo;
neg. ikkallo}
kalló'chi ggr. of kallochi (make hard)
kallochi to be loud (used with a
preceding verb +kat) (I) [+CPR] [-PR]
{ngr. kallónchi; ygr. kallóyyo'chi} §
Anompolilikat kallochili. I talk
loud. | Ofi'at woochikat kallochi.
The dog is loud, The dog barks
loudly. | Ishtaloowakat ishkallochi'
salami. You sing too loud.
kallochi to make hard (I;3)
[kallo+chi] {ggr. kalló'chi; hngr.

kallohónchi; ngr. kallónchi: to
make harder}
kallochit foyopa to take a deep
breath; to breathe hard (I)
[kallochi+t] § Kallochit foyopali. I
take a deep breath.
kallohónchi hngr. of kallochi (make
hard)
kallónchi ngr. of kallochi (make
hard, loud)
kallot binohli to be lumpy (of a
mattress) (3) [kallo+t]
kallot íbbalhto to be lumpy (of gravy)
(3) [kallo+t]
kallóyyo'chi ygr. of kallochi (loud)
kalh kalh kalh aachi, ka'lh ka'lh
ka'lh aachi to make the sound of
knocking, pounding, or hammering
(expressive) (I) {kalhak kalhak
kalhak aachi, <kalha'chi>}
kalha to have pus or fluid come out
(of a wound, blister, etc.) (3) {v2.
kalhali} § Salbakat kalhatok. My
hand had pus come out of it.
kalha' pus, discharge [kalha+']
kalha'at áyyalhto for there to be pus
in (—;3) [kalha'+at] § Kalha'at
salbak ayyalhto. There's pus in my
(infected) hand.
<kalha'chi> in ittikalha'chi {klgr.
<kálhlhakli'chi>; rcgr. kalhalhá'chi;
kalh kalh kalh aachi, kalhak kalhak
kalhak aachi}
kalhaháma hngr. of kalhama
kalhak kalhak kalhak aachi to make
a knocking, pounding, or
hammering sound; to make the
sound of wagon wheels turning
(expressive) (I) {kalh kalh kalh
aachi, <kalha'chi>}
kalhali to make pus or liquid come
out of (an infected area): burst (a
blister), lance (a boil), squeeze (a
pimple) (I;3) {v1. kalha} § Hichi'

kalhalhá'chi

kalhalilitok. I lanced the boil.
kalhalhá'chi to make a noise like
wood bumping or being bumped
(3)—rcgr. of <kalha'chi>
kalhama to be smelly (like urine) (II)
{ggr. kálhlha'ma; hngr. kalhaháma;
ygr. kalháyya'ma}
kalháyya'ma ygr. of kalhama
kalhafa, kalhafa' phlegm (IIIp)
kalhafa' see kalhafa
kalhká'ki ggr. of kalhkaki
kalhkáhha'ki hgr. of kalhkaki
kalhkaki to be corrugated, like a
washboard; to be bumpy, rocky (of a
road or field); to have skin that is
corrugated (like an okra) (II) {ggr.
kalhká'ki; hgr. kalhkáhha'ki; ygr.
kalhkáyya'ki}
kalhkáyya'ki ygr. of kalhkaki
kálhlha'ma ggr. of kalhama
<kálhlhakli'chi> in
ittikálhlhakli'chi—klgr. of
<kalha'chi>
kalho'chi to rub (for instance, on a
washboard); to wash (clothes) (I;3)
[-SC] {hgr. kalho'lihínchi; ngr.
kalho'línchi}
kalho'lihínchi hngr. of kalho'chi
kalho'línchi ngr. of kalho'chi
<kama'chi> in ittikama'chi {klgr.
kámmakli'chi; rcgr. <kamamá'chi>}
kamahássa hngr. of kamassa
<kamamá'chi> in ittikamamá'chi—
rcgr. of <kama'chi>
kamassa to be old (II) {ggr.
kámmassa; hngr. kamahássa; ngr.
kamássa; ygr. kamáyya'sa}
kamassa' old one, old person, elder
[kamassa+']
kamassachi to get old (II)
[kamassa+chi] {ngr. kamassánchi}
kamassánchi ngr. of kamassachi
kamassaa-asha' old people's home
[kamassa' aa-asha']

kamáyya'sa ygr. of kamassa
kamaa to be striped, especially with
wide stripes (II) [+CPR] [+PR] {ggr.
kámma'ha, kámma'a; ngr. kamáa}
kamaachi to stripe, paint different
colors (I;II) [kamaa+chi] {hngr.
kamaahánchi}
kamaahánchi hngr. of kamaachi
kamáa ngr. of kamaa
kamássa ngr. of kamassa
kámma'ha, kámma'a ggr. of kamaa
kámmakli'chi to hit on the head
(I;II)—klgr. of <kama'chi> [+SC]
kámmassa ggr. of kamassa
kamohóshli hngr. of kamoshli
kamosha to be tickled; to be
nauseated (II) {v2. kamoshli; ygr.
kamóyyo'sha}
kamoshachi to nauseate (I;II)
[kamosha+chi]
kamoshli to tickle (I;II) {v1. kamosha;
hngr. kamohóshli}
kamóyyo'sha ygr. of kamosha
kana someone (nonsubj.),
someone's; who, whom (inf.)
(nonsubj.), whose (inf.) {int. kata} §
Kana inchipotaho ofi'at kisitoka
ithanali. I know whose child the
dog bit.
kana'li to change position, move
around (pl. subj.) (I) {sg. kanalli}
kanahmat someone (subj.)
[kana+hmat] {inf. kanahoot; int.
katahaat}
kanahma someone (nonsubj.)
[kana+hma] {inf. kanaho; int.
katahta} § Kanahma issolikat
ithanali. I know I hit someone.
kanahookano, kanookano someone,
somebody (unspecified) (subj.,
nonsubj.) [kana+hookano] §
Kanahookano
ishtihaalalla'chihaakayniha'ni.
You'll marry someone.

kanahookya, kanookya everyone, everybody; (in a negative sentence) no one, nobody, anyone, anybody (subj., nonsubj.) [kana+hookya] § Kanahookya ishka̲ imalhkaniya' ki'yo. No one forgets his mother. | Ishkaat kanahookya ikimalhkani'yokitok. His mother didn't forget anyone.
kanahoot who (inf.) (subj.) [kana+hoot] {ind. kanahmat; int. katahaat} § Ithanali kanahoot taloowaka̲. I know who's singing.
kanaho̲ who, whom (inf.) (nonsubj.) [kana+ho̲] {ind. kanahma̲; int. katahta} § Kanaho̲ issolikat ithanali. I know who I hit.
kanalli, kanatli to move to a new location, leave (sg. subj.) (I) {ggr. kánnalli: to have been moved (3); rmgr. kannanáli; pl. kana'li}
kanallichi to take away (I;II) [kanalli+chi]
kanannak green striped lizard about six or seven inches long
kanatli see kanalli
kanchi to sell (sg.-dl.-tpl. obj.); to throw away, get rid of, let off (sg. obj.) (I;II) {hngr. kahánchi; ngr. kánchi; dl. obj. (throw away, let off) fimmi; tpl. obj. (throw away, let off) lhatabli, lha̲'li; inkanchi: to sell to; ká̲shcha aya; ka̲'shcha kaniya}
kánchi ngr. of kanchi {ká̲shcha aya}
kani'mi to be in a certain configuration; to be how, in what configuration (inf.) (I) [+HM], <kani̲'> {int. kati'mi} § Iikani'mikat kiliyatok. A certain number, proportion, subgroup of us went. | Kani̲'toka akitha'no. I don't know how it went together. | Ofi' kani̲'kat Lynn lhiyohtok. A few dogs (a certain group of dogs) chased Lynn.

kani'mihmat in a certain configuration of (I) (subj.) [kani'mi+hmat] {inf. kani'mihoot; int. kati'mihaat}
kani'mihma̲ in a certain configuration of (I) (nonsubj.) [kani'mi+hma̲] {inf. kani'miho̲; int. kati'mihta} § Charlesat iikani'mihma̲ popi̲stok. Charles knows a number of us.
kani'mihoot in what configuration of (I) (subj.) (inf.) [kani'mi+hoot] {ind. kani'mihmat; int. kati'mihaat}
kani'miho̲ in what configuration of (nonsubj.) (inf.) [kani'mi+ho̲] {ind. kani'mihma̲; int. kati'mihta}
kani'militokat see kani̲'tokat immo'ma
kanihíya hngr. of kaniya
kanihmi to happen (of something), to happen (of what) (inf.) (3); to do (something) (ind.), to do (what) (inf.) (I;3); to have (something) happen to one; to have (what) happen to one (inf.) (II;3-at) [+HM], <kani̲h> {int. katihmi} § Nanna kanihmili. I'm doing something. | Nannakat sakanihtokat iksamalhpi'so. I'm sad that something happened to me. | Nannaho̲ ishkanihmikya.... No matter what you do.... | Nannaho̲ ishkanihka ithanali. I know what you're doing. | Nannahmat kanihna malitok. Something happened and he ran.
kanihmi some kind of, what kind of (inf.) (nonsubj.); of some kind, of what kind (inf.) (possr.) {int. katihmi}
kanihmihmat some kind of (subj.) [kanihmi+hmat] {inf. kanihmihoot; int. katihmihaat} § Ofi' kanihmihmat kisitok. Some kind of

kanihmihma

dog bit him.
kanihmihma some kind of (nonsubj.) [kanihmi+hma] {inf. kanihmiho; int. katihmihta}
kanihmihma, nannakat kanihmihma, nannahmat kanihmihma for some reason, because something happened [(nanna+kat/hmat) kanihmi+hma] {inf. kanihmiho; int. katihmihta} § Nannakat kanihmihma ikimalhpi'so, Kanihmihma ikimalhpi'so. She's sad for some reason, Something made her sad.
kanihmihoot what kind of (inf.) (subj.) [kanihmi+hoot] {ind. kanihmihmat; int. katihmihaat} § Ofi' kanihmihoot Charles sakisilitoka ithanali. I know what kind of dog bit Charles.
kanihmiho what kind of (inf.) (nonsubj.) {ind. kanihmihma; int. katihmihta} § Charlesat ofi' kanihmiho pistoka ithanali. I know what kind of dog Charles saw.
kanihmiho, nannakat kanihmiho, nannahoot kanihmiho why (inf.) [kanihmi+ho] {ind. kanihmihma; int. katihmihta} § Kanihmiho ishiyyatoka akitha'no. I don't know why you went.
kanihmikya see ikkanihmikya
kanihmo'si to be just a little, just a few (3) (mainly subord.) [kanihmi+o'si] § Yappakot kanihmo'sika imayya chaahakat. He's just a little taller than the other one. | Kanihmo'sikat ashtok. A little was left. | Kanihmo'sna momaho ishtayatok. There was just a little and he took it all. | Bala'at kanihmo'si. There's a few beans (not enough to cook).
kanimpi a certain (one); which (one)

(inf.) (nonsubj.); of a certain (one), of which (one) (inf.) (possr.) {int. katimpi} § Chipota kanimpi imofi'at sakisilitok. One of the children's dog bit me.
kanimpi to be a certain (one); to be which one (inf.) (I) (sg. reference, used with pl. agreement; with lexical dl. or pl. verb, refers to a pair) {int. katimpi} § Ofi'at kanimpikat sakisilitok. A certain dog bit me. | Kiikanimpitok. It was one of us.
kanimpihmat a certain (one), a certain one of (I) (sg. reference, used with pl. agreement; with lexical dl. or pl. verb, refers to a pair) (subj.) [kanimpi+hmat] {inf. kanimpihoot; int. katimpihaat} § Ofi' kanimpihmat sakisilitok. A certain dog bit me.
kanimpihma a certain (one), a certain one of (I) (sg. reference, used with pl. agreement; with lexical dl. or pl. verb, refers to a pair) (nonsubj.) [kanimpi+hma] {inf. kanimpiho; int. katimpihta} § Kiikanimpihma ofi'at pokisilitok. The dog bit one of us.
kanimpihoot which (one), which (one) of (I) (sg. reference, used with pl. agreement; with lexical dl. or pl. verb, refers to a pair) (inf.) (subj.) [kanimpi+hoot] {ind. kanimpihmat; int. katimpihaat} § Hashkanimpihoot hashiyyatoka ithanali. I know which of you went.
kanimpiho which (one), which (one) of (I) (sg. reference, used with pl. agreement; with lexical dl. or pl. verb, refers to a pair) (inf.) (nonsubj.) [kanimpi+ho] {ind. kanimpihma; int. katimihta} § Ithanali kanimpiho inkashtoka. I know which one he sold it to. |

Iikanimpiho ofi'at pokisilitoka ishithanata? Do you know which one of us the dog bit? **kaniya** to go away, to be gone, to vanish (sg. subj.) (I); to be lost, directionless (sg. subj.) (II) {hngr. kanihíya; ngr. kaníya; ggr. kánni'ya: a little, kind of (aux.); pl. subj. tamowa; inkaniya: to lose} § Kaniyali. I went away. | Sakaniya. I am lost, I don't know where to go. **kaniya fokha** to be to a certain (notable) extent (ind.); to be how (inf.), to be to what degree (inf.) (aux., used with preceding verb +kat); to weigh how much (inf.) (I) {int. katiya fokha} § Chaahakat kaniya fokha. He's certainly tall. | Lynnat chaahakat kaniya fokhakat ithana. Lynn knows how tall she is. | Kaniya ishfokhaka ithanali. I know how much you weigh. **kaniya fokhahmat** some amount of, some (very large or uncountable) number of (subj.) [fokha+hmat] {inf. kaniya fokhahoot; int. kaniya fokhahaat} **kaniya fokhahma** some amount of, some (very large or uncountable) number of (nonsubj.) [kaniya fokha +hma] {inf. kaniya fokhaho; int. katiya fokhahta} § Benjieat naachampoli' kaniya fokhahma apatok. Benjie ate some of the candy. **kaniya fokhahoot** how much, how many (of a very large or uncountable number) (subj.) (inf.) [kaniya fokha +hoot] {ind. kaniya fokhahmat; int. katiya fokhahaat} § Kaniya fokhahoot lhatapaka ithanali. I know how much spilled. **kaniya fokhaho** how much, how many (of a very large or

uncountable number) (nonsubj.) (inf.) [fokha+ho] {ind. kaniya fokhahma; int. katiya fokhahta} § Kaniya fokhaho apatoka akitha'no. I don't know how much he ate. **kaniya fokhaho** when (nonpast) (inf.) [kaniya fokha +ho] {ind. kaniya fokhakmak; int. katiya fokhakmak} § Kaniya fokhaho pisa'chika ithanali. I know when he's going to see it. | Kaniya fokhaho alaka ithanali. I know when she comes. **kaniya fokhakaash** some time ago, at some time (in the past) [fokha+kaash] {inf. kaniya fokhakaasho; int. katiya fokhakaash} § Kaniya fokhakaash pistok. He saw him some time ago, at some point in the past. **kaniya fokhakaasho** when (past) (inf.) [fokha+kaash+ho] {ind. kaniya fokhakaash; int. katiya fokhakaash} § Kaniya fokhakaasho alatoka amanoli. Tell me when she got here. **kaniya fokhakmak, kaniya fokhakma** sometime, sometimes (nonpast), at some time (not in the past) [kaniya fokha +kmak/kma] {inf. kaniya fokhaho; int. katiya fokhakmak} § Kaniya fokhakma pisala'chihaakayni. I'll see him sometime. **kaniya fokhakma** see kaniya fokhakmak **kaniya', kaniya'ma, kaniya'mak** somewhere, someplace (specified) [kaniya'+hma/hmak] {inf. kaniya'o; int. katiyakta} § Kaniya' ayatok. He went somewhere. | Yappa' kaniya'ma ti'wa'ni. It must be lying here somewhere. **kaniya'ko** see kaniya'o (where)

kaniya'mak see kaniya'
kaniya'mako see kaniya'o (where)
kaniya'mat someone, somebody:
especially, someone known but not
identified (subj.) [kaniya'+hmat]
{inf. kaniya'oot}
kaniya'ma someone, somebody:
especially, someone known but
unidentified (nonsubj.)
[kaniya'+hma] {inf. kaniya'o}
kaniya'ma see kaniya'
kaniya'ookano, kaniyookano
somewhere, someplace
(unspecified); someone, somebody
(unspecified) (subj., nonsubj.)
[kaniya'+hookano] § Kaniyookano
omba. It's raining somewhere. |
Kaniya'ookano
ishtihaalalla'chihaakayniha'ni.
You'll marry someone. |
Kaniya'ookano
achipiila'chihaakayniha'ni.
Someone will take care of you.
kaniya'ookya, kaniyookya
everyplace, everywhere, everybody,
everyone; (in a negative sentence)
nowhere, nobody, no one, anyplace,
anywhere, anybody, anyone (subj.,
nonsubj.) [kaniya'+hookya]
kaniya'oot someone, somebody
(unidentified); who (inf.) (subj.)
[kaniya'+hoot] {ind. kaniya'mat} §
Kaniya'oot aya'chi. Somebody (we
don't know who) is going. |
Kaniya'oot aya'chika akitha'no. I
don't know who's going.
kaniya'o someone, somebody
(unidentified); who, whom (inf.)
(nonsubj.) [kaniya'+ho] {ind.
kaniya'ma} § Lynnat kaniya'o
ayoppanchika ishithanata? Do you
know who Lynn likes?
kaniya'o, kaniya'mako, kaniya'ko
where (inf.) [kaniya+ho] {ind.

kaniya'; int. katiyakta} § Kaniyaho
ayatoka ithanali. I know where he
went.
kaniyookano see kaniya'ookano
kaniyookya see kaniya'ookya
<kani'> [HM] of kani'mi
kani'tokat immo'ma, kani'tokat
ishtayya'ma, kani'tokat i'ma to be
the same (I) (note that with an 'I'
subj. the first word is
kani'militokat); to be the same (II)
[*kani'mi+tokat] § Ishkani'tokat
i'ma, Chikani'tokat i'ma. You're
the same.
kani'tokat ishtayya'ma see kani'tokat
immo'ma
kani'tokat i'ma see kani'tokat
immo'ma
<kanih> [HM] of kanihmi
kanihchi to do (something); to do
(what) (inf.) (I;3); to do (something)
to °; to do (what) to ° (inf.) (I;II;3)
[<kanih>+chi] {int. katihchi} §
Nannama sakanihshtok. He did
something to me.
kanihchihma somehow, for some
reason: especially, because of
something (someone, not the subj.
of the following sentence) did (I)
[kanihchi+hma] {inf. kanihchiho;
int. katihchihta} § Kanihchihma
ayatok. It goes somehow (said about
a windup toy). | Ishkanihchihma
ayatok. It goes because of something
you did.
kanihchihoot see kanihsht (how)
kanihchiho why, for what reason:
especially, because of what that
(someone, not the subj. of the
following sentence) did (I) (inf.)
[kanihchi+ho] {ind. kanihchihma;
int. katihchihta} § Kanihchiho
ayatoka akitha'no. I don't know
why it goes (said about a windup

<kánnoh>

toy). | Ishkanichiho ayatoka
akitha'no. I don't know what you
did so that it goes.
kanihkaash at some point, sometime
(in the past) {inf. kanihkaasho, int.
katihkaash} § Kanihkaash
ootpisatok. He went to see it at
some point.
kanihkaasho when (in the past) (inf.)
{ind. kanihkaash; int. katihkaash} §
Kanihkaasho pislitokat ithanali. I
know when I saw him.
kanihka really, very [<kanih>+ka] §
Kanihka chissikopa. You're very
mean. | Chipotaat kanihka
sahalhlhi. The baby really kicks me.
kanihkmak, kanihkma at some
point, sometime, sometimes
(nonpast) [<kanih>+kmak/kma]
{int. katihkmak} § Kanihkma
taloowali. Sometimes I sing.
kanihkma see kanihkmak
kanihsht in some way, somehow
[kanihchi+t] {inf. kanihsht, int.
katihsht}
kanihsht, kanihchihoot how (inf.)
[kanihchi+t] {ind. kanihsht; int.
katihsht} § Kanihsht
ishmintila'chikat akitha'nohoot
ayala'chi. I don't know how I'll
come back with it, but I'm going.
kaniht some way; finally (often used
with ggr.); how, in what way (inf.)
[<kanih>+t] {int. katiht} § Kaniht
onala'nikat ithanali. I know how to
get there. | Kaniht acho'lila' ki'yo.
There's no way I can sew it. |
Kaniht tallo'watok. She finally sang.
kaníya ngr. of kaniya
kankishniha' issosh tomato worm
(WB) [kanka' isht niha+']
kanka' short form of akanka'
kanka'simpa' type of chicken (CC)
[akanka'+a'si impa+' ?]

kánnakli to jerk, make a sudden
movement, dodge (I)
kánnalli to have been moved (3)—
ggr. of kanalli
kannanáli to move around, keep
moving (I)—rmgr. of kanalli
kánni'ya a little, kind of, somewhat
(aux. used after II or III subj.
verbs)—ggr. of kaniya § Hoshontit
kanni'ya. It's a little cloudy. |
Anchokmat kanni'ya. I feel kind of
good.
kánnohmi to be a few, several, a
small group (pl. subj.); to have a
split personality (sg. subj.); to be
how many (pl. subj.) (inf.) (I) [+HM],
<kánnoh> [+PR] [+CPR] {int.
káttohmi} § Kannohmikat ayatok.
Several of them went. |
Kiikannohmi. There are several of
us. | Charlesat iikannohmika
popistok. Charles saw several of us.
kannohmihmat a few, several, some;
a few, several, some of (I) (subj.)
[kannohmi+hmat] {inf.
kannohmihoot, int. kattohmihaat}
kannohmihma a few, several, some;
a few, several, some of (I) (nonsubj.)
[kannohmi+hma] {inf.
kannohmiho; int. kattohmihta}
kannohmihoot how many; how
many of (I) (inf.) (subj.)
[kannohmi+hoot] {ind.
kannohmihmat; int. kattohmihaat}
§ Ilithana iikannohmihoot
iliya'chikat. We know how many of
us are going. | Ofi' kannohmihoot
Lynn lhiyohtoka ithanali. I know
how many dogs chased Lynn.
kannohmiho how many; how many
of (I) (inf.) (nonsubj.)
[kannohmi+ho] {ind.
kannohmihma; int. kattohmihta}
<kánnoh> [HM] of kánnohmi

<kano'mi>

<kano'mi> in inkano'mi
<kanomi> in ishtakanomi
kanookano see kanahookano
kanookya see kanahookya
kantak type of briar plant
(greenbrier?)
kantak ishto' type of large briar
(greenbrier?) [ishto+']
Kantak Abookoshi Briar Creek
kanti' bala' see bala' kanti'
kapahássa hngr. of kapassa
kapali to put in one's mouth (I;II); to
dip (snuff), chew (tobacco) (I;3) {ggr.
káppa'li: to have in one's mouth}
<kapasa> var. grade base for kapassa
{ngr. kapása; ygr. kapáyya'sa; prt.
kapast}
kapassa to be cold (II) [+PR] [-CPR]
{v2. kapassali; ggr. káppassa; hngr.
kapahássa; ngr. kapássa, kapása; ygr.
kapáyya'ssa, kapáyya'sa; prt. kapast,
kapassat; inkapassa: to feel cold;
<kapasa>}
kapassachi to be cool (II)
[kapassa+chi] {ngr. kapassánchi}
kapassali to make cold (I;II) {v1.
kapassa; ngr. kapassáli: to make
colder}
kapassánchi ngr. of kapassachi
kapassat prt. of kapassa
kapassáli to make colder—ngr. of
kapassali
kapast prt. of kapassa, <kapasa>
kapast ala to turn cold (of the
weather) (—); to have it turn cold
(of a place) (3) § Oklahomma'at
kapast alatok. It turned cold in
Oklahoma.
kapáyya'ssa, kapáyya'sa ygr. of
kapassa, <kapasa>
kapássa, kapása ngr. of kapassa,
<kapasa>
<kapittani'> see inkapittani' [from
English captain or Spanish capitán]

kapko' hackberry
kapko' ani' wartlike growths on
hackberry bark that are burned to
make ashes used to flavor banaha
kapochcha', (WB) kabochcha', (AW)
kapachcha stickball; stickball stick
káppa'li to have in one's mouth—
ggr. of kapali
káppassa ggr. of kapassa {inkappassa:
to feel cold}
kas kas kas aachi, ka's ka's ka's aachi
to make the sound of high-pitched
clanking or knocking (especially, on
metal) or the sound of chewing ice
(expressive) (I) {kasa'chi}
kasa'chi to make a sound with a
wooden object (castanets, sticks,
knocking on a door); to pop gum (I)
[±SC] {hngr. kasa'lihínchi; klgr.
<kássakli'chi>; ngr. kasa'línchi;
rcgr. kasasá'chi; inkasa'chi: to knock
on (someone's) door; kas kas kas
aachi, kasak kasak kasak aachi}
kasa'lihínchi hngr. of kasa'chi
kasa'línchi ngr. of kasa'chi
kasak kasak kasak aachi to make the
sound of high-pitched clanking or
knocking (especially, on metal) or
the sound of chewing ice
(expressive) (I) {kasa'chi}
kasasá'chi to keep making a
knocking sound (I)—rcgr. of
kasa'chi [+SC]
kasbi yard, open area near a house
kasbi itti' yard tree (of any variety,
especially ornamental)
kaso' type of weed with small
triangular stickers
kasofa to be bald (II) (AB) {masofa}
<kássakli'chi> in ittikássakli'chi—
klgr. of kasa'chi
kash kash kash aachi, ka'sh ka'sh
ka'sh aachi to make the noise of
eating crunchy things (expressive)

(I)
<kasha'chi> in ittikasha'chi {klgr.
<káshshakli'chi>; rcgr.
<kashashá'chi>; kash kash kash
aachi, kashak kashak kashak aachi}
kashabli to give away, share (with
another) (I;3) {v1. kashapa; ggr.
káshshabli; hngr. kashahámbli; ngr.
kashámbli; kashkoli: to share with
many; inkashabli: to share with}
kashahámbli hngr. of kashabli
kashahámpa hngr. of kashapa
kashahᶏma hngr. of kashama
kashak kashak kashak aachi to make
the noise of eating crunchy things
(expressive) (I)
kashama to smell like something
burning (3) {ggr. káshsha'ma; hngr.
kashahᶏma; ngr. kashᶏma; ygr.
kasháyya'ma}
kashámbli ngr. of kashabli
kashámpa ngr. of kashapa
kashapa to be divided (into a
relatively small number of parts); to
be a part, be a class (in a school); to
split off (as of a religious sect) (I) {v2.
kashabli; ggr. káshsha'pa; hngr.
kashahámpa; ngr. kashámpa;
kashkowa: to be divided among
many; akashapa, inkashapa}
<kashashá'chi> in ittikashashá'chi—
rcgr. of <kasha'chi>
kasháyya'ma ygr. of kashama
kashᶏfa, shᶏfa to make a noise like a
scared horse (3)
kashᶏma ngr. of kashama
kashiiho', kashiiyo' in ihoo
kashiiho'
kashkó'li ggr. of kashkoli
kashkohᶐli hngr. of kashkoli
kashkoli to divide up (among many),
share out (I;II) {v1. kashkowa; ggr.
kashkó'li; hngr. kashkohᶐli; ngr.
kashkᶐli; kashabli: to share with a

few; inkashkoli, ittakashkoli}
kashkowa to be split up, divided
(into many parts, or among many)
(I) {v2. kashkoli; kashapa: to be
divided among few; ittakashkowa}
kashkᶐli ngr. of kashkoli
kasho'chi, kashoochi to wipe (I;II)
[-SC] {v1. kasho'kalhchi,
kasho'walhchi; hngr.
kasholihínchi; ngr. kasholínchi}
kasho'kalhchi to be wiped (of a
nonhum.) (3) [+T] {v2. kasho'chi;
kasho'walhchi}
kasho'walhchi to be wiped (3) {v2.
kasho'chi; kasho'kalhchi}
kashofa to be clean (3) [+CPR] [+PR]
{v2. kashoffi; ggr. káshsho'fa; ngr.
kashᶐfa; ygr. kashóyyo'fa}
kashoffi to clean (I;II) {v1. kashofa;
hngr. kashohᶐffi}
kashohᶐffi hngr. of kashoffi
kasholihínchi hngr. of kasho'chi
kasholínchi ngr. of kasho'chi
kashóyyo'fa ygr. of kashofa
kashoochi see kasho'chi
kashᶐfa ngr. of kashofa
káshsha'ma ggr. of kashama
káshsha'pa ggr. of kashapa
káshshabli ggr. of kashabli
<káshshakli'chi> in
ittikáshshakli'chi—klgr. of
<kasha'chi>
káshsho'fa ggr. of kashofa
kashti flea
kata who, whom (nonsubj.); whose
(int.) {ind.-inf. kana} § Kata
inkonihat Lynn kisitok? Whose
skunk bit Lynn?
<katabli> in inkatabli
katahaat who (subj.) (int.) [kata+haat]
{ind. kanahmat; inf. kanahoot} §
Katahaat Lynn pisa? Who saw
Lynn?
katahta who, whom (nonsubj.) (int.)

katahto

[kata+hta] (ind. kanahma; inf. kanaho) § Katahta Charlesat pisa?, Charlesat katahta pisa? Who did Charles see? **katahto** who is it? [kata+hto] <katapa> in inkatapa <katapo'li> in inkatapo'li **kati, kati api', itti' kati** honey locust tree **kati'mi** to be how, in what configuration (3) (int.) [+HM], <kati'> (ind.-inf. kani'mi) § Yappakot kati'tam? How did this one go on? **katihími** hngr. of katihmi **katihmi** to do (what) (I;3); to happen (of what) (3); to have (what) happen to (II;3-at) (int.); to be doing how, to be feeling better (in a greeting) (II) [+HM], <katih> (hngr. katihími; ind.-inf. kanihmi) § Nantahta ishkatihma'ni? What can you do? | Nantahaat chikatihmi? What happened to you? | Nantahaat katihtok? What happened? § Chikatihta? How are you doing? Are you feeling better? | Lynnat katihta? How's Lynn doing? **katihmi** what kind of (nonsubj.), of what kind of (possr.) (int.) (ind.-inf. kanihmi) § Hattak katihmi chiya? What kind of person are you? **katihmihaat** what kind of (subj.) [katihmi+hat] (ind. kanihmihmat; inf. kanihmihoot) § Ofi' katihmihaat Charles kisitok? What kind of dog bit Charles? **katihmihaat** see katiht **katihmihta** what kind of (nonsubj.) [katihmi+hta] (ind. kanihmihma; inf. kanihmiho) **katihmihta, nantahaat katihmihta** why? (int.) [katihmi+hta] § Katihmihta ishiya? Why are you

going? | Nantahaat katihmihta malitok? Why did he run? **katimpi** to be which of, to be which one of (sg. reference, used with pl. agreement) (I) (int.) (subj. is unmarked unless followed by yammat or yappat) (ind.-inf. kanimpi) § Hashkatimpitok? Which (one) of you was it? | Hattak katimpa'chi? Which man will it be? | Hattak yappat katimpitok? Which (one) of these men was it? **katimpi** which, which one (nonsubj.), which one's (int.) (ind.-inf. kanimpi) § Katimpi imofi'at chikisilitok? Which one's dog bit you? **katimpihaat** which, which (one) of (subj.) (I) (int.) (used with pl. affix but sg. reference; refers to a pair when used with a lexical dl. or pl. verb) [katimpi+haat] (ind. kanimpihmat; inf. kanimpihoot) § Hashtochchi'nakat hashkatimpihaat hashmalitok? Which (one) of the three of you ran? **katimpihta** which, which (one) of (nonsubj.) (I) (int.) (used with pl. affix but sg. reference; refers to a pair when used with lexical dl. or pl. verb) [katimpi+hta] (ind. kanimpihma; inf. kanimpiho) § Katimpihta ofi' inchompatok? Which one's dog did he buy?, Which one did he buy the dog from? | Kiikatimpihta ishpopistok? Which (one) of us did you see? **katimpihto** which is it? [katimpi+hto] **katiya** where? (used alone) (int.) (katiyak) **katiya fokha** how, to what degree (aux., preceded by verb +kat) (int.)

{ind.-inf. kaniya fokha} § Chipalhkikat katiya fokha? How fast are you? **katiya fokhahaat** how much, how many (of a very large or uncountable number) (subj.) (int.) [(katiya fokha)+hat] {ind. kaniya fokhahmat; inf. kaniya fokhahoot} § Oka' katiya fokhahaat lhatapa? How much water spilled? | Hattak katiya fokhahaat ayya'shtok? How many people were there (in the crowd)? | Chimofi'at ofishik katiya fokhahaat imayya'sha? How many puppies did your dog have? **katiya fokhahta** how much, how many (of a very large or uncountable number) (nonsubj.), how much (adv.) (int.) [(katiya fokha)+hta] {ind. kaniya fokhahma; inf. kaniya fokhaho} § Paska champoli' katiya fokhahta Benjieat apatok? How much of the cake did Benjie eat? | Katiya fokhahta lhabanka? How much does he snore? **katiya fokhakaash** when (in the past) (int.) [(katiya fokha)+kaash] {ind. kaniya fokhakaash; inf. kaniya fokhakaasho} § Katiya fokhakaash ishonatok? When did you get there? **katiya fokhakmak** when (nonpast) (int.) [(katiya fokha)+kma] {ind. kaniya fokhakmak; inf. kaniya fokhaho} § Katiya fokhakmak ishona'chi? When will you get there? **katiya'mak** see katiyak **katiya'makta** see katiyak **katiyak, katiyakta, katiya'mak, katiya'makta** where [katiya+ak(+ta)] {ind. kaniya'; inf. kaniya'o} § Katiyakta pitmalili?

Where is he running to? | Abooha anonka' katiyakta ishbohtok? Where in the house did you put it down? **katiyakta** see katiyak <kati'> [HM] of kati'mi <katih> [HM] of katihmi **katihchi** to do (what) to ° (I;II;3); to do what to (I;II) (int.) [<katih>+chi] {ind. kanihchi} § Ishkatihshta? What are you doing to him? | Nanta sakatihchim? What did he do to me? **katihchihaat** see katihsht **katihchihta** why: especially, what did (someone, not the subj. of the following verb) do so that (I) [katihchi+hta] {ind. kanihchihma; inf. kanihchiho} § Brenda'at katihchihta issotok? Why did Brenda hit him?, What did he do so that Brenda would hit him? | Ishkatihchihta apatok? What did you do so that he would eat it? **katihkaash, katihkaasht, katihkaashta** when (in the past) (int.) [<katih>+kaash(+hta)] {ind. kanihkaash; inf. kanihkaasho} § Katihkaash ishiyyatok?, Katihkaash ishiyyam? When did you go? **katihkmak** when (nonpast) (int.) [<katih>+kmak] {ind. kanihkma} § Katihkmak ishpisa'chi? When are you going to see him? **katihsht, katihchihaat** how, in what manner (int.) [katihchi+t/haat] {ind.-inf. kanihsht} § Katihsht acho'lila'chi? How should I sew it (in what style)? | Katihchihaat abitok Mikeat? How did Mike kill her? **katiht, katihmihaat** how, in what way (int.) [<katih>+t/katihmi+haat] {ind.-inf. kaniht} § Katiht

acho'lila'chi? How am I going to
sew it (I don't even have a
machine)?
katohólhlhi hngr. of katolhlhi
katolha to be cut, cut off (pl. subj.) (3)
{v2. katolhlhi; sg. tapa}
katolhlhi to cut , cut off (pl. obj.); to
cut (something long) crosswise
more than once (I;II) {v1. katolha;
ggr. káttolhlhi; hngr. katohólhlhi;
ngr. katólhlhi; sg. obj. tabli}
katólhlhi ngr. of katolhlhi
káttohmi to be how many, to be how
many of (I) (int.) [+HM], <kátto̲h>
{ind.-inf. kánnohmi} §
Kilookatto̲htam? How many of us
were there? | Hattakat
kattohma'chi? How many men will
there be?
kattohmi how many, how many of
(nonsubj.) (int.) {ind.-inf.
kannohmihta} § Ofi' kattohmi
ishpi̲stok? How many dogs did you
see?
kattohmihaat how many, how many
of (subj.) (I) (int.) [kattohmi+haat]
{ind. kannohmihmat; inf.
kannohmihoot} § Ofi' kattohmihaat
chikisilim? How many dogs bit
you? | Hashkattohmihaat
hashla'chi? How many of you are
going?
kattohmihta how many, how many
of (obj.), of how many (poss.) (I)
(int.) [kattohmi+hta] {ind.
kannohmihma̲; inf. kannohmiho̲}
§ Hashkattohmihta hachipi̲stok?
How many of you did he see? | Ofi'
kattohmihta ishpi̲sam? How many
dogs did you see? | Hattak
kattohmihta inchokka' ona JPat?
How many people's houses did JP
go to?
káttolhlhi ggr. of katolhlhi

<kátto̲h> [HM] of kattohmi
kawa to be broken (so as to fit) (pl.
subj.) (3) [+T] {v2. kawwi}
kawaski to be hard (like granite) (3)
[+CPR] [+PR] {ggr. káwwaski; ngr.
kawa̲ski; ygr. kawáyya'ski}
kawaskichi to harden (I;3)
[kawaski+chi]
kawáyya'ski ygr. of kawaski
kawa̲ski ngr. of kawaski
kawwana in iyyaat kawwana, iyyi'
kawwana', iyyincha̲maat kawwana
{xgr. kawwánna'a}
kawwánna'a to be bowlegged (I); to
be bowlegged in (a place) (I;3)—xgr.
of kawwana § Yammako̲
kawanna'alitok. I was there,
bowlegged.
káwwaski ggr. of kawaski
kawwi to break (sticks, for instance)
to make them short enough to fit
(pl. obj.) (I;3) {v1. kawa; ggr. ká'wwi;
hngr. kaha̲wwi; ngr. ka̲wwi}
kayya to be full (after eating) (II); to be
full of (a food or drink) (II;3) [-PR]
[-CPR] {ggr. ká'yya; hgr. káhhayya;
ngr. ka̲yya} § Tako̲lo sakayyatok. I'm
full of peaches.
káyya'a, káyya'ha to lie down, be
lying (I); to lie down in (a location)
(I;3) (dl. subj.) {sg. ti'wa; tpl. kahat
ma̲a}—ygr. of <kaha> § Topa
iikáyya'ha. The two of us are lying
in bed.
káyya'ha see káyya'a
káyya'llo ygr. of kallo
kayyachi to fill up (with food—
especially, a pet or baby) (I;II)
[kayya+chi]
kayyachit abi to kill (nonhum. obj.—
baby birds, for instance) by
overfeeding (I;3) [kayyachi+t]
kaa, kaar, kaa' car [from the English]
kaa aawayaachi' garage (for one car)

[kaa aa+wayaachi+']
kaa aawayoochi' parking lot (for many cars) [aa+wayoochi+']
kaa iksaachi' mechanic [iksaachi+']
kaa ishpa̲achi', kaa ishtaapa̲a', kaa ishtaapa̲achi' car horn [isht (aa+)pa̲a+chi+']
kaa ishtachifa' chamois, car cloth [isht achifa+']
kaa ishtaapa̲a' see kaa ishpa̲achi'
kaa ishtaapa̲achi' see kaa ishpa̲achi'
kaa' see kaa
kaa-at imilli to have one's car battery die (III) [kaa+at]
kaafaafoloha' coffee grinder [kaafi' aa+foloha+']
kaafaaishkimpatha' saucer [kaaf-aaishko' im+patha+']
kaafaaishko' coffee cup, teacup [kaafi' aa+ishko+']
kaafaaishko' aayo'kli' coffee cup handle
kaafaawalhahli', kaafaawalhaali' coffeepot [kaafi' aa+walhahli+']
kaafaawalhahli' ibichchala' coffeepot spout
kaafi' coffee [from the English?]
kaafi' ani' coffee beans
kaafi' bota' instant coffee; (ER) ground coffee [bota+']
kaafi' foloha' see kaafi' folowa'
kaafi' folowa', kaafi' foloha' ground coffee [folowa+']
kaafi' lakchi' dregs of coffee
kaafi' losa' black coffee [losa+']
kaafi' nihi' coffee beans
kaafishfoloha' coffee grinder [kaafi' isht foloha+']
kaak kaak kaak aachi, ka'k ka'k ka'k aachi to make a sound like a crow (expressive) (I)
kaala' collar [from the English]
kaala' cha̲la' removable starched shirt collar [cha̲la+']

kaalli to call on the phone (I;II) (the beginning of this word is pronounced like English call) [from English call] § Issakaallitok. You called me.
kaalhkaha to cluck
kaar see kaa
kaawa, (WB) ka̲wa to bark like a fox (I)
Kaayowa name of an Oklahoma Indian tribe (CC) [from English Kiowa]
ka̲'shcha kaniya to abandon, go off and leave (permanently) (I;II , I) (cha expression; includes kanchi) § Issaka̲'shcha ishkaniyatok. You abandoned me.
ká̲ha, ká̲a to be there, stay, be left (dl. subj.) (I)—ngr. of kaha {sg. tó̲wa; tpl. á̲sha; á̲shwa}
ká̲hli hngr. of kahli
ká̲llo ngr. of kallo
kalhkaha to make a chicken's noise (3) {hngr. kalhkahá̲a}
kalhkahá̲a hngr. of kalhkaha
<ká̲na> in inká̲na
ká̲shcha aya to leave behind, go off from (temporarily) (I;II , I) (cha expression; includes ká̲nchi) (see aya) § Saka̲shcha ayatok. He left me behind. | Issaka̲shcha ishiyyatok. You left me behind.
ká̲wwi ngr. of kawwi
ká̲yya ngr. of kayya
kendi' candy [from the English]
kendi' bala' see bala' kendi'
kendi' kallo' hard candy, rock candy [kallo+']
<ki'> in inki'
kí'nni ggr. of kinni
ki'yo no; not, be not (aux.); to not be (3;3C) (requires overt preceding complement noun; followed by +ki before certain suffixes) § Itha̲nali

kidi'

ano' ki'yoka. I know it's not me. | Lynnat ishtikayoppo alikchi' ki'yokat. Lynn is sad that she is not a doctor. | Lynnat alikchi' ki'yokita? Isn't Lynn a doctor?

kidi' cat (CC) [from English kitty]

kifaháa hngr. of kifaa

kifaa, (AW) kifaa, (EH) kifaha to groan, grunt (with pain or exertion) (I) {hngr. kifaháa} § Ikkifa'o. He didn't groan.

kihíli hngr. of kihli

kihílhlhi hngr. of kilhlhi

kihísli hngr. of kisli

kihli to wipe oneself (after defecation or urination) (I) {hngr. kihíli; ngr. kíhli}

kilaa to burn, be burning, flame (II) [-PR] [-CPR] {v2. kilili; ngr. kiláha: to burn with a flame}

kiláha to burn with a flame—ngr. of kilaa

kilihímpi hngr. of kilimpi

kilihíha hngr. of kiliha

kilihíya hngr. of kiliha

kilili to set afire; to strike (a match) (I;II) {akiliili; v1. kilaa}

kilimpi to be strong (II) {ggr. kílli'pi: to be solid; hngr. kilihímpi; ngr. kilímpi; ygr. kilíyyi'pi; kallo, inkilish}

<kilish> in inkilish

kilíyyi'pi ygr. of kilimpi

kiliha, kiliya to growl, roar (I) [+CPR] [-PR] {hngr. kilihíha, kilihíya}

kilihachi to make growl (I;II) [kiliha+chi]

kiliya see kiliha

kílli'pi to be solid—ggr. of kilimpi

kilhlhi to bite on, gnaw (I;II) {hngr. kihílhlhi; ngr. kílhlhi} § Kintaat itti' kilhlhi. The beaver is gnawing the wood.

kina to be transplanted, set out (rare)

(3) [+T] {v2. kinni}

kiná'ffi ggr. of kinaffi

kinafa to lean, fall over (sg. subj.) (3) {v2. kinaffi; hngr. kinaháfa; pl. kinahli}

kinaffi to push over, make fall (sg. obj.) (I;3) {v1. kinafa; ggr. kínnaffi, kiná'ffi; hngr. kinaháffi; pl. obj. kinaachi}

kinaháfa hngr. of kinafa

kinaháffi hngr. of kinaffi

kinaháli hngr. of kinahli

kinahchi see kinaachi

kinahli to fall down (pl. subj.) (3) {hngr. kinaháli; sg. kinafa}

kinaachi, kinahchi to knock down (pl. obj.) (I;3) [-SC] [kinahli+chi] {sg. obj. kinaffi} § Ikkina'chokitok, Ikkinahchokitok. He didn't knock them down.

kínnaffi ggr. of kinaffi

kinni to transplant (I;3) {v1. kina; ggr. kí'nni}

kinta beaver

kisafa to be cracked (sg. subj.), to have one crack (3) {pl. kisahli}

kisaháli hngr. of kisahli

kisahli to be cracked (pl. subj.), to have lots of little cracks (3) {hngr. kisaháli; ngr. kisáhli; sg. kisafa}

kisáhli ngr. of kisahli

kisichi to make ˚ bite ˚ (I;II;3) [-SC] [kisili+chi] {hngr. kisilihínchi, kisiihínchi} § Josephineat Lynn sakisilishtok. Josephine made Lynn bite me, Josephine made me bite Lynn.

kisili to bite (especially, once), take a bite out of (mainly sg. obj., mainly sg. subj.) (I;II) [-OPR] {hngr. kisihíli; pl. obj., subj. kisli}

kisilihínchi, kisiihínchi hngrs. of kisichi

kisit toshaffi to bite a piece out of (I;II)

kobaffi

[kisili+t] § Kisit satoshaffitok. He bit a piece out of me.
kisli to gnash one's teeth, bite (like a dog); to bite more than once; to bite (pl. obj.); to bite (pl. subj.) (I;II) {hngr. kihísli; sg. obj., sg. subj. kisili}
kitafa to be cracked, to have a crack (of the ground, for example— mainly sg. subj.) (3) {pl. kitahli}
kitaháli hngr. of kitahli
kitahli to be cracked (pl. subj.) (3) {hngr. kitaháli; sg. kitafa}
kitiini horned owl, great horned owl
kitoba bottle, jar (made of glass)
kitoba aapishi', kitobaapishi' nipple (on a baby bottle) [kitoba aa+pishi+']
kitoba holba' plastic bottle
kitoba ibish pump dispenser on a soap or lotion bottle (with a bend at the top)
kitoba ishtokshili'ta' cork (for a bottle) [isht okshilitta+']
kitoba nanna-aalhto' mason jar
kitoba nannalhto' canned goods
kitobabihli to can, put up (especially, large round things like peaches or tomatoes) (I;3) [kitoba *abihli] {kitobani} § Takolo
kitobabihlila'chi. I'm going to can the peaches.
kitobacho'sha' type of plant with purple blooms on a long stalk [kitoba achoosha+' ?]
kitobalhiipi'ya' bottle cap; canning jar lid and ring [kitoba alhiipi'ya']
kitobani to can, put up (especially, small things like beans) (I;3) [kitoba *ani] {kitobani} § Bala' kitoba ishannitam? Did you can the beans?
kitobaa-abihli to can some of (peaches, for instance) (I;3) [kitoba *aa-abihli] § Takolo yappako kitobaa-abihlila'chi. I'm going to can some of these peaches.

kitobaa-ani to can some of (beans, for instance) (I;3) [kitoba *aa-ani] § Bala' yappako kitoba ishaa-anitam? Did you can some of these beans?
kitobaapishi' see kitoba aapishi'
kitobishtiwwi' bottle opener [kitoba isht tiwwi+']
kitoboshi' little bottle [kitoba oshi']
kitti' wooden mortar for grinding corn
kii oh! (exclamation of surprise)
kiihi hey! (exclamation indicating indignation); whew! (exclamation indicating tiredness or exhaustion)
kiitatak spotted sawyer beetle (WB)
kiiyoho', (TJ) kiiyo'o' girlie, sister (used about a girl in the family— often as a term of address)
kíhli ngr. of kihli
kílhlhi ngr. of kilhlhi
ko' exclamation of surprise (OC) (Ct)
ko'b ko'b ko'b aachi see kob kob kob aachi
kó'lli ggr. of kolli
ko'm ko'm ko'm aachi see kom kom kom aachi
kó'wa ggr. of kowa
kob kob kob aachi, ko'b ko'b ko'b aachi to make the sound of something inside a hollow container, or the sound of wood being hit (expressive) (I) {<kobo'chi>}
kobá'ffi ggr. of kobaffi
kobafa to break, be broken (of something long) (sg. subj.) (3); to be broke, out of cash (II) [+PR] [+CPR] {v2. kobaffi; ggr. kóbba'fa; hngr. kobaháfa; pl. kobahli; kowa: to break (of something round)}
kobaffi to break (a sg. long obj.); to impoverish (I;II) {v1. kobafa; ggr. kóbbaffi, kobá'ffi; hngr. kobaháffi; pl. obj. kobbi, kobaachi; kooli: to break

223

kobaháfa

(a round obj.)} § anompa kobaffi: to
break one's word | nannalhpisa'
kobaffi: to break the law
kobaháfa hngr. of kobafa
kobaháffi hngr. of kobaffi
kobaháli hngr. of kobahli
kobahli to break, be broken (of long
obj.) (pl. subj.), to be all broken (3)
{hngr. kobaháli; sg. kobafa; kobbi,
kobaachi}
kobahlihínchi hngr. of kobaachi
kobaachi to break (pl. long obj.) (I;3)
[+SC] [kobahli+chi] {hngr.
kobahlihínchi; sg. obj. kobaffi;
kobbi}
kóbba'fa ggr. of kobafa
kóbbaffi ggr. of kobaffi
kobbi to break (pl. long obj.) (I;3)
{hngr. kohómbi; sg. obj. kobaffi;
kobahli; kobaachi}
<kóbbokli'chi> in ittikóbbokli'chi—
klgr. of <kobo'chi>
kóbbokshi to be hunched over,
doubled up—ggr. of kobokshi
kóbbossa ggr. of kobossa
<kobo'chi> in ittikobo'chi {klgr.
<kóbbokli'chi>; rcgr. <kobobó'chi>;
kob kob kob aachi, kobok kobok
kobok aachi, kobo'kachi; kobokshi,
<koboli>, kobolli', kobossa}
kobo'kachi to make a bumping noise
(3) {<kobo'chi>}
<kobobó'chi> in ittikobobó'chi—
rcgr. of <kobo'chi>
kobohósa hngr. of kobossa, <kobosa>
kobok kobok kobok aachi to make
the sound of something inside a
hollow container, or of wood being
hit (expressive) (I) {<kobo'chi>}
kobokshi to be humped up; to have a
hump (II) {ggr. kóbbokshi: to be
hunched over, doubled up; ygr.
kobóyyokshi; <koboli>, kobolli'} §
issoba kobokshi': camel

<koboli> in oshkoboli, yalhkobo'li'
kobolli' bunch of little things
{chipota kobolli'; itti' kobolli';
tanchi' kobolli'} § Kobolli' poya.
We're little.
<kobosa> var. grade base for kobossa
{hngr. kobohósa}
kobossa to have a convex shape
relative to a horizontal surface:
especially, of something whose
edges have warped up, but which
has been turned over (3) {ggr.
kóbbossa; hngr. kobohósa; ygr.
kobóyyo'ssa; <kobosa>}
kobóyyo'ssa ygr. of kobossa
kobóyyokshi ygr. of kobokshi
kochcha to go out, come out (of a
person, or of the sun or moon), rise
(of the sun or moon), be out (in
baseball) (I) [+PR] [-CPR] [+taha] {v2.
kochchi; ggr. kôchcha; hngr.
kohónchcha; ngr. kónchcha;
kochchi; aakochcha: to go out of} §
Ishkochcha! You're out!
kôchcha ggr. of kochcha
kochcha' outside, the outside
[kochcha+'] § Kochcha'at palli.
Outside it's hot. | Kochchaak
wayyayaalitok. I'm outside on my
hands and knees pulling grass.
kochcha' aya to go out, go outside; to
go to the bathroom (euphemistic) (I)
kochcha' pitkanchi to throw out,
kick out (I;II) [pit *kanchi]
kochchat minti to come up (of the
sun) (3) [kochcha+t]
kochchaafokka' clearing, valley—an
open place out in the middle of
nowhere [kochcha' aa+fokha+']
kochchaakaali to take out, put out
(pl. obj.) (I;II) {sg. obj. ishkochcha}
<kochchaalínchi> in kochchaalisht
kochchaalisht being outside—prt. of
<kochchaalínchi>

224

kochchali' (moving) outside {kochcha'} § Kochchali' aatok. He went along outside (the fence, for instance).

kochchi to take out one's penis (I) {v1. kochcha; hngr. kohónchchi; ngr. kónchchi; kochcha}

kochchí'chi ggr. of kochchichi

kochchichi to put out, to make (someone) go out: especially, to impeach, vote out of office; to evict (I;II) [kochcha/kochchi+chi] {ggr. kochchí'chi}

kóffolli ggr. of kofolli

kofi quail

kofishto' pheasant [kofi oshi']

kofó'lli ggr. of kofolli

kofohólli hngr. of kofolli

kofohóllit prt. of kofohólli—can be used to refer to a person [kofoholli+t] § Kofohollit hikki'yalitok. I stood there steaming.

kofolli, kofotli to steam (of water, hot food, one's breath on a cold day) (3) {ggr. kóffolli, kofó'lli; hngr. kofohólli; ngr. kofólli}

kofollichi to make (a liquid) steam (I;3) [kofolli+chi]

kof-oshi' little quail [kofi oshi']

kofotli see kofolli

kofólli ngr. of kofolli

kohómbi hngr. of kobbi

kohónchcha hngr. of kochcha

kohónchchi hngr. of kochchi

kohónta hngr. of konta

kohóli hngr. of kooli

kohólli hngr. of kolli

kola to be dug (3) {v2. kolli}

kolli to dig (I;3) {v1. kola; ggr. kó'lli; hngr. kohólli; ngr. kólli} § Akkollo. I didn't dig it.

kóllo'fa ggr. of kolofa

kolofa to be cut, cut off (II) {v2.

koloffi; ggr. kóllo'fa; kolohli}

koloffi to cut (especially, with a knife), to cut off, break off a part of (I;II) {v1. kolofa; ngr. kolófi} § aakoloffi: to break off a part of I inkoloffi: to break off a part for

kolohli to have knife cuts all over one, to be cut up (II) {kolofa}

kolófi ngr. of koloffi

kom kom kom aachi, ko'm ko'm ko'm aachi to make a banging sound (expressive) (I) {komo'chi}

kombo' okra [from English gumbo]

kombo' awaalhaali' fried okra [awaalhaali+']

kómmokli'chi to hit (making a noise) (I;II)—klgr. of komo'chi

komo'chi to make a big noise (I) [±SC] {klgr. kómmokli'chi; rcgr. komomó'chi; kom kom kom aachi, komok komok komok aachi}

komoha to have pains (II)

komok komok komok aachi to make the sound of banging or hitting (expressive) (I) {komo'chi}

komomó'chi to go along making a clanging noise (I)—rcgr. of komo'chi {ngr. komomo'chi; komo'chi}

komomó'chi ngr. of komomó'chi

komoochi to have rheumatism, arthritis; to have an ache in the bones, perhaps from standing in very cold water (II) [-SC] [komoha+chi]

komoowachi to buzz (like a bee) (I) {ngr. komoowánchi}

komoowánchi ngr. of komoowachi

kónchcha in ootkónchcha—ngr. of kochcha

kónchchi ngr. of kochchi

koni skunk

koni chokcho' civet cat; small striped skunk

koni hollisso

koni hollisso small spotted skunk (MC)
<kónno'fa> in akónno'fa, ittakónno'fa
konta to whistle (with the lips or a blade of grass—not with an instrument) (I); to whistle (a tune) (I;3) [+CPR] [-PR] {ggr. kó̱'ta; hngr. kohónta; inkonta: to whistle at} § "Amazing Grace" kontalitok. I whistled "Amazing Grace".
kontá'chi ggr. of kontachi
kontachi to make (someone) whistle (I;II) [konta+chi] {ggr. kontá'chi}
kosóhho'ma hgr. of kosoma
kosoh ó̱ma hngr. of kosoma
kosoma to be smelly (II) [+CPR] [+PR] {ggr. kósso'ma; hgr. kosóhho'ma; hngr. kosoh ó̱ma; ngr. kos ó̱ma; ygr. kosóyyo'ma} § issi' kosoma': goat
kosomachi to make smelly (I;II) [kosoma+chi] {hngr. kosomahánchi}
kosomahánchi hngr. of kosomachi
kosomoshi' little stinker (a pet name) (MJ) [kosoma+' oshi']
kosóyyo'ma ygr. of kosoma
kos ó̱ma ngr. of kosoma
kósso'ma ggr. of kosoma
kostí'ni in ootkosti'ni—ggr. of kostini
kostini to come to one's senses, sober up (II) {ggr. kostí'ni; ngr. kost ị́ni: to behave; to be sober; ygr. kostíyyi'ni; neg. ikkosti'no: be funny}
kostinichi to tame (a wild horse, for example), to sober (someone) up (I;II) [kostini+chi]
kostíyyi'ni ygr. of kostini
kostíyyi'ni ki'yo to be wild, kind of crazy (II)
kost ị́ni to behave, sit quietly (I / II); to be sober (II) [+PR] [+CPR] —ngr. of kostini

koshibba', (ER, ML) koshobba' poke salad, poke weed
koshibba' hakshish poke root (used for medicine)
kotoh ó̱ma hngr. of kotoma
kotoma to be bad smelling, rancid (of oil, grease) (II) {ggr. kótto'ma; hngr. kotoh ó̱ma; ngr. kot ó̱ma; ygr. kotóyyo'ma}
kotóyyo'ma ygr. of kotoma
kótto'ma ggr. of kotoma
kot ó̱ma ngr. of kotoma
kowa to break, crack; to be broken (of a round obj.) (3) [-CPR] [+PR] {v2. kooli; ggr. kó'wa}
kow-as ị̱'bish type of roadside plant with tall green stalks [kowi' hasimbish]
kowi' cat
kowi' hasimbish cattail (ER, CC, CP, LF), catnip (WB)
kowi' imimpa' see kowimpa'
kowi' oshpishichi' mother cat with nursing kittens
kowi-homma' cow-killer (insect sp.) [kowi' homma+']
kow-imilhlha' wildcat [kowi' imilhlha+']
kowimpa', kowi' imimpa' cat food [kowi' (im+)impa+']
kowinchosh bobcat [kowi' <akchosh>]
kowinchosh losa' type of bobcat [losa+']
kowi-p a̱achi' mountain boomer—large lizard sp. [kowi' p a̱a+chi+']
kowishki' mother cat [kowi' ishki']
kowishtapa' large maggot [kowishto' apa+' ?]
kowishto, kowishto', (JC, CC) kow-ishto', (ER) kowi' ishto' lion, tiger, mountain lion, wildcat [kowi' ishto+']
kowishto' see kowishto

lalli

kowishto' losa' panther [losa+']
kowishto' shiwaa' tiger [shiwaa+']
kow-oshi' kitten [kowi' oshi']
koyofa to be striped with one stripe
going around the body (of a hog, for
example) (II) [+PR] [+CPR] {v2.
koyoffi}
koyoffi to make a stripe around the
body of (I;II) {v1. koyofa}
koyoha, (MJ, LF) koyowa to be
wrinkled (of clothes, paper) (3) {v2.
koyohli; ggr. kóyyo'ha; ngr. koyǫ́ha}
koyohli to wrinkle, ball up
(something) (I;II) {v1. koyoha; hngr.
koyohǫ́li} § ishkin koyohli: to rub
one's eyes
koyohǫ́li hngr. of koyohli
koyota (LR), (PBr) koyita to be
wrinkled {koyoha}
koyǫ́ha ngr. of koyoha

kóyyo'ha ggr. of koyoha
kookoli to break (compact obj.) (pl.
obj.) (for instance, to crack nuts) (I;3)
[+OPR] {v1. kookowa; sg. obj. kooli}
kookowa to break, be broken (of
compact obj.) (pl. subj.) (3) {v2.
kookoli; sg. kowa}
kookowa to make a noise like a
squirrel (ER)
kooli to break, crack (a compact obj.)
(I;3) (for instance, to crack a nut or
break a dish) [+OPR] {v1. kowa; ggr.
kó'li; hngr. kohǫ́li; ngr. kǫ́li; pl. obj.
kookoli} § Charlesak amposhi'
inkoolilitok. I broke Charles's dish.
kǫ́'ta ggr. of konta
kǫ́li ngr. of kooli
kǫ́lli ngr. of kolli
koshchi' dogwood (CP)

1

lá'lli ggr. of lalli
la's la's la's aachi see las las las aachi
lá'wa ggr. of lawa
lá'wwi ggr. of lawwi
labaachi to talk all the time [-SC] (I)
{hngr. labaahánchi; labbi ?}
labaahánchi hngr. of labaachi
labbi to lick (I;3) (rare alternative to
pitlabbi) § Ishlabbinna! Don't lick it!
labbit pisa to taste by taking a little
lick (I;3) [labbi+t] § Ashiila labbit
pisalitok. I tasted the soup.
lahángna hngr. of lakna
lahǫ́lli hngr. of lalli
lahǫ́wwi hngr. of lawwi
láhhakna hgr. of lakna
láhhashpa to be barely warm—hgr.
of lashpa
lakchi' dregs, remainder (for

instance, what's left in the sifter
after you're done sifting) (normally
preceded by another noun) § kaafi'
lakchi': coffee dregs
lakna to be yellow, brown, gold (II)
[+CPR] {ggr. lâkna; hgr. láhhakna;
hngr. lahángna; ngr. lángna; ygr.
láyyakna}
lâkna ggr. of lakna
lakna losayyi to be dark yellow,
brown (3) [lakna+t]
laknachi to make brown, yellow (I;II)
[lakna+chi] {ngr. laknánchi: to make
browner}
laknánchi to make browner,
yellower—ngr. of laknachi
laknaak howita to vomit bile (II / I)
[lakna'+ak]
lalli, latli to chop up (meat, or

227

lángna

slippery elm or other bark for
medicine—usually not with an an.
obj.) (I;II) {v1. lata; ggr. lá'lli; hngr.
lahálli; lataffi}
lángna ngr. of lakna
lapaháli hngr. of lapali
lapali to stick (of rice in a pan, for
instance) (3); to have sexual
intercourse with (a woman) (of a
man) (I;II) {ggr. láppa'li: to stick on
(sg.); hngr. lapaháli; ngr. lapáli: to be
left sticking; rmgr. lappapáli}
lapaachi to stick on, stick onto (sg.
obj.) (I;II) [±SC] [lapali+chi] {hngr.
lapaahánchi, lapaalihínchi; ngr.
lapáanchi, lapaalínchi; pl. obj.
lapoochi}
lapaahánchi, lapaalihínchi hngr. of
lapali
lapaalínchi, lapáanchi ngr. of
lapaachi
lapáli to be left sticking (of
something in a pan) (3)—ngr. of
lapali
lapish horn; antenna, feeler (IIp);
instrument made from an animal's
horn
lapish falaa, lapish falaa' buck with
well-developed antlers; longhorn
steer [lapish falaa+']
lapish falaa' see lapish falaa
lapish falowa' macaroni (CC)
lapish kolofa' horn (instrument or
powder horn—usually, one made
from an animal's horn) [kolofa+']
<lapohli> in lapoht máa, lapoochi
{ggr. láppohli; hngr. lapohóli; ngr.
lapóhli; rmgr. lappopóli; ittilapoli}
lapohóli hngr. of <lapohli>, láppohli
lapoht máa, lapoot máa to stick on,
be sticking to (pl. subj.) (I;3)
[<lapohli>+t] {sg. láppa'li; dl.
láppohli} § Lapoht kiimaatok. We
are sticking on it.

lapoochi to stick on, stick onto (pl.
obj.) (I;II) [±SC] [<lapohli>+chi] {sg.
obj. lapaachi}
lapoot máa see lapoht máa
lapóhli to be left sticking (dl.) (3)—
ngr. of <lapohli>, láppohli
láppa'li to stick on, be sticking to (sg.
subj.) (I;3)—ggr. of lapali {dl.
láppohli; tpl. lapoht máa}
lappapáli to climb up (a tree, a house)
(sg. subj.) (I;3)—rmgr. of lapali {dl.
lappopóli}
láppohli to stick on, be sticking to (dl.
subj.) (I;3)—ggr. of <lapohli> {hngr.
lapohóli; ngr. lapóhli: to be left
sticking; rmgr. lappopóli; sg.
láppa'li; tpl. lapoht máa}
lappopóli to climb up (a tree, house)
(dl. subj.) (I;3)—rmgr. of <lapohli>,
láppohli {sg. lappapáli}
las las las aachi, la's la's la's aachi to
make a smacking noise while eating
(expressive) (I) {<lasa'chi>}
<lasa'chi> in ittilasa'chi {klgr.
<lássakli'chi>; rcgr. <lasasá'chi>; las
las las aachi, lasak lasak lasak aachi}
lasak lasak lasak aachi to make a
smacking noise while eating
(expressive) (I) {<lasa'chi>}
<lasasá'chi> in ittilasasá'chi—rcgr. of
<lasa'chi>
<lássakli'chi> in ittilássakli'chi—
klgr. of <lasa'chi>
lashpa to be warm (of a solid, not a
liquid) (II) [+PR] [+CPR] {hgr.
láhhashpa: to be barely warm; ngr.
láshpa; ygr. láyya'shpa}
lashpachi to warm (something) (I;II)
[lashpa+chi] {ngr. lashpánchi: to
make warmer}
lashpánchi ngr. of lashpachi
lata to be chopped (3) [+T] {v2. lalli}
latafa to be hurt, pinched, stubbed (II)
{v2. lataffi}

lataffi to step on, stub (toes), to smash (hands with a hammer, for example) (I;II) {v1. latafa; hngr. latahá̱ffi; lalli} § Sayyi' lataffilitok. I stubbed my toe.
latahá̱ffi hngr. of lataffi
latahá̱ssa, latahá̱sa hngr. of latassa, <latasa>
<latasa> var. grade base for latassa {hngr. latahá̱sa; ngr. latá̱sa; ygr. latáyya'sa}
latassa to be flat (II) {v2. latassali; ggr. láttassa: to be flat-chested, skinny, all by oneself (I); hngr. latahá̱ssa, latahá̱sa; ngr. latá̱ssa, latá̱sa; ygr. latáyya'ssa, latáyya'sa; pl. latastowa; <latasa>}
latassachi to flatten, squash; to let the air out of (sg. obj.) (I;II) [latassa+chi] {pl. obj. latastowachi}
latassali to flatten (sg. obj.) (I;II) {v1. latassa; pl. obj. latastowachi}
latastowa to be flat (pl. subj.) (3) (Ct?) {sg. latassa}
latastowachi to flatten (pl. obj.) (I;3) {sg. obj. latassachi, latassali}
latáyya'ssa, latáyya'sa ygr. of latassa, <latasa>
latá̱ssa, latá̱sa ngr. of latassa, <latasa>
latli see lalli
láttassa to be flat-chested, skinny; to be all alone by oneself (I)—ggr. of latassa
lawa to be many, to be a lot, to be a bunch (I); to be a lot in (a place) (3;3) [+PR] [+CPR] {ggr. lá'wa; ngr. lá̱wa: to be more; ygr. láyya'wa} § Hattakat chincokkaako̱ lawa. There's a lot of people there. I Kiilawa. There are a lot of us.
lawachi to accumulate (a lot of) (I;3) [lawa+chi]
lawashki to be warm (of a liquid) (3) [+PR] [+CPR] {ggr. láwwashki; ngr.

lawá̱shki; ygr. lawáyya'shki}
lawashkichi to warm (a liquid) (I;3) [lawashki+chi] {hngr. lawashkihínchi; ngr. lawashkínchi: to make warmer}
lawashkihínchi hngr. of lawashkichi
lawashkínchi to make warmer—ngr. of lawashkichi
lawáyya'shki ygr. of lawashki
lawá̱shki ngr. of lawashki
<lawichi> {ggr. láwwi'chi}
láwwashki ggr. of lawashki
lawwi to sting (of salt, acid, alcohol on a wound) (3); to stain (of a plant substance) (3;3); to be stained with (3;3) {ggr. lá'wwi; hngr. lahá̱wwi; ngr. lá̱wwi; i̱lawwi; alawwichi} § Tako̱laat naafka̱ lawwitaha. The peach (juice) stained the dress. I A̱naafkaat tako̱lo lawwitahatokchayni. My dress got stained with peach (juice).
lawwí'chi ggr. of lawwichi
láwwi'chi to keep up with; to have almost as good a score as (I;II); to be as much as (I;II) [E+kat]—ggr. of <lawichi> {ngr. lawwínchi; neg. iklawwi'cho; lawa, <lawwichi>} § Ishtokat chilawwi'shli. I'm as big as you. I Hopookat chilawwi'shli. I'm as jealous as you. I Intakho'bikat chilawwi'shli. I'm as lazy as you.
lawwichi to stain (something, accidentally) with (a plant substance) (I;3;3) [lawwi+chi] {ggr. lawwí'chi; hngr. lawwihínchi; ngr. lawwínchi} § Benjieat imbalaafka̱ hashshok lawwichitahatok. Benjie got a grass stain on his pants. I Chi̱naafka̱ hashshok ishlawwichitokchayni. You've got a grass stain on your dress.
<lawwichi> in ittilawwichi; var. grade base for láwwi'chi {ngr.

lawwínchi}
lawwihínchi hngr. of lawwichi
lawwínchi ngr. of láwwi'chi,
lawwichi, <lawwichi>
láyya'wa ygr. of lawa
láyyakna ygr. of lakna
láyya'shpa ygr. of lashpa
laa to be plowed (3) [+T] {v2. liili,
liichi}
laay lye [from the English]
láshpa ngr. of lashpa
láwa to be more—ngr. of lawa
láwwi ngr. of lawwi
Leblan Lebanon, Oklahoma [from
the English]
leeti to be late (I) (slang) [from the
English]
lí'li ggr. of liili
líbbo'sha to be limp (like a rag doll,
or a paralyzed child) (II); to be limp
in (a place) (3;3)
likinta to stop, die down (of the
wind) (II / I); to have no wind (of a
place) (3) {ggr. líkki'ta} §
Oklahomma'at likki̱'ta. There's no
wind in Oklahoma.
líkki̱'ta ggr. of likinta
lili' lily (Ct?) [from the English] §
Lili' liilili. I'm hoeing the lilies.
Linho' Chickasaw woman's name
litiha, litiya to be dirty (II) [+PR]
[+CPR] {v2. litihli; ggr. lítti'ha; hngr.
litihí̱ha; ngr. liti̱ha; ygr. litíyyi'ha}
litihí̱ha hngr. of litiha
litihí̱li hngr. of litihli
litihli to get (something) dirty (I;II)
{v1. litiha; hngr. litihí̱li; ngr. liti̱hli:
to make dirtier}
litiya see litiha
litíyyi'ha ygr. of litiha
liti̱ha ngr. of litiha
liti̱hli to make dirtier—ngr. of litihli
lítti'ha ggr. of litiha
liwahá̱li hngr. of liwaali

liwaali to have canker sores (II)
{hngr. liwahá̱li} § Satiat liwaali. My
mouth has canker sores. |
Saliwaatok. I had canker sores.
liichi to plow; to plow under (I;3)
[-SC] [liili+chi] {hngr. liihínchi}
liihínchi hngr. of liichi
liili to hoe (I;3) [laa+li] {v1. laa; ggr.
lí'li; liichi}
ló'hmi ggr. of lohmi
ló'sa ggr. of losa
ló'shka ggr. of loshka
lobahli' in nita' lobahli'
lóbbonni ggr. of lobonni
lobli to plug, stop up, clog
(something) (I;3) {v1. lopa}
<lobo> in lobo' {ngr. lómbo}
lobo' round and firm, like a
hardboiled egg—used only in
complex expressions (akankoshi'
lobo', ishkin lobo', tanchi' lobo')
[<lobo>+'] {lobonni, lombo}
lobó'nni ggr. of lobonni
lobohó̱nni hngr. of lobonni
lobona to be boiled (of a round obj.,
like an egg or a potato), to be
hardboiled (3) (Ct) {lobo'; v2.
lobonni}
lobonni to boil (round things, like
eggs or potatoes) (I;II) {v1. lobona;
ggr. lóbbonni, lobó'nni; hngr.
lobohó̱nni}
lofa to be peeled, shucked (II) {v2.
loffi; hngr. lohó̱fa}
lofalhchi to be peeled, shelled (3) [+T]
{v2. loffichi}
loffi to shuck (corn, for instance) (I;II)
{v1. lofa; hngr. lohó̱ffi}
loffí'chi ggr. of loffichi
loffichi to peel, shell (I;II) {v1.
lofalhchi; ggr. loffí'chi; hngr.
loffihínchi}
loffihínchi hngr. of loffichi
lóhho'sa hgr. of losa

lohmi to hide (something or
someone), to keep (something)
secret (I;II) {v1. loma; ggr. ló'hmi;
hngr. lohómi; ngr. lóhmi; ililohmi:
to hide oneself away; ịlohmi: to
hide (something) from}
lohmit ị'shi to keep a secret (I)
[lohmi+t]
lohómpa hngr. of lopa
lohọ́fa hngr. of lofa
lohọ́ffi hngr. of loffi
lohọ́mi hngr. of lohmi
lohọ́sa hngr. of losa
lohọ́shka hngr. of loshka
lohọ́wa hngr. of lowa
lokchabi to be murky from being
stirred up (of water) (PBr, WB) [<
lokchok biyyi'ka / lokchok abi ?]
lokchok mud
Lokchok Abookoshi see Lokchok
Abookoshi'
Lokchok Abookoshi', Lokchok
Abookoshi Muddy Boggy River
[abookoshi+']
lokchok bíyyi'ka to be muddy (II) §
Lokchok sabiyyi'ka. I'm muddy.
lokchok homma' red clay (AB)
[homma+']
lokfabooha' see lokfi' abooha'
lokfamposhi' pottery bowl [lokfi'
amposhi']
lokfi' dirt
lokfi' abooha', lokfabooha' hogan,
dirt house, mud house; cellar,
storm cellar [abooha+']
lokfi' bíyyi'ka to be dirty, full of dirt
(II) § Lokfi' sabiyyi'ka. I'm dirty.
lokfi' chakissa' clay; putty
[chakissa+']
lokfi' homma', lokfomma' red dirt,
red clay [lokfi' homma+']
lokfi' kaha' grave (where the dirt
sinks in on top) [kaha+']
lokfi' kallo' clod, hunk of dirt

[kallo+']
lokfi' kitoba earthenware jug
lokfi' lakna' yellow clay [lakna+']
lokfi' losa' black dirt [losa+']
lokfi' nona' brick [nona+']
lokfi' nona' abooha see lokfi' nona'
abooha'
lokfi' nona' abooha', lokfi' nona'
abooha brick house [abooha+']
lokfi' shaali' mud dauber (WB)
[shaali+']
lokfi' tali' type of stone made of red
clay — it looks like rock, but can be
easily scraped with a knife
lokfi' to'wa' grave—specifically, the
area where the dirt is piled over a
grave [to'wa+']
lokfi' toba to become dust, dirt; to
corrode (especially of buried obj.,
like pipes or corpses) (I)
lokfi' tohbi' type of white dirt—you
can write with it like chalk [tohbi+']
lokfi' tono'chi' mud dauber (ER)
[tono'chi+']
lokfishkolli' grubbing hoe [lokfi' isht
kolli+']
lokfishpiha' shovel, spade; dustpan
[lokfi' ishpiha']
lokfishshaali' wheelbarrow (CP)
[lokfi' isht shaali+']
lokfi-toba to be rusty (II) [+CPR] [+PR]
[lokfi' toba]
lokfomma' see lokfi' homma'
lókko'li to gather in a bunch in (a
place) (pl. subj.) (I;3)—ggr. of
<lokoli> § Yammakọ iilooko'li. We
gathered there (in a bunch).
<lokoli> in lokoli', chokka' lokoli'
{ggr. lókko'li}
lokoli' neighbors [<lokoli>+']
{chokka' lokoli'}
lokosh gourd
lokosh ishtaka'fa', ishtaka'fa' lokosh
cup made from a gourd

loksapaafohli' type of large bird
[loksi' apakfohli+' ?]
loksi' turtle; hanging or combination
lock; ladybug; (AB) doodlebug
Loksi' Chickasaw man's nickname
loksi' hakshop turtle shell
loksi' hasimbish falaa' loggerhead
turtle (WB) [falaa+']
loksi' ishtashana' hanging or
combination lock [isht ashana+']
loksi' latassa', loksi' patassa' flat
turtle (WB) [latassa/patassa+']
loksi' okokaa-asha' water turtle [oka'
okaa-asha+']
loksi' patassa' see loksi' latassa'
loksimpolona, (WB) loksimpono'lo
type of medicinal plant; (LR, WB)
devil's shoestring [loksi'
im+polona]
loksinto̱'ti' ladybug (CC) [loksi'
im+to̱'ti+']
loksishtincho'li' type of yellow vine
(WB) [loksi' isht incho'li+']
loksishto' snapping turtle (AB, WB)
[loksi' ishto+']
loksittish, (LF) loksosh type of
medicinal plant [loksi' ittish]
loksoshi' little ladybug; baby turtle;
turtle egg [loksi' oshi']
loma to hide, be hidden; to play hide
and seek (I) {v2. lohmi; hngr.
lohómi; ngr. lóma; i̱loma}
<lomaka> in i̱lomaka [loma+ka]
lomat ittimanompoli to talk, meet
secretly, to tryst (especially, of
lovers) (I / IR) [loma+t
*itti+im+anompoli] § Lomat
kiitimanompoli. Let's meet in
secret.
lomat ittipisa to see one another
secretly (I / IR) [loma+t *itti+pisa]
lómbo to be spherical, to have a
rounded bottom; to be whole; to be
in the shell (of an egg) (3)—ngr. of

<lobo> § Yaaknaat lombo. The
world is round.
lombo̱ ishtima see lombo̱shtima
lombo̱ ishtimatobbi to pay in full,
pay in a lump sum (I;III) [lombo+ho̱
isht *imatobbi]
lombo̱shtima, lombo̱ ishtima to pay
in full, to pay in one payment (I;III)
[lombo+ho̱ isht *ima] § Lombo̱
ishtishima'chita? Are you going to
pay in full?
lopa to be stuffed up (of the nose), to
be clogged, plugged, stopped up (3)
[+T] {v2. lobli; hngr. lohompa}
lopi' bone marrow; brain (IIIp) §
salbak lopi': my arm marrow |
chiyyi' lopi': your leg marrow |
ishkobo lopi': brain
loposhki to be soft, thin (3) [+PR]
[+CPR] {ggr. lópposhki; ngr.
lopóshki; ygr. loppóyyo'shki}
lopóshki ngr. of loposhki
lópposhki ggr. of loposhki
lopóyyo'shki ygr. of loposhki
losa to be black; to be a black person,
be an African American (II) {v2.
<losli>; ggr. ló'sa; hgr. lóhho'sa;
hngr. lohósa; ngr. lósa; ygr. lóyyo'sa;
losayyi, lóssakbi, <losoli>}
losa' see hattak losa'
losachi to make black (I;II) [losa+chi]
losahángbi hngr. of lóssakbi,
<losakbi>
losahá̱yyi hngr. of losayyi
<losakbi> see lóssakbi [losa] {ggr.
lóssakbi; hngr. losahángbi; ngr.
losángbi}
losángbi ngr. of lóssakbi, <losakbi>
losáyyakbi ygr. of lóssakbi, <losakbi>
losayyi to be dark, almost black (3)
[losa] {ggr. lóssayyi; hngr. losahá̱yyi}
§ laknat losayyi: to be dark yellow,
brown | hommat losayyi: to be dark
red

los-ihoo' see hattak los-ihoo'
<losli> in apoolosli {v1. losa;
<losoli>}
<losoli> in baklosoli {<losli>}
los-oshi' see hattak los-oshi'
lóssakbi to be really black (with dirt,
for example, not in skin color) (II /
I); to be really black in (a place) (I;3)
[losa]—ggr. of <losakbi> {hngr.
losahángbi; ngr. losángbi; ygr.
losáyyakbi}
lóssayyi ggr. of losayyi
loshka to lie, tell a lie; to gossip, talk
casually, visit (especially when used
with "sit") (I) {ggr. ló'shka; hngr.
lohóshka; ngr. lóshka; ygr.
lóyyo'shka; iloshka: to lie to} §
Bini'cha loshka! Sit and visit a
while!
loshohóma hngr. of loshoma
loshoma to be dead; to die, die out; to
pass away (polite term) (II) [+PR]
{v2. loshommi; ggr. lóshsho'ma;
hngr. loshohóma}
loshommi to kill, wipe out
(especially, pl. obj.) (I;II) {v1.
loshoma; ggr. lóshshommi}
lóshsho'ma ggr. of loshoma
lóshshommi ggr. of loshommi
<lotoha> see lotowa {ggr. lótto'ha;
ygr. lotóyyo'ha}
lotolli, lototli to tenderize, beat
(meat, for example) (I;3) (Ct)
{lotooli} § nip-ishlotolli': meat
chopper
lototli see lotolli
lotowa to be smashed, softened (for
instance, of fruit that has been
banged around in a box—not
usually used of a hum. subj.) (3) {v2.
lotooli; ggr. lótto'ha; ygr. lotóyyo'ha;
<lotoha>}
lotóyyo'ha ygr. of lotowa, <lotoha>
lotooli to smash (a bug or fruit, for

example—not usually used with a
hum. obj.) (I;II) {v1. lotowa,
<lotoha>; lotolli}
lótto'ha ggr. of lotowa, <lotoha>
lowa to burn, catch fire (II) [+PR]
[+CPR] {ggr. ló'wa; hngr. lohówa;
ngr. lówa}
lowachi to burn (something), set on
fire; to sterilize; to cremate (I;II)
[lowa+chi]
lowak fire
lowak aa-apiisachi' fire lookout
tower [aa+apiisachi+']
lowak aainni' heater, fireplace
[aa+inni+']
lowak aaolhti' fireplace; firebox (on a
train); heater [aa+olhti+']
lowak aashobohli' fireplace
lowak chipasli, lowakat chipasli to
emit a spark (of flint, for instance)
(3) § Tali'at lowak chipasli. The rock
has a spark come out of it.
lowak chipaslichi to make a spark (by
striking flint, for example) (I)
[chipasli+chi]
lowak ihínni hngr. of lowak inni
lowak imonti' see chanaa malili'
lowak imonti'
lowak inni to get warm by the fire (I)
{hngr. lowak ihínni; ngr. lowak
ínni}
lowak ishbahli' (WB), (AB, LF, MS)
lowak ishbaali', (LR) baali' poker
(for the fire) [isht bahli+']
lowak ishpiha' coal shovel; dustpan
[isht piha+']
lowak ishshafa', (TJ, TP) lowak shafa',
(VB) lowak ishshaffi' poker (for the
fire) [isht <shafa>+']
lowak ishtabi'chi' poker (for the fire)
(MJ) [isht abi'chi+']
lowak ínni ngr. of lowak inni
lowak moshoochi' fire engine;
fireman [moshoochi+']

233

lowak pak<u>a</u>li'

lowak pak<u>a</u>li' type of poisonous
plant (fireweed?), the same as alba
lowak
lowak toba' matches [toba+']
lowak tobaksi' coal (AB)
lowak tob-api' match tree [lowak
toba' api']
lowak tobaalhto' matchbox, match
book [lowak toba' aalhto']
lowakat chipasli see lowak chipasli
loya' lawyer [from the English]

lóyyo'sa ygr. of losa
lóyyo'shka ygr. of loshka
loolo' doodlebug; white man
(children's word) [naahollo ?]
Loon see Ikloon
l<u>ó</u>hmi ngr. of lohmi
l<u>ó</u>ma ngr. of loma
l<u>ó</u>sa ngr. of losa
l<u>ó</u>shka ngr. of loshka
l<u>ó</u>wa ngr. of lowa

lh

lhabahánka hngr. of lhabanka
lhabanka to snore (I) [-PR] [-CPR]
{hngr. lhabahánka}
lhábbi'ta to be a little muddy—ggr. of
lhabita
lhábbo'cha to be soft, ripe—ggr. of
lhabocha
lhábboshli ggr. of lhaboshli
lhabíhhi'ta hgr. of lhabita
lhabihínta hngr. of lhabita
lhabínta ngr. of lhabita
lhabita to be muddy, soft, slippery (of
ground) (3) [-CPR] [+PR] {ggr.
lhábbi'ta: to be a little muddy; hgr.
lhabíhhi'ta; hngr. lhabihínta; ngr.
lhabínta; ygr. lhabíyyi'ta: to be really
muddy}
Lhabita Abookoshi, Lhabita
Abookoshi' Muddy Boggy River
Lhabita Abookoshi' see Lhabita
Abookoshi
lhabíyyi'ta to be really muddy—ygr.
of lhabita
lhabocha to be cooked, done, boiled
(3) {v2. lhaboshli; ggr. lhábbo'cha: to
be soft, ripe; hngr. lhabohóncha;
ngr. lhabóncha; ygr. lhabóyyo'cha}
lhabohóncha hngr. of lhabocha

lhabóncha ngr. of lhabocha
lhaboshli to cook till done or
overdone (I;II) {v1. lhabocha; ggr.
lhábboshli}
lhabóyyo'cha ygr. of lhabocha
lháchcho'fa ggr. of lhachofa
lhacho'li to mash, crush (for
instance, potatoes, beans) (pl. obj.)
(I;II) {v1. lhacho'wa; sg. obj.
lhachoffi}
lhacho'wa to be mashed, smashed
(pl. subj.) (II) [+T] {v2. lhacho'li; sg.
lhachofa}
lhachofa to be crushed, mashed,
smashed (sg. subj.); to have
difficulty breathing when one's
abdomen appears to cave in due to
illness (II) {v2. lhachoffi; ggr.
lháchcho'fa; pl. lhacho'wa}
lhachoffi to crush, mash, smash (sg.
obj.) (I;II) {v1. lhachofa; hngr.
lhachoh<u>ó</u>ffi; pl. obj. lhacho'li}
lhachoh<u>ó</u>ffi hngr. of lhachoffi
<lhaha> in <u>i</u>lhaha {v2. lhahli}
lháhhakcha hgr. of lhakcha
lháhh<u>a</u>'fa hgr. of lh<u>a</u>'fa
lhahkachi to have lines (of a piece of
notebook paper, for example) (3)

234

{v2. lhahli; lhafa: to have a line}
lhahli to bleed someone, let blood (as
part of an old-time cure, collecting
the blood in a cow horn) (of a
doctor) (I); to scribble on, make lines
on (I;II) {v1. lhahkachi, <lhaha>;
ilhahli: to bleed (someone)}
lhakcha to mope; to be lethargic, not
lively; to be in a daze; to look ready
to die (II) {ggr. lhâkcha; hgr.
lháhhakcha; ygr. lháyyakcha}
lhâkcha ggr. of lhakcha
<lhakofa> {v2. lhakoffi; ngr. lhakófa}
lhakoffi to be cured, healed (II) {v1.
<lhakofa>; hngr. lhakohóffi; ngr.
lhakóffi: to be safe; ilhakoffi: to
avoid}
lhakoffichi to heal, cure (I;II)
[lhakoffi+chi] {ngr. lhakoffínchi: to
spare, save}
lhakoffínchi to spare, save—ngr. of
lhakoffichi
lhakohóffi hngr. of lhakoffi
lhakófa to be one left, to be spared, to
be one alone (II)—ngr. of <lhakofa>
{lhakóffi}
lhakóffi to be safe; to be spared; to
survive—ngr. of lhakoffi {lhakófa} §
Hoolhakóffitok. They were spared.
<lhamalli> in noklhamalli
lhatabli to pour out, dump (a liquid),
to put down in a heap (tpl. or mass
obj.); to throw out (tpl. obj.) (I;3); to
let off (tpl. obj.) (I;II) {v1. lhatapa;
ggr. lháttabli; hngr. lhatahámbli;
ngr. lhatámbli; sg. obj. kanchi (pour
out), bohli (put down); dl. obj.
fimmi (pour out), kahli (put down)}
§ Polhatablitok. He let us off.
lhatahámbli hngr. of lhatabli
lhatahámpa hngr. of lhatapa
lhatámbli ngr. of lhatabli
lhatámpa ngr. of lhatapa
lhatapa to drop, fall (pl. inan. subj.),

to spill (of a liquid) (3) {v2. lhatabli;
hngr. lhatahámpa; ngr. lhatámpa;
sg. inan. (fall) ittola; dl. inan. (fall)
kaha}
lháttabli ggr. of lhatabli
lhayí'lli ggr. of lhayilli
lhayihínta hngr. of lhayita
lhayilli, lhayitli to wash, wet
(something) (I;II) {v1. lhayita; ggr.
lháyyilli, lhayí'lli} § Imbalaafka
lhayillitok. He wet his pants.
lhayínta ngr. of lhayita
lhayita to be wet (II) [+PR] [+CPR] {v2.
lhayilli; ggr. lháyyi'ta; hngr.
lhayihínta; ngr. lhayínta; ygr.
lhayíyyi'ta}
lhayitli see lhayilli
lhayíyyi'ta ygr. of lhayita
lháyyakcha ygr. of lhakcha
lháyyi'ta ggr. of lhayita
lháyyilli ggr. of lhayilli
lha'a to be spilled, to spill, slop over
(3) {v2. lha'li; lhaha}
lha'li to spill (something), to let slop
over; to throw (tpl. obj.) away; to
broadcast (seed) (I;3) {v1. lha'a; hngr.
lhahá'li; sg. obj. kanchi; dl. obj.
fimmi}
lhafa to have a line (3)—usually in
hgr. {v2. lhafi; hgr. lháhha'fa;
lhahkachi: to have lines}
lhafi to make a line on, make a mark
on (I;3) {v1. lhafa}
lhí'ka ggr. of lhihka
lhí'li ggr. of lhili
lhibáfa to be narrower [+T]—ngr. of
lhibafa'si
lhibafa'si to be narrow (3)
[lhibafa+a'si] {ngr. lhibáfa}
lhibafachi to make narrow (I;3)—
usually in ngr. [lhibafa+chi] {ngr.
lhibafánchi}
lhibafánchi to make narrower—ngr.
of lhibafachi

lhíbbokta ggr. of lhibokta
lhibli to wear (something) out (I;3)
[+T] {v1. lhipa} § Chipota yammat
sholosh lhiblitaatok. The children
wore out their shoes.
lhibokta to be round, spherical (sg.
subj.) (II) {ggr. lhíbbokta; ngr.
lhibónkta; pl. lhibowa}
lhiboktachi to roll into a ball, to
make round (sg. obj.) (I;3)
[lhibokta+chi] {ngr. lhiboktánchi: to
make rounder}
lhiboktánchi to make rounder—ngr.
of lhiboktachi
lhibónkta ngr. of lhibokta
lhibowa, (TP) lhobowa to be round,
spherical (pl. subj.) (3) {ngr. lhibówa;
sg. lhibokta}
lhibowachi to make (pl. obj.) round
(I;3) [lhibowa+chi]
lhibówa ngr. of lhibowa
lhíffi'chi ggr. of lhifi'chi
lhíffi'li ggr. of lhifi'li
lhiffifíli to let something (one's feet,
for example) drag while going along
(I)—rmgr. of lhifi'li
lhíffilli, lhíffitli to drag oneself
around slowly, stopping
everywhere (I) {lhifi'li}
lhíffitli see lhíffilli
lhifi'chi to pull, drag (I;II) [±SC]
[lhifi'li+chi] {ggr. lhíffi'chi; ngr.
lhifi'línchi; hngr. lhifi'lihínchi} §
Sayyi' lhiffi'shli, lhiffi'chili. I drag
my feet.
lhifi'li to drag, pull oneself (I) {ggr.
lhíffi'li; rmgr. lhiffifíli; lhíffilli}
lhifi'lihínchi hngr. of lhifi'chi
lhifi'línchi ngr. of lhifi'chi
lhiha to be stripped of leaves (of a
plant) (3) {v2. lhihli; lhịfa, lhoha}
lhihchi to strip (a plant) of leaves
(I;3) [lhihli+chi]
lhíhhi'pa hgr. of lhipa

lhíhhị'ko hgr. of lhinko
lhihímpa hngr. of lhipa
lhihínka hngr. of lhihka
lhihị'ko hngr. of lhinko
lhihịfa hngr. of lhịfa
lhihịli hngr. of lhihli, lhili
lhihka, (AB, MC, CP, LP, TP) lhinka
to blow one's nose (I) {ggr. lhí'ka;
hngr. lhihínka; ngr. lhịhka}
lhihkachi, to help (a child) blow his
nose (I;II) [lhihka+chi] {hngr.
lhihkahánchi}
lhihkahánchi hngr. of lhihkachi
lhihli to strip (a plant) of leaves (for
instance, to make a switch) (I;3) {v1.
lhiha; hngr. lhihịli; lhịfi, lhohli}
lhikiiyachi to wheeze (I) {hngr.
lhikiiyahánchi; ngr. lhikiiyánchi}
lhikiiyahánchi hngr. of lhikiiyachi
lhikiiyánchi ngr. of lhikiiyachi
lhikká'chi ggr. of lhikkachi
lhikkachi to have muscle aches from
exertion (II) {ggr. lhikká'chi; ygr.
lhikkáyya'chi}
lhikkáyya'chi ygr. of lhikkachi
lhikommak, (TJ, MJ) lhikomma', (CP,
TP) lhikomma, (AB) lhokomma'
hummingbird
lhilafa to have torn, cut skin (II); to
be torn (sg. subj.) (3) {v2. lhilaffi;
hngr. lhilaháfa; pl. lhilahli}
lhilaffi to tear, rip (something—
especially, paper) (sg. obj.) (I;II) {v1.
lhilafa; hngr. lhilaháffi; pl. obj.
lhillichi}
lhilaháfa hngr. of lhilafa
lhilaháffi hngr. of lhilaffi
lhilaháli hngr. of lhilahli
lhilahli to be torn (pl. subj.); to be all
torn, scratched up (II) {hngr.
lhilaháli; sg. lhilafa; lhillichi}
lhili to put (medicine) on one's head
or hair and rub it in (I;3) {ggr. lhí'li;
hngr. lhihịli} § Ittịsh lhililitok. I put

<lhóchchokli'chi>

medicine on my hair (or head) and rubbed it in.

lhilichi to apply (a rinse or other preparation) to (someone's°) hair (and rub it in); to blow (medicine, through a hollow reed) onto (someone's°) back (I;II;3) [lhili+chi]

lhillichi to tear into pieces, to tear (pl. obj.) (I;II) [+T] {sg. obj. lhilaffi; lhilahli}

lhimishko to be smooth (3); to have smooth skin (like a child's); to be attractive (slang) (II) [+PR] [+CPR] {ggr. lhímmishko; ngr. lhimíshko; ygr. lhimíyyi'shko}

lhimishkochi to smooth, smooth out (I;II) [lhimishko+chi]

lhimíyyi'shko ygr. of lhimishko

lhimíshko ngr. of lhimishko

lhímmishko ggr. of lhimishko

lhímpa to be lying on the face—ngr. of lhipa (almost always used in prt.) {v2. lhipili}

lhímpat face down—prt. of lhímpa (in lhímpat ittola, lhímpat ti'wa, lhímpat wáyya'a) [lhimpa+t]

lhímpat ittola to fall on one's face (II / I) § Lhimpat sattolatok, Lhimpat ittolalitok. I fell on my face.

lhímpat ti'wa to lie face down (I)

lhímpat wáyya'a to lie face down (I) § Lhimpat ishwayya'a. You're lying face down.

lhinko, (AB) lhanko to be fat (II) [+CPR] [-PR] {hgr. lhíhhi'ko; hngr. lhihí'ko; ygr. lhíyyi'ko}

lhipa to wear out, to be worn out, ragged (II) {v2. lhibli; hgr. lhíhhi'pa; hngr. lhihímpa; ngr. lhímpa: to be lying on the face; ygr. lhíyyi'pa; lhipili}

<**lhipichi**> in lhipichit bohli, lhipisht bohli [lhipili+chi]

lhipichit bohli to turn (someone)

over on his face (I;II) [<lhipichi>+t] {lhipisht bohli} § Lhipichit sabohtok. He turned me over on my face.

lhipili to turn (someone) over on his face (Ct?) (I;3)—usually used in prt. {v1. lhímpa; lhipit bohli}

lhipisht bohli to turn (someone) over on his face (3;3) [<lhipichi>+t] {lhipichit bohli}

lhipit bohli to turn (someone) over on his face (I;3) [lhipili+t]

lhipit wayaachi to turn (mainly inan. obj.) over on its face (vulgar with hum. obj.) (I;II) [lhipili+t]

lhitili' see haksibish lhitili'

lhito'li to squeeze (pl. obj.) (I;3); (MS) to knead {sg. obj. lhitoffi}

<**lhito'wa**> in noklhito'wa

<**lhitofa**> in noklhitofa {v2. lhitoffi}

lhitoffi to squeeze (sg. obj.) (I;II) {v1. <lhitofa>; hngr. lhitohóffi; pl. obj. lhito'li}

lhitohóffi hngr. of lhitoffi

lhiyohli to chase (I;II) {ggr. lhíyyohli; hngr. lhiyohóli; ngr. lhiyóhli}

lhiyóhli ngr. of lhiyohli

lhíyyi'pa ygr. of lhipa

lhíyyi'ko ygr. of lhinko

lhíyyohli ggr. of lhiyohli

lhifa to hang unevenly (of a slip showing or an uneven hem), to hang down (of fruit when a vine or tree is pulled down) (3); to have saggy skin (II) {v2. lhifi; hgr. lhíhhi'fa; hngr. lhihífa; lhiha}

lhifi to remove the leaves and fruit from (a branch or vine, by pulling down on it) (I;3) {v1. lhifa; lhihli}

lhíhka ngr. of lhihka

lho'k lho'k lho'k aachi see lhok lhok lhok aachi

<**lhóchchokli'chi**> in ittilhóchchokli'chi—klgr. of

<lhocho'chi>

<lhocho'chi>
<lhocho'chi> in ittilhocho'chi {klgr.
<lhóchchokli'chi>; rcgr.
<lhochochó'chi>}
<lhochochó'chi> in
ittilhochochó'chi—rcgr. of
<lhocho'chi>
lhoha to be stripped of bark (3) [+T]
{v2. lhohli; lhiha, lh̲o̲fa}
lhohli to strip of bark (I;3) {v1. lhoha;
ngr. lh̲ó̲hli; lhihli}
lhohónka hngr. of lhonka
lhok lhok lhok aachi, lho'k lho'k
lho'k aachi to make the sound of a
flexible obj. (such as a whip, towel,
or clothes on a line) cracking,
slapping, or flapping (expressive) (I)
{<lhoko'chi>, lhokk̲a̲ha}
lhókkakli'chi see lhókkokli'chi
lhokk̲a̲a see lhokk̲a̲ha
lhokk̲a̲ha, lhokk̲a̲a to throw
something flexible (and, usually,
relatively wide, like a towel) at; to
hit repeatedly with something
flexible ((I;II) {lhókkokli'chi}
lhókkokli'chi, lhókkakli'chi to hit
(once) with something flexible, like
a towel (I;II)—klgr. of <lhoko'chi>
{lhokk̲a̲ha}
<lhoko'chi> in ittilhoko'chi {klgr.
lhókkokli'chi; rcgr. <lhokokó'chi>;
lhok lhok lhok aachi, lhokk̲a̲ha}
<lhokokó'chi> in ittilhokokó'chi—
rcgr. of <lhoko'chi>
lhonk lhonk lhonk aachi, lho̲'k lho̲'k
lho̲'k aachi to make a grunting
sound (like a pig) (expressive) (I)
{lhonka}
lhonka to oink, grunt (like a pig) (I)
{ggr. lh̲ó̲'ka; hngr. lhohónka; lhonk
lhonk lhonk aachi, lhonklhowa}
lhonklhoh̲ó̲wa hngr. of lhonklhowa
lhonklhowa to grunt, oink (like a
pig) (I) {hngr. lhonklhoh̲ó̲wa;

lhonka}
lhopo'chi to put through, take
through, put across (pl. location
obj.) (I;3;3) [+SC] [lhopo'li+chi] {sg.
location obj. lhopollichi}
lhopo'li to go through, go across (pl.
obj. or in several places) (I;3) {sg. obj.
lhopolli}
lhopó'lli ggr. of lhopolli
lhopoh̲ó̲lli hngr. of lhopolli
lhopolli, lhopotli to go through, go
across (sg. obj.), to pass (a test) (I;3);
to succeed (I); do throughout (all of
a time period) (aux.) (with
preceding time word +na clause)
{ggr. lhóppolli, lhopó'lli; hngr.
lhopoh̲ó̲lli; rmgr. lhoppop̲ó̲li; pl.
obj. lhopo'li} § Ithanali n̲o̲sl̲i̲ wiik
lhopolla'chika, Ithanali n̲o̲sl̲i̲ wiik
lhopolla'chikat. I know that I'm
going to sleep all week.
lhopollí'chi ggr. of lhopollichi
lhopollichi to put ˚ through, take ˚
through, put ˚ across (sg. location
obj.) (I;II;3) {ggr. lhóppolli'chi,
lhopollí'chi; pl. location obj.
lhopo'chi} [lhopolli+chi] §
Ishholissochi' holisso
lhopollichilitok. I put the pen
through the paper.
lhopollichit p̲í̲sa to see ˚ through
(I;II;3) [lhopolli+chi+t] § Winda'
lhopollichit chip̲i̲sli. I can see you
through the window.
lhopotli see lhopolli
lhóppolli ggr. of lhopolli
lhóppolli'chi ggr. of lhopollichi
lhoppop̲ó̲li to go through all around
(I)—rmgr. of lhopolli
lhotafa to be a fatso, to be fat:
especially, to have wide hips (II)
{ggr. lhótta'fa; hngr. lhotah̲á̲fa; ygr.
lhotáyya'fa}
lhotah̲á̲fa hngr. of lhotafa

lhotáyya'fa ygr. of lhotafa
lhótta'fa ggr. of lhotafa
lho̱'k lho̱'k lho̱'k aachi see lhonk
lhonk lhonk aachi
lhǫ'ka ggr. of lhonka
lho̱fa to shed one's skin (of a snake),
have one's skin pulled off; (CC) to
be naked, to be friendless (II) {v2.

lho̱fi; ililho̱fi; lhohli}
Lho̱fa' type of large hairy mythical
creature found in the woods (like
Bigfoot) [lho̱fa+']
lho̱fi to skin (an animal, for
instance); to pull all the clothes off
(I;II) {v1. lho̱fa}
lhǫhli ngr. of lhohli

m

ma hush! listen! § Ma—haklo!
Hush—listen!
má'hli ggr. of mahli
má'lli ggr. of malli
<ma'sha> in ma'shaak, ma'shaakot,
ma'shaako̱, ma'shaat, ma'sha̱,
mashshaash {mishsha'}
ma'shaak that one; that (rare
emphatic nonsubj.)[<ma'sha>+ak]
ma'shaakot that one; that (rare
emphatic and contrastive nonsubj.);
(What about) that one? (used
elliptically as a question)
[<ma'sha>+akot] § Hattak
ma'shaakot lóyyo'shka. That man is
a real liar.
ma'shaako̱ that one; that (rare,
emphatic and contrastive nonsubj.);
(What about) that one? (used
elliptically as a question)
[<ma'sha>+ako̱]
ma'shaat that one (rare emphatic
subj.) [<ma'sha>+at]
ma'sha̱ (WB) ma'cha! that one; that
(rare emphatic nonsubj.); (CW, WB
only) Look! Look out (for that one)!
[<ma'sha>+a̱]
má'shka ggr. of mashka
mahá̱a, mahá̱ha to go off (in some
other direction) (dpl. subj.) (I)—
hngr. of má̱a

mahá̱ha see mahaa
mahá̱li to kind of blow (of the
wind)—hngr. of mahli
mahá̱lli to skip—hngr. of malli
mahli wind, air (noun); to have
wind blowing, to be windy (of a
place) (3) {ggr. má'hli; hngr. mahá̱li:
to kind of blow, be kind of windy;
ngr. má̱hli; mahlihinchi} § Yammat
mahli. It's windy there.
mahli aloota to have gas; to be blown
up, inflated (like a balloon) (II) §
Mahli asalootatok. I had gas.
mahli ishtikbi' windmill (LR) [isht
ikbi+']
mahli oka' ishtoochi', mahli oka'
oochi' see mahli okoochi'
mahli okoochi', mahli oka' oochi',
mahli oka' ishtoochi', (WB) oka'
ishtoochi' windmill [(isht) oka'
oochi+']
mahlihínchi to blow a little bit, be a
little windy, make a breeze (of an air
conditioner, for instance) (3); to be a
little windy, have a breeze (of a
place) (3) [mahli+chi] §
Oklahomma'at mahlihinchi. It's a
little windy in Oklahoma.
mahlishto', (ER) maalishto' tornado
[mahli ishto+']
mahlishyokachi' windmill [mahli

239

isht yokachi+']
mahya go on! get on! hurry up!
(command only?)
makofa' in yakni' makofa'
makoklhilika see himmakoklhilika
malassa to be shallow (of a container)
(3) {ggr. mállassa}
malashka to be winnowed (3) [+T]
{v2. mashka}
maliassas syrup [from English
molasses]
Maliassas man's nickname
maliassas losa' molasses, sorghum
syrup [losa+']
malichi, maliichi to start (a car), to
make run, run (someone) off (sg.
obj.) (I;II) [±SC] [malili+chi] {hngr.
malihínchi, malilihínchi} §
Samalilishtok, Samaliichitok. He
ran me off.
malihínchi, malilihínchi hngr. of
malichi
malihíli hngr. of malili
malili to run (mainly sg. subj.), to go
(of a machine); to make a run (in
baseball); to run for office (I) [+PR]
[+CPR] {ggr. málli'li; hngr. malihíli;
ngr. malíli; pl. tilhaa; malli}
malili impohónna to trot (3)
{imponna}
malin type of plant (WB) [from
English mullein ?]
malit afoolopa to make a run (in
baseball) (I) [malili+t]
malit aakaniya to run away from
someone or something, run away
from home (I) [malili+t]
malit folota to make a run (in
baseball) (I) [malili+t]
malit inkaniya to run away from
(someone) (I;III) [malili+t] § Lynn
imofi'at malit ankaniya. Lynn's dog
ran away from me.
malit kaniya to run away (I)

[malili+t]
maliichi see malichi
malíli to run, start (of a car)—ngr. of
malili
mállassa ggr. of malassa
malli to jump; to jump rope (I); to
beat fast, palpitate (of the heart) (3)
[-CPR] [+PR] {ggr. má'lli; hngr.
mahálli: to skip; malili,mallittakali}
mallichi to make jump; to bounce,
dance (a baby) (I;II) [malli+chi]
mallittahángli to skip, jump
around—especially, like a chicken
with its head cut off (I); to skip,
jump around in (a place) (I;3) {ngr.
mallittángli; mallittakali}—hngr. of
<mallittakli> §
Ishmallittahánglitok. You jumped
around like a chicken with its head
cut off.
mallittakali to jump back (I) [malli+t
takaali ?] {<mallittakli>; malli} §
Ikmallittaka'lokitok. He didn't
jump back.
<mallittakli> {hngr. mallittahángli;
ngr. mallittángli; mallittakali}
mallittángli ngr. of <mallittakli>—
see mallittahángli
malhaha see malhaa
malhahánta hngr. of malhata
malhaháa hngr. of malhaa
malhallichi to scare (especially, by
doing something scary) (I;II) [-OPR]
{v1. malhata; hngr. malhallihínchi}
malhallihínchi hngr. of malhallichi
malhánta ngr. of malhata
malhata to be surprised and happy,
astonished, nervous, scared (II) {v2.
malhallichi; hngr. malhahánta; ngr.
malhánta; ggr. málhlha'ta}
malháyya'ha ygr. of malhaa
malhaa, malhaha to be spoiled, badly
behaved, ornery; to be angry (II)
[+CPR] [+PR] {ggr. málhlha'ha; ygr.

malháyya'ha; ngr. malhaháa}
málhlha'ha ggr. of malhaa
málhlha'ta in ishmálhlha'ta—ggr. of
malhata
mani' money [from the English]
manki' monkey [from the English]
manki' ishkobo' speckled peas (ER)
[ishkobo+']
mankokchi' iodine, mercurochrome,
merthiolate: "monkey blood"
[manki' okchi']
mano where is (used in simple
questions with preceding unsuffixed
noun; cannot be suffixed or
embedded) § Catherine mano?
Where is Catherine? | Ofi' mano?
Where is the dog?
ma-pila that way [yamma pila]
masachi to cure (someone) (I;II) [+SC]
[masali+chi] {hngr. masalihínchi;
masaachi} § Samasalishtok. He
cured me.
masali to be cured; to fade (in the
sun), have the color run (in water)
(II) [+PR] [+CPR] {ggr. mássa'li; ygr.
masáyya'li; masachi, masaachi}
masalihínchi hngr. of masachi
masáyya'li ygr. of masali
masaachi to fade (something) (I;3)
[-SC] [masali+chi] {hngr.
masaahánchi; ngr. masáanchi;
masachi}
masaahánchi hngr. of masaachi
masáanchi ngr. of masaachi
masóhho'fa hgr. of masofa
masohófa hngr. of mssofa
masóyyo'fa ygr. of masofa
masofa to be bald (II) [+PR] [+CPR]
{v2. masofi; ggr. másso'fa; hgr.
masóhho'fa; hngr. masohófa; ngr.
masófa; ygr. masóyyo'fa}
masofachi to make (someone) bald
(I;II) [masofa+chi]
masofi to shave (someone's) head

(I;II) {v1. masofa; ggr. másso'fi, ngr.
masófi} § Akchimaso'fokitok. I
didn't shave your head.
masófi ngr. of masofi
mássa'li ggr. of masali
másso'fa ggr. of masofa
másso'fi ggr. of masofi
mastat mustard [from the English]
mastat imilhlha' wild mustard
[imilhlha+']
mastat nihi' mustard seed
mashka to winnow (I;II) {v1.
malashka; ggr. má'shka; ngr.
máshka}
Mashkookanompa',
Mashkookimanompa' Creek
language, Creek-Seminole language
[Mashkooki' (im+)anompa']
Mashkooki' Creek, Seminole
Mashkookimanompa' see
Mashkookanompa'
Mashkookiyaakni' the Creek Nation
of Oklahoma [Mashkooki'
im+yaakni']
mashshaash from long ago (used
only with a preceding noun phrase)
[<ma'sha'>+aash] {subj.
mashshaashoot; nonsubj.
mashshaasho} § Sarah mashshaash:
Sarah (I used to know her) | ihoo
yamma mashshaash: that woman
(from the past)
mashshaashoot from long ago (subj.;
used only with a preceding noun
phrase) [mashshaash+oot] § Sarah
mashshaashoot alatok. Sarah (the
one we used to know) came.
mashshaasho in, on (used with long-
ago time expressions); from long
ago (nonsubj.; used only with a
preceding noun phrase)
[mashshaash+o] § afammi yamma
mashshaasho: in that (long-ago)
year | 1947 mashshaasho alalittook.

241

I was born in 1947. | Ihoo yamma mashshaash<u>o</u> p<u>i</u>slitok. I saw that woman (from the past).
<mayya> in <u>i</u>mayya
mayyoka' in different directions, every which way, one by one [<ayyoka>] § Mayyoka' iliyyatok. We went off in different directions.
maabil, (WB, CM) maabal marble (toy) [from the English]
maalihinchi to blow a little
maami', maama' mother (IIIp) [from English mama, mommy]
maap mop [from the English]
m<u>á</u>a to go off (I); to get (following verbs taking I subjs.) (I) [E+t]; get (aux. used following verbs taking II or III subjs.); (aux. for positional or orientational verbs with an. subjs.) {hngr. mah<u>á</u>a (dpl.); ishm<u>á</u>a} § P<u>a</u>lhkit m<u>a</u>ali, p<u>a</u>lhkit ishm<u>a</u>ali. I'm getting faster. | Sasipongnit ishm<u>a</u>a. I'm getting older. | Kahat kiim<u>a</u>a. We are lying down.
m<u>á</u>hli ngr. of mahli
m<u>á</u>shka ngr. of mashka
mi he, she, they (used as predicate); her, him, them (primarily as predicate); the same, the original one or ones (primarily as predicate) § Mi chiya ki'yo. You're not the same one, You're not him, You're not he.
mi alhiha', mihalhiha' they (as predicate); them (mainly as predicate) § Mi alhiha'. It's them, It is they.
mi finha' the original one, the genuine article, the real thing; original (of a photocopy) § Mih finhaakot chongma. The original one is better. | Mih finha' saya. I'm the real thing.
mí'lli ggr. of milli

mi't mi't mi't aachi see mit mit mit aachi
miha, miya to say about oneself (I); to try (I); to mean (3) [E] {hngr. mih<u>í</u>ha; <u>i</u>miha} § Hilha mihalitok. I tried to dance. § Hooala'chi mihatok. They said they would come. | Hilhala'ni mihalitok. I said I could dance. | Nantata miha? What does it mean?
mihachi in ilimihachi, <u>i</u>mihachi, <u>i</u>n<u>a</u>mihachi, n<u>a</u>na mihachi
mihalhiha' see mi alhiha'
mihaash the same one [mi+aash] § Mihaash chiya ki'yo. You're not the same one.
mihaash ikholbo not to be the same (IN) § Mihaash akholbo. I'm not the same, I've changed.
mihaashayni same [mihaash ayni] § Hattak mihaashaynit ala! The same man came back!
<mihchi> in yakmihchi, yamihchi
mihínti to come (dpl.)—hngr. of minti
mih<u>í</u>ha hngr. of miha
mih<u>í</u>li very (aux.); even (aux., with preceding negative) § Iksapi'so mih<u>i</u>li. He didn't even see me. | Sapisa mih<u>i</u>li ki'yo. He doesn't see me very much, very often. | Sipokni mih<u>í</u>cha tikahbi. She's very old and she's tired.
mihoot he, she, they; the same one (subj.) [mi+hoot] § Mihoot ayatok. She left.
mih<u>o</u> him, her, them (obj.) [mi+h<u>o</u>] § Lynnat mih<u>o</u> pistok. Lynn saw him.
mikya'ba okay, all right, no problem, forget it (used, for instance, after receiving a negative response to one's request)
milínka to be near, close—most often, in a physical sense (I;II); near to (aux.—preceded by verb +a'chik<u>a</u>

or +a'chikat) {imilínka: to be near, close—most often, in a nonphysical sense} § Ith<u>a</u>nali salla'chik<u>a</u> milinkakat, Ith<u>a</u>nali salla'chikat milinkakat. I know that I'm near death.
milinkachi to bring near (I;3) [milinka+chi] {ngr. milinkánchi}
milinkánchi ngr. of milinkachi
milli, mitli to make little holes in (for instance, to shoot full of holes) (I;II) {ggr. mí'lli; hngr. mih<u>í</u>lli; mitaffi: to make one little hole in; mitahli}
mina habitually, always; for a considerable while (aux.) (when embedded, becomes <-n<u>á</u>a>) § Hilhali minattook. I used to dance. I Yappak<u>o</u> aaishkoli mina'chi. I'll always drink from this one. I Anompoh<u>o</u>n<u>a</u>acha tikahbitahatok. He was talking so much that he got tired.
<minko> in aaminko, minko'
minko' chief, governor, president, king [<minko>+']
Minko' Holiitopa' President of the United States [holiitopa+']
minkoshto' big chief [minko' ishto+']
minnat minutes (of a meeting) [from the English]
minti to come, be on the way, move in this direction, approach (I); to come to (I;3) [+taha] {ggr. mí'ti; hngr. mihínti: to come (dpl.); ygr. míyy<u>i</u>'ti; hashtaht minti, onnat minti} § Anchokkaak minti. He's coming to my house. I Onnat minti. Dawn is coming.
missíhhi'la hgr. of missila
missih<u>í</u>la hngr. of missila
missila to have a big stomach, be round (of a sugar bowl, for instance)

(II) {v2. missilili; ggr. missí'la; hgr. missíhhi'la; hngr. missih<u>í</u>la; rigr. missilm<u>í</u>ya; xgr. missílli'ya; ygr. missíyyi'la}
missilili to inflate: especially, to enlarge the stomach of (an inflatable animal, for instance) (I;3) {v1. missila}
missílli'ya to have a really big stomach, be kind of round; to bulge (of the cheeks, for instance) (II)— xgr. of missila
missilm<u>í</u>ya to sway when one walks, with one's fat rolling around (I)— rigr. of missila
Missipi' Mississippi [from the English]
Missipi' Chahta' Mississippi Choctaw person (either from Mississippi or a Mississippi Choctaw of Oklahoma)
misha' that visible over there (used with a preceding noun phrase) {<ma'sha>} § Janat naafka ikbitok misha'at litiha. The dress over there that Jan made is dirty. I Naafka misha'<u>a</u> p<u>i</u>sli. I saw that dress over there.
misha' fonka that way, in that direction (nearer than misha' pila)
misha' intannap see mishintannap
misha' pila, misha' p<u>í</u>lla visible (moving) over there, up ahead; that way, in that direction (farther than misha' fonka); to be visible (usually moving) way over there, up ahead (inan. subj.) (3)
misha' p<u>í</u>llakaash long ago [misha' pilla+kaash] § Misha' pillakaash attook. It was long ago, It happened long ago.
mishintannap, misha' intannap just on the other side of (preceded by a clause, not a simple noun phrase)

mishshakma

[misha' intannap] § Issi' ishaa-
abikaash mishintannapako
aapislitok. I saw him just on the
other side of where you killed the
deer. | Aattalika mishintannapako
anta. She lives just on the other
side of me, of where I live.
mishshakma see onna mishshakma
mishshaash, mishshaasho,
mishshakaash see oblaashaash
mishshaash
mit mit mit aachi, mi't mi't mi't
aachi to make the sound of walking
without shoes or hitting pillows
(expressive) (I) {miti'chi}
mitafa to have one little hole (3) {v2.
mitaffi; ggr. mítta'fa; mitahli: to be
full of little holes}
mitaffi to make a little hole or
opening in, to pierce (I;3) {v1.
mitafa; hngr. mitaháffi; milli: make
little holes in}
mitaháffi hngr. of mitaffi
mitaháli hngr. of mitahli
mitahli to have a bunch of little
holes (3) {hngr. mitaháli; mitafa: to
have a little hole in; milli}
mitaachi to make more than one
little hole in, perforate (I;II) [-SC]
[mitahli+chi] {ngr. mitaalínchi;
mitaffi: make a little hole in}
mitaalínchi ngr. of mitaachi
miti'chi to hit (without noise, thus,
for instance, with a pillow) (I;II)
[±SC] {klgr. míttikli'chi; rcgr.
mitití'chi; mit mit mit aachi,
mittiha}
mitití'chi to make the sound of
hitting soft things: to beat on a
pillow; to walk around without
shoes (I)—rcgr. of miti'chi [-SC]
mitli see milli
mítta'fa ggr. of mitafa
míttikli'chi to hit with the fist (I;II)—

klgr. of miti'chi
mittiha to punch, pummel (I;II)
{miti'chi} § Ikmitti'hokitok. She
didn't punch him.
miya see miha
míyyi'ti ygr. of minti
Mí'tabi' name of a mineral spring
near Durant (CP) [mi'ti abi+']
mí'ti ggr. of minti
móchcho'li to close the eyes tight—
ggr. of mocholi
<mochi> in omochi
mocholi to close the eyes (I) [-PR]
[-CPR] {ggr. móchcho'li: to close the
eyes tight}
mokofa to be rubbed raw (II) {v2.
mokoffi}
mokoffi to rub raw (3;II) {v1. mokofa;
hngr. mokohóffi}
mokohóffi hngr. of mokoffi
<molhchi> in omolhchi
<mosak> in ilbak imosak
moshmohóli hngr. of moshmoli
moshmoli to blink, wink (I) [-CPR]
[-PR] {hngr. moshmohóli}
moshoochi to put out, extinguish (a
fire, lamp), to turn off (the gas) (I;3)
[±SC] [moshooli+chi] {hngr.
moshoohónchi}
moshoohónchi hngr. of moshoochi
moshoohóli hngr. of moshooli
moshooli to go out (of fire, candle),
to die out (of a tribe) (II) [+PR]
[+CPR] {hngr. moshoohóli;
amóshsho'li}
moyoshki to be mushy, watery, soft,
overripe; to be mashed; to be
muddy, watery (of land) (3) {ggr.
móyyoshki}
moyoshkichi to mash (potatoes, for
example) (I;3) [moyoshki+chi]
móyyoshki ggr. of moyoshki
móyyo'ma ygr. of móma (Ct)
mooha to moo (of a cow) (WB)

244

mooshan motion (in a meeting)
[from the English]
móma to be all; to be complete, intact
(for instance, of a newborn baby) (I);
more, another (subr. modifier only)
[+CPR] [+PR] {ygr. móyyo̱'ma (Ct);
ishti̱móma; mo̱t} § Naafka toklo
momaho̱ chompalitok. I bought
two more dresses, I bought another
two dresses. I Chipotaat ilbakoshi'at

mo̱ma. All of the child's fingers are
there, The child has all his fingers.
<mo̱machi> in i̱mo̱machit táyya'ha
[mo̱ma+chi] {ngr. mo̱mánchi}
mo̱mánchi to do all, to want all (I); to
go with all, a lot of (men or women)
(I;3)—ngr. of <mo̱machi>
mo̱shi' uncle (vocative) (IIIp)
mo̱t all (subj.) [mo̱ma+t] § Mo̱t
hilhatok. They all danced.

n

ná'lli ggr. of nalli
ná'lha ggr. of nalha
ná'lhlhi ggr. of nalhlhi
na'm na'm na'm aachi see nam nam
nam aachi
nahá̱lha hngr. of nalha
nahá̱lhlhi hngr. of nalhlhi
náhhakbi hgr. of nakbi
nakbatiipoli', (TP, CP) nakbitiipoli',
(MC) nakbotiipoli', (ML)
tikbatiipoli' rainbow [naki' ?; hina'
?; nakbi ?; aba' ? atiipoli+']
nakbi to be set on a slanted surface
(of a movable inan. obj. with a flat
bottom) (3) {hgr. náhhakbi; ygr.
náyyakbi}
nakbí'chi ggr. of nakbichi
nakbichi to set (a movable inan. obj.
with a flat bottom) on a slant (I;3)
[nakbi+chi] {ggr. nakbí'chi}
<nakfi'> in i̱nakfi'
nakfish younger sibling of the same
sex as oneself: younger sister (of a
woman), younger brother (of a
man); younger cousin of the same
sex as oneself (IIp) {i̱nakfi'}
nakfish iklanna' younger half-sibling
of the same sex as oneself (IIp)
[iklanna+']

nakfish toba' younger step-sibling of
the same sex as oneself (IIp)
naki' bullet; arrowhead; arrow
naki' aabilili' melting pot (for
melting lead for bullets) [aabilili+']
naki' bila' lead (metal) [bila+']
naki' hakshop shell casing
naki' ishtayachi' gunpowder
[<ishtayachi>+']
naki' i̱haloppa' sharp, pointed tip of
an arrow [im+haloppa+']
naki' i̱hottok, naki̱hottok
gunpowder [naki' im+hottok]
naki' kawaski' silver bullet
[kawaski+']
naki' lohmi' hide the bullet (an old
game) [lohmi+']
naki' oshkibili' arrowhead (or
possibly the whole arrow)
[oshkibili+']
naki' palli' bad spell placed on
someone by an Indian doctor (AJ)
[palli+']
nakishtikbi' bullet mold [naki' isht
ikbi+']
naki̱hottok see naki' i̱hottok
nakni to act like a man (only used in
the negative) (male subj.) (II)
{iknakno} § Chinakni ki'yo. You

245

nakni'

didn't act like a man.
nakni' male, man
nakni' banna to want a man; to be in heat (of a female animal) (II)
nak-oshi' little shell, little bullet [naki' oshi']
nakoshik BBs, shot [naki' <oshik>]
naksabasali' icicle [naksi']
naksi' rib (IIp)
naksika' side, edge (IIp); on the side, edge (II) [naksi'+ka'] {naksikali'} § abooha' naksika' wall | sanaksika' my side; on my side
naksikali' (moving) on the side, edge (3) {naksika'} § Onchaba naksikali' aatok. He was going along on the side of the mountain.
naksish branch—only used in complex expressions like itti' naksish, naksish filammi'
naksish filammi' branch of a tree (cln.)
nakshobi to be smelly (like a dog) (II); to smell like (a dog, blood, fish) (II;3C) {ygr. nakshóyyo'bi; ngr. nakshómbi; hgr. nakshóhho'bi} § Ofi' chinakshobi. You smell like a dog.
nakshóhho'bi hgr. of nakshobi
nakshómbi ngr. of nakshobi
nakshóyyo'bi ygr. of nakshobi
naktoomi to be moonlight (—) [ninak toomi] {ninak toomi} § Iknakto'mokitok. It wasn't moonlight, There was no moon.
naktoomi chokma to be full moonlight (so that it's easy to see) (—); to have full moonlight (of a place) (3) § Saudi Arabia'at naktoomi chokmatok. It was full moonlight in Saudi Arabia, Saudi Arabia had full moonlight.
nalli to swallow quickly, swallow (pl. obj.) (I;3) {ggr. ná'lli; sg. obj.

nannabli}
nalha to be shot (II) {v2. nalhlhi; ggr. ná'lha; hngr. nahálha}
nalhchaba, (ER) nalhchoba, (CC) nalhchiba, (TP) nashchaba back (of the body) (IIp)
nalhchaba foni' spine, backbone
nalhchaba kobokshi' hunchback [kobokshi+']
nalhlhi to shoot and hit, to sting (I;II) {v1. nalha; ggr. na'lhlhi; hngr. nahálhlhi}
nam nam nam aachi, na'm na'm na'm aachi to make the sound of chewing or lip smacking (as when something tastes good, or to interest a baby in eating) (expressive) (I)
nambilama' perfume, incense [nanna bilama+']
nambosholli' trash, garbage [nanna imbosholli+']
nambosholli' ayowa' garbage man [ayowa+']
nambosholli' shaali' garbage truck [shaali+']
nampakali' flower [nanna pakali+']
nampakali' aaholokchi' flowerpot [aa+holokchi+']
nampakali' aalhto' vase
nampakali' balalli', (WB) pakali balalli' flowering vine [balalli+']
nampakali' imilhlha' wildflower [imilhlha+']
nampakali' poshi' pollen
nampanaa' string, twine, yarn, crochet cotton [nanna panaa+']
nampila to fix, take care of, adjust, put on (something) (I;3) [*nanna <pila>] {ngr. nampíla; inampila; pitnampíla}
nampíla to get better, easier (of pain) (3); to take care of a problem (I)— ngr. of nampila
nampofalli' lint [nanna pofalli+']

246

namposhi' vegetables, produce (still in the garden); garden [nanna poshi']

nanchampoli' sweets, sweet stuff—candy, jam, jelly, molasses [nanna champoli+']

nanchanahli' pinwheel [nanna chanahli+']

nanchofalli' person who keeps things clean [nanna chofalli+']

nanchompa, nanna chompa to shop (I) [nanna *chompa] § Nannishchompatam? Were you shopping?

nani' fish

nani' aayoka' fishnet (TJ) [aa+yoka+']

nani' fochik starfish

nani' hotost aya to go fishing (I) [hotosi+t] {nanishholhtosi'} § Nani' hotost ishiyyatam? Did you go fishing?

nani' ishhokaffi' see nanishhokaffi'

nani' ishhokaachi' fishnet (CP) [isht hokaachi+']

nani' ishtayowa', nanishtayowa' fishnet [nani' isht ayowa+']

nani' ishhokaffi' see nanishhokaffi'

nani' ishyokachi', nanishyokachi' fishnet [nani' isht yokachi+']

nani' ifanalhchi' fish's fin [im+fanalhchi']

nani' kallo' gar fish [kallo+']

Nani' Kallo' Hilha' Gar Dance, also called "Hard Fish"—name of a Chickasaw dance

nani' lakna' mudcat (fish) (WB) [lakna+']

nani' patassa', patassa' flatfish, perch [patassa+']

nani' patassa' lhibokta' bluegill (fish) (WB) [lhibokta+']

nani' patassa' sotko' goggle-eyed perch (WB) [sotko+']

nani' sinti', (CC) sinti' nani' eel

nani' takha' trout

nanishhokaffi', nani' ishhokaffi', nanishtokaffi', nani' ishtokaffi' fishnet [isht hokaffi/okaffi+']

nanishholhtosi' fishing pole, rod, (TP) fishnet [nani' isht holhtosi+'] {nani' hotost aya}

nanishtayowa' see nani' ishtayowa'

nanishto' whale [nani' ishto+']

nanishtokaffi' see nanishhokaffi'

nanishyokachi' see nani' ishyokachi'

nankanchi' salesman, auctioneer [nanna kanchi+']

nanna, (Ct?) nana something; what (inf.) (nonsubj.); something's; of what (inf.) (may be used as a cln.; see nannakat, nannaka) {int. nanta; nannahmat, nannahma, nannahoot, nannaho} § Nanna hommaho pisli. I saw something red. | Nanna chiya. You're something. | Nanna hakshopookano Lynnat hommachitok. Lynn dyed some skin (the skin of something) red.

nanna maybe, perhaps, whether, if (aux., preceded by verb +kma) § Alhlhikma nanna. Maybe it's true. | Ayakma nannatok. Maybe he went. | Ayalikma nanna'chikat akitha'no. I don't know if I'm going. | Hilhalikma nannatokat akitha'no. I don't know if I danced. | Ishiyyakma nannatoka akitha'no. I don't know if you went.

nanna albani' barbecue, barbecued meat [albani+']

nanna apoolosa' plaster (WB) [<apoolosa>+']

nanna asonnak tobbaalhto' canned goods [asonnak tobbi' aalhto']

nanna ashshachi see nannashshachi'

nanna ashshachi' see nannashshachi'

nanna ataklama' intoba

nanna ataklama' intoba to have
something bad or annoying come
up (III) [ataklama+' *im+toba] §
Nanna ataklama' antobatokat
sanokhanglo. I'm sad that I had
something bad come up.
nanna ayya peace (Bible word)
[<ayya> ?] {ittinannayya,
<nannayya>}
nanna ayya bíyyi'ka to be peaceful (of
a place or situation), have peace (3)
nanna ayya bíyyi'kanokfilli to be
peaceful (of a person), to be a
peaceful person (I) [(nanna ayya
biyyi'ka) *anokfilli]
nanna aa-ashshachika', nannaa-
ashshachika' hell
[aa+ashshachi+ka']
nanna aabaani' grill [aa+abaani+']
nanna aaishko' earthenware jug (CC)
[aaishko+']
nanna aalowachi' sacrificial altar
[aa+lowachi+']
nanna aalhto' chest of drawers,
dresser
nanna chompa see nanchompa
nanna holokchi' cultivated plant or
vegetable [holokchi+']
nanna ilitobasht nowa' witch
[ilitobachi+t nowa+']
nanna imaalami see nannimaalami
nanna ishshaali', nannishshaali'
truck [isht shaali+']
nanna ishtithana' holisso,
nannishtithana' holisso deed
(document), diploma [isht ithana+']
nanna ihollo see nannihollo
nanna loma' mystery, secret [loma+']
nanna mihachi, namihachi to
complain about (I;II) (a II prefix may
go either before or after nanna or
na; a I;II prefix combination must go
only before na) [nanna *mihachi] §
Nanna samihachi, Nasamihachi,

sanamihachi. He complained about
me. I Nanchimihachi. He
complained about you. I
Issanamihashtok. You complained
about me.
nanna móma everything (cln.) §
nanna momakat: everything (subj.)
I nanna momaka: everything
(nonsubj.)
nanna ontalla'a' hot-plate mat
nanna pokta' something split in two
parts that are still attached
nanna poshi' something powdery;
powdery substance
nanna shila' dry cereal [shila+']
nanna shombachi' bugs in grain or
cereal [shombachi+']
nanna ta'osso ishtaaponta'
pawnshop [isht aa+ponta+']
nanna wakaa' parachute [wakaa+']
nanna washaachi' rattle (noun)
[washaachi+']
nanna yamma that thing there (see
yamma)
nanna yappa this thing here (see
yappa)
nanna'chihchi I wonder if, could it
be that (about a future event—used
with a preceding verb +kma)
[nanna+a'chi+hchi] § Alalikma
nanna'chihchi. I wonder if I'll go.
nanna'chikyásha, nanna'chikya ásha
if nothing happens (used to express
'might', with preceding verb +kma)
[nanna+a'chi+kya asha] § Ayalikma
nanna'chikyásha. I might go (if
nothing happens).
nannabli to swallow (sg. or hum.
obj., solid or liquid); to take (a pill)
(I;II) [*nanna apa ?] {ggr. nannâbli;
hngr. nannahámbli; pl. obj. nalli} §
Ishnannablitok. You swallowed it.
nannâbli ggr. of nannabli
nannafaana'chi' detective [nanna

248

afaana'chi+']
nannahámbli hngr. of nannabli
nannahánchi hngr. of nannaachi
nannahchi I wonder if, could it be
that (about a present event—used
with a preceding verb +kma)
[nanna+hchi] § Ayakma nannahchi.
I wonder if he's going.
nannahmat something (subj.)
[nanna+hmat] (inf. nannahoot; int.
nantahaat; nannakat)
nannahmat kanihmi to have
something happen to one (II)
[+HM], <nannahmat kanih> (inf.
nannahoot kanihmi; int. nantahaat
katihmi)
nannahmat kanihmihma see
kanihmihma
<**nannahmat kanih**> [HM] of
nannahmat kanihmi
nannahma something (nonsubj.)
[nanna+hma] (inf. nannaho; int.
nantahta) § Nannahma pislitok. I
saw something.
nannahookano, nannookano
something (unspecified) (subj., obj.)
[nanna+hookano] § Nannahookano
kanihma'chi. Something's going to
happen. | Nannahookano pislitok. I
saw something.
nannahookya, nannookya, nannakya
everything; (in negative sentence)
anything, nothing (subj., obj.)
[nanna+hookya]
nannahoot what (inf.), thing (subj.)
[nanna+hoot] (ind. nannahmat; int.
nantahaat) § Lynnat nannahoot
kisitoka ikitha'no. Lynn doesn't
know what bit her. | Nannahoot
sassokmat ishtotok. The thing that
hit me was big, What hit me was
big.
nannahoot ishtimaawí'ki ggr. of
nannahoot ishtimaawiiki

nannahoot ishtimaawiiki to have
what bothering one (III) (inf.) (ggr.
nannahoot ishtimaawí'ki; ind.
nannakat ishtimaawiiki; int.
nantahaat ishtimaawiiki) §
Nannahoot ishchimaawi'kika
ithanali. I know what's bothering
you.
nannahoot kanihmi to have what
happen to one (II) (inf.) [+HM],
<nannahoot kanih> (ind.
nannahmat kanihmi; int.
nantahaat katihmi) § Nannahoot
kanihtokat ithana Lynnat. Lynn
knows what happened to her.
nannahoot kanihmiho see
kanihmiho
<**nannahoot kanih**> [HM] of
nannahoot kanihmi
nannaho what (thing) (inf.); what
(one), which (inf.); thing (nonsubj.)
[nanna+ho] (ind. nannahma; int.
nantahta) § Lynnat nannaho
pistokat ithana. Lynn knows what
she saw. | Ofi' nannaho ishpistoka
ithanali. I know what dog you saw.
nannakat something; what (inf.)
(subj.; cln. variant of nannahmat)
[nanna+kat] § Nannakat kanihmi.
Something happened.
nannakat aafinha for it to be
necessary, important (often subr.) §
Nannakat aafinhahootoko
ayala'chi. I must go, I am going
because it is necessary.
nannakat finha for there to be a
miracle, for something to occur
miraculously (naafinha)
nannakat imoktani to have a vision
of something, know something in
advance (III) § Nannakat amoktani.
I had a vision of it, I knew in
advance.
nannakat ishtimaakallo to have it be

hard on one (III) [isht im+aa+kallo]
§ Nannakat ishtamaakallo haklola'
ki'yohootokot. It's hard on me that
I can't hear.
nannakat ishtimaawí'ki ggr. of
nannakat ishtimaawiiki
nannakat ishtimaawiiki to have
something bothering one (III) {ggr.
nannakat ishtimaawí'ki; inf.
nannahoot ishtimaawiiki; int.
nantahaat ishtimaawiiki} §
Nannakat ishtimaawi'kitokoot
ayatok. There was something
bothering him, so he left.
nannakat kanihmihma see
kanihmihma
nannakat kanihmiho see kanihmiho
nannaka something; what (inf.)
(nonsubj.; cln. variant of nanna,
nannahma) [nanna+ka] § Nannaka
apatok. He ate something.
nannaka ihollo see nannihollo
nannakya see nannahookya
**nannakya ikimiksho, nannookya
ikimiksho** not to have, to have
nothing in the way of (III;3)
[nanna+kya/ookya] § Ta'osso
nannakya iksamiksho. I have no
money. | Hattak nannakya
ikchimiksho. You don't have a
husband.
**nannakya iksho, nannookya iksho,
nanniksho** for there to be nothing
in, for there to be none of
(something) (—;3); for there to be
none of (something) in (a place) (—
;3;3); for there to be no (ER, TP) (3)
[nanna+kya/ookya *iksho] §
Talhpaka nannakya iksho. There's
nothing in the basket, The basket is
empty. | Tii nannakya iksho.
There's no tea. | Chahta nanniksho
yappa. There are no Choctaws here.
| (ER, TP) Chahtaat nanniksho.

There are no Choctaws.
nannalhiipi'ya' cover specially made
to fit something (such as a car cover)
[nanna alhiipi'ya']
nannalhpisa', naalhpisa' law [nanna
alhpisa+']
nannalhpisa' abooha see nannaa-
apiisa' abooha
nannalhpisa' ikbi, naalhpisa' ikbi to
make a law (I)
**nannalhpisa' kobaffi, naalhpisa'
kobaffi** to break the law (I)
Nannalhpisa' Pokko'li' the Ten
Commandments
nannalhpooba' see naalhpooba
nannannoya' story [nanna annoya+']
nannanokfillikat chokma bíyyi'ka to
be peaceful (I , — , —) [nanna
anokfilli+kat]
nannanokfillikat toklo to be unable
to make up one's mind, be in two
minds about (I , —) [nanna
*anokfilli+kat] §
Nannishanokfillikat toklo. You
can't make up your mind.
nannanokfillit aatapichi to think too
much about something, worry (I)
[nanna anokfilli+t]
nannanoli' reporter [nanna anoli+']
Nannapiisa' Congress, Legislature
[nanna apiisa+']
nannashshachi, nanna ashshachi to
sin, commit a sin (I) [nanna
*ashshachi] §
Nannishashshachitok. You sinned.
nannashshachi', nanna ashshachi'
sin; sinner [nannashshachi+']
nannatobbi to be punished, pay (for
something) (I) [nanna *atobbi] §
Nannikatobbo. He hasn't been
punished.
nannatokchi, nannootokchi I
wonder if, could it be that (about a
past event) (used with preceding

verb +kma) [nanna+tok+hchi] §
Malilikma nannatokchi. I wonder if
he ran, Could it be that he ran? |
Ishpisakma nannatokchi. I wonder
if you saw it.
nannawaa', naawaa' fruit,
vegetables, produce (already
harvested) [nanna waa+']
nannayolhlha to have good luck,
have things come to one (II) [nanna
*ayolhlha] § Nannasayolhlha. I
have good luck.
<nannayya> in ittinannayya [nanna
ayya]
nannaa-asha' place where stuff is
[nanna aa-asha']
nannaa-apiisa' abooha, nannalhpisa'
abooha courthouse, legislature
[nanna apiisa+']
nannaa-apiisachi' lookout (place),
watchtower [nanna aa+apiisachi+']
nannaa-ashshachika' see nanna aa-
ashshachika'
nannaabachi' teacher (IIIp:
nannimaabachi') [nanna
(im)aabachi+'] § nannamaabachi':
my teacher | nannapomaabachi',
nampomaabachi': our teacher
nannaabilili' melting pot (for
melting lead, for example) [nanna
aa+bilili+']
nannaabilhpoha', nannaabilhpowa'
pocket [nanna aa+abilhpoha+']
nannaachi to make noise (I) [nanna
*aachi] {hngr. nannahánchi;
nannookahánchi} §
Nannishaachinna! Don't make
noise!
nannaachiifa' sink [nanna
aa+achiifa+']
nannaahalma' ironing board [nanna
aa+halma+']
nannaahammi' ironing board
[nanna aa+hammi+']

nannaaholhponi' pressure cooker
[nanna aa+holhponi+']
nannaahosa' target [nanna
aa+hosa+']
nannaaiksaa' see nannaaiksaachi'
nannaaiksaachi', nannaaiksaa'
factory [nanna aa+iksaachi/iksaa+']
nannaaishko' beer joint, saloon
[nanna aa+ishko+']
nannaaishshachi' sin [nanna
<aaishshachi>+']
nannaaithana' college [nanna
aa+ithana+']
nannaakalho'chi' washboard [nanna
aa+kalho'chi+']
nannaakanchi' booth, stand; auction
[nanna aa+kanchi+']
nannaakapassali' refrigerator car (on
a train) [nanna aa+kapassali+']
nannaalhchifa', nanna aalhchifa'
washing machine [nanna
aa+alhchifa+']
nannaalhpi' handle [nanna aalhpi']
nannaalhto' pocket, bag, drawer
[nanna aalhto+']
nannaashana', nannaashanni'
wringer [nanna
aa+shana/shanni+']
nannaatanni' knitting machine
[nanna aa+tanni+']
nannaatoba' see aatoba'
nannaawiikichi' scale (for weighing)
[nanna aa+wiikichi+']
nannikaabanno' garbage [nanna
ik+aa+banna+o+']
nanniksaachi' handyman [nanna
iksaachi+']
nanniksho see nannakya iksho
nannimálla'mi ki'yo to have no
business, not to have been supposed
to be (doing something)—negative
ggr. of nannimaalami (III) [nanna
*imalla'mi]
nannimanoli to be a witness for (I;III)

nannimanǫli'

[nanna *im+anǫli] § Chihoowaakot nannamanǫli. God is my witness. **nannimanǫli'** teacher (oIIIp) [nanna im+anǫli+'] § nampomanǫli': our teacher | nannamanǫli': my teacher **nannimapiisa'** governor (of a state) **nannimaabachi'** poss. of nannaabachi' **nannimaaithana'** see inaithana' **nannimaalami, nanna imaalami** to have something to do, to have business; to go to the bathroom (III) [nanna *imaalami] {neg. ggr. nannimálla'mi ki'yo: to have no business} § Nannamaalami. I've got something to do, I have business, I'm going off to the bathroom. **nannimaalami'** businessman [nannimaalami+'] **nannimilhlha'** wild animal [nanna imilhlha+'] **nannimilhlha' aa-asha'** zoo **nannimoktani** to have a vision (III) [nanna *imoktani] § Nanchimoktanitok, Nanna chimoktanitok. You had a vision. **nannimponna** to be smart (III) [nanna *imponna] § Nanchimponna. You're smart. **nannimponna'** knowledge [nannimponna+'] **nanninchokka'** cage [nanna im+chokka'] **nanninkanihmi, nannishtinkanihmi, naaishtinkanihmi** to care (used in the negative, with following ki'yo) (III) [nanna (isht) *inkanihmi] {neg. nannishtikinkanihmo; nanninkanihki'yo} § Nanniksankanihmo, Nannankanihmi ki'yo, Nannishtankanihmi ki'yo, Naaishtankanihmi ki'yo. I don't

care. **nanninkanihki'yo** not to care (III) [nanninkanihmi ki'yo] § Nannankanihki'yo. I don't care. **nannishbookalhchi'** see ishbookalhchi' **nannishchofalli'** vacuum cleaner [nanna isht chofalli+'] **nannishchokoshkomo'** see ishchokoshkomo' **nannishfilito'chi'** spatula [nanna isht filito'chi+'] **nannishhaklo'** hearing aid, stethoscope [nanna isht haklo+'] **nannishhaksi'** see ishhaksi' **nannishhalalli'** tongs [nanna isht halalli+'] **nannishhaloppachi', naaishhaloppachi'**, (WB) naaishhalappachi' file, sharpener [nanna isht haloppachi+'] **nannishholhtosi'** trap [nanna isht holhtosi+'] **nannishkasho'kalhchi'** see ishkasho'kalhchi' **nannishko'** drink: especially, alcoholic beverage [nanna ishko+'] **nannishlhimishkochi'** sandpaper [nanna isht lhimishkochi+'] **nannishshaachi'** grater [nanna isht shaachi+'] **nannishshaali'** see nanna ishshaali' **nannishshokli'** chisel [nanna isht shokli+'] **nannishshoochi'** file (noun) [nanna isht shoochi+'] **nannishtabaawiili'** crane [nanna isht abaawiili+'] **nannishtahalaa** to have something to do with or to say about an affair, to have something be one's business (II) [nanna isht *ahalaa] {ggr. nannishtahálla'a—used primarily in the negative;

ishtahaláa} § Nannishtasahalla'a ki'yo, Nannishtiksahalla'o. It's none of my business, I'm not getting involved.
nannishtahálla'a ggr. of nannishtahalaa
nannishtaháyyo'chi to be mischievous (3) [nanna isht *aháyyo'chi]
nannishtahoobali ki'yo see naaishtahoobali ki'yo
nannishtakli' scoop (noun) [nanna isht takli+']
nannishtalhlhi', nannishtalha' pocket knife [nanna isht alhlhi+']
nannishtalhlhi' see ittishtalhlhi'
nannishtalhpisa' see naaishtalhpisa'
nannishtalhtoko'wa' inner sign, revelation
nannishtanhi to care about (I;II) [nanna isht *anhi] (usually used in the negative: nannishtikanho, nannishtanhi ki'yo) § Charlesat nannishtaponhi ki'yo. Charles doesn't care about us.
nannishtani' see ishtani'
nannishtanni' knitting needle, crochet hook [nanna isht tanni+']
nannishtanompa story (TJ) [nanna isht anompa]
nannishtaponnachi see ishtaponnachi
nannishtasawachi' see ishtasawachi'
nannishtatta to do something, to work (I) [nanna isht *atta] § Nannishtishatta. You're working, You're doing something.
nannishtayowa' vacuum cleaner, suction machine [nanna isht ayowa+']
nannishtaa-asha' amphitheater, outdoor auditorium; city hall [nanna isht aa-asha']
nannishtikinkanihmo,

naaishtikinkanihmo not to care (N+III)—neg. of nannishtinkanihmi [nanna isht *ikinkanihmo] § Nannishtiksankanihmo, Naaishtiksankanihmo. I don't care.
nannishtilayoppa to rejoice (3) (Bible word) [nanna isht *ilayoppa] § Anompa nanna ishtachiyoppa'chiho ishchimallali, hattak momakat nannishtilayoppa'chiho. I bring you words to make you happy, about which all people will rejoice.
nannishtilaayokha to be stingy (I) {ggr. nannishtilaayôkha} § Nannishtilaayokhali. I'm stingy.
nannishtilaayôkha ggr. of nannishtilaayokha
nannishtimatta' lawyer [nanna isht im+atta+']
nannishtinkanihmi see nanninkanihmi
nannishtishko' drinking straw [nanna isht ishko+']
nannishtithana' measuring instrument (compass, thermometer, barometer, etc.) [nanna isht ithana+']
nannishtithana' holisso diploma
nannishtittanaha to organize a meeting about something (pl. subj.) (IR) [nanna isht *ittanaha]
nannishtifinha to be proud of (III;3) [nanna isht *im+finha] § Charlesa nannishtafinhatok. I'm proud of Charles.
nannishwakaa', ishwakaa' hot-air balloon [nanna isht wakaa+']
nannishwilooli' duster [nanna isht wilooli+']
nannishyokachi' trap (noun) [nanna isht yokachi+']
nannittapatkachi' quilt block [nanna

ittapatkachi+']
nannittibalhto' ingredients (usually,
all mixed together) [nanna
itti+ibaa+alhto+']
nannittimapiisa to make an
agreement (I / IR) [nanna
*itti+im+apiisa] §
Nanniitimapiistok. We made an
agreement.
nannittihollo' love (Bible word)
[nanna ittihollo+'] § Nannittihollo'
ikchimikshokmat nanna chiya
ki'yo. If you don't have love you
aren't anything.
nannihollo, nannaka ihollo to be
greedy (III) [nanna(+ka) *ihollo]
{ygr. nannihóyyo'llo} § Nanna
chihollo. You're greedy. | Nannaka
ahollo. I'm greedy.
nannihóyyo'llo ygr. of nannihollo
nannokchamalapa' any insect pest
that eats vegetables
[nannokchamali' apa+']
nannokchamali' vegetables,
especially harvested ones [nanna
okchamali+']
nannokchaa' living thing (animal,
person) [nanna okchaa+']
nannokloha for there to be a miracle
(Ct) [nanna <okloha>] {ygr.
nannoklóyyo'ha}
nannoklóyyo'ha ygr. of nannokloha
nannoktani' revelation [nanna
oktani+']
Nannoktani' Holisso the Book of
Revelation [nanna oktani+']
nannola' music; musical
instrument: piano, whistle, violin,
etc.; record player, radio [nanna
ola+']
nannola' chokoshkomo' musician
[chokoshkomo+']
nannóla' inchokoshkomo' organist
in a church or theater

[im+chokoshkomo+']
nannola' olachi to make music, play
an instrument (I) § Charlesat
hi'lhcha nannola' olashtok. Charles
danced and played music.
nannompatalhpo' bed cover; car
cover; tarpaulin [nanna
om+pattalhpo+']
nannompatkachi' doily, mat [nanna
ompatkachi+']
nannoppolo' monster; poison; trash
heap [nanna oppolo+']
nannoppolo', (MJ, AB) nannokpolo',
(VB) nannoppolo' aalha'li' trash
[aa+lha'li+']
nannoshkannapa to be lucky (MJ)
[nanna *oshkannapa]
nannookahánchi to make noise (I)
[nanna+hook(ano) *ahanchi] {neg.
iknannooka'cho; nannaachi} §
Ishnannookahanchi. You make
noise.
nannookano see nannahookano
nannookya see nannahookya
nannookya ikimiksho see nannakya
ikimiksho
nannookya iksho see nannakya
iksho
nannootokchi see nannatokchi
nanoshik minnow, small fish [nani
<oshik>]
nanta what (nonsubj.), of what
(poss.) (int.) {ind.-inf. nanna} §
Nanta hakshopta ishhommachim?
What skin (the skin of what) did
you dye red? | Nanta ishpisa? What
did you see?
nanta? what (did you say)?
nantahaat what (subj.) (int.) {ind.
nannahmt; inf. nannahoot} §
Nantahaat chikisili? What bit you?
nantahaat inkatihmi to have what be
wrong with one (III) (int.) [+HM],
<nantahaat inkatih> § Nantahaat

chinkatihmi? What's wrong with you?
<nantahaat inkatih> [HM] of nantahaat inkatihmi
nantahaat ishtimaawiiki to have what bothering one (III) {ggr. nantahaat ishtimaawí'ki; ind. nannakat ishtimaawiiki; inf. nannahoot ishtimaawiiki} § Nantahaat ishchimaawi'ki? What's bothering you?
nantahaat katihmi to have what happen to one (anim. subj.) (II) [+HM], <nantahaat katih> § Nantahaat chikatihmi? What happened to you? | Lynnat nantahaat katihmi? What happened to Lynn?
nantahaat katihmihta see katihmihta
<nantahaat katih> [HM] of nantahaat katihmi
nantahánni hngr. of nantanni
nantahta what (nonsubj.) {ind. nannahma; inf. nannaho}
nantahta which, what (nonsubj., used with preceding noun) [influenced by English?] § Ofi' nantahta pistok? Which dog did you see?
nantahto? what is it?
nantanna' crocheted item, something crocheted [nanna tanna+']
nantanna' toba' yarn
nantanni to crochet, knit, embroider (I) [*nanna tanni/ nanna *tanni] {hngr. nantahánni} § Iinantanni, Nankiitanni. We crocheted.
nantokahli' fireworks, caps [nanna tokahli+']
nasi', (ER) nassi' acorn
nasishto' type of acorn with a hairy edging, perhaps from boshto' oak

(burr oak?) [nasi' ishto+']
naslaknapi' type of tree (CC) [nasi' lakna api']
nassano'li', (AB) naasanno'li' praying mantis, devil horse
nassapi' red oak [nasi' api']
nashoba wolf
nashoba homma' coyote [homma+']
nashoba losa' timber wolf [losa+']
nashobattish type of medicinal plant (CC) [nashoba ittish]
nashobaat chomak pofa for it to be foggy (AB) [nashoba+at]
nashob-okchamali' grey wolf [nashoba okchamali+']
nashshaka' back (of the body) (VB) [ashaka']
náyyakbi ygr. of nakbi
naa-achiifa see naachiifa
naa-alhtoka', naalhtoka' policeman, sheriff [nanna alhtoka+']
naa-apiisachi', naapiisachi' guard [nanna apiisachi+']
naachiifa, naa-achiifa to wash clothes, do the wash (I) [*nanna achiifa / nanna *achiifa] § Ishnaachiifa. You do the wash. | Naailachiifa, Iinaa-achiifa. We wash clothes.
naacho'li to sew (I) [*nanna acho'li] § Ishnaacho'li. You sew things.
naafallapa', naafalli' apa' weevil [naafalli' apa+']
naafalli' cotton (plant) [nanna pofalli+'] {nampofalli}
naafalli' apa' see naafallapa'
naafalli' aanihichi' cotton gin [aa+nihichi+']
naafinha miracle {nannakat finha}
naafka see naafokha
naafka aa-apaakotalhchi' see naafkaa-apaakotalhchi'
naafka hasimbish train on a long dress

naafka holiitopa' formal wear (tuxedo, evening gown) [holiitopa+']

naafka ikfo'ko to be naked (IN) {fokha} § Naafka akfo'ko. I'm naked.

naafka loposhki' silk; silk dress [loposhki+']

naafka lo'bo' shirt [lombo+']

naafka shakba' sleeve

naafka shakbifolota' cuff (pl.—a whole lot of cuffs: naafka shakbifoloto'ha', naafka shakbifoloto'wa') [naafka shakba' im+folota+']

naafka shihli to take off one's clothes, get undressed (I)

naafka toba' cloth, fabric (any type, before it is made up) [toba+']

naafka woksho' flannel [woksho+']

naafkaa-achifa' laundry, laundromat [naafka aa+achifa+']

naafkaa-acho'li' sweatshop where sewing is done [naafka aa+acho'li+']

naafkaa-asha' closet; dry-goods store, clothes store [naafka aa-asha']

naafkaachofalli' dry cleaner's [naafka aa+chofalli+']

naafkaaimaaiksaachi' tailor's shop [naafka aa+imaaiksaachi+']

naafkaakanchi' dry-goods store, clothes store [naafka aa+kanchi+']

naafkaalhto' suitcase, grip [naafka aalhto']

naafkaapaakota'lhchi' hem on a dress [naafka aa+apaakotalhchi+']

naafkaataka'li' nail, hook, single hanger—something to hang things on [naafka aa+takali+']

naafkaatakohli' clothesline, clothesrack; hangers [naafka aa+takohli+']

naafkikbi' tailor [naafka ikbi+']

naafkimacho'li' seamstress [naafka imacho'li+']

naafkimaaiksaachi' tailor [naafka imaaiksaachi+']

naafkishtakallochi', naafkishtakallo'chi' clothespin [naafka ishtakallochi'/ naafka ishtakallo'chi']

naafkishto' coat, sweater, jacket [naafka ishto+']

naafkishto' afokhi'chi' vest [afokhi'chi+']

naafkishto' falaa' full-length coat, such as a raincoat or overcoat [falaa+']

naafkishto' tilofa'si jacket

naafkishto' woksho' fur coat [woksho+']

naafkishihli to undress, remove the clothes from (someone) (I;III) [naafka *im+shihli] § Naafka chishihlili. I undress you.

naafokha, naafka dress, clothing [nanna fokha]

naafokha lhipa' old, worn-out clothes [lhipa+']

naafoni' bone (not of one's own body) (IIIp); dice [nanna foni'] § ofi' inaafoni': the dog's bone (to eat)

naafoni' naaishtalhcho'wa', naaishtalhcho'wa' naafoni' bone needle

naafoni' okchi' broth

naahakshop leather [nanna hakshop]

naahalbina' prize, present [nanna halbina+']

naahaloppa' sharp thing (with a point)—pen, knife, dart, fork, pin, thorn [nanna haloppa+']

naaholiitompa' communion (MJ) [nanna holiitompa+']

naaholiitompishtatta', Chihoowa inaaholiitompishtatta' elder, communion server {pl. naaholiitompishtaa-asha'}

naaholiitompishtaa-asha', Chihoowa inaaholiitompishtaa-asha' elders, communion servers {sg. naaholiitompishtatta'}
naaholiitompishtaa-asha' obyaka' impa' communion, the Lord's Supper
naaholbona' package [nanna holbona+']
Naahollanompa' see Naahollimanompa'
naahollihoo' white woman [naahollo ihoo+']
naaholliklanna' half-white person [naahollo iklanna+'] § Naaholliklanna' saya. I'm half white, I'm a half-white.
Naahollimanompa', Naahollanompa' English language [naahollo (im+)anompa+']
naahollimbala' green peas, English peas [naahollo im+bala']
naahollimmi' something white people use, for which there's no Indian name [naahollo immi']
naahollimosak English walnut [naahollo im+osak]
naahollihayi see naahollo ihayi
naahollo, (MJ) naaollo white person, Anglo, white man [nanna ihollo/<hollo>]
naahollo intii' store-bought tea [im+tii']
naahollo ihayi, naahollihayi English walnut [im+naalhpisa']
naahollo inaalhpisa' white men's law; government [im+naalhpisa']
Naahollo Inittak Thanksgiving [im+nittak]
Naahollo Iyaakni' Texas [im+yaakni']
naahollo nannapiisa', naahollo naapiisa' judge [naahollo nanna apiisa+']

naahollo naapiisa' see naahollo nannapiisa'
naaholloshi' white baby [naahollo oshi']
naaholhtina' arithmetic, calculation [nanna holhtina+']
naaholhtina' holisso arithmetic book
naahomi' ammonia [nanna homi+']
naahonkopa' thief, person who will steal anything [nanna honkopa+']
naaishbo'wa' hammer [nanna isht bo'wa+']
naaishchala' starch [nanna isht chala+']
naaishchokoshkomo' game with equipment—checkers, for instance [nanna ishchokoshkomo']
naaishfoloha' drill [nanna isht foloha+']
naaishhaloppachi' see nannishhaloppachi'
naaishhama' iron (for ironing) [nanna isht hama+']
naaishshachi' devil (CP) {nannaaishshachi'}
naaishshachi' isholosh talakchi' devil's shoestring (plant) (CP) [im+sholosh]
naaishtachaakissa' glue [nanna isht achaakissa+']
naaishtacho'li' ilbakoshi' fokha' thimble (WB) [nanna isht acho'li+', fokha+']
naaishtafinni' crowbar [nanna isht afinni+']
naaishtahoobali ki'yo, nannishtahoobali ki'yo not to care about (I;II) [nanna isht ahoobali] § Naaishtasahoobali ki'yo. He doesn't care about me.
naaishtakallishkin, naaishtakallo' ishkin buttonhole [naaishtakallo' ishkin]
naaishtakallo', naashtakallo' button,

257

snap [nanna isht akallo+']

naaishtakallo' ishkin see naaishtakallishkin

naaishtalhcho'wa', chofaakoshi' naaishtalhcho'wa' needle [nanna isht alhcho'wa+']

naaishtalhcho'wa' ishkin eye of a needle

naaishtalhcho'wa' naafoni' see naafoni' naaishtalhcho'wa'

naaishtalhpisa', nannishtalhpisa' something to measure with, such as a tape measure, ruler, yardstick, or bushel basket [nanna isht alhpisa+']

naaishtanalha' nail [nanna isht analha+']

naaishtashana' screw [nanna isht ashana+']

naaishtashanishtiwwi', naaishtashana' ishtiwwi' wrench [naaishtashana' isht tiwwi+']

naaishtashannichi' screwdriver [nanna isht ashannichi+']

naaishtaabachi' in ilbak naaishtaabachi'

naaishtiksaa' trimming: especially, yarn, lace [nanna isht iksaa+']

naaishtimaholiito'pa to be selfish (III) [nanna isht *im+a+holiito'pa] § Naaishtamaholiito'pa. I'm selfish.

naaishtimahómba ki'yo, naaishtimómba ki'yo not to care (III) [nanna isht *im+ahomba] § Naaishtamahomba ki'yo. I don't care.

naaishtimómba ki'yo see naaishtimahómba ki'yo

naaishtinkanihmi see nanninkanihmi

naaishtittilawwichi' level (tool)

naaittapa'ta' sheet or bedspread pieced from several narrow widths of material [nanna <ittapaata>+']

naalhchifa' clean laundry [nanna alhchifa+']

Naalhchifa' Nittak Friday, wash day

naalhila'fa', naalhla'fa' rag; uncut cloth, yardage [nanna lhilafa+'] (naalhilahli')

naalhilahli' rags, pieces of cloth [nanna lhilahli+'] (naalhila'fa')

naalhipa' rag; junk [nanna lhipa+']

naalhipa' aa-asha' junkyard [nanna lhipa+']

naalhla'fa' see naalhila'fa'

naalhopolli' bridge (WB) [nanna lhopolli+']

naalhpisa' see nannalhpisa'

naalhpisa' achapa to break the law, go against the law (I)

naalhpisa' bohli to lay down, make a law (I)

naalhpisa' ikbi see nannalhpisa' ikbi

Naalhpisa' Ikbi' Congress, Legislature; member of Congress, member of the Legislature [ikbi+']

naalhpisa' kobaffi see nannalhpisa' kobaffi

naalhpisa' oppani to break the law (I) § Naalhpisa' ishoppani ishhonkopakmat. If you steal you'll break the law.

Naalhpisa' Pokko'li, Naalhpisa' Pokko'li' the Ten Commandments [pokko'li+']

naalhpooba, nannalhpooba' domestic animal [nanna alhpooba]

naalhpoobimalikchi' veterinarian [naalhpooba im+alikchi']

naalhtoka' election [nanna alhtoka+']

naalhtoka' see naa-alhtoka'

naalhtoka' atookoli to hold elections, have an election (I)

naapiisa to give an order (I) [*nanna apiisa] (inaapiisa: to give an order to) § Ishnaapiisa. You gave an order.

naapiisa' lawmaker, President

[naapiisa+'] § Reaganakot Naapiisa'. Reagan is President.

naapiisachi' see naa-apiisachi'

naashachakla' net material: especially, mosquito net [nanna shachakla+']

naashaali', (WB) naashahli' freight train [nanna shaali+']

naashiha', naashiya' unravelled or dangling threads hanging from a garment or from the edge of a piece of cloth [nanna shiha+']

naashiya' see naashiha'

naashiipa' rubber, elastic [nanna shiipa+']

naashiipa' sholosh aatoba' see sholosh naashiipa' aatoba'

naashombachi' bugs in food [nanna shombachi+']

naashtakallo' see naaishtakallo'

naawaa' see nannawaa'

naayimmi' believer; saint [nanna iyimmi+'] § Chihoowa Inaayimmi' Christian, believer in God

naayimmi' toba to become a believer, become a Christian, be saved (in the Christian sense) (I)

naayoppa happy (MC) (Ct) [nanna ayoppa]

<náa> see mina

naa-alhchi see naalhchi

naachanonkalatta'a' quilt batting [naachi anonka' alatta'a+']

naachi to pick (corn), cut (tree limbs) (pl. obj.) (I;3) [-SC] {v1. naalhchi; hngr. naalihínchi; ngr. naalínchi; sg. obj. nafi}

naachi quilt, blanket [nanna anchi+']

naachi aatanni' weaving loom (for blankets) [aa+tanni+']

naachi shobbokko'li' blanket (of any color) [shobbokko'li+']

naachi shobbokko'li' haloppa' wool blanket [haloppa+']

naachi shobbokko'li' homma' red blanket [homma+']

naachittapatkachi' pieced quilt [naachi ittapatkachi+']

naalihínchi hngr. of naachi

naalínchi ngr. of naachi

naalhchi, naa-alhchi to be picked (of corn), be pruned, be broken but still attached (pl. subj.) (3) {v2. naachi; sg. nafa}

nafa to be broken but still attached (of part of a plant) (sg. subj.) (3) {v1. nafi; pl. naalhchi}

nafi to pick (one ear of corn) or pull off (one branch of a tree) (sg. obj.) (I;3) {v1. nafa; pl. obj. naachi}

namihachi see nanna mihachi

nana see nanna

ní'ha ggr. of niha

nibli to take the arms and legs off, take all apart, dismember (I;II) {nipaachi}

niha grease, fat, lard, shortening; oil, gasoline

niha, niya to be greasy, fatty (II); (TP, ER, OC, MC) to be fat (Ct?) (II) [+CPR] [+PR] {ggr. ní'ha; hngr. nihíha; ngr. níha; ygr. níyyi'ha}

niha akmi' hardened grease, congealed fat [akmi+']

niha finha' pure lard [finha+']

niha losa' asphalt, tar [losa+']

niha shaali', (WB) niha-shahli' tank car (on a train), tanker truck [niha shaali+']

nihachi to grease, oil; to get (something) greasy (I;II) [+OPR] [niha+chi]

nihaakanchi' gas station [niha aa+kanchi+']

nihaakola' oil well [niha aakola']

nihaalhto' butane truck [niha aalhto']

nihi' seed {inihi'}

nihichi to separate the seeds from (cotton) (I;3) [nihi'+chi] § Naafalli' nihishli. I separate the seeds from the cotton. I aanihichi': cotton gin
nihíha hngr. of niha
ninak moon—only used in complex expressions, such as hashi' ninak aa, ninak toomi, ninak yaaha'
ninak ontoomi rainbow (JC)
ninak toomi to be moonlight (—), to have moonlight (of a place) (3) {naktoomi} § Ninak toomikat chokma. The moonlight's pretty, It's moonlight and it's pretty. I Oklahomma'at ninak toomi. It's moonlight in Oklahoma, Oklahoma has moonlight.
ninak yaaha' growth on tree limbs that is sewn in a sack and worn by a child who wakes in the night (MJ) [yaa+']
nipafa to be completely split apart (for instance, of a tree struck by lightning); to have an arm or leg pulled off (of a doll, for instance— not of a person) (3) {v2. nipaffi; nipahli: to have the arms and legs pulled off}
nipaffi to pull off an arm or leg from (I;II) {v1. nipafa; hngr. nipaháffi; nibli, nipaachi: to dismember}
nipaháffi hngr. of nipaffi
nipaháli hngr. of nipahli
nipahchi see nipaachi
nipahli to be all broken to pieces, to have the arms and legs pulled off, to decompose, break apart (II) {hngr. nipaháli; nipafa: to be completely split, to have an arm or leg pulled off; nibli, nipaachi: to dismember}
nipaachi, nipahchi to tear apart, dismember (I;II) [nipahli+chi] {nibli}
nipaafoloha', nipaafolowa' meat grinder [nipi' aa+foloha+']

nipaapalli' frying pan [nipi' aa+palli+']
nipi' meat
nipi' albani' barbecued meat [albani+']
nipi' aa-abaani', nipi' aa-albani' barbecue grill, barbecue pit [aa+abaani/albani+']
nipi' aa-albani' see nipi' aa-abaani'
nipi' aabashli' butcher shop [aa+bashli+']
nipi' aaoshoboochi' smokehouse [aa+oshoboochi+']
nipi' bashli' butcher [bashli+']
nipi' bíyyi'ka to be naked (3) (Ct)
nipi' foloha' sausage [foloha+']
nipi' hapayyima', (MJ) nipi' hapaayma' salt pork, dry salt [hapayyima+']
nipi' hollosi' hash [hollosi+']
nipi' holhponi' stew [holhponi+']
nipi' ishfolohli' meat grinder [isht folohli+']
nipi' okchi' meat broth
nipi' oshobohli' bacon [oshobohli+']
nipi' pasa' jerky [pasa+']
nipi' shila' jerky [shila+']
nipishcha'li' kitchen mallet (for pounding meat) [nipi' isht cha'li+']
nipishlolli' meat chopper [nipi' isht lolli+']
nis nis go potty (word used by children when they wanted to leave a church service, for instance, and go to the bathroom—possibly used just in one family?) (LR)
nita' bear
nita' aakapassaa-asha' polar bear [aa+kapassa aa-asha']
nita' holba' teddy bear
nita' homma' type of small, reddish brown bear [homma+']
nita' kamaa' panda [kamaa+']
nita' lakna' brown bear [lakna+']

nittak nantahta

nita' lobahli' large bush with clusters of small (inedible) bright purple berries (beauty bush?)
nita' losa' black bear [losa+']
nita' sawa'si' koala [sawa'si+']
nita' tish type of medicinal plant (CC)
nita' tohbi' polar bear [tohbi+']
nit-oshi' bear cub [nita' oshi']
nittak day; in the daytime, by day § Nittak nosi. He sleeps in the daytime.
Nittak Ammo'na' Monday (the first day) [ammo'na+']
Nittak Atochchi'na' Wednesday (the third day) [atochchi'na+']
Nittak Atokla' Tuesday (the second day) [atokla+']
Nittak Ayyoshta' Thursday (the fourth day) [ayyoshta+']
nittak chashpo mashshaash see chashpo mashshaash
nittak chashpohma see chashpohma
nittak chiikihma see chiikihma
nittak habina to have a day off (I)
nittak habinachi to give a day off to (I;II)
nittak hashi', (WB) hashi' nittak sun
nittak holitto'pa' religious holiday—Christmas, Sunday, etc. [holitto'pa+']
nittak holiitopa' holiday [holiitopa+']
Nittak Hollishto', (MC, CP) Takhollishto', (VB, WB) Nittak Hollo' Ishto' Christmas [Nittak Hollo' ishto+']
Nittak Hollo' Sunday [<hollo>+']
Nittak Hollo' Aaiklanna', (TP) Nittak Hollo' Iklanna Wednesday [aaiklanna+']
Nittak Hollo' Nakfish Saturday
Nittak Hollo' Nittak Easter (CC)
nittak ima to give a day off to (I;III)

Nittak Ishhanna'li' Saturday (the sixth day) [ishhanna'li+']
Nittak Ishtalhlha'pi' Friday (the fifth day) [ishtalhlha'pi+']
Nittak Ishtayyo'pi', Nittak Istayyopi' Judgment Day, the Last Day [ishtayyo'pi+'] § Nittak Ishtayyo'paat ala'hi. Judgment Day will come.
Nittak Ishtontoklo' Sunday (the seventh day) [ishtontoklo+']
nittak iholiitobli to declare a holiday in honor of (I;III) [im+holiitobli] § Martin Luther King nittak kiliholiitobla'chi. We're going to have a holiday in honor of Martin Luther King.
nittak kanimpihma, nittak kanimpika one day, some day {inf. nittak kanimpiho; int. nittak katimpihta} § Nittak kanimpika onala'chi. I'll go there one day. | Nittak kanimpihma onalitok. I went there one day.
nittak kanimpiho what day (inf.) {ind. nittak kanimpihma; int. nittak katimpihta} § Nittak kanimpiho onalitoka ithana. She knows what day I got there. | Nittak kanimpiho onala'chika ithana. She knows what day I'll get there.
nittak kanimpika see nittak kanimpihma
nittak katimpihta what day (int.) {ind. nittak kanimpihma; inf. nittak kanimpiho} § Nittak katimpihta ala'chi? What day will he come?
nittak nannahma some day, a certain day {inf. nittak nannaho; int. nittak nantahta}
nittak nannaho what day (inf.) {ind. nittak nannahma; int. nittak nantahta}
nittak nantahta what day (int.) {ind.

261

nittaki

nittak nannahma; inf. nittak nannaho)

nittaki early in the morning (usually, before sunup: tomorrow, habitually, or at another time not in the past); to be early in the morning (—) (usually subr.) {ngr. nittánki; níyyi'tako'si} § Nittaki ishlashki. Come early in the morning. | nittaki, nittakikma: early in the morning (tomorrow) | nittaki, nittakiaash: early in the morning (yesterday or in the past) | Nittakikat hashi' ikkochchokisha aatok. He was out early in the morning before the sun was up. | Nittakittook. It was early in the morning.

nittaki hopooni to make breakfast (I)

nittaki impa to eat breakfast (I)

nittaki pakali' type of plant that blooms only in the morning (not morning glory) (CW); (WB, LF, EH, EP, LR, AW) morning glory

nittaki pila before noon § Nittaki pila ootok. It was before noon. | Nittaki pilakma iilatok. We arrived before noon. | Nittaki pilaasho hashi' kanalli pokko'li fokhakaasho pislitok. I saw him at about ten in the morning.

nittakiaash early yesterday (or some other past) morning [nittaki+aash]

nittakikma early tomorrow (or some other future) morning [nittaki+kma]

nittánki ngr. of nittaki

niya see niha

níyyi'ha ygr. of niha

níyyi'tako'si really early in the morning (MJ) [nittaki+o'si]

niini hurt (baby talk)

níha ngr. of niha

nó'na ggr. of nona

nó'si ggr. of nosi

nochi' milkweed

nohóna hngr. of nona

nohósi to fall asleep, drift off—hngr. of nosi

nohówa hngr. of nowa

nokbikichi to give (a child˚) so much of (some soft food like bread) that he chokes (I;II;3) [+SC] [nokbikili+chi]

nokbikili to have something (especially, something soft) stuck in one's throat (II); to gag on, have (something) caught in the throat (II,3) [nok+] § Paska sanokbikitok. I gagged on the bread. | Paskat ishto sala'mina sanokbikitok. The bread was too big so I gagged on it.

nokbiibli to hit and knock the breath out of (sg. obj.) (I;II) [nok+] {v1. nokbiipa; pl. obj. nokbiipo'li}

nokbiipa to have the breath knocked out of one (sg. subj.) (II) [nok+] {v2. nokbiibli; pl. nokbiipo'wa}

nokbiipo'li to knock the breath out of (pl. obj.) (I;II) [nok+] {v1. nokbiipo'wa; sg. obj. nokbiibli}

nokbiipo'wa to have the breath knocked out of one (pl. subj.) (II) [nok+] {v2. nokbiipo'li; sg. nokbiipa}

nokchínto to be calmer—ngr. of nokchito

nokchito to rest, behave oneself, be calm (II) [nok+<chito>] {v2. nokchitoli; ngr. nokchínto; aanokchí'to}

nokchitoli to make rest, make calm (I;II) {v1. nokchito; ngr. nokchitóli}

nokchitóli ngr. of nokchitoli

nokfapa' mudcat (type of fish) (TJ) [lokfi' apa+' ?]

nokfokha to recollect, have come back to one, call to mind (II;3) [nok+fokha] {ngr. nokfónkha: to

remember; ygr. nokfóyyokha}
nokfokhachi to remind (someone to
do something) (I;II); to remind ° of
° (I;II;3) [nokfokha+chi] § Charlesat
Lynna sanokfokhachitok. Charles
reminds me of Lynn, Charles
reminds Lynn of me.
nokfónkha to remember, not forget,
keep in mind (II;3); to remember
(an event) (II)—ngr. of nokfokha
nokfóyyokha ygr. of nokfokha
<nokhamichi> [nok+hammi+chi ?]
{ggr. nokhámmi'chi; hngr.
nokhamihínchi; ngr. nokhamínchi}
nokhamihínchi hngr. of
<nokhamichi>, nokhámmi'chi
nokhamínchi ngr. of <nokhamichi>,
nokhámmi'chi
nokhámmi'chi to be impatient, not
be able to sit still, not to want to
wait; to be in pain, be mourning; to
be overcome by desire (II)—ggr. of
<nokhamichi> [{hngr.
nokhamihínchi; ngr. nokhamínchi}
§ Sanokhammi'shtok. I am
overcome by desire, I am dying for
it (primarily sexually).
nokhánglo to be sad, sorry (II)
[nok+hanglo] {inokhánglo: to be
sorry for, to pity}
nokhanglochi to make sad (I;II)
[nokhanglo+chi] {ngr.
nokhanglónchi}
nokhanglónchi ngr. of nokhanglochi
nokhistap neck (IIp) [nok+]
nokhistap foni' collarbone (CC, ER,
MJ)
nókko'wa to scold, yell, curse, swear
(I)—ggr. of <nokowa> {hngr.
nokohǫ́wa; inókko'wa: to scold
(someone), bawl out}
noklhamá'lli ggr. of noklhamalli
noklhamahą́lli hngr. of noklhamalli
noklhamalli, noklhamatli to inhale,

breathe in (while smoking) (II); to
have (something) go up one's nose
(II;3) [nok+] {ggr. noklhámmalli,
noklhamá'lli; hngr. noklhamahą́lli}
noklhamallichi to choke (someone)
(I;II); to make (someone°) breathe
(something) in (I;II;3)
[noklhamalli+chi]
noklhamatli see noklhamalli
noklhámma'lli ggr. of noklhamalli
noklhíhhi'pa to be lying on one's
face (I) (rare)—hgr. of <noklhipa>
<noklhímpa> in noklhimpat—ngr.
of <noklhipa>
noklhimpat lying on its face—prt. of
<noklhímpa> | Noklhimpat
wayya'a. It's lying on its face.
<noklhipa> [nok+lhipa] {hgr.
noklhíhhi'pa; ngr. <noklhímpa>;
lhímpa}
noklhito'li to choke (someone) (a
little, then release him) (I;II) [nok+
lhito'li] {v1. noklhito'wa;
noklhitofa}
noklhito'wa to be choked a little (II)
[nok+] {v2. noklhito'li; noklhitoffi}
noklhitofa to choke, be choked (II)
[nok+<lhitofa>] {v2. noklhitoffi; ggr.
noklhítto'fa; hngr. noklhitohǫ́fa;
ngr. noklhitǫ́fa; noklhito'wa}
noklhitoffi to choke (someone) (I;II)
[nok+<lhitoffi>] {v1. noklhitofa;
hngr. noklhitohǫ́ffi; noklhito'wa}
noklhitohǫ́fa hngr. of noklhitofa
noklhitohǫ́ffi hngr. of noklhitoffi
noklhitǫ́fa ngr. of noklhitofa
noklhítto'fa ggr. of noklhitofa
noklhitoffit abi to kill by choking, to
hang (as an execution) (I;II)
[noklhitoffi+t]
noklhitoffit illichi to choke
(temporarily), take the breath out of
(I;II) [noklhitoffi+t]
nokohǫ́wa hngr. of nókko'wa,

<nokowa>

<nokowa>
<nokowa> in inokowa {ggr.
nókko'wa; hngr. nokohǫ́wa}
noksí'ta ggr. of noksita
noksíhhi'ta to have something very
tight around one's neck (like a
choke chain)—hgr. of noksita
noksita to be hanged; to choke (II)
[nok+sita] {v2. noksitili; ggr. nosí'ta;
hgr. noksíhhi'ta: to have something
tight around the neck; xgr.
noksítti'ya}
noksitihį́li hngr. of noksitili
noksítti'ya xgr. of noksita
noksitili to hang, to kill by hanging
(I;II) [nok+sitili] {v1. noksita; hngr.
noksitihį́li}
nokshawạli to be clear (of water) (ER)
nokshí'la ggr. of nokshila
nokshila to be hoarse; to be thirsty
(II) [nok+shila] {v2. nokshilili; ggr.
nokshí'la; tokshila}
nokshilili to give (someone) a dry
throat, make someone hoarse (3;II)
[nok+shilili] {v1. nokshila}
nokshiyahą́mmi hngr. of
nokshiyammi
nokshiyammi to have (a liquid) go
down the wrong way, to choke on (a
liquid) (II;3); to have trouble getting
one's breath (while coughing, for
example) (II) [nok+<shiyammi>]
{ggr. nokshíyyammi; hngr.
nokshiyahą́mmi} § Oka'
sanokshiyammikat ithạnali. I know
the water went down the wrong
way.
nokshíyyammi ggr. of nokshiyammi
<nokshoopa> in inokshoopa
noktakaali to have (something solid)
stuck in one's throat (II;3); to gag,
choke on (something solid) (II;3)
[nok+takaali] § Nipi' sanoktakaatok.
I gagged on the meat.

noktala to calm down, get quiet,
comfortable (II) [nok+tala] {v2.
noktalaali; ngr. noktą́la: to be
comfortable, behave, feel better, be
patient; ygr. noktáyya'la}
noktalaali to calm (someone) down,
medicate (I;II) [nok+talaali] {v1.
noktala; ngr. noktalą́li}
noktalą́li ngr. of noktalaali
noktáyya'la ygr. of noktala
noktą́la to be comfortable, behave,
feel better; to be patient, consider
things carefully, bear it—ngr. of
noktala
noktiibli to knock the breath out of,
to hit in the stomach (I;II)
[nok+tiibli] {v1. noktiipa}
noktiipa not to be able to breathe
(because of illness) (II) [nok+tiipa]
{v2. noktiibli}
nokwaya to stay quiet, not to say
anything (especially, for fear of
saying the wrong thing), to be
ashamed to talk (II) [nok+waya]
{ngr. nokwą́ya: to be scared to speak,
to watch one's words; neg.
iknokwayyo; inokwaya}
nokwą́ya to be scared to speak, to
watch one's words—ngr. of
nokwaya
nokyobi to be damp (MJ)
[nok+<yobi>]
nona to be cooked, done, baked; to be
ripe (II) [+CPR] [+PR] {ggr. nó'na;
hngr. nohǫ́na; ngr. nǫ́na; ygr.
nóyyo'na}
nonachi to cook, bake (something);
to fire (pottery) (I;II) [nona+chi]
nosi to sleep, to go to sleep (I / II); to
get numb, be asleep (of an
extremity) (3) [+CPR] [+PR] {ggr.
nó'si; hngr. nohǫ́si; ngr. nǫ́si; prt.
nost}
nosi' fo'kha' pajamas, nightgown

[nosi+' fokha+']
nosi'chi' witch who can put you to sleep and then come into your house [nosichi+']
nosí'lhlha ggr. of nosilhha
nosichi to put to sleep, to anaesthetize (I;II) [nosi+chi]
nosichi' anaesthesiologist [nosichi+']
nosihílhlha hngr. of nosilhha
nosilhha, nosilhlha to be sleepy (II) [*nosi asilhha ?] {ggr. nosí'lhlha, nóssilhha; hngr. nosihílhlha; ygr. nosíyyi'lha, nosíyyi'lhlha} § Sanosilhlha. I'm sleepy.
nosilhhachi, nosilhlhachi to make sleepy (I;II) [nosilhha+chi]
nosilhlha see nosilhha
nosilhlhachi see nosilhhachi
nosíyyi'lha, nosíyyi'lhlha ygr. of nosilhlha
nóssilhha ggr. of nosilhlha
nost prt. of nosi
nost okcha to wake up from a nap (—, II) § Nost achokchata? Did you just wake up?
nostilli to sleep like the dead, not to be able to wake up (II); (LJ) to have a nightmare [(CW) nost *illi / (LJ) *nost illi] § Nossallitok. I slept like the dead, I couldn't wake up. | (LJ) Sanostillitok. I had a nightmare.
noshkó'nna ggr. of noshkonna
noshkohónna hngr. of noshkonna
noshkonna to really like (something) (II;3) [+OPR] {ggr. noshkó'nna; hngr. noshkohónna; ygr. noshkóyyo'nna: to really like, desire (a person)} § Lynn inaafokha sanoshkonnaha!, Lynna naafokha inoshkonnalihí! I really like Lynn's dress!
noshkóyyo'nna to really like, want to go with (a person)—ygr. of noshkonna
nota' bottom, underside (IIp); under,

underneath (II) § Nota' pitbohtok. He put it underneath. | Sanota'at sattopa. My bottom hurts.
nota' aalhipolli' see notaalhipolli'
notakfa jaw, (TP) chin (IIp)
notakfa kallo' lockjaw
notakhish, (WB, MJ, LF) notakshish beard, moustache, whiskers (IIp) [notakfa hishi']
notakhish ishshafi' razor [isht shafi+']
notakhish ishshafi' falaa' straight razor [falaa+']
notaahiyohli' gums (body part) (IIp) [noti' aa+<hiyohli>+']
notaalínchi to go toward underneath, to go the lower way (I); to go underneath at (a place) (I;3) [nota']
notaalhipolli', nota' aalhipolli' underpass [nota' aa+lhipolli+']
notaamá'lli ggr. of notaamalli
notaamalli, notaamatli to go under (I;II) [nota'] {ggr. notaamá'lli}
notaamatli see notaamalli
notali' (moving) underneath § Notali'a ishaalhopolla'hi biyyi'ka. You can go through underneath, by the underneath way. | Aaimpa' notali' mintitok. He came along through underneath the table.
noti', (LF) innoti' tooth (IIp—based on <innoti'>) § sannoti': my tooth | ponnoti': our teeth
noti' holba' false teeth (IIp)
noti' ishchafi'nachi' toothpick (WB)
noti' ittikisilichi to grind one's teeth (IIp , IR) [+SC] § Chinoti' ishtikisilishtam? Did you grind your teeth?
noti' tihli' dentist [tihli+']
notinto'wa' foundation [nota' im+to'wa+']
notishfi'chi', (AB) ishtafi'chi'

265

toothpick [noti' isht fi'chi+']
notishtachifa' toothbrush,
toothpaste, tooth powder [noti' isht achifa+']
notihiyohli' foundation poles or pilings [nota' im+hiyohli+']
nóyyo'na ygr. of nona
nó'wa ggr. of nowa
nóna ngr. of nona
nósi ngr. of nosi
nosit áa to sleepwalk (I , I) [nosi+t] § Ishnosit ishaatok. You walked in your sleep.
nowa to walk (I); to go around E+t] (I) [-CPR] [+PR] {ggr. nó'wa; hngr. nohówa; ngr. nówa} § ishtakanomit nowa: to go around being a clown,

to clown around
nówa ngr. of nowa
nowachi to walk (a dog, for instance), to make walk (I;II) [nowa+chi]
nowat áa to be just walking around (sg. subj.) (I) [nowa+t] {pl. nowat ittanowa}
nowat ibaahaksi to go off and get drunk with or be crazy with; to run around with; to sleep with (I;II) [nowa+t]
nowat ittanohówa see nowat ittanówa
nowat ittanówa, nowat ittanohówa to be just walking around (pl. subj.) (I) [nowa+t] {sg. nowat áa}

O

ó'chi ggr. of oochi
ó'la ggr. of ola
ó'na ggr. of ona
ó'ti ggr. of ooti
oblaashaash yesterday
oblaashaash mishshaash, mishshaash the day before yesterday
oblaashaasho nittaki yesterday morning [oblaashaash+ho]
obya to be evening, especially late evening; to be over (of the day) (3); all day (aux.) (used with a preceding verb +na) {ggr. ôbya; hngr. ohómbya} § Nittakat obyatok. The day is over. | Obyakma pisla'chi. I'll see him this evening. | Ithanali hihilhli obyatokat. I know I danced all day.
ôbya ggr. of obya
obyaka' evening [obya+ka']
obyaka' impa to eat supper (I)
obyaka' impa' supper [(obyaka'

impa)+']
obyaka' pakali' type of flower; (PBr) four-o'clocks
obyaka' pila afternoon § Obyaka' pila hashi' kanalli toklokaasho pislitok. I saw him at two o'clock in the afternoon.
obyaka'aash yesterday evening, (early) last night [obyaka'+aash]
obyakma this evening, (early) tonight [obya+kma]
ofaabli, (TJ) ofaapili, (WB) faapoli ditch
ofaabli ikbi to dig a ditch (I)
ofaabli ikbi' ditch digger [ikbi+']
ofaabli kolli' ditch digger [kolli+']
ofi' dog § sashki' imofi': my mother's dog
ofi' aa-asha' kennel, pound
ofi' aa-ashaachi' pound [aa+ashaachi+']
ofi' falaa' dachshund [falaa+']

ofi' foshi' hoyo' birddog [hoyo+']
ofi' haksibish falaa' hound [falaa+']
ofi' imimpa' see ofimpa'
ofi' imo'ma' Chihuahua; any small dog
ofi' ishki' mother dog
ofi' ishatanni dog tick [im+shatanni]
Ofi' Losa' (bad name to call someone) [losa+']
ofi' naapiisachi' watchdog [nanna apiisachi+']
ofi' oshpishichi' mother dog with nursing pups
ofi' palli' hot dog, frankfurter [palli+'—loan translation from English]
ofi' palhki' greyhound [palhki+']
ofi' sholop ittish medicinal plant with purple flowers and berries
ofi' tish type of medicinal plant (CP) (perhaps the same as ofi' sholop ittish?)
Ofi' Tohbi' Ihina', Ofi' Tohbihina' the Milky Way [tohbi+' im+hina']
Ofi' Tohbihina' see Ofi' Tohbi' Ihina'
ofi' woksho' sheepdog, collie, other long-haired dog [woksho+']
ofi' yokachi' dogcatcher [yokachi+']
ofiminno'chi' see ofinno'chi'
ofimitti', (AW) ofi' imitti' poison oak, poison ivy, poison sumac; (MC, AW) dogwood [ofi' im+itti']
ofimpa', ofi' imimpa' dog food [ofi' im+impa']
ofinchokka' doghouse [ofi' im+chokka']
ofinno'chi', ofiminno'chi' dog collar, dog tag [ofi' (im+)inno'chi']
ofishkobishto', ofi' ishkobishto', (WB) ofi' ishkoboshto' bulldog [ofi' ishkobo ishto+']
ofishkobishtoshi', ofi' ishkobishto' oshi' bulldog puppy [ofishkobishto'

oshi']
ofishik puppy [ofi' <oshik>]
ofiyalhki' pakti' type of white mushrooms that grow in trash (children's expression) [ofi' im+yalhki']
ofolo screech owl
ofolottish type of medicinal plant [ofolo ittish]
óhho'na, óhho'na'si to just barely reach, not to be able to get a grip on (I;3)—hgr. of ona [+a'si] § Ohho'na'sli. I just barely reached it.
óhholhti hgr. of olhti
<ohmi> in yakohmi, yamohmi {hoomi}
ohnochi see onhochi
ohómba hngr. of omba
ohómbya hngr. of obya
ohónchi hngr. of oochi
ohónkcha hngr. of okcha
ohónti hngr. of ooti
ohóla hngr. of ola
ohóna hngr. of ona
ohónna hngr. of onna
ohówwa hngr. of owwa
oka' water; other liquid: especially, liquor
oka' akmi' see okakmi'
oka' apootaka' side of the water, lakeshore
oka' aa-akmichi' freezer [aa+akmichi+']
oka' aabichili' faucet, spout, fountain (Ct?)
oka' aaishko' water glass (VB) [aa+ishko+']
oka' aakatapa' dam [aa+katapa+']
oka' aakolli' maachi' see oka' aamaachi'
oka' aalawashki' see okaalawashki'
oka' aalhatapa', okaalhatapa' waterfall, spillway, faucet, fountain [aa+lhatapa+']

267

oka' aalhto', (CC) oka' aa-alhto'
water container: rain barrel,
reservoir, fire hydrant, pitcher, car
radiator

oka' aamaachi', oka' aakolli' maachi'
windmill (ER) [aa+kolli+'
mahchi+']

oka' aaokaamalli' diving board
[aa+okaamalli+']

oka' aapakali' water lily (CP)
[aa+pakali+']

oka' aaya' gutter [aa+aya+']

oka' aayanahli', oka' aayanalli',
okaayanalli' gutter, ditch
[aa+yanalli/yanahli+']

oka' aayoka' rain barrel, reservoir
[aa+yoka+']

oka' aayokachi' dam, reservoir
[aa+yokachi+']

oka' aayopi' swimming pool
[aa+yopi+'] § amoka' aayopi': my
swimming pool

oka' bakhitibli', oka' bakhitibli
backwater [bakhitibli+']

oka' hapayyima' salt water, brine
[hapayyima+']

oka' homi' whiskey, liquor [homi+']

oka' homi' aaikbi' still, distillery
[aa+ikbi+']

oka' homi' ikbi' bootlegger [ikbi+']

oka' hoyo to divine, look for water
underground (I) [hoyo]

oka' impokpokichi to make bubbles
(in a tub) for, make water bubble for
(I;III) [im+pokpokichi]

oka' ishtahollo' see okishtahollo'

Oka' Ishtakafa' see Ishtaka'fa'

oka' ishtokaayopi' water wings [isht
okaa+yopi+']

oka' ishtokpalali' water wings [isht
okpalali+']

oka' ishtoochi' see okishtoochi'

oka' ishtoochi' inchanaaka' wheel of
a windmill (WB) [im+chanaa+ka']

oka' ishtolha'li' watering can, squirt
gun, clothes sprinkler [isht
on+lha'li+']

oka' ishtoshalalli', okishtoshalalli'
surfboard [isht on+shalalli+']

oka' ishyokachi' cistern, rain barrel
[isht yokachi+']

oka' ittookaaillichi to drown each
other (I / IR) [itti+(oka' okaaillichi)>
oka' *ittookaaillichi] § Oka'
ilittookaaillicha'chi, Oka'
iitokaaillicha'chi. We'll drown each
other.

oka' iyopichi to bathe (someone) for
' (I;III;3)

oka' kapassa' well water; cold water
[kapassa+']

oka' kitobalhto' bottled water [kitoba
alhto+']

oka' lowak firewater (whiskey)—
modern slang [translated from the
English?]

oka' lha'li to water down something
(such as a sidewalk) (I)

oka' nampakali' water lily (CC)

oka' noklhamallit illi to drown (II)
[noklhamalli+t] § Oka'
noklhamallit salla'chi! I'm going to
drown!

oka' okaa-abi to drown (someone)
(I;II) § Oka' issokaa-aba'chi. You'll
drown me.

oka' okaailli to drown (II) § Oka'
asokaaillitok. I drowned.

oka' okaaittánno'wa to wade; to
move, float in the water (of boats,
ducks); to go in a boat (dl. subj.) (I)
{sg. oka' okaanowa (wade), oka'
okaayáa (float, go in a boat); tpl. oka'
okaaittanohówa}

oka' okaaittanohówa to wade; to
move, float in the water (of boats,
ducks); to go in a boat (tpl. subj.) (I)
{sg. oka' okaanowa (wade), oka'

okaayáa (float, go in a boat); dl. oka'
okaaittánno'wa}
oka' okaan**o**wa to wade (sg. subj.) (I)
{dl. oka' okaaittánno'wa; tpl. oka'
okaaittanoh**ó**wa}
oka' okaatákka'li to be (suspended)
in water (I); to float in the water (of
a big boat) (3) (sg. subj.) {dl. oka'
okaatákkohli; tpl. oka' okaatakoht
m**áa**}
oka' okaatákkohli to be (suspended)
in water (dl. subj.) (I) {sg. oka'
okaatákka'li; tpl. oka' okaatakoht
m**áa**}
oka' okaatakoht m**áa** to be
(suspended) in water (tpl. subj.) (I)
[<okaatakohli>+t] {sg. oka'
okaatákka'li; dl. oka' okaatákkohli}
§ Oka' okaatakoht hashm**aa**. You all
are (suspended) in water.
oka' okaay**áa** to move, float in the
water (of a boat, duck); to go in a
boat (sg. subj.) (I) {dl. oka'
okaaittánno'wa; tpl. oka'
okaaittanoh**ó**wa}
oka' omba' see okomba'
oka' omba' aalhto' see okombaalhto'
oka' onashaachi to water (plants) (I;3)
§ Bala'ak oka' onashaashlitok. I
watered the beans.
oka' **o**lh**a**'li to water (the yard,
plants) (I;3)
oka' palli' aalhto' thermos [palli+']
oka' panki' wine
oka' patakshi', oka' potakshi' puddle
(AB) {okpachalhlhi'}
oka' pitokaakanchi to put, push (sg.
obj.) in water (I;II) [pit *okaakanchi]
oka' pitokaawayaachi to put
(nonhum. obj.) into water (I;3) [±SC]
[pit (oka' okaawayya'a)+chi> oka'
pit *okaawayya'a] § Oka'
pitishokaawayaacha'chi. You're
going to put it in the water.

oka' piini' boat (LF, MC)
oka' sinti' water moccasin (CC, CM)
oka' sokbish mouth of a stream;
where two streams come together
oka' taloha' puddle (WB)
oka' taakchaka' shore, beach,
riverbank, side of the water
oka' yopi to bathe, swim (I) § Oka'
ishyopi. You're swimming.
oka' yopichi to bathe (someone) (I;II)
oka'at chaafoochi for it to rain in
little drops, here and there [oka'+at]
{ngr. oka'at chaafoolínchi}
oka'at chaafoolínchi ngr. of oka'at
chaafoochi
oka'at **i**lhatapa to spill water on
oneself, to urinate on oneself (by
accident) (III) [oka'+at im+lhatapa]
okaffi, hokaffi to put a net into the
water to catch (fish), to net (fish) (I;3)
[ok+ ?]
okakmi', oka' akmi' ice [oka'
akmi+']
okakmi' aa-asha' icehouse
okakmi' aalhto', okakmi' aa-alhto'
icebox, ice-cube tray
okakmi' palli' dry ice [translation of
English 'hot ice'; palli+']
okakmi' tosha'fa' ice cube [toshafa+']
okakmishboshollichi' ice pick
[okakmi' isht boshollichi+']
okattola to fall in, fall into (I;3 / II;3)
[okaa+ittola] {imokattola} § Lokchok
okattolalitok. I fell in the mud. |
Apokattolatok. We fell in.
okaa-abi see oka' okaa-abi
okaa-ahánta to live, be in (sg. subj.)
(I;3) [okaa+ahanta] {dl. okaa**á**shwa;
tpl. okaa-áyya'sha} § Okti' okaa-
ahantali. I live in ice.
okaa-áyya'sha to live, be in (tpl. subj.)
(I;3) [okaa+ayya'sha] {sg. okaa-
ahánta; dl. okaa**á**shwa} § Okti'
ilokaa-ayya'sha. We live in ice.

okaaáshwa

okaaáshwa to live, be in (dl. subj.)
(I;3) [okaa+ashwa] {sg. okaa-ahánta;
tpl. okaa-áyya'sha}
okaabaafa to push one's finger into (a
frosted cake, someone's eye, etc.)
(I;3) [okaa+baafa] § Sashkin
okaabaafatok. He stuck his finger in
my eye, He punched me in the eye.
okaabila to melt in, dissolve in (3;3)
[okaa+bila] {v2. okaabilili} §
Ashookolaat oka' okaabilataha. The
sugar dissolved in the water.
okaabilili to melt, dissolve
(something) in (I;3;3) [okaa+bilili]
{v1. okaabila} § Ashookola'a oka'
okaabilililitok. I dissolved the sugar
in the water.
okaabowafa to cave in (from the top),
fall in (of a roof); to settle (of dirt on
top of a grave, for example) (3)
[okaa+bowafa]
okaachiloha', okaachilowa' ditch,
canyon
okaafimmi to put or push (dl. obj.˚)
into (I;II;3) [okaa+fimmi] {sg. obj.
okaakanchi; tpl. obj. okaalha'li}
okaahí'li to stand in, on (dl. subj.)
(I;3) [okaa+hi'li] {sg. okaahíkki'ya;
tpl. okaahiyoht máa}
okaahika to step in (I;3) [+OPR]
[okaa+hika] {okaahíkki'ya}
okaahíkki'ya to stand in, on (sg.
subj.) (I;3) [okaa+hikki'ya] {dl.
okaahí'li; tpl. okaahiyoht máa;
okaahika} § Hashshok
ishokaahikki'yatok. You stood in
the (relatively tall) grass.
okaahilichi to stand, set up (sg. obj.˚)
in, on (I;II;3) [okaa+hilichi] {pl. obj.
okaahiyohchi} § Shinok
achokaahilishli. I stand you up in
the sand.
okaahiyohchi to stand, set up (pl.
obj.) in (I;3;3) [<okaahiyohli>+chi]

{sg. obj. okaahilichi}
<okaahiyohli> in okaahiyoht máa,
okaahiyoochi [okaa+hiyohli]
okaahiyoht máa to stand in, on (pl.
subj.) (I;3) [<okaahiyohli>+t] {sg.
okaahíkki'ya; dl. okaahí'li}
okaahofobi, okaaofobi to sag; to have
a rounded depression, dip; to be
concave (3) [okaa+hofobi] {ggr.
okaaóffo'bi; ygr. okaaofóyyo'bi;
okaaofkobi}
okaahowita to vomit into (I;3)
[+OPR] [okaa+howita] § Shokcha
okaahowitalitok. I threw up into
the sack. I Ishokcha
okaahowitalitok, Shokcha
imokaahowitalitok. I threw up in
her sack.
okaahoyya' eaves (of a roof) [oka'
aa+hoyya+']
okaailli see oka' okaailli
okaaina', (ER) okaahina, (MJ)
aaokaaina', (CP, EP) okaaina down,
downhill (from a high point); (CP)
slough § Okaaina' ayalitok. I went
downhill.
okaaina' pila way down (from a high
point)
okaaittánno'wa, okaatánno'wa to
walk in (a flower bed, for instance)
(dl. subj.) (I;3) [okaa+ittanno'wa] {sg.
okaayáa; tpl. okaaittanohówa; oka'
okaaittánno'wa}
okaaittanohówa, okaatanohówa to
walk in (a flower bed, for instance)
(tpl. subj.) (I;3) [okaa+ittanohowa]
{sg. okaayáa; dl. okaaittánno'wa;
oka' okaaittanohówa}
okaaittashoma to be mixed together,
mixed up (3) [okaa+ittashoma] {v2.
okaaittashommi}
okaaittashommi to mix together,
mix up (I;3) [okaa+ittashommi] {v1.
okaaittashoma}

okaaittichóbbokli'chi to make noise
in the water (I) [+SC] [oka'
aa+ittichobbokli'chi]
okaakanchi to put, push (sg. obj.˚)
into (I;II;3) [okaa+kanchi] {dl. obj.
okaafimmi; tpl. obj. okaalha̱'li}
okaakaniya to go down into (mud,
sand, water, etc.) (II;3); to go into a
group of people, get lost in a crowd
(I;3) [okaa+kaniya]
okaakinafa to be sunken (of a
depressed area over a grave or
disused well, for example) (3)
okaalawashki', oka' aalawashki'
teakettle [oka' aa+lawashki+']
okaalhatabli to pour (one liquid or
mass) in with (something else)
(I;3;3) [okaa+lhatabli] {v1.
okaalhatapa}
okaalhatapa to get mixed up with (of
a liquid or mass, with another) (3;3)
[okaa+lhatapa] {v2. okaalhatabli}
okaalha̱'li to put, push (tpl. obj.˚)
into (I;II;3) [okaa+lha̱'li] {sg. obj.
okaakanchi; dl. obj. okaafimmi}
okaamahli to blow over (—;3)
[okaa+mahli] § Shinok
okaamahtok. It was blowing over
the sand.
okaamahli, okaamaali south [oka'
aa+mahli]
Okaamahli, Okaamahli Hattak, (WB)
Okaamahli Imma' Democrat,
Democratic party; the South (in the
Civil War), southern soldiers
Okaamahli Hattak see Okaamahli
(Democrat)
okaamalli to jump into, dive into
(I;3) [okaa+malli]
okaamaali see okaamahli
okaami to wash one's face (I); to
wash one's face with (a soap or
medicine, for instance) (I;3) [oka'
<mihchi> / yahmi ?]

okaamichi to wash the face of (I;II)
[okaami+chi]
okaano̱wa to walk in (a flower bed,
grass, mud, etc.) (I;3) [okaa+no̱wa]
{oka' okaano̱wa} § Kilokaano̱watok.
We walked in it.
okaaóffo'bi ggr. of okaahofobi,
okaaofobi
okaaofkobi to be full of potholes and
ditches (of a road, for example) (3)
{okaaofobi}
okaaofobi see okaahofobi
okaaofobi' ditch [okaaofobi+']
okaaofóyyo'bi ygr. of okaahofobi,
okaaofobi
okaapisa to look hard, stare at (I;II)
[okaa+pisa]
okaashala'li to ski, slide on; to
wallow in, roll around in (I;3)
[okaa+shala'li] § Lokchok
ishokaashala'tam? Were you
wallowing in the mud?
okaashalalli to slip, slide on (I;3)
[okaa+shalalli]
okaashó'ma ggr. of okaashoma
okaashó'mmi ggr. of okaashommi
okaashoma to be mixed in with (3;3)
[+T] [okaa+<shoma>] {v2.
okaashommi; ggr. okaashó'ma}
okaashommi to mix (one liquid or
mass) together with (another) (I;3;3)
[okaa+<shommi>] {v1. okaashoma;
ggr. okaashó'mmi}
okaatakafa to be hollowed out, to
have part scooped or cut out (of a
melon or a street with a dip) (3)
[okaa+<takafa>] {v2. okaatakaffi}
okaatakaffi to dip out (water, gravy,
or some other liquid): especially, to
dip (liquid) out messily, with one's
hands or the wrong implement (I;3)
[okaa+takaffi] {v1. okaatakafa}
<okaatakaali> [okaa+takaali] {ggr.
okaatákka'li; rmgr. okaatakkaká̱li;

271

okaatákka'li

pl. okaatakohli}
okaatákka'li ggr. of <okaatakaali>—
see oka' okaatákka'li
okaatakkakáli to be suspended on or
in, to swim in (sg. subj.) (I;3)—rmgr.
of <okaatakaali> [okaa+takkakali]
{dl. okaatakkokóli}
okaatákkohli see oka' okaatákkohli
okaatakkokóli to be suspended on or
in, to swim in (dl. subj.) (I;3)—rmgr.
of <okaatakohli> [okaa+takkokoli]
{sg. okaatakkakáli}
<**okaatakohli**> in okaatakoht máa
{ggr. okaatákkohli; rmgr.
okaatakkokóli; sg. okaatakaali}
okaatakoht máa see oka' okaatakoht
máa [<okaatakohli>+t]
okaatalaka to be settled (of sediment
in a liquid); to have the sediment
settled (of a liquid) (3)
[okaa+<talaka>] {v2. okaatalaali}
okaatalaali to put, set (sg. obj. with an
open top) into (water, a box, etc.)
(I;3;3) {v1. okaatalaka; pl. obj.
okaatalooli}
okaatálla'a to be in (sg. subj. with an
open top—for instance, of a small
boat) (I;3) [okaa+talla'a] {dl.
okaatállo'wa; tpl. okaatalowat máa}
okaatállo'wa to be in (dl. subj. with
an open top) (I;3)—ggr. of
<okaatalowa> {sg. okaatálla'a; tpl.
okaatalowat máa}
<**okaatalowa**> in okaatalowat máa
[okaa+talowa] {ggr. okaatállo'wa}
okaatalowat máa to be in (tpl. subj.
with an open top) (I;3)
[<okaatalowa>+t)] {sg. okaatálla'a;
dl. okaatállo'wa}
okaatalooli to put, set (pl. obj. with
open tops) into (I;3;3) [okaa+talooli]
{sg. obj. okaatalaali}
okaatánno'wa see okaaittánno'wa
okaatanohówa see okaaittanohówa

okaatanọwa to move down a slope
(I) [+taha] [okaa+tanọwa]
okaatanọwat aya to go down a slope
(I) [okaatanọwa+t]
okaatanọwat minti to come down a
slope (I) [okaatanọwa+t]
okaatofa to spit in, spit into (I;3;3)
[okaa+tofa] § Aatofa'a chomak
okaatofalitok. I spat tobacco into the
spitoon.
okaatono'li to wallow in, roll around
in (I;3) [okaa+tono'li] § Hashshok
ishokaatono'linna! Don't roll
around in the grass!
<**okaawayaa**> in okaawayaachi
[okaa+<wayaa>] {ggr. okaawáyya'a;
pl. <okaawayowa>}
okaawayaachi to put, set (sg. obj. with
open bottom, sg. four-legged obj., or
sg. obj. on hands and knees°) into
(I;II;3) [<okaawayaa>+chi] {pl. obj.
okaawayoochi}
<**okaawayowa**> in okaawayowat
máa, okaawayoochi
[okaa+<wayowa>] {ggr.
okaawáyyo'wa; sg. <okaawayaa>}
okaawayowat máa to be in (tpl. subj.)
(I;3) [<okaawayowa>+t] {sg.
okaawáyya'a; dl. okaawáyyo'wa}
okaawayoochi to put, set (pl. obj.
with open bottoms, pl. four-legged
obj., or pl. obj. on hands and
knees°) into (I;II;3)
[<okaawayowa>+chi] {sg. obj.
okaawayaachi}
okaawáyya'a to be in (sg. subj.—of an
animal in water, or an overturned
boat) (I;3)—ggr. of <okaawayaa> {dl.
okaawáyyo'wa; tpl. okaawayowat
máa}
okaawáyyo'wa to be in (dl. subj.)
(I;3)—ggr. of <okaawayowa> {sg.
okaawáyya'a; tpl. okaawayowat
máa}

okaayanalli' see oka' aayanahli'
okaayáa to walk in (sg. subj.) (I;3)
[okaa+aa] {dl. okaaittánno'wa; tpl.
okaaittanohówa; oka' okaayáa}
okaayilhihíli hngr. of okaayilhihli
okaayilhihli to completely cave in
(from the sides) (3) [okaa+yilhihi]
{hngr. okaayilhihíli; okaayilhipa}
okaayilhipa to cave in (from the
sides) (3) [ok+aa+yilhipa]
{okaayilhihli}
okaayinoffi to put one's hand in and
grab (something), to grab a handful
of (something) (I;3) [okaa+yinoffi]
okaayopi to take a bath in (I;3)
[okaa+yopi] § Lokchok
hashokaayopitokchayni. You all
wound up taking a bath in the mud.
okcha to wake up (II) [+CPR] [+PR]
{v2. okchali; ggr. ôkcha; hngr.
ohónkcha; ngr. ónkcha; ygr.
óyyokcha: to be awake; okcháa}
ôkcha ggr. of okcha
okchali to wake (someone) up (I;II)
{v1. okcha; hngr. okchafáli; ngr.
okcháli}
okchamachi to make green, blue (I;II)
[okchamali+chi] [-SC] {ngr.
okchamalínchi: to make greener}
okchamali to be green, blue (II); to be
raw (of fruit) (3) [ok+] {ggr.
okchámma'li; hngr. okchamahfáli;
ngr. okchamfáli; ygr. okchamáyya'li}
Okchamali Abookoshi Blue River
okchamalínchi to make greener—
ngr. of okchamachi
okchamáyya'li ygr. of okchamali
okchamáchi to make greener
[okchamáli+chi]
okchamáli to be green, unripe—ngr.
of okchamali
okchámma'li ggr. of okchamali
okchánki to be raw, uncooked (of
eggs, meat, vegetables) (3) §

Okchankina apatok. He ate it raw.
okchaalínchi to bring to life, save,
rescue (I;II)
Okchaalinchi' Savior
[okchaalinchi+']
okchaat lawa see okchi' lawa
okcháa, okcháha to be alive (II)
[+CPR] [+PR] {okcha} § Okchaacha
ilokchina. It was alive and healthy.
okchaat billi'ya' eternal life
[billi'ya+'] § Okchaat billi'ya'
ishtilanompolitok. We talked about
eternal life.
okchi' juice; liquid (associated with
something): for instance, gelatin (on
canned meat) [ok+]
okchi' lawa, okchi'at lawa, okchaat
lawa to be juicy (3) [okchi'+at] §
Takolaat no'nacha okchi' lawa,
Takolaat no'nacha okchi'at lawa.
The peach is ripe and juicy.
okchi'at lawa see okchi' lawa
okfaha to show up, appear (I); to be
exposed, found out, told on (II) {v2.
okfahli}
okfahfáli hngr. of okfahli
okfahchi to show, expose (I;II) [-SC]
[okfahli+chi] {ngr. okfahlínchi} §
Asokfahchitok. He showed me, He
let me be seen.
okfahli to expose (I;II) [ok+fahli ?]{v1.
okfaha; hngr. okfahfáli}
okfahlínchi ngr. of okfahchi
okfíchchibli ggr. of okfichibli
okfichibli to have puddles, be marshy
(of bottomland) (3) [ok+] {ggr.
okfíchchibli} § Pataaschaat
okfichibli. The bottomland is
marshy.
okfincha mink (?); (LF) magic
creature in the water that pulls one
down and eats the ends of one's
hands [ok+]
okfokkol type of snail (CP)

okhisa'

[ok+fokkol]
okhisa' see okkisa'
ok-ima'lak type of green tree frog [oka' ima̲lak]
okishko', (CC) oka' ishko' drunkard, alcoholic [oka' ishko+']
okishko' aa-asha', okishko' aaittafama' alcoholism treatment center [aa+itti+afama+']
Okishko' Hilha' Drunk Dance—name of a Choctaw dance also danced by Chickasaws
okishtahollo', oka' ishtahollo' witch water—area where a river will bubble and rise up toward one if one makes a noise
okishtolhchi', (MC) okaaishtoochi', (AB, TP) oka' ishtolhchi', (ER) oka' ishtoochi', (HS) akostolhchi', (AW) oka' ishto'chi' bucket: especially, wooden well bucket [oka' isht olhchi+']
okishtoochi', oka' ishtoochi' (water) pump; windmill [oka' isht oochi+']
okisht̲oshalalli' see oka' isht̲oshalalli'
okkalali to stare in an angry way; to look sideways (I / II)—often used in prt. [okk+] {ggr. okkálla'li} § Asokkalatok, Okkalalilitok. I looked sideways.
okkalat pisa to look sideways at (I;II) [okkalali+t]
okkálla'li ggr. of okkalali
okkata sea, ocean [oka' <hata>]
okkata foshi' sea gull
okkata tannap, okkatahtannap overseas [okkata(h) tannap]
okkatahapootaka' see okhatapootaka'
okkatahtannap see okhata tannap
okkatapootaka', okkatahapootaka' beach, seashore [okkata(h) apootaka']

okkawá'lli ggr. of okkawalli
okkawahánta hngr. of okkawaata
okkawahá̲lli hngr. of okkawalli
okkawalli, okkawatli to put (pl. obj.) across a gap; to go back and forth across (I;II) [okk+awalli] {ggr. okkáwwalli, okkawá'lli; hngr. okkawahá̲lli; sg. obj. okkawaatali; awalli}
okkawánta ngr. of okkawaata
<okkawatkachi> in okkawatkachit má̲a [okk+awatkachi] {ggr. okkawatkáyya'chi}
okkawatkachit má̲a to lie across (especially, a gap) (tpl. subj.) (I;3) [<okkawatkachi>+t] {sg. okkawátta'a; dl. okkawatkáyya'chi} § Yammak̲o okkawatkachit iimaatok. We all were lying across there.
okkawatkáyya'chi to lie across (especially, a gap) (dl. subj.) (I;3)—ggr. of <okkawatkachi> {sg. okkawátta'a; tpl. okkawatkachit má̲a}
okkawatli see okkowalli
okkawátta'a to lie horizontally (sg. subj.) (I); to lie across (especially, a gap) (sg. subj.) (I;3)—xgr. of okkawaata {dl. okkawatkáyya'chi; tpl. okkawatkachit má̲a; awátta'a}
okkawaata to be sideways (sg. subj.) (I); to be horizontally across (3;3) [okk+awaata] {v2. okkawaatali; ggr. okkáwwa'ta; hngr. okkawahánta; ngr. okkawánta; xgr. okkawátta'a; awaata; ishkinat okkawaata; iwa̲'ta'}
okkawaatali to put sideways, in a horizontal position (sg. obj.) (I;II) [okk+awaatali] {v1. okkawaata, okkawátta'a; pl. obj. okkawalli}
okkáwwa'ta ggr. of okkawaata
okkáwwalli ggr. of okkawalli
okkisa', okhisa' doorframe, doorway;

274

(TP, ER, MC) door (swinging part) [ok+<hisa>+']
okkisa' atooni' doorman, security guard [atooni+']
okkisa' patalhpo' doormat
okkis-oshi' little door; window [okkisa' oshi']
ókkommo ggr. of okommo
okla town
Okla Ishto' Oklahoma City (CP) [ishto+']
okla pila, okla pílla downtown
Oklahomma' Oklahoma [okla (Ct 'people') homma+']
oklattintakla' street [okla ittintakla']
oklattintakla' aashoppala' streetlight
oklóbboshli ggr. of okloboshli
oklobohóshli hngr. of okloboshli
okloboshli to be baptized (by immersion, like a Baptist); to submerge, go under the water; to be dunked, submerged (I) [ok+] {ggr. oklóbboshli; hngr. oklobohóshli}
okloboshlichi to baptize (in the Baptist way); to dunk, push under (I;II) [okloboshli+chi]
okloshi' tribe—may be used alone in a question, but otherwise only used in complex expressions such as okloshi' homma', okloshi' ilayyokha, okloshi' kaniya', Okloshi' Talhlha'pi' [okla oshi'] § Yammakot okloshi' nanta? What tribe is he?
okloshi' homma' Indian tribe (WB) [homma+']
okloshi' ilayyokha another type of person, someone from another tribe or race
okloshi' imilhlha' wild Indians—in other words, not part of the Five Civilized Tribes (LF) [imilhlha+']
okloshi' kaniya' lost tribe (perhaps a group related to the Chickasaws but

not part of the Five Tribes, such as the Alabamas) [kaniya+']
Okloshi' Talhlha'pi' the Five Tribes (traditionally, the Five Civilized Tribes—the Chickasaw, Choctaw, Creek, Seminole, and Cherokee Nations of Oklahoma) [talhlha'pi+']
oklóyyo'ha to be miraculous, to be a miracle (3) (Ct) (EP)—ygr. of <oklǫha> § Nannakat oklóyyo'hattook. What happened was miraculous.
<oklǫha> in nannoklǫha {ygr. oklóyyo'ha}
oklhí'li ggr. of oklhili
oklhí'lli ggr. of oklhílli
oklhíhhi'li hgr. of oklhili
oklhihíli hngr. of oklhili
oklhili night; at night § Oklhili toksali. He works at night.
oklhili to be night, to be dark (3) {ggr. oklhí'li, (var) oklhílli: to be completely dark; hgr. oklhíhhi'li; hngr. oklhihíli; ngr. oklhíli; ygr. oklhíyyi'li}
oklhili hashi' moon
oklhili iklanna see oklhiliklanna
oklhili nǫwa' witch (sg.) [nǫwa+'] {pl. oklhili tanǫwa'}
oklhili shoppalat nǫwa' witch [shoppala+t]
oklhili tanǫwa' witches—pl. of oklhili nǫwa' [<tanǫwa>+']
oklhili toomi to be moonlight in (a place) (3) § Oklahomma'at oklhili toomika pislitok. I saw the moonlight in Oklahoma.
oklhiliaash last night [oklhili+aash]
oklhilichi to get dark (3); to make dark (I;3) [oklhili+chi] § Oklhilishtaha. It got dark.
oklhiliklanna, oklhili iklanna to be midnight (—); to have it be midnight in (a place) (3) §

oklhílli

Oklahommaat oklhiliklanna. It's midnight in Oklahoma.
oklhílli to be completely dark (3)— var. ggr. of oklhili {ggr. oklhí'lli}
oklhiwachi to make all colors, get (something or someone) all dirty (with different colors of dirt) (I;II) [-SC] [oklhiwali+chi] § Asoklhiwachitok. He got me all dirty.
oklhiwali to be all different colors; to be streaked with different colors of dirt, paint (II / I) [ok+ ?] {ggr. oklhíwwa'li}
oklhíwwa'li ggr. of oklhiwali
oklhíyyi'li ygr. of oklhili
oklhíli ngr. of oklhili
okmíllo'li ggr. of okmiloli
okmilohóli hngr. of okmiloli
okmiloli to look at something with interest, be all eyes (I); to be bug-eyed (II); to raise one's eyebrows (I / II) [ok+] {ggr. okmíllo'li; hngr. okmilohóli; ngr. okmilóli; ygr. okmilóyyo'li; onokmiloli: to look at with interest}
okmilóli ngr. of okmiloli
okó'mmo ggr. of okommo
okoffi to precook in a pressure cooker (AB)
ok-okaa-asha' see sinti' ok-okaa-asha'
ok-okaaittanowa' boat (CC)
okomba', oka' omba' rainwater [oka' omba+']
okombaalhto', oka' omba' aalhto' rain barrel or cistern for collecting rainwater
okohómmo hngr. of okommo
okommo to mix (wet ingredients), make (cake, biscuits, mud pies) (I;3) [ok+] {v1. olhkomo; ggr. ókkommo, okó'mmo; hngr. okohómmo}
okoshto, (CP, MJ, WB, ER, TP)

okishto, (MC) okisto to flood, have flooding (3) [oka' ishto] § Abokkoshi'at okoshto. The creek flooded. I Oklahomma'at okoshto. There's flooding in Oklahoma.
okpachalhlhi', (TJ) okpatalhlhi' pond, mudhole, swamp, marsh, area with standing water, (TJ) puddle [ok+]
okpal water lily (MJ) [ok+]
okpalachi to float (something, such as a toy boat) (I;3) [±SC] [okpalali+chi]
okpalali to float, bob (in water) (I) [ok+]
okpalli' in oktaak okpalli'
okpani see oppani
okpolo see oppolo
oksifa ax
oksifoshi' hatchet [oksifa oshi']
oksop, (LF) hoksop bead; (LF) necklace
oksop aahotampi' beading loom
oksop hanaawi'li' beaded sash worn over one shoulder and diagonally across the chest [hanaawi'li+']
oksop inno'chi' bead necklace
oksop toba' uncut gem [toba+']
okshá'lli ggr. of okshalli
okshahálli hngr. of okshalli
okshalli to have (water) come out (of a spring) (3;3) [ok+] {ggr. okshá'lli; hngr. okshahálli} § Kaliat oka' okshalli. The spring has water coming out of it.
okshawali to have light skin (II) {ggr. oksháwwa'li}
oksháwwa'li ggr. of okshawali
okshilihínta hngr. of okshilitta
okshilitta to close (of a door), get stopped up (of a drain) (3) {v2. okshitta; ggr. okshílli'ta: to be closed (of a door); hngr. okshilihínta; ygr. okshilíyyi'ta} § ishtokshili'ta': door

276

(the moving part)
okshilíyyi'ta ygr. of okshilitta
okshílli'ta to be closed (of a door), stopped up (of a drain)—ggr. of okshilitta [+CPR] [+PR]
okshitta to close, plug; to enclose, close in (a porch, for instance) (I;3) {v1. okshilitta}
oktá'ni ggr. of oktani
oktabli to cut off (water, a road) (I;3) [ok+tabli] {v1. oktapa}
oktahani hngr. of oktani
oktáhha'pa hgr. of oktapa
oktani to appear (of a spirit, or in a vision) (I); to be noticed, found out; to be notorious (II) [-CPR] [-PR] [ok+] {ggr. oktá'ni; hngr. oktaháni; ngr. oktáni: to show, be seen, be visible (II)}
oktanichi to show, document; to make (something) appear (of a magician, for instance) (I;II) [oktani+chi] {ggr. oktánni'chi: to make obvious} § Oktanni'chit imanootok. He told him clearly, He made it obvious in telling him.
oktánni'chi to make obvious—ggr. of oktanichi
oktapa to be cut off, blocked (of a road, for example) (3) [ok+tapa] {v2. oktabli; hgr. oktáhha'pa}
oktaak, (CM) ottaak prairie
oktaak chokfi' swamp rabbit (ER)
oktaak foshi' whippoorwill; (WB) meadowlark
oktaak okpalli' water lily (ER)
oktaak pilhchi', (CM) ottaak pilhchi' thistle
oktaak taakchili' prairie wax (type of plant) (WB)
oktaak tofalaa' prairie onion (WB) [atofalla'a']
oktaat shalalli for there to be an avalanche [okti'+at] § Oktaat

shalalli. There was an avalanche.
oktaat wilili for it to hail [okti'+at] § Oktaat wilili. It hailed.
oktáni to show, be showing, be seen, be visible (II)—ngr. of oktani [+CPR] [+PR]
okti' snow, hail [ok+]
okti' abooha igloo
okti' foshi', (ER) oktosha' foshi' snowbird
okti' hattak snowman
okti' ishtokaashalalli' skis; sled (for use on snow) [isht okaashalalli+']
okti' lombo' hailstone [lombo+']
okti' poshi' snowflake
okti' poshi' bíyyi'ka to be soft, newfallen snow (—); to have soft, newfallen snow (of a place) (3) § Oklahomma'at okti' poshi' biyyi'ka. There's soft, newfallen snow in Oklahoma.
okti' shalalli' snowslide, avalanche [shalalli+']
okti' wilili' hail [wilili+']
oktishtoshala'li' skis [okti' isht on+shala'li+']
oktohósha hngr. of oktosha
oktosha to snow (—); to have snow (of a place) (3) [ok+tosha] {hngr. oktohósha} § Oklahomma'at oktosha. It's snowing in Oklahoma.
oktosha' foshi' snowbird; chickadee (?) [oktosha+']
okyobi' dew (TP) [ok+<yobi>+']
ola to ring, sound; to crow (like a rooster) (I) [+PR] {ggr. ó'la; hngr. ohóla}
<ola> in ola' fonka, ola' pila, <olaali>, oláli, olaalínchi, olintannap, osht, oot
ola' fonka this way, in this direction (beckoning or gesturing—to or about someone or something closer than ola' pila, but still some

ola' intannap

distance off) [<ola>+', fokha+' ?]
ola' intannap see olintannap
ola' pila, ola' pílla this way, in this
direction (beckoning or gesturing—
to or about someone or something
closer than ola' fonka) [<ola>+']
olachi to make (something) sound:
to ring (a bell), blow (a horn), play
(an instrument) (I;3) [ola+chi] {hngr.
olahánchi}
olahánchi hngr. of olachi
<olaali> in olaalínchi {ngr. oláli;
<ola>}
olaalínchi in oshtolaalínchi,
pitolaalinchi, olaalínchi ki'yo [ngr.
of <olaali>+chi]
olaalínchi ki'yo to go far away (3)
oláli to be nearby (3) {oshtoláli}
olbi' squash; small pumpkin
olbi' lakna' any yellow squash
[lakna+']
olbi' okchamali' zucchini
[okchamali+']
olbi' tohbi' white squash [tohbi+']
olintannap, ola' intannap just this
side of [<ola>+' intannap] § South
Gate ola' intannapak anta. He lives
just this side of South Gate.
ollaháli hngr. of ollali
olláhha'li hgr. of ollali
ollali to laugh, smile (I); to laugh at
(I;II) [-PR] [-CPR] [ola ?] {hgr.
olláhha'li; hngr. ollaháli; ngr. olláli}
ollalichi to make laugh, to make
smile (I;II); to make (someone)
laugh, smile at (I;3;II) [ollali+chi] §
Irene asollalishtok. He made Irene
laugh at me.
olláli ngr. of ollali
olhchi to be drawn (of water) (3) [+T]
[-CPR] [+PR] {v2. oochi}
olhkomo to be mixed, be all mixed
together (often, in an unpleasant-
looking way, like eggs broken in the

carton or imperfectly canned food)
(3) {v2. okommo}
<olhpi> in aalhpi' {v2. oppi}
olhti to be kindled (3) [-CPR] [+PR]
{v2. ooti; hgr. óhholhti}
olhtipiichi' deacon; (AB) President
omba rain
omba to rain (—); to have rain (3); to
rain in (a place) (—;3) {hngr.
ohómba} § Los Angelesat omba, Los
Angelesa omba. It's raining in Los
Angeles, There is rain in Los
Angeles.
omba fo'kha' raincoat [omba
fokha+']
ombachi to make it rain (I)
[omba+chi] § Ishombachitam? Did
you make it rain?
ombaayo'chi to bounce on (I;II) [-SC]
[on+baayochi]
ombihíntka hngr. of ombitka
ombilhipa to swarm over (of ants on
food or ticks on a person, for
instance), pile up on (of football
players on the ball carrier, for
example) (pl. subj.) (I;II)
[on+<bilhipa>] {ggr. ombílhlhi'pa}
ombílhlhi'pa ggr. of ombilhipa
ombiniili to sit on, ride (sg.-dl.-pl.
subj.) (I;II) [on+biniili]
ombiniichi to set (sg. patient obj.)
down on ˚ (I;II;3) [-SC] [on+biniichi]
§ Apombiniichitok. He set it down
on us.
ombínni'li to sit on: especially, to
ride (a horse) (sg. subj.) (I;II)
[on+binni'li] {dl. onchí'ya;
ombiniili}
ombitihímpa hngr. of ombitiipa
ombitiipa to touch, press down on
(I;II) [on+bitiipa] {ggr. ombítti'pa;
hngr. ombitihímpa}
ombitiipachi to make touch (I;II;3)
[ombitiipa+chi] {abiitippichi}

278

ombitka to press on, massage (I;II)
[on+bitka] {hngr. ombihíntka}
ombítti'pa ggr. of ombitiipa
ombohli to lay, put (sg. patient obj.)
down on ° (I;II;3) [on+bohli] {pl.
patient obj. onkahli, onashaachi} §
Apombohtok. She put it down on
us.
ombowafa to fall on (of a roof, for
example) (3;II) [on+bowafa]
omboyafa to be shed on, to come out
on (of hair) (3;II) [on+boyafa] §
Kowi' hishi'at asomboyafatahatok.
The cat's hair was shed on me.
ompachichi to spray °, splash ° with,
on (I;II;3) [on+pachichi] § Oka'
achompachishli. I splash you with
water, I splash water on you.
ompachili to splash on (3;II); to get
splashed with (II;3-at) (only without
overt subj. in clause) [on+pachiili] §
Oka'at asompachilika ithanali,
Oka'at asompachilikat ithanali. I
know the water splashed on me, I
know I got splashed with water. |
Lynnat ikimalhpi'sokitok oka'at
ompachilikat. Lynn is sad that she
got splashed with water.
ompalli, ompatli to put (flat pl.
patient) on ° (I;II;3) [on+palli] {sg.
patient obj. ompatali} § Asompalli.
They put (flat things) on me.
<ompata> [on+<pata>] {v2. ompatali;
xgr. ompátta'a}
ompatali to put (flat sg. patient) on °
(I;II;3) [on+patali] {v1. ompátta'a,
<ompata>; pl. patient obj. ompalli}
ompatalhpo to be all spread out on
(3;3) {ggr. ompáttalhpo}
<ompatkachi> in nannompatkachi',
ompatkachit máa [on+<patkachi>]
{ygr. ompatkáyya'chi}
ompatkachit máa to be on (tpl. flat
subj.) (of knickknacks on a doily, for

example) (3;3) [<ompatkachi>+t] {sg.
ompátta'a; dl. ompatkáyya'chi}
ompatkáyya'chi to be on (dl. flat
subj.) (3;3)—ygr. of <ompatkachi>
{sg. ompátta'a; tpl. ompatkachit
máa}
ompátta'a to be on (sg. flat subj.) (of a
framed photograph on a doily, for
example) (3;3)—xgr. of <ompata>
{v2. ompatali; dl. ompakáyya'chi;
tpl. ompatkachit máa}
ompáttalhpo ggr. of ompatalhpo
ompihli to sweep off the top of (a
relatively small obj., like a box) (I;3);
to sweep (something) onto ° (I;II;3)
[on+pihli] § Lokfi' asompihli! He's
sweeping dirt onto me!
ompofa to blow (something) at, on °
(I;II;3) [on+pofa] § Alikchaat ittish
achompofa'chi. The doctor will
blow medicine on you.
ona to get there; to suffice, be enough
(I); to get to, arrive at (over there); to
reach, touch (I;3) [+CPR] [+PR]
[+taha] {ggr. ó'na; hgr. óhho'na;
hngr. ohóna; ngr. óna; neg. iko'no:
not to be enough; talhipa chaffaka
óna} § Pam oka' lawakat kaa
ishtachifa'nika onaho ishko. Pam
drank enough water to wash a car. |
Iko'no. It's not enough. | Talhipa
chaffaka ilona. There are a hundred
of us, Our number reaches 100. |
Yamma onatok. He got there. |
Ireneat holisso yamma ona' ki'yo.
Irene can't reach that book.
onachi to make reach (to stretch (a
line) across, for instance) (I;3)
[ona+chi]
onashaachi to put (tpl. patient obj.)
down (especially, in a heap) on °
(I;II;3) [on+ashaachi] {sg. patient obj.
ombohli; dl. patient obj. onkahli} §
Kowi' aponashaashtok. She put the

onáyya'sha

cats on us.

onáyya'sha to be on (tpl. subj.) (I;II)
[on+ayya'sha]

onaa-asha' in paska champoli' onaa-asha'

onáa to walk on, crawl on, go on (I;II)
[on+aa] § Shatannaat achonaana
ishhayoshtam? Did you find any
ticks crawling on you?

onchaba mountain, hill

onchaba hina' aalhopolli', (WB)
onchaba hina-lhopolli' tunnel
[aa+lhopolli+']

onchaba kowi' mountain lion (ER)

onchaffichi to sic on ° (I;II;3)
[on+chaffichi] § Ofi'
asonchaffichitok. He sicked the dog
on me.

onchí'ya to sit on, ride (dl. subj.) (I;II)
[on+chi'ya] {sg. ombínni'li;
ombiniili}

onchokkayahli to drool on (I;II)
[on+chokkayahli] §
Asonchokkayaht ishtahtok. You
drooled on me.

onchokkayalli to drool on (I;II)
[on+chokkayalli] § Ofi'at naachi
onchokkayallitok. The dog drooled
on the quilt.

onchololi to put out new shoots (of a
tree), to grow back (of the leaves of a
tree or a lizard's tail), (LR) to sprout
(3) [+CPR] {v1. <oncholowa>;
ishtaaonchololi'} § Toksila'paat
hasimbishat onchololi. The lizard's
tail grew back.

<oncholowa> in oshi'
ishtaaoncholowa' {v2. onchololi}

onhochi, ohnochi to accuse, blame;
to gossip about (I;II) {hngr.
onnohónchi; ishtonhochi; anompa
kallo' onhochi}

onittola to fall on (sg. subj.) (I;II)
[on+ittola] {dl.<onkaha>; tpl.

olhatapa}

onkaha in onkahat máa,
oshtonkaha, ootonkaha {v2.
onkahli; ygr. onkáyya'a}

onkahat máa to lie on (tpl. subj.) (II =
obj. , I = subj.) [onkaha+t] {sg.
ontí'wa, onto'wa; dl. onkáyya'a} §
Achonkahat iimaatok. We lay on
you.

onkahli to lay, put (pl. patient obj.)
on ° (I;II;3) [on+kahli] {v1. onkaha;
sg. patient obj. ombohli; tpl. obj.
onashaachi: to put (tpl. obj.) down
in a heap on} § Onkahlilitok. I laid
them (dl.) down on it. |
Onkahtahlilitok. I laid them (tpl.)
down on it.

onkáyya'a to lie on (dl. subj.) (I;II)—
ygr. of onkaha {sg. ontí'wa, onto'wa;
tpl. onkahat máa}

ónkcha ngr. of okcha

onkof, (AW) inkof persimmon

onkofollichi to steam (vegetables,
one's face) (I;3) [on+kofollichi]

onna to be the next day, to be
tomorrow (—); to be the next day in
(a place) (3); all night (aux) (used
with a preceding verb +na) {hngr.
ohónna} § onnakma... tomorrow... |
Ithanali toksahalili onnatokat. I
know I worked all night (till the
next day). | Oklahomma'at
onnataha. It's already day in
Oklahoma.

onna mishshakma, mishshakma the
day after tomorrow

onna nittakikma, onnakma nittaki
tomorrow morning [onna+kma,
nittaki+kma]

onna obyakma tomorrow evening
[obya+kma]

onna oklhilikma, onnoklhilikma
tomorrow night [onna
oklhili+kma]

280

onnakma tomorrow [onna+kma]
onnakma nittaki see onna
nittakikma
onnat minti to be after midnight,
before it gets light (—); to be after
midnight in (a place) (3) [onna+t] §
Oklahomma'at onnat minti.
(When it's after ten in California)
it's after midnight in Oklahoma. |
Onnat minti hashi' kanalli
toklokaasho pislitok. I saw him at
two in the morning.
Onnataayi' Chickasaw man's name
onno'sha', (WB) onosha' mattress
onno'sha' kallo' innerspring
mattress [kallo+']
onno'sha' yabofa' feather bed
[yabofa+']
onnohónchi hngr. of onhochi
onnoklhilikma see onna oklhilikma
onobya to have it get to be evening
on one, to have it get dark on one
(hum. subj.) (II) [on+obya] § Lynnat
onobyatok. It got to be evening on
Lynn. | Ithanali asonobyakat. I
know evening snuck up on me.
onoklhili to have it get dark on one
(hum. subj.) (II) [on+oklhili] §
Lynnat onoklhilitok. It got dark on
Lynn.
onokmíllo'li ggr. of onokmiloli
onokmiloli to look at with interest,
ogle (I;II) [on+okmiloli] {ggr.
onokmíllo'li}
onoktosha to snow on (inan. obj.)
(—;3) (used in main clause only); to
be snowed on (II) [on+oktosha] §
Asonoktoshatokat ithanali. I know I
got snowed on. | Aboohaat
onoktosha. The house got snowed
on. | Abooha onoktosha. It snowed
on the house.
onomba to rain on (inan. obj.) (—;3)
(used in main clause only); to be

rained on (II) [on+omba] § Alekat
onombatok. Alex got rained on. |
Asonomba sabanna. I want it to rain
on me. | Osaapa onombatok. It
rained on the fields.
ononna to stay out all night, till
dawn (hum. subj.) (II) [on+onna] §
Asononnatokat ithanali. I know I
stayed out all night.
ontabookoli to have noon creep up
on one (hum. subj.) (II)
[on+tabookoli] § Lynnat
ontabookolitok. Noon crept up on
Lynn, Lynn had noon creep up on
her.
ontalaali to put, place, stand (sg.
patient obj.) on (I;3;3) [on+talaali]
{ggr. ontálla'li: to have placed (sg.
patient obj.) on one; pl. patient obj.
ontalooli} § Nampakali' sapashi'
ontalaalilitok. I put a flower in (on)
my hair.
<ontalkachi> in ittontalkachi
<ontalkáyya'chi> in ittontalkáyya'chi
ontálla'a to be placed, stood on (of a
compact obj. with a closed bottom);
to be sewed on (of a button) (sg.
subj.) (3;3) [on+talla'a] {dl.
ontállo'wa; tpl. ontalowat máa}
ontálla'li to have placed a (sg. patient
obj.) on one—ggr. of ontalaali
ontállo'wa to be placed, stood on (dl.
subj.—of compact objs. with closed
bottoms) (3;3)—ggr. of ontaloha,
ontalowa {sg. ontálla'a; tpl.
ontalowat máa}
ontaloha, ontalowa to be set (of
dishes on the table) (3) [+T]
[on+taloha] {v2. ontalooli; ggr.
ontállo'wa}
ontalowa see ontaloha
ontalowat máa to be placed, stood on
(tpl. subj.—of compact objs. with
closed bottoms) (3;3) [ontalowa+t]

ontalooli

{sg. ontálla'a; dl. ontállo'wa}
ontalooli to put, place, stand (pl.
patient obj.) on (I;3;3) [on+talooli]
{vl. ontaloha; sg. patient obj.
ontalaali}
ontánno'wa to walk on (dl. subj.,
nonhum. obj.) (I;3)—ggr. of
<ontánno'wa> {sg. o̱no̱wa; tpl.
ontanoh<u>ó</u>wa}
ontanoh<u>ó</u>wa to walk on (tpl. subj.,
nonhum. obj.) (I;3)—hngr. of
<ontanowa> {sg. o̱no̱wa; dl.
ontánno'wa}
<ontanowa> [on+<tanowa>] {ggr.
ontánno'wa; hngr. ontanoh<u>ó</u>wa}
ontasahli to scream at (I;II)
[on+tasahli]
ontastachi to talk loudly to (a deaf
person, for instance) (I;II)
[on+tastachi]
ónti ngr. of ooti
ontí'wa to lie on (sg. subj.) (I;II)
[on+ti'wa] {dl. subj. onkáyya'a; tpl.
subj. onkahat m<u>á</u>a; onto'wa}
ontó'wa to lie on (sg. hum. subj.) (I;3)
[on+to'wa] {dl. subj. onkáyya'a; tpl.
subj. onkahat m<u>á</u>a; ontí'wa}
ontochchí'na eight; to be eight in
number (I) [+PR] [on+tochchi'na]
ontochchí'na áyyo'ka to be in groups
of eight (I , —)
ontofa to spit on (I;II) [on+tofa]
ontoklo seven; to be seven in
number (I) [+PR] [on+toklo]
ontoklo áyyo'ka to be in groups of
seven (I , —)
ontono'chi to roll out on (dough on
a table, for instance) (I;3;3) [-SC]
[on+tono'chi] {vl. ontono'kalhchi}
ontono'kalhchi to be rolled out on
(3;3) [on+tono'kalhchi] {v2.
ontono'chi} § Tili'ko'at aaimpa'
ontono'kalhchitaha. The dough is
rolled out on the table.

ontosso'la' handcart (on the railroad)
[on+tossola+']
ontoomi to shine on (3;II); to have
shine on one (II;3-at); to have sun
in one's eyes (II) [on+toomi] §
Hashi'at asontoomi. The sun shines
on me. | Lynnat hashi'at ontoomi.
Lynn has the sun shining on her. |
Hashi'at Lynn ontoomi. The sun is
shining on Lynn.
opa, oopa, (ER, CC) hopa, (JJ) hoopa
short-eared owl; a kind of large
moth
oppá'ni ggr. of oppani
oppani, okpani to break, mess up,
beat up, ruin (I;II) [+OPR] {vl.
oppolo ?; ggr. oppá'ni}
oppi to put a (straight) handle on (I;3)
{vl. <olhpi>; ggr. ôppi; aalhpi'} §
Oks<u>i</u>fa oppitok. He put a handle on
the axe.
ôppi ggr. of oppi
oppó'lo ggr. of oppolo
oppóhho'lo hgr. of oppolo
oppoh<u>ó</u>lo hngr. of oppolo
oppolikmassa'lo' leprosy [oppolo
ik+massa'li+o+']
oppolikmassa'lo' í'shi to have
leprosy (I)
oppóllo'ka ggr. of oppoloka
oppolo, okpolo to be broken, ruined,
no good (II) [+PR] [+CPR] {v2.
oppani?; ggr. oppó'lo; hgr.
oppóhho'lo; hngr. oppoh<u>ó</u>lo; ngr.
opp<u>ó</u>lo; ygr. oppóyyo'lo}
oppolo ishtalakchi' bandage
oppolo lapoochi' bandaid
[lapoochi+']
oppolo'si to be ugly, no good (II)
[oppolo+'si]
oppolohónka hngr. of oppoloka
oppolohónko hngr. of oppolokko
oppoloka to be grouchy, mad all the
time (I) [oppolo+ka] {ggr.

oppóllo'ka; hngr. oppolohónka; ngr. oppolónka; imoppoloka: to answer back}
oppolokko to be warped, not straight; to have the edges curl up (3) [oppolo] {hngr. oppolohónko}
oppolónka ngr. of oppoloka
oppóyyo'lo ygr. of oppolo
oppólo ngr. of oppolo
osak, (WB) oksak hickory nut
osak api' hickory tree
osak falaa' pecan [falaa+']
osak falaa' alhpooba' store-bought or commercially raised pecans [alhpooba+']
osak falaa' api' pecan tree
osak ishkookoli' nutcracker [isht kookoli+']
osak okchi', (CC) sak-okchi' type of fruit (CW): perhaps huckleberry (ER, CC, JC), cherry (CC), or a medicinal plant (CP)
osak takba' kind of walnut, like an English walnut [takba+']
osak tali' hickory nut
osak tanchi' ittalhata' hickory nut hominy
osak tafola' hickory nut hominy (WB) [tafola+']
osaapa' field (under cultivation, not pasture)
osaapa' bala' any peas or beans planted in a field; (ER, ML) field peas
osaapa' tanchi' field corn (WB)
osaapa' toksali' farmer [toksali+']
osaaposhi' garden [osaapa' oshi']
osaaposhi' toksali' gardener [toksali+']
oskapi' cane, bamboo, reed (used for fishing poles, arrows, blowgun tubes) [oski' api']
oski', (WB) oski hollow tube made from oskapi' plant (used to blow on

medicine); arrow shaft; (WB) wild cane
oski' chalhaali' wicker [chalhahli+']
oski' naki' whole arrow—arrowhead and shaft
oski' tannafo' basket (CP) [holhtannafo+']
oski' tapa' blowgun tube [tapa+']
oskola' flute [oski' ola+']
ostahi' squash, cushaw melon [osto ahi']
osto pumpkin
oshaatoba' womb (IIIp) [oshi' aa+toba+']
osha'to' womb (old word); (animal's) pouch, pocket [oshi' alhto+']
oshchahali to have a crest (of a bird); to have a beehive hairdo or pompadour (II) [osh+chaaha] {ggr. oshcháhha'li}
oshcháhha'li ggr. of oshchahali
oshchíllo'li ggr. of oshchiloli
oshchilochi to curl (something), to set (hair), to give a permanent to (I;II) [-SC] [oshchiloli+chi] {hngr. oshchilolihínchi}
oshchilohóli hngr. of oshchiloli
oshchiloli to be curly; to have curly hair (II) [+CPR] [+PR] [osh+<chiloli>] {ggr. oshchíllo'li; hngr. oshchilohóli; ngr. oshchilóli; ygr. oshchilóyyo'li}
oshchilolihínchi hngr. of oshchiloli
oshchilóyyo'li ygr. of oshchiloli
oshchilóli ngr. of oshchiloli
oshchokkowa to come in (I) [osht *chokkowa] § Oshtishchokkowatok. You came in.
oshchónno'li ggr. of oshchonoli
<oshchono> in oshchono' {v2. oshchonoli}
oshchono', oshchono'li' small flower often found growing next to wild onions (it grows bent over)

oshchono'li'

[<oshchono>/oshchonoli+']
oshchono'li' see oshchono'
oshchonochi to bow, bend (someone else's) head (I;II) [-SC] [oshchonoli+chi]
oshchonoli to bow the head, have one's head bent (I) [osh+<chonoli>] {v1. <oshchono>; ggr. oshchónno'li; oshchooni}
oshchooni to nod one's head (I) [osh+<chooni>] {oshchonoli}
oshfaapichi to throw in this direction, to here (sg. obj.) (I;II) [osht *faapichi] {pl. obj. oshfaapo'chi} § Oshtishfaapichitok. You threw it here.
oshfaapo'chi to throw away, to throw in this direction (pl. obj.) (I;II) [-SC] [osht *faapo'chi] {hngr. oshfaapo'lihínchi; ngr. oshfaapo'línchi; sg. obj. oshfaapichi}
oshfaapo'lihínchi hngr. of oshfaapo'chi
oshfaapo'línchi ngr. of oshfaapo'chi
oshfokhi to make (sg. obj.) come in (this way) (I;II) [osht *fokhi] {dl. obj. oshtabihli; tpl. obj. oshtani} § Ossafokhitok. He made me come in.
oshhalili to brush, touch lightly (I;II) [osht *halili] {ngr. oshhalíli}
oshhalíli to brush back and forth— ngr. of oshhalili
oshhíkki'ya to stand (facing this way) (sg. subj.) (I) [osht *hikki'ya]
oshi' son; baby, little one (of an animal) (IIp); interest (on a loan) § asoshi': my son
oshi' aafo'kha' pouch (of a kangaroo) [aa+fokha+']
oshi' aalhto' pouch (of a possum)
oshi' iksho', oshiksho' sterile, barren woman or man; someone without children, who's never had a child [oshi' iksho+']

oshi' iksho' ikbi to spay, fix (a female) (I;II)
oshi' iksho' ilikbi to have oneself sterilized (of a woman), have one's tubes tied (I) [ili+ikbi] § Oshi' iksho' ilikbilitok. I got sterilized.
oshi' ishtaaoncholowa' descendants
oshi' ishtaatiyaka' descendants (Ct?) [isht aatiya+ka+']
oshi' toba' stepson, (TP) nephew (IIp) § achoshi' toba': your stepson
oshi'ak illa atobbi to just pay interest (I) [oshi'+ak]
oshiksho' see oshi' iksho'
oshiitiik daughter (IIp) [oshi' <tiik>] § asoshiitiik: my daughter
oshiitiik toba', (HS) oshiitok toba' stepdaughter, (ER, TP) niece
oshkabachi to give a crew cut or flat top to (I;II) [±SC] [oshkabali+chi] {hngr. oshkabahánchi, oshkabalihínchi}
oshkabahánchi hngr. of oshkabachi
oshkabali to have a crew cut, flattop (II); (TP) to be bald [osh+<kabali>] {ggr. oshkábba'li; ngr. oshkabáli; ygr. oshkabáyya'li}
oshkabalihínchi hngr. of oshkabachi
oshkabáyya'li ygr. of oshkabali
oshkabáli ngr. of oshkabali
oshkábba'li ggr. of oshkabali
oshkanalli to move this way (I) [osht *kanalli] {ngr. oshkanálli} § Oshtishkanallinna! Don't move this way!
oshkanálli ngr. of oshkanalli
oshkanchi to drop (something, in this direction) (I;II) [osht *kanchi]
oshkánna'pa ggr. of oshkannapa
oshkannahámpa hngr. of oshkannapa
oshkannapa, (MC) ishkanna'pa, (CP) ashkónno'pa to have an accident, to be bewitched; (CP) to have bad

284

luck (II) [osh+] {ggr. oshkánna'pa; hngr. oshkannahámpa}
oshkássa'li ggr. of oshpasali, oshkasali
oshkíbbi'li ggr. of oshkibili
oshkibichi to sharpen to a point (I;II) [-SC] [oshkibili+chi] {hngr. oshkibilihínchi}
oshkibili to be pointed (II) [osh+<kibili>] {ggr. oshkíbbi'li; ngr. oshkibíli; ygr. oshkibíyyi'li}
oshkibilihínchi hngr. of oshkibichi
oshkoboli to have a round head (like a pin) (3) [osh+<koboli>]
oshkochcha to come out (in this direction) (I) [osht *kochcha]
oshkóllo'li ggr. of oshkololi
oshkolochi to cut off the top of, to give a flattop haircut to (I;II) [+SC] [oshkololi+chi] {hngr. oshkololihínchi; ngr. oshkololínchi} § Achoshkoloshla'chi. I'll give you a flattop.
oshkololi to be short and stubby, be cut off at the top (I / II)—usually used in ggr. [osh+<kololi>] {ggr. oshkóllo'li}
oshkololihínchi hngr. of oshkolochi
oshkololínchi ngr. of oshkolochi
oshmasholi in ishkobo' oshmasholi [osh+<masholi>]
oshmisohóli hngr. of oshmisoli
oshmisoli; (MJ) oshmisofa to be bald (II) [+CPR] [-PR] [osh+<misoli>] {ggr. oshmísso'li; hngr. oshmisohóli; ngr. oshmisóli; ygr. oshmisóyyo'li; ishkobo' oshmasholi, masofa}
oshmisóyyo'li ygr. of oshmisoli
oshmisóli ngr. of oshmisoli
oshmísso'li ggr. of oshmisoli
osho'ba' in ishkin osho'ba'
oshpasáhha'li hgr. of oshpasali
oshpasachi to make bald (I;II) [-SC]

[oshpasali+chi]
oshpasali, (AB) oshkasali to be bald (II) [osh+<pasali>] {ggr. oshpássa'li, oshkássa'li; hgr. oshpasáhha'li; ngr. oshpasáli}
oshpasáli ngr. of oshpasali
oshpássa'li ggr. of oshpasali
Oshpaananompa',
Oshpaanimanompa' Spanish (language) [Oshpaani' (im+)anompa']
Oshpaani' Mexican, Chicano, Latino, Hispanic person
Oshpaani' imbanaha' tamale [im+banaha']
Oshpaani' Iyaakni', **Oshpaaniyaakni'** Mexico [im+yaakni']
Oshpaanihoo' Mexican woman [Oshpaani' ihoo+']
Oshpaanimanompa' see Oshpaananompa'
oshpaanimbala' refried beans; jumping beans [Oshpaani' im+bala']
oshpaanimimpa', **oshpaanimpa'** Mexican food [Oshpaani' (im+)impa']
oshpaanimpa' see oshpaanimimpa'
oshpaanimpaska tortilla [Oshpaani' im+paska]
Oshpaaniyaakni' see Oshpaani' Iyaakni'
Oshpaanoshi' Mexican child [Oshpaani' oshi']
oshpilachi to send this way (I;II) [osht *pilachi]
oshpishichi' mother: especially, nursing mother; wet nurse [oshi' pishichi+'] § Oshpishichi' saya. I'm a nursing mother, I'm nursing. I kowi' oshpishichi': nursing mother cat, cat with nursing kittens
oshpishínchi to be nursing young (of animals only?) (3) [oshi' pishichi]

285

oshshaachi

oshshaachi to put on the back of ˚ (this way) (I;II;3) [osht *shaachi] § Chipota oshtissashaachi. You put the child on my back.
oshshowahánchi hngr. of oshshowanchi
oshshowanchi, (AW) ishwanchi to smell (something) (I;II) [osh+showa+chi] {ggr. oshshówwa'chi; hngr. oshshowahánchi} § Ikoshshowa'cho. He can't smell it.
oshshowanchichichi to make (someone˚) smell (something) (I;II;3) [oshshowanchi+chichi]
oshshowashpisa to smell (something, especially to see what it's like) (II = obj. , I = subj.) [oshshowanchi+t pisa] § Asoshshowasht ishpisatam? Did you smell me?
oshshowasht hoyo to follow a track by scent (as a dog does) (3) [oshshowanchi+t]
oshshówwa'chi ggr. of oshshowanchi
osht this way, toward the speaker or a point of reference—prt. [<ola>, olaalínchi]
oshta four; to be four in number (I) [+PR] {v2. oshtali}
oshta áyyo'ka to be in (organized) groups of four (I , —) § Kiloshta ayyo'ka. We're in groups of four.
oshta bíyyi'ka to be in (scattered) groups of four (I , —) § Iloshta biyyi'ka. We're in groups of four.
oshtabihli to make (dl. obj.) come in (this way) (I;II) [osht *abihli] {sg. obj. oshfokhi; tpl. obj. oshtani}
oshtali to quarter, divide in four parts (I;3) {v1. oshta}
oshtani to make (tpl., mainly nonhum. obj.) come in (this way)

(I;II) [osht *ani] {sg. obj. oshfokhi; dl. obj. oshtabihli} § Oshtaponi. He made us come in.
oshtimpilachi to send (someone or something) off (this way) to ˚ (I;III;3) [osht *impilachi] § Holisso oshtissampilashtok. You sent the book off to me.
oshtinchaffichi to send to ˚ (this way) (I;III;3) [osht *inchaffichi] § Angel oshponchaffichitok. He sent an angel to us.
oshtifaali see ilbak ifaali
oshtifaapichi to throw (sg. obj.)(in this direction) to ˚ (I;III;3) [osht *ifaapichi] {pl. obj. oshtifaapo'chi}
oshtifaapo'chi to throw (pl. obj.) (in this direction) to ˚ (I;III;3) [osht *ifaapo'chi] {sg. obj. oshtifaapichi}
oshtiwí'li to hold out to—ggr. of oshtiwiili
oshtiwiili to hand (this way) to ˚ (I;III;3) [osht *iwiili] {ggr. oshtiwí'li: to hold out to}
Oshto Chickasaw man's nickname (CC)
oshtolaalínchi to move closer this way (I); to move closer to (something near here) (I;3) [osht *olaalinchi]
oshtoláli to be nearby, not too far off (from here) (3) [osht *oláli]
oshtombohli to put (sg. patient obj.) (this way) on ˚ (I;II;3) [osht *ombohli] {dl. patient obj. oshtonkahli; tpl. patient obj. oshtonashaachi; mass patient obj. oshtolhatabli}
oshtonashaachi to put (tpl. patient obj.) (this way) on ˚ (I;II;3) [osht *onashaachi] {sg. patient obj. oshtombohli; dl. patient obj. oshtonkahli; mass patient obj. oshtolhatabli} §

Oshtachonashaashtok. He put them on you.

oshtonittola to fall (this way) on (sg. subj.) (I;II) [osht *onittola] {dl. oshtonkaha; tpl. oshtolhatapa} § Oshtasonittolatok. He fell (this way) onto me.

oshtonkaha to fall (this way) on (dl. subj.) (I;II) [osht *onkaha] {v2. oshtonkahli; sg. oshtonittola; tpl. oshtolhatapa} § Oshtilonkahatok. We (two) fell (this way) on him.

oshtonkahli to put (dl. patient obj.) (this way) on ° (I;II;3) [osht *onkahli] {v1. oshtonkaha; sg. patient obj. oshtombohli; tpl. patient obj. oshtonashaachi; mass patient obj. oshtolhatabli}

oshtosoli to be bald (II) (CC) [osh+<tosoli>]

oshtoyya to climb (this way) (I) [osht *toyya] § Oshtishtoyyatam? Did you climb up (this way)?

oshtolhatabli to put, pour (mass patient obj.) on ° (this way) (I;II;3) [osht *olhatabli] {v1. oshtolhatapa; sg. patient obj. oshtombohli; dl. patient obj. oshtonkahli; tpl. patient obj. oshtonashaachi} § Shinok halhablit sashshoka' oshtolhatablitok. He kicked sand in my face.

oshtolhatapa to fall (this way) on (I;II) [osht *olhatapa] {v2. oshtolhatabli; sg. oshtonittola; dl. oshtonkaha}

oshwalachi to stick out (one's ears) (of a dog, for example) (I;3); to make (someone's ears) stick out (for instance, by holding them out) (I;II) [±SC] [oshwalali+chi] § Sahaksibish oshwalashlitok. I stuck out my ears. I Achoshwalashla'chi, Achoshwalachila'chi. I make your ears stick out.

oshwalali to have ears that stick up or out (II) [osh+<walali>] {ggr. oshwálla'li}

oshwálla'li ggr. of oshwalali

oshwayaachi to bring (sg. obj. with four legs or with spreading limbs, like a branch) this way, to cause (a branching obj.) to extend this way (I;3) [-SC] [osht *wayaachi] § Oshtishwayaachitok. You brought it (the branch) this way.

oshwayowat máa to stick out, extend this way (tpl. subj.—of, for example, tree limbs or people sticking their heads out the window) (I) [osht wayowat *máa] {sg. oshwáyya'a; dl. oshwáyyo'wa} § Oshwayowat hashmáatok. You all stuck (your heads) out this way.

oshwayoochi to bring (pl. obj. with four legs or with spreading limbs, like branches) this way, cause (branching objs.) to extend this way (I;3) [-SC] [osht *wayoochi] {sg. obj. oshwayaachi}

oshwáyya'a to stick out, extend this way (sg. subj.—of, for example, a tree limb or a person sticking his head out the window) (I) [osht *wayya'a] {dl. oshwáyyo'wa; tpl. oshwayowat máa} § Oshtishwayya'atam? Were you sticking your head out the window?

oshwáyyo'wa to stick out, extend this way (dl. subj.—of tree limbs or people sticking their heads out the window, for example) (I) [osht *wayyo'wa] {sg. oshwáyya'a; tpl. oshwayowat máa}

oshwí'li ggr. of oshwiili

oshwiili to hold straight out (this way) (I;3)—usually used in ggr. [osht *wiili] {ggr. oshwí'li}

287

oshwichaháli hngr. of oshwichali
oshwichali to be bushy, to stick up (of
hair), to have bushy hair (II)
[osh+<wichali>] {ggr. oshwíchcha'li;
hngr. oshwichaháli; ngr.
oshwicháli; ygr. oshwicháyya'li}
oshwicháyya'li ygr. of oshwichali
oshwicháli ngr. of oshwichali
oshwíchcha'li ggr. of oshwichali
ot see oot
owwa to moo (of a cow) (3) {hngr.
ohówwa}

owwá'ta ggr. of owwatta
owwahánta hngr. of owwatta
owwánta ngr. of owwatta
owwatta to hunt, be hunting (I) {ggr.
owwá'ta; hngr. owwahánta; ngr.
owwánta}
owwattat aya to go hunting (I)
[owwatta+t]
<oyya> in toyya {neg. <ikoyyo>}
óyyokcha to be awake, to be
wakeful—ygr. of okcha

OO

oo oh! (exclamation of surprise)
<oo> see a
oochi to draw, draw out (water from
a well), to pump (water) (I;3) {v1.
olhchi; ggr. ó'chi; hngr. ohónchi}
oohaatokma oh, well
ookma in, on (used with future time
expressions) [oo+kma] § Thursday
ookma...: on (this coming)
Thursday... | 1997 ookma...: in
1997...
ookma nannahmat, ookma nannakat
or something, or someone (subj.)
[oo+kma nanna+hmat/kat] § Lynn
ookma nannahmat miyyi'ti. Lynn
or someone is coming.
ookma nannahma, ookma nannaka
or something, or someone
(nonsubj.) [oo+kma
nanna+hma/ka] § Ofi' ookma
nannahma pislitok. I saw a dog or
something.
ooma'shki had better (aux., preceded
by verb +cha) [hoomi+a'shki] §
Ishiksa'shcha ooma'shki. You'd
better fix it. | Ireneat yahmanhicha
ooma'shki. Irene had better be

careful.
oopa see opa
oot, ot, (WB) ont prt. of ona? {<ola>}
ootabaana to flop over, go over on
(that way) (I;II) [oot *abaana]
ootachankahma see achankahma
ootafoolopa to hit a home run, make
a home run (I); to go around (over
there) (I;II) [oot *afoolopa]
ootakkowa to come down, land (over
there) (I) [oot *akkowa] §
Ootishakkowatok. You landed.
ootalawachi to go gather around (pl.
subj.) (I) [oot *alawachi]
ootalokoli to gather over there to see
(I;3) [+T] [oot *alokoli] § Lowak
ootalokolit iitahatok. We all
gathered there to see the fire.
ootalokoochi to gather over there to
see (I;3) [+T] [-SC] [oot *alokoochi]
ootapakfoota to go around (I;II) [oot
*apakfoota]
ootapoota to go over next to (I;II) [oot
*apoota] § Ootasapoota. He went
over next to me.
ootasiita to (go and) hang onto, grab
onto (I;II) [oot *asiita]

ootashaachi to take (tpl. obj.) there (I;II) [oot *ashaachi]

ootawaata to have a fall broken by, come to rest across (that way) (inan. subj.) (3;3) [oot *awaata]

ootaya to go by, pass by (I); to pass (of time) (3) [oot *aya]

ootayyabichi to go beat up (I;II) [oot *ayyabichi]

ootaaittola to fall off, fall through, fall from, fall out of (that way) (sg. subj.) (I;3 / II;3) [oot *aa+ittola] {dl. ootaakaha; tpl. ootaalhatapa} § Itti' ootishaaittolatok. You fell from the tree. | Itti' ootaasattolatok. I fell from the tree.

ootaakaha to fall off, fall through, fall from, fall out of (that way) (dl. subj.) (I;3) [oot *aakaha] {sg. ootaaittola; tpl. ootaalhatapa} § Winda' ootilaakahatok. We (two) fell out of the window.

ootaakkowa to go down on, land on (I;3) [oot *aakkowa]

ootaalhatapa to fall off, fall through, fall from, fall out of (that way) (tpl. subj.) (I;3) [oot *aalhatapa] {sg. ootaaittola; dl. ootaakaha}

ootaalhlhi to die, come to the end; to stop, come to an end, come to an edge (3) [oot *aalhlhi] {ngr. ootálhlhi: to happen, come true} § Hina'at ootaalhlhitok. The road comes to an end, stops.

ootaalhlhi ona to come to the end, reach the end (I)

ootaalhlhika' edge, end (3) [ootaalhlhi+ka']

ootaáyyalhlhi ygr. of ootálhlhi

ootálhlhi to happen, come true, be fulfilled—ngr. of ootaalhlhi [oot *alhlhi] {ygr. ootáyyalhlhi} § Holisso Holitto'paat ootayyalhlhi. The Bible's prophecies are coming to pass.

ootbitiipa to fall, bracing oneself with one's hands in (a place) (I;3)

ootchokkowa to enter, go into (I;3) [oot *chokkowa] § Ootishchokkowatok. You went in.

ootfalama to go and return (I); to go to and return from (I;3) [oot *falama] {ggr. ootfálla'ma} § Lynn inchokka' ootfalamala'chi. I'm going to Lynn's house and back.

ootfálla'ma ggr. of otfalama

ootfimmi to throw out, let go (dl. obj.) (I;II) [oot *fimmi] {sg. obj. ootkanchi; tpl. obj. ootlhatabli; pl. obj. ootlha̲'li}

ootfolota to hit a home run, make a home run (I) [oot *folota]

oothoyo to go and get from there, to pick up (and take somewhere) (I;II) [oot *hoyo]

ooti to kindle, start (a fire) (I;3) {vl. olhti; ggr. ó'ti; hngr. ohónti; ngr. ónti}

ootibaabohli to put ˘ to bed with ˘ (a sg. co-obj.) (I;II;3) [oot *ibaabohli] § Benjie̲a ootsabaabohtok. She put me to bed with Benjie, She put Benjie to bed with me.

ootiksho to go away, die out (3) [oot *iksho]

ootilikostinichi to get saved, become religious (I) [oot *ilikostinichi]

ootimaháya hngr. of ootímmayya

ootimaalhlhi to be about to die, to be almost done for (III) [oot *im+aalhlhi] § Ootamaalhlhitaha. I'm about to die, I'm almost done for.

ootímmayya to pass, get ahead of (I;III) [oot *immayya] {hngr. ootimaháya} § Ootiksammayyokitok. He didn't pass me.

ootímmayya'chi to beat (in a contest), surpass (I;III) [oot *immayya'chi]

ootimokfaha to show up to, appear to (over there) (I;III) [oot *imokfaha]

ootimokkawaatali to run by in front of (over there) (I;III) [oot *im+okkawaatali]

ootimolabi to go and tell to behave (I;III) [oot *imolabi] {ngr. ootimolámbi}

ootimolámbi ngr. of ootimolabi

ootimpilachi to go get and send for ° (I;III;3) [oot impilachi]

ootishtaalhlhi to get to the end; to die, be the last (3) [oot isht *aalhlhi]

ootishtilaatámbli to overdo, be too much (over there) (I) [oot isht *ilaatambli]

ootishtimaatámpa to be mean to (over there) (I;III) [oot isht *imaatampa]

ootishtimalili to run there, taking (something) from (someone°) (I;III;3) [oot isht *im+malili] § Ofi'at Lynn isholosh ootishtamalitok. The dog took Lynn's shoe from me and ran by there.

ootithana to come to, regain consciousness (I) [oot *ithana] § Ootishithana. You came to.

ootittapoota to go up and stand together (IR) [oot *ittapoota]

ootittola to fall off (that way) (sg. subj.) (I / II) [oot *ittola] {dl. ootkaha; tpl. ootlhatapa} § Ootsattolatok, Ootittolalitok. I fell off.

ootkaha to fall off (that way) (dl. subj.) (I) [oot *kaha] {sg. ootittola; tpl. ootlhatapa}

ootkanchi to let go, throw out (that way) (sg. obj.) (I;II) [oot *kanchi] {dl. obj. ootfimmi; tpl. obj. ootlhatabli; pl. obj. ootlha'li}

ootkochcha to come out on the other side, go through, go out the back door; to come out of nowhere, appear (that way) (I) [oot *kochcha] {ggr. ootkôchcha; ngr. ootkónchcha: to stick out, stick up, protrude, show} § Himmonaali' shoboht ootkochcha. Suddenly he appeared in a puff of smoke.

ootkôchcha ggr. of ootkochcha

ootkónchcha to stick out, stick up, protrude; to show (of a slip) [+CPR] [-PR]—ngr. of ootkochcha

ootkostí'ni ggr. of ootkostini

ootkostini to finally realize (II) [oot *kostini] {ggr. ootkostí'ni}

ootlhatabli to let (tpl. obj.) go (in one place, that way) (I;II) [oot *lhatabli] {v1. ootlhatapa; dl. obj. ootfimmi; sg. obj. ootkanchi; pl. obj. ootlha'li}

ootlhatapa to fall off (that way) (tpl. subj.) (I) {v2. ootlhatabli; sg. ootittola; dl. ootkaha}

ootlha'li to let (two or three) go (that way) (paucal pl. obj.) (I;II) [oot *lha'li] {dl. obj. ootfimmi; sg. obj. ootkanchi; tpl. obj. ootlhatabli}

ootlhopolli to go through and come out the other side (I) [oot *lhopolli]

ootokattola to fall into (that way) (I;3 / II;3) [oot *okattola] § Lokchok ootilokattolatok. We fell into the mud.

ootokfaha to show up, appear (over there) (I) [oot *okfaha]

ootokfahli to expose, show up (something, over there) (I;II) [oot *okfahli]

ootoktani to appear, be revealed (over there) (I / II) [oot *oktani]

ootombínni'li to sit down on (I;II) [oot *ombinni'li]

ootombohli to put (sg. patient obj.) down (over there) on ° (I;III;3) [oot

*ombohli] {pl. patient obj.
ootonkahli; tpl. patient obj.
ootonashaachi, ootọlhatabli}
ootonashaachi to put (tpl. patient
obj.) down (especially, in a heap) on
° (I;II;3) [oot *onashaachi] {sg.
patient obj. ootombohli; pl. patient
obj. ootonkahli; ootọlhatabli} §
Ootasonashaashtok. She put them
(in a heap) on me.
ootonittola to fall on (that way) (sg.
subj.) (I;II) [oot *onittola] {dl.
ootonkaha; tpl. ootọlhatapa} §
Ootishonittolatok. You fell on him.
| Ootaponittolatok. He fell on us.
ootonkaha to fall on (dl. subj.) (I;II)
[oot *onkaha] {v2. ootonkahli; sg.
ootonittola; tpl. ootọlhatapa}
ootonkahli to lay, put (pl. patient
obj.) down on ° (I;II;3) [oot
*onkahli] {v1. ootonkaha; sg.
patient obj. ootombohli; tpl. patient

obj. ootonashaachi, ootọlhatabli: to
put down in a heap}
ootọlhatabli to put (a bunch) down
on °, spill (something) down on °
(I;II;3) [oot *ọlhatabli] {v1.
ootọlhatapa; sg. patient obj.
ootombohli; pl. patient obj.
ootonkahli; ootonashaachi}
ootọlhatapa to fall on (tpl. subj.) (I;II)
[oot *ọlhatapa] {v2. ootọlhatabli; sg.
ootonittola; dl. ootonkaha} §
Ootasọlhatapatok. They fell on me.
ootpilachi to take (something) over
and send (it) off (I;II) [oot *pilachi]
ootpisa to go and see (I;II) [oot *pisa] §
Ootchipistok. He went and saw you.
oottakohli to be caught, be hanging
(pl. subj.) (3) [oot *takohli]
oottala to sit there by oneself (of an
obj. with a flat bottom), not to fall
over (3) [oot *tala] § Ootikta'lo. It
went over, It didn't sit there.

ọ

ọfayyí'chi ggr. of ọfayyichi
ọfayyichi to sprinkle (water) on °
(I;II;3) [on+fayyichi] {ggr. ọfayyí'chi}
ọfoyopa to breathe on (I;II)
[on+foyyo'pa] {ggr. ọfóyyo'pa}
ọfóyyo'pa ggr. of ọfoyopa
ọhabishko to sneeze at (I;II)
[on+habishko]
ọhashtahli to have it get light on
one, to have sun in one's eyes (II);
to shine on (someone, of the glory
of God) (3;II) [on+hashtahli] §
Benjieat ọhashtahli. It got light on
Benjie, Benjie had the sun in his
eyes. | Chihoowa
naaishtimaaholitto'paat Mary
ọhashtahtok. The glory of God

shone on Mary.
ọhí'li to stand on (dl. subj.) (I;II)
[on+hi'li] {sg. ọhíkki'ya; tpl.
ọhiyohli, ọhiyoht máa}
ọhika to step on (I;II) [+OPR]
[on+hika]
ọhíkki'ya to stand on (sg. subj.) (I;II)
[on+hikki'ya] {dl. ọhí'li; tpl.
ọhiyohli, ọhiyoht máa} §
Achọhikki'yali. I stand on you (or
on a part of you, for instance, your
foot).
ọhilichi to stand (sg. obj.) on (I;3;3)
[on+hilichi] {pl. obj. ọhiyohchi}
ọhilha to dance on (I;3) [+OPR]
[on+hilha] § Fred Astaireat abooha
naksika'akọ ọhilhatok. Fred Astaire

ohiyohchi

danced on the wall.
ohiyohchi to stand (pl. obj.) on °
(I;II;3) [on+hiyohchi] {sg. obj.
ohilichi}
ohiyohli to stand on (tpl. subj.) (I;II)
[on+<hiyohli>] {sg. ohíkki'ya; dl.
ohí'li; ohiyoht máa} §
Hashohiyohlinna! Don't stand on
it!
ohiyoht máa to stand on (tpl. subj.)
(II = obj. , I) [on+hiyoht maa] {sg.
ohíkki'ya; dl. ohí'li; ohiyohli}
oholissochi to write on (I;3) [+OPR]
[on+holissochi] § Aboohapootaka'
ishoholissochinna! Don't write on
the wall!
ohonkso to fart at (I;II) [on+honkso]
ohoshontikachi see ohoshottikachi
ohoshottika to shade, be shady on
(3;II); to be shaded by (II;3-at —with
overt II prefix only) (usually in ngr.)
[on+hoshottika] {ngr. ohoshottínka}
§ Ithanali ittaat asohoshottinkaka,
Ithanali ittaat asohoshottinkakat. I
know that the tree shades me, I
know that I am shaded by the tree.
ohoshottikachi, ohoshontikachi to
make shade on (I;II)
[on+hoshottikachi]
ohoshottínka ngr. of ohoshottika
ohoshowa to urinate on (I;II)
[on+hoshowa]
ohotolhko to cough on, cough at (I;II)
[on+hotolhko] § Asohotolhko. He
coughed at me.
ohowita to vomit on (I;II)
[on+howita] § Asohowitatok. He
vomited on me.
olabi to want, desire (I;II) {hgr.
oláhha'bi; hngr. olahámbi; imolabi:
to want from; to exact obedience
from; imaaolabi: to get from}
olahámbi hngr. of olabi
oláhha'bi hgr. of olabi

oloshka to lie about (I;II) [on+loshka]
olhatabli to splash on °, spill on °
(I;II;3) [+OPR] [on+lhatabli] § Joyceat
oka' asolhatablitok. Joyce splashed
water on me. | Lynnat Jan inaafka
oka' olhatablitok, Lynnat Jana
naafka oka' imolhatablitok. Lynn
spilled water on Jan's dress.
olhatapa to spill on (3;II); to fall on
(tpl. subj.) (I;II) [on+lhatapa] {sg.
onittola (fall on); dl. ootonkaha (fall
on)} § Oka'at asolhatapatok. The
water spilled on me.
omahli to blow wind on, be windy
on (—;II); to be blown on, have it be
windy on oneself, to feel a draft (II)
[on+mahli] § Alekat omahli, Aleka
omahli. It's blowing on Alex.
omalli to jump on (I;II) [on+malli]
omó'chi ggr. of omochi
omochi to cover ° with (something
loose, like dirt) (I;II;3) {v1.
omolhchi; ggr. omó'chi; hngr.
omohónchi; ngr. omónchi} § Lokfi'
achomochitahlili. I covered you
with dirt.
omohónchi hngr. of omochi
omolhchi to cover up (3;II); to be
covered up (II) [+PR]; to be covered
up with (II;3-at) {v2. omochi} §
Lynnat ithana lokfaat
omolhchitahakat. Lynn knows that
she's covered with dirt. | Ireneat
paskaat imomolhchitaha. Irene's
bread is covered up.
omónchi ngr. of omochi
óna ngr. of ona {talhipa chaffaka óna}
onoli to tell on (I;II) [on+anoli] §
Asonotok. He told on me.
onowa to walk on (sg. subj., mainly
nonhum. obj.) (I;II) [+OPR]
[on+nowa] {dl. ontánno'wa; tpl.
ontanohówa} § Naachi
imonowatok. They're walking on

her blanket.
osi' eagle
osi' ishkobo-homma' type of eagle
[ishkobo' homma+']
osi' ishkobo-tohbi' bald eagle (CP)
[ishkobo' tohbi+']
osi' koyofa' type of eagle (CP)
[koyofa+']
osishto' type of big eagle [osi' ishto+']
ososhi', osi' oshi' baby eagle
<**oshik**> in nakoshik, ofishik, tal-
oshik [oshi']
oshobbichi to sprinkle (water, for
example) on (grass, for instance˚),
to spray ˚ with (I;II;3); to have it
rain or sprinkle on one (II) (only
with overt II prefix) [on+shobbichi]
§ Ithanali asoshobbichitokat. I know
it sprinkled on me.
oshobohchi to smoke, cure with
smoke (I;II); to blow the smoke
from (a substance, such as tobacco)
at ˚ (I;II;3) [-SC] [oshobohli+chi]
{hngr. oshobohlihínchi;
oshobollichi}
oshobohlihínchi hngr. of
oshobohchi
oshobohli to be smoked; to have
smoke on one, be smoke-damaged
(II) [on+shobohli] § shokha' nipi'
oshobohli': bacon, smoked ham
oshobollichi to blow the smoke from
(a substance, such as tobacco) at ˚
(I;II;3) [on+shobollichi]
{oshobohchi} § Chomak

asoshobollichitok. He blew tobacco
smoke at me, He blew smoke from
tobacco at me.
oshoppala to shine on (of a light)
(3;II); to be shone on by (II;3-at); to
have light in one's eyes (II)
[on+shoppala] § Ithanali
aashoppala-at asoshoppalakat,
Ithanali aashoppala-at
asoshoppalaka. I know the light is
shining in my eyes. | Ithanali
asoshoppalakat. I know I have light
in my eyes.
oshoppalali to shine (a light) on ˚
(I;II;3) [on+shoppalali] §
Aashoppala' asoshoppalatok. He
shone a light on me.
owáyya'a to be on (I;II) [on+wayya'a]
oyilhibli to knock (sg. obj.) over on ˚
(I;II;3) [on+yilhibli] {v1. oyilhipa; pl.
obj. oyilhlhichi} § Abooha
asoyilhiblitok. He knocked the
house over on me.
oyilhihli to cave in on (pl. subj.) (3;II)
[+T] [on+yilhihli] {sg. oyilhipa}
oyilhipa to cave in on, fall in on (sg.
subj.) (3;II) [on+yilhipa] {v2.
oyilhibli; pl. oyilhihi} § Abooha
paknaat asoyilhi'pacha
sattopashtok. The roof fell in on me
and hurt me.
oyilhlhichi to knock (pl. obj.) over
on ˚ (I;II;3) [on+yilhlhichi] {sg. obj.
oyilhibli}

p

<**pa**> in pa-pila, yappa
pá'lli ggr. of palli
pá'lhlhi ggr. of palhlhi
pa's pa's pa's aachi see pas pas pas

aachi
pá'ska ggr. of paska
pá'sli ggr. of pasli
pa't pa't pa't aachi see pat pat pat

aachi
pa'w pa'w pa'w aachi see paaw paaw paaw aachi
pachafa to split open (for instance, of a ripened fruit) (sg. subj.) (3) {v2. pachaffi; pl. pachahli}
pachaffi to enable (something, such as a ripened fruit or an overfilled bag) to split open, seemingly by itself (sg. obj.) (I;3) {v1. pachafa; hngr. pacháffi; pl. obj. pachaachi} § Bashlit pachiffi. Cut it open, Cut it so that it can split open.
pacháffi hngr. of pachaffi
pacháli hngr. of pachahli
pachahli to split open (for instance, of ripened fruit) (pl. subj.) (3) {hngr. pacháli; sg. pachafa}
pachahlihínchi hngr. of pachaachi
pachahlínchi ngr. of pachaachi
pachalhpooba', pachi' alhpooba' dove; pet pigeon [alhpooba+']
pachalhpooba' tohbi' white dove [tohbi+']
pachaachi to enable (ripened fruit, or overfilled bags, for example) to split open, seemingly by themselves (for instance, by overfilling bags) (pl. obj.) (I;3) [pachahli+chi] {hngr. pachahlihínchi; ngr. pachahlínchi; sg. obj. pachaffi}
Pachaanosi' name of a Choctaw church [pachi' aa+nosi+']
páchcho'fa ggr. of pachofa
pachi' pigeon
pachi' alhpooba' see pachalhpooba'
pachi' yoshoba', pachi-yoshoba' dove: especially, mourning dove [yoshoba+']
pachí'chi ggr. of pachiichi
pachi-yoshoba' see pachi' yoshoba'
pachiichi to splash, spatter, spray with a liquid (I;II) [+SC] [pachiili+chi] {ggr. pachí'chi} §

Issapachiishtok. You splashed me.
pachiili to splash, spray (of a liquid); to spatter (of hot grease); to sparkle, emit sparks (of fire, a sparkler) (3)
pacho'li to dent (pl. obj.) (I;3) {v1. pacho'wa; sg. obj. pachoffi}
pacho'wa to be dented (pl. subj.) (3) {v2. pacho'li; sg. pachofa; pachohli}
pachofa to be dented; to be really skinny (sg. subj.) (II) {v2. pachoffi; ggr. páchcho'fa; hngr. pachohófa; ngr. pachófa; ygr. pachóyyo'fa; pl. pacho'wa, pachohli}
pachoffi to dent (something) (sg. obj.) (I;II) {v1. pachofa; hngr. pachohóffi; pl. obj. pacho'li}
pachohli to be dented (pl. subj.) (3) {hngr. pachohóli; sg. pachofa; pacho'wa}
pachohófa hngr. of pachofa
pachohóffi hngr. of pachoffi
pachohóli hngr. of pachohli
pachóyyo'fa ygr. of pachofa
pachófa ngr. of pachofa
pahántha hngr. of patha
paháa hngr. of paa
pahálli hngr. of palli
pahálhlhi hngr. of palhlhi
pahálhki hngr. of palhki
páhhalli hgr. of palli
pahhana to be warped, crooked (3) {rigr. pahhanpáa; xgr. pahhánna'a}
pahhánna'a to be warped, crooked (3)—xgr. of pahhana
pahhanpáa to walk crooked (like a duck) (I); to walk crooked in (a place) (I;3)—rigr. of pahhana
páhhatha hgr. of patha
pakaháli hngr. of pakali
Paka'li' Chickasaw woman's name (CP) [pakali+']
pakachi to make bloom (I;3) [pakali+chi] {hngr. pakalihínchi}
pakali to bloom, open (of a flower) (3)

{ggr. pákka'li; hngr. pakaháli}
pakali' flower (of a particular plant—
always preceded by the name of a
plant) (o3p) [pakali+'] § sholop
tilhi'li' pakali': horsemint flower
pakalihínchi hngr. of pakachi
pakka bread (children's word) {paska}
pákka'li ggr. of pakali
pákko'ta to be permanently creased
or folded over, to have a crease
sewed or pressed in (at a hem, for
example) (3)—ggr. of pakota {v2.
pakolli}
pákkolli ggr. of pakolli
pakna' top, ceiling; on top of (II)
{paknaka'; paknali'} § chipakna': on
top of you
paknaka' top; on top of (3) {pakna';
paknakali'}
paknakali' (moving) through, either
on or over the top of (3) [pakna']
paknali' (moving) through, either
on or over the top of (3) [pakna'] §
Aaimpa' paknali' malit lhopollitok.
He ran through on top of the tables.
paknonto'wa' horizontal beams
[pakna' onto'wa+']
pako'li to make a dent in (I;II) {v1.
pako'wa}
pakó'lli ggr. of pakolli
pako'wa to be dented (II) (Ct?) {v2.
pako'li}
pakolli, pakotli to fold over, press a
crease into (I;3) {v1. pakota; ggr.
pákkolli, pakó'lli; ngr. pakólli}
pakota to be folded up (LR) {v2.
pakolli; ggr. pákko'ta; ittapakota}
pakotli see pakolli
pakólli ngr. of pakolli
paktapa' edible mushroom (MJ)
[pakti' apa+']
pakti', (WB, CC, MJ) pakti
mushroom
<palahámmi> in impalahámmi—

hngr. of palammi
palaháska hngr. of palaska
palammi to be serious, bad, difficult
(of an action or experience) (3) {ggr.
pállammi; hngr. <palahámmi>;
impalammi: to be serious for} §
Tannapat pallammi. War is bad.
palaska to be all tangled (of hair) (3)
(usually in ggr.) [+CPR] [-PR] {ggr.
pállaska; hngr. palaháska}
<palaska> in ahi' palaska',
aapalaska', chomak palaska', issosh
palaska', tali' palaska', tanchi'
palaska' {v2. paska}
palassa' in asonnak palassa'
<palata> in impalata
pali' flying squirrel, (EP) flying
mouse
pállammi ggr. of palammi
pállammihma with difficulty
[pallammi+hma] § Pallammihma
hilhashlitok. I got her to dance with
difficulty, It was hard for me to get
her to dance. | Pallammihma
nowali. It's hard for me to walk, I
walk with difficulty.
pállaska ggr. of palaska
palli to be hot; to be angry; to be
sexually aroused (II) [+CPR] [-PR]
{ggr. pá'lli; hgr. páhhalli; hngr.
pahálli; ngr. pálli; ygr. páyya'lli;
impalli}
palli, patli to spread flat, put on the
floor (pl. obj.) (I;3) {ggr. pá'lli; hngr.
pahálli; sg. obj. patali}
pallichi to heat, make hot [palli+chi]
(I;3) {ngr. pallínchi: to make hotter}
pallichit abi to smother (someone)
(I;II) [pallichi+t abi] § Pallichit
sabitok. He smothered me.
pallínchi to make hotter—ngr. of
pallichi
pallit illi to smother (II) [palli+t] §
Pallit sallitok. I smothered.

palha

palha to split, be split (pl. subj.) (3)
[+T] {v2. palhlhi; sg. palhata;
palhahli}
palhá'lli ggr. of palhalli
palhahálli hngr. of palhalli
palhahli to split (pl. subj.) (3) {sg.
palhata; palha}
palhalli, palhatli to chop, split (wood,
for example) (sg. obj.); to cut
(something the long way once); to
split open (something round, once)
(I;II) {v1. palhata; ggr. palhá'lli,
pálhlhalli; hngr. palhahálli; pl. obj.
palhlhi}
palhata to split apart, to break in half
(sg. subj.) (II) {v2. palhalli; pl. palha,
palhahli}
palhatli see palhalli
palhki to be fast (II); to go fast, walk
fast (I) [+PR] [-CPR] {hngr. pahálhki;
ngr. pálhki; ygr. páyya'lhki;
impalhki}
palhkichi to make (something) go
faster (I;II) [palhki+chi] {ngr.
palhkínchi}
palhkínchi ngr. of palhkichi
pálhlhalli ggr. of palhalli
palhlhi to split (pl. obj.); to cut
(something the long way, more
than once); to split open (something
round, more than once) (I;II) {vl.
palha; ggr. pá'lhlhi; hngr.
pahálhlhi; sg. obj. palhalli} §
Paha'lhicha…. He split it and then
he….
panaa to be twisted (3) [+CPR] [+PR]
{v2. paniili; ngr. panáa}
panaachi to twist (something—for
instance, in making thread) (I;3)
[panaa+chi] {hngr. panaahánchi}
panaahánchi hngr. of panaachi
Panaayo'cha' Chickasaw woman's
name
panaayo'li to twist (mainly pl. obj.)

(I;3) {v1. panaayo'wa}
panaayo'wa to go around in a circle
and, at the same time, go up and
down (like a merry-go-round
horse); to walk along thrusting first
one shoulder and then the other
forward; to be all twisted (often pl.
subj.) (I) {v2. panaayo'li; rmgr.
panaayoyówa; panaa}
panaayoyówa to walk along
thrusting the shoulders forward
alternately (I)—rmgr. of
panaayo'wa; usually used in prt. §
Panaayoyowat aalitok. I went along
thrusting my shoulders forward.
panáa ngr. of panaa
paniili to twist (I;II) {v1. panaa}
pankalhfola' see panki' alhfola'
pankapi' grapevine [panki' api']
pankaashoshi', panki' aashoshi'
possum grapes (ER)
panki' grapes
panki' alhfola', pankishtalhfola',
pankalhfola' grape dumpling
[panki' (isht) alhfola']
panki' homma' red grapes:
especially, wine grapes [homma+']
panki' imilhlha' wild grapes
[imilhlha+']
panki' losa' dark purple grapes:
especially, Concord grapes [losa+']
panki' nihiksho' seedless grapes
[nihi' iksho+']
panki' okchamali', pankokchamali'
green grapes [okchamali+']
panki' sawa' possum grapes, a type of
small grapes [<sawa>+']
panki' shila' raisins [shila+']
panki' shobboko'li' type of large
grapes [shobbokoli+']
pankishtalhfola' see panki' alhfola'
pankishto' type of grapes, perhaps
muscadine or a big green grape
[ishto+']

296

pankishan-kachi' growth on
grapevines, boiled and used as
medicine for colic [panki'
im+<shan-kachi>+']
pankokchamali' see panki'
okchamali'
pankokchi' grape juice; wine [panki'
okchi']
pankokchi' hawashko' wine
[hawashko+']
pankoshi' type of little grapes
(another name for panki' sawa')
[panki' oshi']
Pantatak, (CM) Pantattaak Pontotoc,
Oklahoma [< panti' oktaak ?]
pántha ngr. of patha
panti' (AB, CM), (MJ) panto' cattails
Panti' mythical animal with very
beautiful teeth, which it would
trade for a child's discarded baby
teeth (MJ)
pa-pila on this side [<pa> pila]
pas pas pas aachi, pa's pa's pa's aachi
to make a slapping or clapping
sound; to make the sound of big
bare feet (expressive) (I) {pasak
pasak pasak aachi, pasa'chi, passáa,
paska}
pasa to be cut in very thin slices (of
meat, for instance, for jerky) (3) {v2.
pasli}
pasa'chi to clap (the hands), spank,
pat (I;II) [-SC] {klgr. pássakli'chi; rcgr.
pasasá'chi, paska}
pasafa to be cut open; to split open
(mainly sg. subj.) (3) {v2. pasaffi; pl.
pasahli}
pasaffi to cut open (mainly sg. obj.)
(I;II) {v1. pasafa; hngr. pasaháffi; pl.
obj. pasaachi; pasli}
pasaháffi hngr. of pasaffi
pasahli to split open (of a peach or
watermelon, for instance); to be cut
open (pl. subj.) (3) {sg. pasafa}

pasahlínchi ngr. of pasaachi
pasak pasak pasak aachi to make a
slapping sound (expressive) (I) {pas
pas pas aachi}
pasakchala type of medicinal plant
pasasá'chi to clap all the time (for
instance, of an autistic child) (I)—
rcgr. of pasa'chi [+SC]
pasaachi to split, cut open (peaches,
watermelons, for instance) (pl. obj.)
(I;3) [-SC] [pasahli+chi] {ngr.
pasahlínchi; sg. obj. pasaffi}
paska to make bread (I); to make
(baked goods) (I;3); to make into
bread (I;II) {v1. <palaska>; ggr.
pá'ska; pakka, pasa'chi} § Sapaskatok. She made me into
bread. | Tilli'ko' paskalitok. I made
the flour into bread, I made bread
with the flour. | Paska champoli'
paskalitok. I baked cookies.
paska bread, loaf of bread
paska banaa' see banaha'
paska bosholli' crumb [bosholli+']
paska champoli' cake, cookies, pastry
[champoli+']
paska champoli' ibalhto' vanilla
paska champoli' ishbilamachi', paska
ishbilamachi', paskishbilamachi'
flavoring (primarily for baked
goods): especially, vanilla [isht
bilamachi+']
paska champoli' ishhommachi' red
food coloring [isht hommachi+']
paska champoli' onaa-asha' icing,
frosting
paska champoli' pakna' onashaachi'
icing, whipped cream
[onashaachi+']
paska chilili' crumb [chilili+']
paska hakshop crust (of bread)
paska hawashko' sour biscuit
[hawashko+']
paska holiito'pa' communion wafer,

297

paska hoshollo'

bread for communion [holiitopa+']
paska hoshollo' bread crumb
paska ikbi', paskikbi' baker [paska
ikbi+']
paska ishbilamachi' see paska
champoli' ishbilamachi'
paska ishshatabli', paskishshatabli'
baking powder, yeast [isht
shattabli+']
paska ishtontono'kalhchi' see
paskishtontono'kalhchi'
paska kallo' hard, dried-out bread or
biscuits [kallo+']
paska latassa' flat or unleavened
bread, such as tortillas [latassa+']
paska nipi' ittalatta'a' meat
sandwich, hamburger [ittalatta'a+']
paska shatabli' light bread [shatabli+']
paska shila' cracker [shila+']
paska toba' dough (WB) [toba+']
paska toshafa' slice of bread (sg.)
[toshafa+'] {pl. paska toshahli'}
paska toshahli' slices of bread (pl.);
loaf of bread [toshahli+'] {sg. paska
toshafa'}
paskalhfola' corn or flour dumpling
cooked in water [paska alhfola']
paskalhposha' toast; roasted bread
cooked without grease; tortillas:
especially, homemade tortillas
[paska alhposha+']
paskawaalhaali' fried bread [paska
awaalhaali+']
paskawo', (AW, CP) paskabo', (ML)
paskaho' crane (bird)
paskawo' homma' flamingo
[homma+']
paskaa-alhposha' toaster [paska
aa+alhposha+']
paskaaikbi' bakery [paska aa+ikbi+']
paskaalhto' bread box [paska
aalhto+']
paskaanonachi' oven; griddle, cookie
sheet [paska aa+nonachi+']

paskaaposhli', paska aaposhli' toaster
[paska aa+aposhli+']
paskinkano'miksho' bread made
without baking powder (MC,
reported by CW) [paska inkano'mi'
iksho+']
paskishbilamachi' see paska
champoli' ishbilamachi'
paskishkatolhlhi' cookie cutter,
biscuit cutter [paska isht
katolhlhi+']
paskishlatassachi' rolling pin (WB)
[paska isht latassachi+']
paskishtonton'kalhchi', paska
ishtontono'kalhchi', (LR) paska
aatiino'chi', (AB, CM) paska
ishtontono'chi', (ER)
paskaatono'chi', (CP) paska
ontono'chi', (MJ, LP)
paskishtono'chi', (WB)
paskontono'chi', (AW, LF) paska
ishtono'chi' rolling pin [paska isht
ontono'kalhchi+']
paskokchamali' blue corn bread
[paska okchamali+']
pasli to cut (meat, for instance) in
thin slices (for jerky, for example)
(I;II) {v1. pasa; ggr. pá'sli; pasaffi}
passaháa hngr. of passáa
pássakli'chi to slap (I;II)—klgr. of
pasa'chi [+SC] {ittipássakli'chi,
passáa}
passáa, passáha to spank, slap, hit
with the flat of the hand (I;II)
[+OPR] {hngr. passaháa;
pássakli'chi, pasa'chi} §
Ikpassaokitok. She didn't slap him.
passáha see passáa
pashohli to rub, pat, stroke (I;II)
{hngr. pashohóli}
pashohóli hngr. of pashohli
pashshá'na ggr. of pashshana
pashshahána to walk with a swaying
motion (I)—hngr. of pashshana

pashshana to warp in the sun (3); to be swaybacked, bent out of shape (II) {v2. pashshanili; ggr. pashshá'na; hngr. pashshahána: to walk with a swaying motion (I); ngr. pashshána; rigr. pashshanpáa; xgr. pashshánna'a; ygr. pashsháyya'na}

pashshanili to warp (especially, by putting in the sun) (I;II) {v1. pashshana}

pashshánna'a to be all warped (3); to walk with a swaying motion (I)—xgr. of pashshana

pashshanpáa to walk crooked (I)—rigr. of pashshana

pashsháyya'na ygr. of pashshana

pashshána ngr. of pashshana

pat pat pat aachi, pa't pa't pa't aachi to make a popping sound; to make the sound of really big bare feet (expressive) (I) {<pata'chi>; patatá'chi, <páttakli'chi>}

<pata> in hashshok pata' {v2. patali; xgr. pátta'a; patalhpo, patassa, patha}

<pata'chi> in <ittipata'chi> {<klgr. <páttakli'chi>; rcgr. patatá'chi; pat pat pat aachi; pátta'a}

patá'ffi ggr. of pataffi

<patachi> in imaapatachi

patafa to be ripped; to be cut open for disemboweling (mainly sg. subj.) (II) {v2. pataffi; ggr. pátta'fa; pl. patahli}

pataffi to rip (a stitch or row, cloth); to slash, cut open, disembowel (mainly sg. obj.) (I;II) {v1. patafa; ggr. páttaffi, patá'ffi; hngr. patahááffi; pl. obj. pataachi}

patahááffi hngr. of pataffi

patahááli hngr. of patahli, patali

patahássa hngr. of patassa

patahli to be all ripped out; to be ripped out (pl. subj.) (3) {hngr. patahááli; sg. patafa}

patahlínchi ngr. of pataachi

patakshi' in oka' patakshi'

patali to spread flat; to pave; to make (a bed); to put on the floor (sg. obj.) (I;3) {v1. <pata>, pátta'a; hngr. patahááli; pl. obj. palli}

patalínchi to sleep around, to go with a lot of men (of a woman) (I;3)

patalisht hoyo to spread out to look for (a lost child, for instance) (I;II) [patalinchi+t] § Patalisht sahoyotok. They spread out to look for me.

patalhpalhiipi'ya' sheet, bedspread [patalhpo' alhiipiya']

patalhpo to be all spread out, be a covering (usually in ggr.) [+T]; to be made (of a bed) (3) [<pata> +po+] {ggr. páttalhpo; ngr. patáálhpo; ompatalhpo, <pata>}

patalhpo' in akka' patalhpo', patalhpalhiipi'ya', tali' patalhpo' [patalhpo+']

patassa to be flat, mashed (of an originally round obj.) (II) {v2. patassali; ggr. páttassa; hngr. patahássa; ngr. patássa; <pata>}

patassa' see nani' patassa'

patassali to roll out (dough), flatten (I;II) {v1. patassa}

patassoshi' minnow (ER) [patassa' oshi']

patatá'chi to walk without shoes (I)—rcgr. of <pata'chi>

pataachi to rip out (stitches, for example) (pl. obj.) (I;II) [±SC] [patahli+chi] {hngr. pataalihínchi; ngr. patahlínchi; sg. obj. pataffi}

pataalihínchi hngr. of pataachi

pataaschi, pataasachi, (MJ, TP) pataaasachi', (WB) yakni' pataasachi' bottomland

patáálhpo ngr. of patalhpo

patássa ngr. of patassa

patha, (MJ) patta to be wide, broad (II); to be webbed (of feet) (3) {hgr.

páhhatha; hngr. pahánta; ngr. pántha; ygr. páyyatha; <pata>}
pathachi to widen (I;3) [patha+chi] {ngr. pathánchi}
pathánchi ngr. of pathachi
<patkachi> in ompatkachi, patkachit máa {ygr. patkáyya'chi; <apatkachi>}
patkachit máa to just sit around (pl. subj.) (I) [<patkachi>+t] {sg. pátta'a; dl. patkáyya'chi}
patkáyya'chi to just sit around (dl. subj.) (I)—ygr. of <patkachi> {sg. pátta'a; tpl. patkachit máa}
patli see palli
patoksi' mudcat (fish) (AB)
pátta'a to just sit around on the floor, doing nothing; to just lie there (like a throw rug); to be lazy (sg. subj.) (I); to sit around on the floor in (a place) (I;3)—xgr. of <pata> {v2. patali; dl. patkáyya'chi; tpl. patkachit máa}
pátta'fa ggr. of patafa
páttaffi ggr. of pataffi
<páttakli'chi> in ittipáttakli'chi—klgr. of <pata'chi>
pattala to be short, like a midget (3) {rigr. pattalpáa; xgr. pattálla'a}
pattálla'a to be short, like a midget (3)—xgr. of pattala
pattalpáa to be a shorty, be a short one (3)—rigr. of pattala
páttalhpo ggr. of patalhpo
páttassa ggr. of patassa
payofa to be dented, bent out of shape (3) (Ct?); to be ugly looking, hunched over (II) {v2. payoffi; ygr. páyyo'fa; paayo'kachi, paayo'kalhchi}
payoffi to dent, push out of shape; to hit (I;3) (Ct) [+OPR] {v1. payofa; hngr. payohóffi}
payohóffi hngr. of payoffi
páyya'lli ygr. of palli

páyya'lhki ygr. of palhki
páyyatha ygr. of patha
páyyo'fa ggr. of payofa
<paapi'> in impaapi'
paaw paaw paaw aachi, pa'w pa'w pa'w aachi to go "pow", to make the sound of a gun being shot (expressive) (I) [influenced by English?]
paay pie [from the English]
paay hakshop piecrust
paayi' bogeyman (HS) [hopayi']
paayo'kachi to be bent out of shape, warped (of wood, for instance), especially with a wavy shape (3) (Ct?) {baayo'kachi, paayo'kalhchi}
paayo'kalhchi to be wavy, rippling (3) {baayo'kalhchi, payofa, paayo'kachi}
pá'a ggr. of paa
paa, (ER) paha to whoop (like an Indian); to make the noise a bullfrog does (I) {ggr. pá'a; hngr. paháa}
pafi to appoint, choose, select (someone); to make (someone) do something; to challenge, dare (someone) (I;II) § Charlesa pafilitoka aya'chi, Charlesa pafilitok aya'chika. I appointed Charles to go.
pálhki ngr. of palhki
pasita, pasta ribbon; ribbon headdress (IIIp) [ipashi' sita]
pasita ishtalakchi' hair ribbon [isht takchi+']
pashalhiipi'li' see ipashalhiipi'li'
pashi' short form of ipashi'
pashishlhili' hair oil or medicine [pashi' isht lhili+']
pashishtakallo'chi' hair clip, barrette [pashi' isht akallochi+']
pashishyo'kli' hair clip, barrette [pashi' isht yokli+']
pí'la in aba' píla—ggr. of <pila>

pi'scha ishtakaniya to get carried away watching, keep on watching (sg. subj.) (I;3 , I) (cha expression; includes pisa) {ggr. pi'scha ishtakánni'ya; pl. pi'scha ishtatamowa} § TV ishpi'scha ishtishakaniyatok. You got carried away watching TV.

pi'scha ishtakánni'ya ggr. of pi'scha ishtakaniya

pi'scha ishtatamowa to get carried away watching, keep on watching (pl. subj.) (3;3) (cha expression; includes pisa) {sg. pi'scha ishtakaniya}

picha' pitcher [from the English]

pichchaa, pichchaha barn, corncrib, silo

pichifa to splat, be splatted (for example, of a tomato); be crushed with the fingers (of a bug) (sg. subj.) (II) {v2. pichiffi; pl. pichihli}

pichiffi to crush, splat (sg. obj.) (I;II) {v1. pichifa; hngr. pichihíffi; pl. obj. pichihchi; apichiffi}

pichihíffi hngr. of pichiffi

pichihíli hngr. of pichihli

pichihchi to splat, crush (pl. obj.) (I;3) [-SC] [pichihli+chi] {sg. obj. pichiffi}

pichihli to splat, burst (pl. subj.) (3) {hngr. pichihíli; sg. pichifa}

piha to be swept up, swept away (of dirt, for instance) (3) {v2. pihli}

<pihcha> in pihcha', ittapíhhihcha {hgr. píhhihcha; hngr. pihíhcha, pihíncha}

pihcha' shortlegged—only used in complex expressions, such as akank pihcha', hattak pihcha' [<pihcha>+']

pihchi' see pilhchi'

píhhi'la not to do anything, just to be there (I); to be in (a place) doing nothing (I;3)—hgr. of <pila> §

Chinchokkaako pihha'lali. I was in your house just doing nothing.

píhhihcha to be very small, to be a midget (sg. subj.) (I); to be very small, be a midget in (a place) (I;3)— hgr. of <pihcha> {hngr. pihíhcha, pihincha; pl. ittapíhhihcha} § Chincokkakta pihhihcham? Was he there, very small, at your house?

pihíncha, pihíhcha hngr. of píhhihcha, <pihcha>

pihíli hngr. of pihli

pihísa hngr. of pisa

pihli to sweep, sweep up (dirt, the house, fish in a net) (I;3) {v1. piha; hngr. pihíli; ngr. píhli} § Itti' hishi' piht shokolbika' pitashaashlitok. I swept the leaves into the corner, I swept up the leaves, putting them into the corner.

pihlí'chi to preside over, officiate for, lead (I;II) [+SC]—ggr. of <piichi>

pihli'chi' president [pihli'chi+']

pihli'shcha ishtaya to take (pl. obj.) along with one (cha expression; includes <piichi>) (I;3) § Chipota pihli'shlit ishtayalitok. I took the kids along with me.

pihli'sht prt. of <piichi>

pihli'sht áa see piichit áa

pihlínchi to watch (someone's child) (I;3) [+OPR]—ngr. of <piichi> § Anchipota pihlinchi. She's watching my child.

pikkal pickle [from the English]

pikkal abihli to make, put up, can pickles (I)

pikkal champoli' sweet pickle [champoli+']

pikkal wasacha' sour pickle [wasacha+']

piknik picnic [from the English]

pila just, exactly, precisely (always follows a noun specifying location or relationship) {pílla; aba' pila, akka' pila, ma-pila, pa-pila, yamma pila, yappa pila} § Chichonkashat chimalhfabi' pila. Your heart is (precisely there) on the left side. | Sashki' pila. (To be exact about her relationship to me,) she's on my mother's side.

<pila> in pilachi, nampila {ggr. pí'la; hgr. píhhi'la; ngr. <píla>; <aba' pila>, pílla, pit}

pilachi to send (I;II) [<pila>+chi?] {ggr. pílla'chi; hngr. pilahánchi; impilachi}

pilahánchi hngr. of pilachi

pilisa to play with, mess around with (food, dirt, etc.) (I;3) {impilisa}

pílla just, only {pila; aba' pílla; akka' pílla; misha' pílla } § Pilla issolitok. I just hit him (that's all). | Pilla hikki'yatok. He just stood there.

pílla aachi to just say it, not to mean it (I) § Pilla aashlitok. I just said it, I didn't mean it.

pílla'chi ggr. of pilachi

pilhchi', pihchi' sheep sorrel—type of edible weed, like clover {oktaak pilhchi'}

pilhofa to be scraped, to have a scrape (sg. subj.) (II) [+CPR] [-PR] {v2. pilhoffi; pl. pilhohli}

pilhoffi to scrape, skin (one's knee, for example) (sg. obj.) (I;II) {v1. pilhofa; hngr. pilhohǫffi; pl. obj. pilhoochi}

pilhohchi to scuff; to scrape (pl. obj.) (I;II) [±SC] [pilhohli+chi] {hngr. pilhohlihínchi; sg. obj. pilhoffi}

pilhohli to be scuffed; to be scraped (pl. subj.) (II) [+CPR] [-PR] {hngr. pilhohǫli; sg. pilhofa}

pilhohlihínchi hngr. of pilhoochi

pilhohǫffi hngr. of pilhoffi

pilhohǫli hngr. of pilhohli

pinak picnic, packed lunch

pinak aalhto' lunch box

Pinchitokaka' in Aba' Pinchitokaka', Chihoowa Pinchitokaka'

pinha' seed for planting—used only in complex expressions, such as ahi' pinha', tanchi' pinha' {pinhachi}

pinhachi to save for seed (I;II) [pinha'+chi] {hngr. pinnahánchi}

Pinki', Pinki' Chihoowa God our Father [from the Lord's Prayer as in the Choctaw Bible—Pinki' Chihoowa, abaaishbinni'lihma...]

Pinki' Chihoowa Chitokaka' God our Father [Choctaw chito 'big']

pinnahánchi hngr. of pinhachi

pintabi' mouser, mouse killer [pinti' abi+']

pintapa' type of snake that eats mice (MJ) [pinti' apa+']

pinti' mouse

pinti' tohbi' white mouse [tohbi+']

pinti' wakaa' bat [wakaa+']

pintishholhtosi' mousetrap [pinti' isht holhtosi+']

pintishtabi' mouse poison [pinti' isht abi+']

pintishtilli' mouse poison [pinti' isht illi+']

pintishyokachi' mousetrap [pinti' isht yokachi+']

pisa to look at, see (I;II); to try on (used with a preceding prt. referring to the type of garment worn) (I;3) {hngr. pihísa; ngr. písa: to see, look at; neg. ikpi'so: be blind; <hisa>} § fokhat pisa: to try on (a dress) | yaalhipit pisa: to try on (a hat)

pisachi to show ° to ° (I;II;3) [pisa+chi] {ggr. píssa'chi; hngr. pisahánchi}

pisa-chokma, pisa-chokma'si to be pretty, good-looking, beautiful (II) [pisa *chokma+a'si] § Pisa-

chichokma'si. You're pretty.
pisahánchi hngr. of pisachi
pisa-ishtaaíla to look different (II)
[pisa isht *aaila] § Pisa-ishtachiila
chohmi. You look kind of different.
pisa-kanihmi to be what color, to
look like what (II) (inf.) [+HM],
<pisa-kanih> [pisa *kanihmi] {int.
pisa-katihmi} § Pisa-sakanihka
ithana. He knows what I look like.
pisa-kanihmi (of) what color,
looking like what (inf.) (nonsubj.)
{int. pisa-katihmi}
pisa-kanihmihoot (of) what color,
looking like what (inf.) (subj.) [pisa-
kanihmi+hoot] {int. pisa-
katihmihat} § Ofi' pisa-
kanihmihoot chikisilitoka ithanali.
I know what color dog bit you.
pisa-kanihmiho (of) what color,
looking like what (inf.) (nonsubj.)
[pisa-kanihmi+ho] {int. pisa-
katihmihta} § Ofi' pisa-kanihmiho
ishpistoka ithanali. I know what
color dog you saw.
<pisa-kanih> [HM] of pisa-kanihmi
pisa-katihmi to be what color, to look
like what (int.) (II) [+HM], <pisa-
katih> [pisa *katihmi] § Naafkaat
pisa-katihmi? What color is the
dress? | Naafkaat pisa-katihtam?
What color was the dress?, What
color is the dress (if it's now out of
sight)? | Pisa-sakatihmi? What
color am I (for instance, what color
have I been made up to be)?
pisa-katihmi (of) what color, looking
like what (int.) (nonsubj.) {inf. pisa-
kanihmi}
pisa-katihmihat (of) what color,
looking like what (int.) (subj.) [pisa-
katihmi+hat] {inf. pisa-
kanihmihoot} § Ofi' pisa-
katihmihat chikisilitok? What color

dog bit you?
pisa-katihmihta (of) what color,
looking like what (int.) (nonsubj.)
[pisa-katihmi+hta] {inf. pisa-
kanihmiho}
<pisa-katih> [HM] of pisa-katihmi
pis-ayyoba ki'yo to be ugly, bad-
looking (II) [pisa *ayyoba] {ngr. pis-
ayyómba ki'yo} § Pisa-asayyomba
ki'yo. I'm ugly.
pis-ayyómba ki'yo ngr. of pis-ayyoba
ki'yo
pis-ikayyo'bo to be ugly (II) [pisa
*ikayyo'bo] [+CPR] [-PR] {pis-ayyoba
ki'yo} § Pis-iksayyo'bo. I'm ugly.
pisittimilayyoka bíyyi'ka to be all
colors (of a pieced quilt, for
example) (3) [pisa *ittimilayyoka]
pisittimíla to look different (3) [pisa
*ittimila]
píssa'chi ggr. of pisachi
pist prt. of pisa [pisa+t]
pist ala to come to see (II = obj. , I =
subj.) § Sapist ishlatam? Did you
come to see me?
pist aya to go to see (II = obj. , I =
subj.)
pist aat ala to come courting (II =
obj. , — , 3 = subj.) [aa+t] § Sapist aat
alatok. He came courting me.
pishi to suck, nurse (I) [+PR] {ngr.
pishi}
pishichi to suckle, give a bottle to
(I;II) [+OPR] [pishi+chi] {ggr.
píshshi'chi; hngr. pishihínchi; ngr.
pishínchi}
pishihínchi hngr. of pishichi
pishínchi ngr. of pishichi
pishó'ffi ggr. of pishoffi
pishofa to be skinned (of a knee, for
instance), scraped, chafed (sg. subj.)
(II) {v2. pishoffi; pl. pishohli}
pishofa see tashpishofa
Pishofa Hilha' Pishofa Dance

pishoffi

pishoffi to skin (a knee, for instance), scrape, chafe (sg. obj.) (I;II) {v1. pishofa; ggr. pishó'ffi, píshshoffi; hngr. pishohǫ́ffi; pl. obj. pishohchi}
pishohchi to scrape off (thoroughly); to scrape, skin (pl. obj.) (I;II) [-SC] [pishohli+chi] {sg. obj. pishoffi}
pishohli to be all scratched up; to be scraped, skinned (pl. subj.) (II) {sg. pishofa}
pishohǫ́ffi hngr. of pishoffi
pishokchakmi', pishokchi' akmi' ice cream [pishokchi' akmi+']
pishokchaanihachi', pishokchi' aanihachi' see pishokchi' aaniha'
pishokchi' milk (IIIp) [pishi okchi']
psihokchi' akmi' see pishokchakmi'
pishokchi' aaniha', pishokchaanihachi', pishokchi' aanihachi' jar for making butter; churn [pishokchi' aa+niha/nihachi+']
pishokchi' aaniha' okchi', aaniha' okchi' buttermilk
pishokchi' aanihachi' see pishokchaanihachi'
pishokchi' hawashko' sour milk, (ER) cottage cheese [hawashko+']
pishokchi' holba' evaporated milk; dry milk
pishokchi' niha' butter [niha+']
pishokchi' niha' bosholli' cottage cheese [bosholli+']
pishokchi' niha' holba' margarine
pishokchi' nihachi to churn, make butter (I)
pishokchi' pakna' takaali' cream [takaali+']
pishokchi' pakna' takaali' hawashko' sour cream [hawashko+']
pishokchi' palaska' cheese
pishokchi' sotko' clabber, clabbered milk, curds [sotko+']
pishokchi' sotkochi' whey

[sotkochi+']
pishokchi' shila' dry milk [shila+']
pishokchishbo'kalhchi' churn dasher [pishokchi' isht bo'kalhchi+']
pishokchishnihachi' churn dasher [pishokchi' isht nihachi+']
píshshi'chi ggr. of pishichi
píshshoffi ggr. of pishoffi
pit prt.: away from the speaker or a point of reference [<pila>+t ?]
pitahiita to go away behind (I;II) [pit *ahiita] § Pitishahiitatok. You go away behind it.
pitalhko'nacha aya to wrap (something) around oneself (below the waist) and go (cha expression) (I;3) [includes <pit *alhkona>] § Naalhila'fa' pitalhko'nalit ayalitok. I wrapped a piece of cloth around myself and went.
<pitalhkona> in pitalhko'nacha aya [<pit *alhkona>]
pitanchi to cover oneself (for a while) with (I;3) [pit *anchi] § Naachi pitashlitok. I covered myself with the blanket.
pitayyómba to look better (II) [pit *ayyomba] § Pitachiyyomba. You look better.
pitaapisa to see ° (that way) from (I;II;3) [pit *aapisa] § Winda' pitaachipislitok. I saw you from the window.
pitbohli to lay (something) down for a while (over there) (I;II) [pit *bohli] {ngr. pitbǫ́hli}
pitbowafa to sink, settle (down) [pit *bowafa]
pitbǫ́hli ngr. of pitbohli
pitchaffichi to send (sg. obj.) (that way) (I;II) [pit *chaffichi]
pitchokkowa to go (that way) into (I;3) [pit *chokkowa] § Chokka'

pitikchokko'wokitok. He didn't go into the house.

pitfaapo'chi to throw (pl. obj.) (that way) (I;3) [pit *faapo'chi]

pitfokhi to put ˚ in (I;II;3) [pit *fokhi] § Abooha pitsafokhitok. She put me in the house.

pithalalli to pull on (I;II) [pit *halalli] {ngr. pithalálli}

pithalálli ngr. of pithalalli

pithalili to reach (that way) and touch (I;II) [pit *halili]

pithika to step over, step (that way) (I;3) [pit *hika] § Cholok pitishhikanna! Don't step over the hole!

pitibaachaffichi to send ˚ with (a co-obj. or co-subj.˚) (I;II;3) [pit *ibaachaffichi]

pitibaafokhi to put ˚ in with (a co-obj.˚) (I;II;3) [pit *ibaafokhi]

pitilaboknohli to wrap oneself up (quickly or for a while) (I) [pit *ilaboknohli]

pitimbohli to lay (something) down for ˚ (I;III;3) [pit *imbohli] § Pitambohtok. She laid it down for me.

pitinkanihmi to feel better (III) [+HM], <pitinkanih> [pit *inkanihmi] {pitkanihmi}

<pitinkanih> [HM] of pitinkanihmi

pitintalaali to leave (a flat-bottomed obj.) for ˚, give (a flat-bottomed obj.) to ˚ (I;III;3) [pit *intalaali]

pitinampíla to have it (especially, pain) get better for one (III); to take care of it, take care of a problem (I) [pit *inampila] § Pitanampilaakaynitokoot nosilitok. It was getting better for me so I went to sleep. | Pitishinampilakma alala'cho. If you take care of it, I'll come.

pitiwayaachi to leave (a four-footed obj. or one open on the bottom, such as a chair) to ˚, give (a four-footed or open-bottomed obj.) to ˚ (I;III;3) [pit *iwayaachi]

pitiwí'li to hold out to ˚—ggr. of pitiwiili

pitiwiili to hand to ˚ (I;III;3) [pit *iwiili] {ggr. pitiwí'li: to hold out to} § Pitawi'tok. He held it out to me.

pitkanihmi to feel better (II) [+HM], <pitkanih> [pit *kanihmi] {pitinkanihmi} § Pitsakanihmi ki'yo. I'm not feeling better.

<pitkanih> [HM] of pitkanihmi

pitkochcha to go out (that way) (I) [pit *kochcha]

pitlabbi to lick, slurp up (I;3) [pit *labbi] {hgr. pitlahámbi} § Ashiila pitlabbilit ayalitok. I slurped the soup and left.

pitlahámbi hngr. of pitlabbi

pitláwwi'chi to keep up with, pass (someone) (I;II) [+SC] [pit *lawwi'chi]

pitmalili to run to (I;3) [pit *malili] § Inchokkaak pitmalililitok. I ran to his house.

pitnampíla to get better (of a pain) (3); to handle a chore (I) [pit *nampila] {pitinampíla} § Sattopat pitnampilaakaynitoko nosilitok. My pain got better so I went to sleep. | Pitnampilala'cho. I'll handle it.

pitohómmi hngr. of pitommi

pitolaalínchi to move closer to (something over there) (I;3) [pit *olaalínchi]

pitoláli to be nearby, close (I) [pit *olali] § Pitisholala'chi. You'll be near.

pitoma to be sprained (3) {v2. pitommi}

pitommi to sprain (I;3) {v1. pitoma;

pitpilachi

hngr. pitohómmi}
pitpilachi to send (I;II) [pit *pilachi]
pitshóyyo'li ygr. of pitshooli
pitshooli to hold, reach out and hug
(I;II) [pit *shooli] {ngr. pitshóli; ygr.
pitshóyyo'li}
pitshoopalali' light switch (CC)
pitshóli ngr. of pitshooli
pittikíli see tikíli
pittilhiili see pittilhili
pittilhili, pittilhiili to send (pl. obj.)
(that way) (I;II) [pit *tilhili] §
Pitpotilhilitok, Pitpotilhiitok. He
sent us.
pitwalhahli to boil (over there) (3)
[pit *walhahli] {ngr. pitwalhághli}
pitwalhághli ngr. pitwalhahli
pitwaya to stoop down (I) [pit *waya]
§ Pitishwaya. You stoop down.
pitwí'li to hold out—ggr. of pitwiili
pitwiha to move to (I;3) [pit *wiha] §
Lynn inchokkaak pitwihalitok. I
moved to Lynn's house.
pitwiili to hand (something) to
someone (that way) (I;3) [pit *wiili]
{ggr. pitwí'li: to hold out; pitwiili}
<piichi> in apiichi, piichi',
pihli'shcha ishtaya [pihli+chi] {ggr.
pihlí'chi: to preside over, lead; ngr.
pihlínchi: to watch (someone's
child); prt. piichit, pihli'sht}
piichi' leader—usually used only in
complex expressions like iksa'
piichi' [<piichi>+']
piichit prt. of <piichi>
piichit áa, pihli'sht áa to lead around,
attract a following of (I;3) § Hattak
pihli'sht aa. She gets the men to
follow her.
piichit ishtaya to lead (pl. obj.) (I;3) §
Piichit ishtapoyatok. He led us.
piini', (HS, MJ, AW, WB) piini boat;
trough
piini' ishtoobli' paddle (ER) [isht

toobli+']
piini' sawa' little boat, canoe [sawa+']
piini' wakaa' airplane [wakaa+']
piini' wakaa' aahika' airport
[aa+hika+']
piini' wakaa' aakkowa' airport
[aakkowa+']
piinoshi' little boat, canoe (Ct?)
[piini' oshi']
píhli hngr. of pihli
<píla> in nampíla, pílat áa—ngr. of
<pila>
pílat áa to go along showing off or
looking silly (I) [<pila>+t]
písa to see, look at—ngr. of pisa
[-OPR]
píshi ngr. of pishi
pó'lhlhi ggr. of polhlhi
po's po's word little boys would say
to be funny (AB)
pochchoko' in ilbak pochchoko'
pofá'lli ggr. of pofalli
pofahálli hngr. of pofalli
pofalli, pofatli to open (of a cotton
pod); to be light and easily blown
around (like a dandelion's seed) (3)
{ggr. pofá'lli, póffalli; hngr.
pofahálli; nampofalli', naafalli',
poffola}
pofatli see pofalli
pofessa' professor [from the English]
póffalli ggr. of pofalli
póffo'ha ggr. of pofoha
poffola to get inflated, be inflated (3)
{v2. poffololi; xgr. poffóllo'wa; rigr.
poffolpówa; pofalli, poffoola,
pofoha}
poffóllo'wa to be inflated (of a
balloon, paper bag, etc.) (3)—xgr. of
poffola {v2. poffololi; impoffola'}
poffololi to inflate, put air into (I;3)
{v1. poffola}
poffolpówa to puff oneself out like a
toadfrog (I); to puff oneself out in (a

306

place) (I;3)—rigr. of poffola
poffoola to breathe (of a frog or toad)
(3) {poffola}
pofoha, pofowa to be puffed up,
swollen (especially, with dropsy) (II)
{v2. pofohli; ggr. póffo'ha; ygr.
pofóyyo'wa; poffola}
pofohli to swell: especially, to have
hives or small allergic swellings (II)
{v1. pofoha; pofohpoli}
pofohpoli to have swellings (from
hives, for instance) (II) [po+pofohli]
pofowa see pofoha
pofóyyo'wa ygr. of pofowa
pohónta hngr. of ponta
poh̲ó̲fa hngr. of p̲o̲fa
poh̲ó̲lhlhi hngr. of polhlhi
pokkó'li ten; to be ten in number (I)
[+PR]—ggr. of pokoli
pokkó'li awa chaffa see awa chaffa
pokkó'li awa chakká'li see awa
chakká'li
pokkó'li awa hanná'li see awa
hanná'li
pokkó'li awa ontochchí'na see awa
ontochchí'na
pokkó'li awa ontoklo see awa
ontoklo
pokkó'li awa oshta see awa oshta
pokkó'li awa talhlhá'pi see awa
talhlhá'pi
pokkó'li awa tochchí'na see awa
tochchí'na
pokkó'li awa toklo see awa toklo
pokkó'li áyyo'ka to be in groups of
ten (I , —)
pokkosh girlie, sister (usually a term
of address) (VB) {poskosh}
pokolachaffa eleven (CP) {awa chaffa}
pokolachakká'li nineteen (CP) {awa
chakká'li}
pokolahanná'li sixteen (CP) {awa
hanná'li}
pokolatalhlhá'pi fifteen (CP) {awa

talhlhá'pi}
pokolatochchí'na thirteen (CP) {awa
tochchí'na}
pokolatoklo twelve (CP) {awa toklo}
pokoli ten (used only in decade
numbers; see note at pokoli toklo
awa toklo) {ggr. pokkó'li}
pokoli chakká'li ninety; to be ninety
in number (3)
pokoli chakká'li awa hanná'li
ninety-six; to be ninety-six in
number (3)
pokoli chakká'li awa chakká'li
ninety-nine; to be ninety-nine in
number (3)
pokoli hanná'li sixty; to be sixty in
number (3)
pokoli ontochchí'na eighty; to be
eighty in number (3)
pokoli ontoklo seventy; to be seventy
in number (3)
pokoli oshta forty; to be forty in
number (3)
pokoli talhlhá'pi fifty; to be fifty in
number (3)
pokoli tochchí'na thirty; to be thirty
in number (3)
pokoli tochchí'na awa chaffa, (CP)
pokoli tochchí'na achaffa thirty-
one; to be thirty-one in number (3)
pokoli tochchí'na awa tochchí'na,
(CP) pokoli tochchí'na atochchí'na
thirty-three; to be thirty-three in
number (3)
pokoli tochchí'na awa toklo, (CP)
pokoli tochchí'na atoklo thirty-two;
to be thirty-two in number (3)
pokoli toklo twenty; to be twenty in
number (3)
pokoli toklo awa chaffa, (ER) pokoli
toklo akochcha chaffa, (CP) pokoli
toklo achaffa, (EP) pokoli toklo
aachaffa twenty-one; to be twenty-
one in number (3)

pokoli toklo awa chakká'li

pokoli toklo awa chakká'li, (ER) pokoli toklo akochcha chakká'li twenty-nine; to be twenty-nine in number (3)

pokoli toklo awa hanná'li, (ER) pokoli toklo akochcha hanná'li twenty-six; to be twenty-six in number (3)

pokoli toklo awa ontochchí'na, (ER) pokoli toklo akochcha ontochchí'na twenty-eight; to be twenty-eight in number (3)

pokoli toklo awa ontoklo, (ER) pokoli toklo akochcha ontoklo twenty-seven; to be twenty-seven in number (3)

pokoli toklo awa oshta, (ER) pokoli toklo akochcha oshta, (CP) pokoli toklo aoshta, (EP) pokoli toklo aaoshta twenty-four; to be twenty-four in number (3)

pokoli toklo awa talhlhá'pi, (ER) pokoli toklo akochcha talhlhá'pi, (CP) pokoli toklo atalhlhá'pi, (EP) pokoli toklo aatalhlhá'pi twenty-five; to be twenty-five in number (3)

pokoli toklo awa tochchí'na, (ER) pokoli toklo akochcha tochchí'na, (CP) pokoli toklo atochchí'na, (EP) pokoli toklo aatochchí'na twenty-three; to be twenty-three in number (3)

pokoli toklo awa toklo, (ER) pokoli toklo akochcha toklo, (CP) pokoli toklo atoklo, (EP) pokoli toklo aatoklo twenty-two (counting in higher decades works similarly for most speakers: number of tens plus awa plus number of ones); to be twenty-two in number (3)

pokpó'ki ggr. of pokpoki
pokpóhho'ki hgr. of pokpoki
pokpohónki hngr. of pokpoki
pokpoki to be foamy, sudsy (II)

[+CPR] [+PR] {ggr. pokpó'ki; hgr. pokpóhho'ki; hngr. pokpohónki; ygr. pokpóyyo'ki}

pokpoki' bubble (on the surface of a liquid) [pokpoki+']

pokpokichi to make bubbles with, sudse (soap, for example) (I;3) [pokpoki+chi]

pokpóyyo'ki ygr. of pokpoki

pokta' double, grown together—only used in complex expressions such as ahi' pokta', biyyo̲'ka' pokta', hattak pokta', nanna pokta', tanampo pokta'

polla very, really (aux.) (preceded by verb +hma̲); ready to (aux.) (preceded by verb +a'hi; subr. clause only) § Chonnahma̲ polla. He's really skinny. | Kani̲hka̲ hopoolihma̲ pollakat itha̲nali. I know that I'm really very jealous. | Alootolilihma̲ pollatokchayni. I filled it too (very) full. | Yahma'hi polloot hikki'yatok. She stood there ready to do it. | Ayala'hi pollakya akayyokitok. I was ready to go, but I didn't go.

polla to be hardboiled (CC) [probably "very" hard]

pollaho̲ of necessity, necessarily, because it was (preceded by noun (+ak) + ootok or by +ootok clause) [polla+ho̲] § Lynnakootok pollaho̲ ya̲htok. If it wasn't for Lynn, he wouldn't have done it, Because it was Lynn, he did it of necessity. | Jimmyat oshi' ootok pollaho̲ Josephineat ayatok. If it wasn't for the fact that Jimmy was her son, Josephine wouldn't have gone.

<pollichi> in apollichi, aapollichi {vl. <pota>}

polona, (WB) ponola string, thread
polona notinto'wa' bobbin (on a

sewing machine) [nota' in+to'wa']
polonaapakfoha' spool [polona
aa+apakfoha+']
polonaatanni' spinning wheel
[polona aa+tanni+']
polha to be folded (pl. subj., or more
than once) (3) [+T] {v2. polhlhi; sg.
polhoma}
polhkachi to be pleated, folded; to
fold up (like an acordion or kiddy
gate) (pl. subj., or in many pleats or
folds) (3)
polhlhi to pleat, fold up, roll up
(more than once; pl. obj.) (I;3) {v1.
polha, polhkachi; ggr. pó'lhlhi;
hngr. pohólhlhi; ngr. pólhlhi; sg.
obj. polhommi}
pólhlho'ma ggr. of polhoma
pólhlhommi ggr. of polhommi
polhó'mmi ggr. of polhommi
polhohóma hngr. of polhoma
polhohómmi hngr. of polhommi
polhoma to fold, bend; to be folded,
hooked, bent, doubled up (sg. subj.,
or once) (II) {v2. polhommi; ggr.
pólhlho'ma; hngr. polhohóma; pl.
polha}
polhommi to fold, roll (once; sg.
obj.); to face, turn up a hem on (a
garment) (I;II) {v1. polhoma; ggr.
pólhlhommi, polhó'mmi; hngr.
polhohómmi; pl. obj. polhlhi}
<ponna> in imponna, ishtaponnachi
ponta to borrow, rent (I;II); to rent for
(a sum of money) (I;3;3) {hngr.
pohónta; imponta, imaaponta}
[from French emprunter?] §
Chokka' pontalitok ta'osso oshtaho.
I rented a house for four dollars.

ponta' tenant, borrower [ponta+']
poskosh baby, precious baby—term of
endearment (IIIp)
poshi' powdery, soft material—used
only in complex expressions like
hottok poshi', nanna poshi', okti'
poshi', shookola' poshi', tashposhi'
poshi' bíyyi'ka to be powdery (3)
poshichi to grind to powder (I;3)
[+SC] [poshi'+chi] {ggr. póshshi'chi}
poshnaak us (nonsubj.) [poshno'+ak]
poshnaakaynihoot we ourselves
(focus subj.)
[poshno'+aakayni+hoot] §
Poshnaakaynihoot kiihilhatok. We
ourselves danced.
poshnaakayniho us ourselves (focus
nonsubj.) [poshno'+aakayni+ho]
poshnaakot we (emphatic subj.)
[poshno'+akot]
poshnaako us (emphatic nonsubj.)
[poshno'+ako]
poshnaat we (subj., rare)
[poshno'+at]
poshna us (nonsubj., rare)
[poshno'+a]
poshno' us (nonsubj.)
póshshi'chi ggr. of poshichi
<pota> in <apoota> {v2. <pollichi>,
<potoli>}
<potoli> in apootoli {v1. <pota>}
potooni to house sit, take care of (a
house) (I;3) [po+(a)tooni]
pó'fa ggr. of pofa
pofa to smoke (I;3) {ggr. pó'fa; hngr.
pohófa; apofachi} § Chomak pofali.
I'm smoking tobacco.
pólhlhi ngr. of polhlhi

r

raba' rubber (material) [from the English]
raba' ilbak fo'khi' rubber glove

raba' to'wa' rubber ball
<riidi> in iriidi [from English read]

s

sa'k sa'k sa'k aachi see sak sak sak aachi
sahánki hngr. of sakki
sak sak sak aachi, sa'k sa'k sa'k aachi to make the sound of hitting (especially hitting glass or rocks—for instance, marbles hitting together, fingernails on china) (expressive) (I) {saka'chi}
saka'chi to tap (on a wall, for instance) (I) {klgr. sákkakli'chi; rcgr. sakaká'chi, sak sak sak aachi, sakkaha}
sakaká'chi to knock (on something like a table) (I)—rcgr. of saka'chi
sákkakli'chi to hit unexpectedly and knock down; to flick one's finger at (I;II)—klgr. of saka'chi
sakkaa see sakkaha
sakkaha, sakkaa to hit with one's hand; to flick one's finger at: especially, to flick one's finger at the head of (a child) as a mild punshiment; to hit, chop at, strike (with an instrument) (I;II) {saka'chi} § Issasakkahanna! Don't flick my head with your finger!
sakki to catch up with, come even with (I;II) {ggr. sâkki; hngr. sahánki; ngr. sánki}
sâkki ggr. of sakki
sakli' (TJ, ER), (MJ, CM) sakli trout (TJ), sucker (ER, CM, MJ)
sakti bank, hillside

Sakti Tohbi' White Hills (place near McMillan, Oklahoma) [tohbi+']
salakha' liver (IIIp)
salakha' ihomi' gallbladder
salami, (MJ) saláa too much (aux., preceded by verb +') {impa' iksala'mo} § Impali' salami. I ate too much. | Ishimpa' salaminna! Don't eat too much!
salhkona guts, intestines (IIp)
salhkona iskanno' appendix (WB)
salhkona kochcha' hernia, rupture [kochcha+']
salhkona kochcha' í'shi to have a hernia, get a hernia (I)
salhkonachi to gut (I;II) [salhkona+chi]
samánta ngr. of samata
samata to shut up, to be quiet (I) {ggr. sámma'ta; ngr. samánta}
samaachi to ring (a bell) (I); to make a ringing noise (of a doorbell, for instance) (3) {hngr. samaahánchi; ngr. samáanchi; chamaachi}
samaahánchi hngr. of samaachi
samáanchi ngr. of samaachi
sámma'ta ggr. of samata
<sanali> in asanali, aasanali, isanali, isanali' {ggr. <sánna'li>}
sánki ngr. of sakki
<sánna'li> in isánna'li—ggr. of <sanali>
sant homma' see sen homma'
sapontaki', (ML) sapo'taki', (CM)

sapantaki' mosquito
satabli to straighten, stretch (a string, for instance), spread out, unfold (sg. obj.); to hammer out a dent in (I;II) [+OPR] {v1. satapa; ngr. satámbli; pl. obj. satapo'li} § Issatablitam? Did you straighten it?
satámbli ngr. of satabli
satámpa to be straight (of hair) (3) [+CPR][+PR]—ngr. of satapa
satapa to be smoothed, straightened out, stretched, spread out, unfolded (sg. subj.) (3); to be erect, not hunched over, to have one's body straight (I) {v2. satabli; ggr. sátta'pa; ngr. satámpa: to be straight (of hair); pl. satapo'wa}
satapo'li to straighten out, spread out, unfold (pl. obj.); to spread (the wings, of a bird); to hammer out many dents in (I;3) {v1. satapo'wa; sg. obj. satabli; ilisatapo'li: to stretch (onself)}
satapo'wa to stretch oneself (sg.-dl.-pl. subj.), to be unfolded, straightened out (pl. subj.) (I) {v2. satapo'li; sg. satapa}
satappakahchi to jump up, make a sudden movement back (I)
satappakahsht hika to jump up, get up suddenly (I) [satappakahchi+t]
sátta'pa ggr. of satapa
saafki' sofkey (Creek sour corn dish) [from the Creek]
saak saak saak aachi see sak sak sak aachi
saalhkona, (TP, ER, MJ, TJ) saalhkona', (HS) hasalhkona' earthworm, red worm, night crawler
saalhkonishto' really large, long type of earthworm [saalhkona ishto+']
Saaysin Chickasaw woman's name (anglicized as Susan)

<sawa> in hattak sawa', issoba sawa', ishtasawachi, panki' sawa', sawa'si {ngr. sáwa; iabisowa', shawwa}
sáwa ngr. of <sawa>, sawa'si
sawachi to make (pl. obj.) small (I;3) {ngr. sawánchi}
sawa'si to be little (pl. subj.) (II) [+CPR] [-PR] [<sawa>+a'si] {ngr. sáwa}
sawánchi ngr. of sawachi
sela' cellar, storm cellar [from the English]
sen see sent
sent, sen, (WB) sin cent (usually used in expressions like the following) [from the English]
sent chaffa', (AB) sen chaffa penny, one cent [chaffa+']
sent homma' penny, "red cent" [homma+']
sent pokko'li, (WB) simpokko'li, (AB) se'pokko'li dime, ten cents
sent talhlha'pi, (AB) sintalhlha'pi nickel, five cents
Sibi' Chickasaw woman's name
síhhi'pa to be stretched out, be lopsided (I); to be stretched out, lopsided in (a place) (I;3)—hgr. of <siipa> {ngr. sihímpa; ygr. síyyi'pa; siipo'wa}
sihímpa ngr. of síhhi'pa, <siipa>
sihílhlhi hngr. of silhlhi
silhhi see silhlhi
silhlhi, silhhi to research in (I;3) {hngr. sihílhlhi} § Holisso silhlhili. I do research in the book.
sink sink sink aachi see si'k si'k si'k aachi
sinksihíya hngr. of sinksiya
sinksiya to whine (of dogs) (I) {hngr. sinksihíya; si'k si'k si'k aachi}
sinniman cinnamon [from the English]
sinti' snake

sinti' akankosh-apa' chicken snake [akankoshi' apa+']

sinti' basoowa' type of snake with a stripe down its back [basoowa+']

sinti' bo'wa ikkallo' type of snake that's easy to hit [ikkallo+']

sinti' chilambi' copperhead (AW) {chilha'kbi'}

sinti' hakshish snake root (plant) (ER)

sinti' hattak fammi', (LF) hattak fammi' coachwhip snake [fammi+']

Sinti' Hilha' Snake Dance—a Choctaw dance also danced by Chickasaws (usually as the last dance of the night)

sinti' issikopa' copperhead (CM) [issikopa+']

sinti' ittish, sinti' tish, (WB) aasintittish, (AB) sintittish slick vine (medicinal plant)

sinti' kiliha' bull snake (WB) [kiliha+']

sinti' losa' black snake [losa+']

sinti' okchamali', sintokchama'li' green snake, garter snake; (PBr) racer snake [sinti' okchamali+']

sinti' ok-okaa-asha', ok-okaa-asha' water moccasin [oka' okaa-asha+']

sinti' palhki' type of snake; (TJ) horsewhip snake [palhki+']

sinti' tish see sinti' ittish

sinti-nani' eel (CC) [sinti' nani']

sintinchama'chi' snake charmer [sinti' inchama'chi+']

sintinchasha' (rattlesnake's) rattle

sintishtahollo' type of evil snake, perhaps a rattlesnake [sinti' ishtahollo']

sintokchama'li' see sinti' okchamali'

sintoshi' snake egg, baby snake [sinti' oshi']

sipóhhokni hgr. of sipokni

sipohóngni hngr. of sipokni

sipoknabi' syphilis [sipokni abi+'] § Sipoknabi' i'shli. I have syphilis.

sipokni to be old (II) [+CPR] [-PR] {ggr. síppokni; hgr. sipóhhokni; hngr. sipohóngni; ngr. sipóngni; ygr. sipóyyokni}

sipokni' aa-asha' old people's home [sipokni+']

sipokni' inchokka' old people's home [sipokni+']

sipoknichi to make old (I;II) [ispokni+chi] {ngr. sipoknínchi: to make older}

sipoknikat kaniya fokha to be so old, old to a certain degree; to be how old (inf.) (II , — , —) [sipokni+kat] {int. sipoknikat katiya fokha} § Lynnat sipoknikat kaniya fokhakat ithana. Lynn knows how old she is.

sipoknikat katiya fokha to be how old (int.) (II, — , —) [sipokni+kat] {ind.-inf. sipoknikat kaniya fokha} § Chisipoknikat katiya fokha? How old are you?

sipoknínchi to make older—ngr. of sipoknichi

sipóngni ngr. of sipokni

sipóyyokni ygr. of sipokni

síppokni ggr. of sipokni

sita to be braided, fixed, put up (of hair) (3) [+T] {v2. sitili}

sitili to put up, tie back (one's hair) (I;3) {v1. sita; pl. <sitohli>; isitili: to fix (someone's hair)}

<sitohli> in asiitohli {sg. sitili}

síyyi'pa ygr. of síhhi'pa, <siipa>

<siipa> {hgr. síhhi'pa; hngr. sihímpa; ygr. síyyi'pa; siipo'wa, shiipa}

siipo'wa to do exercises, extend one's limbs, stretch (I) {rmgr. siipopówa; síhhi'pa, <siipa>, shiipo'wa}

siipopówa to be stretched out; to keep stretching (3)—rmgr of siipo'wa

Siitan Satan, the devil [from the English]
Siitan imissoba devil horse, praying mantis (WB)
Siitan isholosh talakchi' devil's shoestring (plant) (WB) [im+sholosh]
Siitanat imihoo fammi for Satan to whip his wife: (idiom) for there to be rain and sun at the same time [Siitan+at]
si'k si'k si'k aachi, sink sink sink ʔachi to make the sound of a high-pitched whistle or whine (for instance, of a teakettle or smoke alarm) (expressive) (I) {sinksiya}
sishto, (WB, LF, MJ) sishto', (MC, LR) sintishto' rattlesnake [sinti' ishto]
so'ksok meat skin (children's word) (AB)
So'tko' see Sokko'
soba short form of issoba
soba ishfammi', soba ishfama' see issobishfama'
Soba Losa' man's nickname [losa+']
soba-sawa' see issoba-sawa'
sobompatalhpo' see sontalhpo'
sob-oshi' see issob-oshi'
sokafa to pop, burst (of a small balloon, or one or a few kernels of corn); to be crushed with the fingers (of a bug) (mainly sg. subj.) (3) {v2. sokaffi; pl. sokahli; bokafa: to burst (of a large obj.)}
sokaffi to pop, burst (a small obj.), to crush (a bug, for example) with the fingers (sg. obj.) (I;II) {v1. sokafa; hngr. sokaháffi; pl. obj. sokaachi; bokaffi: to burst (a large obj.); sokli}
sokaháffi hngr. of sokaffi
sokahali hngr. of sokahli
sokahli to pop, burst (of corn, small balloons) (pl. subj.) (3) {sg. sokafa; hngr. sokahali; bokahli: to burst,

pop (of large objs.)}
sokaachi to pop (corn), burst (small things) (pl. obj.) (I;II) [-SC] [sokahli+chi] {ngr. sokaalínchi; sg. obj. sokaffi; bokaachi: burst (large objs.)}
sokaalínchi ngr. of sokaachi
sokbish in oka' sokbish, itti' sokbish, ittakoba-sokbish
sokli to pop, burst (small objs.—such as the little air pockets in plastic packing material) (pl. obj.) (I;3) {sokaffi, sokaachi}
Sokko', Sotko', So'tko' Joseph Pickens's family nickname [sotko+']
soko'chi to thump (on a melon, to see if it is ripe) (AB)
sontalhpo', sobompatalhpo', solhpo' saddle (IIIp) [issoba on+patalhpo+']
sontalhpo' aahalha'bli' stirrups
sontalhpo' filli'tat ombinni'li to ride sidesaddle (I) § Sontalhpo' filli'tat ishombinni'la'chita? Will you ride sidesaddle?
sóntko ngr. of sotko
sotko, (OC) sokko to be thick (3) [+CPR] [-PR] {ngr. sóntko; ygr. sóyyotko}
Sotko' see Sokko'
sotkochi to thicken (gravy, for instance) (I;3) [sotko+chi]
sóyyotko ygr. of sotko
soodi' baking soda [from the English]
Soodi' woman's nickname
solash short form of isolash
solhpo' see sontalhpo'
solhposhkobo' pommel [solhpo' ishkobo']
sosolo' meadowlark; (MJ) yellowhammer
sosh short form of issosh
stokchank see istokchank
stoof see istoof

sh

sha'li to put on, carry on one's back or shoulder (I;II) {ygr. sháyya'li; shaali}

shá'li ggr. of shaali

shá'nni ggr. of shanni

shachahángla hngr. of shachakla

shachahánglat áa to walk along silhouetted against the light, wearing a thin see-through dress (I) [shachahangla+t]

shacháhhakla hgr. of shachakla

shachakla to have big openings or spaces (of the widely spaced side of a comb, for example); to be full of little holes, be loosely woven (of lace, eyelet, a rag, a wicker chair) (3) {ggr. sháchchakla; hgr. shacháhhakla; hngr. shachahángla; ngr. shachángla; ygr. shacháyyakla} § tali' shachchakla': chicken wire

shachángla ngr. of shachakla

shacháyyakla ygr. of shachakla

sháchchakla ggr. of shachakla

<shafa> in lowak ishshafa' {v2. shaffi; shafa}

shaffi to scratch (dirt, like a chicken); to poke (the fire) (I;3) {v1. <shafa>; hngr. shaháffi; shafi}

shaháffi hngr. of shaffi, shafi

shaháli hngr. of shaali

shahánni hngr. of shanni

shahbi, (MJ) shaabi to be cleared (of land) (3) {ngr. sháhbi}

shahbichi to clear (land) (I;3) [shahbi+chi]

sháhha'ba hgr. of shamba

shaka'ki' type of bird (robin?) (AB)

shakabli to make noise, sound (pl. subj.) (I); to make noise in (a place) (pl. subj.) (I;3) [+CPR] [+PR] {ggr. shákkabli; hngr. shakahámbli: to yell}

shakahámbli to yell—hngr. of shakabli

shakaháwa hngr. of shakawa

shakawa to be sandy, dusty (II) {ggr. shákka'wa; hngr. shakaháwa; ngr. shakáwa; ygr. shakáyya'wa}

shakawachi to get sand or dust on (I;II) [shakawa+chi]

shakáyya'wa ygr. of shakawa

<shakali> in bakshakali

shakáwa ngr. of shakawa

shakba' upper arm, shoulder (IIp)

shakba' aaittachakka' shoulder blade (ER)

shakba' ishtalakchi' armband

shakba' imosak wrist (WB)

shakba' nota' armpit (IIp) § sashakba' nota': my armpit

shakbatinna' bobcat (TP, TJ)

shakchi crawfish

shakchifolko', (LF) chokfifolfo' dogwood

shakchikoyyo' buttonbush (WB) [shakchi <ikoyyo>+']

shakchimitti' type of plant [shakchi im+itti']

shakchishto' lobster [shakchi ishto+']

shakili' grasshopper (WB) (Ct)

shákkabli ggr. of shakabli

shákka'wa ggr. of shakawa

shala'chi to drag (I;II) [-SC] [shala'li+chi] {ggr. shala'lí'chi; hngr. shala'lihínchi; ngr. shala'línchi} § Chishala'chilitok. I dragged you.

shala'li to slide (on a slide, for instance) (I / II) {shalalli}

shala'líchi ggr. of shala'chi

shala'lihínchi hngr. of shala'chi

shala'línchi ggr. of shala'chi

shalá'lli ggr. of shalalli

shalahálli hngr. of shalalli

shalahli' see issish shalahli'

314

shalaklak goose, swan
shalaklak okchama'li' grey goose [okchamali+']
shalaklak tohbi' swan [tohbi+']
shalalli, shalatli to slip and fall (I / II) {ggr. shállalli, shalá'lli; hngr. shalahá̲lli; rmgr. shallalá̲li; shala'li}
shalatha', (ER) shalatta' type of bright green grasshopper, (ER) locust
shalatli see shalalli
shalbi'ya' in ilbak shalbi'ya'
shallalá̲li to drag, be dragging (3)—rmgr. of shalalli
shállalli ggr. of shalalli
shamá'lli ggr. of shamalli
<shamali> in shamaachi {ggr. shámma'li; rmgr. shammamá̲li; shamalli}
shamalli, shamatli to squeeze into or through (a tight space); to be stuck in (a place) (sg. subj.) (I;3) {ggr. shamá'lli, shámmalli; rmgr. shammamá̲li; dl. shámmohli; tpl. shamohmá̲a; sg. obj. shamallichi, shamaachi; <shamali>, shamayo'li} § Tali' aaittintaklaako̲ shamallilitok. I squeezed between the rocks.
shamallichi to squeeze (sg. nonhum. obj.) into a tight space (for instance, to squeeze in one more item when packing) (I;3) [shamalli+chi] {hngr. shamallihínchi}
shamallihínchi hngr. of shamallichi
shamatli see shamalli
shamayo'li to hide, to squeeze in (I)
shamaachi to squeeze (sg. nonhum. obj.) into a tight space (for instance, to squeeze in one more item when packing) (I;3); to stick (sg. obj.) into (someone's hair) (I;3;3) [-SC] [<shamali>+chi] {ggr. shámmali'chi: to have (sg. obj.) in (one's hair); hngr. shamaalihínchi;

pl. obj. shamohchi} § Irene ipa̲shi'a̲ ishholissochi' shamaachilitok. I stuck a pencil in Irene's hair.
shamaalihínchi hngr. of shamaachi
shamba to go blind, lose one's sight (II) {ggr. shá̲'ba; hgr. sháhha̲'ba; ngr. shámba; ygr. sháyya̲'ba}
shámba ngr. of shamba
shamba' blind person [shamba+']
shambachi to blind (someone) (I;II) [shamba+chi]
shamíhhi'la to be lame, with one leg shorter than the other (I); to be lame, limping in (a place) (I;3) —hgr. of <shamila> {ggr. shámmi'la; hngr. shamihí̲la; neg. ikshami'lo} § Shamihí̲lali. I'm plame.
shamihí̲la hngr. of <shamila>, shamíhhi'la [+CPR] [-PR]
<shamila> {ggr. shámmi'la; hgr. shamíhhi'la; hngr. shamihí̲la, neg. ikshami'lo}
shámma'li to be stuck in (sg. subj.) (3;3)—ggr. of <shamali> § Nantahat chipa̲shi' shamma'li? What is stuck in your hair?
shámmali'chi to have (something) stuck in (one's hair) (I;3;3)—ggr. of shamaachi § Ishholissochi' sapa̲shi' shammali'shlitok. I had a pencil stuck in my hair.
shámmalli ggr. of shamalli
shammamá̲li to squeeze through, work oneself through (sg. subj.) (I)—rmgr. of <shamali>, shamalli {dl. shammomó̲li}
shámmi'la ggr. of <shamila>, shamíhhi'la
shámmohli to squeeze into or through (a tight place); to be stuck in (dl. subj.) (I;3)—ggr. of <shamohli> {sg. shamalli; ngr. shamó̲hli; tpl. shamohmá̲a; pl. obj.

shamohchi

shamohchi}
shamohchi to squeeze (pl. obj.) in
(I;II); to stick (pl. obj.) into
(someone's hair) (I;3;3) [-SC]
[<shamohli>+chi] {sg. obj.
shamaachi; dl. subj. shámmohli;
tpl. subj. shamohmáa}
<shamohli> in shamohmáa,
shamohchi {ggr. shámmohli: to
squeeze into, be stuck (dl.); ngr.
shamǫ́hli; rmgr. shammomǫ́li}
shamohmáa to squeeze into or
through (a tight place); to be stuck
in (tpl. subj.) (I;3) [<shamohli>+t
*maa] {sg. shamalli; dl. shámmohli;
pl. obj. shamohchi} § Shamoht
iimaatok. We squeezed through.
shammomǫ́li to squeeze through,
work oneself through (dl. subj.)
(I)—rmgr. shammomǫ́li {sg.
shammamáli}
shamǫ́hli ngr. of shámmohli,
<shamohli>
shana to be twisted, wrung out (II)
[+T] {v2. shanni}
shanaháa hngr. of shanaa
shanakha' area between the
shoulders; bone at the top of the
spine (IIIp / (AB) (IIp))
shanáyya'a ygr. of shanaa
shanaa to be off balance, lopsided,
crooked (mainly sg. subj.) (II) {v2.
shaniili; hngr. shanaháa; ngr.
shanáa; ygr. shanáyya'a; pl.
shanaayo'wa}
shanaachi to make crooked (for
example, to cause a shoe to wear
unevenly) (I;II) [shanaa+chi] {hngr.
shanaahánchi}
shanaahánchi hngr. of shanaachi
shanaayo'li to make, put on
(shingles, for instance) crooked (pl.
obj.); to asymmetrically distort the
shape of (of a child sitting on a

cardboard box, for example) (I;3) {v1.
shanaayo'wa; sg. obj. shaniili}
shanaayo'wa to be twisted, crooked
(II); to walk twisted, crookedly (pl.
subj.) (I) {v2. shanaayo'li; hngr.
shanaayohǫ́wa; rmgr.
shanaayoyǫ́wa; sg. shanaa}
shanaayohǫ́wa hngr. of shanaayo'wa
shanaayoyǫ́wa to sway, wiggle when
walking (I)—rmgr. of shanaayo'wa
shanáa ngr. of shanaa
shaniili to make wrong, off balance;
to twist, turn on the side (mainly sg.
obj.) (I;II) {v1. shanaa; pl. obj.
shanayyo'li}
shan-kachi' in pankishan-kachi',
tali' shan-kachi'
shanni to wring, twist (I;II) {v1.
shana; ggr. shá'nni; hngr. shahánni}
shannit tiloffi to wring the neck of
(I;II) [shanni+t] § Shannit
satiloffa'chi. He's going to wring my
neck.
shanti' rat
shanti' losa' type of large rat with a
black back [losa+']
shanti' tohbi' domesticated white rat
[tohbi+']
shapha' flag
shapha' huckleberry (Ct?)
shatabli to rise (of bread, for instance)
(3); to be bloated, have gas (II) §
paska ishshatabli': baking powder |
Shatablit alhtaha bankatok. They
come already risen (of brown-and-
serve rolls).
shatablichi to make rise, cause to rise
(I;3) [shatabli+chi]
shataháli hngr. of shatali
shatahpoli to have a disease
characterized by swelling or little
boils (II) {shatali}
shatali to swell (II) {ggr. shátta'li;
hngr. shataháli; ygr. shatáyya'li;

shatahpoli, shatohli}
shatanni tick (insect)
shatanni afammi' yearling tick
[afammi+']
Shatanni Hilha' Tick Dance—a
Choctaw dance also danced by
Chickasaws
shatanni nihi' seed tick
shatannoshi' little tick, baby tick;
seed tick [shatanni oshi']
shatáyya'li ygr. of shatali
shataachi to make swell (I;II) [-SC]
[shatali+chi] {hngr. shataalihínchi}
shataalihínchi hngr. of shataachi
shatohli to have little bumps or
swellings all over (II) {ngr. shatóhli;
shatali}
shatóhli ngr. of shatohli
shátta'li ggr. of shatali
shawi' raccoon
Shawi' Chickasaw nickname (CP)
shawimpanki' possum grapes (CC,
JC, TP, MJ) [shawi' im+panki']
shawinkabosh see shonkabosh
shawwa in itti' shawwa {<sawa>}
shayofa to be wilted, shriveled; to be
flat, uninflated (of a tire, balloon) (3)
{v2. shayoffi; ggr. sháyyo'fa}
shayoffi to let the air out of (a tire)
(I;3) {v1. shayofa}
shayowachi' sifter {ishhayowalhchi'}
sháyya'li ygr. of sha'li, shaali
sháyya'ba ygr. of shamba
sháyyo'fa ggr. of shayofa
sháa'chi ggr. of shaachi ("to scrape")
and shaachi ("to load")
shaachi to scrape, grate (I;II) [-SC] {v1.
shaalhchi; ggr. sháa'chi, shaalí'chi;
hngr. shaalihínchi; ngr. shaalínchi;
ilishaachi: to scratch oneself}
shaachi to load ° with °, load ° on °
(I;II;3) [shaali+chi] [-SC] {ggr.
shaalí'chi, sháa'chi; hngr.
shaalihínchi, shaahánchi; ngr.

shaalínchi, sháanchi} § Issoba itti'
shaachilitok. I loaded the horse
with wood.
shaahánchi hngr. of shaachi ("to
load")
shaali to haul, be loaded (with) (large
or pl. obj.); to carry (pl. obj.) on
one's shoulder (I;3) {ggr. shá'li;
hngr. sháali; ygr. sháyya'li; sg. obj.
ilabanali: carry on one's shoulder;
sha'li}
shaalí'chi ggr. of shaachi ("to load")
and shaachi ("to scrape")
shaalihínchi hngr. of shaachi ("to
load"), shaachi ("to scrape")
shaalínchi ngr. of shaachi ("to load")
and shaachi ("to scrape")
shaalhchi to be scraped (3) {v2.
shaachi}
sháanchi ngr. of shaachi ("to load")
shaapó'li ggr. of shaapoli
shaapoli to put on (a harness or
backpack) (I;3) {ggr. shaapó'li; ygr.
shaapóyyo'li: to wear (a harness or
backpack), be harnessed}
shaapolichi to harness (a horse, for
instance), to put a backpack on
(someone) (I;II) [shaapoli+chi]
{hngr. shaapolihínchi; ngr.
shaapolínchi}
shaapolihínchi hngr. of shaapolichi
shaapolínchi ngr. of shaapolichi
shaapóyyo'li to be harnessed (I); to
wear a harness or backpack (I;3)—
ygr. of shaapoli
shá'ba ggr. of shamba
shafa to have the hair scraped off (of
pigskin, for example) (3) {v2. shafi}
shafa see kashafa
shafi to shave, scrape off (hair), to
grate (I;II) [+OPR] {v1. shafa; hngr.
shaháfi; ilishafi: to shave oneself;
shaffi} § Charles notakhish
shafilitok, Charlesa notakhish

ishafilitok. I shaved Charles, I
shaved Charles's beard.
shậhbi ngr. of shahbi
shi'f shi'f shi'f aachi see shif shif shif
aachi
shí'lli ggr. of shilli
shibli to pull apart (thin boards or
celery, for instance); to strip the bark
from (pl. obj.) (I;3) {shipaachi}
shif shif shif aachi, shi'f shi'f shi'f
aachi to make the sound of water
on something hot (expressive) (I)
shiha, shiya to unravel, come out (of
threads from a garment or woven
material) (3) {v2. shihli; hngr.
shihiha; shihkachi}
shihchi to hemstitch, pull threads
from (material, to make a fringe or
prepare for embroidery) (I;3)
[shihli+chi]
shihímpa hngr. of shiipa
shihífa hngr. of shifa
shihíha hngr. of shiha
shihíla hngr. of shila
shihíli hngr. of shihli
shihílli hngr. of shilli
shihkachi to run (of stockings),
unravel (of loosely woven cloth,
such as burlap) (3) {ygr.
shihkáyya'chi; shiha}
shihkáyya'chi ygr. of shihkachi
shihli to remove, pull out (threads)
(pl. obj.); to remove completely (I;3)
{v1. shiha, shihkachi; hngr. shihíli;
ngr. shíhli; sg. obj. shifi; shihchi} §
Naafka shihtok. She took off all her
clothes.
shikaishtithana' see hashi' kanalli'
ishtithana'
shikaishtithana' ishtallakchi' see
hashi' kanalli' ishtithana'
ishtallakchi'
shikkilili to be pointed, cone shaped,
pagoda shaped, peaked (of a roof); to

have a tower (of a building); to have
one's head stick up above a wall or
obstruction (seen from a distance)
(3) {ggr. shikkílli'li: to be on tiptoe
(I); rlgr. shikkilli'kíli}
shikkilli'kíli to walk around on
tiptoe (I); to walk around on tiptoe
in (a place) (I;3)—rlgr. of shikkilili
shikkílli'li to be on tiptoe (I); to be
the only one (sticking up visible) in
(a place) (I;3)—ggr. of shikkilili §
Chinchokkaako shikkilli'lilitok. I
was the only one in your house.
shikónno'pa ggr. of shikoonopa
shikonno'pa' old-time story or tale
[shikonno'pa+']
shikonno'pa' anoli to tell a story (I)
shikonno'pa' ishtanompa storybook
[isht anompa]
shikoono'li to tie many knots in; to
tie a knot in (pl. obj.) (I;3) {v1.
shikoono'wa; sg. obj. shikoonobli}
shikoono'wa to be knotted with
many knots; to be knotted (pl. subj.)
(3) {v2. shikoono'li; sg. shikoonopa}
shikoonobli to tie a knot in (sg. obj.)
(I;II) {v1. shikoonopa; pl. obj.
shikoono'li}
shikoonopa to be knotted (sg. subj.)
(II) {v2. shikoonobli; ggr.
shikónno'pa; pl. shikoono'wa}
shila to dry, dry out, to be dry, crisp,
to form a scab (II) [+PR] [+CPR] {v2.
shilili; ggr. shí'la; hngr. shihíla; ngr.
shíla: to be dry (of a baby); xgr.
shílli'ya; ygr. shíyyi'la}
shilili to dry (something) (I;II) {v1.
shila}
shilli, shitli to comb, brush, curry
(hair) (I;3); to comb one's hair (I)
[+OPR] {v1. shita; ggr. shí'lli; hngr.
shihílli; ishilli: to comb (someone's
hair)} § Ishshillitam? Did you comb
your hair?

shippa

shílli'ya to be really dry; to be skinny, bony (II)—xgr. of shila
shillichi to card (wool, cotton, or other fibers) (I;3) [shilli+chi]
shilombish spirit (IIIp)
Shilombish Holitto'pa' the Holy Ghost [holitto'pa+']
Shilombish Ishto' the Great Spirit— old-time Indian expression; (EP) God [ishto+']
shilombish oppolo' bad spirit, devil [oppolo+']
Shimmanooli', (CM) Simmanooli' Seminole § Shimmanooli' ishimanǫli. You're telling the Seminole.
Shimmanoolimanompa' Seminole language [Shimmanooli' im+anompa+']
Shimmanooliyaakni' the Seminole Nation of Oklahoma [Shimmanooli' im+yaakni']
shímmo'ha ggr. of shimoha
shimoha, shimowa to be numb, asleep (for example, of the foot); to have (some part of the body) asleep, numb; to get a shock, tingle (II) {v2. shimohli; ggr. shímmo'ha; ngr. shimǫha; ygr. shimóyyo'ha}
shimohachi to give a shock to (I;II) [shimoha+chi]
shimohli to put to sleep, anesthetize (a part of the body); to give a shock to (I;II) {v1. shimoha}
shimowa see shimoha
shimóyyo'ha ygr. of shimoha
shimoochi to give a shock to (I;II) [-SC] [shimooli+chi]
shimoochit abi to electrocute (I;II) [shimoochi+t]
shimooli see shimohli
shimǫha ngr. of shimoha
shinka noisy big night bird
Shinka Bo'li' Drum Dance—name of

a Choctaw dance also danced by Chickasaws [bo'li+']
shinap in itti' shinap
shinok sand, dirt, dust
shinok aalhto' sandbox
shinok bíyyi'ka to be sandy, full of sand (II)
shinok fokha' desert (Ct?) [fokha+']
shinok holisso, holisso shinok sandpaper
shinok homma' red sand [homma+']
shinok losa' black sand [losa+']
shinok shobolli' sandstorm [shobolli+']
shinok tohbi' white sand [tohbi+']
Shinok Tohbi' White Sands—name of a Choctaw church
shinok tǫshpa' bog, quicksand [tǫshpa+']
shipafa to have splinters sticking out, be splintered (sg. subj.) (3) {v2. shipaffi; pl. shipahli}
shipaffi to pull apart, leaving splinters (sg. obj.) (I;3) {v1. shipafa; hngr. shipaháffi; pl. obj. shipaachi; shibli}
shipaháffi hngr. of shipaffi
shipahǎli hngr. of shipahli
shipahli to come apart (of rotten wood, for instance) (pl. subj.) (3) {hngr. shipahǎli; ngr. shipǎhli; sg. shipafa}
shipaachi to strip (limbs from trees, without cutting them) (pl. obj.) (I;3) [-SC] [shipahli+chi] {ngr. shipaalínchi; sg. obj. shipaffi; shibli}
shipaalínchi ngr. of shipaachi
shipǎhli ngr. of shipahli
shippa to have the water dried out (of a creek, a water tank, or a pan boiled dry), to dry out, boil dry; to be sunken (of eyes) (3) [+T] {v2. shippali; ggr. shîppa; ashippa; yanhakat shippa}

319

shîppa ggr. of shippa
shippachi to have one's fever go
down (II) ; to boil down (jam) (I;3)
[+T] [shippa+chi] {ngr. shippánchi}
shippali to blow on (something, to
cool it); to boil down (jam) (I;3) {v1.
shippa} § Tii shippalilitok. I blew on
the tea.
shippánchi ngr. of shippachi
shita to be combed (3) [+T] {v2. shilli}
shitli see shilli
shiwaháa hngr. of shiwaa
shiwaa to be striped, especially with
narrow stripes (II) [+CPR] [-PR] {ggr.
shíwwa'a; hngr. shiwaháa}
shiwaachi to make stripes on (I;3)
[-SC] [shiwaa+chi] {hngr.
shiwaahánchi}
shiwaahánchi hngr. of shiwaachi
shíwwa'a ggr. of shiwaa
shiya see shiha
<shiyammi> in bakshiyammi,
nokshiyammi
shíyyi'la ygr. of shila
Shiyyo̱'ti', (TP) Shiho̱'ti' Chickasaw
woman's name
shiibli to stretch (something,
especially so that it stays stretched
out) (mainly sg. obj.); to tan
(leather) (I;II) {v1. shiipa; pl. obj.
shiipo'li}
shiiki buzzard
shiiki pakạli' type of medicinal plant
Shiima' nickname for a well-dressed
lady (Ct)
shiipa to be elastic, stretchy; to
stretch; to be stretched out of shape
(mainly sg. subj.) (3) {v2. shiibli;
hngr. shihímpa; pl. shiipo'wa;
<siipa>} § naashiipa': rubber, elastic
shiipo'li to stretch, pull (something
stretchy, like rubber); to pull into
shape (pl. obj.) (I;3) {v1. shiipo'wa;
sg. obj. shiibli}

shiipo'wa to be stretchy, elastic; to be
stretched (pl. subj.) (3) {v2. shiipo'li;
sg. shiipa}
shịfa to come off, come out (3) [+PR]
[-CPR] {v2. shịfi; hngr. shihị́fa} §
Lynn ịsholoshat shịfa, Lynnat
sholoshat ịshịfa. Lynn's shoe came
off.
shịfi to remove, take out, take off (a
single garment); to get out of (a
muzzle or harness); to pull (a single
thread, to unravel it) (I;3) {v1. shịfa;
pl. obj. shihli}
shịla to be dry (of a baby) [-CPR]
[-PR]—ngr. of shila
shị́hli ngr. of shihli
sho'f sho'f sho'f aachi see shof shof
shof aachi
sho'k sho'k sho'k aachi see shok
shok shok aachi
sho'l sho'l sho'l aachi see shol shol
shol aachi
sho'li to carry (especially, a babe in
arms); to give birth to (I;3) {v1.
sho'wa; ygr. shóyyo'li; shooli} §
Chipota sho'tok. She had a baby.
shó'li ggr. of shooli
shó'lli ggr. of sholli
sho'wa to be carried (II) {v2. sho'li;
ygr. shóyyo'wa}
shobbí'chi ggr. of shobbichi
shobbichi, (ER, TJ, MC)
shobommichi, (AW) shombichi to
drizzle, sprinkle, shower (—); to
sprinkle (clothes) (I;3) {ggr.
shobbí'chi; hngr. shobbihínchi}
shobbihínchi hngr. of shobbichi
shobbókko'li ggr. of shobbokoli
shobbokochi to make (something)
grey (I;3) [±SC] [shobbokoli+chi]
shobbokoli to be grey; to be blurry (II)
{ggr. shobbókko'li; ngr. shobbokọ́li}
shobbokọ́li ngr. of shobbokoli
shóbbolli ggr. of shobolli

shobohli to smoke (of a fire, for instance) (3) {hngr. shoboh**ó**li; shobolli}
shobohchi to make (something) smoke (I;3); to make smoke, send smoke signals (I) [-SC] [shobohli+chi]
shobohli, shobooli smoke (noun)
shoboh**ó**nta to make a little cloud of dust or ashes fly (of a chicken scratching or a dusty pillow, for instance) (3)—hngr. of <shobota>
shoboh**ó**li hngr. of shobohli
shoboh**ó**lli hngr. of shobolli
shobohtokahchi see shobottokahchi
shobolli, shobotli to be covered with dust, to have a cloud of dust rise (from overstuffed furniture or certain mushrooms, for example) (II) {v1. <shobota>; ggr. shóbbolli; hngr. shoboh**ó**lli; shobohli}
shobollichi to make a cloud of (dust, sand, smoke) (I;3) [shobolli+chi]
<shobota> {v2. shobolli; hngr. shobohónta}
shobotli see shobolli
shobottokahchi, shobohtokahchi to have something powdery come out suddenly (of certain mushrooms or pillows when they are hit, or a vacuum-packed can when opened) (3) § Alhpishshaat shobottokahshtok. The pillow sent up a cloud of dust.
shobooli see shobohli ("smoke")
shóchchokli'chi to make noise with paper (I)—klgr. of <shocho'chi> {ittishóchchokli'chi}
<shocho'chi> {klgr. shóchchokli'chi; rcgr. shochochó'chi; shochok shochok shochok aachi}
shochochó'chi to drag one's feet while walking; to walk in leaves (I)—rcgr. of shocho'chi

{ittishochochó'chi}
shochok shochok shochok aachi to make the sound of paper crinkling (expressive) (I) {shochochó'chi, <shocho'chi>}
shof shof shof aachi, sho'f sho'f sho'f aachi to make the sound of paper crinkling or of steam being released (expressive) (I) {shofo'chi}
<shóffokli'chi> in ittishóffokli'chi— klgr. of shofo'chi
shofo'chi to sizzle (of a hot stove with water dropped on it); to crinkle (of paper) (3) {klgr. <shóffokli'chi>; rcgr. <shofofó'chi>; ittishofo'chi, shof shof shof aachi}
<shofofó'chi> in ittishofofó'chi— rcgr. of shofo'chi
shoha, showa to smell bad, stink (II); to smell like (a skunk, fish) (II;3C) [+PR] {hngr. shoh**ó**ha; ngr. sh**ó**ha; xgr. shóhho'wa; ygr. shóyyo'ha} § Ith**a**nali koni sashowakat. I know I smell like a skunk.
shohchi to rub, drag along, file (I;3) [-SC] [{v1. shoowalhchi; hngr. shohlihínchi}
shóhho'wa xgr. of shoha
shohlihínchi hngr. of shohchi
shoh**ó**'ka hngr. of sho**͟**ka
shoh**ó**ha hngr. of shoha
shoh**ó**li hngr. of shooli
shoh**ó**lli hngr. of sholli
shok shok shok aachi, sho'k sho'k sho**͟**'k aachi to make the sound of paper or stiff plastic bags crinkling (expressive) (I) {<shoko'chi>}
shoka' short form of ishshoka'
shokafa to chip, be chipped, have a piece (of paint, a scab, etc.) chip off; to have the sole come off (of a shoe) (sg. subj.) (II) [+PR] {v2. shokaffi; hngr. shokah**á**fa; shokahli: have more than one piece chipped off} §

Asholoshat shokafa, Sholoshat ashokafa. The sole's coming off my shoe.

shokaffi to peel, chip off a piece from (sg. obj.) (I;II) {v1. shokafa; hngr. shokaháffi; pl. obj. shokli; shokaachi: chip many pieces off}

shokaháfa hngr. of shokafa

shokaháffi hngr. of shokaffi

shokaháli to peel off easily—hngr. of shokahli

shokahli to be chipped (pl. subj.), have lots of pieces chip off (3) {hngr. shokaháli: to peel off easily; shokafa: have one piece chipped off}

shokaachi to chip (pl. obj.), to chip many pieces off (I;3) [-SC] [shokahli+chi] {hngr. shokaalihínchi; ngr. shokaalínchi; shokaffi: chip one piece off; shokli}

shokaalihínchi hngr. of shokaachi

shokaalínchi ngr. of shokaachi

shokcha sack, bag

shokcha kallo' burlap bag, tow sack [kallo+']

shokchoshi' little bag, pouch [shokcha oshi']

shokha' hog

shokha' chokkayalli', (MJ) shokha' choklhihili', (ML) shokha' chokya'li', (TJ) shokha' chaklhiha'li' possum [chokkayalli+']

shokha' iskano' possum (TP)

shokha' ishoppaya'kalhchi', (CC) shokha' ishoppalakalhchi' hog lights (lungs)

shokha' niha' pork lard

shokha' nipi' pork

shokha' nipi' oshobohli' bacon, smoked ham

shokha' nipi' shila' salt pork, dry salt [shila+']

shokha' saalhkona' chitlins

shokha' sholopha', (CC) shokha' isholopha' hog lights (lungs) [im+sholopha']

shokhalanchi' green fruit on the nassapi' or shokhalanchapi' tree

shokhalanchapi' oak tree with big acorns (another name for nassapi')

shokhata', (CC) shokhati possum (Ct) [shokha' <hata>+']

shokhimpa' hogweed (WB) [shokha' impa']

shokhiskannittish see shokhiskanno' tish

shokhiskanno' tish, shokhiskannittish type of medicinal plant [shokha' iskanno+']

shokhishto' tish type of medicinal plant [shokha' ishto+']

shokhittakoba' pork tripe [shokha' ittakoba']

shokhiyyi' pigs' feet [shokha' iyyi']

shokhiyyobi' ham [shokha' iyyobi']

shokhifalaa' hog lights (lungs) (TP) [shokha' im+falaa+']

shokhok-okaa-asha', (ER) shokha' okaa-asha' hippopotamus [shokha' oka' okaa-asha+']

shokhoshi' pig; baby hog [shokha' oshi']

shokhoshi' ta'ossaalhto' piggy bank [ta'osso aalhto']

shokkawali to be transparent, clear; to glow, shine (3) [+CPR] [+PR] {ggr. shokkáwwa'li; shokmalali}

shokkáwwa'li ggr. of shokkawali

shokkaawi', (AB) shokawwa'li', (MJ: a joke) shokha' hawi' lightning bug, firefly; car with only one headlight working

shokkaawishto' type of large lightning bug [shokkaawi' ishto+']

<shókkokli'chi> in ittishókkoli'chi—klgr. of

<shoko'chi>
shokli to chip (especially, with a chisel or knife) (pl. obj.); to square off the edges of (a log with an axe) (I;3) {shokaachi}
shokmá'lli ggr. of shokmalli
shokmahą́lli hngr. of shokmalli
shokmalachi to shine (something), polish, varnish (I;II) [+SC] [shokmalali+chi] {hngr. shokmalahánchi}
shokmalahánchi hngr. of shokmalachi
shokmalali to be shiny; to shine, sparkle (II) [-CPR] [-PR] {ggr. shokmálla'li: to shine (from a distance); ngr. shokmalą́li; rlgr. shokmalla'mą́li; ygr. shokmaláyya'li; shokkawali, shokmalli, shoppala}
shokmaláyya'li ygr. of shokmalali
shokmálla'li to shine (from a distance)—ggr. of shokmalali
shokmalla'mą́li to be shiny, sparkly; to flash, glitter (II)—rlgr. of shokmalali
shokmallaat isso for lightning to strike (II = obj.) [shokmalli+at] § Shokmallaat sassa'chika ithąnali. I know that lightning's going to strike me, I'm going to get struck by lightning.
shokmalli lightning; to be lightning, to flash (of lightning) (—); to be lightning in (a place) (—;3); to have lightning in (of a place) (rare) (3) {ggr. shokmá'lli; hngr. shokmahą́lli; shokmalali} § Shokmallitok. There was lightning. | Oklahomma'a shokmahąlli. There was lightning in Oklahoma. | Oklahomma'at ombacha shokmallitok. Oklahoma had rain and lightning.
<shoko'chi> in ittishoko'chi {klgr.

<shókkokli'chi>; rcgr. shokokó'chi; shok shok shok aachi}
shokokó'chi to make a noise with paper: especially, to make a noise in a drawer (3)—rcgr. of <shoko'chi>
shokolbika' corner § hattak holba' shokolbika': the corner of the picture
shokolbika' aa-asha to have corners, to be square (of a two-dimensional obj.) (3)
shokolbika' bíyyi'ka to be cube shaped, box shaped (3)
shokolbika' oshta to be four sided (of a two-dimensional figure), have four corners (3)
shokolbika' tochchí'na to be triangular, have three corners (3)
shokshi' gourd (CM)
shokshohǫ́wa hngr. of shokshowa
shokshowa to snort like a deer (3) {hngr. shokshohǫ́wa}
shol shol shol aachi, sho'l sho'l sho'l aachi to make a dragging, scraping, scratching, or rattling sound (especially, of little bells on baby shoes); to make the sound of crickets (expressive) (I) {<shola'chi>, sholo'chi}
<shola'chi> in ittishola.chi {klgr. <shóllakli'chi>; rcgr. <sholalá'chi>; shol shol shol aachi, sholo'chi}
sholá'ffi ggr. of sholaffi
sholafa to be scratched (once) (sg. subj.) (II) {v2. sholaffi; ggr. shólla'fa; pl. sholahli}
sholaffi to scratch (something), claw (once) (sg. obj.) (I;II) {v1. sholafa; ggr. sholá'ffi, shóllaffi; hngr. sholahą́ffi; pl. obj. sholli}
sholahą́ffi hngr. of sholaffi
sholahli to be all scratched up; to be scratched (pl. subj.) (II) {sg. sholafa}
<sholalá'chi> in ittisholalá'chi—

rcgr. of <shola'chi>
shólla'fa ggr. of sholafa
shóllaffi ggr. of sholaffi
<shóllakli'chi> in ittishóllakli'chi—
klgr. of <shola'chi>
{<shóllokli'chi>}
sholli to claw, scratch (more than
once), to pick at (a scab); to scratch
(pl. obj.) (I;II) {ggr. shó'lli; hngr.
shohólli; sg. obj. sholaffi}
<shóllokli'chi> in ittishóllokli'chi
{sholo'chi, <shóllakli'chi>}
sholo'chi to make noise (I) [±SC]
{shol shol shol aachi, <shola'chi>,
<shóllokli'chi>, shololó'chi}
shololó'chi to make a noise (of tin
noisemakers, for example) (3)
{sholo'chi}
sholop ghost (IIp—one's own ghost /
IIIp—a ghost associated with one,
such as a ghost in one's house) §
sasholop: my ghost, the ghost of me
| asholop: my ghost, a ghost in my
house
Sholop Inittak Halloween
[im+nittak]
sholop tilhi'li', shoptilhi'li', (WB)
sholop tilhili' horsemint [tilhili+']
{issoba ishoptilhi'li'}
sholop tilhi'li' iskanno' type of
medicinal plant [<iskanno>+']
sholop tilhi'li' losa', (CP) sholop
tilhili' losa' type of medicinal plant
[losa+']
sholop tilhi'li' tohbi', (CP) sholop
tilhili' tohbi' type of medicinal
plant [tohbi+']
sholopha' lungs (IIp)
sholosh shoe (IIIp)
sholosh alaatali' shoemaker
[alaatali+']
sholosh aa-abihli' shoe rack (for two
shoes) [aa+abihli+']
sholosh aa-albiya' shoe rack (for

more than two shoes)
sholosh aa-asha' shoe store
sholosh aachompa' shoe store
sholosh aakanchi' shoe store
[aa+kanchi+']
sholosh aalhto' shoe rack
sholosh bakshakali shoes with
pointed toes [bakshakali+']
sholosh chaaha' boot; high-topped
shoe or sneaker [chaaha+']
sholosh isolash tongue of a shoe
sholosh ishholo' shoehorn [isht
holo+']
sholosh ishshokmalachi' shoe polish
[isht shokmalachi+']
sholosh ishtalakchi' shoelace,
shoestring [isht talakchi+']
sholosh ishtasitti'ya' shoe buckle
sholosh iyyi' tako'bish heel of a shoe
sholosh iyyi' tako'bish chaaha' high
heels, high-heeled shoes [chaaha+']
sholosh iipatha' sole of a shoe [iyyi'
patha']
sholosh latassa' flat (flat-heeled shoe)
[latassa+']
sholosh naashiipa' aatoba',
naashiipa' sholosh aatoba' rubber
boots [nanna shiipa+' aa+toba+']
sholosh okti' ishtokaashalalli' ice
skates [isht okaashalalli+']
sholosh oktishtoshala'li' ice skates
sholosh pakna' holo'chi' overshoes,
(rain) boots, galoshes [pakna'
holochi+']
sholoshtalhipa musical
instrument—drum, banjo, fiddle,
guitar [probably sholo'chi+t alhipa;
perhaps sholosh isht alhipa or
sholosh talhipa]
sholowi' cricket
sholowi' lakna' brown cricket
[lakna+']
sholowi' losa' black cricket [losa+']
sholoowachi to make noise (of the

wind or little bells on children's shoes, for instance) (3) {hngr. sholoowahánchi; ngr. sholoowánchi; sholo'chi}
sholoowahánchi hngr. of sholoowachi
sholoowánchi ngr. of sholoowachi
<shoma> in ittashoma, okaashoma {v2. <shommi>}
shomba to be eaten by bugs (especially termites or weevils) (3) [+PR]
shombachi to eat (wood) (of termites) (3;3) [shomba+chi]
shommatik low plant with green burrs that later turn brown and stick (larger than hashshok haloppa'—perhaps cockleburr?)
shommatik ani' burrs on the shommatik plant
shommatik ishto' type of plant with big leaves and large burrs that are boiled to make a headache medicine [ishto+']
<shommi> in ittashommi, okaashommi {v1. <shoma>}
shonkabosh, shawinkabosh crabapple; huckleberry [shawi' im+kabosh ?]
shonkabosh ishto' type of big huckleberry or crabapple [ishto+']
shoppá'la ggr. of shoppala
shoppaháya hngr. of shoppaya
shoppala to go on, be lit, be bright (of a light) (3) {v2. shoppalali; ggr. shoppá'la; xgr. shoppálla'a; shokmalali, palli}
shoppala' light: especially, ceiling light [shoppala+']
shoppala' akmi' candle [akmi+']
shoppala' akmi' ishyo'kli' candlestick, candle holder [isht yokli+']
shoppalali to turn on (lights) (I;3)

{v1. shoppala}
shoppálla'a to be on (of a light) (3)— xgr. of shoppala [+CPR] [+PR]
shoppalla'kahchi to give a sudden flash of light (for instance, of lightning or a bulb when it burns out, or of fireworks) (3)
shoppaya to be light (not heavy) (II) {v2. <shoppayali>; hngr. shoppaháya; ngr. shoppáya: to be lighter; xgr. shoppáyya'a; neg. ikshoppayyo}
shoppayachi to make light (in weight) (I;3)—usually in ngr. {ngr. shoppayánchi}
<shoppayali> {v1. shoppaya; ngr. shoppayáli}
shoppayánchi ngr. of shoppayachi
shoppayáli to make lighter (in weight) (3;3)—ngr. of <shoppayali>
shoppáyya'a, (HS) shokpáyya'a to be light (not heavy) (II)—xgr. of shoppaya [+CPR] [+PR]
shoppáya to be lighter (in weight)— ngr. of shoppaya
shoptilhi'li' see sholop tilhi'li'
shoti' churn, crock
shotik sky
shotik ihollokso', (MJ) shotik iholonkso', (CC) shotik ilokso' stinkbug; (MJ) doodlebug [im+hollokso']
showa see shoha
showak urine (IIIp) [shoha, hoshowa]
showak aalhto' bladder (IIIp)
shóyyo'li ygr. of sho'li
shóyyo'wa to be carried (e.g., in the arms, especially of a baby)—ygr. of sho'wa
shoo, shoo' show, movie [from the English] § Shoo pist ayala'chi. I'm going to the show, I'm going to see the show.
shoo ikbi' actor [ikbi+']

shoo ishtikbi'

shoo ishtikbi' movie camera [isht
ikbi+']
shoo' see shoo
shookola' sugar [ultimately from
Spanish azúcar—or French
chocolat?]
shookola' api' sugar cane
shookola' aatoba' sugar cane
[aa+toba+']
shookola' bota' powdered sugar
[bota+']
shookola' holba' saccharin, sugar
substitute
shookola' kallo' sugar lump [kallo+']
shookola' lakna' brown sugar
[lakna+']
shookola' poshi' powdered sugar
shookola' tohbi' white sugar
[tohbi+']

shookolaalhto' sugar bowl
shookolokchi' molasses, syrup
[shookola' okchi']
shooli to hug (I;II) {ggr. shó'li; hngr.
shohǫ́li; ngr. shǫ́li; sho'li}
<shoopa> in inokshoopa
shootko'li', (AB) shootkoli' type of
medicinal plant (perhaps the same
as ampohko'li')
shoowalhchi to be rubbed, scuffed,
shiny from rubbing (3) {v2. shohchi}
shǫ'ka to kiss; to suck (through a
straw, at a bottle, or one's thumb)
(I;II) {hngr. shohǫ́'ka} § ilbak shǫ'ka:
to suck one's thumb
shǫ'kachichi to make ° kiss ° (I;II;3)
[shǫ'ka+chichi]
shǫ́ha ngr. of shoha
shǫ́li ngr. of shooli

t

tá'ha ggr. of taha
tá'hli ggr. of tahli
tá'lhlhi ggr. of talhlhi
tá'nni ggr. of tanni
ta'ossaa-asha' bank (building), vault
[ta'osso aa-asha+']
ta'ossaabohli' bank (for money)
[ta'osso aa+bohli+']
ta'ossaalhto' bank (container),
money box, cash register [ta'osso
aalhto']
ta'ossaaponta' finance company,
lending institution [ta'osso
aa+ponta+']
ta'ossaashaachi' bank (for money)
[ta'osso aa+shaachi+']
ta'ossimponta' money lender,
pawnbroker [ta'osso imponta+']
ta'ossishponta to pawn, borrow
money on (I;3) [ta'osso isht *ponta]

§ Yammak ta'ossishtishpontam?
Did you pawn it?
ta'ossifalammichi to pay taxes to
(I;III) [ta'osso *ifalammichi] §
Ta'ossafalammichi. He pays taxes to
me.
ta'ossishokcha' purse, wallet [ta'osso
im+shokcha+']
ta'osso money; dollar [tali' holisso']
{tali' holisso'}
ta'osso aaishi' welfare office
[aa+ishi+']
ta'osso bosholli' change (money)
[bosholli+']
ta'osso boshollichi to get change, to
cash a check (I)
ta'osso imboshollichi to give change
to, to cash a check for (I;III)
[im+(ta'osso boshollichi)> ta'osso
*imboshollichi] § Ta'osso

326

issambosholliclia'chita? Will you cash a check for me?

ta'osso ishhoyo' collection plate [isht hoyo+']

ta'osso shooli' treasurer [shooli+']

tabashi to be widowed; to be in seclusion and go through ritual mourning after one's husband's death (WB, EP) {bashshi, ilbashsha} § ihoo tabashi': widow

tabashi' widow, widower (MJ), mourning widow (WB) [tabashi+'] {ihoo tabashi'}

tabli to cut, pull apart into two parts, cut off the top of (sg. obj.), to cut (sg. long obj.) across once (I;3) {v1. tapa; pl. obj. katolhlhi}

tabookoli noon, noontime, lunch, lunchtime; to be noon, noontime, lunch, lunchtime (—); to have it be noon (of a place) (3) § New Yorkat tabookoli. It's noon in New York.

tabookoli impa to have a noon meal—dinner (in the Midwestern sense) or lunch (I) § Tabookoli ishimpatam? Did you have lunch?

taha to end, be finished; to be all gone, used up, completed; to be worn out, done for, raggedy; to be worn away, have a worn place (II) [+PR]; accomplish, finish, end, do completely, be completely, be very, be all (aux.—used with II or III subj. verbs or I subj. verbs with no subj. marking); have finished, be in a state resulting from (a motion) (aux., pl. subj. only); now (be able to consume or sense) (aux.) (In aux. uses, taha may appear as a suffix or (rarely) as a separate word following a verb +t. Verbs using taha in the last two meanings above are marked [+taha].) {v2. tahli; ggr. tá'ha; ngr. táha; ygr. táyya'ha} §

Hommataha. It's very red, It's completely red, It's all red. | Satikahbitaha. I'm all tired out. | Antakho'bitaha. I've gotten all lazy. | Hopootaha. He has gotten all jealous. | Ayataha. They are gone. | Ishhanglotaha. Now you hear, Now you can hear. | Takolaat antaha. My peach is all gone.

taháli hngr. of tahli

tahálhlhi hngr. of talhlhi

taháni hngr. of taani

tahánni hngr. of tanni

taháshki hngr. of tashki

táhhakba hgr. of takba

tahli to finish, complete a task (I); to finish: especially, to finish eating; to use up (I;3); to do completely, to do to all (I) [E+t] (used with preceding I subj. verbs only; in this last use, tahli may appear as a suffix or as a separate word following a verb +t) {v2. taha; ggr. tá'hli; hngr. taháli; ngr. táhli; ygr. táyya'hli} § Pobit ishtahla'chi! You're going to kill us all!

taká'chi ggr. of takaachi

<takafa> in aatakafa, ishtaka'fa', okaatakafa {v2. takaffi}

takaffi to dip (a liquid)—usually, just one dip (I;3) {v1. <takafa>; hngr. takaháffi; takli: dip more than once} § Oka' ishtaka'fa' ishtakaffilitok. I dipped water with the cup.

takaháffi hngr. of takaffi

takassali' in bala' takassali'

<takashi'> in intakashi'

takaachi to hang up (sg. obj.); to write (a name, for instance) (I;II); to hang up the telephone (I) [-SC] [takaali+chi] {ggr. tákkali'chi, taká'chi; hngr. takaahánchi, takaalihínchi; ngr. takáanchi; pl. obj. takoochi; holhchifo intakaachi:

takaahánchi

to put (someone's) name down, to
vote for} § Saholhchifo
takaachilitok. I wrote my name.
takaahánchi hngr. of takaachi
takaali to be caught, hung up on (sg.
subj.) (II;3) {ggr. tákka'li: to be
hanging (I); ngr. takáli; rmgr.
takkakáli; pl. takohli; iyyintakaali'}
§ Tali' haloppa' satakaatok. I got
caught on the barbed wire.
takaalihínchi hngr. of takaachi
takáanchi ngr. of takaachi
takaat ittola to trip over (something)
and fall (II;3) [takaali+t] § Nanna
takaat sattolatok. I tripped over
something and fell.
taka'sta', (LF) itti' takastaka', (TJ)
taka'stak, (AW) takasta' redbud tree
takachi to leave hanging (sg. obj.)
(I;3) [takali+chi]
takáli ngr. of takaali {pl. takóhli}
takba to be sour, causing the mouth
to pucker up (like a green
persimmon) (II) {hgr. táhhakba; ygr.
táyyakba; takbiloli}
takbíllo'li ggr. of takbiloli
takbiloli to stick one's lower lip out,
pout (I / II) [tak+] {ggr. takbíllo'li;
hngr. takbilohóli; ngr. takbilóli;
takba}
takchi to tie (something) up (with a
bow or knot); to rope (of a cowboy,
for instance); to bale (hay) (I;II) {v1.
talakchi; intakchi: to brake}
takchi'sha I guess it has to be, it's
bound to be, it has to be that (used
with a preceding future verb)
[takchi ?] § Ishyahma'chi takchi'sha.
I guess you have to do it.
takchit ontalaali to tie a bow on (I;3)
{ggr. takchit ontálla'li}
takchit ontálla'li ggr. of takchit
ontalaali
takha, (MJ, AW) takka, (LF, TJ, AB)

takha' catfish
takholba' see hattak holba'
takilli' see hattak illi'
takilli' shaali' see hattak illi' shaali'
takishpa to be tasteless, to have no
distinct taste (of food) (3) {ggr.
tákkishpa}
tákka'li to hang, be hanging (from
something or in the air, like a
helicopter), to crouch down, squat
(sg. subj.) (I); to hang, crouch down
in (a place) (sg. subj.) (I;3)—ggr. of
takaali {dl. tákkohli; tpl. takoht
máa}
takkakáli to dangle, hang down,
swing in the breeze, hover (sg. subj.)
(I)—rmgr. of takaali {dl. takkokóli}
tákkali'chi ggr. of takaachi
tákkishpa ggr. of takishpa
tákkohli to hang, be hanging, to
crouch down, squat (dl. subj.) (I); to
hang, crouch down in (a place) (dl.
subj) (I;3)—ggr. of takohli {sg.
tákka'li; tpl. takoht máa}
takkokóli to dangle, hang down,
swing in the breeze (dl. subj.) (I)—
rmgr. of takohli {sg. takkakáli}
takla to cluck (of a chicken) (ER)
[tak+] {taktaki, toktowa}
<takla> in <ibaatakla> {ngr. tángla}
takli to dip, dip out (several times, or
to completion) (I;3) {takaffi: dip
once} § Oka' taklilitok. I dipped
water.
taklosa' see hattak losa'
Taklosiyaakni' see Hattak Losa'
Iyaakni'
taklhipachi to open (someone's)
mouth, make (someone) open his
mouth (I;3) [-SC] [taklhipali+chi]
taklhipali to open one's mouth (I)
[tak+] {ggr. taklhíppa'li: to have
one's mouth open}
taklhíppa'li to have one's mouth

hanging open—ggr. of taklhipali
tako'bish in iyyi' tako'bish
takoba bottle (variant of kitoba)
takoba' short form of ittakoba'
takohchi see takoochi
takohli in oottakohli, takoht máa,
takoochi {ggr. tákkohli; ngr. takóhli;
rmgr. takkokóli; sg. takaali}
takohlinchi see takoolinchi
takoht máa to hang, be hanging, to
crouch down, squat (tpl. subj.) (I); to
hang, crouch down in (a place) (tpl.
subj.) (I;3) [takohli+t] {sg. tákka'li; dl.
tákkohli} § Yammako takoht
kiimaatok. We were hanging there.
Takollishto' Holitto'pa' Easter (CP)
[Nittak Hollishto']
takombish falaa' see takolo ibish
falaa'
takoochi, takohchi to hang (pl. obj.)
(I;II); to write a name or date, make
a few marks, write around on a page
(I;3) [-SC] [takohli+chi] {ngr.
takoolínchi, takohlínchi: to leave
hanging; sg. obj. takaachi}
takoolínchi, takohlínchi to leave
hanging (pl. obj.)—ngr. of takoochi
takóhli to be still hanging (pl. subj.)
(3)—ngr. of takohli {sg. takáli}
takola'lhlhi', (AB, TJ, TP) takolo
alhlhi' cling peach [takolo alhlhi+']
takolissish "Indian peach" (they look
more like plums) [takolo issish]
takolo peach
takolo fako'pa' freestone peach
[fakopa+']
takolo fatabli' peach fuzz
takolo finha' peach, true peach
[finha+']
takolo foni' peach stone
takolo haksibish pear (CC)
takolo hishi' peach leaves
takolo holba' crab apple (MJ)
takolo ibish aa-asha' pear [aa-asha+']

takolo ibish falaa', takolobish falaa',
takombish falaa', (MJ) takofalaa',
(MJ) takofalaha' pear [falaa+']
takolo imilhlha' crab apple, wild
apple (MJ) [imilhlha+']
takolo inchakissa' sticky, sweet sap
extruded by peach trees (children's
word) [im+chakissa+']
takolo lakna' yellow peach [lakna+']
takolo maso'fa', takomaso'fa', (WB)
takoso'fa', (OC, EH, HS, MJ)
takoloso'fa' apple [takolo masofa+']
takolo maso'fa' foni' apple core
takolo sawa' crab apple (WB)
[<sawa>+']
takolo tohbi' white peach [tohbi+']
takolo wasacha' green apple; (CC, ER)
crab apple [wasacha+']
takolobish falaa' see takolo ibish
falaa'
takolokchi' sticky, sweet sap extruded
by peach trees [takolo okchi']
takoloshi' plum, (WB) crab apple
[takolo oshi']
takoloshi' imilhlha' wild plum
[imilhlha+']
takoloshi' lakna' type of yellow
plum [lakna+']
takoloshi' shila' prune [shila+']
takomaso'fa' see takolo maso'fa'
takshóllo'li ggr. of takshololi
takshololi to stick out one's lips, to
pucker up (I) [tak+] {ggr.
takshóllo'li}
taktaki to cackle (WB) [tak+] {takla}
tala in noktala, oottala {v2. talaali;
xgr. tálla'a; <talaa>}
talahásbi hngr. of talasbi
<talaka> in okaatalaka {v2. talaali}
talakchi to be tied up, tangled (II) {v2.
takchi; ggr. tállakchi}
talasbi, (MC) talosbi to be slippery (icy
or soapy, for example) (II) {ggr.
tállasbi; hngr. talahásbi; ngr. talásbi;

talasbichi

ygr. taláyya'sbi; halasbi}
talasbichi to make (something) slick,
slippery (I;II) [talasbi+chi]
taláyya'sbi ygr. of talasbi
<talaa> {v2. talaali; ggr. tálla'a; ngr.
taláa; tala, <talaka>}
talaabo'li' anvil [tali' aa+bo'li+']
talaabo'wa' blacksmith's shop [tali'
aa+bo'wa+']
talaali to put down, set down (sg. obj.
with a flat bottom); to bury (I;3); to
put down (sg. obj. with a flat
bottom) in (I;3;3) {v1. tálla'a, tala,
<talaka>, <talaa>; ggr. <tálla'li>;
ngr. találi: to leave (a flat-bottomed
obj.) there; rmgr. tallaláli; pl. obj.
talohli} § Yammako ishtakafa'
talaalilitok. I put the cup down
there.
talaanompa' telephone [tali'
aa+anompa']
talaanompa' aaimanompoli to talk
to on the telephone (I;III)
[aa+im+anompoli] § Talaanompa'
aachimanompolilitok. I talked to
you on the phone.
talaanompa' aaittimanompoli to talk
on the telephone (pl. subj.) (IR)
[aa+itti+im+anompoli] §
Talaanompa' aaiitimanompolitok.
We talked on the phone.
talaanompa' holhtina' telephone
number (IIIp)
talaanompoli' aataka'li' telephone
booth [aa+takaali+']
talaasbo'si to be too slippery to hold
onto (3) [talasbi+os'i]
taláa to be there, be left there (of
something with a flat bottom) (sg.
subj.) (3)—ngr. of tálla'a, <talaa>
{v2. találi; dl. talówa; tpl. ásha}
találi to leave behind, to leave there
(sg. obj.) (I;3)—ngr. of talaali {v1.
taláa}

talásbi ngr. of talasbi
tali' rock; metal; wire; pipe (for
water, for instance)
tali' amposhi' dish made of silver or
some other metal
tali' anompoli' computer
[anompoli+']
tali' aapalaska' outdoor bread oven
[aa+<palaska>+']
tali' bila' mercury [bila+']
tali' bo'li' blacksmith [bo'li+']
tali' bosholli' crushed rock, gravel
(larger than tal-oshik) [bosholli+']
tali' chiffola' hook for lifting bales of
hay [chiffola+']
tali' chipasli' flint [chipasli+']
tali' chofak railroad spike, nail (WB)
(Ct)
tali' cholok aa-asha' (metal) pipe [aa-
asha+']
**tali' fabassa', tali' fabassa' hashshok
ishtalakchi'** baling wire [fabassa+']
tali' fabassa' hashshok ishtalakchi'
see tali' fabassa'
tali' foloha' cement, concrete
[foloha+']
tali' haloppa' barbed wire; dart
[haloppa+']
**tali' haloppa' holitta, tali haloppa'
holitta'** barbed-wire fence
tali' hina' railroad, railroad track
(WB) (Ct)
tali' hina' aabaanabli' railroad
crossing (WB) (Ct)
tali' hina' inkaha' railroad tie (WB)
(Ct)
tali' holisso', (TJ) tali-holisso', tal-isso
(MJ) money: especially, minted
silver (with writing on it) (old
word) [holisso+'] {ta'osso}
tali' holisso' lakna' gold coins
[lakna+']
tali' holitta' barbed-wire, chicken
wire, or chain link fence

<tálla'li>

tali' holiitopa' precious metal, jewel
[holiitopa+']
tali' hoyya' alum [hoyya+']
tali' illi' ohikki'ya' gravestone (pl.
tali' illi' ohiyohli'} [illi+'
on+hikki'ya+']
tali' illi' ohiyohli' gravestones—pl.
of tali' illi' ohikki'ya' [illi+'
on+hiyohli+']
tali' inno'chi' neck chain
tali' ishhalalli' forceps or other tool
for pulling [isht halalli+']
tali' ishholissochi' typewriter [isht
holissochi+']
tali' ishshoppantik type of green rock
that can sudse up and be used for
soap (AB)
tali' ishtapa' see talishtapa'
tali' ishtasiitoha' chain (HS) [isht
<asiitoha>+']
tali' ishtincho'li' branding iron;
printing press; typewriter [isht
incho'li+']
tali' ishtincho'wa' printing press;
printed matter; branding iron;
typewriter [isht incho'wa+']
tali' ittabaana' holitta, tali' ittabaana'
holitta' stone or cement block wall
tali' ittatakali', talittatakali' chain
[ittatakali+']
tali' kawaski' steel [kawaski+']
tali' lakchi' little pieces of rock too
small to pick up easily; gravel
tali' lakna' gold; copper [lakna+']
tali' losa' mole (on the skin) [losa+']
tali' losa'at ontálla'a to have a mole
(on the skin) (II) [(tali' losa')+at] §
Tali' losa'at asontalla'a. I have a
mole.
tali' lowak ishtikbi' flint [isht ikbi+']
tali' nanna aa-albani' barbecue spit
[aa+albani+']
tali' palaska' cement [<palaska>+']
tali' patalhpo' asphalt, paving; any

cement floor
tali' patalhpo' bíyyi'ka to be paved (3)
tali' shachakla' chicken wire; metal
screen [shachakla+']
tali' shan-kachi' see tali' tashan-
kachi'
tali' shokmalali' jewel; diamond
[shokmalali+']
tali' tashan-kachi', tali' shan-kachi'
spring (in a bed or sofa); slinky (toy)
[(tashan-kachi)+']
tali' tohbi' silver [tohbi+']
tali' tokaachi to blast, use dynamite
(I)
talishkolli' pickax; (WB) crowbar
[tali' isht kolli+']
talishtapa', tali' ishtapa' pliers, wire
cutters [tali' isht tapa+']
talishtaatakka'li' door hook [tali' isht
aatakka'li+']
talittatakali' see tali' ittatakali'
<talkachi> in atalkachit máa,
ittontalkachi, yaakni' talkachi'
(ataaya, tala}
<talkáyya'chi> in atalkáyya'chi,
ittontalkáyya'chi
tálla'a to stand, be located, exist (sg.
inan. subj., especially one with a flat
bottom or one thought of as having
open space above a flat bottom, such
as a house or cup) (3); to lie on one's
back (primarily used jokingly) (sg.
subj.) (I); to stand on a flat bottom or
lie on one's back in (a place) (sg.
subj.) (I;3)—ggr. of <talaa>, xgr. of
tala [-CPR] [+PR] {v2. talaali; ngr.
taláa; dl. tállo'wa; tpl. talowat máa;
intálla'a}
tállakchi to be tangled in
something—ggr. of talakchi
(intallakchi: to be braked}
tallaláli to lie on one's back and kick
like a kitten (3)—rmgr. of talaali
<tálla'li> in ontálla'li—ggr. of talaali

25

tállasbi

tállasbi ggr. of talasbi
tállo'wa to stand, be located, exist (dl.
inan. subj. with flat bottoms and
open space above) (3); to lie on
one's backs (dl. subj.) (primarily
used jokingly) (I); to stand on flat
bottoms or lie on one's backs in (a
place) (dl. subj.) (I;3) {v2. talohli;
sg.tálla'a; tpl. talowat máa}
tállo'wa ggr. of taloowa
<taloha>, <talowa> in oka' taloha',
talowat máa {v2. talohli}
talohat máa see talowat máa
talohli to set up (pl. flat-bottomed
inan. obj.) (I;3) {v1. tállo'wa,
<taloha>; sg. obj. talaali}
talohmáa see talowat máa
talohówa hngr. of taloowa
<talop> in intalop
tal-oshik, (ER) taloshik gravel
(smaller than tali' bosholli') [tali'
<oshik>]
<talowa> see <taloha>
talowat máa, talohat máa, talohmáa
to stand, be located, exist (tpl. inan.
subj. with flat bottoms and open
space above) (3); to lie on one's
backs (tpl subj.) (a joke) (I); to stand
on flat bottoms or lie on one's backs
in (a place) (tpl. subj.) (I;3) [<talowa>
/ <taloha>+t] {sg. tálla'a; dl.
tállo'wa}
taloowa to sing (I); to sing (a song)
(I;3) [+PR] [+CPR] {ggr. tállo'wa;
hngr. talohówa; ngr. talówa}
taloowa alhiha choir § Taloowa
alhihaat taloowaka hanglolitok. I
heard the choir sing.
taloowa' song, hymn; singer; singing
event (IIIp) [taloowa+'] § hattak
taloowa': singer
taloowachi to make sing (I;II)
[taloowa+chi] § Sataloowachitok.
She made me sing.

taloowapiichi' song leader, choir
director [taloowa' apiichi+']
talówa ngr. of taloowa
talha to be whittled, to have the sides
cut off, be cut to shape (3) {v2.
talhlhi}
talhipa, (ER) talhlhi'pa hundred
(usually used with another number,
as in the following expressions)
talhipa chaffa one hundred; to be one
hundred in number (3) (mainly
subr.) {talhipa chaffaka óna}
talhipa chaffacha awa chaffa, (EP)
talhipa chaffacha pokko'laachaffa
one hundred eleven; to be one
hundred eleven in number (3)
[chaffa+cha]
talhipa chaffacha chaffa, (AB) talhipa
chaffana chaffa one hundred one;
to be one hundred one in number
(3) [chaffa+cha/na]
talhipa chaffacha pokkó'li, (AB)
talhipa chaffacha pokoli one
hundred ten; to be one hundred ten
in number (3) [chaffa+cha]
talhipa chaffacha tochchí'na one
hundred three; to be one hundred
three in number (3) [chaffa+cha]
talhipa chaffacha toklo, (AB) talhipa
chaffana toklo one hundred two; to
be one hundred two in number (3)
(other expressions for numbers
higher than one hundred are
formed the same way for most
speakers: talhipa plus the number
of hundreds plus cha plus the
number for the tens and ones)
[chaffa+cha/na]
talhipa chaffaka óna to be one
hundred in number, to reach one
hundred in number (I) (óna may be
used to express a non-third-person
subj. of most higher number verbs)
[(talhipa chaffa)+ka] § Talhipa

chaffaka ilona. There are a hundred of us, Our number reaches one hundred.

talhipa hánna'cha chaffa six hundred one; to be six hundred one in number (3) [hanna'li+cha]

talhipa hanná'li six hundred; to be six hundred in number (3)

talhipa toklo two hundred; to be two hundred in number (3)

talhipa toklocha chaffa two hundred one; to be two hundred one in number (3) [toklo+cha]

talhipa sipokni' thousand (usually used with a following number) [sipokni+']

talhipa sipokni' chaffa one thousand; to be one thousand in number (3)

talhipa sipokni' chaffacha chaffa one thousand one; to be one thousand one in number (3) [chaffa+cha]

talhipa sipokni' chaffaka óna to be one thousand in number, to reach one thousand in number (I) [(talhipa sipokni' chaffa)+ka] § Talhipa sipokni' chaffaka ilona. There are a thousand of us.

talhipa sipokni' toklo two thousand; to be two thousand in number (3) (and so on with other numbers)

talhko buckskin (or some other type of leather)

talhlhá'pi five; to be five in number (I) [+PR]

talhlhá'pi áyyo'ka to be in (organized) groups of five (I , —)

talhlhá'pi bíyyi'ka to be in (scattered) groups of five (I , —) § Iitalhlha'pi biyyi'ka. We are in (scattered) groups of five.

talhlhi to whittle (I;3) {v1. talha; ggr. tá'lhlhi; hngr. tahálhlhi; ngr. tálhlhi}

talhlhi'pa see talhipa

tálhlho'fa ggr. of talhofa

talhofa to come loose (for instance, of a rope or something inan.) (sg. subj.) (3) {v2. talhoffi; ggr. tálhlho'fa; sg. obj. talhoffichi; pl. subj. talhohli}

talhoffi to be apart, separated; to be loose, free, to get loose, run loose (sg. subj.) (I / II) [-CPR] [+PR] {v1. talhofa; hngr. talhohóffi; sg. obj. talhoffichi; pl. subj. talhohli; intalhoffi: to pull away from, go off from}

talhoffichi to let (someone) go, release, turn loose (sg. or hum. obj.) (I;II); to loosen (one's belt), unlatch (a door hook) (I;3) [talhoffi+chi] {sg. subj. talhofa, talhoffi} § Potalhoffi'shna iliyyatok. He let us go and we went.

talhohli to get loose (pl. subj.) (3) {hngr. talhohóli; ngr. talhóhli; sg. subj. talhofa, talhoffi; pl. obj. talhoochi}

talhohlínchi ngr. of talhoochi

talhohóffi hngr. of talhoffi

talhohóli hngr. of talhohli

talhoochi to let loose (pl. obj.) (I;3) [+SC] [talhohli+chi] {ngr. talhohlínchi; sg. obj. talhoffichi}

talhóhli ngr. of talhohli

talhpak winnowing basket

talhpakha', (LR, AB, ER, MJ) talhpakka', (LF) takpalhka', (AW) ishtalhpakka' cactus: especially, prickly pear

támmo'wa ggr. of tamowa

tamowa to go away, elope (nonsg. subj.) (I); to be lost (pl. subj.) (II) [+taha] {sg. kaniya; ggr. támmo'wa; intamowa: to lose (pl. obj.)}

tanampaa-asha' gun store, arsenal, armory [tanampo aa-asha']

tanampaahalalli' trigger [tanampo aa+halalli+']

tanampaalhpi' stock (of a gun) [tanampo aalhpi']

tanampalhlhi', tanampo alhlhi' bow [tanampo alhlhi+']

tanampalhlhi' inaki' arrow [im+naki']

tanampincholok muzzle (of a gun) [tanampo im+cholok]

tanampincholok toklo' double-barreled shotgun [toklo+']

tanampiskanno', (CP) tanampo iskanno' .22 shotgun [tanampo <iskanno>+']

tanampishto', (CP) tanamposhto' cannon, machine gun [tanampo ishto+']

tanampishto' inaki', tanampo ishto' inaki' cannonball [im+naki']

tanampishto' inak-oshi' machine gun bullets [im+nak-oshi']

tanampihottok gunpowder [tanampo im+hottok]

tanampishokcha' holster [tanampo im+shokcha']

tanampo gun (tanap)

tanampo alhlhi' see tanampalhlhi'

tanampo falaa' Winchester rifle [falaa+']

tanampo holba' toy gun, squirt gun

tanampo ishto' inaki' see tanampishto' inaki'

tanampo nak-oshi' .22 shotgun (CP)

tanampo nak-oshilawa' shotgun [nak-oshi' ilawa+']

tanampo palhki' machine gun (CP) [palhki+']

tanampo pokoli tochchi'na tochchi'na .30-30 rifle (CP)

tanampo pokta' double-barreled shotgun

tanamposhkololi' handgun: revolver, pistol

tanamposhkololi' inaki' handgun bullet [im+naki']

tanap war (IIIp) {intanap, tanampo, tannap}

tanap turnip [from the English]

tanap homma' beet (WB) [homma+']

tanap imilhlha' wild turnip [imilhlha+']

Tanap Ittibi' some major war: especially, the Civil War, but also World War I, World War II, etc. [ittibi+']

tanchalhfola' see tanchi' alhfola'

tanchalhposha' parched corn, roasted corn [tanchi' alhposha+']

tanchapi' corncob [tanchi' api']

tanchapinka' see tanchi' apinka'

tanchaabotooli' mill; place where corn is ground [tanchi' aa+botooli+']

tanchaafolowa' mill; place where corn is ground [tanchi' aa+folowa+']

tanchaahollosi' flat part of a mortar [tanchi' aa+hollosi+']

tanchaahosi' mortar for grinding corn [tanchi' aa+hosi+']

tanchaalhto' silo, (AB) barn [tanchi' aalhto']

tanchaapalha' place where corn is split [tanchi' aa+palha+']

tanchaashafa' corn grater [tanchi' aa+shafa+']

tanchi' corn (vegetable); corn on the foot

tanchi' alhfola', tanchalhfola' corn on the cob [alhfola+']

tanchi' apinka', tanchapinka' whole corn, corn on the cob [apinka+']

tanchi' bota', tabota home-ground cornmeal , parched corn flour [bota+']

tanchi' champoli' sweet corn [champoli+']

tanchi' chillowa' corn off the cob, corn kernels [chillowa+']

tanchi' folowa' type of cornmeal [folowa+']

tanchi' himona' see tanchi' himona' waa'

tanchi' himona' palaska' fresh corn bread (made with grated raw sweet corn) [<palaska>+'] {tanchi' palaska'}

tanchi' himona waa', tanchi' himona' roasting ears of corn [waa+']

tanchi' hishi' corn shucks

tanchi' holisso' type of corn with kernels of different colors [holisso+']

tanchi' hollapi' corn on the cob

tanchi' holhponi' corn cooked off the cob [holhponi+']

tanchi' homma' red corn [homma+']

tanchi' hoshollo' corn hulls

tanchi' ishmashka', tanchishmashka' winnowing fan [isht mashka+']

tanchi' ihina', tanch-ihina' row of corn [im+hina']

tanchi' kallo' type of solid white hard corn [kallo+']

tanchi' kawaski' Indian corn, a type of corn used for making pishofa or banaha [kawaski+']

tanchi' kobolli' undeveloped corncob (less than three inches long—used for cattle feed)

tanchi' lakchi' corn hulls (burned and used to make coffee)

tanchi' lakna' (LF, MJ, TP), (AB) talakna' yellow corn (AB, TP, MJ); field corn (LF) [tanchi' lakna+']

tanchi' lobo' dried roasted corn (cooked and eaten in the winter); whole corn; hominy

tanchi' okchamali', tanchokchamali' new (green) corn [okchamali+'] {tanchokchama'li'}

tanchi' osaapa aawaa' field corn (ER)

[aa+waa+']

tanchi' palaska' corn bread (made with cornmeal) [<palaska>+']

tanchi' palaska' hawashko' sour corn bread [hawashko+']

tanchi' palaskalhposha' corn bread cooked directly over the fire [tanchi' palaska' alhposha+']

tanchi' palha' grits [palha+']

tanchi' patha' hominy corn (WB) [patha+']

tanchi' pashi', (ER) tanchi' ipashi' corn silk, especially the brown part that sticks out at the end of an unshucked ear [ipashi']

tanchi' pinha' seed corn

tanchi' sokahli', (TP) tanchi' sokwaali', (TP) tasokwaali', (WB) tanchi' tokahli' popcorn [sokahli+']

tanchi' sokahli' champoli' crackerjack [champoli+']

tanchi' tohbi' white corn [tohbi+']

tanchi' walokshi' corn all ready to pick and eat [walokshi+']

tanchi' woksholi' corn silk [woksholi+']

tanchishhayowalhchi' type of basket or colander used for rinsing cleaned corn [tanchi' isht hayowalhchi+']

tanchishhollosi' wooden pestle for pounding corn [tanchi' isht hollosi+']

tanchishmashka' see tanchi' ishmashka'

tanchishpiha' corn shovel [tanchi' ishpiha']

tanchishtani' grain hopper [tanchi' isht ani+']

tanchishtashiila' corn dumpling, cornmeal mush [tanchi' isht ashiila+']

tanchishto', (MJ) tanchi'shto' , (WB) tanchi' hochito' type of large corn; (AB, MJ) field corn [tanchi'

335

tanchįhina'

ishto/hichito+']
tanchįhina' see tanchi' įhina'
tanchokchama'li' blue corn [tanchi'
okchamali+'] {tanchi' okchamali'}
tanchoshi' sweet corn (LF) [tanchi'
oshi']
<tanna> in tanna' {v2. tanni;
nantanna'}
tanna' crocheted or knitted article
[<tanna>+'] § Naafka yappat tanna'
ki'yo. This dress isn't crocheted.
<tannafo'> in oski' tannafo'
{holhtánnaffo, tannasho'}
tannap reverse, other side; on the
other side of, on the far side of;
other (follows the name of a body
part, generally a paired one)
{intannap, tanap} § Tannapat
chokma'si. The other side is pretty.
I Tannapak anta. She lives on the
other side (of the street). I salbak
tannap: my other hand, my hand
on the other side (of my body) I
Holisso tannap bohlili. I put it on
the other (far) side of the book.
tannap pila'si to be on just one side
(3) [pila+a'si]
tannap pila'sit yátto'fa to have a soft
spot (3) [(tannap pila'si)+t]
tannasho', (HS, TP) tannosho', (WB)
tanashsho', (CM) tannisho', (LR)
taanasho' willow
tannasho' pofalli' willow seeds
tanni to weave, darn, crochet, knit
(I;3) {v1. <tanna>; ggr. tá'nni; hngr.
tahánni; nantanni}
tánno'wį, ittánno'wa to pass, go by;
to walk to walk around (dl. subj.)
{T}—ggr. of tanǫ́wa, <tanowa> {sg.
ų tpl. tanohǫ́wa (pass by), tanǫ́wa
(walk)}
tanⱮ .ǫ́wa, ittanohǫ́wa to pass, go by
(tpl. subj.) (I)—hngr. of tanǫ́wa,
<tanowa> {sg. áa; dl. tánno'wa}

<tanowa> [itti+a+nǫwa ?] {ggr.
tánno'wa; hngr. tanohǫ́wa; ngr.
tanǫ́wa}
tanǫ́wa, ittanǫ́wa to walk, walk
around (tpl. subj.) (I)—ngr. of
<tanowa> {ggr. tánno'wa: to pass, go
by, walk (dl. subj.); hngr. tanohǫ́wa:
to pass, go by (tpl. subj.); sg. áa}
tángla while (aux.—used only on
dependent clauses, with a following
subordinator such as +kat or +ka or
+cha)—ngr. of <takla> {aatángla,
ibaatángla} § Hashtaloowatok
kilimpa tanglaka. You sang while
we ate. I Lynnat anompǫli
tanglacha ittolatok. While Lynn was
talking she fell.
tangla' aya, tangla' áa to go with, go
along with (pl. obj.) (II = obj , I =
subj) [tangla+'] § Potangla'
ishiyyatok. You went with us.
tapa to be cut or pulled in two, to be
cut off (sg. subj.) (3) [+PR] [+CPR]
{v2. tabli; pl. subj. katolha}
tapaháski hngr. of tapaski
tapaski to be thin, see-through,
transparent, watery (II) [+CPR] [-PR]
{ggr. táppaski; hngr. tapaháski; ngr.
tapáski}
tapáski ngr. of tapaski
tappak-oshi' basket (LP) [talhpak
oshi']
táppaski ggr. of tapaski
tasá'li ggr. of tasahli
tasaháli hngr. of tasahli
tasahli to scream, yell; to make a
loud, insistent noise (like an alarm
clock, for instance) (I) {ggr. tasá'li;
hngr. tasaháli; ngr. tasáhli;
ontasahli: to scream at; intasahli: to
holler to; tastachi}
tasaachi to make yell (I;II)
[tasahli+chi] § Iktasa'chokitok. He
didn't make him yell.

336

tasáhli ngr. of tasahli
<tasạli> in baktasạli
tasiitili see ittasiitili
tasiitohli see ittasiitohli
tastá'chi ggr. of tastachi
tastachi to talk loudly (I) {ggr.
  tastá'chi; tasahli}
tashan-kachi to coil around, go in the
  shape of a spring (3)
tashayyi' see yaakni' tashayyi'
tashka-chipota', (EP, MJ) tashka-
  chipota, (AB) tashka soldier
  [chipota+']
tashka-chipota' apiichi' officer
tashka-chipota' aya to go join the
  armed forces (I)
tashka-chipota' ibaafóyyokha to be in
  the armed forces, be in the service
  (I)
tashka-chipota' ibaaholhtina to
  enlist, be drafted: to join the army
  or other branch of the armed forces
  (I)
Tashka-chipota' Ịnittak Veterans'
  Day [im+nittak]
tashka-chipota' ịshkoboka' officer,
  general
tashka-chipotaa-asha' barracks
  [tashka-chipota' aa-asha']
tashka-chipotịnaafokha military
  uniform [tashka-chipota'
  im+naafokha]
tashki to lie down (punctual), to go
  to bed (I); to lie down in (a place)
  (I;3) {hngr. tahạshki}
Tataawa name of an Indian tribe (CC)
<tawaa> in tawwalínchi [itti+awa ?]
  {ggr. táwwa'a; ngr. tawạa}
tawạa to be both, to be two (perhaps,
  but not necessarily, together) (often
  subr.) (I); to be both, be two with
  (perhaps, but not necessarily,
  together) (often subr.; logical subj. is
  sg., but marked subj. is collective

dl.) (I;3)—ngr. of táwwa'a, <tawaa>
  § Lynn iitawạakat Charles iipịstok.
  Lynn and I saw Charles (not
  necessarily together).
táwwa'a to be both, to be or do
  together (dl. subj.) (often subr.) (I);
  to live in sin, shack up, be together
  (dl. subj) (I); to do with, be together
  with (often subr.; logical subj. is sg.,
  but marked subj. is collective dl.)
  (I;3); to live in sin with (sg. subj., sg.
  obj.) (I;3); to be partners with (I;3)—
  ggr. of <tawaa> {ngr. tawạa: to be
  both (not necessarily together);
  áwwali'chi, iláwwi'li} § Lynn
  iitawwa'at iihilhatok. Lynn and I
  danced (together). | Charlesat Lynn
  iitawwa'ạ popịstok. Charles saw
  Lynn and me (together). | Lynnakọ
  tawwa'ali. I'm shacking up with
  Lynn.
tawwalínchi to have two (men or
  women) as spouses or lovers at the
  same time (I;II) {<tawaa>;
  áwwali'chi}
tayokhana' in itti' tayokhana'
táyya'ha to be ragged—ygr. of taha
táyya'hli ygr. of tahli
táyyakba ygr. of takba
taa okay, all right, oh, come on!
  (exclamation showing resignation,
  irritation, or even excitement)
taakcha' edge; on the edge of
  {taakchaka'; taakchạli} § Aaimpa'
  taakcha' iksaashlitok. I fixed the
  edge of the table.
taakchaka' edge; selvedge; on the
  edge of {taakcha'; taakchakạli} §
  aaimpa' taakchaka' on the edge of
  the table
taakchakạli' (moving) through along
  the edge of {taakchaka'; taakchạli'}
taakchạli' (moving) through along
  the edge of {taakcha'; taakchakạli} §

337

taakchili'

Iss<u>o</u>shat aaimpa' taakch<u>a</u>li' <u>a</u>atok.
The bug walked along the edge of
the table.
taakchili' chewing gum
taakchili' api' gum tree
taala', daala' dollar [from the
English]
taani to get up, to get out of bed; to
rise from the dead (I) {hngr. tah<u>á</u>ni}
taani' lamb's quarters (plant)
taanichi to get (someone) up (I;II)
[taani+chi]
t<u>a</u>bota see tanchi' bota'
t<u>a</u>fola sofkey (Creek sour corn dish)
[tanchi' folowa] {t<u>a</u>shfolowa'}
t<u>a</u>fola-hawashko' sour sofkey [t<u>a</u>fola
hawashko+']
t<u>á</u>ha ngr. of taha
t<u>a</u>hishi', t<u>a</u>ishi' corn shucks [tanchi'
hishi']
t<u>á</u>hli ngr. of tahli
t<u>a</u>lakna' see tanchi' lakna'
t<u>a</u>lobo any type of cooked whole
corn: especially, hominy [tanchi'
lobo']
t<u>á</u>lhlhi ngr. of talhlhi
t<u>a</u>shfoloha' see t<u>a</u>shfolowa'
t<u>a</u>shfoloha' palaska' see t<u>a</u>shfolowa'
palaska'
t<u>a</u>shfolowa', t<u>a</u>shfoloha' cornmeal
[tanchi' foloha+'] {t<u>a</u>fola}
t<u>a</u>shfolowa' palaska', t<u>a</u>shfoloha'
palaska' corn bread
t<u>a</u>shpishofa, pishofa pishofa (dish
made with split corn cooked with
pork) [tanchi' pishofa]
t<u>a</u>shposhi' cornmeal [tanchi' poshi']
t<u>a</u>shshokkata' type of white
corn[tanchi' shokhata']
ti'f ti'f ti'f aachi see tif tif tif aachi
tí'hli ggr. of tihli
ti'k ti'k ti'k aachi see tik tik tik aachi
ti'p ti'p ti'p aachi see tip tip tip aachi
tí'wa to lie down, to be lying (sg.

subj.); to be located (of a typically
lying subj.—for instance, money in
the bank) (I); to be located lying in (a
place) (I;3) [-CPR] [-PR] {dl. káyya'ha;
tpl. kahat m<u>á</u>a; intí'wa: to give
birth; tó'wa ; ittí'wa}
tí'wa ggr. of tiwa
tí'wwi ggr. of tiwwi
<tiballi> in intiballi, tiballichi
tiballí'chi ggr. of tiballichi
tiballichi to miss (a mark) (I;3) (used
with preceding prt. specifying how
the attempt to hit the mark was
made; prt. may include an obj.
prefix); to strike (in baseball) (I)
[<tiballi>+chi] {ggr. tiballí'chi} §
Issot ishtiballichitok. You missed
(when you hit). | Chissot
tiballichilitok. I missed hitting you.
tibba-takaachi see tikba-takaachi
tibba-takaali' see tikba-takaali'
tif tif tif aachi, ti'f ti'f ti'f aachi to
make the sound of a cat hissing
(expressive) (I)
tiha to be plucked (of a chicken, or a
chicken's feathers); to be pulled (of
weeds); to look plucked, have few
feathers (of a chicken) (3) {v2. tihli;
hngr. tih<u>í</u>ha; sg. t<u>i</u>fa (of one feather,
weed)}
tih<u>í</u>fa hngr. of t<u>i</u>fa
tih<u>í</u>ha hngr. of tiha
tih<u>í</u>li hngr. of tihli
tih<u>í</u>wa hngr. of tiwa
tih<u>í</u>wwi hngr. of tiwwi
tihli to pluck (a chicken), to pull
(teeth, a few at a time, or a lot of
hair, or weeds) (pl. obj.) (I;3) {v1.
tiha; ggr. tí'hli; hngr. tih<u>í</u>li; ngr.
t<u>í</u>hli; sg. obj. t<u>i</u>fi}
tik tik tik aachi, ti'k ti'k ti'k aachi to
make the sound of a clock ticking
(expressive) (I) [influenced by
English?]

338

tikahámbi to be weakly, sickly—
hngr. of tikahbi
tikahbi to be tired (II) [+CPR] [-PR]
{ggr. tíkkahbi; hngr. tikahámbi: to be
weakly, sickly; ngr. tik<u>á</u>hbi; ygr.
tikáyya'hbi}
tikáyya'hbi ygr. of tikahbi
tik<u>á</u>hbi ngr. of tikahbi
<tikba> in intikba, tikba' {ngr.
<tíngba>}
tikba' front; in front of, facing (II);
between the legs, crotch (IIp)
[<tikba>+'] {tikb<u>a</u>li'; tingba'} §
Satikba' hikki'yatok. He's standing
in front of me (either facing or not).
| Chitikba' m<u>o</u>m<u>a</u> pisatok. He's
looking at everything between your
legs, at your whole crotch area.
tikba' afammi last year
tikba' imayya, tikbimayya to lead
(I;III) [tikba' im+ayya] § Tikba'
ishimayyatok. You led them.
tikba' ishtaya to lead, be the leader:
especially, to lead a group in singing
(I) (see ishtaya) {tingba' ishtaya;
tikbishtimayya} § Tikba'
ishtishiyya'chi. You're going to be
the (song) leader.
tikbahihínka hngr. of tikbayka
tikbahínka ngr. of tikbayka
tikba-takálli'chi ggr. of tikba-takaachi
tikba-takaachi, tibba-takaachi to put
on an apron (I) [-SC] [tikba-
takaali'+chi] {ggr. tikba-tákkali'chi,
tikba-takálli'chi} § Iktikba-taka'cho.
She didn't put on an apron.
tikba-takaali', tibba-takaali', (MJ, TJ)
tikba' takaali', (MC, HS) tibbi-
takaali', (VB) tibbi' takaali' apron,
bib, breechcloth (IIIp) [tikba'
takaali+']
tikba-tákkali'chi ggr. of tikba-takaachi
tikbal<u>i</u>sht anokfilli see tikb<u>a</u>li'
anokfilli

tikbáy'ka ggr. of tikbayka
tikbayínka ngr. of tikbayka
tikbayka, tikba-hika to be a dance or
song leader (I) (var. tikba-hika is not
used with endings) [*tikba' hika]
{ggr. tikbáy'ka; hngr. tikbahihínka;
ngr. tikbahínka, tikbayínka} §
Ishtikbaykatam? Were you a dance
leader?
tikb<u>a</u>li' (moving) in front of (II)
{tikba'} § Satikb<u>a</u>li' <u>a</u>atok. He went
on up in front of me.
tikb<u>a</u>li' anokfilli, tingba' anokfilli,
tikbal<u>i</u>sht anokfilli to think ahead,
plan (I)
tikbishtimayya to lead in singing, be
a lead singer for (I;III) [tikba' isht
*imayya] {tikba' ishtaya} §
Tikbishtishpomayyatok. You lead
us in singing.
tikboklhiliaash the night before
(some day in the past), the night
before last [tikba' oklhili+aash]
Tiki'li' Chickasaw woman's name
tikili to cuddle up to (I;II) {ggr.
tíkki'li: to touch, lean against; ngr.
tik<u>í</u>li: to go, be positioned next to;
<tíkkohli>}
tikilihínchi hngr. of tikiichi
tikilínchi ngr. of tikiichi
tikisili' in itti' tikisili' [ittikisili+']
tikiichi to put ° next to, make °
touch, push ° against (I;II;3) [-SC]
[tikili+chi] {hngr. tikiihínchi,
tikilihínchi; ngr. tikilínchi} §
Aboopootaka' satikiichitok. He
pushed me against the wall.
tikiihínchi hngr. of tikiichi
tik<u>í</u>li, pittik<u>í</u>li to go, stand, be
positioned next to—ngr. of tikili
tíkkahbi ggr. of tikahbi
tíkki'li to be right next to, touch, lean
against—ggr. of tikili
tikkit ticket [from the English]

339

<tíkkohli>

<tíkkohli> in ittitíkkohli {tikili}
tili'kishokcha flour sack [tili'ko'
im+shokcha]
tili'ko', (LF, MJ) tilliko', (EP) tilliko
flour; (LF) biscuit [from Spanish
trigo]
tili'ko' aalhkomo', tili'ko'
aaolhkomo' wooden kneading pan
or tray [aa+olhkomo+']
tili'ko' aaolhkomo' see tili'ko'
aalhkomo'
tili'ko' bosholli' pieces of foreign
material in flour that won't go
through a sifter
tili'ko' issatapo'li' rolling pin (CC)
[isht satapo'li+']
tili'ko' lakchi' pieces of foreign
material in flour that won't go
through a sifter
tili'ko' lakna' whole wheat flour
[lakna+']
tili'ko' niha' gravy [niha+']
tili'ko' nihi' wheat
tili'ko' okommo to make biscuits,
bread, or anything using dough (I)
tili'ko' palaska' baking-powder
biscuit
tili'ko' panaa' twisted noodles
[panaa+']
tili'ko' shila' pieces of foreign
material in flour that won't go
through a sifter [shila+']
tili'ko' tohbi' white flour [tohbi+']
tili'kolhkomo' dough, batter [tili'ko'
olhkomo+']
tili'kolhkomo' shila' spaghetti,
macaroni, noodles [shila+']
tilikpi to be round (nonhum. subj.)
(3) {ggr. tíllikpi: to be round, dull,
blunt}
tíllikpi to be round; to be dull (of a
knife); to be blunt (of a pencil)—ggr.
of tilikpi
tíllo'fa ggr. of tilofa'si

Tilobli' Hilha' Jump Dance—a
Choctaw dance also danced by
Chickasaws [from Choctaw tilobli
"jump"+']
tilofa to have the head or top taken
or broken off, to break one's neck
(sg. subj.) (II) {v2. tiloffi; hngr.
tilohófa; ngr. tilófa; pl. tilohli}
tilofánchi see tilofánchi
tiloffi to take, break the head or top
off; to break the neck of (sg. obj.)
(I;II) {v1. tilofa; hngr. tilohóffi; pl.
obj. tilohchi}
tilohchi to take off the tops, heads
(pl. obj.) (I;II) [-SC] [tilohli+chi] {sg.
obj. tiloffi}
tilohli to have the heads or tops
broken off, to have broken necks
(pl. subj.) (II) [+T] {hngr. tilohóli; sg.
tilofa}
tilohófa hngr. of tilofa'si
tilohóffi hngr. of tiloffi
tilohóli hngr. of tilohli
tilófa ngr. of tilofa, tilofa'si
tilofa'si to be short (II) [tilofa+a'si]
{ggr. tíllo'fa; hngr. tilohófa; ngr.
tilófa}
tilofachi to make short, shorten (I;3)
(usually in ngr.) [tilofa+chi] {ngr.
tilofánchi, tilofánchi}
tilofánchi ngr. of tilofachi
tilhaha see tilhaa
tilhaháa hngr. of tilhaa
tilhalhchi to be peeled (of an apple)
(3) [+T] {v2. tilhlhichi}
tilhaa, tilhaha to run, to run for
office (pl. subj.) (I) [+taha] {v2. tilhili;
hngr. tilhaháa; intilhaha: to run
against (AW); sg. malili}
tilhaachi to make run, race (pl. obj.)
(I;II) [+SC] [tilhaa+chi] {hngr.
tilhaahánchi} § Potilhaashtok. He
made us run, He raced us.
tilhaahánchi hngr. of tilhaachi

<tilhiffi> in issot atiilhiffi {v1.
<tílhlhi'fa>}
<tilhiffichi> in issot atiilhiffichi
tilhili, tilhiili to send away, send
back, scare off; to make run, run off;
to fire (pl. obj.) (I;II) {v1. tilhaa; hngr.
tilhihíli; sg. obj. chaffichi (send),
malichi (make run)} § Potilhiitok,
Potilhilitok. He made us run, He
ran us off, He fired us.
tilhihíli hngr. of tilhili
<tílhlhi'fa> in atílhlhi'fa {v2.
<tilhiffi>}
tilhlhichi to peel (an apple) (I;3) {v1.
tilhalhchi}
timimí'chi to make a loud noise
(with, or of, a big drum, for
example) (3) [+SC]
timiiyachi to buzz (of a bee, airplane)
(3) {hngr. timiiyahánchi; ngr.
timiiyánchi}
timiiyahánchi hngr. of timiiyachi
timiiyánchi ngr. of timiiyachi
<tíngba> in tingba'—ngr. of <tikba>
tingba' first, the first one [<tingba>+']
{tikba'} § ahattak tingba': my first
husband
tingba' anokfilli see tikbali' anokfilli
tingba' áyya'sha to be long ago §
Tingba' ayya'shattook. It was a long
time ago. | Tingba' ayya'shahma
ahantattook. He lived long ago.
tingba' ayya'shaka' long ago [(tingba'
ayya'sha)+ka'] § Tingba'
ayya'shakaak attook. It was long
ago.
tingba' ishtaya, tingbishtaya to start
it, start a fight (I) (see ishtaya) {tikba'
ishtaya} § Tingbishthashiyyatok.
You guys started it.
tingba' pílla áyya'sha to be long, long
ago § Tingba' pilla ayya'shattook. It
was very long ago.
<tingbalichi> [tingba'+li+chi] {ngr.

tingbalínchi}
<tingbalínchi> in tingbalísht—ngr.
of <tingbalichi>
tingbalísht see tingbalisht anoli,
tingbalisht aya, tingbalisht imanoli
[<tingbalinchi>+t]
tingbalísht anoli to predict, see in the
future (I); to tell the plans of (I;II) §
Tingbalisht asanotok. He told what I
was going to do.
tingbalísht aya to go on ahead (I) §
Tingbalisht ishiyya'ni. You should
go on ahead.
tingbalísht imanoli to tell the future
to (I;III) [im+(tingbalisht anoli)>
tingbalisht *imanoli § Tingbalisht
amanotok. He told me the future.
tingbishtaya see tingba' ishtaya
tip tip tip aachi, ti'p ti'p ti'p aachi to
make the sound of (relatively
small) bare feet walking or of
fingertips drumming (expressive) (I)
{<bitiipa>, <tipipí'chi>,
<típpikli'chi>, <tiipa>}
<tipipí'chi> in ittitipipí'chi {tip tip
tip aachi, típpikli'chi}
<típpikli'chi> in ittitíppikli'chi
{<tipipí'chi>}
tisho, (CM) tisho' assistant to an
Indian doctor, who watches his
enclosure (IIIp)
Tishohminko', (CM) Tisho' Iminko'
Tishomingo, Oklahoma [tisho
minko']
titta sister (children's word—only
used in one family?) (LR, MS) [from
English sister, perhaps influenced by
tikba' ?]
tiwa to open (by itself) (3) [+CPR]
[+PR] {v2. tiwwi, tiwwichi; ggr.
tí'wa; hngr. tihíwa; ngr. tíwa;
tiwwichi}
tiwa'chi to stir (I;3) [+SC] {v1.
tiwa'kalhchi}

tiwa'kahánchi to move around in a swarm (pl. subj.) (3) {tiwa'kalhchi}

tiwa'kahálhchi hngr. of tiwa'kalhchi

tiwa'kalhchi to be stirred; to agitate (in a washing machine, for example) (3); to mill around, come and go in (a place) (pl. subj.) (I;3) {v2. tiwa'chi; hngr. tiwa'kahálhchi; tiwa'kahánchi}

tiwabli to explode, blow up (something); to let go of (balloons); to tear up, tear the covering or clothes from (I;II); to give a benediction, dismiss a congregation (I); to adjourn (a meeting) (I;3) {v1. tiwapa}

tiwapa to explode (3); to be torn up, beaten up, torn down (3); to be dismissed, given a benediction (pl. subj.) (I); to be over (of a church service) (3); to scatter, go off in all directions, disperse (I) {v2. tiwabli; ggr. tíwwa'pa: to be open, over, to adjourn} § Hashholiitoblikma iitiwwa'pa'chi. If you pass the motion, we'll adjourn.

tíwwa'pa to be open (of a door or umbrella) (3); to be over, closed (3); to adjourn a meeting (I) [+PR] [+CPR]—ggr. of tiwapa

tiwwi to open (something) (I;3) {v1. tiwa; ggr. tí'wwi; hngr. tihíwwi; ngr. tíwwi}

tiwwichi to mess up (paper), open (something) all up, tear down (a house or houses) (I;3) {v1. tiwa}

tiyak , (MJ) ittiyak pine; pine tree

tiyak ani' pinecone

tiyak api' pine tree

tiyak bila' pine pitch [bila+']

tiyak hishi' pine needles

tiyak okchi' pine pitch

tiyak showa', (MJ) takshowa' turpentine [showa+']

tiyya' in itti' tiyya' [toyya+']

tii, tii' tea [from the English]

tii aalhto' teapot

tii aawaalhaali' teapot [aa+waalhaali+']

tii baaksalhto' loose tea [from English box + alhto+']

tii shokcha alhto' see tii shokchalhto'

tii shokchalhto', tii shokcha alhto' tea bag [shokcha alhto+']

tii' see tii

tiibii TB, tuberculosis [from the English]

tiibli to reinjure a sore spot, hurt oneself in the same place again (I); to reinjure (a body part) (I;3) {v1. <tiipa>; tiipo'li: keep on reinjuring a sore spot, noktiibli, <hitibli> ?} § Salbak tiiblilitok. I hurt my hand again.

tiik female—only used in complex expressions like ofi' tiik, issoba tiik {intiik, oshiitiik}

tiika'ti' dirt dauber, mud dauber (wasp)

tiika'ti' losa' type of dirt dauber [losa+']

tiima to spread the tail (of a turkey, peacock, or other bird) (I)

<tiipa> in intiipa, noktiipa {v2. tiibli; ombitiipa, <tiipo'wa>}

tiipo'li to keep on reinjuring oneself in the same place (I); to keep reinjuring (a body part) (I;3) {v1. <tiipo'wa>; tiibli: reinjure a sore spot; <hitiipo'li> ?} § Salbak tiipo'lili. I keep hurting my hand.

<tiipo'wa> in intiipo'wa {v2. tiipo'li; <tiipa>}

tifa to fall out (of a tooth, hair), to be uprooted (of a tree), to be plucked (of a single feather) (sg. subj.) (3) [+CPR] [+PR] {v2. tifi; hngr. tihífa;

pl. tiha}
tifi to pull out by the roots, to pluck, uproot (a single tooth, hair, feather, weed) (sg. obj.) (I;3) {v1. tifa; pl. obj. tihli}
tíhli ngr. of tihli
tish short form of ittish
tish tish tish aachi to make a noise like a bluejay (expressive) (3)
tish hapi epsom salts (WB)
tish ishtilihammichi' rubbing alcohol (WB) [isht ilihammichi+']
tishkila, (LF) ittishkila' bluejay, jaybird
tíwa ngr. of tiwa
tíwwi ngr. of tiwwi
to'f to'f to'f aachi see tof tof tof aachi
to'k to'k to'k aachi see tok tok tok aachi (make a popping sound)
tó'hbi ggr. of tohbi
tó'hno ggr. of tohno
To'kabi' Chickasaw man's name [abi+']
to'li to play ball (I) {to'wa'}
to'li' baseball, any ball game; baseball player [to'li+']
to'li' fo'kha' padding worn by a baseball umpire [fokha+']
to'li' hattak aabinooli' stadium [aa+binohli+']
to'li' inaafokha baseball uniform [im+naafokha]
to'li' iyaalhipa football helmet, baseball player's cap [im+yaalhipa]
to'li' yaalhipa baseball cap
to'p to'p to'p aachi see top top top aachi
tó'shbi ggr. of toshbi
tó'wa to lie down (in order to have sexual intercourse) (sg. subj.) (I); to lie down (for sex) in (a place) (I;3) {ngr. tówa; ti'wa; ontó'wa: to lie on}
to'wa' ball (toy; umpire's call in baseball) {to'li} § To'wa' chaffa,

to'wa' toklo, to'wa' tochchi'na, to'wa' oshta, aya! Ball one, ball two, ball three, ball four, walk!
to'wa' aachokoshkomo' ball field [aa+chokoshkomo+']
to'wa' aachokoshkomo' ishshoka' alhiipi'ya' see ishshoka' alhiipi'ya'
to'wa' aato'li' baseball diamond [aa+to'li+']
to'wa' bo'li' batter (in baseball) [bo'li+']
to'wa' faapo'chi' pitcher (in baseball)
to'wa' isso to hit the ball (in baseball) (I) § To'wa' issa'chi. He's going to hit the ball, He's up. | To'wa' issolitok. I hit the ball, I got a hit.
to'wa' isso' batter (in baseball) (WB) [(to'wa' isso)+']
to'wa' ishbo'li' baseball bat [isht bo'li+']
to'wa' ishbo'wa', to'wishbo'wa baseball bat [isht bo'wa+']
to'wa' ishbokkaa' baseball bat [isht bokkaa+']
to'wa' ishtisso' baseball bat [isht isso+']
to'wa' ishyokachi', to'wishyokachi', ilbak fokhi' to'wishyokachi' baseball glove, mitt [isht yokachi+']
to'wa' ishyokli' baseball glove, mitt [isht yokli+']
to'wa' yokachi' catcher (in baseball) [yokachi+']
to'wa' yokli' catcher, baseman, fielder (in baseball) (WB) [yokli+']
to'wapiisachi' umpire [to'wa' apiisachi+']
to'waalhopo'chi' basketball hoop [to'wa' aa+lhopochi+']
to'wishbo'wa' see to'wa' ishbo'wa'
to'wishyokachi' see to'wa' ishyokachi'
tó'yya ggr. of toyya
toba to become, to appear as, to take

toba'

the form of (I;3C) (requires an overt preceding complement noun) {hgr. tóhho'ba: to substitute for, act as; holisso toba} § Ihoo tobalitok. I became a woman. | Ishno' tobalitok. I became you. | Inki' tobatok. He became a stepfather. | Chikashshanompaat holisso toba'chi. The Chickasaw language will appear in book form. | Chokka' tobatok. The house was built, finished, made, It (what was there before) became a house.

toba' step-relation—only used in complex expressions such as ishki' toba', inki' toba' etc. [toba+']

tobachi to make, create, bring into existence; to beget (Ct?) (I;II) [toba+chi] § Chihoowaat satobachittook. God made me.

tobaksaakola' coal mine [tobaksi' aa+kola+']

tobaksi' coal

tobaksi' bila' volcano, lava [bila+']

tobaksi' kolli' coal miner [kolli+']

tobaksi' losa' coal (fuel) [losa+']

tobaksi' lowa' lava [lowa+']

tobaksi' shaali' coal car [shaali+']

tobbi' in asonnak tobbi' [tohbi+']

tochchí'na three; to be three in number (I) [+PR]

tochchí'na áyyo'ka to be in (organized) groups of three, to go three by three (I , —) § Kiitochchi'na ayyo'katok. We were in groups of three.

tochchí'na bíyyi'ka to be in (scattered) groups of three (I , —)

tof tof tof aachi, to'f to'f to'f aachi to make the sound of a cat spitting (expressive) (I) {tofa}

tofa to spit (once); to spit (sg. subj.) (I); to spit out, spit up; to spit in (a location) (once or sg. subj.) (I;3)

{hngr. toho̱fa; pl. toftowa; tof tof tof aachi}

tofat kanchi to spit out (I;II) [tofa+t] § Tofat saka̱shtok. He spat me out.

tofat kochchi to spit out (something hard) (I;II) [tofa+t] § Tofat sakochchitok. He spat me out.

tofat lhatabli to spit out (a liquid) (I;3) [tofa+t] § Oka' tofat ishlhatablitam? Did you spit out the water?

toftoho̱wa hngr. of toftowa

toftowa to spit more than once (I); to spit out more than once (I;3); to spit (pl. subj.) (I); to spit up, spit out (pl. subj.) (I;3) {hngr. toftoho̱wa; sg. tofa}

tohbi to be white, pale (II) {ggr. tó'hbi; hgr. tóhhohbi; hngr. toho̱mbi; ngr. to̱hbi; ygr. tóyyo'hbi}

tohbichi to bleach, make white (I;II) [tohbi+chi]

tohboklhili see tooboklhili

tóhho'ba to substitute for, act as, serve as (3;3)—hgr. of toba § Holissoot iyyi' tohho'ba. The book serves as a leg (for the table).

tóhho'mi hgr. of toomi

tóhhobli hgr. of toobli

tóhhohbi hgr. of tohbi

tóhhoshbi hgr. of toshbi

tohi' greens (cabbage, lettuce, mustard greens, etc.)

tohi' chaaha', tohi' chaa' collard greens [chaaha+']

tohi' hawashko' sauerkraut [hawashko+']

tohi' ishkobishto', tohishkobishto' cabbage [ishkobo' ishto+']

tohi' ishkobo' cabbage

tohi' okchamali' greens: especially mustard greens, spinach [okchamali+']

tohi' wasacha' salad [wasacha+']

tohno to hire, employ, commission (for an errand or short-term job); to

344

order (to do something) (I;II) {ggr.
tó'hno; hngr. tohóno; ngr. tóhno} §
Charlesat satohnoho ayalitok.
Charles ordered me to go. |
Issatohnotam ayala'chika? Did you
order me to go? | Potooni
satohnotok. He hired me to
housesit.
tohómbi hngr. of tohbi
tohómbli hngr. of toobli
tohófa hngr. of tofa
tohóno hngr. of tohno
tohóshpa hngr. of toshpa
tohówa to lie around (sg. subj.) (I)
{to'wa}
tohóyya hngr. of toyya
tohto', (TP,CC, AB, MJ) tofto' elm
tok tok tok aachi, to'k to'k to'k aachi
to make the sound of popping
(expressive); to make the sound of a
hen clucking (expressive) (I) {tokafa}
tokafa to explode, go off (of a gun,
firecracker, balloon), to crack (of
thunder), to pop (of one corn
kernel), to backfire (once) (sg. subj.)
(3) {v2. tokaffi; hngr. tokahafa; pl.
tokahli; tok tok tok aachi}
tokaffi to fire (a gun), let off (a
firecracker) (sg. obj.) (I;3) {v1. tokafa;
hngr. tokaháffi; pl. obj. tokaachi}
tokaháfa hngr. of tokafa
tokaháffi hngr. of tokaffi
tokaháli hngr. of tokahli
tokahli to pop, explode (pl. subj.), to
backfire (more than once) (3) {hngr.
tokaháli; sg. tokafa}
tokaachi to fire, make (something)
explode (pl. obj.) (I;3) [-SC]
[tokahli+chi] {sg. obj. tokaffi}
tokbakaháli hngr. of tokbakali
tokbakali to be faded, pale, washed
out, (of tea) weak (II) {ggr.
tokbákka'li; hngr. tokbakaháli; ngr.
tokbakáli; ygr. tokbakáyya'li} §

homma tokbakali: pink
tokbakáyya'li ygr. of tokbakali
tokbakáli ngr. of tokbakali
tokbákka'li ggr. of tokbakali
tokbi to be dull, blunt (3)
tokbolhlhichi, (CC) tokboklhichi,
(AB, CM) tobbolhlhichi, (ER)
tokbolhlhachi, (MJ) tokloboshlichi
to gargle (I / II); to gargle with (I;3)
[tok+] § Hapi tokbolhlhichilitok. I
gargled with salt.
tokbolhlhichichi to make gargle (I;II)
[tokbolhlhichi+chi]
tokchana'pa' wart (IIIp)
tokchana'paat ombínni'li to have a
wart (II) [tokchana'pa'+at]
{tokchana'paat onáyya'sha: have
warts} § Tokchana'paat
asombinni'li. I have a wart.
tokchana'paat onáyya'sha to have
warts (II) [tokchana'pa'+at]
{tokchana'paat ombínni'li: have a
wart} § Tokchana'paat
asonayya'shakat ithanali. I know I
have warts.
tokchi'cho I guess so
tokfohli to have one's mouth water,
lick one's lips (II) [tok+fohli] {hngr.
tokfohóli}
tokfohóli hngr. of tokfohli
tokfol, tokhol type of bush or vine
tokhol see tokfol
toklo two; to be two in number (I)
[+PR] {ngr. tónglo}
toklo áyyo'ka to be two by two, to be
in groups of two (I , —) § Kiitoklo
ayyo'katok. We were in groups of
two.
toklo bíyyi'ka to be in (scattered)
groups of two (I , —) § Iitoklo
biyyi'ka. We were scattered around
in pairs.
toklo' twins [toklo+'] § Toklo' poya.
We are twins. | Chipota toklo' ihoo

nakni' tawwa'a. The twins were a boy and a girl.

toklo'chi to have two (especially, two women as lovers at the same time) (I;II) [toklo+chi] {ngr. toklónchi: to sleep with two different women the same day}

toklónchi to sleep with (two different women) the same day—ngr. of toklo'chi

toklhakah̲a̲fa hngr. of toklhak̲a̲fa

toklhak̲a̲fa to play active games, run around (of older children or adults) (I) {hngr. toklhakah̲a̲fa; aatoklha}

toklhak̲a̲fa' old-time party [toklhk̲a̲fa+']

toklhak̲a̲fa' apiisa to give a party (I) § Toklhak̲a̲fa' kilapiistok. We gave a party.

toklhak̲a̲fa' imáyya'sha to have a party (pl. subj.) (III) § Toklhak̲a̲fa' pomayya'shtok. We had a party.

toklhan spider web (CC) {choklhan}

toklhank, (TP) toklhan soot

toksá'li ggr. of toksali

toksala'pa', (CC, VB) toksala̲'pa' type of lizard

toksala'pishto' big lizard, like some of those in California [toksala'pa' ishto+']

toksala'pi̲lapishaa-asha' horned toad [toksala'pa' im+lapish aa-asha+']

toksali to work; to have a job (I) [+CPR] [-PR] {ggr. toksá'li; hngr. toksah̲a̲li; ngr. toks̲a̲li}

toksali' servant, employee, working person, workman, laborer [toksali+']

toksalichi to make work, put to work; to send to prison (I;II) [toksali+chi]

toksalit atobbi to be sent to prison; to work off a sentence (I) [toksali+t] § Toksalit ishatobbitam? Did you

work it off?, Did you go to prison?

toksalit ilatobbi to work off a fine (I)

toksika' hearth, area in front of the fire; (MJ, ER) fireplace

tokshí'la ggr. of tokshila

tokshihi̲la hngr. of tokshila

tokshila to be thirsty (II) [tok+shila] [-CPR] [-PR] {ggr. tokshí'la; hngr. tokshihi̲la; ygr. tokshíyyi'la; nokshila}

tokshilachi to make (someone) thirsty (I;II) [tokshila+chi]

tokshíyyi'la ygr. of tokshila

toktoha, toktowa to cluck, peep (I) [tok+]

toktowa see toktoha

<toloyya> in aatoloyya' {v2. toyya}

<tolhko'> in iyyintolhko'

tolhposhi' in foshi' tolhposhi'

tolhtochi, (LF) tolhto'chi to gallop (of a horse) (3)

tolhtochichi to make (a horse) gallop (I;3) [tolhtochi+chi]

toma' under (Ct)

<tómmokli'chi> in ittitómmokli'chi—klgr. of <tomo'chi>

<tomo'chi> in ittitomo'chi {klgr. <tómmokli'chi>; rcgr. tomomó'chi; toom toom toom aachi, tomok tomok tomok aachi}

tomok tomok tomok aachi to make the sound of beating on a leather-covered drum (I) (expressive) {<tomo'chi>, toom toom toom aachi}

tomomó'chi to beat (of a drum) (3)—rcgr. of <tomo'chi> {ittitomomó'chi}

tonnonónkalhchi to roll around (of a balloon on the floor, for example) (3)—rmgr. of tono'kalhchi

tonnon̲ó̲li to roll around (of a person on the floor, for example) (I)—rmgr.

of tonolli {tonnonónkalhchi}
tono'chi, (LR) tiino͟'chi to roll, roll
out (balls of dough, for instance),
make roll (mainly pl. obj.) (I;II) [-SC]
[tono'li+chi] {sg. obj. tonollichi}
tono'kachi to wobble (of a round
thing on a flat surface); to sway (I)
tono'kalhchi to roll (of a balloon, for
example) (3) {rmgr.
tonnonónkalhchi; tonolli}
tono'li to roll over, roll around
(more than once) (I) {tonolli: to roll
once} § Tono'lilitok. I rolled (more
than once).
tonolli, tonotli to roll over, roll
around (once) (I) {tono'li: to roll
more than once; rmgr. tonnonó͟li;
tonnononkalhchi, tono'kalhchi} §
Iitonollitok. We rolled once.
tonollí'chi ggr. of tonollichi
tonollichi to roll, spin (a sg. long obj.)
(I;II) [tonolli+chi] {ggr. tonollí'chi;
pl. obj. tono'chi} § oshtintonollichi:
to roll (something) to
tonotli see tonolli
tónglo ngr. of toklo
top top top aachi, to'p to'p to'p aachi
to make the sound of cloth or
leather being hit (expressive) (I)
topa bed
topa it hurts (children's word)
[hottopa]
topa lhayilli to wet the bed (I)
topa o͟hoshowa to wet the bed (I)
topa so͟sh bedbug (TU)
topaalhiipi'ya' bedspread, quilt,
bedcover [topa alhiipi'ya']
topishto' big bed, king- or queen-
sized bed [topa ishto+']
topompatalhpo' sheet [topa
ompatalhpo']
top-oshi' little bed, crib [topa oshi']
tossohó͟la hngr. of tossoola
tossola to stoop down, bend over (I)

{v2. <tossololi>; rigr. tossoltó͟wa;
xgr. tossóllo'wa; tossoola}
tossolochi to bend (someone) over
(for instance, when changing a baby)
(I;3) [-SC] [<tossololi>+chi]
<tossololi> in tossolochi {v1. tossola;
ggr. <tossóllo'li>}
<tossóllo'li> ggr. of <tossololi>
{tossollo't bínni'li}
**tossollo't bínni'li, tossollo'wat
bínni'li** to sit Indian style, tailor
style (sg. subj.) (I)
[<tossollo'li>/tossollo'wa+t] {dl.
tossollo'wat chí'ya; tpl. tossollo'wat
binoht má͟a}
tossóllo'wa to curl up, be curled up;
to lie with one's bottom sticking up,
like a baby (I); to curl up, lie with
one's bottom sticking up in (a place)
(I:3)—xgr. of tossola
tossollo'wat bínni'li see tossollo't
bínni'li
tossollo'wat binoht má͟a to sit Indian
style, tailor style (tpl. subj.) (I)
[tossollo'wa+t] {sg. tossollo't
bínni'li; dl. tossollo'wat chí'ya}
tossollo'wat chí'ya to sit Indian style,
tailor style (dl. subj.) (I)
[tossollo'wa+t] {sg. tossollo't
bínni'li; tpl. tossollo'wat binoht
má͟a}
tossoltó͟wa to try to crawl (of a baby,
just learning); to keep bending over
(for instance, when picking up
trash) (I)—rigr. of tossola
tossoola to buck (of a horse); to jump
around (I); to buck, jump around in
(a place) (I;3) {hngr. tossohó͟la;
tossola}
tossoolachi to make (a horse) buck,
make (someone) jump around (I;II)
[tossoola+chi]
<tosha> in oktosha {v2. toshli;
toshafa, toshtowa}

toshafa to have a piece broken off
(mainly sg. subj.) (3) {v2. toshaffi; pl.
toshahli: to break up into pieces;
<tosha>, toshtowa}
toshaffi to break a piece off (mainly
sg. obj.) (I;3) {v1. toshafa; hngr.
toshah**á**ffi; pl. obj. toshaachi; toshli:
to cut into pieces}
toshahá**ffi** hngr. of toshaffi
toshahá**li** hngr. of toshahli
toshahli to break up into pieces, be
broken into pieces, be cut up in
pieces; to have a piece broken off
(pl. subj.) (3) {hngr. toshah**á**li; sg.
toshafa: to have a piece broken off;
toshaachi: to break off many pieces;
toshli: to cut into many pieces; pl.
obj. toshtoli}
toshaachi to break into many pieces;
to break a piece off (pl. obj.) (I;3)
[toshahli+chi] {sg. obj. toshaffi: to
break one piece off; toshtoli}
toshbi to rot; to be rotten, gangrenous
(II) {ggr. t**ó**'shbi; hgr. t**ó**hhoshbi; ygr.
t**ó**yyo'shbi}
toshbichi to rot, ferment
(something), let (something) rot,
ferment (I;3) [toshbi+chi]
toshli to cut (a pie, for instance) into
pieces (I;3) {v1. <tosha>; pl. obj.
toshtoli; toshahli, toshtoli}
toshooli to interpret, translate
(orally), explain, make out, (AW)
read (I;3) {ggr. t**ó**shsho'li} § Toshoot
holissikbitok. He translated it and
wrote it down.
tó**shsho'li** ggr. of toshooli
toshtoli to cut up (pl. obj.) (I;3) (Ct?)
{v1. toshtowa; toshaachi, toshli}
toshtowa to be cut up, all cut up (pl.
subj.) (3) (Ct?) {v2. toshtoli; <tosha>,
toshafa, toshahli}
toyya, (ER) itti' oyya to climb (I); to
climb (something) (I;3) [itti' oyya]

[+taha] [-PR] [-CPR] {v1. <toloyya>;
ggr. t**ó**'yya; hngr. toh**ó**yya; ngr.
t**ó**yya; aatoyya}
toyyachi to make climb, help climb
(I;II) [toyya+chi]
toyyat aya to go up (even if not
climbing) (I) [toyya+t] § Toyyat ayali.
I go up.
tó**yyo'hbi** ygr. of tohbi
tó**yyo'shbi** ygr. of toshbi
tó**yy**o**'shpa** ygr. of t**o**shpa
toobli to push (a button, for
instance), push down (I;II) {hgr.
t**ó**hhobli; hngr. toh**ó**mbli; toopo'li}
tooboklhí**'li** ggr. of tooboklhili
tooboklhili, tohboklhili, (AB)
tikboklhili fog; to be foggy (of a
place) (3) [tohbi oklhili / tikba'
oklhili] {ggr. tooboklh**í**'li}
toom toom toom aachi to make the
sound of beating on a leather-
covered drum (I) (expressive)
{<tomo'chi>, tomok tomok tomok
aachi}
toomi sunshine, sunlight; to be
sunshine, sunlight; to shine, be
bright (of the sun or moon) (3); to be
sunny (of a location) (3) {hgr.
t**ó**hho'mi} § Los Angelesat toomi.
Los Angeles is sunny. |
Oklhilitahakm**a** hashi'at toomi.
The moon shines when it gets dark.
**toomi pallit ishtayya, toompallit
ishtayya** to be spring (—); to have it
be spring in (3) [palli+t] § Los
Angelesat toompallit ishtayya. It's
spring in Los Angeles.
toominni to lie in the sun (I) [toomi
*inni] § Toomi hashinnita? Are you
all lying in the sun?
toompallammo'na' first part of
spring [toompalli' ammo'na+']
toompalli to be summer (—); to have
it be summer in (3) [toomi palli] §

348

Toompallikma ayala'chi. I'll go in the summer. | Los Angelesat toompalli. It's summer in Los Angeles.
toompalli' summer, summertime [toompalli+']
toompallit ishtayya see toomi pallit ishtayya
toopo'li to push against, crowd, push around (often pl. obj.), to keep pushing (I;II) {hngr. toopohóli; rmgr. toopopóli; ittitoopo'li, toobli}
toopohóli hngr. of toopo'li
toopopóli to shove, push repeatedly (I;II)—rmgr. of toopo'li
Toosti' Tuesday (MC) (Ct) [from the English]
To̱'na' Catherine Willmond's childhood nickname [Ct. isht aa(y)+ona+']
to̱'ti to bend one's knees, go up and down (especially, of a baby) (CC, JC)

to̱'tichi to dance (a baby) [to̱'ti+chi] (CC, JC)
to̱falaa' short form of ato̱falla'a'
tóhbi ngr. of tohbi
tóhno ngr. of tohno
to̱shabbi, (MS) toshambi to have the measles (II) [abi]
to̱shabbi' measles [to̱shabbi+']
to̱shabbi' hayoochi to have the measles, to get the measles (I)
to̱shabbi' losa' black measles (a type of measles) [losa+']
to̱shpa to hurry; to do fast (I); to be fast (especially, at getting things done) (II) [-PR] {hngr. tohóshpa; ygr. tóyyo̱'shpa; into̱shpa: to be too fast for}
tówa to be there, be left there, stay there (sg. subj.) (I)—ngr. of tó'wa {dl. káha, áshwa; tpl. ásha; ánta}
tóyya ngr. of toyya

V

vinniga' vinegar [from the English]
voot vote (noun) [from the English]
voot hotihna to count votes (I)
voot ihotihna to count the votes in favor of (a candidate) (I;III) [im+hotihna]
voot kanchi to vote, cast a vote (I) § Voot ishkancha'chi? Are you going

to vote?
voot ka̱sht aya to go vote, to vote (I) [(voot kanchi)+t] § Voot ka̱sht ishiyyatam? Are you going to go vote?
vooti, footi, (MJ) voota to vote (I) [from the English] {imvooti: to vote for}

W

wá'a ggr. of waa
wa'sh wa'sh wa'sh aachi see wash wash wash aachi
wá'ya ggr. of waya

wachokkochi to tickle (I;II) (TJ, TP)
wahánka hngr. of waaka
wahaala to get loose
wáhha'ka hgr. of waaka

wáhhakla hgr. of wakla
wahhala to spread, go outwards (of horns); to be round and spreading (of a hoopskirt); to be cone shaped (3) {v2. wahhalili; rigr. wahhalwáa; xgr. wahhálla'a, wahhaala, wihhila}
wahhalili to spread apart; to make into a cone shape (I;3) {v1. wahhala}
wahhalkachi to raise and lower one's arms at one's sides (I)
wahhálla'a to be wide, spreading outwards (of horns or a hoopskirt) (3)—xgr. of wahhala
wahhalwáa to wear a hoopskirt or other skirt that sways as one walks; to flap one's arms or wings or a cape (I); to wear a hoopskirt or flap one's arms in (a location) (I;3)—rigr. of wahhala
wahhaala to struggle, try to get free (I) {wahhala}
wakaha see wakaa
wakaháa hngr. of wakaa
wakaa, wakaha to fly, to blow away (sg. subj.) (I) [+PR] [-CPR] {v2. wakiili; ggr. wákka'a; hngr. wakaháa; pl. wakoha}
wakaachi to make fly (I;II) [-SC] [wakaa+chi]
wakchahálli hngr. of wakchaalli
wakchalachi to spread (projecting parts of something) apart: especially, to spread (a woman's) legs apart (I;II) [wakchalali+chi]
wakchalali to put one's legs apart, do a split (I); to have one's legs or a similar part apart (for instance, when one walks, or of a fork with crooked tines) (II) {ggr. wakchálla'li; rlgr. wakchalla'wáli; wakchaalli}
wakchálla'li ggr. of wakchalali {prt. wakchalla't}
wakchalla't with the legs apart—prt. of wakchálla'li § Wakchalla't

hikki'yali. I stand with my legs apart.
wakchalla'wáli to have one's feet apart (I)—rlgr. of wakchalali
wakchaalli to kick one's feet in the air (like a baby) (I) {hngr. wakchahálli; wakchalali}
wakiili to fly (an airplane, for example), to make fly (I;II) {v1. wakaa}
wákka'a ggr. of wakaa
wákko'wa ggr. of wakoha
wakla to have a hole or crack (of a window or a table, for example) (3) {hgr. wáhhakla; ngr. wángla; ygr. wáyyakla}
wakoha, wakowa to fly, blow away (pl. subj.) (I) [+taha] {ggr. wákko'wa; hngr. wakohówa; sg. wakaa}
wakohówa hngr. of wakoha
wakowa see wakoha
walaha see walaa
walaháa hngr. of walaa
walaa, walaha to grow, come up (of plants) (3) {hngr. walaháa; ngr. waláa}
waláa ngr. of walaa
walokshi to be tender (of vegetables) (3)—usually used in ngr. {ngr. walónkshi}
walónkshi ngr. of walokshi
walhaháli hngr. of walhahli
walhahchi see walhaachi
walhahli to boil (of a liquid, or something boiled) (3); (CC) to gargle (I) {hngr. walhaháli; ngr. walháhli} § Ahi'at walhahtok. The potatoes were boiled.
walhaachi, walhahchi to boil (something) (I;II); (CC, LF) to gargle (I) [-SC] [walhahli+chi]
walháhli ngr. of walhahli
wangla ngr. of wakla
Wappa-naki' Wapanucka,

Oklahoma

wasacha to be sour (like a lemon or pickle); to be too tart, not quite ripe (3) {ggr. wássa'cha; ngr. wasáncha; ygr. wasáyya'cha}

wasachachi to make sour (perhaps by adding vinegar) (I;3) [wasacha+chi]

wasáncha ngr. of wasacha

wasáyya'cha ygr. of wasacha

wássa'cha ggr. of wasacha

wash wash wash aachi, wa'sh wa'sh wa'sh aachi to make the sound of rattling (especially of a baby rattle) (expressive) (I) {washa'chi}

washa'chi, (MJ) **washoochi** to rattle, shake (something) (I;3) [±SC] {hngr. washa'lihínchi; klgr. <wáshshakli'chi>; rcgr. washashá'chi; washaachi; wash wash wash aachi}

washa'lihínchi hngr. of washa'chi

washashá'chi to rattle, make a rattling sound (I)—rcgr. of washa'chi [+SC]

washaachi to rattle, make a rattling sound (3) {hngr. washaahánchi: make the sound of leaves before a storm; wash wash wash aachi, washa'chi}

washaahánchi to make the sound of leaves before a storm—hngr. of washaachi

washká'bi ggr. of washkabi

washkabi to itch, be itchy; to have mange, be mangy (II) [washko abi] {ggr. washká'bi; hgr. washkáhha'bi; hngr. washkahámbi; ygr. washkáyya'bi}

Washkabi' Chickasaw pet name [washkabi+']

washkabichi to make itch (I;II) [washkabi+chi]

washkahámbi hngr. of washkabi

washkáhha'bi hgr. of washkabi

washkáyya'bi ygr. of washkabi

washko chigger

washo̲'chi' in yakni' washo̲'chi'

washshaháₗla hngr. of washshaala

<wáshshakli'chi> in ittiwáshshakli'chi—klgr. of washa'chi

washshala to have the limbs stick out (of a tree) (3) {v2. washshalili; ngr. washshháₗla; rigr. washshalwáₐa; xgr. washshálla'a; washshaala}

washshalachi to spread (one's hand) (I;3) [washshala+chi] § Salbak washshalashlitok. I spread my hand, spread my fingers.

<washshalaka'> in itti' chanaa inchanaa' iwashshalaka' [washshala+ka']

washshalili to spread (one's fingers, toes) (I;3) {v1. washshala; washshálla'a, washshaala} § Salbak washshalilili. I spread my fingers.

washshálla'a to be spread apart, splayed (of fingers, toes); to stick out all over (of hair); to have no leaves (of a tree); to be bushy (sg. subj.) (3)—xgr. of washshala {dl. washshállo'ha; pl. washshaloha}

washshállo'ha, washshállo'wa to be bushy (dl. subj.)—ggr. of washshaloha {sg. washshálla'a; pl. washshaloha}

washshállo'wa see washshállo'ha

washshaloha to be bushy (pl. subj.) (3) {ggr. washshállo'ha: (dl. subj.); sg. washshálla'a}

washshalwaháₐa hngr. of washshalwáₐa

washshalwáₐa to wave one's arms and legs (or fore- and hind legs) around (of a baby, or a kitten held by the scruff of the neck, for instance), stick one's limbs out every which way (I); to wave one's arms and legs

around in (a place) (I;3)—rigr. of
washshala {hngr. washshalwah<u>á</u>a}
washshaala to wave one's arms and
legs around (I) {hngr. washshah<u>á</u>la;
washshala}
washshaalachi to make (someone or
something) wave its arms and legs
around (I;II) [washshaala+chi]
washsh<u>á</u>la ngr. of washshala
watalhpi to turn on one's back (I); to
turn on one's back in (a place) (I;3)
{ggr. wáttalhpi: to be, lie on one's
back, all stretched out; ngr.
wat<u>á</u>lhpi}
watalhpichi to turn (someone or
something) over on the back (I;II)
[watalhpi+chi]
watalhpichit bohli to turn (a person)
on his back (I;II) [watalhpichi+t] §
Watalhpichit sabohtok. She turned
me on my back.
wat<u>á</u>lhpi ngr. of watalhpi
wat<u>o</u>lo type of crane
wáttalhpi to be, lie on one's back, all
stretched out—ggr. of watalhpi
waya to stoop down (I) {ggr. wá'ya;
xgr. wáyya'a}
wayánchi ngr. of wayaachi
<wayaa> in wayaachi {ggr. wáyya'a;
ngr. way<u>á</u>a; rmgr. wayyay<u>á</u>a; waya}
wayaachi to put up, set up (sg. obj.,
usually one on four legs or with an
open bottom); to park (a car) (I;3); to
make stoop down (I;II) [±SC]
[<wayaa>+chi] {hngr. wayaahánchi;
ngr. wayánchi; pl. obj. wayoochi}
wayaahánchi hngr. of wayaachi
way<u>á</u>a to stay (especially of
something on four legs or with an
open bottom) (sg. subj.) (I) {dl.
way<u>ó</u>wa}—ngr. of <wayaa>, wáyya'a
<wayowa> in wayowat m<u>á</u>a {v1.
<wayooli>; ggr. wáyyo'wa; ngr.
way<u>ó</u>wa; rmgr. wayyoy<u>ó</u>wa}

wayowat m<u>á</u>a to be located, stand,
exist (especially on four feet, or of a
round or shapeless subj.,
particularly one with a relatively
flat top and open space underneath)
(most likely nonhum. subj.—may
be derogatory if applied to humans);
to stoop, crouch down (tpl. subj.) (I);
to stoop, crouch down, be located in
(a place) (tpl. subj.) (I;3)
[<wayo̊wa>+t] {sg. wáyya'a (be
located), waya (stoop), <wayaa>; dl.
wáyyo'wa} § Wayowat iim<u>a</u>a. We
stooped down.
wayoochi to put up, set up (pl. obj.,
especially four-legged or open-
bottomed ones) (I;3); to make stoop
or crouch down (I;II) [-SC]
[<wayooli>+chi] {hngr.
wayoolihínchi; ngr. wayoolínchi; sg.
obj. wayaachi}
<wayooli> in wayoochi {v1.
wáyyo'wa, <wayowa>}
wayoolihínchi hngr. of wayoochi
wayoolínchi ngr. of wayoochi
way<u>ó</u>wa to stay (especially of
something on four legs or with an
open bottom) (dl. subj.) (I) {sg.
way<u>á</u>a}—ngr. of wáyyo'wa,
<wayowa>
wáyya'a to be located, stand, exist
(especially on four feet, or of a
round or shapeless subj.,
particularly one with a relatively
flat top and open space underneath,
such as a table, car, upside-down
cup, or four-legged animal) (most
likely nonhum. subj.—may be
derogatory if applied to humans); to
be upside-down (of an thing usually
thought of as having an open top,
like a cup or box); to lie on one's
stomach, crouch down (with one's
face down) (sg. subj.) (I); to be

located, be upside down, crouch in
(a place) (sg. subj.) (I;3)—ggr. of
<wayaa>, xgr. of waya [+PR] [-CPR]
{ngr. wayáa: to stay; rmgr. wayyayáa;
dl. wáyyo'wa; tpl. wayowat máa;
waya; akka' wáyya'a} §
Yahmishanha'shki—ofi'at wayya'a.
Be careful—there's a dog.
wáyyakla ygr. of wakla
wayyayáa to graze (of a horse, cow);
to go around on one's hands and
knees pulling grass, to bend over
and pull grass (sg. subj.) (I)—rmgr.
of <wayaa>, wáyya'a {dl.
wayyayówa}
wayyayówa to go around on one's
hands and knees pulling grass, to
bend over and pull grass (dl. subj.)
(I)—rmgr. of <wayowa>, wáyyo'wa
{sg. wayyayáa}
wáyyo'wa to be located, stand, exist
(especially on four feet, or of a
round or shapeless subj.,
particularly one with a relatively
flat top and open space underneath)
(may be derogatory if applied to
humans); to stoop, crouch down (dl.
subj.) (I); to stoop, crouch down, be
located in (a place) (dl. subj.) (I;3)—
ggr. of <wayowa> {v2. <wayooli>;
ngr. wayówa: to stay; sg. wáyya'a (be
located), waya (stoop), <wayaa>; tpl.
wayowat máa}
waa, waha, (ER) waaha to have ripe
fruit on (3) [+PR] [-CPR] {ggr. wá'a}
<waa> in iwaa {abaawaa}
waa' pachahli' type of wild fruit that
splits when it's ripe [waa+'
pachahli+']
waachi to ripen, force (plants—for
example, in a greenhouse) (I;3) [-SC]
[waa+chi]
waaka to be spotted (with irregular
spots, like an animal's markings) (3)

[+CPR] [+PR] {hgr. wáhha'ka; hngr.
wahánka}
waaka' cow [from Spanish vaca]
waaka' aabashli' butcher shop
[aa+bashli+']
waaka' hakshop , (VB) waakhakshop
leather, cowhide
waaka' himmita' steer [himmita+']
waaka' imbishlichi' milk cow
[imbishlichi+']
waaka' lapish devil's claw
(medicinal plant)
waaka' lapish faloha' longhorn steer
[faloha+']
waaka' lopi' beef marrow
waaka' nakni' bull
waaka' nakni' ittibi' bullfighter
[ittibi+']
waaka' niha' beef lard [niha+']
waaka' salakha', waakisalakha' beef
liver [waaka' im+salakha']
waaka' shaali', waaka' ishshaali'
cattle car, cattle truck [(isht) shaali+']
waaka' takchi' rodeo; cowboy
[takchi+']
waaka' toksali', waaktoksali' ox
[toksali+']
waakachi to make spots on (I;3)
[waaka+chi]
waakapiisachi' cowherd (person)
[waaka' apiisachi+']
waakaa-abi' slaughterhouse [waaka'
aa+abi+']
waakaatakchi' rodeo grounds
[waaka' aa+takchi+']
waakibilhkan cooked okra (joke)
[waaka' ibilhkan]
waakimbala' type of small plant with
orange and yellow flowers: cowpeas,
field peas (locoweed?) [waaka'
im+bala']
waakimbishlichi to milk a cow (I)
[waaka' imbishlichi] §
Waakishimbishlichitam? Did you

waakimpa'

milk the cow?
waakimpa' cattle feed [waaka' impa+']
waakimpaalhto' silo [waakimpa' aalhto']
waakinchokka' barn (LF) [waaka' im+chokka']
waakipishik cow's teats, udder [waaka' ipishik]
waakishki' mother cow [waaka' ishki']
waakishyokachi', (WB) waakishyokli' cowcatcher (on a train) [isht yokachi/yokli+']
waakittakoba' beef tripe [waaka' ittakoba']
waakihapi salt lick [waaka' im+hapi]
waakisalakha' see waaka' salakha'
waakiyaalhki' manure, fertilizer [waaka' im+yaalhki']
waakombiniili' cowboy [waaka' om+biniili+']
waakoshi' baby cow [waaka' oshi']
waakoshi' nakni' little bull
waakoshpishichi' cow with a nursing calf [waaka' oshpishichi']
waaktoksali' see waaka' toksali'
waalakna' yellow watermelon [waa lakna+']
waash waash waash aachi see wash wash wash aachi
waawa to defecate (baby talk) (I) (Ct?)
waawo' locust
waawo' hakshop, waawo' hakshop shila', (CC) hakshop shila' dried locust shell [shila+']
waawo' hakshop shila' see waawo' hakshop
waawoshto' type of big locust [waawo' ishto+']
<wa'ta'> in iwa'ta'
wi'ha ggr. of wiha
wi'ki ggr. of wiiki
wi'li in iwi'li, oshwi'li, pitwi'li—ggr.

of wiili
wiha to move, change one's home (I) {v2. <wihli>; ggr. wi'ha; aawihli}
wihachi to move (something or someone), change the home of, evacuate (I;II) [wiha+chi]
wihhi'ki hgr. of wiiki
wihhihila hngr. of wihhiila
wihhila to be shaped like an open cone with the large end down (like a lampshade) (3) {v2. wihhilili; ngr. wihhila; rigr. wihhilwiya; xgr. wihhilli'ya; wahhala, wihhiila}
wihhilili to make (something) shaped like an upside-down cone (I;3) {v1. wihhila}
wihhilli'ya to wear a hoopskirt; to have one's arms or wings spread out (I); to wear a hoopskirt, have one's arms or wings spread in (a place) (I;3)—xgr. of wihhila
wihhilwiya to wear a hoopskirt (and have it sway) (I)—rigr. of wihhila
wihhiila to wave one's arms and jump around (to attract someone's attention, for instance) (I) {hngr. wihhihila; iwihhiila, wahhaala, wihhila}
wihhila ngr. of wihhila
wihinki hngr. of wiiki
<wihli> in aawihli, <wiichi> {v1. wiha; wihpoli, wiili}
wihpo'li ggr. of wihpoli
wihpohóli hngr. of wihpoli
wihpoli, (TP) wippolichi, (TP) woppolichi, (ER) woppolichi to rob (I;II) [po+<wihli>] {ggr. wihpó'li; hngr. wihpohóli}
wilichi to make (inan. pl. obj.) fall (for instance, to cut down trees, shake fruits off a tree) (I;3) [±SC] [wilili+chi]
wilihili hngr. of wilili
wilili to fall (inan. pl. subj.) (3)

354

[+CPR] [+PR] {hngr. wilihíli; inan. sg. ittola}
wiloha, wilowa to be shaken out, dusted (3) [+T] {v2. wilooli}
wilohóli hngr. of wilooli
wilowa see wiloha
wilooli to shake (usually, something like a cloth); to dust with a duster (I;3) {v1. wiloha; hngr. wilohóli; iliwilooli: to shake oneself (of a dog)}
wina'kachi in yaaknaat wina'kachi, yaakni' wina'kachi'
winda' window [from the English]
winda' ishtokshili'ta' shutters
winda' takaali' curtain, window shade, window blind [takaali+']
<wini'chi> in ittiwini'chi {rcgr. <wininí'chi>, winiihachi}
<wininí'chi> in ittiwininí'chi—rcgr. of <wini'chi>
winiiyachi to roar, rumble (of thunder, an airplane, a tornado, a large fire, etc.); to sound like a swarm of bees (3) {hngr. winiiyahánchi; ngr. winiiyánchi}
winiiyahánchi hngr. of winiiyachi
winiiyánchi to buzz (VB, ER)—ngr. of winiiyachi
wínki to be heavier (II)—ngr. of wiiki
wíyyi'ki ygr. of wiiki
<wiichi> in ishtibaawiichi [<wihli>+chi]
wiik week [from the English] § wiik chaffa fokhakma: in about a week | wiik atoklakaasho: two weeks ago
wiikaat inkaniya, wiiki'at inkaniya, wiikikat inkaniya to lose weight (III) [wiiki+'+at / wiiki+kat] § Wiikaat ankaniyakat asayoppa. I'm happy I lost weight.
wiiki to be heavy (II); to weigh oneself (I) [+PR] [-CPR] {ggr. wí'ki;

hgr. wíhhi'ki; hngr. wihínki; ngr. wínki; ygr. wíyyi'ki}
wiiki weight; unit of weight, pound (used with a number) § wiiki chaffa': one pound
wiikihínchi hngr. of wiikichi
wiikichi to weigh (I;II) {hngr. wiikihínchi} [wiiki+chi]
wiili in iwiili, pitwiili {ggr. wí'li; abaawiili, <waa>, wihli}
wóhhoksho hgr. of woksho
wohónksho hngr. of woksho
wokkó'la ggr. of wokkola
wokkohóla hngr. of wokkola
wokkola to blister, to be blistered (II) {v2. wokkololi; ggr. wokkó'la; hngr. wokkohóla; ygr. wokkóyyo'la}
wokkolachi to cause a blister for (3;II) [wokkola+chi] § Asholoshat sawokkolashtok. My shoes gave me blisters.
wokkololi to cause a blister for (3;II) {v1. wokkola}
wokkóyyo'la ygr. of wokkola
woksho to be furry, fuzzy, curly (II) [+CPR] [-PR] {v2. woksholi; hgr. wóhhoksho; hngr. wohónksho; ngr. wónksho; ygr. wóyyoksho; bakwosholi, chakwokoli}
wokshó'li ggr. of woksholi
woksholi to bloom (of a pecan tree), put out leaves or green fuzz in the spring (of a tree) (3) {v1. woksho; ggr. wokshó'li} § Osak falaa'at woksholit ishtaya. The pecan is starting to bloom.
wónksho ngr. of woksho
<wosholi> in bakwosholi
woshwó'ki ggr. of woshwoki
woshwohónki hngr. of woshwoki
woshwoki to fizz, bubble (for example, during fermentation) (3) [+PR] [+CPR] {ggr. woshwó'ki; hngr. woshwohónki; woksho}

355

woshwoki'

woshwoki' bubble [woshwoki+']
woshwokichi to make fizz (for
instance, by shaking a can of soda)
(I;3) [woshwoki+chi]
wóyyoksho ygr. of woksho
woochi to bark (I); to bark at (I;II)
[-SC] [-CPR] [-PR] {hngr.
woolihínchi; ngr. woolínchi}
woochichi to make bark (I;3)
[woochi+chi]

wooha, (MJ) woowa to howl (of a
dog) (I) {hngr. woohǫ́ha, woohǫ́wa}
woohachi to make howl (I;II)
[wooha+chi]
woohǫ́ha, woohǫ́wa hngr. of wooha
woolihínchi hngr. of woochi
woolínchi ngr. of woochi
woop oops! (exclamation)
wǫ́lhlha to be wrinkled (II) (ER)

y

<ya> see a ("be")
yá'a ggr. of yaa
yá'nha ggr. of yanha
yábbo'fa ggr. of yabofa
yabbobónka'chi, yabbobónkalhchi to
be round and firm (of a boiled egg or
a balloon) (3)—rmgr. of yabo'kachi
yabbobónkalhchi see yabbobónka'chi
yabo'kachi to be soft and yielding
(like a pillow, a partially inflated
balloon, or a waterbed) (3) {hngr.
yabo'kahánchi; rmgr.
yabbobónka'chi}
yabo'kahánchi hngr. of yabo'kachi
yabofa to be soft (like a pillow or
sponge) (3) {v2. yaboffi; ggr. yábbo'fa;
hngr. yabohǫ́fa; ngr. yabǫ́fa; ygr.
yabóyyo'fa; yabohli}
yaboffi to pound, shake, plump up (a
featherbed or pillow) (I;3) {v1.
yabofa; hngr. yabohǫ́ffi}
yabohli to go down (of a swelling) (3)
{ngr. yabǫ́hli; yabofa}
yabohǫ́fa hngr. of yabofa
yabohǫ́ffi hngr. of yaboffi
yabóyyo'fa ygr. of yabofa
yabǫ́hli ngr. of yabohli
yabǫ́fa ngr. of yabofa
yahánha hngr. of yanha

yáhhammi hgr. of yammi
yahmanhi to be careful, pay attention
(I); to pay attention to, notice (I;3)
[yahmi anhi] § Yahmishanhashki!
Be careful! | Benjieat Irenea
yahmikanhokitok. Benjie didn't
notice Irene.
yahmi to do (I); do, be doing (aux.)
(used with preceding verb +t) ;
might (aux.—used with preceding
verb +a'nikya) [+HM], <yah> {ngr.
yáhmi; yamihchi} § Pila nosilit
yahmi. I'm just sleeping. |
Omba'nikya yahmi. It might rain. |
Hattak kannahǫ ittihalallila'nikya
yahmikat ithanali. I know a man I
might marry.
yahmicha see yahmihma
yahmichichi see yammichichi
yahmihmat see yahmihma
yahmihma, yahmina, yahmihmat,
yahmicha, (LF) mihma then
[yahmi+hma/na/hmat/cha]
yahmina see yahmihma
yakkookay thank you
[yak+<hookay>]
yakkookay imanhi to thank (I;III)
[im+anhi] {ygr. yakkookay
imáyyanhi} § Yakkookay amanhi.

356

He thanked me.
yakkookay imáyyanhi ygr. of
yakkookay imanhi
yakmihchi to do thus, do this way (I);
to do this way with (I;3)
[yak+<mihchi>] {hngr.
yakmihínchi} § Tii ishikbikmat
ishyakmihchi. This is how you
make tea, When you make tea, you
do this. | Holisso yappa
yakmihshtok. He did it this way
with this paper.
yakmihínchi hngr. of yakmihchi
yakni' makofa' gopher (ER) [yaakni']
yakni' shokaawi' type of bug
(perhaps June bug?) (LF) [yaakni']
yakni' washo̲'chi' (WB), (TP) yakni'
yosho̲'chi', (ML) yaknosho̲'chi',
(CC) yakni' yoko̲'chi' mole; (CC)
gopher
yako'mi see yakohmi
yakohmanhi to be careful (I)
[yakohmi *anhi] §
Yakohmishanha'shki. You be
careful.
yakohmi, yako'mi to be this way, to
be like this (I) [+HM], <yako̲h>,
<yako̲'> [yak+<ohmi>] {ggr.
yákkohmi; hngr. yakohó̲mi} §
Yakohmila'chi. This is the way I'm
going to be.
yakohó̲mi hngr. of yakohmi
<yako̲h>, <yako̲'> [HM] of yakohmi
yala locust larva, worm
<yalfolfo'> in iyalfolfo'
yalhki' feces, excrement, manure
(IIIp)
yalhki' bosholli' crumbled dry
manure [bosholli+']
yalhki' tono'chi' tumble bug, (AB,
ER) June bug, (VB) doodlebug
[tono'chi+']
yalhkobo'li' in akanka' yalhkobo'li'
[yalhki' <koboli>+']

yamaska to knead (I;3) (FA, EH, TJ)
yamí'chi ggr. of yamihchi
yamihchi to do (I) [ya(mma)
<mihchi>] {ggr. yamí'chi; ngr.
yamí̲hchi; yahmi}
yamí̲hchi ngr. of yamihchi
yamma yes, indeed, that's it
(response during a speech); here it
is, is this what you wanted?
{yamma}
yamma pila that way
yammak there; that one; that
(oblique nonsubj.) (out of reach or
out of sight) [yamma+ak]
yammakot that; that one, he, she, it;
those; they (contrastive subj.) (out
of reach or out of sight)
[yamma+akot]
yammako̲ that; that one, him, her, it;
those, them (contrastive nonsubj.)
(out of reach or out of sight)
[yamma+ako̲]
yammat that; that one, he, she, it;
those; they (subj.) (out of reach or
out of sight) [yamma+at]
yamma̲, yamma that; him, her, it;
those; them (nonsubj.); there (out of
reach or out of sight) [yamma+a̲]
yammi to be really strong (of coffee,
for instance), to be highly seasoned
(3); to have a strong flavor of (3;3)
{hgr. yáhhammi} § Nipi'at hapi
yammi' salami. The meat tastes too
much of salt.
yammichi to make really strong (I;3);
to season with (I;3;3) [yammi+chi] §
Nipi' hapi yammichilitok. I
seasoned the meat with salt.
yammichichi, yahmichichi to make
(someone) do (I;II) [yahmi+chichci]
yámmohmi to be that way, be like
that (I); to do like (this, that) (I;3)
[+HM], <yámmoh>
[yamma+<ohmi>] § Yammohmili,

357

<yámmọh>

Yammọhli. I'm like that. |
Yammakọ yammohmili. I do it like
that.
<yámmọh> [HM] of yámmohmi
yaná'lli ggr. of yanalli
yanahậlli hngr. of yanalli
yanahli to run down, flow (of water
in a river, for example) (3) {hngr.
yanahậli; yanalli}
yanalli, yanatli to run down, run off,
spread (of a spilled liquid, for
example) (3) {ggr. yaná'lli, yánnalli;
hngr. yanahậlli; yanahli} § oka'
aayanalli, oka' aayanahli: gutter
yanash, (CC) yanosh buffalo
yanatli see yanalli
yanha to have a fever (II) {ggr.
yá'nha; hngr. yahậnha; hoyahno}
yanha ishtithana' thermometer [isht
ithana+']
yanha kobaffi' quinine [kobaffi+']
yanhachi to give a fever to (I;II)
[yanha+chi]
yanhakat chaaha to have a high
fever (II , —) [yanha+kat] §
Sayanhakat chaahatok. I had a high
fever.
yanhakat inchaaha see yanhaat
inchaaha
yanhakat shippa to have one's fever
go down (II , II) [yanha+kat] §
Sayanhakat sashippa. My fever
went down.
yanhaakot inchaaha see yanhaat
inchaaha
yanhaat inchaaha, yanhaakot
inchaaha, yanhakat inchaaha to
have a high fever (III)
[yanha+a(ko)t/kat im+chaaha] §
Yanhaakot anchaaha. I have a high
fever.
yánnalli ggr. of yanalli
yappa here, here it is, this is what
you wanted (exclamation); see

yappa
yappa pila this way
yappak here; this one; this (oblique
nonsubj.) (within reach) [yappa+ak]
Yappakayni Chahta' Native
Choctaw, Oklahoma Choctaw
(Choctaw whose ancestors have
lived in the Choctaw Nation since
before 1850) [yappa+aakayni]
yappakot this; this one, he, she, it;
these; they (contrastive subj.)
(within reach) [yappa+akot]
yappakọ this; this one, him, her, it;
these; them (contrastive nonsubj.)
(within reach) [yappa+akọ]
yáppalli, yáppatli to be slow, lazy,
lackadaisical (I); to be slow, lazy in (a
place) (I;3) [-CPR] [-PR]
yappat this; this one, he, she, it;
these; they (subj.) (within reach)
[yappa+at]
yáppatli see yáppalli
yappạ, yappa this; him, her, it; these;
them (nonsubj.) (within reach);
here [yappa+a]
yato'chi to knead (I;3) [-SC] {v1.
yato'wa; hngr. yato'lihínchi; ngr.
yato'línchi}
yato'lihínchi hngr. of yato'chi
yato'línchi ngr. of yato'chi
yato'wa to be kneaded (3) {v2.
yato'chi}
yatofa to be soft (3) [+PR] [+CPR] {v2.
yatoffi; ggr. yátto'fa; ngr. yatộfa}
yatoffi to plump up (a pillow) (I;3)
{v1. yatofa; hngr. yatohộffi}
yatohộffi hngr. of yatoffi
yatộfa ngr. of yatofa
yátto'fa ggr. of yatofa
yawalli, yawatli to be partly dry (of
cloth) (3) {ggr. yáwwalli; ngr.
yawậlli}
yawallichi to partly dry (clothes, for
instance) (I;3) [yawalli+chi]

yawatli see yawalli
yaw̲álli ngr. of yawalli
yawoochi to be itchy (II) [-SC] {hngr.
yawoolihínchi; ngr. yawoolínchi;
ygr. yawoolíyyi'chi}
yawoolihínchi hngr. of yawoochi
yawoolínchi ngr. of yawoochi
yawoolíyyi'chi ygr. of yawoochi
yawool̲íshnaacha to be itching to (II)
(forms cha expression with
following verb, implying the truth
of that action; includes
[yawoolinchi+naa]) {bannakat
yawoolinchi} § Sayawool̲ishnaacha
issolitok. I was itching to hit him
(and I did).
yáwwalli ggr. of yawalli
yaa, yaaha to cry, weep (I) [+PR]
[-CPR] {hngr. yaah̲áa; ggr. yá'a}
yáa'chi ggr. of yaachi
yaabbis̲owa' see aybis̲owa'
yaachakachi to put (a crown, comb,
headband) on (someone's°) head
(I;II;3) [±SC] [yaachakali+chi] §
Naahaloppa' yaachakachittook.
They crowned him with thorns,
They put thorns around his head
(like a crown).
yaachakali to put (a crown, comb,
headband) on one's head (I;3)
[yaa+chakali] {ggr. yaachákka'li: to
wear (a crown, comb, headband)}
yaachákka'li to wear (a crown, comb,
headband)—ggr. of yaachakali
yaachakka'li' crown; large comb
worn in the hair [yaachakka'li+']
yaachi to make cry (I;II) [-SC]
[yaa+chi] {ggr. yáa'chi; hngr.
yaahánchi}
yaachíkko'li to wear (a turban or hat
that does not cover the neck), to
have (a scarf) on one's head—ggr. of
yaachikoli
yaachiko'li' hat with no brim:

beanie, yarmulke, stocking cap
[yaachikoli+']
yaachikochi to tie (a scarf) over
(someone's) head (I;II;3) [-SC]
[yaachikoli+chi]
yaachikoli to tie (a scarf) over one's
head, to put on (a turban or hat that
does not cover the neck) (I;3) {ggr.
yaachíkko'li: to wear (a scarf, hat,
turban)}
yaachino'ko' back of the head (IIp)
yaaha see yaa
yaahánchi hngr. of yaachi
yaah̲áa hngr. of yaa
yaakas̲ofa to be bald (II) (AB)
yaaknalhpisa' mile (used with a
number) [yaakni' alhpisa+'] §
yaaknalhpisa' chaffa': one mile
yaaknanonka' cave [yaakni' anonka']
yaaknaat ilhko'li for there to be an
earthquake [yaakni'+at] § Yaaknaat
ilhko'tok. There was an earthquake.
yaaknaat wina'kachi for there to be
an earthquake [yaakni'+at] § yaakni'
wina'kachi': earthquake
yaakni' ground, earth; land, property;
country; the earth, the world §
Yaaknaat lombo. The earth is
round.
yaakni' aaittachakkachi' section line
yaakni' aashila', yaakni' shila' desert
[aa+shila+']
yaakni' cholok cave, hole in the
ground
yaakni' cholok abooha' cellar
[abooha+']
yaakni' hayaka' valley, prairie,
desert, open place
Yaakni' I̲minko' President of the
United States [im+minko']
yaakni' kola' hole (in the ground)
[kola+']
yaakni' kolli' ditch digger [kolli+']
yaakni' s̲awa'si' island [s̲awa'si+']

yaakni' shila'

yaakni' shila' see yaakni' aashila'
yaakni' talkachi' group of small
  islands [<talkachi>+']
yaakni' tashayyi', (CP) tishayyi'
  island
yaakni' toshafa' island [toshafa+'] {pl.
  yaakni' toshahli'}
yaakni' toshahli' islands—pl. of
  yaakni' toshafa' [toshahli+']
yaakni' wina'kachi' earthquake
  {yaaknaat wina'kachi}
yaaknishchokmali' fertilizer [yaakni'
  isht chokmali+']
yaaknonkaawaa', (WB)
  yaknanonkaawaa', (CC)
  yakninkaawaa' peanut [yaakni'
  anonka' aa+waa+']
yaaknonkaawaa' bota' peanut butter
  [bota+', perhaps influenced by
  English butter]
yaalhipa, yaalhpa hat (IIIp)
  <yaalhipa> {v2. yaalhipili}
yaalhipa apakfo'ta' hatband
yaalhipa aalhto' hatbox (for more
  than one hat) {yaalhipaafo'kha'}
yaalhipa ibichchalaa-asha' hat with a
  bill (baseball cap, for instance)
  [ibichchala' aa-asha']
yaalhipa kallo' helmet, hard hat
  [kallo+']
yaalhipa patha' hat with a brim
  [patha+']
yaalhipa tanna' straw hat
yaalhipaafo'kha' hatbox (for one hat)
  [yaalhipa aa+fokha+'] {yaalhipa
  aalhto'}
yaalhipaatakohli' hatrack
yaalhipi'li' head covering: scarf, veil,
  headband with feathers (IIIp)
  [yaalhipili+']
yaalhipichi to make (someone°)
  wear (headgear) (I;II;3) [-SC]
  [yaalhipili+chi] {hngr.
  yaalhipilihínchi}

yaalhipichit pisa to try (a hat) on
  (someone) (II = obj , I;3)
  [yaalhipichi+t] § Irenea yaalhipa
  yaalhipichit pisalitok. I tried the hat
  on Irene.
yaalhipihíli hngr. of yaalhipili
yaalhipili to put on (a hat or scarf)
  (I;3) {v1. <yaalhipa>; ggr.
  yaalhíppi'li: to wear (a hat, scarf);
  hngr. yaalhipihíli} § Yaalhipa
  yammat pisa-chokmaha
  ishyaalhippi'lika. That hat looks
  pretty on you, That hat you're
  wearing is pretty.
yaalhipilihínchi hngr. of yaalhipichi
yaalhipimpatha' hat brim [yaalhipa
  im+patha+']
yaalhipishtasiiti'ya' hatpin
yaalhipit pisa to try on (a hat) (I;3)
  [yaalhipili+t]
yaalhíppi'li to wear on one's head, to
  wear (a hat or scarf)—ggr. of
  yaalhipili
yaalhpa see yaalhipa
yaapakna' top of the head (IIp)
yaatala feather ornament for a hat or
  the head, war bonnet
yaatalaachi to put (something:
  especially, a feather) on
  (someone's°) head (I;II;3) [-SC]
  [yaatalaali+chi]
yaatalaali to put a feather on one's
  head (I); to put (a feather or feather
  ornament) on one's head, to carry
  (something) on one's head (I;3)
  [yaatala+li] {ggr. yaatálla'li: to wear a
  feather}
yaatálla'li to have a feather on one's
  head (I); to wear (a feather or feather
  ornament) on one's head (I;3)—ggr.
  of yaatalaali
<yah> [HM] of yahmi
yáhmi ngr. of yahmi
yahtokchi'cho I guess so

[<ya̲h>+tok+]
yáyli see ya̲yli ki'yo (neg. ikyay'lo)
yáyli ki'yo to hate (I;II , —) (ikyay'lo)
§ Chiya̲ylili ki'yo. I hate you.
yí'mmi ggr. of yimmi
yi'ng yi'ng yi'ng aachi see ying ying
ying aachi
yihi̲mmi hngr. of yimmi
yikihi̲lhlha hngr. of yikilhlha
yikilhlha to be wrinkled, gathered,
puckered; to have wrinkled skin (II)
(ggr. yíkkilhlha; hngr. yikihi̲lhlha;
ngr. yiki̲lhlha; ygr. yikíyyi'lhlha)
yikilhlhachi to gather (cloth) (I;3)
[yikilhlha+chi]
yikíyyi'hlha ygr. of yikilhlha
yiki̲lhlha ngr. of yikilhlha
yíkkilhlha ggr. of yikilhlha
yili'chi to make go back and forth, in
a zigzag (I;3) [±SC] (ngr. yili'línchi;
rcgr. yililí'chi; ygr. yili'líyyi'chi;
yili'kachi)
yili'kachi to slither; to wiggle, sway
(while wearing tight pants) (I) (v1.
yili'kalhchi; hngr. yili'kahánchi)
yili'kahánchi hngr. of yili'kachi
yili'kahá̲lhchi hngr. of yili'kalhchi
yili'kalhchi to slither; to wiggle, sway
(while wearing tight pants); to go in
a wavy line, like rickrack or a twisty
road (II) (v2. yili'kachi; hngr.
yili'kahá̲lhchi; rmgr.
yillilínkalhchi)
yili'línchi ngr. of yili'chi
yili'líyyi'chi ygr. of yili'chi
yililí'chi to slither rapidly (of a
snake) (3)—rcgr. of yili'chi
yillilínkalhchi to go in a zigzag (of a
snake or a twisty road) (3)—rmgr. of
yili'kalhchi
yilhibli to knock down (with a
bulldozer, for instance), demolish
(sg. obj.) (I;3) (v1. yilhipa; pl. obj.
yilhlhichi, yilhiichi)

yilhihi̲li hngr. of yilhihli
yilhihchi see yilhiichi
yilhihli to be knocked down,
demolished (pl. subj.) (3) [+T] (hngr.
yilhihi̲li; sg. yilhipa)
yilhipa to collapse, fall down, cave in
(from the sides); to be ruined; to be
knocked down (sg. subj.) (3) [+PR]
[+CPR] (v2. yilhibli; pl. yilhahli)
yilhiichi, yilhihchi to knock down
(pl. obj.) (I;3) [-SC] [yilhihli+chi]
(yilhlhichi)
yilhlhichi to knock down, tear down
(mainly pl. obj.) (I;3) (sg. obj.
yilhibli; yilhiichi)
yimmi to believe (nonhum. obj.)
(II;3); to believe that (preceded by
verb +a'ni/ha'ni or plain verb or
(when this clause has a different
subj. from yimmi by verb +a'chika̲)
(ggr. yí'mmi; hngr. yihi̲mmi;
iyimmi: to believe (a person)) §
Holisso Holiitto'pa' sayimmi. I
believe the Bible. I Ayatok
sayimmi. I believe that she left. I
Chompatahliliha'ni sayimmi. I
believe I'm done shopping. I
Lynnat Charles kisitok aachika̲
poyimmi. We believe (they say) that
Lynn bit Charles.
yimmichi to make (someone)
believe, convince (I;II) [yimmi+chi]
§ Lynnat sayimmichitok Charlesat
ayatok a'shcha. Lynn convinced me
that Charles had left, Lynn
convinced me, saying that Charles
had left.
yinoffi to grab with one's open hand
(I;II) (hngr. yinohó̲ffi; okaayinoffi)
yinohó̲ffi see yinoffi
ying ying ying aachi, yi'ng yi'ng yi'ng
aachi to make the sound of a car
starting (expressive) (I)
yó'ka ggr. of yoka

361

yó'lhkó ggr. of yolhko
yó'pi ggr. of yopi
<yobi> in nokyobi {yohbi}
yoffi to masturbate (MJ)
yohbi to be spring (the season); to
have it be spring (of a place) (3) (Ct)
{<yobi>}
yohbi bíyyi'ka to be peaceful, calm
(— / 3) (Ct)
yohbichi to be spring (ER) [yohbi+chi]
yóhho'ka hgr. of yoka
yóhhokli hgr. of yokli
yohómpi hngr. of yopi
yohónka hngr. of yoka
yohóngli hngr. of yokli
yoka to be in jail, be imprisoned,
confined (II) {v2. yokli; ggr. yó'ka;
hgr. yóhho'ka; hngr. yohónka}
[+PR] [+CPR]
yoka' prisoner, slave [yoka+']
yoka' aa-asha' prison, penitentiary
yokachi to catch, collect, confine; to
rape (pl. obj.) (I;II) [yoka+chi] {ggr.
yókka'chi; sg. obj. yokli}
yókka'chi ggr. of yokachi
yókko'ta ggr. of yokota
yókkolbi ggr. of yokolbi
yokli to catch, hold; to rape (sg. obj.)
(I;II) {v1. yoka; ggr. yôkli; hgr.
yóhhokli; hngr. yohóngli; pl. obj.
yokachi}
yôkli ggr. of yokli
yokó'lli ggr. of yokolli
yokofa to be scalded (II) [yok+] {v2.
yokoffi}
yokoffi to scald (with, or of, a hot
liquid) (I;II) [yok+] {v1. yokofa; hngr.
yokohóffi}
yokohóffi hngr. of yokoffi
yokohólbi hngr. of yokolbi
yokolbi, (EH) yokotbi, (AW) yokobli
to be damp, moist, misty; (AW) to
be soaked (II) [yok+] {ggr. yókkolbi;
hngr. yokohólbi; ngr. yokólbi; ygr.

yokóyyo'lbi}
yokólbi ngr. of yokolbi
yokolbichi to dampen, moisten; to
soak (I;II) [yokolbi+chi]
yokolli, yokotli to shrink
(something) (I;II) [yok+] {v1. yokota;
ggr. yokó'lli; ngr. yokólli}
yokónta ngr. of yokota
yokota to shrink, be shrunk (II)
[+CPR] [+PR] [yok+] {v2. yokolli; ggr.
yókko'ta; ngr. yokónta; ygr.
yokóyyo'ta} § Yokontacha
iskanotok. It shrank up and was
smaller.
yokotli see yokolli
yokóyyo'lbi ygr. of yokolbi
yokóyyo'ta ygr. of yokota
yoko'chi to root in the ground (with
the nose, like a pig) (I); to nuzzle
(like a dog) (I;II) [±SC] {ngr.
yoko'línchi}
yoko'línchi ngr. of yoko'chi
yokólbi ngr. of yokolbi
yokólli ngr. of yokolli
yollichi to shake (from the cold, for
instance), tremble (II) {hngr.
yollihínchi}
yollichichi to make shake, shiver
(3;II) [yollichi+chi] § Oka' homi'at
sayollichishtok. The whiskey made
me shiver.
yollihínchi hngr. of yollichi
yolhaa to be slack, loose (of string,
wire) (3) {ggr. yólhlha'a; ngr. yolháa}
yolhaachi to make slacker, less taut
(for instance, of children sitting on a
wire to bring it down) (I;3)
[yolhaa+chi] [-SC] {hngr.
yolhaahánchi; ngr. yolháanchi}
yolhaahánchi hngr. of yolhaachi
yolháanchi ngr. of yolhaachi
yolháa ngr. of yolhaa
yolhko to get soft or bruised from
being knocked around (of peaches

or tomatoes in a large box, for instance) (3) [+T] {ggr. yó'lhko}
yolhkochi to cause (fruit) to get soft by treating it roughly (I;3); to bruise (I;II) [yolhko+chi]
yolhkon, (MJ) yalhkon mole, gopher
yolhkon ishto' gopher [ishto+']
yólhlha'a ggr. of yolhaa
yómpi ngr. of yopi
yopi to swim, bathe, take a bath (I); to swim, bathe in (a liquid) (I;3) {ggr. yó'pi; hngr. yohómpi; ngr. yómpi; oka' yopi} [+CPR] [+PR]
yopichi to bathe (someone) (I;II) [yopi+chi] {ggr. yóppi'chi; hngr. yopihínchi; ngr. yopínchi}
yopihínchi hngr. of yopichi
yopínchi ngr. of yopichi
yóppi'chi ggr. of yopichi
yoppó'la ggr. of yoppola
yoppohǫ́la hngr. of yoppola
yoppola to make a joke, say something funny (I) [ayoppa ola ?]

{ggr. yoppó'la; hngr. yoppohǫ́la; ngr. yoppǫ́la; iyoppola: to tell a joke to; ishyoppola; ishtayoppolachi; ayoppa}
yoppolachi to make fun of, tease (I;II) [yoppola+chi] {ggr. yoppólla'chi; hngr. yoppolahánchi}
yoppolahánchi hngr. of yoppolachi
yoppólla'chi ggr. of yoppolachi
yoppǫ́la ngr. of yoppola
yoshoba to be lost, mislaid (II) {v2. yoshobli; ggr. yóshsho'ba; hngr. yoshohómba}
yoshobachi to make (someone) lost, get (someone) lost (by abandoning them or giving poor directions, for example) (I;II) [yoshoba+chi]
yoshobli to get (someone) lost, to misdirect (I;II) (Ct?) {v1. yoshoba}
yoshohómba hngr. of yoshoba
yóshsho'ba ggr. of yoshoba
yuuzi to use (I;3) (slang) [from the English]

English-Chickasaw Index

INTRODUCTION

The English-Chickasaw Index is not a dictionary itself, since far less complete information is given here than in the main Chickasaw-English section of this book. When you look up a word in the index you should be sure to check its entry in the main section, especially if more than one Chickasaw equivalent of the English word you are looking up is given. Fine shades of meaning and usage, variant pronunciations, grade forms, and grammatical information are not given in the index. To find out about these things and see examples of how words are used in sentences, it is important to consult the main entry for each word you find in the index in the Chickasaw-English dictionary.

When two or more Chickasaw words appear after an English entry word in the index, they are listed in alphabetical order, not in order of importance, frequency of use, or acceptability. Generally, if more than one Chickasaw word is listed for an English entry, these words are rough equivalents or synonyms. Sometimes the differences among them may be quite great, however, as the main dictionary entries may show. Chickasaw words that are only very peripheral equivalents of the English entry are listed after all the other words, following the English word *also* (in italics).

English words in the index are alphabetized following standard English alphabetical order. They are arranged word by word—thus, all expressions beginning with the simple word **back** (for example, even **back door**) come before any longer word containing **back** (even **backbone**). Commas, hyphens, and apostrophes are ignored in the alphabetization.

a

a certain kanimpi, kanimpihmat, kanimpihma
a certain, to be kanimpi
a few kannohmihmat, kannohmihma
a few, just chaafowa'si, kanihmo'si
a few, to be kánnohmi
a little kánni'ya
abandon, to ka'shcha kaniya
abandoned aachokkillissa'
abandoned child chipotalhtakla'
abide by, to ishtittihállalli
able to do things right, not to be akánni'ya
able to take it, to be achónna'chi
abort, to abi
abortion, to have an chipotabi
about fokha, fokhakaash, fokhakma
about, to be aayimma, fokha, ishtanompa
absentminded, to be imaanokfila-at iksho
absolved, to be inkashofa
abuse sexually, to ishtakaanihmichi
abuse, to ilbashachi
accept, to holiitobli
accepted, to be holiitopa
accident in, to have an aaoshkannapa
accident, to have an ayoppóllo'ka, oshkannapa
accomplish taha
accumulate, to lawachi
accuse falsely, to ahobbichi
accuse, to ishtombohli, ishtonhochi, onhochi
accused, to be falsely ishtonittola
accustomed to, to get imomochi
ache in the bones, to have an komoochi

aches, to have muscle lhikkachi
acorn nasi'
acorn, type of nasishto'
across from, to be straight áchcha'pa
across, to be horizontally okkawaata
across, to come to rest ootawaata
across, to go abaanabli, lhopo'li, lhopolli
across, to go back and forth okkawalli
across, to go straight apissáli
across, to lay awalli, awaatali
across, to lie okkawatkachit máa, okkawatkáyya'chi, okkawátta'a
across, to put abaanali, lhopo'chi, lhopollichi, okkawalli
act as a doctor, to alikchi
act as a midwife, to chipotapooba
act as, to tóhho'ba
act bravely toward, to imaaiklóha
act friendly toward, to inkána
act grouchy toward, to imalhaa
act good, to chokma, chokmat atta
act good to, to chokma imilahobbi
act in a certain way toward, to iyámmohmi
act like a man, to nakni
act like a man, to fail to iknakno
act like friends, to ittinkána
act like, not to ikholbo
act like, to chihmi, chohmi, ilahobbi
act nice to, to ihapashshi
act on, to ayalhlhichi
act silly, to ilihaksichi
act spoiled, to ishtilamákka'li
actor shoo ikbi'
Adam's apple inonkopoolo'
add for, to imalapalínchi
add on another piece, to achaakali
add on, to ibaant hotihna
add on to the side of, to apaatali

369

add some more, to ibaani
add, to ayinínchi, ittibaani
add together, to ittachakli
adder, spreading alhkayya' patha',
  hashaachaffa', hashaapatha'
addict ishhaksi'
addition, to have in ayinínchi
adherent to aayimmi'
adjourn a meeting, to tíwwa'pa
adjourn, to tiwabli
adjust for, to inampila
adjust, to nampila
adopt a child, to chipota habina
adopt out, to ima
adopt out to, to habinachi
adopt, to immit ishi
adoption, to give up a child for
  chipota habinachi
adoption to, to give up a child for
  chipota ima
adult, to become an hofantikat ona
adultery, to commit ittilomaka
adultery with, to commit ibaanowa
affair with, to have an ibaanowa
affected, to be seriously impalammi
afraid of each other, to be
  ittinokshoopa
afraid of, to be inokshoopa
afraid, to be imilhlha
Africa Hattak Losa' Aa-asha', Hattak
  Losa' Iyaakni'
African American hattak losa'
after aballaka', himmaka'
after a while alhchímba
afternoon obyaka' pila
again achankahma, anowa',
  ímmo'ma, ishtáyya'ma, í'ma
again, to do albitili
against, to be aasanali, isanali
agitate, to tiwa'kalhchi
ago, to be long hopaaki
agree, to ittihaalálli, ittihállalli,
  ittibaachaffa
agree, to all aaittibaachaffa

agree with, to aachaffa, imbaatiya
agreement, to come to an
  ittibaanokfilli
agreement, to make an
  nannittimapiisa
ah aa
ahead of, to be ímmayya
ahead of, to get ootímmayya
ahead, to go on tingbalísht aya
Ahloso Aahollonkso', Haalooso
AIDS abikoppolo'
aim at, to apissali'chi, atókkoli'chi
air mahli
air conditioner ishkapassali',
  ishtamaachi'
air out of, to let the latassachi,
  shayoffi
air, to hofka
air, to put one's chin in the
  abakshowali
aired, to be holofka
airhole aafoyopa'
airplane piini' wakaa'
airport piini' wakaa' aahika', piini'
  wakaa' aakkowa'
airs, to put on fínha
akimbo, to have one's arms
  ilombítti'pa
Alabama Indian Albaamo'
alarm clock hashi' kanalli ishithana'
  ola'
alcohol, rubbing foni' hottopa' tish,
  tish ishtilihammichi'
alcoholic okishko'
alcoholic beverage nannishko'
alcoholism treatment center
  okishko' aa-asha'
align the edges of, to ittalalli
aligned, to have the edges
  ittalatkachi
alignment, to be out of hayifa
alive, to be foyohómpa, okcháa
all mot
all alone, to be láttassa

all around bíyyi'ka
all, be taha
all day obya
all gone, to be taha
all of, to have ishtim**ó**ma
all over, to have bíyyi'ka
all people hattak m**o**ma
all right hoomi, mikya'ba, taa
all the time bíyyi'ka
all there, to be im**ó**ma
all, to be m**ó**ma; *also* aalhlhi
all, to do ishtim**ó**ma, m**o**mánchi
all, to do to tahli
all, to want m**o**mánchi
all together, to be ittibalhto, ittib**á**lhto
allergic reaction, to cause a
  fowabbichi
allergic reaction, to have a fowabbi
allergic swellings, to have pofohli
alligator ach**o**'chaba'
alone, to be chaffa bíyyi'ka, chaffa'si,
  illa
alone, to be all láttassa
alone, to be one lhak**ó**fa
along ilawiit
along the edge of, moving
  taakchak**a**li', taakch**a**li
along the side, to go apootakaalínchi
altar aalta', Chihoowa aayoppachi',
  nanna aalowachi'
alter for, to imaaiksaachi
alter, to ittim**i**lachi, **i**lachi, **i**lánch
although chikimba
alum tali' hoyya'
aluminum foil holisso shokmalali'
always bílli'ya, bíyyi'ka, mina
ambitious, to be ishtilibanna
ambulance abika' shaali', hattak illi'
  ishshaali'
ammonia naahomi'
among the company aatangla'
among, to be aatángla, ibaatángla,
  ibaafóyyokha
amphitheater nannishtaa-asha'

amputate, to bashli
amusement arcade aachokoshkomo'
  abooha'
anesthesiologist nosichi'
anesthetic, to give an ishnosichi
anesthetic, type of ishshimohli'
anesthetize, to nosichi, shimohli
andiron aaolhti' **i**hikki'ya'
andirons aaolhti' **i**hi'li'
Anglo naahollo
angry about, to be ishhashaa
angry at, to be **i**hashaa, **i**malhaa
angry, to be hashaa; *also* malhaa,
  palli
angry, to make hashaachi, hashiili
animal *see names of specific animals*
animal, domestic naalhpooba
ankle iyy**i**mosak
announce publically, to annowachi,
  annoyachi
annoy, to imalhchíbba'chi
anoint, to ahammi
anoint with, to ahammi,
  ishtahammi
another m**ó**ma, ittibinka'
another one chaffo', an**o**wa', **i**la'
another time an**o**wa'
answer anompa falama'
answer back, to achapa, imoppoloka
answer the telephone, to ishi
answer, to anompa falammichi,
  anomp**i**falammichi
answer, to get an anompa falama'
  ishi
ant, type of iss**o**sh homma', iss**o**sh
  hommishto', iss**o**sh losa'
antenna lapish, ishtimpashooli'
anvil talaabo'li'
anybody kaniya'ookya, kaniya'ookya
anyone kanahookya, kaniya'ookya
anyplace kaniya'ookya
anything nannahookya
anywhere kaniya'ookya
apart, to be talhoffi

apart, to come shihpahli
apart, to have one's feet
wakchalla'wáli
apart, to have one's legs wakchalali
apart, to spread wakchalachi
apartment house manager
chokkapiisachi'
ape hattak shawi'
apologize, to hábbi'na
apologize to, to ihábbi'na
appear as, to toba
appear, to okfaha, oktani, ootokfaha,
ootoktani, ootkochcha, imokfaha
appear, to make oktanichi
appear to, to ootimokfaha, imoktani
appendix ittakoba' loksi', salhkona
iskanno'
applaud, to impasa'chi
apple takolo maso'fa'—see also
apple, type of
apple core takolo maso'fa' foni'
apple, type of takolo imilhlha',
takolo wasacha'
apply (a rinse) to (someone's) hair, to
lhilichi
appoint a guardian for, to
imatoonichi
appoint each other, to ittaatookoli
appoint oneself, to ilatookoli
appoint, to pafi, atookoli, atookolichi
appointed, to be alhtoka
approach, to minti
apron tikba-takaali'
apron, to put on an tikba-takaachi
arbor chishanko
arbor, to make an hoshontikachi
area between ittintakla', ittintaklaka'
area in the woods, soft hattak
sawintopa
argue, to ittachapo'wa, ittachapa
argue together about, to ishtittachapa
argue with each other, to
ittinokko'wa
argue with, to ishtachapa, achapa

argument, to have an anompa
ishtittimayya ki'yo, anompa
ishtiktimayyo
argument with, to have an anompa
ishtittimayya ki'yo, anompa
ishtiktimayyo
arithmetic naaholhtina'
arithmetic book naaholhtina' holisso
arm ilbak
arm or leg from, to pull off an nipaffi
arm or leg pulled off, to have an
nipafa
armadillo hattak illapa'
armed forces, to be in the tashka-
chipota' ibaafóyyokha
armed forces, to go join the tashka-
chipota' aya
armed forces, to join the tashka-
chipota' ibaaholhtina
armory tanampaa-asha'
armpit aktampi', shakba' nota'
armpit hair aktampi' hishi'
arms and jump around, to wave
one's wihhiila
arms and legs off, to take the
ittanipaachi, nibli
arms and legs pulled off, to have the
nipahli
arms and legs, to wave one's
washshaala, wahshalwáa
arms at the sides, to raise and lower
one's wahhalkachi
arms spread out at the sides, to have
one's wihhílli'ya
around, to be always aayahánta,
aayashahánchi, aayashwahánchi
aroused, to be sexually impalli, palli
arrange, to ittibaakahli, ittibaakaachi
arrive along with, to ibaa-ala
arrive at along with, to ibaaona
arrive at, to ona
arrive, to ala
arrow naki', oski' naki',
tanampalhlhi' inaki'

arrowhead naki', naki' oshkibili'
arsenal tanampaa-asha'
artery issish ihina'
arthritis foni' hottopa
arthritis, to have foni' hottopa i'shi,
komoochi
artificial respiration, to give
foyopachi
as crazy as, to be ibaahaksi
as much as, to be chihmi, ittilawwi
as well ayina
ash tree itti' shinap
ashamed of oneself, to be ilihofahya
ashamed of, to be ishtikímpo,
ihofahya
ashamed, to be hofahya
ashamed to talk, to be nokwaya
ashes hottok, hottok poshi'
ashes fly, to make a cloud of
shobohónta
ashtray hottok aalhto'
ask about, to asilhpowa
ask each other questions, to
ittimasilhpowa
ask for from, to imasilhha
ask for unsuccessfully, to asilhhat
anoktobafa
ask, to asilhha, chokmat asilhha,
imasilhpowa; also imilbashsha
asleep, to be nosi, shimoha
asphalt niha losa', tali' patalhpo'
assemble, to ittafamo'chi, ittafamo'li,
ittanaachi, ittibaachaffa
assembly ittibaachaffa'
assess, to ayalli' ombohli
assist, to apiilánchi
assistance, monetary ishtalhpila'
assistant ishkoboka' apilachi'
assistant to an Indian doctor tisho
associates ittapihaka'a
astonished, to be malhata

asylum, insane haksaa-asha'
asymmetrically, to distort the shape
of shanaayo'li
at night oklhili
at some point kanihkmak
athletic supporter inihi' ishyokli'
attach for, to imalapalínchi
attached, to be ittachákka'a
attached to, to be achákka'a,
achakkachit máa, achakkáyya'chi
attached together, to be ittapótto'wa
attached together, to be closely
ittapotkachit máa, ittapotkáyya'chi
attack, to chímmikli'chi, ittibaayokli
attempt to kill, to atókko'li
attention of, to attract the iwihhiila
attention, to pay yahmanhi
attract a following of, to piichit áa
attract the attention of, to iwihhiila
auction nannaakanchi'
auctioneer nankanchi'
auditorium, outside nannishtaa-
asha'
aunt ishko'si'
automobile itti' chanaa palhki'
avalanche okti' shalalli'
avalanche, for there to be oktaat
shalalli
avoid, to afoolopo'wa, inkanalli,
intiballi, ifolota, ilhakoffi
awake, to be óyyokcha
away from, to be inkaniya
away from, to go inkaniya, intamowa
away, to go kaniya, tamowa
away, to send tilhili
awl chofaak haloppa'
awning hoshottika', ishtalhtipo'
awning over, to put an atiipoli
ax oksifa
ax, type of itti' ishcholha'

b

babble, to anompoli
baby biibi', oshi', poskosh
baby animal *see the name of the animal or the specific type of baby animal ("kitten", "puppy", etc.)*
baby, blue chipotikhofa'to'
baby carrier chipotaafokha'
baby doll chipota holba'
baby, little biibosi'
baby swing chipotimaafa'pa'
baby teeth chipota noti'
baby, to have a chipota sho'li, chipotaat imala, chipotat imatta, chipotat intí'wa
baby-sitter chipotapiisachi'
back aatayya'a', ashaka', nalhchaba, nashshaka'
back and forth, to go fayya'kachi
back and forth, to make go yili'chi
back and forth, to rock fayya'kalhchi
back door abooha ashaka' okkisa'
back door, to go out the ootkochcha
back, middle of the upper chinokko'
back, moving in aballakali'
back of a chair aaombiniili' aatayya'a'
back of the hand ilbak pakna'
back of the head yaachino'ko'
back of, to put on the oshshaachi
back out, to ilihalalli
back, part of the hatip, inchashwa
back, to blow (medicine) onto (someone's) back lhilichi
back, to carry on one's sha'li
back, to come ifalama
back, to grow onchololi
back, to lie on one's tálla'a, wáttalhpi
back to normal, to be aaissa
back, to put falammichi
back, to put on one's sha'li
back, to take falammichi
back to, to give ifalammichi
back, to turn on one's watalhpi

back, to turn over on the watalhpichi, watalhpichit bohli
back together, to bring ittifalammichi
back together, to get ittifalama
back up, to bakhitiblichi
back, upper chonokko'
backbone nalhchaba foni'
backfire, to tokafa, tokahli
backpack on, to put a shaapolichi
backs, to lie on one's tállo'wa, talowat máa
backwards, to go bakhitibli, bakhitiipo'li
backwards, to keep going bakhitiipopóli
backwards, to make go bakhitiipo'chi
backwater oka' bakhitibli'
backwater, to be a bakhitibli
backyard abooha ashaka'
bacon nipi' oshobohli', shokha' nipi' oshobohli'
bad come up, to have something nanna ataklama' intoba
bad language, to use anompoppani, anompoppanichi
bad things about, to say ayyobba'li ki'yo
bad, to be áyyo'ba ki'yo, ikayyo'bo, ishtáyyo'ba ki'yo, ishtikayyo'bo; *also* oppolo, palammi
bad, to feel ikinchokmo, imíla
bad, to smell shoha
bad-looking, to be pis-ayyoba ki'yo
bad-smelling, to be kotoma
badge chofaakoshi' ilontala'li'
badly behaved, to act ishtilamákka'li
badly behaved, to be ishtilamákka'li, malhaa
badly, to treat impalammichi
bag nannaalhto', shokcha—*see also* bag, type of
bag lady ihoo inchokkiksho'

374

bag, type of alikchishokcha,
ishtahollo' ishokcha, shokcha
kallo', shokchoshi'
bail for, to post ato'li, imatooni,
imatoonichi, imimatobbi
bail out of, to aataklit lha'li
bait ishholhtosi'
bake, to aposhli, nonachi, paska
baked, to be alhposha, nona
baker paska ikbi'
bakery paskaaikbi'
baking powder paska ishshatabli'
baking soda soodi'
baking-powder biscuits tili'ko'
palaska'
balcony hoshottika'
bald eagle osi' ishkobo-tohbi'
bald, to be masofa; also ishkobo'
oshmasholi, kasofa, oshmisoli,
oshpasali, oshtosoli, yaakasofa
bald, to make masofachi, oshpasachi
bale, to takchi
ball to'wa'
ball field aato'li', to'wa'
aachokoshkomo'
ball game to'li'
ball in, to play aato'li
ball, rubber raba' to'wa'
ball, to hit the to'wa' isso
ball, to play to'li
ball, to wind into a ittapakfohli,
ittapakfolli
ball up, to bokshikoffi, koyohli
balled up, to be bokshikofa
balloon, hot-air nannishwakaa'
bamboo oskapi'
banaha banaha'
band, brass asonnak ola'
bandage oppolo ishtalakchi'
bandaid oppolo lapoochi'
bandanna innochi' homma'
bandeau ishkobo' apakfo'li'
bang things together, to
ittichámmakli'chi,

ittikámmakli'chi
banging inside, to make the sound of
cham cham cham aachi, chamak
chamak chamak aachi
banging sound, to make a
ittichalha'chi, kom kom kom aachi,
komok komok komok aachi
banging, to make noise
ittikómmokli'chi, ittikomo'chi,
ittikomomó'chi
bangs ibishshachi'
bank sakti, ta'ossaa-asha',
ta'ossaabohli', ta'ossaalhto',
ta'ossaashaachi'
bank, piggy shokhoshi' ta'ossaalhto'
bank, river abookoshi' apotaka'
bantam chicken akankiskanno'
bantam chickens akanksawa'
baptismal font aabaptismochi'
baptismal tank aaokloboshli'
baptistry aaokloboshli'
baptize for, to imbaptismochi
baptize in, to aabaptismochi,
aaokloboshlichi
baptize, to baptismochi, beptaayzi,
okloboshlichi
baptized in, to be aabaptismo,
aaokloboshli
baptized, to be baptismo, okloboshli
bar aaishko'
bar, to afachali, afaanali
barbecue aa-albani', nanna albani'
barbecue equipment nipi' aa-abaani',
tali' nanna aa-albani'
barbecue for, to imambaani
barbecue, to abaani
barbecued meat nanna albani'
barbecued, to be albani
barbed wire tali' haloppa'
barbed-wire fence tali' haloppa'
holitta
barber ipashi' tabli'
barbershop ipashi' aaintapa'
bare feet walking, to make the sound

bare object with something at the top, to be a long

of mit mit mit aachi, pas pas pas
aachi, pat pat pat aachi, tip tip tip
aachi
bare object with something at the top,
to be a long fáhhạ'ko
barefoot, to be iyyi' bíyyi'ka
barefoot, to walk ittipáttakli'chi,
ittitipipí'chi, ittitíppikli'chi,
mitití'chi
bark hakshop
bark chips itti' akchalhpi'
bark for, to ịwoochi
bark like a fox, to kaawa
bark, to woochi
bark, to make woochichi
barn hashshok aa-ashaachi',
issobinchokka', pichchạa,
waakinchokka'
barracks tashka-chipotaa-asha'
barred, to be afáchcha'a, afánnalhchi
barred, to get afacha
barrel itti' kolofa, itti' kolofishto'
barren person oshi' iksho'
barrette ipạshi' ontalla'a,
ipạshishtasiiti'li',
pạshishtakallo'chi', pạshishyo'kli'
barricade against, to put up a
imokkawaatali
barricades against, to put up
imokkawalli
base ishtaaọhikki'ya'
base of the neck chashshanak
baseball to'li'
baseball bat to'wa' ishbo'li', to'wa'
ishbo'wa', to'wa' ishbokkạa', to'wa'
ishtisso'
baseball cap to'li' yaalhipa
baseball diamond aato'li', to'wa'
aato'li'
baseball glove ilbak fokka' to'li',
to'wa' ishyokachi', to'wa' ishyokli'
baseball player to'li'
baseball player's cap to'li' ịyaalhipa
baseball uniform to'li' ịnaafokha

baseman to'wa' yokli'
bashful, to be hofahya
basket oski' tannafo', tappak-oshi'
basket, type of alhpatak,
naaishtalhpisa',
tanchishhayowalhchi'
basket, winnowing talhpak
basketball hoop to'waalhopo'chi'
bat halạ'bosha', pinti' wakaa'
bat, baseball to'wa' ishbo'li', to'wa'
ishbo'wa', to'wa' ishbokkạa', to'wa'
ishtisso'
bath in, to take a okaayopi
bath, to take a yopi
bathe for, to ịyopichi, oka' ịyopichi
bathe, to oka' yopi, oka' yopichi,
yopi, yopichi
bathe with, to ibaayopichi
bathroom abooshi'
bathroom, to go to the abooshi' aya,
imaalami, kochcha' aya,
nannimaalami
bathtub aayopi'
batter tili'kolhkomo', to'wa' bo'li',
to'wa' isso'
battery aashoppala' alhto'
battery die, to have one's car kaa-at
imilli
batting, quilt nạachanonkalatta'a'
bawl out, to ịnókko'wa, ịnokowa,
ịmiha
bawled out, to get ịhiliya
BBs nakọshik
be if any expression containing "be"
(especially one which includes an
English adjective) is not listed here,
see the word which comes after "be"
be a daredevil, to finha
be a good, to chokma
be a group of, to áyya'sha
be among, to ibaafóyyokha,
ibaatángla
be as crazy as, to be ibaahaksi
be away from, to inkaniya

beans, type of

be for, to aachaffa
be friends with, to inkána
be here, not to iksho
be how, to kani'mi
be in a certain configuration, to kani'mi
be in the same group with, to ahiina
be in, to aachaffa, fokha, fóyyokha, okaa-ahánta, okaa-áyya'sha, okaaáshwa, okaatálla'a, okaatállo'wa, okaatalowat máa, okaawáyya'a, okaawáyyo'wa, okaawayowat máa
be in water, to oka' okaatákka'li, oka' okaatakkakáli, oka' okaatákkohli, oka' okaatakkokóli, oka' okaatakoht máa
be in with, to ibalhto
be like that, to yámmohmi
be like this, to yakohmi
be like, to bínka, chihmi, chohmi
be located, to ánta, áyya'sha, áshwa, í'ma, káyya'ha, kahat máa, tálla'a, tállo'wa, talowat máa, tí'wa, wáyya'a, wáyyo'wa, wayowat máa
be not ki'yo
be, not to iksho
be on just one side, to tannap pila'si
be on, to ompatkachit máa, ompatkáyya'chi, ompátta'a, onáyya'sha, owáyya'a
be on top of, to alátta'a
be out of, to intaha
be that way, to ishtaaimóma, ishtaaímmo'ma, yámmohmi
be the only one in, to shkkílli'li
be the same, to aakani'tokat ímmo'ma, ímmo'ma, ittachaffa, ittihooba
be there, just to píhhi'la
be there, to áyya'sha, ánta, káha, taláa, tówa
be this way, to yakohmi
be through with, to aalhopolli,

ishtaalhopolli
be, to a—*if an expression containing "be" (especially one which includes an English adjective) is not listed here, see the word which comes after "be"*
be, to not ki'yo
be together, to táwwa'a
be too much, to aatámpa, ootilaatámbli, ootishtilaatámbli
be which one for, to inkatimpi
be with, to ahiina, ibaa-ánta, ibaa-áyya'sha, ibaaáshwa, ibaachaffa, ibaatángla, ibaayáa, iláwwi'li
be yourself, to ishnaakayni
beach oka' takchaka', okhatapootaka'
bead oksop
beaded sash oksop hanaawi'li'
beading loom oksop aahotampi'
beak fosh-ibichchala', ibichchala'
beak, growth on a turkey's ibilhkan
beams, type of abooha ihiyohli', ishholmo' into'wa', ihiyo'li' onto'wa', paknonto'wa'
bean juice balokchi'
bean pole bala' itti' albilha', balishtalbilha'
bean sprout bala' holhfo', bala' onchololi'
beanie yaachikko'li'
beans bala'—*see also* beans, type of
beans, coffee kaafi' ani', kaafi' nihi'
beans, jumping oshpaanimbala'
beans, row of bala' ihina'
beans, type of bala' alaknachi', bala' albilha', bala' awaalhaali', bala' balalli', bala' bolbo' ahooba'sika', bala' chaaha', bala' falaha' losa', bala' falaa', bala' falaa' ishkin losa', bala' hika', bala' himona', bala' homma', bala' ishkin losa', bala' itti' aatoyya', bala' itti' shawwa aatoyya', bala' kendi', bala' lakna', bala' laalawachi', bala' losa', bala'

377

bear

losayyi', bala' okchamali', bala'
okmiloli', bala' patha', bala' patha'
sawa'si', bala' sinti', bala' shila',
bala' takassali', bala' tohbi', bala'
tohbi' iskano', bala' tohbi' ishto',
bala' tohbi' sawa', bala' tohbi'
sawa'si', bala' woksho', bala-tombi'
iskanno', balishto', chokkala'bolo'
bala', issobimbala', itti' tiyya',
kanka' ishotika', osaapa' bala,
oshpaanimbala'
bear nita'—see also bear, type of
bear cub nit-oshi'
bear fruit, to ani
bear fruit, tree that doesn't itti'
nakni'
bear it, to noktála
bear, polar nita' aakapassaa-asha',
nita' tohbi'
bear, teddy nita' holba'
bear, type of falammi nita', nita'
homma', nita' lakna', nita' losa'
beard notakhish
beard, to have a large chakwokoli
beargrass impisa'
bears fruit, tree that itti' tiik
beat fast, to malli
beat on a leather-covered drum, to
ittitómmokli'chi, ittitomo'chi,
ittitomomó'chi
beat on a pillow, to mitití'chi
beat, to bo'chi, bo'li, ilhko'li,
imambi, lotolli, ootímmayya'chi,
tomomó'chi
beat up again, to ayyabichi,
imayyabichi
beat up along with, to ibaabo'li
beat up, to ayoppanichi, bo'li, bokkaa,
ímmayya'chi, oppani
beat up, to be bo'wa
beat up, to go ootayyabichi
beaten, to be bo'kalhchi, imilli
beaten up, to be tiwapa
beauty bush nita' lobahli'

beater ishbo'chi', ishbo'kalhchi'
beating on a leather drum, to make
the sound of tomok tomok tomok
aachi, toom toom toom aachi
beautiful, to be pisa-chokma
beauty parlor ipashaaiksaachi',
ipashaaoshchilo'chi'
beaver kinta
because it was pollaho
because something happened
kanihmihma
beckon to, to ilbak ishtiwaa
become a Christian, to Iksa'
ibaafokha, naayimmi' toba
become an adult, to hofantikat ona
become clear, to let aloktowachi
become dust, to lokfi' toba
become light, to hashtahli
become religious, to ootilikostinichi
become, to ilahobbi, toba
bed aanosi', topa—see also bed, type
of
bed cover nannompatalhpo'
bed, dry river abookoshi shila'
bed, to get out of taani
bed, to go to tashki
bed, to wet the topa lhayilli, topa
ohoshowa
bed, type of topishto', top-oshi'
bed with, to go imissa
bed with, to put to ootibaabohli
bedbug chinchis, issosh homma',
topa sosh
bedcover topaalhiipi'ya'
bedpan aahoshowa'
bedspread patalhpalhiipi'ya',
topaalhiipi'ya'
bedspread, type of naaittapa'ta'
bee fohi'—see also bee, type of
bee, queen fohi' inkapittani', fohi'
ishki', fohi' iminko'
bee, type of fohi' oshi', fohkol,
hatiimimi'
beef liver waaka' salakha'

378

beef marrow waaka' lopi'
beef tripe waakittakoba'
beehive fohi' ilhpichik
beehive hairdo, to have a oshchaha̲li
beehive, manmade fohinchokka'
beer biya'
beer joint nannaaishko'
bees' nest fohi' ilhpichik
bees, swarm of fohi' wiha'
bees, to sound like a swarm of
   winiiyachi
beeswax fohi' bila'
beet tanap homma'
beetle, type of isso̲sh patha', kiitatak
beets biits
before noon nittaki pila
beg for from, to imasilhha
beg, to imilbashsha, i̲hábbi'na
beget, to tobachi
behave oneself, to nokchito
behave, to kostí̲ni, noktá̲la
behave, to go and tell to ootimo̲labi
behave, to make akkachi
behave well, to chokmat atta
behaved, to act badly ishtilamákka'li
behind ima̲shaka'
behind a closed door, to be
   imokshílli'ta
behind, moving aballaka̲li', a̲shaka̲li'
behind, to be ahiitánka, áwwali'chi,
   iklawwi'cho
behind, to go ahiita
behind, to leave antachínchi,
   biniichi, imá̲sha, impalhki, k̲ashcha
   aya, talá̲li
behind, to make stay antachichi
behold! haatokya
belch, to akiilawa
believe, to i̲yimmi, yimmi
believe, to make yimmichi
believe with, to ibaayimmi
believer naayimmi'
believer in aayimmi'
believer in God Chihoowa

I̲naayimmi'
believer, to become a naayimmi' toba
bell issobinnochi'
bell pepper hommahomma'
   champoli'
bells, to make a noise like little
   ittishololó'chi, ittishóllokli'chi
belong to, to immi
belt askoffa
belt buckle askoffishtasitti'ya',
   askoffontalla'a'
bench aaombiniili' falaa'
bend around, to apaakolli
bend down, to akkoshwayaachi
bend one's knees, to to̲'ti
bend over and pull grass, to
   wayyayá̲a, wayyayó̲wa
bend over, to akka' wayowat má̲a,
   akka' wáyya'a, akka' wáyyo'wa,
   tossola, tossolochi
bend, to bicholli, bichoto'li
   chiffolachi, chiffololi, ittapaakolli,
   polhoma
bending over, to keep tossoltó̲wa
benediction, to give a tiwabli
bent around, to be apaakota
bent into a circle, to be chiffola
bent out of shape, to be pashshana,
   payo'kachi, payofa
bent over, to be chiffola, ittapaakota
bent over to one side, to have one's
   head akassanali
bent, to be bichota, bichoto'wa,
   polhoma
bequeath to, to ima
Bermuda onion ato̲falla'a' homma'
berry, type of bissa', bissa' chaaha',
   bissa' hika'
berry vine bissapi'
beside, moving apootaka̲li'
beside, to be imapátta'li, imaapátta'a
beside, to go along aalaachi
best, to do one's ilamóshsho'li
best, to pick out the chaafo'chit

aayoowa
bet on, to ittasiita
bet, to ittasiita
bet with, to ittasiita
better for one, to have it get
 pitinampíla
better than everyone else, to want to
 be ímmayya banna, ittímmayya'chi
 banna
better, to be ayómba, chóngma,
 ishtayómba
better, to feel noktála, pitinkanihmi,
 pitkanihmi
better, to get nampíla, pitnampíla
better, to look ishtayómba,
 pitayyómba
between ittintakla', ittintaklaka'
between, in ittintakla', ittintaklaka'
between, moving ittintaklali'
between the legs tikba'
bewitch, to ayoshkammi
bewitched and die, to be afiitipat illi
bewitched, to be oshkannapa
bib tikba-takaali'
Bible Holisso Holitto'pa'
bid on, to ayalli' ombohli
big chief minkoshto'
Big Dipper Ishtaka'fa'
big for, to be too imaatámpa, imishto
big openings, to have shachakla
big stomach, to have a missila
big stomach, to have a really
 missílli'ya
big, to be hichito, ishto; also aatámpa
big, to make hichitochi, hichitolichi,
 ishtochichi
big, to make oneself ilishtochichi
big toe iyyishki'
Big Well Kali Chito', Kalishto'
bigger, to be chínto
bigger, to make chintolínchi,
 hichintochínchi, hichintolínchi,
 hichitóli
bile ihomi'

bile, to vomit laknaak howita
bill fosh-ibichchala', ibichchala'
billboard ishtoktani'
billy goat issi', issi' kosoma' nakni',
 issi' nakni'
Biloxi Indian Bilokshi'
bingo hall aachokoshkomo'
binoculars hopaakishpisa'
birch itti' tohbi'
bird foshi'
bird dog foshi-hoyo', ofi' foshi' hoyo'
bird, type of Chahta' losa', chaholo',
 chilanto, cho'ki' losa', foshi' hina',
 foshi' yaaya', fosh-oshi', hankha',
 hilowifoshi', issishkin,
 loksapaafohli', shaka'ki', shinka—
 see also names of specific birds
birdcage foshi' aalhto',
 foshinchokka'
birdhouse foshinchokka'
bird's nest foshilhpichik
birth certificate aattattook holisso
birth control device hobak ishtikbi'
birth control pill ittish lhibowa'
 ishtilihaksichi'
birth, from banka
birth month aafammi hashi'
birthday imaafammi nittak,
 imaafammi'
birthday, to have a afammi
biscuit biskit—see also biscuit, type of
biscuit cutter paskishkatolhlhi'
biscuits, to make tili'ko' okommo
biscuit, type of paska hawashko',
 tili'ko' palaska'
bit, a little chinofa'si
bit, bridle issoba kapali'
bite a piece out of, to kisit toshaffi
bite along with, to ibaakisili
bite each other, to ittikisili
bite on, to kilhlhi
bite, to kisili, kisli
bite, to have an insect hoshonnachi
bite, to make kisichi

bits, four bit oshta
bits, six bit hanna'li
bits, two bit toklo
bitter, to be homi
bitter, to make homichi
bitter weed alba homi', alba lakna'
black child hattak los-oshi'
black coffee kaafi' losa'
black haw chinaafalla'ha'
black man hattak losa' nakni'
black pepper homma' losa'
black person hattak losa'
black person, to be a losa
black, person who is half hattak
losiklanna'
black slave hattak losa' toksali'
black, to be losa
black, to be really lóssakbi
black, to make losachi
black woman hattak los-ihoo'
blackbird chalhha', chalhha' losa'
blackbird, type of chalhha' ishto'
black-eyed susan hattak losishkobo'
blackjack (tree) chiskilik
blackjack oak ash water hottok
hoyya', hottok okchi'
blacksmith tali' bo'li'
blacksmith's shop talaabo'wa'
bladder showak aalhto'
blame each other, to ittonhochi
blame for, to take the imilonhochi
blame oneself, to ilihofahyachi
blame, to ishtonhochi, onhochi
blame, to take the ilonhochi,
ishtilabaanali, ishtilonhochi
blamed, to be ishtonittola,
ishtonti'wa
blanket naachi, naachi shobbokko'li'
blanket, type of issobinaachi,
issobompatalhpo', naachi
shobbokko'li' haloppa', naachi
shobbokko'li' homma'
blaspheme, to Chihoowa kalakshichi
blast, to tali' tokaachi

blaze on the forehead, to have a
baktasali
blaze on the forehead, to put a
baktasachi
blaze, to atalhlhichi
bleach, to tohbichi
bled, to be ilhahli
bleed, to issish aaishi, issish lhatapa,
issishat lhatapa, ilhahli, lhahli
blind in both eyes, to be ishkinat
intamowa
blind person shamba'
blind, to shambachi
blind, to be ikpi'so
blind, to go shamba
blind, window winda' takaali'
blindfold, to ishkin intakchi
blink, to moshmoli
blister, to wokkola
blister, to cause a wokkolachi,
wokkololi
bloated, to be shatabli
block against, to imoktabli
block, quilt nannittapatkachi'
block, to inkatabli
blocked, to be inkatapa, oktapa
blood issish
blood from, to take issish aaishi
blood to clot, for one's issishat hika
blood vessel issish ihina'
bloodclot, type of issish shalahli'
bloodsucker issish ishko', issish
sho'ka'
bloody nose to, to give a ibichchala'
inkooli, ibichchala' kooli
bloom, to pakali, woksholi
bloom, to make pakachi
blow a little bit, to mahlihínchi
blow at each other, to ittaapofachi
blow at, to apofachi, ompofa
blow away, to wakaa, wakoha
blow (medicine) onto (someone's)
back, to lhilichi
blow on for, to ishippali

blow on, to shippali
blow on one's hands, to ilapofachi
blow one's nose, to lhihka
blow out smoke playfully, to chomak
  shoboochi
blow over, to okaamahli
blow the nose, to help lhihkachi
blow the smoke from at, to
  oshobollichi, oshobohchi
blow, to mahli; *also* olachi
blow up for, to impoffololi
blow up, to tiwabli
blow wind on, to omahli
blowing, to have mahli
blown up, to be mahli aloota
blue baby chipotikhofa'to'
blue corn tanchokchama'li'
blue jeans balaafokchamali'
Blue River Okchamali Abookoshi
blue, to be okchamali
blue, to make okchamachi
blueberry bissa' okchamali'
bluebird chaholo'
bluegill nani' patassa' lhibokta'
bluff, to fínha
bluejay tishkila
bluejay, to make a noise like a tish
  tish tish aachi
blunt, to be tokbi, tíllikpi
blurry, to be shobbokoli
board itti' basha'
boast, to aaiklóha
boat oka' piini', ok-okaaittanowa',
  piini'—*see also* boat, type of
boat, to go in a oka' okaaittánno'wa,
  oka' okaaittanohówa
boat, type of piini' sawa', piinoshi'
bob, to okpalali
bobbin polona notinto'wa'
bobby pin ipashishtakallo'chi'
bobcat kowinchosh, shakbatinna'
bobcat, type of kowinchosh losa'
bobtail hasimbish iksho', hasimbish
  tapa'

body haknip
body hair hishi'
bodyguard ihopompoyo'
bog shinok toshpa'
bogeyman boka', hattak sholop,
  paayi'
boil hichi'—*see also* boil, type of
boil come up, to have a hichabbi
boil down, to ashippachi, ashippali,
  shippachi, shippali
boil dry, to shippa
boil over, to abaanabli
boil, to lobonni, pitwalhahli,
  walhahli, walhaachi
boil, to have a hoshonnachi
boil, type of hich-oshi'
boiled away, to be ashippa
boiled, to be alhfola, lobona,
  lhabocha, holhponi
bois d'arc itti' lakna'
bois d'arc fruit itti' laknani'
bolt with, to intilhaa
bond for, to post ato'li
bone foni', naafoni'
bone marrow lopi'
bone marrow of the hand or arm
  ilbak lopi'
bone needle naafoni'
  naaistalhcho'wa'
bones, to have an ache in the
  komoochi
bonnet baanit, ihoo iyaalhipa
bonnet, war yaatala
bony, to be shílli'ya
booger boka'
book holisso
book, arithmetic naaholhtina'
  holisso
bookcase holisso aa-asha', holisso
  aalhto', holisso onaa-asha'
boom, to go bokafa
boondocks, out in the hayaka'
boot sholosh chaaha'
booth nannaakanchi'

bootlegger oka' homi' ikbi'
boots sholosh pakna' holo'chi'
boots, rubber sholosh naashiipa'
aatoba'
bore, to intakho'bichi
bored, to be imalhchíi'ba
born that way, to have been
imaalhpí'sa
born, to be ala, alhpooba, atta, hofanti
born to, to be imalla, imalhpooba,
imatta
borrow from, to imaaponta
borrow money on, to ta'ossishponta
borrow on, to ishponta
borrow, to aaponta, ponta
borrow with, to ibaaponta
borrower ponta'
boss inkapittani'
both, to be táwwa'a
bother each other, to ittaataklammi
bother, to achilita, apistikili,
ataklammi
bothering one, to have something
nannakat ishtimaawiiki
bothering one, to have what
nannahoot ishtimaawiiki,
nantahaat ishtimaawiiki
bottle kitoba, takoba—see also bottle,
type of
bottle cap kitobalhiipi'ya'
bottle opener kitobishtiwwi'
bottle to, to give a pishichi
bottle, type of kitoba holba',
kitoboshi'
bottom ishtaabinili', nota'
bottom of the foot iyyimpatha'
bottom of the hoof iyyi' nota'
bottomland pataaschi
bounce on, to ombaayo'chi
bounce, to baayo'chi, baayo'kalhchi,
imbaayo'chi, mallichi
bounce up and down, to ayobba'li
ki'yo
bouncy, to be baayo'kalhchi

bound to be, it's takchi'sha
bow tanampalhi'
bow on, to tie a takchit ontalaali
bow (someone's) head, to
oshchonochi
bow the head, to oshchonoli
bow tie ilontala'li'
bow to, to ayoppachi, imoshchooni
bowl, pottery lokfamposhi'
bowl, wooden itti' amposhi'
bowlegged person iyyi' kawwana'
bowlegged, to be iyyaat kawwana,
iyyinchaamaat kawwana,
kawwánna'a
box, to ittibo'li
boxing glove ilbak fo'khishtittibi',
ishtittibo'li'
box-shaped, to be shokolbika'
bíyyi'ka
boy chipota nakni', kabi', kabosh
boy, teenage hattak himitta', hattak
himittachi'
(boys' word, little) po's po's
brace oneself with one's hands, to
ootbitiipa
brace, to afina, afin-kachit máa, afin-
káyya'chi, afinni, afínni'ya
brace with, to afiinili
bracelet ilbak apakfo'li'
bracelet, to put on a ilbak apakfo'li'
apakfolli, ilbak apakfo'li'
imapakfolli
brag about to, to ishtimilahobbi
brag, to aaiklóha, imilahobbi
braid, to hotaanaffo, ihotaanaffo
braided, to be holhtánnaffo, sita
brain ishkobo' lopi', lopi'
brake ishtintallakchi'
brake, to intakchi
braked, to be intallakchi
bran hoshollak
branch akaashampa', itti' naksish,
naksish filammi'
branch of, to be a akaashapa

branched, to be falakto
brand new, to be himíyyi'ta
brand, to incho'li
branded, to be incho'wa
branded with, to be ishtincho'wa
branding iron tali' ishtincho'li', tali'
  ishtincho'wa'
brass band asonnak ola'
brave, to be aaiklóha, iknokwayyo
brawl, to ittachapo'wa
bread paska; *also* pakka—*see also*
  bread, type of
bread box paskaalhto'
bread, corn tanchi' palaska'
bread crumb paska hoshollo'
bread for communion paska
  holiito'pa'
bread, fried paskawaalhaali'
bread, light paska shatabli'
bread made with infested flour
  issosh palaska'
bread pan aapalaska'
bread, slice of paska toshafa'
bread, slices of paska toshahli'
bread, to make tili'ko' okommo
bread, type of paska kallo', paska
  latassa', paskalhposha',
  paskinkano'miksho',
  paskokchamali'
break a piece off, to toshaffi,
  toshaachi
break a promise, to anompinkobaffi
break against, to akalhali, akoobaffi,
  akooli
break apart, to nipahli
break for, to inkookoli, inkooli
break in two, to intapa, palhata
break into many pieces, to toshaachi
break off a part of, to koloffi
break off a piece of for, to inkoloffi,
  intoshaffi
break off in, to atiiloffi
break one's fall, to bitiipa
break one's neck, to tilofa

break one's promise, to anompa
  kobaffi
break one's word, to anompa kobaffi,
  anompinkobaffi, imanompa kobaffi
break one's word to, to imanompa
  inkobaffi
break open, to abooshollichi
break (someone's) heart, to really
  hottopánchikat aalhlhi
break the law, to nannalhpisa'
  kobaffi, naalhpisa' achapa,
  naalhpisa' oppani
break the neck of, to tiloffi
break, to inkowa, inkookowa, kawwi,
  kobafa, kobaffi, kobahli, kobaachi,
  kobbi, kowa, kookoli, kookowa,
  kooli, oppani; *also* akalhali,
  hapashshichi
break up into pieces, to toshahli
break up, to cha'li
break wind, to hónkso
breakfast, to eat nittaki impa
breakfast, to make nittaki hopooni
breaking, to make the sound of glass
  cham cham cham aachi, chamak
  chamak chamak aachi
breaking, to make the sound of wood
  bas bas bas aachi, basak basak basak
  aachi
breast hashintak, ipishik
breastbone haship foni'
breasts, area between the haship
breasts, to fondle (a woman's)
  imbishlichi
breath knocked out of one, to have
  the nokbiipa, nokbiipo'wa
breath, to be out of foyopat intaha
breath, to have trouble getting one's
  nokshiyammi
breath, to take a ilifoyopa
breath, to take a deep kallochit
  foyopa
breathe hard, to kallochit foyopa
breathe in, to noklhamalli

breathe in, to make noklhamallichi
breathe, not to be able to noktiipa
breathe on, to ofoyopa
breathe, to foyopa; *also* poffoola
breathe, to make foyopachi
breathing, to be foyohómpa
breathing, to have difficulty lhachofa
breechcloth tikba-takaali'
breed with, to ishtimona
breeze, to make a mahlihínchi
briar kantak, kantak ishto'
Briar Creek Kantak Abookoshi
brick lokfi' nona'
bridge alhchaba; *also* abookoshi'
hina' aalhopolli', aalhopolli', itti'
patalhpo', naalhopolli'
bridge, railroad itti' chanaa' malili'
aa-abaanabli'
bridle issoba kapali' ishhalalli',
issoba kapali' ishtalakchi'
bright, to be hashtahli, shoppala,
toomi
brim, hat yaalhipimpatha'
brine oka' hapayyima'
bring back together, to ittifalammichi
bring down from, to ishtaakkowa
bring down, to akkihci,
akkoshwayaachi, ishtakkowa
bring for, to ishtimalla, ishtimayya,
ishtimona
bring here, to atashaachi, ishtala
bring into a life of prostitution, to
hawichi
bring into existence, to tobachi
bring into, to ishchokkowa
bring near, to milinkachi
bring out, to ishtaakochcha,
ishkochcha
bring the ends of together, to
ittapootoli
bring this way, to oshwayaachi,
oshwayoochi
bring through, to ishtaalhopolli
bring, to help ishtibaawiichi

bring to life, to okchaalínchi
bring to, to ishminti, ishtala, ishtaya,
ishtimalla, ishtimayya, ishtimona,
ishtona
bring together in one place, to
ittanachi
bring together the ends of, to
ittachakli
bring together, to ittachapali, ittapolli
bring up an old issue, to ittachapa
bring up, to hofantichi
broad, to be patha
broadcast, to lha'li
broken but still attached, to be nafa,
naalhchi
broken by, to have one's fall
ootawaata
broken necks, to have tilohli
broken off in, to be atiilofa
broken off, to be atoosháfa
broken off, to have a piece toshafa,
toshahli
broken off, to have the tops tilohli
broken, to be kawa, kobafa, kobahli,
kowa, kookowa, nipahli, oppolo
bronco, bucking issoba malli', issoba
tossoola'
brooch chofaakoshi' ilontala'li',
ishtalhopo'li'
broom ishpiha'
broom weed ishpiha'
broomstick ishpiha' aalhpi'
broth naafoni' okchi'
broth, meat nipi' okchi'
brothel hawi' abooha
brother ittibaapishi, inakfi'
brother, half- intikba iklanna',
ittibaapishi iklanna', inakfiklanna',
nakfish iklanna'
brother, older intikba
brother, younger nakfish
brother-in-law imalak
brown sedge hashshok haloppa'
brown, to be lakna

brown, to be dark lakna losayyi
brown, to make laknachi
bruised, to get yolhko
brush, type of itti' shawwilli'
brush, to halíli, oshhalili, shilli
bubble pokpoki', woshwoki'
bubble, soap ishtalhchifa' pokpoki'
bubble, to woshwoki
bubbles for, to make oka'
impokpokichi
bubbles with, to make pokpokichi
bubbling sound, to make a chobo'chi,
choboowachi
buck issi' nakni'
buck rake hashshok ishkalla'fa'
buck with full-grown horns issi'
lapish faloha', issi' falaa
buck, to tossoola
buck, to make tossoolachi
bucket asonnak tobbi', okishtolhchi'
bucket, type of asonnak tobbi'
okishtolhchi', itti' kolofa
buckeye hahtaayi'; also chalantak
bucking bronco issoba malli', issoba
tossoola'
bucking, to carry while ishtossoola
buckle, belt askoffishtasitti'ya',
askoffontalla'a'
buckskin talhko
budget, to keep a ilatoba
buds come out, to have fakobli
buffalo yanash
bug issǫsh—see also bug, type of
bug spray issǫshtilli'
bug, type of hapaanokfila,
hapaanokfilishto', hatiimimi',
hofanti', kowi-homma', kiitatak,
yakni' shokaawi'—see also names
of specific insects
bug-eyed, to be okmiloli
buggy bagi'
buggy, toy chanalloshi'
bugs in grain or cereal nanna
shombachi'

bugs, to be eaten by shomba
bugs, to have issǫsh bíyyi'ka
build for, to imooti
build log cabin-style, to ittabanni,
ittabannichi
builder abooha ikbi'
building chokkishto'
bulge, to missílli'ya
bull waaka' nakni'—see also bull,
type of
bull nettle fannik
bull snake sinti' kiliha'
bull, type of waakoshi' nakni'
bulldog ofishkobishto'
bulldog puppy ofishkobishtoshi'
bullet naki'—see also bullet, type of
bullet mold nakishtikbi'
bullet, type of naki' kawaski', nak-
oshi', tanampishto' inak-oshi',
tanamposhkololi' inaki'
bullfighter waaka' nakni' ittibi'
bullfrog, to make the noise of a paa
bully, to be a aaiklǫha
bum inchokkiksho'
bumblebee hosiino
bumblebee, to make a noise like a
ittitimimí'chi
bump against, to ilhkoyyokli'chi
bump into each other, to ishtittilisso
bump into, to ishtilisso
bump together, to ishtittilisso
bumping noise, to make a
kobo'kachi
bumpy, to be kalhkaki
bunch ishtaaonchololi'
bunch of little things, a kobolli'
bunch, to be a lawa
bunch, to gather in a lókko'li
bunch up, to ittaboknohli
bundle alhpooyak
bundle, to bokshiko'li, bokshikoffi
bundle, to be in a bokshikofa
bundle up against the cold, to
ilaboknohli

bundled, to be bokshiko'wa, bokshikofa
burden, to ishtimaawiikichi, iwiikichi
burden to, to be a ishtimaawiiki
burden with, to ashiichi
burdened, to be ishtimaawiiki
burdened with, to be ashiiyalhchi
buried, to be holloppi
burlap bag shokcha kallo'
burn, for the sun to hashi'at lowachi
burn off one's hair, to anakshowa, ilanakshooli
burn on, to ashama
burn on, to cause to ashamachi, ashamali
burn oneself on, to holhpa
burn oneself, to ililowachi
burn so as to ignite a large fire, to akiiliili
burn the hair off, to anakshooli
burn, to fannichi, holhpa, holhpali, lowa, lowachi, kilaa
burn up with, to alowa, aloowachi
burned by, to get holhpa
burning, to smell like something kashama
burning, to sound like something basaachi
burp, to akiilawa, akiilawachi
burro haksibish falaa' iskanno'
burrs, type of shommatik ani'
burst against, to akalhali
burst, to bokafa, bokaffi, bokahli, bokahchi, bokli, pichihli, sokafa, sokaffi, sokahli, sokaachi, sokli
bury along with, to ibaahoppi
bury, to bohli, hoppi, talaali
bus bas, hattak shaali'
bush itti' shawwa—see also bush, type of
bush beans itti' tiyya'
bush, beauty nita' lobahli'
bush, type of tokfol

bushel boshshal
bushel basket naaishtalhpisa'
bushy hair, to have oshwichali
bushy, to be abokkoli, ittawashshálla'a, ittawashshállo'ha, oshwichali, washshálla'a, washshállo'ha, washshaloha
business, to have imaalami, nannimaalami
business, to have something be one's nannishtahalaa
businessman hattak nannimaalami', nannimaalami'
busy, to be ataklama
butane truck nihaalhto'
butcher nipi' bashli'
butcher shop nipi' aabashli', waaka' aabashli'
butcher, to help ibaa-abi
butter pishokchi' niha'
butter, to make pishokchi' nihachi
butterfingers ilbak illi'
butterfly hatalhposhik
butterfly net hatalhposhik ishyokachi'
buttermilk aaniha okchi', pishokchi' aaniha' okchi'
buttocks imashaka', ishkish, iyyobi' ishtoka'
button naaishtakallo'
button a button on, to tasiitili
button, to asiitohli, tasiitohli
buttonbush shakchikoyyo'
buttonhole naaishtakallishkin
buy at, to aachompa
buy for in, to aainchompa
buy for, to inchompa
buy for with, to ibaainchompa
buy from in, to aaimaachompa
buy from on credit, to imaahhi'ka
buy from, to aachompa, imaachompa
buy on credit, to ahiika
buy, to chompa
buy, to make chompachi

buy together, to ittibaachompa
buy with, to ibaachompa
buzz, to komoowachi, timiiyachi,
  winiiyánchi
buzzard shiiki
by day nittak

by herself ilapi̲t, ilaapo'
by himself ilapi̲t, ilaapo'
by itself ilapi̲t
by themselves ilaapo'
by, to go tánno'wa, tanohó̲wa

C

cabbage tohi', tohi' ishkobishto',
  tohi' ishkobo'
cabin, log abooha ittabaana',
  aboohattittabaana', itti' ittabaana'
  abooha
cabinet, medicine itti̲sh aa-asha'
caboose itti' chanaa malili'
  hasimbish
cackle, to taktaki
cactus talhpakha'
caesarian section, to deliver a baby by
  bashlicha chipotaaishi
cage nanninchokka', aalhto'
cake paska champoli'
calculation naaholhtina'
calendar hashi' holhtina'
calf of the leg iyyincha̲mo',
  iyyintakaali'
call by name, to hochifo
call for, to inkaali
call on the phone, to kaali
call, to i̲waa
call to mind, to nokfokha
called, the one aachika'
calm down, to akkachi, noktala,
  noktalaali
calm, to be chonkash yohbi,
  nokchito, yohbi bíyyi'ka
calm, to have one's mind be
  imaanokfila-at yohbi bíyyi'ka
calm, to make nokchitoli
calmer, to be nokchínto
camel issoba kobokshi'

camera aaholbachi', ishholbachi'
camera, movie shoo ishtikbi'
camp for, to be a imalbina
camp house aa-albinachi'
camp in, to make aa-albinachi
camp meeting ittanahishto'
camp, to make albinachi', aa-
  albinachi' ikbi
camping place, to be a albina
campsite aa-albinachi'
can, lard asonnak tobbi'
can opener asonnak tobbi' ishtiwwi'
can some of, to kitobaa-abihli,
  kitobaa-ani
can, tin asonnak tobbi',
  asonnaktoshi'
can, to kitobabihli, kitobani
candidate, to be a ilipa̲fi
candle shoppala' akmi'
candle holder shoppala' akmi'
  ishyokli'
candlestick shoppala' akmi' ishyokli'
candy kendi'
candy, type of kendi' kallo'
cane oskapi'
cane, walking ittabi', itti'
  ishtilombitka', itti' ishno̲'wa'
canker sores, to have liwaali
canned food impa' asonnak
  tobbaalhto'
canned goods kitoba nannalhto',
  nanna asonnak tobbaalhto'
cannibal hattak apa'

cannon tanampishto'
cannonball tanampishto' inaki'
cannula ishfoyopa'
canoe piini' sawa', piinoshi'
cantaloupe istokchank bila'ma'
canvas ishtalhtipo'
canyon okaachiloha'
cap, baseball to'li' yaalhipa
cap, baseball player's to'li' iyaalhipa
cap, bottle kitobalhiipi'ya'
cap, stocking yaachiko'li'
cape a'chi'
capricious, to be imaanokfila-at
filito'wa
caps nantokahli'
car itti' chanaa palhki', kaa
car, cattle waaka' shaali'
car cloth kaa ishtachifa'
car cover nannompatalhpo'
car horn kaa ishpaachi'
car starting, to make the sound of a
ying ying ying aachi
car with only one headlight
shokkaawi'
card player chalhka'
card, playing ishchalhka'
card, to shillichi
cardboard holisso kallo'
cardinal foshhommak, foshi'
homma'
cards, to play chalhka
cards in, to play aachalhka
care about, not to naaishtahoobali
ki'yo
care about, to nannishtanhi
care, not to nanninkanihki'yo,
naaishtimahómba ki'yo,
nannishtinkanihmo
care of a problem, to take nampíla,
pitnampíla
care of oneself, to take ilaapichi,
ishtilaapichi
care of, to take apiisachi, holiitobli,
ishtilaapichi, ittahaalahlínchi,

ihapompoyo, nampila
care, to nanninkanihmi
careful with, to be achokmalínchi,
imilipóo, ishtilihopoo
careful, to be aha' anhi, ilihopóo,
yahmanhi, yakohmanhi
caress, to hapashshichi
carouse, to ilihaksichit nowa
carpenter abooha ikbi', abooha
iksaachi', chokkiksaachi'
carpet akka' patalhpo'
carpet beater akka' patalhpo'
ishbo'wa'
carriage bagi'
carried away watching, to get pi'scha
ishtakaaniya, pi'scha ishtataamowa
carried, to be sho'wa
carry off, to ishtáa
carry on one's back, to sha'li
carry on one's head, to yaatalaali
carry on one's shoulders, to ilabanali,
shaali
carry, to sho'li
carry while bucking, to ishtossoola
cartwheels, to turn ishkobo'
hili'shcha filita
cash a check for, to ta'osso
imboshollichi
cash a check, to ta'osso boshollichi
cash register ta'ossaalhto'
casing, shell naki' hakshop
cast a vote, to voot kanchi
castanets ishkasa'chi'
castor bean plant akanka'
ihoshottika'
castor oil ittish bila'
castrate, to imbashli
cat kidi', kowi'
cat, civet koni chokcho'
cat food kowimpa'
cat, mother kowi' oshpishichi',
kowishki'
cataract ishkin hakshop alhiipa'
cataract, to have a ishkinat alhatta,

catch a sickness from, to

ishkinat talha
catch a sickness from, to abika'
imaahalili, abika' ihalili
catch a sickness, to abika' halili
catch by twisting with a stick, to
apannichi
catch fire from, to alowa
catch fire, to lowa
catch in a net, to hokaachi
catch on a hook, to hotosi
catch on a hook, to cause to hotosichi
catch, to hayoochi, yokachi, yokli
catch up with, to sakki
catch with, to ibaayokachi, ibaayokli
catcher to'wa' yokachi', to'wa' yokli'
caterpillar hayowani' woksho'
caterpillar, type of hattak holhpali',
hayowani' holhpali', hayowani'
lhipa'
catfish takha
catnip kowi' hasimbish
cattail hoski, kowi' hasimbish, panti'
cattle car waaka' shaali'
cattle feed waakimpa'
cattle truck waaka' shaali'
caught in one's throat, to have
something nokbikili
caught inside, to be chokkówa
caught on a hook, to be holhtosi
caught, to be oottakohli, takaali
cause a blister, to wokkolachi,
wokkololi
cause an allergic reaction, to
fowabbichi
cause to burn on, to ashamachi,
ashamali
cause to catch on a hook, to hotosichi
cause to get soft, to yolhkochi
cause to shoot at, to hosachi
cave yaaknanonka', yaakni' cholok
cave in completely, to okaayilhihli
cave in on, to oyilhipa, oyilhihli
cave in, to okaabowafa, okaayilhipa,
yilhipa

cayenne pepper hommahomma'
cease, to hika
cedar chowaala'
ceiling aba', abooha pakna', pakna'
cellar lokfi' abooha', sela', yaakni'
cholok abooha'
cement tali' foloha', tali' palaska'
cement floor tali' patalhpo'
census hattak hotihna'
cent sent, sent homma'
cent, one sent chaffa'
cents, fifty bit oshta
cents, five sent talhlha'pi
cents, seventy-five bit hanna'li
cents, ten sent pokko'li
cents, twenty-five bit toklo
centipede iyyi-lawa'
certain, a kanimpi, kanimpihmat,
kanimpihma
certain extent, to be to a kaniya fokha
certain, to be a kanimpi
certificate holisso nannishtithana'
certificate, birth aattattook holisso
chafe, to pishoffi
chain tali' ishtasiitoha', tali'
ittatakali'
chain, neck tali' inno'chi'
chain, to atakalichi
chair aaombiniili'
chair, back of a aaombiniili'
aatayya'a'
chair leg aaombiniili' ihikki'ya',
aaombiniiliyyi'
chair, rocking aaombiniili' faya'kachi
chalk ishholissochi'
chalk, white ishholissochi' tohbi'
challenge, to imiliyimmichi, pafi
chamber pot aahoshowa'
chamois kaa ishtachifa'
chance to iyoba
change ta'osso bosholli'
change around, to ittatobbichi,
ittatobo'chi
change one's home, to wiha

390

change one's mind, to imaanokfila
ilánchi
change oneself, to ililánchi
change position, to kana'li
change the home of, to wihachi
change, to ittimilachi, ilánchi
change, to get ta'osso boshollichi
change to, to give ta'osso
imboshollichi
changeable, to be imaanokfila-at
filito'wa
Changing Partners Ittimolabi' Hilha'
chapped, to be hoshinko
charge high prices for, to ayalli'
chaahachi
charge high prices, to ayalli'
chaahachi, ayalli'at inchaaha,
imayallishto
charge, to ahiika
charley horse halalli'
charley horse, to have a halalli
charm, type of fatpo takaali',
ishtahollo' ishokcha
charm, to inchama'chi
chase oneself, to ililhiyohli
chase, to lhiyohli
chatter like a squirrel, to fikfiya
cheap, to be alhchóna
cheap, to make alhchonachi
cheat each other, to ittihaksichi,
ittihonkopa
cheat out of, to completely
haksi'shcha ayowat intahli
cheat, to ahaksichi, haksichi,
honkopa, ihonkopa
check chek
check for, to cash a ta'osso
imboshollichi
check, to cash a ta'osso boshollichi
checked, to be hólisso
checkers holhtina' ishchokoshkomo'
cheeks ishshoka'
cheer, to ayininchi
cheerleader ayiimillichi

cheese issi' kosomimpishokchi'
niha', pishokchi' palaska'
Cherokee Chalakki'
Cherokee language
Chalakkimanompa'
Cherokee Nation Chalakkiyaakni'
Cherokee person Chalakki'
Cherokee woman Chalakkihoo'
cherry tree ittalikchi'
chest ittoyyo'bi'
chest of drawers nanna aalhto'
chew along with, to ibaahowasa
chew noisily, to ittikáshshakli'chi
chew, to howasa; also kapali
chew, to make howasachi
chewing gum taakchili'
chewing ice, to make the sound of
kas kas kas aachi, kasak kasak kasak
aachi
chewing, to make the sound of nam
nam nam aachi
chewing tobacco chomak pallaska'
chewing tobacco, type of chomak
shana'
Chicano Oshpaani'
chick akankoshi', akankoshi'
hofanti'
chick peas akank imbala'
chickadee oktosha' foshi'
Chickasaw Chikashsha
Chikasaw child Chikashshoshi'
Chickasaw, full-blooded Chikashsha
finha', Chikashsha kallo',
Chikashshalhlhi'
Chickasaw, half Chikashshiklanna'
Chickasaw language
Chikashshanompa'
Chickasaw Nation
Chikashshiyaakni'
Chickasaw person Chikashsha
Chickasaw woman Chickashshihoo'
chicken akanka'—see also chicken,
type of
chicken and dumplings

chicken, bantam

akankishtashiila
chicken, bantam akankiskanno'
chicken dumpling akankishtalhfola'
chicken fat akanka' niha'
chicken feathers akanka' hishi'
chicken, fried akankawaalhaali'
chicken gizzard akankinchakaffa'
chicken hawk akankabi'
chicken house akankinchokka'
chicken liver, gall on akankihomi'
chicken meat akanka' nipi'
chicken pox akankinchakwa'
chicken snake abaksha', akanka'
   sinti', akankapa', akankosh-apa',
   sinti' akankosh-apa'
chicken soup akankishtashiila
chicken, type of akanka' basoowa',
   akanka' chakwokoli', akanka'
   holisso', akanka' lakna', akanka'
   losa', akanka' tohbi', akanka'
   yalhkobo'li', akankhishfili'ta',
   akankimilhlha', akankoshchahali',
   akankoshchiloli', akankpihcha',
   chaloklowa' akanka', kanka'simpa'
chicken wire tali' shachakla'
chickens, bantam akanksawa'
chicken's crop akankimpinak a'lhto',
   akankimpoffola'
chicken's egg akankoshi', akankoshi'
   lombo'
chicken's noise, to make a kalhkaha
chief minko'
chief, big minkoshto'
chigger washko
Chihuahua ofi' imo'ma'
child chipota
child, abandoned chipotalhtakla'
child, illegitimate chipota holhkopa',
   chipota loma', holhkopa'
child, poorly behaved chipotoppolo'
child whose father is not known
   chipota inki' toklo'
child, youngest chipota ishtayyo'pi'
children, someone without oshi'

iksho'
children's ward chipotaa-asha'
chile hommahomma'
chili chili'
chili powder chili' ibalhto'
chill to, to give a ichchokwali
chilled, to be ichchokwa
chimney aaolhti', aashobohli'
chin notakfa
chin in the air, to put one's
   abakshowali
china amposhi' holiitopa'
china cupboard amposhaa-asha'
chink, to apoolosli
chinked, to be apoolosa
chip off a piece from, to shokaffi
chip off, to be a atoosháfa
chip, to shokafa, shokaachi, shokli
chipmunk chilisa'
chipped, to be shokafa, shokahli
chips, wood hakashtap
chisel ittishkola', nannishshokli'
chitlins shokha' saalhkona'
chocolate chaklit, chaklit losa'
chocolate, hot chaklit palli'
Choctaw Chahta'
Choctaw child Chahtoshi'
Choctaw language Chahtanompa'
Choctaw, Louisiana Falanchi'
   Chahta'
Choctaw, Mississippi Missipi'
   Chahta'
Choctaw Nation Chahtiyaakni'
Choctaw, Native Yappakayni
   Chahta'
Choctaw woman Chahtihoo'
choir taloowa alhiha
choir director taloowapiichi'
choke on, to nokshiyammi,
   noktakaali
choke, to nokbikichi,
   noklhamallichi, noklhito'li,
   noklhitofa, noklhittoffi, noklhitoffit
   illichi, noksita

choked a little, to be noklhito'wa
choked, to be noklhitofa
choking, to kill by noklhitoffit abi
choose, to pafi
chop at, to sakkaha
chop, to cha'li, palhalli
chop up, to lalli
chopped, to be lata
chopper, meat nipishlolli'
christen, to baptismochi
christened, to be baptismo
Christian Abaanompa' Yimmi',
  Chihoowa Inannalhpisa' Yimmi',
  Chihoowa Inaayimmi', Iksa'
Christian, to become a Iksa'
  ibaafokha, naayimmi' toba
Christmas Chihoowoshi'
  Imaafammi', Chitokaka'
  Imaafammi', Nittak Hollishto'
church aaittanaha', ittanaha'
church meeting, to have a ittanaha
(church, name of a) Pachaanosi',
  Shinok Tohbi'
church, to join a Iksa' ibaafokha
churn pishokchi' aaniha', shoti'
churn dasher
  pishokchishbo'kalhchi',
  pishokchishnihachi'
churn, to bo'chi, pishokchi' nihachi
cigar chomak pofa' ishto'
cigarette chomak holbona', chomak
  pofa'
cigarette paper chomak aaholbona'
cigarette, to roll a chomak hoboona
cinnamon sinniman
circle around, to form a afoolobli
circle, to be bent into a chiffola
circumcise, to hakshop tabli
circumcised male hakshop tapa'
cistern oka' ishyokachi'
city hall nannishtaa-asha'
civet cat koni chokcho'
Civil War Tanap Ittibi'
clabber pishokchi' sotko'

clam folosh-ata'
clamp ishtakallo'chi'
clan ishtaaoncholoLi'
clan name inchokkachaffa'
  holhchifo
clan, person of a certain old
  Chickasaw Hattak Imosak Cha'a',
  Hattak Inchiisha' Wayya'a', Hattak
  Issi'Inchiisha' Koba'fa', Hattak
  Shawi'
clanging noise, to go along making a
  komomó'chi
clank, to ittichalhalha'chi
clanking sound, to make a
  ittichalha'chi, ittichálhlhakli'chi,
  kas kas kas aachi, kasak kasak kasak
  aachi
clap all the time, to passasa'chi
clap for, to ilbak impasa'chi,
  impasa'chi
clap one's hands, to ittipasa'chi
clap the hands, to ilbak pasa'chi,
  ittipasa'línchi
clap, to pasa'chi
clapping sound, to make a pas pas
  pas aachi
clapping, to make noise ittipasasá'chi
clash, to iktiholbo
class, to be a kashapa
clatter, to chalhaahánchi
clatter, to make a ittikama'chi,
  ittikamamá'chi, ittikámmakli'chi
claw iyyakchosh
claw, to sholaffi, sholli
clay lokfi' chakissa'
clay, type of lokchok homma', lokfi'
  homma', lokfi' lakna'
clean laundry naalhchifa'
clean oneself in the dust, to ayiili
clean, person who keeps things
  nanchofalli'
clean, to chofalli, kashoffi; also
  hayoochi
clean, to be chofata, kashofa

cleaned, to be hayowalhchi
clear one's throat, to inonka'
chokmali
clear up, to bashili
clear, to shahbichi
clear, to be aloktowali, aloktówwa'li,
nokshawali, shokkawali
clear, to let become aloktowachi
cleared, to be shahbi
clearing kochchaafokka'—*see also*
clearing, type of
clearing, to be cut off short in a
ittayoshkóllo'li
clearing, to cut off short in a
ittayoshkolochi
clearing, type of iyaaknasha'
aachokoshkomo', itti' oshkololi',
iyaaknasha' intopa
clever, to be hapoyoksa, imponna,
ishtaponnachi
climb on, to aatoyya
climb, to oshtoyya, toyya
climb, to make toyyachi
climb up, to ashtoyya, lappapáli,
lappopóli
cling peach takola'lhi'
cling to, to achokkobbi, apakchilofa,
atákka'li, atákkohli, atakoht máa
clip ishyo'kli'
clippers, grass hashshok ishkachiili'
clock hashi' kanalli ishtithana'
clock, alarm hashi' kanalli ishithana'
ola'
clod lokfi' kallo'
clog, to lobli
clogged, to be lopa
close against, to imokshitta
close in, to okshitta
close the eyes, to mocholi
close, to ittasiitili, ittasiitohli,
okshilitta, okshitta, tasiitili
close, to be ittitíkki'li, ittimilínka,
milínka, pitoláli
close to, to be imachokkobbi,

imilínka
close to, to be really akónno'fa
closed door, to be behind a
imokshílli'ta
closed in, to be imokshílli'ta
closed, to be okshilitta, tíwwa'pa
closer, to move oshtolaalínchi,
pitolaalínchi
closet abooshi', naafkaa-asha'
clot, for one's blood to issishat hika
cloth naafka toba', naalhila'fa',
naalhilahli'
clothes naafokha
clothes off, to pull all the lhofi
clothes, old naafokha lhipa'
clothes rack naafkaatakohli'
clothes sprinkler oka' ishtolha'li'
clothes store naafkaa-asha',
naafkaakanchi'
clothes, to take off one's naafka
shihli
clothesline naafkaatakohli'
clothespin naafkishtakallochi'
clothing naafokha
cloud hoshonti
cloud of dust fly, to make a
shobohónta
cloud of dust rise, to have a shobolli
cloud of, to make a shobollichi
cloudless, to be bashili
clouds, to be obscured by hoshonti
cloudy, to be hoshonti
cloven, to be falakto
clown ishtakanomi'
clown around in place of, to
ishtimakanomit nowa
clown around, to ishtakanomit
nowa, ishtilihaksichi
clown, to be a ishtakanomi
cluck, to kalhkaha, takla, toktoha
clucking, to make the sound of a hen
tok tok tok aachi
clumsy person ilbak illi'
coachwhip snake sinti' hattak

fammi'
coal lowak tobaksi', tobaksi', tobaksi'
  losa'
coal car tobaksi' shaali'
coal mine tobaksaakola'
coal miner tobaksi' kolli'
coal shovel lowak ishpiha'
coat naafkishto'
coat, type of naafkishto' falaa',
  naafkishto' woksho'
coat, to ashiila
coax, to ihabina
cob, corn- tanchapi'
cob, to be off the chillowa
cob, to be still on the apínka
cock, fighting akanka' ittibi'
cock, to hilichi
cockleburr shommatik
cocoa chaklit, chaklit palli'
coffee kafi'
coffee beans kaafi' ani', kaafi' nihi'
coffee, black kaafi' losa'
coffee cup kaafaaishko'
coffee cup handle kaafaaishko'
  aayo'kli'
coffee, dregs of kaafi' lakchi'
coffee grinder kaafaafoloha',
  kaafishfoloha'
coffee, ground kaafi' folowa'
coffee, instant kaafi' bota'
coffeepot kaafaawalhahli'
coffeepot spout kaafaawalhahli'
  ibichchala'
coffin hattak illi' aafo'kha', hattak
  illintoyyo'bi', ittoyyo'bi'
coil around, to tashan-kachi
coil up, to holbona
coins, gold tali' holisso' lakna'
colander, type of
  tanchishhayowalhchi'
cold, to be kapassa; also ichchokwa,
  inkapassa
cold, to have a ibishshano
cold, to make kapassali

cold, to turn kapast ala
collapse, to yilhipa
collar kaala'
collar, type of iminno'chi',
  issobinno'chi', kaala' chala'
collarbone iwa'ta', nokhistap foni'
collard greens tohi' chaaha'
collect, to ittanahli, yokachi
collection ittahobbi'
collection of, to make a ittahobbi
collection plate ta'osso ishhoyo'
collection, to take up a ittahobbi'
  hoyo
college nannaaithana'
collide, to ishtittilisso
collie ofi' woksho'
color kala'
color run, to have the masali
color, to be what pisa-kanihmi, pisa-
  katihmi
color while ripening, to turn ataachi
colors run together, to have the
  ittimasalichi
colors, to be all pisittimilayyoka
  bíyyi'ka
colors, to make all oklhiwachi
colt issob-oshi'
comb hashintak
comb, fine-tooth issap ishtalbi'
comb one's hair, to shilli
comb, rooster's akankihashintak
comb the hair of, to ishilli
comb, to shilli
comb worn in the hair yaachakka'li'
combed, to be shila
combine, to ittibaani
come and get and send for, to
  atimpilachi
come and get, to athoyo
come and go in, to tiwa'kalhchi
come apart, to shipahli
come back to one, to have nokfokha
come back, to falama, ifalama
come courting, to pist aat ala

come down a slope, to

come down a slope, to okaatanowat
minti
come down, to ashtakkowa,
ootakkowa
come even with, to sakki
come from, to aaminti
come in from, to aaminti
come in to watch for, to impihlínchi
come in, to ashchokkowa,
atchokkowa, oshchokkowa
come loose, to talhofa
come off along with, to ashokafa
come off, to shifa
come off, to have the sole shokafa
come on taa
come out of nowhere, to ootkochcha
come out of, to aaholhfo
come out on the other side, to
ootkochcha
come out on the other side, to go
through and ootlhopolli
come out on, to omboyafa
come out, to atkochcha, kochch,
oshkochcha
come out, to have okshalli
come out, to have something
powdery shobottokahchi
come out, to open the door and
ashkochcha
come see, to pist ala
come, to ala, minti
come to an agreement concerning, to
ishtittibaanokfilli
come to an agreement, to
ittibaanokfilli
come to one's senses, to kostini
come to rest across, to ootawaata
come to the end, to ootaalhlhi,
ootaalhlhi ona
come to, to imalla, minti, ootithana
come to understand, to imithana
come together, to ittapiha,
ittibaachaffa
come true, to ootálhi

come untied, to holhtofa
come up by itself, to ilapit holhfo
come up, to kochchat minti, walaa
come with, to apiha
comet fochik malili'
comfort each other, to ittaapoolhali
comfort, to apoolhachi, apoolhali
comfortable, to be noktála
comfortable, to get apoolha, noktala
comfortable, to make apoolhachi
coming out, to have the hair
boyahálli
commandment, God's Chihoowa
imanompaalhpisa', Chihoowa
inannalhpisa'
Commandments, the Ten
Naalhpisa' Pokko'li, Nannalhpisa'
Pokko'li'
commission, to tohno
commit a sin, to nannashshachi
commit adultery, to ittilomaka
commit adultery with, to ibaanowa
commitment during, to miss a
imambaanapa
commitments, to go back on one's
imaanokfila-at filito'wa
committed, to be ittakánni'ya
communion Chihoowa Imobyaka'
Impa', naaholiitompa',
Naaholiiompishtaa-asha' Obyaka'
Impa'
communion server
naaholiitompishtatta'
communion servers
naaholiitompishtaa-asha'
communion wafer paska holiito'pa'
company, among the aatangla'
compass falammishtithana'
compete against, to achapa
complain about, to nanna mihachi
complain, to ishtilimihachi
complete a task, to tahli
complete, to be móma
completed, to be alhtaha, taha

396

completely, be taha
completely, do taha
completely, to do tahli
computer tali' anompoli'
concave, to be okaahofobi
conceited, to be ilaafinha
concentrate on something, to hopayi
concern, to aayimma
concerned in the matter of, to be
  ishtahaláa
concrete tali' foloha'
conductor chanaa malili' apiisachi',
  hattak apiisachi'
cone shape, to make into a wahhalili,
  wihhilili
cone shaped, to be shikkilili,
  wahhala, wihhila
confess falsely for, to imilonhochi
confess falsely, to ishtilabaanali
confess, to ilanoli, ilonhochi
confession, to make a ilikostinichi
configuration of, in a certain
  kani'mihmat, kani'mihma
configuration of, in what
  kani'mihoot, kani'miho
configuration, to be in a certain
  kani'mi
configuration, to be in what kati'mi,
  kani'mi
confine, to yokachi
confine to the house, to abooha
  fóyyokhi
confined, to be yoka
confuse, to imayoppani'chi
congeal, to akmi
congregation ittanaha'
congregation, to be a ittanaha
congregation, to dismiss a tiwabli
Congress Nannapiisa', Naalhpisa'
  Ikbi'
Congress, member of Naalhpisa'
  Ikbi'
conjunctivitis ishkin homma'
consciousness, to regain ootithana

consider for, to ishtanokfilli
consider precious, to aapichi
constable chokka' naa-alhtoka'
constipated, to be aya' ki'yo
contact lenses ishkin albiha'
container aalhto'
contend for, to aafowa
contend with for, to imaafowa
contend with one another for, to
  ittimaafowa
contestant, to be a ilipafi
converge on a goal, to báyya'ta
convex, to be kobossa
convince, to yimmichi
convulsion, to have a hayoochichi
coo, to anompoli
cook ihopo'ni'
cook in liquid, to alhatali, ittalhatali
cook on the cob, to hollappichi
cook till done, to lhaboshli
cook, to hopooni, nonachi
cook, to make hopoonichi
cooked, to be alhfola, awaalhahli,
  holhponi, lhabocha, nona
cookie cutter paskishkatolhlhi'
cookie sheet aapalaska',
  paskaanonachi'
cookies paska champoli'
cool, to be kapassachi
cool oil aashoppala' niha'
copper tali' lakna'
copperhead chilha'kbi', ishkobo'
  homma', sinti' chilambi', sinti'
  issikopa'
copy from, to aahobachi, hobasht
  imaaishi, imaahobachi
copy, to hobachi, hobasht aaishi
copy, photo- holisso holba'
cord ishtalakchi'
cord, umbilical ittialbish ishtalakchi'
cork kitoba ishtokshilli'ta'
corn tanchi'—see also corn, type of
corn bread tanchi' palaska',
  tashfolowa' palaska'

corn bread, type of tanchi' himona'
palaska', tanchi' palaska'
hawashko', tanchi' palaskalhposha'
corn cooked off the cob tanchi'
holhponi'
corn dumpling tanchishtashiila'
corn flour, parched tanchi' bota'
corn grater tanchaashafa'
corn hulls tanchi' hoshollo', tanchi'
lakchi'
corn, Indian tanchi' kawaski'
corn kernels tanchi' chillowa'
corn off the cob tanchi' chillowa'
corn on the cob tanchi' alhfola',
tanchi' apinka', tanchi' hollapi'
corn, parched tanchalhposha'
corn shovel tanchishpiha'
corn shucks tanchi' hishi', tahishi'
corn silk tanchi' pashi', tanchi'
woksholi'
corn, roasted tanchalhposha'
corn, roasting ears of tanchi' himona
waa'
corn, row of tanchi' ihina'
corn, seed tanchi' pinha'
corn, small ears of hoshollak
corn, sweet tanchi' champoli'
corn, type of tanchi' holisso', tanchi'
homma', tanchi' kallo', tanchi'
kawaski', tanchi' lakna', tanchi'
lobo', tanchi' okchamali', tanchi'
osaapa aawaa', tanchi' patha',
tanchi' tohbi', tanchi' walokshi',
tanchishto', tanchokchamma'li',
tanchoshi', talobo, tashshokkata'
corn, whole tanchi' apinka'
corncob tanchapi'
corncob, undeveloped tanchi'
kobolli'
corncrib pichchaa
corner shokolbika'
corners, to have shokolbika' aa-asha
corners, to have four shokolbika'
oshta

corners, to have three shokolbika'
tochchi'na
corn-grinding place tanchaabotooli',
tanchaapalha'
cornmeal tashfolowa', tashposhi'
cornmeal mush tanchishtashiila'
cornmeal, type of tanchi' bota',
tanchi' folowa'
corpse hattak illi'
correct, to alhpisa'chi, alhpíssa'li
correct, to be alhpí'sa
corrode, to lokfi' toba
corrugated, to be kalhkaki
corset ishtilakallo'chi'
cosign for, to imalapalínchi
cosign, to imalapalinchi
cosmetics ishshoka' albi'
cost, to ayalli
cottage cheese pishokchi' niha'
bosholli'
cotton naafalli'
cotton, crochet nampanaa'
cotton gin aanihichi', naafalli'
aanihichi'
cottonwood itti' tohbi', hashoomala
cottonwood seeds hashoomala
pofalli'
cough for, to ihotolhko
cough medicine hotolhkottish
cough on, to ohotolhko
cough, to hotolhko
cough, to make hotolhkochi
could it be that nanna'chihchi,
nannahchi, nannatokchi
count along with, to ibaahotihna
count in, to ahotihnachi
count in with, to ibaant hotihna
count the votes for, to holisso
ihotihna, voot ihotihna
count, to hotihna
count, to make hotihnachi
count votes, to holisso hotihna, voot
hotihna
counted in, to be aholhtinachi

counted, to be holhtina
country yaakni'
court, to inowoot áa
courthouse abooha nannishtaa-
asha', nannaa-apiisa' abooha
courting, to come pist aat ala
cousin, type of inkano'mi, intikba',
intiik, ittibaapishi, ittibaapishi pila,
inakfi', nakfish
cousins, to be ittinkano'mi
cover alhiipi'ya', nannalhiipi'ya',
nannompatalhpo'
cover oneself, to anchi
cover oneself with, to pitanchi
cover, to alhibli, alhiipili, anchichi,
anchichichi
cover, to have as a áyya'chi
cover up, to omolhchi
cover with, to omochi
covered, to be alhipkachi, alhipkachit
máa, alhipkáyya'chi, alhíppi'ya,
alhiipa, alhtipo, áyya'chi
covered up, to be omolhchi
covered wagon itti' chanaalhtipo'
covered wagon cover itti' chanaa
ishtalhtipo'
covered with dust, to be shobolli
covering hakshop
covering, to be a pattalhpo
cow waaka'
cow, baby waakoshi'
cow, mother waakishki',
waakoshpishichi'
cow, to milk a waakimbishlichi
cowboy issobombinili', waaka'
takchi', waakombinili'
cowcatcher waakishyokachi'
cowherd waakapiisachi'
cowhide waaka' hakshop
cow-killer kowi-homma'
cowlick ifokkol, iyalfolfo'
cowpeas waakimbala'
cow's teats waakipishik
coyote nashoba homma'

crabapple shonkabosh, shonkabosh
ishto', takolo holba', takolo
imilhlha', takolo sawa', takoloshi'
crabgrass hashshok pata'
crack into pieces against, to
aboshollichi
crack into pieces, to boshollichi
crack one's knuckles, to foni' kooli
crack open, to abooshollichi
crack, to basaachi, basasá'chi,
imbosholli, kowa, kooli, tokafa
cracked, to be bosholli, kisafa, kisahli,
kitafa, kitahli
cracker paska shila'
crackerjack tanchi' sokahli'
champoli'
cracking, to make the sound of lhok
lhok lhok aachi
crackling, pork bila' shila'
crackling sound, to make a
ittibasa'chi
cradle chipotintopa
cramp halalli'
cramp, to have a halalli
crane foshi' chaaha',
nannishtabaawiili', paskawo',
watolo
crank ishfilli'chi'
crave for food, to hóppo'ba
crawfish shakchi
crawl on, to onáa
crawl space abooha nota'
crawl, to bala'li
crawl, to make bala'chi
crawl, to try to tossoltówa
crawling, to be always ballaláli
crazy about, to be akaníya
crazy as, to be as ibaahaksi
crazy, not to be imaanokfila-at
imóma, imaanokfila-at móma
crazy over, to go atamowa
crazy, to act ilihaksichi
crazy, to be haksi, haksit kánni'ya,
imaanokfila-at iksho, imaanokfila-

at kaniya, imaanokfilinkaniya,
ishtaatámpa
crazy, to be kind of kostíyyi'ni ki'yo
creak, to basaachi, basasá'chi,
ittibasasá'chi
creaking sound, to make a
ittibasa'chi, ittibássakli'chi
creaking, to make the sound of wood
bas bas bas aachi, basak basak basak
aachi
cream pishokchi' pakna' takaali'
cream, sour pishokchi' pakna'
takaali' hawashko'
crease into, to press a pakolli
creased, to be permanently pákko'ta
create, to ikbi, tobachi
creature, type of mythological
Iyaaknasha', Lhofa'
credit aahiika'
credit for, to extend ahiikachi
credit for, to get on imáhhi'ka
credit, to buy from on imaahi'ka
creek abookoshi'
Creek Mashkooki'
Creek language Mashkookanompa'
Creek Nation Mashkookiyaakni'
Creek-Seminole language
Mashkookanompa'
cremate, to lowachi
crest, to have a oshchahali
crew cut, to have a oshkabali
crew cut to, to give a oshkabachi
crib chipotintopa, top-oshi'
cricket sholowi'
cricket, type of sholowi' lakna',
sholowi' losa'
crickets, to make a noise like
ittishollo'chi
crickets, to make the sound of shol
shol shol aachi
criminal hattak issikopa'
crinkle paper, to ittishofofó'chi,
ittishokokó'chi
crinkle, to ittishóchchokli'chi,

ittishofo'chi, ittishoko'chi
crinkling sound, to make a
ittishofofó'chi
crinkling, to make the sound of paper
ittishóffokli'chi, shof shof shof
aachi, shok shok shok aachi,
shochok shochok shochok aachi
cripple imomoppolo'
crippled, to be imomoppolo
crisp, to shila
criticize (someone's) possessions, to
inamihachi
criticize, to imiha
crochet cotton nampanaa'
crochet hook nannishtanni'
crochet, to nantanni, tanni
crocheted item nantanna', tanna'
crock shoti'
crooked for, to make ishaniili
crooked, to be bichota, bichoto'wa,
chanakbi, pahhánna'a, pahhana,
shanaayo'wa, shanaa
crooked, to lie chiffóllo'wa
crooked, to make shanaayo'li,
shanaachi
crooked, to walk pahhanpáa,
shanaayo'wa
crop ani'
crop, chicken's akankimpinak
a'lhto', akankimpoffola'
crop, fowl's impaalhto', impoffola'
cross itti' tayokhana'
cross one's eyes, to ishkin okkowatali
cross one's legs, to iyyaat ittabánna'a,
iyyi' ittabaanali
cross over, to aalhoppolli
cross paths with, to ayoppitammi
cross, to make ittabaanali
cross-cousin inkano'mi
crossed, for one's eyes to be ishkinat
okkawata
crossed, to be ittaban-kachit máa,
ittabánna'a
cross-eyed, to be ishkinat okkawata

cross-eyed, to make oneself go ishkin okkawatali
crossing guard, railroad itti' basha' tali-hina' aalhopolli' aahiliichi'
crossing, to lay abaanali
crossing, railroad itti' chanaa malili' hina' aabaanapo'li'
crossroad hina' aaittabanna'a'
crossroad in, for there to be a hina'at aaittabanna'a
crotch ịfalakto', tikba'
crotch, to have a falakto
crouch down, to akka' tákka'li, akka' tákkohli, akka' takoht máa, akka' wayowat máa, akka' wáyya'a, akka' wáyyo'wa, tákka'li, takoht máa, wayowat máa, wáyya'a, wáyyo'wa
crouch down, to make wayoochi
crow fala—see also crow, type of
crow for, to imola
crow, to ola
crow, to make a sound like a kaak kaak kaak aachi
crow, type of fala ishto', fal-oshi'
crowbar nannishtafinni'
crowd around, to afoolobli, ayaashachi
crowd, to toopo'li
crown yaachakka'li'
crown, to put on like a yaachakachi, yaachakali
crucified, to be ahonalha
crucifix itti' tayokhana'
crucify, to ahonalhlhichi, itti' tayokhana' aatakaachi, itti' tayokhana' takaachi
cruel, to be issikopa
crumb paska bosholli', paska chilili'
crumbled, to be bosholli
crumbly, to be bosholli, chilili
crumbs of, to make chilichi
crumbs, to be chilili
crumpled up, to be banata
crunchy things, to make a noise

eating ittikasha'chi, ittikashashá'chi, ittikáshshakli'chi
crunchy things, to make the noise of eating kas kas kas aachi, kashak kashak kashak aachi
crush, to alatassachi, bokaffi, lhacho'li, lhachoffi, pichihchi, pichiffi, sokaffi
crushed, to be bokafa, lhachofa, pichifa, sokafa
crust paska hakshop
crusted, to be chilakbi
crutch itti' ishno'wa'
crutches itti' ishtilombitka', ittishnọwa'
cry about, to ishyaa
cry all the time, to bashshi
cry in, to aayaa
cry, to ishtkin okchi' minti, yaa
cry, to make yaachi
crybaby bashshịshokcha'
crybaby, to be a bashshi
crying inside, to be chonkashat yaháa
crying, to make stop apoolhali
crying, to stop apoolha
Cubby Kabi'
cube shaped, to be shokkolbika' bíyyi'ka
cucumber chank haloppa', istokchankapa'
cuddle up to each other, to ittapakchíllo'fa, ittaapakchíllo'fa
cuddle up to, to apakchilofa, tikili
cuddle up, to ittitikili
cuff naafka shakbịfolota'
cultivate, to aliichi
cup aaishko', ishtaka'fa'
cup, type of kaafaaishko', lokosh ishtaka'fa'
curds pishokchi' sotko'
cure with smoke, to ọshobohchi
cure, to lhakoffichi, masachi
cured, to be lhakoffi, masali
curl, to oshchilochi

curl up, to

curl up, to tossóllo'wa
curled up, to be chiffola
curlers ip̱ashishtoshchiloli'
curling iron ip̱ashishtoshchilochi'
curly, to be oshchiloli, woksho
curry, to shilli
curse, to anompimoppani,
anompimoppanichi, anompoppani,
anompoppanichi, nókko'wa
curtain winda' takaali'
curve, to folota
cushaw melon ostahi'
cuss out, to ishtayooba'li ki'yo
(cuss word) chilhilafa
cut a hole and make another hole in,
to amiitaffi
cut for shingles, to be cholha
cut for, to imbashli, inkatolhlhi
cut grass, to hashshok bashli
cut in half for, to intapalhalli
cut in more than two pieces, to
ittapalhlhi
cut in thin slices, to pasli
cut in three or more pieces for, to
intapalhlhi
cut in, to aabashli
cut in, to be aabasha
cut in two, to ittapaalhalli
cut in two, to be tapa
cut in very thin slices, to be pasa
cut into pieces, to toshli
cut into short pieces, to ittakatolhlhi
cut into too much, to aatakaffi
cut off a part of, to aakoloffi, koloffi
cut off along with, to akatolhlhi
cut off at the top, to be oshkololi
cut off evenly, to be atílhlhi'fa

cut off short in a clearing, to
ittayoshkolochi
cut off short in a clearing, to be
ittayoshkóllo'li
cut off the top of, to oshkolochi
cut off, to aakatolhlhi, aatabli,
katolhlhi, kolofa, oktabli
cut off, to be aatapa, katolha, oktapa,
tapa
cut open for disemboweling, to be
patafa
cut open, to pasaffi, pasaachi, pataffi
cut open, to be pasafa, pasahli
cut out, to be kachaha
cut skin, to have lhilafa
cut, to aatabli, bashaffi, bashli,
chalhafa, chalhaffi, chalhlhi,
katolhlhi, koloffi, palhalli, palhlhi,
tabli; also n̲aachi
cut, to be almo, chalha, bashafa,
katolha, kolofa
cut, to be marked with a inchalha
cut, to mark with a inchalhlhi
cut to shape, to be talha
cut tree limbs, to naachi
cut up for, to intoshli
cut up in pieces, to be toshahli
cut up, to toshtoli
cut up, to be chalhahli, kolohli,
toshtowa
cut with a knife, to bashtabli
cut with scissors, to kachiili
cuts all over, to have knife kolohli
cutter ishtamo'
cutter, cookie paskishkatolhlhi'
cyst, to have a chilhlha̲'li

d

dachshund ofi' falaa'
daddy impaapi'

daddy-long-legs abaatalahchaa'
dam baniya, hayip ishto', oka'

aakatapa', oka' aayokachi'
damaged, to be smoke o̱shobohli
dammed, to be baniya
damp, to be nokyobi, yokolbi
dampen, to yokolbichi
dance hilha'
dance for, to i̱hilha
dance ground aahilha'
dance in, to aahilha
dance leader intikbayka'
dance leader for, to be a intikbayka
dance leader, to be a tikbayka
(dance, name of a) Hilha' Falama',
Ishkobo' Toklo Hilha', Ittimo̱labi'
Hilha', Nani' Kallo' Hilha',
Okishko' Hilha', Sinti' Hilha',
Shatanni Hilha', Shinka Bo'li',
Tilobli' Hilha'—see names of
specific dances
dance on, to o̱hilha
dance place aahilha'
dance, to hilha;also mallichi, to̱'tichi
dance, to make hilhachi
dance with, to ibaahilha
dance with, to make ibaahilhachi
dancer hilha'
dandruff, to have fatabli
dangle, to takkaká̱li, takkokó̱li
dare, to pa̱fi
daredevil, to be a fí̱nha, ilifinhachi
dark for, to make it imoklhilichi
dark place aaoklhilika'
dark red, to be homma losayyi
dark, to be losayyi, oklhili
dark, to be completely oklhílli
dark, to get oklhilichi
dark, to have it get onobya, onoklhili
dark, to make oklhilichi
darkroom hattak holba' aaiksaachi'
darn, to tanni
dart tali' haloppa'
dasher, churn
pishokchishbo'kalhchi',
pishokchishnihachi'

dating, to be ibaano̱wa
daub on each other's faces, to
ittaapoolosli
daub on one's face, to apoolosli
daubed all over with, to be
ishtalhpolosa
daubed on, to be alhpolosa
daughter oshiitiik
daughter-in-law ihayya', ipok tiik,
ippolhchihoo', iyyop ihoo'
dawn, to be just before hashtaht
minti, hashtáyyahli,
hashtayyahlo'si
day nittak
day, a certain nittak nannahma̱
day after tomorrow, the onna
mishshakma̱
day, all obya
day before yesterday, the oblaashaash
mishshaash
day off to, to give a nittak habinachi,
nittak ima
day off, to have a nittak habina
day, one nittak kanimpihma̱
day, some nittak kanimpihma̱, nittak
nannahma̱
day, to be the next onna
day, what nittak kanimpiho̱, nittak
katimpihta, nittak nannaho̱, nittak
nantahta
daydream, to binni't ilhpokonna
daze, to be in a lhakcha
deacon iksa' piichi', olhtipiichi'
dead leaves hashtap
dead person hattak illi', illi'
dead, to be loshoma
dead, to fall illit ittola
dead, to rise from the illitokmat
falamat taani, taani
deaf, to be ikhapo̱waklo
death illi'
death, to lose (someone) in i̱loshoma
debate, to ittachapa
debris in a creek bed hashtap

debt ahi'ka'
deceive, to haksichi, i̱loshkat
  haksichi
deceived by, to be i̱haksi
decisions for, to make imanokfilli
declare a holiday in honor of, to
  nittak i̱holiitobli
decompose, to nipahli
decorate, to atahpolichi
dedicate, to holiitoblichi
deed isht̲a̲lhlhi', ishtoktani' holisso,
  nanna ishtith̲a̲na' holisso
deep breath, to take a kallochit
  foyopa
deep, to be hofobi
deep, to make hofobichi
deer issi', issi' imilhlha'
deer, female issi' tiik
deer potatoes issim-ahi'
deer tick issi' i̱shatanni
deface, to ayobba'li ki'yo, ikayobba'lo
defecate in, to alootoli
defecate, to aya, holafa, waawa
defective, not to be imó̲ma
defend oneself against, to ittafama
degrade, to kalakshichi
degraded, to be kalakshi
delay, to ataklammi
delayed, to be ataklama
delegate anompa shaali'
deliver a baby by caesarian section, to
  bashlicha chipotaaishi
deliver a baby, to chipotapooba
deliver of, to imapooba
deliver the baby of, to
  chipotimapooba
deliver, to apooba
delivered, to be alhpooba
demean, to kalakshichi
Democrat Okaamahli
demolish, to yilhibli
demolished, to be yilhihli
denim balaafka' toba'
denominations, different Iksa'

ilayyoka
dent each other, to ittapaakota
dent, to pacho'li, pachoffi, payoffi
dented, to be pacho'wa, pachofa,
  pachohli, pako'wa, payofa
dentist noti' tihli'
department store aachompishto'
depend on, to aanokchi'to
dependent on, to be achokkobbi
depot chanaa malili' aahika', itti'
  chanaa malili' aahika'
depressed, to be impalammi
depression, to be in a aapalammi
descend from, to aakkowa
descend in, to aakkowa
descend, to akka' aya, akkohó̲wa,
  akkowa
descend with, to ibaa-akkowa
descendant ishtaaonchololi',
  ishtaaoncholowa'
descendant of, to be the
  ishtaaoncholowa
descendants aaittapiha', oshi'
  ishtaaoncholowa', oshi'
  ishtaatiyaka'
desert shinok fokha', yaakni'
  aashila', yaakni' hayaka'
deserted, to be hayaka' bíyyi'ka
desire, to anhi, o̲labi
desire, to be overcome by
  nokhámmi'chi
desk aaholissochi'
detective nannafaana'chi'
detective, to be a afaana'chi
detergent ishtalhchifa'
determined, to be alóshsho'ma
develop, to iksaachi
devil naaishshachi', shilombish
  oppolo', Siitan
devil horse nassano'li', Siitan
  imissoba
devil's claw waaka' lapish
devil's power ishtahollifatpo'
devil's shoestring naaishshachi'

isholosh talakchi', Siitan isholosh talakchi'
dew chishak, okyobi'
dewberry bissa' akka' balalli'
diagonally, to wear hanaawi'li
diamond tali' shokmalali'
diaper bakshiyama
diaper, disposable bakshiyama holisso aatoba'
diaper oneself, to bakshiyammi
diaper pin bakshiyamashtasitti'ya'
diaper, to bakshiyammichi
diaper, to have a full alótto'wa, imalótto'wa
diaper, to wear a bakshíyya'mi
diarrhea, to give (someone) alhoopollichi
diarrhea, to have alhoopolli
dice chalhka', foni' lha'li', naafoni'
die along with, to ibaailli
die as a result of witchcraft, to afiitipat illi
die down, to likinta
die from, to ishtilli
die in, to aailli
die of a heart attack, to chonkash hottopat illi
die out, to loshoma, moshooli, ootiksho
die, to illi, loshoma, ootaalhlhi, ootishtaalhlhi
die, to be about to ootimaalhlhi
die, to look ready to lhakcha
different colors, to be all ittashoma
different directions, in mayyoka'
different directions, to go in ittifilamo'li
different from, to be ittimila
different one, a ila'
different, to be ilayyoka, ittimilayyoka, ishtaaila, ishtila, ila
different, to have ittimila
different, to look ishtila, pisa-ishtaaila, pisittimila

different, to make ilachi
difficult place to live, to be a aapalammi
difficult, to be kallo, palammi
difficulty breathing, to have lhachofa
difficulty, with pallammihma
dig a ditch, to ofaabli ikbi
dig along with, to ibaakolli
dig around for, to imimbaakolli
dig, to kolli
dime sent pokko'li
dine, to impa
dingy, to be hotolakna
dinner, to have tabookoli impa
dip out from, to aatakaffi, aatakli
dip out, to okaatakaffi
dip, to takaffi, takli; also kapali
diploma nanna ishtithana' holisso, nannishtithana' holisso
dipped out, to have something aatakafa
dipper ishtaka'fa'
direction, in that misha' fonka, misha' pila
direction, in this ola' fonka, ola' pila
directionless, to be kaniya
directions, in different mayyoka'
directions, to go in diferent ittifilamo'li
director, choir taloowapiichi'
dirt lokfi', shinok—see also dirt, type of
dirt dauber tiika'ti'
dirt dauber, type of tiika'ti' losa'
dirt house lokfi' abooha'
dirt, hunk of lokfi' kallo'
dirt rolling off one's body, to have fatabli
dirt, to become lokfi' toba
dirt, type of lokfi' homma', lokfi' losa', lokfi' tohbi'
dirty face, to have a baklosoli
dirty, to be hotolakna, litiha, lokfi' bíyyi'ka

dirty, to get all

dirty, to get all oklhiwachi
dirty, to make litihli
disappointed by, to be anoktoklo
disease, to have an additional
imalbita
discharge kalha'
disciple inaithana'
disco aahilha'
discourage, to ishtahooba'li ki'yo
discouraged, to be ishtikaaimóno,
ishtikimóno
discussion, to have a anompa
ishtittimayya ki'yo, anompa
ishtiktimayyo
disease, really bad abikoppolo'
disembowel, to pataffi
disemboweling, to be cut open for
patafa
disgusted by, to be inkamosha,
ishtikímpo
disgusting looking, to be ishtáyyo'ba
ki'yo, ishtikayyo'bo
disgusting, to be áyyo'ba ki'yo
dish towel amposhishkasho'kalhchi'
dish, type of amposhi' aaholhponi',
tali' amposhi'
dish, type of prepared ittalhata
dishes amposhi'
dishpan amposhi' aalhchifa',
asonnak palassa', asonnak patha',
asonnak pathassa'
dishrag amposhishtalhchifa'
dishwasher amposhi' aalhchifa'
dishwashing detergent
amposhishtachifa'
dismember inexpertly, to
ittanipaachi
dismember, to nibli, nipaachi
dismiss a congregation, to tiwabli
dismissed, to be tiwapa
disobey, to ikihaklo, ikihapowaklo
dispenser, pump kitoba ibish
disperse, to tiwapa
dissatisfied, to be ishtilimihachi

dissolve in, to okaabila, okaabilili
dissolve, to bila, bilili
distillery oka' homi' aaikbi'
distort the shape of, to
asymmetrically shanaayo'li
distract, to ataapo'chi, ataapolichi
distribute one each, to chaafoochi
ditch ofaabli, oka' aayanahli',
okaachiloha', okaaofobi'
ditch digger ofaabli ikbi', ofaabli
kolli', yaakni' kolli'
ditch, to dig a ofaabli ikbi
ditches, to be full of potholes and
okaaofkobi
dive into, to okaamalli
divide among, to intachaafoochi,
inkashkoli, intakashkoli
divide in four parts, to oshtali
divide itself, to ittifilammichi
divide, to inkashabli
divide up among, to intachaafo'chi
divide up into plots for, to intoshaffi
divide up, to ittachaafo'chi,
ittakashkoli, kashkoli
divided, to be ittakashapa, kashapa,
kashkowa
divine, to oka' hoyo
diving board oka' aaokaamalli'
divorce holisso kashofa'
divorce from, to get a holisso
kashofa' imishi
divorce, to get a holissaat inkashofa,
holisso inkashoffi, holisso kashofa'
ishi, holisso kashoffi
dizzy, to be chokfoloha
dizzy, to make chokfolohli
do a split, to wakchalali
do again, to albitili
do all, to ishtimóma, mománchi
do anything, not to píhhi'la
do as one is told, to ayalhlhichi,
alhlhínchi, imalhlhínchi
do badly by, to ayoppanichi
do completely taha

do completely, to tahli
do everything for, to ishtaapichi
do exercises, to siipo'wa
do fast, to toshpa
do for the first time, to inchaffa
do for the fourth time, to ayyoshtachi
do for the second time, to atoklánchi
do for the third time, to
  atochchi'nachi
do for, to inkanihmi, iyámmohmi;
  also inkatihmi
do it, to really ittakánni'ya
do like, to yámmohmi
do magic tricks, to fatpo
  ishchokoshkomo
do one by one, to chaffa áyyo'ka
do one's best, to ilamóshsho'li
do over and over, to albilli
do poorly, to ayobba'li ki'yo
do right at all, not to ishtayóbba'li
  ki'yo
do something in, to aakanihmi
do something, to nannishtatta
do something, to make atohno
do the same as, to ibaachaffa
do the same back to, to ifalammichi
do the same thing again, to imalbitili
do the wash, to naachiifa
do things right, not to be able to
  akánni'ya
do throughout, to lhopolli
do thus, to yakmihchi
do, to yahmi, yamihchi; *also*
  kanihmi, kaniya'o, kanihchi,
  katihmi
do to all, to tahli
do to excess, to aatabli
do, to have something to
  nannimaalami
do, to know what to
  aakanihma'nikat ithána
do, to really aaikóha
do to, to iyamihchi
do to yourself, to ishnaakayni

do together, to táwwa'a
do too much, to aatabli, aatapichi,
  ishtaatabli, ishtaatapa, ishtaatapichi,
  ishtilaatabli, ishtilaatapichi
do well, not to ayobba'li ki'yo
do well, to aaiklóha
do what in, to aakatihmi
do what one has been told, to
  alhlhínchi
do what to, to katihchi
do with, to ibaayahmi, ibaayamihchi,
  táwwa'a
do work for, to intoksali
doctor alikchi'
doctor each other, to ittimalikchi
doctor, eye ishkin imalikchi'
doctor oneself, to ilimalikchi
doctor, to imalikchi
doctor, to act as a alikchi
doctor who draws blood issish ishko'
doctor, woman alikchihoo'
doctor's assistant, Indian tisho
doctor's medical bag alikchishokcha
doctor's paraphernalia alikchimmi'
document ishtoktani' holisso
document, important ishtalhlhi'
document, to oktanichi
dodge, to imaakana'li, imaakanalli,
  imaakánnakli, inkanalli, kánnakli
doe issi' tiik
dog ofi'—*see also* dog, type of
dog collar iminno'chi', ofinno'chi'
dog food ofimpa'
dog, mother ofi' ishki', ofi'
  oshpishichi'
dog tag ofinno'chi'
dog tags holhchifo inno'chi'
dog tick ofi' ishatanni
dog, type of ofi' imo'ma', ofi'
  naapiisachi', ofi' woksho'
dogcatcher ofi' yokachi'
doghouse ofinchokka'
dogwood koshchi', shakchifolko'
doily nannompatkachi'

doing, be yahmi
doing the right thing, to think one is
  aalhpí'sa
doll hattak holba'
doll, baby chipota holba'
dollar ta'osso, taala'
domestic animal naalhpooba
done for, to be taha
done for, to be almost ootimaalhlhi
done on the inside, not to be chakissa
done, to be alhtaha, awaalhahli, issa,
  lhabocha, nona
donkey haksibish falaa'
donkey, type of haksibish falaa'
  iskanno'
doodlebug loolo'
door abokkisa', ishtokshilitta'
door, back abooha ashaka' okkisa'
door, front abokkisa' tikba'
door hook talishtaatakka'li'
door knocker abokkisishkasa'chi'
door, little okkis-oshi'
doorframe okkisa'
doorknob abokkisaayo'kli',
  ishtokshili'ta' aayo'kli'
doorman okkisa' atooni'
doormat okkisa' patalhpo'
doorstep aaohika'
doorway okkisa'
double over, to ittapaakolli
double potato ahi' pokta'
double, to albitili
double, to make ittalatali
double-barreled shotgun
  tanampincholok toklo', tanampo
  pokta'
doubled over, to be ittapaakota,
  ittalátta'a
doubled up, to be ittalaata,
  kóbbokshi, chiffóllo'wa, polhoma
doubt, to be in anoktoklo
dough paska toba', tili'kolhkomo'
dove pachalhpooba'
dove, type of pachalhpooba' tohbi',

pachi' yoshoba'
down akka', akka' pila, okaaina'
down feathers foshi' hishi' woksho'
down a slope, to come okaatanowat
  minti
down a slope, to go okaatanowat aya
down a slope, to move okaatanowa
down, duck fochosh hishi' woksho'
down, face lhímpat
down, fowl's hishi' loposhki'
down from, to get aakkowa
down in, to go aakkowa
down into, to go okaakaniya
down, moving akkali'
down the wrong way, to have go
  nokshiyammi
down, to bring akihchi,
  akkoshwayaachi
down, to come ootakkowa
down, to go akkohówa, akkowa
down, to have one's fever go
  shippachi, yanhakat shippa
down, to help put ibaa-akkowachi
down, to make go akkowachi
down, to put akkihci, ashaachi,
  talaali
down, to run yanahli, yanalli
down, to turn akkánchi
down, way akka' pilla, okaaina' pila
downhill okaaina'
downstream, to go apissat minti
downtown okla pila
draft, to feel a omahli
drafted, to be tashka-chipota'
  ibaaholhtina
drag along, to shoochi
drag on the ground, to bala'chi
drag one's feet, to shochochó'chi
drag oneself around slowly, to
  lhíffilli
drag, to lhifi'chi, lhifi'li, shala'chi,
  shallalali
drag, to let something lhiffiffli
dragging sound, to make a

ittishola'chi, ittisholalá'chi,
ittishóllakli'chi, ittisholo'chi, shol
shol shol aachi
dragging, to be shallalóli
dragging, to make a noise by
ittifáttakli'chi
dragonfly oka' pakna' tannowa'
draw (water), to oochi
draw a line beside, to apootakachi
drawer nannaalhto'
drawers, chest of nanna aalhto'
drawknife ittishtalha'
drawn, to be olhchi
dream about oneself, to
ishtililhpokonna
dream about, to ishtilhpokonna
dream, to ilhpokonna
dreamer ilhpokonna'
dregs lakchi'
dregs of coffee kaafi' lakchi'
dress naafokha
dress, to fokhachichi
dress up nice, to ilatahpolichi
dress up, to atahpolichi, ilaaiksaachi
dressed up nice, to get ilatahpoli
dresser nanna aalhto'
dried on, to be chilakbi
dried up, to be ashippa
drift off, to nohósi
drill naaishfoloha'
drill, to folohli
drilled, to be foloha
drink nannishko'; also ikko
drink from, to aaishko
drink some of, to aaishko
drink, to ishko
drink, to make ishkochichi
drinking glass amposhi'
shokkawwa'li'
drinking straw nannishtishko'
drip, to bishalhchi, fayyichi, hoyya
drip, to make hoyyachi
drive, to atappichi, ishnọwa, ishtaya,
ishtạa

driver ishnọwa'
drizzle, to shobbichi
drool on, to onchokkayahli,
onchokkayalli
drool, to chokkayahli, chokkayalli
drop into, to imokattola
drop, to akihci, imittola, intalhoffi,
ịlhatapa, lhatapa, oshkanchi
drown each other, to oka'
ittookaaillichi
drown, to oka' okaailli, oka'
noklhamallit illi, oka' okaa-abi
drugstore ittịsh aa-asha', ittịsh
aakanchi'
drum sholoshtalhipa
Drum Dance Shinka Bo'li'
drum, to beat on a leather-covered
ittitómmokli'chi, ittitomo'chi,
ittitomomó'chi
drum, to make the sound of a
leather-covered tomok tomok
tomok aachi, toom toom toom
aachi
Drunk Dance Okishko' Hilha'
drunk for, to get ịhaksi
drunk on, to get ishhaksi
drunk, to be haksi
drunk, to be half chokfóllo'ha
drunk, to get ishkot haksi
drunk with, to get ibaahaksi
drunk with, to go off and get nọwat
ibaahaksi
drunkard okishko'
dry and cracked, to be chilakbi
dry cereal nanna shila'
dry cleaner's naafkaachofalli'
dry ice okakmi' palli'
dry onto, to achiilakbi, ashiila
dry out, to shippa
dry river bed abookoshi shila'
dry salt nipi' hapayyima', shokha'
nipi' shila'
dry throat, to give (someone) a
nokshilili

dry, to shila, shilili
dry, to be shila
dry, to be partly yawalli
dry, to be really shílli'ya
dry, to partly yawallichi
dry-goods store naafkaa-asha',
  naafkaakanchi'
duck fochosh
Duck Dance Fochosh Hilha'
duck down fochosh hishi' woksho'
duck egg fochosh-oshi'
duck, mother fochosh ishki'
duckling fochosh-oshi'
dug, to be kola
dull, to be tokbi, tíllikpi
dump, to lhatabli
dumpling alhfola', ashiila
dumpling, type of panki' alhfola',

paskalhfola', tanchishtashiila'
dumplings from, to make afolli
dunked, to be okloboshli
dust shinok
dust fly, to make a cloud of
  shobohónta
dust on, to get shakawachi
dust rise, to have a cloud of shobolli
dust, to wilooli
dust, to be covered with shobolli
dust, to become lokfi' toba
dusted, to be wiloha
duster aaimpishkasho'kalhchi',
  nannishwilooli'
duster, feather foshi' hishi'
  nannishwilooli'
dustpan lokfishpiha', lowak ishpiha'
dynamite, to use tali' tokaachi

e

each get, to ittachaffa
each of two bínka
eagle osi'—see also eagle, type of
eagle, baby ososhi'
eagle, bald osi' ishkobo-tohbi'
eagle, type of osi' ishkobo-homma',
  osi' ishkobo-tohbi', osi' koyofa',
  osishto'
ear haksibish
ear, area in front of the hakson
ear, part of the haksibish cholok
ear wax haksibish lhitihli'
earlier days, in chashpo,
  chashpohma, chiikihmachiiki'
earlier than expected chiiki'
earlier than expected, to be chiiki
early chiiki'
early for one, to have it be too
  inchiiki
early in the morning nittaki,
  nittakiaash

early in the morning, really
  níyyi'tako'si
early in the morning, to be nittaki
early, to be chiiki, inchiiki
early tomorrow morning nittakikma
earring haksibish takaali'
ears of corn, roasting tanchi' himona
  waa'
ears of corn, small hoshollak
ears that stick out, to have oshwalali
earth yaakni'
earthquake yaakni' wina'kachi'
earthquake, for there to be an
  yaaknaat ilhko'li, yaaknaat
  wina'kachi
earthworm saalhkona
easier, to get nampíla
east hashaakochcha'
Easter Akankoshi' Hoyo' Nittak,
  Akankoshi' Lohmi' Nittak, Iista',
  Takollishto' Holitto'pa', Nittak

Hollo' Nittak
Easter, for it to be Chokfaat Achiili
easy, to be achokmalicho'si
eat along with, to ibaa-apa
eat breakfast, to nittaki impa
eat each other, to ittipa
eat each other's, to ittimappa
eat for each other,to ittimappa
eat for, to imappa
eat greedily, to amosholi
eat in, to aa-apa, aaimpa
eat noisily, to ittilasa'chi,
  ittilasasá'chi, ittilássakli'chi
eat oneself, to ilipa
eat some of, to aa-apa
eat supper, to obyaka' impa
eat, to apa, impa; *also* shombachi
eat too much, not to impa' iksala'mo
eaten by bugs, to be shomba
**eating crunchy things, to make a
  noise** ittikasha'chi,
  ittikashashá'chi, ittikáshshakli'chi
eaves okaahoyya'
echo, to achaamapa
echo, to hear an achaamapa
eclipse hashi' illi'
eclipse, for there to be an hashi'at illi,
  hashi'at ittalata, hashi'at
  ittayoppitammi, hashi'at oklhili,
  hashi'at tilikpi
edge imootaalhlhika', naksika',
  taakcha', taakchaka', ootaalhlhika'
edge of, moving along the
  taakchakali', taakchali'
edge of, to be lined up even with the
  atílhlhi'fa
edge, on the naksika'
edge, to apootakachi
edges curl up, to have the oppolokko
edges lined up, to have the
  ittalatkachi, ittalatkachit máa
edges of, to square off the shokli
eel ayaasinti', nani' sinti', fincha,
  sinti-nani'

egg beater akankoshishbo'kalhchi'
egg, boiled akankoshi' lobo'
egg carton akankoshi' aalhto'
egg, chicken's akankoshi' lombo'
egg, double-yolked akankoshi' toklo'
egg, fried akankoshi' awaalhaali'
egg, hard-boiled akankoshi' lobo',
  akankoshi' lobona'
egg, type of akankoshi' aatahaka'
egg white akankoshintohbi'
egg yolk akankoshilakna'
eggs, scrambled akankoshi'
  bo'kalhchi'
eight ontochchí'na
eight in number, to be ontochchí'na
eight times hiyontochchi'na'
eight, to be in groups of ontochchí'na
  áyyo'ka
eighteen awa ontochchí'na,
  pokolontochchí'na
eighth, to be ishtontochchí'na
eighty pokoli ontochchí'na
eighty in number, to be pokoli
  ontochchí'na
ejaculate, to iminti
elastic naashiipa', shiipo'wa
elastic, to be shiipa
elbow ilbak inkofi'
elbow, the inside of the ilbak
  aapolhoma'
elder kamassa',
  naaholittompishtatta'
elders naaholittompishtaa-asha'
elect, to atookoli
elected, to be alhtoka
election naalhtoka'
elections, to hold naalhtoka' atookoli
electrocute, to shimoochit abi
elephant haksibish ishto', haksibish
  patha'
eleven awa chaffa, pokolachaffa
eleven in number, to be awa chaffa
eleven times hiyyawa chaffa'
elm tohto'

elm, slippery balop
elope, to tamowa
embarrass, to hofahyachi, hofahyali
embarrassed, to be hofahya
embezzle, to ayowa
embroider, to nantanni
emetic ishhowitachi'
emit a spark, to lowak chipasli
emit sparks, to chipasli, pachiili
employ, to tohno
employed person hattak toksali'
employee intoksali', toksali'
empty inside, to be cholok biyyi'ka
enclose, to okshitta
encounter, to afama
end ibitop, ootaalhlhika', taha
end, to taha
end, to come to the ootaalhlhi,
ootaalhlhi ona
end, to get to the ootishtaalhlhi
enemies ittisanali'
enemies, to be ittisánna'li
enemy intanap, isanali'
engine, train ishkobo'
engineer chanaa malili' chaffichi',
chanaa malili ishnowa', chanaa
malili-malichi'
English language
Naahollimanompa'
English peas naahollimbala'
English walnut hayi alhpooba',
naahollo imosak, naahollo ihayi
enjoy, to inchampoli, ishtayiimita
enlarge the stomach of, to missilili
enlist, to tashka-chipota'
ibaaholhtina
enough of, not to get ikimo'no
enough, not to have imóna ki'yo
enough, not to have gotten ikimóno
enough, to be ona
enough, to have imalhpi'sa
enter a contest, to ilipafi
enter, to ashchokkowa, atchokkowa,
ootchokkowa

envious of, to be ishtimalhaa
epidemic abikoppolo'
epsom salts hapi kapassa', tish hapi
equal, to be ittilawwi
erect, to be kallo
erect, to stand fabassa
erection, to have an inkallo
error, to make an ilhakoffi
escape from, to ilhakoffi
Eskimos Hattak Aakapassaa-asha',
Hattak Okakmi' Okaa-asha'
eternal life okchaat billi'ya'
ether ishnosichi'
evacuate, to wihachi
evaluate as, to ishtapiisa
even mihíli
even, to be ittilawwi
even, to make ittilawwichi
even with the edge of, to be lined up
atílhlhi'fa
even with, to be ittilawwi
even with, to come sakki
even with, to get ittillawi'chi
evening obyaka'
evening star fochik ishto'
evening, this himmaka' obyaka,
obyakma
evening, to be obya
evening, to have it get to be onobya
evening, yesterday obyaka'aash
everlastingly bílli'ya
every which way mayyoka'
everybody kanahookya,
kaniya'ookya
everyone hattak moma, kanahookya,
kaniya'ookya
everyplace kaniya'ookya
everything nanna móma,
nannahookya
everywhere kaniya'ookya
evict, to kochchichi
evil, to be ikayyo'bo
exactly pila
excel over, to ímmayya, ímmayya'chi

exchange, to ittima
exchange, to make ittatobbichi
(exclamation) kii, kiihi, ko'—*see also*
specific exclamations
excrement yalhki'
excuse me ạlhakoffitok
exercises, to do siipo'wa
exist, not to iksho
exist, to áyya'sha, ị'ma, tálla'a,
tállo'wa, talowat mạa, wayowat
mạa, wáyya'a, wáyyo'wa (*In
Chickasaw, the notion of existence
is usually expressed by mentioning
the bodily position of the subject.*)
expect, to anhi
expensive, to be ayallishto
explain to, to intoshooli
explain, to toshooli
explode, to tiwabli, tiwapa, tokafa,
tokahli
expose, to okfahli, okfahchi,
ootokfahli
exposed, to be okfaha
extend credit for, to ahiikachi
extend one's limbs, to siipo'wa
extend this way, to oshwayowat mạa,
oshwáyya'a, oshwáyyo'wa
extend this way, to make
oshwayaachi, oshwayoochi
exterminator issọsh abi'

extinguish, to moshoochi
extraordinary, to be ishtaaịla
eye ishkin
eye doctor ishkin imalikchi'
eye, glass ishkin holba'
eye mucus ishkin bakchi'
eye of a needle naaishtalhcho'wa'
ishkin
eyeball ishkin lobo'
eyebrow ishkin hishi', ishkin
osho'ba'
eyebrow pencil ishtilincho'li'
eyebrows, to raise one's okmiloli
eyeglasses ishkin ishpisa'
eyelash ishkin hishi', ishkin
hoshollo'
eyelashes, false ishkin hoshollo'
holba'
eyes crossed, to have one's ishkinat
okkawata
eyes, to be blind in both ishkinat
intamowa
eyes, to close the mocholi
eyes, to cross one's ishkin okkawatali
eyes, to have light in one's
ọshoppala
eyes, to have sun in one's ọhashtahli
eyes water, to have one's ishkin
okchi'at lawa

f

fabric naafka toba'
face ishshoka'
face at, to make a ishshoka' oppanit
pisa
face down lhímpat
face down, to lie lhímpat ti'wa,
lhímpat wayya'a
face each other, to ittachaapa,
ittasaanali

face, lying on the noklhimpat
face mask ishshoka' alhiipi'ya'
face of, to paint the baklosochi
face paint ishshoka' ishtincho'li'
face painted, to have one's baklosoli,
ishshoka'at incho'wa
face powder ishshoka' ishtohbichi'
face, to áchcha'pa, alaatali, asaanali;
also polhommi

413

face, to be lying on one's lhímpa, noklhíhhi'pa
face, to daub on one's apoolosli
face to face, to fight ittasaana
face, to fall on one's lhímpat ittola
face, to have a hairy bakwosholi
face, to have an ugly bokyofoli
face, to paint one's ilibaklosochi
face, to turn over on the lhipa, lhipili, lhipisht bohli, lhipit wayaachi
face, to wash one's okaami
faces, to daub on each other's ittaapoolosli
faces, to make bokyofoli
facing anonkaka' pitpolho'ma', tikba'
factory nannaaiksaachi'
fade, to masali, masaachi
faded, to be tokbakali
fail in asking, to asilhhat anoktobafa
fail to act like a man, to iknakno
fail to do right by, to ayoppanichi
faint, to hayoochichi
faint, to make hayoochichichi
fair, to be aalhpí'sa
fair, to play aalhpi'schokoshkomo
faithful to, to be imálhlhi
fall asleep, to nohósi
fall broken by, to have one's ootawaata
fall dead, to illit ittola
fall down, to akkootittola, akkootkaha, akkootlhatapa, atittola, atkaha, atlhatapa, kinahli, yilhipa
fall down with, to ibaaittola
fall from, to aaittola, ootaaittola, ootaakaha, ootaalhatapa
fall in on, to oyilhipa
fall in, to okaabowafa
fall into, to ootokattola
fall into to get away from, to imokattola
fall off, to ootaaittola, ootaakaha, ootaalhatapa, ootittola, ootkaha, ootlhatapa
fall on each other, to ittoonittola
fall on one's face, to lhímpat ittola
fall on, to ombowafa, onittola, oshtonittola, oshtonkaha, oshtolhatapa, ootonittola, ootonkaha, ootolhatapa, olhatapa
fall out, to ashtittola, boyafa, tifa
fall over, not to oottala
fall over, to kinafa
fall through, to ashtittola
fall, to ittola; also lhatapa, ootbitiipa, wilili
fall, to let imittola
fall, to make wilichi
fall, to slip and shalalli
fall to the ground, to akkootittola, akkootkaha, akkootlhatapa
fall, to trip over and takaat ittola
fall with, to ishtittola
false teeth noti' holba'
falsely, to accuse ahobbichi
family chokka-chaffa', inchokkachaffa', ishtaaoncholomi', imaaokla'
family name holhchifo ishtaalhi'
family of children closely spaced in age chipota kobolli'
famous, to be aaiklóha
fan ishtilamaachi'
fan, electric ishtamaachi'
fan, to amaachi
fan, winnowing tanchi' ishnashka'
far away, to be hopaaki
far away, to go hopaakichi, olaalínchi ki'ya
far side, on the tannap
farmer osaapa' toksali'
fart hollonkso'
fart at, to ohokso
fart, to hónkso
fashionable, to be himitta
fast for, to be too impalhki

fast, to be palhki, toshpa
fast, to do toshpa
fasten one's girdle, to ilashiichi
fastener ishtakallo'chi', ishtasiiti'ya'
faster, to make go palhkichi
fat niha
fat, congealed nihaakmi'
fat, to be lhinko, lhotafa
father inki'; *also* impaapi'
Father, God our Aba' Pinki'
father's brother inko'si'
fatso, to be a lhotafa
fatten, to ilhpitachi
fattened, to ilhpita
fatty, to be niha
faucet ishfilillichi', oka' aabichili',
oka' aalhatapa'
faucet handle ishtaafilito'chi'
favor, to aapichi, holiitómbli,
ishtaapichi
fear, not to imaaiklóha
fearful, to be extremely ilihopoo
feather foshi' hishi', hishi'
feather bed onno'sha' yabofa'
feather duster foshi' hishi'
nannishwilooli'
feather on one's head, to have a
yaatálla'li
feather on one's head, to put a
yaatalaali
feather on (someone's) head, to put a
yaatalachi
feather ornament yaatala
feathers, soft foshi' hishi' woksho'
feathers, to pull out one's iliboyolli
feathers, to shed one's iliboyaffichi
feces yalhki'
feed along with, to ibaaipita
feed, cattle waakimpa'
feed each other, to ittipita
feed to, to ipita
feel bad, to ikinchokmo, imíla
feel better, to noktála, pitinkanihmi,
pitkanihmi

feel fine, to inchokmánka
feel good, to have it ishtinchokmaka
feel hot, to ilashpa
feel like, to chihmi
feel sorry for, to inokhánglo
feel, to halili, halit pisa
feel very sorry, to chonkashat yaháa
feel with one's open hands, to bitka
feeler ishtimpashooli', lapish
feelings hurt, to have one's ikimóno,
imilahchohmi
feet apart, to have one's
wakchalla'wáli
feet in the air, to kick one's
wakchaalli
feet, to drag one's shochochó'chi
feet, to make the sound of big pat pat
pat aachi
feet, to make the sound of big bare
pas pas pas aachi
fellow gang members ittapihaka'a
female ihoo
fence holitta—*see also* fence, type of
fence, barbed-wire tali' haloppa'
holitta
fence in, to holittachi, iholittachi
fence post holitta shokolbika'
ihikki'ya', holittihikki'ya', itti'
palha'
fence, rail itti' palha' holitta
fence, type of itti' ittabaana' holitta'
fence, wire tali' holitta'
fenced in, to be ihóllitta
fenced, to be hóllitta
ferment, to toshbichi
fertilizer waakiyaalhki',
yaaknishchokmali'
fester, to aniichi
fever go down, to have one's
shippachi, yanhakat shippa
fever, to have a yanha
fever, to have a high yanhakat
chaaha, yanhaat inchaaha
fever to, to give a yanhachi

415

few, a kannohmihmat, kannohmihma
few times, a hikannohmi'
few, to be just a chaafoha'si, kanihmo'si
field osaapa'
field peas waakimbala'
fielder to'wa' yokli'
fifteen awa talhlhá'pi, pokolatalhlhá'pi
fifteen in number, to be awa talhlhá'pi
fifth, to be ishtalhlhá'pi
fifty pokoli talhlhá'pi
fifty cents bit oshta
fifty in number, to be pokoli talhlhá'pi
fight all the time, to ittimoppoloka
fight back, to falamat ittibi, falammisht ittibi
fight for, to imittibi
fight in, to aaittibi
fight on, to aaittibi
fight over, to ishtittibi, ittimolabi
fight, to ittibi
fight, to have a ittafama, ittasaana
fight, to make ittibichi
fight, to start a tingba' ishtaya
fight with, to ishtittibi, ittakónno'fa
fighting cock akanka' ittibi'
figure ishtincho'wa'
figure, to hotihna
file nannishhaloppachi', nannishshoochi'
file, to shoochi
fill, to alolli, alótto'wa, aloota
fill up, to alootoli, kayyachi
fill with, to alootoli
film ishholbachi', ishholbachi' fokha'
fin, fish's nani' ifanalhchi'
finally himmaka', kaniht
finance company ta'ossaaponta'
find each other, to ittihayoochi

find out about each other, to ittaakostinichi
find out about, to afaana'chi, akostinichi
find out, to ithana
find, to hayoochi
fine, to be bashili
fine, to feel inchokmánka
fine-tooth comb issap ishtalbi'
finger ilbak-oshi', ilbak-oshi' awaatali'
finger in, to stick one's ibaayakohli
finger, fourth ilbak ayyoshta
finger, index ilbak naaishtaabachi'
finger, little ilbak-oshi'
finger, middle ilbak iklanna'
finger, ring ilbak ilbak shalbi'yaafokha'
fingernail ilbakchosh
fingers, the space between the ilbak-oshi' ittintakla'
fingertips drumming, to make the sound of tip tip tip aachi
finish taha
finish, to issa, tahli
finish up, to atáhli
finished, to be taha
fire lowak
fire ant issosh hommishto'
fire built for one, to have a imolhti
fire dog aaolhti' ihikki'ya'
fire dogs aaolhti' ihi'li'
fire engine lowak moshoochi'
fire escape aatoloyya'
fire hydrant oka' aalhto'
fire lookout tower lowak aa-apiisachi'
fire, to chaffichi, hosa, nonachi, tilhili, tokaffi, tokaachi
fire, to catch lowa
fire, to get warm by the lowak inni
firebox lowak aaolhti'
fired, to get aatoksali'at inkaniya
firefly shokkaawi'

fireman chanaa malili' lowak imooti', hattak lowak moshoochi', lowak moshoochi'
fireplace aashobohli', chimli', lowak aainni', lowak aaolhti', lowak aashobohli'
firewater oka' lowak
fireweed alba lowak, lowak pakali'
firewood itti' olhti'
fireworks nantokahli'
firm, to be kallo
firm, to be round and yabbobónka'chi
first tingba'
first child chipotammo'na'
first cousin ittibaapishi pila
first name holhchifammo'na'
first time, to be the ámmo'na
first time, to do for the inchaffa
first, to be ámmo'na
fish nani'
fish, type of nanoshik, nokfapa'—see also names of specific fish
fishing pole nanishholhtosi'
fishing, to go nani' hotost aya
fishnet nani' aayoka', nani' ishhokaachi', nani' ishtayowa', nani' ishyokachi', nanishhokaffi'
fish's fin nani' ifanalhchi'
fist ilbak pochokko'
fit around, to apakfoota
fit on, to ittifokhi
fit onto, to ittifokha
fit, to alhpí'sa
fit together, to ittabihli
five talhlhá'pi
Five Civilized Tribes Okloshi' Talhlha'pi'
five in number, to be talhlhá'pi
five times hitalhlha'pi'
five, to be in groups of talhlhá'pi áyyo'ka, talhlhá'pi bíyyi'ka
Five Tribes Okloshi' Talhlha'pi'
fix for, to imiksaachi, inampila
fix oneself up, to ilatahpoli,

ilaaiksaachi
fix, to iksaachi, nampila
fix up, to ilatahpolichi
fix up with, to anoshkonna, ishtanoshkonna
fixed, to be sita
fizz, to woshwoki
fizz, to make woshwokichi
flag shapha'
flame, to kilaa
flamingo paskawo' homma'
flannel naafka woksho'
flap in the breeze, to faapo'wa
flap one's arms, cape, or wings, to wahhalwáa
flapping sound, to make a ittifata'chi, ittifatatá'chi, lhok lhok lhok aachi
flash aashoppala'
flash of light, to give a sudden shoppallakahchi
flash, to shokmalli, shokmalla'máli
flashbulb aashoppala'
flat, to be latassa, latastowa, patassa, shayofa
flat, to spread palli
flat-chested, to be láttassa
flat-heeled shoe sholosh latassa'
flatcar chanaa malili-patassa'
flatfish nani' patassa'
flatten against, to alaatassachi
flatten, to ittalaatassachi, latassachi, latassali, patassali
flatulate, to hónkso
flatulation hollonkso'
flavor of, to have a strong yammi
flavor, to be without ikchampo'lo
flavoring ishbilamachi', paska champoli' ishbilamachi'
flea kashti
flexible, to be bicho'kachi
flick one's finger at, to sakkaha, sákkakli'chi
flick, to fayyichi
flimsy, to be bicho'kachi

flint

flint tali' chipasli', tali' lowak
ishtikbi'
flirt, to aatoklha, ittayoshkammi
flirt with, to ayoshkammi
float in the water, to oka'
okaaittánno'wa, oka'
okaaittanohówa, oka' okaatákka'li
float, to okpalachi, okpalali
flood, to okoshto
floor akka'
floor polish akka' ishshokmalachi'
floor, cement tali' patalhpo'
flop across, to abaana
flop over, to ootabaana
flounced, to be awaala'kalhchi
flour tili'ko'—see also flour, type of
flour, pieces of foreign material in
tili'ko' bosholli', tili'ko' lakchi',
tili'ko' shila'
flour sack tili'kishokcha
flour, type of tanchi' bota', tili'ko'
lakna', tili'ko' tohbi'
flow, to yanahli
flower nampakali', pakali'
flower, type of obyaka' pakali',
oshchono'—see also names of
specific flowers
flowerpot nampakali' aaholokchi'
flu, to have the ibishshano
flue aashobohli'
flute oskola'
fly chokaano—see also fly, type of
fly along with, to ibaawakiili
fly egg chokaanoshi'
fly swatter chokaanishtabi'
fly, to wakaa, wakiili, wakoha
fly, to make wakaachi
fly, to make a cloud of dust
shobohónta
fly, type of chokaanokchamali'
flycatcher, scissortailed hilowifoshi'
flying squirrel fani' wakaa', pali'
flying, to make the noise of
ittilhókkokli'chi

flypaper chokaano ishyokachi'
flyspeck chokaani nihi'
foam at the mouth, to itokchaat
pokpoki
foamy, to be pokpoki
fog tooboklhili
foggy, for it to be nashobaat chomak
pofa
foggy, to be tooboklhili
fold around, to apaakolli
fold inside, to apoolhommi
fold line aapolhoma'
fold over, to pakolli
fold, to polhoma, polhommi
fold up, to polhkachi, polhlhi
folded around, to be apaakota
folded inside, to be apólhlho'ma
folded over, to be ittalaata
folded, to be polha, polhkachi,
polhoma
folded up, to be pakota
folds between the legs and the trunk
ittakoba' sokbish
follow a squiggly course, to foloto'wa
follow a track by scent, to
oshshowasht hoyo
follow along after, to áwwali'chi
follow around, to achoshkachit máa,
achoshkáyya'chi, achóshsho'wa,
asitti't áa, asitti't tánnowa,
ayyakayya
follow home, to atappichi
follow, to apiha, ayakaa, ayakaat aya,
ayákka'at intánno'wa, ayákko'wat
intánno'wa, ayyakayya
following aballaka', aballakali'
following of, to attract a pihchit áa
fondle (a woman's) breasts, to
imbishlichi
fondle each other, to ittaapollichi
fondle, to apistikili, aapollichi,
impilisa, ishtánta
font, baptismal aabaptismochi'
fontanel chipotinkali

418

food impa'
food, canned impa' asonnak
tobbaalhto', nanna asonnak
tobbaalhto'
food coloring, red paska champoli'
ishhommachi'
food store impa' aa-asha'
fool, to iholbachi
fool with, to ishtánta
foot ishtaaohikki'ya', iyyi'
foot, sole of the iyyimpatha'
foot, to be on akkaanówa, akkaayínka
football helmet to'li' iyaalhipa
footprint iyyi' holba'
for a considerable while mina
for a while ikalhchibo'so
for some reason kanihmihma,
kanihchihma
for sure, to know alhtókko'waka
ithána
for, to be aachaffa
for what reason kanihchiho
forbid activities to, to imihollochi
forbid, to imolabi, inkatabli
forbid to consume, to imihollochi
forbidden, to be imihollo, inkatapa
force, to waachi
forceps tali' ishhalalli'
forearm ilbak api'
forehead ittifon
forehead, to have a high ittifonat
ishto
foreleg iyyi' tikba'
forequarter folop
foreskin ishtaahoshowa' hakshop
forest abokkol-anonka'
forget because of, to ishtimalhkaniya
forget everything while, to
ishtimalhkaniya
forget it mikya'ba
forget, not to nokfónkha
forget oneself, to ilimalhkaniya
forget, to imalhkaniya
forget, to make imalhkaniyachi

forgetful, to be haksit kánni'ya
forgive each other, to ittinannayya
forgive, to inkashoffi
forgiven, to be inkashofa
forgotten, to be alhkaniya
fork chofaak, chofaak ishtimpa'
fork in a road hina' aaittifilammi'
fork, to have a falakto
forked, to be falakto
form a circle around, to afoolobli
form a scab, to shila
form of, to take the toba
formal wear naafka holiitopa'
fortune-teller hopayi'
forty pokoli oshta
forty in number, to be pokoli oshta
foul ball, to hit a faapa, faapichi
found out, to be okfaha, oktani
foundation abooha notinto'wa',
inkaha', notinto'wa'
foundation poles notihiyohli'
fountain oka' aabichili', oka'
aalhatapa'
four oshta
four bits bit oshta
four in number, to be oshta
four parts, to divide in oshtali
four times hiyoshta'
four, to be in groups of oshta ayyoka,
oshta bíyyi'ka
four-sided, to be shokolbika' oshta
fourteen awa oshta, pokoloshta
fourteen in number, to be awa oshta
fourth finger ilbak ayyoshta
fourth time, to do something for a
ayyoshtachi
fourth, to be ayyoshta, ishtayyoshta
fox chola—see also fox, type of
fox squirrel fani' lakna'
fox, to bark like a kaawa
fox, type of chola homma',
cholokchama'li', chol-oshi'
fragrance, to have a bilama
frame, picture hattak holbaafokha'

419

frankfurter ofi' palli'
freckled, to be hóllisso
free, to be talhoffi
free, to try to get wahhaala
freestone peach takolo fako'pa'
freeze onto, to ayakmi
freeze, to akmichi
freeze to, to ayakmichi
freezer oka' aa-akmichi'
freight train naashaali'
french fries ahi' awaalhaali'
French person Falanchi'
Friday Nittak Ishtalhlha'pi',
  Naalhchifa' Nittak
fried bread paskawaalhaali'
fried in, to be aa-awaalhahli,
  ishtawaalhahli
fried, to be awaalhahli
fried with, to be ishtawaalhahli
friend inkana'
friendly, to be ittinkána
friendly towards, to act inkána
friendly with each other, to be
  ittimilínka
friendly with, to be imilínka
friends ittinkana'
friends with, to be inkána
fringe awishipa'
Frisco Falisko'
frisky, to be ilifoyo'chi
frog cho'ti', hoyo'kni'
frog, type of cho'ti' okchamali',
  cho'tishto', haliilawi',
  hoyo'knishto', ok-ima'lak
from birth banka
from long ago mashshaash,
  mashshaashoot, mashshaasho
front tikba'
front door abokkisa' tikba'
front of, in tikba'
front of, moving in tikbali'
front of, to go by in imokkawaatali,
  ootimokkawaatali
front of, to go in ataapolichi

frost hotonti
frost, to have hotonti
frosting paska champoli' onaa-asha'
frozen on, to have ayakmi
frozen, to be akmi
fruit ani', nannawaa'—see also fruit,
  type of
fruit, to bear ani
fruit, to have ripe waa
fruit, tree that bears itti' tiik
fruit, tree that doesn't bear itti'
  nakni'
fruit, type of osak okchi',
  shokhalanchi', waa' pachahli'—see
  also names of specific fruits
fruit fly hashonkani'
fry, to awaalhaachi
frying pan aapallichi', nipaapalli'
fulfilled, to be ootálhi
full blood issish alotto'wa'
full diaper, to have a alótto'wa,
  imalótto'wa
full moon, for there to be a hashi'at
  aloota, hashi'at bolokta, hashi'at
  lhibokta, hashi'at tilikpi
full of dirt, to be lokfi' bíyyi'ka
full of, to be kayya
full, to be alótto'wa, aloota, kayya
full-blooded Indian Hattak Api'
  Homma' alhlhi'
fun of, to make yoppolachi,
  ishtayóbba'li ki'yo
fun, to have ilihaksichit nowa
funeral home hattak illaa-asha'
funnel ishtani'
funny, to be ikkosti'no
funny, to say something yoppola
funny ways, to have ishtaaíla
fur hishi'
fur coat naafkishto' woksho'
furniture abooha nannaa-asha'
furrow ihina'
furry, to be woksho
future to, to tell the tingbalísht

imanoli
future, to be in the himmaka' pila
future, to see in the tingbalísht anoli

fuzz, peach takolo fatabli'
fuzzy, to be woksho

g

gag on, to nokbikili, noktakaali
gag, to iti intakchi, iti takchi
gall ihomi'
gall on chicken liver akankihomi'
gallbladder ifalaaka', salakha' ihomi'
gallop, to abaayo'wa, tolhtochi
gallop, to make abaayo'wachi,
  tolhtochichi
gallows hattak aanoksitili'
galoshes sholosh pakna' holo'chi'
gamble in, to aachalhka
gamble with cards, to chalhka
gambler hattak ittasita'
game, type of akaaballi', naki'
  lohmi', naaishchokoshkomo'—see
  also names of specific games
gamecock akanka' ittibi'
games, to play active toklhakafa
gang aaittapiha', imaaokla'
gangrenous, to be toshbi
gar nani' kallo'
garage kaa aawayaachi'
garbage nambosholli',
  nannikaabanno'
garbage man nambosholli' ayowa'
garbage truck nambosholli' shaali'
garden namposhi', osaaposhi'
gardener osaaposhi' toksali'
garfish nani' kallo'
gargle, to tokbolhlhichi
gargle, to make tokbolhlhichichi
garlic atofalla'a' homi', atofalla'a'
  kosoma'si', issobimatofalla'a'
garter iabisowa' ishtalakchi',
  iabisowa' ishyo'kli'
gas station nihaakanchi'

gas, to have hollonkso' aloota, mahli
  aloota, shatabli
gasoline niha
gather around, to go ootalawachi
gather in a bunch in, to lókko'li
gather over there to see, to
  ootalokoli, ootalokoochi
gather there, to aalokoochi
gather, to alawachi, ayowa,
  ittafamo'li, ittanaachi, ittanaalhchi,
  ittahobbi; also yikilhlhachi
gather, to make ayowachi
gather to see, to alokoochi,
  ootalokoli, ootalokoochi
gathered, to be ittahoba, ittanaalhchi,
  yikilhlha
gathering place, type of hoshottika'
gel, to kallo
gem, uncut oksop toba'
general inkapittani', tashka-chipota'
  ishkoboka'
generation aatiyaka'
genitals, male hakchintalop
gentle with, to be achokmalicho'si
gentleman hattak hapoyoksa'
genuine article, the mi finha'
gesture to, to ilbak ishtimanoli
gesture, to ilbak ishtanoli
get a divorce from, to holisso
  inkashoffi, holisso kashofa' imishi
get a divorce, to holissaat inkashofa,
  holisso kashofa' ishi
get a share of, to ittakashkowa
get a share, to inkashapa
get a shock, to holhpa, shimoha
get a wrong number, to ila'o kaalli

421

get ahead of, to ootímmayya
get all dirty, to oklhiwachi
get an answer, to anompa falama'
ishi
get and send for, to come and
atimpilachi
get and send for, to go and
ootimpilachi
get around fast, to folo'kachi
get as a present from, to imaahabiina
get at, to aahabina
get away from, to inkanalli, ifilammi,
ilhakoffi
get away from, to fall into to
imokattola
get away with it, to let ishtimbaatiya
get back together, to ittifalama
get bawled out, to ihiliya
get before, to try to imaafowa
get better, to nampíla, pitnampíla
get better, to have it pitinampíla
get burned, to holhpa
get carried away watching, to pi'scha
ishtakaniya, pi'scha ishtatamowa
get change, to ta'osso boshollichi
get comfortable, to apoolha
get dark, to oklhilichi
get divorced, to holisso kashoffi
get down from, to aakkowa
get down, to akkowa
get dressed, to fokha
get drunk for, to ihaksi
get drunk on, to ipitat haksichi,
ishhaksi
get drunk with, to ibaahaksi
get drunk, to haksichi, ishkot haksi
get easier, to nampíla
get enough of, not to ikimo'no
get even with, to ittillawi'chi
get everything for oneself, to
ishtilayoppa
get fired, to aatoksali'at inkaniya
get for, to imishi
get from there, to go and oothoyo

get from, to imaaolabi
get greasy, to nihachi
get help, to alhpila' ishi
get here, to ala
get high on, to ishhaksi
get hurt along with, to ibaahottopa
get in front of, to imahiita
get in the way of, to ataapo'chi
get light a long way off, to
hashtáyyahli
get light, to hashtahli
get loose, to talhohli, wahaala
get lost in, to okaakaniya
get lost, to yoshobli
get lost, to make yoshobachi
get mad at, to imoppoloka
get married for, to imittihalalli
get married in, to aaittihalalli
get married, to ittamóshsho'li
get mixed up with, to okaalhatapa
get off, to akkowa, akkohówa
get on credit for, to imáhhi'ka
get one each, to ittachaafowa
get out of bed, to taani
get out of, to shifi
get paid, to imalhtoba
get pregnant, to chipota habina,
chipota hayoochi
get quiet, to noktala
get ready, to atáhli
get religion, to ilikostinichi
get revenge on, to ifalammichi
get revenge, to imaatobbi,
ittillawi'chi
get rid of, to fimmi, kanchi
get sand on, to shakawachi
get saved, to ootilikostinichi
get scared in, to aaimilhlha
get soft, to yolhko
get (someone) used to, to
achokkobbichi
get something for oneself out of, to
ishtilayoppa
get stuck, to kafali, kafohli, kafoht

máa
get stopped up, to okshili'ta
get the job, to alhtoka
get there along with, to ibaaona
get there, to ona
get, to ishi; *also* hayoochi, ishmáa,
máa
get, to come and athoyo
get, to each ittachaffa
get to listen, to haklochi
get to know, to ithana
get to the end, to ootishtaalhlhi
get to, to ona
get, to try to aafowa
get together, to ittafama,
ittamóshsho'li
get undressed, to naafka shihli
get up gidap
get up suddenly, to satappakahsht
hika
get up, to taani
get up, to make taanichi
get used to each other, to
ittimachaaha, ittimachokkobbi
get used to one, to achaahachi
get used to, to aaimomochi,
imachaaha, imachokkobbi,
imomochi
get warm by the fire, to lowak inni
get well, to aaissa
get with, to ibaahabina
ghost sholop
Ghost, the Holy Shilombish
Holitto'pa'
giddyup gidap
gift halbina'
gin, cotton aanihichi', naafalli'
aanihichi'
ginger chincha'
gingerbread chincha' pallaska'
giraffe issoba chaaha', issoba itti'
ibitop aaimpa', issoba nokhistap
falaa'
girdle ishtilakallo'chi'

girdle, to fasten one's ilashiichi
girdled in, to be ashiiyalhchi
girl chipota tiik
girl, teenage ihoo himitta', ihoo
himittachi'
girlie kiiyoho', pokkosh
give a benediction, to tiwabli
give a bloody nose to, to ibichchala'
inkooli, ibichchala' kooli
give a bottle to, to pishichi
give a chill to, to ichchokwali
give a crew cut to, to oshkabachi
give a day off to, to nittak habinachi,
nittak ima
give a fever to, to yahnachi
give a flat top haircut to, to
oshkabachi, oshkolochi
give a good price to on, to
imalhchonachi
give a pain to, to imalhchíbba'chi
give a party, to toklhakafa' apiisa
give a permanent to, to oshchilochi
give a ride to, to ayowa, ayoowa
give a shock to, to holhpali,
shimohachi, shimohli, shimoochi
give a sigh of relief, to fóyyo'pa
give a sudden flash of light, to
shoppalla'kahchi
give along with, to ibaaima
give an anesthetic, to ishnosichi
give an answer, to anompa
falammichi
give an injection to, to ittish ani
give an offering of, to ittahobbi
give an order, to naapiisa
give artificial respiration to, to
foyopachi
give assistance to, to apiilachi
give away, to ittachaafoochi, kashabli
give back to, to ifalammichi
give birth to, to imalla, imalhpooba,
imánta, imatta, imayya'sha, intí'wa,
sho'li
give birth, to chipotaat imala,

chipotaat imatta, chipotaat inti'wa
give change to, to ta'osso
   imboshollichi
give help, to alhpila' ima
give medicine to, to ittish ima
give one's own name, to
   ilaholhchifochi
give one's word to, to anompalhpisa'
   ima
give oneself to, to ilima
give out one each, to chaafoochi
give (someone) a dry throat, to
   nokshilili
give (someone) a laxative, to
   alhoopollichi
give (someone) diarrhea, to
   alhoopollichi
give something to eat or drink to, to
   ipita
give support for, to imapila,
   imapilachi
give the news, to haklochi
give the same name to, to
   ittahoochifochi
give the wrong idea, to imahobbichi
give, to pitintalaali, pitiwayaachi
give to as a present, to habinachi
give to, to ima, inkashabli
give up a child for adoption to, to
   chipota habinachi, chipota ima
give up to for adoption, to habinachi
given a benediction, to be tiwapa
given away, to be halbina
gizzard inchakaffa'
gizzard, chicken akankinchakaffa'
glass amposhi' shokkawwa'li',
   aaishko'
glass eye ishkin holba'
glass, to be all aainchaa' bíyyi'ka
glean, to albillit ayowa
glittering, to be shokmala'máli
glorious place Aaholitto'paka'
glory of God, the Chihoowa
   naaishtimaaholitto'pa'

glove ilbak fo'khi', ilbak lho'fa'
glove, baseball ilbak fokka' to'li',
   to'wa' ishyokachi'
glove, boxing ilbak fo'khishtittibi',
   ishtittibo'li'
glove, rubber ilbak fo'khi' shiipa',
   raba' ilbak fo'khi'
glow, to shokkawali
glowworm hayowani' shoppala'
glue naaishtachaakissa'
glue onto, to achaakissachi
gnash one's teeth, to kisli
gnat bokoffa', hashonkani'
gnaw, to kilhlhi
go across, to abaanabli, lhopo'li,
   lhopolli
go after, to ayakaat aya
go against the law, to naalhpisa'
   achapa
go along beside, to aalaachi
go along different paths to the same
   goal, to báyya'ta
go along in separate rows, to bayalli
go along looking silly, to pílat áa
go along making a clanging noise, to
   komomó'chi
go along on the side, to
   apootakaalínchi
go along showing off, to pílat áa
go along, to abayyachi, áa
go along with authority, to refuse to
   ilaafowa
go along with the crowd, to
   aaiklanna
go along with, to ibaachaffa,
   imbaatiya, imaatiya, ishtimbaatiya,
   tangla' aya
go and get and send for, to
   ootimpilachi
go and get from there, to oothoyo
go and return, to ootfalama
go and see, to ootpisa
go and tell to behave, to ootimolabi
go apart, to ittifilammi

go around in a circle, to panaayo'wa
go around many times, to
  apakfohlihínchi
go around on hands and knees
  pulling grass, to wayyayáa,
  wayyayówa
go around picking fights, to bohpoli
go around, to afoolopa, afoolopo'wa,
  apakfohchi, apakfoota, áa,
  folo'kalhchi, folohónta,
  ootafoolopa, ootapakfoota
go around with, to ishtáa
go away behind, to pitahiita
go away from, to inkaniya, intamowa
go away, to kaniya, ootiksho, tamowa
go away with, to ibaakaniya
go back and forth across, to okkawalli
go back and forth, to faya'kachi
go back and forth, to make yili'chi
go back on one's commitments, to
  imaanokfila-at filito'wa
go backwards, to bakhitiipo'li
go beat up, to ootayyabichi
go behind, to ahiita
go blind, to shamba
go by here, to ataya
go by in front of, to imokkawaatali
go by, to ootaya, ittánno'wa,
  ittanohówa
go crazy over, to atamowa
go down a slope, to okaatanowat aya
go down in, to aakkowa
go down into, to okaakaniya
go down on, to ootaakkowa
go down, to akka, akka' aya,
  akkohówa, akkowa; also yabohli
go down, to make akkowachi
go down with, to ibaa-akkowa
go downstream, to apissat minti
go far away, to hopaakichi, olaalinchi
  ki'yo
go fast, to palhki
go faster, to make palhkichi
go fishing, to nani' hotost aya

go from one to another, to abayya,
  abayyachi, abayyat nowa
go gather around, to ootalawachi
go hunting, to owwattat aya
go in a boat, to oka' okaaittánno'wa,
  oka' okaaittanohówa, oka' okaayáa
go in a wavy line, to yili'kalhchi
go in a zigzag, to yillilínkalhchi
go in different directions, to
  ittifilamo'li
go in front of, to ataapolichi
go in together with, to ibaatobbi
go in with on, to ibaachompa
go into, to chokkohówa, chokkowa,
  okaakaniya, ootchokkowa,
  pitchokkowa
go join the armed forces, to tashka-
  chipota' aya
go look for, to hoyot aya, hoot aya
go off a ways from, to ihopaakichi
go off and get drunk, to nowat
  ibaahaksi
go off and leave, to ka'shcha kaniya
go off from, to ifilamo'li, kashcha aya
go off in all directions, to tiwapa
go off, to intalhoffi, maháa, máa,
  tokafa
go off with, to akaniya, atamowa
go on! mahya
go on ahead, to tingbalísht aya
go on, to onáa, shoppala
go out of, to aakochcha
go out the back door, to ootkochcha
go out through, to aalhopo'li,
  aalhopolli
go out, to kochcha, kochcha' aya,
  moshooli, pitkochcha
go out, to make kochchichi
go out with, to ibaa-aya, ibaanowa
go outwards, to wahhala
go over and over, to abaanahámbli
go over next to, to ootapoota
go over on, to ootabaana
go over one after another, to

425

go over, to

abaanappopóli
go over, to abaanabli, abaanapa,
abaanapo'li
go over, to let imambaanabli
go potty nis nis
go "pow", to paaw paaw paaw aachi
go see, to inowa, pist aya
go straight across, to apissáli
go straight through, to apissat aya
go tell, to imannoyachi
go the lower way, to notaalínchi
go three by three, to tochchí'na
ayyoka
go through all around, to lhoppopóli
go through and come out the other
side, to ootlhopolli
go through hardship with, to
ibaaimpalammi
go through, to lhopo'li, lhopolli,
ootkochcha
go through with, to aalhoppolli
go, to aya; also malili
go to and come back all the time, to
aafálla'ma
go to and return from, to ootfalama
go to bed, to tashki
go to bed with, to imissa
go, to come and tiwa'kalhchi
go to for, to imayya
go, to make ayachi, intohno
go, to refuse to ilaafowa ikbanno
go to school together, to holisso
ittibaapiisa
go to school, to holisso pisa
go to sleep on, to anosi
go to sleep, to nosi
go to the bathroom, to abooshi' aya,
aya, imaalami, kochcha' aya,
nannimaalami
go to, to aya, imona
go, to wrap (something) around
oneself and pitalhko'nacha aya
go toward underneath, to
notaalínchi

go under the water, to okloboshli
go under, to notaamalli
go up and down, to baayo'kachi, to'ti;
also panaayo'wa
go up and stand together, to
ootittapoota
go up, to aba' aya, abaawaa, toyyat aya
go upstairs, to aba' aya
go upstream, to apissat aya
go visit, to inowoot áa
go vote, to voot kasht aya
go with a lot of men, to hattak
ibaanosit nowa, patalinchi
go with all, to mománchi
go with, not to want to imilaafowa
go with, to ahiina, ibaa-aya,
ibaatángla, ibaayáa, tangla aya
goal, to converge on a báyya'ta
goalpost aa-abichi', aailli', ishtaa-abi'
goalposts, stickball itti' aabo'li'
goat issi' kosoma'
goat, billy issi', issi' nakni'
goat, female issi' tiik
goatee issi' kosoma' notakhish
gobble, to chaloklowa
God Chihoowa, Chihoowa Aba'
Binni'li', Chihoowa Pinchitokaka';
also Aba' Binni'li', Aba'
Pinchitokaka', Aba' Pinki',
Chihoowa Chitokaka', Pinki',
Pinki' Chihoowa Chitokaka'
God, the glory of Chihoowa
naaishtimaaholitto'pa'
God, word of abaanompa
God's commandment Chihoowa
imanompaalhpisa'
God's kingdom
Chihoowimaapihlichika'
God's law Chihoowa inannalhpisa'
God's realm Chihoowa
Imaapihlichika'
going with, to be ibaanowa
gold tali' lakna'
gold coins tali' holisso' lakna'

426

gold, to be lakna
gone, to be kaniya, tamowa
gone, to be all taha
good and chokma
good luck, to have ayolhlha,
nannayolhlha
good, to act chokma, chokmat atta
good, to be chokma; *also* ayómba
good, to be a chokma
good, to have it feel ishtinchokmaka
good, to make chokmali
good to, to act chokma imilahobbi
good-bye ayali
good-looking, to be pisa-chokma
goose shalaklak
goose, grey shalaklak okchama'li'
gopher yakni' makofa', yolhkon,
yolhkon ishto'
gospel abaanompa
gospel music abaanompa' taloowa'
gossip anompa chokoshpa', anompa
chokoshpali', anompa falatpo'
gossip about, to
anomponchokoshpali,
inchokoshpachi, inchokoshpali,
ishtonhochi, onhochi
gossip, to anompa chokoshpali,
chokoshpali
gossip, to be falappo
gossip, to spread chokoshpachi
gossip to, to inchokoshpachi,
inchokoshpali
gossiper chokoshpachi'
gourd ishtakafa' toba', lokosh,
shokshi'
government naaholло inaalhpisa'
governor minko', nannimapiisa'
governor, lady ihoo minko'
Governor of the Chickasaw Nation
Chikashshiminko'
grab a handful of, to okaayinoffi
grab and pull down, to halaht
oshwayaachi
grab onto, to ootasiita

grab, to put one's hand in and
okaayinoffi
graduate, to holisso lhopolli
grain hopper tanchishtani'
grandchild ipok
granddaughter ipok ihoo'
grandfather afo'si, imafo'si'
grandfather, great- imafo'sishto'
Grandma Appo'si'
grandmother ippo'si'
Grandmother Appo'si'
grandmother, great- ippo'sishto'
grandson ipok nakni'
Granny Appo'si'
grape dumpling panki' alhfola'
grape juice pankokchi'
grapes panki'—*see also* grapes, type
of
grapes, possum pankaashoshi',
panki' sawa', shawimpanki'
grapes, seedless panki' nihiksho'
grapes, type of hashtola-panki',
panki' homma', panki' imilhlha',
panki' losa', panki' okchamali',
panki' sawa', panki' shobboko'li',
pankishto', pankoshi'
grapevine pankapi'
grapevine, growth on a pankishan-
kachi'
grass hashshok—*see also* grass, type
of
grass clippers hashshok ishkachiili'
grass cutter hashshok ishtamo'
grass, to bend over and pull
wayyayáa, wayyayówa
grass, type of hashshan, hashshok
holokchi', hashshok kallo',
hashshok loposhki', hashshok pata'
grasshopper hatafo, shakili'
grasshopper, type of shalatha'
grate, to shaachi, shafi
grater nannishshaachi'
grater, corn tanchaashafa'
grave lokfi' kaha', lokfi' to'wa'

"grave digger" hattak illapa'
gravel tali' lakchi', tal-oshik
gravestone hattak illi' ohikki'ya',
  tali' illi' ohikki'ya'
gravestones hattak illi' ohiyohli',
  tali' illi' ohiyohli'
graveyard aaholloppi', hattak illi' aa-
  asha'
gravy tilli'ko' niha'
graze, to wayyayáa
grease niha
grease for, to inihachi
grease, hardened nihaakmi'
grease, to aabi, nihachi
greased up, to be albi
greasy, to be niha
great horned owl kitiini
Great Spirit Shilombish Ishto'
great with child, to be chakali
great-grandfather imafo'sishto'
Great-grandma Appo'sishto'
great-grandmother ippo'sishto'
Great-grandmother Appo'sishto'
greedy for, to be amosholi
greedy, to be amosholi, nannihollo
green hattak sawintopa
green onion atofalaa' himona'
green peas naahollimbala'
green, to be okchamali
green, to make okchamachi
greenbrier kantak, kantak ishto'
greens tohi', tohi' okchamali'
greens, collard tohi' chaaha'
greet each other, to ittaayoppachi
greet, to ayoppachi
greet, to make ayoppachichi
grey, to be shobbokoli
grey, to make shobbokochi
grey wolf nashob-okchamali'
greyhound ofi' palhki'
griddle aapalaska', paskaanonachi'
grill nanna aabaani', nipi' aa-abaani'
grin, to choklhiili
grind fine, to botoli

grind one's teeth, to noti' ittikisilichi
grind, to folohli
grinder, coffee kaafaafoloha',
  kaafishfoloha'
grinder, meat nipaafoloha', nipi'
  ishfolohli'
grits tanchi' palha'
groan, to haha, kifaa
groceries impa'
groom, to ishilli
grouchy, to be oppoloka
grouchy toward, to act imalhaa
ground yakni'
ground up, to be bota, foloha
ground, hole in the yakni' cholok
ground, to inkatabli
ground, to root in the yoko'chi
grounded, to be inkatapa
group imaaokla'
group, in the aatangla'
group of, to be a áyya'sha
groups, to put into separate
  ittifilamo'chi
grout ishtaabi'
grow a little, to áchcha'ka
grow back, to onchololi
grow on the ground, to balalli
grow out at the sides, to ilalawachi
grow over, to abalalli, atobachi
grow taller, to chaahakat achaaka
grow, to achaaka, hofanti, holhfo,
  walaa; also falaachi, faliili,
  holhfochi
grow together, to ittabalalli
grow together with, to abalalli
growl, to kiliha
growl, to make kilihachi
grown up, to be hofantikat ona
growth, new ittonchololi'
growth on a turkey's beak ibilhkan
growth on hackberry bark kapko'
  ani'
growth on tree limbs ninak yaaha'
grubbing hoe itti' haksishcha'ha',

lokfishkolli'
grunt at, to i̱lhonklhowa
grunt, to ha̱ha, kifa̱a, lhonka, lhonklhowa
grunting sound, to make a lhonk lhonk lhonk aachi
guarantor for, to be a imalapalinchi
guard naa-apiisachi'
guard for, to imatooni
guard, security okkisaatooni'
guard, to atooni
guardian atooni'
guardian for, to appoint a imatoonichi
guardian, to make a atoonichi
guess it has to be, I takchi'sha̱
guess so, I tokchi'cho̱, ya̱htokchi'cho̱
guest chokkaalaa'
guilty, to be ilonhochi
guinea fowl akankholisso'

gum, chewing taakchili'
gum tree taakchili' api'
gums notaahiyohli'
gun tanampo—see also gun, type of
gun, machine tanampishto, tanampo palhki'
gun, squirt oka' ishto̱lha'li'
gun store tanampaa-asha'
gun, toy tanampo holba'
gun, type of tanampo falaa'—see also names of specific guns
gunpowder naki' ishtayachi', naki' i̱hottok, tanampi̱hottok
gurgling sound, to make a chobo'chi, choboowachi
gut, to salhkonachi
guts salhkona
gutter oka' aaya', oka' aayanahli'
gymnasium aatoklhaka̱fa'
gypsy chipsi', hopayi'

h

habit, to have a imo̱mochi
habitually mina
hackberry kapko'
hackberry bark growths kapko' ani'
had better ooma'shki
hail bachali, okti', okti' wilili'
hail, for it to oktaat wilili
hail on a roof, to make the noise of ittibakahánchi, ittichamahánchi
hailstone okti' lombo'
hair ipa̱shi'
hair, body hishi'
hair clip pa̱shishtakallo'chi', pa̱shishyo'kli'
hair coming out, to have the boyahálli
hair fall out, to have the boyafa, boyahli
hair grows from, place where the

ishkobo' folfo', i̱yalfolfo'
hair oil pa̱shishlhili'
hair on the legs iyyi' hishi'
hair, pubic hakchish
hair ribbon pa̱sita' ishtakchi'
hair scraped off, to have the sha̱fa
hair, to apply (a rinse) to (someone's) lhilichi
hair, to burn off one's anakshowa, ilanakshooli
hair, to comb one's shilli
hair, to have bushy oshwichali
hair, to scratch out one's iliboyaachi
hair, to singe off one's anakshowa, ilanakshooli
hair, to wash one's ayiili
hair, to wash (someone's) ayiichi
hairdo, to have a beehive oshchaha̱li
hairline, to have a high ittifonat

ishto
hairnet ip̲ashi' alhiipi'li'
hairpiece ip̲ashi' holba'
hairpin ip̲ashishtakallo'chi'
hairy face, to have a bakwosholi
half black, person who is hattak
losiklanna'
half moon hashi' alootiklanna
half moon, for there to be a hashi'at
iklanna'si
half one's body paralyzed, to have
haknip tannapat illi
half past, to be iklanna
half, to be iklanna, iklanna'si
half, to break in palhata
half-breed iklanna'
half-brother intikba iklanna',
ittibaapishi iklanna', i̲nakfiklanna',
nakfish iklanna'
half-sibling ittibaapishi iklanna'
half-sibling, older intikba iklanna
half-sibling, younger nakfish
iklanna'
half-sister intikba iklanna', intiik
iklanna', ittibaapishi iklanna',
nakfish iklanna'
half-slip alhkona' iklanna'si
half-white person naaholliklanna'
hall aboohattintakla'
Halloween Sholop I̲nittak
ham iyyobi', shokhiyyobi'
ham, smoked shokha' nipi'
o̲shobohli'
hamburger paska nipi' ittalatta'a'
hammer naaishbo'wa'
hammer out many dents in, to
satapo'li
hammer out one dent in, to satabli
hammer, to bakaká'chi
hammering sound, to make a bak
bak bak aachi, kab kab kab aachi,
kabak kabak kabak aachi, kababá'chi,
kalh kalh kalh aachi, kalhak kalhak
kalhak aachi

hammock aafa'pa'
hamstring iyyobi' hakshish
hand ilbak
hand and foot, to wait on ishtaapichi
hand, back of the ilbak pakna'
hand, to put into (someone's) ilbak
i̲fokhi
hand to someone, to pitwiili
hand, to take by the hala'li
hand to, to i̲wiili, oshti̲wiili
handcart ontosso'la'
handcuffs ilbak ishtalakchi'
handcuffs on, to put ilbak takchi
handful ilbak alotto'wa, ilbak a̲lhto
handful, double ilbak tokl̲o alotto'wa
handful of, to grab a okaayinoffi
handgun tanamposhkololi'
handgun bullet tanamposhkololi'
i̲naki'
handkerchief innochi'
handle nannalhpi'
handle a chore, to pitnampíla
handle, candle ishtaahala'li'
handle, curved aayo'kli'
handle, faucet ishtaafilito'chi'
handle on, to put a straight oppi
handle, to hold by the hállalli
handle, to take by the hala'li
handlebars aayo'kli'
hands, to blow on one's ilapo̲fachi
hand, to brace oneself with one's
ootbitiipa
hands, to hold hálla'li, ittihállalli
hands, to wash one's ilbachifa
hands, to wash (someone's)
ilbachifachi
hands with, to hold hállalli
handwritten material ilbak
ishtincho'wa'
handyman nanniksaachi'
hang down, to lhi̲fa, takkaká̲li,
takkokó̲li
hang from, to atákka'li
hang onto, to apakchilofa, asítti'ya,

asiita, asotkachit máa, asotkáyya'chi,
atákka'li, atákkohli, atakohmáa,
atakoht máa, ataakakáli, ataakokóli,
aatakaali, holiitobli, ootasiita
hang unevenly, to lhifa
hang, to tákka'li, tákkohli, takoht
máa, takoochi; also faapo'wa,
noklhitoffit abi, noksitili
hang up, to takaachi
hanged, to be noksita
hanger naafkaataka'li'
hangers naafkaatakohli'
hanging, ring for ishtaatakaali'
hanging, to be oottakohli, tákka'li,
tákkohli, takoht máa
hanging, to leave takachi
happen in, to aakanihmi
happen once, to himonna'si
happen quickly, to himonali
happen to iyoba
happen, to kanihmi, katihmi,
ootálhi
happen to one, to have something
nannahmat kanihmi
happen to one, to have what
nannahoot kanihmi, nantahaat
katihmi
happens, if nothing nanna'chikyásha
happy naayoppa
happy about a situation, to be
ishtayiimita
happy about, to be ishtayoppa
happy, to be ayoppa, ilokchina
happy, to be surprised and
ishmalhata
hard for, to make things ataapolichi
hard hat yaalhipa kallo'
hard on one, to have it be nannakat
ishtimaakallo
hard on, to be really inkallo
hard, to be kallo, kawaski
hard, to make kallochi
hard, to try amóshsho'li
hardboiled, to be polla

harden, to kawaskichi
hardheaded person ishkobo' kallo'
hardhearted, to be ilikallochi
harness issoba shaapoli'
harness, to shaapolichi
harnessed, to be shaapóyyo'li
hash nipi' hollosi'
hasten the end of, to chashpochi
hat yaalhipa—see also hat, type of
hat brim yaalhimpatha'
hat, to put on a yaachikoli
hat, to wear a yaachíkko'li
hat, type of yaachiko'li', yaalhipa
ibichchalaa-asha', yaalhipa patha',
yaalhipa tanna'
hatband yaalhipa apakfo'ta'
hatbox yaalhipa aalhto',
yaalhipaafo'kha'
hatch, to hofanti
hatchet oksifoshi'
hate each other, to ikittiyay'lo
hate oneself, to ikiliyay'lo
hate, to ikyay'lo, yáyli ki'yo
hate to talk to, to inokwaya
hatpin yaalhipishtasiiti'ya'
hatrack yaalhipaatakohli'
haul, to shaali
haunted, to be aaholba
Hauwani Creek Hayowani'
Abookoshi
have a baby, to chipota sho'li,
chipotaat imala, chipotaat imatta,
chipotaat inti'wa
have a beehive hairdo, to oshchahali
have a big stomach, to missila
have a birthday, to afammi
have a blaze on the forehead, to
baktasali
have a boil come up, to hichabbi
have a boil, to hoshonnachi
have a broken heart, to ishhottómpa
have a cataract, to ishkinat alhatta,
ishkinat talha
have a charley horse, to halalli

have a cloud of dust rise, to shobolli
have a cold, to ibishshano
have a conversation with, to ibaa-
anompoli
have a convulsion, to hayoochichi
have a cover on, to áyya'chi
have a crack, to kisafa, kitafa
have a crest, to oshchahali
have a crew cut, to oshkabali
have a cyst, to chilhlha'li
have a day off, to nittak habina
have a diaper on, to bakshíyya'mi
have a dip, to aatakafa
have a dirty face, to baklosoli
have a discussion, to anompa
ishtittimayya ki'yo, anompa
ishtiktimayyo
have a fall broken by, to ootawaata
have a feather on one's head, to
yaatálla'li
have a fever, to yanha
have a fight, to ittafama
have a fire built for one, to imolhti
have a fork, to falakto
have a fragrance, to bilama
have a full diaper, to alotto'wa,
imalotto'wa
have a habit, to imomochi
have a hairy face, to bakwosholi
have a headache, to ishkobo'at
hottopa
have a heart attack, to
abikimilhkooli, chonkash hottopa'
hayochi, chonkashat hottopa
have a hernia, to salhkona kochcha'
í'shi
have a high fever, to yanhakat
chaaha, yanhaat inchaaha
have a high forehead, to ittifonat
ishto
have a high price, to ayallit chaaha
have a hole, to wakla
have a homosexual relationship
with, to ihoo intoba

have a hump, to kobokshi
have a husband, to hattakat
imayya'sha
have a job, to toksali
have a large beard, to chakwokoli
have a line, to lhafa
have a lot of holes, to cholok biyyi'ka
have a meal for, to imimpa
have a meal, to impa
have a meeting about, to ishtittanaha
have a meeting, to ittafama
have a memorial service for, to aa-
akshochi, imaa-akshochi, ishtimaa-
akshochi
have a memorial service, to aa-
akshochi' imáyya'sha, aa-akshochi'
ishtáyya'sha
have a miscarriage, to chipotaat
imilli, chipotaat inkaniya
have a mole, to tali' losa'at ontalla'a
have a nightmare, to iholba
have a noon meal, to tabookoli impa
have a nosebleed, to ibichchala'
issish lhatapa
have a pain, to hottopa
have a party, to toklhakafa'
imáyya'sha
have a period, to issish lhatapa
have a piece broken off, to toshafa,
toshahli
have a piece chip off, to shokafa
have a pompadour, to oshchahali
have a really big stomach, to
missílli'ya
have a relapse, to aafilima
have a relationship, to ittihaalálli
have a round head, to oshkoboli
have a rounded bottom, to lómbo
have a rounded depression, to
okaahofobi
have a runny nose, to ibilhkanat
lhatapa
have (a scarf) on one's head, to
yaachíkko'li

have a serious illness, to abikakat
impallammi
have a shaking fit, to abikimilhkooli
have a soft spot, to tannap pila'sit
yátto'fa
have a sore throat, to inonka'
hottopa
have a splinter, to ashiyama,
hashiyama, hofkaa
have a split personality, to
kánnohmi
have a sticker, to hofkaa
have a strong flavor of, to yammi
have a swelling disease, to
shatahpoli
have a taste, to champoli
have a tower, to shikkilili
have a vision of, to nannakat
imoktani
have a vision, to iholba,
nannimoktani
have a wart, to tokchana'paat
ombínni'li
have a wife, to ihooat imáyya'sha
have a woman over, to ihooat
ootimokfaha
have a worn place, to taha
have all of, to ishtimóma
have all over, to bíyyi'ka
have allergic swellings, to pofohli
have an abortion, to chipotabi
have an accident in, to
aaoshkannapa
have an accident, to ayoppolo'ka,
oshkannapa
have an ache in the bones, to
komoochi
have an additional disease, to
imalbita
have an affair with, to ibaanowa
have an allergic reaction, to fowabbi
have an argument, to anompa
ishtittimayya ki'yo, anompa
ishtiktimayyo

have an arm or leg pulled off, to
nipafa
have an election, to naalhtoka'
atookoli
have an erection, to inkallo
have an insect bite, to hoshonnachi
have an operation in, to aabasha
have an operation, to basha
have an ugly face, to bokyofoli
have arthritis, to foni' hottopa i'shi,
komoochi
have as a leftover, to imaatámpa
have as a secret lover, to ilomaka
have as an additional sexual partner,
to ayinínchi
have as one's second, to atoklónchi
have been born that way, to
imaalhpí'sa
have big openings, to shachakla
have blocked, to imoktapa
have broken necks, to tilohli
have buds come out, to fakobli
have bugs, to issosh bíyyi'ka
have bushy hair, to oshwichali
have business, to imaalami,
nannimaalami
have canker sores, to liwaali
have come back to one, to nokfokha
have come out, to okshalli
have corners, to shokolbika' aa-asha
have cracks, to kisahli, kitahli
have curly hair, to oshchiloli
have dandruff, to fatabli
have diarrhea, to alhoopolli
have different, to ittimíla
have difficulty breathing, to lhachofa
have dirt rolling off one's body, to
fatabli
have ears that stick out, to oshwalali
have enough, not to imóna ki'yo
have enough, to imalhpi'sa
have everything be okay, to
ishtinchokmaka
have finished taha

have four corners, to shokolbika'
oshta
have fun, to ilihaksichit nowa
have funny ways, to ishtaaíla
have gas, to hollonkso' aloota, mahli
aloota, shatabli
have good luck, to ayolhlha,
nannayolhlha
have gotten enough, not to ikimóno
have hives, to pofohli
have how many, to inkánnohmi,
inkáttohmi
have in addition, to ayiimillichi,
ayinínchi
have in one's hands, to í'shi
have in one's mouth, to káppa'li
have in with, to imimbalhto
have internal bleeding, to issish
lhatapa
have it be hard on one, to nannakat
ishtimaakallo
have it be too early for one, to
inchiiki
have it feel good, to ishtinchokmaka
have it get better for one, to
pitinampíla
have it get dark on one, to onobya,
onoklhili, ohashtahli
have it get to be evening on one, to
onobya
have it rain on one, to oshobbichi
have it seem like, to imahooba
have knife cuts all over, to kolohli
have left, to imásha
have leprosy, to oppolikmassa'lo'
í'shi
have light in one's eyes, to
oshoppala
have light skin, to okshawali
have lines, to lhahkachi
have little holes, to mitahli
have lots of pieces chip off, to
shokahli
have magical powers, to fatpo í'shi

have mange, to washkabi
have marks, to holisso
have mercy on, to inokhánglo
have more than one hole, to baha
have muscle aches, to lhikkachi
have nightmares about, to ishtiholba
have no distinct taste, to takishpa
have no leaves, to washshalla'a
have no wind, to likinta
have noon creep up on one, to
ontabookoli
have on (a belt), to askofféyya'chi
have one leg shorter than hayifa
have one leg shorter, to iyyi'
tannapat falaakat iklawwi'cho, iyyi'
tannapat tilofa'si
have one little hole, to mitafa
have one, to ittichaffa
have one's arms spread out
wihhílli'ya
have (one's candidate) lose, to
inkaniya
have one's car battery die, to kaa-at
imilli
have one's comment ignored, to
imanompaat kobafa
have one's eyes water, to ishkin
okchi'at lawa
have one's feelings hurt, to ikimóno,
imilahchohmi
have one's feet apart, to
wakchalla'wáli
have one's fever go down, to
shippachi, yanhakat shippa
have one's hair singed off, to
anakshowa
have one's head bent over to one
side, to akassanali
have one's head bent, to oshchonoli
have one's head on, to alhpíyyi'shi
have one's head ring, to achaamapa
have one's head stick up, to
shikkilili
have one's legs or a similar part

apart, to wakchalali
have one's mind be calm, to
imaanokfila-at yohbi bíyyi'ka
have one's mind keep turning
around, to imaanokfila-at
fashkalamo'wa
have one's mind made up, to
alóshsho'ma
have one's mouth water, to tokfohli
have one's picture turn out good, to
holba'at chokmaho toba
have one's skin pulled off, to lhofa
have one's skirt be too short, to
inchawwala
have one's time be up, to hashi'
kanallaat imambaanapa, hashi'
kanallaat intaha
have one's tubes tied, to oshi' iksho'
ilikbi
have one's wings spread out, to
wihhílli'ya
have oneself sterilized, to oshi'
iksho' ilikbi
have open for, to intiwa
have over, to ittifammichi
have pains, to komoha
have paint on, to albi
have peace, to nannayya biyyi'ka
have pinned onto one, to asítti'ya
have pins and needles, to hofkachi
have puddles, to okfichibli
have pus come out, to kalha
have pus, to aniichi
have rheumatism, to komoochi
have ringworm, to halambabi
have ripe fruit, to waa
have run out of, to intaha
have saggy skin, to lhifa
have several, to inkánnohmi
have sexual intercourse with, to
hosha, lapali
have sexual intercourse with, to lie
down to into'wa
have smooth skin, to lhimishko

have something bad come up, to
nanna ataklama' intoba
have something be one's business, to
nannishtahalaa
have (something) be too heavy for
one, to iwiiki
have something bothering one, to
nannakat istimaawiiki
have something caught in one's
throat, to nokbikili
have (something) go down the wrong
way, to nokshiyammi
have (something) go up one's nose,
to noklhamalli
have something good happen, to
ayolhlha
have something happen to one, to
nannahmat kanihmi
have something powdery come out,
to shobottokahchi
have something stuck in one's
throat, to nokbikili, noktalaali
have something tight around one's
neck, to noksíhhi'ta
have something to do with, to
ishtahaláa, nannishtahalaa
have something to do, to
nannimaalami
have something twisted in one's
hair, to atannalhchi
have splinters, to shipafa
have sticking into one, to hofkaa
have sticking onto one, to ashiila
have stitches, to alhcho'wa
have stuck in one's throat, to
noktakaali
have stuck in, to shámmali'chi
have sun in one's eyes, to ontoomi,
ohashtahli
have swellings, to pofohpoli
have tangled, to atannalhchi
have the arms and legs pulled off, to
nipahli
have the breath knocked out of one,

435

have the color run, to

to nokbiipa, nokbiipo'wa
have the color run, to masali
have the edges curl up, to oppolokko
have the edges lined up, to
  ittalatkachi, ittalatkachit máa
have the flu, to ibishshano
have the hair coming out, to
  boyahálli
have the hair fall out, to boyafa,
  boyahli
have the hair scraped off, to shafa
have the limbs stick out, to
  washshala
have the measles, to toshabbi,
  toshabbi' hayochi
have the same name as, to
  aholhchi'fo
have the same (parent), to ittinchaffa
have the say-so, to aachi
have the sediment settled, to
  okaatalaka
have the sides cut off, to talha
have the sole come of, to shokafa
have the top taken off, to tilofa
have the tops broken off, to tilohli
have the water dried out, to shippa
have three corners, to shokolbika'
  tochchí'na
have tied on, to ashiiyalhchi
have (time), to imambaanapa
have, to imánta, imáyya'sha,
  imáshwa, imi'ma, immi, intálla'a,
  intállo'wa, intalowat máa, intí'wa,
  ishtáyya'sha, í'ma, iwáyya'a,
  iwáyyo'wa, iwayowat máa; also
  hayoochi, í'shi, and other
  expressions listed here beginning
  with have
have torn skin, to lhilafa
have trouble getting one's breath, to
  nokshiyammi
have two lovers or spouses at the
  same time, to tawwalínchi
have two, to toklo'chi

have warts, to tokchana'paat
  onáyya'sha
have watery eyes, to ishkin okchi'at
  lawa
have what be wrong with one, to
  nantahaat inkatihmi
have what bothering one, to
  nannahoot ishtimaawiiki,
  nantahaat ishtimaawiiki
have what happen to one, to
  nannahoot kanihmi, nantahaat
  katihmi
have whooping cough, to
  hotolhkilli' í'shi
have wind blowing, to mahli
have with one, to ishtáa
have worms, to issosh ilawa
have wrapped around, to
  apakfóyyo'li
have wrinkled skin, to yikilhlha
haw, black chinaafalla'ha'
hawk akankabi'—see also hawk, type
  of
hawk, chicken akankabi'
hawk, red-tailed akankabi'
  hasimbish homma'
hawk, type of akankabiskanno'
hay hashshok; also hashshok shila'
hay, bale of hashshok talakchi'
hay barn hashshok aa-ashaachi'
hayloft hashshok aa-asha'
hazy, to be hoshontichi
he yammakot, yammat, yappakot,
  yappat; also mi, mihoot
he and he alone ilaapakilloot
he himself ilaapakaynihaat,
  ilaapakaynihoot
he himself also ilaapakya
head ishkobo', ishkoboka',
  inkapittani'
head, back of the yaachino'ko'
head bent over to one side, to have
  one's akassanali
head bent, to have one's oshchonoli

436

head covering yaalhippi'li'
head in a pimple, hard ishkin
head off, to inkatabli
head off, to take the tiloffi
head over, to make (someone) lean
  his akassanachi
head stick up, to have one's
  shikkilili
head taken off, to have the tilofa
head, to bow (someone's)
  oshchonochi
head, to bow the oshchonoli
head, to carry on one's yaatalaali
head, to have a feather on one's
  yaatálla'li
head, to have a round oshkoboli
head, to have (a scarf) on one's
  yaachíkko'li
head, to nod one's oshchooni
head, to put (medicine) on one's lhili
head, to put a feather on one's
  yaatalaali
head, to put on (someone's)
  yaachakaachi, yaatalachi
head, to put on one's yaachakaali,
  yaatalaali
head, to shave (someone's) mas<u>o</u>fi
head, to tie a scarf over (someone's)
  yaachikochi
head, to toss one's abakshowakli
head, to turn one's filita, filito'wa
head, to wear on one's yaalhíppi'li,
  yaatálla'li
head, top of the yaapakna'
head way back, to put one's
  abakshowali
headache, to have a ishkobo'at
  hottopa
headband ishkobo' apakfo'li',
  yaalhippi'li'
headed off, to be inkatabli
headlight aashoppala'
headlight, car with only one
  shokkaawi'

heads broken off, to have the tilohli
heads, to take off the tilohchi
heal, to aaissa, lhakoffichi
healed, to be <u>i</u>masali, lhakoffi
healthy looking, to be ilokchina
healthy, to be ilokchina, inchokma,
  inchokmishto
hear along with, to ibaahaklo
hear an echo, to achaamapa
hear from, to imaahaklo
hear, to haklo, hánglo, hap<u>o</u>waklo
hear, to make haklochichi
hearing aid nannishhaklo'
heart chonkash
heart attack chonkash hottopa'
heart attack, to have a
  abikimilhkooli, chonkash hottopa'
  hayochi, chonkash hottopat illi,
  chonkashat hottopa
heart shape chonkash holba'
heart, to have a broken ishhottómpa
hearth toksika'
heat, to pallichi
heat, to be in nakni' banna
heater aaolhti', lowak aainni', lowak
  aaolhti'
heater, wall aalashpali'
Heaven Aba' Chaaha', Aba' Yakni',
  Aaholitto'paka', Aaokch<u>a</u>a',
  Chihoowa Imaapihlichika'
heavy, to be wiiki
heel iyyi' tako'bish
heel of a shoe sholosh iyyi' tako'bish
heels, high sholosh iyyi' tako'bish
  chaaha'
held up, to be ataklama
hell aaishshachika', aaoklhilika',
  aaoppoloka', aayoppoloka', nanna
  aa-ashshachika'
hellfire aalowa', aayoppoloka'
hello ba' ishlata, chinchokma,
  chokmata, hallito
helmet yaalhipa kallo'
helmet, football to'li' <u>i</u>yaalhipa

437

help

help alhpila'
help blow the nose, to lhihkachi
help bring, to ishtibaawiichi
help butcher, to ibaa-abi
help catch along with, to ibaayokachi,
 ibaayokli
help count, to ibaahotihna
help make play, to
 ibaachokoshkomochi
help make sit, to ibaabiniichi
help move, to ishtibaawiichi
help oneself, to ilapila
help out with, to imapila, imapilachi
help pick, to ibaa-ayowa
help put down, to ibaa-akkowaachi,
 ibaabohli
help shoulder, to ilabanachi
help spank, to ibaapassáa
help, to apila
help, to get alhpila' ishi
help, to give alhpila' ima
help, to make apilachi
help with, to ibaa-apila
helper apila'
helper, to take on as a ilapilachi
hem on a dress
 naafkaapaakota'lhchi'
hem on, to turn up a polhommi
hem, to apakollichi, apaakollichi
hemmed, to be apaakotalhchi
hemstitch, to shihchi
hen akanka' tiik
hen, guinea akank holisso'
hen, mother akankishki'
hen, setting akankalaata'
her mi, miho, yammako, yamma,
 yappako, yappa
her herself ilaapakayni
herd, to atappichi
here yappa, yappak, yappa
here it is yamma, yappa
here, not to be iksho
here, to be ala
here, to get ala

hermaphrodite hattak ihoo iklanna'
hernia salhkona kochcha'
hernia, to have a salhkona kochcha'
 í'shi
herself ilaapo'
herself, by ilapit
hey! kiihi
hiccup, to chokfiyammi,
hickory nut osak, osak tali'
hickory nut hominy osak tanchi'
 ittalhata', osak tafola'
hickory tree osak api'
hidden by, to be ahiitánka
hidden from, to be iloma
hidden, to be loma
hide along with, to ibaalohmi
hide from each other, to ittiloma
hide from in, to imaaloma
hide from, to ilohmi, iloma
hide in, to aalohmi, aaloma
hide oneself away, to ililohmi
hide the bullet naki' lohmi'
hide, to fóyyokhi, lohmi, loma,
 shamayo'li
hiding place aaloma'
high fever, to have a yanhakat
 chaaha, yanhaat inchaaha
high forehead, to have a ittifonat
 ishto
high heels sholosh iyyi' tako'bish
 chaaha'
high on, to get ishhaksi
high priced, to be ayallit chaaha
high prices, to charge ayalli'
 chaahachi, ayalli'at inchaaha,
 imayallishto
high, to be chaaha
high, to make chaahachi
high, to sing chaaha taloowa
higher, to be achánka
highchair chipotimaaombiniili'
 chaaha'
high-heeled shoe sholosh iyyi'
 tako'bish chaaha'

highly seasoned, to be yammi
high-topped shoe sholosh chaaha'
highway hinishto'
hill onchaba
hillside sakti
him mi, miho̱, yammako̱, yamma̱,
yappako̱, yappa̱
him himself ilaapakayni
himself ilaapo'
himself, by ilapi̱t
hind leg iyyi' a̱shaka'
hinge ishtaatakaali'
hip, outer part of the iyyobi'
ishtaachoosho'wa'
hipbone iyyobi' aaittachakka'a'
hippopotamus shokhok-okaa-asha'
hips hatip, i̱wa̱'ta'
hire, to tohno
Hispanic Oshpaani'
hissing, to make the sound of a cat tif
tif tif aachi
hit a foul ball, to faapa, faapichi
hit a home run, to ootafoolopa,
ootfolota
hit along with, to ibaaisso
hit and knock down, to sákkakli'chi
hit and knock the breath out of, to
nokbiibli
hit back, to falammisht isso
hit each other, to ittibo'li
hit each other with, to ishtittibo'li,
ishtittilisso
hit himself, to make ilissochichi
hit in the stomach, to issot
ittapakolli, noktiibli
hit in, to aaisso
hit on the head, to kámmakli'chi
hit oneself, to ilibo'li, ilisso
hit repeatedly, to lhokka̱ha
hit suddenly, to chímmikli'chi
hit the ball, to to'wa' isso
hit the wrong way, to issot tiballichi
hit, to bo'li, isso; also bákkakli'chi,
bokka̱a, kómmokli'chi,

lhókkokli'chi, miti'chi, payoffi,
sakka̱ha
hit, to make issochichi
hit, to make the sound of cloth being
top top top aachi
hit together and make noise, to
chamapa
hit with one's hand, to sakka̱ha
hit with, something to ishbo'wa'
hit with the fist, to míttikli'chi
hit with the flat of the hand, to
passa̱a
hit without knocking down, to issot
anoktobaffi, issot atiilhiffi, issot
atiilhiffichi
hit wrong, to issot tiballichi
hitch to, to halallichi
hitchhike, to aakaayinkat a̱a
hitting pillows, to make the sound of
mit mit mit aachi
hitting soft things, to make the sound
of mititi'chi
hitting, to make the sound of komok
komok komok aachi, sak sak sak
aachi
hives, to have pofohli
hoard, to i̱holiitopa
hoarse, to be nokshila
hoarse, to make nokshilili
hobo inchokkiksho'
hoe ishlaa'
hoe, grubbing itti' haksishcha̱'ha',
lokfishkolli'
hoe handle ishlaa' aalhpi'
hoe, to apihchi, liili
hog shokha'; also choocho'
hog, baby shokhoshi'
hog lights shokha'
i̱shoppaya'kalhchi', shokha'
sholopha', shokhi̱falaa'
hogan lokfi' abooha'
hogweed shokhimpa'
hold by the handle, to hállalli
hold dear, to i̱holitto'pa

439

hold elections, to naalhtoka' atookoli
hold hands, to hálla'li, ittihállalli
hold hands with, to hállalli
hold onto, to aatákka'li, aatákkohli,
  aatakohmáa
hold out to, to pitiwí'li, oshtiwí'li
hold out, to pitwí'li
hold straight out, to oshwiili
hold, to í'shi, pitshooli, yokli
hold to, to ishtittihállalli
hold up, to ataklammi, intíkki'li,
  ihíkki'ya
holder aabilhpowa'
hole cholok, yakni' kola'
hole in the ground yakni' cholok
hole in, to make a little mitaffi
hole in, to make more than one little
  mitaachi
hole, to have more than one baha
hole, to have one little mitafa
hole while making another hole, to
  cut a amiitaffi
holes in, to make little milli
holes, to be full of little shachakla
holes, to have a lot of cholok biyyi'ka
holes, to have little mitahli
holiday nittak holiitopa'—see also
  names of specific holidays
holiday in honor of, to declare a
  nittak iholiitobli
holiday, religious Chihoowa inittak
  holitto'pa, nittak holitto'pa'
holler, to intasahli
hollow tube oski'
hollow, to be cholok biyyi'ka
hollowed out, to be okaatakafa
holly, type of foshiyyi'
holster tanampishokcha'
Holy Ghost Shilombish Holitto'pa'
holy person holitto'pa'
holy place aaholitto'pa'
holy, to be holítto'pa
home inchokka'
home in, to make one's aa-asha,

aashwa, aatta, inchokka' aaikbi
home of, to change the wihachi
home run, to make a ootafoolopa,
  ootfolota
home, to change one's wiha
home, to run away from malit
  aakaniya
homemade, something ilaapit ikbi'
homesick, to be ikacha'ho
hominy tanchi' lobo', talobo
hominy, hickory nut osak tanchi'
  ittalhata', osak tafola'
homosexual man hattak ihoo toba'
homosexual woman ihoo hattak
  ilahobbi'
honey fohi', fohinchampoli'
honey locust itti' kati, kati
honeycomb fohi' ilhpichik
hoof iyyakchosh
hoof, bottom of the iyyi' nota'
hook naafkaataka'li'
hook, to atakalichi
hook, type of tali' chiffola',
  talishtaatakka'li'
hooked, to be atákka'li, polhoma
hoop, basketball to'waalhopo'chi'
hoop, hula ishchokkaamala'
hoopskirt alhkona' wahhala',
  alhkona' wihhila'
hoopskirt, to wear a wahhalwáa,
  wihhílli'ya, wihhilwíya
hoorah for, to say ayiimillichi'
hope, to anhi
hopper, grain tanchishtani'
horizontal, to put okkawaatali
horizontally across, to be okkawaata
horn lapish; also lapish kolofa'
horn, car kaa ishpaachi'
horned owl kitiini
horned toad toksala'pilapishaa-asha'
horse issoba
horse apple issobintakolo
horse, baby issob-oshi'
horse blanket issobinaachi

horse collar issobinno'chi'
horse, mother issoba ishki', issoba oshpishichi'
horse, to make a noise like a scared kashafa
horse trough issoba aaipita' piini'
horse, wild issobimilhlha'
horsefly holhaano, issobinchokkaana
horsemint sholop tilhi'li'; *also* issoba ishoptilhi'li'
horseshoe issobintali' lapali', issobisholosh, issoba isholosh
horsewhip issobishfama'
hospital abikaa-asha'
hot and spicy, to be homi
hot chocolate chaklit palli'
hot dog ofi' palli'
hot, to be impalli, palli
hot, to feel ilashpa
hot, to make pallichi
hot-air balloon nannishwakaa'
hotel aanosi' abooha
hot-plate mat nanna ontalla'a'
hound ofi' haksibish falaa'
hour hashi' kanalli
house abooha, chokka'—*see also* house, type of
house cleaner abooha chofalli'
house, in back of the abooha ashaka'
house, little abooshi'
house of prostitution hawi' abooha
house, old abooha lhipa'
house paint aboohalbi'
house, side of the aboohapootaka'
house sit, to potooni
house, type of lokfi' abooha'
houses in a bunch chokka' lokoli'
hover, to takkakáli
how kanihsht, katiya fokha, katihsht, kaniht, katiht
how are you? chinchokma, chokmata
how many kaniya fokhahoot, kaniya fokhaho, kannohmihoot,

kannohmiho, katiya fokhahat, katiya fokhahta, kattohmi, kattohmihat, kattohmihta
how many times hikannohmi', hikattohmi'
how many, to be káttohmi
how many, to have inkánnohmi, inkáttohmi
how much kaniya fokhahoot, kaniya fokhaho, katiya fokhahat, katiya fokhahta
how old, to be afammi kánnohmi, afammi káttohmi, sipoknikat kaniya fokha, sipoknikat katiya fokha
how, to be kani'mi, kaniya fokha, kati'mi
how, to be doing katihmi
howl, to wooha; *also* fohómmi
howl, to make woohachi
huckleberry shapha', shonkabosh, shonkabosh ishto'
huff, to be in a imilahchohmi
hug, to shooli
hug, to reach out and pitshooli
hug with, to ibaashooli
hula hoop ishchokkaamala'
hulls, corn tanchi' hoshollo', tanchi' lakchi'
hulls of grain hoshollak
humble oneself, to ilakkaalíncho'si
humble, to akkaalínchi
humble, to be akkálo'si, chonkash akkálo'si
hummingbird lhikommak
hump, to have a kobokshi
humped up, to be kobokshi
hunchback nalhchaba kobokshi'
hunched over, to be ittapaakota, kóbbokshi, payofa
hundred talhipa
hundred, one talhipa chaffa
hundred, two talhipa toklo
hung up, to be takaali, takohli

hungry, to be hopoba
hunt for the benefit of, to imowwatta
hunt in, to aaowwata
hunt, to hoyo, hoyot aya, hoot aya,
   owwatta
hunt with, to ibaaowwatta
hunting, to go owwattat aya
hurry each other, to ittaatoshpalichi
hurry, to toshpa
hurry, to make atoshpalichi
hurry up! mahya
hurt niini
hurt along with, to get ibaahottopa
hurt each other, to ittihottopachi
hurt oneself in the same place again,
   to tiibli
hurt oneself, to ilihottopachi
hurt, to hottopa, hottopachi

hurt, to be latafa
hurt, to be deeply ishhottómpa
hurt, to be really hottómpakat
   aalhlhi
hurt, to have one's feelings ikimóno,
   imilahchohmi
hurting, to keep on tiipo'li
hurts, it topa
husband ihattak
husband, to have a hattakat
   imáyya'sha
husbands at the same time, to have
   two tawwalínchi
hush! ma!
hymn aba' ishtaloowa', taloowa'
hysterical, to be abikimilhkooli
hysterical, to make abikimilhkoochi

i

I ana'akot, ana'at
I beg your pardon? haa
I guess it has to be takchi'sha
I guess so tokchi'cho, yahtokchi'cho
I. Hunter Pickens Aayahanta'
I myself ana'aakaynihaat,
   ana'aakaynihoot
I wonder if nanna'chihchi,
   nannahchi, nannatokchi
ice okakmi'
ice cream pishokchakmi'
ice cube okakmi' tosha'fa'
ice-cube tray okakmi' aalhto'
ice, dry okakmi' palli'
ice pick chofaak haloppa',
   okakmishboshollichi'
ice skates sholosh okti'
   ishtokaashalalli', sholosh
   oktishtoshala'li'
icebox okakmi' aalhto
icehouse okakmi' aa-asha'

icicle naksabasali'
icing paska champoli' onaa-asha',
   paska champoli' pakna'
   onashaachi'
ideas ignored, to have one's
   imanompaat kobafa
if nothing happens nanna'chikyásha
igloo okti' abooha
ignored, to have one's ideas
   imanompaat kobafa
illegitimate child chipota holhkopa',
   chipota loma', holhkopa'
illness, to have a serious abikakat
   impállammi
imagine, to imahooba
imitate, to hobachi
imitation holba'
impatient, to be nokhámmi'chi,
   ishnokhámmi'chi
impeach, to kochchichi
important, for it to be nannakat

442

aafinha
important, to be aafinha
impose a serious responsibility on, to
anompa kallo' onhochi
impoverish, to kobaffi
impoverished, to be ilbashsha
impress, to inkostini
imprisoned, to be yoka, yoka' oot
ahánta
improve, to chokmali
in a daze, to be lhakcha
in a certain configuration, to be
kani'mi
in a group together, to be all
aaittibaachaffa
in (a time) aash, mashshaasho,
ookma
in back ashaka'
in between ittintaklaka', ittintakla'
in charge, to be aachi
in charge of, to put apihchi
in different directions mayyoka'
in doubt, to be anoktoklo
in earlier days chiikihmachiiki'
in front of tikba'
in front of, moving tikbali'
in front of, to be imahiita
in front of, to get imahiita
in front of, to go ataapolichi,
imokkawaata
in heat, to be nakni' banna
in jail, to be yoka
in labor, to be chipoti'sha'chit abika
in, moving anonkali', anonkakali'
in pain, to be nokhámmi'chi
in some way kanihsht
in that direction misha' fonka,
misha' pila
in the group aatangla'
in the same group with, to be ahiina
in the shell, to be lómbo
in there with them, to be aaiklanna
in this direction ola' fonka, ola' pila
in, to be aachaffa, fokha, fóyyokha,

okaa-ahánta, okaa-áyya'sha,
okaaáshwa, okaatálla'a,
okaatállo'wa, okaatalowat máa,
okaawáyya'a, okaawáyyo'wa,
okaawayowat máa
in water, to be oka' okaatákka'li, oka'
okaatakkakáli, oka' okaatákkohli,
oka' okaatakkokóli, oka' okaatakoht
máa
in what manner katihsht
in what way kaniht, katiht
in with, to be aaibaachaffa, ibalhto
incense nambilama'
include in the count, to ahotihnachi
increase, to achaakáli, chaahachi
increased, to be achánka
indeed yamma
index finger ilbak naaishtaabachi'
Indian Hattak Api' Homma'—*see
also* Indian, type of
Indian corn tanchi' kawaski'
Indian doctor's assistant tisho
Indian, full-blooded Hattak Api'
Homma' alhlhi'
Indian home hattak api'
homminchokka'
Indian judge hattak api' homma'
naapiisa'
Indian reservation hattak api'
homma' aa-asha'
Indian sign language, to use ilbak
ishtanoli
Indian spirit guide hattak sawa'
Indian style, to sit tossollo't bínni'li,
tossollo'wat binoht máa,
tossollo'wat chí'ya
Indian Territory Hattak Api'
Homma' Iyaakni'
Indian tribe okloshi' homma'
Indian, type of Kaayowa, Tataawa
Indian, wild hattak imilhlha'
Indians, wild okloshi' imilhlha'
indulge in self-pity, to iliposilhlha
inexpensive, to be alhchóna

infertile person or animal hobak
inflate for, to impoffololi
inflate, to missilili, poffololi
inflated, to be mahli aloota, poffola,
  poffóllo'wa
inflated, to get poffola
ingredients nannittibaalhto'
inhale, to ilafoyopa, ilifoyopa,
  noklhamalli
injection, to give an ittish ani
insane asylum haksaa-asha'
insane, to be haksi
insect issosh—see also insect, type of
insect bite, to have an hoshonnachi
insect pest nannokchamalapa'
insect, type of hapaanokfila,
  hapaanokfilishto', hatiimimi',
  hofanti', kowi-homma', yakni'
  shokaawi'—see also names of
  specific insects
inside anonka', anonkaka'
inside, moving anonkakali',
  anonkali'
inside, not to be done on the chakissa
inside out, to be anokpilifa,
  fashkálla'ma, fashkalamo'wa,
  fili'ta, fílli'ta
inside out, to turn anokpiliffi,
  fashkalammi, fashkalamo'li
inside, to be álhto
inside, to be caught chokkówa
inside, way anonkaka'
insistent noise, to make a loud
  tasahli
instant coffee kaafi' bota'
instep iyyi' pakna'
instrument, musical nannola'
instrument, type of musical lapish,
  lapish kolofa', sholoshtalhipa
(insult, type of) chihaksibish patha,
  chihasimbish, chihasimbish falaa,
  chishkish!, chishkish losa,
  chifalakto', haksibish patha',
  ishkish, ishkish losa'

intact, to be móma
intercourse with, to have sexual
  hosha, lapali
intercourse, to have sexual
  ittayoshkammi, ittihosha, ittilapali
interest, to look at something with
  okmiloli
interest, to look at with onokmiloli
interest, to pay oshi'ak illa atobbi
interpret for, to imimanompoli,
  intoshooli
interpret, to toshooli
interpreter for iminaanooli'
interpreter for, to be an iminaanoli
interrupt, to imayoppani'chi
intersection aafalakto', hina'
  aaittabanna'a'
intersection in, for there to be an
  hina'at aaittabánna'a
intestines salhkona
introduce oneselves, to ittithana
introduce, to ittithanachi
investigate each other, to
  ittaafaana'chi
investigate, to afaana'chi
invite, to ittafamachi, ittafammi'chi,
  ittifamo'chi
involved with, to be ahiina
iodine ittish homma', mankokchi'
iron naaishhama'
iron, branding tali' ishtincho'li', tali'
  ishtincho'wa'
iron, to hammi
ironed, to be halma
ironing board nannaahalma',
  nannaahammi'
irritate skin, to hoshinkochi
irritate, to imalhchíbba'chi
is it okay? chokma imalhta
is this what you wanted? yamma
island yaakni' sawa'si', yaakni'
  tashayyi', yaakni' toshafa'
islands, group of small yaakni'
  talkachi'

it yammakot, yammako̲, yammat,
  yamma̲, yappakot, yappako̲, yappat,
  yappa̲
it has to be that way chii takchi'sha̲
it hurts topa
itch, to washkabi
itch, to make washkabichi
itching to, to be bannakat

yawoolínchi, yawooli̲shnaacha
itchy, to be washkabi, yawoochi
itchy, to make hoshinkochi
it's bound to be takchi'sha̲
it's really different a̲lhlhi i̲la
itself ilaapo'
itself, by ilapi̲t
ivy, poison ofimitti'

j

jacket naafkishto', naafkishto'
  tilo̲fa'si
jackrabbit chokfi haksobish falaa',
  chokfi palhki'
jackrabbit, type of chokfi haksobish
  falaa' okchamali'
jail abooha kallo'
jail, to be in yoka
janitor abooha chofalli'
jar kitoba
jar for making butter pishokchi'
  aaniha'
jar lid kitobalhiipi'ya'
jar, mason kitoba nanna-aalhto'
jaw notakfa
jaybird ti̲shkila
jealous of with regard to, to be
  ahopoochi
jealous of, to be hopoo, ishhashaa,
  ishtahopoochi
jealous of, to make hopoochi
jealous over, to be ishmalhaa
jealous, to be hopoo
jelly cheli'
jelly beans bala' kendi'
jerk around, to fata'chi
jerk, to faapo'chi, hállakli'chi,
  ilhkóyyokli, ilhkoyyokli'chi,
  kánnakli
jerky nipi' pasa', nipi' shila'
Jesus Chihoowoshi', Chiisas, Hattak

Oshi'
jewel tali' holiitopa', tali'
  shokmalali'
job, to have a toksali
jock strap i̲nihi' ishyokli'
join a church, to Iksa' ibaafokha
join the armed forces, to tashka-
  chipota' ibaaholhtina
join the armed forces, to go tashka-
  chipota' aya
join with, to ibaaholhtina
joint aaittachakkachi'
joke about, to ishtayoppolachi
joke around with, to aatoklha
joke, to make a yoppola
joke to, to tell a iyoppola
judge hattak i̲naapiisa', nannapiisa',
  naahollo nannapiisa'
judge as, to ishtapiisa
judge, Indian hattak api' homma'
  naapiisa'
Judgment Day Nittak Ishtayyo'pi'
jug lokfi' kitoba, nanna aaishko'
juice okchi'
juicy, to be okchi' lawa, okchi'at lawa
jump along carrying, to ishmalli
jump along with, to ibaamalli
jump along with, to make
  ibaamallichi
jump around, to mallittahángli,
  tossoola

445

jump around, to make tossoolachi
jump around, to wave one's arms
  and wihhiila
jump back, to mallittakali
Jump Dance Tilobli' Hilha'
jump down, to ashmalli
jump for, to imalli
jump from, to aamalli
jump into, to okaamalli
jump into with, to ibaaokaamalli
jump off, to aamalli, aamallittakali
jump on in, to aaomalli
jump on, to omalli
jump out of, to aamalli,
  aamallittakali
jump rope, to ishtalakchi' malli,
  malli
jump, to hállakli'chi, malli
jump, to make mallichi

jump up and down, to ayiimita,
  ishtayímmi'ta
jump up, to satappakahchi,
  satappakahsht hika
jumping beans bala' malli',
  oshpaanimbala'
June bug chaloklowa' imissap,
  hatiimimi'
junk naalhipa'
junkyard naalhipa' aa-asha'
just pila, pilla
just a few, to be kanihmo'si
just a little chohmo'si
just a little, to be kanihmo'si
just a while, to be ikalhchibo'so
just now himmako'sa
just say it, to pílla aachi
just, to be biika, illa
just to be there píhhi'la

k

Kalihoma Kali Homma'
keep a budget, to ilatoba
keep a house of prostitution, to
  hawi' abooha apiisachi
keep a secret, to lohmit í'shi
keep being reinjured in, to
  intiipo'wa
keep for, to imí'shi, imbóyyohli
keep from doing, to imolabi
keep going backwards, to
  bakhitiipopóli
keep going on, to chonkash yohbi
keep in mind, to nokfónkha
keep in the house, to abooha
  fóyyokhi
keep in, to fóyyokhi
keep on reinjuring, to intiipo'li,
  tiipo'li
keep on, to achónna'chi, chilita
keep on watching, to pi'scha

ishtakaaniya, pi'scha ishtataamowa
keep pushing, to toopo'li
keep secret, to lohmi
keep, to bóyyohli, í'shi
keep turning, to folototó'chi
keep up with, to láwwi'chi,
  pitlawwi'chi
keep with one for, to imiláwwi'li
kennel ofi' aa-asha'
ketchup akankishniha' okchi'
kettle, type of iyyaa-asha'
keyhole cholok ishtiwa'
  ishtaafilito'chi'
kick around, to ahalhlhichi
kick for, to ihalhabli
kick like a kitten, to tallalálí
kick one's feet in the air, to
  wakchaalli
kick out, to kochcha' pitkanchi
kick, to halhabli, halhlhi

kicked, to be halha, halhapa
kid, to iyoppola
kidnap, to honkopa
kidney ilbolbo'
kidney beans bala' bolbo'
   ahooba'sika'
kill along with, to ibaa-abi
kill by choking, to noklhitoffit abi
kill by hanging, to noksitili
kill by overfeeding, to kayyachit abi
kill deliberately, to illichi
kill each other, to ittibi, ittillichi
kill for, to imambi
kill in, to aa-abi
kill oneself, to ilibi
kill some of, to aa-abi
kill, to abi, issot bohli, loshommi
kill, to attempt to atókko'li
kin, to be ittapiha
kin, younger aaittapiha'
kind of chohmi, kánni'ya
kind, to be akkálo'si
kind to, to be imakkálo'si
kindle, to ooti
kindled, to be olhti
king minko'
kingdom imaapihlichika'
kiss himself, to make (someone)
   ilisho'kachichi
kiss in, to aasho'ka
kiss, to imbasmo, sho'ka
kiss, to make sho'kachichi
kitchen aalhponi', aaholhponi'
kitchen shelves amposhaa-asha'
kitten kow-oshi'
kleenex ishkasho'kalhchi'
knead, to yamaska, yato'chi
knee iyyinto'lhka'
kneel down, to achokmilhka
kneel in, to aa-achokmilhka
kneel, to achokmihilhkat bínni'li,
   achokmihilhkat chí'ya, bílhlhi'pa,
   achokmihilhkat binohmáa
kneel, to make achokmilhkachi

kneel to, to imachokmilhka
kneeler aachokmilhka'
kneeling, to be achokmihilhka
knees, to bend one's to'ti
knees, to get on one's achokmilhka
knickknacks ishtasawachi'
knife bashpo—see also knife, type of
knife cuts all over, to have kolohli
knife handle bashpaalhpi'
knife, pocket nannishtalhlhi'
knife, to cut with a bashtabli
knife, type of bashpo chakchaki',
   bashpo falaa', bashposhi', bashpo
   ishtimpa'
knife-blade edge bashpihaloppa'
knit, to nantanni, tanni
knitted article tanna'
knitting machine nannaatanni'
knitting needle nannishtanni'
knock down, to kinaachi, yilhibli,
   yilhiichi, yilhlhichi
knock down, to hit and sákkakli'chi
knock into, to ishtilibo'li
knock on, to imbaka'chi, imbo'li,
   inkaba'chi, inkasa'chi
knock out, to issot illichi
knock over on, to oyilhibli,
   oyilhlhichi
knock the breath out of, to issot
   noktiibli, issot nokbiibli,
   nokbiipo'li, noktiibli
knock the breath out of, to hit and
   nokbiibli
knock things together, to
   ittikábbakli'chi
knock, to sakaká'chi
knocked down, to be yilhihli, yilhipa
knocker, door abokkisishkasa'chi'
knocking sound, to keep making a
   kassasa'chi
knocking sound, to make a bak bak
   bak aachi, ittibaka'chi,
   ittibakaká'chi, ittikaba'chi,
   ittikababá'chi, ittikábbakli'chi, kab

447

knot in, to tie a

kab kab aachi, kabak kabak kabak
aachi, kababá'chi, kalhak kalhak
kalhak aachi, kalh kalh kalh aachi,
kas kas kas aachi, kasak kasak kasak
aachi
knot in, to tie a shikoonobli
knot onto, to ashiikoono'li
knot together, to ittashiikoono'li
knots in, to tie many shikoono'li
knotted onto, to be ashiikoono'wa
knotted, to be shikoono'wa,
shikoonopa
knotted together, to be
ittasiikoono'wa
know for sure, to alhtókko'waka

ithána
know how to do, to imponna
know one's way around, to aaithána
know, to ithána; *also* imannoya
know what to do, to
aakanihma'nikat ithána
know with, to ibaaithána
knowledge nannimponna'
known, to be annowa, annoya
knuckle ilbak aaittachakkachi'
knuckle joint, the inside of the ilbak-
oshi' aapolhoma'
knuckles, to crack one's foni' kooli
koala nita' sawa'si'

1

labor pains, to feel hottopakmat
nokhammi'chi
labor, to be in abika, chipoti'sha'chit
abika
laborer toksali'
lace nannishtiksaa'
lace oneself up, to ilashiichi
lace up, to ashiichi
laced up with, to be ashiiyalhchi
lackadaisical, to be yáppalli
ladder aatoloyya'
ladybug ahi' imissosh, issosh loksi',
loksi', loksinto'ti'
ladybug, type of loksoshi'
laid across, to be awatkachit máa,
awatkáyya'chi, awátta'a
laid out in, to be aato'wa
laid out, to be aakahat máa,
aakáyya'ha, aatí'wa
lake hayip, hayip ishto'
lakeshore oka' apootaka'
lamb chokfalhpooboshi'
lamb's quarters taani'
lame, to be shamíhhi'la

lamp aashoppala'
lamp oil aashoppala' niha'
lampshade aashoppala' alhiipi'ya',
aashoppala' owayya'a'
lance, to kalhali
land yaakni'
land, bottom- pataaschi
land on, to ootaakkowa
land, to ootakkowa
landlord chokkimponta', hattak
chokkimponta'
language anompa—*see also names
of specific languages*
language, to use bad anompoppani,
anompoppanichi
lantern aashoppala' talakchi'
lap, to labbi
lard niha—*see also* lard, type of
lard can asonnak tobbi'
lard can lid asonnak tobbalhiipi'ya'
lard, type of niha finha', shokha'
niha', waaka' niha'
larva, locust yala
last child in a family aballakshi'

Last Day Nittak Ishtayyo'pi'
last name holhchifo ishtaalhi'
last night oklhiliaash, obyaka'aash
last one ishtaalhlhi'
last quarter, for the moon to be in its hashi'at kaniyat ishtaya
last, the ishtayyo'pi
last, to be aballaka' finha, ishtáyyo'pi
last, to be the aalhlhi, ootishtaalhlhi
last year tikba' afammi
latch, to atakalichi
late, to be alhchiba, imalhchiba, leeti
late, to make imalhchibachi
later, to be alhchímba
lath aaittachakkachi' ompatkachi'
Latino Oshpaani'
laugh at each other, to ittollali
laugh at himself, to make (someone) ilollalichi
laugh at in, to aaollali
laugh at oneself, to ilollali
laugh in, to aaollali
laugh, to ollali
laugh, to make ollalichi
laundromat naafkaa-achifa'
laundry naafkaa-achifa'
laundry, clean naalhchifa'
lava tobaksi' bila', tobaksi' lowa'
law nannalhpisa'
law, old-time Indian Ishki' Oshta'
law, to break the nannalhpisa' kobaffi, naalhpisa' achapa, naalhpisa' oppani
law, to make a nannalhpisa' ikbi, naalhpisa' bohli
lawmaker naapiisa'
lawn hashshok holokchi'
lawyer loya', nannishtimatta'
laxative ishtalhopolli', ishtalhoopollichi'
laxative, to give (someone) a alhoopollichi
lay across, to abanni, abaanali, awalli, awaatali

lay down for, to imbohli, pitimbohli
lay down on, to abaanali, ombohli, ootonkahli
lay down, to bohli, kahli, pitbohli
lay down together, to ittibaakahli
lay down with, to ibaakahli
lay off, to chaffichi
lay on, to onkahli
lay one's head on, to alhpishshi
lay out, to kahli
lay, to achiili, chiili
lay together, to ittapolli
layer, to be put on over another albítti'ya
lazy, to be intakho'bi, pátta'a, yáppalli
lazy, to make intakho'bichi
lazy with, to be ibaaintakho'bi
lead naki' bila'
lead around, to pihchit áa
lead in singing, to intaloowa, tikbishtimayya
lead singer for, to be tikbishtimayya
lead, to halaht ishtona, pihchit ishtaya, tikba' imayya, tikba' ishtaya
leader ishkoboka'
leader, dance intikbayka'
leader for, to be a dance or song intikbayka
leader in, to be a aaminko
leader, song taloowapiichi'
leader, to be a dance or song tikbayka
leader, to be the tikba' ishtaya
leader, to make a apihchi
leaf hishi'
leaf of a table aaimpa' ittintakla'
leaf, tree itti'shi'
lean against each other, to ittaatáyya'a
lean against, to atalkachit máa, atalkáyya'chi, atáyya'a, ataaya, ataayali
lean his head over, to make (someone) akassanachi

lean one's head to one side, to

lean one's head to one side, to
  akassanali
lean, to kinafa
lean-to hoshottika'
learn about, to akostinichi
learn from, to imaaithana
learn one's way around, to aaithana
learn to, to ithana
leash ishtalakchi'
leather naahakshop, waaka' hakshop
leather, imitation asiita holba'
leather, tanned asiita
leather, to tan asiita iksaachi
leave after, to ayakaa
leave behind, to antachínchi,
  biniichi, imásha, impalhki, kashcha
  aya, találi
leave behind with, to ibaa-antachichi
leave for, to imambíhli, imáni,
  intaláli, intalóli, ifónkhi,
  pitintalaali, pitiwayaachi
leave hanging, to takachi
leave on a light for, to ishoppaláli
leave some for, to imáni
leave some, to áni
leave there, to találi
leave, to aaissachi, inkáa, intaláa,
  intalówa, intówa, ifilammi,
  ifilamo'li, iwayáa, iwayówa, kanalli
leave, to go off and ka'shcha kaniya
leave to in one's will, to ima
leave tracks on, to aanowa
leave with, to imantachínchi
leaves before a storm, to make the
  sound of washaahánchi
leaves, to have no washshálla'a
Lebanon Leblan
leech fokkol, hosolo, issish ishko',
  issish sho'ka'
left alhfabi'
left side alhfa'bika', imalhfabi'
left standing, to be hikíya
left sticking, to be lapáli, lapóhli
left there, to be taláa, tówa

left, to be ásha, áshwa, káha
left, to be one lhakófa
left, to the alhfabi' pila
left-handed, to be alhfa'bi
leftover, to have as a imaatámpa
leg iyyi'
leg, calf of the iyyinchaamo',
  iyyintakaali'
leg, chair aaombiniili' ihikki'ya',
  aaombiniiliyyi'
leg from, to pull off an arm or a
  nipaffi
leg, hind iyyi' ashaka'
leg, lower iyyapi', iyyinchamo'
leg pulled off, to have an arm or
  nipafa
leg shorter, to have one iyyi'
  tannapat falaakat iklawwi'cho, iyyi'
  tannapat tilofa'si
leg, table aai'piyyi'
leg, to show a lot of chawwala,
  chawwálla'a
leg, wooden iyyi' holba'
Legislature Naalhpisa' Ikbi',
  Nannapiisa'
legislature nannaa-apiisa' abooha
Legislature, member of the
  Naalhpisa' Ikbi'
legs apart, to put one's wakchalali
legs apart, with the wakchalla't
legs, between the tikba'
legs for, to spread one's iwakchalali
legs, hair on the iyyi' hishi'
legs off, to take the arms and
  ittanipaachi, nibli
legs pulled off, to have the arms and
  nipahli
legs, to cross one's iyyaat ittabánna'a,
  iyyi' ittabaanali
legs, to wave one's arms and
  washshaala, washshalwáa
lend, to imponta
lending institution ta'ossaaponta'
lengthen, to achaakáli, falaachi,

faliili, falohachi
leprechaun hattak s<u>a</u>wa', <u>i</u>yaaknasha'
leprosy oppolikmassa'lo'
lesbian ihoo hattak ilahobbi'
less, to do hínka
lessen, to akka' aya
let become clear, to aloktow<u>a</u>chi
let blood, to lhahli
let do something, to imissa
let fall, to imittola, intalhoffi
let get away with it, to ishtimbaatiya
let go of, to tiwabli
let go, to ootfimmi, ootkanchi,
   ootlhatabli, ootlh<u>a</u>'li, talhoffichi
let hear, to haklochi
let loose, to talhoochi, kanchi,
   lhatabli, tokaffi
let out, to fimmi
let rest in, to aafohachi
let rest, to fohachi
let slop over, to lh<u>a</u>'li
let something drag, to lhiffif<u>í</u>li
let stand, to aloktow<u>a</u>chi
let the air out of, to latassachi,
   shayoffi
lethargic, to be lhakcha
letter opener holisso ishtiwwi'
lettuce tohi'
level naaishtittilawwichi'
level, to be ittil<u>á</u>wi
library holisso aa-asha'
license nannishtith<u>a</u>na'
license, marriage ittihaalalli' holisso
lick one's lips, to tokfohli
lick, to fohli, pitlabbi
lick, to taste by taking a labbit pisa
lid alhiipi'ya'
lie about each other, to itt<u>o</u>loshka
lie about, to ishtaloshkachi, <u>o</u>loshka
lie across, to okkawatkachit m<u>á</u>a,
   okkawatk<u>á</u>yya'chi, okkaw<u>á</u>tta'a
lie around on one's side, to
   achaknahaaski
lie around, to aw<u>á</u>tta'a, toh<u>ó</u>wa

lie crooked, to chiffollo'wa
lie doubled up, to chiffollo'wa
lie down, to kahat m<u>á</u>a, k<u>á</u>yya'a,
   tashki, tí'wa, t<u>ó</u>'wa
lie down to have sexual intercourse
   with, to into'wa
lie down, to make kahli
lie face down, to lhímpat ti'wa,
   lhímpat wayya'a
lie in the sun, to toominnni
lie in wait for, to imayyachi
lie in, to aato'wa
lie next to, to aaittí'wa
lie on one's back and kick like a
   kitten, to tallal<u>á</u>li
lie on one's back, to t<u>á</u>lla'a, w<u>á</u>ttalhpi
lie on one's backs, to t<u>á</u>llo'wa,
   talowat m<u>á</u>a
lie on one's side in, to achaknah<u>á</u>ski
lie on one's side, to achaknaski
lie on one's stomach, to w<u>á</u>yya'a
lie on, to onkahat m<u>á</u>a, onk<u>á</u>yya'a,
   ontí'wa, ont<u>ó</u>'wa
lie there, to just p<u>á</u>tta'a
lie, to tell a loshka
lie to, to <u>i</u>loshka
lie with one's bottom sticking up, to
   toss<u>ó</u>llo'wa
lie with, to ibaakahat m<u>á</u>a,
   ibaak<u>á</u>yya'ha, ibaatí'wa
lie with, to each ishkahat m<u>á</u>a,
   ishk<u>á</u>yya'ha
lies about, to suggest aloshkachi
life everlasting ahalla'ta'
life, eternal okch<u>a</u>at billi'ya'
life, to bring to okchaalínchi
lift, to abaawiili
light aashoppala', shoppala'
light and easily blown, to be pofalli
light and shadow stretching between
   clouds and the earth, for there to be
   bars of hashi'at oka' oochi
light bread paska shatabli'
light bulb aashoppala'

light for, to leave on a ishoppaláli
light for, to make ishoppayachi
light in one's eyes, to have oshoppala
light on one, to have it get ohashtahli
light skin, to have okshawali
light switch pitshoopalali'
light, to be shoppaya, shoppáyya'a
light, to be before it gets onnat minti
light, to get hashtahli
light, to give a sudden flash of shoppalla'kahchi
lighter, to make shoppayáli
lightning shokmalli
lightning bug issosh shoppala', shokkaawi'
lightning bug, type of shokkaawishto'
lightning, to be shokmalli
lightning to strike, for shokmallaat isso
lights ishoppaya'
like as a possible mate for, to anoshkonna
like each other, to ittayoppánchi
like for, to ishtanoshkonna
like it, to ishtinchokmaka
like, not to ikimahooba'lo
like oneself, to make (someone) ilachokkobbichi
like that, to be yámmohmi
like the taste of, to inchampoli
like this, to be yakohmi
like, to anhínchi, ayoppánchi; also imanhínchi, imayoppánchi, ishtachaaha, inoshkonna
like, to be binka, chihmi, chohmi
like, to really noshkonna
like to, to inchokma
lily lili'
lily, water oka' nampakali', okpal, oktaak okpalli'
lima beans issobimbala'

limber, to be bicho'kachi, ikkallo
limbs cut from a tree itti' shawwa
limbs stick out, to have the washshala
limbs, to cut tree naachi
limp, to be líbbo'sha
limp, to walk with a hayihífa
limping, to be shamíhhi'la
line on, to make a lhafi
line, section yaakni' aaittachakkachi'
line, to alaatali
line, to have a lhafa
line up in, to bayalli
line up with, to apolli
lined up even with the edge of, to be atílhlhi'fa
lined up side by side, to be ittimaapatohli
lined up, to be ittayákko'wa, ittayakowa
lines, to go along in separate bayalli
lines, to have lhahkachi
liniment, red ishkobo' homma' tish, ittish homma'
lining anonkalatta'a'
lint nampofalli'
lion kowishto
lip ittialbi'
lip of a pitcher aabichili'
lip smacking, to make the sound of nam nam nam aachi
lip, to stick out one's lower ittialbi' falaa, takbiloli
lips, to lick one's tokfohli
lips, to stick out one's takshololi
lipstick ittialbishhommachi'
liquid okchi', oka'
liquor oka', oka' homi'
listen, not to ikihaklo
listen to and obey, to ihaklo
listen to himself, to make ilihaklochichi
listen to, to haklo, hánglo, hapowánglo, imaatiya

listen! ma
lit, to be shoppala
littermate ittibaapishi
littermates, to be ittibaapishi
little animal *see the name of the animal*
little bit, a chinofa'si
little one immo'ma', oshi'
little stinker kosomoshi'
little things, a bunch of kobolli'
little, to be chipota'si, iskanno'si, sawa'si
little, to be just a kanihmo'si
little while, a alhchimba'si
live close together, to ittimilínka
live in sin, to táwwa'a
live in, to ashwa, atta, okaa-ahánta, okaa-áyya'sha, okaaáshwa
live there, to áyya'sha
live, to ánta, aa-asha, aashwa, aatta
live together, to ittibaa-áyya'sha, ittihayoochi
live with in a homosexual relationship, to ihoo intoba
live with, to ibaa-ánta, ibaa-atta, iláwwi'li
lively, not to be lhakcha
lively, to be ilokchina
liver salakha'
liver, beef waaka' salakha'
living room hattak aabinohli'
living thing nannokchaa'
lizard, type of halambo, kanannak, kowi-paachi', toksala'pa'
lo! haatokya
load, to abihpoli
load with, to shaachi
loaded, to be áyyalhto, shaali
loaf of bread paska, paska toshahli'
located beside, to be imaapátta'a
located, to be ánta, áyya'sha, áshwa, í'ma, káyya'ha, kahat máa, tálla'a, tállo'wa, talowat máa, tí'wa, wayowat máa, wáyya'a, wáyyo'wa

lock ishtasha'na', ishtaasha'na'; *also* loksi', loksi' ishtashana'
lock, to ashannichi
lock up, to imashannichi
locked in, to be imashana, imashanalhchi
locked, to be ashana, ashanalhchi, intallakchi
lockjaw notakfa kallo'
locksmith ishtiwa' ikbi'
locoweed waakimbala'
locust waawo'—*see also* locust, type of
locust, honey itti' kati, kati
locust larva yala
locust shell, dried waawo' hakshop
locust tree kati
locust, type of waawoshto'
log itti' lombo', itti' tapa'
log cabin abooha ittabaana', aboohattittabaana', itti' ittabaana' abooha
loggerhead turtle loksi' hasimbish falaa'
lonely place aachokkillissa'
lonely, to be ilaapilla, imalhchíi'ba, inchokkillissa
lonesome, to be ikacha'ho
long ago chashpo, chashpohma, misha' pillakaash, tingba' ayya'shaka'
long ago, from mashshaash, mashshaashoot, mashshaasho
long ago, to be hopaaki, tingba' áyya'sha
long bare object with something coming out at the top, to be a fáhha'ko
long in the thighs, to be chawwálla'a
long, long ago, to be tingba' pilla áyya'sha
long time, to be a alhchiba
long, to be falaa, faloha
long, to make falaachi, faliili,

falohachi
longer, to be achánka
longer, to make achaakali, achakli, falaahánchi
longhorn steer lapish falaa, waaka' lapish faloha'
look! haatokya, ma'sha
look around, to hapompoyo
look at books, to holisso pisa
look at each other, to ittipisachi
look at each other with interest, to ittayokmíllo'li, ittoonokmiloli
look at secretly, to ahaalaachi
look at, to pisa
look at with interest, to onokmiloli
look behind one, to hapompoyo
look better, to ishtayyómba, pitayyómba
look different, to ishtíla, pisa-ishtaaíla, pisittimíla
look for along with, to ibaahoyo
look for each other, to ittihoyo
look for each other, to make ittihoyochi
look for, to bitkat hoyo, hoyo
look for, to go hoyot aya
look for, to spread out to patalisht hoyo
look for water underground, to oka' hoyo
look hard, to okaapisa
look into something carefully, to chokmat asilhlha
look like vomit, to hollashki
look like, to ahooba
look like what, to pisa-kanihmi, pisa-katihmi
look out! ma'sha
look ready to die, to lhakcha
look sideways at, to okkalat pisa
look sideways, to okkalali
look up, to hoyo
looking like what pisa-kanihmi, pisa-kanihmihoot, pisa-kanihmiho,

pisa-katihmi, pisa-katihmihat, pisa-katihmihta
looking silly, to go along pílat áa
lookout nannaa-apiisachi'
lookout tower, fire lowak aa-apiisachi'
loom naachi aatanni'
loom, type of oksop aahotampi'
loose, to be aatámpa, ikkallo, talhoffi, yolhaa
loose, to get talhofa, talhohli, wahaala
loose, to let talhoochi
loose, to turn talhoffichi
loosen, to talhoffichi
lopsided, to be hayifa, síhhi'pa, shanaa
lopsided, to make hayiffi
Lord, Our Aba' Pinchitokaka'
Lord's Supper Chihoowa Imobyaka' Impa', naaholittompishtaa-asha' obyaka' impa'
lose all one's money, to imayoppolo'ka
lose in death, to iloshoma
lose one's job, to aatoksali'at inkaniya
lose one's sight, to shamba
lose, to imilli, inkaniya, intamowa
lose, to have one's candidate inkaniya
lose weight, to wiikat inkaniya
lost in, to get okaakaniya
lost, to be kaniya, tamowa, yoshoba
lost, to make get yoshobachi
lost tribe okloshi' kaniya'
lot of, a mománchi
lot, to be a lawa
loud, insistent noise, to make a tasahli
loud noise, to make a timimí'chi
loud, to be kallochi
loudly, to talk tastachi
loudly to, to talk ontastachi

454

Louisiana Choctaw Falanchi'
 Chahta'
louse issap
louse eggs issap nihi'
love nannittihollo'
love each other, to ittihollo
love each other, to make ittihollochi
love, to anhínchi, ihollo; *also*
 achokkobbi, akaníya, anhi,
 ayoppánchi, holiitobli,
 imachokkobbi, ishtachaaha
lover, to have as a secret ilomaka
lovers at the same time, to have two
 tawwalínchi
low, to sing akka'si taloowa
lower leg iyyapi'
lower one's arms at the sides, to raise
 and wahhalkachi
lower, to akkachi
lower way, to go the notaalínchi
lowest of the low, to be kalakshi
loyal to, to be ibaachaffa, imbaatiya
luck, to have good ayolhlha,
 nannayolhlha
lucky, to be ayolhlha,

nannoshkannapa
luggage alhpooyak
lump sum, to pay in a lombo
 ishtimatobbi
lumpy, to be kallot binohli, kallot
 íbbalhto
lunch tabookoli
lunch box pinak aalhto'
lunch, packed pinak
lunch, to have tabookoli impa
lunchtime tabookoli
lungs ishoppaya', sholopha'
lye laay
lye soap ishtalhchifa' homi'
lying in, to be aato'wa
lying on its face noklhimpat
lying on one's side, to be
 achaknaháski
lying on the face, to be lhímpa,
 noklhíhhi'pa
lying on, to be aban-kachit máa,
 aban-káyya'chi, abánna'a
lying, to be aakahat máa, aakáyya'ha,
 aatí'wa, káyya'a, tí'wa

m

macaroni lapish falowa',
 tili'kolhkomo' shila'
machine gun tanampishto',
 tanampo palhki'
machine gun bullets tanampishto'
 inak-oshi'
mad all the time, to be oppoloka
mad at each other, to be
 ittimoppoloka
mad at, to get imoppoloka
madam ihoo hawi' apiisachi'
made for, to be imiksaa
made from, to be aatoba
made of a number of different items,

to be ittachakkachi
made, to be iksaa, patalhpo
made up, to be ishshoka'at incho'wa
made with wood stacked with
 overlapping ends, to be ittabaana
maggot, type of chokaanoshi',
 kowishtapa'
Magi, the Hattak Hapoyoksa'
magic fatpo
magic, bad ishtahollifatpo'
magic, to do fatpo ishchokoshkomo
magical item alikchimmi'
magical power fatpo
magical powers, to have fatpo í'shi

455

magician

magician fatpo shaali'
magnifying glass hichitolishpisa'
mail truck holisso shaali'
mailbag holisso aalhto', holisso
ishshaali'
mailbox holisso aalhto'
main road hinishto'
make a banging sound, to kom kom
kom aachi
make a big noise, to komo'chi
make a breeze, to mahlihínchi
make a bubbling sound, to chobo'chi,
choboowachi
make a bumping noise, to
kobo'kachi
make a camp, to albinachi
make a chicken's noise, to kalhkaha
make a clanking sound, to
ittichalhalhá'chi
make a clatter, to ittikama'chi,
ittikamamá'chi, ittikámmakli'chi
make a cloud of dust fly, to
shobohónta
make a cloud of, to shobollichi
make a collection of, to ittahobbi
make a confession, to ilikostinichi
make a creaking sound, to
ittibasa'chi, ittibássakli'chi
make a crinkling sound, to
ittishofofó'chi
make a dent in, to pako'li
make a dragging noise, to
ittishola'chi, ittisholalá'chi,
ittishóllakli'chi, ittisholo'chi, shol
shol shol aachi
make a face at, to ishshoka' oppanit
pisa
make a few marks, to takoochi
make a flapping sound, to
ittifatatá'chi
make a grunting sound, to lhonk
lhonk lhonk aachi
make a guardian, to atoonichi
make a hammering sound, to

ittibaka'chi, ittibakaká'chi
make a hole in while making
another hole in, to amiitaffi
make a home run, to immo't folota,
ootafoolopa, ootfolota
make a joke, to yoppola
make a knocking sound, to bak bak
bak aachi, ittibaka'chi,
ittibakaká'chi, ittikaba'chi,
ittikababá'chi, ittikábbakli'chi,
kababá'chi, kalhak kalhak kalhak
aachi
make a law, to nannalhpisa' ikbi,
naalhpisa' bohli
make a leader, to apihchi
make a line on, to lhafi
make a little hole in, to mitaffi
make a little noise by clapping or
slapping, to ittipasasá'chi
make a little noise, to ittipasa'línchi
make a loud noise, to tasahli,
timimí'chi
make a mark on, to lhafi
make a mistake, to ilhakoffi
make a noise by dragging, to
ittifáttakli'chi
make a noise eating crunchy things,
to ittikasha'chi, ittikashashá'chi,
ittikáshshakli'chi
make a noise flapping, to ittifata'chi
make a noise inside a wooden box, to
ittikóbbokli'chi, ittikobo'chi,
ittikobobó'chi
make a noise like a bluejay, to tish
tish tish aachi
make a noise like a bumblebee, to
ittitimimí'chi
make a noise like a scared horse, to
kashafa
make a noise like a squirrel, to fikfiya
make a noise like a tornado, to
fomoowachi
make a noise like a wagon, to
ittibakahánchi

456

make a noise like hail on a roof, to
ittibakahánchi, ittichamahánchi

make a noise like little bells, to
ittishóllokli'chi, ittishololó'chi

make a noise like wood bumping, to
kalhalhá'chi

make a noise shaking something, to
ittifata'chi, ittifatatá'chi,
ittifáttakli'chi

make a noise, to ittiwasha'chi,
shololó'chi

make a noise with marbles, to
ittikasa'chi, ittikasasá'chi,
ittikássakli'chi, ittisaka'chi,
ittisakaká'chi, ittisákkakli'chi

make a noise with metal, to
chamamá'chi, inchama'chi

make a noise with paper, to
ittishókkokli'chi, shokokó'chi

make a noise with wood, to baka'chi,
bakaká'chi

make a photocopy, to holisso
holbachi

make a pig out of oneself, to
amosholi

make a pile of, to ittanahli

make a popping sound, to pat pat pat
aachi

make a rattle, to ittichálhlhakli'chi

make a rattling sound, to chash
chash chash aachi, chashak chashak
chashak aachi, ittichalha'chi,
ittichalhalhá'chi, ittichasha'chi,
ittichashashá'chi, ittiwashasha'chi,
ittiwáshshakli'chi, washaahanchi,
washshashá'chi

make a ringing sound, to samaachi

make a run, to holhtina-chaffaho
ikbi, malili, malit afoolopa, malit
folota

make a running sound, to
ittimiti'chi

make a rustling sound with for, to
intishoko'chi

make a rustling sound with, to
ittishoko'chi

make a slapping or clapping sound, to
pas pas pas aachi

make a slapping sound, to pasak
pasak pasak aachi

make a slurping noise, to
ittilhóchchokli'chi, ittilhocho'chi,
ittilhochochó'chi

make a smacking noise, to las las las
aachi

make a sound like a crow, to kaak
kaak kaak aachi

make a sound with a metal object, to
chama'chi

make a sound with a wooden object,
to kasa'chi

make a sound with one's feet, to
ittipatatá'chi

make a sound with paper, to
itticháshshakli'chi

make a spark, to lowak chipaslichi

make a splashing sound, to chob
chob chob aachi, chobok chobok
chobok aachi, ittichóbbokli'chi,
ittichobo'chi, ittichobobó'chi

make a spoken agreement, to
aanompishtombohli

make a stripe around the body of, to
koyoffi

make a sudden movement back, to
satappakahchi

make a sudden movement, to
ilhkóyyokli, kánnakli

make a tent, to atiipoli

make a type of noise, to
ittibákkakli'chi, ittikalha'chi,
ittikalhalhá'chi, ittikálhlhakli'chi,
ittipássakli'chi

make a whistling sound, to si'k si'k
si'k aachi

make a will for, to holissimikbi

make a will, to holissikbi

make all colors, to oklhiwachi

make along with, to ibaaikbi
make an agreement, to
nannittimapiisa
make an arbor, to hoshontikachi
make an error, to ilhakoffi
make an offering, to ima
make angry, to hashaachi, hashiili
make appear, to oktanichi
make bald, to masofachi, oshpasachi
make bark, to woochichi
make behave, to akkachi
make believe, to yimmichi
make big, to hichitochi, hichitolichi,
ishtochichi
make bigger, to chintolínchi,
hichintochínchi, hichintolínchi,
hichitóli
make biscuits, to tili'ko' okommo
make bite, to kisichi
make bitter, to homichi
make black, to losachi
make bloom, to pakachi
make blue, to okchamachi
make bread, to paska
make breakfast, to nittaki hopooni
make breathe in, to noklhamallichi
make breathe, to foyopachi
make brown, to laknachi
make bubbles for, to oka'
impokpokichi
make bubbles with, to pokpokichi
make buck, to tossoolachi
make burp, to akiilawachi
make butter, to pishokchi' nihachi
make buy, to chompachi
make calm, to nokchitoli
make camp in, to aa-albinachi,
imalbina
make camp, to albinachi, aa-
albinachi' ikbi
make cheap, to alhchonachi
make chew, to howasachi
make climb, to toyyachi
make cold, to kapassali

make colder, to kapassáli
make come in, to oshfokhi,
oshtabihli, oshtani
make comfortable, to apoolhachi
make cook, to hopoonichi
make cough, to hotolhkochi
make count, to hotihnachi
make crawl, to bala'chi
make crooked for, to ishaniili
make crooked, to shanaayo'li,
shanaachi
make crumbs of, to chilichi
make cry, to yaachi
make dance, to hilhachi
make dance with, to ibaahilhachi
make dark, to oklhilichi
make decisions for, to imanokfilli
make deep, to hofobichi
make different, to ittimilachi, ilachi,
ilánchi
make dirty, to litihli
make dizzy, to chokfolohli
make do something, to atohno
make do, to yammichichi
make double, to ittalaatali
make drink, to ishkochichi
make drip, to hoyyachi
make dumplings from, to afolli
make (ears) stick out, to oshwalachi
make eat, to impachichi
make even, to ittilawwichi
make explode, to tokaachi
make extend this way, to
oshwayaachi, oshwayoochi
make eyes at, to ishkin tannap pila
ishpisa
make face, to asaanalichi
make faces, to bokyofoli
make faint, to hayoochichichi
make fall, to kinaffi, wilichi
make fight, to ittibichi
make fizz, to woshwokichi
make fly, to wakaachi, wakiili
make for in, to aaimiksaachi,

aaimaaiksaachi
make for, to imikbi, imiksaachi
make forget, to imalhkaniyachi
make from, to aaikbi
make fun of, to ayoppolachi,
  ishtahooba'li ki'yo, ishtayóbba'li
  ki'yo, ishtikahooba'lo, yoppolachi
make gallop, to abaayo'wachi,
  tolhtochichi
make gargle, to tokbolhlhichichi
make gather, to ayowachi
make get lost, to yoshobachi
make get used to oneself, to
  ilachokkobbichi
make go back and forth, to yili'chi
make go backwards, to bakhitiipo'chi
make go faster, to palhkichi
make go out, to kochchichi
make go, to ayachi,
  chokoshkomochi, intohno
make good, to chokmali
make green, to okchamachi
make greet, to ayoppachichi
make grey, to shobbokochi
make grow for, to iwaachi
make growl, to kilihachi
make happy with, to ishtayoppali
make hard, to kallochi
make hear, to haklochi
make high, to chaahachi
make hit himself, to ilissochichi
make hit, to issochichi
make hoarse, to nokshilili
make hot, to pallichi
make howl, to woohachi
make hurry, to atoshpalichi
make hysterical, to abikimilhkoochi
make in, to aaiksaachi
make into a prostitute, to hawi' ikbi
make into shingles, to cholhlhi
make it dark for, to imoklhilichi
make it rain, to ombachi
make it work, to ittakánni'ya
make it worse for, to imayyabichi

make itch, to washkabichi
make itchy, to hoshinkochi
make jealous of, to hopoochi
make jump along with, to
  ibaamallichi
make jump around, to tossoolachi
make jump, to mallichi
make kiss himself, to ilisho'kachichi
make kiss, to sho'kachichi
make kneel, to achokmilhkachi
make late, to imalhchibachi
make laugh at himself, to ilollalichi
make laugh, to ollalichi
make lazy, to intakho'bichi
make lie down, to kahli
make light for, to ishoppayachi
make lighter, to shoppayáli
make listen to himself, to
  ilihaklochichi
make little holes in, to milli
make long, to falaachi, faliili,
  falohachi
make longer, to achaakali, achakli,
  falaahánchi
make look at each other, to
  ittipisachi
make look for each other, to
  ittihoyochi
make lopsided, to hayiffi
make love each other, to ittihollochi
make love, to ittayoshkammi
make mean, to issikopachi,
  issikopalichi
make mind, to ihapowanglochi
make miss, to intiballichi
make more than one little hole in, to
  mitaachi
make muddy, to hayimachi
make music, to nannola' olachi
make narrow, to lhibafachi
make noise banging, to
  ittikómmokli'chi, ittikomo'chi,
  ittikomomó'chi
make noise for, to imola

make noise in the water, to
okaaittichóbbokli'chi
make noise, to ánchi, chalha'chi,
chalhaachi, chalhaahánchi,
chamapa, chámmakli'chi,
nannaachi, nannookahánchi,
shakabli, sholo'chi, sholoowachi—
*see also words describing specific
noises*
make noise with paper, to
shóchchokli'chi
make noise with wood, to kaba'chi
make obvious, to oktánni'chi
make old, to sipoknichi
make one's home in, to aa-asha,
aashwa, aatta, inchokka' aaikbi
make one's mark on, to holisso i̱lhafi
make oneself big, to ilishtochichi
make oneself go cross-eyed, to ishkin
okkowatali
make oneself white, to ilitohbichi
make out, to toshooli
make over for, to imaaiksaachi,
imiksaachi
make over, to himittachi
make overlap, to ittayoppitammichi
make pay, to atobbichi
make peace, to itti̱nannayya
make (people) pass each other
without stopping, to
ittayoppitammichi
make pickles, to pikkal abihli
make play, to chokoshkomochi
make play with, to
ibaachokoshkomochi
make pus come out of, to kalhali
make quiet, to chokkilissachi
make race, to ittimpalammichi
make reach, to onachi
make red, to hommachi
make resemble, to ahoobachi
make rest, to fohachi, nokchitoli
make right, to alhpisa'chi, alhpíssa'li
make rise, to shatablichi

make roll, to chanaachi, tono'chi
make round, to lhiboktachi,
lhibowachi
make run, to malichi, tilhaachi,
tilhili
make sad, to alhkayyachi,
nokhanglochi
make say, to hochifochi
make shade for, to i̱hoshottikachi
make shade on, to o̱hoshottikachi
make shake hands with, to
ayoppachichi
make shake, to yollichichi
make short, to tilofachi, chawwalili
make sick, to abikachi
make sing for, to intaloowachi
make sing, to taloowachi
make sing with, to ibaataloowachi
make sit down, to biniichi, binohchi
make sit together, to ittibaabinohchi
make sit with, to ibaabiniichi,
ibaabinohchi
make slacker, to yolhaachi
make sleepy, to nosilhhachi
make slippery, to talasbichi
make small, to iskannochi
make smell good, to bilamachi
make smell himself, to
iloshshowanchichichi
make smell, to oshshowanchichichi
make smelly, to kosomachi
make smile, to ollalichi
make smoke, to shobohchi
make smooth, to ittilawwichi
make sneeze, to habishkochi
make (someone) lean his head over,
to akassanachi
make (someone) like oneself, to
ilachakkobbichi
make (someone) open his mouth, to
taklhipachi
make (someone) pass without
speaking, to ayoppitammichi
make (something) the third, to

atochchi'nachi
make sound, to olachi
make sour, to hawashkochi,
wasachachi
make spicy, to homichi
make spin, to chanaachi
make spots on, to waakachi
make stab, to baafachi
make stand up, to hilichi, hiyohchi
make stay behind, to antachichi
make stay with, to ahiinachi
make steam for, to inkofollichi
make steam, to kofollichi
make sticky, to chakissachi
make stoop, to wayoochi
make stop crying, to apoolhali
make stripes on, to shiwaachi
make swell, to shataachi
make talk, to anompolichi
make tall, to chaahachi
make the noise of a bullfrog, to paa
make the noise of eating crunchy
things, to kas kas kas aachi, kashak
kashak kashak aachi
make the noise of something flying,
to ittilhókkokli'chi
make the noise of something in a
box, to ittilhoko'chi,
ittilhokokó'chi
make the sound of a car starting, to
ying ying ying aachi
make the sound of a cat hissing, to tif
tif tif aachi
make the sound of a cat spitting, to
tof tof tof aachi
make the sound of a clock ticking, to
tik tik tik aachi
make the sound of a flexible object, to
lhok lhok lhok aachi
make the sound of a gunshot, to
paaw paaw paaw aachi
make the sound of a hen clucking, to
tok tok tok aachi
make the sound of a high-pitched

whistle, to si'k si'k si'k aachi
make the sound of banging or hitting,
to komok komok komok aachi
make the sound of a leather-covered
drum, to tomok tomok tomok
aachi, toom toom toom aachi
make the sound of bare feet walking,
to tip tip tip aachi
make the sound of big bare feet, to
pas pas pas aachi, pat pat pat aachi
make the sound of chewing, to nam
nam nam aachi
make the sound of clanking or
knocking, to kas kas kas aachi,
kasak kasak kasak aachi
make the sound of cloth being hit, to
top top top aachi
make the sound of crickets, to shol
shol shol aachi
make the sound of dishes rattling, to
ittichama'chi, ittichamamá'chi
make the sound of glass breaking, to
cham cham cham aachi, chamak
chamak chamak aachi
make the sound of hitting, to sak sak
sak aachi
make the sound of hitting soft things,
to mitití'chi
make the sound of knocking, to kab
kab kab aachi, kabak kabak kabak
aachi, kalh kalh kalh aachi
make the sound of leaves before a
storm washaahánchi
make the sound of little parts rattling,
to chalh chalh chalh aachi, chalhak
chalhak chalhak aachi
make the sound of paper crinkling, to
ittishóffokli'chi, shof shof shof
aachi, shok shok shok aachi,
shochok shochok shochok aachi
make the sound of popping, to tok
tok tok aachi
make the sound of rattling, to wash
wash wash aachi

make the sound of something in a
hollow container, to kob kob kob
aachi, kobok kobok kobok aachi
make the sound of steam being
released, to shof shof shof aachi
make the sound of walking without
shoes, to ittimitití'chi,
ittimíttikli'chi, mit mit mit aachi
make the sound of water on
something hot, to shif shif shif
aachi
make the sound of wood creaking or
breaking, to bas bas bas aachi, basak
basak basak aachi
make things hard for, to ataapolichi
make thirsty, to tokshilachi
make tired along with, to
ibaatikahbichi
make, to ikbi, iksaachi; *also* tobachi
make too much noise for, to
haksobachi
make touch each other, to
ittitikoochi, ittitikilichi
make touch, to halichi, haliichi,
ombitiipachi, tikiichi
make up a pair with, to ittachaabli
make up one's mind, not to be able to
imaanokfila-at fashkalamo'wa
make up one's mind, to imaanokfila-
at toklo
make up, to ittinkana
make vomit, to howitachi
make walk, to nowachi
make want, to bannachi
make wave the arms and legs, to
washshaalachi
make waves in, to bo'chi
make wear, to yaalhipichi
make whip, to fammichi
make whistle, to kontachi
make white, to tohbichi
make wider, to achakali, achakli
make work, to toksalichi
make work with, to ibaatoksalichi

make wrong, to shaniili
make yell, to tasaachi
make yellow, to laknachi
make young, to himittachi
makeup ishshoka' albi', ishshoka'
ishtincho'li', ishtilaaiksaachi'
makeup, to put on ishshoka' incho'li
male nakni'
male person hattak, hattak nakni'
mallet nipishcha'li'
mallet, kitchen ishcha'li'
man hattak, hattak nakni', nakni'
man, to act like a nakni
man, to fail to act like a iknakno
man, to want a nakni' banna
man, young hattak himitta'
manager naapiisachi'
mane issoba ipashi'
mange, to have washkabi
mangy, to be washkabi
mannequin hattak holba'
(man's name) Bani', Baatambi',
Boshto, Chiklin, Ikloon
(man's nickname) Book, Chokfi
mantis, praying nassano'li'
manure waakiyaalhki', yalhki'
manure, type of yalhki' bosholli'
many, to be lawa
marble maabil
marbles, to make a noise with
ittikasa'chi, ittikasasá'chi,
ittikássakli'chi, ittisaka'chi,
ittisakaká'chi, ittisákkakli'chi
marbles, to play ittikássakli'chi
march, to ittilawwichit tanówa
margarine pishokchi' niha' holba'
marijuana alboppolo'
mark on, to make a lhafi
mark on, to make one's holisso ilhafi
mark, to incho'li
mark with a cut, to inchalhlhi
marked with a cut, to be inchalha
marked with a number, to be
holhtina

marked, to be incho'wa, ishtincho'wa
marks, to make a few takoochi
maroon, to be homma losayyi, hommayyi
marriage license ittihaalalli' holisso
married for, to get imittihaalalli
married in, to get aaittihaalalli
married, to be hattakat imáyya'sha, ihooat imáyya'sha, ittihaalalli, ittamóshsho'li
married, to get ittihaalalli
married, woman who has never been ihoo hattak ikimiksho'
marrow, beef waaka' lopi'
marrow of a leg or foot bone iyyi' lopi'
marry, to ittihaalalli, ittihaalallichi
marsh okpachalhlhi'
marshy, to be okfichibli
martin cho̱'ki'
mash, to lhacho'li, lhachoffi, moyoshkichi
mashed, to be lhacho'wa, lhachofa, moyoshki, patassa
mask ishshoka' holba'
mask, type of ibichchala' alhiipi'ya', ishshoka' alhiipi'ya'
mason jar kitoba nanna-aalhto'
mass, to alawachi
massage parlor aaombitka'
massage, to ombitka
masturbate, to bilo'chi, biloffi, ilibilo'chi, imbiloffi, yoffi
mat nannompatkachi'
mat, hot-plate nanna ontalla'a'
match, not to iktiholbo
match, to ittihó̱lba
match tree lowak tobapi'
matchbook lowak tobaalhto'
matchbox lowak tobaalhto'
matches lowak toba'
mate chaffo', ittacha'pa'
mate with, to hosha

maternity ward chipotishki' aa-asha'
mattress onno'sha'
mattress, type of onno'sha' kallo'
mayapple falaanosi'
maybe nanna
me ana'ak, ana'ako̱, ana'a̱, ano'
me myself ana'aakayniho̱, ana'aakaynihta̱
meadowlark so̱solo'
meal for, to have a imimpa
mean hoyopa
mean a lot to, to i̱holitto'pa
mean it, not to pila aachi
mean, to aachi, miha
mean, to be issikopa; also aaikló̱ha, hoyopa, imilahobbi
mean, to make issikopachi, issikopalichi
mean, to teach to be issikopachi
mean to, to be imaaikló̱ha, imissikopa, imoppoloka, impalata, ishtayóbba'li ki'yo, ishtimaatapa, ootishtimaatámpa
mean to, to talk imbachali
measles hoshonnachi', to̱shabbi'
measles, black to̱shabbi' losa'
measles, to have the to̱shabbi, to̱shabbi' hayoochi
measure, tape naaishtalhpisa'
measure, to apiisa
measure with, something to naaishtalhpisa'
measured, to be alhpisa
measuring cup ishtaka'fa' naaishtapiisa'
measuring instrument nannishtithana'
meat nipi'
meat, barbecued nanna albani', nipi' albani'
meat broth nipi' okchi'
meat chopper nipishlolli'
meat grinder nipaafoloha', nipi' ishfolohli'

meat sandwich paska nipi' ittalatta'a'
meat skin so'ksok
mechanic kaa iksaachi'
medal chofaakoshi' ishtilontala'li'
medicate, to ittish ima, noktalaali
medicinal plant, type of ahalla'ta',
basho'kchi', chalokloha' ittish,
hahtok, haksibish falaha', halambo
tish, issimittish, issoba
ishoptilhi'li', ishkobo' homma'
pakali', itti' okchama'li', koshibba'
hakshish, loksimpolona, loksittish,
nashobattish, nita' tish, ofi' sholop
ittish, ofi' tish, ofolottish,
pasakchala, shokhiskanno' tish,
shiiki pakali', shokhishto' tish,
sholop tilhi'li' iskanno', sholop
tilhi'li' losa', sholop tilhi'li' tohbi',
shootko'li', waaka' lapish
medicine ittish—see also medicine,
type of and names of specific
medicines
medicine cabinet ittish aa-asha'
medicine, cough hotolhkottish
medicine, hair pashishlhili'
medicine to, to give ittish ima
medicine, type of holhtina hanna'li'
tochchi'na, ninak yaaha',
pankishan-kachi', sinti' ittish—see
also medicinal plant, type of
meet along with, to ibaa-afama
meet face to face and go on by, to
ittayoppitammi
meet face to face, to ayoppitammi
meet in, to aa-afama, aaittafama
meet secretly, to lomat
ittimanompoli
meet, to afama, afaama, ittafama
meeting ittanaha', ishtittanaha'
meeting about, to have a ishtittanaha
meeting, religious
abaanompittanaha'
meeting, to have a ittafama
meeting, to have a church ittanaha

meeting, to organize a
nannishtittanaha
melt into, to ashiila, okaabila,
okaabilili
melt onto, to abila, abilachi
melt, to bila, bilili
melt together, to ittabila, ittabilachi,
ittabilili
melted, to be bila
melting pot naki' aabilili',
nannaabilili'
member aachaffa'
member of Congress Naalhpisa' Ikbi'
member of the Legislature
Naalhpisa' Ikbi'
memorial service aa-aksho', aa-
akshochi'
memorial service for, to have a aa-
akshochi, imaa-akshochi, ishtimaa-
akshochi
memorial service, to have a aa-
akshochi' imáyya'sha, aa-akshochi'
ishtáyya'sha, aakshochi
men, to go with a lot of patalinchi
menstrual period hashi' abika', ihoo
imambiika'
menstruate, to hashi' abika, issish
lhatapa
menstruating, to be abika
mercurochrome mankokchi'
mercury tali' bila'
mercy on, to have inokhánglo
merely pila
merthiolate mankokchi'
mess around with, to pilisa
mess up for, to imayoppani'chi,
ishaniili
mess up, to ayóbba'li ki'yo, ayiimita,
ayoppanichi, ikayobba'lo, oppani,
tiwwichi
metal tali'
metal, precious tali' holiitopa'
metal, to make a noise with
chama'chi, chamamá'chi,

inchama'chi
meteor fochik malili'
Mexican Oshpaani'
Mexican child Oshpaanoshi'
Mexican food oshpaanimimpa'
Mexican woman Oshpaanihoo'
Mexico Oshpaani' Iyaakni'
middle of the upper back chinokko'
middle, to be in the iklanna
midget hattak immo'ma', hattak
    pihcha', immo'ma'
midget, to be a píhhihcha
midgets, to be ittapíhhihcha
middle finger ilbak iklanna'
midnight, to be oklhiliklanna
midnight, to be after hashtaht minti,
    onnat minti
midwife chipota ippo'si'
midwife, to act as a chipotapooba
might ásha, nanna'chikyásha, ahmi
mile yaaknalhpisa'
milk chiichi', pishokchi'—see also
    milk, type of
milk a cow, to waakimbishlichi
milk, to imbishlichi
milk, type of pishokchi' holba',
    pishokchi' shila'
milked, to be imbishalhchi
milkweed nochi'
Milky Way Ofi' Tohbi' Ihina'
mill tanchaabotooli', tanchaafolowa'
mill around in, to tiwa'kalhchi
mill around, to ittabállalli
milt intakashshi'
mind imaanokfila
mind be calm, to have one's
    imaanokfila-at yohbi bíyyi'ka
mind is set, person whose chonkash
    kallo
mind made up, to have one's
    alóshsho'ma
mind, to hapowaklo, ihapowánglo
mind, to be completely out of one's
    imaanokfila-at ikimiksho

mind, to be unable to make up one's
    imaanokfila-at toklo,
    nannanokfillikat toklo
mind, to change one's imaanokfila
    ilánchi
mind, to make ihapowanglochi
mine, coal tobaksaakola'
miner, coal tobaksi' kolli'
minister abaanompishtanompoli',
    abaanompi'shi'
mink okfincha
minnow nanoshik, patassoshi'
mint, type of chaloklowa' ittish,
    sholop tilhi'li'
minutes minnat
miracle naafinha
miracle, for there to be a nannakat
    finha, nannokloha
miracle, to be a oklóyyo'ha
mirage, to see a iholba
mirror aailipisa, aainchaa'
miscarriage, to have a chipotaat
    imilli, chipotaat inkaniya
mischievous, to be
    nannishtaháyyo'chi
misdirect, to imayoppani'chi,
    yoshobli
mislaid, to be yoshoba
miss a commitment during, to
    imambaanapa
miss in throwing, to anoktobaffichi
miss, not to atókkoli'chi
miss, to anokfilli, intiballi, tiballichi
missionary abaanompi'shi'
Mississippi Missipi'
Mississippi Choctaw Missipi'
    Chahta'
mistake, to make a ilhakoffi
mistletoe fanishapha'
mistreat, to ilbashachi
misty, to be yokolbi
mitt to'wa' ishyokachi', to'wa'
    ishyokli'
mitten ilbak fokhi'

mix in while talking, to

mix in while talking, to ittashommit
anompoli, ittibaakaachit anompoli
mix, to ittayokommochi,
ittayolhkomochi, ittibaakaachi,
ittibaani, okommo
mix together, to ittibakaachi,
okaaittashommi
mix together with, to okaashommi
mix up, to ittashommi,
ittayokommo
mixed group, to be a ittashoma
mixed in with, to be okaashoma
mixed, to be olhkomo
mixed together, to be okaaittashoma
mixed up, to be ittashoma,
ittayolhkomo, ittibalhto
mixed up with, to get okaalhatapa
mixer ishbo'chi'
moccasins hattak api'
hommisholosh
mock, to ishtahooba'li ki'yo,
ishtikahooba'lo
mockingbird fosh-ato'chi', foshi'
taloowa'
moist, to be yokolbi
moisten, to yokolbichi
molasses shookolokchi', maliassas
losa'
mold, to have green hakboli
moldy, to be hakboli
mole yakni' washo'chi', yolhkon—
see also mole, type of
mole on the skin tali' losa'
mole on the skin, to have a tali'
losa'at ontalla'a
mole, type of hakson wakla'
molest, to impilisa
Monday Nittak Ammo'na'
monetary assistance ishtalhpila'
money mani', ta'osso, tali' holisso'
money box ta'ossaalhto'
money lender ta'ossimponta'
money, paper holisso loposhki'
monkey hattak shawi', manki'

monster nannoppolo'
month hashi', hashittakashkowa'
moo, to mooha, owwa
moon hashi', hashi' ninak aa',
ninak, oklhili hashi'
moon, for there to be a full hashi'at
aloota, hashi'at bolokta, hashi'at
lhibokta, hashi'at tilikpi
moon, for there to be a half hashi'at
iklanna'si
moon, for there to be a new hashi'at
awaata, hashi'at himona' awaata
moon, for there to be no hashi'at
kaniya
moon, half hashi' alootiklanna
moon, new hashi' awaata', hashi'
himoona
moon, ring around the
hashaakonoli'
moon to be in its last quarter, for the
hashi'at kaniyat ishtaya
moonlight in, to be oklhili toomi
moonlight, to be ninak toomi
mop aboohishtachifa', maap
mope lhakcha
more móma
more in, to put some ibaani
more than, to be ímmayya
morning star fochik ishto'
morning, early in the nittaki
morning, early tomorrow
nittakikma
morning glory baafalallak, nittaki
pakali'
morning, really early in the
níyyi'tako'si
morning, this himmaka' nittakika
morning, to be early in the nittaki
mortar, flat part of a tanchaahollosi'
mortar, to apoolosli
mortar, type of kitti', tanchaahosi'
mortgage for, to ishtatochi
mortgage, to atochi, ishtatooni
mosquito sapontaki'

mosquito, type of bokoffa'
moth hatalhposhik—*see also* moth, type of
moth balls iss<u>o</u>shtilli'
moth, type of opa
mother ishki'—*also* chipotishki', <u>i</u>maami', maami', oshpishichi'
mother cat kowishki', kowi' oshpishichi'
mother dog ofi' ishki', ofi' oshpishichi'
mother hen akankishki'
mother, unfit ishki' holba'
mother who doesn't take care of her kids ishki' holba'
mother's brother <u>i</u>m<u>o</u>shi'
motion mooshan
mountain onchaba; *also* alhchoba
mountain boomer kowi-p<u>a</u>achi'
mountain lion kowishto, onchaba kowi'
mourn, to ishyaa
mourning, to be impalammi, nokhámmi'chi
mourning, to go through ritual tabashi
mouse pinti'
mouse poison pintishtabi', pintishtilli'
mouser pintabi'
mousetrap pintishholhtosi', pintishyokachi'
moustache notakhish
mouth iti, ittiya
mouth of a stream oka' sokbish
mouth, to open one's taklhipali
mouth, to put in one's kapali
mouth water, to have one's tokfohli
move around in a swarm, to tiwa'kahánchi
move around, to kana'li, kannan<u>á</u>li
move aside, to aakana'li, aakanalli
move away from, to imaakana'li, imaakanalli

move back, to bakhitibli
move closer to, to oshtolaalínchi, pitolaalínchi
move down a slope, to okaatan<u>o</u>wa
move in the water, to oka' okaaittánno'wa, oka' okaaittanoh<u>ó</u>wa, oka' okaay<u>á</u>a
move in this direction, to minti
move out of the way, to aakana'li, aakanalli, aakánnakli
move out of, to aakochcha, aawiha
move this way, to ashkanalli, oshkanalli
move, to ilhko'k<u>ó</u>li, ilhko'li, kanalli, wiha, wihachi
move, to help ishtibaawiichi
move to, to pitwiha
moved, to have been kannalli
movement, to make a sudden ilhk<u>ó</u>yyokli, kánnakli
movie shoo
movie camera shoo ishtikbi'
moving along the edge of taakchak<u>a</u>li', taakch<u>a</u>li'
moving behind aballak<u>a</u>li', <u>a</u>shak<u>a</u>li'
moving beside apootak<u>a</u>li'
moving between ittintakl<u>a</u>li'
moving down akk<u>a</u>li'
moving following aballak<u>a</u>li'
moving in anonkak<u>a</u>li', anonk<u>a</u>li'
moving in front of tikb<u>a</u>li'
moving inside anonkak<u>a</u>li', anonk<u>a</u>li'
moving on paknak<u>a</u>li', pakn<u>a</u>li'
moving on the side naksik<u>a</u>li'
moving outside kochch<u>a</u>li'
moving over paknak<u>a</u>li', pakn<u>a</u>li'
moving, to keep kannan<u>á</u>li
moving underneath not<u>a</u>li'
mow along with, to ibaa-amo
mow for, to imammo
mow grass, to hashshok bashli
mow, to amo, bashli
mowed, to be almo

mower ishtamo'
much, how kaniya fokhahoot,
kaniya fokha͟o, katiya fokhahat,
katiya fokhahta
much, not to eat too impa' iksala'mo
much, to be too aatámpa,
ootilaatámbli, ootishtilaatámbli
much, to do too aatapichi, ishtaatabli,
ishtaatapa, ishtaatapichi,
ishtilaatabli, ishtilaatapichi
much, too aatapa, salami
mucus, eye ishkin bakchi'
mud lokchok
mud dauber lokfi' shaali', lokfi'
tono'chi', tiika͟'ti'
mud house lokfabooha'
mudcat nani' lakna', nokfapa',
patoksi'
Muddy Boggy River Lokchok
Abookoshi, Lhabita Abookoshi
muddy, to be hayima, lokchok
bíyyi'ka, lhabita, moyoshki
muddy, to make hayimachi
mudhole okpachalhlhi'
muff ilbak aabihli', ilbak fokhi'
mulberry bihi'

mulberry tree bihi' api'
murderer hattak abi'
murky, to be lokchabi
muscle aches, to have lhikkachi
mush ashiila
mushroom pakti'
mushroom, type of paktapa',
ofiyalhki' pakti'
mushy, to be bishalhchi,
hayi'kalhchi, moyoshki
music nannola'
music, gospel abaanompa' taloowa'
music, to make nannola' olachi
musical instrument nannola',
sholoshtalhipa
musician nannola' chokoshkomo'
mustard mastat
mustard greens tohi', tohi'
okchamali'
mustard seed mastat nihi'
mustard, wild mastat imilhlha'
muzzle tanampincholok
myself ana'akaynit
mystery nanna loma'
mythical creature, type of
Iyaaknasha', Panti', Lho͟fa'

n

nail naafkaataka'li', naaishtanalha',
tali' chofak
nail clippers ilbakchosh ishkatolhlhi'
nail file ilbakchosh ishshoochi'
nail polish ilbakchosh
ishhommachi'
nail scissors ishkalasha' iskanno'si'
nail to, to analhlhichi
nailed on, to be aanalha
nailed, to be analha
naked, to be chakbakali, haknip
bíyyi'ka, naafka ikfo'ko, nipi'
bíyyi'ka

name holhchifo—see also specific
names under (name,...) and
(nickname,...)
name after each other, to
ittaaholhchifochi
name after oneself, to ilahoochifochi
name after, to aholhchifochi,
ahoochifochi
(name, bad) Issoba Losa', Ofi' Losa'
(name, Chickasaw family) Filli'ta',
Ishaaki'
(name, Chickasaw men's) Boshto,
Chaali', Ikloon, Kabi', Onnataayi',

To'kabi'
(name, Chickasaw pet) Haksibish
Patha', Into'lhka-losishto',
Washkabi'—*see also* (nickname)
(name, Chickasaw women's)
Impaka̱'li', Iili', Linho', Paka̱'li',
Panaayo'cha', Saaysin, Sibi',
Shiyo̱'ti', Tiki'li', To̱'na'
name down, to put a holhchifo
intakaachi
name, family holhchifo ishtaalhi'
name, first holhchifammo'na'
name, last holhchifo ishtaalhi'
name oneself, to ilaholhchifochi
name, to hochifo
name to a team, to hochifo
name, to call by hochifo
name, to sign one's holhchifo
intakaachi
name to, to give the same
ittahoochifochi
named after, to be aholhchi'fo
named, to be holhchifo
nanny goat issi' tiik
nape of the neck chashshanak
napkin ishtilikasho'chi'
narcotic itti̱sh oppolo'
narrow, to be lhiba̱fa'si
narrow, to make lhiba̱fachi
narrower, to be lhibá̱fa
Native Choctaw Yappakayni Chahta'
nauseate, to kamoshachi
nauseated by, to be inkamosha
nauseated, to be kamosha
navel ittialbish
near each other, to be ittimilínka
near to milínka
near, to be milínka
near, to bring milinkachi
nearby, to be olá̱li, oshtolá̱li, pitolá̱li
necessarily pollaho̱
necessary, for it to be nannakat
aafinha
necessity, of pollaho̱

neck nokhistap
neck, base of the chashshanak
neck chain tali' inno'chi'
neck, nape of the chashshanak
neck of, to break the tiloffi
neck of, to wring the shannit tiloffi
neck, to break one's tilofa
neck, to have something tight around
one's noksíhhi'ta
necklace iminno'chi', inno'chi'
necks, to have broken tilohli
necktie inno'chi'
need, to really aabanna finha
needle naaishtalhcho'wa'; *also* hishi'
needle, bone naafoni'
naaistalhcho'wa'
needle, eye of a naaishtalhcho'wa'
ishkin
needle, pine tiyak hishi'
neighbor inchokkaponta'
neighbors chokka' lokoli', lokoli'
neighbors, to be close itti̱milínka
nephew ibayyi
nervous, to be malhata
nest ilhpichik
nest, type of fohi' ilhpichik,
fochchanashik ilhpichik
net material naashachakla'
net, to okaffi
nettle, type of fannik, fannik ishto'
never ámmohmi
never satisfied, to be ilamákka'li,
ishtamákka'li
new growth ittonchololi'
new moon hashi' awaata', hashi'
himoona
new moon, for there to be a hashi'at
awaata, hashi'at himona' awaata
new, to be himitta
new, to be brand himíyyitta
New Year Afammi Himitta'
New Year's Day Afammi Himitta'
newborn himonala'
newly hatched homonofanti'

469

newspaper anompa chokoshpa',
holisso chokoshpa'
next day, to be the onna
next to apantat, aponta', apootaka'
next to one another, to be ittitíkki'li
next to, to be apátta'a, apónta,
apotkachit máa, apotkáyya'chi,
apótto'wa
next to, to go over ootapoota
next to, to put apaatali, apootoli
nice, to be chokma
nice to, to act ihapashshi
nickel sent talhlha'pi
(nickname, Chickasaw) Iyyinto'lhka'
Losishto', Shawi', Washkabi'—see
also (name, Chickasaw pet)
(nickname, Chickasaw men's)
Chabi', Chokfi, Loksi', Maliassas,
Oshto, Soba Losa', Sokko'
(nickname, Chickasaw women's)
Soodi', Shiima'
niece ibayyi, ibayyihoo'
night oklhili
night before last, the tikboklhiliaash
night crawler saalhkona
night, last oklhiliaash
night, to be oklhili
night, to stay the albinachi
nightgown nosi' fokha'
nightmare, to have a iholba
nightmares about, to have ishtiholba
nine chakká'li
nine in number, to be chakká'li
nine times hichakka'li'
nine, to be in groups of chakká'li
áyyo'ka
nineteen awa chakká'li,
pokolachakká'li
nineteen in number, to be awa
chakká'li
ninety pokoli chakká'li
ninety in number, to be pokoli
chakká'li
ninety-nine pokoli chakká'li awa

chakká'li
ninety-nine in number, to be pokoli
chakká'li awa chakká'li
ninety-six pokoli chakká'li awa
hanná'li
ninety-six in number, to be pokoli
chakká'li awa hanná'li
ninth, to be ishchakká'li
nip playfully, to chokoshkomo
nipple aasho'ka', ipishik ibitop,
kitoba aapishi'
nipple on a baby bottle chipotaapishi'
nits issap nihi'
no ha'aa, ki'yo
no for an answer, person who won't
take ishkobo' kallo'
no good, to be oppolo, oppolo'si
no matter what ikkanihmikya
no moon, for there to be hashi'at
kaniya
no one kanahookya, kaniya'ookya
no place kaniya'ookya
no problem mikya'ba
nobody kanahookya, kaniya'ookya
nod at, to imoshchooni
nod one's head, to oshchooni
noise see also index entries under
words describing specific noises
noise for, to make imola
noise for, to make too much
haksobachi
noise in the water, to make
okaaittichóbbokli'chi
noise like a tornado, to make a
fomoowachi
noise shaking something, to make a
ittifata'chi, ittifatatá'chi,
ittifáttakli'chi
noise, to hit together and make
chamapa
noise, to make ánchi, chalha'chi,
chalhaachi, chalhaahánchi,
chámmakli'chi, nannaachi,
nannookahánchi, shakabli,

sholo'chi, shololó'chi, sholoowachi,
timimí'chi
noise, to make a loud, insistent
tasahli
noise, to make a type of
ittibákkakli'chi, ittikalha'chi,
ittikalhalhá'chi, ittikálhlhakli'chi,
ittipasasá'chi, ittipássakli'chi
noise with wood, to make a
bakaká'chi
nominate, to atookoli
noodles tili'kolhkomo' shila'
noodles, type of tili'ko' panaa'
noon tabookoli
noon, before nittaki pila
noon creep up on one, to have
ontabookoli
noon meal, to have a tabookoli impa
noon, to be tabookoli
normal, to be back to aaissa
north falammi, falammi pila
North Pole Falammi Pilla
North Star Falammi Fochik
North, the Falammi
Northern soldiers Falammi
nose ibichchala'
nose, to blow one's lhihka
nose, to have a runny ibilhkanat
lhatapa
**nose, to have (something) go up
one's** noklhamalli
nose, to pick one's ibichchala'
ibayakohli
nose to, to give a bloody ibichchala'
inkooli, ibichchala' kooli
nosebleed, to have a ibichchala'
issish lhatapa
nostril ibichchala' cholok
nosy, to be afánnali'chi
not ki'yo
not be, to ki'yo
not enough iko'no
not for long ikalhchibo'so
not to act like, to ikholbo

not to be iksho
not to be able to breathe noktiipa
not to be able to do things right
akánni'ya
not to be able to make up one's mind
imaanokfila-at fashkalamo'wa
not to be able to sit still
nokhámmi'chi
**not to be able to stand what happens
to** ikimachonna'cho
not to be crazy imaanokfila-at
imóma, imaanokfila-at móma
not to be defective imóma
not to be done on the inside chakissa
not to be here iksho
not to be lively lhakcha
not to be retarded imaanokfila-at
imóma, imaanokfila-at móma
not to be serious about ishyoppola
not to be the same mihaash ikholbo
not to be there iksho
not to care nanninkanihki'yo,
nannishtinkanihmo,
naaishtimahómba ki'yo
not to care about naaishtahoobali
ki'yo
not to do anything píhhi'la
not to do right at all ishtayóbba'li
ki'yo
not to do well ayobba'li ki'yo
not to eat too much impa' iksala'mo
not to exist iksho
not to fall over oottala
not to fear imaaiklóha
not to forget nokfónkha
not to get enough of ikimo'no
not to have enough imóna ki'yo
not to have gotten enough ikimóno
not to lie flat abáwwa'a
not to like ikimahooba'lo
not to listen ikihaklo
not to match iktiholbo
not to mean it pila aachi
not to miss atókkoli'chi

not to say anything

not to say anything nokwaya
not to spend much on oneself ilatoba
not to think anything akánni'ya
not to want to go with imilaafowa
not to want to wait nokhámmi'chi
nothing nannahookya—*also*
  chikimba
nothing in, for there to be nannakya
  iksho
nothing, to talk about bachali
notice, to yahmanhi
noticed, to be oktani
noticing, to have (time) pass without
  one's imambaanapa
notorious, to be oktani
now himmaka', himmaka'ma
now, just himmako'sa
now, right himmako'si finha

nowhere kaniya'ookya
nowhere, to come out of ootkochcha
numb, to be shimoha
numb, to get nosi
number holhtina'—*see also names*
  of specific numbers
number of times, a hikannohmi'
number, roll iholhtina'
numbered, to be holhtina
numbered with, to be ibaaholhtina
nun ihoo holitto'pa'
nurse abik-apiisachi'
nurse from, to impishi
nurse, to pishi
nurse with, to ibaapishi
nursing young, to be oshpishínchi
nutcracker osak ishkookoli'
nuzzle, to yoko'chi

O

oak, poison ofimitti'
oak, type of boshto', chiskilik,
  chisha', nassapi', shokhalanchapi'
obey, to ayalhlhichi, alhlhínchi,
  hapowaklo, imayalhlhínchi,
  imalhlhínchi, ihapowánglo
obey, to listen to and ihaklo
obscene, to be ikayyo'bo
obscured by clouds, to be hoshonti
obstinate toward, to be imilaafowa
obvious, to make oktánni'chi
ocean okhata
o'clock, to be hashi' kanalli
of necessity pollaho
of what color pisa-kanihmi
off balance, to be shanaa
off limits, to be imihollo
off the cob, to be chillowa
offering ittahobbi'
offering, to make an ima
offering, to take up an ittahobbi'

hoyo
office, to run for tilhaa
officer tashka-chipota' apiichi',
  tashka-chipota' ishkoboka'
ogle each other, to ittoonokmiloli
ogle, to onokmiloli
oh aa, kii, oo, taa
oh well oohaatokma
oil niha
oil, cool aashoppala' niha'
oil, lamp aashoppala' niha'
oil, to nihachi
oil well nihaakola'
oink, to lhonka, lhonklhowa
okay chokmahookay, ho'mi,
  mikya'ba, taa
okay, to have everything be
  ishtinchokmaka
Oklahoma Oklahomma'
Oklahoma Choctaw Yappakayni
  Chahta'

472

Oklahoma City Okla Ishto'
okra kombo'
okra, type of kombo' awaalhaali';
  also waak ibilhkan
old clothes naafokha lhipa'
old house abooha lhipa'
old one kamassa'
old people's home kamassaa-asha',
  sipokni' aa-asha', sipokni'
  inchokka'
old, to be kamassa, sipokni
old, to be how afammi kánnohmi,
  afammi káttohmi, sipoknikat
  kaniya fokha, sipoknikat katiya
  fokha
old, to be so sipoknikat kaniya fokha
old, to be so many years afammi
  kánnohmi
old, to get kamassachi
old, to make sipoknichi, sipoknikat
  kaniya fokha
old woman ihoo kashiiho'
older brother intikba
older half-sibling of the same sex as
  oneself intikba iklanna'
older sibling of the same sex as
  oneself intikba
older sister intikba
older step-sibling of the same sex as
  oneself intikba toba'
oldest child chipota ammo'na'
oldest, the ammo'na'
oldest, to be ámmo'na
on aash, mashshaasho, ookma
on foot, to be akkaanówa, akkaayínka
on her own ilaapo'
on his own ilaapo'
on the edge naksika'
on the edge of taakcha'
on the far side tannap
on the left alhfabi' pila
on the other side tannap
on the other side of intannap
on the same ittinchaffali'

on the side naksika'
on the side, moving naksikali'
on the way, to be minti
on their own ilaapo'
on this side pa-pila
on, to be ompatkachit máa,
  ompatkáyya'chi, ompátta'a,
  onáyya'sha, owayya'a; *also*
  shoppálla'a, shoppálla'a
on top pakna'
on top of paknaka'
on top of, moving paknakali',
  paknali'
on top of the other, to be one
  ittalatkáyya'chi
on top of, to be alátta'a
on welfare, to be alhpila' ishi
on wrong, to be fili'ta, ittifili'ta,
  ittishanaa
once himonna'
once, to happen himonna'si
once upon a time... chiiki
  áyya'shahmat..., himonnahma...,
  hopaaki áyya'shahmat...
one chaffa
one alone, to be lhakófa
one by one mayyoka'
one by one, to do chaffa áyyo'ka
one day nittak kanimpihma
one each, to be chaffa áyyo'ka
one hundred talhipa chaffa
one hundred eleven talhipa
  chaffacha awa chaffa
one hundred eleven in number, to be
  talhipa chaffacha awa chaffa
one hundred in number, to be
  talhipa chaffa, talhipa chaffaka óna
one hundred one talhipa chaffacha
  chaffa
one hundred one in number, to be
  talhipa chaffacha chaffa
one hundred ten talhipa chaffacha
  pokkó'li
one hundred ten in number, to be

473

talhipa chaffacha pokkó'li
one hundred three talhipa chaffacha
tochchí'na
one hundred three in number, to be
talhipa chaffacha tochchí'na
one hundred two talhipa chaffacha
toklo
one hundred two in number, to be
talhipa chaffacha toklo
one in number, to be chaffa, ilachaffa
one in, to be the only shikkílli'li
one left, to be lhakófa
one of aachaffa'
one of a group ila'
one of the same type as binka'
one removed from the present, to be
atokla
one thousand talhipa sipokni' chaffa
one thousand in number, to be
talhipa sipokni' chaffa, talhipa
sipokni' chaffaka óna
one thousand one talhipa sipokni'
chaffacha chaffa
one thousand one in number, to be
talhipa sipokni' chaffacha chaffa
one, to be the only chaffa, ilachaffa
one, to have ittichaffa
one year old, to be afammi chaffa'si
one-eyed, to be ishkinat tannap
pila'si
one-way, to be aya' chaffa
onion atofalla'a'
onion, type of atofalla'a' himona',
atofalla'a' homma', atofalla'a'
imilhlha', atofalla'a' imilhlha'
hishi' patha', atofalla'a' lakna',
atofalla'a' okchamali', atofalla'a'
shobbokoli', atofalla'a' tohbi',
hashtola' atofalla'a'
only pilla
only child, to be an ilachaffa
only one chaffa'si
only one in, to be the shikkílli'li
only one, to be chaffa'si

only one, to be the chaffa, ilachaffa
only, to be biika, illa
oops! woop
open all up, to tiwwichi
open area near a house kasbi
open for, to intiwwi
open his mouth, to make (someone)
taklhipachi
open one's mouth, to taklhipali
open place yaakni' hayaka'
open the door and come in, to
ashchokkowa
open the door and come out, to
ashkochcha
open, to tiwa, tiwwi; also fachopa,
fakohli, fakopa, pofalli
open, to be tíwwa'pa; also
fáchcho'pa, fachobli
opener, bottle kitobishtiwwi'
openings, to have big shachakla
operate on in, to aabashli
operate on, to bashli
operated on in, to be aabasha
operated on, to be basha
opossum chakwihili'
opponents, to be ittisánna'li
opposed to, to be aasanali, isanali
optometrist ishkin imalikchi'
or ba'
or someone ookma nannahmat,
ookma nannahma
or something ookma nannahmat,
ookma nannahma
order, to atohno, atohnochi, imanoli,
inaapiisa
order, to give an aachi, naapiisa
organ, sex immi', ishkish
organist nannola' inchokoshkomo'
organize a meeting, to
nannishtittanaha
organize, to imáyya'sha, ishtáyya'sha
original holisso mi finha'
original, the mi, mi finha'
originally banka

ornament ishtilatahpoli'
ornament, feather yaatala
ornament, to atannichi
ornamented with twists, to be
  atannalhchi
ornaments ishtasawachi'
ornery, to be malhaa
orphan alhtakla', chipotalhtakla'
orphanage alhtaklaa-asha'
orphaned, to be alhtakla
other tannap
other one, the chaffo'
other room, in the abooha tannap
other room, the abooha chaffo'
other side tannap
other side of, just on the
  mishintannap
other side of, on the intannap
other side of the house, on the
  abooha tannap
other side, on the other tannap
other side, to come out on the
  ootkochcha
other, the anowa'
other, to be the chaffa
ouch alii, aliiho
Our God Aba' Pinchitokaka'
Our Lord Aba' Pinchitokaka'
out in the boondocks hayaka'
out of alignment, to be abáwwa'a
out of breath, to be foyopat intaha
out of it, to be ámmohmi
out of one's mind, to be imaanokfila-
  at ikimiksho
out of shape, to be hayifa
out of shape, to be bent pashshana,
  payo'kachi, payofa
out of, to be intaha
out of, to bring ishtaakkowa

out of, to go aakochcha
out, to be annowa, annoya
outhouse abooshi', aahola'fa'
outside kochcha'
outside, being kochchaalisht
outside, moving kochchali'
outsmart, to inkostini, ihapoyoksa
outwalk, to impalhki
outwards, to go wahhala
oven paskaanonachi'
oven, type of tali' aapalaska'
over and over, to do albilli
over, moving paknakali', paknali'
over there, visible misha' pila
over, to be obya, tiwapa, tíwwa'pa
overcome by desire, to be
  nokhámmi'chi
overdo, to ootishtilaatámbli
overdone, to cook until lhaboshli
overfeeding, to kill by kayyachit abi
overlap, to make ittayoppitammichi
overlapping on the ends, to be laid
  ittaban-kachit máa
overlapping, to be made of wood
  stacked with the ends ittabaana
overpass hina' aa-abaanabli', hina'
  aalhopolli'
overripe, to be moyoshki
overseas okkata tannap
overshoes sholosh pakna' holo'chi'
owe on, to áhhi'ka
owe to on, to imáhhi'ka
owl, type of hoopa, ofolo, kitiini, opa;
  also chokkala'bolo'
own ilaapo', aakaynihoot, aakayniho
own, to immi
ox waaka' toksali'
oxygen tube ishfoyopa'

p

pack for, to imambihpoli
pack, to abihli, abihpoli
package naaholbona'
packed in, to be ittaakallohónchi
packed lunch pinak
packed, to be abilhpowa
padding worn by a baseball umpire
  to'li' fo'kha'
paddle piini' ishtoobli'
page holisso
pagoda shaped, to be ittashikkílli'li,
  shikkilili
paid for, to be alhtoba, ishtalhtoba
paid to, to be imalhtoba,
  ishtimalhtoba
pain, to be in nokhámmi'chi
pain, to have a hottopa
pain to, to give a imalhchíbba'chi
painful, to be hofkachi
pains, to have komoha
paint albi'
paint a blaze on the forehead of, to
  baktasachi
paint for, to imaabi
paint, house aboohalbi'
paint one's face, to ilibaklosochi
paint the face of, to baklosochi
paint, to aabi, baklosochi, ishtaabi
painted on, to be albi
painted, to have one's face baklosoli
pairs, to be sorted into ittachapo'wa
pairs, to sort into ittachapo'li,
  ittachaafoochi
pair with, to make up a ittachaabli
pajamas nosi' fo'kha'
pale, to be tohbi, tokbakali
pallet akka' patalhpo'
palm of the hand ilbak impatha'
palomino issoba lakna'
palpitate, to malli
pan lid asonnak pathalhiipi'ya'
pan, frying nipaapalli'

pan, type of asonnak patha'
pancake turner ishfilillichi',
  ishfilito'chi'
panda nita' kamaa'
pant, to hahka
panther kowishto' losa'
pants balaafokha'
pants, blue balaafokchamali'
pants, to wet one's imbalaafka',
  ohoshowa
panty hose ihoo imiabisowa'
paper holisso
paper clip holisso ishtakallo'chi'
paper money holisso loposhki'
paper plate holissamposhi'
paper, to be in the holisso fóyyokha
paper, to make noise with
  ittishókkokli'chi, shóchchokli'chi
parachute nanna wakaa',
  ishtakkowa'
parallel, to be ittapótto'wa
paralyzed on half of one's body, to be
  haknip tannapat illi
paralyzed person hattak haknip illi'
paralyzed, to be haknip illi' hayoochi
parasol ishtiloshontika'chi'
parch, to aposhli
parched corn tanchalhposha'
parched corn flour tanchi' bota'
park hattak aa-asha'
park, to wayaachi
parking lot kaa aawayoochi'
parrot foshi' anompoli'
part of, to be a atoosháfa
part one's hair, to akaniili
part, to akanaachi, akaniili,
  imakanaachi, imakaniili
part, to be a kashapa
parted, to be akanaa
partner aaittawwa'a'
partners, to be aaittáwwa'a,
  ittibaaishi

partners with, to be táwwa'a
parts, private iyyobittintakla'
party, Democratic Okaamahli
party, Republican Falammi
party, to give a toklhakafa' apiisa
party, to have a toklhakafa'
imáyya'sha
party, type of toklhakafa'
pass away, to loshoma
pass gas, to hónkso
pass going in opposite directions, to
ittayoppitammi
pass off as, to ishtapiisa
pass, to abaanapa, ímmayya'chi,
lhopolli, ootaya, ootímmayya,
pitlawwi'chi, ittánno'wa,
ittanohówa; also holiitobli
pass, to have (time) imambaanapa
pass without speaking, to make
(someone) ayoppitammichi
pass without stopping, to make
(people) ittayoppitammichi
passed, to be holiitopa
passenger car hattak shaali'
pastry paska champoli'
pat, to pasa'chi, pashohli
patch, to alalli, alaatali
patched, to be alaata
path hin-oshi'
paths to the same goal, to go along
different báyya'ta
patient, to be noktála
pave, to patali
paved, to be tali' patalhpo' bíyyi'ka
paving tali' patalhpo'
paw iyyimpatha'
pawn, to ta'ossishponta
pawnbroker ta'ossimponta'
pawnshop nanna ta'osso
ishtaaponta'
pay attention, to yahmanhi
pay attention to, to yahmanhi
pay back, to imatobbi
pay for oneself, to ilatobbi

pay for, to atobbi, imimatobbi
pay for with, to ibaachompa,
ibaatobbi
pay in full, to lombo ishtimatobbi,
lomboshtima
pay interest, to oshi'ak illa atobbi
pay off a debt for, to atobbit inkashoffi
pay taxes to, to ta'ossifalammichi
pay, to ishtatobbi, nannatobbi
pay, to make atobbichi
pay to, to imaatobbi
pay with, to ishtimaatobbi
peace nanna ayya
peace, to have nanna ayya bíyyi'ka,
ittinannayya
peaceful heart, to have a chonkash
yohbi
peaceful, to be nanna ayya bíyyi'ka,
nanna ayya bíyyi'ka nokfilli,
nannanokfillikat chokma bíyyi'ka,
yohbi bíyyi'ka
peaceful, to have one's mind be
imaanokfila-at yohbi bíyyi'ka
peach takolo, takolo finha'—see also
peach, type of
peach, cling takola'lhlhi'
peach, freestone takolo fako'pa'
peach fuzz takolo fattabli'
peach leaves takolo hishi'
peach stone takolo foni'
peach, type of takolissish, takolo
lakna', takolo tohbi'
peach-colored, to be homma
tokbakali
peacock chaloklowokchamali'
peaked, to be shikkilili
peanut yaaknonkaawaa'
peanut butter yaaknonkaawaa' bota'
pear takolo haksibish, takolo ibish
aa-asha', takolo ibish falaa'
pearl folosh-ata' aatoba'
peas bala'
peas, type of akankimbala', bala'
falaa', bala' falaa' ittitikili', bala'

falaa' shobookoli', bala' hakshop losa', bala' hakshop okchamali', bala' holisso', bala' ittakallochi', bala' lhibowa', bala' shiwaa', bala' shotik pila', bala' tohbi' sawa', bala' waaka', manki' ishkobo', osaapa' bala', waakimbala'
pecan osak falaa'—*see also* pecan, type of
pecan tree osak falaa' api'
pecan, type of osak falaa' alhpooba'
peck like a woodpecker, to bákkaka'chi
pedal aahalhabli'
pedal, to halhlhi
pedestal ishtaaohikki'ya'
peel, to loffichi, shokaffi, tilhlhichi
peeled, to be lofa, lofalhchi, tilhalhchi
peep at, to ahaalaachi
peep, to toktoha
pen ishholissochi'
pen, quill foshi' hishi' ishholissochi'
pencil ishholissochi'
penis hakchin, inkilish, ishtaahoshowa'
penis, to take out one's kochchi
penitentiary aatoksali', yoka' aa- asha'
penny sent chaffa', sent homma'
pension, to be on a ilhpita
people imaaokla'
people, all hattak moma
pepper hommahomma' ani'—*see also* pepper, type of
pepper shaker homma' losaalhto'
pepper, type of homma' losa', hommahomma', hommahomma' champoli', hommahomma' homi', hommahomma' lakna', hommahomma' okchamali'
perch nani' pathassa'
perch, type of nani' patassa' sotko'
perforate, to mitaachi

perform an abortion on, to chipotimaaishi
perfume ishtilibilamachi', nambilama'
perfume, to bilamachi
perfume, to put on ilibilamachi
perhaps nanna
period, menstrual hashi' abika', ihoo imambiika'
period, to have a menstrual hashi' abika, issish lhatapa
permanent to, to give a oshchilochi
perpendicular to, to be aban-kachit máa, aban-káyya'chi, abánna'a
persevere, to achónna'chi, chilita
persimmon onkof
person hattak *see also* person, type of *and words which would be used to describe specific types of person in English*
person in charge atooni'
person, type of chonkash kallo, ishkobo' kallo', okloshi' ilayyokha
pest, insect nannokchamalapa'
pester, to achilita, apistikili, ataklammi
pet name *for specific pet names, see* (name, Chickasaw pet)
pet, to hapashshichi
petition against, to achapa
petrified wood itti' tali'
petticoat anonkalhko'na'
pew aaombiniili' falaa'
pheasant kofishto'
phlegm kalhafa
phone, to call on the kaali
photocopy holisso holba'
photocopy, to make a holisso holbachi
photograph holba'
photograph album holba'
photograph, to holbachi
photograph well, to holba'at chokmaho toba

photographed, to be holba
photography studio aaholbachi'
piano nannola'
pick a fight with, to imiliyimmichi
pick at, to sholli
pick on, to ishtapistíkki'li
pick one's nose, to ibichchala'
  ibayakohli
pick (one's teeth), to fi'chi,
  ishchafi'nachi
pick out the best, to chaafoochit
  aayoowa
pick the best one, to chaafoochi
pick, to ayowa; also naachi, nafi
pick up, to abaawiili, afaama, ayowa,
  ayoowa, oothoyo
pick with, to ibaa-ayowa
picked over, to be hayowalhchi
picked, to be naalhchi
Pickens, I. Hunter Aayahanta'
picking fights, to go around bohpoli
pickle istokchankapa', pikkal
pickle, type of pikkal champoli',
  pikkal wasacha'
pickles, to make pikkal abihli
picnic piknik, pinak
picture hattak holba', holba'
picture frame hattak holbaafokha'
picture turn out good, to have one's
  holba'at chokmaho toba
pie paay
piece together, to ittapalli
pieced quilt ittapalli', ittapatkachi'
pieced together, to be ittapatkachi
pieces, to cut into toshli
piecrust paay hakshop
pierce, to mitaffi
pig shokhoshi'
pigeon pachi'
pigeon, type of pachalhpooba'
piggy bank shokhoshi' ta'ossaalhto'
pigheaded, to be ilapóla
pigs' feet shokhiyyi'
pile up around, to aaittanaachi

pile up on, to ombilhipa
pile up, to chikkibichi, ittanaalhchi
piled up, to be chikkibbi, ittahoba,
  ittalatkachi, ittalatkachit máa,
  ittalátta'a, ittalbitkachi
pilings, foundation notihiyohli'
pill ittish lhibowa'
pill, birth control hobak ishtikbi',
  ittish lhibowa' ishtilihaksichi'
pill, sleeping ishnosi'
pillow alhpishshi'
pillow case alhpishshi' ishokcha
pillow one's head on, to alhpishshi
pillow (someone's) head, to
  alhpishichi
pillow, to beat on a mitití'chi
pillows, to make the sound of hitting
  mit mit mit aachi
pimp ihoo hawi' piichi', ihoo hawi'
  intoksali', ihoo hawi' ittanahli'
pimple, to have a hoshonachi
pin chofaakoshi', chofaakoshi'
  ilontala'li', ishtalhopo'li'
pin, bobby ipashishtakallo'chi'
pin on, to asilli, asiitili, asiitohli
pin to, to aaittasiitilichi
pin, safety bakshiyamashtasitti'ya',
  chofaakoshi'
pin, straight chofaakoshi' oshkibbi'li'
pin, to tasiitohli
pinch chinofa'si
pinch a lot, to chino'li
pinch, to chino'li, chinoffi
pinched a lot, to be chino'wa
pinched, to be chino'wa, chinofa,
  latafa
pincushion chofaakoshi'
  aachoshkachi'
pine tiyak
pine needle tiyak hishi'
pine pitch tiyak bila', tiyak okchi'
pine tree tiyak api'
pinecone tiyak ani'
pink, to be homma tokbakali,

pinkeye

ilokchina
pinkeye ishkin homma'
pinking shears ishkalasha'
chakchaki'
pinned on, to be asitkáyya'chi,
asítti'ya, asiitowat máa
pinned onto one, to have asítti'ya
pins and needles, to have hofkachi
pinwheel nanchanahli'
pipe aashobohli', chomak aapofa',
chomak shoti', tali', tali' cholok aa-
asha'
pipe, type of kali foloha'
pishofa tashpishofa
Pishofa Dance Pishofa Hilha'
pistol tanamposhkololi'
pitch, pine tiyak bila'
pitcher oka' aalhto', picha', to'wa'
faapo'chi'
pitchfork chofaak
pitiful, to be ilbashsha
pity, to inokhánglo
place crosswise on, to afinni, afiinili
place for, to intalaali, intalooli,
iwayaachi, iwayoochi
place mat amposhi' ontalla'a',
aaimpompatkachi'
place on, to ontalaali, ontalooli
place one's hands on one's waist, to
ilombítti'pa
place the hair grows from ishkobo'
folfo', iyalfolfo'
place to stay, to be a albina
place where corn is ground
tanchaafolowa'
place where stuff is nannaa-asha', aa-
asha'
placed crosswise on, to be afin-kachit
máa, afin-káyya'chi
placed on, to be ontálla'a, ontállo'wa,
ontalowat máa
plague abikoppolo'
plan a work party, to iikowa' apiisa
plan, to apiisa, tikbaalisht anokfilli,

tikbali' anokfilli
plane ittishshafi', ittishtalha',
nannishtalhlhi'
plank itti' basha'
plant alba—see also plant, type of
plant for, to ihilichi, ihiyohchi
plant sap albokchi'
plant sap, white albimpishokchi'
plant, to hiyohchi, hokchi
plant, type of akankittibi'chi', alba
haloppa', alba homi', alba lakna',
alba lowak, chalokloha' ittish,
chokfisholosh, falaanosi', fani'
hasimbish, fannik, fannik sawa',
hakshish apissa'li', hashshok
haloppa', homma' losa' api', issim-
ahi', ishkobo' homma',
kitobacho'sha', kow-asi'bish,
loksishtincho'li', lowak pakali',
malin, nanna holokchi', nita'
lobahli', nittaki pakali', oktaak
taakchili', oshchono', pilhchi',
shakchimitti', shommatik,
shommatik ishto', tokfol,
waakimbala'—see also plant, type of
medicinal and names of specific
plants and types of plants
plant, type of medicinal ahalla'ta',
basho'kchi', chalokloha' ittish,
hahtok, haksibish falaha', halambo
tish, issimittish, issoba
ishoptilhi'li', ishkobo' homma'
pakali', itti' okchama'li', koshibba'
hakshish, loksimpolona, loksittish,
nashobattish, nita' tish, ofi' sholop
ittish, ofi' tish, ofolottish,
pasakchala, shiiki pakali',
shokhiskanno' tish, shokhishto'
tish, sholop tilhi'li' iskanno',
sholop tilhi'li' losa', sholop tilhi'li'
tohbi', shootko'li', waaka' lapish—
see also names of specific medicinal
plants
planted, to be holokchi

plaster nanna apoolosa'
plaster, to apoolosli
plate amposhimpatha'
plate, paper holissamposhi'
platform itti' patalhpo'
platter amposhi' falaa'
play active games, to toklhak̲afa
play akaaballi' in, to aa-akaaballi
play akaaballi', to akaaballi,
 akaaballichi
play along with, to
 ibaachokoshkomo
play an instrument, to nannola'
 olachi
play around with, to ishyoppola
play ball in, to aato'li
play ball, to to'li
play cards for money with, to
 ibaachalhka
play cards in, to aachalhka
play cards, to chalhka
play fair, to alhpi'schokoshkomo
play hide and seek, to ittiloma, loma
play marbles, to ittikássakli'chi
play, to chokoshkomo; also olachi
play, to make chokoshkomochi
play with sexually, to aapollichi
play with, to aatoklha, chiko'li,
 impilisa, pilisa
play with, to make
 ibaachokoshkomochi
playground aachokoshkomo'
playhouse abooha aachokoshkomo',
 aachokoshkomo' abooha'
playing card ishchalhka'
playpen chipotaachokoshkomo'
please with, to ishtayoppali
pleased for, to be ishtimachaaha
pleat, to polhlhi
pleated, to be polhkachi
Pleiades Fochik Ontoklo'
pliers talishtapa'
plow issobishliichi', issobishliili',
 ishliichi'

plow, to liichi
plowed, to be laa
pluck, to tihli, tifi
plucked, to be tiha, tifa
plug ishtakallochi'
plug into, to achoshli, achoosholi
plug, to lobli, okshitta
plugged into, to be achoshkachit
 m̲áa, achoshkáyya'chi,
 achóshsho'wa
plugged, to be lopa
plum tak̲oloshi'
plum, type of tak̲olo lakna',
 tak̲oloshi' imilhlha'
plump up, to yaboffi, yatoffi
pneumonia hashtola' yanha'
pneumonia, to have hashtola'
 yanha' í'shi
pocket nannaabilhpoha',
 nannaalhto'
pocket knife nannishtalhlhi'
point at, to aabachi
point, to sharpen to a oshkibichi
pointed, to be bakshak̲ali,
 ittashikkílli'li, oshkibili, shikkilili
pointer itti' ishtaabachi'
poison itt̲ish oppolo', nannoppolo'
poison ivy ofimitti'
poison oak ofimitti'
poison sumac ofimitti'
poke into things, to afánnali'chi
poke root koshibba' hakshish
poke salad koshibba'
poke, to abi'chi, bahli, shaffi
poke weed koshibba'
poker ishtabi'chi', lowak ishbahli',
 lowak ishshafa', lowak ishtabi'chi'
polar bear falammi nita', nita'
 aakapassaa-asha', nita' tohbi'
pole, bean bala' itti' albilha',
 balishtalbilha'
pole beans bala' albilha', itti' tiyya'
pole, fishing nanishholhtosi'
poles, to be trained on albilha

poles, type of hoshottokihiyohli', itti' ihiyohli', notihiyohli'
police station aayokachi'
policeman naa-alhtoka'
polish, to shokmalachi
polka-dotted, to be chisiya
pollen nampakali' poshi'
pommel solhposhkobo'
pompadour, to have a oshchahali
pond hayip, okpachalhlhi'
Pontotoc Pantatak
pony issoba sawa'
pony, Shetland issoba imo'ma'
pool, swimming oka' aayopi'
poor thing ilbashsha'
poor, to be ilbashsha
poorly behaved child chipotoppolo'
pop sokahli
pop gum, to ittilasa'chi, ittilasasá'chi, ittilássakli'chi
pop open, to bokahli
pop, to sokafa, sokaffi, sokaachi, sokli, tokafa, tokahli
popcorn tanchi' sokahli'
popping sound, to make a pat pat pat aachi
popping, to make the sound of tok tok tok aachi
porch hoshottika', itti' patalhpo'
porch pole hoshottikihiyohli'
pork shokha' nipi'
pork crackling bila' shila'
pork, salt nipi' hapayyima', shokha' nipi' shila'
pork tripe shokhittakoba'
position, to change kana'li
possession immi'
possum chakwihili', shokha' chokkayalli', shokha' iskano', shokhata'
possum grapes pankaashoshi', panki' sawa', shawimpanki'
post bail for oneself, to ilatobbi
post bail for, to ato'li, imatooni, imatoonichi, imimaatobbi

post oak chisha'
post office holissaaishi', holissaaittola'
post office box holisso aaishi', holisso aalhto'
post office box number holisso aaishi' holhtina'
pot asonnak aaholhponi', aaholhponi'
pot, coffee- kaafaawalhahli'
pot, tea- tii aalhto', tii aawaalhaali'
potato ahi' —see also potatoes, type of
potato bug ahi' imissosh, issosh loksi'
potato, double ahi' pokta'
potato, eye of a ahi' ishkin
potato masher ahishlhacho'li'
potato patch ahi' aaholokchi'
potato vine ahi' api'
potatoes, freshly dug ahi' himona'
potatoes, Irish ahi' lhibowa'
potatoes, seed ahi' pinha'
potatoes, sweet ahi' lhobowa' champoli'
potatoes, type of ahi' alhlhi', ahi' homma', ahi' palaska', ahi' tohbi'
potholes and ditches, to be full of okaaofkobi
pottery bowl lokfamposhi'
pouch osha'to', oshi' aafo'kha', oshi' aalhto', shokchoshi'
pound wiiki
pound, dog ofi' aa-asha', ofi' aa-ashaachi'
pound, to bo'li, cha'li, hosi, yaboffi
pounded, to be cha'a, hollosi
pounding sound, to make a kalhak kalhak kalhak aachi
pounding, to make the sound of kalh kalh kalh aachi
pour for in, to aaimanni
pour for, to imanni, imbichili

pour in with, to okaalhatabli
pour on, to oshtǫlhatabli
pour out, to lhatabli
pour some of into, to aa-ani
pour, to ani, bichili
pout, to takbiloli, ittialbi' falaa
Pouty face! Chittialbi' falaa!
pow, to go paaw paaw paaw aachi
powder nanna poshi'
powder puff ishtilitohbichi'
powder, talcum ishtilitohbichi'
powder, to put on face ilitohbichi'
powdered sugar shookola' bota'
powdery come out, to have
  something shobottokahchi
powdery substance nanna poshi'
powdery, to be poshi' bíyyi'ka
power, magical fatpo
practice, to imaabalhchi
prairie oktaak, yaakni' hayaka'
prairie onion oktaak tǫfalaa'
prairie wax oktaak taakchili'
praise, to ayoppachi
prance, to ilokchina
pray for, to
  anompilbashshimanompoli
pray, to anompilbashshanompoli,
  anompilbashshasilhlha
pray to, to
  anompilbashshishtanompoli
prayer anompilbashsha'
prayer meeting abaanompittanaha'
praying mantis nassano'li', Siitan
  imissoba
preach, to abaanompa' anǫli,
  abaanompishtanompoli
preach to, to
  abaanompishtimanompoli,
  holissintoshooli
preacher aba' anompishtanompoli',
  abaanompa' toshooli',
  abaanompishtanompoli', holisso
  toshooli', holitto'pa'
preacher, lady ihoo

abaanompishtanompoli'
preacher, male hattak
  abaanompishtanompoli'
precious baby poskosh
precious, to be holítto'pa, iholítto'pa
precious, to consider aapichi
precipitating, to stop ayoli
precisely pila
precook, to okoffi
predict, to tingbalísht anooli
prefer, to holiitómbli
pregnant, to be chakali, chipotishtáa
pregnant, to get chipota habina,
  chipota hayoochi
prepare, to atahli
present halbina', naahalbina'
present day, the himmaka' nittak
present from, to get as a imaahabiina
preserve, to bóyyohli
preserves cheli'
president inkapittani', minko',
  naapiisa', pihli'chi'
president in, to be aaminko
president, lady ihoo minko'
President of the United States
  Minko' Holiitopa', Yaakni' Iminko'
president, vice- apiilanchi'
press a crease into, to pakolli
press against, to abiitippichi
press down for, to imambiitippichi
press down on, to abiitippichi,
  ombitiipa
press down with one's open hands, to
  bitka
press flat against, to alaatassachi
press on one's skin, to ilombitka
press on, to ombitka
press, to hammi
press together, to ittalaatassachi
pressure cooker nannaaholhponi'
pretend ahobbichi
pretend, to ilahobbi
pretend to be, to ahobbichi
pretentious, to be ilahobbi

pretty, to be chokma'si, inchokma'si, pisa-chokma
price ayalli'
price, to ayalli' imombohli, ayalli' ombohli
price, to have a high ayalli' chaaha
price to on, to give a good imalhchonachi
prices, to charge high ayalli' chaahachi, ayalli'at inchaaha, imayallishto
prickly pear talhpakha'
printed matter tali' ishtincho'wa'
printing press tali' ishtincho'li', tali' ishtincho'wa'
prison aatoksali', yoka' aa-asha'
prison, to be sent to toksalit atobbi
prison, to send to toksalichi
prisoner hattak yoka', yoka'
prisoner, female ihoo yoka'
private parts iyyobittintakla'
prize naahalbina'
problem, to take care of a nampíla, pitnampíla
produce ani', namposhi', nannawaa'
produce, to ani
professor pofessa'
projection from a roundish object ibish
promiscuous, to be bilo'chit nowa, hattak ibaanosit nowa, ihoo ibaanosit nowa
promise anompalhpisa'
promise each other, to anompittimapiisa
promise, to anompalhpisa' ima, anompapiisa, anompimapiisa, imapiisa
promise, to break one's anompa kobaffi, anompinkobaffi
promise, to keep an old ishtittihállalli
prop up with, to intikiichi
proper, to be alhpí'sa

property yaakni'
prophecy Chihoowaak inaanooli'
prophet Chihoowa inaanoli', hopayi', holitto'pa'
propose, to apiisa, imapiisa
proscribed, to be imihollo
prostitute hawi', ihoo hawi'
prostitute, male hattak hawi'
prostitute, to hawichi
prostitute, to make into a hawi' ikbi
prostitution, house of hawi' abooha
prostitution, to keep a house of hawi' abooha apiisachi
protrude, to ootkónchcha
proud of oneself, to be ilafinha
proud of, to be imayoppánchi, ishtayoppa, nannishtifinha
proud, to be ilahobbi, ilifaya'chi, ilifinhachi, ilifoyo'chi
prune takoloshi' shila'
pruned, to be naalhchi
pruning shears ittishkatolhlhi'
Psalms, Book of Aataloowa' Holisso
psych oneself up, to iliyimmichi
psychiatrist alikchi' hattak yokolli'
pubic hair hakchish
public assistance ishtalhpila'
pucker up, to takshololi
puckered, to be yikilhlha
puddle oka' patakshi', oka' taloha'
puddles, to have okfichibli
puff oneself out, to poffolpówa
puffed up, to be pofoha
pull all the clothes off, to lhofi
pull along with, to ibaahalalli
pull apart into two parts, to tabli
pull apart, to shibli, shipaffi
pull around, to folollichi
pull away from, to intalhoffi
pull back, to ilaafowa
pull down on, to halaht lhifi
pull down, to akkowachi
pull down, to grab and halaht oshwayaachi

pull each other's hair, to ittichiko'li
pull grass, to bend over and
   wayyayáa, wayyayǫ́wa
pull into shape, to shiipo'li
pull off an arm or leg from, to nipaffi
pull off, to naafi
pull on hair, to chiko'li
pull on, to pithalalli
pull oneself, to lhifi'li
pull out by the roots, to tifi
pull out hair, to boyaffi
pull out one's feathers, to iliboyolli
pull out, to halaht ishkochchi,
   ilihalalli, shihli
pull threads from, to shihchi
pull, to halalli; also halahli,
   hállakli'chi, lhifi'chi, shiipo'li, shifi,
   tihli
pull up, to abaawiili, halaht abaawiili
pulled apart in two, to be tapa
pulled off, to have an arm or leg
   nipafa
pulled off, to have one's skin lhǫfa
pulled off, to have the arms and legs
   nipahli
pulled, to be tiha
pulling grass, to go around on hands
   and knees wayyayáa, wayyayǫ́wa
pulpit aaǫhikki'ya'
pummel, to mittiha
pump dispenser kitoba ibish
pump (one's breasts), to bishlichi
pump, water okishtoochi'
pumpkin osto
pumpkin, small olbi'
punch in the eye, to ishkin
   imokaabaafa
punch more than one hole in, to
   bahli
punch, to baafa, mittiha
punish, to ittabánna'li
punished, to be atobbi, nannatobbi
puppy ofishik
purple martin chǫ'ki'

purse ta'ossishokcha'
pus kalha'
pus come out, to have kalha
pus come out, to make kalhali
pus in, for there to be kalha'at
   áyyalhto
pus, to have aniichi
push against each other, to
   ittitoopo'li
push against, to tikiichi, toopo'li
push and shove each other, to
   ittitoopopǫ́li
push back, to bakhitiipo'chi
push down on, to baayo'chi
push each other's heads to the side, to
   ittaakassanachi
push in a swing, to faapichi,
   faapo'chi, ifaapo'chi
push in water, to oka' pitokaakanchi
push into, to okaafimmi,
   okaakanchi, okaalha'li
push one's finger into, to okaabaafa
push out of shape, to payoffi
push over, to kinaffi
push repeatedly, to toopopǫ́li
push (someone's) head over to one
   side, to akassanachi
push, to faya'chi, toobli
push to get into a crowded space, to
   chikkibbi
put a backpack on, to shaapolichi
put a bracelet on, to ilbak apakfo'li'
   imapakfolli
put a chain on, to atakalichi
put a diaper on oneself, to
   bakshiyammi
put a diaper on, to bakshiyammichi
put a feather on one's head, to
   yaatalaali
put a net into the water, to okaffi
put a price on, to ayalli' imombohli,
   ayalli' ombohli
put a roof on for, to ihomo
put a ruffle on, to awaala'chi

put a spell on, to ayoshkammi
put a straight handle on, to oppi
put a tail on, to atakchichi
put across, to abaanali, lhopo'chi,
  lhopollichi, okkawalli
put an additional on, to imalbitili
put an awning over, to atiipoli
put another on, to intalbitili
put around, to afooloblichi,
  apakfohchi
put aside, to ilatoba
put away in the wrong place, to
  ittashommi
put back, to falammichi
put dirt on, to apihchi
put down along with, to ibaa-
  akkowachi, ibaabohli
put down in a heap, to lhatabli
put down in, to talaali
put down on, to onashaachi,
  ootombohli, ootonashaachi,
  ootonkahli, oot<u>o</u>lhatabli
put down, to akkaalínchi, akkihci,
  akkowachi, ashaachi, bohli,
  ikahooba'lo, talaali
put down, to help ibaa-akkowachi
put handcuffs on, to ilbak intakchi,
  ilbak takchi
put in a pile, to ashaachi
put in along with, to ibaa-ani,
  ibaafokhi
put in charge of, to apihchi
put in for, to imambihli, <u>i</u>fokhi
put in one's mouth, to káppa'li
put in the bank, to bohli
put in the dark, to imoklhilichi
put in or into, to abihli, fokhi,
  okaafimmi, okaakanchi, okaalh<u>a</u>'li,
  okaatalaali, okaatalooli,
  okaawayaachi, okaawayoochi,
  pitfokhi
put in, to be albí'ha, albihat m<u>á</u>a,
  fokha
put in water, to oka' pitokaakanchi,

oka' pitokaawayaachi
put in with, to pitibaafokhi
put into a container, to be alhto
put into (someone's) hand, to ilbak
  <u>i</u>fokhi
put into, to ani
put (medicine) on one's head, to lhili
put more in for, to imbaani
put more than one additional on, to
  imalbilli, intalbitli
put next to each other, to ittapootoli
put next to, to apaatali, apootoli,
  imaapatachi, tikiichi
put on (a backpack), to shaapoli
put on (a belt), to askoffachi
put on a bracelet, to ilbak apakfo'li'
  apakfolli
put on (a hat), to yaalhipili
put on (a sash), to hanaawi'li,
  hanaawiichi
put on (a turban), to yaachikoli
put on airs, to fínha
put on an additional, to ittalbitili
put on an apron, to tikba-takaachi
put on another, to albitili
put on crooked, to shanaayo'li
put on each other, to ittoonashaachi
put on face powder, to ilitohbichi
put on (gloves), to fokhi
put on makeup, to ishshoka' incho'li
put on more than one additional, to
  albilli, ittalbilli
put on one's back, to sha'li
put on one's face, to apoolosli
put on one's head, to yaachakali,
  yaatalaali
put on oneself, to ilontalaali
put on over another layer, to be
  albítti'ya
put on over others, to be albitkachi
put on perfume, to ilibilamachi
put on (shoes) holo, holochi
put on (someone's) head, to
  yaachakachi, yaatalaachi

put on the back of, to oshshaachi
put on the floor, to palli, patali
put on, to fokha, inampila, nampila, ompalli, ompatali, ontalaali, ontalooli, oshtombohli, oshtonashaachi, oshtonkahli
put on war paint, to ilincho'li, ishshoka' incho'li
put on wrong, to ittishaniili
put one on top of the other, to ittalalli, ittalaatali
put one's arms around, to apakfoota
put one's chin in the air, to abakshowali
put one's hand in and grab, to okaayinoffi
put one's head up, to abáwwa'a
put one's head way back, to abakshowa'li
put one's legs apart, to wakchalali
put out a hand to break one's fall, to bitiipa
put out for, to intalaali, intalooli
put out leaves, to woksholi
put out new shoots, to onchololi
put out of one's mind, to imalhkaniya
put out, to kochchaakaali, kochchichi, moshoochi

put over, to abaanappichi
put sideways, to okkawaatali
put some more in, to ibaani
put stripes on, to basoowachi
put the facts in the paper, to annowachi, annoyachi
put through, to aalhopollichi, lhopo'chi, lhopollichi
put, to oshtolhatabli
put to bed, to bohli
put to bed with, to ootibaabohli
put to sleep, to ishnosichi, nosichi, shimohli
put to sleep with, to ibaanosichi
put together, to ittachakali, ittachakli, ittibaakaachi, ittibaani
put up a barricade against, to imokkawaatali
put up a shade, to hoshottikachi
put up as security, to atochi
put up barricades against, to imokkawalli
put up (dirt) to guard new plants, to apiichi
put up, to apihlínchi, ashaachi, sitili, wayaachi, wayoochi
put up, to be sita
put whiskers on, to bakwoshochi
putty lokfi' chakissa'

q

quail kofi
quail, type of kof-oshi'
quarter, for the moon to be in its last hashi'at kaniyat ishtaya
quarter, to oshtali
queen ihoo minko'
queen bee fohi' inkapittani', fohi' ishki', fohi' iminko'
question carefully, to chokmat imasilhha

quicker than expected, to be chiiki
quickly chiiko'si'
quickly, to happen himonali
quicksand shinok toshpa'
quiet for, to imapoolhali
quiet, to apoolhali
quiet, to be chokkilissa, samata
quiet, to get noktala
quiet, to make chokkilissachi
quill pen foshi' hishi' ishholissochi'

quilt

quilt naachi, topaalhiipi'ya'—*see
also* quilt, type of
quilt batting naachanonkalatta'a'
quilt block nannittapatkachi'

quilt, pieced ittapalli', ittapatkachi'
quilt, type of naachittapatkachi'
quinine ittish homi', yanha kobaffi'
quit, to aaissachi

r

rabbit chokfi
rabbit, type of chokfi lakna', chokfi
loma', chokfokchamali', chokfoshi',
chokfoshtaka'li', oktaak chokfi'
rabbit's foot chokfiyyi'
raccoon shawi'
race against each other, to ittintilhaa,
ittintilhili
race, to ittimayyachi, ittimpalammi,
ittimpalammichi, ittintilhaa,
tilhaachi
racially mixed group, to be a
ittashoma
radiator, car oka' aalhto'
radio nannola'
rafters ishholmo' ihiyohli'
ragged, to be lhipa, táyya'ha
raggedy, to be taha
rag naalhila'fa', naalhipa'
rags naalhilahli'
rail fence itti' palha' holitta
railing aayo'kli'
railroad tali' hina'
railroad bridge itti' chanaa malili' aa-
abaanabli'
railroad crossing itti' chanaa malili'
hina' aabaanapo'li', tali' hina'
aabaanabli'
railroad crossing guard itti' basha'
tali-hina' aalhopolli' aahiliichi'
railroad spike tali' chofak
railroad station chanaa malili'
aahika', itti' chanaa malili' aahika'
railroad tie itti' chanaa malili' ihina'
inkaha', tali' hina' inkaha'

railroad track itti' chanaa malili'
ihina', tali' hina'
railroad train itti' chanaa malili'
rain omba
rain and sun at the same time, for
there to be Siitanat imihoo fammi
rain barrel oka' aalhto', oka' aayoka',
oka' ishyokachi', okombaalhto'
rain in little drops, for it to oka'at
chaafoochi
rain on one, to have it oshobbichi
rain on, to onomba
rain, to omba
rain, to make it ombachi
rainbow Chihoowa inaalhpisa',
hashaanokpila', nakbatiipoli',
ninak ontoomi
raincoat omba fo'kha'
rained on, to be onomba
rainwater okomba'
raise and lower one's arms at the
sides, to wahhalkachi
raise one's eyebrows, to okmiloli
raise, to aba' pilachi, abaawaachi,
abaawiili, apooba, hofantichi
raise with, to ibaahofantichi
raisins panki' shila'
rake ishkala'fa'
rake, buck hashshok ishkala'fa'
rake handle ishkala'fa' aalhpi'
rake, to kalaffi
rally ishtittanaha'
ramp aatoyya'
rancid, to be kotoma
rape, to yokachi, yokli

488

rash, to have a hoshonnachi
rat shanti'
rat, type of shanti' losa', shanti'
 tohbi'
rattle nanna washaachi',
 ittiwasha'chi', ittiwashasha'chi',
 sintinchasha'
rattle around and make noise, to
 ittichalhaahánchi
rattle, baby's ishtittichaalha'chi'
rattle, to chalha'chi, chalhaahánchi,
 ittiwashashá'chi, ittichalhalhá'chi,
 ittichámmakli'chi, washa'chi,
 washaachi, washashá'chi
rattlesnake ittiwasha'chi',
 ittiwashanchi', sintishtahollo',
 sishto'
rattling inside, to make the sound of
 cham cham cham aachi, chamak
 chamak chamak aachi
rattling sound, to make a chash
 chash chash aachi, chashak chashak
 chashak aachi, ittichalha'chi,
 ittichálhlhakli'chi, ittichasha'chi,
 ittichashashá'chi, ittiwashashá'chi,
 ittiwáshshakli'chi, shol shol shol
 aachi, wash wash wash aachi
rattling, to make the sound of dishes
 ittichama'chi, ittichamamá'chi
rattling, to make the sound of little
 parts chalh chalh chalh aachi,
 chalhak chalhak chalhak aachi
raven fala ishto'
raw, to be okchánki
raw, to be rubbed mokofa
raw, to rub mokoffi
rawhide hakshop okchanki'
razor ishtilishafi', notakhish
 ishshafi'
razor, straight notakhish ishshafi'
 falaa'
razor strop aahaloppachi',
 ishtilishafi' aahaloppachi'
reach and touch, to pithalili

reach out and hug, to pitshooli
reach out to touch, to halili
reach, to ona
reach, to just barely óhho'na
reach, to make onachi
read in the paper, to anompa pisa
read to, to imittimanompoli, iriidi
read, to ittimanompoli; *also*
 holissintoshooli, holisso toshooli
ready to polla
ready, to be alhtaha, imalhtaha
ready to die, to look lhakcha
ready, to get atáhli
real thing, the mi finha'
realize, to finally ootkostini
really chokma, kanihka, polla
really do it, to ittakánni'ya
realm imaapihlichika'
rear end imashaka', ishtaabinili'
rear with, to ibaahofantichi
rear, to hofantichi
reason, for some kanihmihma,
 kanihchihma
reason, for what kanihchiho
recede, to akka
receipt ishtalhlhi'
receive along with, to ibaahabina
receive at, to aahabina
receive for, to ihabina
receive, to habina, inkashapa
recognize, to ithana
recollect, to nokfokha
reconcile, to ittinkana, ittifalama,
 ittifalammichi
record player nannola'
recorded with, to have one's name
 ibaaholisso
rectum ishkish cholok
red all over, to be hommakbi
red light aashoppala' homma'
red liniment ittish homma'
red onion atofalla'a' homma'
red pepper hommahomma'
Red River Abookoshi Homma'

489

red root

red root hahtok
Red Spring Kali Homma'
red, to be homma
red, to be dark hommayyi
red, to make hommachi
red worm saalhkona
redbird foshhommak, foshi'
  hommak
redbud tree taka'staa'
red-tailed hawk akankabi' hasimbish
  homma'
reduce the price of, to alhchonachi
reed oskapi'
reel aapakfoha'
referee chokoshkomo-apiisachi'
refrain from doing something, to
  ilihalalli
refried beans bala' awaalhaali',
  oshpaanimbala'
refrigerator car nannaakapassali'
refuse things, to always ilimihachi
refuse to change one's mind, to
  chonkash kallochi
refuse to go along with authority, to
  ilaafowa
refuse to go, to ilaafowa ikbanno
regain consciousness, to ootithana
registered together with, to be
  ittibaaholisso
registered with, to be ibaaholisso
rehearse, to imaabalhchi
reinjure a sore spot, to intiibli
reinjure one's own sore spot, to
  intiipa
reinjure, to intiipa, tiibli
reinjured in, to keep being
  intiipo'wa
reinjuring, to keep on intiipo'li,
  tiipo'li
rejoice, to nannishtilayoppa
relapse, to have a aafilima
related, to be ittapiha
relationship, to have a ittihaalálli
relationship with, to have a

homosexual ihoo intoba
relatives ittapihaka'a
release, to talhoffichi
released, to be holhtofa
religion, old-time Indian Ishki'
  Oshta'
religion, to get ilikostinichi
religious holiday Chihoowa inittak
  holitto'pa, nittak holitto'pa'
religious meeting
  abaanompittanaha'
religious service, old-time Indian
  Ishki' Oshta' aaittanaha'
religious, to become ootilikostinichi
reluctant to talk to, to be inokwaya
remain, to ahánta, álhto, ásha, áshwa
remainder lakchi'
remember, to nokfónkha
remind, to nokfokhachi
remove along with, to ashokaffi
remove the leaves and fruit from, to
  lhifi
remove, to shihli, shifi
renew, to himittachi
renovate, to himittachi, himonachi
rent, to ponta
rent to, to imponta
renter hattak chokkimponta'
repeat once, to albitili
repent, to ilikostinichi
reporter nannanoli'
repossess things from, to awihpoli
representation holba'
representation of someone hattak
  holba'
reproach oneself, to ilihofahyachi
reproduce oneself, to ilatobachi
Republican party Falammi
rescued, to be okchaalínchi
research in, to silhlhi
resemble, to ahooba
resemble, to make ahoobachi
reservation, Indian hattak api'
  homma' aa-asha

490

reserve for, to imilatómba
reservoir oka' aalhto', oka' aayoka',
oka' aayokachi'
resist, to ilaafowa, ilaafowa ikbanno,
imilaafowa
responsibility on, to impose a serious
anompa kallo' onhochi
rest across, to come to ootawaata
rest in, to aafoha
rest in, to let aafohachi
rest stop aafoha'
rest, to aafoha, foha, nokchito
rest, to make fohachi, nokchitoli
restrict oneself, to ilatoba
Resurrection, the Illit Falamat Taani'
retarded, not to be imaanokfila-at
imóma, imaanokfila-at móma
retire, to foha
retire, to make fohachi
retriever foshi-hoyo'
return from, to go to and ootfalama
return, to falama, falammichi,
falamo'chi
return to, to ifalama, ifalammichi
rev, to ittiwininí'chi, ittiwini'chi
reveal to, to imoktanichi
revealed, to be ootoktani
revelation nannishtalhtoko'wa',
nannoktani'
Revelation, Book of Nannoktani'
Holisso
revenge, to get imaatobbi,
ittillawi'chi
reverse tannap
revolver tanamposhkololi'
rheumatism, to have komoochi
Rhode Island Red akanka' homma'
rib naksi'
ribbon pasita
ribbon, hair pasita ishtalakchi'
ribbon headdress pasita
rice haaloshi'
rich, to be alhpísa, holiitopa
rick itti' alhpisa'

ride sidesaddle, to sontalhpo' filli'tat
ombinni'li
ride, to ombiniili, ombínni'li,
onchí'ya
ride to, to give a ayowa
rifle, .22 tanampiskanno'
rifle, Winchester tanampo falaa'
right aalhpi'sa'
right behind, to be awwali'chi
right now himmako'si finha
right thing, to think one is doing the
aalhpí'sa
right, to be alhpí'sa
right, to make alhpisa'chi, alhpissa'li
righteous, to be aalhpí'sa
rind hakshop
ring ilbak shalbi'ya'
ring around the moon
hashaakonoli'
ring finger ilbak ilbak
shalbi'yaafokha'
ring for hanging ishtaatakaali'
ring, to chamamá'chi, chamaachi,
ola, olachi, samaachi
ring, to have one's head achaamapa
ringworm, to have halambabi
rinse, to achifachi, albitichi, albitit
achifa
rip out, to pataachi
rip the clothes off, to chakbakachi
rip, to lhilaffi, pataffi
ripe fruit, to have waa
ripe, to be lhábbo'cha, nona
ripen, to alaknachi, waachi
ripening, to turn color while ataachi
ripped out, to be patahli
ripped, to be patafa
rippling, to be payo'kalhchi
rise from the dead, to illitokmat
falamat taani, illitokoot falamat
taani, taani
rise, for the dead to illitokoot falamat
taani
rise, for the sun to hashi'at kochcha

rise, to abaawaa, kochcha, shatabli
rise, to have a clous of dust shobolli
rise, to make shatablichi
river abookoshi'—*see also names of specific rivers*
river bed, dry abookoshi' shila'
riverbank abookoshi' apotaka', oka' takchaka'
road hina'
road with a dip in it hina' aatakafa'
roadrunner foshi' palhki'
roar, to kiliha, winiiyachi
roast each other, to ittaaposhli
roast, to aposhli
roasted corn tanchalhposha'
roasted, to be alhposha
roasting pan asonnak patha'
rob, to wihpoli
rob using, to ishwihpoli
rock tali'—*see also* rock, type of
rock back and forth, to fayya'kalhchi
rock, little pieces of tali' lakchi'
rock salt hapi kallo'
rock, to imbaayo'chi, ifaya'chi
rock, type of tali' bosholli', tali' ishshoppantik
rocking chair aabiniili' tono'chi', aaombiniili' faya'kachi'
rocks, to throw bohpoli
rocky, to be kalhkaki
rod, fishing nanishholhtosi'
rod with something at the top, to be a bare fáhha'ko
rodeo waaka' takchi'
rodeo grounds waakaatakchi'
rodeo rider issobombinili'
roll a cigarette, to chomak hoboona
roll around in, to aatono'li, aatonolli, okaashala'li, okaatono'li
roll around, to tonnonónkalhchi, tonnonóli
roll into a ball, to lhiboktachi
roll number iholhtina'
roll oneself up in, to ilaboknohli, ilapakfolli
roll out on, to ontono'chi
roll out, to patassali
roll, to bánnalli, chanahli, chanalli, chanallichi, chanaa, intono'chi, polhommi, tono'chi, tono'kalhchi, tono'li, tonolli, tonollichi
roll, to make chanaachi, tono'chi
roll up, to banalli, banallichi, polhlhi
rolled out on, to be ontono'kalhchi
rolled up in, to be ilapakfóyyo'lli
rolled up, to be banaa
rolling pin paskishtonton'kalhchi', tili'ko' issatapo'li'
roof abooha pakna', chokka' pakna'
roof beams ishholmo' into'wa'
roof on for, to put a ihomo
roof, to homo
roofed outdoor gathering place hoshottika'
roofed, to be holmo
roofing material ishholmo'
room abooha
room, in the other abooha tannap
room, side abooha lapa'li'
room, the other abooha chaffo'
room with, to ibaa-atta
rooster akanka' nakni'
rooster spurs akanka' ishtimittibi', akankinchofak
rooster's comb akankihashintak
root hakshish, ishtaahikki'ya'—*see also* root, type of
root in the ground, to yoko'chi
root of a tree itti' hakshish
root, red hahtok
root, type of hakshish falakto'
rope ishtalakchi'
rope, to takchi
rope, to jump ishtalakchi' malli, malli
rot, to toshbi, toshbichi
rotate, to chanahli
rotten, to be toshbi

rotten, to smell hawashko
rough, to be chilabli
roughen chilablichi
round and firm lobo'
round and firm, to be yabbobónka'chi
round and spreading, to be wahhala
round head, to have a oshkoboli
round projection ibish
round, to be bolokta, lhibokta, lhibowa, missila, tilikpi
round, to be kind of missílli'ya
round, to make lhiboktachi, lhibowachi
rounded bottom, to have a lómbo
rouse, to inkaba'chi, inkasa'chi
row ihina'
rows, to go along in separate bayalli
rub (medicine) on one's head, to lhili
rub in, to ilaabi
rub on, to aabi
rub one's eyes, to ishkin koyohli
rub raw, to mokoffi
rub, to kalho'chi, pashohli, shoochi
rub together, to ishtittishoochi
rubbed raw, to be mokofa
rubbed, to be shoowalhchi
rubber naashiipa', raba'
rubber ball raba' to'wa'
rubber boots sholosh naashiipa' aatoba'
rubber glove ilbak fo'khi' shiipa', raba' ilbak fo'khi'
rubbing alcohol foni' hottopa' tish, tish ishtilihammichi'
rude to, to be ishtayóbba'li ki'yo
ruffle, to awaala'chi
ruffled, to be awaala'kachi, awaala'kalhchi
rug akka' patalhpo'
ruin for, to imayoppani'chi
ruin, to oppani
ruined, to be ayoppolo'ka, bosholli, imayoppóllo'ka, oppolo, yilhipa
ruler naaishtalhpisa'

rumble, to ittiwininí'chi, ittiwini'chi, winiiyachi
rumor anompa chokoshpa'
rumor, for there to be a anompaat chokoshpa
rumor, to be the anompaat inchokoshpa
rumored about, to be anompinchokoshpa
rumors about, to spread anompinchokoshpali
rumors, to spread anompa chokoshpali
run against one another, to ittintilhaa, ittintilhaachi, ittintilhili
run against, to aasanali, intilhaa
run around like crazy, to ittolat folo'kachi
run around, to bilo'chit nowa, toklhakafa
run around with, to nowat ibaahaksi
run away from, to imalili, malit inkaniya
run away, to malit aakaniya, malit kaniya
run by in front of, to ootimokkawaatali
run by, to take from and ootishtimalili
run down, to yanahli, yanalli
run for office, to malili, tilhaa
run from, to intilhaa
run off from, to intilhili
run off, to chaffichi, malichi, tilhili; also yanalli
run off together, to ishtittaamowa
run onto, to amasali
run out of, to have intaha
run over, to abaanapa, abaanappichi
run, to malili, tilhaa; also malíli
run, to have the color masali
run, to make malichi, tilhaachi, tilhili
run, to make a holhtina-chaffaho

493

run, to make a home

ikbi, malili, malit afoolopa, malit
folota
run, to make a home immo̲'t folota,
ootafoolopa, ootfolota
run to, to pitmalili
run together, to have the colors
ittimasalichi
rung aao̲hika'
running sound, to make a
ittimiti'chi
runny nose, to have a ibilhkanat

lhatapa
rupture salhkona kochcha'
rustle, to ittishoko'chi
rustling sound with for, to make a
intishoko'chi
rustling sound, to make a chash
chash chash aachi, chashak chashak
chashak aachi, ittichasha'chi,
ittichashashá'chi
rusty, to be lokfi-toba

S

saccharin shookola' holba'
sack shokcha
sack, flour tili'ki̲shokcha
sad about, to be ishtikimalhpi'so
sad, to be ikimalhpi'so, nokhánglo;
also alhkayya, inchokkillissa,
ishtikayoppo
sad, to make alhkayyachi,
nokhanglochi
sad with, to be ibaanokhánglo
saddle issobompatalhpo', sontalhpo'
saddle blanket issobompatalhpo'
safe from, to be i̲lhakoffi
safe, to be lhako̲fi
safety pin bakshiyamashtasitti'ya',
chofaakoshi'
sag, to okaahofobi
saggy skin, to have lhi̲fa
saint naayimmi'
salad tohi' wasacha'
salesman nankanchi'
saliva itokchi'
salivate, to itokchaat lawa
salivate, to make itokchi' lawachi
saloon aaishko', nannaaishko'
salt hapi, hapi poshi'
salt, a pinch of hapi chino'fa'si
salt lick hapi aafohli', waaki̲hapi

salt pork nipi' hapayyima', shokha'
nipi' shila'
salt, rock hapi kallo'
salt shaker hapi aalhto'
salt, to hapayyimmi
salt water oka' hapayyima'
salty, to be hapayyima, hapi homi
same mihaashayni
same back to, to do the i̲falammichi
same, not to be the mihaash ikholbo
same, on the ittinchaffa̲li'
same one, the mihaash, mihoot
same, the mi
same, to be the aakani̲'tokat
ímmo'ma, ímmo'ma, ishtáyya'ma,
ittihooba, i̲'ma, kani̲'tokat
ímmo'ma
same, to have the ittachaffa,
ittichaffa, ittinchaffa
San Francisco Falisko'
sand shinok—*see also* sand, type of
sand on, to get shakawachi
sand, type of shinok homma',
shinok losa', shinok tohbi'
sandbox shinok aalhto'
sandpaper holisso
nannishtilawwichi',
nannishlhimishkochi', shinok

494

holisso
sandstorm shinok shobolli'
sandwich, meat paska nipi'
  ittalatta'a'
sandy, to be shinok bíyyi'ka
sandy, to taste shakawa
sap itti' okchi'
sap from peach trees tak<u>o</u>lokchi',
  tak<u>o</u>lo inchakissa'
sap, plant albokchi'
sap, white plant albimpishokchi'
sash hanaawi'li'
sash, beaded oksop hanaawi'li'
sass at, to achapa
sassafras kafi'
sassafras tree itti' kafi'
Satan Siitan
satisfied, to be never ilamákka'li
Saturday Nittak Hollo' Nakfish,
  Nittak Ishhanna'li'
saucer kaafaaishkimpatha'
sauerkraut tohi' hawashko'
sausage nipi' foloha'
save for seed pinhachi
save for, to imilatómba
save, to ilatoba, lhakoffínchi,
  okchaalínchi
saved, to be ilikostinichi, naayimmi'
  toba
saved, to get ootilikostinichi
Savior Okchaalinchi'
saw ittishbasha'
saw, to bashli
sawdust itti' bosholli'
sawed, to be basha
sawhorse issoba, itti' aabashli'
sawmill ittaabasha', itti' aabashli'
sawteeth ittishbasha' noti'
sawtoothed pattern, to make a
  chakchakichi
sawtoothed, to be chakchaki
sawyer beetle, spotted kiitatak
say about oneself, to miha
say anything, not to nokwaya

say bad things about, to ayyobba'li
  ki'yo
say hoorah for, to ayiimillichi
say it, to just pila aachi
say something funny, to yoppola
say suggestive things to, to
  ishtakaanihmichi
say things without foundation, to
  chokoshpali
say, to aachi; also anompoli, miha
say to each other, to ittimaachi
say, to make hochifochi
say to, to imaachi
scab hakshop shila'
scab, to form a shila
scald, to yokoffi
scalded, to be yokofa
scale nannaawiikichi'
scallop, to chakchakichi
scalloped, to be chakchaki
scare each other, to ittimalhallichi,
  ittimilhlhali, itt<u>i</u>malhata
scare off, to imilhlhali, tilhili
scare, to imilhlhali, malhallichi
scarecrow fala imilhlhali'
scared in, to get aaimilhlha
scared of each other, to be itt<u>i</u>malhata
scared of, to be <u>i</u>malhata
scared, to be imilhlha, malhata
scared to speak, to be nokw<u>á</u>ya
scared with, to be ibaaimilhlha
scaredycat imilhlhabi'
scaredycat, to be a imilhlhabi
scarf innochi', yaalhipi'li'
scatter all over, to ittafimobli
scatter, to tiwapa
scattered bíyyi'ka
scattered all over, to be fímmo'pa,
  ittafímmo'pa, ittafimopa
scattered around alone, to be
  ilachaffa bíyyi'ka
school holissaapisa'
school, to go to holisso pisa
schoolteacher holisso-pisachi'

scissors ishkalasha'
scissors, small ishkalasha'
iskanno'si'
scissors, to cut with kachiili
scissortail foshi' ishkalasha'
hasimbish, hilowifoshi'
scold, to nókko'wa
scoop nannishtakli'
scooped out, to have part okaatakafa
scorch, to ashama, ashamachi,
ashamali, hoshbali
scorched, to be hoshba
score as, to have almost as good a
láwwi'chi
score, to holhtina-chaffaho ikbi
score, to have a ittillawwi
score, to have a tie ittatalakchi
scorpion hasimbish chanaa'
scramble up, to fattaala
scrape off, to pishoochi, shafi
scrape, to pilhoffi, pilhohchi, pishoffi,
pishohchi, shaachi
scraped off, to have the hair shafa
scraped, to be pilhofa, pilhohli,
pishohli, shaalhchi
scraping sound, to make a
ittishola'chi, ittisholalá'chi,
ittishóllakli'chi, shol shol shol
aachi
scratch an itch, to ilishaachi
scratch oneself, to ilikalli, ilishaachi
scratch out one's hair, to iliboyaachi
scratch, to inkalli, kalli, shaffi,
sholaffi, sholli
scratched, to be lhilahli, pishohli,
sholafa, sholahli
scratching sound, to make a
ittishóllakli'chi, shol shol shol
aachi
scratchy, to be haloppa
scream at, to ontasahli
scream, to tasahli
scream to, to intasahli
screech owl ofolo

screen tali' shachakla'
screw naaishtashana'
screwdriver naaishtashannichi'
scuff, to pilhohchi
scuffed, to be pilhohli, shoowalhchi
scythe hashshok ishtamo'
sea okkata
seagull okkata foshi'
seamstress naafkimacho'li'
seashore okkatapootaka'
season with, to ayammi, yammichi
seasoned, to be highly yammi
seat ishtaabini'li'
seclusion, to be in tabashi
second one for, to be a imatoklanchi
second time, to be the atóngla
second time, to do for the atoklánchi
second, to be ishtatokla
second, to be the atokla
second, to have as one's atoklónchi
secret nanna loma'
secret lover, to have as a ilomaka
secret, to keep lohmi
secret, to keep a lohmit í'shi
secretary holissochi'
section line yaakni' aaittachakkachi'
security for, to use as ishponta
security guard okkisa' atooni'
sedative ishnosi'
sedge, brown hashshok haloppa'
sediment settled, to have the
okaatalaka
seduce, to hotosi, ihaksina ibaanosi,
ishtakaanihmichi
seduce, to cause to hotosichi
seduced with a medicinal charm, to
be holhtosi
see a mirage, to iholba
see by touch, to bitkat pisa
see each other in, to aaittipisa
see each other, to ittipisa
see from, to aapisa, pitaapisa
see in the future, to tingbalísht anoli
see in, to aapisa

see one another secretly, to lomat
ittipisa
see oneself in, to aailipisa
see oneself, to ilipisa
see through, to lhopollichit písa
see, to pisa, písa
see, to come pist ala
see, to gather to alokoochi,
ootalokoli, ootalokoochi
see, to go ootpisa, pist aya
see with one's own eyes, to ishkin
ishpísa
see with, to ibaapísa
see-through, to be tapaski
seed nihi'
seed corn tanchi' pinha'
seed tick shatanni nihi',
shatannoshi'
seed, to save for pinhachi
seedless grapes panki' nihiksho'
seeds from, to separate the nihichi
seem like, to ahooba, chihmi
seem like, to have it imahooba
seen, to be oktáni
seesaw, to ittimbaayo'chi
seine, to hokaachi
seizure, to have a hayoochichi
select for a team, to ayowa, ayoowa
select from a group, to aayoowa
select, to hochifo, pafi
selfish, to be naaishtimaholiito'pa
sell, to kanchi
sell to, to inkanchi
selvedge taakchaka'
Seminole Mashkooki',
Shimmanooli'
Seminole language
Shimmanoolimanompa'
Seminole language, Creek-
Mashkookanompa'
Seminole Nation
Shimmanooliyaakni'
send an answer to, to
anompifalammichi

send away, to chaffichi, tilhili
send back, to tilhili
send for, to come and get and
atimpilachi
send for, to go and get and
ootimpilachi
send off, to ayachi
send off, to take over and ootpilachi
send off to, to oshtimpilachi
send oneself, to ilipilachi
send oneself to, to imilipilachi
send smoke signals, to shobohchi
send smoke signals to, to ishobohchi
send this way, to oshpilachi
send, to pilachi, pitchaffichi,
pittilhili, pitpilachi
send to each other, to ittimpilachi
send to oneself, to ilimpilachi
send to prison, to toksalichi
send to, to impilachi, oshtinchaffichi
send with, to ibaachaffichi,
ibaapilachi, pitibaachaffichi
senses, to come to one's kostini
sensitive to the presence of spirits, to
be imaaholba
sent to prison, to be toksalit atobbi
sentence, to anompa kallo' onhochi
sentence to do something, to
inaapiisa
separate from, to ifilammi,
ifilamo'chi
separate rows, to go along in bayalli
separate the seeds from, to nihichi
separate, to ittachaafoochi,
ittifilammi, ittifilammichi,
ittifilamo'chi, ittifilamo'li
separated, to be talhoffi
serious about, not to be ishyoppola
serious, to be palammi
seriously affected, to be impalammi
servant toksali'
serve as, to tóhho'ba
serves you right ahaa
service for, to have a memorial aa-

497

akshochi
service, memorial aa-aksho', aa-
akshochi'
service, to be in the tashka-chipota'
ibaafóyyokha
service, to have a ittanaha
set afire, to kilili
set down on, to ombiniichi
set down, to akkowachi, binohchi,
talaali
set, for the table to be amposhi'at
ontalowa
set into, to okaatalaali, okaatalooli,
okaawayaachi, okaawayoochi
set next to, to ibaatalaali
set on a slant, to nakbichi
set on a slanted surface nakbi
set on fire, to lowachi
set out, to be kina
set, person whose mind is chonkash
kallo'
set the table, to amposhi' ontalohli
set, to ittilawwichi, kallo
set, to be ittilawwi, ontaloha
set up in, to okaahilichi,
okaahiyohchi
set up on a flat bottom, to be tálla'a
set up on flat bottoms, to be tállo'wa,
talowat máa
set up, to talohli, wayaachi, wayoochi
set up with, to ibaatalaali
setting hen akankalaata'
settle, to bowafa, okaabowafa,
pitbowafa
settled, to have the sediment
okaatalaka
seven ontoklo
seven in number, to be ontoklo
Seven Stars Fochik Ontoklo'
seven times hiyontoklo'
seven, to be in groups of ontoklo
áyyo'ka
seventeen awa ontoklo,
pokolontoklo

seventeen in number, to be awa
ontoklo
seventh, to be ishtontoklo
seventy pokoli ontoklo
seventy in number, to be pokoli
ontoklo
seventy-five cents bit hanna'li
several kánnohmi, kannohmihmat,
kannohmihma
several, to have inkannohmi
sew a zigzag stitch, to falamo'sht
acho'li
sew for, to imacho'li
sew, to acho'li, naacho'li
sew together, to ittapaatali, ittashiichi
sewed on, to be ontálla'a
sewed, to be alhcho'wa
sewed together, to be ittapatkachi,
ittapátta'a
sewed up wrong, to be ittashiiyalhchi
sewn, to be alhcho'wa
sex organ immi', ishkish
sex-crazed, to be haksit kánni'ya
sexual intercourse, to have ittihosha,
ittilapali, ittayoshkammi
sexual intercourse with, to have
hosha, lapali
sexual intercourse with, to lie down
to have into'wa
sexual partner, to have as an
additional ayinínchi
sexually aroused, to be impalli, palli
shack up, to ittihayoochi, táwwa'a
shack up with, to iláwwi'li
shade for, to make ihoshottikachi
shade on, to make ohoshottikachi
shade oneself, to ilohoshontikachi
shade, to ohoshottika
shade, to make hoshontikachi
shade, to put up a hoshottikachi
shade, window winda' takaali'
shaded by, to be ohoshottika
shadow hoshontikachi'
shadow stretching between clouds

and the earth, for there to be bars of
bashi'at oka' oochi
shady area aahoshottika'
shady on, to be ohoshottika
shady, to be aahoshottínka,
hoshottika
shake hands with, to make
ayoppachichi
shake oneself, to fatatá'chi,
ilifata'chi, ittifatatá'chi, iliwilooli
shake, to fahli, fata'chi, faya'chi,
ilhko'chi, ilhko'kóli, ilhko'li,
washa'chi, wilooli, yaboffi, yollichi
shake, to make yollichichi
shaken out, to be wiloha
shaking fit, to have a abikimilhkooli
shaking, to make a noise ittifata'chi,
ittifatatá'chi, ittifáttakli'chi
shallow, to be malassa
shampoo ishtayili'
shape, to be out of hayifa
share (clothes) with, to ibaafokha
share expenses on, to ittibaatobbi
share of, to get a ittakashkowa
share out, to kashkoli
share, to ittakaashabli, ittakashkoli,
kashabli
share, to get a inkashapa
share with, to inkashabli
Sharkey Ishaaki'
sharp thing naahaloppa'
sharp, to be haloppa
sharpen, to bakshakachi, haloppachi
sharpen to a point, to oshkibichi
sharpener nannishhaloppachi'
sharpening, stone for aahaloppachi'
shatter against, to abooshollichi
shatter, to imbosholli
shave in, to aailishafi
shave (someone's) head, to masofi
shave, to ilishafi, shafi
shawl a'chi'
she mi, mihoot, yammakot, yammat,
yappakot, yappat

she and she alone ilaapakilloot
she herself ilaapakaynihaat,
ilaapakaynihoot
she herself also ilaapakya
shears, pinking ishkalasha'
chakchaki'
shears, pruning ittishkatolhlhi'
shed hoshottika'
shed on, to be omboyafa
shed one's feathers, to iliboyaffichi
shed one's skin, to lhofa, ililhofi
shed, to boyafa, boyahli
sheep chokfalhpooba', chokfi, chokfi
ishto'—see also sheep, type of
sheep sorrel pilhchi'
sheep, type of chokfi hishi' falaa',
chokfi losa', chokfi woksho'
sheepdog ofi' woksho'
sheet patalhpalhiipi'ya',
topompatalhpo'
sheet, type of naaittapa'ta'
shell hakshop
shell casing naki' hakshop
shell, little nak-oshi'
shell, to chilokka, loffichi
shell, to be in the lómbo
shell, turtle loksi' hakshop
shelled, to be lofalhchi
shelter hoshottika' hattak aa-asha'
shelter, women's hoshottika' ihoo
aa-asha'
shelves, kitchen amposhaa-asha'
shepherd chokfalhpoobapiisachi'
sheriff naa-alhtoka'
sheriff's badge fochik ilontalaali'
Shetland pony issoba imo'ma'
shield ishtittibi'
shimmer in the heat, to bin-kachi
shin iyyinchamo'
shine on, to ontoomi, ohashtahli,
oshoppala, oshoppalali
shine, to shokkawali, shokmalachi,
shokmalali, shokmálla'li, toomi
shingles itti' cholha'

shiny from rubbing, to be
shoowalhchi
shiny, to be aainchaa' bíyyi'ka,
shokmalla'máli, shokmalali
shirt naafka lo'bo'
shiver, to make yollichichi
shock, to get a holhpa, shimoha
shock, to give a shimohli
shock to, to give a holhpali,
shimohachi, shimoochi
shoe sholosh—see also shoe, type of
shoe buckle sholosh ishtasitti'ya'
shoe, heel of a sholosh iyyi' tako'bish
shoe polish sholosh ishshokmalachi'
shoe rack sholosh aa-abihli', sholosh
aa-albiya', sholosh aalhto'
shoe, sole of a sholosh iipatha'
shoe store sholosh aa-asha', sholosh
aachompa', sholosh aakanchi'
shoe, tongue of a sholosh isolash
shoe, type of itti' sholosh, sholosh
chaaha', sholosh iyyi' tako'bish
chaaha', sholosh latassa'
shoehorn sholosh ishholo'
shoelace sholosh ishtalakchi'
shoemaker sholosh alaatali'
shoes, high-heeled sholosh iyyi'
takho'bish chaaha'
shoes with pointed toes sholosh
bakshakali
shoestring sholosh ishtalakchi'
shoo away from, to intilhili
shoot along with, to ibaahosa,
ibaanalhlhi
shoot and hit, to nalhlhi
shoot at, to hosa
shoot at, to cause to hosachi
shooting star fochik malili'
shoots, to put out new onchololi
shop, butcher nipi' aabashli'
shop for, to inchompa
shop, tailor's naafkaaimaaiksaachi'
shop, to nanchompa
shore oka' takchaka'

short and stubby, to be oshkololi
short one, to be a pattalpáa
short, to be ikcha'ho, ikfala'o,
tilofa'si, pattala, pattálla'a
short, to be too chawwala,
chawwálla'a
short, to have one's skirt be too
inchawwala
short, to make tilofachi, chawwalili
shortcut, to take a apissat aya
shorten, to chashpochi, tilofachi
shortening niha
shorts balaafka' chawwala'
shorty, to be a pattalpáa
shot nakoshik
shot along with, to be ibaanalha
shot, to be nalha
shot, to give a ittish ani
shot, to make the sound of a gun
being paaw paaw paaw aachi
shotgun tanampo nakoshilawa'
shotgun, double-barreled
tanampincholok toklo', tanampo
pokta'
shoulder folop, ittaalhchi', shakba'
shoulder blade ittaalhchi' foni',
shakba' aaittachakka'
shoulder straps ishtilabanna'li'
shoulder, to ilabaanali
shoulder, to carry on one's ilabanali,
sha'li
shoulder, to help ilabanachi
shoulders, area between the
inchashwa, shanakha'
shoulders forward while walking, to
thrust one's panaayo'wa,
panaayoyówa
shoulders, to carry on one's ilabanali
shoulders, to walk with arms around
each other's ittishoyyo't tanówa
shove, to toopopóli
shovel lokfishpiha'
shovel, coal lowak ishpiha'
shovel, corn tanchishpiha'

show shoo
show a lot of leg, to chawwala, chawwálla'a
show books to, to holisso pisachi
show how to sing, to intaloowa
show off, to fínha, ilihaksichi, iloktanichi, ishtilahobbi
show off to, to imilahobbi, ishtimilahobbi
show oneself naked, to ilipisachi
show, to okfahchi, oktanichi, oktáni, ootkónchcha
show to each other, to ittipisachi
show to himself, to ilipisachi
show to, to pisachi
show up in front of, to imokfaha
show up to, to ootimokfaha
show up with unexpectedly, to ishtihaksi
show up, to okfaha, ootokfaha, ootokfahli
shower, to shobbichi
showing off, to go along pílat áa
showing, to be oktáni
shrink, to yokolli, yokota
shriveled, to be shayofa
shuck, to loffi
shucked, to be lofa
shucks, corn tanchi' hishi', tahishi'
shuffle, to ittashommi
shuffled, to be ittashoma
shut up, to chokilissachi, samata
shut up, to be albí'ha, albihat máa, alhto
shutter ishtokshilitta'
shutters winda' ishtokshilli'ta'
shy, to be hofahya
Siamese twins hattak pokta'
sibling ittibaapishi
sibling, half- ittibaapishi iklanna'
sibling, older intikba
sibling, younger nakfish
siblings, to be ittibaapishi
sic on each other, to ittaatohnochi

sic on, to atohnochi, onchaffichi
sick after overeating, to be imashama
sick all the time, to be abiikami
sick along with, to be ibaa-abika
sick as a result of contact with a menstruating woman or one who has just given birth, to be hollabi
sick for, to be imambiika
sick of, to be imintakho'bi
sick person abika'
sick, to be abika
sick, to make abikachi
sickly, to be abiikami, ilabiika'si bílli'ya, tikahámbi
sickness abika'
sickness from, to catch a abika' imaahalili, abika' ihalili
sickness, to catch a abika' halili
side apootaka', naksika'
side by side, to be ittitíkki'li
side by side, to be lined up ittimaapatohli
side in, to lie on one's achoknahaski
side of, just on the other mishintannap
side of, just on this olintannap
side of, on the other intannap
side of the house aboohapootaka'
side of the water oka' takchaka'
side of, to add on to the apaatali
side, on the naksika'
side, on the far tannap
side, on the other tannap
side, other tannap
side room abooha lapa'li'
side, to be lying on one's achaknaháski
side, to be on just one tannap pila'si
side, to go along the apootakaalínchi
side, to lean one's head to one akassanali
side, to lie on one's achaknaski
side, to make (someone) lean his head to one akassanachi

side, to turn on one's achaknaski
side, to turn on the achaknaskichi,
  achaknaskichit bohli
sides cut off, to have the talha
sidesaddle, to ride sontalhpo' filli'tat
  ombínni'li
sidewalk hattak aaittan<u>o</u>wa'
sideways, to be okkawaata
sideways, to look okkalali
sideways, to put okkawaatali
sift, to hayoochi
sifted, to be hayoha, hayowalhchi
sifter ishhayowalhchi', ishhayoochi',
  shayowachi'
sigh of relief, to give a fóyyo'pa
sign incho'wa', ishtoktani'
sign a document, to anomp<u>i</u>lh<u>a</u>fi
sign, inner nannishtalhtoko'wa'
Sign Language, to use American
  ilbak ishtanompoli
sign language, to use Indian ilbak
  ishtan<u>o</u>li
sign one's name, to holhchifo
  intakaachi
sign, to holisso <u>i</u>lh<u>a</u>fi
sign to, to ilbak ishtimanompoli
signals, to send smoke shoboochi
silk naafka loposhki'
silk, corn tanchi' p<u>a</u>shi', tanchi'
  woksholi'
silly, to act ilihaksichi
silly, to be imaanokfila-at iksho
silly, to go along looking p<u>í</u>lat <u>á</u>a
silo pichch<u>a</u>a, tanchaalhto',
  waakimpaalhto'
silver tali' tohbi'
silver bullet naki' kawaski'
similar one to, a ittibinka'
sin aaishshachika', nannashshachi'
sin against, to imashshachi
sin, to ashshachi, nannashshachi
sinew, type of inchashwa'
sing about, to ishtaloowa
sing for along with, to ibaaintaloowa

sing for, to intaloowa
sing for, to make intaloowachi
sing high, to chaah<u>a</u> taloowa
sing low, to akka's<u>i</u> taloowa
sing, to taloowa
sing to in, to aaintaloowa
sing to oneself, to ilintaloowa
sing with, to ibaataloowa
sing with, to make ibaataloowachi
singe off one's hair, to anakshowa,
  ilanakshooli
singe the hair off, to anakshooli
singer hattak taloowa', taloowa'
singer for, to be the lead
  tikbishtimayya
singing event taloowa'
singing, to lead in tikbishtimayya
single file, to be in ittayakowa
sink aaoka'mi', nannaachiifa'
sink, to bowafa, pitbowafa
sinner hattak yoshoba',
  nannashshachi'
sissy, to be a iknakno
sister intiik, ittibaapishi; *also* chitta',
  kiiyoho', pokkosh, titta, *and other*
  words below
sister, half- intikba iklanna', intiik
  iklanna', ittibaapishi iklanna',
  nakfish iklanna'
sister, older intikba
sister, younger nakfish
sister-in-law im<u>a</u>lako'si'
sit and rest in, to aafoha
sit around, to binnin<u>í</u>li, chih<u>í</u>ya,
  imbínni'li, imbinohm<u>á</u>a, inch<u>í</u>'ya
sit around, to just patkachit m<u>á</u>a,
  patkáyya'chi, pátta'a
sit by while (someone) works, to
  inch<u>í</u>'ya
sit by, to imbínni'li, imbinohm<u>á</u>a
Sit down! Hobinili!
Sit down and tell lies! Bini'cha
  loshka!
sit down on, to ootombínni'li

502

sit down, to biniili, binohli
sit down, to make biniichi, binohchi
sit dreaming, to binni't ilhpokonna
sit Indian style, to tossollo't bínni'li, tossollo'wat binoht máa, tossollo'wat chí'ya
sit on one's haunches, to akka' tákka'li, akka' tákkohli, akka' takoht máa
sit on one's heels, to achokmihilhkat bínni'li, achokmihilhkat binohmáa, achokmihilhkat chí'ya
sit on, to ombiniili, ombínni'li, onchí'ya
sit quietly, to kostíni
sit still, not to be able to nokhámmi'chi
sit there by oneself, to oottala
sit, to bínni'li, binohmáa, chí'ya
sit together, to make ittibaabinoochi
sit up high, to aba' bínni'li
sit with, to make ibaabiniichi, ibaabinoochi
sitting down, to be bínni'li, binohmáa, chí'ya
sitting so that just the heads are visible, to be ittashikkílli'li
sitting, to be bínni'li, chí'ya
six hanná'li
six bits bit hanna'li
six hundred talhipa hanná'li
six hundred in number, to be talhipa hanná'li
six hundred one talhipa hánna'cha chaffa
six hundred one in number, to be talhipa hánna'cha chaffa
six in number, to be hanná'li
666 medicine holhtina hanna'li' tochchi'na
six times hihanna'li'
six, to be in groups of hanná'li áyyo'ka
sixteen awa hanná'li, pokolahanná'li

sixteen in number, to be awa hanná'li
sixth, to be ishhanná'li
sixty pokoli hanná'li
sixty in number, to be pokoli hanná'li
sizzle, to ittishofo'chi, shofo'chi
skates, ice sholosh okti' ishtokaashalalli', sholosh oktishtoshala'li'
skeleton foni' bíyyi'ka, foni' illa, hattak foni'
ski, to okaashala'li
skim from, to aatakaffi
skin hakshop
skin and bones foni' illa
skin, meat so'ksok
skin, to lhofi, pilhoffi, pishoffi, pishohchi
skin, to have light okshawali
skin, to have wrinkled yikilhlha
skin, to press on one's ilombitka
skin, to shed one's ililhofi, lhofa
skin, untanned hakshop okchanki'
skinned, to be pishofa, pishohli
skinny, to be chonna, láttassa, shílli'ya
skinny, to be really pachofa
skip, to mallittahángli
skirt alhkona'
skirt be too short, to have one's inchawwala
skirt, hoop- alhkona' wahhala', alhkona' wihhila'
skirt, to wear a alhkóyyo'na
skirt, to wear a swaying wahhalwáa
skirts too short, to wear chawwálla'a
skis okti' ishtokaashalalli', oktishtoshala'li'
skull ishkobo' foni'
skunk koni
skunk, type of koni chokcho', koni hollisso
sky shotik

503

slack, to be yolhaa
slacker, to make yolhaachi
slant, to be set on a nakbi
slant, to set on a nakbichi
slap, to pássakli'chi, passáa
slapping sound, to make a lhok lhok
lhok aachi, pas pas pas aachi, pasak
pasak pasak aachi
slapping, to make noise ittipasasá'chi
slash, to pataffi
slather with, to ishtapoolosli
slathered on, to be ishtalhpóllo'sa
slathered with, to be ishtalhpolosa
slaughterhouse waakaa-abi'
slave hattak yoka', intoksali', yoka'
slave, black hattak losa' toksali'
sled itti' shalalli', okti'
ishtokaashalalli'
sleep around, to patalinchi
sleep around with women, to ihoo
ibaanosit nowa
sleep like the dead, to nostilli
sleep next to, to anosi
sleep, to nosi
sleep, to put to shimohli
sleep together, to ittibaanosi
sleep with, to ibaanosi, ibaatí'wa,
nowat ibaahaksi
sleeping pill ishnosi'
sleepwalk, to nosit áa
sleepy, to be nosilhha
sleepy, to make nosilhhachi
sleet, to bachalosha
sleeve naafka shakba'
slice of bread paska toshafa'
slices of bread paska toshahli'
slices, to be cut in very thin pasa
slices, to cut in thin pasli
slick elm balop
slick, to make talasbichi
slick vine sinti' ittish
slide aashala'li'
slide on, to okaashala'li, okaashalalli
slide, to shala'li

sliding board aashala'li'
slimy, to be hollashki
sling ilbak ishtalakchi'
slingshot itti' falakto'
slinky tali' tashan-kachi'
slip anonkalhko'na'
slip and fall, to shalalli
slip back, to bakhitibli
slip on, to okaashalalli
slip, half- alhkona' iklanna'si
slippery elm balop
slippery, to be lhabita, talasbi; also
halasbi
slippery to hold onto, to be too
talaasbo'si
slippery, to make talasbichi
slither rapidly, to yililí'chi
slither, to chiffolfówa, chiffolkachi,
yili'kachi, yili'kalhchi
slobber, to chokkayalli
slop over, to lha'a
slop over, to let lha'li
slop with, to ishtapoolosli
slosh in, to hayiyí'chi
slow, to be alhchibachi, iktoshpo,
imalhchiba, yáppalli
slowed down by, to be
ishtimalhchiba
slurp, to ittilhóchchokli'chi,
ittilhocho'chi, ittilhochochó'chi
slurp up, to pitlabbi
smack one's lips, to ittilasa'chi,
ittilasasá'chi, ittilássakli'chi
smacking nose, to make a las las las
aachi, lasak lasak lasak aachi, nam
nam nam aachi
small of the back hatip
small, to be iskanno'si, ittapíhhihcha
small, to be very píhhihcha
small, to make iskannochi, sawachi
smaller, to be chipónta
smart person hattak hapoyoksa'
smart, to be imponna,
ishtaponnachi, nannimponna

smart-aleck, to be a ilifinhachi, iliyimmi, immayya banna
smart-alecks, to be ittimmayya'chi banna
smart-alecky, to be ilahobbi
smash, to lataffi, lotooli, lhachoffi
smashed, to be lotowa, lhacho'wa, lhachofa
smear for, to imaabi
smear with, to aabi, ishtaabi
smell bad, to shoha
smell good, to bilama
smell good, to make bilamachi
smell himself, to make (someone) iloshshowanchichichi
smell like something burning, to kashama
smell like, to nakshobi, shoha
smell sour, to hawashko
smell, to oshshowanchi, oshshowashpisa
smelly, to be kalhama, kosoma, nakshobi
smelly, to make kosomachi
smile, to choklhiili, ollali
smile, to make ollalichi
smoke pofa, shobohli
smoke from at, to blow the oshobollichi
smoke on one, to have oshobohli
smoke out, to ishobohchi
smoke rings, to blow chomak shobohchi
smoke signals, to send shobohchi
smoke signals to, to send ishobohchi
smoke, to chomak pofa, oshobohchi, shobohli
smoke, to make shobohchi
smoked ham shokha' nipi' oshobohli'
smoked, to be oshobohli
smoke-damaged, to be oshobohli
smokehouse nipi' aaoshoboochi'
smokestack aashobohli'

smoking star fochik shobohli'
smooth out, to isatabli
smooth, to lhimishkochi
smooth, to be lhimishko
smooth, to make ittilawwichi
smoothed, to be satapa
smother, to pallichit abi, pallit illi
snail hosolo
snail, type of fokkol, okfokkol
Snake Dance Sinti' Hilha'
snake ittiwashanchi', sinti'—see also snake, type of
snake, baby sintoshi'
snake charmer sintinchama'chi'
snake, chicken abaksha', akanka' sinti', akankapa', akankosh-apa', sinti' akankosh-apa'
snake egg sintoshi'
snake root sinti' hakshish
snake, type of pintapa', sinti' basoowa', sinti' bo'wa ikkallo', sinti' hattak fammi', sinti' kiliha', sinti' losa', sinti' okchamali', sinti' ok-okaa-asha', sinti' palhki', sintishtahollo'—see also names of specific snakes
snap naaishtakallo'
snap beans bala' homona'
snarl, to atannichi
snarled in ones hair, to have something atannalhchi
sneak up on each other, to ittayaapahli, ittaayaapahli
sneak up on, to ayaapaali
sneaker, high-topped sholosh chaaha'
sneeze at, to ohabishko
sneeze, to habishko
sneeze, to make habishkochi
snore, to lhabanka
snort, to shokshowa
snot ibilhkan
snow okti', oktosha
snow in the mountains ahalla'ta'

505

snow, to be soft

snow, to be soft okti' poshi' bíyyi'ka
snowbird foshi' tolhposhi', okti'
  foshi'
snowed on, to be onoktosha
snowflake okti' poshi'
snowman okti' hattak
snowslide okti' shalalli'
snuff chomak bota'
so ba'
so many years old, to be afammi
  kánnohmi
so there ahaa
so you've come! ba' ishlata!
soak, to yokolbichi
soap ishtachifa', ishtalhchifa'
soap bubble ishtalhchifa' pokpoki'
soap, lye ishtalhchifa' homi'
sober up, to kostini, kostinichi
sober, to be kostíni
socks iabisowa'
socks, silk iabisowa' loposhki'
soda, baking sodi'
sofa aaombiniili' falaa'
sofkey saafki', tafola
sofkey, type of tafola-hawashko'
soft spot chipotinkali
soft spot, to have a tannap pila'sit
  yátto'fa
soft, to be hayi'kalhchi, iklawwi'cho,
  loposhki, lhábbo'cha, lhabita,
  moyoshki, yabo'kachi, yabofa, yatofa
soft, to cause to get yolhkochi
soft, to get yolhko
softened, to be lotowa
solder onto, to abila, abilachi, abilili
solder together, to ittayakmichi
solder, to ayakmichi
soldier tashka-chipota'
soldiers, Northern Falammi
sole come off, to have the shokafa
sole of a shoe sholosh iipatha'
sole of the foot iyyimpatha'
solid, to be kílli'pi
some kannohmihmat,

kannohmihma
some amount of kaniya fokhahmat,
  kaniya fokhahma
some day nittak kanimpihma, nittak
  nannahma
some kind of kanihmi,
  kanihmihmat, kanihmihma
some number of kaniya fokhahmat,
  kaniya fokhahma
some point, at kanihkaash
some time ago kaniya fokhakaash
some time, at kaniya fokhaho,
  kaniya fokhakmak
some, to be chaafowa'si
some way kaniht
somebody kaniya'mat, kaniya'ma,
  kaniya'oot, kaniya'o, kanahookano,
  kaniya'ookano
somehow kanihchihma, kanihsht
someone kana, kanahmat, kanahma,
  kanakookano, kaniya'mat,
  kaniya'ma, kaniya'ookano,
  kaniya'oot, kaniya'o
someone, or ookma nannahmat,
  ookma nannahma
someone standing aahikki'ya'
someone's kana
someplace kaniya', kaniya'ookano
somersault, to turn a ishkobo'
  hili'shcha filita
something nanna, nannahmat,
  nannahma, nannakat,
  nannahookano
something, or ookma nannahmat,
  ookma nannahma
something white people use
  naahollimmi'
something's nanna
sometime kaniya fokhakmak,
  kanihkaash, kanihkmak
sometimes kaniya fokhakmak,
  kanihkmak
somewhat kánni'ya
somewhere kaniya', kaniya'ookano

son oshi'
Son of God, the Chihoowoshi'
song taloowa'
song book holisso aataloowa'
song leader taloowapihchi'
song leader for, to be a intikbayka
song leader, to be a tikbayka
song sheet holisso aataloowa'
son-in-law ippolhchi', iyyop
sonny kabi'
soot toklhank
sore throat, to have a inonka' hottopa
sores, to have canker liwaali
sorghum syrup maliassas losa'
sorry for oneself, to be ishtiliposilhha
sorry, to be nokhánglo
sorry, to feel very chonkashat yaháa
sort into pairs, to ittachapo'li, ittachaafoochi
sorted into pairs, to be ittachapo'wa
sound like a cow, to make a kaak kaak kaak aachi
sound like a swarm of bees, to winiiyachi
sound like something burning, to basaachi
sound of a car starting, to make the ying ying ying aachi
sound of a cat hissing, to make the tif tif tif aachi
sound of a cat spitting, to make the tof tof tof aachi
sound of a clock ticking, to make the tik tik tik aachi
sound of a hen clucking, to make the tok tok tok aachi
sound of a leather-covered drum, to make the tom tom tom aachi, tomok tomok tomok aachi
sound of bare feet walking, to make the tip tip tip aachi
sound of cloth being hit, to make the top top top aachi

sound of leaves before a storm, to make the washaahánchi
sound of popping, to make the tok tok tok aachi
sound of rattling, to make the wash wash wash aachi
sound with paper, to make a itticháshshakli'chi
sound, to ola, shakabli
sound, to make olachi
soup ashiila
soup spoon folosh chinto'
sour cream pishokchi' pakna' takaali' hawashko'
sour milk pishokchi' hawashko'
sour, to be hawashko, takba, wasacha
sour, to make hawashkochi, wasachachi
source of a spring kali walhaali'
south hashaatabookoli', okaamahli
South, the Hashaatobookoli' Imma', Okaamahli
spaces, to have big shachakla
spade lokfishpiha'
spaghetti tili'kolhkomo' shila'
Spanish Oshpaananompa'
spank along with, to ibaapassáa
spank, to pasa'chi, passáa
spare, to lhakoffínchi
spared, to be lhakófa, lhakófi
spark, to emit a lowak chipasli
spark, to make a lowak chipaslichi
sparkle, to pachiili, shokmalali
sparkly, to be shokmalla'máli
sparks chibaali
sparks, to emit chipasli, pachiili
sparrow aachompa' foshi'
spatter, to pachiichi, pachiili
spatula ishfilillichi', ishfilito'chi', nannishfilito'chi'
spay, to oshi' iksho' ikbi
speak in tongues, to anompila anompoli, Chihoowimanompa anompoli

507

speak nonsensically, to anompaat intayolhkommo
speak, to anompoli
speak to each other, to ittayoppachi
speak to, to ayoppachi
spell on, to put a ayoshkammi
spell, someone under a hattak oppani'
spell, type of naki' palli'
spend much on oneself, not to ilatoba
spherical, to be bolokta, lómbo, lhibokta, lhibowa
spicy, to be hot and homi
spicy, to make homichi
spider cholhkan
spider, type of cholhkan ishto', cholhkan losa', cholhkan oshi'
spider wasp cholhkan apa'
spider web cholhkan hala'li', toklhan
spill from, to aalhatabli, aalhatapa
spill on oneself, to ilolhatabli
spill on the ground, to akka' lhatabli
spill on, to ootolhatabli, olhatabli, olhatapa
spill, to ilhatapa, ilha'a, lhatapa, lha'a, lha'li
spill water on oneself, to oka'at ilhatapa
spilled, to be lha'a
spillway oka' aalhatapa'
spin around in, to aachokfanni, aachokkaamala
spin around, to chokfanni, chokfannichi, chokkaamala
spin for, to ihilhachi
spin, to chanahli, chanallichi, chanaa, hilha, hilhachi, tonollichi
spin, to make chanaachi
spinach tohi' okchamali'
spine nalhchaba foni'
spine, bone at the top of the shanakha'

spinning wheel polonaatanni'
spirit shilombish
spirit, bad shilombish oppolo'
spirit companion iyaaknasha'
Spirit, the Great Shilombish Ishto'
spirits, to be sensitive to the presence of imaaholba
spit, barbecue tali' nanna aa-albani'
spit in, to aatofa, okaatofa
spit on, to ontofa
spit out, to tofat kanchi, tofat kochchi, tofat lhatabli
spit, to tofa, toftowa
spitoon aatofa', aatoftowa'
spitting, to make the sound of a cat tof tof tof aachi
splash around, to bo'chit lha'li
splash on, to ompachili, olhatabli
splash, to chobo'chi, pachiichi, pachiili
splash with, to ompachichi
splashed, to be bo'kalhchi
splashing sound, to make a chob chob chob aachi, chobok chobok chobok aachi, ittichobo'chi, ittichobobó'chi, ittichóbbokli'chi
splat on, to apiichiffi
splat, to pichifa, pichiffi, pichihchi, pichihli
splayed, to be washshalla'a
spleen intakashi'
splinter itti' shipafa'
splinter in one, to have a hofkaa
splinter, to shipaffi
splinter, to have a ashiyama
splintered, to be shipafa
splinters, to have shipafa
split apart, to palhata
split apart, to be completely nipafa
split in more than two, to ittapalhlhi
split in two, to ittapaalhalli
split off from, to akaashapa
split off, to kashapa
split open against, to apaalhalli

split open, to pachafa, pachaffi,
pachahli, pachaachi, pasafa, pasahli
split, to palha, palhahli, palhalli,
palhlhi, pasaachi
split, to be falakto
split, to do a wakchalali
split up among oneselves, to
ittakashkowa
split up, to ittakashapa
split up, to be kashkowa
spoil, to ishtaapichi
spoiled, to act ishtilamákka'li
spoiled, to be ishtikayyo'bo, malhaa
spoke of a wheel itti' chanaa
inchanaa' iwashshalaka'
sponge ishtachifa'
spool aapakfoha', polonaapakfoha'
spoon folosh
spoon, type of alhpash, folosh
chinto', folosh falaa', folosh
ishtimpa', folosh naaishtapiisa',
folosh-oshi', itti' folosh
spotted, to be chisiya, holisso, waaka
spots on, to make waakachi
spouses at the same time, to have two
tawwalínchi
spout aabichili', oka' aabichili'
spout, coffeepot kaafaawalhahli'
ibichchala'
sprain, to pitommi
sprained, to be pitoma
spray, to oshobbichi, pachiichi,
pachiili
spray with, to ompachichi
spread apart, to wahhalili,
wakchalachi
spread apart, to be washshalla'a
spread flat, to palli, patali
spread gossip, to anompa chokoshpa'
anoli, chokoshpachi
spread the wings, to ilisatapo'li
spread one's legs for, to iwakchalali
spread out at the sides, to have one's
arms or wings wihhílli'ya

spread out on, to be all ompatalhpo
spread out, to satabli, satapo'li
spread out, to be satapa
spread out, to be all patalhpo
spread out to look for, to patalisht
hoyo
spread rumors about, to
anompinchokoshpali
spread rumors, to anompa
chokoshpali
spread stories about, to
anompittimapiisa, anompombohli
spread the tail, to tiima
spread, to aaikbichi, wahhala,
washshalachi, washshalili, yanalli
spreading adder alhkayya' patha',
hashaachaffa', hashaapatha'
spreading outwards, to be wahhálla'a
spreading, to be round and wahhala
spring kali okshalli', tali' tashan-
kachi'
spring, hot kali palli', kali walhaali'
(spring, name of a) Mi'tabi'
spring, source of a kali walhaali'
spring, the first part of
toompallammo'na'
spring, to be toomi pallit ishtayya,
yohbi, yohbichi
sprinkle on one, to have it
oshobbichi
sprinkle on, to ofayyichi, oshobbichi
sprinkle, to shobbichi
sprinkler, clothes oka' ishtolha'li'
sprout from, to aaholhfo
sprout, to achaaka, holhfo
spun around, to be chokfanni,
chokkaamalachi
spurs chofaak yaalhfowa'
spurs, rooster akanka' ishtimittibi',
akankinchofak
spy hapompoyo'
spy on, to apollichi
square off the edges of, to shokli
square, to be shokolbika' aa-asha

squash, to latassachi
squash, type of olbi', olbi' lakna',
olbi' tohbi', ostahi'
squat, to tákka'li, takoht máa
squeeze in, to shamallichi,
shamayo'li, shamaachi, shamohchi
squeeze into, to shamalli,
shámmohli, shamohmáa
squeeze out milk from, to
imbishlichi
squeeze out, to bishlichi
squeeze through, to shamalli,
shammamáli, shámmohli,
shammomóli, shamohmáa
squeeze, to lhitoffi
squirrel fani'—see also squirrel, type
of
squirrel, flying chilisa', pali'
squirrel, to make a noise like a
fikfiya, kookowa
squirrel, type of falakna', fani' lakna',
fani' losa', fani' shobboko'li',
fanokchama'li', fan-oshi'
squirt gun oka' ishtolha'li', tanampo
holba'
stab, to bahli, baafa
stab, to make baafachi
stack, to ittalalli
stacked, to be ittalbitkachi,
ittontalkachi, ittontalkachit máa,
ittontalkáyya'chi
stacked with the ends overlapping, to
be made of wood ittabaana
stadium to'li' hattak aabinooli'
stage makeup, to put on ilincho'li
stain, to alawwi, alawwichi, lawwi
stain with, to lawwichi
stairs aatoloyya'
stalk, to ayaapaali
stamp holisso ishtaya'
stand nannaakanchi'
stand and walk around, to hikkikíya
stand around, to hihíli
stand back, to hikíya

stand erect, to fabassa
stand in, to okaahilichi, okaahí'li,
okaahíkki'ya, okaahiyoht máa
stand it, to achónna'chi
stand on, to ishtohikki'ya, ontalaali,
ontalooli, ohí'li, ohíkki'ya, ohilichi,
ohiyohchi, ohiyohli, ohiyoht máa
stand, to hí'li, híkki'ya, hiyohmáa,
hiyoht máa; also oshhíkki'ya,
tálla'a, tállo'wa, talowat máa,
wáyya'a
stand together, to go up and
ootittapoota
stand up for, to ihilichi, ihiyohchi
stand up in, to okaahiyohchi
stand up, to hika, hilichi, hiyohchi
stand up, to make hiyohchi
stand up to, to imaaiklóha
stand what happens to, not to be able
to ikimachonna'cho
stand with, to ibaahí'li, ibaahíkki'ya,
ibaahiyohmáa
stander ishtaahikki'ya'
standing up, to be hí'li, híkki'ya,
hiyohmáa, hiyoht máa
staple holisso ishtakallo'chi'
star fochik
star, evening fochik ishto'
star, morning fochik ishto'
Star, North Falammi Fochik
star shape fochik holba'
star, shooting fochik malili'
star, smoking fochik shobohli'
starch naaishchala'
starch, to chalachi
starched, to be chala
stare at, to okaapisa
stare, to okkalali
starfish nani' fochik
start a fire with, to akiiliili
start it, to tingba' ishtaya
start, to malichi, malíli
startle, to hállakli'chi
starve, to hopoba, hopobachi

starve to death, to hopobachit abi,
   hopobat illi
station, railroad itti' chanaa malili'
   aahika'
statue hattak holba', holba'
stay all night with, to imalbinachi
stay around, to aayahánta,
   aayashahánchi, aayashwahánchi
stay at home out of fear, to
   ishtilihopoo
stay back, to hikíya
stay behind, to make antachichi
stay home alone, to imalhchíi'ba
stay in the house all the time, to
   ililohmi
stay out all night, to ononna
stay quiet, to nokwaya
stay the night, to albinachi
stay there, to áyya'sha, tówa
stay, to ahánta, ánta, ásha, áshwa,
   káha, wayáa, wayówa
stay together, to ittahiina
stay watching, to aayahánta,
   aayashahánchi, aayashwahánchi
stay with, to achokkobbi, iláwwi'li
stay with, to make ahiinachi
steal from, to aahonkopa,
   imaahonkopa, ihonkopa
steal little by little, to ayowa
steal, to honkopa
steam being released, to make the
   sound of shof shof shof aachi
steam for, to make inkofollichi
steam, to kofolli
steam, to make kofollichi
steamroller hina'
   ishtontono'kalhchi'
steel tali' kawaski'
steer waaka' himmita'
steer, longhorn lapish falaa, waaka'
   lapish faloha'
steer, to folotó'chi
steering wheel ishfolota'
stem api'

step in, to okaahika
step on, to lataffi, ohika
step over, to pithika
step, to hika
step-sibling, younger nakfish toba'
stepbrother ittibaapishi toba', inakfi'
   toba'
stepdaughter oshiitiik toba'
stepfather inki' toba'
stepmother ishki' toba'
stepsister intiik toba', ittibaapishi
   toba'
stepson oshi' toba'
sterile hobak
sterile person oshi' iksho'
sterilization method hobak ishtikbi'
sterilize, to hobak ikbi, lowachi
sterilized, to have oneself oshi'
   iksho' ilikbi
stethoscope foyopishtithana',
   nannishhaklo'
stew ashiila, nipi' holhponi'
stick itti'
stick in, to achoshli, achoosha,
   achoosholi, afinni, shamaachi,
   shamohchi
stick on, to lapaachi, lapoht máa,
   lapoochi, láppa'li, láppohli
stick one's finger in, to ibaayakohli
stick onto, to achaakissa,
   achaakissachi, ashiila
stick out all over, to washshalla'a
stick out (one's ears), to oshwalachi
stick out one's limbs, to
   washshalwáa
stick out one's lips, to takshololi
stick out one's lower lip, to ittialbi'
   falaa, takbiloli
stick out one's tongue at, to isolash
   ifaliili
stick out one's tongue, to isolash
   falaa, isolash faliili
stick out this way, to oshwayowat
   máa, oshwáyya'a, oshwáyyo'wa

511

stick out, to ootkónchcha
stick out, to have ears that oshwalali
stick out, to have the limbs
washshala
stick out, to make (ears) oshwalachi
stick, stickball kapochcha'
stick, to ashama, lapali
stick to, to achoshkachit máa,
achoshkáyya'chi, achóshsho'wa
stick together, to ittachaakissa,
ittahiina
stick up for, to ibaahí'li, ibaahíkki'ya,
ibaahiyohmáa
stick up, to oshwichali, ootkónchcha
stick up, to have one's head
shikkilili
stick, walking ishtilombitka'
stick with something at the top, to be
a bare fáhha'ko
stickball kapochcha'
stickball goalposts itti' aabo'li'
stickball stick kapochcha'
sticker in one, to have a hofkaa
sticking in one, to have hofkaa
sticking onto one, to have ashiila
sticking, to be left lapáli, lapóhli
sticking to, to be lapoht máa, láppa'li,
láppohli
sticking up, to be chiko'wa
sticky, to be chakissa
sticky, to make chakissachi
stiff, to be kallo
stiff with dirt, to be chala
still ímmo'ma, í'ma, ishtáyya'ma,
oka' homi' aaikbi'
still okay chokma immo'ma
stilts ittishnowa', itti' ishno'wa'
sting, to fannichi, ilawwi, lawwi,
nalhlhi
stinging plant fannik
stingy, to be nannishtilaayokha,
ilaayokha
stingy with, to be ishtilaayokha,
iholiitopa, ihollo, ihollochi,

ishtilayyokha
stink, to shoha
stinkbug shotik ihollokso'
stinker, little kosomoshi'
stir, to tiwa'chi
stirred, to be tiwa'kalhchi
stirrup aahalhabli', sontalhpo'
aahalha'bli'
stitches, to have alhcho'wa
stock (of a gun) tanampaalhpi'
stocking cap yaachikko'li'
stockings ihoo imiabisowa',
iabisowa'
stockings, silk ihoo imiabisowa'
loposhki', iabisowa' loposhki'
stolen, something holhkopa'
stomach ittakoba'
stomach ache ittakoba' kisili'
stomach ache, to get a ittakoba' kisili'
hayoochi, ittakoba' kisili' i'shi
stomach of, to enlarge the missilili
stomach, to have a big missila,
missílli'ya
stomach, to lie on one's wáyya'a
stomach ulcer ittakoba' loksi',
ittakoba' malli'
stomp, to hayi'chi
stone, type of aahaloppachi', lokfi'
tali'
stood on, to be ontálla'a, ontállo'wa,
ontalowat máa
stoop down, to pitwaya, tossola, waya
stoop over, to akka' wayowat máa,
akka' wáyya'a, akka' wáyyo'wa
stoop, to wayowat máa
stoop, to make wayoochi
stop at, to hika
stop by, to folota
stop crying, to apoolha
stop crying, to make apoolhali
stop in, to hika
stop precipitating, to ayoli
stop, to hika, hilichi, inkatabli,
intakchi, likinta, ootaalhlhi

512

stop, to try to inkatapo'li,
inkatapo'chi
stop up, to lobli
stop up with, to ishtakallochi
stoplight aashoppala' homma'
stopped up, to be lopa, okshilitta
stopped up, to get okshilitta
stopped, to be imoktapa
stopper ishtakallochi'
stopping place aahika'
stopping, without immo̲'t
store aachompa'—see also store, type
of
store, food impa' aa-asha'
store, shoe sholosh aa-asha', sholosh
aachompa', sholosh aakanchi'
store, type of aachompishto',
naafkaa-asha', naafkaakanchi'—see
also names of specific stores
storm cellar lokfi' abooha', sela'
storm, to make the sound of leaves
before a washaahánchi
story chokoshpa, ishtannowa,
nannannoya', nannishtanompa,
shikonno'pa'
story, to tell a shikonno'pa' ano̲li
storybook shikonno'pa' ishtanompa
stove aaholhponi', istoof
straddle, to kafali, kafohli, kafoht
má̲a
straight across, to go apissá̲li
straight on immo̲'t
straight pin chofaakoshi' oshkibbi'li'
straight razor notakhish ishsha̲fi'
falaa'
straight through, to go apissa̲t aya
straight, to be apissa, fabassa, satámpa
straighten, to alhpisa'chi, alhpíssa'li,
apissali, i̲satabli, satabli, satapo'li
straightened out, to be satapa,
satapo'wa
strain through, to hoyya
strain, to bishlichi, hoyyachi
strap aahala'li'

straps, shoulder ishtilabanna'li'
straw hat yaalhipa tanna'
strawberry biyyo̲'ka'
streaked, to be oklhiwali
stream, mouth of a oka' sokbish
street oklattintakla'
streetlight oklattintakla' aashoppala'
streets, to walk the hawit no̲wa
stretch oneself, to satapo'wa
stretch, to ilisatapo'li, satabli,
siipo'wa, shiibli, shiipa, shiipo'li
stretched out of shape, to be shiipa
stretched out, to be síhhi'pa,
siipopó̲wa
stretched out, to lie watalhpi
stretched, to be satapa, shiipo'wa
stretching, to keep siipopó̲wa
stretchy, to be shiipa, shiipo'wa
strike (a match) kilili
strike, for lightning to shokmallaat
isso
strike, to faapa, faapichi, sakka̲ha
string nampanaa', polona
string, type of inchashwa'
string, to hotampi
stringy, to be hollashki
strip naked, to ilichakbakachi
strip of bark, to lhohli
strip the bark from, to shibli
strip the fruit from, to halaht lhi̲fi
strip the leaves from, to alhiichi,
halaht lhi̲fi, lhihli, lhihchi
strip, to shipaachi
stripe, to basoowachi, kamaachi,
koyoffi
striped, to be basoowa, kamaa,
koyofa, shiwaa
stripes on, to make shiwaachi
stripped of bark, to be lhoha
stripped of leaves, to be lhiha
stripper ilichakbakachi'
stroke, to hapa̲shshichi, pashohli
stroller chipotaafokha'
strong, to be kilimpi

513

strong-tasting, to be homi, yammi
strong-tasting, to make really
  yammichi
strop, razor aahaloppachi',
  ishtilishafi' aahaloppachi'
struggle, to wahhaala
strung, to be holhtapi
stub one's toe, to ililataffi
stub, to lataffi
stubbed, to be latafa
stubborn person ishkobo' kallo'
stubborn, to be ilapóla, ilaafowa
  ikbanno
stubborn toward, to be imilaafowa
stucco, to apoolosli
stuck in one's throat, to have
  noktakaali
stuck in, to be achoshkachit máa,
  achoshkáyya'chi, achóshsho'wa,
  afina, afínni'ya, shamalli,
  shámma'li, shámmohli,
  shamohmáa
stuck in, to have shámmali'chi
stuck into, to get achoosha
stuck onto, to be achaakissa
stuck, to be akallo
stuck, to get kafali, kafohli, kafoht
  máa
stuck with, to be ishtimalhchiba
student holisso pisa'
studio, photography aaholbachi'
study, to holisso pisa
stuffed up, to be lopa
stump ittibikolofa
sty in the eye ishkin afo'pa'
stylish, to be himitta
subject of rumor, to be the anompaat
  inchokoshpa
submerge, to okloboshli
substitute for, to tóhho'ba
subtract, to aaishi
succeed, to lhopolli
suck himself, to make
  ilisho'kachichi

suck in, to ilafoyopa
suck one's thumb, to ilbak sho'ka
suck, to pishi, sho'ka
suck with, to ibaapishi
sucker chalbakko', sakli'
suckle, to pishichi
suction machine nannishtayowa'
sudden movement back, to make a
  satappakahchi
sudden movement, to make a
  ilhkóyyokli, kánnakli
suddenly himonali'
suddenly, to get up satappakahsht
  hika
sudse, to pokpokichi
sudsy, to be pokpoki
suffice, to ona
sugar shookola'—see also sugar, type
  of
sugar bowl shookolaalhto'
sugar cane shookola' api', shookola'
  aatoba'
sugar lump shookola' kallo'
sugar, powdered shookola' bota'
sugar substitute shookola' holba'
sugar, type of shookola' lakna',
  shookola' tohbi', shookola' poshi'
suggest falsehoods about, to
  aloshkachi
suggest incorrectly to, to imahobbichi
suggestive things to, to say
  ishtakaanihmichi
suitcase hachik, naafkaalhto'
sulphur hottok lakna'
Sulphur Kali Showa'
sumac bashanchik
sumac, type of bashanchik homma',
  bashanchik tohbi', bati', ofimitti'
summer toompalli'
summer, to be toompalli
sun hashi'
sun at the same time, for there to be
  rain and Siitanat imihoo fammi
sun in one's eyes, to have ontoomi,

ohashtahli
sun, in the aatoomika'
sun to burn, for the hashi'at lowachi
sun, to lie in the toominni
sun to rise, for the hashi'at kochcha
sun to shine, for the hashi'at toomi
sun worshipper hashi' ayoppachi'
sunbonnet baanit
Sunday Nittak Hollo', Nittak Ishtontoklo'
sunflower hashi' pakali'
sunglasses ishkin ishpisa' losa'
sunken, to be shippa, okaakinafa
sunlight toomi
sunny, to be hashi'at toomi, toomi
sunshine toomi
sunshine, to be toomi
supermarket aachompishto'
supper obyaka' impa'
supper, to eat obyaka' impa
support a rejected candidate, to ittachapa
support for, to give imapila, imapilachi
support, to apiilachi, ittibaayôkli, ihíkki'ya
supposedly chikimba
sure, to know for alhtókko'waka ithána
surfboard oka' ishtoshalalli'
surgeon hattak bashli'
surgical mask ibichchala' alhiipi'ya'
surpass, to ootímmayya'chi
surprised and happy, to be ishmalhata, malhata
surprised by, to be imalhata
survive, to lhakófi
suspect, to hopoo
suspended in, to be okaatakkakáli, okaatakkokóli
suspenders ishtilabanna'li'
suspicious, to be hopoo, ilihopoo
swaddle in, to aboknohli
swaddled in, to be aboknoha

swagger, to ilifaya'chi, ilifoyo'chi
swallow along with, to ibaanalli, ibaanannabli
swallow, to nalli, nannabli
swamp okpachalhlhi'
swamp rabbit oktaak chokfi'
swan shalaklak, shalaklak tohbi'
swarm around, to ayaashachi
swarm of bees fohi' wiha'
swarm of bees, to sound like a winiiyachi
swarm over, to ombilhipa
swarm, to tiwa'kahánchi
sway, to faya'kalhchi, tono'kachi, yili'kachi, yili'kalhchi
sway when one walks, to missilmíya, pashánna'a, shanaayoyówa
swaybacked, to be pashshana
swaying skirt, to wear a wahhalwáa
swear, to anompoppani, anompoppanichi, nókko'wa
sweat, to hoyahno
sweater naafkishto'
sweatshop naafkaa-acho'li'
sweep off the top of, to ompihli
sweep onto, to ompihli
sweep, to pihli
sweet corn tanchi' champoli'
sweet peas bala' champoli'
sweet potato ahi' champoli'
sweet potatoes, mashed ahi' palaska'
sweet stuff nanchampoli'
sweet, to be champoli
sweeten, to champolichi
sweetheart chonkash champoli'
sweets nanchampoli'
swell, to pofohli, shatali
swell, to make shataachi
swelling disease, to have a shatahpoli
swelling, to have a hard chilhlha'li
swellings, to have pofohpoli
swept away, to be piha
swept, to be piha

swim for in, to imaayopi
swim for, to iyopi
swim in, to aayopi, okaatakkak\u00e1li,
  okaatakkok\u00f3li
swim, to oka' yopi, yopi
swim with in, to ibaayopi
swimming pool aayopi', oka' aayopi'
swing aafa'pa'
swing around, to faapo'chi
swing from side to side while
  walking, to ilifoyo'chi
swing in the breeze, to faapop\u00f3wa,
  takkak\u00e1li, takkok\u00f3li
swing, to fata'kalhchi, faapa,
  faapichi, faapo'wa

switch ishfama'—see also switch,
  type of
switch back and forth between, to
  ittatobo'chi
switch, light pitshoopalali'
switch, type of ishfama' falaa'
swollen, to be pofoha
sword bashpo falaa' ishtittibi',
  ishtittibi'
sycamore itti' tohbi'
sympathize with, to ibaanokh\u00e1nglo
sympathy, to try to get iliposilhlha
syphilis sipoknabi'
syrup maliassas, shookolokchi'
syrup, sorghum maliassas losa'

t

table aaimpa'
table leg aaimpiyyi'
table to be set, for the amposhi'at
  ontalowa
table, to set the amposhi' ontalohli
tablecloth aaimpalhiipi'ya'
tablespoon folosh chinto'
tadpole hata'lobo'
tags, dog holhchifo inno'chi'
tail hasimbish
tail, to put on a atakchichi
tail, to spread the tiima
tailbone hasimbish foni'
tailor naafkikbi', naafkimaaiksaachi'
tailor style, to sit tossollo't b\u00ednni'li,
  tossollo'wat binoht m\u00e1a,
  tossollo'wat ch\u00ed'ya
tailor's shop naafkaaimaaiksaachi'
take a bath for, to iyopi
take a bath in, to okaayopi
take a bath, to yopi
take a bite out of, to kisili
take a breath, to ilifoyopa
take a deep breath, to kallochit

foyopa
take a picture of, to hobachi
take (a pill), to nannabli
take a shortcut, to apissat aya
take across, to ishlhopolli
take all apart, to nibli
take along, to isht\u00e1a
take along with one, to pihli'shcha
  ishtaya
take along with, to ibaaishi
take an offering, to ittahobbi' hoyo
take apart, to ittashokaffi,
  ittashokaachi
take away from, to imaaishi,
  imaaolabi, ishtihopaakichi,
  ifilammichi, ifilamo'chi
take away, to aaishi, ishhopaakachi,
  kanallichi
take back, to falammichi, falamo'chi
take blood from, to issish aaishi
take by the hand or handle, to hala'li
take care of a problem, to namp\u00edla,
  pitnamp\u00edla
take care of oneself, to ilaapichi

take care of, to apiisachi, holiitobli,
ishtilaapichi, ittahaalahlínchi,
ihapompoyo, nampila
take each other's hands, to ittihala'li
take for, to imishi, ishtimayya
take from and run by, to
ootishtimalili
take from, to aawihli, aawihpoli,
imishi
take good care of one's things, to
ilatoba
take in turn, to ittatobo'chi
take it, to be able to achónna'chi
take (liquid medicine), to ishko
take off one's clothes in front of each
other, to ittipisachi
take off one's clothes, to naafka
shihli
take off the hulls from, to fakohchi
take off the tops, to tilohchi
take off, to imaaishi, shifi
take on as a helper, to ilapilachi
take one's time, to alhchibachi
take out one's penis, to kochchi
take out, to ishkochcha,
kochchaakaali, shifi
take over and send off, to ootpilachi
take the arms and legs off, to
ittanipaachi, nibli
take the blame for, to imilonhochi
take the blame, to ilonhochi,
ishtilabaanali, ishtilonhochi
take the breath out of, to noklhitoffit
illichi
take the form of, to toba
take the Lord's name in vain, to
Chihoowa kalakshichi
take the name of, to aholhchi'fo
take the name, to ilaholhchifochi
take the top off, to tiloffi
take there, to ootashaachi
take through, to ishlhopolli,
lhopo'chi, lhopollichi
take, to ishi

take to, to ishtaya, ishtimaya,
ishtimona, ishtona
take too much time, to abaanappichi
take turns, to ittalhtobo'wa,
ittatobo'wa
take turns with, to ittatobo'chi
take up a collection, to ittahobbi'
hoyo
talcum powder ishtilitohbichi'
talk about nothing, to bachali
talk about, to anompinchokoshpali,
ishtanompoli
talk all the time, to labaachi
talk at once, to all ittachapo'wa
talk back to, to achapa
talk bad about, to ikayyobba'lo
talk casually, to loshka
talk loudly, to tastachi
talk loudly to, to ontastachi
talk mean to, to imbachali
talk on the telephone, to
talaanompa' aaittimanompoli
talk secretly, to lomat ittimanompoli
talk, to anompoli; also fatpoli
talk to about, to ishtimanompoli
talk, to be ashamed to nokwaya
talk to for, to imimanompoli
talk, to make anompolichi
talk to on the telephone, to
talaanompa' aaimanompoli
talk to oneself, to ilimanompoli
talk to, to imanompoli; also ifatpoli
talk together, to ittimanompoli,
ittifatpoli
talk too long, to hashi' kanallaat
imambaanapa, hashi' kanallaat
intaha
talk too much, to bachali
talk with, to ibaa-anompoli
talked about, to be ishtannowa,
ishtanompa
talking, to mix in while ittashommit
anompoli, ittibaakaachit anompoli
tall, to be chaaha

tall, to be very chawwala,
chawwálla'a
tall, to make chaahachi
taller, to grow chaahakat achaaka
tamale Oshpaani' imbanaha'
tame one hapashshi'
tame, to hapashhsichi, kostinichi
tame, to be hapashshi
tan leather, to asiita iksaachi
tan, to shiibli
tan, to be hotolakna
tangle, to have a atannalhchi
tangle up, to ittaboknohli,
ittaaboknohli
tangled around, to be apakfowalhchi
tangled, to be ittaboknowa,
ittapakfohkachi, ittashiikoono'wa,
ittashiiyalhchi, ittatakali,
ittaaboknowa, talakchi, palaska
tank hayip
tank car niha shaali'
tanker truck niha shaali'
tanned leather asiita
tap, to saka'chi
tape measure naaishtalhpisa'
tar niha losa'
target nannaahosa'
target, to atókko'li
tarpaulin nannompatalhpo'
taste by taking a lick, to labbit pisa
taste good, to champoli
taste of, to like the inchampoli
taste, to apat pisa
tasteless, to be ikchampo'lo,
takkishpa
tattered, to be chalhahli
tattletale anompa chokoshpali'
tattoo, to incho'li
tattooed, to be incho'wa,
ishtincho'wa
taut, to make less yolhaachi
taxes to, to pay ta'ossifalammichi
TB tiibii
tea tii

tea bag tii shokchalhto'
tea, type of naahollo intii', tii
baaksalhto'
teach, to holisso pisachi, imaabachi;
also imanoli, imponnaci
teach to be mean, to issikopachi
teacher holisso toshooli',
nannaabachi', nannimanoli'
teacup kaafaaishko'
teakettle okaalawashki'
teapot tii aalhto', tii aawaalhaali'
tear ishkin okchi'
tear apart, to nipaachi, tiwwichi,
yilhlhichi
tear, to lhilaffi, lhillichi
tear up, to tiwabli
tease, to apistikili, ayoppolachi,
chiko'li, iyoppola, ishtapistíkki'li,
yoppolachi
teased, to be chiko'wa
teats, cow's waakipishik
teddy bear nita' holba'
teenage boy hattak himitta', hattak
himittachi'
teenage girl ihoo himitta', ihoo
himittachi'
teenager, to be a himitta'si
teenager, to have become a
himittachi
teeth, baby chipota noti'
teeth, false noti' holba'
teeth, to grind one's noti' ittikisilichi
telephone talaanompa'
telephone booth talaanompoli'
aataka'li'
telephone number talaanompa'
holhtina'
telephone pole itti' chaaha'
telephone, to answer the ishi
telephone, to talk on the
talaanompa' aaittimanompoli
telephone, to talk to on the
talaanompa' aaimanompoli
telescope hopaakishpisa'

television hattak holba' aapisa'
tell (someone's) fortune, to i̱hopayi
tell a joke to, to iyoppola
tell a lie, to loshka
tell a story, to shikonno'pa' anooli
tell an untrue story, to anompa
 chokoshpa' anooli
tell half-truths about, to aloshkachi
tell in full, to alootolit anooli
tell jokes about, to ayoppolo'ka
tell off, to imbachali, i̱mihachi,
 i̱namihachi
tell on oneself, to ilano̱li
tell on, to o̱nooli
tell the future to, to tingbalísht
 imanooli
tell the plans of, to tingbalísht anooli
tell the truth, to a̱lhlhi, a̱lhlhi' ano̱li
tell the whole story, to alootolit
 anooli
tell, to ano̱li, haklochi
tell to behave, to imo̱labi
tell to behave, to go and ootimo̱labi
tell, to go imannoyachi
tell to go backwards, to bakhitiipo'chi
tell to, to imano̱li
tempt with, to bannachi
ten pokkó'li—also pokoli
ten in number, to be pokkó'li
Ten Commandments, the
 Nannalhpisa' Pokko'li', Naalhpisa'
 Pokko'li
ten times hipokko'li'
tenant ponta'
tender, to be walokshi
tenderize, to lotolli
tendon hakshish
tent alhtipo', aa-albinachi'
 ishtalhtipo', ishtalhtipo'
tent caterpillar hayowani' lhipa'
tent for living in ishtalhtipo' abooha
tent over, to put a atiipoli
tent, to make a atiipoli
tented, to be alhtipo

tenth ishpokko'li'
tenth, to be ishpokkó'li
termite isso̱sh itti' apa', isso̱sh itti'
 toshbichi'
testicles intalop, i̱nihi'
Texas Naahollo I̱yaakni'
thank, to yakkookay imanhi
thank you yakkookay
Thanksgiving Naahollo I̱nittak
that yammak, yammakot, yammako̱,
 yammat, yamma̱; also ma'shaak,
 ma'shaakot, ma'shaako̱, ma'shaat,
 ma'sha̱
that direction, in misha' fonka,
 misha' pila
that one yammak, yammakot,
 yammako̱, yammat, yamma̱; also
 ma'shaak, ma'shaakot, ma'shaako̱,
 ma'shaat, ma'sha̱
that thing there nanna yamma
that visible over there misha'
that way misha' fonka, misha' pila,
 yamma pila
that way, to be ishtaaímmo'ma,
 ishtaaimó̱ma, yámmohmi
that's it yamma
thaw, to bila, bilili
the first time, to be ámmo'na
the night before tikboklhiliaash
them yammako̱, yamma̱, yappako̱,
 yappa̱; also mi, mi alhiha', miho̱
them themselves ilaapakayni
themselves ilaapo'
then yahmihma̱
there yammak, yamma̱
there, not to be iksho
there, to be áyya'sha, ká̱ha, ánta,
 talá̱a, tó̱wa
there, to get ona
there, to leave talá̱li
there, visible over misha' pila
thermometer yanha ishtithana'
thermos oka' palli' aalhto'
these yappakot, yappako̱, yappat,

yappa
they yammakot, yammat, yappakot,
  yappat; also mi, mi alhiha', mihoot
they and they alone ilaapakilloot
they themselves ilaapakaynihaat,
  ilaapakaynihoot
they themselves also ilaapakya
thick, to be sotko
thicken, to sotkochi
thickener issotkochi'
thicket abokkoli'
thief honkopa', naahonkopa'
thigh iyyobi'
thigh, top of the iyyobi' aaishto'
thighs, to be long in the chawwálla'a
thimble chofaakoshi' ishtoopo'li',
  naaishtacho'li' ilbakoshi' fokha'
thin, to be fabassa, loposhki, tapaski
thing immi', nannahoot, nannaho
think about each other, to
  ishtittaanokfilli
think about something in one's
  heart, to chonkash ishtanokfilli,
  imichonkash ishtanokfilli
think about something together, to
  ittibaa-anokfilli
think about, to anokfilli,
  ishtanokfilli, ishtimanokfila
think ahead, to tikbali' anokfilli
think for, to imanokfilli
think one can do anything, to
  ilifinhachi, iliyimmi
think one has seen, to ishtiholba
think one is better, to imayya banna
think one is doing the right thing, to
  aalhpí'sa
think one is too good for things, to
  ilimihachi
think oneselves to be better, to
  ittímmayya'chi banna
think only about one thing, to
  imaanokfila-at kaniya
think poorly of, to ikahooba'lo
think, to anokfilli, imahooba

think too much about something, to
  nannanokfillit aatapichi
think with, to ibaa-anokfilli
third time, to do for the
  atochchi'nachi
third, to be ishtatochchí'na
third, to be the atochchí'na
third, to make the atochchi'nachi
thirsty, to be nokshila, tokshila
thirsty, to make tokshilachi
thirteen awa tochchí'na,
  pokolatochchí'na
thirteen in number, to be awa
  tochchí'na
thirty pokoli tochchí'na
thirty in number, to be pokoli
  tochchí'na
thirty-one pokoli tochchí'na awa
  chaffa
thirty-one in number, to be pokoli
  tochchí'na awa chaffa
thirty-three pokoli tochchí'na awa
  tochchí'na
thirty-three in number, to be pokoli
  tochchí'na awa tochchí'na
thirty-two pokoli tochchí'na awa
  toklo
thirty-two in number, to be pokoli
  tochchí'na awa toklo
thirty-thirty rifle tanampo pokoli
  tochchí'na tochchí'na
this yappak, yappakot, yappako,
  yappat, yappa
this evening himmaka' obyaka,
  obyakma
this is what you wanted yappa
this morning himmaka' nittakika
this one yappak, yappakot, yappako,
  yappat, yappa
this side of, just olintannap
this side, on pa-pila
this thing here nanna yappa
this way ola' fonka, ola' pila, osht,
  yappa pila

this way, to be yakohmi
this way, to do yakmihchi
this way, to move ashkanalli,
oshkanalli
this year afammi himona'
thistle oktaak pilhchi'
thorn in one, to have a hofkaa
those yammakot, yammak<u>o</u>,
yammat, yamm<u>a</u>
thousand talhipa sipokni'
thousand, one talhipa sipokni' chaffa
thousand, two talhipa sipokni' toklo
thread polona
threads naashiha'
threads from, to pull shihchi
three tochchí'na
three by three, to go tochchí'na
ayyoka
three in number, to be tochchí'na
three times hitochchi'na'
three, to be in groups of tochchí'na
áyyo'ka, tochchí'na bíyyi'ka
throat inonkopoolo'
throat, to clear one's inonka'
chokmali
throat, to give (someone) a dry
nokshilili
throat, to have a sore inonka'
hottopa
throat, to have something stuck in
one's nokbikili
throat, to have stuck in one's
noktakaali
throb, to bin-kachi
through, to go lhopolli, ootkochcha,
ootlhopolli
through, to put aalhopollichi,
lhopo'chi, lhopollichi
through, to see lhopollichit p<u>í</u>sa
through with, to be aalhopolli,
ishtaalhopolli
throughout, to do lhopolli
throw across, to abanni
throw around, to faapichi

throw at, to achoshli, achoosholi,
lhokk<u>a</u>ha
throw away, to kanchi, lh<u>a</u>'li,
oshfaapo'chi
throw in this direction, to
oshfaapichi, oshfaapo'chi
throw one's head back, to
abakshowakli
throw on each other, to itt<u>o</u>lha'chi
throw out, to fimmi, intohno,
kochcha' pitkanchi, lhatabli,
ootfimmi, ootkanchi
throw rocks, to bohpoli
throw that way, to pitfaapo'chi
throw, to faapichi, faapo'chi
throw to, to osht<u>i</u>faapichi,
osht<u>i</u>faapo'chi
thrust shoulders forward while
walking, to panaayo'wa,
panaayoy<u>ó</u>wa
thumb ilbakshki', ilbak inki'
thumb, to suck one's ilbak sh<u>o</u>'ka
thump on, to soko'chi
thunder hiloha
thunder, to hiloha
Thursday Ayyoshta', Nittak
Ayyoshta'
thus, to do yakmihchi
tick shatanni—see also tick, type of
Tick Dance Shatanni Hilha'
tick, type of issi' <u>i</u>shatanni, ofi'
<u>i</u>shatanni, shatanni afammi',
shatanni nihi', shatannoshi'
ticket tikkit
ticking, to make the sound of a clock
tik tik tik aachi
tickle, to kamoshli, wachokkochi
tickled, to be kamosha
tie a bow on, to takchit ontalaali
tie a knot in, to shikoonobli
tie a scarf over (someone's) head, to
yaachikochi
tie a scarf over one's head, to
yaachikoli

521

tie back, to

tie back, to sitili
tie for, to intakchi
tie in, to ashiichi
tie many knots in, to shikoono'li
tie on, to asiitili
tie, railroad itti' chanaa malili' ịhina'
  inkaha'
tie score, to have a ittatalakchi
tie score with, to have a ittilawwi,
  ittillawi'chi
tie something onto, to atakchichi
tie to, to ashiichi
tie together, to aaittasiitilichi,
  ittashiichi, ittatakchichi
tie up, to takchi
tie with, to ishtakchi
tied into ashiiyalhchi
tied, to be asítti'ya
tied together, to be ittashiiyalhchi
tied up, to be talakchi
tied with each other, to be
  ittatalakchi
tiger kowishto', kowishto' shiwaa'
tight around one's neck, to have
  something noksíhhi'ta
tight fit for, to be a akallo
tight, to be akallo, kallo
tight with, to be ishtimaholítto'pa
tighten, to akallochi, ashannichi
tightwad, to be a ishtimaholítto'pa
timber wolf nashoba losa'
time hashi' kanalli
time be up, to have one's time hashi'
  kanallaat imambaanapa, hashi'
  kanallaat intaha
time, for it to be what hashi' kanalli
  kaniya fokha, hashi' kanalli
  kánnohmi, hashi' kanalli katiya
  fokha, hashi' kanalli káttohmi
time to be up, for the hashi'
  kanallaat taha
time, to take too much abaanappichi
times, a few hikannohmi'
times, how many hikannohmi'

timid, to be hofahya
tin asonnak
tin can asonnak tobbi', asonnaktoshi'
tin plate asonnak amposhi'
tinfoil holisso shokmalali'
tingle, to shimoha
tinkling, to make the sound of cham
  cham cham aachi, chamak chamak
  chamak aachi
tip of an arrow, sharp naki' ịhaloppa'
tiptoe, to be on shikkílli'li
tiptoe, to walk around on
  shikkilli'kịli
tire inchanaa'
tired of, to be imintakho'bi
tired, to be tikahbi; also imaalhlhi
tired with, to be ibaatikahbi
tired with, to make ibaatikahbichi
Tishomingo Tishohminko'
to the left alhfabi' pila
to what degree katiya fokha
toad chọ'tishto', hoyo'kni'—see also
  toad, type of
toad frog chọ'tishto', hoyo'kni'
toad, horned toksala'pịlapishaa-asha'
toad, type of hoyo'knishto'
toast paskalhposha'
toast, to aposhli
toasted, to be alhposha
toaster paskaa-alhposha',
  paskaaposhli'
tobacco chomak—see also tobacco,
  type of
tobacco leaves chomak hishi'
tobacco pouch chomak ịshokcha
tobacco, type of chomak pallaska',
  chomak shana'
today himmaka' nittak
today in the morning
  himmaka'nittakika̲
toe iyyoshi'
toe, big iyyishki'
toe out, to iyyaat ittịfili'ta
toenail iyyakchosh

522

toes out, to turn one's iyyaat ittifílli'ta
together, to be cho'mi, ittihaalálli, ittihállalli, táwwa'a
together, to be all ittibalhto, ittibálhto
together, to bring ittachapali, ittapolli
together, to bring back ittifalammichi
together, to do táwwa'a
together, to get back ittifalama
toilet aaombinili'
toilet paper ishkihli'
told about, to be annowa, annoya
told on, to be ishtannowa, okfaha
told, to be imannoya
told, to do as one is ayalhlhichi
tomato akanka' inchoka'to', akankimimpa', akankintakoloshi', akankishniha', chaka'to'
tomato worm chomak apa', kankishniha' issosh
tomorrow onnakma
tomorrow evening onna obyakma
tomorrow morning onna nittakikma
tomorrow morning, early nittakikma
tomorrow night onna oklhilikma
tomorrow, the day after onna mishshakma
tomorrow, to be onna
tongs nannishhalalli'
tongue isolash
tongue at, to stick out one's isolash ifalili
tongue of a shoe sholosh isolash
tongue, to stick out one's isolash falaa, isolash falili
tonight himmakoklhilika, obyakma
too aatapa, ayili, finha, ishtaatabli, ishtaatapa
too big for, to be imaatámpa, imishto
too many, to be aatámpa
too much aatapa, salami
too much, not to eat impa' iksala'mo
too much, to be aatámpa,

ootilaatámbli, ootishtilaatámbli
too much, to do aatapichi, ishtaatabli, ishtaatapa, ishtaatapichi, ishtilaatabli, ishtilaatapichi
too, to be ayina
tool, type of ittishtalha', tali' ishhalalli'—see also names of specific tools
tooth noti'
tooth powder notishtachifa'
toothbrush notishtachifa'
toothpaste notishtachifa'
toothpick noti' ishchafi'nachi', notishfi'chi'
top alhiipi'ya', pakna', paknaka'; also hilha'chi'
top of the head yaapakna'
top of, to be on alátta'a
top of, to cut off the tabli
top off, to take the tiloffi
top taken off, to have the tilofa
tops broken off, to have the tilohli
tops, to take off the tilohchi
torn down, to be tiwapa
torn skin, to have lhilafa
torn, to be lhilafa, lhilahli, lhilahli
torn up, to be tiwapa
tornado mahlishto'
tornado, to make a noise like a fomoowachi
tortilla oshpaanimpaska
tortillas paskalhposha'
toss one's head, to abakshowakli
touch along with, to ibaahalili
touch each other, to ittihaliili
touch each other, to make ittitikoochi, ittitikilichi
touch for, to ihalili
touch lightly, to oshhalili
touch, to apistikili, halili, intikili, ombitiipa, ona
touch, to make halichi, haliichi, ombitiipachi
touch, to reach and pithalili

touch with, to halichi, haliichi
touching each other, to be ittitikili,
  ittitikohli, ittitikoht máa
tow sack shokcha kallo'
toward the speaker osht
towel ishkasho'kalhchi',
  ishtilikasho'chi'
towel, dish
  amposhishkasho'kalhchi'
tower, to have a shikkilili
town aachompa', okla—see also
  names of specific towns
toy ishchokoshkomo'
toy gun tanampo holba'
toy with, to ishtánta, ishyoppola
track, railroad itti' chanaa malili'
  ihina', tali' hina'
tractor ishtoksali'
trade off, to ittalhtobo'wa,
  ittatobo'wa
trade to for, to ittatoba
trading post aachompa'
traffic signal aashoppala' homma'
trail hin-oshi'
train itti' chanaa malili'
train car, type of nannaakapassali'—
  see also names of specific types of
  train cars
train engine ishkobo'
train, freight naashaali'
train on a dress naafka hasimbish
train on stakes, to abilhlhi
trained on poles, to be albilha
trained, to be imaabalhchi
trampoline aaombaayo'chi',
  aaomalli'
translate for, to intoshooli
translate, to anompintoshooli,
  toshooli
translator anompa toshooli'
transparent, to be aloktowáli,
  shokkawali, tapaski
transplant, to kinni
transplanted, to be kina

transvestite hattak ihoo ilahobbi',
  hattak ihoo toba'
trap ishholhtosi', nannishholhtosi',
  nannishyokachi'
trap along with, to ibaainkatabli
trap, to inkatabli
trapped along with, to be
  ibaainkatapa
trash aayoppolo', hakashtap,
  hayompolo', haayonkpolo',
  nambosholli', nannoppolo'
trash can asonnak tobbi'
trash heap nannoppolo'
treadle aahalhlhi'
treasure, to holiitobli
treasurer ta'osso shooli'
treat badly along with, to
  ibaaimpalammichi
treat badly, to impalammichi
treat each other well, to
  ittaachokmalichi
treat like, to chihmihchi
treat well, to achokmalichi,
  achokmalínchi
tree itti'—see also tree, type of
tree, branch of a naksish filammi'
tree growths, type of kapko' ani'
Tree of Life Aaokchaa' Itti'
tree root itti' hakshish
tree that bears fruit itti' tiik
tree that doesn't bear fruit itti' nakni'
tree trunk itti' api'
tree, type of itti' hobak, itti'
  holokchi', itti' tikisili', kapko', kasbi
  itti', lowak tobapi', naslaknapi',
  taka'staa'—see also names of
  specific trees
tree-trunk bottom itti' sokbish
tremble, to yollichi
triangular, to be shokolbika'
  tochchí'na
tribe okloshi'
tribe, Indian okloshi' homma'
tribe, lost okloshi' kaniya'

(tribe, name of a) Tataawa—*see also names of specific tribes*
Tribes, Five Okloshi' Talhlha'pi'
trick, to haksichi
trigger tanampaahalalli'
trimming naaishtiksa'
Trinity, the Inki' Oshi' Shilombish Tochchi'na
trip over and fall, to takaat ittola
tripe ittakoba'
tripe, type of shokhittakoba', waakittakoba'
trot, to malili impohóna, tolhtochi
trough piini'
trough, horse issoba aaipita' piini'
trousers balaafokha'
trout nani' takha', sakli'
truck nanna ishshaali'
truck, type of holisso shaali', nambosholli' shaali', waaka' shaali'
true, to be álhlhi
true, to be really ayalhlhi
true, to come ootálhlhi
true to, to be imálhlhi
trumpet vine ampohko'li', shootko'li'
trunk api', ittoyyo'bi'
trunk, tree itti' api'
trust, to iyimmi
truth alhlhi'
truth, to tell the alhlhi' anoli
try hard, to amóshsho'li, ittamóshsho'li
try on, to fokhachisht pisa, fokhat pisa, holot pisa, pisa, yaalhipichit pisa, yaalhipit pisa
try to attract attention, to iloktanichi
try to crawl, to tossoltówa
try to get before, to imaafowa
try to get free, to wahhaala
try to get sympathy, to iliposilhlha
try to get, to aafowa
try to get used to a situation, to ilachaahachi

try to stop, to inkatapo'li, inkatapo'chi
try, to chilita, miha
tryst, to lomat ittimanompoli
tuba asonnak banna'ta'
tuberculosis tiibii
tubes tied, to have one's oshi' iksho' ilikbi
Tuesday Nittak Atokla', Toosti'
tug, to halahli
tumblebug yalhki' tono'chi'
tumbleweed alba tono'li'
tunnel hina' aalhopolli', onchaba hina' aalhopolli'
turkey chaloklowa', fakit
Turkey Dance Chaloklowa' Hilha'
turkey wattles chaloklowa' ibilhkan
turkey, wild chaloklowa' imilhlha'
turn a somersault, to ishkobo' hili'shcha filita
turn all the time, to folottoto'chi
turn around in different directions, to fashkalamo'wa
turn around quickly, to filíhta, filihtikahchi, folohtokahchi
turn around, to falama, filita, filillichi, folota
turn cartwheels, to ishkobo' hili'shcha filita
turn cold, to kapast ala
turn color while ripening, to ataachi
turn down, to akkánchi
turn in at, to folota
turn inside out, to anokpiliffi, fashkalammi, fashkalamo'li
turn loose, to talhoffichi
turn off, to filillichi, moshoochi
turn on one's back, to watalhpi
turn on one's side, to achaknaski
turn on the back, to watalhpichit bohli
turn on the side, to achaknaskichi, achaknaskichit bohli, shaniili
turn on, to filillichi, shoppalali

turn one's head, to

turn one's head, to filita, filito'wa
turn one's toes out, to iyyaat ittifili'ta
turn oneself in, to iliyokachi
turn oneself into, to ilitobachi
turn over and over, to filitotówa
turn over on the back, to watalhpichi
turn over on the face, to lhipit
  wayaachi
turn over, to fashkalammi,
  fashkalamo'li, filillichi, filita
turn quickly, to filíhta
turn so as to avoid, to ifolota
turn (someone) over on his face, to
  lhipichit bohli, lhipili, lhipisht
  bohli, lhipit bohli
turn, to filillichi, filita, filito'chi,
  fili'chi, filito'wa, folollichi, folota,
  folototówa
turn up a hem on, to polhommi
turn upside down, to
  akchomakpilachi
turn yellow, to alaknachi
turned around, to be filita, fili'ta
turned inside out, to be
  fashkalamo'wa
turned on, to be fili'ta
turned out, to be ittifili'ta
turned over, to be fashkalamo'wa,
  fashkálla'ma, filita
turning on one's side, to keep
  achaknaháski
turning, to keep filitotó'chi,
  filitotówa
turnip tanap
turnip, wild tanap imilhlha'
turpentine tiyak showa'
turtle loksi'—see also turtle, type of
turtle egg loksoshi'
turtle, loggerhead loksi' hakshop
turtle shell loksi' hakshop
turtle, type of halowa, loksi' latassa',
  loksi' okokaa-asha', loksishto',
  loksoshi'
tweezers ishkin hishi' ishtihli'

twelve awa toklo, pokolatoklo
twelve in number, to be awa toklo
twenty pokoli toklo
twenty in number, to be pokoli toklo
twenty-eight pokoli toklo awa
  ontochchí'na
twenty-eight in number, to be pokoli
  toklo awa ontochchí'na
twenty-five pokoli toklo awa
  talhlhá'pi
twenty-five cents bit toklo
twenty-five in number, to be pokoli
  toklo awa talhlhá'pi
twenty-four pokoli toklo awa oshta
twenty-four in number, to be pokoli
  toklo awa oshta
twenty-nine pokoli toklo awa
  chakká'li
twenty-nine in number, to be pokoli
  toklo awa chakká'li
twenty-one pokoli toklo awa chaffa
twenty-one in number, to be pokoli
  toklo awa chaffa
twenty-seven pokoli toklo awa
  ontoklo
twenty-seven in number, to be
  pokoli toklo awa ontoklo
twenty-six pokoli toklo awa hanná'li
twenty-six in number, to be pokoli
  toklo awa hanná'li
twenty-three pokoli toklo awa
  tochchí'na
twenty-three in number, to be pokoli
  toklo awa tochchí'na
twenty-two pokoli toklo awa toklo
twenty-two in number, to be pokoli
  toklo awa toklo
.22 rifle tanampiskanno', tanampo
  nak-oshi'
twice hitokla'
twigs itti' kobolli'
twin boys chipota nakni' toklo'
twin girls chipota tiik toklo'
Twin Wells Kali Toklo'

twin women ihoo toklo'
twine nampanaa'
twins chipota toklo', hattak toklo', toklo'
twins, Siamese hattak pokta'
twist around, to apaaniili, ishtapanni, ishtapaaniili
twist in, to atannichi
twist shut, to ashannichi
twist (someone's) arm, to ilbak ishanni, ilbak shanni
twist, to afannichi, apannichi, ittapanaachi, panaayo'li, panaachi, paniili, shaniili, shanni
twist together, to ittapanaachi, ittapanni, ittapaaniili
twist up, to apanaachi
twisted around, to be apanaa
twisted, to be filita, panaa, shana, shanaayo'wa; also panayyo'wa
twisted together, to be ittapanaa
two toklo
two attached parts, something split in nanna pokta'
two bits bit toklo

two by two, to be toklo ayyoka
two different colors, to be ittimíla toklo
two hundred talhipa toklo
two hundred in number, to be talhipa toklo
two hundred one talhipa toklocha chaffa
two hundred one in number, to be talhipa toklocha chaffa
two in number, to be toklo
two minds about, to be of imaanokfila-at toklo
two or more alhiha'
two parts, to cut in tabli
two thousand talhipa sipokni' toklo
two thousand in number, to be talhipa sipokni' toklo
two, to be cut in tapa
two, to be in groups of toklo áyyo'ka, toklo bíyyi'ka
two, to have toklo'chi
two-tone, to be ittimíla toklo
typewriter tali' ishholissochi', tali' ishtincho'li', tali' ishtincho'wa'

u

udder waakipishik
ugly face, to have an bokyofóli
ugly looking, to be payofa
ugly, to be ayyabi, oppolo'si, pis-ayoba ki'yo, pis-ikayyo'bo
ulcer, stomach ittakoba' loksi', ittakoba' malli'
umbilical cord ittialbish ishtalakchi'
umbrella ishtiloshontika'chi'
umpire to'wapiisachi'
unable to breathe, to be afiitipa
unable to make up one's mind, to be imaanokfila-at toklo, nannanokfillikat toklo

unafraid, to be iknokwayyo
uncertain about, to be anoktoklo
uncle inko'si', imoshi', moshi'
uncooked, to be okchánki
uncut gem oksop toba'
under nota', toma'
under the water, to go okloboshli
under, to go notaamalli
underneath nota'
underneath, moving notali'
underneath, to go toward notaalínchi
underpants balaafokha'
underpass hina' aalhopolli',

527

underside

notaalhipolli'
underside nota'
understand, to imitháŋa, itháŋa
understand, to come to imithana
undertaker hattak illi' shaali'
underwear anonka' fokha'
undeveloped corncob tanchi'
  kobolli'
undisciplined, to be iknokchi'to
undress, to naafkịshihli
undressed, to get naafka shihli
uneven, to be ittimayya
unexpectedly haksịsht
unexpectedly, to show up ishtịhaksi
unfit mother ishki' holba'
unfold, to satabli, satapo'li
unfolded, to be satapa, satapo'wa
uniform, baseball to'li' ịnaafokha
uniform, military tashka-
  chipotịnaafokha
uninflated, to be shayofa
unique one, a ịla'
unit akaashampa'
United States, President of the
  Yaakni' Ịminko'
unlatch, to talhoffichi
unmatched, to be ịla
unravel, to shiha, shihkachi
unresponsive, to be ilikallochi
unripe, to be okchamáli
untie, to hotoffi, hotohchi
untied, to be holhtofa, hotohli
untrue story, to tell an anompa
  chokoshpa' anooli
untrue, to be falappo
unusual, to be ishtaaịla, ịla
unyielding person chonkash kallo
up aba', aba' pila
up ahead misha' pila
up the hill aapakna'
up there, way aapakna' pílla
up, to be aba' pílla
up, to get taani
up, to go abaawaa, aba' aya, toyyat aya

up, to make get taanichi
up, to put aba' pilachi, ashaachi
up, way aba' pílla
upper arm shakba'
upper back chonokko'
upper floor abooha aba'
uproot, to tịfi
uprooted, to be tịfa
upside down, to be akchomakpí'la,
  wáyya'a
upside down, to turn akchomakpila
upstairs aba', abooha aba'
upstream, to go apissat aya
urethra ishtaahoshowa'
urinal aahoshowa'
urinate on oneself, to ilọhoshowa,
  oka'at ịlhatapa
urinate on, to ọhoshowa
urinate, to hoshowa
urination, organ for ishtaahoshowa'
urine showak
us poshnaak, poshnaakọ, poshno';
  also haposhnaak, haposhnaakọ,
  haposhno'
us ourselves poshnaakaynihọ; also
  haposhnaakaynihọ,
  haposhnaakaynihta
use American Sign Language, to
  ilbak ishtanompoli
use as security for, to ishponta
use bad language, to anompoppani,
  anompoppanichi
use Indian sign language, to ilbak
  ishtanọli
use, to yuuzi
use up, to tahli
used only to, to be achokkobbi
used to a situation, to try to get
  ilachaahachi
used to each other, to be
  ittachokkobbi, ittaachokkobbi
used to each other, to get
  ittimachaaha, ittimachokkobbi
used to it, to be ishtimọmochi,

imomachit táyya'ha
used to oneself, to make (someone)
get ilachokkobbichi
used to, to be achaaha, ishtimomochi
used to, to get achokkobbichi,

aaimomochi, imomochi
used up, to be taha
usher hattak binoochi'
uvula isolash-oshi'

V

vaccinate, to ittish ani
vacuum cleaner aboohishpihli',
nannishtayowa', nannishchofalli'
vagina hasi'
valley kochchaafokka', yaakni'
hayaka'
vandalize, to incho'li,
ishtakaanihmichi
vandalized, to be incho'wa
vanilla paska champoli' ibalhto',
paskishbilamachi'
vanilla bean bala' bilama'
vanish, to kaniya
varnish, to shokmalachi
vase nampakali' aalhto'
vasectomy on, to perform a imbashli
vault ta'ossaa-asha'
vegetable nanna holokchi',
namposhi', nannawaa',
nannokchamali'—see also names
of specific vegetables
vegetarian hattak nannokchamalapa'
veil yaalhipi'li'
vein issish ihina'
vent aafoyopa'
very kanihka, mihíli, polla
very, be taha
very shortly himmako'si finha
vest naafkishto' afokhi'chi'
Veterans' Day Tashka-chipota'
Inittak
veterinarian naalhpoobimalikchi'
vibrate and make a noise, to

achaamapa
vibrate, to ilhko'li
vice-president apiilanchi'
vicious, to be hoyopa, issikopa
vine alba balalli', balalli'
vine, type of itti' okchama'li',
loksishtincho'li', nampakali'
balalli', tokfol
vinegar vinniga'
violin nannola'
virgin hattak ikhali'lo'
visible over there misha' pila
visible way over there, to be misha'
pila
visible, to be oktáni
vision of, to have a nannakat
imoktani
vision, to have a iholba,
nannimoktani
visit, to inchokkaalaa, inowa; also
loshka
visitor chokkaalaa'
voice inonka'
volcano tobaksi' bila'
volunteer, to ilatookoli
vomit bile, to laknaak howita
vomit into, to okaahowita
vomit on, to ohowita
vomit, to howita
vomit, to look like hollashki
vomit, to make howitachi
vote voot
vote against, to achapa
vote for, to apila, holisso ilhafi,

holhchifo intakaachi, imvooti
vote out of office, to kochchichi
vote, to foota, voot kanchi, voot
kasht aya, vooti

votes for, to count the holisso
ihotihna, voot ihotihna
votes, to count holisso hotihna, voot
hotihna

W

wade, to oka' okaaittánno'wa, oka'
okaaittanohówa, oka' okaanowa
wafer, Communion paska holiito'pa'
wag, to fahli
wagon itti' chanaa, itti' chanaa ishto'
wagon, covered itti' chanaalhtipo'
wagon, little itti' chanaa oshi'
wagon, to make a noise like a
ittibakaanchi
wagon, toy chanalloshi'
wagon wheel itti' chanaa inchanaa'
wait for, to ihimóna
wait on hand and foot, to ishtaapichi
wait, to himóna
wake each other up, to ittokchali
wake up from a nap, to nost okcha
wake up, not to be able to nostilli
wake up, to okcha, okchali
wakeful, to be óyyokcha
walk along in a thin dress, to
hayahankat áa, shachahánglat áa
walk along thrusting the shoulders
forward, to panaayo'wa,
panaayoyówa
walk along with, to ibaanowa
walk around aimlessly, to ittabállalli
walk around in a group, to ittabállalli
walk around on tiptoe, to
shikkilli'kili
walk around, to apakfoota,
ittánno'wa, ittanówa, nowat
ittanówa
walk around without shoes, to
mitití'chi
walk backward, to bakhitiipo'li

walk barefoot, to ittipáttakli'chi,
ittitipipí'chi, ittitíppikli'chi
walk crooked, to pahhanpáa,
shanaayo'wa
walk fast, to palhki
walk in leaves, to shochochó'chi
walk in step, to ittilawwichit tanówa
walk in, to aanowa, hayiyí'chi,
okaaittánno'wa, okaaittanohówa,
okaanowa, okaayáa
walk like a penguin, to fattalfáa
walk on, to aanowa, onáa,
ontánno'wa, ontanohówa, onowa
walk the streets, to hawit nowa
walk, to nowa; also aya, áa,
ibaanowachi, nowachi, ittánno'wa,
ittanówa
walk, to make nowachi
walk twisted, to shanaayo'wa
walk with a swaying motion, to
missilmíya, pashánna'a
walk with a wiggle ilishanaayo'chi
walk with arms around each other's
shoulders, to ittishoyyo't tanówa
walk with the hips and shoulders
swinging, to fattalfáa
walk without shoes, to patatá'chi
walker ishno'wa'
walkie-talkie aaittimanompoli'
walking around, to be just nowat áa,
nowat ittanówa
walking stick ishtilombitka', ittabi'
walking, to be akkaanówa,
akkaayínka
walking without shoes, to make the

sound of ittimititi'chi, ittimíttikli'chi, mit mit mit aachi
wall abooha naksika', aboohapootaka', holitta—*see also* wall, type of
wall heater aalashpali'
wall, type of tali' ittabaana' holitta
wallet ta'ossishokcha'
wallow in, to okaashala'li, okaatono'li
wallpaper abooha holisso lapali'
walnut hayi
walnut, type of hayi alhpooba', hayi api', hayi imilhlha', naahollimosak, naahollo ihayi, osak takba'
want a man, to nakni' banna
want all, to mománchi
want for, to ishbanna
want from, to aabanna, imaabanna, imolabi
want, to banna; *also* anhi, olabi
want to be better than everyone, to ímmayya banna, ittímmayya'chi banna
want to be better, to imayya banna
want to do in place of, to ishtilibanna
want to go with, not to imilaafowa
want, to make bannachi
Wapanucka Wappa-naki'
war intanap, tanap
war, a major Tanap Ittibi'
war bonnet yaatala
war paint ishshoka' ishtincho'li'
war paint, to put on ilincho'li, ishshoka' incho'li
warm by the fire, to get lowak inni
warm, to lashpachi, lawashkichi
warm, to be lashpa, lawashki
warp in the sun, to pashshana
warp, to pashshanili
warped and turned over, to be kobossa
warped, to be oppolokko, pahhánna'a, pahhana,

pashshánna'a, payo'kachi
wart tokchana'pa'
wart, to have a tokchana'paat ombínni'li
warts, to have tokchana'paat onáyya'sha
wash again, to albitit achifa
wash along with, to ibaa-achifa
wash clothes, to naachiifa
wash day Naalhchifa' Nittak
wash each other's faces, to ittokaamichi, ittookaamichi
wash hair, to ayichi
wash in, to aa-achifa
wash off, to achifachi
wash one's face in, to aaokaami
wash one's face, to okaami
wash one's hair, to ayiili
wash one's hands, to ilbachifa
wash out, to achifachi
wash (someone's) face, to okaamichi
wash (someone's) hair, to ayiichi
wash (someone's) hands, to ilbachifachi
wash, to achifa; *also* ishilli, kalho'chi, lhayilli
wash with, to ishtachifa
washbasin aaoka'mi'
washboard nannaakalho'chi'
washcloth ishtachifa', ishtilachifa'
washed in, to be aa-alhchifa, ishtalhchifa
washed out, to be tokbakali
washed, to be alhchifa
washed with, to be ishtalhchifa
washing machine nannaalhchifa'
Washington, D. C. Abooha Tohbi'
washrag ishtachifa'
wasp fochchanashik—*see also* wasp, type of
wasp nest fochchanashik ilhpichik, fohi' ilhpichik
wasp, type of cholhkan apa'
waste time, to alhchibachi

watch hashi' kanalli ishtithana'
watch for, to impotooni
watch one's words, to nokwáya
watch oneself around, to imilipóo
watch out for, to ihapompoyo
watch out, to hapompoyo
watch, to apiisachi; *also*
   ittahaalahlínchi, pihlínchi
watch with, to ibaa-apiisachi
watchband hashi' kanalli ishtithana'
   ishtalakchi'
watchdog naapiisachi'
watching, to get carried away pi'scha
   ishtakaniya, pi'scha ishtatamowa
watching, to stay aayahánta,
   aayashahánchi, aayashwahánchi
watchtower nannaa-apiisachi'
water oka'—*see also* water, type of
water, bottled oka' kitobalhto'
water container oka' aalhto'
water creature, type of hason
water down something, to oka' lha'li
water glass oka' aaishko'
water lily oka' aapakali', oka'
   nampakali', okpal, oktaak okpalli'
water moccasin chona'sha', oka'
   sinti', sinti' ok-okaa-asha'
water on something hot, to make the
   sound of shif shif shif aachi
water, salt oka' hapayyima'
water, side of the oka' apootaka',
   oka' taakchaka'
water, to oka' olha'li, oka'
   onashaachi
water, to be in oka' okaatákka'li, oka'
   okaatakkakáli, oka' okaatákkohli,
   oka' okaatakkokóli, oka' okaatakoht
   máa
water, to go under the okloboshli
water, to have one's eyes ishkin
   okchi'at lawa
water, to have one's mouth tokfohli
water, to move in the oka'
   okaaittánno'wa, oka'

okaaittanohówa, oka' okaayáa
water, type of oka' kapassa'
water wings oka' ishtokaayopi', oka'
   ishtokpalali'
water, witch okishtahollo'
watery eyes, to have ishkin okchi'at
   lawa
waterfall oka' aalhatapa'
watering can oka' ishtolha'li'
watermelon istokchank—*see also*
   water, type of
watermelon seeds istokchank nihi'
watermelon, type of istokchank
   kallo', istokchanglakna', waalakna'
watery, to be moyoshki, tapaski
wattles, turkey chaloklowa' ibilhkan
wave one's arms and jump around,
   to wihhiila
wave one's arms and legs, to
   washshalwáa, washshaala
wave the arms and legs, to make
   washshaalachi
wave, to fahli, fata'kalhchi,
   faapopówa, faapa, faapo'wa
wave to, to ilbak ifahli
waves in, to make bo'chi
waves, to come in bo'kalhchi
wavy line, to go in a yili'kalhchi
wavy, to be payo'kalhchi
wax akka' ishshokmalachi'
wax, ear haksibish lhitihli'
way down akka' pílla, okaaina' pila
way inside anonkaka'
way off somewhere hayaka'
way up aba' pílla
way up there aapakna' pílla
we poshnaakot, poshnaat; *also*
   haposhnaakot, haposhnaat
we ourselves poshnaakaynihoot;
   also haposhnaakaynihaat,
   haposhnaakayihoot
weak, to be tokbakali
weakly, to be tikahámbi
weapon ishhottopachi'

wear (a backpack or harness), to
  shaapóyyo'li
wear (a hat), to yaachíkko'li,
  yaalhíppi'li
wear (a hoopskirt), to wahhalwáa,
  wihhílli'ya, wihhilwíya
wear (a necklace), to innóyyo'chi
wear (a scarf), to innóyyo'chi,
  yaachíkko'li
wear (a skirt), to alhkóyyo'na
wear (a swaying skirt), to wahhalwáa
wear (a turban), to yaachíkko'li
wear (gloves), to fóyyokhi
wear on one's head, to yaachákka'li,
  yaalhíppi'li, yaatálla'li
wear on oneself, to ilontálla'li
wear one another's clothes, to
  ittibaafokha
wear out, to ibaatikahbichi,
  imaalhlhichi, intakho'bichi, lhibli,
  lhipa
wear over one shoulder and across
  the chest, to hanaawi'li
wear (shoes), to hóyyo'lo
wear skirts too short, to chawwálla'a
wear the same as, to ibaafokha
wear, to fóyyokha
wear underneath, to afokhi'chi
wear wrapped around, to
  apakfóyyo'li
weave, to folototówa, tanni
web, spider cholhkan hala'li',
  toklhan
webbed, to be patha
Wednesday Nittak Atochchi'na',
  Nittak Hollo' Aaiklanna'
weed alba, alboppolo', hayompolo'
weed, type of basho'kchi', chomak
  holba', hapo'lo', hashshan, kaso'
week wiik
weep, to yaa
weevil naafallapa'
weigh oneself, to iliwiikichi, wiiki
weigh, to wiikichi

weight wiiki
weight, to lose wiikaat inkaniya
welfare ishtalhpila'
welfare office ta'osso aaishi'
welfare, to be on alhpila' ishi
well chokma
well, oh oohaatokma
well, to be inchóngma
well, type of kali hofobi', kalishto'
well, water kali
well-behaved person hattak
  hapoyoksa'
well-known, to be annowishto
west hashaakottola', hashaaobya'
wet nurse oshpishichi'
wet one's pants, to imbalaafka'
  ohoshowa
wet the bed, to topa lhayilli, topa
  ohoshowa
wet, to lhayilli
wet, to be lhayita
whale nanishto'
what nanna, nannahoot, nannaho,
  nannakat, nanta, nanta, nantahaat,
  nantahta, nantahta
what? haa
what about that one? ma'shaako
what be wrong with one, to have
  nantahaat inkatihmi
what bothering one, to have
  nantahaat ishtimaawiiki
what color (of) pisa-kanihmihoot,
  pisa-kanihmiho, pisa-katihmi, pisa-
  katihmihat, pisa-katihmihta
what color, to be pisa-kanihmi, pisa-
  katihmi
what configuration, to be in kani'mi,
  kati'mi
what day nittak kanimpiho, nittak
  katimpihta, nittak nannaho, nittak
  nantahta
what degree, to katiya fokha
what degree, to be to kaniya fokha
what happen to one, to have

nannahoot kanihmi, nantahaat katihmi
what in, to do aakatihmi
what is it? nantahto?
what kind of kanihmi, kanihmihoot, kanihmiho, katihmi, katihmihat, katihmihta
what, looking like pisa-kanihmihoot, pisa-kanihmiho, pisa-katihmi, pisa-katihmihat, pisa-katihmihta
what manner, in katihsht
what nothing!—you heard me haa chikimba
what, of nanna, nanta
what time, for it to be hashi' kanalli kaniya fokha, hashi' kanalli kánnohmi, hashi' kanalli katiya fokha, hashi' kanalli káttohmi
what to do, to know aakanihma'nikat ithána
what, to look like pisa-katihmi
what way, in katiht
wheat tili'ko' nihi'
wheat flour, whole- tili'ko' lakna'
wheel inchanaa'
wheel of a windmill oka' ishtoochi' inchnaaka'
wheel, spinning polonaatanni'
wheel, spoke of itti' chanaa inchanaa' iwashshalaka'
wheel, wagon itti' chanaa inchanaa'
wheelbarrow itti' chanaa oshi', lokfishshaali'
wheelchair aaombiniili' chanalli'
wheeze, to lhikiiyachi
when kaniya fokhaho, kaniya fokhakaasho, kanihkaasho, katiya fokhakaash, katiya fokhakmak, katihkaash, katihkmak
where kaniya'o, katiya, katiyak
where is mano
whether nanna
whether, to be yakohmi

whew! kiihi
whey pishokchi' sotkochi'
which kanimpi, kanimpihoot, kanimpiho, katimpi, katimpihat, katimpihta, nannaho, nantahta
which is it? katimpihto
which of, to be katimpi
which one for, to be inkatimpi
which one, to be kanimpi
which way, every mayyoka'
while ittintángla, tángla
while, a little alhchimba'si
while, for a ikalhchibo'so
while, to be just a ikalhchibo'so
whine, to sinksiya
whining sound, to make a sink sink sink aachi
whip ishfama' falaa'
whip along with, to ibaafammi
whip, to fammi
whip, to make fammichi
whipped along with, to be ibaafama
whipped cream paska champoli' pakna' onashaachi'
whipped, to be fama
whippoorwill chokkala'bolo', oktaak foshi'
whirlwind, type of hapaanokfila, hapaanokfilishto'
whiskers notakhish
whiskers on, to put bakwoshochi
whiskey oka' homi'
whistle nannola'
whistle at, to inkonta
whistle, to konta
whistle, to make kontachi
whistling sound, to make a si'k si'k si'k aachi
white baby naaholloshi'
white corn tanchi' tohbi'
white dove pachalhpooba' tohbi'
White Hills Sakti Tohbi'
White House, the Abooha Tohbi'
white men's law naahollo

inaalhpisa'
white people use, something
naahollimmi'
white person loolo', naahollo
White Sands Shinok Tohbi'
white, to be tohbi
white, to make tohbichi
white, to make oneself ilitohbichi
white woman naahollihoo'
whittle, to talhlhi
whittled, to be talha
who kana, kanahoot, kanaho,
  kaniya'oot, kaniya'o, kata, katahaat,
  katahta
who is it? katahto
whoa! hika!
whole world, the Chihoowa iyaakni'
whole, to be lómbo
whole-wheat flour tili'ko' lakna'
whom kana, kanaho, kaniya'o, kata,
  katahta
whoop, to paa
whooping cough hotolhkilli'
whooping cough, to have
  hotolhkilli' i'shi
whose kana, kata
why kanihmiho, kanihchiho,
  katihchihta
why? katihmihta
wick aakilaa'
wicker oski' chalhaali'
wide area across one's body iwa'ta'
wide, to be patha, wahhálla'a
widen, to pathachi
wider, to make achaakali, achakli
widow alhtakla', ihoo alhtakla', ihoo
  hattak imilli', ihoo tabashi', tabashi'
widowed, to be alhtakla, tabashi
wife imihoo
wife, to have a ihooat imayya'sha
wig ipashi' holba'
wiggle, to chiffoola, yili'kachi,
  yili'kalhchi
wiggle when walking, to

shanaayoyówa
wiggle, to walk with a
  ilishanaayo'chi
wild animal nannimilhlha'
wild apple takolo imilhlha'
wild onion atofalla'a' imilhlha'
wild plum takoloshi' imilhlha'
wild, to be iknokchi'to, imilhlha,
  kostíyyi'ni ki'yo
wildcat kow-imilhlha', kowishto
wilderness ittannonka'
wildflower alba pakali', nampakali'
  imilhlha'
will holisso nanna ishtalhlhi'
will for, to make a holissimikbi
will, to make a holissikbi
willow chishanko toba', tannasho'
willow seeds tannasho' pofalli'
wilted, to be shayofa
win the affection of, to hotosi
win, to imambi
Winchester rifle tanampo falaa'
wind mahli
wind around, to apakfohli,
  apakfohchi
wind into a ball, to ittapakfohli,
  ittapakfolli
wind on, to blow omahli
wind, to folo'kalhchi; also
  oshannichi
wind, to have no likinta
wind up, to apakfolli,
  chokoshkomochi
windmill mahli ishtikbi', mahli
  okoochi', mahlishyokachi', oka'
  aamaachi', oka' ishtoochi'
windmill wheel oka' ishtoochi'
  inchnaaka'
window aahashtahli', okkis-oshi',
  winda'
window shade winda' takaali'
windy on, to be omahli
windy, to be mahli
windy, to be a little mahlihínchi

wine oka' panki', pankokchi' hawashko', pankokchi'

wing fanalhchi'

wings spread out at the sides, to have one's wihhílli'ya

wings, to spread the ilisatapo'li

wink at, to ishkin inkan̲i̲'chi, ishkin tannap pila ishpisa, i̲mocholi, i̲moshmoli

wink, to moshmoli

winnow, to mashka

winnowed, to be malashka

winnowing basket talhpak

winnowing basket, type of alhpatak

winnowing fan tanchi' ishmashka'

winter hashtola'

winter onion ato̲falla'a' ililawachi', hashtola' ato̲falla'a'

winter, the beginning of hashtolammo'na'

winterberry foshiyyi'

wipe after defecation, to inkihli

wipe oneself off, to ilikasho'chi

wipe oneself, to kihli

wipe out, to loshommi

wipe, to kasho'chi

wiped, to be kasho'kalhchi, kasho'walhchi

wire tali'—see also wire, type of

wire cutters talishtapa'

wire fence tali' holitta'

wire, type of tali' fabassa', tali' haloppa', tali' shachakla'

wise man hattak hapoyoksa', hattak nannithana'

wise, to be hapoyoksa

wish, to anhi, anhit anokfilli

wish well, to imanhi

witch ishtahollo', nanna ilitobasht no̲wa', oklhili no̲wa', oklhili shoppalat no̲wa'

witch, type of ilitobasht no̲wa', ishtaholloppolo', nosi'chi'

witch water okishtahollo'

witchcraft, to die as a result of afiitipat illi

witches oklhili tano̲wa'

with difficulty pallammihm̲a̲

with, to be ahiina, ibaa-ánta, ibaa-áyya'sha, ibaafóyyokha, ibaatángla, ibaayáa, iláwwi'li

with, to go ahiina, ibaayáa, tangla aya

withdraw, to aaponta

without ikshokat, iksho̲

without stopping immo̲'t

witness i̲naano̲li'

witness for imi̲naano̲li'

witness for, to be a ibaapísa, imi̲naano̲li, nannimano̲li

wobble, to tono'kachi

wolf nashoba

wolf, type of nashoba losa', nashob-okchamali'

woman ihoo

woman, homeless ihoo inchokkiksho'

woman, old ihoo kashiiho'

woman over, to have a ihooat ootimokfaha

woman who has never been married ihoo hattak ikimiksho'

woman, young ihoo himitta'

womb oshaatoba', osha̲'to'

women, to have ihoo toklo'

wonder if, I nanna'chihch̲i̲, nannahch̲i̲, nannatokch̲i̲

wood itti'

wood being hit, to make the sound of kob kob kob aachi, kobok kobok kobok aachi

wood chips hakashtap

wood, petrified itti' tali'

wood, split itti' palha'

wood, to make a noise with baka'chi, bakkaka'chi

wooden bowl itti' amposhi'

wooden floor itti' patalhpo'

wooden leg iyyi' holba'

wooden pestle for pounding corn
tanchishhollosi'
wooden shoe itti' sholosh
woodpecker bakbak; *also* aboowa
bo'li'
woodpecker, type of bakbak ishkobo'
homma', bakbak ishto', chapchap,
itti' cha̲'li'
word anompa
word of God abaanompa
(word used by little boys) po's po's
(word used to call chickens) chik
work along with, to ibaatoksali
work for, to intoksali
work hard, to ilamóshsho'li
work in, to aatoksali
work off a fine, to toksalit ilatobbi
work off a sentence, to toksalit atobbi
work oneself through, to
shammamáli
work out for, to intoksali
work party iikowa'
work, to nannishtatta, toksali
work, to make toksalichi
work together, to ittapila
work with, to make ibaatoksalichi
worker hattak toksali'
working person toksali'
workman toksali'
world hattak mo̲ma, yaakni'
world, the whole Chihoowa i̲yaakni'
worm hayowani', isso̲sh, yala
worm, type of chomak apa', itti'
toshbi' isso̲sh, saalhkona,
saalhkonishto'
worms, to have isso̲sh i̲lawa
worn away, to be taha
worn out, to be imaalhlhi, lhipa,
taha
worry about, to ishtimanokfila
worry, to nannanokfillit aatapichi
worse for, to make it imayyabichi
worsen the condition of, to ayyabichi
worship, to ayoppachi

wound around, to be apakfoha,
apakfohkáyya'chi, apakfowalhchi,
apakfowat má̲a, apanaa
wound up, to be folohónta
woven, to be loosely shachakla
wrap hoboona
wrap around, to apakfolli,
apakfóyyo'ta, apakolli, apakolli
wrap oneself up in, to aboknoha,
ilaboknohli
wrap oneself up, to pitilaboknohli
wrap (something) around oneself and
go, to pitalhko'nacha aya
wrap up in, to aboknohli
wrapped around, to be aboknoha,
apakfohkachit má̲a, apakfowalhchi,
apakfowat má̲a, apakfóyyo'ta
wrapped around, to have
apakfóyyo'li
wrapped, to be apakfohkáyya'chi,
ayoppolo'ka
wrapped up in, to be aboknoha
wrapped up, to be holbona
wrecked, to be ayoppolo'ka
wrench naaishtashanishtiwwi'
wrestle, to ittishooli, ittiyokli
wring the neck of, to shannit tiloffi
wring, to shanni
wringer nannaashana'
wrinkle, to koyohli
wrinkled, to be banata, koyoha,
koyota, wó̲lha, yikilhlha
wrist ilbak i̲mosak, shakba' i̲mosak
write for, to i̲holissochi
write in, to aaholissochi, holissochi
write on on top of, to aao̲holissochi
write, to holissochi; *also* takaachi,
takoochi
write to, to i̲holissochi
written, to be holisso
wrong idea, to give the imahobbichi
wrong number, to get a ila'o̲ kaali
wrong place, to put away in the
ittashommi

wrong, to be

wrong, to be ikalhpi'so
wrong, to be on itt_ifilli'ta, itt_ishanaa,
  _ifili'ta
wrong, to hit issot tiballichi
wrong, to make shaniili

wrong, to put on itt_ishaniili
wrong with one, to have what be
  nantahaat inkatihmi
wrung out, to be shana

x

Xerox copy holisso holba'

Xerox, to make a holisso holbachi

y

yam ahi' champoli'
yard alhpisa, kasbi
yard tree kasbi itti'
yardage naalhila'fa'
yardstick naaishtalhpisa'
yarmulke yaachikko'li'
yarn ishtalakchi', nantanna' toba',
  naaishtiksaa'
yaupon foshiyyi'
yawn, to afaapo'wa
year afammi
year, last tikba' afammi
year old, to be another afammi
year, this afammi himona'
yearling tick shatanni afammi'
yeast paska ishshatabli'
yell at, to _inókko'wa, _inokowa
yell, to nókko'wa, shakahámbli,
  tasahli
yell, to make tasaachi
yellow, to be lakna
yellow, to be dark lakna losayyi
yellow, to make laknachi
yellow, to turn alaknachi
yellow weed alba lakna'
yellowed, to be hotolakna
yellowhammer fottatak, s_osolo'
yellowjacket fohi' lakna'
yes _ii; _also_ _ah_aa, hoo, ho'mi, yamma

yes, I've come _ii alali
yesterday oblaashaash
yesterday evening obyaka'aash
yesterday morning oblaashaash_o
  nittaki
yesterday, the day before oblaashaash
  mishshaash
yielding, to be soft and
  yabbokahánchi
yoke itti' falakto'
yoked, to be itti' falakto' innoyyo'chi
you ishnaak, ishnaat, ishnaakot,
  ishnaak_o, ishn_a, ishno'
you all hachishnaak, hachishnaakot,
  hachishnaak_o, hachishnaat,
  hachishn_a, hachishno'
you guys hachishnaak,
  hachishnaakot, hachishnaak_o,
  hachishnaat, hachishn_a, hachishno'
You pouter! Chittialbi' falaa!
you yourself ishnaakayhihaat,
  ishnaakaynihoot, ishnaakaynih_o,
  ishnaakayniht_a
you yourselves
  hachishnaakaynihaat,
  hachishnaakaynihoot,
  hachishnaakaynih_o,
  hachishnaakayniht_a
young man hattak himitta'

young, to be chipota'si, himitta
young, to make himittachi
younger half-sibling nakfish iklanna'
younger sibling nakfish
younger step-sibling nakfish toba'

younger, to be chipónta, himittánchi
youngest child chipota ishtayyo'pi'
you're welcome chokmahookay,
ho'mi

z

zebra issoba basoowa', issoba kamaa',
issoba shiwaa'
zigzag, to foloto'wa
zigzag, to go in a yillilínkalhchi

zigzag, to make yili'chi
zoo nannimilhlha' aa-asha'
zucchini olbi' okchamali'